Hoover's Online is your source for business information that works.

Millions of businesspeople use Hoover's Online every day for research, analysis, and prospecting. Hoover's updates information daily on thousands of companies and hundreds of industries worldwide.

USE HOOVER'S ONLINE FOR:

- **COMPANY RESEARCH**
  Overview
  History
  Competitors
  News
  Products
  Location(s)
  Financials
  Stock data

- **INDUSTRY RESEARCH**
  Quick synopsis
  Leading companies
  Analysis of trends
  Associations
  Glossary of terms
  Research reports

- **PROSPECTING**
  Search by industry,
  location, sales, keyword
  Full officer lists
  Company history
  Financials

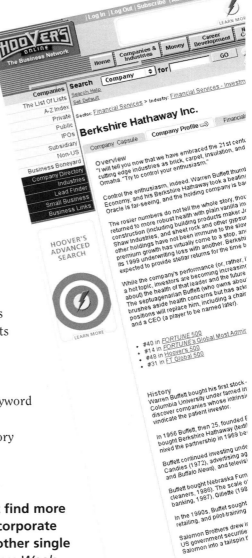

You simply can't find more information on corporate America in any other single source." —*Business Week*

For accurate online business information, visit us at www.hoovers.com

Hoover's
Handbooks
Index

2002

HOOVER'S
BUSINESS PRESS
Austin, Texas

BUSINESS PRESS

10 9 8 7 6 5 4 3 2 1

Publishers Cataloging-In-Publication Data

Hoover's Handbooks Index 2002

   Includes indexes.

     1. Business enterprises — Directories. 2. Corporations — Directories.

HF3010   338.7

   Hoover's Company Information is also available on America Online, Bloomberg Financial Network, CNBC on MSN Money, EBSCO, Factiva, FORTUNE, Hoover's Online, LexisNexis, NewsEdge, ProQuest, The Washington Post, and other Web sites.

   A catalog of Hoover's products is available on the World Wide Web at www.hoovers.com.

   ISBN 1-57311-076-0

   ISSN 1097-7864

   The Hoover's Handbook series is edited by George Sutton and produced for Hoover's Business Press by Sycamore Productions, Inc., Austin, Texas, using Quark, Inc.'s QuarkXPress 4.04; EM Software, Inc.'s Xtags 4.1; and fonts from Adobe's Clearface, Futura, and Myriad families. Cover design is by Shawn Harrington. Electronic prepress and printing were done by Edwards Brothers Incorporated, Ann Arbor, Michigan. Text paper is 60# Arbor.

US AND WORLD DIRECT SALES

Hoover's, Inc.
5800 Airport Blvd.
Austin, TX 78752
Phone: 512-374-4500
Fax: 512-374-4501
e-mail: orders@hoovers.com

EUROPE

William Snyder Publishing Associates
5 Five Mile Drive
Oxford OX2 8HT
England
Phone & fax: +44-186-551-3186
e-mail: snyderpub@cs.com

HOOVER'S, INC.

Founder: Gary Hoover
Chairman: Patrick J. Spain
President and CEO: Jeffrey Tarr
EVP Corporate Strategy and Development: Carl G. Shepherd
SVP Product Management: Russell Secker

EDITORIAL

Managing Editor: Nancy Regent
Assistant Managing Editor: Valerie Pearcy
Editorial Operations Manager: Ashley Schrump
Director, Financial Information: Dennis Sutton
Senior Editors: Rachel Brush, Margaret Claughton, Paul Geary, Joe Grey, Kathleen Kelly, Mary Mickle Morales
Assistant Senior Editors: Larry Bills, Angela Boeckman, Joe Bramhall, Michaela Drapes, Chris Huston, Joe Simonetta
Associate Editors: Joy Aiken, Sally Alt, Graham Baker, Jason Cother, Bobby Duncan, Carrie Geis, Todd Gernert, Allan Gill, Gregg Gordon, Melanie Hall, Matt Saucedo, Vanita Trippe, Randy Williams, David Woodruff
Contributing Editor: Travis Brown
Senior Writers: David Hamerly, Stuart Hampton, Guy Holland, Josh Lower
Writers: Linnea Anderson, James Bryant, Ryan Caione, Jason Cella, Danny Cummings, Tom Elia, Laura Ivy, Andreas Knutsen, Julie Krippel, Anne Law, Diane Lee, John MacAyeal, Nell Newton, Sheri Olander, Amanda Palm, Elizabeth Paukstis, Rob Reynolds, Amy Schein, Seth Shafer, Tim Walker, Chris Zappone
Financial Editors: Adi Anand, Troy Bryant, John Flynn, Chris Huston, Joel Sensat, Matt Taylor
Chief Copyeditor: Emily Weida Domaschk
QA Editors: Anthony Staats, John Willis
Assistant Editors: Tommy Ates, Lesley Epperson Dings, Jeanette Herman, Michael McLellan, David Ramirez, Christopher Sovine, Daysha Taylor
Editorial Assistants: Daniel Croll, Jana Cummings, Jay Koenig, Michelle Medina, Anna Porlas, Kcevin Rob
Research Coordinator: Jim Harris
Library Coordinator: Kris Stephenson

PRINT PRODUCTS DIVISION

Director, Print Products: Dana Smith
Distribution Manager: Rhonda Mitchell
Fulfillment and Shipping Manager: Michael Febonio
Shipping Clerk: James H. Taylor IV

ABOUT HOOVER'S, INC.

Hoover's, Inc. (Nasdaq: HOOV) provides online business information and tools to help business-people get their jobs done. Hoover's information is available through its destination site Hoover's Online (http://www.hoovers.com), through co-branding agreements with other online services, and through customized applications developed for enterprise information portals. Hoover's investors include AOL Time Warner (NYSE: AOL), Media General (AMEX: MEGA), and Knowledge Universe, through its Knowledge Net Holdings and Nextera Enterprises (Nasdaq: NXRA) units. Hoover's is headquartered in Austin, Texas, and has offices in New York City and San Francisco.

Contents

About *Hoover's Handbooks Index 2002* ix

Using the Index...x

Index of Companies by Industry 1

Index of Companies by Headquarters Location 23

Index of Brands, Companies, and People 47

ABOUT *HOOVER'S HANDBOOKS INDEX 2002*

This volume is made up of the combined indexes from the 2002 editions of the Hoover's Handbooks series — our comprehensive multivolume set of reference works that covers the world of business, from the largest and the most valuable to the most interesting business enterprises, public and private, US and non-US.

The 2002 series of handbooks — which covers 2,325 public, private, US, and global enterprises — includes:

- *Hoover's Handbook of American Business* (two volumes)
- *Hoover's Handbook of Emerging Companies*
- *Hoover's Handbook of World Business*
- *Hoover's Handbook of Private Companies*

The information in this combined index is organized into three separate sections. The first two list the profiled companies organized by industry group and by headquarters location. The main index includes all of the brand names, companies, and people mentioned in the profiles and in our briefer capsules.

In addition to the companies featured in our handbooks, coverage of some 12 million business enterprises is available in electronic format on our Web site, Hoover's Online: The Business Network (www.hoovers.com).

Our goal is to provide one site that meets all the needs of business professionals. Hoover's has partnered with other prestigious business information and service providers to bring you all the right business information, services, and links in one place, including information on the IPO market.

Additionally, Hoover's Company Information is available on other sites on the Internet, including The Washington Post, LexisNexis, and online services Bloomberg Financial Network, Factiva, and America Online.

We believe anyone who buys from, sells to, invests in, lends to, competes with, interviews with, or works for a company should know about that enterprise. Taken together, Hoover's products and resources represent the most complete source of basic corporate information readily available to the general public.

We welcome the recognition we have received as the premier provider of high-quality company information — online, electronically, and in print — and we continue to look for ways to make our products more available and more helpful to you.

We hope you find our books useful. We invite your comments by phone (512-374-4500), fax (512-374-4501), mail (5800 Airport Blvd., Austin, TX 78752), or e-mail (comments@hoovers.com).

The Editors
Austin, Texas
February 2002

USING THE INDEX

PAGE NUMBERS

The letter preceding each page number of an index entry indicates the handbook volume that is being referenced:

A=American Business
E=Emerging Companies
P=Private Companies
W=World Business

(For convenience, this list of handbook titles and the corresponding letters are also included at the bottom of every index page.)

Boldfaced numbers indicate the page on which a company's profile appears. Numbers in regular type indicate other references to a company.

ALPHABETIZATION

English-language articles (a, an, the) are ignored when they appear at the beginning of a company or product name, but foreign articles are not ignored and are alphabetized as they appear. Ampersands are treated as though they are spelled out, as are the abbreviations Ft., Mt., and St.

If a company name is also a person's name, such as Edward J. DeBartolo or Mary Kay, it will be alphabetized under the first name; if the company name starts with initials, for example, L.L. Bean or S.C. Johnson, look for it under the combined initials (in the above examples, LL and SC, respectively).

Initials or words indicating limited liability appearing at the beginning of international company names (AB, A/S, NV, P.T., S.A., AS, Industrias, Gesellschaft, Koninklijke, Kongl, and Oy) are ignored and the company is sorted on the following word. Similarly, foreign-language words (Grupo, Gruppo, Compagnie, Sociedad, etc.) that begin foreign company names are ignored and the names are sorted by the key word that follows.

SPECIAL CONVENTIONS

If additional information appears in parentheses, i.e., "Clean Pride (janitorial supplies)," it indicates that the reference it modifies (Clean Pride) is a company name. If the explanation is not in parentheses, i.e., "Crouse-Hinds electrical fixtures," it indicates that the reference is to a product name rather than a company.

INDUSTRY INDEX

Companies are listed alphabetically within industry types. Similar types are grouped under industry categories. For example, the Heavy Construction industry is found along with the Aggregates, Concrete & Cement industry and other construction-related industries under the category Materials & Construction. For your convenience, a listing of Hoover's industry categories and the pages on which each begins can be found on page 2.

Hoover's Handbooks Index

INDUSTRY INDEX

Note: Page numbers in **boldface** indicate the company's profile.

INDUSTRY CATEGORIES

Aerospace & Defense	2
Automotive & Transport Equipment	2
Banking	2
Chemicals	3
Computer Hardware	4
Computer Software & Services	4
Conglomerates	5
Consumer Products — Durables	5
Consumer Products — Non-Durables	5
Diversified Services	6
Drugs	7
Electronics & Miscellaneous Technology	8
Energy	8
Financial Services	9
Food, Beverage & Tobacco	10
Health Products & Services	11
Insurance	12
Leisure	13
Manufacturing	14
Materials & Construction	15
Media	16
Metals & Mining	16
Real Estate	17
Retail	17
Specialty Retail	18
Telecommunications	19
Transportation	20
Utilities	20

AEROSPACE & DEFENSE

Maintenance & Service
United Space Alliance P**754**

Major Diversified
Airbus S.A.S. W**70**
BAE SYSTEMS W**110**
The Boeing Company A**272**
Bombardier Inc. W**132**
General Dynamics Corporation A**644**
Lockheed Martin Corporation A**882**
Northrop Grumman Corporation A**1044**
Raytheon Company A**1190**

Products
Alliant Techsystems Inc. A**120**
CFM International, Inc. P**572**
Comptek Research, Inc. E**183**
Goodrich Corporation A**662**
HEICO Corporation E**67**, E**212**
Herley Industries, Inc. E**68**, E**214**
Honeywell International Inc. A**728**
ITT Industries, Inc. A**780**
Rolls-Royce plc W**496**
United Technologies Corporation A**1432**
Vought Aircraft Industries, Inc. P**766**

AUTOMOTIVE & TRANSPORT EQUIPMENT

Auto Manufacturers
AB Volvo W**632**
Bayerische Motoren Werke AG W**120**
DaimlerChrysler AG W**188**
Dr. Ing. h. c. F. Porsche AG W**458**
Fiat S.p.A. W**226**
Ford Motor Company A**616**
General Motors Corporation A**650**
Honda Motor Co., Ltd. W**264**
Isuzu Motors Limited W**294**
Mazda Motor Corporation W**362**
New United Motor Manufacturing, Inc. P**366**, P**687**
Nissan Motor Co., Ltd. W**402**
PSA Peugeot Citroën S.A. W**442**
Renault S.A. W**480**
Suzuki Motor Corporation W**560**
Toyota Motor Corporation W**614**
Volkswagen AG W**630**

Auto Parts
ArvinMeritor, Inc. A**198**
BorgWarner Inc. A**278**
BREED Technologies, Inc. P**561**
Cardone Industries Inc. P**565**

Collins & Aikman Corporation A**388**
Cummins, Inc. A**456**
Dana Corporation A**460**
Delco Remy International, Inc. P**152**, P**590**
Delphi Automotive Systems Corporation A**476**
Eagle-Picher Industries, Inc. P**600**
Federal-Mogul Corporation A**584**
Johnson Controls, Inc. A**802**
Lear Corporation A**856**
Mark IV Industries, Inc. P**310**, P**664**
Meridian Automotive Systems, Inc. P**673**
Metaldyne Corporation P**673**
Oxford Automotive, Inc. P**695**
Penske Corporation P**390**, P**699**
Robert Bosch GmbH W**490**
Tenneco Automotive Inc. A**1368**
TRW Inc. A**1412**
UIS, Inc. P**752**
Venture Industries P**764**

Motorcycles & Other Small-Engine Vehicles
Harley-Davidson, Inc. A**682**

Pleasure Boats
Brunswick Corporation A**298**
Genmar Holdings, Inc. P**614**

Rail & Trucking Equipment
Duchossois Industries, Inc. P**598**
Great Dane Limited Partnership P**621**
Trinity Industries, Inc. A**1406**

Shipbuilding & Related Services
McDermott International, Inc. A**940**

Trucks, Buses & Other Vehicles
Navistar International Corporation A**1010**
PACCAR Inc A**1078**

BANKING

Asia & Australia
National Australia Bank Limited W**382**

Canada
Bank of Montreal W**112**
Canadian Imperial Bank of Commerce W**156**
RBC Financial Group W**474**
The Toronto-Dominion Bank W**608**

Europe
Allied Irish Banks, p.l.c. W**86**
Espírito Santo Financial Group S.A. W**224**
National Bank of Greece S.A. W**384**
UBS AG W**616**

Money Center Banks

ABN AMRO Holding N.V. W56
Bank of America
  Corporation A226
The Bank of New York Company,
  Inc. A228
BANK ONE
  CORPORATION A230
Barclays PLC W114
BNP Paribas W130
Citigroup Inc. A370
Crédit Lyonnais W182
Credit Suisse Group W184
Deutsche Bank AG W200
Federal Reserve Bank of New
  York P607
Federal Reserve System P186,
  P607
FleetBoston Financial
  Corporation A602
HSBC Holdings plc W268
J.P. Morgan Chase & Co. A808
Mizuho Holdings, Inc. W374
Santander Central Hispano
  S.A. W512
Wells Fargo & Company A1508

Other Banking Services

NetBank, Inc. E251

US Mid-Atlantic

Chevy Chase Bank, F.S.B. P574
Columbia Bancorp E182
Commerce Bancorp, Inc. E182
Lakeland Bancorp, Inc. E231
The PNC Financial Services
  Group, Inc. A1146
Yardville National
  Bancorp E320

US Midwest

Capitol Bancorp Ltd. E171
Citizens Banking
  Corporation E179
Comerica Incorporated A394
Fifth Third Bancorp A592
First Defiance Financial
  Corp. E204
KeyCorp A822
MB Financial, Inc. E239
National City
  Corporation A1000
Northern Trust
  Corporation A1042
U.S. Bancorp A1444
Vail Banks, Inc. E310
Wintrust Financial
  Corporation E318

US Northeast

Boston Private Financial
  Holdings, Inc. E165
Capital Crossing Bank E170
Chittenden Corporation E178
First Niagara Financial Group,
  Inc. E205
Mellon Financial
  Corporation A954
NBT Bancorp Inc. E250
Roslyn Bancorp, Inc. E281

Seacoast Financial Services
  Corporation E285
Staten Island Bancorp,
  Inc. E293
Sterling Financial
  Corporation E294
Sun Bancorp, Inc. E295
Thistle Group Holdings,
  Co. E301
Tompkins County Trustco,
  Inc. E302
Waypoint Financial
  Corporation E315

US Southeast

AmSouth Bancorporation A166
BancorpSouth, Inc. E162
First Bancorp E204
Main Street Banks, Inc. E236
The South Financial Group,
  Inc. E291
Southern Financial Bancorp,
  Inc. E291
SouthTrust Corporation A1308
SunTrust Banks, Inc. A1346
Superior Financial Corp. E296
Wachovia Corporation A1486

US Southwest

First Banks America, Inc. E204
Prosperity Bancshares,
  Inc. E271
Southwest Bancorporation of
  Texas, Inc. E291

US Territories

R&G Financial
  Corporation E275
W Holding Company, Inc. E314

US West

Banner Corporation E162
CoBiz Inc. E181
Downey Financial Corp. E194
Golden West Financial
  Corporation A658
Greater Bay Bancorp E209
Heritage Commerce Corp E213
Heritage Financial
  Corporation E213
Humboldt Bancorp E216
Navy Federal Credit Union P686
Silicon Valley Bancshares E122,
  E288
Umpqua Holdings
  Corporation E307
VIB Corp E312
Washington Mutual, Inc. A1500
Westcorp E316

CHEMICALS

Agricultural Chemicals

Agrium Inc. W66
CF Industries, Inc. P572
IMC Global Inc. A752
Monsanto Company A984
Royster-Clark, Inc. P718

Basic & Intermediate Chemicals
& Petrochemicals

Ashland Inc. A200
Chevron Phillips Chemical
  Company LP P574
Crompton Corporation A450
Lyondell Chemical
  Company A900
Sinopec Shanghai Petrochemical
  Company Limited W542
Texas Petrochemicals LP P745

Diversified

Air Products and Chemicals,
  Inc. A100
Akzo Nobel N.V. W72
BASF Aktiengesellschaft W116
Bayer AG W118
Cabot Microelectronics
  Corporation E168
The Dow Chemical
  Company A504
Dow Corning
  Corporation P164, P596
E. I. du Pont de Nemours and
  Company A534
Eastman Chemical
  Company A522
Ecolab Inc. A530
Engelhard Corporation A550
Henkel KGaA W256
Huntsman Corporation P238,
  P636
ICC Industries Inc. P637
Imperial Chemical Industries
  PLC W278
Millennium Chemicals
  Inc. A974
Minnesota Mining and
  Manufacturing Company A976
Noveon, Inc. P691
Olin Corporation A1060
OM Group, Inc. A257
Praxair, Inc. A1156
Rohm and Haas
  Company A1212
Solutia Inc. A1300
W. R. Grace & Co. A1536

Paints, Coatings & Other
Finishing Products

Contran Corporation P583
PPG Industries, Inc. A1152
The Sherwin-Williams
  Company A1278

Plastics & Fibers

Carpenter Co. P568
Equistar Chemicals, LP P604
Formosa Plastics
  Corporation W228

Specialty Chemicals

Borden, Inc. P90, P558
Flint Ink Corporation P608
Hercules Incorporated A704
International Flavors &
  Fragrances Inc. A766
J. M. Huber Corporation P645

COMPUTER HARDWARE

Computer Peripherals

Canon Inc. W158
InFocus Corporation E73, E220
Lexmark International,
Inc. A870
Logitech International
S.A. W338
ViewSonic Corporation P765

Data Storage Devices

Advanced Digital Information
Corporation E23, E148
EMC Corporation A542
Imation Corp. A750
Iomega Corporation A778
Maxtor Corporation A928
Quantum Corporation A1184
Seagate Technology,
Inc. A1260, P440, P725
Silicon Graphics, Inc. A1284
Storage Technology
Corporation A1336
Western Digital
Corporation A1514

Diversified Computer Products

CASIO COMPUTER CO.,
LTD. W168
Fujitsu Limited W236
Hewlett-Packard
Company A712
International Business Machines
Corporation A764
NEC Corporation W386
Oki Electric Industry Company,
Limited W420
SANYO Electric Co., Ltd. W514
SBS Technologies, Inc. E284
Seiko Epson Corporation W530
Sun Microsystems, Inc. A1342
Toshiba Corporation W610

Electronic Business Equipment

Danka Business Systems
PLC W190
Diebold, Incorporated A488
IKON Office Solutions,
Inc. A746
Minolta Co., Ltd. W368
NCR Corporation A1012
Pitney Bowes Inc. A1142
Ricoh Company, Ltd. W486
Tidel Technologies, Inc. E301
Xerox Corporation A1544

Miscellaneous Computer-Based Systems

Mercury Computer Systems,
Inc. E241
NYFIX, Inc. E256

Networking & Communication Devices

3Com Corporation A54
Brocade Communications
Systems, Inc. E166
Cisco Systems, Inc. A368
Foundry Networks, Inc. E206
JNI Corporation E226

Juniper Networks, Inc. E226
McDATA Corporation E239
QLogic Corporation E272
SonicWALL, Inc. E290

Personal Computers

Acer Inc. W60
Apple Computer, Inc. A186
Compaq Computer
Corporation A398
Dell Computer
Corporation A472
Gateway, Inc. A636
MicronPC, LLC P676

COMPUTER SOFTWARE & SERVICES

Communications Software

Inet Technologies, Inc. E219
SignalSoft Corporation E287
Ulticom, Inc. E307

Computer Products Distribution & Support

The ASCII Group, Inc. P544
ASI Corp. P545
Black Box Corporation E164
Comark, Inc. P136, P580
CompuCom Systems, Inc. A400
Computacenter plc W176
Corporate Software &
Technology, Inc. P584
Ingram Micro Inc. A758
MA Laboratories, Inc. P662
Merisel, Inc. A958
Tech Data Corporation A1356
Westcon Group, Inc. P771

Corporate, Professional & Financial Software

Advent Software, Inc. E25, E149
BMC Software, Inc. A270
Click Commerce, Inc. E180
Dendrite International,
Inc. E191
Manhattan Associates,
Inc. E236
MatrixOne, Inc. E237
MetaSolv, Inc. E243
PeopleSoft, Inc. A1098
SAP Aktiengesellschaft W516
SAS Institute Inc. P430, P721

Data Processing Software & Services

Innodata Corporation E221

Database & File Management Software

Embarcadero Technologies,
Inc. E197
Oracle Corporation A1066

Development Tools, Operating Systems & Utility Software

Mercury Interactive
Corporation E91, E242
Microsoft Corporation A972
Rational Software
Corporation E110, E276

SERENA Software, Inc. E286

Diversified Software

Computer Associates
International, Inc. A402
Compuware Corporation A406

Document Management Software

Actuate Corporation E22, E148
T/R Systems, Inc. E303
Verity, Inc. E134, E311

Educational Software

Renaissance Learning,
Inc. E278

Entertainment & Games Software

Take-Two Interactive Software,
Inc. E298

Information Technology Consulting Services

Answerthink, inc. E157
Atos Origin W100
Bull W150
Cap Gemini Ernst &
Young W160
Carreker Corporation E172
Cognizant Technology Solutions
Corporation E181
Computer Sciences
Corporation A404
DynCorp P599
Electronic Data Systems
Corporation A538
Inforte Corp. E220
Jack Henry & Associates,
Inc. E77, E225
NAVIDEC, Inc. E249
NetSolve, Incorporated E252
Perot Systems
Corporation A1112
Science Applications
International
Corporation P438, P724
Unisys Corporation A1424

Internet & Intranet Software & Services

Art Technology Group,
Inc. E159
F5 Networks, Inc. E201
PCTEL, Inc. E261

Multimedia Production, Graphics & Publishing Software

Adobe Systems
Incorporated A76
Macromedia, Inc. E86, E235
Roxio, Inc. E281

Networking & Connectivity Software

BEA Systems, Inc. E33, E163
Citrix Systems, Inc. E42, E179
Micromuse Inc. E245
Novell, Inc. A1050

Other Application Software

Vitria Technology, Inc. E313

A=AMERICAN BUSINESS • E=EMERGING COMPANIES • P=PRIVATE COMPANIES • W=WORLD BUSINESS

Security Software & Services
Digimarc Corporation E**192**
Internet Security Systems,
  Inc. E**222**
Netegrity, Inc. E**96**, E251
RSA Security Inc. E**114**, E281

CONGLOMERATES
Conglomerates
Accor W**58**
Carlson Companies, Inc. P**106**,
  P567
Diageo plc W**206**
E.ON AG W**218**
EBSCO Industries Inc. P**170**,
  P601
Ergon, Inc. P**605**
General Electric Company A**646**
Hitachi, Ltd. W**260**
Hutchison Whampoa
  Limited W**272**
Hyundai Group W**274**
ITOCHU Corporation W**296**
Koç Holding A.S. W**318**
Koch Industries, Inc. A**834**,
  P**280**, P653
Koor Industries Ltd. W**322**
LG Group W**334**
The Marmon Group, Inc. P**312**,
  P665
Marubeni Corporation W**358**
Metromedia Company P**332**,
  P674
Mitsubishi Corporation W**370**
Nissho Iwai Corporation W**404**
Norsk Hydro ASA W**410**
Pacific Dunlop Limited W**428**
Preussag AG W**460**
RWE AG W**504**
Sammons Enterprises,
  Inc. P**720**
Samsung Group W**508**
Siemens AG W**536**
Sime Darby Berhad W**538**
Six Continents PLC W**544**
Suez W**558**
Swire Pacific Limited W**564**
Tata Enterprises W**566**
Textron Inc. A**1380**
Thermo Electron
  Corporation A**1382**
TOMEN Corporation W**602**
Tomkins PLC W**604**
Virgin Group Ltd. W**622**
Whitbread PLC W**638**
The Yucaipa Companies
  LLC P**524**, P777
Trading Companies
Jardine Matheson Holdings
  Limited W**306**
Mitsui & Co., Ltd. W**372**

CONSUMER PRODUCTS — DURABLES
Appliances
AB Electrolux W**210**
Conair Corporation P**580**
Goodman Manufacturing
  Company, L.P. P**618**
Maytag Corporation A**934**
Salton, Inc. E**116**, E283
Singer N.V. P**729**
Whirlpool Corporation A**1520**
Consumer Electronics
Bose Corporation P**92**, P559
Emerson Radio Corp. E**58**,
  E198
Koninklijke Philips Electronics
  N.V. W**444**
Matsushita Electric Industrial
  Co., Ltd. W**360**
Pioneer Corporation W**448**
Sony Corporation W**550**
Home Furnishings
Ashley Furniture Industries,
  Inc. P**544**
Furniture Brands International,
  Inc. A**630**
Klaussner Furniture Industries,
  Inc. P**652**
La-Z-Boy Incorporated A**854**
Leggett & Platt,
  Incorporated A**858**
LifeStyle Furnishings
  International Ltd. P**298**, P659
Newell Rubbermaid Inc. A**1022**
Pillowtex Corporation A**1134**
Sealy Corporation P**442**, P725
Serta, Inc. P**727**
Springs Industries, Inc. A**1316**,
  P**452**, P733
Housewares & Accessories
The Longaberger
  Company P**660**
Tupperware Corporation A**1414**
Waterford Wedgwood plc W**636**
WKI Holding Company,
  Inc. P**775**
The Yankee Candle Company,
  Inc. E**143**, E320
Jewelry, Watches & Clocks
Seiko Corporation W**528**
The Swatch Group Ltd. W**562**
**Lawn & Garden Equipment
& Small Tools & Accessories**
The Black & Decker
  Corporation A**264**
MTD Products Inc. P**679**
Snap-on Incorporated A**1294**
The Stanley Works A**1322**
The Toro Company A**1392**
**Miscellaneous Durable
Consumer Goods**
Jostens, Inc. P**262**, P647

**Office & Business Furniture
& Fixtures**
Falcon Products, Inc. E**202**
Haworth Inc. P**222**, P627
Herman Miller, Inc. A**706**
HON INDUSTRIES Inc. A**726**
Knoll, Inc. P**276**, P652
Lane Industries, Inc. P**655**
Steelcase Inc. A**1334**
**Photographic Equipment
& Supplies**
Concord Camera Corp. E**184**
Eastman Kodak Company A**524**
Fuji Photo Film Co., Ltd. W**234**
Polaroid Corporation A**1148**
**Professional Sports Gear
& Apparel**
adidas-Salomon AG W**62**
Reebok International
  Ltd. A**1194**
Russell Corporation A**1220**
The Topps Company, Inc. E**130**,
  E303
Sporting Goods
Colt's Manufacturing Company,
  Inc. P**132**, P578
Direct Focus, Inc. E**193**
ICON Health & Fitness,
  Inc. P**637**
**Toys, Games & Other
Recreational Goods**
Hasbro, Inc. A**692**
JAKKS Pacific, Inc. E**225**
LEGO Company W**332**
Mattel, Inc. A**926**
Nintendo Co., Ltd. W**394**
SEGA Corporation W**526**
Ty Inc. P**486**, P751
The Vermont Teddy Bear Co.,
  Inc. E**135**, E311
Yamaha Corporation W**648**

CONSUMER PRODUCTS — NON-DURABLES
Apparel
Benetton Group S.p.A. W**124**
Calvin Klein, Inc. P**100**, P564
Converse Inc. P**142**, P583
Hartmarx Corporation A**690**
Jones Apparel Group, Inc. A**804**
Kenneth Cole Productions,
  Inc. E**78**, E227
Levi Strauss & Co. A**868**, P**292**,
  P657
Liz Claiborne, Inc. A**880**
New Balance Athletic Shoe,
  Inc. P**686**
NIKE, Inc. A**1032**
Oakley, Inc. E**99**, E257
OshKosh B'Gosh, Inc. A**1068**
Polo Ralph Lauren
  Corporation A**1150**
Skechers U.S.A., Inc. E**289**
Steven Madden, Ltd. E**294**

Tommy Hilfiger
Corporation W**606**
Tropical Sportswear Int'l
Corporation E**305**
VF Corporation A**1474**
The Warnaco Group, Inc. A**1498**
Williamson-Dickie
Manufacturing Company P**773**

Business Forms & Other Office Supplies
Avery Dennison
Corporation A**210**
Deluxe Corporation A**480**
Moore Corporation
Limited W**378**

Cleaning Products
Church & Dwight Co.,
Inc. A**358**
The Clorox Company A**374**
Colgate-Palmolive
Company A**386**
The Dial Corporation A**486**
Kao Corporation W**308**
The Procter & Gamble
Company A**1164**
Reckitt Benckiser plc W**476**
S.C. Johnson & Son,
Inc. A**1246**, P**432**, P**722**

Luxury Goods
Gucci Group N.V. W**250**
LVMH Moët Hennessy Louis
Vuitton SA W**348**
Tiffany & Co. A**1384**

Miscellaneous Non-Durable Consumer Goods
Doane Pet Care Company P**595**
The Hartz Mountain
Corporation P**626**
Solo Cup Company P**731**

Personal Care Products
Avon Products, Inc. A**216**
The Estée Lauder Companies
Inc. A**564**
The Gillette Company A**656**
Kimberly-Clark
Corporation A**826**
L'Oréal SA W**342**
MacAndrews & Forbes Holdings
Inc. A**902**, P**304**, P**663**
Mary Kay Inc. P**316**, P**666**
Revlon, Inc. A**1200**
Shiseido Company,
Limited W**534**

DIVERSIFIED SERVICES

Accounting, Bookkeeping, Collection & Credit Reporting
Andersen A**172**, P**48**, P**540**,
W**90**
Deloitte Touche
Tohmatsu A**474**, P**154**, P**590**,
W**196**
Equifax Inc. A**558**
Ernst & Young
International A**562**, P**182**,
P**605**, W**222**

Grant Thornton
International P**206**, P**620**
H&R Block, Inc. A**680**
KPMG International A**840**,
P**286**, P**654**, W**324**
NCO Group, Inc. E**250**
PricewaterhouseCoopers A**1158**,
P**400–401**, P**705**, W**462**

Advertising
Bcom3 Group, Inc. P**72**, P**551**
Dentsu Inc. W**198**
The Interpublic Group of
Companies, Inc. A**772**
Omnicom Group Inc. A**1062**
Publicis Groupe S.A. W**466**
WPP Group plc W**646**

Building Maintenance & Related Services
Asplundh Tree Expert Co. P**545**
Encompass Services
Corporation A**548**
SC Johnson Commercial
Markets, Inc. P**722**
The ServiceMaster
Company A**1272**

Car & Truck Rental
AMERCO A**134**
Avis Group Holdings, Inc. A**212**
Budget Group, Inc. A**300**
Enterprise Rent-A-Car P**178**,
P**603**
Frank Consolidated
Enterprises P**611**
The Hertz Corporation A**710**

Charitable Organizations
American Cancer Society,
Inc. P**40**, P**537**
The American Red Cross P**44**,
P**538**
Goodwill Industries
International, Inc. P**618**
The Rockefeller
Foundation P**414**, P**715**
Salvation Army USA P**426**, P**720**
UJC of North America P**752**
United Way of America P**492**,
P**755**
YMCA of the USA P**777**

Consumer Services
AAA P**528**
Holberg Industries, Inc. P**236**,
P**633**

Foundations & Cultural Institutions
The Andrew W. Mellon
Foundation P**541**
Bill & Melinda Gates
Foundation P**78**, P**555**
The Ford Foundation P**194**,
P**610**
National Geographic
Society P**358**, P**683**
The Robert Wood Johnson
Foundation P**715**
Smithsonian Institution P**450**,
P**731**

W.K. Kellogg Foundation P**520**,
P**774**

Legal Services
Baker & McKenzie A**220**, P**66**,
P**548**
Pre-Paid Legal Services,
Inc. E**107**, E**269**
Skadden, Arps, Slate, Meagher &
Flom LLP A**1288**, P**446**, P**730**

Management Consulting Services
Arthur D. Little, Inc. P**54**, P**543**
Bain & Company P**64**, P**548**
Booz-Allen & Hamilton
Inc. P**88**, P**558**
The Boston Consulting
Group P**94**, P**559**
The Corporate Executive Board
Company E**186**
Hewitt Associates LLC P**631**
The Management Network
Group, Inc. E**236**
MAXIMUS, Inc. E**88**, E**238**
McKinsey & Company A**948**,
P**326**, P**670**
Towers Perrin P**480**, P**746**

Market & Business Research Services
ACNielsen Corporation A**66**
Forrester Research, Inc. E**63**,
E**205**
NetRatings, Inc. E**251**
The Source Information
Management Company E**290**

Marketing & Public Relations Services
PDI, Inc. E**261**
Vertis Inc. P**506**, P**765**

Membership Organizations
AARP P**28**, P**529**
AFL-CIO P**34**, P**532**
International Brotherhood of
Teamsters P**246**, P**641**
Rotary International P**420**,
P**718**

Miscellaneous Business Services
4Kids Entertainment, Inc. E**147**
Automatic Data Processing,
Inc. A**204**
Cintas Corporation A**364**
Copart, Inc. E**45**, E**185**
CTN Media Group, Inc. E**188**
eBay Inc. E**54**, E**196**
eMerge Interactive, Inc. E**197**
The Freeman Companies P**611**
F.Y.I. Incorporated E**207**
International Management
Group P**250**, P**641**
Muzak LLC P**350**, P**681**
Sotheby's Holdings, Inc. A**1304**
Viad Corp A**1478**

Personal Services
Regis Corporation A**1196**
Service Corporation
International A**1268**

A=AMERICAN BUSINESS · E=EMERGING COMPANIES · P=PRIVATE COMPANIES · W=WORLD BUSINESS

**Printing, Photocopying
& Graphic Design**

Dai Nippon Printing Co.,
Ltd. **W186**
Kinko's, Inc. **P274**, P651
Quad/Graphics, Inc. **P404**, P708
Taylor Corporation **P742**

**Schools & Educational
Services — Colleges
& Universities**

Boston University **P560**
California State University **P98**,
P564
The City University of New
York **P128**, P576
Columbia University **P134**,
P579
Cornell University **P584**
Duke University **P598**
Emory University **P602**
Harvard University **P220**, P626
Indiana University **P638**
The Johns Hopkins
University **P646**
Louisiana State University
System **P661**
Loyola University of
Chicago **P661**
Massachusetts Institute of
Technology **P667**
New York University **P689**
Northwestern University **P378**,
P691
The Ohio State University **P382**,
P693
The Pennsylvania State
University **P699**
Stanford University **P456**, P735
State University of New
York **P460**, P736
The Texas A&M University
System **P470**, P743
The University of Alabama
System **P755**
University of California **P494**,
P755
The University of Chicago **P496**,
P756
University of Florida **P756**
University of Illinois **P756**
The University of Iowa **P757**
The University of
Kentucky **P757**
University of
Massachusetts **P757**
The University of
Michigan **P758**
University of Minnesota **P758**
University of Missouri
System **P758**
The University of
Nebraska **P759**
The University of
Pennsylvania **P759**
University of Phoenix
Online **E309**

University of Pittsburgh of the
Commonwealth System of
Higher Education **P759**
University of Rochester **P760**
University of Southern
California **P760**
University of Tennessee **P760**
The University of Texas
System **P498**, P761
University of Virginia **P761**
University of Washington **P761**
The University of Wisconsin
System **P500**, P762
University System of
Maryland **P762**
Vanderbilt University **P763**
Washington University in St.
Louis **P769**
Yale University **P776**

**Schools & Educational
Services — Education & Training
Services**

Canterbury Consulting Group,
Inc. **E36**, E170
Career Education
Corporation **E172**
New Horizons Worldwide,
Inc. **E252**

**Security & Protection Products
& Services**

Armor Holdings, Inc. **E29**, E158
Cornell Companies, Inc. **E186**
Securitas AB **W524**
The Wackenhut
Corporation **A1488**
Wackenhut Corrections
Corporation **E138**, E314

**Staffing, Outsourcing & Other
Human Resources**

Administaff, Inc. **A74**
Ceridian Corporation **A342**
EPIX Holdings
Corporation **P603**
Express Personnel
Services **P606**
Hall, Kinion & Associates,
Inc. **E210**
Kelly Services, Inc. **A818**
Manpower Inc. **A910**
MSX International, Inc. **P679**
Robert Half International
Inc. **A1208**
TAC Worldwide
Companies **P741**
TeamStaff, Inc. **E125**, E299
TTC Illinois, Inc. **P750**

**Technical & Scientific Research
Services**

Battelle Memorial Institute **P70**,
P551
SEMATECH, Inc. **P444**, P726
SRI International **P454**, P734

**Telemarketing, Call Centers
& Other Direct Marketing**

RMH Teleservices, Inc. **E113**,
E280

TeleTech Holdings, Inc. **E127**,
E300

DRUGS

Biotechnology — Medicine

Albany Molecular Research,
Inc. **E150**
Amgen Inc. **A160**
Celgene Corporation **E174**
Enzon, Inc. **E199**
Genentech, Inc. **A640**
IDEC Pharmaceuticals
Corporation **E217**
Immunex Corporation **E71**,
E218
MedImmune, Inc. **E90**, E240

Biotechnology — Research

Applera Corporation **P542**
Diversa Corporation **E193**

Diagnostic Substances

Cytyc Corporation **E50**, E190
Dade Behring Inc. **P587**

Drug Delivery Systems

Andrx Corporation **E156**
Noven Pharmaceuticals,
Inc. **E255**

Drug Manufacturers

Abbott Laboratories **A58**
Allergan, Inc. **A118**
American Home Products
Corporation **A148**
Aventis **W102**
Bristol-Myers Squibb
Company **A290**
Connetics Corporation **E184**
Eli Lilly and Company **A540**
GlaxoSmithKline plc **W246**
Johnson & Johnson **A800**
King Pharmaceuticals,
Inc. **E229**
Medicis Pharmaceutical
Corporation **E89**, E240
Merck & Co., Inc. **A956**
Novartis AG **W414**
Novo Nordisk A/S **W416**
Pfizer Inc **A1118**
Pharmacia Corporation **A1122**
PolyMedica Corporation **E105**,
E268
Purdue Pharma L.P. **P707**
Roche Group **W492**
Salix Pharmaceuticals,
Ltd. **E283**
Schering-Plough
Corporation **A1250**
TAP Pharmaceutical Products
Inc. **P741**

Drugs & Sundries — Wholesale

AmerisourceBergen
Corporation **A156**
Cardinal Health, Inc. **A320**
Kinray, Inc. **P651**
McKesson Corporation **A946**
Priority Healthcare
Corporation **E270**

Quality King Distributors
Inc. **P709**

Vitamins, Nutritionals & Other Health-Related Products

Nikken Global Inc. **P689**

ELECTRONICS & MISCELLANEOUS TECHNOLOGY

Computer Boards, Cards & Connector Products

Creative Technology Ltd. **W180**
Dataram Corporation **E190**
Molex Incorporated **A982**
RadiSys Corporation **E109**, **E274**
SimpleTech, Inc. **E289**

Contract Electronics Manufacturing

DDi Corp. **E191**
Jabil Circuit, Inc. **A782**
Pemstar Inc. **E262**
Plexus Corp. **E104**, **E267**
Sanmina Corporation **A1240**
SCI Systems, Inc. **A1256**
Solectron Corporation **A1298**
SYNNEX Information
Technologies, Inc. **P740**
TTM Technologies, Inc. **E306**

Diversified Electronics

Alcoa Fujikura Ltd. **P535**
CTS Corporation **E189**
Diodes Incorporated **E192**
International Rectifier
Corporation **E74**, **E222**
Sharp Corporation **W532**
Spectrum Control, Inc. **E124**, **E292**
Tatung Co. **W570**
TDK Corporation **W572**
Vishay Intertechnology,
Inc. **A1482**

Electronic Test & Measurement Instruments

Agilent Technologies, Inc. **A98**
Frequency Electronics,
Inc. **E206**
Ixia **E224**
Newport Corporation **E253**
Photon Dynamics, Inc. **E266**
Sunrise Telecom
Incorporated **E296**
Symmetricom, Inc. **E297**
Tektronix, Inc. **A1358**
Teradyne, Inc. **A1372**
Tollgrade Communications,
Inc. **E302**

Electronics Distribution

All American Semiconductor,
Inc. **E151**
Arrow Electronics, Inc. **A196**
Avnet, Inc. **A214**
Nu Horizons Electronics
Corp. **E97**, **E256**

Pioneer-Standard Electronics,
Inc. **A1140**
Reptron Electronics, Inc. **E278**
ScanSource, Inc. **E118**, **E284**
Somera Communications,
Inc. **E290**
TTI, Inc. **P750**

Miscellaneous Electronics

BEI Technologies, Inc. **E164**
L-3 Communications Holdings,
Inc. **A846**
PECO II, Inc. **E261**

Scientific & Technical Instruments

FEI Company **E203**
Fisher Scientific International
Inc. **A600**
Measurement Specialties,
Inc. **E240**
Mykrolis Corporation **E248**
PerkinElmer, Inc. **A1110**

Semiconductor — Broad Line

Advanced Micro Devices,
Inc. **A82**
Intel Corporation **A760**
National Semiconductor
Corporation **A1002**
Semtech Corporation **E119**,
E286
STMicroelectronics N.V. **W554**
Texas Instruments
Incorporated **A1378**

Semiconductor Equipment & Materials

Advanced Energy Industries,
Inc. **E24**, **E149**
Amkor Technology, Inc. **A162**
Applied Materials, Inc. **A188**
Asyst Technologies, Inc. **E31**,
E160
ATMI, Inc. **E160**
Axcelis Technologies, Inc. **E161**
AXT, Inc. **E162**
Brooks Automation, Inc. **E35**,
E166
Cohu, Inc. **E44**, **E182**
Credence Systems
Corporation **E46**, **E187**
Cymer, Inc. **E49**, **E189**
Electro Scientific Industries,
Inc. **E56**, **E196**
Electroglas, Inc. **E57**, **E197**
Helix Technology
Corporation **E213**
inTEST Corporation **E223**
Kopin Corporation **E229**
Kulicke and Soffa Industries,
Inc. **E81**, **E230**
Metron Technology N.V. **E244**
MKS Instruments, Inc. **E246**
Nanometrics Incorporated **E248**
Nikon Corporation **W392**
QuickLogic Corporation **E273**
Rudolph Technologies,
Inc. **E282**
Therma-Wave, Inc. **E300**

Tokyo Electron Limited **W600**
Varian Semiconductor
Equipment Associates,
Inc. **E133**, **E310**

Semiconductor — Integrated Circuits

ANADIGICS, Inc. **E28**, **E156**
Analog Devices, Inc. **A170**
Centillium Communications,
Inc. **E174**
Conexant Systems, Inc. **A410**
Elantec Semiconductor,
Inc. **E55**, **E196**
Linear Technology
Corporation **E84**, **E233**
Micrel, Incorporated **E92**, **E244**
Pericom Semiconductor
Corporation **E263**
Silicon Laboratories Inc. **E288**
TranSwitch Corporation **E304**
Vitesse Semiconductor
Corporation **E136**, **E313**

Semiconductor — Memory Chips

Catalyst Semiconductor,
Inc. **E173**
Kingston Technology
Company **P272**, **P651**
Micron Technology, Inc. **A970**
SanDisk Corporation **E117**,
E284
Silicon Storage Technology,
Inc. **E121**, **E288**
Virage Logic Corporation **E313**
White Electronic Designs
Corporation **E317**

Semiconductor — Specialized

Alpha Industries, Inc. **E152**
Aware, Inc. **E161**
Cree, Inc. **E47**, **E188**
DSP Group, Inc. **E194**
II-VI Incorporated **E20**, **E146**
IXYS Corporation **E76**, **E224**
Lattice Semiconductor
Corporation **E82**, **E232**
LSI Logic Corporation **A894**
Microchip Technology
Incorporated **E93**, **E245**
Multilink Technology
Corporation **E247**
NVIDIA Corporation **E256**
Oak Technology, Inc. **E98**, **E257**
Pixelworks, Inc. **E267**
PLX Technology, Inc. **E267**
QUALCOMM
Incorporated **A1182**
RF Micro Devices, Inc. **E280**
TriQuint Semiconductor,
Inc. **E305**
WJ Communications, Inc. **E318**

ENERGY

Integrated Oil & Gas

Amerada Hess
Corporation **A132**
BP p.l.c. **W136**

A=AMERICAN BUSINESS • E=EMERGING COMPANIES • P=PRIVATE COMPANIES • W=WORLD BUSINESS

Chevron Corporation A352
Conoco Inc. A412
Eni S.p.A. W216
Exxon Mobil Corporation A576
Imperial Oil Limited W280
OAO LUKOIL W346
OMV Aktiengesellschaft W424
PETRÓLEO BRASILEIRO S.A. - PETROBRAS W436
Petróleos de Venezuela S.A. W438
Petróleos Mexicanos W440
Phillips Petroleum Company A1128
Repsol YPF, S.A. W482
Royal Dutch/Shell Group W500
Shell Oil Company A1276
Texaco Inc. A1376
TOTAL FINA ELF S.A. W612
USX-Marathon Group A1460
YPF, S.A. W650

Oil & Gas Equipment
Baker Hughes Incorporated A222
FMC Corporation A612

Oil & Gas Exploration & Production
3TEC Energy Corporation E146
Anadarko Petroleum Corporation A168
Apache Corporation A184
Barnwell Industries, Inc. E163
Berry Petroleum Company E164
Burlington Resources Inc. A310
Cabot Oil & Gas Corporation E168
Carrizo Oil & Gas, Inc. E173
Chesapeake Energy Corporation E39, E176
Clayton Williams Energy, Inc. E180
Comstock Resources, Inc. E183
Denbury Resources Inc. E191
Devon Energy Corporation A482
Equity Oil Company E199
Evergreen Resources, Inc. E200
EXCO Resources, Inc. E200
The Exploration Company of Delaware, Inc. E201
Forest Oil Corporation E62, E205
Goodrich Petroleum Corporation E209
Greka Energy Corporation E209
The Houston Exploration Company E216
Hunt Consolidated Inc. P635
Kerr-McGee Corporation A820
Key Production Company, Inc. E228
Louis Dreyfus Natural Gas Corp. E234
Magnum Hunter Resources, Inc. E235

Maynard Oil Company E238
The Meridian Resource Corporation E242
Mitchell Energy & Development Corp. A978
Newfield Exploration Company E253
North Coast Energy, Inc. E254
OAO Gazprom W242
Occidental Petroleum Corporation A1054
PANACO, Inc. E260
Parallel Petroleum Corporation E260
Patina Oil & Gas Corporation E260
Penn Virginia Corporation E262
PetroCorp Incorporated E264
Petroleum Development Corporation E264
PetroQuest Energy, Inc. E264
Pogo Producing Company E268
Prima Energy Corporation E270
Prize Energy Corp. E270
Pure Resources, Inc. E272
Quicksilver Resources Inc. E273
Remington Oil and Gas Corporation E278
Spinnaker Exploration Company E292
St. Mary Land & Exploration Company E282
Stone Energy Corporation E295
Swift Energy Company E297
Tom Brown, Inc. E129, E302
Ultra Petroleum Corporation E307
United States Exploration, Inc. E308
Unocal Corporation A1438
Vintage Petroleum, Inc. E312
Westport Resources Corporation E316
XTO Energy Inc. E319

Oil & Gas Pipelines & Storage
El Paso Corporation A536
EOTT Energy Partners, L.P. A556
Kinder Morgan Energy Partners, L.P. E228
Plains Resources Inc. A1144
Sunoco Logistics Partners L.P. P738
TC PipeLines, LP E298
The Williams Companies, Inc. A1528

Oil & Gas Refining & Marketing
Adams Resources & Energy, Inc. A68
Crown Central Petroleum Corporation P586
Duke Energy Field Services Corporation P598
Equilon Enterprises LLC P604

George E. Warren Corporation P614
Marathon Ashland Petroleum LLC P664
Motiva Enterprises LLC P344, P679
ONEOK Inc. A1064
Pennzoil-Quaker State Company A1096
Polski Koncern Naftowy ORLEN S.A. W456
Premcor Inc. P704
Red Apple Group, Inc. P712
Sinclair Oil Corporation P729
Sunoco, Inc. A1344
Tesoro Petroleum Corporation A1374
Valero Energy Corporation A1466

Oil & Gas Services
Arctic Slope Regional Corporation P542
Halliburton Company A676
Hanover Compressor Company E210
Key Energy Services, Inc. E79, E227
MarkWest Hydrocarbon, Inc. E237
Schlumberger Limited A1252
TMBR/Sharp Drilling, Inc. E301
Unit Corporation E308

Petroleum Product Distribution
Apex Oil Company, Inc. P542
Chemoil Corporation P574
Chesapeake Utilities Corporation E177
Global Companies LLC P616
Gulf Oil, L.P. P624
Tauber Oil Company P742
Transammonia, Inc. P748
Truman Arnold Companies P749
Warren Equities Inc. P769

FINANCIAL SERVICES
Asset Management
Affiliated Managers Group, Inc. E149
American Century Companies, Inc. P537
AXA Financial, Inc. A218
California Public Employees' Retirement System A314, P96, P563
Eaton Vance Corp. E53, E195
FMR Corp. A614, P190, P609
Gabelli Asset Management Inc. E65, E207
Teachers Insurance and Annuity Association-College Retirement Equities Fund A1354, P466, P742
The Vanguard Group, Inc. A1468, P504, P764
Waddell & Reed Financial, Inc. E315

Commercial Lending
AgAmerica, FCB P**533**
AgFirst Farm Credit Bank P**533**
AgriBank, FCB P**533**
Allied Capital Corporation E**151**
National Rural Utilities
 Cooperative Finance
 Corporation P**685**

Consumer Loans
AmeriCredit Corp. E**27**, E154
Capital One Financial
 Corporation A**318**
CompuCredit Corporation E**183**
Household International,
 Inc. A**734**
MasterCard International
 Incorporated A**924**, P**322**,
 P**668**
MBNA Corporation A**936**
Providian Financial
 Corporation A**1170**
USA Education, Inc. A**1448**
Visa International A**1480**, P**508**,
 P**766**
WFS Financial Inc. E**317**

**Investment Banking
& Brokerage**
A.G. Edwards, Inc. A**94**
The Bear Stearns Companies
 Inc. A**238**
Cantor Fitzgerald, L.P. P**565**
The Charles Schwab
 Corporation A**348**
Credit Suisse First Boston A**448**
E*TRADE Group, Inc. A**566**
The Goldman Sachs Group,
 Inc. A**660**
The Jones Financial Companies,
 L.P., LLP P**260**, P646
Ladenburg Thalmann Financial
 Services Inc. E**231**
Lehman Brothers Holdings
 Inc. A**860**
Linsco/Private Ledger
 Corp. P**659**
Merrill Lynch & Co., Inc. A**960**
Morgan Stanley Dean Witter &
 Co. A**988**
Nomura Holdings, Inc. W**408**
Siebert Financial Corp. E**287**
Tucker Anthony Sutro E**132**,
 E306

Investment Firms
Berkshire Hathaway Inc. A**252**
The Carlyle Group P**110**, P567
The Dyson-Kissner-Moran
 Corporation P**600**
Equity Group Investments,
 L.L.C. A**560**, P**180**, P**604**
Gores Technology Group P**619**
Hicks, Muse, Tate & Furst
 Incorporated A**714**, P**232**,
 P631
Knowledge Universe, Inc. P**278**,
 P652
Kohlberg Kravis Roberts &
 Co. A**836**, P**282**, P**653**

Michigan Avenue Partners P**675**
Platinum Equity Holdings P**703**
Safeguard Scientifics,
 Inc. A**1232**
SOFTBANK CORP. W**548**
Texas Pacific Group P**474**, P**744**
Tracinda Corporation P**747**
Vulcan Northwest Inc. P**510**,
 P767
Wingate Partners P**518**, P**774**

Leasing
Comdisco, Inc. A**392**
GATX Corporation A**638**
National Equipment Services,
 Inc. E**249**
TTX Company P**751**

Miscellaneous Financial Services
Actrade Financial Technologies,
 Ltd. E**21**, E148
A-Mark Financial
 Corporation P**536**
American Stock Exchange,
 Inc. P**46**, P539
Asta Funding, Inc. E**159**
Clark/Bardes, Inc. E**180**
Investors Financial Services
 Corp. E**223**
LaBranche & Co Inc. E**230**
National Association of
 Securities Dealers, Inc. A**996**,
 P**352**, P682
New York Stock Exchange,
 Inc. A**1018**, P**374**, P**688**

**Mortgage Banking & Related
Services**
American Business Financial
 Services, Inc. E**153**
American Home Mortgage
 Holdings, Inc. E**154**
Charter Municipal Mortgage
 Acceptance Company E**176**
Countrywide Credit Industries,
 Inc. A**438**
Doral Financial
 Corporation E**193**
Fannie Mae A**580**
Federal Agricultural Mortgage
 Corporation E**203**
Freddie Mac A**626**

Royalty Trusts
BP Prudhoe Bay Royalty
 Trust E**166**
Permian Basin Royalty
 Trust E**263**
San Juan Basin Royalty
 Trust E**283**

Services to Financial Companies
First Data Corporation A**596**
State Street Corporation A**1332**
U.S. Central Credit Union P**763**

FOOD, BEVERAGE
& TOBACCO
**Agricultural Operations
& Products**
Archer Daniels Midland
 Company A**192**
Bartlett and Company P**549**
Chiquita Brands International,
 Inc. A**354**
ContiGroup Companies,
 Inc. A**426**, P**140**, P583
Dole Food Company, Inc. A**494**
Farmland Industries, Inc. A**582**,
 P**184**, P606
J.R. Simplot Company P**264**,
 P648
King Ranch, Inc. A**828**, P**270**,
 P650
Michael Foods, Inc. P**674**
Southern States Cooperative,
 Incorporated P**732**
Sunkist Growers, Inc. P**464**,
 P738

Agricultural Services
Ag Processing Inc P**36**, P**532**
Agway Inc. P**38**, P**534**
Cargill, Incorporated A**324**,
 P**104**, P**566**
Cenex Harvest States
 Cooperatives P**122**, P571
DeBruce Grain, Inc. P**589**
Dunavant Enterprises,
 Inc. P**599**
GROWMARK, Inc. P**622**
Riceland Foods, Inc. P**714**
The Scoular Company P**724**
Staple Cotton Cooperative
 Association P**735**

Agriculture — Biotechnology
Wilbur-Ellis Company P**772**

**Bottlers & Wholesale
Distributors**
Coca-Cola Bottling Company of
 Chicago P**577**
Coca-Cola Enterprises
 Inc. A**384**
Dr Pepper/Seven Up Bottling
 Group, Inc. P**597**
Glazer's Wholesale Drug
 Company Inc. P**616**
Honickman Affiliates P**634**
National Distributing Company,
 Inc. P**682**
The Pepsi Bottling Group,
 Inc. A**1102**
PepsiAmericas, Inc. A**1104**
Southern Wine & Spirits of
 America, Inc. P**732**
Sunbelt Beverage
 Corporation P**738**
Topa Equities, Ltd. P**746**
Wirtz Corporation P**774**
Young's Market Company,
 LLC P**777**

Brewers
Adolph Coors Company A**78**

Anheuser-Busch Companies,
Inc. A174
Carlsberg A/S W162
Foster's Group Limited W230
Heineken N.V. W254
Interbrew S.A. W288
Kirin Brewery Company,
Limited W314
Molson Inc. W376
San Miguel Corporation W510
S&P Company P428, P721
South African Breweries
plc W552

Canned & Frozen Foods
Del Monte Foods
Company A470
Schwan's Sales Enterprises,
Inc. P436, P724

Dairy Products
Associated Milk Producers
Incorporated P58, P546
California Dairies Inc. P563
Dairy Farmers of America P148,
P587
Dairylea Cooperative Inc. P588
Dean Foods Company A466
Dreyer's Grand Ice Cream,
Inc. A510
Foremost Farms USA,
Cooperative P610
Groupe Danone W192
Land O'Lakes, Inc. A850, P288,
P654
Leprino Foods Company P657
Prairie Farms Dairy Inc. P704
Quality Chekd Dairies,
Inc. P708
Schreiber Foods, Inc. P723
Suiza Foods Corporation A1338
Suprema Specialties, Inc. E296
WestFarm Foods P771

Distillers
Allied Domecq PLC W84
Bacardi Limited W108
Brown-Forman
Corporation A296

Diversified Foods — Major
Campbell Soup Company A316
ConAgra Foods, Inc. A408
General Mills, Inc. A648
H.J. Heinz Company A722
Kraft Foods Inc. A842
Nestlé S.A. W388
PepsiCo, Inc. A1106
The Pillsbury Company A1136
The Quaker Oats
Company A1180
Sara Lee Corporation A1242
Unilever W618

Diversified Foods — Other
Goya Foods, Inc. P204, P619
Rich Products
Corporation P714

Food Wholesale — to Grocers
Advantage/ESM Ferolie P530

Alex Lee, Inc. P535
Associated Food Stores,
Inc. P545
Associated Grocers, Inc. P546
Associated Wholesale Grocers,
Inc. P62, P547
Associated Wholesalers,
Inc. P547
Bozzuto's Inc. P560
C&S Wholesale Grocers,
Inc. P102, P565
Core-Mark International,
Inc. P584
Di Giorgio Corporation P592
Eby-Brown Company P601
Fleming Companies, Inc. A606
Grocers Supply Co., Inc. P622
GSC Enterprises, Inc. P623
H.T. Hackney Co. P635
Nash Finch Company A994
Purity Wholesale Grocers,
Inc. P708
Roundy's, Inc. P422, P718
Shamrock Foods
Company P728
Spartan Stores, Inc. A1312
SUPERVALU INC. A1348
Topco Associates, Inc. P478,
P746
Unified Western Grocers,
Inc. P488, P752
Wakefern Food
Corporation A1490, P514,
P768

Food Wholesale — to Restaurants
Ben E. Keith Company P553
Dot Foods, Inc. P596
Golden State Foods P202, P617
Gordon Food Service P618
International Multifoods
Corporation A768
Keystone Foods LLC P650
The Martin-Brower Company,
L.L.C. P665
MBM Corporation P669
Performance Food Group
Company A1108
Reyes Holdings LLC P713
Services Group of
America P727
SYSCO Corporation A1350

Grains, Breads & Cereals
The Connell Company P581
Flowers Foods, Inc. A608
Interstate Bakeries
Corporation A774
Keebler Foods Company A814
Kellogg Company A816
McKee Foods Corporation P669

Meat Products
Foster Farms P610
Gold Kist Inc. P200, P616
Hormel Foods
Corporation A730
IBP, Inc. A742

Perdue Farms
Incorporated P392, P700
Pilgrim's Pride
Corporation A1132
Rosen's Diversified, Inc. P717
Smithfield Foods, Inc. A1290
Tyson Foods, Inc. A1418
Wolverine Packing
Company P775

Other Processed & Packaged Goods
McCormick & Company,
Incorporated A938
Monterey Pasta Company E247

Soft Drinks
The Coca-Cola Company A382
Ocean Spray Cranberries,
Inc. P380, P692

Sugar & Confectionery
American Crystal Sugar
Company P538
Cadbury Schweppes plc W154
Hershey Foods
Corporation A708
Mars, Incorporated A914, P314,
P665
Russell Stover Candies
Inc. P424, P719
Tate & Lyle PLC W568
Wm. Wrigley Jr.
Company A1526

Tobacco Products
British American Tobacco
p.l.c. W142
DIMON Incorporated A492
Gallaher Group Plc W240
Imperial Tobacco Group
PLC W282
Japan Tobacco Inc. W304
Philip Morris Companies
Inc. A1126
R.J. Reynolds Tobacco Holdings,
Inc. A1204
Star Scientific, Inc. E293
Universal Corporation A1436
UST Inc. A1458

Wineries
Constellation Brands, Inc. A422
E. & J. Gallo Winery A520,
P168, P600

HEALTH PRODUCTS & SERVICES
Health Care Plans
Aetna Inc. A90
Anthem Insurance Companies,
Inc. A178
Blue Cross and Blue Shield
Association A268, P82, P556
Blue Cross and Blue Shield of
Massachusetts, Inc. P84, P557
Blue Cross Blue Shield of
Michigan P86, P557
Cerulean Companies, Inc. P572

Delta Dental Plan of
California P**591**
Empire HealthChoice,
Inc. P**174**, P**602**
Group Health Cooperative of
Puget Sound P**622**
Harvard Pilgrim Health Care,
Inc. P**626**
Health Insurance Plan of Greater
New York P**628**
Health Net, Inc. A**696**
Highmark Inc. A**716**, P**234**,
P**632**
Humana Inc. A**738**
Kaiser Foundation Health Plan,
Inc. A**810**, P**266**, P**649**
Oxford Health Plans,
Inc. A**1076**
PacifiCare Health Systems,
Inc. A**1080**
Tufts Associated Health Plans,
Inc. P**751**
UnitedHealth Group
Incorporated A**1434**
WellPoint Health Networks
Inc. A**1506**

Home Health Care
Amedisys, Inc. E**152**

Hospitals
Adventist Health P**530**
Advocate Health Care P**531**
Allina Health System P**536**
Ascension Health P**56**, P**544**
Banner Health System P**549**
Baylor Health Care
System P**551**
BJC Health System P**555**
Bon Secours Health System,
Inc. P**557**
CareGroup, Inc. P**566**
Carilion Health System P**566**
Carondelet Health System P**568**
Catholic Health East P**114**,
P**569**
Catholic Health
Initiatives P**116**, P**569**
Catholic Healthcare
Network P**570**
Catholic Healthcare
Partners P**570**
Catholic Healthcare West P**118**,
P**570**
CHRISTUS Health P**575**
Detroit Medical Center P**591**
HCA, Inc. A**694**
Health Midwest P**629**
Henry Ford Health
System P**630**
IASIS Healthcare
Corporation P**637**
Inova Health System P**639**
Intermountain Health
Care P**640**
Johns Hopkins Medicine P**645**
Manor Care, Inc. A**908**
Mayo Foundation P**324**, P**668**
MedStar Health P**671**

Memorial Hermann Healthcare
System P**671**
Memorial Sloan-Kettering
Cancer Center P**672**
Montefiore Medical
Center P**678**
New York City Health and
Hospitals Corporation P**368**,
P**687**
North Shore-Long Island Jewish
Health System P**690**
Novant Health, Inc. P**691**
OhioHealth P**694**
Partners HealthCare System,
Inc. P**697**
Presbyterian Healthcare
Services P**704**
Provena Health P**706**
Providence Health System P**706**
Province Healthcare
Company E**271**
Rush System for Health P**719**
Sentara Healthcare P**726**
Sisters of Charity of
Leavenworth Health Services
Corporation P**729**
Sisters of Mercy Health System-
St. Louis P**730**
SSM Health Care System
Inc. P**734**
Sutter Health P**739**
Tenet Healthcare
Corporation A**1366**
Texas Health Resources P**744**
Trinity Health P**748**
Wake Forest University Baptist
Medical Center P**768**
William Beaumont
Hospital P**773**

Long-Term Care Facilities
Beverly Enterprises, Inc. A**258**
Life Care Centers of
America P**658**
Select Medical
Corporation E**286**
Sun Healthcare Group,
Inc. A**1340**
Sunrise Assisted Living,
Inc. E**295**

Medical Appliances & Equipment
ArthroCare Corporation E**159**
Beckman Coulter, Inc. A**242**
Hillenbrand Industries,
Inc. A**718**
Imatron Inc. E**218**
INAMED Corporation E**219**
Medtronic, Inc. A**952**
Medtronic MiniMed E**241**
Vasomedical, Inc. E**311**
ZOLL Medical
Corporation E**144**, E**320**

Medical Instruments & Supplies
Bausch & Lomb
Incorporated A**234**
Baxter International Inc. A**236**
Becton, Dickinson and
Company A**244**

Boston Scientific
Corporation A**282**
C. R. Bard, Inc. A**444**
Guidant Corporation A**674**
Medline Industries, Inc. P**670**
North American Scientific,
Inc. E**254**
ResMed Inc. E**112**, E**279**

Medical Laboratories & Research
IMPATH Inc. E**72**, E**218**

**Medical Practice Management
& Services**
AdvancePCS, Inc. A**84**
American Dental Partners,
Inc. E**153**
AmeriPath, Inc. E**155**
Express Scripts, Inc. A**574**
NovaMed Eyecare, Inc. E**255**
OrthAlliance, Inc. E**259**
RehabCare Group, Inc. E**111**,
E**277**
Team Health, Inc. P**743**

Medical Products Distribution
Caremark Rx, Inc. A**322**
Owens & Minor, Inc. A**1070**

Specialized Health Services
Accredo Health,
Incorporated E**147**
America Service Group
Inc. E**153**
AmSurg Corp. E**155**
Continucare Corporation E**185**
Dynacq International, Inc. E**195**
HEALTHSOUTH
Corporation A**698**
Magellan Health Services,
Inc. A**904**
Metropolitan Health Networks,
Inc. E**244**
UniHealth Foundation P**753**

INSURANCE
Accident & Health Insurance
AFLAC Incorporated A**92**
Conseco, Inc. A**414**
Golden Rule Insurance
Company P**617**
Health Care Service
Corporation P**226**, P**628**
HealthExtras, Inc. E**211**

Insurance Brokers
Aon Corporation A**182**
Marsh & McLennan Companies,
Inc. A**916**
Security Benefit Group,
Inc. P**725**

Life Insurance
Aid Association for
Lutherans/Lutheran
Brotherhood P**534**
AMP Limited W**88**
The Guardian Life Insurance
Company of America P**214**,
P**623**

Jefferson-Pilot
Corporation A**794**
John Hancock Financial
Services, Inc. A**798**
Massachusetts Mutual Life
Insurance Company A**922**,
P**320**, P**667**
Metropolitan Life Insurance
Company A**964**
Minnesota Mutual Companies,
Inc. P**677**
The MONY Group Inc. A**986**
New York Life Insurance
Company A**1016**, P**370**, P**688**
Nippon Life Insurance
Company W**396**
Northwestern Mutual A**1048**,
P**376**, P**690**
Pacific Mutual Holding
Company P**384**, P**695**
Penn Mutual Life Insurance
Co. P**698**
The Principal Financial
Group A**1162**
Prudential Financial A**1172**
Torchmark Corporation A**1390**
The Union Central Life
Insurance Company P**753**
Universal American Financial
Corp. E**309**

Multiline Insurance
AEGON N.V. W**64**
Allianz AG W**82**
Allmerica Financial
Corporation A**124**
American International Group,
Inc. A**150**
American United Life Insurance
Company P**539**
Amica Mutual Insurance
Company P**540**
Assicurazioni Generali
S.p.A. W**98**
AXA W**104**
Ceres Group, Inc. E**175**
CIGNA Corporation A**360**
CNA Financial
Corporation A**378**
The Hartford Financial Services
Group, Inc. A**688**
ING Groep N.V. W**286**
Liberty Mutual Insurance
Companies A**874**, P**294**, P**658**
Lincoln National
Corporation A**878**
Lloyd's of London W**336**
Loews Corporation A**884**
MEEMIC Holdings, Inc. E**241**
The Mutual of Omaha
Companies P**348**, P**680**
National Life Insurance
Co. P**684**
Nationwide A**1008**, P**364**, P**685**
Ohio Farmers Insurance
Company P**693**
Prudential plc W**464**
SAFECO Corporation A**1230**

Sentry Insurance, A Mutual
Company P**726**
Trustmark Insurance
Company P**750**
The Union Labor Life Insurance
Company P**754**
UNUMProvident A**1440**
USAA A**1452**, P**502**, P**763**
Zurich Financial Services W**652**

Property/Casualty Insurance
The Allstate Corporation A**126**
American Family Insurance
Group P**42**, P**538**
American Financial Group,
Inc. A**144**
The Chubb Corporation A**356**
Kemper Insurance
Companies P**268**, P**650**
Philadelphia Consolidated
Holding Corp. E**265**
The Progressive
Corporation A**1168**
The St. Paul Companies,
Inc. A**1236**
State Farm Insurance
Companies A**1330**, P**458**, P**735**
The Tokio Marine and Fire
Insurance Company,
Limited W**596**

Reinsurance
Münchener Rückversicherungs-
Gesellschaft
Aktiengesellschaft W**380**

**Surety, Title & Miscellaneous
Insurance**
Federated Insurance
Companies P**607**
Fidelity National Financial,
Inc. A**590**
The First American
Corporation A**594**
Pension Benefit Guaranty
Corporation P**388**, P**699**
Radian Group Inc. E**108**, E**274**

LEISURE
Gambling Resorts & Casinos
Black Hawk Gaming &
Development Company,
Inc. E**165**
Harrah's Entertainment,
Inc. A**684**
Horseshoe Gaming Holding
Corp. P**634**
Mandalay Resort Group A**906**
Mashantucket Pequot Gaming
Enterprise Inc. P**318**, P**667**
MGM Mirage A**966**
MTR Gaming Group, Inc. E**247**
Park Place Entertainment
Corporation A**1086**
Penn National Gaming,
Inc. E**262**

Gaming Activities
California State Lottery
Commission P**564**

Churchill Downs
Incorporated E**40**, E**178**
Connecticut Lottery
Corporation P**581**
Georgia Lottery
Corporation P**615**
Hilton Group plc W**258**
Illinois Department of the
Lottery P**638**
Maryland State Lottery
Agency P**666**
Massachusetts State Lottery
Commission P**668**
Michigan Lottery P**675**
Multi-State Lottery
Association P**680**
New Jersey State Lottery
Commission P**687**
New York State Lottery P**372**,
P**688**
Ohio Lottery Commission P**693**
The Pennsylvania Lottery P**698**
State of Florida Department of
the Lottery P**736**
Texas Lottery
Commission P**472**, P**744**
Virginia State Lottery P**766**

Lodging
Candlewood Hotel Company,
Inc. E**169**
Cendant Corporation A**338**
Club Méditerranée S.A. W**170**
Extended Stay America,
Inc. E**59**, E**201**
Hilton Hotels Corporation A**720**
Hyatt Corporation A**740**, P**240**,
P**636**
Marriott International,
Inc. A**912**
ResortQuest International,
Inc. E**279**
Starwood Hotels & Resorts
Worldwide, Inc. A**1328**
Strategic Hotel Capital
LLC P**737**
Wyndham International,
Inc. A**1540**

Miscellaneous Entertainment
Feld Entertainment, Inc. P**188**,
P**608**

**Professional Sports Teams
& Organizations**
Boston Celtics Limited
Partnership A**280**
The Edward J. DeBartolo
Corporation P**172**, P**602**
The Green Bay Packers,
Inc. A**672**, P**210**, P**621**
Major League Baseball P**306**,
P**663**
National Association for Stock
Car Auto Racing P**681**
National Basketball
Association P**354**, P**682**
National Football League P**356**,
P**683**
National Hockey League P**360**,
P**684**

World Wrestling Federation
Entertainment, Inc. **E141**,
E319

Restaurants

Advantica Restaurant Group,
Inc. **A86**

Brinker International,
Inc. **A288**

BUCA, Inc. **E167**

Buffets, Inc. **P562**

Burger King Corporation **A302**

Chick-fil-A Inc. **P124**, **P575**

Darden Restaurants, Inc. **A464**

Dave & Buster's, Inc. **E51**, **E190**

Doctor's Associates Inc. **P160**,
P595

Domino's Inc. **A500**, **P162**,
P595

Investors Management
Corp. **P642**

Jack in the Box Inc. **A784**

McDonald's Corporation **A942**

Nathan's Famous, Inc. **E95**,
E249

P.F. Chang's China Bistro,
Inc. **E265**

Shoney's, Inc. **A1280**

Triarc Companies, Inc. **A1400**

TRICON Global Restaurants,
Inc. **A1404**

Waffle House Inc. **P512**, **P767**

Wendy's International,
Inc. **A1510**

White Castle System, Inc. **P516**,
P772

**Specialty Eateries & Catering
Services**

ARAMARK Corporation **A190**

Compass Group PLC **W174**

Delaware North Companies
Inc. **P590**

Krispy Kreme Doughnuts,
Inc. **E80**, **E230**

New World Restaurant Group,
Inc. **E253**

Sodexho Alliance **W546**

Sodexho, Inc. **A1296**

Starbucks Corporation **A1326**

Sporting Activities

24 Hour Fitness Worldwide
Inc. **P528**

ClubCorp, Inc. **P130**, **P577**

International Speedway
Corporation **E75**, **E222**

**Travel Agencies, Tour Operators
& Other Travel Services**

American Express
Company **A142**

Carlson Wagonlit Travel **A328**,
P108, **P567**

Carnival Corporation **A330**

Hotel Reservations Network,
Inc. **E215**

Liberty Travel, Inc. **P296**, **P658**

Maritz Inc. **P308**, **P664**

Navigant International
Inc. **E250**

Rosenbluth International **P418**,
P717

Royal Caribbean Cruises
Ltd. **A1216**

Sabre Inc. **A1228**

WorldTravel BTI **P776**

MANUFACTURING

Agricultural Machinery

AGCO Corporation **A96**

Deere & Company **A468**

Kubota Corporation **W326**

**Construction, Mining & Other
Heavy Machinery**

Caterpillar Inc. **A332**

Komatsu Ltd. **W320**

NACCO Industries, Inc. **A992**

Diversified Machinery

AMSTED Industries
Incorporated **P540**

Connell Limited
Partnership **P581**

Dover Corporation **A502**

Illinois Tool Works Inc. **A748**

Ingersoll-Rand Company **A754**

Joy Global Inc. **A806**

MAN Aktiengesellschaft **W350**

NESCO, Inc. **P686**

**Fluid Control Equipment, Pumps,
Seals & Valves**

Colfax Corporation **P578**

Parker Hannifin
Corporation **A1088**

Swagelok **P739**

Glass & Clay Products

Ball Corporation **A224**

Ceradyne, Inc. **E175**

Compagnie de Saint-
Gobain **W506**

Guardian Industries
Corp. **P212**, **P623**

Hardware & Fasteners

Questron Technology, Inc. **E273**

**Industrial Automation Products
& Industrial Controls**

Cognex Corporation **E43**, **E181**

CyberOptics Corporation **E48**,
E189

Danaher Corporation **A462**

Rockwell International
Corporation **A1210**

**Industrial Equipment & Products
Distribution**

Anixter International Inc. **A176**

CHEMCENTRAL
Corporation **P573**

Consolidated Electrical
Distributors Inc. **P582**

Graybar Electric Company,
Inc. **P208**, **P620**

Richton International
Corporation **E280**

WESCO International,
Inc. **A1512**

W.W. Grainger, Inc. **A1538**

Lighting & Other Fixtures

Genlyte Thomas Group
LLC **P613**

National Service Industries,
Inc. **A1004**

**Machine Tools, Components
& Accessories**

Harbour Group Industries,
Inc. **P625**

NN, Inc. **E254**

The Timken Company **A1386**

Material Handling Machinery

Crown Equipment
Corporation **P586**

Metal Fabrication

Mobile Mini, Inc. **E246**

Tower Automotive, Inc. **A1394**

**Miscellaneous & Diversified
Industrial Products**

CoorsTek, Inc. **E185**

Crane Co. **A446**

Invensys plc **W290**

**Miscellaneous Electrical
Products**

C&D Technologies, Inc. **E169**

Cooper Industries, Inc. **A430**

Emerson **A546**

Exide Technologies **A572**

Kyocera Corporation **W328**

Power-One, Inc. **E269**

SPX Corporation **A1320**

**Miscellaneous General & Special
Machinery**

Allied Devices Corporation **E26**,
E151

Briggs & Stratton
Corporation **A286**

BTU International, Inc. **E167**

Packaging & Containers

Bemis Company, Inc. **A250**

Crown Cork & Seal Company,
Inc. **A452**

Dart Container
Corporation **P150**, **P588**

Graham Packaging Company,
L. P. **P620**

Green Bay Packaging Inc. **P621**

Owens-Illinois, Inc. **A1074**

Plastipak Packaging, Inc. **P702**

Printpack, Inc. **P705**

Sealed Air Corporation **A1262**

The SF Holdings Group,
Inc. **P727**

U.S. Can Corporation **P762**

Paper & Paper Products

Boise Cascade
Corporation **A274**

Bowater Incorporated **A284**

Central National-Gottesman
Inc. **P571**

International Paper
  Company A**770**
The Mead Corporation A**950**
Menasha Corporation P**673**
The Newark Group P**689**
Parsons & Whittemore,
  Incorporated P**696**
Riverwood International
  Corporation P**715**
Smurfit-Stone Container
  Corporation A**1292**
Sonoco Products
  Company A**1302**
Stora Enso Oyj W**556**
Temple-Inland Inc. A**1364**
Westvaco Corporation A**1516**
Willamette Industries,
  Inc. A**1524**

Rubber & Plastic Products
Bridgestone Corporation W**138**
Carlisle Companies
  Incorporated A**326**
Compagnie Générale des Étab-
  lissements Michelin W**366**
Cooper Tire & Rubber
  Company A**432**
The Goodyear Tire & Rubber
  Company A**664**
PW Eagle, Inc. E**272**
Reunion Industries, Inc. E**279**
Trex Company, Inc. E**305**
Woodbridge Group P**776**

Textile Manufacturing
Beaulieu Of America, LLC P**552**
Burlington Industries,
  Inc. A**306**
Milliken & Company Inc. P**342**,
  P**677**
Mohawk Industries, Inc. A**980**
Parkdale Mills, Inc. P**696**
R. B. Pamplin Corp. P**711**
W. L. Gore & Associates,
  Inc. P**522**, P**775**

**Turbines, Transformers & Other
Electrical Generation Equipment**
Capstone Turbine
  Corporation E**171**
Eaton Corporation A**526**
Schneider Electric SA W**520**

Wire & Cable
General Cable
  Corporation A**642**
Jordan Industries, Inc. P**647**
Pirelli S.p.A. W**450**

MATERIALS
& CONSTRUCTION
Aggregates, Concrete & Cement
Hanson PLC W**252**
Lafarge North America
  Inc. A**848**
U.S. Concrete, Inc. E**309**
Vulcan Materials
  Company A**1484**

Diversified Building Materials
Fortune Brands, Inc. A**618**
Owens Corning A**1072**
U.S. Industries, Inc. A**1446**
USG Corporation A**1456**

**Engineering & Architectural
Services**
AECOM Technology
  Corporation P**531**
Barton Malow Company P**550**
BE&K Inc. P**552**
Black & Veatch P**556**
CH2M Hill Companies,
  Ltd. P**573**
The Day & Zimmermann Group,
  Inc. P**589**
The Keith Companies,
  Inc. E**226**
Parsons Brinckerhoff Inc. P**696**
Skidmore Owings & Merrill
  LLP P**448**, P**730**

Environmental Services
Synagro Technologies,
  Inc. E**297**
Tetra Tech, Inc. E**128**, E**300**
TRC Companies, Inc. E**131**,
  E**304**

Heavy Construction
ABB Ltd. W**54**
Austin Industries Inc. P**547**
Bechtel Group, Inc. A**240**, P**74**,
  P**552**
The Beck Group P**553**
Bouygues S.A. W**134**
Brasfield & Gorrie, LLC P**560**
Charles Pankow Builders,
  Ltd. P**573**
Clark Enterprises, Inc. P**576**
Devcon Construction
  Incorporated P**592**
Dick Corporation P**593**
Dillingham Construction
  Corporation P**593**
DPR Construction, Inc. P**597**
Dunn Industries, Inc. P**599**
Dycom Industries, Inc. E**52**,
  E**195**
Fisher Development, Inc. P**608**
Fluor Corporation A**610**
Foster Wheeler Ltd. A**620**
Gilbane, Inc. P**615**
H. B. Zachry Company P**627**
Hensel Phelps Construction
  Co. P**630**
Hoffman Corporation P**632**
Hopewell Holdings
  Limited W**266**
Hunt Construction Group P**635**
J. F. Shea Co., Inc. P**643**
Jacobs Engineering Group
  Inc. A**786**
J.S. Alberici Construction Co.,
  Inc. P**649**
M. A. Mortenson
  Company P**663**
McCarthy P**669**

Modern Continental Companies,
  Inc. P**678**
Parsons Corporation P**386**,
  P**697**
Pepper Construction Group,
  LLC P**700**
Peter Kiewit Sons', Inc. A**1114**,
  P**396**, P**701**
Rooney Brothers
  Company P**716**
Rudolph and Sletten, Inc. P**719**
The Structure Tone
  Organization P**737**
Swinerton Incorporated P**740**
TIC Holdings Inc. P**745**
The Walsh Group P**768**
Washington Group
  International, Inc. P**769**
The Whiting-Turner Contracting
  Company P**772**

**Lumber, Wood Production
& Timber Operations**
Columbia Forest Products
  Inc. P**579**
Georgia-Pacific
  Corporation A**654**
Louisiana-Pacific
  Corporation A**890**
Lumbermens Merchandising
  Corporation P**662**
Sierra Pacific Industries P**728**
Weyerhaeuser Company A**1518**

Manufactured Buildings
Champion Enterprises,
  Inc. A**346**
Fleetwood Enterprises,
  Inc. A**604**
Modtech Holdings, Inc. E**94**,
  E**246**

Miscellaneous Building Materials
Andersen Corporation P**50**,
  P**541**
Armstrong Holdings, Inc. A**194**
G-I Holdings, Inc. P**612**
JELD-WEN, inc. P**643**
National Gypsum
  Company P**683**
Pella Corporation P**698**

Plumbing & HVAC Equipment
American Standard Companies
  Inc. A**152**
Engineered Support Systems,
  Inc. E**198**
Kohler Co. P**284**, P**653**
Lennox International Inc. A**864**
Masco Corporation A**920**
York International
  Corporation A**1550**

**Specialty Contracting
& Industrial Maintenance**
EMCOR Group, Inc. A**544**

Waste Management & Recycling
Allied Waste Industries,
  Inc. A**122**
Scope Industries E**285**
Stericycle, Inc. E**293**

Waste Connections, Inc. E**139**, E**315**
Waste Management, Inc. A**1504**

MEDIA

Information Collection & Delivery Services

The Associated Press P**60**, P**546**
Bloomberg L.P. P**80**, P**556**
The Dun & Bradstreet Corporation A**516**
FactSet Research Systems Inc. E**61**, E**202**
HyperFeed Technologies, Inc. E**70**, E**217**
OneSource Information Services, Inc. E**100**, E**258**
Reuters Group PLC W**484**

Internet & Online Content Providers

Yahoo! Inc. A**1546**

Media

AOL Time Warner Inc. A**180**
Bertelsmann AG W**126**
Cox Enterprises, Inc. A**442**, P**146**, P**585**
Fox Entertainment Group, Inc. A**622**
Grupo Televisa, S.A. W**582**
The Hearst Corporation A**700**, P**228**, P**629**
Lagardère SCA W**330**
Liberty Media Corporation A**872**
National Amusements Inc. P**681**
The News Corporation Limited W**390**
Pearson plc W**430**
Quebecor Inc. W**470**
R. R. Donnelley & Sons Company A**1218**
The Thomson Corporation W**592**
Tribune Company A**1402**
USA Networks, Inc. A**1450**
Viacom Inc. A**1476**
Vivendi Universal S.A. W**624**
VNU N.V. W**626**
The Walt Disney Company A**1496**

Motion Picture & Video Production & Distribution

DreamWorks SKG P**166**, P**597**
Lucasfilm Ltd. P**302**, P**661**
Metro-Goldwyn-Mayer Inc. A**962**
Pixar Animation Studios E**103**, E**266**

Movie, Television & Music Production Services & Products

Mackie Designs Inc. E**85**, E**234**
Macrovision Corporation E**235**
The Rank Group PLC W**472**

Movie Theaters

Cinemark USA, Inc. P**126**, P**575**
Regal Cinemas, Inc. P**412**, P**712**

Music Production & Publishing

EMI Group plc W**212**

Publishing

Advance Publications, Inc. A**80**, P**32**, P**530**
American Greetings Corporation A**146**
Asahi Shimbun Publishing Company W**96**
Axel Springer Verlag AG W**106**
Consumers Union of United States, Inc. P**138**, P**582**
Dow Jones & Company, Inc. A**506**
The E. W. Scripps Company A**568**
Encyclopædia Britannica, Inc. P**176**, P**603**
Freedom Communications, Inc. P**611**
The Future Network plc W**238**
Gannett Co., Inc. A**632**
Hallmark Cards, Inc. A**678**, P**216**, P**625**
Hollinger Inc. W**262**
International Data Group P**248**, P**641**
Johnson Publishing Company, Inc. P**258**, P**646**
Journal Communications Inc. P**648**
Knight Ridder Inc. A**832**
Landmark Communications, Inc. P**655**
Martha Stewart Living Omnimedia Inc. A**918**
The McGraw-Hill Companies, Inc. A**944**
MediaNews Group, Inc. P**670**
The New York Times Company A**1020**
Penton Media, Inc. E**102**, E**263**
PRIMEDIA, Inc. A**1160**
Rand McNally & Company P**408**, P**711**
The Reader's Digest Association, Inc. A**1192**
Reed Elsevier plc W**478**
Scholastic Corporation A**1254**
United Business Media PLC W**620**
The Washington Post Company A**1502**
Wolters Kluwer nv W**642**

Radio Broadcasting & Programming

Clear Channel Communications, Inc. A**372**
Entercom Communications Corp. E**199**
Regent Communications, Inc. E**277**
Westwood One, Inc. E**140**, E**317**

Television Production, Programming & Distribution

Harpo, Inc. P**218**, P**625**

TV Broadcasting

ABC, Inc. A**60**
British Broadcasting Corporation W**144**
CBS Television Network A**334**
Corporation for Public Broadcasting P**144**, P**585**
Discovery Communications, Inc. P**158**, P**594**
Emmis Communications Corporation E**198**
ESPN, Inc. P**605**
Granada plc W**248**
Hearst-Argyle Television, Inc. E**212**
National Broadcasting Company, Inc. A**998**

METALS & MINING

Aluminum

Alcan Inc. W**74**
Alcoa Inc. A**112**
MAXXAM Inc. A**930**
Pechiney W**432**

Coal

AEI Resources, Inc. P**531**
CONSOL Energy Inc. A**416**

Copper

Freeport-McMoRan Copper & Gold Inc. A**628**

Diversified Mining & Metals

Allegheny Technologies Incorporated A**116**
Anglo American plc W**92**
BHP Billiton W**128**
Inco Limited W**284**
Phelps Dodge Corporation A**1124**
Quexco Incorporated P**709**
Rio Tinto plc W**488**
Stillwater Mining Company E**294**
WMC Limited W**640**

Gold & Silver & Other Precious Metals

Lonmin Plc W**340**
Meridian Gold Inc. E**242**
Newmont Mining Corporation A**1024**
Placer Dome Inc. W**452**

Metals & Alloys Distribution

O'Neal Steel, Inc. P**694**
Ryerson Tull, Inc. A**1224**
Tang Industries, Inc. P**741**

Miscellaneous Mining & Metals Processing

Soave Enterprises L.L.C. P**731**

Steel Production

AK Steel Holding Corporation A**104**
Bethlehem Steel Corporation A**256**
Commercial Metals Company A**396**

Corus Group plc W**178**
Earle M. Jorgensen
  Company P**601**
Ispat International N.V. W**292**
The LTV Corporation A**896**
Maverick Tube
  Corporation E**87**, E**238**
National Steel
  Corporation A**1006**
Nippon Steel Corporation W**398**
Nucor Corporation A**1052**
OmniSource Corporation P**694**
Pohang Iron & Steel Co.,
  Ltd. W**454**
Renco Group Inc. P**712**
Republic Technologies
  International, LLC P**713**
Southwire Company P**733**
ThyssenKrupp AG W**594**
USX-U.S. Steel Group A**1462**

REAL ESTATE
Miscellaneous Real Estate Services
  CB Richard Ellis Services,
    Inc. P**120**, P**571**
  Colliers International Property
    Consultants Inc. P**578**
  Cushman & Wakefield
    Inc. P**587**
  HomeServices.Com Inc. E**215**

**Property Investment
& Management**
  American Real Estate Partners,
    L.P. E**154**
  Berwind Group P**554**
  Catellus Development
    Corporation E**37**, E**173**
  Equivest Finance, Inc. E**200**
  Gale & Wentworth, L.L.C. P**613**
  Helmsley Enterprises,
    Inc. P**230**, P**629**
  Intergroup Corporation E**221**
  JMB Realty Corporation P**645**
  Kennedy-Wilson, Inc. E**227**
  LNR Property
    Corporation E**234**
  Municipal Mortgage and Equity,
    LLC E**248**
  NRT Incorporated P**692**
  Security Capital Group
    Incorporated E**285**
  Tarragon Realty Investors,
    Inc. E**298**
  Trammell Crow
    Company A**1398**
  Trammell Crow
    Residential P**747**
  The Trump
    Organization A**1408**, P**482**,
    P**749**

Real Estate Development
  California Coastal Communities,
    Inc. E**169**
  Consolidated-Tomoka Land
    Co. E**184**
  Heartland Partners, L.P. E**212**

The Irvine Company Inc. P**252**,
  P**642**
JPI P**648**
The Lefrak Organization P**290**,
  P**656**
Lincoln Property
  Company P**659**
Opus Corporation P**695**
The St. Joe Company E**115**,
  E**282**
Tishman Realty & Construction
  Co. Inc. P**476**, P**745**
Trendwest Resorts, Inc. E**304**
WCI Communities, Inc. P**770**

REIT
  Acadia Realty Trust E**147**
  Alexander's, Inc. E**150**
  Alexandria Real Estate Equities,
    Inc. E**150**
  America First Mortgage
    Investments, Inc. E**152**
  AMRESCO Capital Trust E**155**
  Anthracite Capital, Inc. E**157**
  Avalonbay Communities,
    Inc. E**161**
  Bedford Property Investors,
    Inc. E**163**
  Boston Properties, Inc. E**34**,
    E**165**
  Cabot Industrial Trust E**167**
  Capital Automotive REIT E**170**
  Charles E. Smith Residential
    Realty, Inc. E**175**
  Cornerstone Realty Income
    Trust, Inc. E**186**
  Corporate Office Properties
    Trust E**187**
  Correctional Properties
    Trust E**187**
  Duke Realty Corporation E**194**
  Health Care Property Investors,
    Inc. E**211**
  Healthcare Realty Trust
    Incorporated E**211**
  Home Properties of New York,
    Inc. E**214**
  Host Marriott Corporation A**732**
  Humphrey Hospitality Trust,
    Inc. E**216**
  Income Opportunity Realty
    Investors, Inc. E**219**
  Investors Real Estate
    Trust E**223**
  iStar Financial Inc. E**224**
  Jameson Inns, Inc. E**225**
  Keystone Property Trust E**228**
  Kramont Realty Trust E**229**
  LaSalle Hotel Properties E**231**
  Mission West Properties,
    Inc. E**245**
  New Plan Excel Realty Trust,
    Inc. E**252**
  Pacific Gulf Properties
    Inc. E**259**
  Philips International Realty
    Corp. E**266**
  PS Business Parks, Inc. E**271**
  RAIT Investment Trust E**275**

Reckson Associates Realty
  Corp. E**276**
Regency Centers
  Corporation E**276**
Simon Property Group,
  Inc. A**1286**
SL Green Realty Corp. E**289**
Transcontinental Realty
  Investors, Inc. E**303**
Vornado Realty Trust E**137**,
  E**314**

Residential Construction
  A. G. Spanos Companies P**532**
  Capital Pacific Holdings,
    Inc. E**171**
  Centex Corporation A**340**
  David Weekley Homes P**588**
  D.R. Horton, Inc. A**508**
  KB Home A**812**
  Lennar Corporation A**862**
  Meritage Corporation E**243**
  Pulte Homes, Inc. A**1178**
  The Ryland Group, Inc. A**1226**

RETAIL
Auto Parts Retail & Wholesale
  AutoZone, Inc. A**208**
  CARQUEST Corporation P**112**,
    P**569**
  Discount Tire Co. P**594**
  General Parts, Inc. P**613**
  Genuine Parts Company A**652**
  Heafner Tire Group, Inc. P**628**
  LDI, Ltd. P**656**
  Les Schwab Tire Centers P**657**
  The Pep Boys - Manny, Moe &
    Jack A**1100**

**Building Materials & Gardening
Supplies Retail & Wholesale**
  84 Lumber Company P**26**, P**528**
  Ace Hardware Corporation A**64**,
    P**30**, P**529**
  American Builders &
    Contractors Supply Co.,
    Inc. P**537**
  Builder Marts of America,
    Inc. P**562**
  Builders FirstSource, Inc. P**562**
  Do it Best Corp. P**594**
  Hines Horticulture, Inc. E**214**
  The Home Depot, Inc. A**724**
  Kingfisher plc W**312**
  Lanoga Corporation P**655**
  Lowe's Companies, Inc. A**892**
  Menard, Inc. P**330**, P**672**
  North Pacific Group, Inc. P**690**
  Payless Cashways, Inc. A**1090**
  Primus, Inc. P**705**
  Quality Stores, Inc. P**406**, P**709**
  Sutherland Lumber Company,
    L.P. P**739**
  TruServ Corporation A**1410**,
    P**484**, P**749**

**Clothing, Shoe & Accessory
Retail & Wholesale**
  Abercrombie & Fitch Co. A**62**

American Retail Group
  Inc. **P539**
Brown Shoe Company,
  Inc. **A294**
Burlington Coat Factory
  Warehouse Corporation **A304**
Charlotte Russe Holding,
  Inc. **E176**
Chico's FAS, Inc. **E177**
The Children's Place Retail
  Stores, Inc. **E177**
Christopher & Banks
  Corporation **E178**
Factory 2-U Stores, Inc. **E60**,
  E202
The Gap, Inc. **A634**
Goody's Family Clothing,
  Inc. **A666**
Hot Topic, Inc. **E69**, E215
Intimate Brands, Inc. **A776**
J. Crew Group, Inc. **P254**, P642
Lands' End, Inc. **A852**
The Limited, Inc. **A876**
L.L. Bean, Inc. **P300**, P660
Pacific Sunwear of California,
  Inc. **E101**, E259
Payless ShoeSource, Inc. **A1092**
Retail Brand Alliance, Inc. **P713**
Spiegel, Inc. **A1314**
The TJX Companies, Inc. **A1388**

**Consumer Electronics
& Appliance**

Best Buy Co., Inc. **A254**
Circuit City Group **A366**
P.C. Richard & Son **P697**
RadioShack Corporation **A1188**
Tweeter Home Entertainment
  Group, Inc. **E306**

**Convenience Stores & Gas
Stations**

7-Eleven, Inc. **A56**
Clark Retail Group, Inc. **P577**
Cumberland Farms, Inc. **P586**
Flying J Inc. **P609**
Hale-Halsell Co. **P624**
Holiday Companies **P633**
Ito-Yokado Co., Ltd. **W298**
The Pantry, Inc. **A1084**
Petro Stopping Centers,
  L.P. **P701**
Pilot Corporation **P702**
QuikTrip Corporation **P710**
RaceTrac Petroleum, Inc. **P710**
Sheetz, Inc. **P728**
Swifty Serve Corporation **P740**
TravelCenters of America,
  Inc. **P745**
Wawa Inc. **P770**

Department Stores

Belk, Inc. **P76**, P553
Boscov's Department
  Stores **P559**
Dillard's, Inc. **A490**
Federated Department Stores,
  Inc. **A586**
Hudson's Bay Company **W270**

J. C. Penney Company,
  Inc. **A790**
Karstadt Quelle AG **W310**
Kohl's Corporation **A838**
Marks and Spencer p.l.c. **W356**
The May Department Stores
  Company **A932**
The Neiman Marcus Group,
  Inc. **A1014**
Nordstrom, Inc. **A1036**
Pinault-Printemps-
  Redoute **W446**
Saks Incorporated **A1238**
Sears, Roebuck and Co. **A1264**
Wal-Mart de México, S.A. de
  C.V. **W634**

Discount & Variety

Ames Department Stores,
  Inc. **A158**
Army and Air Force Exchange
  Service **P52**, P543
Big Lots, Inc. **A260**
BJ's Wholesale Club, Inc. **A262**
Costco Wholesale
  Corporation **A436**
Dollar General
  Corporation **A496**
Family Dollar Stores, Inc. **A578**
Kmart Corporation **A830**
Navy Exchange Service
  Command **P685**
Ross Stores, Inc. **A1214**
Service Merchandise Company,
  Inc. **A1270**
ShopKo Stores, Inc. **A1282**
Target Corporation **A1352**
Wal-Mart Stores, Inc. **A1494**

Drug, Health & Beauty Products

1-800 CONTACTS, INC. **E146**
Alberto-Culver Company **A108**
Alticor Inc. **P536**
CVS Corporation **A458**
Longs Drug Stores
  Corporation **A886**
Rite Aid Corporation **A1202**
Walgreen Co. **A1492**

Grocery

Albertson's, Inc. **A110**
Bashas' Inc. **P550**
Big V Supermarkets, Inc. **P554**
Big Y Foods, Inc. **P554**
Brookshire Grocery
  Company **P561**
Carrefour SA **W164**
Casino Guichard-
  Perrachon **W166**
Coles Myer Ltd. **W172**
Delhaize "Le Lion" S.A. **W194**
Demoulas Super Markets
  Inc. **P591**
Furrs Supermarkets, Inc. **P612**
George Weston Limited **W244**
Giant Eagle Inc. **P198**, P615
The Golub Corporation **P617**
The Great Atlantic & Pacific Tea
  Company, Inc. **A670**

H. E. Butt Grocery
  Company **P224**, P627
Houchens Industries Inc. **P634**
Hy-Vee, Inc. **P636**
IGA, INC. **A744**, P242, P638
Inserra Supermarkets,
  Inc. **P640**
J Sainsbury plc **W300**
Jitney-Jungle Stores of America,
  Inc. **P644**
The Kroger Co. **A844**
K-VA-T Food Stores, Inc. **P654**
Meijer, Inc. **P328**, P671
METRO AG **W364**
Minyard Food Stores, Inc. **P677**
The Penn Traffic
  Company **A1094**
Publix Super Markets,
  Inc. **A1176**, P402, P707
Raley's Inc. **P710**
Royal Ahold N.V. **W498**
Safeway Inc. **A1234**
Save Mart Supermarkets **P722**
Schnuck Markets, Inc. **P723**
Stater Bros. Holdings
  Inc. **P462**, P736
Tengelmann
  Warenhandelsgesellschaft
  OHG **W588**
Tesco PLC **W590**
Trader Joe's Company **P747**
Wegmans Food Markets,
  Inc. **P771**
Whole Foods Market,
  Inc. **A1522**
WinCo Foods, Inc. **P773**
Winn-Dixie Stores, Inc. **A1532**
Woolworths Limited **W644**

Home Furnishings & Housewares

Abbey Carpet Company,
  Inc. **P529**
Bed Bath & Beyond Inc. **A246**
Carpet Co-op Association of
  America **P568**
Heilig-Meyers Company **A702**
IKEA International A/S **W276**
Pier 1 Imports, Inc. **A1130**
Rooms To Go **P716**
Williams-Sonoma, Inc. **A1530**

Non-Store Retailing

Otto Versand Gmbh &
  Co. **W426**

SPECIALTY RETAIL

Auto Dealers & Distributors

Asbury Automotive Group,
  Inc. **P543**
AutoNation, Inc. **A206**
Bill Heard Enterprises **P555**
Brown Automotive Group
  Ltd. **P561**
Burt Automotive Network **P563**
Crown Group, Inc. **E188**
David Wilson's Automotive
  Group **P589**
Don Massey Cadillac, Inc. **P596**

The Faulkner
Organization **P606**
Gulf States Toyota, Inc. **P624**
Hendrick Automotive
Group **P630**
The Herb Chambers
Companies **P631**
Holman Enterprises **P633**
Jim Koons Automotive **P644**
JM Family Enterprises,
Inc. **P256**, P644
Jordan Automotive Group **P647**
Larry H. Miller Group **P656**
Marty Franich Auto
Center **P666**
Morse Operations, Inc. **P678**
Planet Automotive Group,
Inc. **P702**
Prospect Motors, Inc. **P706**
Rosenthal Automotive
Companies **P717**
Santa Monica Ford
Corporation **P721**
Spitzer Management, Inc. **P733**
VT Inc. **P767**

Computer & Software
CDW Computer Centers,
Inc. **A336**
Fry's Electronics, Inc. **P196**,
P612
MCSi, Inc. **E239**
Micro Electronics, Inc. **P336**,
P675
Micro Warehouse, Inc. **P338**,
P676

Jewelry Retail & Wholesale
M. Fabrikant & Sons **P662**
Zale Corporation **A1552**

Miscellaneous Retail
DFS Group Limited **P156**, P592
FTD.COM INC. **E207**
Guitar Center, Inc. **E66**, E210
Jo-Ann Stores, Inc. **A796**
MarineMax, Inc. **E237**
Petco Animal Supplies,
Inc. **P394**, P701
PETsMART, Inc. **A1116**
Ritz Camera Centers, Inc. **P714**
Roll International
Corporation **P416**, P716
Sharper Image
Corporation **A1274**, E120,
E287

**Music, Video, Book
& Entertainment**
Amazon.com, Inc. **A130**
Anderson News Company **P541**
Baker & Taylor
Corporation **P68**, P548
Barnes & Noble College
Bookstores, Inc. **P549**
Barnes & Noble, Inc. **A232**
Blockbuster Inc. **A266**
Borders Group, Inc. **A276**
Columbia House
Company **P579**

Follett Corporation **P192**, P609
Ingram Entertainment Holdings
Inc. **P639**
Ingram Industries Inc. **A756**,
P244, P639
MTS, Incorporated **P346**, P680

**Office Products Retail
& Distribution**
Global Imaging Systems,
Inc. **E208**
Gould Paper Corporation **P619**
Office Depot, Inc. **A1056**
OfficeMax, Inc. **A1058**
Staples, Inc. **A1324**
United Stationers Inc. **A1430**

Sporting Goods
Bass Pro Shops, Inc. **P550**
Dick's Sporting Goods,
Inc. **P593**
Recreational Equipment,
Inc. **P410**, P711
Venator Group, Inc. **A1470**

Toy & Hobby Retail & Wholesale
Hobby Lobby Stores, Inc. **P632**
K-B Toys **P649**
Michaels Stores, Inc. **A968**
Toys "R" Us, Inc. **A1396**

TELECOMMUNICATIONS

Cable TV & Satellite Systems
Adelphia Communications
Corporation **A72**
British Sky Broadcasting Group
plc **W146**
Cablevision Systems
Corporation **A312**
Charter Communications,
Inc. **A350**
Comcast Corporation **A390**
EchoStar Communications
Corporation **A528**
Hughes Electronics
Corporation **A736**
Intelsat, Ltd. **P640**

**Communications Processing
Equipment**
Anaren Microwave, Inc. **E156**
Applied Innovation Inc. **E157**
Digital Lightwave, Inc. **E192**
Gentner Communications
Corporation **E208**
Polycom, Inc. **E268**

**Diversified Telecom Service
Providers**
Cable and Wireless plc **W152**
Deutsche Telekom AG **W204**
Telstra Corporation
Limited **W586**

**Internet & Online Service
Providers**
Infonet Services
Corporation **E220**
Interland, Inc. **A762**

**Local Telecom & Private
Transmission Services**
ALLTEL Corporation **A128**
BCE Inc. **W122**
BellSouth Corporation **A248**
Broadwing Inc. **A292**
BT Group plc **W148**
Compañía de
Telecomunicaciones de Chile
S.A. **W576**
France Telecom **W232**
Nippon Telegraph and Telephone
Corporation **W400**
NTELOS Inc. **E255**
Olivetti S.p.A. **W422**
Qwest Communications
International Inc. **A1186**
Royal KPN N.V. **W502**
SBC Communications
Inc. **A1244**
Telecom Italia S.p.A. **W574**
Telefónica, S.A. **W578**
Teléfonos de México, S.A. de
C.V. **W580**
Telia AB **W584**
Verizon Communications
Inc. **A1472**

Long-Distance Carriers
AT&T Corp. **A202**
Level 3 Communications,
Inc. **A866**
Sprint Corporation **A1318**
WorldCom, Inc. **A1534**

**Miscellaneous End-User
Communications Services**
Concert Communications
Company **P580**
VarTec Telecom, Inc. **P764**

**Miscellaneous Services to
Communication Providers**
Arguss Communications,
Inc. **E158**
Illuminet Holdings, Inc. **E217**
International FiberCom,
Inc. **E221**
LCC International, Inc. **E232**
Lexent Inc. **E233**
Lightbridge, Inc. **E83**, E233
Metro One Telecommunications,
Inc. **E243**
Wireless Facilities, Inc. **E318**

**Switching & Transmission
Equipment**
ADC Telecommunications,
Inc. **A70**
Alcatel **W76**
ARRIS Group, Inc. **E30**, E158
Carrier Access
Corporation **E172**
CIENA Corporation **E41**, E179
Corning Incorporated **A434**
FiberCore, Inc. **E203**
Harris Corporation **A686**
JDS Uniphase Corporation **A792**
Lucent Technologies Inc. **A898**
Marconi plc **W354**

Nortel Networks
Corporation **W412**
Optical Communication
Products, Inc. **E258**
Scientific-Atlanta, Inc. **A1258**
Tekelec **E126, E299**
Tellabs, Inc. **A1362**
UTStarcom, Inc. **E310**
XETA Technologies, Inc. **E142,
E319**

**Wireless Communications
Services**

Centennial Communications
Corp. **E38, E174**
Cingular Wireless **P576**
Leap Wireless International,
Inc. **E232**
Mannesmann AG **W352**
Nextel Communications,
Inc. **A1026**
NTT DoCoMo, Inc. **W418**
Rogers Communications
Inc. **W494**
TeleCorp PCS, Inc. **E299**
Telephone and Data Systems,
Inc. **A1360**
Verizon Wireless Inc. **P765**
Vodafone Group PLC **W628**

**Wireless, Satellite & Microwave
Communications Equipment**

California Amplifier, Inc. **E168**
Loral Space & Communications
Ltd. **A888**
Motorola, Inc. **A990**
Nokia Corporation **W406**
Powerwave Technologies,
Inc. **E106, E269**
Radyne ComStream Inc. **E274**
REMEC, Inc. **E277**
Spectrian Corporation **E123,
E292**
Telefonaktiebolaget LM
Ericsson **W220**
ViaSat, Inc. **E312**
Western Multiplex
Corporation **E316**

TRANSPORTATION

**Air Delivery, Freight & Parcel
Services**

Airborne, Inc. **A102**
Atlas Air Worldwide Holdings,
Inc. **E32, E160**
CNF Inc. **A380**
Deutsche Post AG **W202**
DHL Worldwide Express,
Inc. **A484**
FedEx Corporation **A588**
United Parcel Service,
Inc. **A1426**
United Shipping & Technology,
Inc. **E308**
United States Postal
Service **A1428, P490, P754**

Airlines

Air Wisconsin Airlines
Corporation **P534**
Alaska Air Group, Inc. **A106**
Alitalia - Linee Aeree Italiane
S.p.A. **W78**
All Nippon Airways Co.,
Ltd. **W80**
America West Holdings
Corporation **A138**
AMR Corporation **A164**
British Airways Plc **W140**
Continental Airlines, Inc. **A428**
Delta Air Lines, Inc. **A478**
Deutsche Lufthansa AG **W344**
Frontier Airlines, Inc. **E64,
E206**
Japan Airlines Company,
Ltd. **W302**
KLM Royal Dutch
Airlines **W316**
Northwest Airlines
Corporation **A1046**
Qantas Airways Limited **W468**
SAS AB **W518**
Singapore Airlines
Limited **W540**
Société Air France **W68**
Southwest Airlines Co. **A1310**
UAL Corporation **A1420**
US Airways Group, Inc. **A1442**

**Bus, Taxi & Other Passenger
Services**

Metropolitan Transportation
Authority **P334, P674**
The Port Authority of New York
and New Jersey **P398, P703**

**Logistics & Other Transportation
Services**

Allied Worldwide, Inc. **P535**
GeoLogistics Corporation **P614**
Penske Truck Leasing **P700**
Ryder System, Inc. **A1222**
Stevedoring Services of America
Inc. **P737**

Railroads

Burlington Northern Santa Fe
Corporation **A308**
Conrail Inc. **P582**
CSX Corporation **A454**
National Railroad Passenger
Corporation **P362, P684**
Norfolk Southern
Corporation **A1038**
RailAmerica, Inc. **E275**
Union Pacific
Corporation **A1422**

Shipping

A.P. Møller **W94**
Crowley Maritime
Corporation **P585**
General Maritime
Corporation **E208**
The Peninsular and Oriental
Steam Navigation
Company **W434**

Trucking

C.H. Robinson Worldwide,
Inc. **A344**
Consolidated Freightways
Corporation **A420**
J.B. Hunt Transport Services,
Inc. **A788**
Roadway Corporation **A1206**
Schneider National, Inc. **P434,
P723**
UniGroup, Inc. **P753**
USFreightways
Corporation **A1454**
Watkins Associated
Industries **P770**
Yellow Corporation **A1548**

UTILITIES

Diversified Utilities

Ameren Corporation **A136**
Cinergy Corp. **A362**
CMS Energy Corporation **A376**
Consolidated Edison, Inc. **A418**
Constellation Energy Group,
Inc. **A424**
Dominion Resources, Inc. **A498**
JEA **P643**
Memphis Light, Gas and Water
Division **P672**
MidAmerican Energy Holdings
Company **P340, P676**
NiSource Inc. **A1034**
Public Service Enterprise Group
Incorporated **A1174**
SCANA Corporation **A1248**
Scottish Power plc **W522**
Sempra Energy **A1266**
TXU Corp. **A1416**
UtiliCorp United Inc. **A1464**
Xcel Energy Inc. **A1542**

Electric Utilities

Allegheny Energy, Inc. **A114**
American Electric Power
Company, Inc. **A140**
Bonneville Power
Administration **P558**
DTE Energy Company **A512**
Edison International **A532**
Electricité de France **W208**
Enel S.p.A. **W214**
Entergy Corporation **A554**
Exelon Corporation **A570**
FirstEnergy Corp. **A598**
FPL Group, Inc. **A624**
GPU, Inc. **A668**
Los Angeles Department of
Water and Power **P660**
Niagara Mohawk Holdings
Inc. **A1028**
Northeast Utilities **A1040**
Oglethorpe Power
Corporation **P692**
PacifiCorp **A1082**
Pinnacle West Capital
Corporation **A1138**
Power Authority of the State of
New York **P703**

PPL Corporation A**1154**
Progress Energy, Inc. A**1166**
Puerto Rico Electric Power
 Authority P**707**
Sacramento Municipal Utility
 District P**720**
South Carolina Public Service
 Authority P**732**
Southern Company A**1306**
SRP P**734**
Tennessee Valley
 Authority A**1370**, P**468**, P743

The Tokyo Electric Power
 Company, Incorporated W**598**
Gas Utilities
 KeySpan Corporation A**824**
 Nicor Inc. A**1030**
**Independent Power Producers
& Marketers**
 The AES Corporation A**88**
 Covanta Energy
  Corporation A**440**
 Duke Energy Corporation A**514**

Dynegy Inc. A**518**
Enron Corp. A**552**
Orion Power Holdings,
 Inc. E**258**
PG&E Corporation A**1120**
Reliant Energy,
 Incorporated A**1198**
Water Utilities
 American Water Works
  Company, Inc. A**154**
 Philadelphia Suburban
  Corporation E**265**

Hoover's Handbooks Index

HEADQUARTERS INDEX

Note: Page numbers in **boldface** indicate the company's profile.

ARGENTINA

Buenos Aires
YPF, S.A. **W650**

AUSTRALIA

Mascot
Qantas Airways Limited **W468**
Melbourne
BHP Billiton **W128**
National Australia Bank
Limited **W382**
Telstra Corporation
Limited **W586**
Richmond
Pacific Dunlop Limited **W428**
Southbank
Foster's Group Limited **W230**
WMC Limited **W640**
Sydney
AMP Limited **W88**
The News Corporation
Limited **W390**
Woolworths Limited **W644**
Tooronga
Coles Myer Ltd. **W172**

AUSTRIA

Vienna
OMV Aktiengesellschaft **W424**

BELGIUM

Brussels
Delhaize "Le Lion" S.A. **W194**
Leuven
Interbrew S.A. **W288**

BERMUDA

Pembroke
Bacardi Limited **W108**

BRAZIL

Rio de Janeiro
PETRÓLEO BRASILEIRO S.A. -
PETROBRAS **W436**

CANADA

Brampton
Nortel Networks
Corporation **W412**
Calgary
Agrium Inc. **W66**
Montreal
Alcan Inc. **W74**
Bank of Montreal **W112**
BCE Inc. **W122**

Bombardier Inc. **W132**
Molson Inc. **W376**
Quebecor Inc. **W470**
Toronto
Canadian Imperial Bank of
Commerce **W156**
George Weston Limited **W244**
Hollinger Inc. **W262**
Hudson's Bay Company **W270**
Imperial Oil Limited **W280**
Inco Limited **W284**
Moore Corporation
Limited **W378**
RBC Financial Group **W474**
Rogers Communications
Inc. **W494**
The Thomson Corporation **W592**
The Toronto-Dominion
Bank **W608**
Vancouver
Placer Dome Inc. **W452**

CHILE

Santiago
Compañía de Telecomunicaciones
de Chile S.A. **W576**

CHINA

Shanghai
Sinopec Shanghai Petrochemical
Company Limited **W542**

DENMARK

Bagsværd
Novo Nordisk A/S **W416**
Billund
LEGO Company **W332**
Copenhagen
A.P. Møller **W94**
Humlebaek
IKEA International A/S **W276**
Valby
Carlsberg A/S **W162**

FINLAND

Espoo
Nokia Corporation **W406**
Helsinki
Stora Enso Oyj **W556**

FRANCE

Blagnac
Airbus S.A.S. **W70**
Boulogne-Billancourt
Renault S.A. **W480**
Clermont-Ferrand
Compagnie Générale des Établissements Michelin **W366**
Clichy
L'Oréal SA **W342**

Courbevoie
TOTAL FINA ELF S.A. **W612**
Evry
Accor **W58**
La Défense
Atos Origin **W100**
Louveciennes
Bull **W150**
Montigny-le-Bretonneux
Sodexho Alliance **W546**
Paris
Alcatel **W76**
AXA **W104**
BNP Paribas **W130**
Cap Gemini Ernst &
Young **W160**
Carrefour SA **W164**
Club Méditerranée S.A. **W170**
Compagnie de Saint-
Gobain **W506**
Crédit Lyonnais **W182**
Electricité de France **W208**
France Telecom **W232**
Groupe Danone **W192**
Lagardère SCA **W330**
LVMH Moët Hennessy Louis
Vuitton SA **W348**
Pechiney **W432**
Pinault-Printemps-
Redoute **W446**
PSA Peugeot Citroën S.A. **W442**
Publicis Groupe S.A. **W466**
Suez **W558**
Vivendi Universal S.A. **W624**
Roissy
Société Air France **W68**
Rueil-Malmaison
Schneider Electric SA **W520**
Saint-Etienne
Casino Guichard-
Perrachon **W166**
Saint-Quentin-en-Yvelines
Bouygues S.A. **W134**
Schiltigheim
Aventis **W102**

GERMANY

Bonn
Deutsche Post AG **W202**
Deutsche Telekom AG **W204**
Cologne
Deutsche Lufthansa AG **W344**
Düsseldorf
E.ON AG **W218**
Henkel KGaA **W256**
Mannesmann AG **W352**
METRO AG **W364**
ThyssenKrupp AG **W594**
Essen
Karstadt Quelle AG **W310**
RWE AG **W504**

Frankfurt
Deutsche Bank AG W200
Gerlingen-Schillerhöhe
Robert Bosch GmbH W490
Gütersloh
Bertelsmann AG W126
Hamburg
Axel Springer Verlag AG W106
Otto Versand Gmbh & Co. W426
Hanover
Preussag AG W460
Herzogenaurach
adidas-Salomon AG W62
Leverkusen
Bayer AG W118
Ludwigshafen
BASF Aktiengesellschaft W116
Mülheim an der Ruhr
Tengelmann
Warenhandelsgesellschaft
OHG W588
Munich
Allianz AG W82
Bayerische Motoren Werke
AG W120
MAN Aktiengesellschaft W350
Münchener Rückversicherungs-
Gesellschaft
Aktiengesellschaft W380
Siemens AG W536
Stuttgart
DaimlerChrysler AG W188
Dr. Ing. h. c. F. Porsche
AG W458
Walldorf
SAP Aktiengesellschaft W516
Wolfsburg
Volkswagen AG W630

GREECE

Athens
National Bank of Greece
S.A. W384

HONG KONG

Hopewell Holdings
Limited W266
Hutchison Whampoa
Limited W272
Jardine Matheson Holdings
Limited W306
Swire Pacific Limited W564
Kowloon
Tommy Hilfiger
Corporation W606

INDIA

Mumbai
Tata Enterprises W566

IRELAND

Dublin
Allied Irish Banks, p.l.c. W86
Waterford Wedgwood plc W636

ISRAEL

Tel Aviv
Koor Industries Ltd. W322

ITALY

Ivrea
Olivetti S.p.A. W422
Milan
Pirelli S.p.A. W450
Ponzano Veneto
Benetton Group S.p.A. W124
Rome
Alitalia - Linee Aeree Italiane
S.p.A. W78
Enel S.p.A. W214
Eni S.p.A. W216
Telecom Italia S.p.A. W574
Trieste
Assicurazioni Generali
S.p.A. W98
Turin
Fiat S.p.A. W226

JAPAN

Hamamatsu
Suzuki Motor Corporation W560
Yamaha Corporation W648
Hiroshima
Mazda Motor Corporation W362
Kadoma
Matsushita Electric Industrial
Co., Ltd. W360
Kyoto
Kyocera Corporation W328
Nintendo Co., Ltd. W394
Moriguchi
SANYO Electric Co., Ltd. W514
Osaka
Kubota Corporation W326
Minolta Co., Ltd. W368
Nippon Life Insurance
Company W396
Sharp Corporation W532
Suwa
Seiko Epson Corporation W530
Tokyo
All Nippon Airways Co., Ltd. W80
Asahi Shimbun Publishing
Company W96
Bridgestone Corporation W138
Canon Inc. W158
CASIO COMPUTER CO.,
LTD. W168
Dai Nippon Printing Co.,
Ltd. W186

Dentsu Inc. W198
Fuji Photo Film Co., Ltd. W234
Fujitsu Limited W236
Hitachi, Ltd. W260
Honda Motor Co., Ltd. W264
Isuzu Motors Limited W294
ITOCHU Corporation W296
Ito-Yokado Co., Ltd. W298
Japan Airlines Company,
Ltd. W302
Japan Tobacco Inc. W304
Kao Corporation W308
Kirin Brewery Company,
Limited W314
Komatsu Ltd. W320
Marubeni Corporation W358
Mitsubishi Corporation W370
Mitsui & Co., Ltd. W372
Mizuho Holdings, Inc. W374
NEC Corporation W386
Nikon Corporation W392
Nippon Steel Corporation W398
Nippon Telegraph and Telephone
Corporation W400
Nissan Motor Co., Ltd. W402
Nissho Iwai Corporation W404
Nomura Holdings, Inc. W408
NTT DoCoMo, Inc. W418
Oki Electric Industry Company,
Limited W420
Pioneer Corporation W448
Ricoh Company, Ltd. W486
SEGA Corporation W526
Seiko Corporation W528
Shiseido Company,
Limited W534
SOFTBANK CORP. W548
Sony Corporation W550
TDK Corporation W572
The Tokio Marine and Fire
Insurance Company,
Limited W596
The Tokyo Electric Power
Company, Incorporated W598
Tokyo Electron Limited W600
TOMEN Corporation W602
Toshiba Corporation W610
Toyota
Toyota Motor Corporation W614

LUXEMBOURG

Espírito Santo Financial Group
S.A. W224

MALAYSIA

Kuala Lumpur
Sime Darby Berhad W538

MEXICO

México, D.F.
Petróleos Mexicanos W440
Teléfonos de México, S.A. de
C.V. W580
Grupo Televisa, S.A. W582
Wal-Mart de México, S.A. de
C.V. W634

A=AMERICAN BUSINESS · E=EMERGING COMPANIES · P=PRIVATE COMPANIES · W=WORLD BUSINESS

THE NETHERLANDS

Amstelveen
KLM Royal Dutch Airlines W316
Amsterdam
ABN AMRO Holding N.V. W56
Gucci Group N.V. W250
Heineken N.V. W254
ING Groep N.V. W286
Koninklijke Philips Electronics
N.V. W444
Wolters Kluwer nv W642
Arnhem
Akzo Nobel N.V. W72
Haarlem
VNU N.V. W626
The Hague
AEGON N.V. W64
Royal Dutch/Shell Group W500
Royal KPN N.V. W502
Rotterdam
Ispat International N.V. W292
Zaandam
Royal Ahold N.V. W498

NORWAY

Oslo
Norsk Hydro ASA W410

PHILIPPINES

Mandaluyong City
San Miguel Corporation W510

POLAND

Plock
Polski Koncern Naftowy ORLEN
S.A. W456

RUSSIA

Moscow
OAO Gazprom W242
OAO LUKOIL W346

SINGAPORE

Creative Technology Ltd. W180
Singapore Airlines Limited W540

SOUTH KOREA

Pohang
Pohang Iron & Steel Co.,
Ltd. W454
Seoul
Hyundai Group W274
LG Group W334
Samsung Group W508

SPAIN

Madrid
Repsol YPF, S.A. W482
Santander Central Hispano
S.A. W512

Telefónica, S.A. W578

SWEDEN

Farsta
Telia AB W584
Gothenburg
AB Volvo W632
Stockholm
AB Electrolux W210
SAS AB W518
Securitas AB W524
Telefonaktiebolaget LM
Ericsson W220

SWITZERLAND

Basel
Novartis AG W414
Roche Group W492
Biel
The Swatch Group Ltd. W562
Geneva
STMicroelectronics N.V. W554
Romanel-sur-Morges
Logitech International
S.A. W338
Vevey
Nestlé S.A. W388
Zurich
ABB Ltd. W54
Credit Suisse Group W184
UBS AG W616
Zurich Financial Services W652

TAIWAN

Hsichih
Acer Inc. W60
Taipei
Formosa Plastics
Corporation W228
Tatung Co. W570

TURKEY

Istanbul
Koç Holding A.S. W318

UNITED KINGDOM

Bath
The Future Network plc W238
Bristol
Allied Domecq PLC W84
Imperial Tobacco Group
PLC W282
Chertsey
Compass Group PLC W174
Cheshunt
Tesco PLC W590
Farnborough
BAE SYSTEMS W110

Glasgow
Scottish Power plc W522
Greenford
GlaxoSmithKline plc W246
Hatfield
Computacenter plc W176
Isleworth
British Sky Broadcasting Group
plc W146
London
Anglo American plc W92
Barclays PLC W114
BP p.l.c. W136
British Airways Plc W140
British American Tobacco
p.l.c. W142
British Broadcasting
Corporation W144
BT Group plc W148
Cable and Wireless plc W152
Cadbury Schweppes plc W154
Corus Group plc W178
Danka Business Systems
PLC W190
Diageo plc W206
EMI Group plc W212
Granada plc W248
Hanson PLC W252
HSBC Holdings plc W268
Imperial Chemical Industries
PLC W278
Invensys plc W290
J Sainsbury plc W300
Kingfisher plc W312
Lloyd's of London W336
Lonmin Plc W340
Marconi plc W354
Marks and Spencer p.l.c. W356
Pearson plc W430
The Peninsular and Oriental
Steam Navigation
Company W434
Prudential plc W464
The Rank Group PLC W472
Reed Elsevier plc W478
Reuters Group PLC W484
Rio Tinto plc W488
Rolls-Royce plc W496
Six Continents PLC W544
South African Breweries
plc W552
Tate & Lyle PLC W568
Tomkins PLC W604
Unilever W618
United Business Media
PLC W620
Virgin Group Ltd. W622
Whitbread PLC W638
WPP Group plc W646
Newbury
Vodafone Group PLC W628
Slough
Reckitt Benckiser plc W476

Watford
Hilton Group plc W258
Weybridge
Gallaher Group Plc W240

US

ALABAMA
Alexander City
Russell Corporation A1220
Birmingham
AmSouth Bancorporation A166
BE&K Inc. P552
Brasfield & Gorrie, LLC P560
Caremark Rx, Inc. A322
EBSCO Industries Inc. P170, P601
HEALTHSOUTH Corporation A698
O'Neal Steel, Inc. P694
Saks Incorporated A1238
SouthTrust Corporation A1308
Torchmark Corporation A1390
Vulcan Materials Company A1484
Huntsville
SCI Systems, Inc. A1256
Tuscaloosa
The University of Alabama System P755

ALASKA
Anchorage
Arctic Slope Regional Corporation P542

ARIZONA
Chandler
Bashas' Inc. P550
Microchip Technology Incorporated E93, E245
Phoenix
Avnet, Inc. A214
International FiberCom, Inc. E221
PETsMART, Inc. A1116
Phelps Dodge Corporation A1124
Pinnacle West Capital Corporation A1138
Radyne ComStream Inc. E274
Shamrock Foods Company P728
University of Phoenix Online E309
Viad Corp A1478
White Electronic Designs Corporation E317
Scottsdale
Allied Waste Industries, Inc. A122
The Dial Corporation A486
Discount Tire Co. P594
Medicis Pharmaceutical Corporation E89, E240

Meritage Corporation E243
P.F. Chang's China Bistro, Inc. E265
Tempe
America West Holdings Corporation A138
Mobile Mini, Inc. E246
SRP P734

ARKANSAS
Bentonville
Wal-Mart Stores, Inc. A1494
Fort Smith
Beverly Enterprises, Inc. A258
Little Rock
ALLTEL Corporation A128
Dillard's, Inc. A490
Superior Financial Corp. E296
Lowell
J.B. Hunt Transport Services, Inc. A788
Springdale
Tyson Foods, Inc. A1418
Stuttgart
Riceland Foods, Inc. P714

CALIFORNIA
Alameda
UTStarcom, Inc. E310
Aliso Viejo
Fluor Corporation A610
QLogic Corporation E272
Altadena
Charles Pankow Builders, Ltd. P573
Anaheim
DDi Corp. E191
Pacific Sunwear of California, Inc. E101, E259
Anderson
Sierra Pacific Industries P728
Artesia
California Dairies Inc. P563
Benicia
Copart, Inc. E45, E185
Beverly Hills
Hilton Hotels Corporation A720
Kennedy-Wilson, Inc. E227
Tracinda Corporation P747
Brea
Earle M. Jorgensen Company P601
Burbank
The Walt Disney Company A1496
Burlingame
Metron Technology N.V. E244
SERENA Software, Inc. E286

Calabasas
Countrywide Credit Industries, Inc. A438
Ixia E224
The Ryland Group, Inc. A1226
Tekelec E126, E299
Camarillo
California Amplifier, Inc. E168
Power-One, Inc. E269
Vitesse Semiconductor Corporation E136, E313
Carlsbad
ViaSat, Inc. E312
Chatsworth
Capstone Turbine Corporation E171
North American Scientific, Inc. E254
Optical Communication Products, Inc. E258
City of Industry
Hot Topic, Inc. E69, E215
Colton
Stater Bros. Holdings Inc. P462, P736
Commerce
Unified Western Grocers, Inc. P488, P752
Costa Mesa
Ceradyne, Inc. E175
The Keith Companies, Inc. E226
Cupertino
Apple Computer, Inc. A186
Mission West Properties, Inc. E245
Rational Software Corporation E110, E276
El Centro
VIB Corp E312
El Segundo
CB Richard Ellis Services, Inc. P120, P571
Computer Sciences Corporation A404
Hughes Electronics Corporation A736
Infonet Services Corporation E220
International Rectifier Corporation E74, E222
Mattel, Inc. A926
Merisel, Inc. A958
Unocal Corporation A1438
Emeryville
Pixar Animation Studios E103, E266
Eureka
Humboldt Bancorp E216
Folsom
Waste Connections, Inc. E139, E315

Foothill Ranch
Oakley, Inc. E**99**, E257

Foster City
Rudolph and Sletten, Inc. P**719**
Visa International A**1480**, P**508**, P766

Fountain Valley
Kingston Technology
Company P**272**, P651

Fremont
ASI Corp. P**545**
Asyst Technologies, Inc. E**31**, E160
AXT, Inc. E**162**
Centillium Communications, Inc. E**174**
Credence Systems Corporation E**46**, E187
New United Motor Manufacturing, Inc. P**366**, P687
SYNNEX Information Technologies, Inc. P**740**
Therma-Wave, Inc. E**300**
Virage Logic Corporation E**313**

Fullerton
Beckman Coulter, Inc. A**242**

Glendale
DreamWorks SKG P**166**, P597
PS Business Parks, Inc. E**271**

Irvine
Allergan, Inc. A**118**
California Coastal Communities, Inc. E**169**
Fidelity National Financial, Inc. A**590**
Freedom Communications, Inc. P**611**
Golden State Foods P**202**, P617
Hines Horticulture, Inc. E**214**
Newport Corporation E**253**
Nikken Global Inc. P**689**
Westcorp E**316**
WFS Financial Inc. E**317**

Jackson
Prospect Motors, Inc. P**706**

Lafayette
Bedford Property Investors, Inc. E**163**

Lake Forest
Western Digital Corporation A**1514**

Livingston
Foster Farms P**610**

Long Beach
California State University P**98**, P564

Los Angeles
AECOM Technology Corporation P**531**
Gores Technology Group P**619**
Intergroup Corporation E**221**
KB Home A**812**

Los Angeles Department of Water and Power P**660**
Northrop Grumman Corporation A**1044**
Occidental Petroleum Corporation A**1054**
Platinum Equity Holdings P**703**
Roll International Corporation P**416**, P716
Topa Equities, Ltd. P**746**
University of Southern California P**760**
The Yucaipa Companies LLC P**524**, P777

Malibu
JAKKS Pacific, Inc. E**225**

Manhattan Beach
Skechers U.S.A., Inc. E**289**

Menlo Park
E*TRADE Group, Inc. A**566**
Knowledge Universe, Inc. P**278**, P652
Robert Half International Inc. A**1208**
SRI International P**454**, P734

Mill Valley
S&P Company P**428**, P721

Milpitas
Devcon Construction Incorporated P**592**
Elantec Semiconductor, Inc. E**55**, E196
Linear Technology Corporation E**84**, E233
LSI Logic Corporation A**894**
Maxtor Corporation A**928**
Nanometrics Incorporated E**248**
NetRatings, Inc. E**251**
PCTEL, Inc. E**261**
Polycom, Inc. E**268**
Quantum Corporation A**1184**
Roxio, Inc. E**281**
Solectron Corporation A**1298**

Modesto
E. & J. Gallo Winery A**520**, P**168**, P600
Save Mart Supermarkets P**722**

Monrovia
Trader Joe's Company P**747**

Mountain View
Silicon Graphics, Inc. A**1284**

Newark
Ross Stores, Inc. A**1214**

Newbury Park
Semtech Corporation E**119**, E286

Newport Beach
Capital Pacific Holdings, Inc. E**171**
Conexant Systems, Inc. A**410**
Downey Financial Corp. E**194**
Health Care Property Investors, Inc. E**211**

The Irvine Company Inc. P**252**, P642
Pacific Gulf Properties Inc. E**259**
Pacific Mutual Holding Company P**384**, P695

Nicasio
Lucasfilm Ltd. P**302**, P661

Northridge
Medtronic MiniMed E**241**

Oakland
The Clorox Company A**374**
Crowley Maritime Corporation P**585**
Dreyer's Grand Ice Cream, Inc. A**510**
Golden West Financial Corporation A**658**
Kaiser Foundation Health Plan, Inc. A**810**, P**266**, P649
University of California P**494**, P755

Orange
David Wilson's Automotive Group P**589**
Young's Market Company, LLC P**777**

Palo Alto
Agilent Technologies, Inc. A**98**
CNF Inc. A**380**
Connetics Corporation E**184**
Greater Bay Bancorp E**209**
Hewlett-Packard Company A**712**
Sun Microsystems, Inc. A**1342**

Pasadena
Alexandria Real Estate Equities, Inc. E**150**
Avery Dennison Corporation A**210**
Jacobs Engineering Group Inc. A**786**
Parsons Corporation P**386**, P697
Tetra Tech, Inc. E**128**, E300

Perris
Modtech Holdings, Inc. E**94**, E246

Pleasanton
Dillingham Construction Corporation P**593**
PeopleSoft, Inc. A**1098**
Safeway Inc. A**1234**

Poway
ResMed Inc. E**112**, E279

Redwood City
DPR Construction, Inc. P**597**
Oracle Corporation A**1066**

Riverside
Fleetwood Enterprises, Inc. A**604**

Rosemead
Edison International A**532**

Roseville
Adventist Health P**530**

Sacramento
AgAmerica, FCB P**533**
California Public Employees'
  Retirement System A**314**, P**96**,
  P**563**
California State Lottery
  Commission P**564**
Sacramento Municipal Utility
  District P**720**
Sutter Health P**739**
Salinas
Monterey Pasta Company E**247**
San Diego
Charlotte Russe Holding,
  Inc. E**176**
Cohu, Inc. E**44**, E182
Cymer, Inc. E**49**, E189
Diversa Corporation E**193**
Factory 2-U Stores, Inc. E**60**,
  E202
Gateway, Inc. A**636**
IDEC Pharmaceuticals
  Corporation E**217**
Jack in the Box Inc. A**784**
JNI Corporation E**226**
Leap Wireless International,
  Inc. E**232**
Linsco/Private Ledger
  Corp. P**659**
Petco Animal Supplies,
  Inc. P**394**, P**701**
QUALCOMM Incorporated A**1182**
REMEC, Inc. E**277**
Science Applications
  International
  Corporation P**438**, P724
Sempra Energy A**1266**
Wireless Facilities, Inc. E**318**

San Francisco
24 Hour Fitness Worldwide
  Inc. P**528**
Advent Software, Inc. E**25**, E149
Bechtel Group, Inc. A**240**, P**74**,
  P**552**
BEI Technologies, Inc. E**164**
Catellus Development
  Corporation E**37**, E173
Catholic Healthcare West P**118**,
  P**570**
The Charles Schwab
  Corporation A**348**
Chemoil Corporation P**574**
Chevron Corporation A**352**
Del Monte Foods Company A**470**
Delta Dental Plan of
  California P**591**
DFS Group Limited P**156**, P592
DHL Worldwide Express,
  Inc. A**484**
Embarcadero Technologies,
  Inc. E**197**
Fisher Development, Inc. P**608**
The Gap, Inc. A**634**
Hall, Kinion & Associates,
  Inc. E**210**
Levi Strauss & Co. A**868**, P**292**,
  P**657**

Macromedia, Inc. E**86**, E235
McKesson Corporation A**946**
Micromuse Inc. E**245**
PG&E Corporation A**1120**
Providian Financial
  Corporation A**1170**
Sharper Image
  Corporation A**1274**, E**120**,
  E**287**
Swinerton Incorporated P**740**
Wells Fargo & Company A**1508**
Wilbur-Ellis Company P**772**
Williams-Sonoma, Inc. A**1530**

San Jose
Adobe Systems Incorporated A**76**
BEA Systems, Inc. E**33**, E163
Brocade Communications
  Systems, Inc. E**166**
Cisco Systems, Inc. A**368**
eBay Inc. E**54**, E196
Electroglas, Inc. E**57**, E197
Foundry Networks, Inc. E**206**
Fry's Electronics, Inc. P**196**,
  P**612**
Heritage Commerce Corp E**213**
JDS Uniphase Corporation A**792**
Knight Ridder Inc. A**832**
MA Laboratories, Inc. P**662**
Micrel, Incorporated E**92**, E244
Pericom Semiconductor
  Corporation E**263**
Photon Dynamics, Inc. E**266**
Sanmina Corporation A**1240**
Sunrise Telecom
  Incorporated E**296**
Symmetricom, Inc. E**297**
WJ Communications, Inc. E**318**

Santa Ana
The First American
  Corporation A**594**
GeoLogistics Corporation P**614**
Ingram Micro Inc. A**758**
New Horizons Worldwide,
  Inc. E**252**
PacifiCare Health Systems,
  Inc. A**1080**
Powerwave Technologies,
  Inc. E**106**, E269
SimpleTech, Inc. E**289**

Santa Barbara
INAMED Corporation E**219**
Somera Communications,
  Inc. E**290**
Tenet Healthcare
  Corporation A**1366**

Santa Clara
3Com Corporation A**54**
Applied Materials, Inc. A**188**
DSP Group, Inc. E**194**
Intel Corporation A**760**
IXYS Corporation E**76**, E224
National Semiconductor
  Corporation A**1002**
NVIDIA Corporation E**256**
Silicon Valley Bancshares E**122**,
  E**288**

Santa Monica
A-Mark Financial
  Corporation P**536**
Metro-Goldwyn-Mayer Inc. A**962**
Santa Monica Ford
  Corporation P**721**
Scope Industries E**285**
Scotts Valley
Seagate Technology, Inc. A**1260**,
  P**440**, P**725**
Sherman Oaks
Sunkist Growers, Inc. P**464**,
  P**738**
South San Francisco
Actuate Corporation E**22**, E148
Core-Mark International,
  Inc. P**584**
Genentech, Inc. A**640**
Imatron Inc. E**218**
Stanford
Stanford University P**456**, P735
Stockton
A. G. Spanos Companies P**532**
Sunnyvale
Advanced Micro Devices,
  Inc. A**82**
ArthroCare Corporation E**159**
Catalyst Semiconductor,
  Inc. E**173**
Juniper Networks, Inc. E**226**
Macrovision Corporation E**235**
Mercury Interactive
  Corporation E**91**, E242
Oak Technology, Inc. E**98**, E257
PLX Technology, Inc. E**267**
QuickLogic Corporation E**273**
SanDisk Corporation E**117**, E284
Silicon Storage Technology,
  Inc. E**121**, E288
SonicWALL, Inc. E**290**
Spectrian Corporation E**123**,
  E**292**
Verity, Inc. E**134**, E311
Vitria Technology, Inc. E**313**
Western Multiplex
  Corporation E**316**
Yahoo! Inc. A**1546**
Taft
Berry Petroleum Company E**164**
Thousand Oaks
Amgen Inc. A**160**
WellPoint Health Networks
  Inc. A**1506**
Torrance
OrthAlliance, Inc. E**259**
Ventura
Kinko's, Inc. P**274**, P**651**
Walnut
J. F. Shea Co., Inc. P**643**
ViewSonic Corporation P**765**
Walnut Creek
Longs Drug Stores
  Corporation A**886**

Watsonville
Marty Franich Auto Center P666

West Sacramento
MTS, Incorporated P346, P680
Raley's Inc. P710

Westlake Village
Consolidated Electrical
  Distributors Inc. P582
Diodes Incorporated E192
Dole Food Company, Inc. A494
Guitar Center, Inc. E66, E210

Woodland Hills
Health Net, Inc. A696
UniHealth Foundation P753

COLORADO
Black Hawk
Black Hawk Gaming &
  Development Company,
  Inc. E165

Boulder
Carrier Access Corporation E172
SignalSoft Corporation E287

Broomfield
Ball Corporation A224
Level 3 Communications,
  Inc. A866
McDATA Corporation E239

Denver
Catholic Health Initiatives P116,
  P569
CoBiz Inc. E181
Duke Energy Field Services
  Corporation P598
Evergreen Resources, Inc. E200
Forest Oil Corporation E62,
  E205
Frontier Airlines, Inc. E64, E206
Key Production Company,
  Inc. E228
Leprino Foods Company P657
MediaNews Group, Inc. P670
Newmont Mining
  Corporation A1024
Patina Oil & Gas
  Corporation E260
Prima Energy Corporation E270
Qwest Communications
  International Inc. A1186
St. Mary Land & Exploration
  Company E282
TeleTech Holdings, Inc. E127,
  E300
Tom Brown, Inc. E129, E302
United States Exploration,
  Inc. E308
Westport Resources
  Corporation E316

Englewood
Burt Automotive Network P563
Liberty Media Corporation A872
MarkWest Hydrocarbon,
  Inc. E237
Navigant International Inc. E250

Fort Collins
Advanced Energy Industries,
  Inc. E24, E149

Golden
Adolph Coors Company A78
CoorsTek, Inc. E185

Greeley
Hensel Phelps Construction
  Co. P630

Greenwood Village
CH2M Hill Companies,
  Ltd. P573
First Data Corporation A596
NAVIDEC, Inc. E249

Lakewood
CARQUEST Corporation P112,
  P569

Littleton
EchoStar Communications
  Corporation A528

Louisville
Storage Technology
  Corporation A1336

Steamboat Springs
TIC Holdings Inc. P745

Vail
Vail Banks, Inc. E310

CONNECTICUT
Bristol
ESPN, Inc. P605

Cheshire
Bozzuto's Inc. P560

Danbury
ATMI, Inc. E160
Praxair, Inc. A1156

Enfield
Retail Brand Alliance, Inc. P713

Fairfield
General Electric Company A646

Greenwich
Crompton Corporation A450
Equivest Finance, Inc. E200
FactSet Research Systems
  Inc. E61, E202
Holberg Industries, Inc. P236,
  P633
UST Inc. A1458

Hartford
Aetna Inc. A90
The Hartford Financial Services
  Group, Inc. A688
United Technologies
  Corporation A1432

Mashantucket
Mashantucket Pequot Gaming
  Enterprise Inc. P318, P667

Milford
Doctor's Associates Inc. P160,
  P595

New Britain
Connecticut Lottery
  Corporation P581
The Stanley Works A1322

New Haven
Yale University P776

Norwalk
Applera Corporation P542
EMCOR Group, Inc. A544
Micro Warehouse, Inc. P338,
  P676
Olin Corporation A1060

Rocky Hill
Ames Department Stores,
  Inc. A158

Shelton
TranSwitch Corporation E304

Stamford
ACNielsen Corporation A66
Asbury Automotive Group,
  Inc. P543
Conair Corporation P580
Crane Co. A446
International Paper
  Company A770
NYFIX, Inc. E256
Pitney Bowes Inc. A1142
Purdue Pharma L.P. P707
World Wrestling Federation
  Entertainment, Inc. E141,
  E319
Xerox Corporation A1544

Trumbull
Oxford Health Plans, Inc. A1076

West Hartford
Colt's Manufacturing Company,
  Inc. P132, P578

Windsor
TRC Companies, Inc. E131,
  E304

DELAWARE
Dover
Chesapeake Utilities
  Corporation E177

Newark
W. L. Gore & Associates,
  Inc. P522, P775

Wilmington
E. I. du Pont de Nemours and
  Company A534
Hercules Incorporated A704
MBNA Corporation A936

DISTRICT OF COLUMBIA
Newark
AARP P28, P529
AFL-CIO P34, P532
The American Red Cross P44,
  P538
The Carlyle Group P110, P567
Corporation for Public
  Broadcasting P144, P585

Federal Reserve System P186, P607
Intelsat, Ltd. P640
International Brotherhood of Teamsters P246, P641
National Geographic Society P358, P683
National Railroad Passenger Corporation P362, P684
Pension Benefit Guaranty Corporation P388, P699
Smithsonian Institution P450, P731
The Union Labor Life Insurance Company P754

Washington
Allied Capital Corporation E151
The Corporate Executive Board Company E186
Danaher Corporation A462
Fannie Mae A580
Federal Agricultural Mortgage Corporation E203
National Association of Securities Dealers, Inc. A996, P352, P682
United States Postal Service A1428, P490, P754
The Washington Post Company A1502

FLORIDA
Boca Raton
Purity Wholesale Grocers, Inc. P708
Questron Technology, Inc. E273
RailAmerica, Inc. E275

Bonita Springs
Abbey Carpet Company, Inc. P529
WCI Communities, Inc. P770

Clearwater
Digital Lightwave, Inc. E192
MarineMax, Inc. E237
Tech Data Corporation A1356

Coral Gables
Planet Automotive Group, Inc. P702

Daytona Beach
Budget Group, Inc. A300
Consolidated-Tomoka Land Co. E184
International Speedway Corporation E75, E222
National Association for Stock Car Auto Racing P681

Deerfield Beach
JM Family Enterprises, Inc. P256, P644

Delray Beach
Office Depot, Inc. A1056

Fort Lauderdale
Andrx Corporation E156
AutoNation, Inc. A206
Citrix Systems, Inc. E42, E179

Morse Operations, Inc. P678
Fort Myers
Chico's FAS, Inc. E177
Gainesville
University of Florida P756
Heathrow
AAA P528
Hollywood
Concord Camera Corp. E184
HEICO Corporation E67, E212
Jacksonville
Armor Holdings, Inc. E29, E158
JEA P643
Regency Centers Corporation E276
The St. Joe Company E115, E282
Winn-Dixie Stores, Inc. A1532
Juno Beach
FPL Group, Inc. A624
Lake Mary
Priority Healthcare Corporation E270
Lakeland
BREED Technologies, Inc. P561
Publix Super Markets, Inc. A1176, P402, P707
Melbourne
Harris Corporation A686
Miami
All American Semiconductor, Inc. E151
Answerthink, inc. E157
Burger King Corporation A302
Carnival Corporation A330
Continucare Corporation E185
Lennar Corporation A862
LNR Property Corporation E234
Noven Pharmaceuticals, Inc. E255
Royal Caribbean Cruises Ltd. A1216
Ryder System, Inc. A1222
Southern Wine & Spirits of America, Inc. P732
Orlando
Darden Restaurants, Inc. A464
Tupperware Corporation A1414
Palm Beach Gardens
Correctional Properties Trust E187
Dycom Industries, Inc. E52, E195
The Wackenhut Corporation A1488
Wackenhut Corrections Corporation E138, E314
Riviera Beach
AmeriPath, Inc. E155
Sebastian
eMerge Interactive, Inc. E197

Seffner
Rooms To Go P716
St. Petersburg
Jabil Circuit, Inc. A782
Tallahassee
State of Florida Department of the Lottery P736
Tampa
EPIX Holdings Corporation P603
Global Imaging Systems, Inc. E208
Reptron Electronics, Inc. E278
Tropical Sportswear Int'l Corporation E305
Vero Beach
George E. Warren Corporation P614
West Palm Beach
Metropolitan Health Networks, Inc. E244

GEORGIA
Alpharetta
NetBank, Inc. E251
Atlanta
American Cancer Society, Inc. P40, P537
BellSouth Corporation A248
Carpet Co-op Association of America P568
Cerulean Companies, Inc. P572
Chick-fil-A Inc. P124, P575
Cingular Wireless P576
The Coca-Cola Company A382
Coca-Cola Enterprises Inc. A384
CompuCredit Corporation E183
Cox Enterprises, Inc. A442, P146, P585
CTN Media Group, Inc. E188
Delta Air Lines, Inc. A478
Emory University P602
Equifax Inc. A558
Genuine Parts Company A652
Georgia Lottery Corporation P615
Georgia-Pacific Corporation A654
Gold Kist Inc. P200, P616
The Home Depot, Inc. A724
Interland, Inc. A762
Internet Security Systems, Inc. E222
Jameson Inns, Inc. E225
Manhattan Associates, Inc. E236
National Distributing Company, Inc. P682
National Service Industries, Inc. A1004
Printpack, Inc. P705
Riverwood International Corporation P715
Southern Company A1306
SunTrust Banks, Inc. A1346
Trammell Crow Residential P747

United Parcel Service,
Inc. **A1426**
Watkins Associated
Industries **P770**
WorldTravel BTI **P776**

Calhoun
Mohawk Industries, Inc. **A980**

Carrollton
Southwire Company **P733**

Columbus
AFLAC Incorporated **A92**
Bill Heard Enterprises **P555**

Dalton .
Beaulieu Of America, LLC **P552**

Duluth
AGCO Corporation **A96**
ARRIS Group, Inc. **E30, E158**

Kennesaw
Main Street Banks, Inc. **E236**

Lawrenceville
Scientific-Atlanta, Inc. **A1258**

Norcross
American Retail Group Inc. **P539**
T/R Systems, Inc. **E303**
Waffle House Inc. **P512, P767**

Savannah
Great Dane Limited
Partnership **P621**

Smyrna
RaceTrac Petroleum, Inc. **P710**

Thomasville
Flowers Foods, Inc. **A608**

Tucker
Oglethorpe Power
Corporation **P692**

HAWAII
Honolulu
Barnwell Industries, Inc. **E163**

IDAHO
Boise
Albertson's, Inc. **A110**
Boise Cascade Corporation **A274**
J.R. Simplot Company **P264,**
P648
Micron Technology, Inc. **A970**
Washington Group International,
Inc. **P769**
WinCo Foods, Inc. **P773**

Nampa
MicronPC, LLC **P676**

ILLINOIS
Abbott Park
Abbott Laboratories **A58**

Aurora
Cabot Microelectronics
Corporation **E168**

Bedford Park
CHEMCENTRAL
Corporation **P573**

Bloomingdale
Comark, Inc. **P136**, P580

Bloomington
GROWMARK, Inc. **P622**
State Farm Insurance
Companies **A1330, P458**, P735

Carlinville
Prairie Farms Dairy Inc. **P704**

Chicago
AMSTED Industries
Incorporated **P540**
Andersen **A172, P48**, P540, **W90**
Aon Corporation **A182**
Baker & McKenzie **A220, P66,**
P548
BANK ONE
CORPORATION **A230**
Bcom3 Group, Inc. **P72**, P551
Blue Cross and Blue Shield
Association **A268, P82**, P556
The Boeing Company **A272**
BorgWarner Inc. **A278**
Click Commerce, Inc. **E180**
CNA Financial Corporation **A378**
Encyclopædia Britannica,
Inc. **P176**, P603
Equity Group Investments,
L.L.C. **A560, P180**, P604
Exelon Corporation **A570**
FMC Corporation **A612**
GATX Corporation **A638**
Grant Thornton
International **P206**, P620
Harpo, Inc. **P218**, P625
Hartmarx Corporation **A690**
Health Care Service
Corporation **P226**, P628
Heartland Partners, L.P. **E212**
Hyatt Corporation **A740, P240,**
P636
HyperFeed Technologies,
Inc. **E70, E217**
IGA, INC. **A744, P242**, P638
Inforte Corp. **E220**
JMB Realty Corporation **P645**
Johnson Publishing Company,
Inc. **P258**, P646
Loyola University of
Chicago **P661**
The Marmon Group, Inc. **P312,**
P665
MB Financial, Inc. **E239**
Navistar International
Corporation **A1010**
Northern Trust
Corporation **A1042**
NovaMed Eyecare, Inc. **E255**
Pepper Construction Group,
LLC **P700**
The Quaker Oats
Company **A1180**
R. R. Donnelley & Sons
Company **A1218**

Rush System for Health **P719**
Ryerson Tull, Inc. **A1224**
Sara Lee Corporation **A1242**
Smurfit-Stone Container
Corporation **A1292**
Strategic Hotel Capital
LLC **P737**
Telephone and Data Systems,
Inc. **A1360**
Tribune Company **A1402**
TruServ Corporation **A1410,**
P484, P749
TTX Company **P751**
The University of Chicago **P496,**
P756
USFreightways
Corporation **A1454**
USG Corporation **A1456**
The Walsh Group **P768**
Wirtz Corporation **P774**
Wm. Wrigley Jr. Company **A1526**
YMCA of the USA **P777**

Decatur
Archer Daniels Midland
Company **A192**

Deerfield
Baxter International Inc. **A236**
Dade Behring Inc. **P587**
Jordan Industries, Inc. **P647**
Walgreen Co. **A1492**

Des Plaines
Frank Consolidated
Enterprises **P611**
United Stationers Inc. **A1430**

Downers Grove
FTD.COM INC. **E207**
The ServiceMaster
Company **A1272**
Spiegel, Inc. **A1314**

Elk Grove Township
UAL Corporation **A1420**

Elmhurst
Duchossois Industries, Inc. **P598**
Keebler Foods Company **A814**

Evanston
National Equipment Services,
Inc. **E249**
Northwestern University **P378,**
P691
Rotary International **P420**, P718

Frankfort
Provena Health **P706**

Franklin Park
Dean Foods Company **A466**

Freeport
Newell Rubbermaid Inc. **A1022**

Glenview
Illinois Tool Works Inc. **A748**

Highland Park
Solo Cup Company **P731**

Hoffman Estates
Career Education
Corporation E**172**
Sears, Roebuck and Co. A**1264**

Itasca
Serta, Inc. P**727**

Joliet
Horseshoe Gaming Holding
Corp. P**634**

Kankakee
TTC Illinois, Inc. P**750**

Lake Forest
Brunswick Corporation A**298**
IMC Global Inc. A**752**
Reyes Holdings LLC P**713**
Stericycle, Inc. E**293**
TAP Pharmaceutical Products
Inc. P**741**
Tenneco Automotive Inc. A**1368**
Trustmark Insurance
Company P**750**
Wintrust Financial
Corporation E**318**
W.W. Grainger, Inc. A**1538**

Lawrenceville
Golden Rule Insurance
Company P**617**

Lincolnshire
Fortune Brands, Inc. A**618**
Hewitt Associates LLC P**631**

Lisle
Molex Incorporated A**982**
Tellabs, Inc. A**1362**

Lombard
The Martin-Brower Company,
L.L.C. P**665**
U.S. Can Corporation P**762**

Long Grove
CF Industries, Inc. P**572**
Kemper Insurance
Companies P**268**, P650

McCook
Michigan Avenue Partners P**675**

Melrose Park
Alberto-Culver Company A**108**

Moline
Deere & Company A**468**

Mount Prospect
Salton, Inc. E**116**, E283

Mount Sterling
Dot Foods, Inc. P**596**

Mundelein
Medline Industries, Inc. P**670**

Naperville
Eby-Brown Company P**601**
Nicor Inc. A**1030**
Quality Chekd Dairies, Inc. P**708**

Niles
Coca-Cola Bottling Company of
Chicago P**577**

North Barrington
Clark/Bardes, Inc. E**180**

Northbrook
The Allstate Corporation A**126**
Lane Industries, Inc. P**655**

Northfield
Kraft Foods Inc. A**842**

Oak Brook
Ace Hardware Corporation A**64**,
P30, P529
Advocate Health Care P**531**
Clark Retail Group, Inc. P**577**
McDonald's Corporation A**942**

Peoria
Caterpillar Inc. A**332**

Prospect Heights
Household International,
Inc. A**734**

River Grove
Follett Corporation P**192**, P609

Rosemont
Comdisco, Inc. A**392**

Schaumburg
Motorola, Inc. A**990**

Skokie
Anixter International Inc. A**176**
Rand McNally & Company P**408**,
P711
Topco Associates, Inc. P**478**,
P746

Springfield
Illinois Department of the
Lottery P**638**

Urbana
University of Illinois P**756**

Vernon Hills
CDW Computer Centers,
Inc. A**336**

Westmont
Ty Inc. P**486**, P751

INDIANA

Anderson
Delco Remy International,
Inc. P**152**, P590

Batesville
Hillenbrand Industries,
Inc. A**718**

Bloomington
Indiana University P**638**

Carmel
Conseco, Inc. A**414**

Columbus
Cummins, Inc. A**456**

Elkhart
CTS Corporation E**189**

Fort Wayne
Allied Worldwide, Inc. P**535**
Do it Best Corp. P**594**

OmniSource Corporation P**694**

Indianapolis
American United Life Insurance
Company P**539**
Anthem Insurance Companies,
Inc. A**178**
Duke Realty Corporation E**194**
Eli Lilly and Company A**540**
Emmis Communications
Corporation E**198**
Guidant Corporation A**674**
Hunt Construction Group P**635**
LDI, Ltd. P**656**
Simon Property Group,
Inc. A**1286**

Merrillville
NiSource Inc. A**1034**

Mishawaka
Jordan Automotive Group P**647**
National Steel
Corporation A**1006**

IOWA

Des Moines
MidAmerican Energy Holdings
Company P**340**, P676
The Principal Financial
Group A**1162**

Iowa City
The University of Iowa P**757**

Muscatine
HON INDUSTRIES Inc. A**726**

Newton
Maytag Corporation A**934**

Pella
Pella Corporation P**698**

West Des Moines
Hy-Vee, Inc. P**636**
Multi-State Lottery
Association P**680**

KANSAS

Kansas City
Associated Wholesale Grocers,
Inc. P**62**, P547

Leavenworth
Sisters of Charity of Leavenworth
Health Services
Corporation P**729**

Merriam
VT Inc. P**767**

Overland Park
The Management Network Group,
Inc. E**236**
U.S. Central Credit Union P**763**
Waddell & Reed Financial,
Inc. E**315**
Yellow Corporation A**1548**

Topeka
Payless ShoeSource, Inc. A**1092**
Security Benefit Group,
Inc. P**725**

Westwood
Sprint Corporation A1318
Wichita
Candlewood Hotel Company, Inc. E169
Koch Industries, Inc. A834, P280, P653

KENTUCKY
Ashland
AEI Resources, Inc. P531
Bowling Green
Houchens Industries Inc. P634
Covington
Ashland Inc. A200
Regent Communications, Inc. E277
Highland Heights
General Cable Corporation A642
Lexington
Lexmark International, Inc. A870
The University of Kentucky P757
Louisville
Brown-Forman Corporation A296
Churchill Downs Incorporated E40, E178
Genlyte Thomas Group LLC P613
Humana Inc. A738
TRICON Global Restaurants, Inc. A1404

LOUISIANA
Baton Rouge
Amedisys, Inc. E152
Louisiana State University System P661
Lafayette
PetroQuest Energy, Inc. E264
Stone Energy Corporation E295
New Orleans
Entergy Corporation A554
Freeport-McMoRan Copper & Gold Inc. A628
McDermott International, Inc. A940

MAINE
Freeport
L.L. Bean, Inc. P300, P660
Portland
UNUMProvident A1440

MARYLAND
Adelphi
University System of Maryland P762
Baltimore
Constellation Energy Group, Inc. A424

Crown Central Petroleum Corporation P586
Johns Hopkins Medicine P645
The Johns Hopkins University P646
Maryland State Lottery Agency P666
Municipal Mortgage and Equity, LLC E248
Orion Power Holdings, Inc. E258
Sunbelt Beverage Corporation P738
Vertis Inc. P506, P765
The Whiting-Turner Contracting Company P772
Beltsville
Ritz Camera Centers, Inc. P714
Bethesda
The ASCII Group, Inc. P544
Clark Enterprises, Inc. P576
Discovery Communications, Inc. P158, P594
Goodwill Industries International, Inc. P618
Host Marriott Corporation A732
LaSalle Hotel Properties E231
Lockheed Martin Corporation A882
Marriott International, Inc. A912
Chevy Chase
Chevy Chase Bank, F.S.B. P574
Columbia
Columbia Bancorp E182
Corporate Office Properties Trust E187
Humphrey Hospitality Trust, Inc. E216
Magellan Health Services, Inc. A904
MedStar Health P671
W. R. Grace & Co. A1536
Gaithersburg
MedImmune, Inc. E90, E240
Sodexho, Inc. A1296
Hagerstown
Allegheny Energy, Inc. A114
Linthicum
CIENA Corporation E41, E179
Marriottsville
Bon Secours Health System, Inc. P557
Rockville
Arguss Communications, Inc. E158
HealthExtras, Inc. E211
Salisbury
Perdue Farms Incorporated P392, P700
Sparks
McCormick & Company, Incorporated A938

Towson
The Black & Decker Corporation A264

MASSACHUSETTS
Andover
MKS Instruments, Inc. E246
Bedford
Aware, Inc. E161
Mykrolis Corporation E248
RSA Security Inc. E114, E281
Beverly
Axcelis Technologies, Inc. E161
Boston
Affiliated Managers Group, Inc. E149
Bain & Company P64, P548
Blue Cross and Blue Shield of Massachusetts, Inc. P84, P557
Boston Celtics Limited Partnership A280
The Boston Consulting Group P94, P559
Boston Private Financial Holdings, Inc. E165
Boston Properties, Inc. E34, E165
Boston University P560
Cabot Industrial Trust E167
Capital Crossing Bank E170
CareGroup, Inc. P566
Colliers International Property Consultants Inc. P578
Connell Limited Partnership P581
Eaton Vance Corp. E53, E195
FleetBoston Financial Corporation A602
FMR Corp. A614, P190, P609
The Gillette Company A656
International Data Group P248, P641
Investors Financial Services Corp. E223
John Hancock Financial Services, Inc. A798
Liberty Mutual Insurance Companies A874, P294, P658
New Balance Athletic Shoe, Inc. P686
Partners HealthCare System, Inc. P697
State Street Corporation A1332
Teradyne, Inc. A1372
Tucker Anthony Sutro E132, E306
University of Massachusetts P757
Boxborough
Cytyc Corporation E50, E190
Braintree
Massachusetts State Lottery Commission P668
Burlington
Lightbridge, Inc. E83, E233

ZOLL Medical Corporation E**144**, E**320**

Cambridge
Art Technology Group, Inc. E**159**
Arthur D. Little, Inc. P**54**, P**543**
Forrester Research, Inc. E**63**, E**205**
Harvard University P**220**, P626
Massachusetts Institute of Technology P**667**
Modern Continental Companies, Inc. P**678**
Polaroid Corporation A**1148**

Canton
Cumberland Farms, Inc. P**586**
Reebok International Ltd. A**1194**
Tweeter Home Entertainment Group, Inc. E**306**

Charlton
FiberCore, Inc. E**203**

Chelmsford
Brooks Automation, Inc. E**35**, E166
MatrixOne, Inc. E**237**
Mercury Computer Systems, Inc. E**241**

Chelsea
Gulf Oil, L.P. P**624**

Concord
OneSource Information Services, Inc. E**100**, E258

Dedham
National Amusements Inc. P**681**

Framingham
Bose Corporation P**92**, P559
Staples, Inc. A**1324**
The TJX Companies, Inc. A**1388**

Gloucester
Varian Semiconductor Equipment Associates, Inc. E**133**, E310

Hopkinton
EMC Corporation A**542**

Lakeville-Middleboro
Ocean Spray Cranberries, Inc. P**380**, P692

Lexington
Raytheon Company A**1190**

Mansfield
Helix Technology Corporation E**213**

Natick
BJ's Wholesale Club, Inc. A**262**
Boston Scientific Corporation A**282**
Cognex Corporation E**43**, E181

New Bedford
Seacoast Financial Services Corporation E**285**

Newton
TAC Worldwide Companies P**741**

North Billerica
BTU International, Inc. E**167**

North Reading
Converse Inc. P**142**, P583

Norwood
Analog Devices, Inc. A**170**
Corporate Software & Technology, Inc. P**584**

Pittsfield
K-B Toys P**649**

Somerville
The Herb Chambers Companies P**631**

Springfield
Big Y Foods, Inc. P**554**
Massachusetts Mutual Life Insurance Company A**922**, P**320**, P667

Taunton
Kopin Corporation E**229**

Tewksbury
Demoulas Super Markets Inc. P**591**

Wakefield
American Dental Partners, Inc. E**153**

Waltham
Global Companies LLC P**616**
Netegrity, Inc. E**96**, E251
Thermo Electron Corporation A**1382**
Tufts Associated Health Plans, Inc. P**751**

Wellesley
Harvard Pilgrim Health Care, Inc. P**626**
PerkinElmer, Inc. A**1110**

West Springfield
Northeast Utilities A**1040**

Westborough
TC PipeLines, LP E**298**

Whately
The Yankee Candle Company, Inc. E**143**, E320

Woburn
Alpha Industries, Inc. E**152**
PolyMedica Corporation E**105**, E268

Worcester
Allmerica Financial Corporation A**124**

MICHIGAN
Ada
Alticor Inc. P**536**

Ann Arbor
Borders Group, Inc. A**276**
Domino's Inc. A**500**, P**162**, P595
Flint Ink Corporation P**608**
The University of Michigan P**758**

Auburn Hills
Champion Enterprises, Inc. A**346**
Guardian Industries Corp. P**212**, P623
MEEMIC Holdings, Inc. E**241**
MSX International, Inc. P**679**

Battle Creek
Kellogg Company A**816**
W.K. Kellogg Foundation P**520**, P774

Benton Harbor
Whirlpool Corporation A**1520**

Bloomfield Hills
Pulte Homes, Inc. A**1178**

Dearborn
CMS Energy Corporation A**376**
Ford Motor Company A**616**
Meridian Automotive Systems, Inc. P**673**

Detroit
Blue Cross Blue Shield of Michigan P**86**, P557
Comerica Incorporated A**394**
Detroit Medical Center P**591**
DTE Energy Company A**512**
General Motors Corporation A**650**
Henry Ford Health System P**630**
Penske Corporation P**390**, P699
Soave Enterprises L.L.C. P**731**
Wolverine Packing Company P**775**

Farmington Hills
Compuware Corporation A**406**
Trinity Health P**748**

Flint
Citizens Banking Corporation E**179**

Fraser
Venture Industries P**764**

Grand Rapids
Gordon Food Service P**618**
Meijer, Inc. P**328**, P671
Spartan Stores, Inc. A**1312**
Steelcase Inc. A**1334**

Holland
Haworth Inc. P**222**, P627

Lansing
Capitol Bancorp Ltd. E**171**
Michigan Lottery P**675**

Mason
Dart Container Corporation P**150**, P588

Midland
The Dow Chemical Company A**504**
Dow Corning Corporation P**164**, P596

Monroe
La-Z-Boy Incorporated A**854**

Muskegon
Quality Stores, Inc. P406, P709
SPX Corporation A1320

Plymouth
Don Massey Cadillac, Inc. P596
Metaldyne Corporation P673
Plastipak Packaging, Inc. P702

Royal Oak
William Beaumont
Hospital P773

Southfield
Barton Malow Company P550
Federal-Mogul Corporation A584
Lear Corporation A856

Taylor
Masco Corporation A920

Troy
ArvinMeritor, Inc. A198
Collins & Aikman
Corporation A388
Delphi Automotive Systems
Corporation A476
Kelly Services, Inc. A818
Kmart Corporation A830
Oxford Automotive, Inc. P695
Woodbridge Group P776

Zeeland
Herman Miller, Inc. A706

MINNESOTA

Arden Hills
Land O'Lakes, Inc. A850, P288,
P654

Austin
Hormel Foods Corporation A730

Bayport
Andersen Corporation P50, P541

Bloomington
Holiday Companies P633
The Toro Company A1392

Eagan
Buffets, Inc. P562
Northwest Airlines
Corporation A1046

Eden Prairie
Best Buy Co., Inc. A254
C.H. Robinson Worldwide,
Inc. A344
SUPERVALU INC. A1348

Edina
Alliant Techsystems Inc. A120
HomeServices.Com Inc. E215
Regis Corporation A1196

Fairmont
Rosen's Diversified, Inc. P717

Inver Grove Heights
Cenex Harvest States
Cooperatives P122, P571

Marshall
Schwan's Sales Enterprises,
Inc. P436, P724

Minneapolis
Aid Association for
Lutherans/Lutheran
Brotherhood P534
Bemis Company, Inc. A250
BUCA, Inc. E167
Carlson Companies, Inc. P106,
P567
Ceridian Corporation A342
CyberOptics Corporation E48,
E189
General Mills, Inc. A648
Genmar Holdings, Inc. P614
Jostens, Inc. P262, P647
M. A. Mortenson Company P663
Medtronic, Inc. A952
Michael Foods, Inc. P674
Nash Finch Company A994
PepsiAmericas, Inc. A1104
The Pillsbury Company A1136
PW Eagle, Inc. E272
Target Corporation A1352
Tower Automotive, Inc. A1394
United Shipping & Technology,
Inc. E308
University of Minnesota P758
U.S. Bancorp A1444
Xcel Energy Inc. A1542

Minnetonka
ADC Telecommunications,
Inc. A70
Allina Health System P536
International Multifoods
Corporation A768
Opus Corporation P695
UnitedHealth Group
Incorporated A1434

Moorhead
American Crystal Sugar
Company P538

New Ulm
Associated Milk Producers
Incorporated P58, P546

North Mankato
Taylor Corporation P742

Oakdale
Imation Corp. A750

Owatonna
Federated Insurance
Companies P607

Plymouth
Carlson Wagonlit Travel A328,
P108, P567
Christopher & Banks
Corporation E178

Rochester
Mayo Foundation P324, P668
Pemstar Inc. E262

Shoreview
Deluxe Corporation A480

St. Paul
AgriBank, FCB P533
Ecolab Inc. A530

Minnesota Mining and
Manufacturing Company A976
Minnesota Mutual Companies,
Inc. P677
The St. Paul Companies,
Inc. A1236

Wayzata
Cargill, Incorporated A324,
P104, P566

MISSISSIPPI

Clinton
WorldCom, Inc. A1534

Greenwood
Staple Cotton Cooperative
Association P735

Jackson
Ergon, Inc. P605
Jitney-Jungle Stores of America,
Inc. P644

Tupelo
BancorpSouth, Inc. E162

MISSOURI

Carthage
Leggett & Platt,
Incorporated A858

Chesterfield
Maverick Tube Corporation E87,
E238

Clayton
First Banks America, Inc. E204
Graybar Electric Company,
Inc. P208, P620

Columbia
University of Missouri
System P758

Des Peres
The Jones Financial Companies,
L.P., LLP P260, P646

Fenton
Maritz Inc. P308, P664
UniGroup, Inc. P753

Kansas City
American Century Companies,
Inc. P537
Bartlett and Company P549
Black & Veatch P556
Dairy Farmers of America P148,
P587
DeBruce Grain, Inc. P589
Dunn Industries, Inc. P599
Farmland Industries, Inc. A582,
P184, P606
H&R Block, Inc. A680
Hallmark Cards, Inc. A678,
P216, P625
Health Midwest P629
Interstate Bakeries
Corporation A774
Russell Stover Candies
Inc. P424, P719

Sutherland Lumber Company, L.P. **P739**

UtiliCorp United Inc. **A1464**

Lee's Summit

Payless Cashways, Inc. **A1090**

Maryland Heights

Express Scripts, Inc. **A574**

Monett

Jack Henry & Associates, Inc. **E77, E225**

Springfield

Bass Pro Shops, Inc. **P550**

St. Louis

A.G. Edwards, Inc. **A94**

Ameren Corporation **A136**

Anheuser-Busch Companies, Inc. **A174**

Apex Oil Company, Inc. **P542**

Ascension Health **P56, P544**

BJC Health System **P555**

Brown Shoe Company, Inc. **A294**

Carondelet Health System **P568**

Charter Communications, Inc. **A350**

Emerson **A546**

Engineered Support Systems, Inc. **E198**

Enterprise Rent-A-Car **P178, P603**

Falcon Products, Inc. **E202**

Furniture Brands International, Inc. **A630**

Harbour Group Industries, Inc. **P625**

J.S. Alberici Construction Co., Inc. **P649**

The May Department Stores Company **A932**

McCarthy **P669**

Monsanto Company **A984**

Premcor Inc. **P704**

RehabCare Group, Inc. **E111, E277**

Schnuck Markets, Inc. **P723**

Sisters of Mercy Health System-St. Louis **P730**

Solutia Inc. **A1300**

The Source Information Management Company **E290**

SSM Health Care System Inc. **P734**

Washington University in St. Louis **P769**

MONTANA

Columbus

Stillwater Mining Company **E294**

NEBRASKA

Lincoln

The University of Nebraska **P759**

Omaha

Ag Processing Inc **P36, P532**

Berkshire Hathaway Inc. **A252**

ConAgra Foods, Inc. **A408**

The Mutual of Omaha Companies **P348, P680**

Peter Kiewit Sons', Inc. **A1114, P396, P701**

The Scoular Company **P724**

Union Pacific Corporation **A1422**

NEVADA

Las Vegas

Harrah's Entertainment, Inc. **A684**

Mandalay Resort Group **A906**

MGM Mirage **A966**

Park Place Entertainment Corporation **A1086**

Tang Industries, Inc. **P741**

Reno

AMERCO **A134**

Meridian Gold Inc. **E242**

NEW HAMPSHIRE

Hampton

Fisher Scientific International Inc. **A600**

NEW JERSEY

Bedminster

Verizon Wireless Inc. **P765**

Berkeley Heights

The Connell Company **P581**

Burlington

Burlington Coat Factory Warehouse Corporation **A304**

Camden

Campbell Soup Company **A316**

Carteret

Di Giorgio Corporation **P592**

Cherry Hill

Commerce Bancorp, Inc. **E182**

inTEST Corporation **E223**

Clinton

Foster Wheeler Ltd. **A620**

Cranford

The Newark Group **P689**

East Rutherford

Metromedia Company **P332, P674**

Eatontown

New World Restaurant Group, Inc. **E253**

Edison

J. M. Huber Corporation **P645**

Elizabeth

Wakefern Food Corporation **A1490, P514, P768**

Englewood Cliffs

Asta Funding, Inc. **E159**

Fairfield

Covanta Energy Corporation **A440**

Measurement Specialties, Inc. **E240**

Flanders

Rudolph Technologies, Inc. **E282**

Florham Park

Gale & Wentworth, L.L.C. **P613**

Franklin Lakes

Becton, Dickinson and Company **A244**

Hackensack

Innodata Corporation **E221**

Hamilton Square

Yardville National Bancorp **E320**

Iselin

Engelhard Corporation **A550**

U.S. Industries, Inc. **A1446**

Jersey City

Lehman Brothers Holdings Inc. **A860**

The Port Authority of New York and New Jersey **P398, P703**

UIS, Inc. **P752**

Lawrenceville

New Jersey State Lottery Commission **P687**

Madison

American Home Products Corporation **A148**

Schering-Plough Corporation **A1250**

Mahwah

Inserra Supermarkets, Inc. **P640**

Medford

Canterbury Consulting Group, Inc. **E36, E170**

Montvale

Advantage/ESM Ferolie **P530**

The Great Atlantic & Pacific Tea Company, Inc. **A670**

Morristown

Dendrite International, Inc. **E191**

GPU, Inc. **A668**

Honeywell International Inc. **A728**

Mt. Laurel

Ulticom, Inc. **E307**

Murray Hill

C. R. Bard, Inc. **A444**

The Dun & Bradstreet Corporation **A516**

Lucent Technologies Inc. **A898**

New Brunswick

Johnson & Johnson **A800**

Newark

Prudential Financial **A1172**

Public Service Enterprise Group Incorporated **A1174**

Oak Ridge
Lakeland Bancorp, Inc. E**231**
Paramus
Toys "R" Us, Inc. A**1396**
Vornado Realty Trust E**137**, E314
Park Ridge
The Hertz Corporation A**710**
Parsippany
Emerson Radio Corp. E**58**, E198
NRT Incorporated P**692**
Paterson
Suprema Specialties, Inc. E**296**
Peapack
Pharmacia Corporation A**1122**
Pennsauken
Holman Enterprises P**633**
Honickman Affiliates P**634**
Piscataway
American Standard Companies Inc. A**152**
Enzon, Inc. E**199**
Princeton
Church & Dwight Co., Inc. A**358**
Dataram Corporation E**190**
Exide Technologies A**572**
The Robert Wood Johnson Foundation P**715**
Ramsey
Liberty Travel, Inc. P**296**, P658
Red Bank
Millennium Chemicals Inc. A**974**
Rochelle Park
Cantor Fitzgerald, L.P. P**565**
Roseland
Automatic Data Processing, Inc. A**204**
Saddle Brook
Alexander's, Inc. E**150**
Sealed Air Corporation A**1262**
Secaucus
The Children's Place Retail Stores, Inc. E**177**
Goya Foods, Inc. P**204**, P619
The Hartz Mountain Corporation P**626**
Somerset
Multilink Technology Corporation E**247**
TeamStaff, Inc. E**125**, E299
Teaneck
Cognizant Technology Solutions Corporation E**181**
Union
Bed Bath & Beyond Inc. A**246**
Upper Saddle River
PDI, Inc. E**261**
Vineland
Sun Bancorp, Inc. E**295**
Voorhees
American Water Works Company, Inc. A**154**
Wall
Centennial Communications Corp. E**38**, E174
Warren
ANADIGICS, Inc. E**28**, E156
Celgene Corporation E**174**
The Chubb Corporation A**356**
Wayne
G-I Holdings, Inc. P**612**
Whitehouse Station
Merck & Co., Inc. A**956**
Woodcliff Lake
Ingersoll-Rand Company A**754**

NEW MEXICO

Albuquerque
Furrs Supermarkets, Inc. P**612**
Presbyterian Healthcare Services P**704**
SBS Technologies, Inc. E**284**
Sun Healthcare Group, Inc. A**1340**
Santa Fe
Security Capital Group Incorporated E**285**

NEW YORK

Albany
Albany Molecular Research, Inc. E**150**
State University of New York P**460**, P736
Amherst
Mark IV Industries, Inc. P**310**, P664
Armonk
International Business Machines Corporation A**764**
Bethpage
Cablevision Systems Corporation A**312**
Ladenburg Thalmann Financial Services Inc. E**231**
Bronx
Montefiore Medical Center P**678**
Brooklyn
KeySpan Corporation A**824**
Buffalo
Comptek Research, Inc. E**183**
Delaware North Companies Inc. P**590**
Rich Products Corporation P**714**
Corning
Corning Incorporated A**434**
DeWitt
Agway Inc. P**38**, P534
East Syracuse
Anaren Microwave, Inc. E**156**
Dairylea Cooperative Inc. P**588**
Elmira
WKI Holding Company, Inc. P**775**
Fairport
Constellation Brands, Inc. A**422**
Farmingdale
P.C. Richard & Son P**697**
Florida
Big V Supermarkets, Inc. P**554**
Garden City
Avis Group Holdings, Inc. A**212**
Great Neck
North Shore-Long Island Jewish Health System P**690**
Hicksville
Allied Devices Corporation E**26**, E151
Islandia
Computer Associates International, Inc. A**402**
Ithaca
Cornell University P**584**
Tompkins County Trustco, Inc. E**302**
Jericho
Roslyn Bancorp, Inc. E**281**
Lockport
First Niagara Financial Group, Inc. E**205**
Long Island City
Steven Madden, Ltd. E**294**
Melville
American Home Mortgage Holdings, Inc. E**154**
Arrow Electronics, Inc. A**196**
Nu Horizons Electronics Corp. E**97**, E256
Reckson Associates Realty Corp. E**276**
Mitchel Field
Frequency Electronics, Inc. E**206**
Mount Kisco
American Real Estate Partners, L.P. E**154**
New York City
4Kids Entertainment, Inc. E**147**
ABC, Inc. A**60**
Actrade Financial Technologies, Ltd. E**21**, E148
Amerada Hess Corporation A**132**
America First Mortgage Investments, Inc. E**152**
American Express Company A**142**
American International Group, Inc. A**150**
American Stock Exchange, Inc. P**46**, P539
The Andrew W. Mellon Foundation P**541**

A=AMERICAN BUSINESS • E=EMERGING COMPANIES • P=PRIVATE COMPANIES • W=WORLD BUSINESS

Anthracite Capital, Inc. **E157**
AOL Time Warner Inc. **A180**
The Associated Press **P60**, P546
AT&T Corp. **A202**
Avon Products, Inc. **A216**
AXA Financial, Inc. **A218**
The Bank of New York Company,
  Inc. **A228**
Barnes & Noble College
  Bookstores, Inc. **P549**
Barnes & Noble, Inc. **A232**
The Bear Stearns Companies
  Inc. **A238**
Bloomberg L.P. **P80**, P556
BP Prudhoe Bay Royalty
  Trust **E166**
Bristol-Myers Squibb
  Company **A290**
Calvin Klein, Inc. **P100**, P564
Catholic Healthcare
  Network **P570**
CBS Television Network **A334**
Cendant Corporation **A338**
Charter Municipal Mortgage
  Acceptance Company **E176**
Citigroup Inc. **A370**
The City University of New
  York **P128**, P576
Colgate-Palmolive
  Company **A386**
Columbia House Company **P579**
Columbia University **P134**, P579
Consolidated Edison, Inc. **A418**
ContiGroup Companies,
  Inc. **A426**, **P140**, P583
Credit Suisse First Boston **A448**
Cushman & Wakefield Inc. **P587**
Deloitte Touche Tohmatsu **A474**,
  P154, P590, **W196**
Dover Corporation **A502**
Dow Jones & Company,
  Inc. **A506**
The Dyson-Kissner-Moran
  Corporation **P600**
Empire HealthChoice, Inc. **P174**,
  P602
Ernst & Young
  International **A562**, **P182**,
  P605, **W222**
The Estée Lauder Companies
  Inc. **A564**
Federal Reserve Bank of New
  York **P607**
The Ford Foundation **P194**,
  P610
Fox Entertainment Group,
  Inc. **A622**
General Maritime
  Corporation **E208**
The Goldman Sachs Group,
  Inc. **A660**
Gould Paper Corporation **P619**
Greka Energy Corporation **E209**
The Guardian Life Insurance
  Company of America **P214**,
  P623
Health Insurance Plan of Greater
  New York **P628**

Hearst-Argyle Television,
  Inc. **E212**
The Hearst Corporation **A700**,
  P228, P629
Helmsley Enterprises, Inc. **P230**,
  P629
ICC Industries Inc. **P637**
IMPATH Inc. **E72**, E218
International Flavors &
  Fragrances Inc. **A766**
The Interpublic Group of
  Companies, Inc. **A772**
iStar Financial Inc. **E224**
J. Crew Group, Inc. **P254**, P642
J.P. Morgan Chase & Co. **A808**
Kenneth Cole Productions,
  Inc. **E78**, E227
Kohlberg Kravis Roberts &
  Co. **A836**, **P282**, P653
KPMG International **A840**, **P286**,
  P654, **W324**
L-3 Communications Holdings,
  Inc. **A846**
LaBranche & Co Inc. **E230**
Lexent Inc. **E233**
Liz Claiborne, Inc. **A880**
Loews Corporation **A884**
Loral Space & Communications
  Ltd. **A888**
M. Fabrikant & Sons **P662**
MacAndrews & Forbes Holdings
  Inc. **A902**, **P304**, P663
Major League Baseball **P306**,
  P663
Marsh & McLennan Companies,
  Inc. **A916**
Martha Stewart Living
  Omnimedia Inc. **A918**
The McGraw-Hill Companies,
  Inc. **A944**
McKinsey & Company **A948**,
  P326, P670
Memorial Sloan-Kettering Cancer
  Center **P672**
Merrill Lynch & Co., Inc. **A960**
Metropolitan Life Insurance
  Company **A964**
Metropolitan Transportation
  Authority **P334**, P674
The MONY Group Inc. **A986**
Morgan Stanley Dean Witter &
  Co. **A988**
National Basketball
  Association **P354**, P682
National Broadcasting Company,
  Inc. **A998**
National Football League **P356**,
  P683
National Hockey League **P360**,
  P684
New Plan Excel Realty Trust,
  Inc. **E252**
New York City Health and
  Hospitals Corporation **P368**,
  P687
New York Life Insurance
  Company **A1016**, **P370**, P688
New York Stock Exchange,
  Inc. **A1018**, **P374**, P688

The New York Times
  Company **A1020**
New York University **P689**
Omnicom Group Inc. **A1062**
Parsons Brinckerhoff Inc. **P696**
Pfizer Inc **A1118**
Philip Morris Companies
  Inc. **A1126**
Philips International Realty
  Corp. **E266**
Polo Ralph Lauren
  Corporation **A1150**
PricewaterhouseCoopers **A1158**,
  P400-401, P705, **W462**
PRIMEDIA, Inc. **A1160**
Red Apple Group, Inc. **P712**
Renco Group Inc. **P712**
Revlon, Inc. **A1200**
Richton International
  Corporation **E280**
The Rockefeller
  Foundation **P414**, P715
Royster-Clark, Inc. **P718**
Schlumberger Limited **A1252**
Scholastic Corporation **A1254**
The SF Holdings Group,
  Inc. **P727**
Siebert Financial Corp. **E287**
Singer N.V. **P729**
Skadden, Arps, Slate, Meagher &
  Flom LLP **A1288**, **P446**, P730
Skidmore Owings & Merrill
  LLP **P448**, P730
SL Green Realty Corp. **E289**
Sotheby's Holdings, Inc. **A1304**
The Structure Tone
  Organization **P737**
Take-Two Interactive Software,
  Inc. **E298**
Tarragon Realty Investors,
  Inc. **E298**
Teachers Insurance and Annuity
  Association-College Retirement
  Equities Fund **A1354**, **P466**,
  P742
Tiffany & Co. **A1384**
Tishman Realty & Construction
  Co. Inc. **P476**, P745
The Topps Company, Inc. **E130**,
  E303
Towers Perrin **P480**, P746
Transammonia, Inc. **P748**
Triarc Companies, Inc. **A1400**
The Trump Organization **A1408**,
  P482, P749
UJC of North America **P752**
USA Networks, Inc. **A1450**
Venator Group, Inc. **A1470**
Verizon Communications
  Inc. **A1472**
Viacom Inc. **A1476**
The Warnaco Group, Inc. **A1498**
Westvaco Corporation **A1516**
Westwood One, Inc. **E140**, E317

Norwich
NBT Bancorp Inc. **E250**

Pleasantville
The Reader's Digest Association, Inc. A1192

Port Washington
Acadia Realty Trust E147

Purchase
Atlas Air Worldwide Holdings, Inc. E32, E160
Central National-Gottesman Inc. P571
MasterCard International Incorporated A924, P322, P668
PepsiCo, Inc. A1106

Rego Park
The Lefrak Organization P290, P656

Rochester
Bausch & Lomb Incorporated A234
Eastman Kodak Company A524
Home Properties of New York, Inc. E214
University of Rochester P760
Wegmans Food Markets, Inc. P771

Ronkonkoma
Quality King Distributors Inc. P709

Rye
Gabelli Asset Management Inc. E65, E207

Rye Brook
Parsons & Whittemore, Incorporated P696
Universal American Financial Corp. E309

Schenectady
The Golub Corporation P617
New York State Lottery P372, P688

Somers
The Pepsi Bottling Group, Inc. A1102

Staten Island
Advance Publications, Inc. A80, P32, P530
Staten Island Bancorp, Inc. E293

Syracuse
Carlisle Companies Incorporated A326
Niagara Mohawk Holdings Inc. A1028
The Penn Traffic Company A1094

Tarrytown
Westcon Group, Inc. P771

Westbury
Nathan's Famous, Inc. E95, E249
Vasomedical, Inc. E311

White Plains
ITT Industries, Inc. A780

Power Authority of the State of New York P703
Starwood Hotels & Resorts Worldwide, Inc. A1328
Texaco Inc. A1376

Whitestone
Kinray, Inc. P651

Yonkers
Consumers Union of United States, Inc. P138, P582

NORTH CAROLINA

Asheboro
Klaussner Furniture Industries, Inc. P652

Cary
SAS Institute Inc. P430, P721

Charlotte
Baker & Taylor Corporation P68, P548
Bank of America Corporation A226
Belk, Inc. P76, P553
Duke Energy Corporation A514
Goodrich Corporation A662
Hendrick Automotive Group P630
National Gypsum Company P683
Nucor Corporation A1052
Wachovia Corporation A1486

Durham
Cree, Inc. E47, E188
Duke University P598
Swifty Serve Corporation P740

Gastonia
Parkdale Mills, Inc. P696

Greensboro
Burlington Industries, Inc. A306
Jefferson-Pilot Corporation A794
RF Micro Devices, Inc. E280
VF Corporation A1474

Hickory
Alex Lee, Inc. P535

High Point
LifeStyle Furnishings International Ltd. P298, P659

Huntersville
Heafner Tire Group, Inc. P628

Matthews
Family Dollar Stores, Inc. A578

Raleigh
General Parts, Inc. P613
Investors Management Corp. P642
Progress Energy, Inc. A1166
Salix Pharmaceuticals, Ltd. E283

Rocky Mount
MBM Corporation P669

Sanford
The Pantry, Inc. A1084

Trinity
Sealy Corporation P442, P725

Troy
First Bancorp E204

Wilkesboro
Lowe's Companies, Inc. A892

Winston-Salem
Krispy Kreme Doughnuts, Inc. E80, E230
Novant Health, Inc. P691
R.J. Reynolds Tobacco Holdings, Inc. A1204
Wake Forest University Baptist Medical Center P768

NORTH DAKOTA

Fargo
Banner Health System P549

Minot
Investors Real Estate Trust E223

OHIO

Akron
FirstEnergy Corp. A598
The Goodyear Tire & Rubber Company A664
Republic Technologies International, LLC P713
Roadway Corporation A1206

Canton
The Timken Company A1386

Cincinnati
American Financial Group, Inc. A144
Broadwing Inc. A292
Catholic Healthcare Partners P570
CFM International, Inc. P572
Chiquita Brands International, Inc. A354
Cinergy Corp. A362
Cintas Corporation A364
The E. W. Scripps Company A568
Eagle-Picher Industries, Inc. P600
Federated Department Stores, Inc. A586
Fifth Third Bancorp A592
The Kroger Co. A844
The Procter & Gamble Company A1164
The Union Central Life Insurance Company P753

Cleveland
American Greetings Corporation A146
Ceres Group, Inc. E175
Eaton Corporation A526
International Management Group P250, P641
KeyCorp A822
The LTV Corporation A896
National City Corporation A1000

Noveon, Inc. P691
Ohio Lottery Commission P693
OM Group, Inc. E257
Parker Hannifin
Corporation A1088
Penton Media, Inc. E102, E263
Pioneer-Standard Electronics,
Inc. A1140
The Sherwin-Williams
Company A1278
TRW Inc. A1412

Columbus
American Electric Power
Company, Inc. A140
Battelle Memorial Institute P70,
P551
Big Lots, Inc. A260
Borden, Inc. P90, P558
Intimate Brands, Inc. A776
The Limited, Inc. A876
Nationwide A1008, P364, P685
The Ohio State University P382,
P693
OhioHealth P694
White Castle System, Inc. P516,
P772

Dayton
MCSi, Inc. E239
The Mead Corporation A950
NCR Corporation A1012
Primus, Inc. P705

Defiance
First Defiance Financial
Corp. E204

Dublin
Applied Innovation Inc. E157
Cardinal Health, Inc. A320
Wendy's International,
Inc. A1510

Elyria
Spitzer Management, Inc. P733

Findlay
Cooper Tire & Rubber
Company A432
Marathon Ashland Petroleum
LLC P664

Galion
PECO II, Inc. E261

Hilliard
Micro Electronics, Inc. P336,
P675

Hudson
Jo-Ann Stores, Inc. A796

Mayfield Heights
NACCO Industries, Inc. A992
NESCO, Inc. P686

Mayfield Village
The Progressive
Corporation A1168

Middletown
AK Steel Holding
Corporation A104

New Albany
Abercrombie & Fitch Co. A62

New Bremen
Crown Equipment
Corporation P586

Newark
The Longaberger Company P660

North Canton
Diebold, Incorporated A488

Shaker Heights
OfficeMax, Inc. A1058

Solon
Swagelok P739

Toledo
Dana Corporation A460
Manor Care, Inc. A908
Owens Corning A1072
Owens-Illinois, Inc. A1074

Twinsburg
North Coast Energy, Inc. E254

Valley City
MTD Products Inc. P679

Westfield Center
Ohio Farmers Insurance
Company P693

Westlake
TravelCenters of America,
Inc. P748

Youngstown
The Edward J. DeBartolo
Corporation P172, P602

OKLAHOMA
Ada
Pre-Paid Legal Services,
Inc. E107, E269

Bartlesville
Phillips Petroleum
Company A1128

Broken Arrow
XETA Technologies, Inc. E142,
E319

Oklahoma City
Chesapeake Energy
Corporation E39, E176
Devon Energy Corporation A482
Express Personnel Services P606
Hobby Lobby Stores, Inc. P632
Kerr-McGee Corporation A820
Louis Dreyfus Natural Gas
Corp. E234

Tulsa
Hale-Halsell Co. P624
ONEOK Inc. A1064
PetroCorp Incorporated E264
QuikTrip Corporation P710
Rooney Brothers Company P716
Unit Corporation E308
Vintage Petroleum, Inc. E312
The Williams Companies,
Inc. A1528

OREGON
Beaverton
Metro One Telecommunications,
Inc. E243
NIKE, Inc. A1032
Tektronix, Inc. A1358

Hillsboro
FEI Company E203
Lattice Semiconductor
Corporation E82, E232
RadiSys Corporation E109, E274
TriQuint Semiconductor,
Inc. E305

Klamath Falls
JELD-WEN, inc. P643

Portland
Bonneville Power
Administration P558
Columbia Forest Products
Inc. P579
Electro Scientific Industries,
Inc. E56, E196
Hoffman Corporation P632
Louisiana-Pacific
Corporation A890
North Pacific Group, Inc. P690
PacifiCorp A1082
R. B. Pamplin Corp. P711
Umpqua Holdings
Corporation E307
Willamette Industries,
Inc. A1524

Prineville
Les Schwab Tire Centers P657

Tualatin
Digimarc Corporation E192
Pixelworks, Inc. E267

Wilsonville
InFocus Corporation E73, E220

PENNSYLVANIA
Allentown
Air Products and Chemicals,
Inc. A100
PPL Corporation A1154

Altoona
Sheetz, Inc. P728

Bala Cynwyd
American Business Financial
Services, Inc. E153
Entercom Communications
Corp. E199
Keystone Foods LLC P650
Philadelphia Consolidated
Holding Corp. E265

Bethlehem
Bethlehem Steel
Corporation A256

Blue Bell
C&D Technologies, Inc. E169
Unisys Corporation A1424

Bristol

Jones Apparel Group, Inc. **A804**

Bryn Mawr

Philadelphia Suburban
Corporation **E265**

RMH Teleservices, Inc. **E113**,
E280

Camp Hill

Rite Aid Corporation **A1202**

Chesterbrook

AmerisourceBergen
Corporation **A156**

Cheswick

Tollgrade Communications,
Inc. **E302**

Coudersport

Adelphia Communications
Corporation **A72**

East Greenville

Knoll, Inc. **P276**, **P652**

Eighty Four

84 Lumber Company **P26**, **P528**

Fairview

Spectrum Control, Inc. **E124**,
E292

Fort Washington

NCO Group, Inc. **E250**

Harrisburg

Waypoint Financial
Corporation **E315**

Hershey

Hershey Foods Corporation **A708**

Horsham

Penn Mutual Life Insurance
Co. **P698**

Lancaster

Armstrong Holdings, Inc. **A194**

Herley Industries, Inc. **E68**,
E214

Sterling Financial
Corporation **E294**

Lawrence

Black Box Corporation **E164**

Malvern

IKON Office Solutions, Inc. **A746**

The Vanguard Group,
Inc. **A1468**, **P504**, **P764**

Vishay Intertechnology,
Inc. **A1482**

Mechanicsburg

Select Medical Corporation **E286**

Middletown

The Pennsylvania Lottery **P698**

Newtown Square

Catholic Health East **P114**, **P569**

Philadelphia

ARAMARK Corporation **A190**

Berwind Group **P554**

Cardone Industries Inc. **P565**

CIGNA Corporation **A360**

Comcast Corporation **A390**

Conrail Inc. **P582**

Crown Cork & Seal Company,
Inc. **A452**

The Day & Zimmermann Group,
Inc. **P589**

Lincoln National
Corporation **A878**

The Pep Boys - Manny, Moe &
Jack **A1100**

Radian Group Inc. **E108**, **E274**

RAIT Investment Trust **E275**

Rohm and Haas Company **A1212**

Rosenbluth International **P418**,
P717

Sunoco, Inc. **A1344**

Sunoco Logistics Partners
L.P. **P738**

Thistle Group Holdings,
Co. **E301**

The University of
Pennsylvania **P759**

Pittsburgh

Alcoa Inc. **A112**

Allegheny Technologies
Incorporated **A116**

CONSOL Energy Inc. **A416**

Dick Corporation **P593**

Dick's Sporting Goods, Inc. **P593**

Giant Eagle Inc. **P198**, **P615**

Highmark Inc. **A716**, **P234**,
P632

H.J. Heinz Company **A722**

Mellon Financial
Corporation **A954**

The PNC Financial Services
Group, Inc. **A1146**

PPG Industries, Inc. **A1152**

Reunion Industries, Inc. **E279**

University of Pittsburgh of the
Commonwealth System of
Higher Education **P759**

USX-U.S. Steel Group **A1462**

WESCO International,
Inc. **A1512**

Plymouth Meeting

Kramont Realty Trust **E229**

Radnor

Penn Virginia Corporation **E262**

Reading

Boscov's Department
Stores **P559**

Penske Truck Leasing **P700**

Robesonia

Associated Wholesalers,
Inc. **P547**

Saxonburg

II-VI Incorporated **E20**, **E146**

Trevose

The Faulkner Organization **P606**

University Park

The Pennsylvania State
University **P699**

Wawa

Wawa Inc. **P770**

Wayne

Lumbermens Merchandising
Corporation **P662**

Safeguard Scientifics, Inc. **A1232**

West Chester

Amkor Technology, Inc. **A162**

West Conshohocken

Keystone Property Trust **E228**

Willow Grove

Asplundh Tree Expert Co. **P545**

Kulicke and Soffa Industries,
Inc. **E81**, **E230**

Wyomissing

Penn National Gaming,
Inc. **E262**

York

Graham Packaging Company,
L. P. **P620**

York International
Corporation **A1550**

PUERTO RICO

Mayaguez

W Holding Company, Inc. **E314**

San Juan

Doral Financial
Corporation **E193**

R&G Financial
Corporation **E275**

San Turce

Puerto Rico Electric Power
Authority **P707**

RHODE ISLAND

Lincoln

Amica Mutual Insurance
Company **P540**

Pawtucket

Hasbro, Inc. **A692**

Providence

Gilbane, Inc. **P615**

Textron Inc. **A1380**

Warren Equities Inc. **P769**

Woonsocket

CVS Corporation **A458**

SOUTH CAROLINA

Columbia

AgFirst Farm Credit Bank **P533**

SCANA Corporation **A1248**

Fort Mill

Muzak LLC **P350**, **P681**

Springs Industries, Inc. **A1316**,
P452, **P733**

Greenville

Bowater Incorporated **A284**

Builder Marts of America,
Inc. **P562**

ScanSource, Inc. **E118**, **E284**

A=AMERICAN BUSINESS • E=EMERGING COMPANIES • P=PRIVATE COMPANIES • W=WORLD BUSINESS

The South Financial Group,
Inc. E**291**
Hartsville
Sonoco Products
Company A**1302**
Moncks Corner
South Carolina Public Service
Authority P**732**
Spartanburg
Advantica Restaurant Group,
Inc. A**86**
Extended Stay America,
Inc. E**59**, E**201**
Milliken & Company Inc. P**342**,
P**677**

SOUTH DAKOTA
Dakota Dunes
IBP, Inc. A**742**

TENNESSEE
Brentwood
America Service Group
Inc. E**153**
Doane Pet Care Company P**595**
Province Healthcare
Company E**271**
Service Merchandise Company,
Inc. A**1270**
Bristol
King Pharmaceuticals, Inc. E**229**
Cleveland
Life Care Centers of
America P**658**
Collegedale
McKee Foods Corporation P**669**
Franklin
Alcoa Fujikura Ltd. P**535**
IASIS Healthcare
Corporation P**637**
Goodlettsville
Dollar General Corporation A**496**
Johnson City
NN, Inc. E**254**
Kingsport
Eastman Chemical
Company A**522**
Knoxville
Anderson News Company P**541**
Goody's Family Clothing,
Inc. A**666**
H.T. Hackney Co. P**635**
Pilot Corporation P**702**
Regal Cinemas, Inc. P**412**, P**712**
Team Health, Inc. P**743**
Tennessee Valley
Authority A**1370**, P**468**, P743
University of Tennessee P**760**
La Vergne
Ingram Entertainment Holdings
Inc. P**639**

Memphis
Accredo Health,
Incorporated E**147**
AutoZone, Inc. A**208**
Dunavant Enterprises, Inc. P**599**
FedEx Corporation A**588**
Memphis Light, Gas and Water
Division P**672**
ResortQuest International,
Inc. E**279**
Nashville
AmSurg Corp. E**155**
HCA, Inc. A**694**
Healthcare Realty Trust
Incorporated E**211**
Ingram Industries Inc. A**756**,
P**244**, P639
Shoney's, Inc. A**1280**
Vanderbilt University P**763**

TEXAS
Addison
Mary Kay Inc. P**316**, P666
Arlington
D.R. Horton, Inc. A**508**
Texas Health Resources P**744**
Austin
NetSolve, Incorporated E**252**
SEMATECH, Inc. P**444**, P726
Silicon Laboratories Inc. E**288**
Temple-Inland Inc. A**1364**
Texas Lottery Commission P**472**,
P744
The University of Texas
System P**498**, P761
Whole Foods Market, Inc. A**1522**
College Station
The Texas A&M University
System P**470**, P743
Coppell
Minyard Food Stores, Inc. P**677**
Dallas
7-Eleven, Inc. A**56**
AMRESCO Capital Trust E**155**
Army and Air Force Exchange
Service P**52**, P543
Austin Industries Inc. P**547**
Baylor Health Care System P**551**
The Beck Group P**553**
Blockbuster Inc. A**266**
Brinker International, Inc. A**288**
Builders FirstSource, Inc. P**562**
Carreker Corporation E**172**
Centex Corporation A**340**
ClubCorp, Inc. P**130**, P577
Commercial Metals
Company A**396**
CompuCom Systems, Inc. A**400**
Contran Corporation P**583**
Dave & Buster's, Inc. E**51**, E190
Dr Pepper/Seven Up Bottling
Group, Inc. P**597**
EXCO Resources, Inc. E**200**
The Freeman Companies P**611**

F.Y.I. Incorporated E**207**
Glazer's Wholesale Drug
Company Inc. P**616**
Halliburton Company A**676**
Hicks, Muse, Tate & Furst
Incorporated A**714**, P**232**,
P631
Hotel Reservations Network,
Inc. E**215**
Hunt Consolidated Inc. P**635**
Income Opportunity Realty
Investors, Inc. E**219**
Lincoln Property Company P**659**
Maynard Oil Company E**238**
The Neiman Marcus Group,
Inc. A**1014**
Permian Basin Royalty
Trust E**263**
Perot Systems
Corporation A**1112**
Pillowtex Corporation A**1134**
Quexco Incorporated P**709**
Remington Oil and Gas
Corporation E**278**
Sammons Enterprises, Inc. P**720**
Southwest Airlines Co. A**1310**
Suiza Foods Corporation A**1338**
Texas Instruments
Incorporated A**1378**
Trammell Crow Company A**1398**
Transcontinental Realty Investors,
Inc. E**303**
Trinity Industries, Inc. A**1406**
TXU Corp. A**1416**
VarTec Telecom, Inc. P**764**
Vought Aircraft Industries,
Inc. P**766**
Wingate Partners P**518**, P774
Wyndham International,
Inc. A**1540**
El Paso
Petro Stopping Centers,
L.P. P**701**
Fort Worth
AmeriCredit Corp. E**27**, E154
AMR Corporation A**164**
Ben E. Keith Company P**553**
Burlington Northern Santa Fe
Corporation A**308**
Pier 1 Imports, Inc. A**1130**
Quicksilver Resources Inc. E**273**
RadioShack Corporation A**1188**
Sabre Inc. A**1228**
San Juan Basin Royalty
Trust E**283**
Texas Pacific Group P**474**, P744
TTI, Inc. P**750**
Williamson-Dickie Manufacturing
Company P**773**
XTO Energy Inc. E**319**
Frisco
Comstock Resources, Inc. E**183**
Grapevine
Prize Energy Corp. E**270**
Houston
3TEC Energy Corporation E**146**

Adams Resources & Energy, Inc. **A68**
Anadarko Petroleum Corporation **A168**
Apache Corporation **A184**
Baker Hughes Incorporated **A222**
BMC Software, Inc. **A270**
Burlington Resources Inc. **A310**
Cabot Oil & Gas Corporation **E168**
Carrizo Oil & Gas, Inc. **E173**
Chevron Phillips Chemical Company LP **P574**
Compaq Computer Corporation **A398**
Conoco Inc. **A412**
Continental Airlines, Inc. **A428**
Cooper Industries, Inc. **A430**
Cornell Companies, Inc. **E186**
David Weekley Homes **P588**
Dynacq International, Inc. **E195**
Dynegy Inc. **A518**
El Paso Corporation **A536**
Encompass Services Corporation **A548**
Enron Corp. **A552**
EOTT Energy Partners, L.P. **A556**
Equilon Enterprises LLC **P604**
Equistar Chemicals, LP **P604**
Goodman Manufacturing Company, L.P. **P618**
Goodrich Petroleum Corporation **E209**
Grocers Supply Co., Inc. **P622**
Gulf States Toyota, Inc. **P624**
Hanover Compressor Company **E210**
The Houston Exploration Company **E216**
Kinder Morgan Energy Partners, L.P. **E228**
King Ranch, Inc. **A828, P270, P650**
Lyondell Chemical Company **A900**
MAXXAM Inc. **A930**
Memorial Hermann Healthcare System **P671**
The Meridian Resource Corporation **E242**
Motiva Enterprises LLC **P344, P679**
Newfield Exploration Company **E253**
PANACO, Inc. **E260**
Pennzoil-Quaker State Company **A1096**
Plains Resources Inc. **A1144**
Pogo Producing Company **E268**
Prosperity Bancshares, Inc. **E271**
Reliant Energy, Incorporated **A1198**
Service Corporation International **A1268**
Shell Oil Company **A1276**
Southwest Bancorporation of Texas, Inc. **E291**

Spinnaker Exploration Company **E292**
Swift Energy Company **E297**
Synagro Technologies, Inc. **E297**
SYSCO Corporation **A1350**
Tauber Oil Company **P742**
Texas Petrochemicals LP **P745**
Tidel Technologies, Inc. **E301**
Ultra Petroleum Corporation **E307**
United Space Alliance **P754**
U.S. Concrete, Inc. **E309**
USX-Marathon Group **A1460**
Waste Management, Inc. **A1504**

Irving
AdvancePCS, Inc. **A84**
CHRISTUS Health **P575**
Crown Group, Inc. **E188**
Exxon Mobil Corporation **A576**
JPI **P648**
Kimberly-Clark Corporation **A826**
Magnum Hunter Resources, Inc. **E235**
Michaels Stores, Inc. **A968**
Zale Corporation **A1552**

Kingwood
Administaff, Inc. **A74**

Lewisville
Fleming Companies, Inc. **A606**

Midland
Clayton Williams Energy, Inc. **E180**
Key Energy Services, Inc. **E79, E227**
Parallel Petroleum Corporation **E260**
Pure Resources, Inc. **E272**
TMBR/Sharp Drilling, Inc. **E301**

Pittsburg
Pilgrim's Pride Corporation **A1132**

Plano
Cinemark USA, Inc. **P126, P575**
Denbury Resources Inc. **E191**
Electronic Data Systems Corporation **A538**
J. C. Penney Company, Inc. **A790**
MetaSolv, Inc. **E243**

Richardson
Inet Technologies, Inc. **E219**
Lennox International Inc. **A864**

Round Rock
Dell Computer Corporation **A472**

San Antonio
Clear Channel Communications, Inc. **A372**
The Exploration Company of Delaware, Inc. **E201**
H. B. Zachry Company **P627**
H. E. Butt Grocery Company **P224, P627**
SBC Communications Inc. **A1244**

Tesoro Petroleum Corporation **A1374**
USAA **A1452, P502, P763**
Valero Energy Corporation **A1466**

Sulphur Springs
GSC Enterprises, Inc. **P623**

Texarkana
Truman Arnold Companies **P749**

Tyler
Brookshire Grocery Company **P561**

The Woodlands
Mitchell Energy & Development Corp. **A978**

UTAH
Draper
1-800 CONTACTS, INC. **E146**

Logan
ICON Health & Fitness, Inc. **P637**

Murray
Larry H. Miller Group **P656**

Ogden
Flying J Inc. **P609**

Provo
Novell, Inc. **A1050**

Roy
Iomega Corporation **A778**

Salt Lake City
Associated Food Stores, Inc. **P545**
Equity Oil Company **E199**
Gentner Communications Corporation **E208**
Huntsman Corporation **P238, P636**
Intermountain Health Care **P640**
Sinclair Oil Corporation **P729**

VERMONT
Brattleboro
C&S Wholesale Grocers, Inc. **P102, P565**

Burlington
Chittenden Corporation **E178**

Montpelier
National Life Insurance Co. **P684**

Shelburne
The Vermont Teddy Bear Co., Inc. **E135, E311**

VIRGINIA
Abingdon
K-VA-T Food Stores, Inc. **P654**

Alexandria
Avalonbay Communities, Inc. **E161**
Salvation Army USA **P426, P720**

United Way of America P492, P755

Arlington
The AES Corporation A88
Charles E. Smith Residential Realty, Inc. E175
Gannett Co., Inc. A632
Rosenthal Automotive Companies P717
TeleCorp PCS, Inc. E299
US Airways Group, Inc. A1442

Charlottesville
University of Virginia P761

Chester
Star Scientific, Inc. E293

Danville
DIMON Incorporated A492

Fairfax
Brown Automotive Group Ltd. P561

Falls Church
Capital One Financial Corporation A318
General Dynamics Corporation A644
Inova Health System P639

Glen Allen
Owens & Minor, Inc. A1070

Herndon
Lafarge North America Inc. A848
National Rural Utilities Cooperative Finance Corporation P685

McLean
Booz-Allen & Hamilton Inc. P88, P558
Capital Automotive REIT E170
Freddie Mac A626
LCC International, Inc. E232
Mars, Incorporated A914, P314, P665
Sunrise Assisted Living, Inc. E295

Norfolk
Landmark Communications, Inc. P655
Norfolk Southern Corporation A1038
Sentara Healthcare P726

Reston
Concert Communications Company P580
DynCorp P599
MAXIMUS, Inc. E88, E238
Nextel Communications, Inc. A1026
USA Education, Inc. A1448

Richmond
Carpenter Co. P568
Circuit City Group A366
Colfax Corporation P578
Cornerstone Realty Income Trust, Inc. E186

CSX Corporation A454
Dominion Resources, Inc. A498
Heilig-Meyers Company A702
Performance Food Group Company A1108
Southern States Cooperative, Incorporated P732
Universal Corporation A1436
Virginia State Lottery P766

Roanoke
Carilion Health System P566

Smithfield
Smithfield Foods, Inc. A1290

Vienna
Feld Entertainment, Inc. P188, P608
Jim Koons Automotive P644
Navy Federal Credit Union P686

Virginia Beach
Navy Exchange Service Command P685

Warrenton
Southern Financial Bancorp, Inc. E291

Waynesboro
NTELOS Inc. E255

Winchester
Trex Company, Inc. E305

WASHINGTON

Bellevue
PACCAR Inc A1078
Vulcan Northwest Inc. P510, P767

Issaquah
Costco Wholesale Corporation A436

Kent
Recreational Equipment, Inc. P410, P711

Lacey
Illuminet Holdings, Inc. E217

Olympia
Heritage Financial Corporation E213

Redmond
Advanced Digital Information Corporation E23, E148
Lanoga Corporation P655
Microsoft Corporation A972
Trendwest Resorts, Inc. E304
TTM Technologies, Inc. E306

Seattle
Airborne, Inc. A102
Alaska Air Group, Inc. A106
Amazon.com, Inc. A130
Associated Grocers, Inc. P546
Bill & Melinda Gates Foundation P78, P555
F5 Networks, Inc. E201
Group Health Cooperative of Puget Sound P622

Immunex Corporation E71, E218
Nordstrom, Inc. A1036
Providence Health System P706
SAFECO Corporation A1230
Services Group of America P727
Starbucks Corporation A1326
Stevedoring Services of America Inc. P737
University of Washington P761
Washington Mutual, Inc. A1500
WestFarm Foods P771

Tacoma
Weyerhaeuser Company A1518

Vancouver
Consolidated Freightways Corporation A420
Direct Focus, Inc. E193

Walla Walla
Banner Corporation E162

Woodinville
Mackie Designs Inc. E85, E234

WEST VIRGINIA

Bridgeport
Petroleum Development Corporation E264

Chester
MTR Gaming Group, Inc. E247

WISCONSIN

Appleton
Air Wisconsin Airlines Corporation P534

Arcadia
Ashley Furniture Industries, Inc. P544

Baraboo
Foremost Farms USA, Cooperative P610

Beloit
American Builders & Contractors Supply Co., Inc. P537

Dodgeville
Lands' End, Inc. A852

Eau Claire
Menard, Inc. P330, P672

Green Bay
Green Bay Packaging Inc. P621
The Green Bay Packers, Inc. A672, P210, P621
Schneider National, Inc. P434, P723
Schreiber Foods, Inc. P723
ShopKo Stores, Inc. A1282

Kohler
Kohler Co. P284, P653

Madison
American Family Insurance Group P42, P538

The University of Wisconsin
   System P**500**, P762
Menomonee Falls
   Kohl's Corporation A**838**
Milwaukee
   Harley-Davidson, Inc. A**682**
   Johnson Controls, Inc. A**802**
   Journal Communications
      Inc. P**648**
   Joy Global Inc. A**806**
   Manpower Inc. A**910**
   Northwestern Mutual A**1048**,
      P**376**, P690
   Rockwell International
      Corporation A**1210**

Neenah
   Menasha Corporation P**673**
   Plexus Corp. E**104**, E267
Oshkosh
   OshKosh B'Gosh, Inc. A**1068**
Pewaukee
   Quad/Graphics, Inc. P**404**, P708
   Roundy's, Inc. P**422**, P718
Pleasant Prairie
   Snap-on Incorporated A**1294**
Racine
   S.C. Johnson & Son, Inc. A**1246**,
      P**432**, P722

Stevens Point
   Sentry Insurance, A Mutual
      Company P**726**
Sturtevant
   SC Johnson Commercial Markets,
      Inc. P**722**
Wauwatosa
   Briggs & Stratton
      Corporation A**286**
Wisconsin Rapids
   Renaissance Learning, Inc. E**278**

VENEZUELA

Caracas
   Petróleos de Venezuela
      S.A. W**438**

Hoover's Handbooks Index

Main Index

Note: Page numbers in **boldface** indicate the company's profile.

SYMBOLS

02-DO paging service W419
10 Yen-Mail cellular e-mail W419
1-800 CONTACTS, Inc. E146
1-800 LETS MEET conference calling service E208
180096hotel.com E215
The 1901 Corporation A659
1912 (company) W94
II-VI Inc. E**20, E146**
20 Mule Team cleaning and laundry products A486, A487
2000 HR Service Center Survey (publications) P481
21st Century Toys E225
24 Hour Fitness Worldwide Inc. P258
24/7 Media (marketing). *See* 24/7 Real Media
24/7 Real Media A999, P506
24seven W208
3 For The Money lottery game P675
3 Musketeers candy A914, A915, P314, P315, P665
3 Suisses France International W426, W427
3000 Xtra desktop information system W484, W485
The 30-Second Seduction (educational video) P139
33 Export beer W255
360 Communications Company A128, A1318, E38
365biz.com E113, E280
3Com Corporation A**54-A55**, A958, A1357, E263, E288, P137, P545, P662
3D snacks A1107
3D World (magazine) W239
3i Group plc (venture capital) W626
3M. *See* Minnesota Mining and Manufacturing Company
3TEC Energy Corporation E146
40 Wall Street A1408, A1409, P482, P483
401k Company A1009
4Front Technologies A1012
4Kids Entertainment, Inc. E147
4Runner vehicle W615
4Tel telephone system testing device A1372
501 brand jeans A869, P293
55 ALIVE/Mature Driving P29
5th Avenue candy A709
60 Minutes A334, A602
607486 Alberta Ltd. A575
$64,000 Question (TV show) A334, A1200
7 UP soft drink A714, A1102, A1103, A1104, A1105, P110, P232, P597, P634, W154, W155, W544
76 gas products A1128, A1438
77 Sunset Strip (TV show) A60

7dream.com W298
7-Eleven, Inc. A**56-A57**, A142, A1338, P728, W298, W299
8 à Huit convenience stores W164, W165
8000 Plus (magazine) W238
800.com (online retailer) P511
84 Lumber Company P**26-P27**, P528
9 1/2 weeks (movie) A804
9 & Company clothing A805
9-Lives pet food A722, A723

A

A. Ahlstrom Oy W556
A. Schilling & Company (spices and flavorings) A938
A to Z Equipment (construction trailers) A544
A.1. steak sauce A843
A-10 Warthog anti-tank planes A120
AA Interfinance B. V. W57
AA Rentals (equipment leasing) A710
AAA P528
AAA Homes A340
Aachener und Munchener W98, W99
AAdvantage frequent flier program A164
AAE Cargo (rail car lessors) A638, A639
AAGUS Financial Services Group N.V. W57
AAL Bank and Trust P534
Aalaei, Faraj E174
The A&B Group (starters and alternators) P152
A&C International (casual shirts) A1220
A&E Television Networks A60, A61, A700, A999, P228, P229, P629
A&F. *See* Abercrombie & Fitch
A&J Hospital Supply A1070
A&M Records W444
A&P grocery stores A670, A671, P103, P198, P224, P592, W588, W589
A&W restaurants and root beer A354, A385, P597, W154, W155
Aanonsen, Fred G. A705
Aardman Animations P166
Aaron Brothers art supply stores A968
Aaron, Daniel A390
Aaron, Roger S. P447
AARP A688, A1016, A1434, P**28-P29**, P370, P529, P688
AB, A/S. *See* entry under primary company name
A.B. Dick A1544
ABA (Swedish airline) W518
Abacus Concepts P430
ABACUS International Holdings (computerized reservations) A1228, W540

Abarelix drug A160, A161
Abarth (car) W226
Abaton (online tools) A947
ABB Ltd. E76, E224, W**54-W55**, W92, W116, W188
Abbagnaro, Louis A503
Abbany, Zul P431
Abbas, Jeffrey A73
Abbey Carpet Company, Inc. P529
Abbey Life (insurance) W652
Abbey National plc A438, A936
Abbinante, Christopher A591
Abbokinase drug A58
Abbot Mead Vickers A1062
Abbott, Carole A305
Abbott, Catherine G. A1035
Abbott, Donald A975
Abbott Laboratories A**58-A59**, A100, A160, A220, A282, E90, E236, P66, P741, W116, W492
Abbott, Wallace A58
ABC, Inc. A**60-A61**, A334, A1450, A1496, A1497, E212, P166, P218, P228, P229, P360, P605, P682, P684
ABC Markets P524, P777
ABC Supply P537
ABCO Desert Markets Inc. A606, A1234
Abe, Katsuhiro W449
Abe, Sadao W535
Abel, Gregory E. P341
Abele, John A282
Abend-AID software A406
Aber Resources (diamonds) A1384
Abercrombie & Fitch Company A**62-A63**, A876, P254
Abercrombie, David A62
Abercrombie, George B. W493
Abernathy, Robert E. A827
Abex (aircraft parts) A612, A902, P304
Abex Friction Products (brake materials) A430
Abex NWL (aerospace) A1088
Abfalter, Dan P710
ABG pavers A755
Abgenix E72
Abinder, Susan P637
Abington, Bill P670
Abitibi-Consolidated Inc. A284, A1292, A1430, P696, W470
Able, James E. A1155
Ablon, Ralph A440
Ablon, Richard A440
ABN AMRO Holding N.V. A370, A1142, W**56-W57**, W114, W286, W382
Abney, Kelly R. A1091
About.com P282
AboveNet Communications, Inc. P333
ABR Information Services A342
Abraham & Straus stores A586
Abrahamsen, Rob J. N. W317
Abrahamson, James R. A721
Abramo, Guy P. A759

Abramowicz, Daniel A. A453
Abrams, Sharlene E91, E242
Abrams, Steve L. A925, P323
Abramsky, Jenny W145
Abramsom, Richard P455
Abril-Martorell Hernández,
  Fernando W579
ABRY Partners P350, P681
A.B.S. by Allen Schwartz (active
  wear) A1498
Abshire, Richard B. A69
Absolut liquor A618, W315
ABT Building Products
  Corporation A890
Abu Dhabi Petroleum Investments
  L.L.C. W425
Abuhoff, Jack E221
Abuzz Technologies A1020
ABX Air, Inc. A102
A.C. Ernst A746
A.C. Monk A492
Academy Awards A962, A1158,
  E103, P166, P218, P302, P400,
  P597, P661, W462
Acadia Partners A968
Acadia Realty Trust E147
ACC Consumer Finance A734
Accamando, Anthony, Jr. A73
Accardi, Larry J. A1351
Accel E305
Accel Partners A836, P282
Accelerated Reader software E278
Accenture Ltd. A172, A840, A1050,
  A1222, E180, P48, P286, P540,
  W90, W324
Access Blue (managed care
  plan) P84, P85, P558
Access Business Network P536
Access Health, Inc. (Web site) A947
Access Logix software A543
Access software A973
AccessAtlanta.com A442, P146
Accessible Space, Inc. A1076
AccessMax E297
AccessNurse P743
Acciai Speciali Terni (steel) W594
The Accident Fund Company P87
ACCO World A618, A619
Accommodation (steamboat) W376
Accor A328, P106, P108, P567,
  W58-W59, W546
Accord car W264, W265, W403
Accord Energy (energy
  marketer) A518
Accountemps (temporary
  help) A1208, A1209
Accredo Health, Inc. E147
AccuBanc Mortgage A1000
AccuData System W493
Accudyne Corporation A120
Accuride Corporation A837, A1124,
  P283
Accusearch (information
  retrieval) P642
Accutane drug W492, W493
ACD Tridon (automotive
  parts) W604

Ace Auto Parts P112
ACE bandages A244
Ace Beverage P746
Ace glass products P212
Ace Hardware
  Corporation **A64-A65**, A1410,
  P30-P31, P212, P479, P484, P529,
  P565, P594, P623, P749
Ace Insurance Agency A64, P30
ACE Limited A360, W336
Ace Scavenger Service A1504
Acela train service P362, P684
ACENET P30
Acer Inc. A82, A162, A1378,
  W60-W61
Acer Semiconductor
  Manufacturing W60
AcerLand stores W60
Acford, Joanne P. A799
Achex (payment systems) A596
Achira, Hideo W397
Achleitner, Paul W83
Aciennes Mutuelles Accidents W104
Acierno, Ann A777
Acima (biocides) A1212
Aciphex drug A801
Grupo Acir
  Communicaciones A373, W582
Ackel, Rick R. A1241
Ackerman, F. Duane A249
Ackerman, Roger G. A434
Ackerman, Val P355
Ackermann, Josef W201
Ackland, Gary A. A183
Acklands Ltd. (automotive after
  market products) A1538, P112
Acklands-Grainger Inc. A1539
Ackley Manufacturing and Sales
  (hydraulic tools) A1322
Ackley, Robert W. A451
Acktion Corporation P112
Acme Can A452
Acme Corrugated Cases A284
Acme Display A1004
Acme Markets A110, A111, P198
Acme Overall & Rag Laundry A364
Acme Quality Paints A1278
Acme Quilting and Bed
  Covers A1134
Acme Steel P741
Acme-Cleveland Corporation
  (process/environmental
  controls) A462, A463
AcmePet.com A1116
A-CMI (auto parts) A112
ACNielsen Corporation **A66-A67**,
  A516, E181, W626
ACO Brokerage A1508
Acone, Adam P361
A:Copy PLC A746
Acordia, Inc. (property/casualty
  insurance) A178, A1508
Acordis bv (fibers) W72
Acorn Computers Group W422
The Acorn Development Group,
  Inc. A719
Acosta, Alan P457

Acoustic Wave speakers P93
Acoustimass speakers P93
AcoustiSeal A856
ACOUSTONE ceiling panels A1457
Acquavella Modern Art A1305
Acquilina, Michelle P311, P664
Acquisition Capability
  (company) E21
Acre, Marlene E20, E146
Acrilan fibers A984, A1122, A1300
Acrimo home decor
  products A1023
Acrobat Reader software A76, A77
Acry-Glo paint A1279
Act III (theaters) A836, P282, P412
Act One Uniform Rentals A364
Actava Group P332
Actebis Holding W426, W427
Actibrush toothbrush A387
Actimel dairy products W193
Action Against the BNP Raid
  Cartel W130
Action Direct (brokerage) W474
Action Express, Inc. A1548
Action Office modular
  systems A706, A707
Action Wheelers toys W333
Activase drug A640, A641, W493
Active Life medical devices A291
Activelle drug W416, W417
ACTIVENT fabrics P523
Activitrax pacemaker A952
Activity Booths W527
Actrade Financial Technologies,
  Ltd. **E21**, E148
Actuarial Sciences Associates A182
Actuate Corporation **E22**, E148
Acular ophthalmic products A119
Acuma Labs (software) E85
Acumen E43
Acura car P138, P733, W264, W265
Acushnet A618
Acute Care Medical Management,
  Inc. A323
Acutex (solenoid valves) A1320
ACUVUE A800
ACX Technologies A78, A452, E49,
  E185. *See also* Graphic Packaging
  International
Acxion Corporation A480
AD Delhaize W194, W195
A.D. Makepeace Company P380
Ada Crude Oil Company A69
Ada Oil A68
Ada programming language E110
ADAC Laboratories, Inc. W444
ADAGEN drug E199
Adair, A. Jayson E45
Adair, Robert L., III E155
Adam Opel A650
Adam, Phillippe W175
Adami, Norman J. W553
Adamo, Victor T. E241
Adams, Alton W. A1459
Adams, Austin A. A231
Adams, Barbara P611

Adams, Charles A1190
Adams, Denis W469
Adams, Ed (Enterprise Rent-A-Car) P179, P603
Adams, Edward S. (Navigant) E250
Adams, Eula A597
Adams, Jacob P542
Adams, John B. (American Home Products) A149
Adams, John (former President) P220
Adams, John L. (Trinity Industries) A1407
Adams, John Quincy (former President) P220
Adams, John (RSA Security) E114
Adams, Johnston C., Jr. A208
Adams, J. Phillip P609
Adams, Kirby C. W129
Adams, K. S., Jr. "Bud" A68, A69
Adams, Linda J. A867
Adams, Michael D. (Chesapeake Utilities) E177
Adams, Michael T. (AK Steel) A105
Adams, Pam P175
Adams, Paul W143
Adams Resources & Energy, Inc. A68-A69
Adams, Richard C. P71
Adams, Robert W489
Adams, Staci P594
Adams Super Food Stores P560
Adams, Thomas R. A1205
Adams, Valencia I. A249
Adamson, James B. A86, A87
Adamson, Reggie D. A795
Adamson, Terrence B. P359
Adap A208
Adaptec A170, E281, P137, W554
ADC Telecommunications, Inc. A70-A71, E172
Adderley, Terence E. A818, A819
Addis, Paul D. A141
Addison Energy E200
Addison Wesley Longman (publisher) W430
Addis-Wechsler & Associates A772
Additional Securities Ltd. W337
Addoms, Samuel D. E64, E206
Adecco (employment services) A910
Adelaide Steamship group W644
Adel-Meguid, Tarek F. A989
Adelphia Business Solutions, Inc. A571
Adelphia Communications Corporation A72-A73, A390
Adelson, Richard P. E72
Adelt, Bruno W631
ADI. See Analog Devices, Inc.
ADIC. See Advanced Digital Information Corporation
adidas-Salomon AG A839, A1194, E60, P686, W62-W63
Adik, Stephen P. A1035
Adjemian, Harry A920
Adjemian, Vart K. A427, P141
Adjmi, Norma P719

Adkerson, Richard C. A629
ADL. See Arthur D. Little, Inc.
Adler, Nadia C. A445
Adley Express (trucking) A1548
ADM. See Archer Daniels Midland Company
ADM Chemical A200
The Admar Group, Inc. A1162, A1163
Administaff, Inc. A74-A75
Admiral appliances A934, A935, A1210, A1521
Admiral Cruises A1216
Adobe Systems Inc. A76-A77, A524, E192, E311
Adolph Coors Company A78-A79, E185, P428, W376
AdOne Classified Network A80, P32
ADP. See Automatic Data Processing, Inc.
AdriaVita S.p.A. W99
Adria-Wien Pipeline Gesellschaft m.b.H. W425
AdSEND digital ad delivery P546
Adshead, John E. W301
ADT Automotive P146
ADT Security Services, Inc. A206
Adtranz W132, W188
Advance Alliance A202
Advance Holding Corporation A1264
Advance Online (training) P279
Advance Paradigm A84, A1202
Advance Publications, Inc. A60, A80-A81, A1020, P32-P33, P530
Advance Techniques hair care A217
Advanced Auctions LLC A1332
Advanced Cardiovascular Systems A674
Advanced Care Partners, Inc. A739
Advanced Digital Information Corporation E23, E148
Advanced Energy Industries, Inc. E24, E149
Advanced Logic Research A636
Advanced Machine Programming E31
Advanced Marketing Services, Inc. A772
Advanced Micro Devices, Inc. A82-A83, A162, A188, A760, A928, A970, A1002, E82, E222, E313, P444, P445, P662, P726, W236, W532, W536, W600
Advanced Photo System E184, W234, W368
Advanced Polymer P164
Advanced Power Center brand A527
Advanced Power Systems A546
Advanced Protection Systems A340
Advanced Radio Telecom A1186
Advanced Research Projects Agency P444
Advanced Research & Technology Institute P638
Advanced Semiconductor Engineering, Inc. E230

Advanced Technology Materials, Inc. See ATMI, Inc.
Advance/Newhouse Communications P158, P594
AdvancePCS, Inc. A84-A85, A574
Advanta Corporation A142, A602, A808, E113, E280
Advantage 10 vegetarian foods A408
Advantage brand A527
Advantage Foods (poultry processor) P392
Advantage Health Corporation A699
Advantage Insurance Network A124
Advantage Learning Systems. See Renaissance Learning, Inc.
Advantage Sales & Marketing P530
Advantage toothbrush A657
Advantages/ESM Ferolie P530
Advantica Restaurant Group, Inc. A86-A87, A836, P282
Advantrust A516
Advantus Capital Management P677
Advent Browser Reporting software E25
Advent International Corporation W212
Advent Software, Inc. E25, E149
Adventist Health P530
Adventure (magazine) P358, P359
Adventure of the Seas (cruise ship) A1217
Advertising Age (magazine) A1126
The Advest Group, Inc. A986
Advil over-the-counter drug A148, A149
The Advisory Board Company E186
Adweek (magazine) W626
Adwers, James R. A445
AE. See Allegheny Energy, Inc.
A E Staley Manufacturing W568
AEA Investors Inc. A434, P408, P691, P711
AEG appliances W210, W536
Aegis Group Plc W478
AEGON N.V. A790, A1170, W64-W65, W104
Aeon (aluminum substrates) A1260, P440
AEON Company, Ltd. (retailer) A880, A1058
AEP. See American Electric Power
AEP Industries Inc. P90
Aer Lingus W71
Aera Energy LLC A577, A1276, A1277
AERA (magazine) W96, W97
Aerial Communications A1360
Aero International W110
AeroKinetics E67
Aerolinas Argentinas W79
Aerologic A484, W344
AeroMexico A478, A1228, W68
Aeron office seating A707
Aeronca Electronics E35
Aeroquip (air conditioning) A1088
Aeroquip-Vickers, Inc. A526

The Aerospace Corporation P438
Aerospatiale Matra W70, W76, W110, W330
Aerowings (video game) W527
Aertker, Gayle A1057
AES China Generating Company A88
The AES Corporation **A88-A89**, A1174, A1198, A1382, W612
Aestix (e-commerce) P88
Aether Systems (wireless technology) A1480, P508, W484
Aetna Heiwa Life A922, P320
Aetna, Inc. A90-A91, A370, A414, A878, A904, A1016, A1506, E228, P226, P370, W98, W286
Aetna/Generali International Office W99
Afable, Mark V. P43
Afable, Richard F. P115
AFC Enterprises, Inc. P124, P575
AFCO (do-it-yourself products) A1364
Affeldt, Kathleen J. A871
Affilated Computer Services A882
Affilated Paper Companies of Alabama A1109
Affiliated Managers Group, Inc. E149
Affiliated Publications A1020
The Affiliates (temporary help) A1208, A1209
Affiliation Networks W238
AFFLAB brand A1109
AFFLINK brand A1109
AFG. *See* American Financial Group, Inc.
AFI Food Service Distributors, Inc. A1109
AFLAC Inc. A92-A93
AFL-CIO A946, P34-P35, P246, P492, P532, P754
AFN Communications A114, A115
Afore Banamex AEGON S.A. W65
African Life (insurance) W92
Africatours W58
Afrin nasal spray A1250, A1251
A.G. Edwards, Inc. A94-A95
AG Industries (retail displays) A147
Ag Processing Inc. P36-P37, P532
A.G. Spanos Companies P532
Ag States Agency P122, P123
AgAmerica, FCB P533
AG&E. *See* American Gas & Electric
Agar Manufacturing A770
Agarwal, Bhikam C. W293
Agathen, Paul A. A137
AGB Italia Group (market research) W646
Agbayani, Arnold P. E76, E224
AG-BIO W66
Ag-Chem Equipment A96
AGCO Corporation A96-A97
AGCOSTAR farm equipment A97
Age Defying cosmetics A1200
AGE International, Inc. A95
Ageco A668

Agee, Mark E142
AGENCY.COM Ltd. A1062
Agent Server software E311
Ager, Rowley S. W591
Agere Systems (microelectronics) A898, E161, E223, P444, P445, P726
Agfa-Gevaert A686, E184, W118
AgFirst Farm Credit Bank P534
AG/Fleming Northwest P546
Aggarwal, Kamal K. A1003
Aggers, Jane A797
Aggies of Texas A&M University P471
AGI-Camelot, Inc. A259
Agilent Technologies, Inc. **A98-A99**, A712, A1358, E162, E224, W444, W555, W600
AgileVision E241
AgileVision (electronics) E104
Agip SpA A310
Agip/AgipPetroli SpA W216, W217
AGL Resources Inc. A498
Agnelli family W170, W192
Agnelli, Giovanni W226, W227
Agnelli, Giovanni, II W226
Agnes, Bob A1359
Agnesi (pasta) W192
Agnew Nickel Mine W640
AGO Holding W64
Agora Foods W244
Agouron Pharmaceuticals, Inc. W304
AGP. *See* Ag Processing Inc.
AGP Grain Cooperative P37
Agracetus A1536
AgraTrade Financing, Inc. P200, P201
Agree hair products A1246, P432
Ågren, Anders A1295
Ågren, Christer W557
Agress, Amy E221
AgrEvo P104
Agri International P200
AgriAmerica radio network E198
AgriBank, FCB P534
AgriBioTech, Inc. P264
Agribrands International, Inc. A324, P104
Agrico Chemical A1528
Agricultural and Mechanical College of Texas for Colored Youth P470, P743
Agricultural and Mechanical College of the Kentucky University P757
Agricultural Marketing Act (1929) A582, P184
Agriholding A994
Agriliance, LLC A582, A583, P122, P123, P184, P185
Agrilink Foods A466, A470
Agrippina (insurance) W652
AgriRecycle P392
Agri-Service Centers P123
Agrium Inc. W66-W67
Agroindustrial Del Noroste A1291

Agrolinz Melamin GmbH W424, W425
Agroservicios Pampeanos W67
Aguallo, Robert A315, P97
Aguerrevere, Leopoldo W439
Aguila beer W255
Aguirre, DeeAnne P89, P558
Aguirre, Gastón W653
Agut Bonsfills, Joaquim W579
Agway Energy Products LLC P38, P39
Agway Inc. P38-P39, P535
A.H. Robins A148
AH Software A76
Aharoni, Amos E21, E148
Ahaus Alstatter Eisenbahn A639
AHC Realty Corporation A65, P31
A.H.C. Store Development Corporation P31
AHI Healthcare Corporation A1507
AHK Air Hong Kong Ltd. W565
Ahlers, Linda L. A1353
Ahlstrom Corporation W520
Ahlström, Krister W557
Ahlstrom Paper A620
Ahmed, Riaz W609
Ahold Czech Republic W498
Ahold USA A208, P479
AHP. *See* American Home Products
Ahrens & Ott A152
AHS Blue Cross P174
Ahuja, Parkash P. A349
Ahura Mazda W362
AIB. *See* Allied Irish Banks, PLC
AIB International Financial Services W87
Aiba, Hiroshi W449
Aid Association for Lutherans/Lutheran Brotherhood P534
Aida Corporation A1372
Aida (cruise line) W434
Aidekman, Al A1490, P515
Aidekman, Sam A1490
Aiello, Larry, Jr. A435
AIG. *See* American International Group
AIG Star Life Insurance A150
Aihara, Hironori W371
Aija tobacco W143
Aijala, Ainar D., Jr. A475, P155, W197
Aikawa, Yoshisuke W402
Aiken, Philip S. W129
Aikenhead Hardware A724, W376
Aikens, Peter A423
Aikman, Charles A388
AIL Systems (electronics) A526
AIM Management Group E210
Aimco auto parts A461
Ainsley, Christopher W643
Oy Air Botnia Ab W518, W519
Air Canada A164, A218, A1420, A1421, W71, W79, W80, W344, W518
Air China E32
Air Europa, Lineas-Aereas S.A. W79

Air Express International
Corporation W202, W203
Société Air France A428, A478,
W68-W69, W71, W78, W303
Air France Holidays P658
Air Fresh home care W476
Air Gate PCS A1319
Air India A1228, W566
Air Inter W68
Air Jamaica A478
Air Jordan shoes A1032, A1194
Air Liberté W140
Air Line Pilots Association P34
Air Littoral W316
Air Micronesia A428
Air New Zealand Limited A1421,
W468, W541
Air Nippon W80
Air Nostrum W132
Air Orient W68
Air Pacific W468, W469
Air Partner A428, P474
Air Products and Chemicals,
Inc. A100-A101
Air Southwest A1310
Air Step shoes A295
Air System Components W605
Air Transport World
(magazine) E102, E263
Air Union W68
Air Wick home care W476, W477
Air Wisconsin Airlines
Corporation P534
AirBaltic W519
Airborne Air Park A102
Airborne Express. See Airborne, Inc.
Airborne Flower Traffic
Association A102
Airborne Freight Corporation P545
Airborne, Inc. A102-A103
Airborne shoes A295
airborne@home A102
Airbus S.A.S. A662, W70-W71,
W110, W132, W330
AirCap A1262
Airco (chemicals and plastics) A100
Aircraft Service International
(fueling) A1478
Aircraft Transport and Travel W140
Airetool power tools A430, A431
Airflex brand A527
Airfone A1534
Airline Deregulation Act
(1978) A106
Airlines of Britain Holdings W518
Airlink Pty. Ltd. W468, W469
Airport Parking Company of
America P236
AirShields (infant incubators) A718
Airtel Movil W628
Airtex (automotive products) P113
AirTouch Communications A1472,
W628
Airtours A330
Airtron A548
Airwaves gum A1527

Aisin Seiki Company, Ltd. (auto
parts) E55
Aitken Campbell (stock market
maker) A348
Aitken, Kevin S. A397
AITS. See American International
Travel Service
A. J. Metler & Rigging (glass
transport) P434
A.J. Wright stores A1388, A1389
Ajax cleanser A386, A387
AJ's Fine Foods P550
AK Steel Holding
Corporation A104-A105
Akademiai Kiadó (tax and business
information) W643
Akamai E96
Akashi, Yasuo W329
Akashic Memories (disks) W326
Akatsuka, Noriaki W603
Aker, David O. A1425
Akeroyd, Richard P79
Akers, John A764
Akers, Joseph A. W119
Akerson, Daniel F. A1026
Akhurst, Bruce J. W587
Akikusa, Naoyuki W236, W237
Akilian, Elie S. E219
Akin, Cathy B. E312
Akin, Steven P. A615, P191
Akins, Robert P. E49, E189
Akron Electric Light and Power
Company A598
Akron (Ohio) Beacon Journal A832,
A833
Akron Traction and Electric
Company A598
AKT (flatpanel displays) A188
Akutsu, Makoto W597
Akzo Nobel N.V. A324, A504, A1152,
A1300, P104, W72-W73, W116
A.L. Hyde Company
(process/environmental
controls) A462, A463
Al Khaily, Mohamed Naser W425
Ala laundry soap W619
Alabama Bancorp P170
Alabama Financial Group A1308
Alabama Power Company A1306,
A1307
Alabama River Newprint P696
Alabama Traction Light &
Power A1306
Alabama-Tennessee Health Network,
Inc. A695
Aladdin carpets A980, A981
Aladdin (movie) P166
Aladdin Steel Products
(stoves) A726
Alagem, Beny W508
Alahuhta, Matti W407
Alamo Market P489
Alamo Rent A Car A206
Alamo Title Company A590, A591
Alan Flusser brand A691
Ala-Pietilä, Pekka W407
Alarko Alsim (contractor) W358

Alarm Systems Holding E29
Alascom (long distance) A1082
Alaska Air Group, Inc. A106-A107,
A1046, A1047, W469
Alaska Native Claims Settlement
Act P542
Alaska Native Wireless P542
Alathon (high-density
polyethylene) A900
Alba paint W278
Alba watches W528, W529, W530
Albany brand A209
Albany Life Assurance A964
Albany Molecular Research,
Inc. E150
Albany (New York) Times
Union A701, P229
Albany Normal School P460
Albaugh, James F. A273
Alber, Laura J. A1531
Albergo, Margaret A. A313
Albert Einstein College of
Medicine P678, P690
Albert E. Reed & Company W478
Albert Heijn supermarkets W498,
W499
Alberta Energy Company Ltd. W66
Alberthal, Lester A538
Albertian, Edward P565
Alberto VO5 A108, A109
Alberto-Culver
Company A108-A109
Albert's Foods P122
Albertson, Bruce A778, A779
Albertson, J. A. "Joe" A110
Albertson, Kathryn A110
Albertson, Marty P. E66, E210
Albertson's, Inc. A110-A111, A276,
A670, A886, A1532, P462, P736
Albion Industries, Inc. P313
Albrecht, Karl P747
Albrecht, Mariel C. A721
Albrecht, Theo A110, P747
Albrethsen, Svend Erik W163
Albright & Wilson plc
(chemicals) A1368
Albright, David L. A317
Albright, Michael S. A341
The Albuquerque (New Mexico)
Tribune A569
Alcan Aluminium Limited W432
Alcan Inc. A112, W74-W75, W410
Alcan-Pechiney-Algroup W74
Alcantara, Carlos T. A1097
Alcântara (sugar) W568, W569
Alcatel A170, A792, A888, A894,
A1002, A1240, A1298, A1362,
A1372, E191, E192, E220, E247,
E258, E273, E277, E304, E305,
E313, W76-W77, W152, W532,
W554
Alchin, John R. A391
Alco Oil and Chemical A746
Alco Standard A156, A746
Alcoa Fujikura Ltd. P535
Alcoa Inc. A112-A113, A120, A224,
A954, A988, P535, P627, W74,
W128, W410, W640

Alcoa World Alumina and Chemicals W640
Alcon Laboratories (ophthalmology products) E255, W388
Alconix (nonferrous marketing) W404
Aldana, Cherie E261
Aldebaran mines W452
Alden Merrell (frozen desserts) A722
Aldens A1314
Alder, Kenton K. E306
Alderman, Don A109
Alderman, Ken P615
Alderson, Sandy P307
ALDI Group (supermarkets) A110, P747, W644
Aldinger, William F. A734, A735
Aldrich, David J. E152
Aldrich, James P422
Aldridge, David A1273
Aldus (software) A76
Alea Group Holdings AG A837, P283
Alegent Health Systems P116, P348
Alehouse Company W638
Alekperov, Vagit Y. W346, W347
Alenia W110
Alesio, Steve A517
Alessandro, Victor T. A671
Aleve drug W492, W493
Alex. Brown & Sons P110
Alex Lee, Inc. P535
Alexander & Alexander Services Inc. A182, A356
Alexander, Anthony (Imperial Tobacco) W283
Alexander, Anthony J. (FirstEnergy) A599
Alexander, Clifford, Jr. A516
Alexander Grant & Company (accounting) P206
Alexander, Gregory A1275, E120
Alexander Hamilton Life Insurance Company A734, A794
Alexander, Isaac E244
Alexander, Jim P588
Alexander Julian furniture P298, P299
Alexander Keith's beer W289
Alexander, Mark K. A763
Alexander, Mary S. A1179
Alexander McQueen brand W251
Alexander, R. David, Jr. A579
Alexander Smith carpets A980, A981
Alexander, Stephen B. E41
Alexander, S. Tyrone A717, P235, P632
Alexander's, Inc. E137, E150, E314
Alexandre, Patrick W69
Alexandria Real Estate Equities, Inc. E150
Alexis de Tocqueville Society P492
Alexopoulos, Pantelis S. A929
Alfa Holdings A440
Alfa Laval (industrial flow) A446

Alfa Romeo car A650, W226, W227
AlfaBeta (investment publication) P481
Alfa-Beta stores W194, W195
Alfani brand clothing A587
Alfano, Susan A. A923, P321, P667
Alfa-Wasserman E283
Alfieri, John A471
Alfiero, Salvatore H. P310
Alford, Mack L. P735
Alfpha-Beta Vassilopoulos W194
Alfred Erickson (advertising) A772
Alfred I. du Pont Testamentary Trust E115, E282
Alfred Wall AG (packaging) A1516
Alfri-Loder A420
Algeco SA (portable buildings) W460
Algemeene Friesche W64
Algemene Bank Nederland W56
Algemene Kunstzijde-Unie W72
Algroup. See Alusuisse Lonza Group
Alhambra car W631
Alhambra water A946, W193
Alhand, Elizabeth P734
Ali, Irfin A55
Aliant Communications, Inc. A128
Alias, Patrick A. E43
Alias Research (software) A1284
Alice White wines A422
Alierta Izuel, César W579
Alifin A1144
Alighn-Rite (photomask maker) A686
Aligned Agency Group (advertising) A773
Alim, Ahmed A1097
Alimenta Processing P200
Alitalia-Linee Aeree Italiane S.p.A. A428, A1046, W71, W78-W79, W302, W316
Alkaline-ion no Mizu soft drink W315
Alka-Seltzer W118
All About Eve (movie) A622
All America Cables and Radio E38
All American Aviation A1442
All American Communications, Inc. W430
All American Pipeline A664, A1144
All American Semiconductor, Inc. E151
All Bar One restaurants W545
All Conditions Gear (shoes) A1032
All Energy A518
All England Lawn Tennis & Croquet Club P251
All for One stores A260
All in the Family (TV show) A334
all laundry detergent W619
All News Radio P60
All Nippon Airways Company, Ltd. A1421, W80-W81, W302, W344, W518
All Skins cosmetics A564
All Sport drink A1103, A1104, A1106

All Staff (staffing) E111
All Things Considered (radio program) P144
All Wound Up toys and novelties A276
Allaire Corporation (software) E86
Allaire, Paul A. A1544, A1545, P195
Allaire, Yvan W133
All-American chain A1176, P402
All-American Football Conference P356
Allami Biztosito W64
Allan, Alexander R. C. A383
Allan candy W155
Allan Home Health Care and Hospice A908
Allan, Michael A1157
Allavena, Jean-Luc W331
All-Bran cereal A816, A817
Allchin, James E. A973
All-Clad Inc. (cookware) W636, W637
All-Crop harvester A96
ALLDATA A208, A209
Allders International P156
Alldredge, William T. A1023
Allegany Health System P114
Allegheny Airlines, Inc. See US Airways Group, Inc.
Allegheny Communications Connect A114
Allegheny Corporation W56
Allegheny Energy, Inc. A114-A115
Allegheny Health, Education & Research Foundation A1366
Allegheny Heat Treating A396
Allegheny International A1152
Allegheny Ludlum Steel Company A116
Allegheny Power System A598
Allegheny Rodney A117
Allegheny Technologies Inc. A116-A117
Allegheny Teledyne A116, A256, A1044
Allegheny Ventures A114
Allegiance Corporation (health products) A236, A320, A321
Allegiance Telecom, Inc. E243
Allegis Corporation. See UAL Corporation
Allegra drug A1506, E150, W102, W103
Allegro Coffee Company A1522
Allemang, Arnold A. A505
Allen, Andrew W. P568
Allen, Anne E. A1019, P375
Allen, Bob D. E184
Allen, Bradley D. A751
Allen, Bruce M. A687
Allen, Charles Lamb (Granada) W248, W249
Allen, Charles (National Australia Bank) W383
Allen, Charlie (Ogden Corp.) A440
Allen, C. Richard P359

Allen Envelope of
  Philadelphia A1004
Allen, George A1094
Allen, Herbert P252
Allen, Horatio A1038
Allen, James P88
Allen, John H. E44, E182
Allen, L. Nash, Jr. E162
The Allen Manufacturing Company
  (tools and components) A462,
  A463
Allen, Michael B. (R. R. Donnelley &
  Sons) A1219
Allen, Michael (Macromedia) E86
Allen, Patrick E. A1211
Allen, Paul G. (Charter
  Communications) A350, A351
Allen, Paul G. (Microsoft) A972,
  A1450, A1496, P166, P312, P510,
  P511, P597, P767
Allen, Randy L. A831
Allen, Robert A. P584
Allen, Ronald A478
Allen, R. Scott A723
Allen Systems Group A406
Allen, Wayne A1128
Allen, Wes P657
Allen, William L. (National
  Geographic) P359
Allen, William S. (Atlas Air
  Worldwide) E32, E160
Allenbaugh, Bruce A1231
Allen-Bradley (industrial
  electronics) A1210
Allende, Salvador W576
Allender, Patrick W. A463
AllerCare pillow and mattress
  covers A1246, A1247, P432, P433
Allergan, Inc. A118-A119, E261
Allergan Ligand Retinoid
  Therapeutics A118
Alley, Allen H. E267
Alley Cat pet food P626
Allfirst Bank W86, W87
Allford, Susan P225, P627
Allgemeine Deutsche
  Direktbank W286
Alliance Beverage
  Distribution P616, P738
Alliance Capital Management
  Holding L.P. A218, A219
Alliance Data Systems
  Corporation A666, A876
Alliance Entertainment
  Corporation P524, P525, P777
Alliance for Cervical Cancer
  Prevention P79
Alliance Forest Products Inc. A284
Alliance Imaging, Inc. (MRI
  service) A837, P283
Alliance Regional Transmission
  Organization A598
Alliance Tire & Rubber W322
Alliances Ventures, Inc. A717, P235,
  P632
Alliant Energy Corporation A1542
Alliant Exchange Inc. W498

Alliant Techsystems Inc. A112,
  A120-A121, A704
Allianz AG P384, P695, W82-W83,
  W130, W182, W200, W201, W380,
  W504, W652
Allied Bakeries W244
Allied Bakery Products A608
Allied Breweries W84
Allied Capital Corporation E151
Allied chain A1498
Allied Chemical & Dye
  Corporation A728
Allied Corporation A600, A728,
  P142
Allied Devices Corporation E26,
  E151
Allied Domecq PLC A252, P474,
  W84-W85, W108, W162, W544,
  W638
Allied Dunbar Assurance W652,
  W653
Allied Electronics A214
Allied Fibers (carpets) A980
Allied Group (fireplaces) A726
Allied Group (multiline
  insurance) A1008, A1009, P364,
  P365
Allied Holdings, Inc. (automotive
  carrier) A1222
Allied Irish Banks, PLC W86-W87
Allied Labs (pharmaceuticals) A504
Allied Maintenance (janitor
  services) A440
Allied Mills A426, P140
Allied Power & Light A376
Allied Safety A1538
Allied Specialty Care Services,
  Inc. A905
Allied Stores A586, P172
Allied Telephone A128
Allied Van Lines P535
Allied Waste Industries,
  Inc. A122-A123, A1504, E139,
  E293, W564
Allied Westminster & Company,
  Ltd. A879
Allied Worldwide, Inc. P535
Allied Zurich W142, W652
Allied-Lyons W84, W162
AlliedSignal Inc. See Honeywell
  International Inc.
Allina Health System P536
Allis, Edward A96
Allis-Chalmers Company A96, A780
Allison, Christian L. E302
Allison Engine W496
Allison hardware and tools A1023
Allison, Joel T. P551
Allison, Mike E297
Allison, M. Jay E183
Allison, Ralph A70
Allison, Robert J. A169
Allison Transmission A650
Allison-Fisher International W621
Allman, Bill P159
Allman, Michael W. A1267
Allmanna Svenska Electriska
  Aktiebolaget W54

Allmaps Canada Limited P408
Allmerica Financial
  Corporation A124-A125
Allmerica Property &
  Casualty A124
Alloptic (fiber-optic) W450
Allred, Douglas C. A369
Allspach, Eugene R. A901
All-Star Game (baseball) P306
The Allstate
  Corporation A126-A127, A378,
  A794, A884, A964, A988, A1168,
  A1264, A1440
Allstate tires A1264
Allsteel (office furniture) A726
ALLTEL Corporation A128-A129,
  A1318, E38, E290
Alltrans (trucking) A1454
Alltrista Corporation A224
Alltus Foods A1180
Allum, Brian J. E86
Allure (magazine) P33, P530
ALLWEILER (pumps) P578
ALM Antillean Airlines W316
Alm, John R. A385
Almacenas Paris stores A790
Almaden wines A422, A423
Alman, Rex, III A169
Almay cosmetics A1200, A1201
Almeida, Geoff W149
Almet France W433
Almgren, Ake E171
Almonate Complex A417
Almond Joy candy P314, W154
Aloe (medical supplies) A298
Alper Ink Group A950
Alpert, Bruce N. E65
Alpert, Leon A888
Alpert, Warren P769
Alpex A1142
Alpha Bank S.A. W384
Alpha Beta stores A606, P462,
  P478, P524
Alpha Corporation A1072
Alpha Distributors P236
Alpha G. See Gabelli Asset
  Management Inc.
Alpha Healthcare Ltd. (nursing
  homes) A1340
Alpha Industries, Inc. E152
Alpha Tube Corporation A104
Alphagan ophthalmic
  products A118, A119
Alpha/Owens-Corning A1072
Alphasem (semiconductors) A502
Alpina (insurance) W652
Alpine Capital (investments) E283
Alpine Lace brand cheeses A850,
  P288, P289
Alpo pet food W388
ALRT. See Allergan Ligand Retinoid
  Therapeutics
Al's Auto Supply A1078
Alsmar, Karl W221
Alsons showers A921
Alspaugh, Robert W. A841, P287,
  W325

Alstadt, Steven W. A631
ALSTOM W54, W76, W226, W354
Alta Dena Certified Dairy A466, A467
Alta Energy A482
Altabef, Peter A1113
Altair International Inc. (microcomputer) A972
AltaVista Company A398
Altec Electronics A896
AlterEgo Networks (wireless networking) P455
Alternative Living Services A908
Alternative Market Operations (insurance brokerage) A183
Alterra Healthcare Corporation A908
Althaver, Brian A783
Althin Medical (dialysis) A236
Althoff, Theodor W310
Althouse Chemical Company A450
Altia A296
Alticor Inc. P536
Altima car W402, W403
Altissimo (automotive accessories) A780
Altman, Judith J. A307
Altman, Steven R. A1183
Alto van W560, W561
Altoids mints A842, A843
Alton Geoscience E131
Altos Computer Systems W60
Altos Hornos de Mexico A1224
Altos Semiconductor E92
Altra EV car W403
Altron A1240
Altruda, Vincent E. A277
Altschuler, Lena E161
Altsys (software) E86
Altura Energy A1054, A1276, W136
Altwegg, Markus W493
Alum Rock Foodservice A768
Alumax A112
Aluminium Limited W74
Aluminum Company of America A112, W74
Aluminum of Korea W74
Alumni Association of Georgetown University A936
Alusuisse Lonza Group A112, W74, W432
Alvarado, Joe W293
Alvarez Cienfuegos, Antonio Hernández-Gil W483
Alvarez, David R. A1171
Alvarez, Eduardo M. P89
Alvarez, Guillermo A1101
Alvarez-Pallete Lopéz, José Maria W579
al-Waleed bin Talal, Saudi Prince P110
Always Low Price Stores P62
Always Save brands P62, P63
Always Tender pork A730, A731
Aly, Sherine A641

ALZA Corporation (pharmaceutical research) A58, A800, E90
AM Chicago (TV show) P218
A-M Handling (melting and assaying) P536
A.M. Lewis (grocery distributor) A436
A.M. Tenney Associates A522
AMA. See American Medical Association
Amadeus Global Travel Distribution, S.A. (computer reservations) A428
Amador Motors P706
Amadori, Nicholas A. A1459
Amalfi shoes A804
Amalgamated Electric W412
Amalgamated Metal Corporation PLC W461
Amalgamated Retail W552
Amana Appliance A934
Amana Heating and Air Conditioning P618
Amana Refrigeration A1190
Amann, James J. A587
Amarex International A102
Amarillo Gear Company P313
A-Mark Financial Corporation P536
Amaryl drug W102, W103
Amateur Hockey Association of Canada P360
Amati Communications A1378
Amazon.com, Inc. A130-A131, A180, A276, A1116, A1304, A1396, P68
AMB Aachener und Muenchener W98
AMB Generali Holding AG W98
Ambassador greeting cards A678, A679, P216, P217, P625
Ambassador liquors A296
Ambassador Oil A168
Ambassador table linens P343
Ambassadorial Scholarships P421
Ambe Attar, Isidoro W581
Amber Leaf tobacco W241
Amber Milling P122
Amber Networks W406
AmBev A174, W376
Ambi office seating A707
Ambiance in parking P237
Ambien drug A1122
Amblard, Michel W191
Ambrosia Cake A774
Ambrosio, Anthony A335
AMCIS A1300
Amcoal W92
Amcol International W116
Amcot P735
Amcraft brand P537
AMD. See Advanced Micro Devices, Inc.
Amdahl Corporation A1002, A1066, W236
Amdocs W412
AMEC plc A340, A440
Ameche, H. Kathleen A1403

Amedco (casket maker) A1268
Amedisys, Inc. E152
Amelineau, Laurent W171
Amelio, Gilbert A186, A1002
Amelio, William J. A473
Amell, John P223, P627
Amemiya, Koichi W265
Amen, Robert M. A771
AMER World Research A66
Amerada Hess Corporation A132-A133, A556, A1460, W216, W438
Amerada Petroleum A132
AMERCO A134-A135, A300
Amerco Real Estate Company A135
Ameren Corporation A136-A137
AmerenCIPS (Illinois utility) A136, A137
AmerenUE (Missouri utility) A136, A137
AmerGen Energy Company, LLC A570, A571, A668
America At Risk: A History of Consumer Protest (educational video) P139
America First Companies E152
America First Mortgage Investments, Inc. E152
America Fore Group A378
America Latina Companhia de Seguros (insurance) W597
América Móvil (wireless) W580
America Online Inc. See AOL Time Warner Inc.
America Securities Capital Partners A86
America Service Group Inc. E153
America West Airlines. See America West Holdings Corporation
America West Arena A1478
America West Holdings Corporation (airline) A138-A139, P474, P475, W71
American Agricultural Chemicals A412
American Airlines Center (sports arena) P547
American Airlines, Inc. A106, A164, A272, A428, A478, A1228, A1538, P54, W68, W70, W71, W140, W302, W468, W469, W497
American Alliance of Family Owned Businesses A922, P320
American Annuity Group A1268
American Appliance Company A1190
American Arithmometer A1424
American Asiatic Underwriters A150
American Asset Management P294
American Association for Community Associations P492
American Association of Retired Persons. See AARP
American Association of the Red Cross. See The American Red Cross

American Messenger
Company A1426
American Metal Products A856
American Microwave
Technology E68, E123
American Motorists Insurance
Company P268
American Motors
Corporation W480
American Movie Classics cable
network A312, A313, A872, A962,
A999
American Music Group E66, E210
The American National Bank &
Trust A166
American National Can Group,
Inc. W432
American National Financial,
Inc. A590
American of Martinsville
furniture A854
American Oil Company W136
American Olean (ceramic tile) A194
American Pad and Paper P742
American Paging A1360
American Personal
Communications
(wireless) A1502
American Petroleum
Exchange A308
American Portable Telecom A1360
American Potash & Chemical A820
American Power & Light
Company A624, A1138
American Precision Industries Inc.
(motion controls) A462
American Premier
Underwriters A144, A642
American Professional Football
Association A672, P211, P356,
P683
American Protection
Industries P416
American Protection
Insurance P268
American Public Television P145
American Radiator A152
American Re. See American
Reinsurance
American Real Estate Partners,
L.P. E154
American Realty Investors,
Inc. E219, E303
The American Red Cross P44-P45,
P493, P538
American Rehability Services A698
American Reinsurance A90, W380
American Residential Services,
Inc. A1272, A1273
American Retail Group Inc. P539
American Rod & Gun P550
American Rolling Mill A104
American Rug Craftsmen A980
American Savings Bank
(California) A1500
American Savings (Colorado) A658
American Seaway Foods P198
American Self-Service A1092

American Society for the Control of
Cancer P40
American Standard Companies
Inc. A152-A153, A198, A1550
American Standard Insurance
Company P42, P43
American States Financial
Corporation A878, A1230, A1231
American States Life Insurance
Company A1231
American Steamship
Company A638, A639
American Steel Foundries P540
The American Stock Exchange,
Inc. A396, A806, A996, A997,
A1018, A1130, A1382, P46-P47,
P352, P353, P374, P539, P682
American Stores Company A66,
A110, A670, A886, A1094, A1234,
P462, W634
American Stroke Association E111
American Telecasting A1318
American Telephone and
Telegraph A202, A898
American Tobacco Company A514,
A618, A814, A1436, P598, W142,
W240, W282, W652
American Tobacco Trust A1204
American Tourister A718
American Tradition motor
homes A605
American Transmission Systems,
Inc. A598, A599
American Trust Company A226
American United Life Insurance
Company P539
American Viscose (rayon and
cellophane) A612, A984, A1122,
A1300
American Water Works Company,
Inc. A154-A155
American Water Works & Electric
Company A114, A154, A156
American Weavers (carpets) A980
American Wilderness Experience
(zoo) A440
American Wireless Telegraph A802
American Woodworker
(magazine) A1193
American Xtal Technology. *See* AXT,
Inc.
American-Marietta Company A882
AmeriCare Health A696
America's Best Homes A604
America's Car-Mart E188
America's Choice foods A671
America's Cup (yacht racing) P250,
P251
America's Fiber Network LLC A114
America's Tire Company P594
Americatours W58
AMERICOM Wireless
Services A1298
AmeriCredit Corporation A808,
E27, E154
Ameridrives couplings P578
Amerifee Corporation A318
AmeriGas Partners A1034

AmeriGas Propane A1128
AmeriHost Inns A338
AmeriLink Corporation (cable
installer) A1188
Amerimark Building
Products A1072
Amerin Guaranty E108, E274
AmeriPath, Inc. E155
AmeriServ Food Company. *See*
AmeriServe Food Distribution
AmeriServe Food
Distribution A302, A1404, P236,
P633
AmeriSource Health Corporation.
See AmerisourceBergen
Corporation
AmerisourceBergen
Corporation A156-A157, A320,
A458, A946, A958, A1070, A1354,
P466
AmeriSpec (home
inspections) A1273
AmeriStar Financial Services,
Inc. A863
AmeriState Mobile Medical
Services P518
Ameritech Corporation A176, A206,
A1182, A1244, A1245, W122
Ameritrade Holding
Corporation A348
Amerman, John A926
Amerock cabinet hardware A1022,
A1023
Amerotron A1380
Amersil (fused quartz) A550
Ames Department Stores,
Inc. A158-A159, A1388, E147
Ames (tools) A1446, A1447
Ames Worsted Textile
Company A158
Amescua, Sergio W635
Ametex furniture P299, P659
AmEx. *See* American Express
Company
AMEX. *See* The American Stock
Exchange, Inc.
Amex Airlines A164
AMF. *See* American Machine and
Foundry
A.M.F. (bowling equipment) A298
Amfac Health Care A320
AMFM Inc. (radio station
operator) A372, A714, P232,
P350, P631
Amgen Inc. A160-A161, E71, W314
Amherst College P78
AMI Community Hospital (Santa
Cruz, CA) P118
Amic (company) W92
Amica Mutual Insurance
Company P540
Amicar drug E71
Amiga Format (magazine) W238
Amiraian, Donna P461, P736
Amiry, Reda H. A453
Amistad (movie) P166, P167
AMK A354

Amkor Technology, Inc. A162-A163
Ammirati Puris Lintas A772
Ammon, Donald R. P530
Ammon, Theodore P506, W378
Amoco. *See* BP Amoco p.l.c.; BP p.l.c.
Amoco Chemicals W136
Amore, John W653
Amory, Louis P65
Amos, Daniel P. A92, A93
Amos, John A92
Amos, Paul S. A92
Amos, William A92
Amoy foods W193
AMP, Inc. E124
AMP Limited (investments) A1464, W88-W89
Ampacet A900
Ampex A1066
Amphenol Corporation (cables and connectors) A837, P283
Amphora tobacco A1242, W282, W283
AMPI. *See* Associated Milk Producers Inc.
AMPLICOR HIV-1 Test W493
Amplifon A234
AMR Corporation A164-A165, A478, A1228, A1310, W140
AMRESCO Capital Trust E155
Amrion (nutraceuticals) A1522
Am-Safe, Inc. P313
AmSouth Bancorporation A166-A167, A1308
Amstar Sugar Corporation A500, P162, W568
Amsted Industries Inc. P540
Amstel beer W254, W255, W552
Amsterdam (ship) A331
Amsterdam-Rotterdam Bank W56
Amstrad Action (magazine) W238
Amstrad PLC W490
AmSurg Corporation E155
Amtel (integrated circuits) A1482
Amtrak. *See* National Railroad Passenger Corporation
Amundsen, Chris P492
Amundson, Joy A. A59
Amurol Confections Company A1526, A1527
Amusategui, Jose Maria W512
AMVEST Vastgoed B.V. W65
Amway Corporation A1164, P536
Amy & Isabelle (movie) P219
Amylum (sweeteners and starches) W568
ANA Hotels W80
ANA Sports W80
Anacin over-the-counter drug A148
Anacostia Museum and Center for African American History & Culture (Washington, DC) P450, P451
Anadarko Petroleum Corporation A168-A169
Anadarko pipeline A536

ANADIGICS, Inc. E28, E156, E229
Anadol car W318
Anadrill (drilling) A1252
Anaheim Angels (baseball team) A1496, A1497, P307
Analog Devices, Inc. A170-A171, E161
The Analysts (computerized mud logging) A1252
Anam Group A162
Anam Semiconductor, Inc. A162
Anania, Andrea A361
Anapamu wine A521, P169
Anaren Microwave, Inc. E156
Anbuma Group (steel tubing) P312
ANC Rental Corporation A206
Anchor Blue Clothing P539
Anchor Chemical A100
Anchor Glass A1074
Anchor Hocking glassware A1022, A1023, E60
Anchor Oil A1128
Ancienne Mutuelle of Calvados W104
Ancienne Mutuelle of Orleans W104
ANCIRC Pharmaceuticals E156
Anco brand A585
Ancona, Edgar D. A735
Ancona, Henry W151
Ancure blood vessel patch A674
A & K Petroleum A820
Andenaes, Henrik W411
Anders Wilhelmsen (shipping) A1216
Andersen A172, A172-A173, A220, A840, A1424, P48-P49, P66, P206, P286, P540, P620, P705, W90, W90-W91, W324
Andersen, Arthur A172, P48, W90
Andersen, Carl M. A659
Andersen Consulting. *See* Accenture
Andersen Corporation P50-P51, P541
Andersen, Darl J. P550
Andersen, Fred P50
Andersen, Hans P50
Andersen, Herbert P50
Andersen, Jørgen Kristian W411
Andersen, Nils Smedegaard W163
Andersen, Ole A1551
Andersen, Sarah J. P51
Andersen, Vagn W417
Andersen Worldwide. *See* Andersen
Anderson, Abram A316
Anderson, A. D. A742
Anderson & Cromwell A614, P190
Anderson & Kerr Drilling Company A820
Anderson, Arthur B. (PepsiCo) A1107
Anderson, Arthur (Peninsular and Oriental) W434
Anderson Box Company A1364
Anderson, Bradbury H. A255
Anderson, Brian (ContiGroup) A427, P141

Anderson, Brian P. (Baxter) A237
Anderson, Bruce C. A125
Anderson, Byron J. A99
Anderson, Charles (Anderson News) P541
Anderson, Charles A. (Trammell Crow) A1399
Anderson, Chris W238, W239
Anderson Clayton (company) A1180
Anderson Copper and Brass Company P313
Anderson, Craig P725
Anderson, David C. (Airborne Freight) A103
Anderson, David (Charter Communications) A351
Anderson, David G. (HCA) A695
Anderson, David (Lennox) A864
Anderson, David R. (American Family Insurance) P43
Anderson, David (SEMATECH) P445
Anderson, Ed A400
Anderson Exploration A482
Anderson, Fred D. A187
Anderson, Gary E. (Dow Corning) P165, P596
Anderson, Gary R. (Storage Technology) A1337
Anderson, Gerard M. A513
Anderson, Gordon W. A1479
Anderson, Greg P471
Anderson, Herbert W., Jr. A1045
Anderson Hickey (office furniture) P222
Anderson, James E., Jr. (Ingram Micro) A759
Anderson, James (Kerr-McGee) A820
Anderson, J. C. A1521
Anderson, John E. P746
Anderson, Kenneth (Modern Continental) P678
Anderson, Ken (Novell) A1051
Anderson, Kerrii B. A1511
Anderson, Lee Ann E283
Anderson, Lloyd P410, P711
Anderson, Mary P410, P711
Anderson News Company A190, P541
Anderson, Paul M. W128, W129
Anderson, Richard C. (Lands' End) A852, A853
Anderson, Richard (Encyclopaedia Britannica) P177, P603
Anderson, Richard H. (Northwest Airlines) A1046, A1047
Anderson, R. John A869, P293
Anderson, Robert A198
Anderson School of Business P746
Anderson, Thomas R. E272
Anderson, Timothy E172
Anderson, Truman A184
Anderson, Walter A81, P33, P516
Anderson, William D. (BCE) W123
Anderson, William (NCR) A1012
Anderson, William (Raley's) P710

Anderson, William (Trinity Health) P748
Anderson-Bargrover (food growing and processing equipment) A612
Anderson-Prichard Oil A200
Andersson, Bengt W211
Andersson, Curt J. A1387
Andersson, Rune W211
Andert, Mary A1197
Andhurst brand P77
Ando, Göran A1123
Ando, Kunitake W551
Ando, Toshio W409
Andolino, Joseph F. A663
André champagne A521, P169
Andreae, Jan G. W499
Andreas, Dwayne O. A192, A193
Andreas, G. Allen A192, A193
Andreas, Martin L. A193
Andreas, Michaels A192
Andretta, Thierry W251
Andreu, Jean-Louis W521
Andrew Corporation E168
Andrew Jergens (skin care) A234, W308
The Andrew W. Mellon Foundation P541
Andrews, Charles P777
Andrews, Dick P750
Andrews, Duane P. P439
Andrews, Harry C. A977
Andrews, J. Michael A643
Andrews, John V. A117
Andrews, Paul E., Jr. P750
Andrews, Steven R. A1105
Andrews, Timothy M. A1161
Andriani, Marino E58
Andritz W568
Andronico's Markets P489
Andrukonis, David A. A627
Andrus, Ethel P28
Andrus Foundation P28, P29
Andrx Corporation E156
Añejo Rum W109
Anell, Lars W633
AneuRx A952
Anew skin care A217
Anfinson's P406
Ang, Ramon S. W511
Angeion Corporation A674
Angel, Michael D. E123, E292
Angel Soft paper products A654
Angel, Spencer J. E185
Angel, Stephen A1157
Angelilli, Lawrence A341
Angello, Matthew J. A195
Angiomed GmbH A445
Angle-Spring brand A527
Anglia Television W249
Anglo American plc W92-W93, W340, W500
Anglogold A1024, W92
Anglo-Persian Oil W136, W612
Anglophile A776
Anglo-Swiss Condensed Milk Company W388

Anglovaal Mining W92
Angress, David E66
ANGUS Chemical A504
Angus, William A., III E49, E189
Anheuser, Eberhard A174
Anheuser-Busch Companies, Inc. A78, A174-A175, A1062, A1074, A1164, P72, P428, P553, P715, W162, W288, W314
Anido, Armando E90
Animal Planet (cable channel) P158, P159, P594
Animex S.A. A1290, A1291
Animorphs (books and TV show) A1255
Anixter Brothers (wire and cable) A176
Anixter International Inc. A176-A177, A560, A561, E30, P180, P181
Ann J. Kellogg School P520
Ann Sacks art tiles P284, P285, P653
The Annals of America (books) P176, P177, P603
Anne Cole brand lingerie A1499
Annenberg, Walter P144, P492
The Annenberg/CPB Projects P144, P145
Annenburg School for Communication P759
Annes, Michael D. A1181
Annexstad, Al P607
Annis, Rick P570
AnnTaylor Stores Corporation A586, A634
Compañia Anonima Nacional Telefonos de Venezuela A88
ANR (pipeline) A537
Anraku, Kanemitsu W403
Ansata (publishing) W107
The Anschutz Corporation E62
Anschutz, Philip F. A836, A1186, A1187, A1422, E62, E205, P232, P412, P712
Ansell Brewery W84
Ansell Healthcare Inc. W428, W429
Anselmo L. Morvillo (printing) P404
Ansett Australia (airline) A138, A1421, W468, W540
Anson, Charles W259
Anson, Mark P97
Anstandig, Marshall A833
Anstice, David W. A957
Answer Financial A1448
Answer office furniture A1335
Answer Products Inc. P656
Answerthink, Inc. E157
Companhia Antarctica Paulista Industria Brasileira de Bebidas e Conexo A1174
Antares Capital Corporation A922, A923, P321
ANTEC Corporation A176, A873, E30, E158
Antell, Richard H. E83

Antero Health Plans, Inc. A1081
Anthem Insurance Companies, Inc. A178-A179, A268, A1506, P82, P84, P226
Anthony, Barbara Cox A442, P146
Anthony, Ross P692
Anthony's pasta P91
Anthracite Capital, Inc. E157
Antinonin pesticide W118
Antioco, John F. A266, A267
Antoine, Richard L. A1165
Antonini, Joseph A830
Antonio, Franklin P. A1183
Antonson, Steve P565
Antron carpet fibers A534
Antz (movie) P166, P167
Anzai, Takashi W299
Anzaki, Satoru W320, W321
Anzilotti, Maria A519
A. O. Smith Corporation A1394
A. O. Smith Data Systems A480
A. O. Smith Motor Wheel A286, A1550
Aoki Corporation (construction) A1328
Aoki, Datoshi W265
Aoki, Takashi W599
Aoki, Toshiharu W401
AOL Canada W474
AOL MovieFone, Inc. A180
AOL Time Warner Inc. A60, A76, A80, A130, A146, A180-A181, A202, A206, A226, A266, A312, A334, A370, A390, A566, A636, A680, A736, A832, A872, A976, A1000, A1002, A1198, A1258, A1268, A1284, A1342, A1450, A1494, A1496, A1500, A1502, A1534, A1546, E86, E197, E206, E235, E242, E245, P32, P33, P80, P248, P346, P356, P416, P510, P579, P682, P756, W126, W212, W238, W296, W342, W418, W426, W448, W550, W610, W624
AOLTV A1002
Aon Corporation A182-A183, A356, W652
Aoyagi, Kazuhiro W321
Aozora Bank, Ltd. W396, W548
AP. See The Associated Press
A.P. Møller A454, W94-W95
AP Radio Network P60
AP WirePhoto Network P60
APAC, Inc. (asphalt and highway materials) A200
Apache Corporation A184-A185, A1054, A1276
Apache helicopters A120, E175
Apallas, Yeoryios P429
Apatoff, Robert S. A127
Apax Partners & Company A714, E193, P232, W148, W238, W290
APCOA/Standard Parking P236, P633
APD auto parts delivery service A1100
Apex cameras E184

Apex Global Information Services A128
Apex Oil Company, Inc. P542, P586
Apex Orchards (almonds and pistachios) P416
Apex sockets A430
Apex Supply Company, Inc. A724
Apicerno, Kenneth J. A1383
APL Limited (shipping) A1422
APlus convenience stores A1344
Apollo Advisors A338, P692
Apollo Computers A712
Apollo Group, Inc. E309
Apollo Investment Fund A630
Apollo Management A548, P577
Apollo Presentation Products A618
Apollo reservation system W316
Apollo space program A198, A272, A370, A542, A572, A1044, A1210, W392
Apollo Technologies A530
Apomate E254
Apostrophe brand A1265
Appalachian Power Company A140
Apparatebau Hundsbach (electronic sensors) A430
Apparelmaster A364
Appel, Laurence B. A725
APPI (machined components) E26
Apple Computer, Inc. A186-A187, A972, A990, A1002, A1184, A1256, A1356, A1357, A1544, E86, E235, E245, E263, E266, P430, P597, P719, W60, W180, W338, W532, W538, W550
Apple Jacks cereal A817
Apple Market P62, P63, P488
Applebaum, Jay I. P519
Appleby, Anne F. P692
Appleby, David A. P701
Applera Corporation P542
Appletiser soft drink W552, W553
Appleton & Lange (publisher) A944
Appleton, Steven R. A970, A971
Applica Inc. A264
Société d' Applications des Machines Mortices A1412
Applied Biosystems Group P542
Applied Color Systems A194
Applied Energy Services A88
Applied Immune Sciences W102
Applied Innovation Inc. E157
Applied Intelligent Systems E56
Applied Komatsu Technology. See AKT (flat panel displays)
Applied Materials, Inc. A188-A189, E24, E149, E185, E213, E246, E248, W600
Applied Molecular Genetics A160
Applied Science and Technology, Inc. E246
Appomattox Trustees A498
Aprati, Robert L. A301
APS Energy Services Company, Inc. A1139
APS Holding Corporation P112
Apted, William R. A453

Apter, C. Victoria A1355, P467
APTN. See Associated Press Television Network
APV Chemical Machinery A450
APW Limited P581
Aqua Velva body care A1243
Aquafina water A382, A1102, A1103, A1105, A1107
Aquafresh toothpaste W246
Aquair toiletries W535
Aqualon Group A704
Aquamarine cosmetics A1201
AquaPenn Spring Water Company, Inc. W192
Aquarius Travel P418
AquaTraxx irrigation tape A1393
Aquila, Inc. A668, A1464, A1465
Aquila Steel W128
Aquino, Corazon W510
Aquino, Richard A. A545
A. R. Baron Company A238
A. R. Brasch Marketing A1320
Arab Finagrain A426, P140
Arab Potash A786
Arabian American Oil Company. See Aramco
Aragones, Mercedes W635
Arai, Takao W397
Arai, Yoshikazu W315
Araki, Hiroshi W599
Araki, Ryuji W615
Aral service stations W218
Aramaki, Koichiro W315
ARAMARK Corporation A190-A191, A440, A1350, A1478, P541
Arambula, Frank P760
Aramco A352, A576, W500
Aramis fragrance A564, A565
Aramis, Inc. W607
Aramony, William P492
Aramoto, Magohiro W533
Aranda, Anai-i E247
ARANESP drug A160
Arango Arias, Jéronimo W634
Arango Arias, Manuel W634
Arango Arias, Plácido W634
Aranovich, Julio A. A189
Arany Aszok beer W553
Arappco Homes A509
Arata, Tatsuo W327
Arathoon, W. Robert A641
Araujo Ramirez, Felix José W583
Arava drug W103
Arbelaez, Maurice E111
Arbenz, Jacobo A354
Arbitron A342
Arbor Drugs A458
Arbor Mist wines A423
Arborland Management Company, Inc. A259
Arby's fast food A1400, P669
Arcanet (telecom) W150
Arce, David W513
Arçelik (appliances) W318
Arceneaux, William A1448

Arch Chemicals, Inc. A1060
Arch Coal, Inc. A416
Arch Communications Group A248
Arch Deluxe sandwich A942
Arch Mineral A200
Archabal, Daniel A. A173, P49
Archbold, Michael N. A233
Archer Daniels Midland Company A192-A193, A582, A742, A768, A1132, A1536, P36, P122, P184, P200, P532, P565, P622, W308, W568
Archer Farms brand foods A1352
Archer, George A192
Archer, Richard W177
Archer Western Contractors P768
Archibald, Ed P331
Archibald, Nolan D. A264, A265
Archidocese of New York P570
Archinaco, Frank A. A1153
Archipelago Holdings ECN A960, A996, P352
Architect Software P248
Architectural Digest (magazine) A80, P32, P33
Architectural Record (magazine) A945
Archives of American Art P451
Archstone Communities E175, E285
Arciniega, Tomas A. P99
ARCO Chemical Company A900, A1128
ARCO gasoline W136
Arcodan (headend systems) A1258
Arcor (Internet provider) W352
Arctic Alaska Fisheries A1418
Arctic Slope Regional Corporation P542
Arcuri, Catherine E293
Ardagh PLC (containers) A1074
Arden Courts (assisted living) A908
Arden International Kitchens (frozen foods) P723
Ardent Software, Inc. (computer graphics) W326
Area Agencies on Aging P698
Arechabala family W108
Arela wax A375
Arenas, Andrea-Teresa P501
Arendt, William G. A1027
ARES (property management) A986
Arethusa (Off-Shore) Limited A884
Argo Communications A128
Argonaut Insurance A116
Argonne National Laboratory P496, P497
Argos (retailer) W142
Argosy Gaming Company P634
Arguello Inc. A1145
Argus (breweries) W262
Argus cameras E184
Argus, Don R. W128, W129
Arguss Communications, Inc. E158
Argyll Group A1234, W300
Aria card A1170
Aria Services for Physicians P719

Ariba, Inc. A764, A1228, E242
Aricept drug A1118, A1119
Arison, Micky A330, A331
Arison, Ted A330
Arista Records W126
Aristech Chemical
  Corporation A1344
Aristokraft cabinets A618, A619
Arithmos (integrated
  circuits) W554
Arius Finance W131
Arizona Business Bank E181
Arizona Cardinals (football
  team) P356, P357
Arizona Chemical Company A770
Arizona Copper A1124
Arizona Diamondbacks (baseball
  team) A1478, P307
Arizona Edison A1138
Arizona Electric Power Competition
  Act A1138
Arizona Grocery (stores) A1234
Arizona Jean Company A790, A791
Arizona Public Service
  Company A1138, A1139
Arizona Republic A632
Arizpe, A. Steve A75
Ark, Jennifer A673, P211
Ark Life Assurance Company
  Limited Life W87
Arkansas Power & Light A554
Arkla A1199
Arlans discount stores A246
Arlauskas, Robert A. A1131
Arledge, David A. A537
Arledge, Roone A61
Arleigh-Burke (destroyer) E183
Arline, Marcella K. A709
Arlington International Racecourse
  (Chicago) E40, E178, P598
Arlington Memorial Hospital
  Foundation P744
Arlington State College P470
Arlotta, John J. A323
ARM & HAMMER baking
  soda A358, A359
Armacost, Samuel H. P455
Armadale W262
Armament Systems A645
Armani brand P100
Armbrust, Rick W291
Armco, Inc. A104
Armed Forces Financial
  Network P686
Armijo, Ralph E249
Armistead, David M. A161
Armitage, Leslie L. P111
Armitage Shanks A153
ArmKel A358
Armor All Products
  Corporation A374, A946
Armor Holdings, Inc. E29, E158
Armour & Company P392
Armour Food Company A408,
  A486, A1478
Armour, Mark W479

Armour Meat Packing A408, A409,
  A486, A916
Armour, Philip A1042
Armour Star A487
Armour-Dial A486
Armstrong Air A864
Armstrong air conditioning A865
Armstrong Brothers (cork
  cutting) A194
Armstrong Brothers Tool A462
Armstrong, C. Michael A202, A203
Armstrong Furnace A864
Armstrong Holdings,
  Inc. A**194**-A**195**
Armstrong, Mark F. A432
Armstrong, Michael T. A736
Armstrong, Synetta S. P57
Armstrong, Thomas A194
Armstrong Tire W450
Armstrong Tools, Inc. A463
Armstrong Whitworth
  (aircraft) W110
Armstrong World Industries A194,
  A630
Armtek (automotive
  products) P310
Armus LLC A358
Army and Air Force Exchange
  Service P**52**-P**53**, P543
Army Math Research Center P500
Army of Stars (radio and TV
  shows) P426
Arnault, Bernard W134, W348,
  W349
Arndt, Terrence D. A575
Arneault, Edson R. "Ted" E247
Arnesen, Mark R. A595
Arnett, James W376
Arnett, Lonnie A. A257
Arnette Optic Illusions
  (sunglasses) A234
Arning, Robert F. A841, P287, W325
Arnold, Craig A527
Arnold Foods (baked goods) A426,
  P140
Arnold, Greg P749
Arnold Industries, Inc. A1206
Arnold, James W. A1395
Arnold, Joel A1187
Arnold, Kurt W185
Arnold, Linda E116, E283
Arnold, Lugman W617
Arnold, Michael C. (Timken) A1387
Arnold, Michael J. (Freeport-
  McMoRan) A629
Arnold, Neal E. A593
Arnold, Steven P. A763
Arnold, Thomas G. A1337
Arnold Transportation
  Services A1206
Arnold's pickles A467
Aroma coffee shops A943
Aroma Ltd. coffee shops A942
Aron, Gary M. A235
Aron, Mark G. A455
Aronson, Laurence A1201
Arosa car W631

Arovas, Bob P614
ARPANET computer network P454
Arpey, Gerard J. A165
Arps, Leslie A1288, P446
Arras, Richard K. A1281
Array Technology (storage
  products) A542
ARR/CRS (kitchen
  equipment) A530
Arrid antiperspirant A358
Arrigo, Joseph F. P752
Arrington, David J. A1029
ARRIS Group, Inc. E30, E158
Arrison, Clement P310
Arriva tires A664
Arrojo, José Manuel W513
Arrow Electronics,
  Inc. A**196**-A**197**, A214, A958,
  A1140, E222
Arrow Hart electrical
  products A431
Arrow Industries (flexible
  packaging) A250
Arrow Radio A196
Arrowmint gum A1527
Arrowstreet Capital A314, P96
Arroyo, Gloria W511
Art Collection (office
  furniture) P222
The Art of the Comeback
  (book) P482
The Art of the Deal (book) P482
Art Shokai service station W264
Art Technology Group, Inc. E159
Artal Luxembourg A608, A814
Artemis (holding company) W446
Arterial Vascular Engineering,
  Inc. A952
ArthroCare Corporation E159
Arthur Andersen & Company. *See*
  Andersen
Arthur D. Little, Inc. P**54**-P**55**, P94,
  P543
Arthur Frommer's Budget Travel
  (books) A1502
Arthur, Gary L., Jr. A1467
Arthur, H. Thomas A1249
Arthur, Meagan M. A905
Arthur M. Sackler Gallery P451
Arthur, Rita P704
Arthur, Steve A757, P245
Arthur Treacher's Fish &
  Chips A1510, E95, E249
Arthur, Yoko P145
Arthur Young (accounting) A562,
  P182, W222
Arthur's pasta products E247
Artis, Curtis R. A899
Artois, Sebastien W288
Artois-Piedboeuf-Interbrew W288
Arts & Entertainment cable
  network. *See* A&E cable network
Arts and Industries Building P451
Artzt, Russell M. A403
Arvey (paper) A770
Arvida Realty Services E115
Arvin Industries A198, P310

ArvinMeritor, Inc. A**198**-A**199**
Arzco Medical Systems P312
As The World Turns (TV show) A1164, A1165
A. S. Watson & Company, Limited (holding company) W272, W273
ASA Holdings, Inc. A478
Asada, Atsushi W395
Asada, Kazuo W401
Asada, Okihiro W327
Asahi Breweries W231, W314
Asahi Camera (magazine) W97
Asahi Chemical Industry Company W228, W304
Asahi (communications equipment) W168
Asahi Evening News W96, W97
Asahi Glass Company, Ltd. W370, W371
Asahi Mutual Life Insurance Company W596
Asahi Shimbun Publishing Company W**96**-W**97**
Asahi-Dow A504
Asakura, Masaaki A57
Asano, Naomichi W315
ASARCO Inc. A1124
Asatsu-DK, Inc. (advertising) W646
Asbeck, Katherine A. A435
Asbury Automotive Group, LLC P156, P543
Asbury, Mel P691
ASC Network Corporation A699
Ascend Communications, Inc. (network hardware) A898
Ascension Health P**56**-P**57**, P544, P569
Ascent Entertainment Group, Inc. A872
Aschenbrenner, John E. A1163
Aschenbroich, Jacques W507
Ascher, Michael C. P335
The ASCII Group, Inc. P544
Ascom Holding E224
Ascot Plc A504
ASD Specialty Healthcare A155
ASDA Group Limited (supermarkets) A1494, A1495, W300, W312, W588
ASEA AB W54, W210
Asea Brown Boveri. *See* ABB Ltd.
Asesoria Administrativa de Logistica, S.A. de C.V. A789
ASG (freight forwarder) W202
Asgrow brand A985
Ash, Bruce A497
Ash, Darron A715, P233, P631
Ash, Mary Kay P316, P666
Ashanti Goldfields Company W340, W341
Ashbourne (long-term care providers) A1340
Ashburn, Carolyn P656
Ashby, Bruce A1443
Ashby, James A83
Ashby, William S. A103
Ashcraft's Markets A1312

Ashcroft, Charles W213
Ashcroft, Tim E272
Ashen, Frank Z. A1019, P375, P688
Ashenhurst, Harry J. A865
Asher Edelman A620, A1090
Asher, J. Burke E278
Asher, Noah S. E113, E280
Asheville Power & Light A1166
Ashland Inc. A**200**-A**201**, A1460, P664
Ashley Furniture Industries, Inc. P544
Ashley, Richard A530
Ashley, Roger P530
Ashraff, M. H. W567
Ashton Mining W488
Ashton, William L. A161
Ashwill, Terry M. E318
Ashworth, Ronald B. P730
ASI Corporation P545
ASI Holding A152
Asia Airfreight Terminal Company Ltd. W541
Asia Broadcasting and Communications Network W296
Asia Medical Supplies Company, Ltd. A1071
Asian Development Bank A314, P96
Asian Industries A427
Asian Infrastructure Fund A150
Asian Roadway Express A1206
The Asian Wall Street Journal A506, A507
Asiana (airline) W469
AsiaSat I satellite W272
Asiatic Petroleum W500
Asietours W58
Asimus, Stewart F., Jr. A1189
ASIX Systems E46
ASK Group (network software) A402
Ask Jeeves, Inc. (Web site) E201
Ask Mr. Foster Travel A328, P106, P108, P567
Askanas, Mark S. A1215
Askey Computer E261
Askin, David J. E21
Askin, Richard H., Jr. A1403
askMartha (radio and newspaper) A918, A919
Asko Deutsche Kaufhaus (supermarkets) W364
Askren, Stanley A. A727
Aslami, Mohd A. E203
Asleep At the Wheel (music group) P167
ASM Lithography Holding N.V. E189, W392, W444
Aso, Kotaro W235
ASP World Conference & Expo P249
Aspen Institute P416
Aspen Litharne W238
Aspen Peripherals A1336
Aspen Publishers W642, W643
Aspen Research P50
Aspera A1520

Aspire personal computers W60
Aspire Visa credit card E183
Asplundh, Scott P545
Asplundh Tree Expert Company P545
Aspril cosmetics W535
ASSA-ABLOY AB (locks) W524
Assault (racehorse) A828, P270
Asscher, Jean-Claude E126, E299
Assembly Solutions A1240
Assembly Technologies E81
Asset Investment & Financial Group A325
Asset One (loan servicing) E227
Assicurazioni Generali S.p.A. W**98**-W**99**
Associated Aviation Underwriters A356
Associated Biscuit W244
Associated British Foods W244, W590
Associated British Picture Corporation W212
Associated Bulk Carriers W434
Associated Chemists, Inc. A890
Associated Dairy Products P596
Associated Dry Goods A932
Associated Electrical Industries W354
Associated Food Stores, Inc. P545
Associated Gas & Electric Company A668
Associated Grocers Company P62
Associated Grocers, Inc. P546
Associated Grocers of Arizona A606
Associated Grocers of Michigan A1312
The Associated Group, Inc. A872
Associated Hospital Service P174
Associated Insurance Companies A178
Associated Medical Care Plans A268, P82
Associated Merchandising Corporation A1352, A1353
Associated Merchants A932
Associated Milk Producers Inc. P**58**-P**59**, P546
Associated Physical Therapy Practitioners, Inc. A259
Associated Press A568
The Associated Press P**60**-P**61**, P546
Associated Press Television Network P60, P61, P546
Associated Securities Corporation P385
Associated Stationers P518
Associated Unit Companies A638
Associated Wholesale Grocers, Inc. P**62**-P**63**, P547
Associated Wholesalers, Inc. P547
Associates First Capital Corporation A370, A616, A790, A822, A1380, A1552
Association for Asian Studies P610
Association of America's Public Television Stations P145

Association of Blue Shield Plans A268, P82

Assurances Générales de France A688, W82

Compagnie d'Assurances Mutuelles contre l'incendie W104

AST (computers) W508

AST Research, Inc. P272

Asta Funding, Inc. E159

Astaris LLC A612, A1300

Astec Industries, Inc. A116, A546

ASTeX. See Applied Science and Technology

Astika beer W289

Aston Martin car A616

Astra CAPSA (oil and gas exploration). See Astra Compania Argentina de Petroleo S.A.

Astra Compania Argentina de Petroleo S.A. W482, W483, W650

Astra Group (satellites) W146

Astrakhanneft (oil exploration) W346

Astral tobacco A1458, A1459

Astralwerks recording label W213

AstraZeneca PLC A540, E193, W414, W492

Astrolink (global broadband satellite) A1412

Aström, Håkan A1123

AstroPower, Inc. (solar power) A668, A669

AstroTurf A984, A1122, A1300

Astrum International A718

ASUAG (watchmaker) W562

Asulab (research and watch development) W563

PT Asuransi Jiwa Principal Indonesia A1163

ASV (aluminum) W410

Asymetrix (multimedia software) P510

Asyst Technologies, Inc. E31, E160

At Home Corporation A202

A.T. Kearney & Company, Inc. A538, A948, P326

A.T. Massey Coal A610

A.T. Mays, the Travel Agents A328, P108

El-Ata, Ahmad Abu W185

Atack, Jonathan W545

At-A-Glance appointment books and calendars A950

Ataka W296

AT&T 00 Info E243

AT&T Broadband A72, A202, A312, A350, A390, A442, A528, A832, A872, A1450, A1472, E30, E158, P146, P158, P737, W390, W582

AT&T Capital. See Newcourt Financial

AT&T Corporation A70, A72, A98, A128, A180, A202-A203, A213, A248, A292, A312, A404, A636, A646, A736, A780, A872, A888, A898, A916, A972, A982, A1012, A1050, A1082, A1182, A1184, A1186, A1222, A1244, A1258, A1318, A1342, A1362, A1472, A1534, E117, E221, E224, E230, E233, E252, E300, E316, E318, P88, P106, P208, P580, P772, W76, W122, W148, W160, W204, W334, W338, W400, W406, W412, W422, W444, W486, W502, W580, W584, W586, W646

AT&T Corporation Center (Chicago) P449

AT&T Wireless Services, Inc. A202, A570, A842, A1026, E83, E126, E210, E233, E243, E287, E299, P542, W418, W494

Atari Corporation (game systems) A1298, W394

Atay, Ternel W319

Atchison, Topeka & Santa Fe (railroad) A308

ATCO Gas A310

Atecs Mannesmann AG W352, W490, W536

Ateliers (drapery hardware) A1022

Athenos cheese A843

Athens Outlet Stores A666

Athens Stock Exchange W384

Atherton, Peter R. A727

The Athletic and Swim Club at Equitable Center (New York City) P131

The Athletic Shoe Factory stores A1214

Athlon microprocessor A82, A970

@Home A1284

ATI Technologies Inc. E256

ATI Telecom International E41

Atir, Yiftach W323

Atitech (maintenance) W79

ATK. See Alliant Techsystems Inc.

Atkin, Mary V. A95

Atkins, Howard I. A1509

Atkins, Orin A200

Atkins pickles A467

Atkins, Steve P635

Atkinson, Graham W. A1421

Atkinson, Peter Y. W263

Atkinson, Ray P764

Atkinson, Richard C. P494, P495, P755

Atkinson, Sharon E46, E187

ATL Products, Inc. A1184

ATL Ultrasound W444

Atlanta Baking Company A608

Atlanta Beat (soccer team) A443

Atlanta Braves (baseball team) A180, A181, P307

Atlanta Capital Management E53

Atlanta Falcons (football team) P357

Atlanta Hawks (basketball team) A180, P355

The Atlanta Journal-Constitution A442, A443, P146, P147, P585

Atlanta Paper A950

Atlanta Thrashers (hockey team) A180, P361

Atlantic Bank and Trust. See Capital Crossing Bank

Atlantic Bank of New York W384, W385

Atlantic City Hilton Casino Resort A1086, A1087

Atlantic City Showboat casino A685

Atlantic Coast Line Railroad A454

Atlantic Dairy Cooperative A850, P288

Atlantic Envelope Company A1004, A1005

Atlantic Industries A450

Atlantic, Mississippi & Ohio (railroad) A1038

Atlantic Mortgage & Investment Corporation A1142, W56

Atlantic Petroleum A1344

Atlantic Precision Products E26

Atlantic Rayon A1380

Atlantic Richfield Company A900, P238, P488, W136, W296

Atlantic Seaboard Dispatch A638

Atlantic Shores Healthcare, Inc. A1489

Atlantic Southeast Airlines, Inc. A478, A479

The Atlantic Superstore W245

Atlas Advisors, Inc. A659

Atlas Air Worldwide Holdings, Inc. E32, E160

Atlas Automation (automation equipment) A1088

Atlas Bolt & Screw Company P313

Atlas Commerce (software) A1233

Atlas Crankshaft A456, W594

Atlas ordering system P316

Atlas Powder A704

Atlas rockets A1412

Atlas Securities, Inc. A659

AtLee, Frank V., III A985

ATM Technologies E36

ATM Ventures, LLC A567

Atmaramani, K. N. W567

ATM/Canterbury (business travel consulting) E36, E170

@McKinsey A948, P326

ATMI, Inc. E160

ATOFINA (chemicals) W256, W613

AtomFilms E86, E235

AtomicTangerine (information security) P454, P455

AtomShockwave E86, E235

Atos Origin A1112, W100-W101

Atra razor A657

Atrasentan drug A58

Atria hotels W59

@Rosenbluth (business travel management) P418, P419

Attack detergent W308, W309

Attanasio, Raymond C. A63

Atterbury, Rennie, III A333

Attic Treasures P486, P487
Attisholz Holding A826
Attol Testware E110
Attwood, Frank A1151
Attwood, James A., Jr. P111
Atwater (casino developer) A906
Atwood, Charles A685
ATx Telecom Systems A1258
Au Bon Pain bakery/cafe W174
Au Printemps W446
Aube, Gregory R. A1315
Aubert, Lucien W104
Auburn Steel A1052
Auction Web E54
Aud, Jody A905
Audet (publishing) W626
Audi automobiles A616, W188,
  W340, W362, W630, W631
Audier, Agnès W625
Audio Communications
  Network P350
Audio Development Company A70
Audiofina W430
Audits & Surveys Worldwide
  (market research). See RoperASW
Auer W536
Auerbach, Red A280
Augmentin drug W246
August Max stores P713
Augustin, Jean-Luc W479
Augustine, Cynthia H. A1021
Augustus Barnett liquor stores W84
Aulbaugh, Carrol P671
Aulen, Kenneth L. A201
Auletta, Patrick V. A823
Ault, Frank H. A1267
Ault, John L. A1279
Aunt Jane's pickles A467
Aunt Jemima Mills A1180
Aunt Jemima pancake mix A1106,
  A1107, A1181
"Auntie". See British Broadcasting
  Corporation
Aupres cosmetics W535
AURATONE ceiling panels A1457
Aurelio, Richard A. E133, E310
Auréole hair color W342
Aurora Foods Inc. A816
Aurora (insurance) W98
Aurora Modular Industries E94
Aurrerá Bolivar discount
  store W634
Aurrerá hypermarkets W635
AUSSAT satellite W586
Aussedat Rey A770
Austar United
  Communications W586
Austell, Alfred A1486
Austell, Barbara A. A191
Austin, Adam W177
Austin Company A492
Austin, Edward L. A1511
Austin E. Knowlton School of
  Architecture P382, P383, P693
Austin, Eula P572
Austin, Gene A271
Austin, Glenn T., Jr. A581

Austin, H. Brent A537
Austin, Ian G. W453
Austin Industries Inc. P547
Austin, John D. A1109
Austin, J. Paul P87
Austin, Karen P690
Austin, Maureen F. A463
Austin Motor W402
Austin Quality Foods A814
Austin Reed women's clothes A690,
  A691
Austin, Roxanne S. A737
Austin, S. J. A133
Austin, Steve "Stone Cold" E141,
  E319
Austin, Susie P251, P641
Austin (Texas) American-
  Statesman A443, P147
Austin Ventures E243, E288
Austotel Trust (hotels) W230
Australia Airlines W468
Australia and New Zealand Banking
  Group Limited W382
Australia Postmaster-General's
  Department W586
Australia-Asia Airlines W468
Australian and Overseas
  Telecommunications
  Corporation W586
Australian Competition and
  Consumer Commission W382
Australian Independent
  Wholesalers W644, W645
Australian Iron and Steel W128
Australian Leisure and
  Hospitality W230
Australian Mutual Provident
  Society. See AMP Limited
Australian (newspaper) W390
Australian Radio Network A372,
  A373
Australian Regional Airlines Pty.
  Ltd. W469
Australian Stock Exchange E112,
  P80, W644
Australian Telecommunications
  Commission W586
AUSTRIA Mineralöl GmbH W425
Austria Tabak W240
Austrian Airlines Group A478,
  A1421, W80, W518
Austrian Mineral Oil
  Administration W424
Austro-Hellenique S.A. A492, A493
Authentic fitness
  (swimwear) A1498
Authority pet food A1117
Authorware E86
Auto Buggy truck A1010
Auto Marine Terminal P399
Auto Palace A208
Auto Parts Wholesale P113
Auto Shack A208
Grupo Auto Todo SA de CV A652,
  A653
Auto Union W188, W630
AutoAlliance International,
  Inc. W363

AutoCyte E50
Autogrill SpA A732
AutoInfo, Inc. A204
Autokonszern Rt. W560
Autolatina W630
Autoline Industries P113
Autoliv, Inc. A662
Automated Vehicle Systems A612
Automated Wagering
  International P698
Automatic Binding Bricks W332
Automatic Data Processing,
  Inc. **A204**-**A205**
Automatic Liquid Packaging A320
Automatic Payrolls A204
Automatic Retailers of
  America A190
Automatic Signals/Eagle
  Signal P310
Automation (vision systems) E56
Automobile Dacia SA W480
Automobile Mutual Insurance
  Company of America P540
Automobili Lamborghini Holding
  S.p.A. W630, W631
Automotive Components Group
  Worldwide A476
Automotive Hall of Fame P644
Automotive Industries A856
Automotive Moulding P212
Automotive Products
  Company A1394
Automotive Research
  Associates A1110
Automotive Resources
  International P633
Automotive Satellite Television
  Network A1160, A1161
Automotive Warehouse, Inc. P113
AutoNation, Inc. **A206**-**A207**, A266,
  A548, E201, P256
AutoSet flow generator E112
Autoshade car care products A1097
Autoshift brand A527
AutoSimulations E35
Auto-Soft (automation) E35
AutoTrader.com L.L.C. A442, A443,
  P146, P147, P585
AutoVantage (online car
  buying) A206
AutoWay (vehicle
  dealerships) A206, A207
Autozam Inc. W363
AutoZone, Inc. A198, **A208**-**A209**,
  A802, A1100, P112, P152, P590
Autry, Glenn T. P608
Auvil, Paul R., III E313
Société Auxiliaire de Distribution
  d'Eau W624
Auxton Computer A292
A.V. Roe (aircraft) W110
Avadex brand A985
Availability Reservisor A1228
Avakian, Laura P667
Avalon Cable A350
Avalon car W615
Avalon Foundation P541
Avalon Imaging E43

Avalon water A1105
Avalonbay Communities, Inc. E161
Avalox drug W118
Avantek (communications) A98
AvantGo, Inc. A76
Avaya Inc. (communications) A898, E142, E319
AVCO. *See* Aviation Corporation
Avco Corporation (aerospace and financial) A1380
Avdel (metal fastenings) A1380
Aved Display Technologies E151
Aveda cosmetics A564, A565
Aveeno skin care A800, A801, A1246, P432
Avenir office furniture A1334, A1335
Avenor (newsprint) A284
Aventis CropScience W118
Aventis (pharmaceuticals) A160, A534, A956, A974, E89, E150, E193, E240, E255, W102-W103, W118, W160, W416, W612
Averill, Meredith S. P415
Avert (employment screening) A204
Avery, David A845
Avery Dennison Corporation A210-A211
Avery, Sewell A1456
Avery, Stanton A210
Avery, William J. A452
AvestPolarit (steel) E257
Aviation Capital Group P385
Aviation Corporation A164
Aviation Week (magazine) A944, A945
Avicola Pilgrim's Pride de Mexico, S.A. DE C.V. A1132
Avidtek W180
AViiON servers A543
Aviles, Alan D. P369
Avilés, Dionel E. P471
Avion Coach A604, A605
Avion Corporation A1044
Avionics Power A662
Avir S.p.A. (glass) A1074
Avis Europe W472
Avis Group Holdings, Inc. A212-A213, A300, A338, A339, P178, P666, W130
Avis, Robert G. A95
Avis, Warren A212
AvMed Health Plan A810, P266
Avnet, Charles A214
Avnet, Inc. A196, A214-A215, A1140
Avnet, Lester A214
Avnet, Robert A214
Avocet Hardware Plc (locks and hardware) A920
The Avon Centre day spa A216
Avon Color cosmetics A216, A217
Avon Products, Inc. A216-A217, A880, A1384, A1414, P316, P666
Avon Tyres Limited A432
Avondale shipyard A440

AVP (equipment maker) W290
Avro RJ jets W110, W111
AvtoVAZ (auto maker) A650
AVW Audio Visual P611
AVX Corporation (ceramic capacitors) W328
A. W. Sijthoff W642
AWA. *See* America West Airlines
AWAC. *See* Alcoa World Alumina and Chemicals
Award (disposable contact lens) A234
Aware, Inc. E161
Away From Home (food service) A316
Aweida, Jesse A1336
AWG. *See* Associated Wholesale Grocers, Inc.
AXA A218, W104-W105, W182, W286, W472, W652
AXA Financial, Inc. A218-A219, A1008, A1236, A1240, P364, W98, W104, W105
Axcelis Technologies, Inc. A526, E133, E161, E310
Axe deodorant W618, W619
Axel Springer Verlag AG W106-W107
Axelrod, Mikhail W243
AXENT/AEGON Leven N.V. W65
Axime (IT services) W100
Axiom Technology E46
Axion cleanser A387
Axius car care products A1096
Axle and Case Company A198
Axminster carpets A980
Axsys Technologies, Inc. A982
AXT, Inc. E162
Axys software E25, E149
Ayalon, Eli E194
Aycock, H. David A1052
AYDIN (electronic products) A846
Ayer, Ramani A689
Ayer, William S. A107
Ayers, Robert L. A781
Ayers, Ronald W. A921
Ayerst Laboratories A148
Aylesworth, William A. A1379
Ayling, Bob W140
Aymar, Michael A. A761
Aymie, Marion A911
Aymoré biscuits W193
AYP Capital (holding company) A114
Ayr-Way A1352
Ayura cosmetics W535
Azaria, Pierre W76
Azcárraga Jean, Emilio W582, W583
Azcárraga Milmo, Emilio W582
Azcárraga Vidaurreta, Emilio W582
AZCO Inc. (mining) A1124
Azedo, Gabriel P207
Azelex acne treatment A118
Azerty (distribution centers) A1430
AZO over-the-counter drug E105, E268

Azonix Corporation (control systems) A447
AZP Group A1138
Azteca Stadium W582, W583
Aztex Enterprises P635
Azurix Corporation A154, A552
Azzurra Air W78, W79

B

B. Dalton Bookseller A232, A233, A1352
B. Green & Company A994
BA. *See* British Airways Plc
B.A. Pargh (office products) A1270
Baan Company N.V. (software) W290
Babb, Douglas J. A259
Babb, Ralph W., Jr. A395
Babbage's Etc. video games and software A232, A233
Babbio, Lawrence T., Jr. A1473
Babcock & Wilcox A940
Babcock Borsig W460
Babcock, Havilah A826
Babcock, Jeffrey C. P431
Babich, George, Jr. A1101
Babies "R" Us A1396, A1397
Babrowski, Claire A943
Baby Bells A70, A202, A248, A312, A1186, A1244, A1318, A1472, P438, P724
Baby Depot A304, A305
Baby Magic A386
Baby Mickey toys W333
Baby Ruth candy bar W388
Baby Superstore A1396
Baby Togs stores A880
BabyCenter, Inc. (online parenting resource) A800
babyGap A634, A635
The Baby-Sitters Club (books and TV show) A1254, A1255
Bacardi Limited A296, P616, P777, W108-W109
Bacardi y Maso, Emilio W108
Bacardi y Maso, Facundo W108
Bacardi y Maso, Jose W108
Bacchieri, Gregg A937
Bach, Herbert W381
Bache & Company A930
The Bache Group A1172
Bachelder, Cheryl A1405
Bacherman, Renee A271
Bachey, John A1075
Bachiddu, Gianni A621
Bachman, Brian R. E161
Bachman, John W. P260, P261, P646
Bachmann, Karen A785
Bachmann, Lisa A159
Bachmann, Mark R. A1005
Bachmann, Peter W185
Bäck, Ragnar W221
Backberg, Bruce A. A1237
Backman, Brent E24
Backman, Cathy L. W609

Backstreet Boys (music group) W213
Bacon, Donald G. A1465
Bacon, Kenneth J. A581
Bacon, Michael J. A1525
Bacon, William Gordon W285
Bacot, J. Carter A1470, A1471
Bacova Guild (rugs) A306
Badalotti, Enzo W575
Baden, Colin E99
Badgett, Guy M., III A1485
Badin, Adrien W432
Badinter, Elisabeth W466, W467
Badinter, Simon W467
Badische Anilin & Soda-Fabrik W116
Badoit water W193
Baduini, Paul J. A1213
BAE SYSTEMS A404, A882, A1190, W70, W110-W111, W120, W330, W354, W536
BAE SYSTEMS CANADA A456
Baedeker, Frederick M., Jr. E40
Baelen (tobacco) W282
Baer, Arthur H. A197
Baer, Donald A. P159
Baer, Jerome I. A183
Baer, Robert J. P753
Bærnholdt, Jesper W163
Bagby, Candice W. A167
Bagby, Robert L. A94, A95
Baggies plastic bags A1368
Bagley biscuits W193
Bagley, E. S., Jr. P363
Bagley, George D. A106, A107
Bagnell Dam A136
Bahadori, Hamid R. E22
Bahadurian, Armen J. A261
Bahama Breeze restaurants A464, A465, P669
Bahash, Robert J. A945
Bahl, Tracy L. A1435
Bahler, Gary M. A1471
Bahlmann, Jerome R. P71
Bahnam, John W639
Bahorich, Michael A185
Bahr, Ira H. A529
Bahr, Mark A. P550
Bahrain Telecommunications Company B.S.C. W153
Bailar, Gregor S. A997
Bailey Banks & Biddle Fine Jewelers A1552, A1553
Bailey, Bary G. A1081
Bailey, C. Stanley E296
Bailey, David A778
Bailey, James P188
Bailey, Keith E. A1529
Bailey, Lee A1467
Bailey, Michael J. (Compass Group) W174, W175
Bailey, Michael L. (Jostens) P263
Bailey, Mike (SC Johnson Commercial Markets) P722
Bailey Mine A417
Bailey, Richard A1123

Bailey, Robert D. (Smithsonian) P451
Bailey, Robert J. (Hertz) A711
Bailey, Robert J. (Pioneer-Standard) A1141
Bailey, Rose A995
Bailey's liqueurs W206
Bailis, David P. A597
Baillie, A. Charles W609
Bailly nuclear plant A1034
Bailye, John E. E191
Bain & Company P64-P65, P474, P548
Bain, Bill P64
Bain Capital A260, A500, A702, A1242, E207, P64, P162, P238, P442, P595, P637, P649, P725
Bain de Soleil sun care A1250
Bain, Douglas G. A273
bainlab (startup consulting) P548
Bains, Harrison M., Jr. A291
Bair, Michael A273
Baird, Anna M. E164
Baird, D. Euan A1253
Baird, Michael B. A209
Baird, William W356
Baity, John C. P41
Baja boats A298, A299
Bajenski, Richard J. A431
Baker & Company (platinum) A550
Baker & McKenzie A220-A221, P66-P67, P548
Baker & Taylor Corporation A1536, P68-P69, P548
Baker Canning A774
Baker, Carl A222
Baker Casing Shoe Company A222
Baker, Charles D., Jr. P626
Baker, D. A531
Baker, Dan R. A417
Baker, David A. A1025
Baker, Debra A1459
Baker, Donald I. P463
Baker, D. W. W269
Baker Extract A938
Baker, George (West Side Lighting) A532
Baker, H. Gene A491
Baker, Howard P760
Baker Hughes Inc. A116, A222-A223, A1252, A1382, W650
Baker Industries (armored transport) A278
Baker, James A., III (Carlyle Group) P110, P111, P567
Baker, James (Baker & Taylor) P68
Baker, Joffre B. A641
Baker, John P336, P337, P675
Baker, Jonathan B. A1263
Baker, Leonard E300
Baker, Leslie M., Jr. A1487
Baker, Lloyd W. E162
Baker, Looe A344
Baker, Lorenzo A354
Baker, Mark R. A725
Baker, Martin R. E82

Baker, Michael A. (ArthroCare) E159
Baker, Michael D. (Fifth Third Bancorp) A593
Baker Oil Tools A222, A223
Baker Perkins (printing machinery) A1210
Baker Petrolite A222, A223
Baker, Reid P696
Baker, Robert W. A165
Baker, Ronald M. P643
Baker, R. Pierce, III A435
Baker, Russell A220, P66, P548
Baker, Samuel A1304
Baker small engines P284
Baker, Ted A690
Baker, Tom A1417
Baker, Vernon G., II A199
Baker, Warren J. P99
Baker, Wendy W337
Baker, William A1198
Baker, W. Randolph A175
Baker's chocolate A842
Baker's Secret cookware P91, P775
Baker's Supermarkets A606
Bakersfield Memorial hospital P118
Bakhsh, Abdullah Taha A690
Bakke, Dennis W. A88, A89
Bakken, Earl A952
Bakker, R. H. W627
Bal, Dileep G. P41
Balachandran, Madhavan A161
Balagna, Jeffrey A. A953
Balance Bar Company (energy snack) A842
Balanced Budget Act of 1997 A1366
Balbinot, Sergio W99
Balboa Insurance Company A438
Balboa Life and Casualty A438
Balch, Benjamin A124
Balchunas, Michael J. A849
Balco (engine diagnostic) A1294
BALCO, Inc. A544
Bald Mountain mine W453
Baldanza, B. Ben A1443
Baldauf, Sari W407
Baldi, John F. A607
Baldi, Salvator E26
Baldridge, Richard A. E312
Balduino, Michael J. A771
Baldwin, Dick P123, P571
Baldwin hardware A921
Baldwin, Jerry A1326
Baldwin, L. Blake E122
Baldwin, Louis G. E319
Baldwin, Robert H. A967
Baldwin United Company A964
Baldwin, W. Preston, III A1459
Baldwin-Lima Hamilton (locomotives) A1478
Baledge, Les R. A1419
Baleno car W561
Bales for Food P489
Balfe, Edward T. A849
Bali, Ashish A475, P155, W197

Bali window furnishings A1316,
A1317, P452, P453, P733
Balint, Judy A567
Balk, Thomas A615, P191
Balkan Airlines W79
Balke, Julius A298
Balkins, A. James, III A275
Ball Aerospace & Technological
Corporation A224
Ball Corporation A224-A225, W506
Ball, Edward E115
Ball, F. Michael A119
Ball, Frank A224
Ball, George A1172
Ball Industries (janitorial
supplies) A1538
Ball, J. Fred P63
Ball, Lucille P218
Ball Park packaged meats A1242,
A1243
Ball, Robert L. W75
Ball, Tony W146, W147
Ball Western Can Company A224
Ballam, Sam A154
Ballantine brewery P428
Ballantine's scotch W84, W85
Ballantyne, Richard L. A687
Ballarat Banking Company W382
Ballard and Ballard Flour
Company A1136
Ballard, David R. A687
Ballard Medical Products A826
Ballard, Robert A. A1335
Ballarpur Industries (glass) A1074
Ballast Nedam Construction W110
Ballatore champagne A521, P169
Ballentine Stores A1532
Ball-Foster Glass Container A224
Balli (steel trader) W218
Ballmer, Steven A. A972, A973
Balloon Zone balloons A146, A147
Balloun, James S. A1004, A1005
Bally Entertainment
Corporation A720, A906, A966,
A1086
Bally Management Ltd. (shoes and
accessories) P474, P475
Bally's Casino Resort A720, A1086,
A1087
Balmuth, Michael A. A1214, A1215
Balsamo, Salvatore P741
Baltic International (airline) W518
Baltika beer W163
Baltimore & Ohio A454
Baltimore Colts (football
team) P356
Baltimore Gas and Electric
Company A424, A425, E187
Baltimore Orioles (baseball
team) P307, P666
Baltimore Ravens (football
team) P356, P357
The Baltimore Sun A1402
Bamelis, Pol W119
Bamford, Peter R. W629
Banacci. *See* Banamex-Accival
Banamex A1424

Banamex-Accival A370
Banana Republic A634, A635, P608
Banaski, Robert E170
Banc of America Marketplace (e-
commerce) A226
Banc of America Securities,
LLC A226
Banc One Capital Markets A230
BANC ONE CORPORATION A230,
A1508
Banc One Financial
Corporation A231
Banc One Payment Services A596
Banca di Gestione
Patrimoniale W185
BancData Solutions E77
Banco. *See* Northwest Bancorp
Banco ABN AMRO Real S.A. W57
Banco Ambrosiano W422
Banco Best. *See* Banco Electrónico
de Serviço Total
Banco Bilbao Vizcaya Argentaria
S.A. W112
Banco Boavista-
InterAtlantico W224, W225
Banco Central
Hispanoamerica W512
Banco Comercial de Lisboa W224
Banco de Investimentos
Garantia W184
Banco do Estado de São Paulo
S.A. W512
Banco Electrónico de Serviço
Total W224
Banco Español de Credito W512
Banco Espirito Santo de
Investimento SA W225
Banco Espirito Santo e Comercial
de Lisboa SA W224, W225
Banco Hispano Americano W512
Banco Internacional de Credito
SA W224, W225
Banco Meridional W512
Banco Nacional de Cuba W474
Banco Nacional de Mexico A230
Banco Real W56
Banco Santander-Chile W512
Banco Santiago W512
BancOhio A1000
Bancomer SA A1478
Bancorp Financial Services E216
BancorpSouth, Inc. E162
Bancroft Family A506
BancTec, Inc. E77
Group BancWest
Corporation W130, W131
Bandai Company, Ltd. (toys) W526
Band-Aids A800, A801
B&B liqueur W109
Bandepe (bank) W56
B&G Foods, Inc. A1136
B&H Supply Company A108
Bandier, Martin W213
Bandit motorcycle W561
Bandit PTCA catheter A282
B&M baked beans A1136
Bandolino shoes A804, A805

B&Q do-it-yourself stores W312,
W313
B&R Foods A1109
B&S electrical products A431
B&T. *See* Baker & Taylor
Corporation
Bane, Dan P747
Bane, Keith J. A991
Bane, Lonnie D. A139
Banespa. *See* Banco do Estado de
São Paulo
Banesto. *See* Santander Central
Hispano S.A.
Bangel, Edward P588
Bangert, Richard E., II A1079
Bangert, Steven E181
Bangkok Elevated Road and Train
System W266
Bangkok Metropolitan Bank W268
Bangs, Lawrence N. A735
Bangs, Nelson A. A1015
Banham, John W313
Banis, William J. P379
Banister, Gaurdie E. A1277
Banjo-Kazooie (video game) W395
Bank Alliance Program E153
PT Bank CL Indonesia W183
Bank Hofmann W185
Bank Holding Company Act
(1956) A1444
Bank Leu W185
Bank Mart A592
Bank of America building (San
Francisco) P449
Bank of America Corporation A204,
A226-A227, A348, A484, A626,
A808, A822, A902, A924, A936,
A1170, A1480, A1486, A1508,
P304, P322, P350, P508, W114,
W200, W512, W616
Bank of British Columbia W156,
W268
Bank of Canada W112
The Bank of Castile E302
Bank of China W464
The Bank of East Alabama A166
Bank of Hanover and Trust E294
Bank of Ireland A1112, W86
Bank of Italy A226
Bank of Lancaster County E294
Bank of Los Altos E213
Bank of Manhattan A808
Bank of Montreal A228,
W112-W113, W156, W608
Bank of New England A602, A836,
P282
The Bank of New York Company,
Inc. A228-A229, A808, A954,
A1018, E166, P374
Bank of New Zealand W382, W383
The Bank of Nova Scotia W474
Bank of San Francisco E204
Bank of Stockdale E312
Bank of Tampa A166
Bank of the Ohio Valley A592
Bank of the People W112
Bank of the United States P476

Bank of Tidewater A1308
Bank of Toggenburg W616
The Bank of Tokyo-Mitsubishi Ltd. *See* Mitsubishi Tokyo Financial Group
Bank of Toronto W608
Bank of Virginia A318
The Bank of Western Massachusetts E178
Bank of Winterthur W616
Bank One Ballpark A1478
BANK ONE Corporation A74, **A230-A231**, A566, A596, A734, A936, A1486, W474, W596
Bank Slaski W286
Bank United Corporation A488, A1500
Bank Zachodni S.A. W86, W87
Bank Zachodni WBK W86
BankAmerica. *See* Bank of America Corporation
BankAmerica Capital Corporation P518
BankAmericard charge card A230, A924, A1146, A1480, P322, P508, W114
BankBoston Corporation A602, A1508
Banker, James M. A105
Bankers, Eugene E. A159
Bankers Life Association A1162
Bankers National Life Insurance Company A414
Bankers Trust Australia Group A1162
Bankers Trust Corporation A414, A614, P190, W114, W200
Banking Research Center P379
Bankinter, S.A. W512
Bankmont Financial Corporation W113
Banks, Arthur E. P85
Banks, David R. A259
Banks, Donna J. A817
Banks, Lee A1089
Banks of Iowa A1444
Banks, Robert K. A111
Banks, Tyra P250, P251, P641
Banner Corporation E162
Banner Health System P118, P549
Banner Packaging, Inc. A250, A251
Bannick, Matthew E54
Banos, Len P65, P548
Banque Arabe W130
Banque Bruxelles Lambert W286
Banque de l'Ile de France W183
Banque du Caire W130
Banque du Groupe Casino W167
Banque Hervet W268
Banque Indosuez W558
Banque Lambert building (Brussels) P449
Banque Lehman Brothers S.A. A861
Banque Nationale de Grèce W385
Banque Nationale de Paris. *See* BNP Paribas Group

Banque National pour le Commerce et l'Industrie W130
Banque PSA Finance W442
Banque Worms W104, W200
Banquet frozen foods A408
Banta, Vivian L. A1173
Bantam Books A144, W126
Bantle, Louis A1458
Banton, Julian W. A1309
Banucci, Eugene G. E160
Banucci, Phyllis E160
Baptist Health System P56
Bar codes P70
Barad, Jill A926
Barasch, Richard A. E309
Barash, Anthony H. A285
Barbakow, Jeffrey C. A1366, A1367
Barbara Ann Karmanos Cancer Institute P591
Barbassa, Almir Guilherme W437
Barbee, J. Ray A891
Barbee-Fletcher, Sharon P389, P699
Barber, B. B. P68
Barber, Kevin A411
Barber, Rigel P645
Barber, Walter C. A787
Barber-Colman (controls) W290
Barberio, Mark G. P311, P664
Barber's dairy products A467
The Barbers, Hairstyling for Men & Women, Inc. A1196
Barbey, J. E. A1474
Barbey, John A1474
Barbie dolls (toys and products) A294, A692, A926, A927, E60
Barbier, Aristide W366
Barboas, José Coutinho W437
BarbWire restaurants A1280
Barcelo, Ana E221
Barclay cigarettes W143
Barclay, James W114
Barclay Jewelers A844, A845
Barclay, Richard P544
Barclays Bank (Canada) W156
Barclays, Bevan & Tritton W114
Barclays de Zoete Wedd W114
Barclays Global Investors E223
Barclays PLC A228, W56, **W114-W115**, W152, W268
Barcrest (amusement machines) W544
Bard, Charles Russell A444
Barden, Ron A703
Barefoot Inc. (lawn care) A1272
Barefoot, Marrinan & Associates (banking consultants) A840, P286, W324
Bareuther, James L. A297
Barfitt, John D. A205
Barford, David G. A351
Bargain World stores A158
Bargerm Donald G., Jr. A1549
Bargonetti, Arthur W607
Barham, Thomas P776
Baril, W. Barry E46

Barings Bank W286
Barker, Clarence W. P253
Barker, Francis B. P111
Barker, Myra O. P317
Barkey, Dennis P709
Barkin, Ellen A902, P304
Barkla, Andrew A1099
Barkley, James M. A1287
Barkov, Anatoly A. W347
Barksdale Inc. (switches and transducers) A447
Barkus, Bruce E. A579
Bärlocher, Urs W415
Barlow, Charles P729
Barlow, Frank W430
Barman, Bruce G. P443
The Barn Markets grocery stores A670, A671
Barna, Peter A451
Barnaba, Constance Hall A75
Barnard College P134
Barnard, Glen A813
Barnard, Patricia A. A655
Barnes & Noble College Bookstores, Inc. P549
Barnes & Noble, Inc. A130, **A232-A233**, A756, A1326, A1352, P192, P244, P549
Barnes, Ben P472
Barnes, Charles A232, P192
Barnes, David G. A79
Barnes, David (Mellon Financial) A954
Barnes, Galen R. A1009, P365
Barnes, James E44
Barnes, Jesse A397
Barnes, Keith L. E46
Barnes, Leroy T. A1121
Barnes, Leslie A1222
Barnes, Paul D. A905
Barnes, R. E. A915, P315, P665
Barnes, Richard A. W637
Barnes, Terry A1451
Barnes, William (Barnes & Noble) A232, P192
Barnes, William C. (Vintage Petroleum) E312
Barnes, W. Michael A1211
barnesandnoble.com A232, A233, P68, W127
Barnes-Jewish, Inc. P555
Barnett Banks A226
Barnett, Charles L. P57
Barnett, Hoyt R. A1177, P403
Barnett, Preston B. A443, P147
Barnett, Robert L. A991
Barnevik, Percy N. W54
Barney, James W. A643
Barney, Steven P734
Barney (TV show and products) A926
Barney's clothing stores A690, A790
Barnhart, Christy E187
Barnhill, Carl L. A79
Barnholt, Brandon K. P577
Barnholt, Edward W. A98, A99
Barnickol, Karl R. A1301

Barnicle, Mike A1020
Barnsley, John C. A1159, P401, W463
Barnum & Bailey circus P188
Barnum's Animal Crackers A843
Barnum's Kaleidoscape P188, P189, P608
Barnwell Industries, Inc. E163
Baron, Ronald A908
Baron, Thomas H. A1029
Barone, Angela A. E248
Barone, Anthony A1395
Barone, Frank J. E82
Barq's soft drink A382, A383, A384, A385, P577
Barr, D. Scott A1025
Barr, James, III (Telephone and Data Systems) A1361
Barr, J. James (America Water Works) A154, A155
Barr, Wallace R. A1087
Barr, William P. A1473
Barracuda disk drive P441
Barratt, Simon W639
Barre, Steven C. A1447
Barrera, Norma J. E206
Barrett, Colleen C. A1310, A1311
Barrett, Craig R. A760, A761
Barrett, David J. A701, E212, P229
Barrett Equipment (automotive brakes) A612
Barrett, Matthew W. W112, W114, W115
Barrett (mattress) P442, P725
Barrett Resources (natural gas) A482, A1276, A1528, W500
Barrett, Robert A. (PerkinElmer) A1111
Barrett, Robert M. (Advantica) A87
Barretto y de Ycaza, Don Enrique W510
Barrick Gold Corporation A1024, E242
Barrick, Kathy L. E157
Barrie Pace women's clothes A690, A691
Barrington Bank and Trust E318
Barrington, Michael R. E27, E154
Barrington, William J. A299
Barrist, Michael J. E250
Barron, Arnold S. A1389
Barron, Clarence A506
Barron, Harold S. A1425
Barron, Millard E. A1090, A1091
Barron's (publication) A506, A507
Barros, Diego W577
Barrow, Wade, Guthrie (accounting) A840, P286, W324
Barr's department store A932
Barry, Alan H. A921
Barry, Cliff P579
Barry, G. C. A133
Barry, John J. P35
Barry, June B. A705
Barry, Melissa E242
Barry, Pete E29, E158
Barsab (investment) W552

BART. See San Francisco Bay Area Rapid Transit
Bart, Todd R. E260
Barta, J. Joseph A641
Bartell, Mark C. A675
Bartels, Juergen P106
Bartes, Brian P775
Barth, John M. A803
Bartle Bogle Hegarty P73
Bartles & James wine coolers A520, A521, P168, P169
Bartlett and Company P549
Bartlett, Jerry P537
Bartlett, Linda A. A913
Bartlett, Mark R. P87, P557
Bartlett, Thomas (State University of New York) P460
Bartlett, Tom (Verizon) A1473
Bartner, Robert P338
Bartoli, Henry E. A621
Barton, Clara P44
Barton, C. O. P550
Barton Creek Resort and Country Club (Texas) P131
Barton, Enos P208
Barton, Glen A. A332, A333
Barton, Joel B. A1313
Barton liquors A423
Barton Malow Company P550
Barton, Robert H. P673
Bartoszewski, Thomas S. A775
Bartow, P. K. E26
Bartsh, Richard L. A469
Bartzokas, R. J. A133
Barusch, Ronald P447
Baryshnikov, Mikhail P251
Basch, Jeffrey W. A1169
BASCO (auto body hardware) A286
Bascom, John P500
Bascomb, Stuart L. A575
The Baseball Academy P251
Basel AG W414
Baseler, Theodor P. A1459
BASF Aktiengesellschaft A58, A148, A1072, A1212, P573, **W116-W117**, W118, W278, W500
Basha, Edward N., Jr. P550
Basha, James P62
Bashas' Inc. P550
Bashaw, Gerald E94
Basic Capital Management E219, E303
Basic Instinct (movie) W448
BASIC software language A972, P510
Basile, Diane A1111
BASILEA Pharmaceutica W492
Basin Exploration E295
Basis Petroleum, Inc. A1466
Baske, James R. A897
Basketball Association of America A280, P354
Baskin-Robbins ice cream A354, A466, W84, W85
Baskins, Ann O. A713
Bass Ale W162, W288, W289
Bass, Arthur A380

Bass family A778, A1496, P230
Bass Fishing (video game) W527
Bass Hotels & Resorts W544
Bass, James K. A185
Bass, Michael W544
Bass, Paul M. A263
Bass PLC. See Six Continents
Bass Pro Shops, Inc. P550
Bass, Robert (Acadia Partners) A968
Bass, Robert M. (Keystone) P456, P457, P474, P518, P603, W252
Bass, Sid A1498
Bass, William (Lands' End) A853
Bass, William (Six Continents) W544
Bassett bedding P442, P443
Bassett candy W155
Bassett, Richard E237
Bassi, Peter A. A1405
Bastani, Bami E28, E156
Bastiaens, F. Guillaume A325, P105
Bastian, Edward H. A479
Bastianen, Ben C. M. A803
Baston Patiño, Jose Antonio W583
Bastrop Pulp & Paper A770
B.A.T. Industries. See British American Tobacco p.l.c.
Batch Embedder software E192
Batchelder, E. L. A1129
Batchelder, Lewis W. A193
Batchelor, Paul W89
Batchelors soups A316
Bateman, Barry R. J. A615, P191
Bateman, Giles A436
Bateman (health care) W174, W175
Bateman, Maureen S. A1333
Bates, Barry P52
Bates, Robert D. A795
Bates, Tony W213
Batesville Casket Company A718, A719
Batey, Brian J. A389
Batey Holding (advertising) W646
Bath & Body Works, Inc. personal care products A776, A777, A876, A877, W534
Bath Iron Works Corporation A644, A645
Bathgate Industrial Park P399
Bati-Service A812
Batista, Fulgencio W108
Batman action figures A693
Batson, Homer A1170
Batt, Michael P107
Battelle, Gordon P70, P551
Battelle Memorial Institute A1544, **P70-P71**, P382, P551
Batten, Barton, Durstine & Osborn (advertising) A1062
Batten, Bruce E. E48
Batten, Frank, Jr. P655
Batten, Richard D. P750
Battenberg, J. T., III A476, A477
Battenfeld Gloucester Engineering A450

Battery Park housing
development P290, P656
Batting, Douglas A. P269
Battle Creek Sanitarium P520
Battle Creek Toasted Corn Flake
Company A816, P520
Battle, J. Michael A1309
Battle Mountain Gold A1024
The Battle of the Network Stars (TV
show) P250
Battle, Thomas P. A979
Batu Hijau (copper and gold
mine) A1024
BATUS A838
Baty, Roderick R. E254
Baucom, Early W. A799
Bauder, Lillian A921
Baudin, Jerry J. P661
Baudin, Remí W547
Bauer, Alan R. A1169
Bauer, Brett A1369
Bauer, Elaine P115
Bauer, Eugene P457
Bauer, Kenneth P335
Bauer NIKE Hockey, Inc. A1032
Bauer, Stephen C. A1231
Bauer, W. Neil A889
Bauer, Wolf Otto W381
Baugh, Jammie A1037
Baugh, John A1350
Bauhaus USA furniture A854
Bauknecht appliances A1520
Baukol, Ronald O. A977
Baum, Herbert M. A486, A487,
A1096
Baum, Michael H. E278
Baum, Stephen L. A1267
Baumann, Brian K. P713
Baumann, Ernst W121
Baumann, Karl-Hermann W537
Baumel-Eisner Neuromedical
Institute A84
Baumgartner, Vito H. A333
Baunton, Michael J. A333
Baur, Hans W459
Baur, Michael L. E118, E284
Bausback, Scott A1359
Bausch & Lomb, Inc. A118,
A234-A235, W308
Bausch, Jacob A234
Bausch, William A234
Bavaria beer W376
Bavarian Brewery A174
Bavely, Donald B. P717
Baxendale, Brian M. A1143
Baxley, W. R. A1533
Baxter, Bob P75
Baxter, Donald A236
Baxter International Inc. A58,
A236-A237, A244, A290, A976,
P164
Baxter, Raymond A. W245
Bay Area Practice Management
Group, Inc. A323
Bay department stores W270, W271
Bay Harbour (investments) P740

Bay Meadows Operating Company
(racetrack) A1540
Bay Networks, Inc. W412
Bay Petroleum A1368
Bay Ridge Co-op (New York) P291
Bay State Gas Company A1034,
A1035
Bay State Milling P123
Bayas Tudjas W104
BayCare Health Systems P115
Baycol drug W118
Bayer AG A450, A686, A820, A900,
A984, A1122, A1300, E105, E261,
W102, W116, **W118-W119**, W278,
W568
Bayer, Friedrich W118
Bayer, Gregory A905
Bayer, James W. A901
Bayerische BrauHolding W254
Bayerische Hypotheken und
Vereinsbank W64, W82
Bayerische Motoren Werke
AG A584, A616, A856, E170,
P631, P633, P764, **W120-W121**,
W496, W538, W630
Bayerische Vereinsbank W64
Bayern Atomkraft W504
Bayernwerk (utility) W218
Bayliner boats A298, A299
Baylor College of Dentistry P470,
P471
Baylor Health Care System A1070,
P551
Baylor University P82, P551
Baylor University Hospital P86,
P174, P226
Bayman, James L. A1140, A1141
Bayne, Bill P336
Bayonne Bridge P399
Bayonne (New Jersey) *Times* A80,
P32
Bayou City Pipelines, Inc. A69
Bayou Steel Corporation P709
Bays, James W291
Bazhenov, Vladislav P. W347
Bazooka bubble gum E130
Bazzani, Craig S. P756
BB Biotech E240
BBC. *See* British Broadcasting
Corporation
BBC America (cable channel) P158,
P159, W144
BBC Brown Boveri W54
BBDO Worldwide
(advertising) A1062, A1063
BBVA Bancomer W112
B.C. Hydro (rail freight line) A176
BC Life & Health Insurance
Company A1507
BC Partners P310, P664
BCBSM Foundation P87
BCC electronics stores W313
BCD Holdings P776
BCE Inc. A1245, **W122-W123**,
W412, W494, W592
BCE PubliTech (printing) W470
BCH. *See* Santander Central
Hispano S.A.

BCI. *See* Bell Canada International
BCI Holdings A384
BCLP. *See* Boston Celtics Limited
Partnership
BCO Technologies (wafers) A170
Bcom3 Group, Inc. **P72-P73**, P551,
W198, W199
BD. *See* Becton, Dickinson and
Company
BDB Holding Corporation A232
BDM (advertising). *See* Bcom3
Group; Bcom3 Group, Inc.
BDM International (information
technology) A1412, P110
BEA. *See* British European Airways
BEA Systems, Inc. **E33**, E163, E249
Beach Federal Savings A658
Beach, Milo C. P451
Beach, Roger C. A1438
Beacon Hill furniture P298
Beacon Insurance P693
Beacon Manufacturing
Company A1134, A1135
Beacon's Information A1161
Beadie, Karen R. A751
Beaird Industries (rail cars) A1406
Beale, Susan M. A513
Beall, Don A410, A1210
Beals, Vaughn A682
Beaman, Rick A1339
Bean, Francis A768
Bean, John A612
Bean, Leon Leonwood P300, P660
Bean, Roger E172
Bean Spray Pump Company A612
BE&K Inc. P552
Beanie Babies E54, P486, P487,
P751
Bear (archery) A1446
Bear, Joseph A238
The Bear Stearns Companies
Inc. A84, **A238-A239**, A714,
A808, A836, P232, P282
Beard, James R. (Nucor) A1053
Beard, James S. (Caterpillar) A333
Beard, John R. A901
Beardsley, Paul A1320
Bear-Grams E135, E311
Bearing Specialty A652
Beartrack mine E242
Beasley, Gerry E. W157
Beasley, John P700
Beasley, Lynn J. A1205
Beatles (music group) W213
Beatrice, Dennis P455
Beatrice Foods A212, A408, A618,
A836, E80, P282, W278
Beatt, Bruce H. A1323
Beattie, Don E87
Beatty, Sarah H. A1451
Beau Brummel of New York A1150
Beau Interconnects A982
Beau Rivage (hotel and
casino) A966, A967
Beauchamp, Lee A. A69
Beauchamp, Robert E. A270, A271
Beauchesne, Sheila A919

Beauchet, Jacques W165
Beaudin, Timothy J. E37
Beaudoin, Laurent W132, W133
Beaudrault, Peter J. W472, W473
Beaulieu, David R. E35
Beaulieu, Michael E. A321
Beaulieu of America, LLC P552
Beaumont, Ronald A1535
Beaute cosmetics W535
BeautiControl (skin care
  products) A1414, A1415
Beauty and the Beast (ice
  show) P188, P189, P608
Beauty Express stores A1196
Beauty Star mail order P258
Beauty Systems Group A108
Beauvais, Edward A138
Beaver, Betty Anne P678
Beaver, David L. A929
Beaver, Hugh W206
Beaver Lumber A64, P30, W376
Beaver Street Fisheries A1350
Beaver Valley nuclear plant A598
Beaver, William S. A1517
Beazer Homes USA, Inc. A549
Beazer PLC (construction) W252
Beban. Gary J. P121
Bébéar, Claude W104, W105
Bebee, Gary R. A1527
BEC Energy A554
Becel cooking products W619
Becerly, W. Michael P53
Bech, Alexandra W411
Becherer, Hans A468
Bechhofer, David P65
Becht, Bart W476, W477
Becht, Sue A. A515
Bechtel, Charles J. A489
Bechtel Group, Inc. A240-A241,
  A1120, E318, P74-P75, P386,
  P438, P552, W500
Bechtel, Riley P. A240, A241, P74,
  P75, P552
Bechtel, Steve A240, P74
Bechtel, Steve, Jr. A240, A241, P74,
  P75
Bechtel, Warren A240, P74
Bechtel-McCone-Parsons
  Corporation P386
Bechtolsheim, Andreas A1342
Beck, Andrew J. E26
Beck, Barbara A369
Beck, Deborah A. A1049, P377
The Beck Group P553
Beck, Henry P553
Beck, Richard P. E24, E149
Beck, S. Fred P637
Beckel, Daniel D. A173, P49, W91
Becker, Clark A255
Becker, Donald E. A845
Becker, Gary P496
Becker Group LLC (auto
  components) A388, A802
Becker, Joseph P670
Becker, Kenneth A. P115
Becker, Michael J. A1047

Becker Minerals W252
Becker, Robert M. P692
Becker, Steven P732
Beckerman, Neil W619
Beckers, Pierre-Olivier W195
Beckley, William H. A1049, P377
Beckman, Arnold A242
Beckman Coulter, Inc. **A242-A243**
Beckman, Jerry P609
Beckner, Larry W. A1179
Beck's beer W288
Beckwitt, Richard A508
Becton, Dickinson and
  Company **A244-A245**
Becton, Henry A244
Becton, Maxwell A244
Bed Bath & Beyond
  Inc. **A246-A247**
bed n bath linen stores A246
Bed Time mattresses P443
Bedard, Kipp A. A971
Bedat & Company W251
Bedell-Pearce, Keith W465
Bedford, Peter B. E163
Bedford Property Investors,
  Inc. E163
Bedrosian, John A1366
beeb Ventures (Internet
  company) W144, W145
Beebe, Kevin L. A129
Beebe, Mike A405
Beebe, Skip P121
Beebe, Stephen A. P264, P265,
  P648
Beech Aircraft A1190, A1191
Beecham Group A118, A242
Beecher, Gregory A1373
Beechwood
  (telecommunications) W160
Beed, Jill A. P325
Beeder, John A679, P217
Beefeater gin W84, W85
Beefeater restaurants W638, W639
Beefsteak bread A775
Beefy-T knitwear A1243
Beegle, Ronald R. A635
Beene, Betty S. P492
Beep-A-Call (paging) W322
Beer Chang W163
Beer, Gary P451
Beer Shokunin W315
Beer, William L. A935
Beers Construction P716
Beery, James W247
Beery, Joseph A139
Beeson, Thomas P93
Beeston, Paul P307
Beetle car W630, W631
Beevers, Edward A. A263
Beffa, Jean-Louis W507
Before & After software A1148
Before Women Had Wings
  (movie) P219
Begelman, Mark A1056
Beggs, John P478
Beggs, Lyman P442

Begley, Christopher A59
Begor, Mark A999
Beguwala, Moiz M. A411
Beha, Ralph P107
Behm, Londell J. P423
Behn, Sosthenes A780, W220,
  W580
Behnke, Michael C. P497
Behr Process Corporation
  (coatings) A725, A920
Behrendt, William P566
Behrens, George M. A1031
Behrens (pharmaceutical
  distribution) A320
Behring, Kenneth P450
Behrman, Philip G. A1461
Behrouzi, Massued A1299
BEI Technologies, Inc. E164
Beier, Anita P. A1443
Beijing Airport Inflight Kitchen
  Limited W541
Beijing Huilian Food Company,
  Ltd. P313
Beilby's (stores) W172
Bein, Andrew A1193
Beindorff, Gerhard W185
Beinner, David M. A257
Beira pipeline W340
Beisheim, Otto W364
Beittel, David R. A147
Beketic, Ralph D. P423
The Bekins Company (moving
  vans) P614
Bekkers, John P201, P616
Bel Air Investment Advisors A1332
Bel Air Markets P488, P710
Bel Arbor wines A297
Belanger, Richard C. E63
Belco Oil & Gas E316
Belco Petroleum A552, A556
Belcor lingerie W475
Belda, Alain J. A112, A113
Belden & Blake Corporation (oil and
  gas) P474, P475
Belden brand A585
Belden Electronics P208
Belgacom W502
Belgam tobacco W143
Belgian Beer Cafe W288
Belk Brothers P76
Belk, Henderson P76
Belk, H. W. McKay P76, P77
Belk, Inc. P**76**-P**77**, P553
Belk, Irwin P76
Belk, John M. P76, P77, P553
Belk, John R. P76, P77, P553
Belk National Bank P76
Belk, Sarah P76
Belk, Thomas M., Jr. P77
Belk, Tim P76
Belk, Tom P76
Belk, William Henry P76
Belk, William Henry, Jr. P76
Belkamp, Inc. (automotive
  parts) A652, A653
Bell, Albert J. A261

Bell, Alexander Graham A202, A248, A898, P208, P358, W122, W220, W232, W576
Bell & Gossett (pumps) A780
Bell & Howell Company A524, A1142, E100, P308
Bell, Andrew P176
Bell Atlantic A128, A312, A400, A1182, A1362, A1472, P765, W628
Bell, Bonnie P744
Bell, Bradley J. A1213
Bell Cablemedia W152
Bell Canada Enterprises. See BCE Inc.
Bell Canada International W122, W581
Bell, Chris W259
Bell Dairy A466
Bell, David A. (Interpublic) A773
Bell, David (Pearson) W431
Bell, Ernie A1491, P515, P768
Bell family A70
Bell, George F. A405
Bell, Glenn A1404
Bell Globemedia W122, W123, W592, W593
Bell Helicopter A1380
Bell Industries A196
Bell, James (General Mills) A648
Bell, James R., III (National City) A1001
Bell, John Hickman W539
Bell Laboratories A202, A242, A898, A1358, A1362, E20, E117
Bell, Lawrence T. A531
Bell Markets A845
Bell, Michael A. (Pacific Mutual) P385
Bell, Michael J. (Swire Pacific) W565
Bell, Michael W. (CIGNA) A361
Bell Mobility W122
Bell Nexxia W122
Bell, Paul D. (Dell) A473
Bell, Paul R. (Merck) A957
Bell, Richard E. P714
Bell Savings Banc A658
Bell Sports (bicycles) A298
Bell, Stanley R. A275
Bell Systems A572
Bell Telephone A202, A898
Bell Telephone Company of Canada W412
Bell Telephone Company of Missouri A1244
Bell Telephone of Boston A292
Bell, Vincent G. A1233
Bell, William J. A313
Bella Pasta restaurants W638, W639
Bellagio (hotel and casino) A966, A967
Bellamy, Adrian P156
Bellcore research consortium A1244, A1472, P438
Belle Epoque champagne W85
Belle, Russell J. A1301

Bellemead Development Corporation A356
Bellens, Didier W127
Beller, Gary A. A965
Belleville (Illinois) News-Democrat A833
Belle-Vue beer W288, W289
Bellevue Hospital Center P369
Bellinida legwear A1243
Bellomy, Gregory F. E111
Bellon, Pierre A1296, W546, W547
Belloni, Antonio W349
Bellow, Saul P560, P756
BellSouth Corporation A248-A249, A538, A1244, A1318, E106, E195, P535, P576
BellSouth New Zealand W628
Belluzzo, Richard A973, A1284
Belmont Industries A902, P304
Belmont Plaza hotel A884
Belmont Plaza shopping center P172
Beloit (papermaking equipment) A806
Beloved (movie) P218, P219, P625
Belridge Oil A1276
Belsito, Jack W155
Belton, Y. Marc A649
Beltrame, James M. A1281
Belz, Raymond T. A1457
Bemburg fabrics P343
Bemis Company, Inc. A250-A251
Bemis, Daniel A73
Bemis, Judson Moss A250
Bemis, Stephen A250
BeMusic W127
Ben & Jerry's Homemade, Inc. (ice cream) A262, A510, W618, W619
Ben Arnold-Sunbelt Beverage P738
Ben Bridge Jeweler A252
Ben E. Keith Company P553
Ben Franklin variety stores A734, A968, A1006, A1494
Benadryl antihistamine A1118
Benaich, Pierre W467
Benanav, Gary G. A1017, P371
BenchCraft furniture P298, P299, P659
Benchmark Capital A1036, A1396
Benchmark Insurance Company P63
BenchTop tools A831
Benckiser A358, W476
Benckiser, Johann A. W476
Bender, Brian W. A1283
Bender, Jeffrey M. A185
Bender, John C. (Boise Cascade) A275
Bender, John (Pizza Hut) A1404
Bendir, Arthur W258
Bendix Aviation A214, A736
Bendix Corporation A728, A836, A882, P282
Bendix Electronics W536
Bendoraitis, Thomas A905
Bendure, Raymond L. A359
Benecol margarine A800

Benedetti, Laura L. E183
Benedict, Forest C. P661
Benedictine liqueur W109
Benedictine Sisters of Mother of God Monastery P117
Beneficial Corporation A734, A1314
Beneficial Finance W114
Beneficial Standard Life A414
Benenson, Harvey A313
Benetton, Carlo W124, W125
Benetton family W423, W450, W574
Benetton, Gilberto W124, W423, W575
Benetton, Giuliana W124
Benetton Group S.p.A. W124-W125
Benetton, Luciano W124, W125
Benetton, Mauro W125
BenGay rub A1118, A1119
Bengston, David C. A161
Bengtsson, Lars W557
Bengü, Hasan W319
Benhamou, Eric A. A55
Benito y Monjardin (brokerage) W224
Benjamin, Harvey E. P355
Benjamin Jacobson & Sons A660
Benjamin, James P69
Benjamin Moore & Company (paints) A252, A253
Benjamin Polakoff & Son (food wholesalers) A1350
Benjumea, Ignacio W513
Benmore A608
Benmosche, Robert H. A965
Bennack, Frank A., Jr. A700, A701, P228, P229, P629
Benne, Paul P704
Bennett, Alan A91
Bennett, Carl L. P405
Bennett, Dale A1551
The Bennett Funding Group E200
Bennett, Glenn W63
Bennett, James P. A699
Bennett, Jana P159
Bennett, Joel M. E225
Bennett, Lerone, Jr. P259
Bennett, Michael L. A173, W91
Bennett, Patrick E200
Bennett, R. E. T. W269
Bennett, Richard W., III A933
Bennett, Robert R. A873
Bennett, Scott L. A945
Bennett, Tim P219
Bennett, Tommy A403
Bennett, Val E306
Bennett, William A906, P278
Bennett's sauces A467
Bennigan's restaurants P332, P333, P674
Bennink, Jan W193
Benoit, James P373
Benoliel, Joel A437
Benrubi, Steven H. A347
Bensen, Richard A. A333
Bensinger, B. E. A298

Bensinger, Bob A298
Bensinger, Moses A298
Bensinger, Ted A298
Benson & Hedges cigarettes A1126, W142, W143, W240, W241, W282
Benson, Bruce D. E308
Benson, David H. A1473
Benson, Glenwyn W145
Benson, James B. (Automatic Data Processing) A205
Benson, James M. (Metropolitan Life) A965
Benson, John W. A977
Benson, Richard W240
Benson, Stanley M. A161
Bensonhurst Co-op (New York) P291
Bent, Ritchie W307
Bentas, Lily H. P586
Bentley, C. Alan P740
Bentley Health Care P678
Bentley, Julia A. A1239
Bentley Motor Company W120, W496, W631
Bentley-Harris brand A585
Benton & Bowles Advertising P72, P176
Benton, Jesse L. A1177
Benton, William (Benton & Bowles Advertising) P72, P176
Benton, William (Muzak) P350
Benzaquen, Maurice W171
Benzer, Jody A583, P185
Benzing, Bill A745, P243
Bepanthen skin care W493
Beracha, Barry H. A1243
Beran, John R. A395
Berardi, John F. A583, P185, P606
Berardino, Joseph A173, P49, P540, W91
Berardy, Ricky P721
Berberian Enterprises, Inc. P489
Berce, Daniel E. E27, E154
Berden, Robert J. A1049, P377
Berdini, Marie E307
Berenguel, Rhonda E288
Berey, Catherine A. A159
Berg, Carl E. E245
Berg, Charles G. A1077
Berg, Donald C. (Brown-Forman) A297
Berg, Don (Land O'Lakes) A851
Berg, Don (Land O'Lakes) P289
Berg, Egon E. A149
Berg Electronics A714, P232
Berg, Eric A. A665
Bergant, Paul R. A789
Bergdorf Goodman department stores A1014, A1015, P100
Bergdorf, Herman A1014
Bergen Brunswig Drug Company. See AmerisourceBergen Corporation
Bergen, David G. A869, P293
Bergen gas engine W496
Bergenbier W289
Berger, David W627

Berger, Jean-Pierre W167
Berger, Walter Z. E198
Bergerac, Michel A1200
Bergeron, Kayla P399
Bergeron, Stephanie W. A665
Berges, James G. A547
Berggren, Bo Erik W519
Berglund, Thomas W525
Bergly, Kris A1197
Bergman, Ron P674
Bergmark, Edward A1435
Bergner's department stores A1238
Bergquist, Rick A1099
Bergstresser, Charles A506
Bergstrom, Stephen W. A519
Bergt, Neil A106
Berhman, Grant E236
Beringer Wine Estates Holdings P474
Beringer wines W230, W231, W388
Berk, Alexander L. A423
Berk, Jeffrey L. A1471
Berk, Jim W472
Berke, Richard C. A205
Berkel, Susan L. A1081
Berkeley, Alfred R., III A997, P353
Berkeley building (New York City) P230
Berkeley, Edmund P248
Berkeley Farms dairy products A466, A467
Berkeley Superkings cigarettes W240, W241
Berkeley, Vince A303
Berkley & Jensen A262
Berkley Petroleum A168
Berkley, Stephen A1184
Berkline furniture P298, P299, P659
Berkman, Mehmet Ali W319
Berkshire Hathaway Inc. A142, **A252-A253**, A382, A516, A656, A680, A804, A880, E215, P340, P676, W84, W336
Berkshire International (hosiery) A1474
Berkshire Life Insurance Company of America P214, P215
Berkshire Partners P611, P762
Berland, Joseph E231
Berle, Milton A1376
Berlei tires W428
Berlin, Jacob E115
Berlin, Richard A700, P228
Berlin, Ronald G. A1369
Berlin, Steven R. E264
Berliner Morgenpost (newspaper) W106, W107
Berliner Wasserbetriebe W504
Berling, Henry A. A1071
Berman, Bridget Ryan A1151
Berman, Gail A622, A623
Berman, Harris A. P751
Berman, Michael A283
Berman, Richard K. A245
Berman, Stephen E225
Bermingham, Robert P. P525

Bernabe, Franco W216, W574
Bernard, Betsy J. A203
Bernard, Daniel W164, W165
Bernard M. Baruch College P129
Bernard, Richard P. A1019, P375
Bernard, Robert E. (The Limited) A877
Bernard, Robert (J.Crew) P254
Bernardi, Dan E212
Bernardo, Thomas P. A339
Bernauer, David W. A1493
Bernd, David L. P726
Berner, Mary G. A81, P33
Berney, Rand C. A1129
Bernhard, Alexander P93
Bernheim, Antoine W99, W349
Bernheimer-Leader department store A932
Bernick, Carol L. A108, A109
Bernick, Howard B. A108, A109
Berning, Allen J. E262
Bernis, Valérie W559
Bernon, Alan J. A1339
Bernon family A1338
Bernotat, Wulf H. W219
Bernoulli Box disk drive A778
Bernstein, Alan A. (Amerada Hess) A133
Bernstein, Alan B. (Wackenhut) A1489
Bernstein, Alexander W248
Bernstein, Alison R. P195
Bernstein, Carl A1502
Bernstein, Cecil W248
Bernstein, David H. E110
Bernstein, Kenneth F. E147
Bernstein, Sidney (Granada) W248
Bernstein, Sidney R. (EMCOR) A545
Berol office products A1023
Berra, J. M. A547
Berrard, Steven A266
Berresford, Susan V. P194, P195, P610
Berrios Enterprises furniture stores A702
Berry, Antony A910
Berry Bearing A652
Berry, Charles W523
Berry, Fred P573
Berry, G. Dennis A443, P147
Berry Industries (garage doors) A1322
Berry, Ken A212
Berry, L. Wilson P340
Berry, Michael P. A233
Berry Petroleum Company E164
Berry, Robert E. A889
Berry, Stephen J. A481
Berry, W. B. A1129
Berry, William (Dominion Resources) A498
Berry, William E. (Heafner Tire) P628
Bersani Decree (Italy) W214
Berschied, John R., Jr. A109
Berstein, Vicki Vann A759

Bert Grant's Ale A1459
Bert, James A278
Bertasso, Michael J. A723
Bertea (flight controls) A1088
Bertelli, James R. E241
Bertelsmann AG A232, A700, P32,
   P228, W126-W127, W212, W430
Bertelsmann, Carl W126
Bertière, François W135
Bertko, John M. A739
Bertolini, Mark T. A361
Bertsch, Robert A585
Bertucci, John R. E246
Berube, Edward M. A415
Berube, S. Neal P545
Berwanger, Robert M. E113
Berwind Group P554
Besancon, Michael A1523
Besen, Peter D. E98
Beshears, Cletes A1338
Besnier Group P264
Bessant, Catherine P. A227
Besse, Georges W480
Besse, Kim P131
Bessemer (small engines) A430
Bessire, Michael J. A1235
Bessler, Joni P89
Best & Company P428
Best Apparel stores A1036
Best Buy cigarettes P584
Best Buy Company,
   Inc. A254-A255, A366, A870
Best Buys for Your Home
   (book) P139
Best Choice brands P62, P63
Best, Derek E121
Best Ice beer W289
Best, Jacob P428
Best, Lawrence C. A283
Best (magazine) A701
Best Power A1320, W290
Best Products (catalog sales) A1270
Best, Robert O. A1441
Best Tractor A332
Best Travel Deals (book) P139
Best, Tyler A301
Best Value cigarettes A1205
Best Western International Inc.
   (hotels) E215
Bestfoods W618
Bestfoods Baking W244
Bestform Intimates
   (lingerie) A1474, A1475, W607
Best's Kosher meats A1243
Bestway brand foods P560
Bestway (trucking) A1454
BestYet brand foods A607
Beswick, Hugh G. A347
BET Holdings A872, A1476
Betadine antiseptic P707
Betamax video W514, W550
Betcher, Carl D. A605
Beth Israel Deaconess P566
Bethancourt, John E. A1377
Bethany Medical Center P729
BethForge A256

Bethlehem Steel Corporation A116,
   A256-A257, A954, A1224, A1406,
   P418
Bethune, Gordon M. A429
Betrix A902, P304
BeTrusted (Internet
   security) A1158, P400, W462
Betsch, Philip P645
Bettacchi, Robert J. A1537
Bettcher, T. E. A547
Bettencourt, Anthony J., III E134
Bettencourt, Liliane W342
Better Baked Pizza P436
Better Brands (liquors) P777
Better Business Bureau P196
Better Homes A604
Better Homes and Gardens A1218
Better Method Oil Well Cementing
   Company A676
Bettiga, Michael J. A1283
Bettman, Gary B. P360, P361, P684
Betts, Gene M. A1319
Betts, Kathleen V. E83, E233
Betty Crocker A648, A649
Betty Crocker's Picture Cook
   Book A944
Betty Crocker Tree House
   Restaurant A464
Betz Laboratories A1536
BetzDearborn (water
   treatment) A704
Beumer, Richard E. A787
Bevans, Patty P573
Bevcon (consortium) W552
Beverage World (magazine) W626
Beveridge, Crawford A1343
Beverido Lomelín, Rafael W441
Beverly Enterprises,
   Inc. A258-A259
The Beverly Hillbillies (TV
   show) A334
Beverly Hills Hotel P553
Beverly Hills Travel P308
Bevilacqua, Diego W619
Bevilacqua, Thomas A. A567
Bevis Custom Furniture A726
BEWAG Aktiengesellschaft
   (utility) A1306, W218
Bewley, Peter D. A375
BEXXAR drug E217
Bey Soo Khiang W541
Beyer, Richard M. E55, E196
Beyond Buttondowns men's
   clothing catalog A853
Beyond Color cosmetics A217
Beystehner, John J. A1427
Beyster, J. Robert P438, P439, P724
Bezos, Jeffrey P. A130, A131
B.F. Goodrich Aerospace A326
BFG. See The Bennett Funding
   Group
The BFGoodrich Company A272,
   A660, A662, A1190, P142, W367,
   W538
BFI. See Browning-Ferris Industries
BFP Holdings P506
BG Group plc A824, A1374

BG plc W500
B.G. Sulzle, Inc. P313
BG Wholesale. See Houchens
   Industries Inc.
BGC Finance A734
BGE Home Products & Services,
   Inc. A424, A425
BGS Healthcare, Inc. A323
BGS Systems (software) A270
Bhattal, Jasjit S. A861
BHC Communications A1476
BHF-Bank W286
Bhowmick, Subir W567
BHP Billiton Plc A112, A1052,
   A1374, A1512, W128-W129,
   W230
BHS tabletop AG W201
Bias, Len A280
Bibendum the Michelin Man W366
Bible, Geoffrey C. A843, A1127
Bible, Michael P614
BICC Data Networks A54
BICC General (US) W450
BICC Group Plc A434, A642
Bickford, Michael T. P47
Bick's condiments A768
Bid.com E237
Bidulka, Brian W377
Bidzos, D. James E114
Biebl, Anthony W. A375
Biedenharn, William L. A951
Bieffe Medital (blood therapy) A236
Biegler, David W. A1417
Biel, Walter A217
Biel watch W562
Bielanski, Andrew S. A439
Bienen, Henry S. P378, P379, P691
Bierbaum, John F. A1105
Bierman, R. Craig A653
Bies, Susan Schmidt P187
Big Bear Farm Stores P406, P478
Big Bear supermarkets A1094
"Big Blue". See International
   Business Machines Corporation
The Big Bopper (performer) P188
Big Bowl restaurants A288, A289
Big Boy restaurants A1280
Big Brothers/Big Sisters of
   America P492, P493, P755
Big Brother (TV show) A334
Big C stores W166, W167
The Big Dig. See Central Artery
   Tunnel (Boston)
Big Flower Holdings. See Vertis Inc.
Big Game Lottery P372, P638,
   P668, P675, P687, P766
BIG Internet search engine P176
Big Joe ice cream cones A110
Big K convenience stores A1084,
   A1085
Big King sandwich A303
Big Kmart stores A830
Big League Chew gum A1527
Big Lots, Inc. A260-A261
Big Mac sandwich A942
Big Mac sauce P202, P617
Big Pond (Internet portal) W586

Big Red gum A1526, A1527
Big Screen City stores E306
Big Spin (TV show) P564
Big Star grocery stores A670
Big Stone (canned vegetables) A466
Big Value brands P201
Big V Supermarkets, Inc. A1094, A1490, A1491, P514, P515, P554, P768
Big W stores W644, W645
Big Y Foods, Inc. P103, P479, P554
Bigelow carpets A980, A981, P568
Biggar, John R. A1155
Biggs Continent stores W165
bigg's food stores A1348, A1349
Biggs, John H. A1354, A1355, P466, P467, P742
Bigheart Pipe Line P280
BIG/ip controller E201
BIGLOBE (Internet provider) W386
Bigsby, Elisabetta W475
Bihary, Kristen M. A527
Bil Mar Foods A1242
Biland, Alan T. A1295
Bilawsky, Mark A. A359
Bild am Sonntag (magazine) W107
Bild der Frau (magazine) W106
Bild (newspaper) W106, W107
Bilek, Paul J. A1157
Bill & Melinda Gates Children's Vaccine Program P78
Bill & Melinda Gates Foundation A540, P**78-P79**, P555
Bill Blass Ltd. E60, E305
Bill Communications W626
Bill Heard Enterprises P555
Billabong International Ltd. (clothing) E101, E259
Billboard (magazine) W626
Biller, Leslie S. A1509
Billerud (forestry) W556
Billick, Steven M. A1141
Billig, E. H. P153
Billings, David A. A103
Billingsley, Henry A1398
Billingsley, Lucy Crow A1398
Billington, Timothy B. E93
BillingZone A1112
Billiton plc W128
Billmaier, Jim P511
Bill's Drugs stores A886
Bill's Lake Tahoe casino A685
Bi-Lo Foods A1094, W172
BI-LO Foods stores W498, W499
Bilodeau, Kathy E131, E304
Bilous, O. B. P444, P445
The (Biloxi, MS) *Sun Herald* A833
Bim Bim candy W155
Bimblick, Warren A1161
bin Nik Yaacob, Tan Sri Nik Mohamed W539
bin Tunku Yahaya, Tunku, Tan Sri Dato' Seri Ahmad W539
Binder, Regis F. A115
Binder, Steven G. A731
Bindley Western Industries (pharmaceuticals) A320, E270

Bing, Richard F. P311
Bingay, James S. A823
Bingham Financial A1508
Bingham, Hiram P358
Bingham, Paul M. A605
Bingham, Tony P177
Bing-Lear Manufacturing A856
Binion, Jack P634
Binkley, David A. A1521
Binkowski, Roman W457
Binks Sames (spray painting) A748
Binney & Smith, Inc. (crayons) A678, A679, P216, P217, P625
Bins Transfer & Storage P434
Binyon, Bryan A812
Bio dairy products W193
Bio Gro E297
Bioblock Scientific (instruments) A600
BioClinical Partners E72
Biogen E147
Biomedical Research Alliance of New York P690
Bio-Medicus (centrifugal blood pumps) A952
bioMérieux-Pierre Fabre (pharmaceuticals) W72
Biomni Limited (software) W176
Biondolillo, Michael A. P698
Biore skin care W308, W309
Biorex Laboratories E283
Biotherm W342, W343
Biovitrum drug A1122
Biran, Danny W323
Birch, Bryan P175
Birch, Cristin P389
Birch, Stephen W488
Birch Telecom Inc. A837, P283
Birchtree Financial Services, Inc. A681
Birck, Michael J. A1362, A1363
Bird Corporation (roofing materials) W506
Bird, Karen H. A87
Bird, Larry A280, P354
Birds Eye A466, W618, W619
Birds, John G. A103
Birdsall, Doug A1047
Birdseye, Clarence A842
Bi-Rite brand foods A1348, A1349
Birk, David R. A215
Birkel, Bernard L. A931
Birkeland, Kristian W410
Birkholm, Michael B. A147
Birks, Ian W241
Birle, James A388
The Birmingham (Alabama) *News* A81, P33
Birmingham (Alabama) *Post-Herald* A569
Birmingham Slag A1484
Birmingham Trust and Savings Company A1308
Birnbaum, Richard S. A367
Birra Moretti (brewery) W254
Birt, John W144

Birth of a Nation (movie) A962
Bischoff, Manfred W71, W189
Bischoff, Winfried F. W. W153
Bisco Products P164
Bishop, Bradford E139
Bishop, Derry E. A219
Bishop, Robert R. A1284, A1285
Bismuth, Pierre E. A1253
Bisone, Loris W423
Bisquick A648, A649
Bisswanger, Mark A1227
Bitech (oil exploration) W346
Bitel Participações S.A. W575
Bitito, Robert J. E179
Bitner, Livia P69
BITOR (mines) W438
BITService W176
Bittenbender, Charles A. A993
Bitting, William M. P429
Bitumenes Orinocco, SA W439
Bitzer, Marc A1521
Biumi, Bonnie S. A1217
Bix office furniture A1335
Bixby, James A. A1263
Bixler, R. Jeffrey A909
BizJet A1420
BizMart office products A1058
biztravel.com P418, P419, P717
bizzport (Internet portal) A74
B.J. Johnson Soap Company A386
BJ Services (pumping) A222
BJC Health System P555
Bjorkmans (tubing products) P310
BJ's Wholesale Club, Inc. A**262-A263**, P103
Bjurstrom, Edward E. A161
BK Broiler sandwich A302, A303
The Black & Decker Corporation A152, A**264-A265**, A462, A920, A1148
Black, Andrew K. (LEGO) W333
Black, Andrew W. (Jostens) P263
Black Angus Beef P185
Black, Barbara A. W263
Black Bear deli items A1491, P515
Black, Bill R. A1525
Black Box Corporation E164
Black, Cathleen P. A701, P229
Black, Clyde A979
Black, Conrad M. W262, W263
Black, Craig A. A527
Black, Duncan A264
Black, Eli A354
Black Entertainment Television. *See* BET Holdings
Black Flag insecticide A374, W476
Black Hawk Gaming & Development Company, Inc. E165
Black Ice beer W377
Black, Joseph E31, E160
Black, Julie E243
Black Label pork A731
Black, Leo F. P325
Black, Leon P142

Black Magic car care products A1097
Black, Mary E201
Black Mountain Gas (utility) A1543
Black Pearls fragrance A766
Black, Richard B. E98
Black, Robert W. A1335
Black rum W109
Black, Sherman A1261
Black, Thomas M. A1031
Black Velvet whiskey A422, A423
Black, William A840, P286, W324
Black World (magazine) P258
Blackbund E25
Blackburn, Richard W. A515
Blackfoot Logistics Ltd. A421
Blackhawk helicopters E175
Blackjack lottery game P373
Blackmore, Peter A399
BlackRock Financial Management E157
BlackRock, Inc. A1147
BlackRock Income Trust A1146
Blackstone Capital Partners A388, A1422, P238, W472
Blackstone Group L.P. A150, A338, A732, A1178, A1396, E38, E174, P620, P704
Blackstone Management Associates P713
Blacksville Mine A417
Blackthorn cider A423
Blackwell, H. Pryor A1399
Blackwell, Jean S. A457
Blackwell, Ron P35
Blackwell, Todd V. A1353
Blackwolf Run golf course P285
Blackwood and Nichols A482
Blackwood, Len A329, P109
Blades, Judith A. A689
Blagden PLC P90
Blagg, Joe W. A1410, A1411, P485
Blagg, Shannan A745, P243
Blaha, Karl L. E219
Blaine, Jack A. A1425
Blair, Brett P535
Blair, Bryce E161
Blair, Cary P693
Blair, Donald W. A1033
Blair, Thomas E211
BlairLake (e-commerce) A406
Blairstow, Jeffrey J. A697
Blake, Brian W251
Blake, Isaac Elder A412
Blake, Mary Pat A351
Blake, Norman P., Jr. A392, A393
Blake, William A. P517, P772
Blakely, Kevin M. A823
Blakely, Robert T. A901
Blakely, Ron P604
Blalock, Paul H. A1027
Blanc, Christian W68
Blanc, Gerard W71
Blanchard, Daniel G. E129, E302
Blanchard, Eric A. A467
Blanchard, Gus A480

Blanchard, Matthew A1293
Blancpain watch W562, W563
Bland, Christopher W149
Bland, Jeff A1189
Blanes, Ana P707
Blank, Arthur M. A724
Blanks, Judith Jones P589
Blass, Bill A1316, P452
Blast Bike A682
Blaster CD-RW W181
Blaszyk, Michael P119, P570
Blatt, Gregory R. A919
Blatt, Lee N. E68, E214
Blauer, Roy A303
Blaupunkt (car radios) W490
Blavier, Philippe W131
Blaw-Knox Construction Equipment A754, A755
Blayau, Pierre W446
Blazer Energy A200
BLC (performance improvement) P308
Blédina foods W193
Bledsoe, Oscar P735
Blencke, Charles D. A275
Blenner, Joel W. E63
Blessing Verlag W127
Bleustein, Jeffrey L. A683
Bleustein-Blanchet, Marcel W466
Bleustein-Blanchet, Michele W466
Blickman, Fred P628
Bligh, Philip S. E220
B-Line Systems (electrical and telecom) A430
Blinn, Mark A. A341
Blitz, Gérard W170
Blixt, Charles A. A1205
Bloch, Henry W. A680, A681
Bloch, Richard A680
Bloch, Thomas A680
Block, Ann E. E64, E206
Block Financial Corporation A681
Block Industries A1004
Block, L. E. A1224
Block Medical (home infusion therapies) A718
Block, Philip W. A201
Block, Richard H. A1517
Block, Stephen A. A767
Blockbuster Inc. A206, A266-A267, A1188, A1476, A1477, A1480, E59, E201, E300, P508, P639, P681, W270
Blockson Chemical A1060
Blodgett (commercial cooking equipment) A934, A935
Bloem, James H. A739
Blomqvist, Carl Olof W221
Bloodgood, Sharp, Buster, and Kaufman Meeks (architecture) A1227
Bloom, Jaryn E78
Bloom, Rochelle A565
Bloom, Steven E. P179
Bloomberg L.P. A506, P80-P81, P556

Bloomberg, Michael R. P80, P81, P556
Bloomberg Money (magazine) P80
Bloomberg, Stuart A61
Bloomer, Jonathan W465
Bloomingdale Insane Asylum P134
Bloomingdale, Samuel A586
Bloomingdale's stores A586, A587, A1068, A1150, P404, P708
Blount College P760
Blount, Daniel J. P715
Blount, Frank W586
Blount, W. Houston A1485
Blowers, Carl H. P263
Blue Arrow (temporary employment) A910
Blue Bell (clothing manufacturer) A1474
Blue Bird baked goods A609
Blue Bonnet tablespread A409
Blue Care Elect-Preferred (managed care plan) P85
Blue Care Network (HMO) P86, P87, P557
Blue Chip computers W274
Blue Chip Venture Company E277
Blue Choice New England P84, P85, P557
Blue Choice (point of service) P87
Blue Circle (bathroom fixtures) A152
Blue Coral car care products A1096, A1097
Blue Cross and Blue Shield Association A84, A178, A268-A269, A904, A1506, A1507, E251, P82-P83, P84, P174, P226, P556, P557
Blue Cross and Blue Shield of Colorado A178
Blue Cross and Blue Shield of Connecticut A178
Blue Cross and Blue Shield of Georgia P572
Blue Cross and Blue Shield of Maine A178
Blue Cross and Blue Shield of Massachusetts, Inc. P84-P85, P557
Blue Cross and Blue Shield of Minnesota A268, P82
Blue Cross and Blue Shield of New Jersey A178
Blue Cross and Blue Shield of Rhode Island A178
Blue Cross and Blue Shield of Texas Inc. P226, P628
Blue Cross Blue Shield of Illinois. See Health Care Service Corporation
Blue Cross Blue Shield of Michigan P86-P87, P557
Blue Cross Blue Shield of New Mexico P226
Blue Cross of Connecticut P82
Blue Cross of Indiana A178
Blue Cross of Northeastern New York P174

Blue Cross of Western
Pennsylvania A716, P234
Blue Label Air Service A1426
Blue Moon Belgian White Ale A78, A79
Blue Network A60
Blue Note recording label W212, W213
Blue Point Capital Partners A1378
Blue Preferred P557
Blue Ribbon potatoes P265
Blue Ribbon Sports A1032
Blue Ridge Nursing Homes A1202
Blue Ridge Paper Products A1516
Blue Shield Association P84, P174
Blue Shield of Indiana A178
Blue Shield of Pennsylvania A716
Blue Square-Israel Ltd. P479, W276
Blue Stamps P198
Blue Star Business Supplies
Group A274
Blue Star Oil and Gas E201
Blue Stream pipeline W242
Blue Sunoco A1344
Blue Valley Federal Savings A658
Bluebell detergent A375
Bluebird car W403
Bluebird Toys A926
BlueCard Worldwide (health
insurance) A269, P83
Bluegum Group A1298
BlueLight.com, L.L.C. A830, A918, A919
Blues of Greater New York P174
BluesCONNECT (health
insurance) A268, A269, P82, P83
Bluestone Software, Inc. A712
Bluetooth modules E189
Bluetooth Special Interest Group
(wireless technology) A54, A764, W220, W338, W406
BlueWater seafood W618
Bluffs Run Casino A685
Bluhm, Neil P645
Blum, Bradley D. A465
BLUM Capital Parnters L.P. A904, P120
Blum, Eva T. A1147
Blum, Jonathan D. A1405
Blum, Melvyn H. E137
Blum, Paul E78
Blum, Richard P120
Blum, Stephen D. A487
Blumenfeld, Alan P. A531
Blumenthal, Michael A1424
Blurton, Jerry H. A677
Bly, Stanley A118
Blystone, John B. A1320, A1321
Blyth, Lord W207
Blythe, John C. A621
BMC Software, Inc. **A270-A271**, E22, E148
BMG Entertainment W126, W127, W212
BMO Financial, Inc. W113
BMO Ireland Finance
Company W113

BMW. *See* Bayerischen Motoren
Werke
BN Leasing Corporation A309
BNFL (nuclear energy) W54
BNP Cooper Neff W131
BNP Paribas Group A212, A914,
P314, W104, **W130-W131**, W182, W224
BNSF. *See* Burlington Northern
Santa Fe Corporation
BNSF Acquisition A309
BNY. *See* The Bank of New York
Company
BNY Capital Markets, Inc. A228
BOAC (airline) W541
Boakye, Kwame A. A687
Boardman, Robert A. A1011
Boardwalk Hotel and Casino A966, A967
Boater's World Marine
Centers P714
Boatmen's Bancshares A226
Bob Timberlake furniture P299
Bobak, Mark T. A175
Bobbi Brown *essentials*
cosmetics A564, A565
Bobby Jones golf wear A690, A691
Bobby, Theodore N. A723
Bobcat excavators A754, A755
Bobeff, Peter A. W231
Bober, Joanne L. A357
Bobowicz, Jay A701, P229
Bobro Products P112
Bobrow, Richard S. A563, P183, W223
Bob's Big Boy restaurants A732
Bob's Stores clothes and
shoes A458
Bobula, Renee E273
The BOC Group A100, A244
Boca Burger soy burger A842, A843
Boccardi, Louis D. P60, P61, P546
Boccio, Frank M. P371
Bock, Daniel M. P112, P113
Bock, Dieter W340
Bock, Klaus W163
Bock, Steven A217
Böckel, Jens-Juergen W589
Bockhausen, Christian J. A407
Bocklet & Company E230
Bocklet, Charles J., Jr. A1019, P375
Boddingtons beer W289
Bode, Margaret P615
Bodega Aurrerá discount
warehouses W634, W635
Bodeker Drug Company A1070
Boden, David W473
Bodenheimer, George W. A61, P605
Bodin, Fred W633
Bodinger, Bill P651
Bodnar, Anne Donovan P481, P746
Bodnar, J. Michael A1280, A1281
Body by Victoria brand A776
The Body Shop International
PLC A776, A876
Bodyslimmers lingerie A1498, A1499

Bodzewski, Michael C. A65, P31
Boeckmann, Alan L. A611
Boehm, Marty P389
Boehne, Richard A. A569
Boehnen, David L. A1349
Boeing, Bill A272, A1420
The Boeing Company A98, A120,
A190, **A272-A273**, A274, A662,
A736, A1190, A1210, A1372,
A1402, A1432, E222, E273, P110,
P430, P438, P649, P675, P754,
P766, W70, W110, W132, W303
Boeken, Richard A1126
Boerstler, Barry L. A593
Boesky, Ivan A930
Boesky, Stuart J. E176
Boeve, Roger L. A1109
Bofill, Carlos E38
Bofors W72
Bogan, Thomas F. E110
Bogatyreva, Irina Nikolaevna W243
Boger, Jim P584
Boggs, Brucie P566
Bogle, John A1468, P504
Bogle, Nigel P73
Boglioli, Anthony J. P47
Bognanno, Paul F. A1163
Bohane, M. John A1193
Bohannon, Robert H. A1479
Bohemia beer W289
Bohemia, Inc. (timberlands) A1524
Bohlen, Bruce P399
Bohlen, Kenneth C. A1381
Bohlinger's beer W553
Bohlmann, Thomas W427
Bohn refrigeration A864
Bohn, Robert D. P53
Bohr, Bernd W491
Bohren, Deborah L. P175
Bohrer, Ralph T. E89
Boike, James E A1531
Boillot, Jean W443
Boinet, Sven W59
Boireau, Christian W69
Boireau Group A710
Boise Cascade
Corporation **A274-A275**, A654,
A950, A1302
Boise Payette Lumber
Company A274
Boisi, Geoffrey T. A809
Boistue, W. W. A645
Boisvert, Andre P430
Boitmann, Paul G. A1023
Boivin, Pierre W377
Bokach, Peter M. A201
Bokar coffee A670
Bolch, Carl P710
Bolch, Carl E., Jr. P710
Bold Venture (racehorse) A828, P270
Bolding, Jay D. A409
Bolding, Louann E180
Bolduc, J. P. A1536
Bolen, David E. A797
Bolen, Michael D. P669
Bolender, David F. E56

Bolero lingerie A1474
Bolger, David P. A231
Bolinder-Munktell (farm machinery) W632
Bolinger, Jennifer L. E176
Bo-Linn, George P119
Bolio, Wayne A421
Bolla wines A296, A297
Bollenbach, Stephen F. A720, A721, A1087
Bollgard brand A985
Bollinger, Lee C. P135, P758
Bologna, Nancy C. A255
Bolotin, Andra A1149
Bolster, William A999
Bolton, Michael A1233
Bolton, Roger A91
Bolvig, Peter P552
Bombardier Inc. W132-W133, W188
Bombardier, Joseph-Armand W132
Bombardier, J. R. Andre W133
Bombay gin W108, W109, W206
Bomber Bait (company) P170
Bombril S.A. A374
Bompreço supermarkets W499
The Bon Marche stores A586, A587, A1552
Bon, Michel W164, W233
Bon Secours Health System, Inc. P557
Bonahoom, Alfred J. "Jim" P775
Bonaiuto, Paul M. P648
Bonanni, Fabrizio A161
Bonanza Steakhouse A968, P332, P333, P674
Bonavia, Paul J. A1543
Bond, Barbara J. E236
Bond, Bob W. A1089
Bond Corporation Chile W576
Bond, David F. A1235
Bond, Ed P728
Bond, John M., Jr. (Columbia Bancorp) E182
Bond, John R. H. (HSBC Holdings) W269
Bond, Richard L. (IBP) A743
Bond, Ritchie L. (Dimon) A493
Bonda, Ted P236
Bonderman, David E191, P474, P475, P744
Bondi, Enrico W423, W574, W575
Bonds, Barry P306
Bonds tires W428
Bonfield, Peter W149
Bongiorno, John J. A1011
Bongiorno, Joseph N. A1471
Bongo van W363
Bonham, Derek C. W155, W283, W354, W355
Bonhoeffer, Klaus W344
Boniface, Barry A249
Bonini, Richard F. E193
Bonner, Glenn D. A967
Bonneville Power Administration P558
Bonney, Jeffrey A. E234

Bonnie Maid Premium Veal P775
Bonno, Anthony J. P385, P695
Bonora, Anthony C. E31
Bonsall, James J., Jr. A897
Bonsall, Mark B. P734
Bonsignore, Francis N. A917
Bonsignore, Michael A728
Bonso Electronics E240
Bontems, G. Bart A469
Bonvino, Frank W. A769
Bonwit Teller department stores A1384, P100
Booch, Grady E110
Boogaarts Food Stores A606
Booher, Matthew W. A293
Book Inventory Systems A276
Book, Jonathan D. A905
Book of Virtues P278
Book TV cable channel W186
Book Wholesalers, Inc. P192, P193
Booke, Keith D. A1467
Bookmyer, Joseph R. P415
Books etc. bookstores A276
Books-A-Million, Inc. (bookstores) P541
Bookstar stores A232, A233
Books-To-Go P237
Bookstop stores A232, A233
Boole & Babbage, Inc. (software) A270
Booma, Stephen R. P85, P349
Boomtown Biloxi casino E262
Boon, Harry W429
Boone International (presentation products) A618
Boone National Bank P260
Boone, Pam E87, E238
Boone, Thomas H. A439
Boone Valley Cooperative P36
Boone's Farm wines A520, A521, P168, P169
Boonstra, Cor W444
Boor, David A. A455
Booth, Clement W381
Booth, Mark W146
Booth, Melvin D. E90
Booth Newspapers P32
Booth, Newton P384
Booth, Randall A1113
Booth, Robert L. P359
Booth, William P426
Boothby, David M. A1315
Boothe Financial Corporation A1208
Boots & Coots International Well Control, Inc. A676
Boots the Chemist (drugmaker and retailer) W116, W246, W312
Booxtra (electronic media) W106
Booz, Edwin P88
Booz-Allen & Hamilton Inc. P88-P89, P558
Boozer, Renea P125, P575
Bora car W631
Borateem cleaning and laundry products A486, A487
Boratynski, Nicholas E128

Boraxo soap A487
Borches, Susan M. A1277
Bordeaux, LeRoy A. A1007
Borden, Gail, Jr. P90, W388
Borden Inc. A722, A836, A837, A1106, A1278, P90-P91, P148, P282, P283, P558
Bordenave, Philipe W131
Borden/Meadow Gold Dairies P90
Borders Group, Inc. A130, A276-A277, A756, A830, E290, P244
Borders, Louis A276
Borders, Tom A276
Borealis (polyolefin) W424
Borel Bank & Trust E165
Borel, Daniel V. W338, W339
Boren, Thomas G. A1121
Boretz, J. Craig A381
Borg & Beck A278
Borg, Frank A741, P241, P636
Borgata (resort) A966
Borgelt, James A74
Borghetti, John W469
Borg-Warner Automotive A278
BorgWarner Inc. A222, A278-A279, A526, A1550
Borg-Warner Security P518
Bories, Christel W433
Bories, Jean-Louis A1003
Boris, Howard P291
Bork, Daniel P. A871
Borland Software A1050, A1356
Borlik, Robert W. A1349
Borman, Mark P. A71
Borne, William F. E152
Bornhoft, LaDonna A1419
Bornmann, David E. A1177
Bornstein, Steven M. A60, A61, A1497
Borofsky, Mark H. A245
Borok, Gil A495
Boromisa, Jeffrey M. A817
Borough of Manhattan Community College P129
Bors, Kimberly A299
Börsig, Clemens W201
Borsodchem W242
Bortolussi, Pierluigi W125
Bortz, Jon E. E231
Boruch, Daniel M. P61
Boruch, John N. A163
Bos, Jerry P149, P587
Bosack, Leonard A368
Bosch. See Robert Bosch GmbH
Bosch, Carl W116
Bosch, Robert P699, W490
Bosch-Siemens Hausferate GmbH E222
Boscia, Jon A. A879
Boscov, Solomon P559
Boscov's Department Stores P559
Bose, Amar G. P92, P93, P559
Bose Corporation P92-P93, P559
Bosford gin W109
Boshart, James S., III A231
Boshart, Mike P411

Bosma, Roger E231
Bosman, Cees P. W503
Bosowski, Edward M. A1457
Bosselmann, Rainer H. E158
Bossert Industrial Supply A1538
Bossidy, Larry A728
Bossman, Lori L. A65, P31
Bostic, James E., Jr. A655
Bostik adhesives A264
Bostitch A1322
Bostock, Ray P72
Boston auto parts A461
Boston Bruins (hockey team) P360, P361, P590
Boston Celtics Limited Partnership A**280**-A**281**, P355
Boston Chicken A942
Boston Club liquor W315
Boston Communications (customer relations) E127
Boston Compania Argentina de Seguros SA A1441
The Boston Company, Inc. A596, A954, A955
The Boston Consulting Group P64, P**94**-P**95**, P559
Boston Federal Reserve Bank P46
Boston Financial Data Services A1332, A1333
Boston FleetCenter arena P590
Boston Fruit Company A354
Boston Garden A280
Boston Gas A824
Boston Gear power transmission P578
The Boston Globe A252, A1020, A1021
Boston Management and Research E195
Boston Marathon W636
Boston Market restaurants A942, A943, A1296
Boston Old Colony Insurance Company A379
Boston Private Financial Holdings, Inc. E165
Boston Properties, Inc. E**34**, E165
Boston Public (TV show) A622
Boston Red Sox (baseball team) P307
Boston Roman Catholic P56
Boston Safe Deposit and Trust Company A955, P94
Boston Scientific Corporation A**282**-A**283**, A674, E159
Boston Store department stores A1238
Boston, Terry A1371, P469
Boston Trader children's clothing A1068
Boston University P560
Boston vision care A235
Boston Whaler boats A298, A299, A1194, E237
BostonCoach A615, P191, P609
Boston.com A1020
Bostrom, Susan L. A369

Boswell, John P694
Boswell, Robert S. E62, E205
Botín, Emilio W512
Botín Rios, Emilio W512
Botín-Sanz de Sautuola, Emilio W512
Botín-Sanz, Emilio W513
Botín-Sanz, Jaime W513
Botox drug A118, A119
Botsford, Jon D. A1335
Bottega Veneta (leather goods) W251
Botter, Jennifer A1341
Bottini, Giancarlo W125
Bouchard, Jeffrey B. E267
Boucher, Donald R. E144
Boucheron (jewelry) W250
Bouchut, Pierre W167
Bouck, Steven F. E139, E315
Bouckaert, Alfred W105
Bouckaert, Carl P552
Bouckaert, Mieke P552
Boudier, Marc W69
Boudreau, Donald L. A925, P323
Boudreau, Thomas M. A575
Bougie, Jacques W74
Boulden, Al P443
Boulett, Scott A270
Boulouri, Chahram W413
Boult, Michael P419
Boultbee, Jack A. W263
Boulton, Richard E. S. A173, W91
Bounce laundry product A1165
Bounce (magazine) P347
Bounce pet food A915, P315
Bounder motor homes A605
Bounty candy A915, P315
Bounty paper products A1164, A1165
Bouquet d'Or candy W155
Bourdais de Charbonniere, Eric W367
Bourdier, Jean-Pierre W209
Bourgault, T. E158
Bourgeron, Thierry W167
Bourguignon, Philippe W170, W171
Bourigeaud, Bernard W100, W101
Bourke, Patrick W621
Bourland, Ron P744
Bourne, Richard W434
Bouruet-Aubertot, Alain A849
Bousbib, Ari A1433
Boushy, John M. A685
Bousquet-Chavanne, Patrick A565
Bousquette, Matthew C. A927
Boussois (glassmaker) W192
Boutwell, Wayne A. P732
Bouwfonds Nederlandse Gemeenten (mortgages) W56
Bouwman, T. G. G. W627
Bouygues, Francis W134
Bouygues, Martin W134, W135
Bouygues, Olivier W134, W135
Bouygues S.A. W**134**-W**135**
Bovender, Jack O., Jr. A695

Boveri, Walter W54
Bovis Construction W434
Bowater, Eric A284
Bowater Home Centers A724
Bowater Inc. A**284**-A**285**, A654
Bowater Southern (newsprint mill) A284
Bowater, William A284
Bowcutt, A. Jay A1053
Bowden, Travis J. A1307
Bowe, William J. P177, P603
Bowen, Charlie P88
Bowen, Henry A378
Bowen, Jim C. A1303
Bowen, Lane P658
Bowen, Ray M. P471
Bowen, Robert L. E50, E190
Bowen, Terrell L. A859
Bowen, William G. P541
Bower, Curtis A. P387, P697
Bower, Dorothy E. A. W67
Bower, Marvin A948, P326
Bower Roller Bearing Company A584
Bowerman, Bill A1032
Bowerman shoe A1032
Bowers, Christopher D. A1421
Bowers, Dave E97
Bowers, Deborah P613
Bowers, Robert E. E251
Bowers, Scott E99
Bowers, Tom P445
Bowes, Joseph A1065
Bowes, Walter A1142
Bowflex fitness equipment E193
Bowick, Susan D. A713
Bowker, Gordon A1326
Bowl Appetit! frozen foods A649
Bowler, M. Kenneth A1119
Bowles, Chester P72
Bowles, Crandall Close A1316, A1317, P452, P453, P733
Bowlin, John D. A1127
Bowling, Bill J. A1387
Bowling, Daniel S. A385
Bowlus, Bradford A. A1081
Bowman bakery A814
Bowman Dam A240, P74
Bowman, Dennis J. A367
Bowman, Ed H., Jr. E207
Bowman, Kenneth R. A936
Bowman, Philip (Allied Domecq) W84, W85
Bowman, Philip (Coles Myer) W172
Bowman, Roberta B. A515
Bowman, Robert A. P307
Bowman, Steven P. E27
Bowmar Instrument E317
Bowyer, Chris P165
Box Clever (TV rentals) W249
Box Energy. See Remington Oil and Gas Corporation
Box Office Attraction Company A622
Boxer, Leonard A880
Boxer, Scott J. A865

Boxster car W458, W459
Boy Scouts of America P492, P493, P755
Boychuk, Michael T. W123
Boyd, Arthur A. A817
Boyd, Barton K. A1497
Boyd, Bert P479
Boyd, Cecil E. E126
Boyd, Frolly A91
Boyd Gaming A966
Boyd, James R. A201
Boyd, Jessica E188
Boyd, John E. A419
Boyd, Joseph A. (Harris) A687
Boyd, Joseph (Perot Systems) A1113
Boyd, Mitchell A1280
Boyd, Norman L. A97
Boyd, Rodney A. A1407
Boyd, Stephen P771
Boyd, William A. P350, P351, P681
Boyds Bears A679, P217
The Boyds Collection, Ltd. A837, P283
Boyer, Herbert W. A119, A640
Boyer, Jeffrey N. A831
Boykin, Edward P. A405
Boylan, Christopher P. P335
Boyle, Bernard C. "Brian" E261
Boyle, Douglas S. A1097
Boyle, Marsilia P291
Boyle, Robert E. P398
Boyle, Timothy J. E57
Boyle-Midway W476
Boynton, John W. E63
Boynton, Judith G. W501
Boyoud, Emile W432
Boys, Jack P142, P143, P583
Boys Markets P488
Boyum, Ronald L. E130
Bozard, Richard F. A1071
Bozek, Mark A1451
Bozell (advertising) A772
Bozell, Jacobs, Kenyon & Eckhardt W466
Bozicno beer W289
Bozynski, David A. A585
Bozzelli, Richard L. P171, P601
Bozzone, Robert P. A116, A117
Bozzuto, John P560
Bozzuto, Michael A. P560
Bozzuto's Inc. P243, P560
BP Amoco p.l.c. See BP p.l.c.
BP Amoco p.l.c. E166
BP p.l.c. A132, A168, A184, A352, A576, A582, A612, A820, A1054, A1276, A1374, A1376, P184, P438, **W136**-W137, W152, W176, W218, W296, W488, W542, W612, W640
BP Prudhoe Bay Royalty Trust E166
BPI Communications (publishing) W626
BPI, Inc. (panel systems) A726
Braathens ASA (airline) W317
Brabeck-Letmathe, Peter W388, W389
Brabham, Sherry F. P129, P576

BRACC. See Budget Rent-a-Car Corporation
Brace, Raymond A709
Brace, Robert A515
Bracken, Thomas A. E295
Bradbury, R. Douglas A867
Braden copper mine W488
Braden Winch A1078
Bradham, Caleb A1102, A1106, A1404
Bradlees stores A838
Bradley armored personnel carriers A612
Bradley, Carolyn A1371, P469
Bradley, Cathy L. A1027
Bradley, Charles E., Sr. E279
Bradley, David R. A689
Bradley Fighting Vehicle A120
Bradley, Glen W415
Bradley, James H. A819
Bradley, Karen P689
Bradley, Kathleen G. P277
Bradley, Michael A. A1373
Bradley, Rickford D. P576
Bradley, Steve W645
Bradley, Thomas A. A1237
Bradner, Lawrence A1259
Brador beer W377
Bradshaw, A. W341
Bradshaw, Robert C. A1257
Bradstreet, John M. A516
Brady, Anthony A418
Brady, Janet M. A375
Brady, Mike A73
Brady, Patrick J. A421
Brady, Sharon M. A1295
Brady, Stephen J. A1297
Brady, Thomas F. A425
Brady, Timothy A1547
Brailer, Daniel A. A1513
BrainPlay.com A260
Brajer, Richard O. A245
Brakel, C. J. W642
Brakken, William P655
Bram, Stephen B. A419
Bramalea Homes (home builders) A862
Bramble, Frank P. W87
Brammell, Stephen A685
Bran Buds cereal A817
Bran Flakes cereal A816
Branca, Michael E278
Brancella, Diane P297
Branch Cabell & Company E306
Brancheau, Joan M. A819
Brancher A864
Brand, Myles P638
Brand, Stephen R. A1129
Brandaris tobacco W283
BrandDirect Marketing A1192
Brandeis Brokers Limited W433
Brandes Investment Partners W306
Brandgaard, Jesper W417
Brandolini d'Adda, Tiberto Ruy W171

Brandon, David A. A500, A501, P162, P163, P595
Brandon, John A187
Brandon tobacco W282
Brandow, Peter B. P413
Brandstatter, Richard P. E212
Brandt, Andrew A673, P211
Brandt, Donald E. A137
Brandt, Eric K. A119
Brandt, Werner W517
Brandy, Jo Etta A595
Brandywine Foods A1418
Braniff Airlines A740, A896, A1310, P240, P312
Brannigan, Mike W177
Brannoch men's clothes A691
Brannon, Robert A. E59
Branson, Richard W212, W330, W622, W623
Brasfield & Gorrie, LLC P560
Brasfield, Thomas C. P560
Brashear, James F. A1229
Brasier, Barbara L. A951
Companhia Brasileira de Distribuição W166, W167
BrasilPrev Previdencia Privada S.A. A1163
Brass Bell Bakery P642
Brassard, Michael R. A263
BrassCraft components A921
Brassies Kronenbourg (brewery) W192
Brasso home care W477
BrassRing A1402
Brasswell, Gale P542
Brastemp appliances A1521
Braswell, G. Thomas A653
Braswell Motor Freight Lines A1548
Bratcher, Harlan P101
Brauer, Keith E. A675
Brauerei BECK GmbH & Company W288
BrauHolding International W254
Braun, Beatrice P29
Braun (electric shavers) A656
Braun, Kathy A1514
Braun, Kurt M. A871
Braun, Lloyd A61
Braun Oral-B A657
Brauner, Josef W205
Braun's bread A775
Braun's Fashions. See Christopher & Banks Corporation
Bravell (claims management) A1282
Braveman, John P457
BravePoint (consulting and software) E177
Braverman, Alan N. A61
Bravo cable network A312, A313
Brawny paper products A654
Bray, Michael E. A1155
Brazier, Robert G. A103
Bread & Circus stores A1522
Bread du Jour A775

Bread of Life natural foods markets A1522
The Breadman (infomercial) E116
Break the Bank lottery game P473
Breakdown brand clothing E259
Breakfast at Tiffany's (book and movie) A1384
Breakstone's butter P149
Breard, Jack H., Jr. P171
Breath Savers A708, A709
Bréchon, Jean W151
Breci, Robert J. A653
Breck body, hair, skin care A486, A487
Breco Collision Repair System A1294
Breco Holding P524
Breed, Richard A140
Breeden, Richard C. E200
Breedlove, John P. A1349
Breen, Bernard J. A405
Breen, John G. A1278
Breen, Thia A565
BreezeBoard paperboard P689
Bregar, Raymond E. E119
Bregman, Mitchell S. A573
Breguet watch W562, W563
Brehm, Rodney A. A57
Breit, Martha A829, P271, P650
Breitbach, J. Paul E80
Breitman, Wallace E. E49, E189
Brekkies pet food A915, P315
Bremer, John M. A1049, P377
Bremkamp, Detlev W83
Bremner, David W300
Bren, Donald L. P252, P253, P642
Brendsel, Leland C. A627
Brenn, James E. A287
Brennan, Christine P580
Brennan College Service P192
Brennan, Edward J. P156, P157, P592
Brennan, John J. A1468, A1469, P504, P505, P764
Brennan, Joseph P. A491
Brennan, Timothy A. E110, E276
Brennen, Susan P297, P658
Brenner, George A813, A987
Brenninkmeyer, Hans P539
Brent, John A. A263
Brentjens, Joep W626
Breseke, Nancy P45, P538
Breslawsky, Marc C. A1143
Breslin, Brian P329
Bresnan Communications (cable) A350
Bresnan, Thomas J. E252
Bress, Joseph M. P363
Bressler, Richard (Burlington Northern) A310
Bressler, Richard J. (Viacom) A1477
Bresson, Bernard W233
Société Bretonne de Salaisons A1290, A1291
Brett, Barbara S. A1509
Brett, Larry A73
Bretthauer, Vicki A485

Brettner, Donald M. A82
Breu, Raymund W415
Breuer, Marcel P276
Breuer, Rolf E. W201
Brewer, Rob P547
Brewer Sand W252
Brewers Fayre pubs W638
Brewington, James K. A899
Brewpole W254
Brewster, Lewis C. A411
Brewster, P. Timothy A247
Brewster Transport (tours) A1478, A1479
Bre-X Minerals A628
Breyers Ice Cream A510, W618, W619
Breyers yogurt A843
Brezenoff, Stanley P368
Briar Hall Country Club (NY) A1409, P483
Briatico, Thomas A. A935
Brick, Kathy P763
Bricker, William H. A897
Brickley, Peter W143
Brico Dépôt do-it-yourself stores W312, W313
Bride's (magazine) P33
Brideshead Revisited (TV show) W248
Bridge Casket A718
Bridge Communications A54
Bridge Information Systems, Inc. A204, A506, E70, P80, W484
Bridgestone Corporation A616, A664, P628, W138-W139, W366, W450
Bridgestone/Firestone tires A616
Bridport plc P312, P313
Brierley Investments W230, W262
Briët, Franswillem C. W. W178
Briggs & Stratton Corporation A286-A287
Briggs, C. John A1197
Briggs Equipment (trucks) P720
Briggs, Fred A1535
Briggs, John P636
Briggs, Kendice K. E194
Briggs, Paul P568
Briggs, Philip P175
Briggs, Robert E. A1137
Briggs, Stephen Foster A286
Briggs-Weaver (industrial equipment) P720
Brigham and Women's Hospital P697
Bright, Neil A573
Bright Station (online research info) W592
BrightLane (online payroll) E125
Brightpoint, Inc. E228
BrightReasons restaurants W638
Brigitte (magazine) W126
Brill, John D. P399
Brill Media Ventures P282
Brill, Ronald A724
Brill, Steve A1160, A1161
Brill, Tony G. A1391

Brillance brass finish A921
Brillet, René W165
Brillo cleanser A358, A359, A486
Brill's Content (publication) A1160
Brim Healthcare E271
Brinckerhoff, A. C. P488
Brindle, Ian A1159, P401, W463
Briner, Michael S. E121
Bringuel, Michael E54, E196
Brinker International, Inc. A288-A289
Brinker, Norman E. A288, A289
Brinkerhodd, James E290
Brinkley, Amy A227
Brinkman, Stephen L. E247
Brinsford, Michael W. A405
Brinson Canada W616
Briones Alonso y Martin (attorneys) A220, P66
Brisk, Tabra E199
Brisk tea W619
Briskman, Louis A335
Brisky, Lauren J. P763
Bristol Aeroplane W110
Bristol Compressors A1550, A1551
Bristol Farms Markets, Inc. P489
Bristol Hotels & Resorts W544
Bristol West Insurance Group A837, P283
Bristol, William A290
Bristol-Myers Squibb Company A148, A290-A291, A534, A956, A976, A1060, A1164, E72, E191, P164, W342, W414, W416, W534
Bristol-Siddley Engines W496
Brita water filtration A374, A375
Britannia biscuits W192, W193
Britannia Holdings E201
Britannica First Edition Replica Set (encyclopedia) P177
Britannica.com P176
British Aerospace. *See* BAE SYSTEMS
British Air Marine Navigation W140
British Aircraft Corporation W110
British Airways Plc A138, A164, A1420, A1442, W68, W78, W140-W141, W302, W316, W344, W468, W469, W622
British American Tobacco p.l.c. A618, A838, A1352, W82, W142-W143, W240, W282, W304, W608, W652
British Association of Toy Retailers W332
British Aviation Group A356
British Bank of North America W112
British Bank of the Middle East W268
British Broadcasting Act W146
British Broadcasting Corporation P158, W144-W145, W146, W212, W522
British Caledonian (airline) W140
British Columbia Packers W244

British Commonwealth Pacific
Airlines W468
British Dyestuffs W278
British Energy plc A570, A571,
W174
British European Airways W78,
W140
British Gas A518, A824
British Home Stores W300
British India Steam Navigation
Company W434
British Industries A214
British Interactive
Broadcasting W146
British Library P134
British Mergers and Monopolies
Commission W340
British Midland plc (airline) A1421,
W78, W344, W518, W519
British Monopolies
Commission W246
British National Films W472
British Overseas Airways
Corporation W140, W540
British Parliament W144
British Petroleum. See BP p.l.c.
British Post Office W148
British Rail W174
British Sales Limited A470
British Satellite Broadcasting. See
British Sky Broadcasting Group
British Sky Broadcasting Group
plc E28, W146-W147, W248,
W390, W624
British Steel Act of 1988 W178
British Steel Corporation. See
Corus Group plc
British Telecommunications
plc E219. See BT Group plc
British Trademark Registration Act
(1875) W544
British-Borneo Oil & Gas W216
Britt, Anita A805
Britt Lumber Company, Inc. A931
Brittain Brothers (auto parts) A652
Brittain, John S., Jr. A1027
Brittania Sportswear A1474, A1475
Brittin, Louis A1046
Britto, Mark J. A131
Britton, Ted G. P407, P709
Britts, William C. E23
Britvic soft drink W544, W545
Britz, Robert G. A1019, P375
Brizel, Michael A. A1193
BRL Hardy Limited (wines) A422
Broad, Eli A812
Broad Inc. A812
Broad River Power Company A1248
Broadband Access Systems A70
Broadband Communication
Products A792
Broadband Office A560, P180
Broadband Partners A350, P510
BroadbandNOW A114
Broadbent, Guy A1383
Broadcast Microwave Services E44,
E182
Broadcast Systems Software P506

Broadcaster Argyle Television A700,
P228
Broadcom Corporation A1258,
E313
Broadgate Development
(London) P449
Broadhead, James L. A625
Broadhead, Paul P126
Broadley, Philip W465
Broadnax, Hazel P389
Broadview Central Texas,
Ltd. A1399
BroadVision, Inc. (software) E210,
E311
Broadway Stores, Inc. A560, A586,
P180
Broadwing Inc. A**292**-A**293**
Broadxent W180
Brocade Communications Systems,
Inc. E166
Brock, Jim A1547
Brock, John F. W155
Brock Telecom Limited A1256
Brockett, Francesca L. A1397
Brockovich, Erin A1120
Brockton Public Market P478
Brodeur Worldwide (public
relations) A1063
Brodie, Nancy S. P698
Brodin, Bob A1047
Brodsky, Bernard A305
Brodsky, Howard P568
Brodsky, Julian A. A390, A391
Brody Brothers Dry Goods A1238
Brody, Jack P406
Brody, Rae P406
Brody, William R. P646
Broekaert, Jan W569
Brogan, Terance P729
Brogoch, Gary A. A153
The Broken Hill Proprietary Group.
See BHP Billiton
Brokke, Gregory D. A1115, P397
Brolick, Emil A1405
Brolick, Tony A1087
Bromet, Steven M. A261
Bromhard, Stefan A303
Bromley Communications P73
Bromley, Ernest P73
Bronczek, David J. A589
Bronfman, Charles F. W322, W323
Bronfman, Edgar M., Jr. W625
Brongniart, Philippe W559
Bronneck, John D. A1207
Brons, Paul K. W73
Bronson, John S. A1531
Bronson, Joseph R. A189
Bronsweig, David A109
Bronx Community College P128,
P129
Bronzelite lighting P613
Brooke, F. Dixon, Jr. P171
Brooke Group A1126
Brookes, Bernie W645
Brookes, Nick W143
Brookfield Properties E37

Brookhaven Country Club
(Dallas) P130
Brookhaven National
Laboratories P438
Brookhaven Science Associates P70
Brooklyn College P128, P129
Brooklyn Gas Light Company A824
Brooklyn Rapid Transit P334
Brooklyn Staten Island Family
Health Network P369
Brooklyn Union Exploration
Company A824
Brooklyn Union Gas Company A824
Brooklyn-Port Authority Marine
Terminal P399
Brookpark Plastics A326
Brooks Automation, Inc. E**35**, E166
Brooks, Brian W647
Brooks Brothers stores A586,
A1150, P713, W356, W357
Brooks, C. A669
Brooks, Clint D. A767
Brooks convenience stores A606
Brooks, Craig L. A161
Brooks, David P200
Brooks, Diana A1304
Brooks, Douglas H. A289
Brooks, Garth W213
Brooks, George H. P501, P762
Brooks, Jeffrey W355
Brooks, John A856
Brooks, Norman E35
Brook's Pharmacy A1312
Brooks, Rhonda L. A1073
Brooks, Robert P210
Brooksher, Robert R. E264
Brookshire Grocery Company P561
Brookshire, Tim P561
Brookstone stores A1274, A1530
Brooktree Corporation A410
Brookwood Medical Center of
Gulfport, Inc. A695
Broome, Anne C. P495
Broon, Kristie E191
Brose, Bryan P607
Brosig, Thomas J. A1087
Brosnan, Timothy P307
Bross, Richard A. A731
Brossard baked goods A1243
Brossman, Douglas S. A195
Broster, Stuart W259
Brostowitz, James M. A683
Brother, Thomas E. A111
Brotherhood of All Railway
Employees P750
Brotman, Jeffrey H. A436, A437
Broughton Foods (milk
processor) A1338
Broughton, Joan P411
Broughton, Martin F. W142, W143
Brouillard, Jack C. P225, P627
Broun, Elizabeth P451
Brouse, John S. A717, P235, P632
Broussard, Susan E265
Brouwer, Aart A161
Brover, Barry P549
Brower, Paul G. P201

Brown & Root Energy
Services A676, A677, A1198
Brown & Williamson
Industries A838, E293, W142
Brown Automotive Group
Ltd. P561
Brown, Bailey & Pikus
(consulting) E36
Brown, Bart R. A637
Brown, Bernard E295
Brown, Boveri, and Company W54
Brown, Bruce S. A1127
Brown, Carol M. E138
Brown, Charles (Brown,
Boveri) W54
Brown, Charles E. (Office Depot,
Inc.) A1057
Brown, Charles R., II (Vulcan
Materials) A1485
Brown, Charles S. (Eastman
Kodak) A525
Brown, Christopher A. A995
Brown, Cleyson A1318
Brown, Colin
(Computacenter) W177
Brown, Collin (JM Family
Enterprises) P257
Brown, Craig D. P72, P73
Brown, Dale P337, P675
Brown, David (Quantum
Corporation) A1184
Brown, David T. (Owens
Corning) A1073
Brown, Dick W152
Brown, Edward (Bemis) A250
Brown, Edward, III (Bank of
America) A227
Brown, Emily S. P732
Brown, Eric A. A731
Brown Fintube Company A835,
P281
Brown, Fleming & Murray
(accounting) A562, P182, W222
Brown, Francis A1250
Brown, G. Michael "Mickey" P318
Brown, Gary H. A1471
Brown, George (Brown-
Forman) A296
Brown, George (Brown Shoe) A294
Brown, George (Rockefeller
Foundation) P415
Brown, George V. (Duke
Energy) A515
Brown, Gifford E. P165, P596
Brown, Gregory Q. E245
Brown Group A294
Brown, H. P. W586
Brown, Harris, Stevens (real
estate) P230
Brown, Herbert G. P421
Brown, J. Frank A1159, P401, W463
Brown, Jack E. (ACNielsen) A67
Brown, Jack H. (Stater Brothers
Holdings) P462, P463, P736
Brown, Jacob A1318
Brown, James M. (Cohu) E44
Brown, James R. (Adelphia
Communications) A73

Brown, James R. (Becton,
Dickinson) A245
Brown, JoBeth G. A175
Brown, Julian W523
Brown, Karen C. E95, E249
Brown, Kathleen J. A145
Brown, L. Don A79
Brown, LaRay P369
Brown, Larry A589
Brown, Lee A296
Brown, Loren A329, P109
Brown, Mark E. A1521
Brown, Mary Rose A1467
Brown, Michael A. A1184, A1185
Brown, Owsley, II A296, A297
Brown Pagoda shoe sales A294
Brown Paper Mill A1060
Brown, Paul F. P609
Brown, Peter D. (Venator) A1471
Brown, Peter (Yellow) A1549
Brown Printing A1004
Brown, Randall A179
Brown, Reed A779
Brown, Richard (Health
Midwest) P629
Brown, Richard H. (Electronic Data
Systems) A538, A539
Brown, Robert E.
(Bombardier) W133
Brown, Robert T. (State University
of New York) P461
Brown, Ronald C. (Starwood
Hotels) A1329
Brown, Ronald (Oxford
Health) A1077
Brown, Ronald (Sotheby's) A1304
Brown, Ron (US Commerce
Secretary) P386, W54
Brown, Ross A171
Brown, Sandy J. P363
Brown, Scott D. A783
Brown Shoe Company,
Inc. A294-A295
Brown, Stephen (Carlson
Companies) P107
Brown, Stephen F. (Tenet
Healthcare) A1367
Brown, Teresa E70
Brown, Thomas C. (TMBR/Sharp
Drilling) E301
Brown, Thomas D. (Abbott
Laboratories) A59
Brown, Tina A80, P32
Brown, Tom (Tom Brown,
Inc.) E129
Brown, Tracy A1531
Brown, Treg S. A653
Brown University P382, P763
Brown, Vincent P. A315, P97, P563
Brown, W. Douglas A101
Brown, Walter A280
Browne, Joe P357
Browne, John P. W136, W137
Browne, Michael P672
Brownell, James A. A1531

Brown-Forman
Corporation A296-A297, A922,
P320, P616, P777, W108
Browning, Jay D. A1467
Browning, John P132
Browning, Jonathan A1329
Browning, Peter A1302
Browning, Robert B. A1465
Browning, Stuart E197
Browning-Ferris Industries,
Inc. A122, A206, A1504, E139,
E293, W558
Brownley, John F. A1511
Brownlie, William R. E128
Brownling rods and reels A298
Brown's Dairy A1339
Browns restaurants W545
Brown-Service (funeral
insurance) A1390
Broyhill Furniture Industries A630
Broyhill, J. E. A630
Brozowski, Patricia D. A613
Bru, Abelardo E. A1107
Brubeck, Patrick W339
Bruce, Ailsa Mellon P541
Bruce, Peter W. A1049, P377
Bruce, Tom P708
Bruckmann, Rosser, Sherill &
Company P644
Bruffet, Stephen L. A1549
Brugman (home improvement
products) A920
Brugnoli, Giampaolo W99
Brumley, Elizabeth D. A931
Brummett, Larry A1065
Brune, David A. A425
Brune Reiseburo (travel
agency) A328, P108
Brunelli, Massimo W575
Brunetti, Wayne H. A1543
Brunini, Bob W271
Brunk, J. Dale A1125
Brunner, John W121
Brunner, Kim M. A1331, P459
Brunner, Mond and Company
(chemicals) W278
Bruno, Rosemarie E157
Bruno's Supermarkets, Inc. A836,
P282, P644, W498
Brunson, Curtis A847
Brunswick Building (Chicago) P449
Brunswick
Corporation A298-A299, E237
Brunswick, John A298
Brunswick nuclear plant A1166
Brunswick Pulp and Paper A654
Brunswick records A298
Brunswick-Balke-Collender
Company A298
Brunton, Thomas E. E57, E197
Bruse, Anders W585
Brush Electric Light
Company A570, A1028
Brush, Victoria S. A785
The Bruss Company (steaks) A742,
A743
Brust, Robert H. A525

Bruton, Steve A1241
Groupe Bruxelles Lambert W126
Bryan, A. Bradford, Jr. A913
Bryan, Alvin A294
Bryan, Brown and Company A294
Bryan Foods A1242, A1243
Bryan, John H. A1242, A1243
Bryan, L. Merill, Jr. A1423
Bryan, Lowell L. P327
Bryan, Michelle V. A1443
Bryan, Pendleton, Swats &
 McCallister, LLC A1509
Bryant, Andrew (Avnet) A215
Bryant, Andy D. (Intel) A761
Bryant, Dave P652
Bryant, Ernest A864
Bryant, John M. W178, W350
Bryant, Warren F. A845
Bryantt, Diane K. E223
Bryce, M. James A1101
Brydon, Donald W105
Brylane (catalog sales) A876,
 A1388, W446
Brylcreem body care A1243
Bryn Mawr Stereo & Video
 stores E306
Bryson, Jeffery A. E118, E284
Bryson, Michael A. A955
BSH Bosch und Siemens
 Hausgeräte GmbH (household
 appliances) A920, W490, W536
BSI Holdings A920
BSkyB. See British Sky
 Broadcasting
BSN Emballage (glassmaker) W192
BSpringer W127
BT Cellnet W148, W149
BT Funds Management A1163
BT Group plc A202, A714, A1534,
 P580, W146, **W148-W149**, W152,
 W176, W334, W494, W502, W578,
 W584, W628
BT Openworld (Internet
 services) W149
BTM Capital A1146
BTNB Corporation A1308
BTR Fatati Limited (automotive
 carpet) A388, A856
BTR plc A1074, W290
BTrieve Technologies A1050
BTU International, Inc. E167
Buback, Ken P739
Bubble Mask E112
Bubble Tape gum A1526, A1527
Bubble Wrap packaging A1262
Bubble Yum gum A708, A709, A843
Bubbs, Roy H. A987
Bublitz, Maxwell E. A415
BUCA di BEPPO restaurants E167
BUCA, Inc. E167
Bucci, David A489
Bucciarelli, Edward A881
Buchan, Colin W617
Buchan, H. Carl A892
Buchanan, James P760
Buchanan, John G. S. W137
Buchanan Mine A417

Bucher Holdings of
 Switzerland A264
Bucher (publishing) W107
Buck Consultants, Inc. A954, A955,
 P480
Buck, James E. A1019, P375
Buck, Peter P160, P161, P595
Buck, Robert R. A365
Buckberg, Joel R. A339
Buckcherry (performer) P167
Buckel, David A. A763
Bucker, William A. A325
Buckeye (potato chips) P90
Buckeye power tools A430
The Buckeye Union Insurance
 Company A379
Buckhead Beef Company A1350
Buckhorn restaurants P748
Buckler beer W255
Buckler, Robert J. A513
Buckley Acquisition A86
Buckley, George W. A299
Buckley, J. Edward A545
Buckley, John A581
Buckley, Mary Kate A1033
Buckley, Michael W87
Buckley Mining Corporation A69
Buckley, William F., Jr. P776
Buckly, Ronald W. E126
Buckman, Fred A1082
Buckman, James E. A339
Buckman, Michael A. P776
Bucknall, William L., Jr. A1433
Buckner, William A. P105
Bucks, Thomas E. E38
Bucyrus Erie W320
Bud Light beer A174, A175
Budd Company (steel) A1482
Budd, John A791
Budd, Wayne A. A799
Budde, David E109
Buddies supermarkets A1532
Budget Gourmet (frozen
 foods) A722
Budget Group, Inc. **A300-A301**,
 A616, A1222
Budget Rent-a-Car
 Corporation P666
Budig, Renee A1185
Budney, Albert J., Jr. A1029
Budreau, Karen P249, P641
Bud's Discount City A1494
Budweiser beer A174, A175, A224,
 W289, W314
Budweiser Wuhan International
 Brewing A174
Buechner, Klaus M. W413
Buell, Erik F. A683
Buell Motorcycle Company A682,
 A683
Buena Vista (film
 distribution) A1497
Buena Vista Television A60, A61
Buenaslor, Naomi P777
Buensuceso, Ma. Bellen C. W511
Buente, Stephen M. A527
Bueti, Antonio P372

Bufacchi, Alessandro W215
Buffalo Bills (football team) P357
Buffalo Bill's (hotel and
 casino) A966, A967
Buffalo Bisons (baseball team) P714
Buffalo (New York) *News* A252
Buffalo, Niagara and Eastern
 Power A1028
Buffalo Sabres (hockey team) A72,
 P361
Buffenbarger, R. Thomas P35
Bufferd, Allan S. P667
Buffet Partnership A252
Buffet, Patrick W559
Buffets, Inc. P562
Buffett, Howard A252
Buffett, Susan A252
Buffett, Warren E. A142, A252,
 A253, A382, A462, A516, A638,
 A656, A680, A804, A880, A1346,
 A1456, A1502, P340, P474, P510,
 P676, W84
Buffington, Melissa A497
Buford, Anne A1151
Bug City candy A1527
Bugaj, Czeslaw Adam W457
Bugatti sports cars W630
Bugles snack food A649
Bugs Burger Bug Killers A1246,
 P432
A Bug's Life (movie) E103, E266
Buhler & Partners P73
Buhrmaster, Robert C. P262, P263,
 P647
Buick Motors A476, A584, A650,
 P596, P606, P706, P733, W188,
 W294
Builder Homesite A508
Builder (magazine) A340
Builder Marts of America, Inc. A64,
 P30, P212, P562, P623
Builders Emporium A388, P406
Builders FirstSource, Inc. P562
Builders Square A830
Builder's Transport (trucking) P434
Building Materials Corporation of
 America P612
Building One Services A548
Building Technology, Inc. A545
Buisson, Jean-René W193
Buitenhuis, André W499
Buiter, Wilbert J. M. A1013
Buitoni pasta W388
Bujakowski, Mike E293
Bukatko, Aurelian P695
Bulcao, Gilberto D. A245
Bulfin, John J. E138
Bulgari S.p.A. (jeweler) A912
Bulger, William M. P757
Bulgurlu, Bülent W319
Bulkeley, Eliphalet A90
Bulkeley, Morgan A90
Bull A488, **W150-W151**, W160,
 W386, W406
Bull & Bear Group W474
Bull, Christopher R. H. W489
Bull, Fredrik W150

Bull, George W301
Bull Information Technology A782
The Bull Tractor Company A1392
Bulldog fasteners A1022
Bulldog office seating P277
Bullhead brand clothing E259
Bullock & Jones catalogs A1238
Bullock, Donald A527
Bullock, Lee W. P363
Bullock's stores A586
Bulls Eye golf balls A618
Bullwhackers Casino
  (Colorado) E262
Bullwinkel, George B. A1249
Bulmer, Chris W639
Bulova Corporation
  (watches) A884, A885, A1384
Bulpitt, Nigel W241
Bulwark work wear A1474, A1475
Bumble and Bumble (hair
  salons) A564, A565
Bumble Bee tuna A408, A409
Bumin Mutual Savings & Finance
  Corporation W335
Bunch, Charles E. A1153
Bundaberg (sugar) W568
Bundespost. See Deutsche Post AG
  and Deutsch Telekom AG
Bundy, McGeorge P194
Bundy, Steve P601
Bunge, Johann Peter Gottlieb P565
Bunger, Richard E246
Bunger, Steven G. E246
Bungie Software Products A972
Bunker Ramo (bank
  automation) A204, W422
Bunnell, Ron P549
Bunney, Graham E44
Bunny baked goods A609
Bunshaft, Gordon P448
Bunte, Mark A421
Bunting, W. Clark P159
Bunton, Collette W339
Buntrock, Dean A1504
Buonaiuto, Joseph M. A141
Buongiorno, Joseph A1459
Buora, Carlo W423, W451
Buoy, Howard E. A193
BUPHENYL drug E89
Burbage, C. T. A883
Burberry's clothing A690, A691
Burch, Larry P345
Burchfield, Robert R. A1005
Burck, R. D. P498, P499, P761
Burd, Steven A. A1234, A1235
Burdakin, David C. A727
Burden, David W469
Burden, Eugene A1375
Burden family (Starwood Hotels &
  Resorts Worldwide) A1328
Burdick, Don A437
Burdines stores A586, A587
Bureau en Gross stores A1325
Bureau of Business Practice
  (publishing) W642
Burg, H. Peter A599

Burg, Robert H. P715
OOO Burgaz W243
Burgdoerfer, Stuart A877
Burgdorf, Lawrence P436
Burger, Andrew A271
Burger, Joachim W267
Burger King Corporation A86,
  A288, A302-A303, A608, A942,
  A1046, A1136, A1404, A1470,
  A1488, A1510, P72, P124, P516,
  P669, P704, W174, W206, W207,
  W304
Burger, Martha A. E39, E176
Burgess, Claude B. A711
Burgess, Gary L. A453
Burgess, Ian G. R. W88, W641
Burgess, J. Joseph A441
Burgess, Kimberly S. E209
Burgess, Richard S. A1395
Burgess, Robert K.
  (Macromedia) E86
Burgess, Robert K. (Pulte
  Homes) A1179
Burgestahler, Robert J. A977
Burgmans, Antony W619
Burgo, Raymond P199
Burk group of companies A1302
Burkart, Phillip A. A1393
Burke, George B. A1391
Burke, James J. E142
Burke, John P. (Trump
  Organization) A1409, P483
Burke, John R. (Church &
  Dwight) A359
Burke, Joseph J. A637
Burke, Ken E180
Burke, Kevin A419
Burke, Michael A556
Burke, Richard A1434
Burke, Robert E. (American Home
  Mortgage) E154
Burke, Robert E. (Boston
  Properties) E34
Burke, Sheila P451
Burke, Stephen B. A391
Burke, Thomas A. (Telephone and
  Data Systems) A1361
Burke, Thomas J. (Thermo
  Electron) A1383
Burkett, Charles L. P87
Burkett, Lawrence V., Jr. A923,
  P321
Burkhard, Mark E53, E195
The Burkhardt Company
  (binders) P170
Burkhardt, Glenn S. E128
Burkhart, William R. A1387
Burkhead, Gary A615
Burkhead, J. Gary P191
Burkitt, Paul J. E113
Burkle, Joe P462
Burkle, Ronald W. P462, P524,
  P525, P777
Burks Pumps A446
Burleigh, William A568
Burlington, Alec E250
Burlington Biscuits W192

Burlington Coat
  Factory A304-A305
Burlington House interior
  furnishings A306
Burlington Industries, Inc. A304,
  A306-A307, P696
Burlington Klopman Fabrics A306
Burlington Mills A306
Burlington Northern Santa Fe
  Corporation A308-A309, A536,
  A788, A916, A1222, A1422, A1478,
  P751
Burlington Resources Inc. A308,
  A310-A311, E263, E283
Burlington Zephyr (passenger
  train) A308
Burlwood wine A521, P169
Burmah Castrol A644, W136
Burne, Phil A147
Burnell, Karen P542
Burner, David L. A662, A663
Burnet, Thomas P. A297
Burnett, Charles V. A437
Burnett, G. Kent A491
Burnett, Leo P72
Burnett, Robert J. A637
Burnham, Daniel P. A1190, A1191
Burnham, Dick P632
Burnham, Duane A58
Burnham, Lem P357
Burnham, Tom A119
Burns, Edward P678
Burns Fry (brokerage) W112
Burns Harbor Division A256, A257
Burns, Iain W141
Burns International Services
  Corporation A278, W524, W525
Burns, Jenny E193
Burns, Jules W249
Burns, Keith B. A993
Burns, Kevin A1299
Burns, Laurie A465
Burns, Lewis E. A503
Burns, M. Anthony A1222, A1223
Burns, Michael B. (Crown Cork &
  Seal) A453
Burns, Michael J. (General
  Motors) A651
Burns, M. Michele A479
Burns, Patrick E135
Burns, Philp (spices and
  flavorings) A938
Burns, Robert A767
Burns, Robin R. A777, A877
Burns, Roland O. E183
Burns, Stephanie P165
Burns, William M. W493
Burnside, Franklin T. A433
Burnside, Terry D. A887
Burr, Aaron A808
Burr, Kevin A77
Burr-Brown A1378
Burrell Communications
  Group W466
Burrell, Rebecca A. E260
The Burridge Group E149
Burris, John C. E42

Burroughs Corporation A1424
Burroughs, Silas W246
Burroughs Wellcome and Company W246
Burrows, Brian W. A1457
Burson-Marsteller (public relations) W646
Burstein, Mark P135
Burstell, Ed A877
Burt Automotive Network P563
Burt, Donald B. W495
Burt, Robert N. A613
Burton, B. Kent A441
Burton, Diana E. A1447
Burton, James E. A315, P97, P563
Burton, Richard N. A1517
Burton, Robert G. W378, W379
Busang gold mine A628
Busby, Elsie P427
Busby, John P427, P720
Buscarinio, Carolyn M. A1017, P371
Busch, Adolphus A174
Busch, August A. A174
Busch, August A., III A174, A175
Busch beer A174, A175
Busch, David C. P423
Busch Gardens theme park A174
Busch Grand National racing circuit P681
Busch Light beer A175
Busch, Robert E. A1175
Bush Boake Allen A766, A770
Bush, George H. W. (former US President) A1096, P110, P186, P567, P776
Bush, George W. (US President) A676, E129, P110
Bush, John (Brown Shoe) A294
Bush, John (Sodexho) A1297
Bush, Robert J. A1025
Bushaw, Dewey P. P385
Bushy, David S. A479
Business 2.0 (magazine) W238
Business and Career Publications W626
Business Browser (Web site) E100, E258
The Business Depot stores A1324, A1325
Business Express P418
Business Forum P338
Business Integration Group P587
Business Loan Express E151
Business Men's Assurance Company of America W99
Business Travelers' Briefcase Atlas (book) P409
Business Travel International (BTI) P776
Business Trends Group (general staffing) A818
Business Week (magazine) A944, A945, P378, P454
Businessland (computer resale) A544
BusinessLink software A588

BusinessWare suite software E313
BuSpar drug A290, A291
Busquet, Anne M. A143
Buss electrical products A431
Bussells, Walter P. P643
Bussien, Aldo W339
Buster Brown children's shoes A294
Bustos, Alejandro W635
Busy Bees day care centers W638
BUT electronics stores W312, W313
Butcher, Ernesto L. P399
Butler, Bruce W. P85
Butler Capital P202, P406
Butler, Clifford E. A1133
Butler, Clive W619
Butler, David T., III A847
Butler, Gary C. A205
Butler, James E., Jr. P764
Butler, John D. A1381
Butler, Kevin M. A477
Butler, Patrick A1503
Butler, Robert C. A111
Butler, Ronald P. A1373
Butler shoes A1552
Butler, Stephen G. A841, P287, W325
Butler, William J.(Danaher) A463
Butler, William T. (Lyondell) A901
Butlins (resorts) W472
Butson's food stores A1349
Butt, Charles C. P224, P225, P627
Butt, Florence P224
Butt, Howard, Jr. P224
Butt, Howard, Sr. P224
Butter Cream Baking A774
Butterball turkey A409
Butterbrodt, John P58
Butterfield & Swire W564
Butterfield, Richard W564
Butterfield, Stewart W249
Butterfields (auctions) E54, E196
Butterfinger candy bar W388
ButterKrust baked goods A608, A609
Butterley Brick W252
Butterley (company) A100
Buttermaid bread A775
Butternut bread A774, A775
Butterworth, William A468
Buttigieg, Joseph J., III A395
The Buttonwood Agreement (1792) A1018, P374
Buttrey Food and Drug Stores A110
Butzer, Bart A1353
Butzow, Barry W. A345
Buxton, Andrew W114
Buxton, Mark J. A471
Buy Me That! A Kid's Survival Guide to TV Advertising (educational video) P139
Buy, Richard B. A553
Buyer Profile (online inventory) E45
Buyers' Choice brands P423
Buy-n-Save grocery stores A995

Buys, Ernest A85
Buystream (software) A1233
Buytenhuys, Darroll A271
Buz, Carl W350
buzz (airline) W316, W317
Buzz Lightyear of Star Command: The Adventure Begins (movie) E103
Buzzard, James A. A1517
Buzzard, Maura A1401
Buzzcuts (cards) A147
Buzzell, Michael L. E100
Buzzeo, John P357, P683
B.V. Tabak Export & Import Compagnie A492
Bvlgari brand W637
BVR Systems W323
BW Holdings P90, P558
BWP Distributor, Inc. P113
BX (Base Exchange) P52
Byars, Michael D. W195
Bycoff, Barry N. E96, E251
Byerlotzer, James J. E79
Byers, David F. A681
Byers, Debbie P479
Byerwalter, Mariann P457, P735
Byfield Travel P308
Byford, Mark W145
Bygge, Johan W211
Byington, Sue P706
Bykerk, Cecil D. P349
BYL Bancorp E204
Byllesby, Henry A1542
Bynum, Joseph R. A1371, P469
Byom, John E. A769
Byrd, Benjamin C., III A1149
Byrd, Don P675
Byrne, Stephen A. A1249
Byrnes, Bruce L. A1165
Byrnes, James J. E302
Byrnes, Thomas J. A213
Byron, Carla A. A355
Byron's barbecue P714
B.Z. W107
BZ Gruppe Holding W492
BZW. *See* Barclays de Zoete Wedd

C

C. & E. Cooper A430
C. Itoh & Company A744, P242, W296, W358, W398, W560
C. Jespersen (accounting) A840, P286, W324
C. Lee Cook (compressor seals and piston rings) A502
C2it online payment system A370
C3, Inc. (lab created gems) E47
CA One Services (airport food) P590
Cabañas, Francisco W577
Cabbage Patch Kids toys A692, A927
Cabiallavetta, Mathis A917, W616
Cabin cigarettes W305
Cable and Wireless HKT W152

Cable and Wireless plc A538, A1252, A1534, W122, W134, W**152**-W**153**, W218, W272, W400
Cable Atlantic W494
Cable Car Beverage A1400
Cable, Dale A. A147
Cable Educational Network P158
Cable ONE, Inc. A1503
Cable USA, Inc. P313
Cable World A1161
CABLESPAN network delivery system A1362, A1363
Cablevisión W582, W583
Cablevision Lightpath A312
CableVision S.A. A714, P232
Cablevision Systems Corporation A72, A**312**-A**313**, A350, A962
Cabot, Cabot & Forbes E34
Cabot Corporation E168
Cabot Industrial Trust E167
Cabot LNG (energy) W559
Cabot Microelectronics Corporation E168
Cabot Oil & Gas Corporation E168
Cabriolet car W631
Caccini, Gianpolo W507
Cacharel fragrances W343
Cache Valley cheese P723
Cachet office furniture A1335
Cacique lingerie A776, A876
Cactus Company (oil and gas machinery) A756, P244
Cadadia supermarkets W498
Cadbury candy A708, A709, W155
Cadbury, Dominic W154
Cadbury, John W154
Cadbury Schweppes plc A382, A384, A842, A914, A1102, A1400, E42, P110, P314, P597, P634, W**154**-W**155**, W244, W552, W553
Caddell, Lynn M. A1549
Caddy car W631
Caddy-Home (delivery service) W194
Cade Industries A1432
Cadec Systems A456
Caden, Grace A403
Cadence Design Systems A754, A894, P278
Cadence Network (energy management) A362
Cadet Uniform Services A364
Cadi soft drink W315
Cadieux, Chester P710
Cadillac car A476, A650, P92, P152, P316, P555, P596, P606, P631, P656, P706, P733
Cadima, Manny P613
Cadnetix A238
Cadnica battery W514
Cadogan, William A70
CAE Systems A1358
Caesars Gauteng A1087
Caesars Palace resort and casino A1086, A1087, A1328
Caesars World A720

Caetano, Marcelo W224
Café do Ponto coffee A1243
Café Flo W174
Café Goya beverage P205
Cafe Perdue chicken P392
Café Rouge restaurants W638, W639
Caffe Starbucks online store A1326
Caffey, William R. A835, P281
Caffrey's beer W289
Cafri beer W289
Cahill, Douglas J. P595
Cahill, Frank E218
Cahill, Gerald R. A331
Cahill, John T. A1102, A1103
Cahill, Patricia A. P116, P117, P569
Cahners Business Information W478, W479
Cahoon, Keith P347
Cahouet, Frank A954
Cailler (candy) W388
Cain Chemical A1054
Cain, Gary M. A1163
Cain, Gordon A548
Caine, Franklyn A. A1191
Caio, Francesco W422
Cairn Energy USA E242
CAIS Internet Inc. A837, P283
Caisse de Dépôt et Placement du Québec (public pensions) W470
Caja de Ahorro de Asturias (bank) A1416
Cajun Joe's fast food P160
Cal Fed Bancorp A902, P304
Cala Foods A845
Calabrese, Wayne H. E138
Calado, Miguel A1339
Calamity Association of Accident Insurance Companies W82
Calapco. *See* Central Arizona Light & Power
Calarco, Vincent A. A451
Calavia, Philippe W69
CALC/Canterbury (technology training) E36, E170
Calder, Frank P360
Calder Race Course (Miami) E40, E178
Caldera, Louis E. P99
Caldera, Rafael W438
Calderin, Rob A303
Calderoni, Frank E117, E284
Caldor stores A158, A838, A932
Caldwell bedding and towels A1135
Caldwell, James R. A813
Caldwell, Kim A. A211
Caldwell, Nanci A1099
Calello, Paul A449
Calendar Club A232
CalEnergy Company. *See* MidAmerican Energy Holdings Company
CalFarm Insurance A1008, A1009, P364, P365
Calgary Flames (hockey team) P361
Calgary Sun W471
Calgene (biotech) A984, A1122

Calgon dishwashing and fabric care W476, W477, W558
Calgonit dishwashing and fabric care W476, W477
Calhoon, Donald F. A1511
Calhoon, J. Richard A859
Calhoun, David L. A647
Calhoun, George A672, P210
Calhoun, Jay S. A1017, P371, P688
Calhoun, N. Anthony P389, P699
Cali, Philip S. A1031
Calianese, Elizabeth J. E58, E198
Caliber Logistics (trucking) A1206
Caliber System (trucking) A588, A1206
Calibre filing cabinets P277
Calico clothing A805
California Adventure A1496
California Amplifier, Inc. E168
California Blue Cross A1506
California Closets A1530
California Coastal Communities, Inc. E169
California Compensation Insurance A696
California Culinary Academy E172
California Dairies Inc. P563
California Department of Personnel Administration A314, P96
California Department of Water Resources A424
California Digital Library P494
California Electric Light A1120
California Electric Power A532
California Energy P340
California Financial Holding A1364
California Fruit Canners Association A470
California Fuel Cell Partnership A576
California Gold (dairies) P148
California HealthCare Foundation A1506
California Healthcare System P739
California Institute of Technology A242
California Insurance Department P268
California Jockey Club A1540
California Maritime Academy P99
California Medical Association A696, A1506
California Microwave A846, A1044
California Milk Producers P563
California Oregon Power A1082
California Perfume Company A216
California Public Employees' Retirement System A**314**-A**315**, A836, E37, P**96**-P**97**, P120, P282, P563
California Public Utilities Commission A532, A1120, A1266
California State Lottery Commission A558, P564
California State Polytechnic University P98, P99
Trustees of the California State University P**98**-P**99**, P564

California-American Water
Company A155
CaliforniaCare A1506
California-Texas Oil Company. *See*
Caltex Corporation
Calise, William J., Jr. A1211
Call, Harry A666
Call, Jay P609
Call, John G. A1215
Callaghan, Michael W. A293
Callahan, Bernard B. P359
Callahan, Dennis S. P215
Callahan, Maureen E144, E320
Callahan, Patricia R. A1509
Callahan, Robert F. A60
Callahan, Timothy J. A1071
Callaway Golf A1446
Callaway nuclear plant A136
Callaway wines W85
Callen, Daniel F. A337
Callera, Gilberto W217
Callier, James P518
Call-Net Enterprises Inc. A1318
Calman Australia (cleaning and
chemical supplies) A1004
CALMAR plastic sprayer W506
CalMat A1484
Calorex (water heaters) A152
Caloric (stoves) A1190, P618
Calpak (canning) A470
CalPERS. *See* California Public
Employees' Retirement System
Calphalon cookware A1022, A1023
Calpine A824
CAL-PURE (marketing co-op) P416
CalTech. *See* California Institute of
Technology
Caltex Corporation A352, A1376,
A1377, W334
Caltex Gas Company W335
Caltex Oil Corporation W335
Calton Homes A340
Calumet & Arizona Mining A1124
Calumet Electric A1034
Calumet Florida, Inc. A1145
Calumet Lubricants A1096
Calumet Steel A278
Caluori, Vince A693
Calvé brand food W619
Calvert Cliffs nuclear plant A424
Calvert, Phyllis J. A87
Calvert, Stanton C. P471
Calvet, Jacques W442
Calvin, John P585
Calvin Klein, Inc. A1498, A1499,
E236, **P100**-**P101**, P564, W618,
W619
Caly Online W166, W167
Camardo, Michael F. A883
Camarena, Guillermo W582
Camatriaín Corbi, María
Belén W579
Cambex Corporation A542
Cambre, Ronald C. A1024, A1025
Cambria, Christopher C. A847
Cambria Iron A1094
Cambria motor homes A604

Cambridge Consultants
Limited P55
Cambridge Homes A509
Cambridge men's clothes A691
Cambridge Properties A508
Cambridge Silicon Radio P55
Cambridge Soundworks, Inc.
(speakers) W180, W181
Cambridge Suites by Candlewood
(hotels) E169
Cambridge Technology Partners,
Inc. A1232
Cambridge, Thomas R. E260
Cambridge University Press P134
Camco International Inc. (drilling
services) A1252
Camden, Carl T. A819
Camden Graphics A146
Camden Yards stadium (New
Jersey) P576, P666
Camel cigarettes A492, A1204,
A1205, W240, W241, W304, W305
Camelo Martínez, Julio W441
Camelot Group plc
(lotteries) W154, W622
Camera, Nicholas J. A773
The Camera Shop P714
Cameron, Allan C. (General
Dynamics) A645
Cameron, Allan E. (Dana
Corporation) A461
Cameron Ashley Building Products,
Inc. P212, P565, P623
Cameron, Charles P40
Cameron, Edward D. E213
Cameron Forged Products A430
Cameron Iron Works (oil drilling
equipment) A430
Camerote, Mark A. A1101
CAMI Automotive W560
Camilleri, Louis C. A1127
Caminiti, Vincent F. A479
Camino Real tequila W109
Cammack, Randy P247
Cammaker, Sheldon I. A545
Cammarata, Bernard A1388, A1389
Cammarata, David J. E72, E218
Cammidge, John P457, P735
Camminton Technology P272
Camp Creek (activewear) A1220,
A1221
Camp Hyatt (children's
activities) A740, A741, P240,
P241, P636
Camp, Kenneth A. A719
Camp, Robert A1130
Camp, Walter P356
Camp, William H. A193
Campagna, Richard J. A1077
Campanaro, Gary C. E226
Campanaro, Leonard A. A195
Campbell, Christian L. A1405
Campbell, C. Keith P29
Campbell, David D. (Fortune
Brands) A619
Campbell, David W. (Iomega) A779
Campbell, Donald G. A1389

Campbell, Douglas C. W587
Campbell, Dugald K. A1394, A1395
Campbell, Eric B. P371
Campbell, G. Anthony A609
Campbell, George K. A615, P191
Campbell, James (DynCorp) P599
Campbell, James E. (Nucor) A1053
Campbell, J. Michael A921
Campbell, Joe (Associated Wholesale
Grocers) P63
Campbell, John (Anderson
News) P541
Campbell, John B. (Ag
Processing) P37
Campbell, John D. (American Red
Cross) P45, P538
Campbell, Joseph (Campbell
Soup) A316
Campbell, J. Patrick A997, P353
Campbell, Judith E. A1017, P371
Campbell, Keith M. P677
Campbell, Kermit A706
Campbell Kids A316
Campbell, Lewis B. A1380, A1381
Campbell, Michael H. (Continental
Airlines) A429
Campbell, Michael L. (Regal
Cinemas) P412, P413, P712
Campbell Red Lakes Mines W452,
W453
Campbell, Robert (Holman) P633
Campbell, Robert (Sunoco) A1344
Campbell, Robin D. A161
Campbell Soup
Company A**316**-A**317**, A426,
A466, A510, A1096, E143, P140,
W618
Campbell, Steven G. A1515
Campbell Taggart (baked
goods) A174
Campbell-Sell Baking A774
Campeau Corporation A586
Campeau, Robert P172
Camperdown Corporation A1237
Campmany, Domingo
Goenaga A643
Campo, Javier W165
Campos, Mauro Orofino W437
Campos Verdes body, hair, skin
care A487
Campsa (oil distribution) W482
Campto drug W103
Camptosar drug A1122
Campus Services book stores P192
Campus Solutions (software) A1098
Camry car W403, W614, W615
Camus, Philippe W331
Can Can Mine W452
Can Do canned foods A471
Canac kitchen and bath
cabinets P284, P285
Canada & Dominion Sugar
Company W568
Canada Cement Company A848
Canada Dry soft drink A382, A383,
A384, A385, A1102, A1103, A1105,
A1204, P597, P634, W154, W155
Canada Trust W608

Canadair A644, W132, W496
Canadair jets P534
Canadian Airlines International A164, W78, W518
Canadian Bank of Commerce W156
Canadian beer W377
Canadian Cablevision W494
Canadian Canners Limited A470
Canadian Club whiskey W85
Canadian Copper Company W284
Canadian Freightways, Limited A380, A420, A421
Canadian Imperial Bank of Commerce A342, W112, W114, **W156-W157**, W608
Canadian International Paper A770
Canadian LTD whiskey A423
Canadian Mist whiskey A296, A297
Canadian National Railway Company A308
Canadian Niagara Power Company Limited A1029
Canadian Occidental A1054
Canadian Pacific Railway Limited W284
Canadian Regional Jet W132
Canadian Sufferance Warehouses A420
Canadian Vickers W132
Canal Fox A623
Canales A873
CANAL+ W624, W625
CanalSatellite W330, W331, W624
Canandaigua Brands. *See* Constellation Brands, Inc.
Canavan, Beth O. A1385
C&C. *See* Castle & Cooke
C&D Technologies, Inc. A802, E169
Canderel artificial sweetener A984, A1122
Candie's fragrances A880
Candie's shoes E78
C&K Components A780
Candler, Asa A382
Candlestick Park, San Francisco CA A54
Candlewood Hotel Company, Inc. E169
Candlish, Malcolm P442
C&M Steel A396
C&N (tour company) P106
C&N Touristic. *See* Thomas Cook AG
C&S Choices stores A1410, P484, P749
C&S Wholesale Grocers, Inc. P**102-P103**, P565
Candy Land game A692
Canfield, Charles F. (oil driller) W440
Cangialosi, Loretta V. A1119
Canion, Joseph "Red" A398
Canja, Esther P29
Canji (gene therapy research) A1250
Cannataro, James A1315
Cannatelli, Vincenzo W215

Cannavino, James A1112
Cannella, Gina P659
Cannito, Peter A. P335
Cannon bedding and towels A1134, A1135, P696
Cannon, Charles H., Jr. A613
Cannon Electric A780
Cannon, Jan E304
Cannon, John H. (Venator) A1471
Cannon, John, III (CIGNA) A361
Cannon, Marc A207
Cannon, Michael R. A928, A929
Cannon, Robert P555
Cannon, Victor E52, E195
Cannon, W. Stephen A367
Cannondale (bicycles) W606, W607
canoe.com W470
Canon Inc. A524, A746, A747, A971, E189, E239, P137, W**158-W159**, W190, W191, W328, W358, W368, W392
Canova, Tony E166
CANPET Energy A1144
Canpotex Limited W67
Canstar Sports A1032
Cantalupo, James R. A943
Cantarella, Paolo W227
Canteen food services A86
Canteen Vending W174, W175
Cantel (telecommunications) W494
Canter, Kassie A999
Canter, Stephen E. A955
Canterbury Consulting Group, Inc. E**36**, E170
Cantor Fitzgerald, L.P. P565
Cantrell, Duane L. A1093
Cantrell, W. Alan A407
CANTV. *See* (Compañía) Anonima Nacional Telefonos de Venezuela
Canty, D. Peter E295
CanWest Global Communications W262
Canyon Resources A1124
Canyon River Blues brand A1265
Caorso nuclear plant W214
Cap Gemini Ernst & Young A562, E180, W**160-W161**, W222
Cap Gemini Group P182, P605
C.A.P. (software) W160
CAP Warehouse P113
Capatides, Michael W157
CAPCO Automotive Products A526
CAPCO Inc. P132, P192
Cape Cod Cranberry Company P380
Cape, Olwen B. A1071
Capek, John M. A675
Capell, Peter J. A649
Capellas, Michael D. A398, A399
Caperan, Loïc W209
Capezio brand A805
Capin Mercantile E60
Capistar stores A1312
Capital Airlines A1420
Capital Automotive REIT E170, P717
Capital Cities/ABC A252, A700, A720, A1496, P228

Capital Cities Communications A60
Capital Crossing Bank E170
Capital Financial Services A378
Capital Group International E300
Capital Holding. *See* Providian Financial Corporation
Capital One Financial Corporation A**318-A319**
Capital Pacific Holdings, Inc. E171
Capital Partners A928
Capital Research and Management Company A468
Capital Thrift & Loan E216
Capital Trust, Inc. A561, P181
Capital Valley Bank E216
Capital Z Partners (investments) E309
CapitalOnePlace.com A318
Capitan tequila A423
Capitol Bancorp Ltd. E171
Capitol Records W212, W213
Capizzi, Thomas A. E261
Caplan, Gary G. P335, P674
Caplan, Mitchell H. A567
Caple, Bill P754
Cap'n Crunch cereal A1106, A1107, A1180, A1181
Capote, Truman A1384
Capoten drug A290, A291
Capozide drug A291
Capozzi, Lou P73
Cappaert, Steven M. A1431
Cappiello, William A791
Capps Digital P73
Capps, Rick P73
Capps, Thomas E. A498, A499
Cappuccio, Paul T. A181
Capri cigarettes W143
Capri lighting P613
Capri Sun juice A843
Capri wines A423
Caprock Industries A325
Capsa (energy) A536
Capstar P350
Capstar Partners W130
Capstone Turbine Corporation E171, P510
Capsure Holdings A378
Captain Black tobacco W143
Captain D's quick-service seafood A1280, A1281
Captain Morgan rum W84
Captiva camera A1148
Capture carpet cleaning P343
Caputo, Louise P571
Car & Driver (magazine) W330
Caraballo, Malcolm J. E318
Caradine Hat P308
Caragajal, Esther E248
Carambar candy W155
Caramello candy A709
Carando breads and specialty meats P185
Carapelli foods A730
Carasso, Daniel W192
Carasso, Isaac W192

Caraustar Industries (building products) A1364
Caravella liqueurs A423
Caravelle commercial vehicle W631
Carbine guns P133
CarboGen Laboratories A1300
Carbonari, Bruce A. A619
Carbone, Anthony J. A505
Carbone, Richard J. A1173
Carbozulia, SA W439
Carburos Metalicos A100
CarCare P237
Carcelle, Yves W349
Card Capture Services, Inc. A566
Card, Larry J. P385
Card, Wesley R. A805
Cardani, Antonio W215
Cardarelli, Donald P. P39, P534
Cardarone drug A148
Cardean University P496
Cardell Corporation (automotive connectors) A982
Cardenas Cruz, Paulino W441
Cárdenas, Lázaro W440
Cardew & Company W340
Cardiac Assist Division of St. Jude Medical A444
Cardiac Pacemakers A674
Cardiac Rhythm Management Laboratory A674
Cardillo, James G. A1079
Cardillo, Salvatore W215
Cardinal beer W163
Cardinal Food Group A320, P422
Cardinal Health, Inc. A156, A236, A320-A321, A600, A1070, E240
Cardinal River Mine A417
Cardinale, Dora Braschi A919
CardioThoracic Systems A674
Cardiovascular Dynamics A674
Cardizem drug E156
Cardone Industries Inc. (automotive products) P113, P565
Cardone, Michael, Jr. P565
Cardone, Richard P689
Cardoso, Mário A. F. W225
Cardwell, J. A., Sr. "Jack" P701
Cardwell, Jim P701
Care Bears (cartoon characters) A146
Care Choices HMO P748
CARE (Cups Are REcyclable Program) P151
Care Free Homes A346
Care Management Resources A905
Career Education Corporation E172
CareerBuilder (online recruitment) A832, A1402
CareerPath.com A442, A832, P146
CareerStaff Unlimited, Inc. A1340, A1341
CareFlorida Health Systems A696
Care*Free gum A708
CareGroup, Inc. P566
Carel, Cecily P419, P717

Caremark Rx, Inc. A236, A322-A323, A1366, P84
CareNetwork (HMO) A738
Carey, Chase A623, W391
Carey, Dennis J. A725
Carey, Dorothy A. A1019, P375
Carey, Earl T. A599
Carey, James J. (Conseco) A415
Carey, Jim H. (CompuCom Systems) A401
Carey, J. Paul A1449
Carey, Kevin P. A1281
Carey, Mariah W212, W213
Carey, Michael J. A801
Carey, Ronald P246
Carey-McFall (window furnishings) A1316, P452
Cargile, Charles F. E253
Cargill AgHorizons A325
Cargill Animal Nutrition A325
Cargill, Austen S., II A325
Cargill, Inc. A96, A192, A324-A325, A426, A752, A834, A984, A1122, A1132, A1350, A1418, E227, P36, P104-P105, P122, P123, P140, P280, P565, P566, P653
Cargill, James A324, P104
Cargill, Sam A324, P104
Cargill, William S. A324, P104
Cargill, William W. A324, P104
Cargo Carriers A325, P105
Cargo Express housewares chain A796
Cargo Furniture stores A1130
Caribbean Classics beverage W109
Caribbean Ispat W292
Caride, Eduardo W579
Carilion Health System P566
Carita cosmetics W535
Caritas Christi Health Care System P56
Carl Domino Associates LP A1042
Carl, John L. A127
Carl Upmann cigars W283
Carl Zeiss (cameras and lenses) W328
Carless Refining & Marketing W482
Carli, Claudio W79
Carlile, Thomas E. A275
Carlin, Edward R. A667
Carlin, George A1020
Carlin Trend A1024
Carling beer W288, W289, W544, W552
Carling O'Keefe Breweries W230, W376
Carlino, Peter M. E262
Carlisle Companies, Inc. A326-A327, P310
Carlisle, Douglas R. A739
Carlisle Tire and Rubber Company A326
Carlo Rossi wine A520, A521, P168, P169, P600
Carlos, Chris P682
Carlos I brandy W85
Carlos, John A. P682

Carlos, Juan, King of Spain W650
Carlos Santana shoes A294
Carl's Jr. fast food A590
Carlsberg A/S W84, W162-W163, W289, W553
Carlsberg Brewery Hong Kong Ltd. W564
Carlson, Arleen P106
Carlson, Chester A1544, P70
Carlson Companies, Inc. A296, A328, P106-P107, P108, P567, W58
Carlson Craft (printing) P742
Carlson, Curtis (Carlson Companies) A328, P106, P567
Carlson, Curtis R. (SRI International) P455, P734
Carlson, Deborah A. A995
Carlson, James R. A1243
Carlson, Jeff A1047
Carlson, Jennie P. A1445
Carlson, John S. A1351
Carlson, LeRoy T. A1360, A1361
Carlson, LeRoy T., Jr. A1360, A1361
Carlson, Margaret P578
Carlson, Terrence L. A1111
Carlson Wagonlit Travel A328-A329, P106, P108-P109, P567, P776, W58, W59
Carlton & Smith Agency (advertising) W646
Carlton and United Breweries Proprietary W230, W231
Carlton Cards A146, A147
Carlton cigarettes W143
Carlton Communications W248, W620
Carlton House (New York City) P629
Carlton, William James W646
Carlucci, Frank C. (Carlyle Group) P110, P111, P567
Carlucci, Frank (Nortel) W412
Carlucci, Paul W391
The Carlyle Group A338, A612, A644, A1044, A1110, A1380, P68, P110-P111, P120, P548, P567, P597, P766, W154
Carlzon, Jan W518
Carma (insurance) W164
Carman, Stephen F. E320
Carman, Ted A913
Carman, Thomas W. A699
CarMax Group A366
Carmean, C. William A975
Carmen Sandiego software A926
Carmichael, David R. P385
Carmichael Lynch A772, A773
Carmichael, Scott P361
Carmola, John J. A663
Carmony, Robert F. P127
Carnahan, Karen L. A365
Carnaroli, Craig P759
Carnation W388
CarnaudMetalbox (packaging) A452
Carneal, Drew St. J. A1071
Carnegie, Andrew A1462

Carnegie Foundation for the Advancement of Teaching A1354, P466
Carnegie Steel A1462, A1550
Carnes, James E. P455
Carney, Brian P. A797
Carney, Christopher M. P557
Carney, Dan A1404
Carney, Frank A1404
Carney Hospital (Boston) P56
Carney, Jeffrey R. P191
Carney, Thomas D. A277
Carniaux, Bob A693
Carnival Corporation A**330**-A**331**, A1216, W434
Carnival Destiny (ship) A331
Carnival Food Stores P677
Carnival Spirit (ship) A331
Carnival Victory (ship) A331
Carnwath, Richard K. A1485
Caro Foods, Inc. A1109
Carol Cable Company A642
Carol, David J. P363
Carol Wire & Cable A214
Carolan, Doug P62
Carolco Pictures W448
Carolina Eastman Company A522
Carolina Fiber A1302
Carolina First Bank E291
Carolina Fleets (trucking) A1222
Carolina Golden Products P200
Carolina Hurricanes (hockey team) A406, P361
Carolina Medicorp P691
Carolina Panthers (football team) A86, P357
Carolina Power & Light A1166, A1167
Caroline Records W213
Carondelet Health System P568
Caronia (ship) A330, A331
Caroselli, John A. A219
Carp, Daniel A. A524, A525
Carpenter, Charles J. A155
Carpenter Company P568
Carpenter, David R. P753
Carpenter, Glenn L. E259
Carpenter, Jenny L. A467
Carpenter, John A. A717, P235
Carpenter, Michael A. A371
Carpenter Paper A770
Carpenter, R. Elliot E281
Carpenter, William M. A234
Carpentier, Elisabeth W547
Carpet Co-op Association of America P568
Carpet One stores P568
CARQUEST Corporation P**112**-P**113**, P569, P613
Carr, Cassandra C. A1245
Carr, J. Robert P29, P529
Carr, Michael A661
Carr, Robert B. A1207
Carrasco, Jorge A155
Carrefour SA A870, A1056, A1116, P593, W130, W**164**-W**165**

Carreker Corporation E172
Carreker, James A1540
Carreker, John D., Jr. "Denny" E172
Carreon, Michael R. A139
Carrera car W459
Carrera, Margaret E88
Carrera-MAXIMUS E88
Carreras, Jose P251
Carr-Gottstein Foods Company A1234
Carrico, Stephen J. P630
Carrier Access Corporation E172
Carrier, Carol P758
Carrier Corporation (HVAC) A1432, A1433, A1550
Carriere, Margaret A677
Carrig, John A. A1129
Carrig, Kenneth J. A1351
Carrington, Edward V. A705
Carrington-Chase brand P442, P443
Carrion, Esperanza P205
Carrizo Oil & Gas, Inc. E173
Carrizosa, Fernando A1489
Carroll, Charles P523, P775
Carroll County Foods A1109
Carroll, David (Horseshoe Gaming) P634
Carroll, David L. (LTV) A897
Carroll, David M. (Wachovia) A1487
Carroll, David W. (Lafarge) A849
Carroll, Jim P149
Carroll, Mary Beth A599
Carroll, Matt P69
Carroll McEntee & McGinley (securities) W268
Carroll, Philip A610
Carroll, Philip J., Jr. A610, A611
Carroll, Thomas A. A1553
Carroll, William J. A461
Carroll's Foods, Inc. A1290
Carrow, John C. A1425
Carrows restaurants A86
Carr's crackers A814, A815
Carruth, John Campbell "Cam" A1454
Carry vehicle W561
Carsey, Marcy P218
Grupo Carso Global Telecom S.A. de C.V. W580
Grupo Carso, S.A. de C.V. A1244
Carson, Charles G. A1463
Carson (ethnic beauty products) W342
Carson Group (investor relations) W592
Carson, Johnny A854
Carson Pirie Scott & Company (department stores) A1238
Carson, Randy W. A527
Carta Blanca rum W109
Carta, Giuseppe W215
CarTemps USA A206
Carter Automotive (fuel pumps) A584
Carter brand A585
Carter, Bruce E. P682

Carter, Calvin H., Jr. E47
Carter, Christopher A449
Carter, C. Michael A495
Carter, Daniel T. E176
Carter, Diane E. A997, P353, P682
Carter Hawley Hale A932, A1014
Carter Holt Harvey A770
Carter, Ian A265
Carter, Jay W. A899
Carter, Jerome N. A771
Carter, Jimmy A1380, P186
Carter, John (Bechtel) A241, P75
Carter, John (Moore) W378
Carter, Ken W. P718
Carter, Larry R. A369
Carter, Marshall N. A1332
Carter, Martin W411
Carter, Mary Ann P115
Carter, Matthew E. A1105
Carter, Pamela F. A457
Carter, Paul (Foster Farms) P610
Carter, Paul R. (Wal-Mart) A1495
Carter, Rebecca C. A553
Carter, Robert B. A589
Carter, Sandra J. P85
Carter, Stephen J. (Imation) A751
Carter, Stephen M. (Cingular Wireless) P576
Carter, Terry P710
Carter, Vince P251
Carter, William H. P91, P558
Carter's brand A839
Carter-Wallace, Inc. A358
Cartmill, Colleen E208
Cartographic and Information Services P408
Carton, Bernard W547
Cartoon Network A180
Cartoonbank.com A81, P33
Cartwright, Carolyn A1347
Cartwright Williams (marketing) P73
Carty, Donald J. A164, A165
Carty, Douglas A. E32, E160
Carusello, Mike P596
Caruso, Joseph A. P215
Caruso, Nick J. A1277
Carver P92
Carvette, Anthony P737
Carville, James P661
Carvin, Joseph W. A1177
CASA W70
Casa Ley A1234
Casado, Francisco W635
Casal, Carolina P204
Casale, Carl A985
Casale, Karen P770
Casalee Group (tobacco processor) A1436
Casas Guzmán, Francisco W441
Casazza, William J. A91
Cascade dishwashing product A1164, A1165
Cascade Imperial Mills P690
Cascade Lumber Company A274

Cascadian Farms organic
foods A649
Casco Nobel A1152
Case (agricultural
equipment) W226, W227
Case Dunlop (marketing) A1063
Case, Edward R. A195
Case, John J. A855
Case New Holland. *See* CNH Global
Case, Stephen M. (AOL Time
Warner) A180, A181
Case, Steven K. (CyberOptics) E48,
E189
Case Technologies A1372
Case, Weldon A128
Casein (glue) P90
Casey, Don L. (Pep Boys) A1101
Casey, Donnis L. (A.G.
Edwards) A95
Casey, Gregory M. A1187
Casey, Jim A1426
Casey, John M. A1373
Casey, Julianna P115
Casey, Katie P47, P539
Casey, Mary Beth P73
Casey, Michael A1327
Cash America (pawnshop) E27
Cash and Carry warehouse
stores P488
Cash Flurries lottery game P373
Cash in Hand lottery game P666
Cash Management Account A230
Cash, Marta E239
Cash, Roberta P678
Cash Saver stores P62, P63
Cashword lottery game P675
Casino Guichard-
Perrachon W166-W167
Casino Magic Bay St. Louis
(Mississippi) E262
Casino Nova Scotia-Halifax A1087
Casino Rouge Riverboat
(Louisiana) E262
Casino Windsor A1087
CASIO COMPUTER CO., LTD. A170,
W168-W169
Casio, Inc. W603
Cason, Marsden P143
Casper, Gerhard P456
Caspers, Freddy W477
Caspersen, Curt A. A595
Caspian Oil Company W346
Cassard, Christopher D. P690
Cassava chips P204
Cassel, Sandy E274
Cassidy, Frank A1175
Cassidy, Henry J. A627
Cassidy, John F. A293, A1433
CASSIOPEIA handheld PC W168
Cassis, Jeffrey A. E35
Cassutt, Mark P263
Castagna, Eugene A. A247
Castagna, Vanessa A791
Castaigne, Robert W613
Castañer, Francisco W389
Casteen, John T., III P761
Castella cigars W283

Castella, José C. C. W225
Castellani, Frederick C. A923, P321
Castelli, Michael J. A151
Castelli (office furniture) P222
Castellini, Clateo A245
Castellini, Daniel J. A569
Caster cigarettes W304, W305
Castillo del Barrio
supermarkets W498
Castillo, Richard A. E256
Castillo rum W109
Casting Service A116
Castle & Cooke, Inc. A494
Castle beer W552
Castle Computing P338
Castle Creek A280
Castle Energy Corporation E201
Castle, Samuel A494
Castleberry, Michael P622
Castonguay, Brenda A1167
Castonguay, Maurice L. E237
Castorama-Dubois Investissements
(do-it-yourself stores) W312,
W313, W376
Castro, Fidel W108
Castro, Manuel, Sr. A1407
Castrol oil W136
Casual Corner Group, Inc.
(stores) P713
Caswell, Peter M. E25, E149
Catacosinos, William A824
Catalano, Michael E153
Cataligent (consulting) P55
Catalina Marketing A66
A Catalog for Cooks A1530
Catalyst Semiconductor, Inc. E173
Catalyst Telecom E118
Catalyst test A1373
Catamount Dairy Holdings P38
Catawba Power Company A514
Catell, Robert B. A824, A825
Catelli pasta P91
Catellus Development
Corporation E37, E173
Caterair International P110
Caterpillar China Investment
Company Ltd. A332
Caterpillar Inc. A332-A333, A546,
A584, A612, A1078, P590, P600,
W320, W538
Cates pickles A467
Cathay Pacific Airways Ltd. A164,
W140, W268, W540, W564, W565
Cathcart, Silas A748
Cathcart, W. Alun W472, W473
Cathelineau, André W233
Catherwood, Johnathon F. A1511
Catheter Innovations A282
Catholic Charities USA P492, P493,
P755
Catholic Health Association P115
Catholic Health Corporation of
Omaha P116, P569
Catholic Health East P114-P115,
P116, P569
Catholic Health Initiatives P114,
P116-P117, P569

Catholic Health Ministries P748
Catholic Health System (Buffalo,
NY) P115
Catholic Healthcare Audit
Network P116
Catholic Healthcare Network P570
Catholic Healthcare Partners P570
Catholic Healthcare West P56,
P118-P119, P570, P753
Catholic Managed Care
Consortium P115
Catholic Relief Services P56
Cathy, Dan T. P124, P125
Cathy, Donald M. P125
Cathy, S. Truett P124, P125, P575
Cativen W167
Catmull, Edwin E. E103
Catsimatidis, John A. P712
Catsoulis, Elizabeth E167
Catt, Lynn E155
CattleInfoNet.com E197
Catucci, William V. A559
Caudill, Edward B. A1079
Causey, Richard A. A553
Cauz, Jorge P177
Cavalier, Lynn M. A599
Cavalier, Michael P127
Cavallaro, Rosanna W495
Cavallero, Michael J. A495
Cavanaugh, Andrew J. A565
Cavanaugh, Daniel A965
Cavanaugh, Robert B. A791
Cavanaugh, Steven M. A909
Cavanaugh, William, III A1167
Cavanna, Anthony J. E305
Cavarra, Mary K. A757, P245
Cavco Industries, LLC
(manufactured homes) A340
Caviar hard drives A1515
Cawdron, Peter E. B. W175
Cawley, Charles M. A936, A937
Caxton-Iseman Capital P562
Cayenne SUV W458
Cayne, James E. A238, A239
Cayuga Bank E205
Cazalot, Clarence P., Jr. A1461
CB Richard Ellis Services,
Inc. P120-P121, P571
CBE Technologies E280
CBRE Stewardship P121
CBS Records W550
CBS Telenoticias P80
CBS Television Network A60,
A334-A335, A390, A546, A884,
A918, A948, A998, A1192, A1408,
A1476, A1477, A1496, P80, P178,
P218, P326, P356, P681, W536
C. C. Butt Grocery P224
CC Industries P621
CC&S. *See* Crown Cork & Seal
Company
CCI-MAXIMUS E88, E238
CCI/Triad Systems Corporation
(computer systems) P233
CCM International Ltd. A438
C-Cube Microsystems Inc. A894

C. D. Kenny Company (coffee, tea, and sugar) A1242
C.D. Smith Healthcare, Inc. A155
CDB Infotek A558
CDC. *See* Control Data Corporation
C-Dilla (CD-ROM copy protection) E235
CDiscount.com W166
CDME (electrical equipment) W446
CDnow P579, W126, W127
CD-ROM WAREHOUSE (catalogs) P338
CDW Computer Centers, Inc. **A336-A337**
CEAG electrical products A431
CEA-Industrie W554
Ceanothe Holdings (picture frames) A1022
Cearlock, Dennis B. P71
Cebema (publishing) W626
Cebra Inc. W113
Cece, Sam E33
Cecere, Andrew A1445
Cecil, Joe D. A1439
Cecillion, J. F. W527
CeCorr (corrugated sheets) A654
Cedax drug A1250, A1251
Cederberg, Barbara M. A751
Cederroth International A108
CEDIS (retailer) W166
Cedric car W403
Cedrone, Nicholas E44
Cefalo, Romeo R. A111
Cefiro car W403
Cefobid drug A1118
Cegelec (engineering) W76
Cegetel (telecommunications) W352, W624
Cegos Informatique W100
CEI Citicorp Holding A715, P233
Cela, José W653
Celanese A100
Celballos Soberanis, José A. W441
Çelebican, Kutsan W319
Celebration (ship) A331
Celebrex drug A984, A1119, A1122
Celebrity Cruises A1216
Celentano, Eugene G. A1377
Celera Genomics Group P542
Celeritas Technologies A1210
Celerity loop qualification A1373
Celeron microprocessor A760, A1002
Celeron Oil A664
Celerra software A543
Celestica A1240, A1298, E206, E226, E237
Celey, Floyd P318
Celgene Corporation E174
Celica car W614, W615
Celine fashions W348
Cella, Frank W389
Cella wines A296
Cellarmaster Wines (wine club) W230
Cellco Partnership A1473, W629

Cellnet A1252, W628
Cellular Communications International W352
Cellular Communications of Puerto Rico W580
Cellular One E245
Cellular Telecommunications Industry Association A1182
Celluvisc ophthalmic products A119
Celoni, Daniel L. A401
Celsius W460
Cemax-Icon (medical imaging) A750
CEMIG. *See* (Companhia) Energetica de Minas Gerais
Cendant Corporation A212, **A338-A339**, A562, A872, A873, W222, W624
Cendoya Mendez de Vigo, Juan Mañuel W513
Ceneca Communications (Web toolmaker) A76
Cenergy (petroleum) A340
Cenex Harvest States Cooperatives A582, A583, A850, P**122-P123**, P184, P185, P288, P571, P572
CENIT Bancorp A1308
CENTEC A256
Centel Corporation A1318
Centennial Communications Corporation **E38**, E174
Center for Biomedical Ethics P457
Center for Computer Research in Music and Acoustics P457
Center for Elephant Conservation P188
Center for Folklife Programs and Cultural Heritage P451
Center for Human Genetics P560
Center for Integrated Facilities Engineering P457
Center for International Legal Studies P194
Center for Space Physics P560
Center for the Study of Language and Information P457
Centerior Energy Corporation A598
Centerman, Jörgen W54, W55
Centerpiece paper products P727
Centers for Disease Control and Prevention W102
Centex Corporation **A340-A341**, A549
Centex Homes A508, A1178
Centigram Communications Corporation A70
Centillium Communications, Inc. E174
Centipede (video game) W527
Centocor drug A800, A1250
Central and South West utility holding company A140
Central Area Power Coordination Group A598
Central Arizona Light & Power A1138

Central Arkansas Provider Network, Inc. A695
Central Artery Tunnel (Boston) P678, P696
Central Carolina Power A1166
Central Farmers Fertilizer Company P572
Central Finance A734
Central Florida Division Practice, Inc. A695
Central Guaranty Trust W608
Central Hockey League P361
Central Holding W92
Central Homes A604
Central Illinois Public Service A136
Central Market P224, P225, P627
Central Mississippi Manufactured Housing A346
Central National-Gottesman Inc. P571
Central National Life Insurance Company P174
Central Newspapers, Inc. A632
Central New York Power Corporation A1028
Central Pacific Railroad A1422, P384, P456
Central Power and Light Company A1198
Central States Indemnity (credit insurance) A252
Central Tennessee Hospital Corporation A695
Central Tractor Farm & Country P406, P709
Centrala Produktow Naftowych W456
Centre Capital (investments) P350
Centre National d'Etudes des Télécommunications W232
Centre Partners (buyout firm) E116, E283
Centrefile (payroll processing) A343
Centrewrite Ltd. (insurance) W337
Centric Group P178, P603
Centric Software, Inc. A837, P283
Centrica plc A310, A1266
CENTRICITEE ceiling grid A1457
Centrilift (submersible pumps) A223
Centriplex (storage) A542
Centro Elettrotecnico Sperimetale Italiano W215
Centro Nazionale de Controllo W214
Centrum Communications A54
Centrum department stores W310
Centrum multivitamin A148, A149
Centura Banks of North Carolina W474
Centura Software A406
Centurion Furniture A854
Century 21 (real estate) A86, A338, A964, P692
Century cigarettes A1204, A1205
Century Communications (cable TV) A72, E38
Century (cruise ship) A1217

Century of Progress
Exposition P448
Century Products P518
Century Telephone A1082
Century Title Agency, Inc. A508,
A509
CenturyTel, Inc.
(telecommunications) A128,
A1082
Ceppos, Jerry A833
Cepravin drug A1251
Cepsa (oil refiner) W482
Ceradyne, Inc. E175
Cerchiai, Fabio W99
Cereal Partners Worldwide A648,
W388
Cerent (fiber-optic network
equipment) A368
Ceres Fruit Juices W552
Ceres Group, Inc. E175
Ceres Integrated Solutions A1012
Cerestar P104
Cereti, Fausto W79
Cerezo Pérez, Adolfo W581
Ceridian Corporation A342-A343,
A644, W608
Cernugel, William J. A109
Cerny, Gary M. A1199
Cerprobe Corporation E81
Cerro Corporation P312
Cerro Metal Products
Company P313
Cerro Negro P386
Cerrone, Stephen A303
Cerrudo, Maraget M. A1245
CertainTeed (building
materials) W506
Certegy A558
Certified Grocers of
California P488, P752
Certified Systems (payroll
processing) A1272
Certina watch W563
Certs breath mint A1118
Cerulean Companies, Inc. A1506,
A1507, P572
Compañía Cervecarías Unidas
S.A. A174
Cervino, Paul M. E26, E151
Cesar pet food A915, P315
Cescau, Patrick J. W619
CESI SpA (research) W215
Cesky Telecom W502, W503
Cessna Aircraft A644, A1380
Cestaro, David A305
CET (electric utility) A1198
Cetec (audio equipment) P310
Cetlin, Joan E252
Cetnar, Krzysztof Piotr W457
Cetti, Carlo E. A785
CF AirFreight A380, A420, A421
CF Industries, Inc. P572, P622
CF MotorFreight A380, A420
C.F. Property Managment
Company A593
CF&I Steel A446
CFAO (distributor) W446, W447

CFIHC, Inc. A415
CFM International, Inc. P572
CFRB radio station W494
CFS Continental (food
distribution) A1350
CFW Communications. See
NTELOS Inc.
CG&E. See The Cincinnati Gas &
Electric Company
CGC. See ContiGroup Companies
CGE. See (Compagnie) Générale
d'Électricité SA
CGI Equities P126
CGI Group P154, W196
CGNU plc A688
CGR (medical equipment) A646
CH Energy Group, Inc. A518
C.H. Masland & Sons (automotive
carpet) A306
CH Mortgage Company A509
C.H. Patrick (textiles) A1400
C.H. Robinson, Inc. (produce
brokerage) A994
C.H. Robinson Worldwide,
Inc. A344-A345
CH2M Hill Companies, Ltd. P573
Cha Chi-Soo W275
Chabraja, Nicholas D. A644, A645
Chacon, Humberto E121, E288
Chaddick, Steve W. E41
Chaden, Lee A. A1243
Chadwick, Rod W428
Chadwick's of-Boston (catalog
sales) A1388
Chaffin, G. Patrick E291
Chafkin, Jeremiah H. A349
Chai, Jay W. W295
Chaifetz, David H. A1157
Chain Level Trading Areas A67
Chaine, Jacques W182
Chairmans ESB beer W553
Chait, Ben P198
Chalifoux, Michael T. A367
Chalker, John R. P309
Challenger 600 jet W132
Challenger brand A527
Chamberlain Group keyless entry
systems P598
Chamberlain, Wilt P354
Chambers, Anne Cox A442, P146
Chambers catalogs A1530, A1531
Chambers Development
Corporation A1504
Chambers, Edward P770
Chambers, Elizabeth G. A1193
Chambers, Herbert G. P631
Chambers, Jeff P431, P721
Chambers, John T. A368, A369
Chambers, Lamar M. A201
Chambliss, Darrell W. E139
Chambolle, Thierry W559
Chameleon kiosks E301
Chamillard, George W. A1372,
A1373
Champ, Joseph A1541
Champagne, Kevin G. E285
Champagne, Paul T. A1155

Champagne Perrier-Jouet W84
Champeaux, Jacques W233
Champion athletic wear A1242,
A1243
Champion auto parts A585
Champion batteries W428
Champion Enterprises,
Inc. A346-A347, A604, E60
Champion International
Corporation (paper) A770
Champion, John L. E170
Champion Laboratories P752
Champion Mortgage A822
Champion Spark Plug A430
Champion supermarkets W164,
W165
Champion tobacco W283
Champions Choice A325
Championship Auto Racing
Teams P390
Champlain & St. Lawrence
(railroad) W112
Champley, Michael E. A513
Champness, Jerilyn A885
Champs Sports stores A1470, E99,
E257
CHAMPUS A696, A1080, P52, P174
Champy, James A1113
Chan, Chiu Moon E195
Chan, Lilian W565
Chan, L. L. A133
Chan, Nelson E117
Chan, Philip E195
Chan, Timothy P381, P692
Chance, David W146
Chance Vought Corporation
(airplanes) A896, A1432
Chancellor, Christopher A284
Chancellor Media (radio) A714,
P232
Chandeleur Homes, Inc. A346,
A347
Chandler, Harry A1402
Chandler Hill clothing A666
Chandler, J. Harold A1440, A1441
Chandler, Jim A757, P245
Chandler, John T. A559
Chandler Medical Center P757
Chandler, Michael E. A645
The Chandler Trust A1402
Chandra, Ashok K. E134
Chandra, Kim E184
Chandran, Robert V. P574
Chanel A564
Chaney, J. Wesley A605
Chaney, William R. A1384, A1385
Chang, Diane A63
Chang, Erh-Hsun W339
Chang, JoMei E313
Chang, Karen W. A349
Chang, Lily S. E25
Chang, Paul Ker-Chin E296
Chang Soo Kim W335
Change Your Life TV P218
ChangeMan software E286
Chango, Ronald F. A257
Channel 5 W621

Channel, Karen P624
Channel Management Application
 Suite software E180
Channel One Network A1160,
 A1161, P460, P653
Channel Tunnel. *See* Chunnel
ChannelMax E118
Channelview petrochemical
 complex A900
Channon, Gordon W177
Chao, Elaine P492
Chao, Stephen A1451
Chapela Castañares, Gustavo W441
Chapelle Darblay (paper) W446
Chaplin, Harvey P732
Chapman, Byrne W. P43
Chapman, Clare W591
Chapman Drug Company A320
Chapman, Fay L. A1501
Chapman Hall Center for Children
 and the Laborartory
 Schools P497
Chapman, John B. A1115, P397,
 P701
Chapman, Thomas F. A559
Chapman, William P239, P636
Chapman-Pincher, Pat A1535
Chappel Brothers A914, P314
Chappell, Robert E. P698
Chappie pet food A915, P315
Chapple, Thomas L. A633
Chaps by Ralph Lauren A1150,
 A1498, A1499
Charaf, Anthony N. A479
Chareton W164
Charger Inc. (trucking) A788
Chargeurs W146
Charisma bedding and
 towels A1135
Charles de Gaulle Airport
 (Paris) W68, W134
Charles E. Smith Residential Realty,
 Inc. E137, E175, E314
Charles II, King of England W270
Charles Pankow Builders, Ltd. P573
Charles Pfizer Company A428,
 A1118
Charles, Prince of Wales W244
Charles River Data Systems A170
Charles River Laboratories
 International, Inc. A234
Charles, Saul P254
The Charles Schwab
 Corporation A228, **A348-A349**,
 A566, A614, A960, E70, E245,
 P190, W608
Charles Schwab Tokio Marine
 Securities W596, W597
Charles Town Entertainment
 Complex (West Virginia) E262
Charles Volner champagne W109
Charlesbank Equity Fund IV P628
Charleston Consolidated Railway,
 Gas and Electric Company A1248
Charleston Electric Light
 Company A1248
Charleston Gas Light
 Company A1248

Charlie Brown (cartoon
 character) A568
Charlie Chalk Fun Factories W638
Charlie fragrance A1200, A1201
Charlie's Angels (TV show) A60
Charlotte Hornets (basketball
 team) P355
The Charlotte (North Carolina)
 Observer A833
Charlotte Russe Holding, Inc. E176
Charlotte Sting (basketball
 team) P355
Charlotte's Room stores E176
Charlson, Alan E. A933
Charlson Broadcast
 Technologies E40
Charlton, R. Scott A1177
Char-Lynn A527
Charm Tred Mills A306
Charmer Industries, Inc. P738
Charmin Paper Mills A1164, A1165
Charming Shoppes, Inc. A876
Charrington United
 (brewery) W544
Charron, Paul R. A880, A881
Chart House Enterprises, Inc.
 (restaurants) A561, P181
Charter Behavioral
 Corporation A904, A905
Charter Club brand clothing A587
Charter Collection clothing A852
Charter Communications Inc.
 (cable TV systems) **A350-A351**,
 A1258, E158, P510, P511
Charter Financial A1508
Charter House retirement
 community (Rochester, NY) P325
Charter Mac. *See* Charter Municipal
 Mortgage Acceptance Company
Charter Medical A904
Charter Municipal Mortgage
 Acceptance Company E176
Charter Mutual Benefit Health &
 Accident Association P348
Charter Oak Capital
 Management A922
Charter School USA P279
Charterhouse Securities W286
Charters (food services) W175
Chartwell Investments A806
Chartwell Land W313
Chartwells (food services) W174,
 W175
Chase & Sanborn coffee A1243
Chase Capital Partners P250
Chase, Jacqueline A. A751
Chase Limogere sparkling
 wines A423
The Chase Manhattan Bank A809
Chase Manhattan Capital A1084
Chase Manhattan
 Corporation A220, A238, A474,
 A626, A808, A1146, A1172, W88.
 See also J.P. Morgan Chase &
 Company
Chase Manhattan Corporation
 building (New York) P449
Chase, Mike A521, P169, P600

Chase National Bank A448
Chase, Rodney F. W137
Chase, Ron P621
Chase, Salmon A808
Chase, Walter P480
Chase-Pitkin Home & Garden
 Centers P771
Chastelet, Gerry E192
Château d'Yqem winery W348
Chateau Latour winery W430
Chateau Ste. Michelle wine A1458,
 A1459
Chateau St. Jean wines W231
Chatel, Marc P584
Chatlain, Dean F. A795
Chatterjee, Nirmal A101
Chatwinds Group E279
Chau, Micheline P303, P661
Chaubin, Alden J., Jr. E55
Chaudhri, M. Javade A637
Chaudhuri, Asok K. A455
Chaukar, Kishor W567
Chaumet watches W348
Groupe Chauvin A234
Chauvin, Jacques W209
Chavannes, Marc A1262
Chavez, Hugo W438
Chavez, Lloyd G. P563
Chavez-Thompson, Linda P35
Chay Kwong Soon W180
Chazen, Jerome A880
Chazen, Stephen I. A1055
Cheap Tickets, Inc. A338
Cheaper Liquor stores W644, W645
Cheatham, Owen A654
Checchi, Alfred A1046
Check Point Software Technologies
 Ltd. A176, E96, E251
Checker, Chubby P188
Checkerboard animal feeds A324,
 P104
Checkfree A438
CheckOut Entertainment
 Network P524
CheckOut.com P777
Cheek, Michael V. A297
Cheer laundry product A1165
Cheerios A648, A649
Cheers (TV show) A998
Cheetah disk drive P441
Cheetos snacks A1107
Cheez Whiz A843
Cheez-It crackers A814, A815, A816
Chef Boyardee Quality Foods A148,
 A408, A409, A714, A232
Chef Francisco soups A723
Cheffins, John W497
Chef's Catalog A1014, A1015
Chef's Choice brands P393
Chef's Express food A1491, P515,
 P768
Chef's Orchid (airline
 catering) A440
Chef-way oil and shortening P714
Chehayl, Peter W. E38, E174
Cheil Communications, Inc.
 (advertising) W509

Cheil Industries Inc.
(textiles) W509
Cheil Sugar Company W508
Chelberg, Bruce A1104
Chell, Beverly C. A1161
Chellgren, Paul W. A200, A201
*Chelsea - The Official
Magazine* W239
Chelsea Products A460
Chelsea (soccer team) W238
CHEMCENTRAL Corporation P573
ChemConnect, Inc. A1156
Chemdal International W116
Chemetron W116
Chemfab (polymenrs) W506
Chemical Bank A808, A1146
Chemical Process Company A278
Chemical Waste
Management A1504
Chemie Linz W424
Gesellschaft für Chemische
Industrie Basel W414
Chemische Werke Hüls W218
ChemLawn (lawn care) A530,
A1272
Chemline Industries A194
Chem-Nuclear Systems A1504
Chemoil Corporation P574
Chemplex Australia Limited P238
Chemstrand (synthetic fiber) A984,
A1122, A1300
Chemurgic Corporation A786
Chen, C. H. E192
Chen, James L. M. A489
Chen, Lincoln C. P415
Chen, Mabel F. A575
Chen, Winston A1298
Chenault, Kenneth I. A142, A143
Chenevert, William J. A909
Chenevich, William L. A1445
Cheney, Dick A676, A952
Cheney, Jeffery P. P285, P653
Cheney, Philip W. A1191
Cheng, K. C. A103
Cheng Lock, Tun Tan W538
Chenille carpets A980
Cheong Chan (food) A316
Cheong Choong Kong W541
Cheplin Biological Labs A290
Chernin, Peter A623, W391
Chernobyl nuclear plant A240, P74,
P552, W214
Chernomyrdin, Viktor W242
Chero-Cola soft drink A1400
Cherokee Cream Company A510
Cherry, Dean E. W379
Cherry, James C. A1487
Cherry, Joseph A. A445
Cherry, Neil P65
Cherry, Wendell A738
Chesapeake & Ohio (railroad) A454
Chesapeake Corporation A1364
Chesapeake Energy
Corporation E39, E176
Chesapeake Paper Products A498,
A654
Chesapeake Publishing A1502

Chesapeake Utilities
Corporation E177
Chesebrough-Ponds skin and beauty
aids W618
Cheshire data systems W355
Cheshire, Ian W313
Cheskin, Steve P159
Chesko, John T. A955
Chesney, Alan P760
Chesney, Michael K. A1361
Chess King clothing store A458
Chesser, Leicle E. A545
Chesser, Michael J. A669
Chessie System (railroad) A454
Chester, E. B. E310
Chester Fried Chicken P623
Chester, Kay E310
Chesterfield cigarettes A1126
Chestnut, James E. A383
Chestnut, Kathie T. A1511
Cheung, Cassian K. S. A1181
Cheung, Derek A1211
Cheung Kong Infrastructure
Holdings Limited A1082, W268,
W272, W273
Cheval Ordex (office
products) A210
Chevalier, Alain W348
Chevalier, Jacques W151
Chevallier, Jean A1253
Chevassus, Jerry P411
Chevrolet A650, P92, P308, P366,
P390, P555, P596, P606, P656,
P687, P706, P717, P733
Chevrolet, Louis A650
Chevron Corporation A352-A353,
A518, A538, A984, A1054, A1096,
A1122, A1128, A1144, A1344,
A1376, A1377, W280, W346,
W500. *See also* ChevronTexaco
Chevron Phillips Chemical
Company LP A352, A1128, P574
ChevronTexaco E208, P345, P416,
P418, P574, P604, P630, P679,
P717, W94. *See also* Chevron
Corporation *and* Texaco Inc.
Chevy Chase Bank, F.S.B. P574
Chevy Luv truck W294
Chevy Nova P366
Chew, Albert E., III P131, P577
Chew Choon Seng W541
Chew, Dan A869
Chew, Lewis A1003
Chew, S. B. A573
Chewens, Michael J. E250
Chewning, Thomas N. A499
Chex cereal A649
Chex Mix snack food A648
Chex-Systems (account
verification) A480
Cheyenne Light, Fuel & Power
Company A1542, A1543
Cheyenne Software, Inc. (network
management) A402
CHFI radio station W494
CHI. *See* Catholic Health Initiatives
Chiapetta, Robert P540
Chiapetta, Susan S. P684

Chiarolanza, Biagio W125
Chiasson, William B. A869, P293,
P657
Chiat, Jay A1062
Chiat/Day (advertising) A1062
Chiba, Masato W387
Chibuku beer W553
Chic jeans A1474, A1475
Chicago & Alton (railroad) A1422
Chicago and North Western
Railway A412
Chicago and Southern
Airlines A478
Chicago Bears Football Club,
Inc. P356, P357
Chicago Beverage Systems P713
Chicago Blackhawks (hockey
team) P361, P774
Chicago Board of Exchange E249
Chicago Board Options
Exchange P46, P539
Chicago Bridge & Iron Company,
N.V. A1156
Chicago Brothers Pizza P436
Chicago Bulls (basketball
team) P355, P774
Chicago, Burlington & Quincy
(railroad) A308
Chicago Corporation A1368
Chicago Cubs (baseball
team) A1402, A1403, A1526, P307
Chicago Cutlery P91, P775
Chicago Directory Company A1218
Chicago Group (newspapers) W263
Chicago Laser Systems E56
Chicago Medical College P378
Chicago Pacific (furniture) A934
Chicago Research & Training A226
Chicago Stockyards A638
Chicago Style Pizza P623
Chicago Sun-Times A1408, P482,
W262, W263, W390
Chicago Title and Trust A590, A878
Chicago Title Corporation A590,
A591
Chicago Town pizza P436, P437
Chicago Tribune A1402, P88, P378,
P408
Chicago White Sox Ltd. (baseball
team) P306, P307
Chi-Chi's Mexican Food A731,
A784, P110
Chicken McNuggets A942, P650
Chicken Run (movie) P124, P166,
P167
Chick-fil-A Inc. P124-P125, P575,
P669
Chico Pardo, Jaime W581
Chicopee Manufacturing
(gauze) A800
Chico's FAS, Inc. E177
Chico's Outlet stores E177
Chico-San foods A1180
Chida, Hideo W315
Chidsey, John W. A339
Chidsey, Peter P139
Chief Auto Parts A208
Chieftain International P635

Chieger, Kathryn J. A299
Chiel, Jonathan A799
Chien, Chester Lin A1299
Chihaya, Akira W399
Chikasha Cotton Oil Company W603
Chila, Dan A. E295
Child Guidance toys E225
Child World stores A1396
Childers, Charles W413
Children's Discovery Centers P278
Children's Health Matters P115
The Children's Place Retail Stores, Inc. E177
Children's Supermart A1396
Children's World Learning Centers A190, A191
Childs, David M. P448
Chili's Grill & Bar A288, A289
Chillemi, Diane E231
Chilquinta Energia A1174
Chilton (credit) A278
Société Chiminique des Usines du Rhône W102
China Airlines E32, E160
China Coast restaurants A464
China Comfort (travel agency) P418
China Computer Reseller World (magazine) P248
China Construction Bank A988
China Eastern Airlines A164
China Industrial Exchange A674
China International Trust & Investment W272
China Martini liqueur W109
China Merchants Shekou Port Service A1398
China Mobile (Hong Kong) Limited W628
China National Aerotechnology Import and Export Corporation W338
China National Oil & Gas Exploration & Development A184
China Navigation Company W564
China Petroleum & Chemical Corporation W542
China Resources Snowflake Brewery W314
China Securities Investment Trust W268
China Southern Airlines Company Limited A478, E32, W71
China Telecom W152
China Unicom Limited A1182
Chindex A674
Ching, David T. A1235
Chinn, Neil E272
Chinni, Charles A791
Chinnici, Joseph R. E41, E179
ChipCenter A196, A214, A1140
Chipcom Corporation A54
Chiplogic A170
Chipotle Mexican Grill A942, A943
Chipperfield, Lynn A631
Chippewa Logging A756, P244

Chips Ahoy! cookies A814, A842, A843
Chips Deluxe cookies A815, A816
Chiquet, Maureen A635
Chiquita Brands International, Inc. A144, A145, A354-A355, A494, A632
Chiron (biotech) W118, W414
Chiron (vision) A234
Chisholm Manufacturing (meat processing) W644
Chisholm, Sam W146
Chittenden Corporation E178
Chitwood, James L. A523
Chitwood, Noel L. A855
Chivas Regal liquor W315
Chivo dairy A467
Chiyoda Kogaku Seiko (Optics and Fine Engineering) A676, W368
Chiyoda Mutual Life Insurance Company A150
Chizen, Bruce R. A76, A77
Chlada, John P393
Chloe W251
Chloride (batteries) W428
Chlor-Trimeton drug A1250, A1251
Chmara, Harold J. W271
CHO Energy W215
Cho, Fujio W614, W615
Cho, Kendall P689
Choate, Chris A. E27
Choate, Jerry A126
Chock full o'Nuts Corporation (coffee) A1242
Chocolate Kisses A708
Chodron de Courcel, Georges W131
Choël, Patrick W349
Choi Kwang-Woong W455
Choi Sung-Rai W509
Choi, Y. M. W275
Choice Ride insurance program A1452, P502
ChoiceCare/Humana Cincinnati A739
Choicelinx A574
Choicepoint (insurance services) A558
Chokel, Charles A415
Chokey, James A. A807
Choksi, Sureel A. A867
Choppin, S. Walker E153
Choquette, Paul J., Jr. P615
Chorengel, Bernd A741, P241
Chorus Communications (telephone service) A1360
Chou, Rebecca P740
Chou, Silas K. F. W606, W607
Chouinard, Marc W271
Chow, Dean P721
Chow, Joseph W. A1333
Chow, Peter T. C. A1455
Chow, Ricky P662
Chow Woo, Susan M. F. W273
Chowdry, Michael E32, E160
CHR. *See* C.H. Robinson Worldwide, Inc.
Chrenc, Robert J. A67

Chris-Craft Industries, Inc. A622, A1476, W390
Christ, Chris T. P521
Christ, William F. A709
Christal, Nancy R. A459
Christenbury, Edward S. A1371, P469
Christensen, Mariann S. W417
Christensen, Paul S. A1069
Christensen, Ralph N. A679, P217, P625
Christensen, Roy A258
Christenson, Arne L. A581
Christenson, Gary P698
Christenson, James E. A707
Christenson, Ronald L. A325, P105
Christian Dior brands A804, W348
Christian Hansen Holding A450
Christian Health Systems P555
Christian Lacroix fashion house W348, W349
Christiano, Matthew E235
Christiansen, George D. A821
Christiansen, Godtfred W332
Christiansen, Ole Kirk W332
Christie, James L. A687
Christie, L. Ray E300
Christie, Mitchell & Mitchell A978
Christie, Robert S. W593
Christie, Tod S. A1263
Christie's International plc A1304, W446
Christman, Linda E306
Christmas, Harold Percival W644
Christodoulou, James C. E208
Christodoulou, P. W385
Christopher & Banks Corporation E178
Christopher, David A1189
Christopher, Gary R. E264
Christopoul, Thomas D. A339
Christus Health P575
Christy, Michael P. A105
Christy's stores A56
ChromaVision Medical Systems, Inc. A1232, A1233
Chronicle Publishing P228
Chrysalis recording label W212, W213
The Chrysler Building East (New York City) P737
Chrysler Corporation A198, A920, A1052, A1420, P86, P88, P258, P338, P666, P706, P733, P747, W188, W264, W370, W442, W480. *See also* DaimlerChrysler AG
Chrysler Defense A644
Chrysler, Walter W188
Chrysler's Van Pool Services A300
Chrzan, Janet C. A879
CHS. *See* Cenex Harvest States Cooperatives
CHS Electronics Inc. (computer products distribution) A958, A1356
CHS Management, Inc. A323
Chu, James P765

Chua, C.T. A1257
Chuang, Alfred S. E33, E163
The Chubb Corporation A150, A**356**-A**357**, W336
Chubb Life Insurance Company of America A794, E211
Chubb, Percy A356
Chubb Re (international reinsurance) A356
Chubb, Thomas C. A356
Chuck Taylor All Star basketball sneaker P142, P583
Chuckles candy A709
Chun King foods A409, A1204
Chung Chai-Kwan W275
Chung Goo-Lee W275
Chung Hee Park W454
Chung Ju-Yung W274
Chung Mong Koo W275
Chung, Po A484
Chung, Tzau A299
Chunghwa Picture Tubes W570
The Chunnel A240, P74, W56, W134, W434
The Chuo Mitsui Trust and Banking Company, Ltd. W372, W373
Chuo Mitsui Trust & Banking A1332
Chur, Wolfgang W491
Church & Dwight Company, Inc. A**358**-A**359**, A486
Church, Austin A358
Church, James A358
Church, Kenneth E. A855
Church, Leroy A1218
Church of Jesus Christ of Latter-day Saints P238, P640
Church of Scientology A220, P66
Church, Steven C. A215
Churchfield, John W. P165
Churchill, David A1359
Churchill Distributors P738
Churchill Downs Inc. (race course) E**40**, E178, P598
Churchill Insurance W88
Churchill, William M. A1369
Churchill, Winston W144
Churchs fast food A1084, P124, P516, P575
Churney, Lila J. A611
Churrubusco Studios W582
Chutes and Ladders game A692
Chvala, Vicki L. P43, P538
CHW. *See* Catholic Healthcare West
Chylko, Peter E175
Chyna (WWFE star) E141, E319
C.I. Foods Systems Company, Ltd. P243
Ciaccio, Don P750
Cialis drug A540
Cialone, Henry J. P71
Ciancio, Ronald J. A639
Ciara fragrance A1201
Ciba Specialty Chemicals W116
CIBA Vision A234, W414
Cibacen drug W415
Ciba-Geigy AG A386, A612, W414

CIBC World Markets W156, W157
Cibrone, Frank A897
Ciby 2000 (film production) W134
CIC, Inc. A595
Cicconi, James W. A203
Cicinnati Concrete Pipe W252
Cicutto, Francis J. W383
CIED W439
Cielo appliances A1520, A1521
CIENA Corporation (telecom equipment) A792, A1362, E**41**, E179
Cieply, Jeff A673, P211
Cif household care products W619
Cifra. *See* Wal-Mart de México; Wal-Mart de México, S.A. de C.V.
Ciga (hotel operator) A1328
CIGNA Corporation A**360**-A**361**, A878, P290
CII-Honeywell Bull W150
Cilag-Chemie A800
CILCORP (utility holding company) A88
Cilva Holdings A212
Cima car W403
Cimber Air W518
Cinader, Arthur P254, P642
Cinader, Mitchell P254
Cincinnati and Suburban Bell Telephone A292
Cincinnati Bell Public Communications Inc. A293
Cincinnati Bengals (football team) P357
Cincinnati Electric Light A362
Cincinnati Financial Corporation A592
The Cincinnati Gas & Electric Company A362
Cincinnati Milacron (plastics) A802
The Cincinnati (Ohio) *Enquirer* A144, A632, A633
The Cincinnati Post A569
Cincinnati Reds baseball stadium A144
Cincinnati Reds (baseball team) P307
Cincinnati Red Stockings (baseball team) P306
Cinemark USA, Inc. P**126**-P**127**, P412, P575
Cinemascope lens A234
Cineplex Odeon W550
Cinergy Corporation A**362**-A**363**, A554, A668
Cinergy Global Resources, Inc. A363
Cinergy Solutions, Inc. A363
Cingano, Francesco W99
Cingular Wireless A248, A1026, A1062, A1244, A1245, E126, E316, E318, P576
Cintas Corporation A190, A**364**-A**365**
Cintron, Alfredo Padilla E314
Cinven (buyout specialist) W472, W478, W624
CIO (magazine) P248, P249, P641

Cipriani, Jack P247
Cipro drug W118
CIPSCO Investment Company A136, A137
Circle Four Farms A1290
Circle K A144, A496, A1128, A1338
Circles (interactive media) A701, P229
Circuit City Group A254, A**366**-A**367**, P697
Circus Circus hotel and casino (Las Vegas) A720, A740, A906, A907, P240
Cirillo, Frank J. P369
Cirone, Frank A393
Cirrus (ATM network) A924, P322, P323, P668
Cirrus Logic, Inc. (integrated chips) E97, W328
Cisco Systems, Inc. A98, A**368**-A**369**, A434, A747, A758, A764, A782, A840, A898, A990, A1298, A1357, A1482, E122, E173, E192, E224, E226, E245, E247, E252, E258, E263, E267, E269, E274, E289, E304, E313, P136, P137, P250, P251, P286, P454, P592, P654, W160, W324, W412, W450, W490
CISE Tecnologie Innovative Srl (research) W215
Ciskowski, Michael S. A1467
Cisneros Group P229
Cisneros, Henry A812
Cisneros, Sandy A837, P283, P653
CIT Alcatel W76
Citadel Cement A848
Citadel Group (credit card services) E183
CITGO Petroleum Corporation A56, A556, A900, W438, W439
Citibank, N.A. A370, A371, A958, A1202, P298, P659, W608
CITIC Group (investments) W306, W464, W564
Citicasters Inc. A144
Citicorp Inc. A602, A1550, E250, P110, P260
Citicorp Venture Capital A156, A1264, A1446, P152, P590, P679
Cities Service Company (fuel) A252, A1054, W438
Citigroup Center (Boston) E34
Citigroup Inc. A142, A226, A230, A356, A**370**-A**371**, A734, A808, A822, A936, A954, A958, A960, A1270, A1332, A1346, A1486, A1508, E300, W82, W200, W578
CitiPower A140, A554
Citizen Kane (movie) A700, E212, P228
Citizens Banking Corporation E179
Citizens Bank & Trust Company A166
Citizens Cellular E38
Citizens Communications A154
Citizens Financial Group, Inc. A954
Citizens Insurance Company of Illinois A124

Citizens Power A532, A1416
Citizens Telephone A292
Citizens Utilities A128, A154
Citla (automotive belts and hoses) P310
Citrix Systems, Inc. A747, E**42**, E179
Citroën, André W442
Citroën cars W366, W442
Citroën do Brasil W442
Citrus Bank E291
Citrus Colloids A704
Citrus Corporation A552
Citrus Hill juice A1105
Cittadini, Peter I. E22, E148
City and Suburban Telegraph Association A292
City and Village Mutual Automobile Insurance A1330, P458
City Bank of Cleveland A1000
City Brewery P428
City College P129
City Homes A340
City Market Food & Pharmacy A844, A845
The City Meat Markets Ltd. A1532
City National Bank and Trust A230
City National Bank of Commerce A230
City University Governance and Financing Act (1979) P128
The City University of New York P**128**-P**129**, P576
cityhopper W316
Cityplaza shopping center (Hong Kong) W564
CitySearch, Inc. (Web site) A1116, A1450
Citystate Holdings A875, P294
Cityvision video chain A266
Civic car W264, W265
Civil War (TV documentary) P144
Civilian Health and Medical Program for the Uniformed. *See* CHAMPUS
C.J. Banks stores E178
C. J. Root Glass Company A382
CJC Leasing, Inc. A69
cK apparel P100, P101
ck Watches W563
CK Witco A450
CKC Corporation A591
CKE Restaurants, Inc. A86, A590
CL Europe SA W183
CL Marchés de Capitaux W183
Claasen (publishing) W107
Claassen, Jürgen W595
Clabes, Judith G. A569
Claflin, Bruce L. A54, A55
Claiborne clothing A691, A880, A881
Claiborne, Liz A880
Clair, Michel W131
Clairol A108, A290, A1164
Clairs, Reg W644
Clamato juice P732, W155
Clamon, Jean W131

Clan of the Cave Bear (movie) A804
Clan tobacco W143
Clancy, Gregory J. A1449
Clancy, Tom W430
Clapp, Richard L. A633
CLARCOR Inc. P310
Clare, Peter J. P111
Clarent Hospital Corporation P637
Clarey, Patricia A697
Claricom Holdings (telecommunications) A1324
Clariden Bank W185
Claridge Hotel and Casino (Atlantic City) A1086
Claridge Israel W322
Clarify Inc. (customer relations software) W412
CLARiiON data storage A543
Grupo Clarin W578
Clarinex drug A1250
Clarins A564
Clarion A1182
Clarion Marketing & Communications P73
Claris W338
Claris software A186, A1356
Claritin drug A956, A1250, A1251
Clarity Vision, Inc. A717, P235
Clark, A. James P576
Clark, Alan W553
Clark, Amy A499
Clark Bar candy P752
Clark, Bernard F. A979
Clark, Bruce G. A209
Clark, Caroline A461
Clark, Charles C. (Caremark) A323
Clark, Charles (Kimberly-Clark) A826
Clark, Donald A734
Clark Enterprises, Inc. P576
Clark Equipment A754
Clark, F. Lamar A133
Clark Foodservice A1350
Clark, G. Edmond A589
Clark, Gerald A965
Clark, Gregory J. P279
Clark, H. Craig E62
Clark, Jack M. (Owens & Minor, Inc.) A1071
Clark, James A1284, P456
Clark, J. Coley A539
Clark, J. Lance P259
Clark, Joan P643
Clark, John M., III (National Semiconductor) A1003
Clark, John W. (Providian) A1171
Clark, Karen K. A1083
Clark, Kevin P. A601
Clark, Mike A. C. W155
Clark, M. Lewis E40
Clark, Paul G. A1001
Clark Retail Group, Inc. P577
Clark, Richard T. (Merck) A957
Clark, Rick D. (Devon Energy) A483
Clark, R. Kerry A1165
Clark, Robert F. A753

Clark, Roger A1451
Clark stores P577
Clark, Stuart P445, P726
Clark, Thomas A. A599
Clark USA (oil refiner) P577
Clark, W. Edmund W609
Clark, Wesley M. A1539
Clark Wilson (construction) E171
Clark/Bardes, Inc. E180
Clarke, David H. A1446, A1447
Clarke, Jeff A399
Clarke, Kenneth H. W143
Clarke, Michael A1241, P584
Clarke, Philip A. W591
Clarke, Robert E. A391
Clarke, Thomas E. A1033
Clarke, Tim W545
Clarke, Vaughn A. A627
Clarke, Wade P., Jr. A469
Clarkeson, John S. P95
Clark-Hurth Components (drivetrains) A460, A754
Clark-Johnson, Susan A633
Clark-Schwebel Fiber Glass A1316, P452
Clarksville Natural Grocery A1522
Clason, Roy, Jr. A91
Class, Fran W467
Class, Robert W. A1209
Classen, Peter K. A1147
Classic Car Wax A1096, A1097
Classic CD (magazine) W238
Classic City Homes A604
Classic Coal Corporation A69
Classic Crest writing paper A826
Classic lawn equipment A287
Classic Pooh bedding and towels A1135
Classic Residence by Hyatt (retirement communities) A740, A741, P240, P241, P636
Classic Resources E146
Classico pasta sauce P90, P91
Classified Ventures (online classifieds) A832, A1402
Clausen, R. A. A1301
Clauson, Joe P349
Clauss, Phil A1510
Claussen, John H. E131
Claussen pickles A843
Clavel, Alexander W414
Clawson, Carolyn E246
Clay, John W., Jr. A1347
Clay, Landon E53
Claypool, Jeffrey C. P443, P725
Clayton, Dubilier & Rice, Inc. (investments) A870, A1512, P274, P535, P651, P715
Clayton, John W., Jr. A1539
Clayton, R. Bruce A653
Clayton Williams Energy, Inc. E180
Cle de Peau cosmetics W534, W535
Clean Air Act (1990) A114, A140, A362, A598, A1370, P468
Clean Car AG W201
Clean Shower cleanser A358, A359
Clean Water Act A466

CleanStream vacuum cleaner filters P523
Clear Channel Communications, Inc. A372-A373, A560, A714, P180, P232, P350, P631, P681
Clearasil beauty care A1164
Clearfield cheese P723
Clearing de Informes of Montevideo, Uruguay A558
Clearly Canadian water A1194
ClearPath A1424, A1425
Clearskin skin care products A217
ClearTint dye P343
Clearview Cinema Group A312
ClearWorks Technologies A1178
Cleary Gull Reiland & McDevitt E132
Cleary, James J. A537
Cleavelin, Rinn P445
Cleberg, H. D. "Harry" A582, P184
Cleburg, Anthony S. A347
Cleghorn, John W474
Clemens, Peter J., III (Vulcan) A1485
Clemens, Peter J., IV (Caremark) A323
Clement, James H. A828, A829, P270, P271
Clement, Philip W473
Clement, Robert M. A787
Clemente, C. L. A1119
Clements, Donald M., Jr. A141
Clements, Paul B. A441
Clements, Rita Crocker P499
Clemons, Lori E216
Clemson University P124
Clendenin, John L. E106
Cleopatra (movie) A622
Clestra Hauserman A1334
Cletrac Corporation A132
Cleveland & Western Coal A992
Cleveland Browns (football team) P356, P357
Cleveland Cap Screw Company A1412
Cleveland Cavaliers (basketball team) P355
The Cleveland Electric Illuminating Company A598, A599
Cleveland Fabric store A796
Cleveland Hopkins International Airport P236
Cleveland Indians (baseball team) P307
Cleveland, Joseph R. A883
Cleveland Rams (football team) P356
Cleveland Rockers (basketball team) P355
Cleveland-Cliffs A896
Clevite auto parts A461
Clexane drug W103
Cleza, Pedro A1247, P433
Click Commerce, Inc. E180
ClientLink A400
Cliffdale Farms A730
Clifford & Wills (apparel catalog) A1314, A1315, P254

Clifford Chance LLP (attorneys) A220, P66, P548
Clifford, James R. A1265
Clifford, R. Leigh W489
Clifford the Big Red Dog (books and TV show) A1254, A1255
Clifford, William E262
Cliffs and Associates, Limited A896
CliffsNotes study guides P248
Clin d'Oeil (publication) W471
Clincher herbicides A504
Cline, Linda P445, P726
Cline, Robert S. A103
Cline, Roy L. A1115, P397
Cline, Stephanie E. A785
Cline, Thomas G. P379
Cline, William C. A279
Clingman, James F. P224, P225
Clinique skin care products A564, A565
CliniShare home health services P753
Clinoril drug A956
ClinPharm International A1434
Clinton, Bill A258, A1288, A1330, P186, P388, P446, P458, P630
Clinton Drug and Discount stores A458
Clinton, Hillary Rodham A848, A918
Clinton nuclear plant A570
Clinton Pharmaceutical A290
Clio car W480, W481
Clissitt, David W337
Clizbe, John P45
Cloathbond (clothing manufacturer) A1220
Cloer, Dan A270
Cloninger, Kriss, III A93
Clonotech Laboratories (genetic tests) A244
Clorisol bleach A375
The Clorox Company A374-A375, A946, A1152, A1246, P432, W256
Clos du Bois wines W85
Close family A1316, P452, P733
Close, William A1316, P452
Close-Up toothpaste W619
Cloth World stores A294, A796
Cloud, Linda P472, P473, P744
Clough, DeWitt A58
Clough, Suzanne M. A221, P67
Clouser, Christopher E. A303
Cloutier, Roger R., II P614
Clow, Lee A1062, A1063
Clowe, C. Thomas P473
Clown College P188
Clozaril drug W415
CLT-Ufa W126, W127, W430
CLTV News (regional cable) A1402
Club Aquarius resorts W170
Club Aurrerá warehouse outlets W634
Club beer W553
Club Car (golf cars) A754
Club Corporation of America P130
Club crackers A815

Club House spices and flavorings A938
Club Méditerranée S.A. W170-W171
Club Monaco stores A1150
ClubCorp, Inc. P130-P131, P577
Clubhouse hotels A1540
ClubLink P130, P577
ClubMom (Web site for mothers) P524
Clupak kraft paper A1516
Clutterbuck, Robert T. A823
Clydesdale Bank PLC W382, W383
C.M. Life Insurance Company A923, P321
C-MAC Industries A1298
CMAC Investments. See Radian Group Inc.
CMC. See Commercial Metals Company
CMC Electronics Inc. W110
CMG Health Inc. A905
CMG plc (computer engineering) W100
CMGI, Inc. A1160, P282
CMP Media LLC (publisher) P248, W620, W621
CMS Capital Ventures, Inc. A699
CMS Energy Corporation A376-A377, A512, A514, A536, A598, A1542
CMT. See Country Music Television
CMT Holdings, Inc. A395
CNA Financial Corporation A378-A379, A884, A885, E107, E315, W380
CNA Surety Corporation A560, P180
CNB Bancshares of Indiana A592
CNB Capital Trust I A593
CNB Financial E250
CNBC cable network A312, A506, A998, A999
CNET Networks, Inc. A998, A999, P80, W548
CNF Inc. A380-A381
CNF Transportation A420
CNG. See Consolidated Natural Gas
CNH Global N.V. A96, A456, A468, A616, W226
CNN News Group A180, A181, E188
CNNfn E289
Coach Leatherware International A1242
Coach Specialties Company A604
Coallier, Robert W377
Coalport brand W637
Coan, R. Thomas A1239
Coast soap A487, A1164
Coast to Coast hardware stores A734, A1410, P484, P485, P749
The Coastal Corporation A536, A552, A556, A1344, W296
Coastal Modular Buildings E94
Coastal States Gas Corporation A1466
Coastal Vintners wines A423

Coates, Vincent E248
Cobalt Networks A1342
Cobb, Anne L. A1481, P509
Cobb, Bernard A376
Cobb, Marett P773
Cobb, M. Zita A793
Cobb Theatres P412
Cobb, Tom A1189
Cobb Vantress (chicken supplier) A1419
Cobblestone Mill baked goods A608, A609
COBEE A1542
CoBiz Inc. E181
Coblation tissue removal E159
Coblin, James M. A1053
Cobra golf clubs A618
COBRAS INTEGRA analysers W493
Cobre Cerrillos Sociedad Anonima A1125
Cobre Mining A1124
Coburg dairy product A467
Coburn, Gordon E181
Coburn, Steven E201
Coca-Cola Amatil W510
Coca-Cola Bottling Company of Chicago P577
Coca-Cola Bottling Company of Indianapolis P577
The Coca-Cola Company A252, A253, A382-A383, A384, A452, A772, A934, A1014, A1102, A1106, A1164, A1346, A1510, E186, P72, P354, P381, P416, P417, P512, P715, W154, W314, W466, W552, W553, W564
Coca-Cola Enterprises Inc. A224, A384-A385
Coca-Cola Nordic Beverages A/S W162
Coca-Cola Philippines W511
Coccari, Gregg P417
Cocchiola, Mark E296
Cochell, Roger P773
Cochlear (company) W428
Cochran, Carol P720
Cochran, David A1059
Cochran, J. Guyton, Jr. P733
Cochran, John R. III A937
Cochran, Michael D. A169
Cochrane, James L. A1019, P375
COCIFEM (communications) W559
Cockerham, Haven E. A1219
Cockrell, Mel P553
Cocoa Krispies cereal A817
Cocoa Puffs cereal A649
Coconut Creek Lexus Dealership P256
Cocoran, J. Timothy A1383
Coco's restaurants A86
Cocroft, Duncan H. A339
Cocuzza, Frank P700
Coden, Daniel J. P373
Coditel (cable TV) A1360
Codon, Dennis P. R. A1439
Cody Company E168
Cody, Douglas R. P107

Coe, George P69
Coen, Janet E265
Cofer, James E. P758
Coffee Rich nondairy creamer P714
Coffey, Bruce A847
Coffey, Frank W. A775
Coffey, John P. A1331, P459
Coffin, Charles A646
Coffman, Vance D. A883
Cofoni, Paul M. A405
Cofreth (heating systems) W558
Cogan, Andrew B. P276, P277, P652
Cogdill, Richard A. A1133
Cogels, Renaud W195
Cogen South LLC A1248
Cogent (investments) W89
Coggin, James A. A1239
Coghlan, John P. A349
Coghlan, Michael P. A385
Coghlan, Paul E84, E233
Cognetta, Gary A81, P33
Cognex Corporation E43, E181, W321
Cognis B.V. (chemicals) W256
Cognizant. See Nielsen Media Research
Cognizant Technology Solutions Corporation E181
Cogswell, Theresa S. A775
Cohen, Alan (Boston Celtics) A280
Cohen, Alan P. (Andrx) E156
Cohen, Arnold P254
Cohen, Benjamin W59
Cohen, Betsy Z. E275
Cohen, Collin E25
Cohen, David P135
Cohen, Gary M. A245
Cohen, Ilyse A305
Cohen, Israel P102
Cohen, Jack W590
Cohen, Jay M. A1077
Cohen, Jim P102
Cohen, Kenneth P. A577
Cohen, Larry A987
Cohen, Leonard A1366
Cohen, Lester P102
Cohen, Michael S. A107
Cohen, Mitchell M. E287
Cohen, Richard B. (C&S Wholesale Grocers) P102, P103, P565
Cohen, Richard I. (Allstate) A127
Cohen, Stuart F. E109
Cohen-Hatfield Industries A902, P304
Cohera software A1098
Coherent Communications A1232, A1362
Cohn, John D. A1211
Cohn, Michael P275
Cohne, Brett E27, E154
Cohoes Fashions clothing store A304, A305
Cohu, Inc. E44, E182
Cohu, La Motte E44
Coit, Janet A986
Coit, Lynde H. A441

Cojuangco, Eduardo M., Jr. W510, W511
Coke Southwest A384
Coken, Carl A271
Coker, Charles A1302
Coker, Charles W. A1302, A1303
Coker, James A1302
Coker, James, Jr. A1302
Cola, Michael A1233
Colagiacomo, Dario A1415
Colalillo, Claudia J. A1031
Colaninno, Roberto W422, W450, W574, W575
Colas, Giles W507
Colas S.A. (road construction) W134, W135
COLAZAL drug E283
Colbert, Heather P253
Colbert, Kenneth S. A359
Colbert, Kitty Carroll P359
Colborn, Mark R. A125
Colbourne, Bill A269, P83, P556
Colburn, David M. A181
Colburn, Keith W. P582
Colburn, Martin P. A581
Colby, David C. A1507
Colby, Ronald A1435
Cold Fusion E210
Coldicott, Jayne W435
Coldman, John W337
Coldplay (music group) W213
Coldwell Banker A338, A1264, P110, P120, P692
Coldwell, Colbert P120
Cole, Alan D. P299, P659
Cole, Brady P686
Cole, Daniel F. A137
Cole, Diane M. P533
Cole, Glen P164
Cole Haan Holdings Inc. A1032
Cole, Jonathan R. P135
Cole, Kenneth D. E78, E227
Cole, Micheal J. P359
Cole, M. Mark A347
Cole, Natalie P757
Cole, Nat "King" W212
Cole, Richard T. P87
Cole, Robert E. A931
Cole, Tom A587
Cole, Vincent J. A871
Coleco A692
The Coleman Company, Inc. A902, P304, P663
Coleman, Edward A400, A401
Coleman, Gary L. A1391
Coleman, Gracie P. A1317, P453, P733
Coleman, Gregory G. A1547
Coleman, James E. A521, P169, P600
Coleman, John P93
Coleman, Kenneth L. A1285
Coleman, Lester L. A677
Coleman, Mary Sue P757
Coleman, Michael J. A633
Coleman, Owen W. A773

Coleman, Peter J. A1141
Coleman trailers A604
Coleman, Wesley A. A1247, P433
Coleman, William T., III E33
Coler/Goldwater Memorial
  Hospital P369
Coles, George James W172
Coles, Martin A637
Coles Myer Ltd. A830,
  W**172**-W**173**, W644
Coley, Thomas H. A1309
Colf, Richard W. A1115, P397
Colfax Corporation A460, P578
Colgan, Celeste A677
Colgate, Jessie M. P371
Colgate, Samuel A386
Colgate, William A386
Colgate-Palmolive
  Company A**386**-A**387**, W256,
  W516
Colgate-Palmolive-Peet A386
Grupo Collado A1224
Collard, Kevin R. P604
Collazo, José A. E220
Colleagues (direct
  marketing) W378
Collee, Dolf W57
College Bookstore (Web site) A1494
The College Channel P460
College of Staten Island P128, P129
College Retirement Equities
  Fund A1354, P466
College Television Network. *See*
  CTN Media Group, Inc.
Collender, H. W. A298
Collett, David P659
Collett Dickenson Pearce
  (advertising) W198
Collett, William C. A511
Colley, Jerry A1057
Colli, Bart J. A191
Collier, Calvin J. A843
Collier Enterprises A828, P270
Collier, J. Douglas A779
Collier, Richard T. A1123
Collier, William L., III A629
Colliers International Property
  Consultants Inc. P580
Colliers Jardine P578
Colliers Macauley Nicolls P578
Collin, Jacques W161
Colling, Dennis P697
Collins & Aikman
  Corporation A**388**-A**389**, A1380
Collins, Arthur D., Jr. A953
Collins, Christopher D. W253
Collins, Colin C. A923, P321
Collins, Crispian W617
Collins, Duane E. A1088, A1089
Collins (foodservice) A1350
Collins, Gary L. A199
Collins, Howard A1055
Collins, J. Barclay, II A133
Collins, J. Mitchell E279
Collins, Joan A974, W252
Collins, Joanne B. A879
Collins, John (Arthur D. Little) P55

Collins, John J., Jr. (Champion
  Enterprises) A347
Collins, John W., III (Alcoa) A113
Collins, Jonathan W307
Collins, Kathleen M. A595
Collins, Keith V. P431
Collins, Kevin R. E200
Collins, Marshall J. W499
Collins, Michael P. (Avis) A213
Collins, Michael (Trammell
  Crow) P747
Collins, Paul J. W407
Collins Publishers W390
Collins Radio A538, A1210
Collins, Timothy R. P171
Collins, William (Collins &
  Aikman) A388
Collins, William J. (AgriBank) P533
Collister, Richard A. A395
Collman mustard W619
Colloc'h, Françoise W105
Collomb, Bertrand P. A848, A849
Collombert, Marie-Tatiana W101
Colloredo-Mansfield,
  Ferdinand E167
Colloredo-Mansfield, Franz E167
Colman, James W476
Colman, Jeremiah W476
Colman, Michael W476
Colman mustard W476
Colman, Robert L. A479
Colmart discount store W172
Colombo bread A774, A775
Colombo Gas SpA W214, W215
Colombo yogurt A648, A649
Colomer, Carlos A1200
Colon, Conrad O. P205
Colon fabric care W477
Colonel Lee Bourbon A423
Colonial Bank W114
Colonial Gas A824
Colonial Group P294
Colonial Insurance of
  California A1008, P364
Colonial Life and Accident
  Insurance Company A356, A1441
Colonial Mutual Funds P295
Colonial Penn Group A624
Colonial Penn Insurance P28
Colonial Tradition brand A1109
Colony Capital E227, P474
Colony, George Forrester E63,
  E205
Colony Hotels P106
The Color Purple (movie) P218
Color Trend cosmetics A217
Colorado Avalanche (hockey
  team) P361
Colorado Bankers Life Insurance
  Company P227
The Colorado Belle Hotel and
  Casino A906, A907
Colorado Business Bankshares. *See*
  CoBiz Inc.
Colorado Casualty P295
Colorado Healthcare Management,
  LLC A695

Colorado Interstate Gas A537, E200
Colorado Rockies baseball
  stadium A78
Colorado Rockies (baseball
  team) P307
Colorama cosmetics A1200, W342
Colorsilk cosmetics A1201
ColorStay cosmetics A1200, A1201
ColorStream P506
Colorworks cosmetics A216
Colosi, Michael A1109
Colotti, Raymond L. A205
Colowyo Coal Company W488
Colpo, Charles C. A1071
ColRich Communities (home
  builders) A862
Colson Caster Corporation P313
Colson Company A740, P240, P312
Colson, Daniel W. W263
Colt 45 beer P721
Colt, Edward H. E242
Colt, Samuel P132, P578
COLT Telecom Group plc A615,
  A866, P190, P191, P609
Coltec Industries (aerospace
  components) A278, A460, A662
Colter, Gary A841, P287, W325
Coltharp, Douglas E. A1239
Coltman, Edward P145
Colton, Donald G. A1261
Colton, S. David A1125
Colt's Manufacturing Company,
  Inc. P**132**-P**133**, P578
Columbia Bancorp E182
The Columbia Bank
  (Maryland) E182
Columbia brand A839
Columbia Broadcasting System. *See*
  CBS Television Network
Columbia Capital Medical Center
  Limited Partnership A695
Columbia Casualty Company A379
Columbia Crest wine A1458, A1459
Columbia Electric Light A570
Columbia Electric Street Railway,
  Light and Power Company A1248
Columbia Energy Group A200,
  A1034
Columbia Energy Resources,
  Inc. A1035
Columbia Forest Products
  Inc. P579
Columbia Gas & Electric A362
Columbia Gas Light
  Company A1248
Columbia Gas System A200
Columbia Hospital
  Corporation A694
Columbia House Company P579,
  W550
Columbia lighting A1447
Columbia Management
  Company A602
Columbia Phonograph Broadcasting
  System A334
Columbia Pictures A382, W550
Columbia Presbyterian Medical
  Center A1076

Columbia Propane A1034, A1400
The (Columbia, SC) *State* A833
Columbia Steel A104
Columbia Tower Club
(Washington) P131
Columbia TriStar Television
Group W550
Columbia University P**134**-P**135**,
P579
Columbia wines A422
Columbia Winnelson
(plumbing) P705
Columbia/HCA Healthcare. *See*
HCA, Inc.
Columbian National Life A688
Columbian Peanut A192
Columbia-Presbyterian Medical
Center P134
Columbine JDS Systems P506
Columbus Blue Jackets (hockey
team) P360, P361, P684
Columbus Coated Fabrics P90
Columbus (Georgia) *Ledger-
Enquirer* A833
Columbus Plastics A1010
Columbus Southern Power
Company A140
Colwell Systems (medical business
forms) A480
Colyear Motor Sales A652
Comair, Inc. A478, A479, W141
Comanche Peak nuclear
plant A1416
Comark, Inc. P**136**-P**137**, P580
Comas, Daniel L. A463
Comau S.p.A. (robotics) W226,
W480
Combat insecticide A374
Combes, James H. P748
Combet, Jacques W77
CombiChem, Inc. (biotech
research) A534
Combined Communications
Corporation A632
Combined Federal Campaign P492
Combined Insurance Company of
America A182, A183
Combined Registry Company A182
Combined Specialty A182
Combos snacks A914, A915, P314,
P315, P665
Combot, Pierre W135
Combs, Colleen E305
Combs, H. Lee E75
Combs, Mark A403
Combs, Samuel, III A1065
Comcast Corporation A72, A202,
A**390**-A**391**, A442, A1232, A1244,
E195, P146, P332
ComCore Semiconductor A1002
Comdata (trucking
information) A342, A343
COMDEX trade shows W548
Comdisco, Inc. A**392**-A**393**
Comeau, Susan A1333
ComEd (utility) A570, A571
Comedy Central cable
network A1476

Comer, Gary C. A852, A853
Comercializadora Internacional de
Cargo S.A. de C.V. A789
Comerford, Janet D. E185
Comerica Inc. A**394**-A**395**, A936
Comet cleanser A1165
Comet electronics stores W312,
W313
Comet Transport (trucking) A1454
Comexter (transportation) A344
Comforel bedding and
towels A1135
Comfort Inn E216
Comfort laundry soap W619
Comforto (office chair) P222
ComfortPLUS ophthalmic
products A119
Comgas W500
Cominco Ltd. W66
Coming Home catalog A853
Command Audio (audio on
demand) P511
Commander-Larabee (flour
milling) A192
Commando guns P133
Commerce Bancorp, Inc. E182
Commerce Clearing House
(CCH) W642
Commerce One, Inc. A1066, W292,
W516, W608
The Commercial Appeal
(Memphis) A568, A569
Commercial Aviation Leasing
Ltd. W519
Commercial Banking
Company W382
Commercial Bank of Albany A822
Commercial Credit Company A342
Commercial Management,
Inc. A259
Commercial Metals
Company A**396**-A**397**
Commercial Metals Europa A396
Commercial National Bank (North
Carolina) A226
Commercial National Bank
(Ohio) A230
Commercial Traveller's Savings
Bank A1346
Commerfin SpA (door
systems) A802
Commerzbank AG W98, W200,
W512
Commisary Operations A1280
CommNet Cellular Inc. W628
Commodore Hotel A1408, P482
Common Fund P518
Common School Fund P638
Commonwealth and Southern
(utility) A376, A598, A1306
Commonwealth Bank E154
Commonwealth Bank of
Australia W382, W644
Commonwealth Edison
(utility) A570
Commonwealth Energy A1306
Commonwealth Insurance A1170

Commonwealth Mortgage
Assurance E108
Commonwealth of Independent
States W242
Commonwealth of
Pennsylvania A1424
Commonwealth Oil Refining
Company A1374
Commonwealth Power A376
Commonwealth System of Higher
Education P759
Commonwealth Telephone
Enterprises, Inc. A128, A866,
A1114, P396
CommSite Development
Corporation E128
CommSouth (prepaid phone
service) W580
CommTech (software) A70
Commtron (videocassettes) A756,
P244
Communications Construction
Group E52
Communications Consulting
Worldwide A1062
Communications Marketing P136
Community Bankshares,
Inc. A1308
Community Blue (PPO) P87
Community Care, Inc. A259
Community Chest P492
Community Economic
Assistance P118
Community Energy
Alternatives A1174
Community Group
(newspapers) W263
Community Medical Care P174
Community Mutual
(insurance) A178
Community of Science (research
network) P279
Community Reinvestment Act A964
Community-Based Public Health
Initiative P520
Commuter Express P731
CommWorks A54
ComNet (event) P249
ComNet Mortgage Holdings E154
Comod supermarkets W164
CompactFlash memory E117,
E121, E288, P273
Compagnia, Compagnie, Compañía.
See entry under primary company
name
CompAir W290
Companion Life Insurance
Company P349
Companion Mortgage
Corporation A681
Companion systems home
theater P92
The Company Doctor A699
Company for the Development of
People's Cars W630

Compaq Computer
Corporation A54, A82, A170,
A**398**-A**399**, A400, A406, A472,
A542, A636, A712, A747, A758,
A760, A870, A894, A928, A958,
A970, A1002, A1050, A1062,
A1080, A1140, A1184, A1188,
A1260, A1284, A1298, A1336,
A1357, A1424, A1514, A1544, E73,
E166, E180, E189, E190, E222,
E226, E256, E261, E267, E272,
E273, E286, E287, E306, P136,
P137, P338, P580, P740, W60,
W100, W180, W338, W530, W646
Compass Bancshares A166
Compass Bank for Savings E285
Compass Foods, Inc. A670
Compass Group plc A190, A1478,
W**174**-W**175**, W248, W546
Compass (standing order
service) P69
CompCare. See Comprehensive
Care Corporation
Comper, F. Anthony W112, W113
Competition Tire West E75
Components Agents A196
Comprehensive Care
Corporation E111
Comprehensive Integrated
Marketing Services A1507
Comprehensive Major Medical
(health plan) P85
Compressed Industrial Gases A100
Compris Technologies A1012
Comptek Research, Inc. (electronic
defense systems) A1044, E183
Comptoir National d'Escompte de
Paris W130
Comptoirs Modernes
supermarkets W164
Compton, Jim A429
Compton, William W. E305
Comptonix A1240
Compton's MultiMedia
Encyclopedia (CD-Rom) P176
CompuBank E251
Comp-U-Card America A338
CompuCessory office
products A652
CompuCom Systems,
Inc. A**400**-A**401**, A1188, A1232,
A1233
CompuCredit Corporation E183
Compugraphic W118
Compumat (computer
systems) A544
Compumech Technologies A1140
CompUSA Inc. A472, A758, A870,
A1058, A1188
CompuServe Interactive Services,
Inc. A180, A366, A566, A680
CompuShop A400
Computacenter plc W**176**-W**177**
Computasoft (software) W176
Computational Systems A546
Computer 2000 A1356
Computer Aided Real Estate Data,
Inc. A595

Computer Animated Production
System E103
Computer Applications Learning
Center E36
Computer Associates International,
Inc. A**402**-A**403**, A404, A758,
A1378, P136, P584
Computer City stores A1188
Computer Discount
Corporation A392
Computer Discount
Warehouse A336
Computer Music (magazine) W239
Computer Power (data
processing) A128
Computer Research, Inc. A1012
Computer Reseller News
(magazine) P136
Computer Resources Trust W378
Computer Sciences
Corporation A400, A402,
A**404**-A**405**, A840, P286, W120,
W324
Computer Shoppe stores A1270
Computerized Applications
Programming (software) W160
ComputerLand stores A958
Computerm Corporation A1320
Computers and Automation
(magazine) P248
Computersbynet.com P338
Computerworld (magazine) P248,
P249
Computing Devices
International A342
Computing Publications W626
Computing Strategy (research) E63
Computing-Tabulating-Recording
Company A764
Compuware
Corporation A**406**-A**407**
CompX International Inc. P583
COMSAT Corporation A882
Comsat General W110
Comstock Canada Ltd. A544, A545
Comstock funds E65
Comstock Group A544
Comstock Resources, Inc. E183
Comstor P771
Comsumers Energy A1542
ComTrain (testing and training
software) A818
Comverse Technology E307
Conaghan, Thomas B. A585
ConAgra Foods, Inc. A324,
A**408**-A**409**, A486, A714, A816,
P104, P232, P406, P566
ConAgra Grocery Products A224,
A510
Conair Corporation P580
Conant, Douglas R. A316, A317
Conard, Bruce R. W285
Conarty, Thomas J., Jr. A257
Conaty, William J. A647
Conaway, Charles C. A830, A831
Conaway, J. Edwin A381
Concannon, William F. A1399
Conceptronic E158

Concepts and Creative Analogies
(book) A130
Concert Communications
Company P580
Concert Communications
Services A202, A1534, W148,
W149
Concerta drug A800
Concha, Mario A655
Concierge.com A80, A81, P32
Conco Industries A600
Concord Camera Corporation E184
Concorde Acceptance (mortgage
lender) E188
Concorde air plane W68, W110,
W140, W496
Condake-Pulte A1178
Condé Nast Building (New York
City) A875, P294
Condé Nast Publications A80, A81,
P32, P33, P404
Condé Nast Traveler
(magazine) P33
CONDEA-Huntsman GmbH &
Company KG P239
Condit, Linda F. A1097
Condit, Philip M. A273
Condon, James E. A691
Condon, Kenneth P560
Condon Supply P236
Condor (charter airline) W344
Condor tobacco W241
Condos, George A1511
condosaver.com E215
Condrin, J. Paul, III A875, P295,
P658
Condron, Christopher M. A219,
W105
Conduct (network
management) E91
Condux (concrete pipe) W252
Condy, Charles P340
Cone Lumber Company A1524
ConEd. See Consolidated Edison,
Inc.
Conely, John L., Sr. A779
Conestoga Enterprises
(telecommunications) E255
Conexant Spinco. See Mindspeed
Technologies
Conexant Systems,
Inc. A**410**-A**411**, A1210, E229,
P444, P445, P726
Coney Island Hospital P368, P369
Confederation Life Insurance
Company P384
Conforama (furniture and
appliances) W446, W447
Conforti, Leopoldo W79
Conforti, Thomas G. A812
Congdon, Jeffrey D. A300
Congoleum Corporation A980,
A1048, P376
Congregation of the Dominican
Sisters of St. Catherine of
Siena P117
Congress Life Insurance A230

Congress of Industrial
Organizations A716, P34, P234
Congressional Quarterly A1502
Conifer Group A602
Conish, Mark G. A359
Coniston Partners (investment
firm) A86, A1420
Conklyn, Elizabeth A1453, P503,
P763
Conley, E. Renae A555
Conley, Frances M. P411
Conley, Terence P. A339
Conliffe, Roy R. W245
Conlin, Kelly P. P249, P641
Conlin, Paul A1077
Conn Creek wine A1458
Connectics Corporation E184
Connecticut General A360
Connecticut Light and Power
Company A1040, A1041
Connecticut Lottery
Corporation P581
Connecticut Mutual Life
Insurance A90, A922
Connecticut Power A1040
Connecticut Yankee nuclear
plant A240, A1040, P74
Connecticut-American Water
Company A155
Connections for Independent
Living P29
Connectiv A1542
Connectix W338
Connectrix fibre channel
switches A543
Connell Brothers P772
The Connell Company P581
Connell, Dennis A241
Connell, Grover P581
Connell, Kathleen P96
Connell, Kevin B. A289
Connell Limited Partnership P581
Connell, Terry P581
Connell, William F. P581
Connelly, Jim P357
Connelly, Marjorie M. A319
Connelly, Michael D. P570
Connelly, Patrick O. A1357
Connelly, Thomas M. A535
Conner, Finis A1260, P440
Conner Peripherals, Inc. A1260,
P440
Conners Brothers
(packaging) W244
Conners, John B. A875, P295
Connex (network storage) A1514
Connexion (in-flight Internet
services) A272
Connick, Mary P119
Connie women's shoes A294, A295
Conniff, George A241, P75
Conning Corporation A964, A965
Connolly, Brian (Avon) A217
Connolly, Brian P.
(Lightbridge) E83
Connolly, George A. E262

Connolly, John P. A475, P155,
W197
Connolly, Patrick J. A1531
Connolly, Peter W607
Connolly, Robert A1495
Connor, Christopher M. A1278,
A1279
Connor, John A728
Connor, P. Eric P341
Connor, Sandra J. E142
Connor, Terry L. A875, P295
Connors, Dennis A55
Connors, John G. A973
Connors, Joseph C. A1251
Connors, Mary Jean A833
Connors, Michael P. A67, W627
Connors, Richard E. A987
Connors Steel A396
Conoco Inc. A132, **A412-A413**,
A416, A534, A978, A1128, A1460,
P729, W346, W410
Conophy, Thomas M. A1329
Conophy, Tony W177
Conorada Petroleum. *See* Oasis (oil)
Conover, Donna D. A1311
Conover, James A362
Conover, Lisa P534
Conover, Pamela C. A331
Conowingo Hydroelectric
Station A570
Conphoebus Scrl (research) W215
Conquest (advertising) W646
Conrac (electronic displays) P310
Conrad, Bob A171
Conrad, Carl A174
Conrad, Christy P179
Conrad, Conrad A. A487
Conrad International Hotels A720,
A721
Conrad Jupiters Goald Coast A1087
Conrad, Lucius C. P574
Conrad, Michael B. P73
Conrad Resort and Casino Punta del
Este A1086
Conrail A454, A1038
Conrail Inc. P582
Conroy, Alexandre A245
Conroy, J. Patrick P391, P699
Conseco, Inc. **A414-A415**, A1408,
P482
Conservation and Research
Center P451
Considine, John R. A245
Consiglio, Bob P579
Consilium (software) A188, A189
CONSOL Energy Inc. A412,
A416-A417, W504
Consolidated Apparel Group A690
Consolidated Business Systems
(forms) A488
Consolidated Cigar Holdings A902,
P304, P663
Consolidated Citrus Limited
Partnership A829, P271
Consolidated Coal A628
Consolidated Container Company
LLC A452, A1114, A1338, P396

Consolidated Controls (precision
instruments) A526
Consolidated Devices (torque
application and
measuring) A1294
Consolidated Edison Company of
New York A1306
Consolidated Edison,
Inc. **A418-A419**, A424, A554,
A824, A1040
Consolidated Electrical Distributors
Inc. P582
Consolidated Electric Power
Asia W266
Consolidated Foods
Corporation A1242, W210
Consolidated Freightways
Corporation A380, **A420-A421**
Consolidated Gas Company of
Baltimore A424
Consolidated Gas Company of New
York A418
Consolidated Gas Electric Light and
Power Company A424
Consolidated Gold Fields W92
Consolidated Grocers A1242
Consolidated Las Vegas Medical
Centers A695
Consolidated Lumber
Company A446
Consolidated Mills A408
The Consolidated Mining and
Smelting Company of Canada
Limited W66
Consolidated National Life
Insurance A414
Consolidated Natural Gas
Company A498
Consolidated Nutrition commercial
feeds P36, P37, P532
Consolidated Papers W556
Consolidated Press Holdings P238,
P239
Consolidated Rail P582
Consolidated Sewing Machine P712
Consolidated Stores A260
Consolidated Truck Lines A380,
A420
Consolidated TVX Mining
Corporation W284, W452
Consolidated Vultee Aircraft A644
Consolidated Zinc W488
Consolidated-Bathhurst
(newsprint) A1292
Consolidated-Tomoka Land
Company E184
Consolidation Coal. *See* CONSOL
Energy Inc.
Consolidation Services P535
Consorcio Minero Benito Juarez
Pena Colorada SA de CV W293
Consort hair care products A108
Consortium Rhodanien de
Réalisations W183
CONSTAR International (plastic
containers) A452
Constellation Brands,
Inc. **A422-A423**

Constellation Energy Group,
  Inc. A**424**-A**425**, A1028, E258
Constellation Real Estate E187
Construcciones Aeronauticas
  SA W330
Constructors & Associates P737
Consul appliances A1521
Consultas N.V. W57
Consulting Magazine P94
Consumer Marketplace Report A67
Consumer Policy Institute P138,
  P582
Consumer Reports (magazine) P92,
  P138, P139, P332, P582, P710,
  W294, W560
Consumer Value Store A458
Consumer*Facts A67
Consumerfirst A518
Consumers Cooperative
  Association A582, P184
Consumers Energy Company A376,
  A377, A512
Consumers Food & Drug
  stores A606
Consumers Gas Group A376
Consumers Ice A56
Consumers International P138
Consumers Light & Power A1166
Consumers Power Company A1542
Consumers Power Railway & Light
  Company A376
Consumers Union of United States,
  Inc. P**138**-P**139**, P582, W560
Contac cold medicine W246
Contact East (electric tools) A1322
Contadina Foods, Inc. A470, A471,
  W388
Container Corporation of
  America A1292
CONTAX copy machines and
  printers W328
Conte, Steven A. A1025
Contempo Casuals A1014
Contentnea, Inc. A493
Contentville A1160
Conti, Fulvio W215
Conti, Richard T. A375
ContiBeef LLC P140
ContiGroup Companies,
  Inc. A**426**-A**427**, P**140**-P**141**,
  P583
Continental AG W201
Continental Airlines, Inc. A74,
  A106, A138, A**428**-A**429**, A478,
  A1046, A1442, E64, P474, P744,
  W68, W78, W79, W518
Continental (automotive) A780,
  W188
Continental Baking A774
Continental Cablevision A700, P228
Continental Can Company. *See*
  Consolidated Container Company
  LLC
Continental Capital E275
Continental Coffee Products A1180
Continental Conveyor &
  Equipment P686
The Continental Corporation A378

Continental Deli Foods A743
Continental Express A428
Continental Grain A426, P104,
  P140, W542
Continental Homes, Inc. A508,
  A509
The Continental Insurance
  Company A378, A379
Continental Investment
  Corporation A1390
Continental jet W132
Continental Land Title A1436
Continental Medical Systems A698
Continental Micronesia, Inc. A428,
  A429
Continental Mobile Home
  Brokerage Corporation A438
Continental Mortgage and Equity
  Trust E303
Continental Mutual Savings
  Bank A1500
Continental Oil & Transportation.
  See Conoco Inc.
Continental Research A342
The Continental Spirits
  Company W230
Continental Telephone A1362
Continental Teves (automotive
  systems) E164
Compagnie Continentale
  d'Assurances W99
Contino, Francis A. A939
Continucare Corporation E185
The Continuum Company, Inc.
  (insurance services) A404
ContiSea A426
Contour cars A616
Contour Medical (nursing
  homes) A1340
Contour Software, Inc. A595
Contra Costa Academy P494
Contra Costa Electric, Inc. A545
Contra Costa Newspapers
  (California) A833
Contractor Supply stores A1090,
  A1091
ContractorHub.com P434
Contran Corporation P583
Contreras Maza, Oswaldo W438
Control Cells (aerospace
  research) A224
Control Corporation of
  America A1512
Control Data Corporation A342,
  A370, A782
Control Delivery Systems A234
Control Displays (flight deck
  equipment) A526
Control Systems A1258
Control Video A180
Controladora Comercial
  Mexicana A436, A437
ControlCenter software A543
Controlled Substance Act P220
Controneo, Frank J. A681
Convair A644
Convenience Clubs P488

ConvergeNet (storage area network
  equipment) A472
Convergent Group A1252
Convergent workstations A1424
Convergys E127, E300
Converium (reinsurance) W652
Converse Inc. A630, E60,
  P**142**-P**143**, P583
Converse, Marquis P142
Convertibles and
  Convertiwalls A1334
Convery, Joseph W235
Conway, Craig A. A1098, A1099
Conway, Daniel J. A357
Conway, Gordon R. P414, P415,
  P715
Conway, James J. A451
Conway, John K. (Kemper
  Insurance) P269
Conway, John W. (Crown Cork &
  Seal) A452, A453
Conway, Kenneth A. A1271
Conway, Mary E. A1265
Conway, Michael A. (Aon) A183
Conway, Michael (American
  West) A138
Con-Way Transportation
  Services A380, A381, A420
Conway, William E., Jr. (Carlyle
  Group) P110, P111
Conway, William E., Jr.
  (Nextel) A1027
Conwed Designscape A1072
Conwood A1458
Conzemius, Peter A. P663
Conzinc Riotinto of Australia W488
Coogan, Robert C. A293
Cook, Brian J. (USG Corp.) A1457
Cook, Brian R. (Direct Focus) E193
Cook, David A266
Cook, Donald A140
Cook, Ian M. A387
Cook, James (Berwind Group) P554
Cook, James D. (Computer
  Sciences) A405
Cook, James M. (Manhattan
  Associates) E236
Cook, Jerry E69
Cook, John R., Jr. A1009, P365
Cook, Michael A474, P154, W196
Cook Paint and Varnish A1278
Cook, Paul H. E290
Cook, Richard A1497
Cook, Robert E. W211
Cook, Rodney W89
Cook, Susan J. A527
Cook, Timothy D. A187
Cooke, Amos A494
Cooke, Art P431
Cooke, Jennifer P592
Cooke, Kevann M. A183
Cooke, Paul N. W289
Cooke, Peter H. A849
Cookin' Good brands P393
Cook's meats A408
Cook's sparkling wines A422, A423
Cookson Group A770

Cool Cat lottery game P693
Cool Crunch gum A1527
Cool Whip dessert topping A843
Cooley, Bradford S. E56
Cooley, Cheryl P599
Cooley, Hugh P345
Cooley, James A. A493
Cooley, Jeffrey E. A1023
Coolidge Mutual Savings
 Bank A1500
Coombe, John W247
Coombe, Mary Ellen A557
Coon, Allan E68
Coon, Jonathan C. E146
Cooney, Charles C. A1362
Cooney, Lynne M. A629
Coonfield, David A301
Coonrod, Robert T. P144, P145,
 P585
Coop Atlantique W164
Cooper, Brian S. A1431
Cooper Brothers A1158, P400,
 W462
Cooper Cameron (petroleum
 equipment) A430, W496
Cooper, Charles (Cooper
 Industries) A430
Cooper cheese P723
Cooper, Cheryl P29
Cooper, Chuck (Boston
 Celtics) A280
Cooper Companies (eye care) A1250
The Cooper Corporation A432
Cooper Health System P114
Cooper Industries, Inc. **A430-A431**,
 A462, A584
Cooper, Ira A432
Cooper, Jackie A744, P242
Cooper, Janet K. E239
Cooper, Jean P417
Cooper, Jerry P553
Cooper, Joe R. (Big Lots) A261
Cooper, Joseph P. (Medicis
 Pharmaceutical) E89
Cooper, Marvin D. A1525
Cooper, Michael P393, P700
Cooper, Patty E219
Cooper, Ray W213
Cooper, Raymond S. (Salvation
 Army USA) P427
Cooper, Roger A1285
Cooper, Sherry S. W113
Cooper Tire & Rubber
 Company **A432-A433**, W450
Cooper, William A1158, P400,
 W462
Cooperative Grange League
 Federation Exchange P38
Co-operative Grocers P488
Cooper-Bessemer A430
Cooper-Hewitt, National Design
 Museum P451
Cooperman, Daniel A1067
Coopers & Lybrand
 International A562, A840, A1158,
 P182, P286, P400, P705, W222,
 W324, W462

Cooper/T. Smith Corporation A826
Coordinated Health Services A190
Coords, Robert H. A1347
Coors, Adolph A78
Coors, Adolph, III A78
Coors, Adolph, Jr. A78
Coors Brewing Company A78,
 A875, P294, P428, P634, W230,
 W376, W377
Coors Ceramics. *See* Coorstek, Inc.
Coors Field P663
Coors, Joe A78
Coors, John K. E185
Coors, Peter H. A78, A79
Coors, William K. A78, A79
Coorstek, Inc. E185
Coot Industries (ATVs) A456
Copart, Inc. E**45**, E185
CoPartfinder E45
Copaxone drug W103
Cope A1174
Copeba (company) W552
Copebras A1124
Copeland, F. Dean A1441
Copeland, James E., Jr. A474, A475,
 P154, P155, P590, W196, W197
Copeland, John D. A1419
Copeland, Richard P. P37
Copeland, William W314
Copenhagen tobacco A1458, A1459
Copes-Vulcan A1320
Copley W262
Copper & Brass Sales, Inc. W594
Copper Mountain Networks E174
Copper-7 IUD A1122
Copperbond A1060
Copperidge by E&J Gallo
 wines A521, P169
Coppertone sun care A1250, A1251
Copperweld A896
Coppieters 't Wallant, Jean-
 Claude W195
Copple, Robert D. P127, P575
Coppley men's clothes A691
Coppola, Francis Ford P302
The Copps Corporation P422
Copymaster copier W368
CopyMax printing A1058
Coqueiro canned fish A1181
Cora hypermarkets W164
Cora SA (retailer) W166
Coral betting shops W258, W544
Coral Energy, L.P. A1276, A1277
Corange (diagnostics) W492
Corbett, Gary A. A467
Corbett, Gerald M. N. W313
Corbett, Jeff A485
Corbett, Joseph P640
Corbett, Larry R. A493
Corbett, Luke R. A821
Corbett, Roger C. W644, W645
Corbiere, Adrian B. A627
Corbin Russwin (architectural
 hardware) A264
Corbin, William R. A1519
Corbo, Vincent J. A704

Corbusier, Drue A491
Corby, Brian W464
Corby, Kenneth A. E58, E198
Corcoran, Alison Gregg A1149
Corcoran, Elizabeth P65, P548
Corcoran, John F. A1039
Corcoran, Philip E. P136, P137,
 P580
Corcoran, Thomas A. A116
Corcoran, William M. A1537
Corcóstegui Guraya, Ángel W513
Cord, E. L. A164
Cordano, Mike A929
Cordant Technologies Inc. A112
Cordaro, Robert A. A1475
Cordarone drug A149
Cordero, Alfonso E106
Cordero Mining Company A1344,
 W488
Cordes, Eckhard W189
Cordiant Communications Group
 plc W467
Cordis Corporation (heart disease
 products) A674, A800
Cordon-Cardo, Carlos E72
Core Materials Corporation A1010
Core Pacific Development Company
 Ltd. P126
Corel Corporation (software) A758,
 A972, A1050, A1356, E192, E311
Corelle dinnerware P90, P91, P558,
 P775
Core-Mark International, Inc. P584
Coreson, Dave A1359
CoreStates Financial
 Corporation A954, A1486
CoreWare A894
Corgard drug A290
Corian A534
Coricidin cold medicine A1250
Corinth hydroelectric project A770
Corio, Inc. E179
Corixa Corporation
 (pharmaceuticals) E217
Corlett, E. S. A1410, P484
Corley, James W. "Buster" E51
Corley, Terry B. P53, P543
Corliss steam engine A430
Corman, Judith A. A1255
Cormier & Gaudet (caskets) A718
Corn Flakes cereal A816, A817
Corn Pops cereal A817
Corn Sweeteners A192
Corneel Geerts International A420
Cornelio, Charles C. A795
Cornélis, François W613
Cornelius, James A674
Cornelius, Michael A. A1515
CORNELL auto care
 products A1101
Cornell Companies, Inc. E186
Cornell, Harry M., Jr. A858, A859
Cornell, Howland and Hayes and
 Merryfield plus Hill P573
Cornell, Jim P275
Cornell University P460, P496,
 P584

Corner Bakery Cafe A288, A289
Cornerstone Construction &
  Materials W252
Cornerstone Equity Investors A264
Cornerstone Properties Inc. A560,
  P180
Cornerstone Real Estate Advisers,
  Inc. A922, A923, P320, P321,
  P667
Cornerstone Realty Income Trust,
  Inc. E186
Cornerstone Title Company A1227
Cornhill Insurance PLC W82
Cornhuskers of University of
  Nebraska P759
Cornice Holdings Company,
  Inc. A955
Corning Consumer Products. *See*
  World Kitchen (housewares)
Corning Glass Works A1072
Corning Inc. **A434**-**A435**, A504,
  A898, A1022, P164, P558, P596,
  W450
CorningWare P90, P91, P775
Cornish, Jeffrey L. P702
Cornnuts snack A843
Cornog, Robert A. A1294, A1295
Cornucopia bone china W637
Corolla car P366, P367, P687,
  W614, W615
Corona beer A174, A422, A423,
  P746, W254
Corona car W614
Corona, George S. A819
Corona, Jesús W635
Coronado, William J. A1437
Coronation Street (TV show) W249
Coronet paper products A654
Corporate Brand Foods
  America A742
Corporate Centre Mannesmann
  AG W353
The Corporate Executive Board
  Company E186
Corporate Express (office
  supplies) A1058
Corporate Food Services A1297
Corporate My Yahoo! (intranet
  services) A1546
Corporate Network eCom P763
Corporate Office Properties
  Trust E187
Corporate Property Investors A1286
Corporate Sales Micro Center P336
Corporate Software & Technology,
  Inc. A1218, P584
Corporate Technology Information
  Services E100
Corporation for Public
  Broadcasting P**144**-P**145**, P585
Corporation for the Promotion of
  Production W576
Corpoven W438
CorpTech. *See* Corporate
  Technology Information Services
Corpus Christi State
  University P470
Corpus dairy products W193

Corr, Thomas L. P614
Corrado, Fred A671
Corran, Tom W477
Correctional Foodservice
  Management A190
Correctional Properties Trust E187
Corrections Corporation of
  America E138, E314, W546
Correll, Alston D. A655
Correnti, John A1052
Correze, Jacques W342
Corrie, Jack A315, P97
Corrigan, Fredric W. A325, P105
Corrigan, Jack E. E271
Corrigan, Wilfred J. A894, A895
Corrigan-Davis, Mary Ann A147
Corrigan's jewelers A1552
Corriveau, David O. E51, E190
Corrugados La Colmena A1524
Corsair airplanes A1432
Corsair Communications, Inc. E83,
  E233
Corsiglia, Nancy E. E203
Corso, Patrick A. P131
Corsten, Ralf W461
CORT Business Services (furniture
  rental) A252
Cortese, Edward P291
Cortez Mine W452, W453
Corti, Robert J. A217
Cortina de Alcocer, Alfonso W483,
  W650, W651
Cortland Savings BAnk E205
Cortright, Lynn M. A1089
Corus Brands (wines) A422
Corus Entertainment Inc. A872
Corus Group plc A896, W160,
  W178-**W179**
Corvaia, Joseph D. A1449
Corvair Auto Stores A260
Corvallis Lumber Company A1524
Corvis Corporation A292
Corvita Corporation A283
Cory Corporation A740, P240
Corzine, Jon A660
COS China (Web portal) P278
Cosby, Bill P26, P757
Cosby, Mark S. A1405
The Cosby Show (TV show) A998
Cosgrave, Ronald F. A107
Cosgrove, William P739
Cosmair (hair care) W342
The Cosmetic Center, Inc. A1200
Cosmo car W362
Cosmopolitan (magazine) A700,
  A701, P228, P229, P248, P629
Cosmos Bottling W511
Coso Project geothermal P340
Cost Care, Inc. A1507
Cost Cutters hair salons A1196
Cost Plus, Inc. (stores) A1130
Costa Classica (ship) A331
Costa Crociere (cruise line) A330
Costa Marina (ship) A331
Costa restaurants W639
Costa Riviera (ship) A331

Costantini, William A671
Costas, Bob P250, P251, P641
Costas, John W617
Costco Wholesale
  Corporation A252, A262,
  A436-**A437**, A822, A1348, A1396,
  E247, W164
Costello, Albert A1536
Costello, Ellen M. W113
Costello, Joe P278
Costello, Kevin S. A1125
Costello, Lawrence A153
Costello, Thomas E. (International
  Paper) A771
Costello, Thomas, Jr.
  (Compuware) A407
Coster, Donald A946
Coster, Peter A917
Costley, Gary E. A768, A769
COSUN (sugar) A1436
Cosworth (auto engines) A616,
  W630
Cote, David M. A1412, A1413
Cote, Richard E72
Cote, William O. P489
Cotone, Pierpaolo W575
Cotros, Charles H. A1350, A1351
Cotsakos, Charles M. A567
Cotsakos, Christos A566
Cottee's beverage W155
Cotter & Company A1410, P484,
  P749
Cotter, John A1410, P484
Cotter, Robert F. A1329
Cottle, Gail A. A1037
Cotton, Al A1299
Cotton Bowl (Dallas) P553
Cotton, Richard A999
Cottonelle paper products A826,
  A827
Cotton's Holsum bread A775
Cottrell, Michael W. P557
Coty Awards A1150
Coty (cosmetics) A1118
Couder, Alain A99
Coudurier, Thierry W367
Cougar Valves and Fittings A1088
Couger, Patti P471, P743
Coughlin, Christopher J. A1123
Coughlin, Deborah J. A403
Coughlin, Sue A. P269, P650
Coughlin, Thomas M. A1495
Coull, Ian W301
Coulombe, Joe P747
Coulter Corporation A243
Coulter Counter cell analyzer A242
Coulter, David A226
Coulter Electronics A242
Coulter, James P474
Coulter, Joe A242
Coulter, Wallace A242
Council for Jewish
  Federations P752
Council, Ivy D. A1215
Country Best brands P38, P534
Country Casuals stores A1214
Country Club Malt Liquor P428

Country Clubs, Inc. P130
Country Crock margarine W618, W619
Country Cupboard stores P740
Country Energy, LLC A582, A583, P122, P123, P184
Country Fair gas stations P712
Country Fresh food brand A1338, A1339
Country General Stores P406
Country Hearth baked goods A609
Country Hedging, Inc. P123
Country Inn Specialties A817
Country Inns & Suites by Carlson P106, P107, P567
Country Kitchen Foods A374
Country Kitchen International P106
Country Living (magazine) P229
Country Market stores P198
Country Mart stores P62, P63, P547
Country Miss clothing A690
Country Music Television A334, A1476
Country Pride meats A408, A409
Country Pride restaurants P748
Country Products Group P534
Country Roadhouse Buffet & Grill P562
Country Road stores W172
Country Time lemonade A843, A1105, W155
Countrymark Cooperative P622
Countrywide Credit Industries, Inc. A438-A439
County Classic Dairies P771
County Post P406
County Seat clothing stores A1348
Couper, John W272
Courage & Barclay (brewery) W282
Courage Breweries W162, W230
The Courier-Journal (Louisville, KY) A633
Court TV cable network A180, A872, A873
Société de Courtage d'Assurance Universal W131
Courtaulds Textiles A1242, W72, W114
Courtepaille (restaurants) W58, W59
Courter, Craig A221, P67
Courtesy Insurance Company P257
Courtesy Motors P256
Courtesy Products (coffee and tea) P178
Courtney, Lisa P743
Courtois, Jean-Phillipe A973
Courtot, Philippe E134
Courtright, Geoffrey B. A121
Courtyard by Marriott A732, A912, A913, A1296, W639
Courvoisier cognac W84, W85
Cousteau, Jacques P290, W392
Cousy, Bob A280, P354
Coutinho, Simone A959
Coutte, Didier F. W175

Coutts, Robert B. A883
Couvreux, Christian P. W167
Covad Communications Group, Inc. A1186, A1244
Covance Inc. A434, A600
Covanta Energy Corporation A190, A440-A441
Covarrubias Fernandez, Julio W577
Covenant Health Systems P570
Coveney, Elizabeth P761
Coventry Corporation A1162
Coventry, Mary A. A1263
Cover Girl cosmetics A1164, A1165, A1200, W342
Covert, Geoffrey J. A845
Covey Run wines A422
Covey, Stan A1090
Covia Partnership A1420, A1442, W316
Coviello, Arthur W., Jr. E114, E281
Covington, Graham L. A275
Covitz, David S. A159
COW TECH training programs P708
Cowan, Charles G. W263
Cowart, John R. A1317, P453
Cowboy handgun P578
Cowden, Barbara A1331, P459
Cowdray, Lord A132
Cowen, Bruce E131
Cowens, Dave A280
Cowlan, Richard P297, P658
Cowles Business Media E289
Cowles Media A1160, A1192, A1502
Cowsill, Kevin A407
Cox, Carol M. A1117
Cox, Carrie Smith A1123
Cox Communications, Inc. A390, A442, A632, A1138, E30, E158, E221, E243, P146, P147, P158, P585, P594
Cox, David A. A1039
Cox Enterprises, Inc. A442-A443, P146-P147, P585
Cox, Greg W89
Cox, James Kennedy A442, P146
Cox, James Middleton A442, P146
Cox, John W. A271
Cox, Kathleen P145
Cox, Kermitt L. A93
Cox, Kevin L. A1103
Cox, R. M., Jr. A547
Cox, Roxanne E285
Cox, Samuel W. P618
Cox, Terry L. A845
Coyle, Dennis P. A625
Coyle, Maryanna P117
Coyle, Thomas E. A1075
Coyne, Martin M., II A525
Coyne, William E. A977
Cozaar drug A541, A956
Cozymel's Coastal Mexican Grill A288, A289
Cozza, Patrick A. A735
CP Chem. See Chevron Phillips Chemical Company LP
CP Kelco A704

CP&L Energy A1166
CPB. See Corporation for Public Broadcasting
CPI Qualified Plan Consultants, Inc. A95
CPM Energy P333
CPN. See Centrala Produktow Naftowych
CPR Engineering A786
CPS (gift wrap) A147
C. R. Bard, Inc. A444-A445, A674, A770
CR New Car Price Service P139
CR Technology (X-ray systems) E266
CRA (company) W488
Crabb, Nancy P501
Crabbe Huston A875, P294
Cracchiolo, Anthony P399
Cracchiolo, James M. A143
Cracker Barrel cheese A843
Cracker Jack snack A1106, P90
Cracking the Japanese Market (book) A188
Cracklin' Oat Bran cereal A817
Craddock-Terry Shoe stores A1092
Craft, Harold D., Jr. P584
Crafts & More stores A158
Craftsman tools A462, A1265
Craftsman Truck racing circuit P681
Cragg, Suzanne P611
Craig, B. Jeff A569
Craig Corporation P462
Craig, Timothy P. A871
Craighead, Michael D. E263
Crain, Alan R. A223
Crain, B. J. P471
Craisins dried cranberries P380, P381
Cramb, Charles W. A657
Cramer Electronics A196
Cramer-Klett, Theodor W380
Cranberry Canners P380
Cranberry King P380
Crandall, Bob A164
Crandall, L. Dale A811, P267
Crane Company A446-A447, E23
Crane, Dale A792
Crane, Elsie A981
The Crane Fund A446
Crane, Kelly P560
Crane Nuclear, Inc. (fluid handling) A457
Crane, Richard Teller A446
Crane, Robert C. (Cummins Engine) A457
Crane, Robert M. (Kaiser Foundation) A811, P267
Cranford, Alan N. A1367
Cranford, Mary E155
Cranor, Timothy W. A775
Crary, Bradley V. A71
Crary, Shirley P709
Crate & Barrel (housewares stores) P608, W426, W427
Crate, Darrell W. E149

Craven, John A. W340, W341
Craver, Theodore F., Jr. A533
Craves, Robert E. A437
Crawford Consulting. *See* CCI-MAXIMUS
Crawford, Daniel Eldon A1535
Crawford, Edwin M. "Mac" A322, A323, A904
Crawford, Jim P772
Crawford, Stephen S. A989
Crawford Supply (prison supply) P178
Cray Research Inc. A342, A1284, A1342, W386
Cray, Seymour A342
Crayola A678, A679, P216, P217, P625
Crazy Eddie store A366
Crazy Horse clothing A791, A880, A881
Crazy Prices stores W644, W645
Crazy Taxi (video game) W527
CRC Protective Life Insurance A922, P320
Cream Ale W377
Cream corn starch A487
Cream of Wheat cereal A843
Cream o' Weber dairy product A467
Creamette pasta P90, P91
Creamland Dairy A466, A467
Crean, John A604
Creaney, Martyn A. W453
Creasey, Frederick A. W263
Creative Associates W199
Creative Business Concepts E280
Creative Card P742
Creative Control Designs (HVAC and lighting controls) A802
Creative Design Solutions A928
The Creative Group (advertising) A1208, A1209
Creative Products Resource W256
Creative Publications (greeting cards) A678, P216
Creative Rivets A1322
Creative Technology Ltd. E256, **W180-W181**
CREDCO (mortgage credit reporting) A594
Credence, Inc. A559
Credence Systems Corporation E**46**, E187
Credico (consumer lender) A602
Credisol, S.A. A1509
Crédit Agricole (bank) W182, W224
Credit and Financial Services W447
Credit Card Center E301
Crédit Commercial de France SA W268, W286
Crédit Lyonnais A962, P747, W100, W130, W**182**-W**183**, W384
Credit Management Solutions A594
Credit Mobilier A1422
Credit Reports, Inc. A591
Credit Suisse First Boston A348, A**448**-A**449**, W114, W184, W185

Credit Suisse First Boston (USA), Inc. A90, A218, A234, A448, A449, A600, A614, P190, P595, W184, W185
Credit Suisse Group A448, P637, W88, W**184**-W**185**, W464, W616
Credit Technologies. *See* Lightbridge, Inc.
Credle, Eric P. E204
Credor watches W528, W529
Cree, Drew A595
Cree, Inc. E**47**, E123, E188
Cregg, Roger A. A1179
Creighton, John (Weyerhaeuser) A1518
Creighton, John W., Jr. (Unocal) A1439
Creighton, Lorenzo A1087
Crellin, Alan W. A1443
Créme Egg candy W154
Cremers, F. J. G. M. W627
Cremora brand P90
Crenshaw, Gordon L. A1436, A1437
Crenshaw, W. Edwin A1177, P403
Creole Petroleum W438
Creran, Heather E72
Cresap, McCormick & Paget P480
Crescendo Communications A368
Crescent Market Project A1484
Crescent Operating, Inc. A904
Crescent Resources (real estate) A514
Crescent Vert (artificial gems) W328
Crescent wrenches A430
Crespo, Iván W439
Crest Communities A1227
Crest Hotel W544
Crest Ridge Homes, Inc. A346, A347
Crest toothpaste A1164, A1165
Crestar Financial A936, A1346
Crestline Capital Corporation (retirement properties) A732
Creuzet, Gérard W209
Crew, Spencer R. P451
Crews, Jesse V. A639
Crews, Terrell K. A985
Cribari wines A423
Cricket Communications E232
Cricket disposable lighters A656
Criqui, Robert P355, P682
Crisco shortening A1164, A1165
Crisp, David J. W271
Crisp, Linda E184
Crispix cereal A817
Criss, C. C. P348
Criss, Mabel P348
Criss, Neil P348
Cristal cleaning and laundry products A487
Cristallo, Peter P. E81, E230
Criswell, James A1059
Critchfield, James V. A365
Critelli, Michael J. A1142, A1143
Criterion office furniture A1334, A1335

Critical Care America of New York, Inc. A695
Critical Path, Inc. A1546
Crittenden, Bruce A. A415
Crittenden, Gary A143
Crixivan drug A956, A957
CRK Advertising P100
Croatia Airlines W79
Crocker, Charles E164, P384
Crockett, Gary E126
Crockett, Joan M. A127
Croft & Barrow A838, A839
Croissan'wich A302, A303
Cromb, Barbara I. W609
Cromme, Gerhard W595
Crompton & Knowles A450, W118
Crompton Corporation A**450**-A**451**
Crompton Loom Works A450
Crompton, William A450
Cronin, Kelly E231
Cronin, Mary P221, P626
Cronin, Patrick G. A1013
Cronin, William L. A365
Cronk, William F., III A510, A511
Crook, Carl R. P689
Crook, Dennis R. A1085
Crook, Robert E248
Crooke, Edward A. A425
Crooker, Colleen M. P135, P579
Crop Production Services, Inc. W66, W67
Crosby, Arthur P480
Crosby, Gary L. A309
Crosby, Ralph D., Jr. A1045
Crose, Daniel J. A993
Crosfield (catalysts and silicas) A1536, W278
Croskrey, Stephen E. E29
Cross, Bruce A. A995
Cross Creek (activewear) A1220, A1221
Cross, Gregory A721
Cross Stitch (magazine) W238
Cross, Thomas W. A1159, P401, W463
Cross Timbers Oil. *See* XTO Energy, Inc.
Cross Trainer shoes A1032
CrossAction toothbrush A657
Crossland Economy Studios E59, E201
Crossmark (food broker) A1136
Crosson, Jay A1057
Crossroads brand A1265
Crossroads Cuisine A1296
Crossroads Pipeline Company A1034
CROSSTECH fabrics P523
Crothall Services (health care) W174
Crotty, W. Garrett E75
Crouch, E. C. A133
Crouch, Kenneth W. A821
Crouse-Hinds (electrical materials) A430, A431
Crouzet Automatismes W520
Crouzet, Phillippe W507

Crovitz, Charles K. A635
Crovitz, L. Gordon A507
Crow family P747
Crow, Harlan A1398
Crow, Michael M. P135
Crow, Trammell A1398, P659
Crow/Billingsley
 Investments A1398
Crowe, James Q. A866, A867
Crowe, John C. A723
Crowell, Craven A1370, A1371,
 P468
Crowell, Gary P645
Crowell, Henry A1180
Crowl, Dave A373
Crowley, Dan A696
Crowley, Geoffrey T. P534
Crowley Maritime
 Corporation P585
Crowley, Richard D., Jr. E92, E244
Crowley, Ruth M. A683
Crowley, Thomas P585
Crowley, Thomas B., Jr. P585
Crown Can Hong Kong Ltd. W565
Crown car W614
Crown Center Hyatt Regency
 hotel A678, P216
Crown Center
 Redevelopment A679, P217
Crown Central Petroleum
 Corporation P586
Crown Cork & Seal Company,
 Inc. A452-A453, A1302, W564
Crown Crafts (woven
 bedding) A980
Crown Equipment
 Corporation P586
Crown family A644
Crown Group, Inc. E188
Crown, Henry P621
Crown, John R. A1109
Crown Lager beer W231
Crown, Lester A1484
Crown Media A350, A678, P216
Crown Pumps A446
Crown Royal whiskey W206
Crowne Plaza hotels W544, W545
Crozier, Scott A. A1117
CRS Sirrine Engineers A786
CRSS Constructors A786
Crucial Technology A971
Cruciotti, Augustine M. A1187
Crüesemann, Michael E. W427
Cruesli cereal A1181
Cruise America camper
 rentals A300
Crum, Fred C. A1309
Crum, Gregory N. A1311
Crum, John A. A185
Crum, Terry L. A221
Crumley, Theodore A275
Crummey, John A612
Crump-Caine, Lynn A943
Crumrine, Thomas L. A1009, P365
Crunch candy bar W388
Crusa, Jack D. A859
Crusader Insurance A360

Crush soft drink A383, W155
Crutcher, Michael B. A297
Crutchfield, C. Richard A559
Crutchfield Edward A1486
Cruttenden Roth (investment
 bank) A590
Cruz, Frank H. P144, P145
Cruz, Jane E69, E215
Cruz, Zoe A989
Cruzcampo beer W254, W255
Cryovac packaging A1262
Crystal Brands A648
Crystal Computer Services
 software A1260, P440
Crystal Decisions software P440,
 P441
Crystal Holidays travel
 agency A1478
Crystal Lake Bank and Trust E318
Crystal Light beverages W155
Crystal Palace vodka A423
Crystal, Richard P. A877
Crystal Springs water W193
Crystal sugar P538
Crystal water A946, W193
Crystallex International
 Corporation W452
CrystalPleat window
 furnishings A1317, P453
C. S. Brooks (bath
 furnishings) A1316, P452
CS First Boston Pacific A448, W184
C.S. Green International A344
CSA knitwear A1475
CSA-Czech (airline) W79
CSC. See Computer Sciences
 Corporation
CSFB. See Credit Suisse First
 Boston
CSFBdirect Inc. A449
Csige, Geza A758
CSK Auto Corporation A1078
CSK Corporation W526
CSM (engineering) E131
CSM nv A722
CSR Ltd. A1518
CSU (food retailer) W498
CSW. See Central and South West
CSX Corporation A454-A455,
 A1038
CSX (railroad) P582
C.T. Bowring Reinsurance A916
CT Farm & Country P406
CT Financial Services Inc. W608
CTC Distribution Direct (parcel
 mailing) A1218
C-TEC. See Commonwealth
 Telephone Enterprises, Inc.
CTI Authority E118
CTI Holdings, S.A. A1473
CTI Logistx Inc. A454
CTI-Cryogenics On-Board E213
CTN Media Group, Inc. E188
CTS Corporation E189
CTV Inc. (broadcast TV) W122,
 W123, W593

CTX Mortgage Company A340,
 A341
CU. See Consumers Union of United
 States, Inc.
Cub Cadet lawn equipment P679
Cub Foods stores A1348, A1349,
 P773, W194, W195
Cub motorcycle W264
Cuba (book) P359
Cuba Libre mixed drink W108
Cuban American Oil
 Company A930
Cubbage, Allen P379
Cubbon, M. W565
Cube car W403
CUC International Inc. A338
Cucchi, Gregory A571
Cuccorelli, Albert A305
Cuddihy, Rita M. A1443
Cuff, Kimberly L. E119, E286
Cugine, Steven P. A359
Cuisinart appliances P91, P580
Culhane, Noreen M. A1019, P375
Culinar A774
Culinary Foods A1418, A1419
Cullen, John A373
Cullen, Michael A844
Culligan, Elizabeth R. A670, A671
Culligan, Thomas M. A1191
Culligan Water A618, A752
Cullinan, Joe A1376
Cullinet software A402
Cullman, Joseph A1126
Cullman Ventures A950
Cullo, Leonard A. A723
Cullum Companies
 (supermarkets) A1494
Culp, Dorie A1233
Culp, E. Ronald A1265
Culp, H. Lawrence, Jr. A462, A463
Culpepper, Bruce P345, P604, P679
Culturelle dietary
 supplements A408
Cultus Petroleum W424
Culver, Blaine A108
Culver, David W74
Culver, Robert L. P776
Cumberland Diagnostic & Treament
 Center P369
Cumberland Farms, Inc. P586
Cumberland Pipeline A200
Cumberland Telephone and
 Telegraph A248
Cummings, Bruce P213, P623
Cummings, Candace S. A1475
Cummings, Daniel P111
Cummings, Debra P693
Cummings, Linda M. (Lin) A199
Cummings, Mark E41
Cummings, Nathan A1242
Cummings, Steve E. A1487
Cummins, Andrew E. A101
Cummins, Clessie A456
Cummins Engine Company,
 Inc. A456-A457, A584, W320,
 W326, W594
Cummins, James L. E189

Cummins Wartsila A456
Cummis, Clive S. A1087
Cuna, Claudio W239
Cunard Cruise Line A330, P60
Cundiff, Rich A1523
Cunningham, A. Patrick A503
Cunningham Graphics A204
Cunningham, Jack L., Jr. (Trinity Industries) A1407
Cunningham, J. Dawson A1207
Cunningham, John Patrick (Citrix Systems) E42, E179
Cunningham, Larry H. A193
Cunningham, Norma E47, E188
Cunningham, Tom P299
Cunningham, William H. P498
Cunnion, Robert J., III A1227
CUNY. *See* The City University of New York
Cuomo, Mario E78
Cupid Cash lottery game P473
Cupp, B. Garland A271
Cupp, Kenneth W. A275
Cupps, Peter M. A1471
Cuprinol coatings A1278
CuraGen (genomics) W118
Curatek Pharmaceuticals P741
The Curb P46
Cure 81 ham A730, A731
Curel lotion A234, W308, W309
Curemaster ham A731
Curin, Joanne W435
Curlander, Paul J. A870, A871
Curler, Jeffrey H. A251
Curley, John J. A632
Curley, Thomas A633
Curme, Oliver E267
Curran, Brian M. A1207
Curran, Michael R. A1231
Curran, Ray A1293
Curran, Timothy J. A1357
Current (catalogs) P742
Current (greeting cards) A480
Current Technology, Inc. (process/environmental controls) A462
Currents office furniture systems P276, P277, P652
Currie, Nancy Sherlock P382
Currie, Peter W. W475
Currie, Richard J. W245
Curry, Barbara B. A1417
Curry, William W241
Curtice Burns Foods P38
Curtin Matheson Scientific (diagnostic equipment) A600
Curtis Circulation W330
Curtis, Jim P558
Curtis, Miranda A873
Curtiss, Jeffrey E. A1269
CURVATURA ceiling systems A1457
Curwin, Ronald A247
Curwood, Inc. (medical product packaging) A250, A251
Cusano, Sam A1270, A1271
Cushman & Wakefield Inc. P587
Cushman, J. Clydesdale P587

Cushman, Mark A487
Cushman transports A1380
Custody World (publication) P481
Custom Cable Industries A1334
Custom Cleaner (home dry cleaning) W256
Custom Edge A398
The Customer Comes Second (book) P418
Customers' Afternoon Letter A506
Custom-Res (global reservation system) P418, P419
Custom-Touch compilers E313
Custos (investments) W632
Cutex cosmetics A1201
Cuthbert, Tom A110
Cutillas, Manuel Jorge W108
Cutlass airplanes A1432
Cutler, Alexander A527
Cutler, James E139
Cutler-Hammer (electronics) A526, A527
Cutrer, Michael E254
Cutting, Allen A406
Cuyamel Fruit Company A354
CV Reit E229
CVC Capital Partners W72, W192
CVP. *See* Venezuelan Petroleum Corporation
CVS Corporation A**458**-A**459**, A830, A946, A956, A1202, A1492, A1494
CVS.com A178
CW Lease Nederland B.V. W287
CWR Properties E146
Cyanamid W116
Cyanamid Agricultural Products A148
Cybear Group E156
CyberCare, Inc. (customer relations) E127
CyberCash, Inc. A596, W100
CyBerCorp A348
CyberDisplay LCD's E229
Cyberex, Inc. (process/environmental controls) A463
Cyberian Outpost, Inc. P196
Cybermaster toys W333
Cybernet Electronics (CB radio) W328
Cybernetic Systems E56
CyberOptics Corporation E**48**, E189
Cyberslam toys W333
CyberSource Corporation P511
CyberStar A888
CyberT, Inc. A349
CyberTrader, Inc. A348
Cycle & Carriage Ltd. W307
Cycle pet food A723
Cycle-Sat (telecommunications) A1528
Cycling Plus (magazine) W238, W239
Cygan, Thomas S. A1225
Cygnus, Inc. A244

Cymer, Inc. E**49**, E189
Cymerys, Edward C. A1081
Cymrex watches P308
Cynergy A1028
The Cypress Group A1512, P130, P474, W190
Cypress Merchant Banking Partners P126, P575
Cyprus Amax Minerals Company A1124
Cyprus Eurowings (airline) W79
Cyprus, Nicholas S. A203
Cyras Systems (fiber-optics) E41
Cyrillus (sportswear) W446
Cyrix Corporation A1002
Cyrk (marketing). *See* Simon Worldwide, Inc.
Cyrus, Michael J. A363
CytoGam drug E90, E240
CytoSystems A400
Cytyc Corporation E**50**, E190
Czuba, Richard S. P69

D

D' Ambrose, Michael A1397
D. Connelly Boiler A620
D2 (mobile communications) W628
Da Gama Textiles W552
Da Vinci Re (reinsurance) P458
Dabah, Ezra E177
Dabbiere, Alan E236
Dabek, John P419
Daberko, David A. A1001
Daboo, Jamshed S. W567
Dacco P647
Dachowski, Peter W507
Dacier, Paul T. A543
DACODA P418, P419, P717
Dacom (telecommunications) W334
Dacron A534, A1135
Daddario, Richard A987
Dade Behring Inc. P587
Daewoo Group A476, A616, A1408, P482, W226
DAF Trucks A1078, A1079
Daffy Duck cartoon character A1480, P508
Daft, Douglas N. A382, A383
Daft Punk (music group) W213
Dages, Peter F. A1293
OOO Dagestangasprom W243
Dagnon, James B. A273
Dahan, Rene A577
Dahl, Daryl D. P37
Dahl, W. Robert P111
Dahlbäck, Claes W557
Dahlberg (hearing aids) A234
Dahlberg, Kenneth C. A645
Dahlen, Patrik A1111
Dahlen, Tom A607
Dähler, Erich W225
Dahlstrand, Harold A1314
Dahlvig, Anders W276, W277
Dahmen, David S. A1003
Dai Nippon Brewery W314

Dai Nippon Printing Company, Ltd. **W186-W187**
Dai Nippon Toryo Company, Ltd. W371
Daido Boeki W358
Daifuku America E35
Daigle, Michael A601
Daihatsu (minivehicles) W614
The Dai-Ichi Kangyo Bank, Limited A228, W200, W374
Dai-ichi Mutual Life Insurance Company A92, A878, W396
Daiken Company W358
Daiko Advertising W96, W97
Daikuma discount stores W299
Dailey, John P451
Dailey, Joseph P449, P730
Dailey pickles A467
Daily Camera (Boulder) A569
Daily Chronicle (newspaper) A284, W620
The Daily Comet (Thibodaux, Louisiana) A1021
Daily Herald Company A1502
Daily Mail (London) A284
Daily Mirror (London) A284
Daily News (newspaper) A1402, W620
Daily Racing Form (publication) A1160, P144
The Daily Telegraph (London) W262, W263
Daimler Airways W140
Daimler-Benz A380, A616, A1482, W71, W160, W200, W458, W536, W562, W566, W630. *See also* DaimlerChrysler AG
DaimlerChrysler Aerospace W70, W330
DaimlerChrysler AG A104, A152, A278, A332, A380, A388, A460, A476, A549, A572, A584, A802, A856, A1010, A1044, A1062, A1078, A1190, A1394, A1412, A1482, P390, P560, P563, P644, P649, P673, P679, P695, P706, P713, P747, P764, P71, W132, W160, **W188-W189**, W200, W201, W204, W370, W536, W566, W614, W632. *See also* Chrysler Corporation *and* Daimler-Benz
Dain Rauscher Corporation. *See* RBC Dain Rauscher
Dain Rauscher Wessels W474
Daini Seikosha Company W528, W530
Daini-Denden (Second Phone Company) W328
Dainippon Celluloid Company W234
Dairy Brand A730
Dairy Export P771
Dairy Express A466
Dairy Farmers of America A850, A1338, P58, P90, **P148-P149**, P288, P587, P588, P654
Dairy Farm International Holdings Ltd. W306, W307, W644
Dairy Milk candy bar W154

Dairy Queen P702
Dairylea Cooperative Inc. P588
Dairyman's Cooperative Creamery Association A850, P288
Dairymen P58
Dais, Seigfried W491
Daisy Kingdom home furnishings A1317, P453
Daisy Systems A238
Daisy Systems (electronic automation) E91
Daiwa Kogyo Ltd. W528, W530
Daka International W174
Dakil, David E272
Dakin stuffed animals P486
Dal Pino, Paolo W423
Dalby, Alan J. W476, W477
Dale Electronics A1482
Daleo, Robert D. W593
Dales, James E. A539
D'Alessandris, Joseph P. E21, E148
D'Alessandro, David F. A799
D'Alessandro, Robert T. A1459
Daley, Clayton C., Jr. A1165
Daley, Leo J. A101
Daley, Michael T. A1163
Daley, Robert W. A461
Dalgety W388
Dalkia Holdings W208, W209
Dalkon Shield A148
D'Allaird stores W356
Dallas Community Newspaper Group A568
Dallas Cowboys Football Club, Ltd. P357
Dallas Decorative Center A1398
Dallas Homefurnishing Mart A1398
Dallas Lumber and Supply A1524
Dallas Market Center Company Ltd. A1398
Dallas Mavericks (basketball team) P355
Dallas Power & Light A1416
Dallas Stars (hockey team) P361
Dallas Tank Company A1406
Dallas, Terry G. A1439
Dallas World Trade Center A1398
Dalle, François W342
Dalley, Robert R. A1083
D'Almada, Peter A531
Dalmazia Trieste SpA (real estate) W215
D'Aloia, G. Peter A153
Dalsey, Adrian A484
Dalton, James F. A1359
Dalton, Richard J. E181
Dalton, William R. P. W269
Dalton's Weekly (classified advertising) W621
Daly, Ann P167
Daly, Kevin C. A1185
Daly, Pablo A217
Daly, Richard J. A205
Daly, Ronald E. A1219
Daly, Thomas M. A605
Daly, William P361
Dalzell, Richard L. A131

Dam, S. Peter A387
D'Amato, Anthony P90
D'Amato, Janice M. A1079
D'Ambra, Thomas E. E150
D'Amelio, Frank A. A899
Dames & Moore Group A504
Damlamian, Jean-Jacques W233
Dammerman, Dennis D. A647
Dammeyer, Rod F. A176
d'Amore, Massimo F. A1107
D'Amour, Charles P479
D'Amour, Donald H. P554
D'Amour, Gerald P554
D'Amour, Paul P554
Dampskibsselskabet af 1912, Aktieselskabet W94
Aktieselskabet Dampskibsselskabet Svendborg W94
Damrow Denmark A326
Damrow USA A326
Dan H. Bomar Company A916
Dan Murphy liquor stores W644, W645
Dana auto parts P112, P113, P569
Dana Buchman clothing A880, A881
Dana, Charles A460
Dana Corporation **A460-A461**, A1088, A1320
Dana-Farber Cancer Institute P697
Danaher Corporation A430, **A462-A463**
Danair (airline) W518
Danaklon Group A704
Danao dairy products W193
Danbor Service A/S W95
Dancall Telecom W490
D&B. *See* The Dun & Bradstreet Corporation
D&B HealthCare Information A516
D&D Homes A604
Dando, Stephen W145
D'Angelo Law Library P497
Dangremond, Robert N. A807
Daniel, Charles A610
Daniel, Chris, Jr. A743
Daniel, D. Ronald P221
Daniel Hechter brand A691
Daniel Industries (flow-control) A546
Daniel International (engineering and construction) A610
Daniel, James R. A1117
Daniel, Mark J. W285
Daniel, Ronald A948, P326
Daniel, William D. (Ingram Entertainment) P639
Daniel, William K. (ArvinMeritor) A199
Daniell, Bob A1432
D'Aniello, Daniel A. (Baker & Taylor) P69
D'Aniello, Daniel A. (Carlyle Group) P110, P111
Daniels & Fischer department store A932
Daniels, Bob A169

Daniels, Diana M. A1503
Daniels, Gerald E. A273
Daniels, Iris D. E72
Daniels, John A192
Daniels Linseed Company A192
Daniels, Mitchell E., Jr. A541
Daniels, Pamela H. A259
Daniels, Randy A. P461
Daniels, Steve B. A493
Daniels, Tony W429
Danimals Drinkables dairy
  products W193
Danis, Peter G. A1091
Danish Creamery Association P563
Danish Kitchen frozen foods A609
Dank, Denise E194
Danka Business Systems
  PLC W190-W191
Danka Services International A1142
Dankberg, Mark D. E312
Danly Die Set P581
Dannehl, William B. A683
Danner, Bryant C. A533
Danner Foods A1280
Danner, Ray A1280
Dannewitz, Charles V. A1357
Danon, Lawrence W447
Danon, Pierre W149
Groupe Danone A648, A842, A946,
  W192-W193
Dan's Supreme Supermarkets,
  Inc. P545
Dansikring A/S W525
Dansk Industri Syndikat A/S W95
Dansk International Designs
  (crystal and flatware) A296, A297
Dansk Undergrunds
  Consortium W94
D'Antoni, David J. A201
Danzas Holding AG W202, W203
DAP (caulking) A1456
Dapper, L. Robert A1435
Dapsco P705
D'Aquino, Nuno W231
Darbee, Peter A. A1121
Darbelnet, Robert L. P528
D'Arbeloff, Alexander V. A1372
Darby, Henry W538
D'Arcy Masius Benton &
  Bowles P72, P73, P551
Darcy, Thomas E. P439, P724
D'Arcy, William P72, W136
Darden, Bill A464
Darden, Calvin A1427
Darden, Glenn M. E273
Darden Restaurants,
  Inc. A464-A465, P669
Darden, Thomas E273
Darigold Farm stores P771
Dark, Jerry A567
Darken, Michele E237
Darkie/Darlie toothpaste A386
Darling, Bruce B. P495
Darling, Michele S. A1173
Darman, Richard P110, P567
Darnaby, Rick E290
Darretta, Robert J. A801

Darrow, Kurt L. A855
Darsey, James R. A1053
Dart and Kraft, Inc. A842, A1414,
  A1520
Dart Container
  Corporation P150-P151, P588
Dart Energy P150
Dart Group A1234
Dart Industries A842
Dart, Kenneth B. P150, P151, P588
Dart, Robert C. P150, P151
Dart, Tom P150
Dart Truck A326
Dart, William A. P150, P151
Dart, William F. P150
Darty electronics stores W312,
  W313
Darwin, Charles W636
Darwin Magazine P249
Das, Santanu E304
Dasani water A382, A385
Dasburg, John H. A302, A303,
  A1046, W207
DaSilva, Moacyr E72
Dassault Aviation P766
Dassault Industries W76, W330
Dassler, Adi W62
Dassler, Rudi W62
DAT Motors W402
Data & Metering Specialties A136
Data Broadcasting
  Corporation P350, W430
Data CommWAREHOUSE
  (catalogs) P338
Data Corporation A950
Data Discman CD player W550
Data Exchange E25
Data General Corporation A542
Data Insight P430
Data Packaging, Ltd. E279
Data Processing Resources A406
Data Technology E98
Data Terminal Systems A1002
Data Trace Information
  Services A594
Data Tree (property records) A594
Datachecker A1002
DataFlash memory P273
Dataline (financial
  information) A950
Datamec (out sourcing) A1424
DataMosaic International E36
DataPath Systems (communication
  chips) A894
Dataram Corporation E190
DATAS II (Delta reservaton
  system) A1046
DataSafe (Maxtor servers) A778,
  A779
Datatec P771
DataTools (software) A270
Dataworks (software) A1012
DateWorks (calendars) A146, A147
D'Atri, Justin W. P712
Datsun car W402
Dattilo, Thomas A. A433
Datz, Linda P655

Daubrée, Edouard W366
Daugherty, Arthur A716, P234
Daugherty, Jack E27
Daugherty, Tim R. A583, P185
Daughters of Charity National
  Health System P56, P116, P544
Daughters of Charity, Province of
  the West P118, P119
Dauk, Regis A. P679
Daultresme, Béatrice W343
Dauman, Philippe P. A1477
Daurer, Herta W425
Daurès, Pierre W135
Dauska, Walter J. P621
Davco, Inc. (engine
  accessories) P391
Dave & Buster's, Inc. E51, E190
Davel Communications Group,
  Inc. A561, P181
Davenport Cement A848
Davenport, Don W175
Davenport, Gary B. W271
Davenport Insulation Group A920
Davenport, Lynn E. (Edward J.
  DeBartolo Corp.) P173, P602
Davenport, Lynn P.
  (MAXIMUS) E88
Davenport, Margaret P617
Davenport, Peter J. C. A1193
David Aaron shoes E294
David and Lisa (movie) P219
David Brown Group plc (industrial
  gears) A1380
David, Daryl A1501
David, Doug P690
David, George A1432, A1433
David J. Johnson Company P731
David L. Babson & Company,
  Inc. A922, A923, P320, P321,
  P667
The David Leadbetter Golf
  Academy P251
David Lloyd Leisure club W638,
  W639
David Sarnoff Research
  Center P454
David Weekley Homes P589
David Wilson's Automotive
  Group P589
Davidowski, Ronald P597
David's Bridal shops A932
Davids Ltd. P243
Davidson & Associates, Inc.
  (software) A338
Davidson, Ann D. A121
Davidson, Arthur A682
Davidson, Carolyn A1032
Davidson, Davre A190
Davidson, H. Clint, Jr. P598
Davidson, Janet A899
Davidson, J. Kenneth A1261
Davidson, Richard K. A1423
Davidson, Sheila K. A1017, P371
Davidson, Sue H. A1553
Davidson Supply A108
Davidson, Walter A682

Davidson, William (Guardian Industries) P212, P213, P623
Davidson, William (Harley-Davidson) A682
Davie, Ron A1221
Davies, Chris W341
Davies, Clive B. E84
Davies, Curtis W469
Davies, Gavyn W145
Davies, G. Basil A897
Davies, Geraldine W465
Davies, Robert A., III A358, A359
Davies, Ronald W. A937
Davignon, Etienne W59
Dávila, Luis W439
Dávila Urcullu, Jaime W583
Davis, A. D. A1532
Davis, A. Dano A1532, A1533
Davis, Alan S. A1311
Davis, Alfred P682
Davis & Company (wine auctioneers) A1304
Davis, Andy P615
Davis, Angela P552
Davis, Arthur A112, W74
Davis, Bruce (Digimarc) E192
Davis, Bruce G. (IMC Global) A753
Davis, Charles A. A917
Davis, Christopher J. A1233
Davis, Craig S. A1501
Davis, Crispin W478, W479
Davis, Curtis A171
Davis, Darrell P740
Davis, Don H., Jr. (Rockwell) A1210, A1211
Davis, Don K. (Progress Energy) A1167
Davis, D. Scott A1427
Davis, Edward W74
Davis, Erica T. A1071
Davis, Erin D. E298
Davis, E. Stephen A607
Davis, Gareth W282, W283
Davis, Gary L. A791
Davis, George (Applied Materials) A189
Davis, George E. (Lincoln National) A879
Davis, George F. (Hershey) A709
Davis, Jack E. A1139
Davis, Jacob A868, P292
Davis, James S. (New Balance Athletic Shoe) P686
Davis, Jane G. A1551
Davis, Jay M. P682
Davis, J. B. P652
Davis, J. E. A1532
Davis, Jean E. A1487
Davis, Jim (SAS Institute) P431
Davis, Jocelyn P29, P529
Davis, John (Allmerica) A124
Davis, John L. (National Steel) A1007
Davis, John (Rank Group) W472
Davis, Joseph D. P253
Davis, Karyll A. A723
Davis, Leonard (ANADIGICS) P28

Davis, Leon (Rio Tinto) W488
Davis, Lynn D. (Allegheny Technologies) A117
Davis, Lynn J. (ADC Telecommunications) A71
Davis, Marvin A622, A1420
Davis, M. Austin A1532
Davis, Milton L. A397
Davis, Nancy P659
Davis, Peter W300, W301
Davis, Raymond P. E307
Davis, Rebecca C. A93
Davis, Reginald E. A1487
Davis, Richard K. (US Bancorp) A1445
Davis, Richard (Rand McNally) P408
Davis, Robert A. (NCR) A1013
Davis, Robert G. (USAA) A1453, P503, P763
Davis, Robert S. (Wyndham) A1541
Davis, Robert T. (United States Postal Service) A1429, P491
Davis, Robert (Winn-Dixie) A1532
Davis, Roger W115
Davis, Stephen W. A969
Davis, Susan F. A803
Davis, Terry J. W231
Davis, Thomas, III (BJ's) A263
Davis, Thomas W. (Merrill Lynch) A961
Davis, Tine A1532
Davis, Tom E. (RehabCare Group) E111
Davis Vision, Inc. A717, P235
Davis Wholesale stores A158
Davis, William E. (Niagara Mohawk) A1029
Davis, William L. (R. R. Donnelley) A1218, A1219
Davis, William (Table Supply) A1532
Davison, Barry E. W93
Davison Chemical A1536
Davison, Terri E67, E212
Davisson, Bill P622
Davis-Standard (plastic and rubber extrusion) A450
Davnet Telecommunications Pty Ltd. W400, W401
Davol Inc. A444, A445, A770
Davon (concrete) W252
Davtel W401
Daw Drug A1202
Dawes, Alan S. A477
Dawley, Claude A56
Dawson, Chuck P443
Dawson Home Fashions A1316
Dawson Production Services, Inc. E79
The Day & Zimmermann Group, Inc. P589
Day, Bruce D. W495
Day, Colin W477
Day, Fred N., IV A1167
Day, Guy A1062
Day, Randy P393

Day, Thomas R. A731
Dayco Industrial Power Transmission A326, P310, P664
Daymarc E44
Days Inn A338, A339
DaySpring (greeting cards) A678, A679, P216, P217
Daystar International A344
Daystrom (electronics maker) A1252
Day-Timers personal planners A618
Dayton Engineering Laboratories P152
Dayton Flexible Products A236
Dayton, George A1352
Dayton Hudson Corporation A158, A232, A490, A1352
Dayton (Ohio) *Daily News* A442, A443, P146
Dayton Tire & Rubber W138
Dayton Winfastener P705
Daytona International Speedway Corporation E75, E222
DAYTONA USA (theme park) E75, E222
DB Capital Partners P691
DB Leben (insurance) W200
DBA (bowling) A298
DBI Insurance Company Ltd. W99
DBKOM (telecom network) W352
DBV-Winterthur Group W185
DC Card Company, Ltd. W371
DC Comics A180
D.C. Cook nuclear plant A140
D. C. Heath (textbooks) A1190
d-Con home care W476, W477
DDB Needham Worldwide (advertising) P372
DDB Worldwide (advertising) A1062, A1063
DDi Corporation (wireless telecom) E191, W328, W418
DDJ Capital Management A1094
DDL (Danish airline) W518
de Aguiar Teixeira, Carlo A. W437
de A. Mayer, Ricardo W377
de Angoitia Noriega, Alfonso W583
de Bedout, Juan Ernesto A827
De Beers (diamonds) P776, W92, W348, W349, W488
De Benedetti, Carlo W422
De Benedetti, Marco W423, W575
de Bergia González, Francisco W579
De Beukelaer biscuits W193
de Brier, Donald P. A1055
de Campos Meirelles, Henrique A603
de Castries, Henri A219, W105
de Chalendar, Pierre-André W507
de Combret, Bernard W613
de Croisset, Charles W269
de Cure, Marc W89
de Espírito Santo Silva, José W224
de Espírito Santo Silva, José Maria W224

de Espírito Santo Silva, Ricardo W224
de Gaulle, Charles W130
de Goya y Lucientes, Francisco José P204
de Havilland aircraft W132
de Hegedus, Coloman A387
de Herrera, Leonor W439
De Hooiberg Brewery (The Haystack) W254
de Izaguirre, Pascal W69
de Jong, Jan Maarten W57
De Keersmaecker, Guido W257
De Keersmaeker, Paul W288
de Kool, L. M. A1243
de La Chapelle, Philippe A1499
de La Martinière, Gérard W105
De La Riva, Juan L. A199
de la Rivière, Bruno A517
de Larosiére, Jacques W131
de Lasa, Jose M. A59
de las Morenas López, Carmelo W483, W651
de La Vaissière, Vincent W447
de Leeuw, Fred L. E32
de Lesseps, Ferdinand W558
De Lisi, Nancy J. A1127
De Lorean car A260
De Luca (entree maker) P392
De Luca, Guerrino W338, W339
De Luca, Michael P167
D.E. Makepeace (gold and silver) A550
de Margerie, Christophe W613
de Margerie, Philippe W559
de Marillac, Louise (Saint) P56
de Mars, Susan A85
de Mevius family W288
de Molina, Alvaro G. A227
de Munnik, Hans A841, P287, W325
de Navarro, Jose Francisco A754
de Panafieu, Guy W150, W151
De Paul, Vincent (Saint) P56
de Pesquidoux, Hubert W77
De Pree, D. J. A706
De Pree, Hugh A706
De Pree, Max A706
De Prycker, Martin W77
de Puppi, Luigi W124, W125
de rigueur footwear E101
de Ruiter, Hendrikus W179, W499
De Santi, Dan P247
de Sarrau, Xavier A173, W91
de Seze, Amaury-Daniel W131
D.E. Shaw & Company (hedge fund) A130, A226, A960
de Silguy, Yves-Thibault W559
De Simone, Lawrence E. A1155
de Smedt, Pierre-Alain W481
De Sole, Domenico W250, W251
de Souza Gonçalves, Albano W437
de Souza, Teresa W225
De Spaarnestad (publishing) W626
de Spoelberch family W288
de Swaan, Tom W57

De Tuinen natural products stores W498
de Uriarte, Héctor M. W635
de Vasconcelos Lima, José J. W437
de Vaucleroy, Gui W195
de Virville, Michel W481
de Weck, Pierre W617
de Weert, Arnaud A1323
De Wilde, Julien W77
De Witte, Jaak W289
de Ybarra y Churruca, Emilio W483
DealerTrack (online auto lending) E27
Dealing 3000 workstation W485
Deam, William A67
Dean, Alan A703
Dean, Donna J. P415
Dean Foods Company A466-A467, A850, A1094, A1338, P148, P288
Dean, Hilton A563, P183, P605, W223
Dean, Howard M. A466, A467
Dean, James W458
Dean, John C. (Silicon Valley Bancshares) E122
Dean, John S. (Steelcase) A1335
Dean, Lloyd H. P119, P570
Dean, Richard H. P768
Dean, Sam A466
Dean Tire A432
Dean, Warren M. A787
Dean Witter, Discover A226, A988
Dean Witter Reynolds A204, A988, A1264
DeAngelis, Frederick J. E34
DeAngelo, Dominick J. A293
Dear America (books and TV show) A1255
Dearborn Mid-West Conveyor Company W605
Deardorff, J. Richard A1207
Dearlove, A., James E262
Deason, David S. A233
Deats, James L. A1091
Deavenport, Earnest W., Jr. A523
Deavens, Greg A361
Deaver, Scott A213
DeBartolo, Edward J., Jr. A1286, P172, P602
DeBartolo, Edward J., Sr. A490, P172
DeBartolo Entertainment P172
DeBenedictis, Nicholas E265
DeBerry, Donna A1541
DeBiasi, Glenn P535
Debica tires A664
Debis Air-Finance W188
Debis Systemhaus (information technology) W204
DeBlasio, Michael P. A889
DeBoer, Bruce R. E129
DeBoer, Jack P. E169
Debon, Pascal W413
Debrodt, Donna A407
DeBruce Grain, Inc. P589
DeBruce, Paul P589
Debry, Jean-Luc A1263

Debswana Diamond W92
DeBuck, Donald G. A405
DEC. See Dyrekcja Eksploatacji Cystern
DeCamp, Dodd W. A1129
DeCanniere, Dan P631
DeCarlo, Anthony J. P662
DeCarlo, Don D. A483
DeCaro, Thomas C. A969
Decelle clothing store A304, A305
Dechow, Mary A1313
DeCiccio, John M. A799
Decillion A1072
Decker, Alonzo A264
Decker, Dwight W. A410, A411
Decker foods A409
Decker, Glenn J. A1225
Decker, Harold P44, P45
Decker, Michael B. P519
Decker, Robert L. E40, E178
Decker, Susan A1547
DeClouet, Gladys A785
Decor Concepts commercial furniture E202
Décoration Chez-Soi (publication) W471
DeCordova, Bryan M. A969
DeCota, William R. P399
Deddens, Carl J. A1499
Dedman, Robert H., Jr. P131, P577
Dedman, Robert H., Sr. P130, P131
Dedrick, Gregg R. A1405
Deeds, Edward A1012
Deemer, Barbara A. A1449
Deep Blue supercomputer A764
Deep Impact (movie) P166, P167
Deep Rock Oil A820
Deep Woods OFF repellents A1247, P433
DeepTech International A536
Deepwater cogeneration plant A88
Deer Park Refining Limited Partnership A1277
Deer Valley wines A423
Deerbrook Insurance Company A126
Deere & Company A468-A469, E280
Deere, Charles A468
Deere, John A468
Deering, Barbara A1161
Deering Harvester A1010, P342
Deering, Mari-Ann E172
Deering, William P342
Dees, Robert E., Jr. A1505
Deese, George E. A609
DeFabis, Mike P62
DeFalco, Stephen P. A1111
Defender handgun P578
Defense Electronics A342
Deffebach, Harry L. A793
Deffenbaugh, Ted A929
Defforey, Louis W164
Definity 2 trifocals A800
DeFrancisco, Margaret R. P372, P373, P688
DeFranco, James A528, A529

Defratus, Kellie P597
Degas, Hilaire Germain
  Edgar A1304
Deggendorfer Werft und
  Eisenbau W351
DeGiovanni, Frank F. P195
Degn, Doug A1495
Degnan, John J. A357
DeGolyer, Everette A132
DeGraan, Edward F. A656, A657
DeGrande, JoAnn A1501
Degree deodorant W618, W619
DeGregorio, Bob A851, P289
Degrémont (water) W558
DeGroote, Michael (Laidlaw) A206
Degussa Metals Catalyst
  Cerdec E257
Degussa-Hüls AG (chemicals) A236,
  W218, W219
Deignan, D. Michael E311
Deily, Linnet F. A349
De-Ion brand A527
Dejouany, Guy W624
DEK Energy Company A184, A185
DEKALB Energy A184
DEKALB Genetics A984, A985,
  A1122
Dekkers, Marijn A1383
DeKuyper cordials A618
Del Monte Foods
  Company A470-A471, A1204,
  P474, P475
Del Moro, Robert J. P413
del Rio, Xavier W635
del Salto, Carlos A237
del Valle, José Luis W513
Del Vecchio, Claudio P713
Del Webb Corporation (home
  builder) A1178, A1179, P643
Delabrière, Yann W443
Delainey, Dave A553
Delaney, Dennis A757, P245, P639
Delaney, James M. A1225
Delaney, Michael V. A1459
Delaney, Rory A. A1137
Delano, Harley J. P489
DeLany & Company A172, W90
DeLany, Clarence A172, P48, W90
Delaplane, Thomas M. A511
DeLapp, Jeffery A743
Delark, Robert J. E52
Delaware Management
  Holdings A878
Delaware North Companies
  Inc. P590
Delchamps stores P644
Delco Electronics A476, A736
Delco Remy International,
  Inc. A1012, P152-P153, P590
DeLeo, Richard A439
Delfino, Angelo W215
DelGrosso, Douglas A857
Delhaize, Adolphe W194
Delhaize, Edouard W194
Delhaize, Jules W194
Delhaize "Le Lion"
  S.A. W194-W195

Deli XL (food supplier) W498
Deliberto, Robert A329, P109
Delicare detergent A358, A359
Delicates brand A791
Deli-Fast Foods P623
Deli-Maatschappij A1436
Delimex Holdings, Inc. (frozen
  Mexican foods) A722
Delisle dairy products W193
Delk, R. Mitchell A627
Delker, Wayne L. A375
Delker, Wilfried A153
Dell Computer Corporation A74,
  A248, A398, A472-A473, A636,
  A760, A782, A928, A1050, A1062,
  A1336, E190, E201, E256, E263,
  E267, E272, E281, P338, W180
Dell, Michael S. A472, A473, A636,
  A762, A984, A1122
Della Penta, David T. A601
della Sala, Umberto A621
Dell'Antonia, Jon C. A1069
Delmarva Power & Light A1174
Delmas, Philippe W71
DeLoach, Harris E., Jr. A1302,
  A1303
Deloitte Consulting A808
Deloitte Touche Tohmatsu A204,
  A474-A475, P154-P155, P206,
  P590, P620, P776, W196-W197
Deloitte, William A474, P154, W196
DeLorenzo, David A. A495
Delperdang, Janice E193
Delphi Automotive Systems
  Corporation A460, A476-A477,
  A650, A736, A856, A1412
Delprat, Guillaume W128
Delta Air Lines, Inc. A272, A364,
  A428, A478-A479, A698, A1012,
  A1046, A1420, E96, P94, W68,
  W71, W78, W132, W140, W540
Delta and Pine Land Company
  (cotton seed) A984
Delta Center arena P656
Delta Communications A1362
Delta Consolidated Industries, Inc.
  (tools and components) A462
Delta Dental Plan of
  California P591
Delta Design E44, E182
Delta Express A478
Delta faucets A920, A921, P298
Delta rockets A120, A272
Delta Steel, Inc. W461
Delta Tube W293
Delta Woodside Industries,
  Inc. P342
Deltaven W439
DeLuca Anthony T. A215
DeLuca, Carmela P161, P595
DeLuca, Charles E203
DeLuca, Frederick A. P160, P161,
  P595
Deluxe Corporation A480-A481
Deluxe Entertainment
  Services W472, W473
Deluxe Film Laboratories (film
  processing) W473

Deluxe Paper Payment
  Systems A480
Delvag Luftfahrt-Versicherungs-AG
  (insurance) W345
Delvita stores W194, W195
Demag Krauss-Maffei
  (engineering) W352
Demag (machinery) W352
DeMarco, Frederick L. P145
DeMarco, John P313
DeMars, Jerry V. A1053
Demartini, Gretchen A595
DeMartini, Richard M. A227
DeMartino, Frank A. P387
Dematic (engineering) W352
Demax Software A792
Demeritt, Stephen R. A649
Demerling, Donna J. A1387
DeMerlis, Jim A1535
Demers, Pat E190
Demetrion, James T. P451
Demetriou, Steven J. P691
Demicell, Dan A1471
Demilio, Mark S. A905
DeMillo, Richard A. A713
DEMINEX (oil exploration) W218
Demio car W363
Demo, Murray A77
d.e.m.o. stores E101, E259
Demon Internet W522
Demorest, Harry L. P579
Demoulas, George P591
Demoulas, Mike P591
Demoulas Super Markets Inc. P591
Dempsey & Company A566
Dempsey, Dennis A171
Dempsey, Jack A744, P242
Dempsey, Paul S. E64
Dempsey, William G. A59
Dempster, Charles K. A1465
DeMuro, Gerard J. A645
Demuynck, Guy G. M. W445
den Bergh, Jurgens W618
den Bergh, Van W618
Den Horen Brewery W288
Denaro, Robert P. P409
Denbury Resources Inc. (oil and
  gas) E191, P475
Dendrite International, Inc. E191
Deng Xiaoping W542
Denis, Bertrand A911
Denis, Roberto A625
Denison, David F. P191
Denison, John G. A1311
Denka Grace. See Grace Chemicals
  K.K.
Dennard, Richard L. A1135
Denner, Stephen G. A1007
Denningham, Wayne A. A111
Dennis, David L. A1367
Dennis, Felix P338
Dennis, Kenneth D. A289
Dennison, Aaron A210
Dennison, Andrew A210
Dennison, Eliphalet Whorf A210
Dennison, Henry A210

Dennison Manufacturing
  Company A210
Denny, Charles A70
Denny, Diane S. P115
Denny, Dwight D. A1223
Denny, Michelle W181
Denny, Robert M. A405
Denny's Restaurants A86, A836,
  P282, W298, W299
Deno, David A1405
DENSO CORPORATION W226
Denson, Charles D. A1033
Denson, William F., III A1485
Dent, Hawthorne A1230
Dental Blue P85
The Dental Concern, Inc. A739
Dental-Net, Inc. A1163
Denti-Cal P591
Dent-Kannon, Pinkie A1503
Denton, Robert E. A425
Dentsu Inc. P72, P551,
  W198-W199, W394
DENTSUmarchFIRST (Internet
  services) W198, W199
Dentyne gum A1118
Denver Broncos Football Club P357
Denver International Airport P663
Denver Nuggets (basketball
  team) P355
The Denver Post A568, P670
*Denver Rocky Mountain
  News* A568, A569
Deo Deo (retailer) A1056
Deoras, Sudhir W567
DEP (hair products) A1246, P432
Depakote drug A58
dePalo, Armand M. P215
Depend undergarments A826, A827
Deposit Interest Retention Tax
  (DIRT) W86
Depot convenience stores A1084
Depot Food Store A1084, A1085
DePuy Inc. A800
Dequest water treatment
  chemicals A1301
Derbesse, Michel W135
Derbyshire, Adam C. E283
Derhofer, George A1475
Derieg, Thomas F. A1505
Dermatological Research
  Laboratories A58
Dermigny, Nicholas P. E287
Deromedi, Roger K. A842, A843,
  A1127
DeRoy, Craig I. A595
Derrick, James V., Jr. A553
Derrico, Georgia S. E291
D'Errico, John J. A895
Deruluft (airline) W344
DeRusha, William A702
deS Couch, David A1313
DES (diethylstilbestrol) drug A540
Desai, H. K. E272
DeSalvo, Daniel R. P43
DeSanctis, Ellen R. A311
DeSanto, Joseph A1233
Desbarats-Bollet, Bruno W467

Desc SA A450
Descarpentries, Jean-Marie W150
d'Escatha, Yannick W209
Deschamps, Bruno A531
Descheemaeker, Stéfan W289
Desenex over-the-counter
  medication W414, W415
Deseret Medical A244
Desert Classic men's clothes A691
Desert Inn A1328
Desert Partners A1456
Desert Peak geothermal P340
Desford Steel Tubes A1386
Desfosses International
  (media) W348
Design Studio stores A1530, A1531
Designer Checks (company) A480
Designer Holdings
  (sportswear) A1498, P100
Designers' Collection
  (stationery) A146, A147
DesignTex (fabrics) A1334
DesignWare (party goods) A146,
  A147
DeSimone, L.D. A976
Desitin A1118
Desjardins, Daniel W133
Desmarest, Thierry W612, W613
Desmond, Mick W249
Desmond-Hellmann, Susan
  D. A641
Desnouee, Jean P. A101
Desnoyers, Jerome A294
DeSoto A1278
DeSoto Mills A1220
Desser, Ed P355
De-Sta-Co (clamps and
  valves) A502
d'Estaing, Antoine Giscard W521
d'Estaing, Henri Giscard W171
Destec Energy, Inc. A88, A504,
  A518
DeStefano, Gary M. A1033
Destileria Serralles W84
Detailleur, J. M. W643
Details (magazine) A80, A81, P32,
  P33
Deterding, Henri W500
Detergentes Bombril S.A. A374
Detharding, Herbert W117
Detroit Bank A394
Detroit Diesel (motor
  manufacturing) A1010, P390,
  P699, W188
The Detroit Edison Company A512,
  A513
Detroit Free Press A832, A833
Detroit Lions (football team) P262,
  P357
Detroit Medical Center A406, P591
Detroit Metropolitan Airport P731
The Detroit News A633, A832
The Detroit Pistons Basketball
  Company P212, P355, P623
Detroit Race Course W258
Detroit Red Wings (hockey
  team) P361

Detroit Savings Bank A394
Detroit Savings Fund
  Institute A394
Detroit Shock (basketball
  team) P355
Detroit Tigers, Inc. (baseball
  team) A500, P162, P307
Detroit White Lead (paint
  maker) A1278
DETROITBANK Corporation A394
Detter, Gerald L. A381
Dettinger, Warren W. A489
Detwiler, John R. E46, E187
Detwiler, W. F. A116
Deull, Charles B. A1255
Deupree, William A1164
Deuster, Robert G. E253
Deutch, John P438
Deutche Post W344
Deutsch (advertising) A772, A773
Deutsch brand A208, A209
Deutsch, Donny J. A773
Deutsch, Robert V. A379
Deutsch, Ted A213
Deutsche Airbus W70
Deutsche Bahn AG (railroad) W352
Deutsche BA Luftfahrtgesellschaft
  mbH W141, W344
Deutsche Banc Alex. Brown P110
Deutsche Bank AG A614, E313,
  P190, W82, W104, W188,
  W200-W201, W352, W374, W380,
  W396, W426, W464, W616, W638,
  W652
Deutsche Beteiligungs AG W201
Deutsche Bundespost W202, W204
Deutsche Hypothekenbank W200
Deutsche Lufthansa AG. *See*
  (Deutsche) Lufthansa AG
Deutsche Perrot-Bremsen
  (brakes) A152
Deutsche Post AG A484,
  W202-W203, W541
Deutsche Postbank W202
Deutsche Reichpost W204
Deutsche SB Kauf food stores W364
Deutsche Telekom AG A1186,
  A1218, A1248, A1318, A1360,
  W76, W106, W134, W152,
  W204-W205, W214, W232, W272,
  W352, W574
Deutsche Tiefbohr-AG W461
Deutsche Treuhand
  (accounting) A840, P286, W324
Deutsche Versicherungs AG
  (insurance) W82
Deutsche Waggonbau (rail
  cars) W132
Deutscher Aero Lloyd
  (airline) W344
Deutsch-Osterreichische
  Mannesmannrohren-Werke W352
DEUTZ AG W201
Deutz Argentina farm
  equipment A96, A97
Deutz-Allis A96
Devany, Stephen W605
Devcon Construction Inc. P592

Development Services of
America P727
Devening, R. Randolph A743
Devereux, Robert W623
Devices for Vascular
Intervention A674
Devil Dogs snacks A774, A775
DeVilbiss A748
Devine, Brian K. P394, P395, P701
Devine, Robert P626
DeVinney, Betty W. A523
Devlin, Gail E. A357
Devlin, George A399
Devlin, Michael T. E110, E276
Devlin, Richard A1319
Devlyn, Frank J. P421, P718
DeVoe, David F. A623, W391
Devon Energy
Corporation A482-A483, A820
Devonshire Custom
Publishing A615
Devonshire, David W. A755
DeVos, Dick M., Jr. P536
DeVos, Richard P536
DeVos, Ronald G. E95, E249
Devtek Electronics
Enclosure A1240
DevX Energy, Inc. E183
DeWALT power tools A264, A265
Dewar's scotch W108, W109, W206
Dewey & Almy Chemical A1536
Dewey, Timothy A418
Dewhurst, Moray A625
DeWitt Media W466
DeWitt, Norman W. E112
DeWitt Wallace-Reader's Digest
Fund A1192
DeWolf, Nicholas A1372
Dexheimer, Brian S. A1261, P441
Dexia W64
Dext (recycling) E285
Dexter Axle W605
Dexter, Charles P422
Dexter Shoe Company A253
DeYonker, Alex J. A1313
DeYoung, John M. W377
DeZurik A1320
DFC Transportation A466
DFG Foods A743
DFS Group Limited P156-P157,
P592, W348, W349
D.H. Baldwin Company P260
Dharia, Arvind E294
Dharma & Greg (TV show) A61
Dhenain, Jean-Michel W547
D'Hinnin, Dominique W331
DHL International A484, W202,
W203, W344, W404
DHL Worldwide Express, Inc. A364,
A484-A485, W302, W404
di Amore liqueurs A423
Di Giorgio Corporation P592
Di Giorno pizza A842, A843
Di health and beauty products
stores W194, W195
Di Lusso salami A731
di Marco, Patrizio W251

Di per Di stores W165
Dia discount stores W164
Dia Met Minerals W128
Dia stores W165
Diabetes Corner A155
Diabetes Shoppe A155
Diabinese drug A1118
Diablo Canyon nuclear plant A1120
Diablo car W631
Diageo plc A296, A302, A316, A648,
A1102, A1136, A1510, W84, W108,
W174, W206-W207, W230, W254,
W624
Diagnostic Health
Corporation A699
Dial (car leasing) W56
The Dial Corporation A358,
A486-A487, A1200, A1478, W256,
W488
Dial, Teresa A. A1509
Dialco supermarkets W498
DIALOG (online full text
service) A832, W592
Diamond, Andrea A881
Diamond beer W377
Diamond, Bernard A1409, P483
Diamond Chain P540
Diamond Crystal Brands
(nutritional products) A730
Diamond Crystal (food
processing) A325
Diamond Crystal salt P566
Diamond, David A. A1009, P365
Diamond department stores A490
Diamond Fields (mining) W284
Diamond, Frank A400, A1232
Diamond, Howard P584
Diamond Offshore Drilling,
Inc. A884, A885
Diamond Oil A1344
Diamond Park Fine Jewelers A1552
DIAMOND plaster A1457
Diamond Products (household
products) A656
Diamond, Richard A81, P33
Diamond, Robert E., Jr. W115
Diamond Rug A980
Diamond Shamrock
Chemicals A1054
DiamondMax disk drives A928,
A929
Diamonds. *See* Dow Jones
Industrial Average unit trusts
Diana, Princess of Wales P416,
P716
Diana (publishing) W107
Diane Von Furstenberg fashion
designs A216
Diapazza, Samuel A. W463
Dias, Ronald J. A1373
Diaz, Anthony J. A619
Diaz, Jacinto W577
Díaz, Porfirio W440
Diaz, Tony P205
Dibelco W552
DiBiasio, Dolf A181
Dible, David A1495

Diboll, J. C. A1364
Dibrell, Alphonso A492
Dibrell Brothers A492
Dibrell, Richard A492
DiCamillo, Gary T. A1148, A1149
DiCarlo bread A775
Dicciana, Nance K. A1213
DiCerchio, Richard D. A437
DiChristina, Michael F. E61
Dick, Brian J. A451
Dick Corporation P593
Dick, David E. P593
Dick, Douglas P593
Dick, Noble P593
Dick, Rollin A414
Dick Smith Electronics
stores W644, W645
Dicke, Allen P586
Dicke, Carl P586
Dicke, James F., II P586
Dickens & Grant cigarettes W240,
W241
Dickens Data Systems
(distributor) A1140
Dickerson, James H., Jr. A323
Dickey, Nancy W. P471
Dickie, Brian N. A1417
Dickies T-shirts P773
Dickinson, Fairleigh A244
Dickinson, Fairleigh, Jr. A244
Dickinson, Inger P601
Dickinson, Robert H. A331
Dickinson School of Law P699
Dickinson, Wright, Moon, Van
Dusen & Freeman A220, P66
Dickoff, Gil A. A447
Dick's Sporting Goods, Inc. P593
Dickson, Allen P275
Dickson, Bruce A509
Dickson, David C. (Administaff) A75
Dickson, David N. (Hormel
Foods) A731
Dickson, John (Roundy's) P422
Dickson, John T. (Lucent) A899
Dickson Licensing Limited (leather
goods) W607
Dickson, Lisa F. A289
Dickson, Lorraine A691
Dictaphone Corporation A1142
Diddy Kong Racing (video
game) W395
Didier, Pascal E49
Didion, James J. P121
DiDonato, Eugene J. E83
DiDonna, Dominick W. A705
Die Welt (newspaper) W106, W107
Diebels (brewery) W288
Diebold, Alain P445
Diebold Bahmann A488
Diebold, Charles A488
Diebold, Inc. A488-A489
Dieckmann, Karl W. E125
DieHard batteries A802, A1265
Diehl, Philip N. A1553
Diehm, Russell C. P559
Diekmann, Michael W83

Dielectric Laboratories (microwave filter) A502
Diem, Ruth A701, P229, P629
Diener, Robert A1451
Dienes, George L. A1361
Dienst, Edward J. A1029
Dierberg, James F. E204
Diercksen, John A1473
Diesel Car (magazine) W239
Diesel, Rudolph A456
Diesel, R. Wayne P461
Diesel Technology (fuel injection systems) P390, P391, P699
Diesen, Magnus W557
Diet Pepsi soft drink A1103, A1105, A1107
Diet Rite soda W155
Dieter, Werner W352
D'Ieteren s.a. W552
Dieterich Standard (instruments) A502
Dietz, Dave P595
Dietz, Garrett L. P481
Dietz, James P. P770
Dietz, Mark W. P131
Dieusaert, Antoon W117
Difco Laboratories A244
Digalen drug W492
Digangi, Diane P487, P751
Di-Gel A1250
Digeo Broadband Inc. A350, P511
DiGeso, Amy A1159, P401, P705, W463
Digex (Web hosting company) A1534
Diggs, James C. A1153
Digicom Systems. *See* Broadxent
Digimarc Corporation E192
Digimon: Digital Monsters shoes A295
DiGiorno pizza P436
Digital City A180
Digital Creators E127
Digital Equipment Corporation A54, A398, A1184, A1256, P444, W100, W528, W530
Digital Island, Inc. (Web hosting) W152
Digital Java Inc. (coffee) E80
Digital Lightwave, Inc. E192
Digital Solutions. *See* TeamStaff, Inc.
Digital Video Express A366
Digital World Services W127
DigitalPersona (fingerprint recognition) W338
DigiTest E302
Dignity Memorial Plan A1268
DiGrazia, Mike A393
Dilacor drug E156
Dilbeck, Ronald A. E109
Dilbert (comic strip) A568
Dildy, Marshall L. E59, E201
DiLeo, Ron P419
Dill brand A527
Dill, Claus M. W105
Dillard, Alex A490, A491

Dillard, Mike A491
Dillard, Richard P343
Dillard, William A490, A491
Dillard, William, II A490, A491
Dillard's Box Office A490
Dillard's Inc. A**490**-A**491**, A586, A690, A880, A932, A1238, P76, P342
Diller, Barry A390, A1450, A1451, E215
Diller, James V. E55
Diller, Kathleen L. A433
Diller, Phyllis A230
Dilling, Troels W95
Dillinger, John A488
Dillingham, Benjamin P593
Dillingham Construction Corporation P593
Dillon, Adrian T. A527
Dillon Companies A844, P479
Dillon, David B. A845
Dillon, John T. A771
Dillon, Lisa M. E310
Dillons (book stores) W212
Dillons Food Stores A844, A845
Dilly, Stephen G. A641
Dilworth Mine A417
Dilworth, Paul C. W379
Dim (hosiery) A1242, A1243
DiMarchi, Richard D. A541
DiMarco, Stephanie G. E25
DiMatteo, Frank A. W495
Dime Bancorp, Inc. A602, A822, A1500
Dimension graphics software A77
DiMicco, Daniel R. A1052, A1053
Dimick, Neil F. A155
Dimling, John A. W627
Dimmer, Dave A1073
DiMola, Nicholas P335
DIMON Inc. A**492**-A**493**
Dimon, James A230, A231
Dimond, Robert B. A995
Dimopoulos, Linda J. A465
DiMuccio, Robert A. P540
DiMuzio, John A401
Dina Camiones (trucks) A1010
Dindo, Kathryn W. A599
Dine pet food A915, P315
Dinea-Gastronomie restaurants W365
Dineen, Edward J. A901
Diners Club A378, W518
Ding-Dongs snacks A775
Dingo Digging Systems A1392, A1393
Dingus, Michael H. R. A1345
Dingwell, Everett P488
DiNicola, Robert J. A1552, A1553
Dintino, Daniel A., Jr. E205
Dinty Moore beef stew A730, A731
Diodes Inc. E192
Dionne, Joseph A944
Dior fashions W348
DiPiazza, Samuel A. A1159, P401, P705
DiPietro, Theresa P693

Dippity-Do hair care A656
Diprolene drug A1251
Diracles, John M., Jr. P107
Direccion Nacional de los Yacimientos Petroliferos Fiscales. *See* YPF, S.A.
DirecPC (Internet access via satellite) A736, A737
Direct Access Arrangement E288
Direct Container Line A1454
Direct Focus, Inc. E193
Direct Safety A1322
Directed Energy, Inc. E76
DirectGroup Bertelsmann W127
Direction Général des Télécommunications W232
Directional Advertising Services P170, P171
DIRECTV, Inc. A266, A528, A650, A736, W186, W390
Dirkes, Mark D. A775
DiRomualdo, Robert F. A276, A277
DIRT. *See* Deposit Interest Retention Tax (DIRT)
Dirt Cheap! Warehouse W172
DirXML software A1051
Disability and Impairment Evaluation Centers of America, Inc. A699
DiSaronno Amaretto W109
Disaster Relief Fund P426
Disbro, Eva L. P669
Discepolo, Michaelanne C. A1161
Dischino, Kirk J. E240
Disclosure (financial information) W626
Disco supermarkets W166, W167
DISCO-Ahold International Holdings W498
Disconto-Gesellschaft (bank) W200
Discount Analysis Containing Optimal Decision Algorithms travel system P418, P419, P717
Discount Tire Company P594
Discover Card A126, A936, A988, A1264
Discover (magazine) P176
Discovery car W120
Discovery Center (data mining) P430
Discovery Communications, Inc. A80, A81, A872, A873, P32, P33, P**158**-P**159**, P358, P530, P593, W144, W145
Discovery motor homes A605
Discovery Toys, Inc. A216
DiscoVision Associates W448
DISCUS (athletic wear) A1220
DISH Network A528
Disk Systems A1336
Disney. *See* The Walt Disney Company
Disney Channel A60, A61, A1496
Disney On Ice (shows) P189, P608
Disney, Roy E. A1496, A1497
Disney, Walt A60, A1496
Disneyland P454
Disney-MGM Studios A1496

Display Films A976
DisplayInspect software E43
Disprin health and personal care W477
Dissinger, Anthony A797
Dissly, Richard L. E266
DiStefano, Ellen E275
DiStefano, Pete A271
Distilling Company of America A974
Distinction Software A1098
Distini, Anthony E296
Distro P705
Distruidora Banquete A722
Ditkoff, James H. A463
Ditori, Melody P598
Ditropan XL drug A800
Dittman, Jay A679, P217
Dittmer Gear A278
Dittmer, Jerald K. A727
Ditto tape backup A778
Ditz, Johannes W425
Diuril drug A956
DIVACO AG & Company KG W201
Divaco investment group W364, W365
Dively, George A686
Diversa Corporation E193
DiverseFoods (condiments) A722
Diversey (chemicals) W376
DiverseyLever cleaning products W618, W619
Diversified Agency Services A1062
Diversified NY IPA, Inc. A575
Diversified Pharmaceutical Services, Inc. A574, A575, A1434
Diversified Services A300
Diversion (publication) P229
Divgi-Warner Limited A278
Dividends office furniture systems P276, P277, P652
Dixie brands A654
Dixie Home Stores A1532
Dixie Toga (flexible packaging) A250
Dixie-Narco (vending machines) A934, A935
Dixon, Diane B. A211
Dixon, Edward J. A127
Dixon, Geoff W469
Dixon, Gregory B. E118
Dixon, James (CompuCom) A400
Dixon, James D. (Bank of America) A227
Dixon, James E., Jr. (SBS Technologies) E284
Dixon, Jennifer P475, P744
Dixon, Karl A1059
Dixon, Maureen P681
Dixon Paper A770
Dixon, Steven C. E39
Dixon Tom-A-Toe A1109
Dixons Group plc (retailer) A870, W312
d'Izarn, Sahut W104
DKB. See The Dai-Ichi Kangyo Bank, Limited

DKNY brand A880, A881, A1243
DKV (insurance) W380
DLJ. See Donaldson, Lufkin & Jenrette
DLT drives A1184, A1185
DLW Aktiengesellschaft A194, A195
DMG (real estate) A462
DMX shoes A1194
DNAX Research Institute A1250
DnC Capital P236
DNL (Norwegian airline) W518
DNN Galvanizing Limited Partnership A1007
DNP. See Dai Nippon Printing Company, Ltd.
Do it Best Corporation A1410, P484, P594
Do It Yourself Network cable network A568
Doan, Christopher A1443
Doane Pet Care Company P595
Dobashi, Yoshikuni W327
Dobbs, Farrell P246
Dobbs International (airline catering) A1478
Dobkin, Robert C. E84
Dobrovich, Linda P714
Dobson Builders A509
Dobson Park Industries A806
Doc Otis' Hard Lemon Flavored Malt Beverage A175
Dockers Outlet by M.O.S.T. P539
Dockers pants A839, A868, A869, P292, P293, P657
Docks Market M165
Docks U.S.A. A1084
DoCoMo. See NTT DoCoMo
Dr. Martens shoes E289
Doctor's Associates Inc. P160-P161, P595
Documation A1336
Documentum, Inc. E311
Docutel (ATM maker) W422
DoD. See US Department of Defense
Dodd, Martin H. E131
Dodds, Christopher V. A349
Dodge cars P647, P666, P706, P733, W188
The Dodge City and Cimarron Valley Railway Company A309
Dodge Ram truck A456
Dodge (training, bearings) A1210
Dodge, William A1124
Dodge/Save Mart 350 race P722
Dodwell Travel A328, P108
DOE. See US Department of Energy
Doe Run (smelting) P712
Doerfler, Ronald J. A701, P229, P629
Doerig, Hans-Ulrich W185
Doerr Companies (electric motors) A1538
Doheny, Dan P713
Doheny, Edward W440
Doherty, Colm W519
Doherty, David P. A1019, P375
Doherty, Harry P. E293

Doherty, Henry A140
Doin, Raynald H. W377
Dokuchayev, Mikhail Vadimovich W243
Dolan, B. F. A1380
Dolan, Charles F. A312, A313
Dolan, James L. A312, A313
Dolan, Kevin P741
Dolan, Michael J. W647
Dolan, Patrick F. A313
Dolan, Peter R. A291
Dolan, Simon P. E98
Dolan, Thomas (Brush Electric Light) A570
Dolan, Thomas C. (Cablevision Systems) A313
Dolan, Thomas J. (Xerox) A1545
Dolan, Thomas (Westcon Group) P771
Dolara, Peter J. A165
Dolberg, Stanley H. E63
Dole, Bob P44, P508
Dole, Elizabeth P44
Dole Food Company, Inc. A470, A494-A495, P416
Dole, Ingram & Kennedy (sawmill) A756, P244
Dole, James A494
Dole juices A1107
Dole, Robert A1480
Dole Valve A526
Doll, Henri A1252
Doll, Mark G. A1049, P377
Dollar (car rental) A300
Dollar General Corporation A496-A497
Dollens, Ronald W. A674, A675
Dollive, James P. A843
Dollond & Aitchison Group (optical services) W240
Dolly Madison snacks A774, A775
Dolmio sauces A915, P315
Dolobid drug A957
Dolomite A153
Dolphin Capital E170
Dolphin Packaging A1262
Dolphin video game system W394
Dols, Terry E82, E232
Dom Pérignon champagne W348, W349
Domaine Ste. Michelle wine A1459
Dome Mines Ltd. W452, W453
Dome Petroleum W136, W156
Domei W198
Domestos household care products W619
Domingo, Placido P250, P251, P641
Dominican Santa Cruz Hospital P118
Dominican Sisters of San Rafael P119
Dominican Sisters of St. Catherine of Siena P118
Dominick, Samuel P., Jr. A1055
Dominick's Finer Foods, Inc. P524
DomiNick's (pizza) A500, P162
Dominick's Supermarkets A1234

Dominion Bank W608
Dominion grocery stores A671
Dominion Metalware
  Industries A718
Dominion Resources,
  Inc. A**498**-A**499**, A514, A598,
  A1040, E234
Dominion Securities W474
Dominion stores A670
Dominion Textile A306
Domino, Fats P188
Domino Sugar A500, P162, W568
Domino's Inc. A**500**-A**501**,
  P**162**-P**163**, P595, P657
Domm, Phyllis P640
Dommelsch beer W289
Domtar (paper) A654, W244
Don Baxter Intravenous
  Products A236
Don Diego cigars P732
Don Massey Cadillac, Inc. P596
Don Pedro brandy W85
Don Tomás tobacco A1458, A1459
Donaghy, Daniel J. A453
Donaghy, Patrick P737
Donahee, Gary R. W413
Donahoe, Jim A373
Donahoe, John P64, P65
Donahoe, Patrick R. A1429, P491
Donahue, James A. E44, E182
Donahue, Michael W131
Donahue, Peter A1120
Donahue, Richard K. A1033
Donahue, Timothy J. (Crown, Cork
  & Seal) A453
Donahue, Timothy M.
  (Nextel) A1026, A1027
Donaldson, A. Gregory P41
Donaldson, Carolyn D. E255
Donaldson, James D. A617
Donaldson, Lufkin & Jenrette. *See*
  Credit Suisse First Boston (USA)
Donaldson, William H. A90
Donatelli, David A. A543
Donatos Pizza A942, A943
Donaway, Carl D. A103
DONCASTERS plc (aircraft
  components) W284
Donches, Stephen G. A257
Donehower, John W. A827
Doney, Bart J. A1365
Dong Woo Deterpan
  (cleaning) A530
Donigan, Heyward A361
Donilon, Thomas E. A581
Donkey Kong (video game) W394,
  W395
Donn ceiling grid A1456, A1457
Donna, James M. P61, P546
Donna Karan International
  Inc. A564, A565, A880, A1243,
  W348
Donnelley Enterprise
  Solutions A1218
Donnelley, Gaylord A1218
Donnelley, James R. A1218
Donnelley, Reuben H. A516

Donnelley, Richard Robert A1218
Donnelley, Thomas A1218
Donnelly Corporation (automotive
  components) A802
Donnelly Meiners Jordan Kline
  (accounting) A680
Donnelly, Robert M. A971
Donnowitz, Vicky P409
D'Onofrio, Anthony B. A831
Donofrio, Nicholas M. A765
Donohue, Mark P390
Donohue Meehan Publishing E102
Donohue (newsprint) W470
Donohue, William C. E102
Donovan, David E. A231
Donovan, Dennis M. A725
Donovan, M. J. W355
Donovan, Paul A283
Donovan, Robert W54
Donovan, Stephen M. E82
Donovan, Timothy R. A1369
Donovan, William J. W413
Donrey Media Group A80, P32
Doody, Joseph G. A1325
Dooley, James T. E56, E196
Dooley, William N. A151
Dooner, John J., Jr. A772, A773
Doosan Group W288
Dooskin, Herbert P206
Döpfner, Mathias W106, W107
Doppelfield, Volker W121
Doppelt, Earl H. W627
Dor, Christian W481
Dorada beer W553
Doral Bank E193
Doral cigarettes A1204, A1205
Doral Financial Corporation E193
Doran, Patrick G. E188
Dorchester cigarettes W240, W241
Dorcy, James R. A995
Doret (office products) A210
Doritos snacks A1106, A1107
Dörken, Uwe R. W203
Dorling Kindersley
  (publishing) W430
Dorman, David W. A203
Dormann, Jürgen W55, W103
Dormer, Michael J. A801
Dormicum drug W493
Dormont, Jean-François W165
Dorn, Clayton Glenville E62
Dorn, Forest Dale E62
Dorn, Gail J. A1353
Dornbusch, Arthur A., II A551
Dorr, Marjorie W. A179
Dorrance, Arthur A316
Dorrance, Bennett A316
Dorrance, John A316
Dorrance, Roy G. A1463
Dorsett, C. Powers A1317, P453
Dorsey, Patrick B. A1385
Dortch, Oscar A752
Dos Equis beer W288, W289
DOS for Dummies (book) P248
Doskocil (pizza toppings) A743
Dossani, Nazir G. A627

Dostie, Daralin E316
Dot Foods, Inc. P596
Dotta, Jim P544
Dotterer, Herb P554
Doty, Michael E219
Doty, Robert D., Jr. A519
Doub, David M. A491
Double Eagle Steel Coating
  Company A1463
Double G Coatings LP A1007
Double Whopper sandwich A303
Doubleday Book Shops A232, A233
Doubleday Publishing W126
Doublemint gum A1526, A1527
Doubletree Hotels A720, A721,
  E169
Douce, Patrice W547
Dougal, Andrew J. H. W253
Dougan, Brady W. A449
Dougan, Paul M. E199
Dougherty, Dennis F. P760
Dougherty, Greg A793
Dougherty, Janice A1116
Dougherty, Jim A1116
Dougherty, Robert J., Jr. A1175
Dougherty, Stephen A1056
Doughtie's Foods A1350
Doughty Hanson & Company W226
Douglas Aircraft Company A190,
  A1044, A1088
Douglas, Edwin P416
Douglas, Gustaf W524, W525
Douglas, Sean P239
Douglas, Stephanie E215
Douglas TV stores E306
Douglass, James B. E72
Douglass, Steven J. A1092, A1093
Douin, Georges W481
Doulding, Karen P736
Doumani, John A317
Douville, Art A771
Douville, Richard A. A205
Douwe Egberts coffee and
  tea A1242
Douwe Egberts Van Nelle W282
DOVatron (circuit board
  assembly) A502
Dove Bar International A914, P314
Dove candy and ice cream A914,
  A915, P314, P315, P665
Dove soap W618, W619
Dover Corporation A**502**-A**503**,
  A748, W594
Dover Downs Race Track A1087
Dover/Ideal (home builders) A812
Dow AgroSciences LLC A504
Dow, Charles A506
The Dow Chemical Company A324,
  A434, A446, A**504**-A**505**, A540,
  A548, A549, A628, A1212, A1246,
  A1252, E193, P104, P164, P238,
  P239, P432, P573, P596, W116
Dow Corning Corporation A270,
  A434, A504, A688, P**164**-P**165**,
  P596
Dow, F. Kerr A723
Dow, Herbert A504

Dow, John A. S. A1025
Dow Jones Industrial Average unit trusts P46, P47
Dow Jones & Company, Inc. A**506**-A**507**, A701, A998, A999, A1018, E61, E202, P60, P80, P229, W484
Dow, Willard P164
Dowa Fire & Marine W396
Dowa Mining W284
DowBrands P432
Dowd, Charles A., Jr. A921
Dowd, Thomas P587
Dowdy, Robert A. A1519
DowElanco A504, A540
dowjones.com (Web portal) A507
Dowling, Anne Melissa A923, P321
Dowling, Glenn P471
Dowling, Michael J. P690
Dowling, Patrick T. W637
Downe, William A. W113
Downey Financial Corporation E194
Downey, Michael S. W377
Downing, Donald S. A1347
Downs, John H., Jr. A385
Downs, Thomas P362
Downtown Manhattan Heliport P399
Downyflake Foods A1104
Doy, Geoff W355
Doyal, Steve A679, P217
Doyle Dane Berbach Group (advertising) A1062
Doyle, Daniel W190
Doyle, David R. A289
Doyle, Dennis M. A355
Doyle, Francis A. A1159, P401, W463
Doyle, John D. P57
Doyle, J. Patrick A501, P163
Doyle, Larry R. P533
Doyle, Patrick T. A737
DPF computer leasing venture A774
DPL Inc. A837, P283
DPR Construction, Inc. P597
DPSUBG. *See* Dr Pepper/Seven Up Bottling Group
DQE, Inc. A598, A1460
Dr. Grabow brand pipes A1458
D.R. Horton, Inc. A**508**-A**509**
The Dr. Laura Program radio program A372
Dr. Martens shoes E289
Dr. Meleghy (auto parts) A1394
Dr. No (movie) A962
Dr. Pat tobacco W283
Dr Pepper Bottling Company of Texas P110
Dr Pepper/Seven Up Bottling Group P597
Dr Pepper soft drink A224, A382, A383, A384, A385, A714, A1102, A1103, A1104, A1105, P110, P232, W154, W155
Dr. Scholl's foot care A1250, A1251

Dr. Scholl's shoes A294
Dr. Susan Smith McKinney Nursing and Rehabilitation Center P369
Drackett A1246, P432
Draft, Howard A773
Dragon 8 beer W163
Dragon Chinese-language terminal W60
Dragonair (airline) E32, W564
Drainville, Gary P. E179
Drake & Scull Engineering Ltd. A544, A545
Drake Beam Morin, Inc. A910
The Drake hotel A884
Drake, John F. A377
Drake, Michael V. P495
Drake's snacks A774, A775
Draloric Electronic A1482
Drano A1247, P433, P722
Dransfield, Graham W253
Draper, E. Linn, Jr. A141
Draper, Lanett P727
Draper, Simeon A964
Drapery Hardware A1022
Drapkin, Donald G A903, P305
The Drawing Board (office supply catalog) A1142
Drax power station A88
Drays, DeeDee A303
Drayton, Harold W620
Drazen, Michael A1393
Dream Angels lingerie A776
Dream motorcycle W264
Dreamcast video game equipment W526, W527
Dreamery Ice Cream A510, A511
Dreamweaver Web design tool E86, E235
DreamWorks SKG P**166**-P**167**, P510, P511, P597
Drechsel, Joop G. W503
Dreher beer W255, W553
Dreier, R. Chad A1227
Dreiling, Richard W. A1235
Dreimann, Leonhard E116, E283
Dreller, Michael J. E202
Dremel tools W490
Dresdner Bank AG W82, W130, W200, W380
Dresdner Kleinwort Benson (investment banking) W200
Dresner, Mark A551
"Dress for Less" stores A1214
Dressel, Daniel M. A467
Dresser Equipment Group A676
Dresser Industries A676, A754, W320
Dresser-Rand Company A676, A754, E210
Dretkiewicz, Andrzej W457
The Drew Carey Show (TV show) A61
Drewery, Eric W55
Drewes, Alfred H. A1103
Drewniak, Michael J. E130
Drewry, June A183

Drexel Burnham Lambert A474, A836, P154, P278, P282, W196
Drexel Heritage furniture P298, P659
Drexler, Mickey A634
Drexler, Millard S. A635
Dreyer, William A510
Dreyer's Grand Ice Cream, Inc. A**510**-A**511**, A1326
The Dreyfuss Corporation A954, A955
Driano, Dominick P717
Driesse, Henry J. A781
Driessen, Christine P605
Drift Golf Club (UK) P131
Dril-Kwik fastening systems A265
Dri-Loc A1262
Dr.ING.h.c.F.Porsche AG. *See* (Dr.ING.h.c.F.)Porsche AG
Drinkward, Cecil W. P632
Driscoll, John W. A1341
DriveOff.com A1508, E249
Drivers International Union P246
Drixoral cold medicine A1250, A1251
Drizd, Alan A177
Drobny, Donald E. A1113
Droessler, Carol P528
Drohan, David F. A237
Dromedary (dates) A494
Dronniberg (farm equipment) A96
Drosdick, John G. A1344, A1345
Droten, Robert J. A679
Drouot (stock insurer) W104
Droxies cookies A814, A815
DRS Industries E60
Drucker, Martin E97
Drucker, Peter A260
Drug Emporium, Inc. A886
The Drug House A156
drugstore.com, inc. A701, A1202, P229, P511
Drum tobacco A1242, W282, W283
Drummey, George L. A263
Drummond, Jere A. A249
Drummond, Kirk G. A1351
Drury, David J. A1163
Drury, John A1504
Drury, Lynn E. A227
Drury, Roger A738
Drusch, Mark A. P. A479
Druskin, Robert A371
Druten, Robert J. P217, P625
Dry Idea antiperspirant A657
Dryden, John A1172
DRYLOFT fabrics P523
Drysch, Marilyn A1081
DSC Communications. *See* Alcatel
DSI Payroll Services E125
DSL (digital subscriber line) A54
DSL Holding AG W203
DSM Chemicals North America W424
DSM (inks) A770
DSP Group, Inc. E194
DST Systems, Inc. (information processing) A1332

DTE Energy Company A376, **A512-A513**

DTEC Inc. (pharmacy management) A1272

DTT. *See* Deloitte Touche Tohmatsu

Du Monceau, John W59

du Peloux, Cyrille W151

du Pont, Alfred I. A534, E115

du Pont de Nemours, Eleuthere Irenee A534

du Pont, Henry A534

Dual-Lite A1320, A1447

Dubay, Eugene N. A1065

Dubilier, Martin A870

Dubinin, Segey Konstantinovich W243

Dublon, Dina A809

Dubois, Guy A1099

Dubois, Lawrence H. P455

Dubow, Craig A633

Dubrish, Robert E. A681

Dubrule, Paul W58, W59

Dubuque, Kenneth R. A1365

Dubuque (processed pork) A730

Ducane heating and air conditioning A864

Ducatelli, Thomas A401

Ducati Motor SpA P474, P475, P744

Ducey, Charles E. A488

Duchek, Karl A1289, P447, P730

DuChene, Todd M. A601

Duchesne, Michel J. A451

Duchossois, Craig J. P598

Duchossois Industries, Inc. E40, P598

Duchossois, Richard E40, E178, P598

Duck Head Apparel (men's clothing) E305

Ducker, Michael L. A589

Ducros Services Rapides SA W203

Grupo Ducros (spices) A938

Dudak, Joseph R. A1007

Duddy, Gail L. A639

Dudek, Michael H. A747

Dudley, Bill A241, P75

Dudley, Brian A1051

Dudley, Diane M. A931

Duet. *See* Sony Music Entertainment

Duet, Nathan P. A1109

Dueweke, Donald G. A1019, P375

Duff, Andrew S. A1445

Duff Brothers (drug wholesaler) A156

Duff, Patricia A902

Duff, Ronald C. A615, P191

Duffey, John P587

Dufficy, James J. A595

Duffield, Al A1098

Duffield, David A. A1098, A1099

Duffy, Dennis J. A1423

Duffy, E. Patrick A285

Duffy, James F. (NYSE) A1019, P375

Duffy, James F. (St. Paul Companies) A1237

Duffy, John A. A1427

Duffy-Mott (applesauce and juice) W154

Dufourcq, Nicolas W233

Dugan, Allan E. A1545

Dugan, John E261

Dugan, Michael T. A529

Dugan (trucking) A1454

Dugand, Helen A1269

Duganier, Barbara J. A173, P49, P540, W91

Duiker Mining Ltd. W340

Duisberg, Carl W118

Dukakis, Michael S. P362, P363

Duke, Dwight B. A1259

Duke Energy Corporation A376, A498, **A514-A515**, A536, A618, A978, A1065, A1128, A1248, A1528, P598, W128

Duke Energy Field Services E260

Duke, James Buchanan A514, A618, P598, W142

Duke, Michael A1495

Duke Nukem (computer game) E298

Duke, Philip J. A883

Duke, Raymond A1197

Duke Realty Corporation E194

Duke University A514, A618, P78, P518, P598

Duke, Washington A618

Duke/Fluor Daniel A514, A515

DukeNet Communications, LLC A514

Dul, John A. A177

Dulac, Sophie W467

Dulce 16 gum A1527

Dulciora candy W155

Duluth (Minnesota) *News-Tribune* A833

Dulux paint W278

Dumas, Jeffrey M. A1337

Dumas, Lawrence B. P379

Dumaya supermarkets W498

Dumbacher, Robert J. P710

Dumesnil, Catherine W151

Dumez (construction) W558

Dumont, Pierre W195

The Dun & Bradstreet Corporation A66, **A516-A517**, A1218, E100, E258

Dun, Robert A516

Dunant, Jean-Henri P44

Dunavant Enterprises, Inc. P599

Dunavant, William, Jr. P599

Duncan, Andy W145

Duncan, C. Robert A1163

Duncan, Cynthia P195

Duncan, David (Koch Industries) A835, P281

Duncan, David S. (Publix) A1177

Duncan, Don R. A1129

Duncan, Douglas G. A589

Duncan, Heather E260

Duncan Hines baking mixes A408, A1164

Duncan, James D. A1293

Duncan, Jeff, Jr. A891

Duncan, Les A797

Duncan, O. Wayne A1351

Duncan, Phillip C. A929

Duncan, R. Foster A363

Duncan, Shelly E270

Dundee home furnishings A1317, P453

Dundee Mills (baby products) A1316, P452

Dundrea, Matthew W. A185

Dungeons and Dragons game A693

Dunham, Archie E. A413

Dunham, Austin A1040

Dunham (boots) P686

Dunham, Duane R. A257

Dunham, John L. A932, A933

Dunham, Truman A1278

Dunhill tobacco products W142, W143

Dunkel, Vernon L. A665

Dunkin' Donuts A252, W84, W85

Dunlap, Ann P660

Dunlap, F. Thomas, Jr. A761

Dunlap, Jennifer P45

Dunlap, Ray P413

Dunlap, Terry L. A117

Dunleavy, Michael F. A453

Dunlop Cox A856

Dunlop, Graeme D. S. W435

Dunlop, John Boyd W428

Dunlop, Nigel W241

Dunlop, Robert A1344

Dunlop Rubber Company A664, W428, W450

Dunn, Brian A255

Dunn, Catherine A. A1525

Dunn, C. Kenneth E40

Dunn, Craig W89

Dunn, David J. A778, A779

Dunn, Edward T. E144

Dunn, E. Paul, Jr. A753

Dunn, Frank A. W412, W413

Dunn, Gregory W. P413

Dunn Industries, Inc. P599

Dunn, Jeffrey T. A383

Dunn, Kevin A943

Dunn, Lydia, Baroness W269

Dunn, Philip J. A367

Dunn, Richard L. E56, E195

Dunn, Robby A1339

Dunn, Sarah W485

Dunn, Shawn E. A1103

Dunn, Terrence P. P599

Dunn, Van P369

Dunne, John A671

Dunnewood wines A423

Dunning Industries (wooden lamps) A492

Dunogué, Jacques W77

Dunoyer, Saint-Gobain W506

Dunphy, T. J. Dermot A1262

Dun's Book A516

Dunsdon, James H. A767

Dunt, Keith S. W143

Duo software E187

DuoDERM medical devices A291

Duo-Fast (pneumatic nailing and stapling) A748
Duofold thermal underwear A1242, A1243
Duo-Glide motorbikes A682
Dupaski, Thomas S. A1387
Dupee, Paul A280
Dupey, Michael A968
DUPLO toys by LEGO W333
DuPont. *See* E.I. du Pont de Nemours and Company
Dupont, Alain W135
duPont, Augustus I. A447, A896
DuPont Canada A1536
Dupont Mexico W441
DuPont Pharmaceuticals A534
duPont, Richard A1442
DuPree, Clifford H. R. A1193
Dupuis, Alain F. W175
DuPuy, Bob P307
Duques, Henry C. A596
Duquesne Light Company. *See* DQE, Inc.
Duquin, James A. A201
Dura Automotive Systems, Inc. A198, A1394
Durabase wallboard P683
Duracell batteries A210, A656, A657, A842, P530
Durack, David T. A245
Duract drug A148
Duralam (plastic film) A250
Duralast brand A208, A209
Duramed Pharmaceuticals, Inc. A148
Durance, Jean-Yves W183
Durand, Patrice W183
Durando, Paul E97, E256
Durant brand A527
Durant, Henry P494
Durant, William A650
Duraswitch Industries, Inc. A476
Dur-A-Vend W538
Durazo, Jesse A1429, P491
Durbin, Dean D. P507, P765
Durcan, D. Mark A971
Durden, Jennifer E183
Durham Downs mine W640
Durham, Michael A1228
Dürheimer, Wolfgang W459
Duricic, Nancy J. E51, E190
Durig, Gregory B. P159, P594
Durik, Michael L. A819
Durity, G. Harry A205
Durkan Patterned Products (carpets) A981
Durkee French spices and flavorings A938
Durkee's Famous Foods A974, W252
Durken, Deborah A. P501, P762
Durkin, G. Michael, Jr. A1105
Durle, Tami L. A179
Durman, Peter W85
DUROCK cement board A1457
Duron microprocessors A82
Durr, John A860

Dursban insecticides A504
Duschdas body care A1243
Dussing, Hilary G. E129
Dustbuster handheld vacuum A264, A265
Dutch Boy paint A1278
Dutch cleaning and laundry products A487
Dutch Housing, Inc. A346, A347
Dutch Ministry for Water, Commerce, and Industry W502
Dutheil, Alain W555
Dutiné, Gottfried W77
Dutta, Rajiv E54, E196
Dutta, Rono J. A1421
Dutton, Michael P319
Duty Free Shoppers. *See* DFS Group Limited
Duval, David P250, P251
Duzan, Steven E71
Dvorak, Kathleen S. A1431
D.W. Burrows (railroad insurance) A916
DW King Services A364
Dwan, John A976
Dwarf Grill P124
Dwarf House diner P124
DWG (holding company) A1400
Dwight, John A358
Dwivedi, Kamalesh A71
Dwyer, Andrew A544
Dwyer, Carrie E. A349
Dwyer, Edward M. A203
Dwyer, Joseph P. P545
Dwyer, Martin A544
Dwyer, Stacey H. A509
Dwyer, Steven M. A1227
Dwyer, Terence E33
Dybal, Alexander W243
Dyckman, David L. E254
Dycom Industries, Inc. E52, E195
Dye, Michael S. A1485
Dye, Molly A97
Dye, Robert J. A185
Dyer, David F. A852, A853
Dyer, Tom E254
dyes (office furniture) P222
Dyk, Thomas W. E129
Dyke, Greg W144, W145
Dykes, Archie R. A1105
Dykes, Ronald M. A249
Dykstra, David A. E318
Dykstra, Karen E. A205
Dykstra, Paul B. A1479
Dymax ultrasound catheter guidance systems A444
Dyna brand motorcycles A683
DYNACIN drug E89, E240
Dynacq International, Inc. E195
Dynalco Controls Corporation A447
Dynalectric Company A544, A545
Dynamark Plastics W604
Dynametal steel products A1386
Dynamic Communications E52
Dynamic Details, Inc. E191
Dynamo software E159

Dynapert (printed circuit boards) A264
Dynapro Systems (touch-screen components) A976
Dynasty (reserve power batteries) E169
Dyna-Traxx brand A527
DynCorp P599
Dynegy, Inc. A88, A352, A518-A519, A1030, A1065, E216
Dyneon LLC A976
Dynner, Alan R. E53
DynTek P599
Dyrbus, Robert W283
Dyrdahl, Melissa A77
Dyrekcja Eksploatacji Cystern A638, A639
Dyson, Brian G. A383
Dyson, Charles P600
Dyson, Ian W473
Dyson, J. David P201
Dyson, Robert R. P600
The Dyson-Kissner-Moran Corporation P600
DyStar W116
Dziedzic, John P769
Dziewisz, Mike A1513
Dziurzynski, Bogdan E90

E

E & B Carpet Mills A194
E & J Brandy A521, P169
E. & J. Gallo Winery A422, A520-A521, P168-P169, P600
E! Entertainment Television A61, A390, A391, A873
E. Machlett & Son A600
E. Maritz Jewelry Manufacturing Company P308
E. Merck AG A956
E Style (mail order catalog) P258
E Walk (entertainment and hotel complex) P476
e2E (electronics) E104
E3 Networks W372
e7th (Internet footwear wholesaler) A902, A903, P305
E.A. Miller (meat) A408
E. A. Pierce A960
Eades, Milton P770
EADS. *See* European Aeronautic Defence and Space Company
Eads, Ralph A537
eAdvisor A566
Eagle Brand condensed milk P90
Eagle cars P666, W188
Eagle Complex A1242
Eagle Credit A682
Eagle Crest resort P643
Eagle engine W497
Eagle Family Discount A496
Eagle Family Foods P90
Eagle Food Centers A1242, P479
Eagle grocery stores P198
Eagle Hardware & Garden Distribution Services, Inc. A892
Eagle Industries A748

Eagle Insurance Group P269, P727
Eagle Managed Care A1202
Eagle One Industries A200
Eagle Pacific Industries. *See* PW
 Eagle, Inc.
Eagle Rubber (toys and sporting
 goods) A294
Eagle Signal Controls P310
Eagle Snacks A174, A1164
Eagle Star Holdings
 (insurance) W82, W652, W653
Eagle STP signal system E126
Eagle tires A664
Eagle Valley brands P198, P199
Eagle-Picher Industries, Inc. P600
Eagles (performers) P166
Eagon, Donald E. A489
Eamer, Richard A1366
Eames, Charles A706
Eames, Don A255
Earhart, Amelia A882
Earl, Johnny R. A289
Earle M. Jorgensen Company P601
Earley, Anthony F., Jr. A513
Earls Court exhibition hall
 (London) W434
Early Bird brands P201
The Early Show (TV show) A919
Early Times whiskey A296, A297
Earnest, Cindy E142, E319
*Earth to Kids: A Guide to Parents
 for a Healthy Planet* (educational
 video) P139
The Earthgrains Company A774,
 A1242
EarthLink, Inc. (Internet service
 provider) A350, A1318
EarthWatch (imaging
 satellites) A780
Easco Hand Tools A462
Easdaq A988, A996, P353
Easley, Brett D. A209
Easley, Warren C. A891
Easley, William K. (Springs
 Industries) A1317, P453
Eason, William E., Jr. (Scientific-
 Atlanta) A1259
East Coast Hockey League P361
East New York Diagnostic &
 Treatment Center P369
East Tennessee Natural Gas
 pipeline A514, A536
East Tennessee, Virginia & Georgia
 (railroad) A1038
East Texas State University P470
Eastbay (footwear) A1470
Easter Enterprises food stores A994
Easterling, V. Edward, Jr. P519
Easterly, David E. A443, P147
Eastern Acoustic Works E85, E234
Eastern Air Lines A138, A428,
 A478, P482, W70
Eastern Airlines Avionics A662
Eastern Australia Airlines Pty.
 Ltd. W468, W469
Eastern Chemical Company,
 Ltd. W603
Eastern Electricity W208

Eastern Energy A1416
Eastern Enterprises A824
Eastern Environmental Services,
 Inc. A1504
Eastern Home Health Supply &
 Equipment Company, Inc. A259
Eastern Idaho Health Services,
 Inc. A695
Eastern Mercy Health System P114
Eastern Mountain Sports, Inc. P539
Eastern Platinum Ltd. W340, W341
Eastern Refining A1096
Eastern Shore Natural Gas E177
Eastern States Farmer
 Exchange P38
Eastern Stores (grocery
 stores) A1234
Eastern Telegraph W152
Eastern Tennessee Medical Services,
 Inc. A695
Eastern Utilities A1306
Eastex Pulp and Paper A1364
Eastgate Technology Park P252
Eastham, Karin E193
Eastland, Woods E. P735
Eastman Chemical
 Company A522-A523, A524,
 A704, A900, P238
Eastman Christensen (drilling
 equipment) A222
Eastman Dry Plate and Film
 Company A522, A524
Eastman, George A522, A524, P760
Eastman Kodak Company A522,
 A524-A525, A750, A764, A944,
 A1148, A1256, A1258, A1544,
 E184, E284, P70, P760, W190,
 W234, W368, W476, W514
Eastman Office Products A1056
Eastman, Robert E66
Eastman School of Music P760
Eastpak back packs A1474, A1475
Eastwood, Clint P565
Easy Bake Oven A693
Easy CD Creator software E281
Easy Off home care W476, W477
Easy Spirit apparel A804, A805
Easy-Pedal brand A527
Eaton & Howard E53
Eaton, Charles F., Jr. E53
Eaton Corporation A278, A286,
 A460, A476, A526-A527, A728,
 A992, A1088, E133, E161
Eaton, Joseph A526
Eaton Vance Corporation E53,
 E195
Eatonite brand A527
Eatzi's Market & Bakery A288, A289
EB beer W255
E.B. Eddy (paper) W244
Ebasco Industries (engineering and
 construction) A274
eBay Inc. E54, E196
Ebbers, Bernard J. A1534, A1535
Ebbing, Karen S. A595
Ebel, David R. P325, P668
Ebel, Gregory L. A569
Ebel watches W348, W349

Ebeling, Thomas W415
Eberhard Faber office
 products A1023
Eberle, Karl M. A683
Ebersman, David A641
Ebersol, Dick A999
Ebersole, Lisa E25, E149
Ebert & Roeper and the Movies (TV
 production) A61
Ebert, Roger L. P340, P345, P679
Ebner, Martin W492
E-Bond Securities A860
Ebony Fashion Fair P259
Ebony Jr! (magazine) P258
Ebony (magazine) P258, P259,
 P646
EBSCO Industries Inc. P170-P171,
 P601
eBusiness TechRankings E205
EBV Group (semiconductors) A214
Eby, Clifford P387
Eby, Tom A82
Eby-Brown Company P601
Ecco Domani wines A521, P169,
 P600
E-Certify A400
Echebarrena, Antonio W635
eChips (sales and marketing) A196
Echlin (auto parts) A460, A1320
Echo car W615
ECHO Real Estate Services
 Company P198
ECHO Suite software A155, A156
Echols, Leldon E. A341
Echosphere A528
EchoStar Communications
 Corporation A528-A529, A650,
 A736, W390
ECI Telecom Ltd. W322, W323
Eck, Dennis K. W172
Eck, John A999
Ecker, H. Allen A1259
Eckerd Corporation
 (drugstores) A66, A790, E147
Eckers family A964
Eckert, Alfred W378
Eckert, Bob (Kraft Foods) A842
Eckert, Peter W653
Eckert, Robert A. (Mattel) A926,
 A927
Eckert, Thomas D. E170
Eckhardt, B. N. A546
Eckhart Library P497
Eckley, Paul A1331, P459
Ecklin, Robert L. A435
Eckrich meats A408, A409
Eckrote, Douglas E. A337
Eckstein, Catherine W. A759
Eckstein, Howard M. E68
Eclipse cigarettes A1204, A1205
Eclipse gum A1526, A1527
Eco Service convenience
 stores W167
ECOAIR (jet engine bearings) A754
Eco-Bat Technologies plc
 (smelting) P709
Ecodyne Limited P313

ECOL Ltd. A1460
Ecolab Inc. A**530**-A**531**, W256
OOO Ecological and Analytical Center of the Gas Industry W243
E-Commerce Industries A1430
ECON + LIST Verlagsgesellschaft (publishing) W106
Econ (publishing) W107
Econofoods grocery stores A994, A995
Economax discount supermarkets P224, P225
Economics Laboratory A530
The Economist (magazine) W430
EcoStar (roofing) A326
EcoWater Systems, Inc. P313
Ecusta Paper A1060
Ed & Joan DeLuca brand P393
Ed stores W165
Grupo EDC A88, A89
Eddie Bauer clothing A648, A1314, A1315
Eddington, Roderick W140, W141
Eddy, Mary Ann P269
Eddy's snacks A775
Ede, Terence W. A503
Edelap (electric company) A88, A1198
Edelman, Asher P332
Edelman, Harriet A217
Edelman, Henry D. E203
Edelman, Robert J. A767
Edelman, Thomas J. E260
Eden, Avi D. A1483
Eden Communications Group A1063
Eden grocery stores A1532
Eden Toys A1068
EDESE (electric company) A1198
Edesur (utility) A554
EDF-Trading W209
EDGAR Online, Inc. (SEC information delivery) E61
Edgar, Richard A. A1019, P375
Edgars stores W552
Edge Diagnostic Systems A1294
Edge in Electronics stores A1188
Edge (magazine) W239
Edge men's grooming products A1246, A1247, P432, P433
Edge Semiconductor E119
Edge Technology Group Inc. (computers) A762
Edgell, Robert M. A533
Edgerly, William S. A1332
Edgerton, David A302
Edgerton, Germeshausen and Grier A1110
Edgerton, Harold A1110
The Edgewater Hotel and Casino A906, A907
Edgewood Tool and Manufacturing A1394
Edicorp (publisher) W238
Edinburgh Portable Compilers A170

Edinger, Daniel J. P39
Edington, Jeff W179
Edison Brothers Stores, Inc. E51
Edison Capital A532
Edison electrical products A431
Edison Electric Illuminating Company of New York A418
Edison (electric power) W214, W216
Edison General Electric A646
Edison Illuminating Company of Detroit A512
Edison International A88, A**532**-A**533**, A1198, W424
Edison Light & Power A1120
Edison Liquor Company P774
Edison Mission Energy A532, A533
Edison, Thomas A418, A434, A572, A646, A1120, A1154, A1248, E58, P164
Éditions CEC W470
Editions Scientifiques et Médicales Elsevier W479
Editor & Publisher Magazine W626
Editorial Televisa W582
Edivisa, S.A. de C.V. (publishing) W582, W583
Edizione Holding W124
EDJ Holding Company, Inc. P261
Edlow, Kenneth L. A239
Edlund, Bjorn W55
Edmonds, David B. A167
Edmonds, William P552
Edmondson, David J. A1189
Edmont (industrial gloves) A244
Edmonton Empire (theater) W248
Edmonton Oilers Hockey Club P361
Edmonton Sun (newspaper) W471
Edmund T. Pratt Jr. School of Engineering P598
Edmunds, John S. E98, E257
Edrick, Alan I. E254
EDS. *See* Electronic Data Systems Corporation
Edsel vehicles A616
Educational Enhancement Trust Fund P736
Educational Television Facilities Act P144
EduTrek International E172
Edward D. Jones & Company, LP P260, P261, P646
The Edward J. DeBartolo Corporation P**172**-P**173**, P602
Edward L. Ginzton Laboratory P457
Edward P. Allis & Co. A96
Edwards, Albert Galatin A94
Edwards, Barry L. E207
Edwards, Benjamin F., III A94, A95
Edwards, Benjamin F., IV A95
Edwards, Benjamin Franklin A94
Edwards, Bruce C. (Powerwave Technologies) E106, E269
Edwards, Bruce J. (International Flavors) A767
Edwards, Carl E., Jr. A865

Edwards, Charlotte P103, P565
Edwards, Christine A. A231
Edwards, C. Webb A1509
Edwards, David M. (GATX) A639
Edwards, David (Salvation Army USA) P427
Edwards Development Corporation A95
Edwards, Edwin P172
Edwards Fine Foods P436
Edwards, Gary W. A413
Edwards Information Network A94
Edwards, James D. A173, W91
Edwards, Jeff A119
Edwards, Jerry A725
Edwards, John K. A457
Edwards, Kim A778
Edwards Lifesciences A236
Edwards, Michael A. (Ford Foundation) P195
Edwards, Michael J. (Jo-Ann Stores) A797
Edwards, Nancy A. A909
Edwards, Ninian A94
Edwards, Paul W469
Edwards, Presley A94
Edwards restaurants W545
Edwards, Robert L. A751
Edwards, S. Eugene A1467
Edwards supermarkets P102
Edwards, Wesley B. A783
Edwards, William F. A1029
Edwards-Finast supermarket A1324
Edwardson, John A. A336, A337
Edy, Joseph A510
Edy's Ice Cream A510
EE Product News (magazine) E102
Eerste Nederlandsche W64
EEX Corporation A1374
E.F. Hutton A204, A596
Effem India (candy) A914
Effird stores P76
Effren, Gary R. A833
EFI Systems W490
EFKA cigarette paper W282, W283
efollett.com P610
EFTC Services, Inc. A782
eFunds Corporation A480
Egan, John M. E30
Egan, Richard J. A542, A543
Egan, Robert A275
Egan, Thomas F. A461, P736
EG&G. *See* Perkinelmer, Inc.
Egawa, Noriyuki W649
Egeck, Mike A1475
Egede-Nissen, Thor P621
Egg Beaters A408, A409
Egg plc (telephone and Internet banking) W464, W465
Egg, William C., Jr. A1145
Eggbeen, Tom P673
Egger, Gary P764
Eggers, Janine Sawaya A697
Eggers, Lonnie A995
Eggers, William D. A435
Egghead.com P196

Eggo waffles A816, A817
EggsPlus A1132
Egreetings Network A146
eGroups (e-mail) A1546
EGS Electrical Group A1320
Ehler, Wes P622
Ehrhorn, William G. A581
Ehrlich, William W. A1501
Ehrling, Marie W519
Ehrmann, Jacques W171
E.I. du Pont de Nemours and
Company A412, A416, A450,
A504, A**534**-A**535**, A550, A612,
A704, A714, A820, A1054, A1060,
A1414, A1550, P122, P232, P418,
P522, P573, P589, P604, P627,
W116, W118, W278, W346, W504
Eichler, Rodney A185
Eick, Karl-Gerhard W205
Eickhoff, John R. A343
Eidelman, Peter E296
Eidgenossische Bank of
Zurich W616
Eidson, Dennis A671
Eidson, Julian W. A1259
Eierhoff, Klaus W127
Eight O'Clock brand A670
E-II Holdings A618
Eijsbouts, A. Jan A. J. W73
Eikrem, Idar W411
Eilers, Ronald E. A481
Eilks, Heinz-Ubbo A461
Eimer & Amend (chemicals) A600
Einstein Bros. Bagels E253
Einstein Papers Project P560
eircom plc
(telecommunications) W502,
W503
Eiref, Zvi A359
EIS, Inc. (electrical
equipment) A653
Eisai A1118
Eisbart, Ben P694
Eisele, Charles R. A1423
Eisen, James J. E37
Eisenberg, Barbara K. P255
Eisenberg, Gregg M. E87, E238
Eisenberg, Joseph B. A451
Eisenberg, Lee A853
Eisenberg, Lewis M. (Port Authority
of New York & New Jersey) P399
Eisenberg, Louie (New York State
lottery winner) P372
Eisenberg, Martin A247
Eisenberg, Phillip A. A987
Eisenberg, Warren A246, A247
Eisenbud, Michael P55, P543
Eisenhardt, William B. P99
Eisenhauer, Gregory J. E111, E277
Eisenhower, David A1385
Eisenhower, Dwight D. A948,
A1068, P74, P134, P326, P492
Eisenhower, M. L. A133
Eisenstein, Joshua J. P571
Eisner, Dean H. A443, P147
Eisner, Michael D. A1496, A1497,
P166

Eisner, Michelle A1419
Eizmendi, Francisco C., Jr. W511
EJ Insurance Agency Holding
LLC P261
E.J. Korvette stores W634
Ejima, Makoto W373
Ek, Jansen B. A1285
Ekanet (broadband
communications) A1422, A1423
Ekati diamond mine W128
Ek-Chai Distribution System
Company Ltd. W591
EKCO Group, Inc. (cookware) P91,
P775
Eklund, George E125
Eklund, Reginald R. A993
El Aguila (brewery) W254
El Al Airlines Limited W496
El Dorado Investment
Company A1138, A1139
El Greco (shoes) E78
El Nuevo Herald (Miami, FL) A833
El Paso Company (oil and
gas) A310
El Paso Energy Corporation A514,
A**536**-A**537**, A1082, A1120,
A1144, A1368, E183
El Paso Natural Gas
Company A310, A536, A537,
A1082
El Peñón mine E242
El Pollo Loco restaurants A86
El Portón restaurants W635
El Puerto de Liverpool, S.A. de
C.V. A830
El Torito-La Fiesta
Restaurants A1536
El Toro tequila A423
Elam, C. Phillip, II A795
Elan Group (IT staffing) A911
Elantec Semiconductor, Inc. E55,
E196
Elation (ship) A331
ELCO Chevrolet Inc. P178, P179
Elco Holdings Limited (electronic
connectors) W328
ELDEC Corporation
(aerospace) A447
Elder, Eric E. A1227
Elder Smith Goldsbrough
Mort W230
ElderMed P753
Elders IXL W230, W282, W376
Eldon, David G. W269
Eldridge, James F. P43
Eleano, Mary S. A1429, P491
Elective Elements office
furniture A1335
Electone electronic organ W648
Electra Fleming
(investments) P740
Electra Glide motorbikes A682
Electra Industrial Company A1392
Electrasol dishwashing W476,
W477
Electric Boat Corporation A644,
A645, W132

Electric Bond and Share
Company A1082, A1154, A1166,
A1198
Electric Clearinghouse A518
Electric Company of America A140
The Electric Corporation of San
Francisco P582
Electric Energy, Inc. A136, A137
Electric Fuels Corporation A1166,
A1167
Electric Power and Light A554
Electric Railway Securities A376
Electric Storage Battery
Company A572
Electric Switch (DVDs) W473
Electric Welding Company A1412
Electrical Lamp Service
Company W212
Electrical Mechanical Corporation.
See EMCOR Group, Inc.
Electricaribe (electric
utility) A1198
Grupo La Electricidad de
Caracas A89
Electricidade de Portugal A1416
Electricité de France A620, A1154,
A1306, W**208**-W**209**, W226, W598
Electriska Aktiebolaget W54
Electro Diesel Rebuild P152
Electro Northern, Inc. A309
Electro Scientific Industries,
Inc. E**56**, E196
Electro-Alkaline Company A374
Electrocomponents plc A214
Electrocosta (electric utility) A1198
Electrodata A1424
Electro-Films (thin film
components) A1482
ElectroGen International A1460
Electroglas, Inc. E**57**, E197
AB Electrolux A286, A618, A934,
A1520, W54, W**210**-W**211**, W220
Electrolux LLC W210
Electrolux Zanussi W124
Société Electrométallurgie
Française W432
Electron debit card A1481, P509
Electronic Arts Inc. P166
Electronic Business and
Information P68
Electronic Darkroom P60
Electronic Data Systems
Corporation A142, A404,
A**538**-A**539**, A650, A1112, A1228,
A1534, W378
Electronic Demand
Publishing P274
Electronic Designs E317
Electronic Measurement W290
Electronic Printing Products,
Inc. A251
Electronic Realty Associates A338,
P692
Electronic Technology
Corporation E92
Electronic Telegraph Web
site W262

The Electronics Boutique plc A162, E298
Electronics Distribution Group A196
Electroquil A514
Electrowatt (utility) W184
Grupo Elektra S.A. de C.V. A366
Kongl. Elektriska Telegraf-Verket W584
Elektromekaniska W210
Elements (chemicals) W538
ELETROBRÁS A88
Eletronet A88
Elettroambiente SpA (waste-to-energy) W215
Elettrogen (electricity generation) W214
Elex (semiconductors) E173
Elexsys International A1240
Elf Aquitaine W116, W342, W410, W612, W613
Elf service stations W612
Elga (coal) W334
Elghandour, Max A. E209
Elgin Watch Company P226
El-Hillow, Michael E213
Eli Lilly and Company A84, A220, A444, A504, A540-A541, A640, A674, A788, A946, A1202, P66, P71, W118, W416
Eli Witt (wholesaler) P635
Elías Ayub, Arturo W581
Elias, Howard D. A399
Eling, Gregory J. A365
Eliot, Charles P220
Elisabeth clothing A880, A881
Elisha, Walter A1316, P452
The Elisra Tadiran Group W322, W323
Elite Information Group, Inc. P438
Elix, Douglas T. A765
ELIXER guitar strings P523
Elixir cosmetics W535
Elizabeth Arden, Inc. (cosmetics) A540, W618
Elizabeth II, Queen of England W144, W250
Eljer (bath and plumbing) A1446, A1447
Elk Creek Complex A417
Elka nail polish A1200
Elkin, Jason E188
Elkin, Lisa A407
Elkington, Kevin W173
Elkins, Alan E. A905
Elkins, John A773
Elkins, Keith P473
Elko, Ed P559
Elle (magazine) W330
Elledge, Patricia R. E301
Ellemtel (research and development) W584
Ellen, Martin M. E168
Ellenberger, Richard G. A292, A293
Eller, Karl A373
Eller Media A372
Eller, Timothy R. A341

Ellingboe, John A1435
Ellington, Donald P753
Elliot, Douglas S. A599
Elliott, Anita C. A261
Elliott, Dale F. A1294, A1295
Elliott, John W230
Elliott, R. Keith A704
Elliott, Robert N. P253
Elliott, Steven G. A955
Elliott, Sue A969
Elliott, Thomas L., III A173, P49, W91
Elliott, William M. A637
Ellis, Bradley L. A447
Ellis, Christopher L. A1455
Ellis, Floyd P772
Ellis, James D. A1245
Ellis, Jeremy W128
Ellis, J. L. (Tiffany) A1384
Ellis, J. N. (Proffitts) A1238
Ellis, Larry T. P756
Ellis, Lisa E103, E266
Ellis, Mark E. A311
Ellis Park Race Course (Kentucky) E40, E178
Ellis, Perry W606
Ellis, Richard A1398
Ellis, Stephen W. R. A573
Ellison, Lawrence J. A1066, A1067, P278, P496, P510, P652
Ellison, Richard D. E131, E304
Ellis-Proffitt Company A1238
Ellspermann, Richard P193, P610
Ellwood, Paul A1434
Ellyn, Lynne A513
Elmer's Products P90, P91, P558
Elmhurst Co-op (New York) P291
Elmhurst Hospital Center P368, P369
Elmira (New York) Gazette A632
Elmot (starters and alternators) P152
E-Loan, Inc. A348
e-logic (e-commerce) W344
Elpida Memory W386
Elsag Bailey (industrial controls) W54
Elsasser, Jon T. A1387
Elsevier Business Information W478, W479, W642
Elsevier Science E221
Elsey, George W469
Elsie the cow P90, P148, P558
Elsmira, Gian E159
Elston, Harold C., Jr. E131, E304
Elton B. Stephens Company. See EBSCO Industries Inc.
Elton, Rosalyn S. A695
Eltra (company) P142
Elvis lottery game P687
Elway, John P563
Ely, Johnnie P372
Elyo (energy) W558
Elzvik, Eric W55
EM Microelectronic-Marin (semiconductors) W563
A/S Em. Z. Svitzer Group W95

Email Ltd. (appliances) W210
Emap PLC (publisher) A1160, W238
e-Maritz (online incentives) P308
eMatrix suite software E237
Embarcadero Center (San Francisco) A1398, E34, E165
Embarcadero Technologies, Inc. E197
Embassy cigarettes W282, W283
Embassy Suites A720, A721
Embassy table linens P343
Embed-It! software E313
Embolic Protection A282
Embraer W132
Embraer (jets) A428
Embree, Steven S., Sr. A1057
EMC Corporation A542-A543, A1184, E166, E226, E239
EMCO Enterprises P50
EMCOR Group, Inc. A544-A545
Emdersa (electric transmission) A668
Emen, Michael S. P47
Emerald Builders A508
Emerald chips E226
Emerge (agricultural land use information software) A408
eMerge Interactive, Inc. A1233, E197
Emergency Food and Shelter National Board Program P492
Emergia Holding N.V. W579
Emerging Companies Market P46
Emerging Sciences. See PolyMedica Corporation
Emerson A332, A446, A488, A546, A546-A547, A1218, A1538, W490, W514
Emerson, Dave S. A783
Emerson Electric Company. See Emerson
Emerson, Frances B. A923, P321
Emerson, H. Garfield W495
Emerson, John A546
Emerson Radio Corporation E58, E198
Emerson, Raeleen E164
Emerson, Richard A973
Emerson, Victor E58
Emery Air Freight A102, A380, A420
Emery (chemicals) W256
Emery, David R. E211
Emery Mine A417
Emery Worldwide A380, P490
Emhart A264
EMI Classics recording label W213
EMI Group plc A180, W212-W213
Emilio Pucci fashion house W348
eMind.com P279
Emma James clothing A880, A881
Emme, Jim A169
Emmerich/Sotheby's A1305
Emmerson, A. A. "Red" P728
Emmerson, Mark P728
Emmerson, R. H. "Curly" P728

Emmick, Gary K. A435
Emmis Communications
  Corporation E198
Emmons, George E., Jr. A823
Emmy Awards A678, P216, P218
Empain Group W520
Emperor Norton A775
EMPHESYS A738, A878
Empire Blue Cross and Blue Shield.
  See Empire HealthChoice
Empire Builder (passenger
  train) A308
Empire District Electric
  Company A1464
Empire HealthChoice A268, P82,
  P174-P175, P602
Empire HealthChoice Assurance
  (HMO) P602
Empire Iron Mining
  Partnership W293
Empire Livestock P588
Empire National Bank A228
Empire Pencil Corporation A692
Empire Seafood Holding A1109
Empire State Building A1408,
  A1409, P230, P231, P482, P483,
  P629, P749
The Empire Strikes Back
  (movie) P302, P303
Empire Trust A228
Empirix (software testing) A1372
Emplit, Janis S. A87
Employee Retirement Income
  Security Act of 1974 A1042,
  A1332, P388
Employer & Occupational Services
  Group, Inc. A697
Employers Insurance of
  Wausau A1008, P294, P364
Employers Reinsurance A646
Empower Group (performance
  evaluation) A911
Empresa de Teléfonos
  Ericsson W580
Empresas Cablevision W580
Empresas Emel A1154
Empress Casino riverboat P634
Empress of Canada (ship) A330
Empson, Jon R. A1465
EMSA Correctional Care E153
E-mu Systems (digital
  sounds) W180
EMVentures (venture capital
  incubator) P279
Emwest Products (electrical switch
  gear) A526
Enagas (natural gas) W482
ENBREL drug A149, E71, E218
Encarta (CD-ROM) P176
Encee, Inc. A1135
Enciclopedia Barsa P176
Encompass Services
  Corporation A548-A549
Encore Books A1202
Encore II, Inc. A509
Encore Media Group A873
ENCORE Program A818
Encore Software P132

Encore tires W367
Encyclopaedia Britannica,
  Inc. P176-P177, P350, P603
Encyclopedia Americana A1254,
  A1255
*The Encyclopedia of Popular
  Music* P177
End, William A852
Endeavour (space shuttle) P92
Endemol (TV producer) W578
Ender, Chris A335
Enders, Larry J. A433
Endesa W214
Endo, Ichiro W159
Endo, Koichi W487
Endonis A530
EndoSonics Corporation A674
Endres, A. R., Jr. A309
Endres, John P617
Endsley, Bruce P253, P642
Endura watch W563
Endurance Specialty (insurance
  underwriter) W652
Endust furniture treatment A1242
Enel S.p.A. W214-W215, W628
Enerchange A1030
Companhia Energetica de Minas
  Gerais A88
Energie Baden-Württemberg
  Aktiengesellschaft W209
Energy America (marketing) A1266
Energy Conservation Center W598
Energy East Corporation A88
Energy Foundation P414
Energy Group PLC A974, A1082,
  A1416, W252
Energy Policy Act (1992) A114,
  A424, A512, A598, A1028, A1154,
  A1542
Energy Systems Industries A544
EnergyNorth A824
EnergyOne A1464
EnergyUSA, Inc. A1034
enews.com A232
Enforcer Products A1004
Engblom, C. P421, P718
Engel, John J. A1111
Engelberg, Steven L. A985
Engelbriet, Mary A679, P217
Engelen, Peter W461
Engelhard, Charles A550
Engelhard, Charles, Jr. A550
Engelhard Corporation A550-A551
Engelstad, Robert J. A581
Engen, James T. E85, E234
Engen, Travis W74, W75
Enger, Thorleif W411
Engers, Scott J. A381
Engibous, Thomas J. A1378, A1379
Engine Synchro Shift transmission
  system A198
Engineered Automation
  Systems E131
Engineered Support Systems,
  Inc. E198
Engineering Measurements
  Company E24

Engineering News Record
  (magazine) A945
Engineering Research
  Associates A342
Engineers Public Service A498
England, Joseph W. A469
England, Rodney D. A855
Englar, John D. A307
Englehart, Jacob W280
Englehorn Frederick W116
Engles, Gregg L. A1338, A1339
English, Edmond J. A1388, A1389
English Electric W110, W354
English, Lawrence W. A151
English, Michela P159
English, Roderick P153, P590
Englund, Lizbeth A. A1231
Engraph (specialty packager) A1302
Engstrom, Bengt C. A1521
Engstrom, Jan W633
Enhance Financial Services Group
  Inc. E108
Enhanced Vision Systems. See
  eMerge Interactive, Inc.
Eni S.p.A. A132, W216-W217,
  W242
ENIAC computer P759
Enichem A504
EniChem SpA W216, W217
Enka. See Nederlandsche
  Kunstzijdebariek
Enlow Fork Mine A417
Ennest, John W. E179
Ennia (insurance) W64
Enoki, Kei-ichi W419
Enola Gay (plane) P450
Enomoto, Toshiaki W599
Enomoto, Yoshio W315
Enos, Thomas L. A1025
Enova Corporation. See Sempra
  Energy
ENPS (electronic news production
  system) P61
ENRAC A1504
Enrcom A1198
Enrico Fermi Institute P496, P497
Enrico, Roger A. A1106, A1107
Enron Corporation A114, A140,
  A154, A314, A404, A552-A553,
  A556, A824, A1120, A1368, E62,
  E260, P96, W216, W278, W460
Enron Field (Houston baseball
  field) A190
Enron Oil Trading &
  Transportation. See EOTT Energy
  Partners, L.P.
EnronOnline A552
Enseco (laboratory services) A434
Ensemble cholesterol reducing
  foods A816
Enserch Environmental A620
ENSERCH (gas) A1416
Ensign, Michael S. A906, A907
Enso Gutzeit Oyj W556
Enso Trasliperi Aktiebolaget W556
Ensoniq (musical instruments). See
  Malvern (electronic musical
  instruments)

Enstone, David G. A573
Ensure nutrition supplement A58, A59
Ente Nazionale Idrocarburi. *See* Eni S.p.A.
Ente Nazionale per l'Energia Elettrica. *See* Enel S.p.A.
Entegris E244
ENTEL (telecommunications) W578
Entenmann's (baked goods) W244, W618
Entercom Communications Corporation E199
Entergy Corporation A554-A555, A624, A834, P280
Entergy-Koch L.P. A835, P281
Entergy-Shaw A554
Enteron A552
Enterprise Bank A1500
Enterprise Capital Management, Inc. A986
Enterprise Diversified Holdings, Inc. A1174
Enterprise hard drives A1515
Enterprise Industrielle (energy) W559
Enterprise Rent-A-Car P178-P179, P603
Enterprise Transport & Distribution d'Électricité W134, W135
EnterpriseSoft E22
EnterpriseWise IT Consulting A292
Entertaining (book) A918, A919
Entertainment Data A66
Entertainment Publications (coupon books) A338
Entertainment UK W312, W313
Enterton Group P506
Entex (gas) A552, A1199
ENTEX Information Services, Inc. A400, A544, W536
Entin, Bruce L. A895
EnTrade A1368
Entrelec Group SA W54
Entreprise Francis Bouygues W134
Entrust Technologies A596
Enviro-Chem brand A985
EnviroFill A1504
EnviroLease A638
Environmental Asset Services, Inc. A1399
Environmental Products USA (water purification) A446
Environmental Safety Systems A340
Environmental Solutions E131
EnviroTech Pumpsystems A222
Envision (brand consultant) A948, P326
Enya, Kenji W393
Enzimax cleaning and laundry products A487
Enzo Angiolini shoes A804, A805
Enzon, Inc. E199
E.ON AG (utility) A196, A214, P474, W137, **W218-W219**
eONE Global A597

EOTT Energy Partners, L.P. A**556-A557**
EP Technologies, Inc. A282, A283
EPA. *See* US Environmental Protection Agency
EPA Einheitspreis discount stores W310
EPCOT (theme park) A1496, P476, P745
Epic Express A420, A421
Epic Records Group W550
Epicor Software, Inc. A1112
Epicurious Web site A80, A81, P32
EPITAXX, Inc. (optical detectors) A792
EPIX Holdings Corporation P603
EPL Japan A86
E-Plus (mobile phones) A248, W502, W503, W504
Epoc operating system W360
Epoch Pharmaceuticals A244
Epoch Systems A542
Epogen drug A160
Epoka W426
Epon (energy) W559
Epperson, Deyonne F. A1073
Eppler, Guerin & Turner A1162
Eppler, W. Durand A1025
EPRO (memory chip testing) E46
Epron, Luc W443
EPSA (electric utility) A1198
Epsilon brand A527
Epson A782, A1356, E284, P136
Epson Electronics America (semiconductors) W530
Epstein, David A1451
Epstein, Max A638
ePublish A1218
EQT Northern Europe (equity firm) W210
Equa office seating A707
Equal artificial sweetener A984, A1122
Equal Employment Opportunity Commission P512
Equant W233
EQUICOR (HMO) A218, A360
Equicor (investments) E95
Equifax, Inc. A**558-A559**
Equilon Enterprises LLC A352, A1276, A1277, A1376, A1377, P340, P604, P679, W500
Equinix, Inc. A240
Equistar Chemicals, LP A900, A974, A1054, P604
Equitable building (New York City) P230
The Equitable Companies W104
Equitable Equipment A1406
The Equitable Life Assurance Society A562, P182, W222
The Equitable Life Assurance Society of the United States A218, A219, A360
Equitable of Iowa (insurance) W286
Equitable Powder A1060
Equitable Real Estate Investment Management A218

Equitable Resources, Inc. E316
Equitable Securities A142, A1346
Equitable Trust A808
Equitas Holdings Ltd. (reinsurance) W336, W337
Equity Corporation International A1268
Equity Financial and Management Company A560, P180
Equity Group Investments, L.L.C. A**560-A561**, P**180-P181**, P604
Equity office furniture systems P276, P277, P652
Equity Oil Company E199
Equity Residential Properties Trust P659
Equiva Services LLC A1277, P340
Equiva Trading Company P340
Equivest Finance, Inc. E200
E. R. Squibb W416
ER (TV show) A998
ERA. *See* Electronic Realty Associates
Erasco (soup) A316
Eraser Mate pens A656
Erede, Sergio W575
Erensen, George B. A1061
e.Reporting Suite software E22
ERF Holdings (trucks) W350
Erfert, Reiner P73
ERG Inc. W128
Ergen, Charles W. A528, A529
ERGO Versicherungsgruppe AG W380
Ergon office seating A706, A707
Erhart, Charles A1118
Erickson, Kim M. A1349
Erickson, Michael A873
Erickson Petroleum P633
Erickson, Richard S. E127
Erickson, Ronald P633
Erickson's Diversified (retailer) A994
Ericson, John A1048, P376
Telefonaktiebolaget LM Ericsson A170, A476, A1256, A1298, A1480, E28, E106, E126, E152, E156, E196, E269, E305, E307, E313, W**220-W221**, W400, W406, W546, W580, W584
Ericsson Energy Systems A546
Ericsson, Lars Magnus W220
Eridania Béghin-Say A730, A938
Erie Technological Products E124
Eriks, Mark C. A1313
Eriksen, Peter B. W417
Eriksson, Andrew W55
Erin Brockovich (movie) A1120
Erinmore tobacco W143
ERISA. *See* Employee Retirement Income Security Act (1974)
Eristoff vodka W109
Erkenbrecher, Andrew A292
Erlandson, Patrick J. A1435
Ermanni, John A407
Ermentrout, Gerald G. A101

Erne, Michael P119
Ernest, E. Robert A445
Ernest Orlando Lawrence Berkeley National Laboratory P495
Ernie Keebler cartoon character A814
Ernst, Alwin A562, P182, W222
Ernst & Ernst A562, A746, P182, W222
Ernst & Whinney A562, P182, W222
Ernst & Young International A220, A338, A474, A**562**-A**563**, A566, A840, P66, P154, P**182**-P**183**, P206, P286, P604, P620, W160, W196, W**222**-W**223**, W324, W474
Ernst, Edgar W203
Ernst, Mark A. A681
Ernst, Robert P227, P628
Ernst, Theodore A562, P182, W222
Erol's video chain A266
Erskine, Peter W149
Ertl (toys) A1446
Ertoil (gas stations) W482
Erwin, Mark A. A429
Erwin, Steven P. A697
Erwin Wasey & Company P72
erythropoietin. See Epogen
ESA. See Extended Stay America, Inc.
E-Sat, Inc. A529
ESB Ray-O-Vac batteries A572, W284
Escada AG A766
Escamez, Antonio W513
Escape theme park W472
Escarra, Vicki B. A479
Eschbach, Joe A77
Escher, Alfred W184
Escher, Sandra A1285
eSchwab (online brokerage) A348, W608
ESCO Electronics A546
ESER. See Espírito Santo Dealer
Eshelman, George C. A395
e-Shopping!Books Web site W298
ESI. See Electro Scientific Industries, Inc.
ESI Canada, Inc. A575
ESI Energy A624
Eskew, Carolyn P649
Eskew, Michael L. A1427
Eskimo Pie snack food P424
Eskofot (office systems) A746
e-Skolar (medical search engine) P456
Eslabon de Lujo appliances A1521
Eslambolchi, Hossein A203
Esmark A182, A212
EsMas.com (Internet portal) W582
ESNR (environmental consulting) P519
E.Solutions A538
ESOTERICA skin creams E89, E240
Espace minivan W330, W481
Espalioux, Jean-Marc W58, W59

Sociedad Española de Automóviles de Turismo. See SEAT S.A. (automobiles)
Espinosa, Maria Margarita E193
Espirit Telecom Group W594
Espírito Santo Dealer W224
Espírito Santo Financial Group S.A. W**224**-W**225**
Espírito Santo Silva, José Manuel P. W225
Espírito Santo Silva Salgado, Ricardo W225
Esplin, J. Kimo P239, P636
ESPN, Inc. A60, A61, A312, A622, A700, A872, A1496, P228, P229, P306, P360, P605, P629, P682, P684
Esposito, Gary R. A735
Esposito, Louis J. A1207
Espy, Mike A1418
Esquire Education Group P192
Esquire (magazine) A700, A701, P228, P229
ESR Exposition Services A1478
Esrey, William T. A1319
Essanelle hair salons A1196
Esselman, Mark S. A1097
Esselman, Paul E72
Essentially Me health and beauty stores W172
Essex AB A1240
Essex Gas A824
Essex Outfitters A1068
Esskay (hot dogs, bacon) A1290
Essner, Robert A. A148, A149
Esso Deutschland GmbH A577
Esso (fuel) A576, W216, W280
Esso Resources Canadian Ltd. W280
Esso Standard (Australia) W128
Esstathiou, Tricia E311
Esstman, Edward H. E27
Estabrook Capital Management A228
Estabrook, Jennifer W379
Estacada Foods, Inc. P489
E-Stamp A1142
Estancia Estates wines A423
Estate Cellars wines A423
Esteban, Manuel A. P99
The Estée Lauder Companies, Inc. A**564**-A**565**, W606, W607
e-steel (online steel trading) P511
Esteem vehicle W561
Estelar Suave rum W109
Estenson, Noel P122
Estenssoro, Jose W650
Estes (home builders) A812
Estrada, Joseph W510
Estrofem drug W417
E.T. The Extra-Terrestrial (movie) P412
Eta salad dressings A723
Etablissements Porcher Paris (bathroom fixtures) A152
Établissements Poulenc Frères W102

Etap Hotel W58, W59
Etchemendy, John P457
ETDE. See Enterprise Transport & Distribution d'Électricité
Etec Systems, Inc. A188, A189
E-Tek Dynamics A792
Eternity fragrance A766, P101
ETEVA (investment bank) W384
Ethan Allen Interiors Inc. A630
Ethel M Chocolates A914, A915, P314, P315
Etherington, Glenn A. E243
Ethernet A54
Ethniki Hellenic Generak Insurance SA W385
Ethospace modular systems A707
Ethridge, Joseph A. P720
Ethyol drug E90, E240
E-Ticket Tracking Solution P419
Etienne, Jean-Michel W467
ETNA convenience stores A1084, A1085
eTopps E130
Etos health and beauty stores W498, W499
etown.com A254
eToys Inc. A1116, P649
ETPM (marine construction) A940
E*TRADE Bank A566, W222
E*TRADE Group, Inc. A150, A562, A**566**-A**567**, A960, P182, W548
ETRAVNET.COM P296
Etter, Gregory V. A1025
Ettinger, Jeffrey M. A731
Ettore, Joseph R. A158, A159
Ettusais cosmetics W535
EU. See European Union
Eubanks, Bob P581
Eubanks, R. Glenn A1309
Euclid Industries A198
Eudermine skin lotion W534
Eudora e-mail software A1182, A1183
Eufemi, Joyce L. A1511
Eugenio Maria de Hostos Community College P129
Eugster, Jack W. A1283
EUK (electronic entertainment) W312
Eukanuba pet foods A1164, A1165, P138
Eulberg, Joe A57
Euller, Steven C. P105
EUnet International A1186
Eurasia Aviation Corporation W344
Eureka appliances W210
Eurelettronica (semiconductors) A196
Eurest International (food services) W174, W175, W546
Euro am Sonntag (newspaper) W107
Euro Belgian Airlines W622
Euro Disney S.C.A. (amusement park) A1496, P110, W170, W174
Euro Lloyd Reiseburo W310
Euro Tunnel. See Chunnel

Eurocan Pulp & Paper W556
Eurocard A924, P322
Eurocom W198
Eurodis Electron A1140
Eurofighter Typhoon jet W111
Eurofly W79
Eurogen (electricity
 generation) W214
Eurohypo (mortgage bank) W200
Euromarche hypermarket W164
Euromaster tires W367
Euronext Brussels S.A./N.V. W288
Euronova (food retailer) W498
Europay A924, P322
Europcar (car rental) W58, W630
Europe 1 radio station W330
European Aeronautic Defence and
 Space Company EADS N.V. W70,
 W110, W330, W331
European American Bank A370
European Automotive Interior
 Systems A388
European Bakers Ltd. (frozen
 foods) A609
European Commission W74, W94,
 W140, W150, W178, W202, W366,
 W482, W518, W624
European Consumer
 Products A1022
European Direct Capital
 Management A1332
European Space Agency W110
European Union A142, A144, A160,
 A354, A494, A728, A1118, A1398,
 A1432, A1480, P508, P509, W86,
 W98, W182, W204, W208, W214,
 W224, W240, W292, W318, W340,
 W432, W492, W520, W578, W632
Société Europeenne de Brasseries
 (brewery) W192
Europe*Star (broadcasting) A888
Eurosar (nursing homes) A1340
Eurotel Praha s.r.o. A1473
Eurotherm W290
Eurotower Holdings W434
Euroweb International
 Corporation W503
Eusden, Alan T. A435
Eustace, Dudley G. W503
eV PRODUCTS E20, E146
EVA Airways A138, W469
Evangeline Maid baked goods A609
Evan-Picone clothing A690, A691,
 A804, A805
Evans, Alna P519, P774
Evans Asset Holding (railcars) A176
Evans Brothers (distributor) P236
Evans, Donald L. (University of
 Texas) P499
Evans, Don (Tom Brown,
 Inc.) E129
Evans, Dwight H. A1307
Evans, Eric W. A897
Evans Forest Products A890
Evans, Gary C. E235
Evans, G. Robert A421
Evans Group W466
Evans, Ivor J. A1423

Evans, James E. (American
 Financial Group) A145
Evans, Jim (Rudolph and
 Sletten) P719
Evans, Joan E229
Evans, John (Payless
 Cashways) A1090
Evans, John R. (Alcan
 Aluminium) W75
Evans, Richard (BAE
 SYSTEMS) W111
Evans, Richard B. (Alcan
 Aluminium) W75
Evans, Robert S. A446, A447
Evans, Scott C. A1355, P467
Evans, Steve P393
Evans, Thomas E. (Collins &
 Aikman) A388, A389
Evans, Thomas Mellon
 (Crane) A446
Evans, Timothy P415
Evans, T. Scott E87
Evanson, Jennifer E236
Evanson, Paul J. A625
Evatt, James W. A273
Evcon A1550
Eveillard, Jean-Marie P294
eVenator (footwear) A1470
Evenflo Company, Inc. A836, A837,
 A1068, P282, P283
Everaert, Pierre Jean W288, W289
Everbach, O. George A827
Everclear (music group) W213
Evercore Partners Inc. A474,
 A1396, P154, P506, P765, W196
Eveready batteries A1190
Eveready battery tester A250
EVEREN Securities A1444
Everest gum A1527
Everett Charles Technologies
 (electronic testing) A502
Everett, Edward P220
Everett, Leslie H. A1121
Everett, Malcolm E., III A1487
Everex Systems Inc. W228
Evergreen Markets, Inc. P489
Evergreen Media A714, P232
Evergreen Resources, Inc. E200
Everhart, George A55
Everitt, Neil W85
Evermore liquor W315
Ever-Sharp mechanical
 pencil W532
Everybody Loves Raymond (TV
 show) A334
Every-Burns, Warwick A375
EveryLash cosmetics A1200
EVI A1078
Evian water A384, A385, W192,
 W193
Evidian W151
Evinrude Outboard Motor
 Company A286, W132, W133
Evista drug A540
Evity (Web monitoring) A270
eVolution Global Partners P64
E. W. Clark (bank) A1038

The E. W. Scripps Company A80,
 A**568**-A**569**, P32, P228
Ewald, Curt R. A1541
Ewalt, Alan R. A1367
Ewing, B. Edward P111
Ewing, Curtis P413
Ewing, Stephen E. A513
Exabyte Corporation (computer
 storage) A928
ExacTech, Inc. (self testing
 system) A59
Exbit Technology E136
Excalibur (hotel and casino) A906,
 A907
Excedrin A290, A291
Excel car W274
Excel Communications, Inc. P764,
 W122, W123
Excel Corporation
 (slaughterhouse) A325, P104,
 P566
Excel Extrusions A112
Excel gum A1527
Excel Realty Trust E252
Excel software A973
Excelan (networking
 software) A1050
Exceler (nursing homes) A1340
Excell Materials (concrete) A1406
Excerpta Medic
 Communications W479
Exchange & Mart (classified
 advertising) W621
Exchange House (London) P449
Exchange Oil and Gas A654
Excite@Home A202, A442, A506,
 A1284, P146, P248
Exclusiv rum W109
EXCO Resources, Inc. E200
Execu-Fit A1080
Execunet (private lines) A1534
ExecuStay Corporation
 (hotels) A912
Executive Choice A262
Executive Incentives & Travel P257
Executive Income Life
 Insurance A414
Executive Jet A252, A253
Executive Leasing P178
Executive Office Group A706
Executive Risk Indemnity Inc. A356
ExecuTrain (technology
 training) P249
Exel beer W377
Exelon Corporation A**570**-A**571**,
 A1550
Exelon drug W415
Exeter Oil A1344
Exhibitgroup/Giltspur A1478,
 A1479
Exide (batteries) W429
Exide Corporation A**572**-A**573**
Exigent International, Inc. A686
ExIn (investors) A700, P228
EXI-PAK molding process P702
Exit Strategy Program E131, E304
Exito supermarkets W166, W167

ExLax laxative W414, W415
Exmark (landscaping
  equipment) A1392
Exodus Communications,
  Inc. E201
Exor (company) W170
EXOR Group P715
Expedia, Inc. (travel service) A1228,
  A1450
Expedition recreational
  vehicles A605
Experian Information
  Solutions A558, A594, A1412,
  E63
Experience Music Project
  (Seattle) P632
The Exploration Company of
  Delaware, Inc. E201
Explorer of the Seas (cruise
  ship) A1217
Explorer sport utility vehicle A616,
  A1394, W138
EXPO Design Centers A724
Export beer W377
Express Access software E36
Express Airlines A1046
Express car W480, W481
Express clothing A876, A877
Express Newspapers W620
Express Parts Service A208
Express Personnel Services P606
Express Ranches P606
Express Scripts, Inc. A**574**-A**575**
Express Stop convenience
  stores A1084, A1085
Express Stores auto parts A208
ExpressClose.com E108
EXPRESSfreighter A588
Expressions containers A1415
ExpressJet Holdings, Inc. A428,
  A429
Exshaw cognac W109
Exsif S.A. P313
Extant (software) A518
Extel (telecommunications) A544
Extended Stay America, Inc. E**59**,
  E201
Extendicare Inc. A738
Extra ETT (automotive
  staffing) A818
Extra food stores W364, W365
Extra gum A1526, A1527
Extra Ordinary Life whole and term
  life insurance P376
Exxon Mobil Corporation A184,
  A352, A412, A514, A552,
  A**576**-A**577**, A620, A770, A772,
  A828, A862, A1138, A1144, A1276,
  A1288, A1368, A1376, A1466,
  E208, E230, E305, P254, P270,
  P408, P416, P446, P701, W116,
  W136, W216, W280, W318, W410,
  W440, W500, W612
Exxon Valdez (ship) A576
Eychmuller, Ing. Wolfgang W491
Eyde, Sam W410
Eye on the Prize (TV
  documentary) P144

Eye-Vision display case A678, P216
Eyewitness to the 20th Century
  (book) P359
Eyler, John H., Jr. A1396, A1397
Eyrich, Keith P253
Eyvazzadeh, Susan P713
EZ Paintr A1022, A1023
E-Z Pass P334, P674
E-Z Serve stores P740
Ezaki, Joichiro W573
EZFibre software E226
Ezy Banking W645

F

F. Hoffmann-La Roche W492
F5 Networks, Inc. E201
FAA. *See* US Federal Aviation
  Administration
F.A.B. (company) P479
Fab detergent A386, A387
Faber, Emmanuel W193
Faber, Joachim W83
Faber, Pam P511, P767
Faber, Terrence A. A177
Faber, Timothy J. A877
Faberge/Elizabeth Arden W618
Faberware (cookware) A1446
Fabia vehicle W631
Fabiano, Joseph M. A209
Fabiano, Rocco J. A735
Fabre, Pierre W572
Fabri-Centers of America A796,
  A1058
Fabry, John J. A673, P211
Fabryka Opakowan Blaszanyck
  (packaging) A452
Faccilongo, Franco W577
Facet air filtration P310
Fachgiven, Rich P413
Façonnable SA A1036, A1037
FACSCalibur cell analysis A244
Fact Plus pregnancy test A59
Factiva A506
Factory 2-U Stores, Inc. E**60**, E202
Factory Mutual Liability Insurance
  Company of America P540
Factorymate brand A527
Facts & Comparisons (health and
  science information) W643
FactSet Research Systems
  Inc. E**61**, E202
Fadem, Bruce A149
Faeyev, Vasiliy Vasilyevich W243
Fafnir bearings A755
FAG Bearings E254
FAG Kugelfischer Georg Schafer
  (needle and cylindrical
  bearing) A754
Fagan, Andrew P431
Fagan, Charles A1151
Fagin, Sherry P753
Fahey, John M., Jr. P358, P359,
  P683
Fahl, John A433
Fahrholz, Bernd W83
Fahrzeugwerke Eisenach
  (cars) W120

Fain, Richard D. A1216, A1217
Fainé Casas, Isidro W579
Fair Housing Act P42
Fair, Isaac & Company A480
Fairbairn, Caroline W145
Fairbairn, Ursula F. A143
Fairbank, Richard D. A318, A319
Fairbanks dessert wine A521, P169
Fairchild Camera &
  Instrument A82, A894
Fairchild Dornier W132
Fairchild Publications, Inc. A60,
  A80, A81, P32, P33, P530
Fairchild Semiconductor
  International, Inc. A760, A1002,
  A1190, E92, W508
Fairchild, Sherman A164
Fairclough Homes Group Ltd. A340
Fairfield Communities (time
  share) A330, A338
Fairfield Inns A732, A912, A913,
  A1296
Fairlane Associates
  (insurance) A394
Fairleigh Dickinson
  University A244
Fairmont Supply Company A416
Fairmount Motor Products A214
Fairway Crude A556
Fairway Foods of Michigan,
  Inc. P633
Faisal, King of Saudi Arabia P74
Faison, Henry J. A1399
Faison, Scott P578
Falco, Randy A999
Falcon Communications
  (cable) A350
Falcon Products, Inc. E202
Falcone, Carmine P345
Falgoust, Dean T. A629
Fali foods W193
Falivene, Rob A1097
Falk, Harry A236
Falk, Ralph A236
Falk, Thomas J. A827
Falkenberg, Martin A281
Faller, Keith R. A179
Falley's stores P62, P63, P524,
  P547, P777
Fallon Hines & O'Connor (real
  estate) A1398
Fallon, James M. A1065
Fallon, Robert J. E88, E238
Fallon Worldwide W466, W467
Falls Rubber Company A432
Falstad, Robert P445
Falstaff beer P428
Falstrup, Asger A759
Faltin, Daniel E. A503
Fame brand foods A995
Famfa Oil A1376
Famicom video game system W394
Famil restaurants W298, W299
Familia car W362, W363
Family Bargain stores E60
Family Circle (magazine) W126

Family Dollar Stores,
  Inc. A**578**-A**579**
Family Fare stores A1312
The Family Handyman
  (magazine) A1193
Family Health Assurance
  (insurance) P174
Family HealthChoice HMO P174
Family Leave Act (1993) P34
Family Pharmacy A155, A156
Family Pure dishwashing
  detergent W308, W309
Family Restaurants A86, A784
Family Service Life
  Insurance A1390
Family Thrift Center grocery
  stores A994, A995
Famous Amos Cookie
  Company A804, A814, A815, A816
The Famous Clothing Store A932
Famous Footwear A294
Famous Recipe Fried Chicken
  restaurants A1280
Famous-Barr department
  stores A932
Fan, John C. C. E229
Fanchi, Louis A. P207, P620
F. & J. Heinz A722
F&G Life A1236
F&G Stores W172
F&M Bank E179
F&M Scientific (analytical
  instruments) A98, A712
F&R Builders A862
F&R Lazarus department
  store A586
Fanella, James A. A1547
Fanfares shoes A295
Fang family A700, P228
Fang, Ted A700, P228
Fani, Robert J. A825
Fanjul, Alfonso W568
Fanjul, J. Pepe W568
Fannie Mae A252, A438,
  A**580**-A**581**, A626, A862, A1448,
  E152, E203
Fannin, David C. A1057
Fanta soft drink A382
Fantasia (movie) A98, A712, A1496
Fantastik cleaner A1247, P433
Fantasy 5 lottery game P564, P736
Fantasy (ship) A331
FAO Schwarz A1396
Far Away fragrance A217
Far East Airlines W80
*Far Eastern Economic
  Review* A506, A507
Faraci, John V. A771
Farady, John T. A799
Farah brand clothing E305
Farah, Roger N. A1151, A1470
Farallon wines A422
Faranda, Joseph A217
Faraone jewelry A1385
Farbacher, Elizabeth A. A717, P235
Farber, John P637

Farberware cookware E116, P91,
  P775
Farell, Dan A1417
Fargo, William A142
Farina P72
Farinon (microwave radio) A686
Farley, Jim P88
Farley, Roger B. P762
Farley, Steven B. A1221
Farley's baby food A723
Farm Bill (1996) P58
The Farm brand A671
Farm Bureau Mutual A1008, P364
The Farm Credit
  Administration E203
Farm Credit Association P122
Farm Credit System P533, P534
Farm Fresh Inc. (food
  stores) A1348, A1349
Farm Frites P264
Farmall tractor A1010
FarmandCountry.com P406
Farman's pickles A467
Farmar, Gary E. A1025
Farmbest meat products A582,
  P184
Farmer, Herschell A364
Farmer Jack grocery stores A670,
  A671, W194
Farmer Mac. *See* Federal
  Agricultural Mortgage
  Corporation
Farmer, Phillip W. A686, A687
Farmer, Richard T. "Doc" A364,
  A365
Farmer, Scott D. A364, A365
Farmer, William J. E48
Farmers and Millers Bank A1444
Farmer's Feed and Seed
  Company A1132
Farmers Group, Inc. (management
  services) W653
Farmers Insurance Group A226,
  W652
Farmers Mutual Automobile
  Insurance P42
Farmers Savings and Trust A230
Farmers Union Central Exchange
  (CENEX) P122
Farmers Union Terminal
  Association P122
Farmhand farm equipment A97
Farmhouse Foods A648
Farmland Foods A583, P184, P185
Farmland Hydro, LP A583, P185
Farmland Industries,
  Inc. A**582**-A**583**, A850, P36,
  P122, P123, P**184**-P**185**, P288,
  P571, P606, P654
Farmland Insurance A1008, A1009,
  P364, P365, P685
Farnsworth, Alan H. A235
Farnsworth, Elon A394
Farnsworth, Susan E. A1537
Farr, David N. A547
Farr, George L. A441
Farr, Kevin M. A927
Farrar, Eileen A1441

Farrar, Stephen D. A1511
Farrel, Donna A983
Farrell, Anthony A1275, E120
Farrell, David A932
Farrell, Edmund J. A1065
Farrell, James A748
Farrell, John (Bcom3) P73
Farrell, John J., Jr. (J.P. Morgan
  Chase) A809
Farrell, Kathie A309
Farrell, Patrick M. A805
Farrell, Peter C. E112, E279
Farrell, Stephen C. E105, E268
Farrell, Thomas F., II A499
Farrell, William F. A581
Farrell, W. James A749
Farrelly, John P291, P656
Farries, David C. E291
Farrington, George A1236
Farrington, Hugh G. W195
Farrington, John A1236
Farris, G. Steven A185
Farshchi, Shawn A485
Farsi, Nicholas A763
Farwell, Peter A1015
Farwell, Simeon A250
Farynowski, Kathryn P223
Fasano, Philip A145
Fascitelli, Michael D. E137
Fashion Effects P342
Fashion Fair cosmetics P258, P259,
  P646
FashionPleat window
  furnishings A1317, P453
Fasola, Kenneth J. A739
Fasold, Mark P301, P660
Fassbind, Renato W55
Fassio, Daniel L. A417
Fassio, James S. A1215
Fasso, Robert V. A1455
Fasson A210
Fast Cash lottery game P473
Fast, Eric C. A447
The Fast Forward MBA in Hiring
  (book) A1208
Fast, John W129
Fast Lane convenience
  stores A1084
Fast, Larry E. A643
Fast Stop convenience stores P622
Fastow, Andrew S. A553
Fat Boy motorbikes A682
Fathom.com P134
Fatjo, Thomas A206
Fattori, Ruth A. A415
Faucet Queen A920
Fauerbach, William V. A1177
Faulders, C. Thomas, III E232
Faulkenberry, David P736
Faulkner Dawkins & Sullivan
  (investments) E61
Faulkner, Duane P565
Faulkner, Hank P606
Faulkner, Henry A606
Faulkner, Larry R. P499
The Faulkner Organization P606

Faulkner, William F. E61
Faure, Patrick W481
Faurecia (auto parts) W442
Faust, Charles R. E128
Faust, James P669
Faust, Thomas E., Jr. E53
Faustino, Alfred L. P53
Faustman, David F. A1235
Favorite Brands P474
Favre & Peret W562
Favre, Brett A672, P210
Fawick brand A527
Fawthrop, Andrew A1439
Fay, Roger L. P712
Fayard, Gary P. A383
Fayne, Henry W. A141
Fay's Inc. (drugstores) A790
Fazio, Peter V., Jr. A1035
Fazzini, Larry P137, P580
FBI. See US Federal Bureau of
 Investigation
FBS Capital I A1445
Groupe FCA (advertising) W466
FCB Group A772, A773
FCB Worldwide (advertising) A1062
FCC. See US Federal
 Communications Commission
FCI Electronics A982
FCI (securities industry
 consulting) A538
FCNB Corporation (credit
 card) A1314
FCX. See Freeport-McMoRan
 Copper & Gold, Inc.
FDA. See US Federal Drug
 Administration
FDB (supermarkets) W94
FDIC. See US Federal Deposit
 Insurance Corporation
FDS feminine deodorant
 spray A108
FDX Corporation A588
FEA. See US Federal Energy
 Administration
Fealy, Robert L. P598
Fear Factor (TV show) A998
Fears, Oscar B., Jr. A1517
Febold, Bill P606
Fedco (automotive heaters) W605
Federal Agricultural Mortgage
 Corporation E203
Federal (automotive
 products) P113
Federal Bearing and Bushing A584
Federal Data (information for US
 government) A1044
Federal Deposit Insurance
 Corporation A1178
Federal Electric A780
Federal Employee Program (health
 insurance) A269, P83
Federal Energy Policy Act
 (1992) A1166
Federal Express Corporation. See
 FedEx Corporation
Federal Family Education Loan
 Program A1449
Federal Filings Business A507

Federal Home Loan Bank A626
Federal Home Loan Mortgage
 Corporation. See Freddie Mac
Federal Insurance Company A356,
 A357
Federal Kemper A178
Federal Kemper Life
 Assurance P268
Federal National Mortgage
 Association. See Fannie Mae
Federal Open Market
 Committee P186
Federal Reserve Act (1913) P186
Federal Reserve Bank of New
 York P607
Federal Reserve System. See US
 Federal Reserve System
Federal Savings and Loan Insurance
 Corporation A1178
Federal Steel Company A1462
Federal Telegraph A780
Federal Telephone & Radio
 Laboratories A780
Federal-Mogul Corporation A430,
 A460, **A584-A585**, P113
Federated Bank Geneva Capital
 Corporation A1444
Federated Department Stores,
 Inc. A490, **A586-A587**, A790,
 A838, A880, A932, A1316, A1498,
 E69, P172, P452
Federated Insurance
 Companies P607
Federico, Richard L. E265
Federle, Louis A. A397
Federman, Irwin E117
FedEx Corporation A102, A380,
 A484, A566, **A588-A589**, A944,
 A1222, A1238, A1428, E147, P490,
 W71, W344
Fed-Mart (discount chain) A436
Fedmart stores A1352
Fedoun, Lionid A. W347
Fedyna, Michael W. P175
Feeback, Cynthia A. A1145
Feeheley, Timothy J. A1431
Feely, Terri E232
Feeney, Charles P156
Feeney, E. K. A546
Feeney, Gordon J. W475
Feeney, John F. P39
Feeny, Steven C. A585
Feeser, Robert A. A951
Feezor, Allen D. A315, P97
Fehrenbach, Franz W491
FEI Company E203
Feidt, Bill A1535
Feigenbaum, Joel A1193
Feigenbaum, Ted C. A1041
Feiger, Mitchell E239
Feinberg, Henry P408
Feiner, Barbara P769
Feiner, Stuart F. W285
Feinstein, Leonard A246, A247
Feinstein, Martin D. W653
Feiwel, Jean L. A1255
Fejes, William T., Jr. A463
Felago, Richard T. A1505

FelCor Suite Hotels A1328
Feld Entertainment,
 Inc. **P188-P189**, P608
Feld, Irving P188, P608
Feld, Israel P188
Feld, Kenneth P188, P189, P608
Feld, Thomas W., Jr. P463
Feldberg, Harley A215
Feldberg, Stanley A1388
Feldberg, Sumner A1388
Feldene drug A1118
Felderman, Douglas C. E60, E202
Feldman, Alan D. A943
Feldman, Jake A396
Feldman, Moses A396
Feldman, Robert J. P649
Feldman, Sally P447
Feldman, Sandra P35
Feldman, Sheila B. A1301
Feldmuhle Nobel W556
Feldner, Ronald A. P555
Feldschlösschen Hürlimann
 (beer) W162, W163
Feldt, James E. A1397
Felicelli, Joseph P. P153
Felicia vehicle W631
Felicity (TV show) A61
Fell, Anthony S. W475
Fell, Fraser M. W453
Feller, Millicent A. A633
Feller, Nancy P. P195
Fellmy, Douglas E. P443
Fellows, David A. A119
Fellows, George A1200
Fellows, John A. (RMH
 Teleservices) E113, E280
Fellows, John (DHL Worldwide
 Express) A485
Fellowship Corporation P520
Fel-Pro (gaskets) A584
Fels Naptha cleaning
 products A487
Fels, Xavier W443
Felsinger, Donald E. A1267
Fels-Werke GmbH W461
Feltz, Guy C. A481
Femme Assise dans un Jardin
 (painting) A1304
Femme Plus (magazine) W471
FEMSA (boxes) A1524
FEMSA Cerveza (beverages) W288
Fender Musical Instruments
 Corporation E210
Fenderson, Albion A521, P169
Fendi fashions W348, W349
Fendt farm equipment A96, A97
Fenestra (doors and springs) P312
Feng Jianping W543
Fenger, Chris A351
Fenichel, Alvin H. A219
Fenix LLC A1422, A1423
Fenn, Grant W469
Fenn, Wade R. A255
Fenner and Beane A960
Fenner Fluid Power A1320
Fenner PLC A1320

Fenton, Charles E. A265
Fenton, Dennis A161
Fenton, Jim E186
Fenwal Labs A236
Fenway Partners
(investments) A722, P406
Fenwick, Lex P81, P556
Feraudo, William K. A825
Ferber, Norman A. A1214, A1215
FERC. *See* US Federal Energy
Regulatory Commission
Ferdon, Ellie P493
Ferembal S.A. A1338
Ferguson, Daniel (Newell
Rubbermaid) A1022
Ferguson, Dan S. (Canadian
Imperial Bank) W157
Ferguson, Fred P545
Ferguson, James M. A1257
Ferguson, J. Brian A523
Ferguson, John J. (Solutia) A1301
Ferguson, John T., II
(Crompton) A451
Ferguson, Larry P723
Ferguson, Leonard A1022
Ferguson Machine Company
SA A446, A447
Ferguson, Peter J. A421
Ferguson, R. Michael A909
Ferguson, Roger W., Jr. P187
Ferguson, Stanley L. A1457
Fergusson, Francis D. P325
Ferko, William G. P613
Ferland, E. James A1175
Ferm, David G. A1161
Fermi, Enrico P496, P756
Fermi nuclear plants A512
Fern, Dave A1490, P514
Fernández, Cesareo W635
Fernández de la Garza, Rafael W441
Fernández de la Vega Sanz,
Jesús W483, W651
Fernandez, Frank L. A725
Fernandez, James N. A1385
Fernandez, Juan C. A1069
Fernandez, Mike A361
Fernandez, Ted A. E157
Fernández-Vidal, Guillermo W579
Ferngas Beteiligungs-
Aktiengesellschaft m.b.H. W425
Ferolie, A. Joseph P530
Ferolie, Lawrence J. P530
Ferrales, Savino A763
Ferramentas Belzer do Brazil (hand
tools) A430
Ferrando, Jonathan P. A207
Ferranti International W354
Ferrara, Peter A373
Ferrari S.p.A. A650, W226, W227
Ferrario, Giovanni W451
Ferrario, Pia A777
Ferraris Piston Service W604
Ferraro, John F. A563, P183, W223
Ferrarone, Joan M. E309
Ferree, Larry P606
Ferreira, Hugo E. I. A461
Ferrell, Susie E211

Ferrellgas A1528
Ferrero, Dominique W183
Ferrero, Mario W423
Ferrick, Patricia E291
Ferrie, John P93, P559
Ferriola, John J. A1053
Ferris, Richard A1420
Ferro Corporation A1300
Ferro, Graciela M. A767
Ferro Manufacturing (auto
seats) A802
Ferro, Michael W., Jr. E180
Ferrone, John G. A1207
Ferrostaal W350, W351
Ferrous Processing & Trading
Company P731
Ferrucci, Richard F. A183
Ferrulmatic (metal parts) A120
Ferry, Pat A1059
Fersch, Richard T. A1315
Ferson Optics A234
Fertman, Don P161
Fery, John A274
Fesler, Larry J. E101
Fessler, Clyde A683
Festival (cruise line) W434
Festivus Maximus II lottery
game P666
Fetah, David A1515
Fetherston, Richard A. P43
Fetsko, Francis M. E302
Fetter, Trevor A1367
Fettig, Jeff M. A1521
Fetzer Vineyards A296, A297
Feuer, Michael A1058, A1059
Feuerhake, Rainer W461
fexofenadine HCL drug E150
Fey, Gwen A75
Fey, Sharlene S. A1375
F.G. Emmett Spice Company of
Philadelphia A938
F.G. Wilson A332, A546
FGH Bank W64
F.H. Faulding & Company
Limited E184
F.H. Tomkins Buckle
Company W604
FHA. *See* US Federal Housing
Administration
FHP International A1080
FHP of Illinois (health plan) A1162
FHP Reinsurance Limited A1081
FHS Life Holdings A697
Fiat S.p.A. A96, A456, A572, A616,
A650, A856, A1394, W100,
W226-W227, W318, W422, W442,
W480
Fiber One (carpets) A980
Fiber Resources P621
FiberCore, Inc. E203
Fiberloid (celluloid) A1300
Fibre Channel E136, E166, E226,
E239, E258, E272
Fibreboard Corporation A356,
A890, A1072
FibreStar E226
Fibrex material P50

Fibrotek (clean room
apparel) A1474
Fichtel & Sachs Industries,
Inc. W352
Fichtner, Werner W. A983
Fick, Jeffrey D. A727
Fickenscher, Gerald H. A451
Fickling, William A904
Ficosa International, Inc. W226
Fidelity Acceptance A1508
The Fidelity & Casualty Company of
New York A379
Fidelity Brokerage Services A566
Fidelity Calvin Corporation A593
Fidelity Daily Income Trust A614
Fidelity Express (money
orders) P623
Fidelity Insurance Agency P257
Fidelity Investments. *See* FMR
Corporation
Fidelity Management and Research.
See FMR Corporation
Fidelity National Financial,
Inc. **A590-A591**
Fidelity Personal Trust
Company A614, P190
Fidelity Technology & Processing
Group A615
Fidelity Title and Trust A954
Fidelity Warranty Services
Inc. P257
Fidenas International E58
Fides appliances A1521
Fides Revision (accounting) A840,
P286, W324
Fiducial Finder II E43
Fiedler, John F. A279
Fiedler, Patrick A359
Field & Stream (magazine) A1402
Field, Benjamin R., III A251
Field Brothers clothing A690
Field family E199
Field, Greg A679, P217
Field, Joseph M. E199
Field, Marshall (Marshall Fields
department stores) A1042, A1352,
P496
Field, Marshall, V
(Teleprompter) P350
Field, Rusty A143
Fieldcrest bedding and towels P696
Fieldcrest Cannon, Inc. A980,
A1134, A1135, E60
Fieldcrest dairy A467
Fielden, Christopher W241
Fielder, Virginia Dodge A833
Fieldfresh Farms (dairy) W244
Fielding, Al A1262
Fielding, Ronald W. A731
Fielding, William G. A583, P185
Fieldmaster brand A1265
Fields, Bill (Blockbuster) A266,
W270
Fields, Bill (Worldcom) A1534
Fields clothing stores W270, W271
Fields, Dave P129
Fields, Macon P413

Fields, Mark W362, W363
Fieldsa, Wayne W. A349
Fieramosca, Charles A1553
Fiesta Texas (theme park) A1452, P502
Fife, Jim A851, P289
Fifth Avenue Bank A228
Fifth National Bank A592
Fifth Quarter steak houses A1280
Fifth Third Bancorp **A592-A593**
Figgie International P94
Figueroa, Lorenzo A305
Figueroa, Luis P707
FileMaker, Inc. (software) A186, A187, A1356
Filene's department stores A586, A932
FileNET Corporation (software) A76
Filer, Anthony J. P57, P544
Fili-Krushel, Patricia A60, A181
Filipacchi Médias W330
Filipek, Joseph J., Jr. A85
Filipps, Frank P. E108, E274
Fill Air packaging A1263
Filler, Gary A1261
Filles d'Aujourd'hui (magazine) W471
Fillzetti, Gary P592
Film-To-Go P237
Filmtrax (music publishing) W212
Filo, David A1546
FINA, Inc. (chemicals) W613
Fin-Ag, Inc. P123
Final Encyclopedia P510
Finalion W183
Finalrealm A715, P333, W192
Finan, Kevin P. A107
Finance Act of 1986 (Ireland) W86
Financial Engines, Inc. A348
Financial Horizons Life A1008, P364
Financial Markets Group A325
Financial News Network A998
Financial Planning Network A1452, P502
Financial Services Technology Consortium A1480, P508
Financial Times (newspaper) A506, W430
Financiera El Sol, S.A. A1509
Societe Financiere de Sucres W568
Compagnie Financiere de Suez W558
Compagnie Financiere Espirito Santo SA (asset management) W225
Compagnie Financiere Richemont W142
Grupo Financiero Banamex W64
Grupo Financiero Bancomer. *See* BBVA Bancomer
Grupo Financiero Santander Mexicano W512
Grupo Financiero Serfin A878
Società Finanziaria Telefonica W574

Finazzo, Kathy P463, P736
Finch, Harold A994
Finch, Harry A994
Finch, H. B. A344
Finding Nemo (movie) E103
Findlater, Richard N. A563, P183, W223
Findlay, Linda D. A1125
Findlay, Rick P479
Findley, Mary Sue A593
Findley, Norman P., III A385
FindMRO.com A1538, A1539
Findus frozen foods W388, W619
Fine, Deborah I. A217
Fine, Gerald J. A435
Fine Living cable network A568
Fine, Peter S. P549
Fine Pitch Technology A1298
Fine, Roger S. A801
Finegold, Aryeh E91
Finelettrica W214
FINELINE ceiling grid A1457
Fineline Steels A257
Finelli, Michael A., Jr. P269
Fineman, S. David A1429, P491
Fingerhut Companies, Inc. A586, A587, P254
Fingleton, Thomas D. A933
Finian's Rainbow (movie) P302
Finishing Systems and Products A748
FinishMaster, Inc. (auto paints) P656
Fink, Chris P299
Fink, Richard H. A835, P281
Fink, Steven B. P279
Finkelman, Daniel B. A877
Finkelstein, Edward A586
Finkelstein, Paul D. A1196, A1197
Finkelstein, William S. A1499
Finlandia Vodka Worldwide A296
Finlay Enterprises, Inc. A1552
Finley, David M. A759
Finley, George S. A223
Finley, Sara J. A323
Finlon, David P69
Finmeccanica SpA W554
Finn, Carolyn A67
Finn, Edwin A., Jr. A507
Finn, Linda T. A1037
Finn, Tim A1471
Finnair Oyj W140, W469, W518
Finnegan, John D. (General Motors) A651
Finneran, John G., Jr. (Capital One) A319
Finney, Jack P. A243
Finn-Filter Oy A1088
Finnigan, Dan A833
Finnigan, Jay P431
Finnish Cable Works W406
Finnish Rubber W406
The FINOVA Group A252, A660
Finsiel-Consulenza e Applicazioni Informatiche S.p.A. W575
Finucane, Anne M. A603

Fiola, Janet S. A953
Fiona Press P338
Fiore, John A. A1333
Fiore, Vito A1485
Fiorello H. LaGuardia Community College P129
Fiori, Giovanni A803
Fiorilli, Matthew A247
Fiorina, Carleton S. A712, A713
Fiorito, Deborah A519
Firdosy, Akbar H. E220
Fire & Ice fragrance A1200, A1201
Fire soft drink W315
Fireman, Paul B. A1194, A1195
Fireman's Fund American Insurance A142
Fireman's Fund Insurance Company W82
Fireman's Insurance Company of Newark, New Jersey A379
Firestone Country Club (Ohio) P131
Firestone, Dan E290
Firestone, Harvey W138
Firestone tires A616, A664, A1394, P628, W138, W366, W450
FireWall-1 software E96, E251
FireWire adapter A1515
Fireworks Web design tool E86, E235
First Affiliate of Alabama Bank Corporation A166
First Albany Companies Inc. (brokerage) A1486
First American Bank A166
The First American Corporation A590, A**594-A595**, A1508
First American Enterprises, Inc. A167
First American Real Estate Solutions A594
First Atlanta bank A1486
First Aviation Services W496
First Banc Group of Ohio A230
First Bancorp E204
First Bancorp of Maryland W86
First Banks America, Inc. E204
First Boston Corporation A448, A714, P232, W184
First Brands Corporation A374
First Building Corporation A1445
First Capital Bank of Arizona E181
First Capital Life P384
First Chicago (bank) A1508
First Chicago Investment A572
First Chicago NBD Corporation A230
First Choice Dental Network P214
First Choice Food Distributors P236
First Choice Haircutters stores A1196
First Choice Holidays (tour operator) A1216, W622
First Colonial Bankshares, Inc. A1444

First Commander Corporation A348
First Commerce Bancshares, Inc. A1509
First Commonwealth, Inc. (dental care) P214, P215
First Consumer National Bank A1314
First DataBank (publication) P229
First Data Corporation A342, A**596**-A**597**, E181
First Defiance Financial Corporation E204
First Deposit Corporation A1170
First Federal Bank of Chattanooga A166
First Federal Bank of the Midwest E204
First Federal Savings and Loan E204
First Financial Management A596
First Franklin Financial Corporation A1000
FIRST (Future in Reservation Systems Technology) P296
First Gibraltar (savings and loan) A902, P304
First Gray Line A212
First Heights savings and loan A1178
First Home Mortgage E154
First Insurance and Investments E204
First Insurance Company of Hawaii, Ltd. A379
First Interstate P110
First Issue boutiques A880, A881
First Mutual Savings Association of Florida A166
The First National Bank of Atlanta A1486
First National Bank of Birmingham A166
First National Bank of Boston A448
First National Bank of Chicago P312, P518
The First National Bank of Cincinnati A1444
First National Bank of Joliet (Illinois) W112
First National Bank of Milwaukee A790, A1444
First National Bank of North East E294
First National Bank of Northern New York E250
First National Bank of Orlando A1346
First National Bank of Pittsburgh A1146
First National Bank of Salem A1486
First National Bank of Wyoming A790
First National Bank (Texas) A714, P232
First National City Corporation A356
First National Insurance Company of America A1230, A1231

First Nationwide (savings and loan) A902, P304
First Niagara Financial Group, Inc. E205
First of America Bank A1000
First Pacific Advisors A346
First Permian E260
First Person women's clothes A853
First Prosperity Bank E271
First Quadrant E149
First Quench Retailing W84, W638
First Reisebuero Management GmbH & Co. KG W460, W461
First Republicbank A226
First Reserve (investments) A676
First SAFECO National Life Insurance Company of New York A1230, A1231
First S&L Shares A658
First Savings & Loan Association of South Holland (IL) E239
First Southeast Banking Corporation A1444
First State Service Corporation A1309
First Sterling Banks. *See* Main Street Banks, Inc.
First System Services, Inc. A1445
First Title Corporation A591
First Travel Corporation P106
First Trust and Deposit A822
First Union Capital Partners A694, A1346, A1508
First Union Center (Philadelphia sports center) A190
First Union Corporation A228, A318, A936, A954, A1170. *See also* Wachovia Corporation
First Unum Life Insurance Company of America A1441
First USA Bank, N.A. A230, A936
First USA Visa cards P348
First Wachovia (bank) A1486
First Washington Bancorp. *See* Banner Corporation
First Wisconsin National Bank of Milwaukee A1444
FirstAir, Inc. A420, A421
Firstar Corporation. *See* U.S. Bancorp
FirstCaribbean International Bank W114
FirstEnergy Corporation A**598**-A**599**
FirstEnergy Trading Corporation A668
FirstGroup (transportation) A1222
FirstMark Communications Europe SA A837, P283
Firtzwerder (ammonia) P748
FIS, Inc. A789
Fischer, A. Charles A505
Fischer, August A. W106, W107
Fischer beer W255
Fischer, Brian J. W281
Fischer, Bruce G. A1345
Fischer, Cathryn M. A665
Fischer, Jurgen W259

Fischer, Robert A., Jr. P39
Fischer, Thomas W201
Fish, W. James A665
Fishbowl restaurants P106, P107
Fishburn, Richard J. A435
Fisher, Aiken A600
Fisher, Andrew S. A443, P147
Fisher, Benjamin A600
Fisher, Charles E. A857
Fisher, Chester A600
Fisher College of Business P693
Fisher Controls International A546
Fisher Development, Inc. P608
Fisher, Donald (Carlson Wagonlit) A328, P108
Fisher, Donald G. (The Gap) A634, A635, P608
Fisher, Doris A634
Fisher (electronics) W514
Fisher, Eric A1467
Fisher, George M. C. A524
Fisher, Herman P699
Fisher, James A600
Fisher, Jerome A804
Fisher, John W. A224, A225
Fisher, Joseph V. A1094, A1095
Fisher, Lawrence N. A611
Fisher, Martyn A475, P155, W197
Fisher, Max M. A1305
Fisher, Oscar A64, P30
Fisher Pierce (process/environmental controls) A463
Fisher, Randall D. A73
Fisher, R. Bruce A153
Fisher Research Laboratory E44, E182
Fisher, Robert S. (Fisher Development) P608
Fisher, Robert (The Gap) A634
Fisher, Ronald D. W549
Fisher Scientific International Inc. A156, A320, A**600**-A**601**, A1070
Fisher, Stephen F. (Entercom Communications) E199
Fisher, Steven P. (Science Applications) P439
Fisher, Thomas E. (Unocal) A1439
Fisher, Thomas L. (Nicor) A1031
Fisher-Price toys A926, A927, A1180, P699
Fishman, Deena S. A1201
Fishman, Jay S. A371
Fishman, Jerald G. A170, A171
Fishman, William A190
Fisk, Gale W. P693
Fisk, Hayward D. A405
Fisons plc (laboratory products) A600
Fister, Michael J. A761
FIT car W265
FITB (IT services) W100
Fitch, Ezra A62
Fitch, Maryla R. A421
Fites, Donald (Caterpillar) A332

Fites, Donald V. (Salvation Army USA) P427
Fit'n Easy chicken P393
Fitschen, Jürgen W201
Fitting, Robert C. E274
Fitts, John R. P171
Fitzgerald, Barbara A. A1117
Fitzgerald dairy product A467
Fitzgerald, James A., Jr. A695
Fitzgerald, J. Darryl A1533
Fitzgerald, Joseph M. A963
Fitzgerald, Lisa A. A853
FitzGerald, Niall W. A. W618, W619
Fitzgerald, Thomas P. A681
Fitzmaurice, Robert A. A1459
Fitzpatrick, Barclay A71
Fitzpatrick, Brian P309
FitzPatrick, David J. A1433
Fitzpatrick, J. Michael A1213
Fitzpatrick, Kenneth F. A403
Fitzpatrick, Maria Z. A1081
Fitzpatrick, Mark S. A89
FitzPatrick, Patrick C. P599
Fitzpatrick, Terri A1075
Fitzpatrick, Thomas J. (USA Education) A1449
Fitzpatrick, Thomas P. (Engelhard) A551
FitzSimmons, Dennis J. A1403
Fitzsimmons, Ellen M. A455
Fitzsimmons, Joseph J. A1495
Fitzsimmons, Peter D. P406, P407, P709
Five Alive beverage A385
Five Star tobacco W283
Fix, Warren D. E169
Fix-a-Flat A1096, A1097
Fizzz soft drink A1105
Fjeldgaard, Kjeld W95
Fjord Seafood A426, P140
Flach, H. B. "Bud" P465, P738
Flack, Gene A744, P242
Flack, Stuart A949, P327
FLAG Telecom Holdings Limited A1472
Flagship Bank and Trust E178
Flagship tobacco W282, W283
Flagstar Companies A86
Flaherty, Gerald S. A333
Flaherty, Joseph A335
Flaim, Theresa A. A1029
Flair motor homes A604, A605
Flamingo Casino-Kansas City A720
Flamingo Hilton casino A1086, A1087
Flanagan, Glenda A1523
Flanagan, Larry A925, P323
Flanders, Howard L. E151
Flanders, Scott P579
Flandre Air W68
Flank Drive wrench A1294
Flash Web design tool E86, E235
FlashVision memory E117
Flatbush Co-op (New York City) P291
Flaten, Alfred A994

Flathead Electric Cooperative A1082
Flatiron building (New York City) P230
Flaum, Russell M. A749
Flavia drinks A915, P315
Flaws, James B. A435
Fleet Aerospace. See Magellan Aerospace
Fleet Call A1026
Fleet Financial Group A602, A680, A734
Fleet Holdings (newspapers) W620
Fleet Meehan Specialist A602
Fleet Mortgage A1500
FleetBoston Financial Corporation A228, **A602-A603**, A734, A836, A875, A1146, A1332, A1500, E207, P294
FleetCenter A280
Fleetguard filtration units A456
FleetMaster P710
Fleet/Norstar A602
Fleetwood Enterprises, Inc. **A604-A605**
Flegel, S. Leslie E290
Fleig, Günther W189
Fleischhacker, James E. A983
Fleischmann's gin A423
Fleischmann's spread A409
Fleishman-Hillard Inc. (public relations) A1062
Fleming Companies, Inc. **A606-A607**, A744, A830, A844, P62, P242, P243, P524, P525, P546, P612, P633, P638
Fleming, Kiley A497
Fleming, Ned A606
Fleming, O. A. A606
Fleming, Paul E265
Fleming, Richard H. A1457
Fleming, Timothy E. A87
Fleming's Sav-U-Foods A1348
Fleming-Wilson Mercantile A606, A744, P242
Flessner, Paul A973
Fleszczynski, Julián W439
Fletcher Challenge Energy A184
Fletcher, Denise K. A925, P323, P668
Fletcher, John E. W172, W173
Fletcher Research E63
Fletcher Stan A. A289
Fleur de Champagne W85
Flex cosmetics A1201
Flexalloy A1380
Flexeril drug A956
Flexible Products Company A504
Flexi-Van Leasing A176, A494
Flexivent windows P50
Flextech plc A873, W144, W145
Flextronics International Ltd. A990, A1240, A1298, E258, W220
Flextronics Photonics P522
Flick, Warren W173
Flicker, Walter E112
Flickinger, Gary D. A467

Flight Dynamics A1210
FlightSafety International, Inc. A252, A253
Flik Flak watch W562, W563
FLIK (food services) W175
Flint, Douglas J. W269
Flint, Eaton A236
Flint, H. Howard, II P608
Flint Ink Corporation P608
Fliss, Tim P435, P723
FLIX cable network A1476
Flocco, Thomas J. A619
Flohr, Thomas A393
Flom, Joseph H. A1288, P446, P447
Flood Data Services A594
Flood, David T. A749
Flood, Frances M. E208
Flood, Gail M. E143
Flood, Tom W645
Flopetrol A1252
Flora, Steven K. E144
Floral City Furniture A854
Florence, Russell V. E199
Flores, Armando B. A1139
Flores, Don A401
Flores, James C. A1144, A1145
Flores, Virginia P746
Florian, Monica P253
Florida Department of Citrus P40
Florida Gas Transmission A552
Florida Insurance Commission A1008, P364
The Florida Marlins (baseball team) P307
Florida Medicaid HMO A738
Florida Panthers Hockey Club P361
Florida Power Corporation A518, A1167
Florida Power & Light A624
Florida Progress Corporation A362, A1166
FLORIDA TODAY (Brevard County) A632, A633
Florimex Worldwide (flower distributor) A492
Florio, Steven T. A81, P33
Florist Distributing P636
Florists' Transworld Delivery. See FTD
FlorJancic, Ronald J. A417
Florman, Carole P145
Florsheim, Jon W147
Florsheim shoes A630
Flo-Sun, Inc. W568
Flowers, Bill A608
Flowers, David J. A. A873
Flowers Ice Cream Company A608
Flowers Industries, Inc. **A608-A609**, A814
Flowers, Joseph A608
Flowers, Langdon A608
Flowers, William A608
Flowserve Corporation A754
Floyd, Chuck A741, P241
Floyd, Israel J. A705
Floyd, Virginia Davis P195
Floyd, William R. A259

Fluharty, Bill A803
Fluid Power Division A278
Fluid Power Systems A1088
Fluke Corporation
  (process/environmental
  controls) A462, A463
Flunker, Bruce G. A1231
Fluno Center for Executive
  Education P500
Fluor Corporation A**610**-A**611**, P74
Fluor Daniel A514, A515, A610
Fluor Global Services E221
Fluor, John Robert A610
Fluor, John Simon A610
Fluor, J. Robert, II A611
Fluor, Rudolph A610
Fluor Signature Services A610
FluShield vaccine A149
Flushing Co-op (New York) P291
Fly, Emerson H. P760
Fly Fishing catalog P301
Flyer's Island Express fast
  food A288
Flyg, William T. A1085
Flying Colors toys E225
Flying J Inc. P609
Flying Tigers freight carrier A588,
  A1420
Flynn, Cary D. A515
Flynn, Charlene P532
Flynn, Gary L. A59
Flynn, John D. A1517
Flynn, Matthew A. A1161
Flynn, Michael T. A129
Flynn, Patrick (International
  Brotherhood of Teamsters) P247
Flynn, Patrick (McDonald's) A943
Flynn, Patrick (PACCAR
  Inc.) A1079
Flynn, Roger W145
Flynn, Timothy P. A841, P287,
  P654, W325
Flynn-White, Dresdene A811, P267,
  P649
FMC Corporation A**612**-A**613**,
  A1294
FMC Technologies, Inc. A612
FMR Corporation A124, A284,
  A348, A**614**-A**615**, A1052, A1468,
  P**190**-P**191**, P504, P609, P764
FN Herstal P132
Fnac (books, music,
  electronics) W446, W447
F. N. Burt W378
FNF Capital, Inc. A590, A591
Foam-Recycling P151
Foamy shaving cream A656, A657
Foate, Dean A. E104
Focon Electronic Systems AS P310
FOCUS fiber-optic network
  systems A1362, A1363
FOCUS package tracking
  system A102
Foden Trucks A1078, A1079
Foerderer, Norma A1409, P483,
  P749
Fogarty, Andrew B. A455

Fogle, Jared P160
Fohrer, Alan J. A533
Fohrman, Monica M. A1219
Foilmark A748
Fok, Canning K. N. W273
Fok, Philip A1299
Folan, McDara P., III A1205
Foldesi, Robert S. P757
Foldie-Morrison, Duncan E. A227
Foley catheter A444
Foley, D. H. P439
Foley, Donald E. A781
Foley, John W637
Foley, Rita V. A1517
Foley, William P., II (Fidelity
  National Financial) A590, A591
Foley, William (Provena
  Health) P706
Foley's department stores A586,
  A932
Folgers Coffee A1164, A1165
Folha Group (printing) P404
Folio (catalogs) A1238
Folio media A1161
Folio (software) A950
Folland Aircraft W110
Follett, Chuck P193
Follett Corporation A232, P68,
  P**192**-P**193**, P609
Follett, C. W. A232, P192
Follett, Dwight P192
Follett, Garth P192
Follett, Robert P192
Follett, Ross P193
Follis, Russ P637
Follit, Evelyn A1189
Follo, James A919
Folmer, Pieter L. W501
Folta, Carl D. A1477
Foltz, William P703
Folz, Dennis C. A1283
Folz, Jean-Martin W442, W443
Corporacion de Fomento de la
  Produccion W576
Foncillas Casáus, Santiago W513
The Fonda Group P727
Fonovisa (records) W583
Fontaine, Jean-Louis W133
Fontaine Modification
  Company P313
Fontana Steel A396
Fontanella, Adrienne A927
Fontanes, A. Alexander A875, P295
Foo, Cedric W541
Food 4 Less supermarkets A606,
  A607, A844, A845, P62, P63, P462,
  P524, P547
Food Barn Stores P62
Food Basics grocery stores A670,
  A671
Food Chief convenience
  stores A1085
Food City supermarkets P550, P654
Food Club brands P198, P478,
  P479, P746
Food Courts P554
Food Dimensions W546

Food Emporium grocery
  stores A670, A671
Food Folks stores A994
Food for Less stores W644, W645
Food Giant stores A1348, W194
Food Lion stores E290, W194,
  W195
Food Machinery Corporation A612
Food Manufacturers A914, P314
Food Maxx stores P722
Food Network cable network A568,
  A919
Food Records recording label W213
Food Service Company (food
  distribution) A1350
Food Services of America P727
Food Service Systems P236
Food Source discount
  warehouse P710
Food Town stores W194
Foodarama Supermarkets,
  Inc. A1491, P515
Foodbrands America, Inc. A742,
  A743
Food.com, Inc. A942, A943
FoodCraft (food equipment) P392
Foodland Associated Ltd. P243
Foodland stores A1349
Foodmaker A784
FoodsCo supermarkets A845
Foodservice Network A1350
Foodtown P103
Foos, Michael R. E139
Foosaner, Robert S. A1027
Foot Locker, Inc. A1470, W312
Foote, Cone & Belding
  Communications W466
Foote, Cone & Belding
  Worldwide A772, A773
Foote Mineral A1024
Foote, W. A. A376
Foote, William C. A1457
FootJoy golf shoes A618
Footquarters stores A1470
Footstar, Inc. (shoe stores) A458
Footsteps (advertising) A1063
Footwear Acquisition, Inc. P142,
  P583
For Dummies selfhelp books P248,
  P641
For Every Dream lottery
  game P687
Foran, Greg W645
Forbes (magazine) A726, A740,
  E305, P80, P130, P218, P308,
  P625
Forbes, Scott E. A339
Forbes, Walter A338
Forbuoys W240
Force Computers A1298
*Forced Into Glory: Abraham
  Lincoln's White Dream*
  (book) P258, P259
Forcenergy E62, E205
Ford Aerospace A616, A888
Ford, Beth A1255
Ford, Brendan A. A321

Ford, David W547
Ford, Edsel A394, A616, P194
The Ford Foundation P**194**-P**195**, P518, P610
Ford, Gerald (former US President) P758
Ford, Gerald J. (MacAndrews & Forbes) A902, P304
Ford, Harrison P450
Ford, Henry (Ford Motor) A616, P194, P630, W138
Ford, Henry, II (Ford Foundation) P194
Ford, Joe T. A128, A129
Ford, John B. (Stanford University) P457
Ford, John (Discovery Communications) P159
Ford, John (PPG Industries) A1152
Ford, Judy P37, P532
Ford, Larry H. (Brinker International) A289
Ford, Larry J. (ADC Telecommunications) A71
Ford, Monte E. A165
Ford Motor Company A104, A170, A278, A300, A388, A456, A460, A476, A550, A572, A584, A**616**-A**617**, A650, A660, A664, A710, A802, A856, A902, A920, A982, A1010, A1052, A1066, A1394, A1412, A1432, A1480, E127, E175, E222, E242, P86, P152, P194, P212, P256, P304, P508, P535, P557, P563, P590, P606, P633, P644, P647, P666, P673, P679, P695, P713, P721, P731, P733, P767, W120, W138, W188, W226, W264, W274, W318, W362, W538, W614, W630, W632, W646, W652
Ford Motor Credit A442, A604, A616, P146
Ford of Orange (California) P589
Ford, Scott T. A129
Ford, Stephen J. A327
Ford, Timothy A1393
Ford, Tom W250, W251
Ford, W. Doug W137
Ford, William C., Jr. A616, A617
Forde, Theresa H. A923, P321
Fordyce, Michael P117, P569
FORE Systems (broadband switching) W354
Forefront Records recording label W213
Foregeard, Noël W71
Forehand, Steve R. A1221
Forehand, Wayne A1167
Foreman, George E116
Foreman, Jerry E. A1271
Foreman, Louise P686
Foreman, Robert B. A1321
Foreman, Spencer P678
Foremost Dairies A946
Foremost Farms USA, Cooperative P58, P610
Foremost Group (insurance) W652
Foremost-McKesson A946

Forese, James J. A746, A747
Forest Hills Co-op (New York) P291
Forest Oil Corporation A1065, E**62**, E205
Forest Park Brewery P428
Forestieri, Teri P591
Foret, Mickey P. A1047
Forethought Financial Services, Inc. A718
Forex (drilling rigs) A1252
Le Groupe Forex (oriented strand board) A890
Forgan, Jeffrey A1275, E120, E287
Forged Steel Products A1294
Forget Me Not (cards) A146
Forlenza, Vincent A. A245
Forman, John A296
Forman, Leonard P. A1021
Formby, Scott P255
Formica Corporation A770
Formosa Asahi Spandex Company, Ltd. W228, W229
Formosa Daikin Advanced Chemicals Company, Ltd. W229
Formosa Komatsu Silicon Corporation W228, W229
Formosa Plastics Corporation W**228**-W**229**
Formpac packaging A1262
Formula 409 cleaning product A374, A375
Formule 1 hotels W58, W59, W552
Fornell, Sten W221
Forrest, Joseph A1402
Forrester Research, Inc. E**63**, E205
Forrester, W. Thomas A1169
Forsee, Gary D. A249
Forsgren, John H. A1041
Forsman, Terry K. E275
Forster, Hans-Erich W595
Forster, H. Walter P480
Forstmann Little & Company (investments) A856, A1278, E143, E320
Forsum, Mike A1227
Forsyth, David W469
Forsythe, Daryl R. E250
Forsythe, John G. A531
Fort Dearborn Life Insurance P227
Fort Garry Brewery W376
Fort James Corporation A654, P530
Fort Mill Manufacturing Company A1316, P452
The (Fort Wayne, IN) *News Sentinel* A833
Fort Wayne National Corp. of Indiana A1000
Fort Worth (Texas) *Star-Telegram* A60, A832, A833
Fortado, Michael G. A1407
Forte, Deborah A. A1255
Forte, Gabriella P100
Forte Hotels W174, W248
Forte, Kate P219
Forté, Mary L. A1553
Forte, Stephen A. A1421
Fortgang, Matthew P662

Fortier, Kimberly A. W263
Fortier, L. Yves W271
Fortin, Raymond D. A1347
Fortino's Supermarkets W245
Fortis B W559
Fortis Financial A688
Fortner, Tom P512
Fortos (company) W546
Fortum Corporation W242
FORTUNE 500 A270, A674, A880, P209, P430
Fortune Brands, Inc. A**618**-A**619**, A754, W240
Fortune Cookie lottery game P373
FORTUNE Group W238
FORTUNE (magazine) A1176, P89, P178, P256, P402, P410, P480, P746, W332
Forum Group (retirement communities) A732, A912
Forums Japan (trade shows) W548
Forward, Frank D. A263
Fosamax drug A956, A957
Foschi, Pier Luigi A331
Foshee, Douglas L. A677
Foss, Eric J. A1103
Foss, Michael E. E127, E300
Fosseys discount stores W172
Fossier, Marc W233
Fossil (watches) W528
Fossum, Lilian W211
Foster, A. Mickelson A975
Foster, Constance P145
Foster, Ernest A620
Foster Farms P610
Foster, Geraldin U. A1251
Foster, Jim P257, P644
Foster, Joe B. (Baker Hughes) A222
Foster, Johnnie M. (Solutia) A1301
Foster, Jonathan F. (Bear Sterns) A239
Foster, Joseph (Reebok) A1194
Foster, Kent B. A758, A759
Foster, LaDoris P259, P646
Foster, Max P610
Foster, Norman P. A93
Foster, Patrick A. A699
Foster, Pell A620
Foster, Richard M. P521
Foster, Robert G. A533
Foster, Ron A1051
Foster, R. R. W230
Foster, Verda P610
Foster, Vince A258
Foster, Ward G. A328, P108
Foster Wheeler Ltd. A**620**-A**621**, P280
Foster, W. Kim A613
Foster, W. M. W230
Foster's Group Limited A78, P474, W128, W**230**-W**231**, W282, W316, W376
Fote, Charles T. A597
Foti, Frances P637
Foti, Richard J. A711
Foti, Salvatore C. P115
Foti, Samuel J. A987

Fotiades, George L. A321
FotoShow (photo capture) A779
Fotsch, Richard J. A287
Foundation Community Health Plan A696
Foundation Health Benefit Life Insurance A696
Foundation Health Systems A84, A696, A1506, E185
Foundation School Fund P472, P744
Foundry (magazine) E102
Foundry Management & Technology (magazine) E263
Foundry Networks, Inc. E206, E310
Fountain Hills (residential development) A931
FountainGlen Properties E259
Fountainhead A770
Four Pillars A210
Four Points Sheraton hotels A1328, A1329
Four Roses liquor W315
Four Seasons Hotel Inc. A732, A906, P106, P486, P737, P751
Four Seasons (promotional products) P170, P171
Four11 (Internet directory specialist) A1546
Fournier, Laura L. A407
Fournier, Marcel W164
Fourrier, Josette W209
Fourtou, Jean-René W102, W103
Fowler, David S. A357
Fowler, James D., Jr. (ITT Industries) A781
Fowler, Jim (naturalist) P348
Fowler, John C. P405, P708
Fowler, Robert (IMC Global) A752
Fowler, Robert R. (Main Street Banks) E236
Fowler, Ted P642
Fowler, William A. A475, P155, P590, W197
Fox & Company P206
Fox Asset management E53
Fox, Bernard A1040
Fox, Brendan P. A541
Fox, Christopher A. (Regis) A1197
Fox, Christopher W. (Agway) P39
Fox, Douglas B. A399
Fox, Edward A. A1449
Fox Entertainment Group, Inc. A334, A**622**-A**623**, A1476, P306, W390, W391
Fox Family Worldwide A60, A622, A623, A1496
Fox, James A967
Fox, Jeffrey H. A129
Fox, John M. (MarkWest Hydrocarbon) E237
Fox, John W., Jr. (Norfolk Southern) A1039
Fox, Louis P62
Fox, Martin A. A1095
Fox, Michael J. P166
Fox, Mitchell A81, P33
Fox Navigation P318, P319

Fox Network P358, P681, P683
Fox Paine & Company E318
Fox Photo stores A524
Fox Plaza (Los Angeles) P254
Fox, Sam P625
Fox Sports Networks A312, A313, A568, A622
Fox Valley Press W262
Fox, Vicente W440
Fox, Wayne C. W157
Fox, William A622
Foxboro Worldwide W290
Fox/Liberty Networks A312, A390, A622, A872, A1450, W146
FoxMeyer Drug (drug distributor) A946, A1006
Fox-Moertl, Kim W185
Foxmoor clothing store A458
Fox's Jewelers A845
FOXTEL (pay TV) W145, W586
Foxwood Store (clothing) A458
Foxwoods Resort Casino P318, P319, P667
Foxworthy, James C. A1365
Foxworthy, Randolph L. A1287
Foy, John T. A631
Foyo, George W. A737
FPL Group, Inc. A554, A**624**-A**625**, P270
Fracalossi, Kim A1479
Fracht AG A420
Fradin, Russell P. A205
Frahm, George P463
Fraikin (vehicle leasing) W226
Frakes, William J. P299, P659
Fraley, Richard E. A311
Fraley, Robert T. A985
Framatome A982, W76, W536
Frame, Mark P425
Frame Technology (software) A76
FrameMaker software A76, A77
Compagnie Française de l'Afrique Occidentale (electrical equipment) W446
Société Francaise de Radiotelephonie W624
Compagnie Française des Pétroles W612
Compagnie Francaise Thomson-Houston W554
France, Bill P681
France, James C. E75
France Telecom A1244, A1318, E296, W150, W174, W204, W205, W214, W**232**-W**233**, W352, W554, W580, W628
France, William C. "Big Bill" E75, E222
Francis, David R. E88
Francis, Gary D. A1337
Francis, George F., III P87, P557
Francis, James L. P739
Francis, J. Stuart A861
Francis, Kathy P307
Francis, Michael R. A1353
Francis, Peter T. P645
Francis, Philip L. A1116, A1117

Franciscan Health Foundation P115
Franciscan Health System of Aston, PA P116, P569
Franciscan Oakville Estate wines A422
Franciscan Sisters Health Care P706
Franciscan Sisters of Allegany P114
Franciscan Sisters of Little Falls (MN) P117
Franciscan Sisters of Mary P734
The Franciscan Sisters of the Poor P570
Franciscan Sisters of the Sacred Heart P119
Franciscan Sisters of St. Joseph P114
Francisco, David H. A1025
Francisco Partners A82
Francis-Vogelsang, Charee A489
Franco, Francisco W482
Franco-American canned pasta A316
François, Emile W507
François-Poncet, Michel W131
Francou, Nicholas A329, P109
Francy, Patricia P135
Franczek, Edward J. A1539
Frandsen, Lau A921
Frangelico liqueur W85
Franich, Martin P666
Franich, Steven "Rocky" P666
Frank A. Blesso, Inc. P208
Frank, Best & Ingram (advertising) P639
Frank, Charles W., Jr. A1515
Frank Consolidated Enterprises P611
Frank, David A. A195
Frank, Greg S. A375
Frank, Howard S. A331
Frank, Jim P611
Frank, J. Louis A1461
Frank, Michael (SUPERVALU) A1349
Frank, Mike (Kmart) A831
Frank Russell Company (brokerage) A1048, A1049, P190, P376, P377, P690
Frank Schaffer Publications A944
Frank, Stephen E. A533
Frank, William P. P447
Frank, Zollie P611
Franke, William A. A138
Frankel & Company W466
Frankel, Michael S. P455
Frankenbach, James T. P719
Frankenberg, Robert A1050
Frankenfield, Michael D. E61
Franklin Automobile A1096
Franklin, Benjamin A1428, P176, P490, P759
Franklin Federal Bancorp P130
Franklin, H. Allen A1307
Franklin, Marc S. P385
Franklin, Marvin A., III A461

The Franklin Mint P416, P716
Franklin Mutual Advisors A1360
Franklin Plastics
  (packaging) A1338
Franklin Rayon Dyeing
  Company A1380
Franklin, Robert M. (Placer
  Dome) W453
Franklin, Robert N. (Pacificare
  Health Systems) A1081
Franklin, Samuel O., III A1347
Franklin Square Agency
  (subscription service) P170
Franklin Storage E228
Franklins Holdings (retailer) W644
Franks, G. William A1239
Franks, Joanne P319, P667
Franks, Mark P151, P588
Franks, Martin A335
Franks, Thomas L. A1323
Franprix supermarkets W166,
  W167
Frantek Computer Products A758
Frantz, Francis X. A129
Frantz, Meg A401
Franz, David G., Jr. E119, E286
Franz, Debbie E278
Franz Haniel & Cie A606, W364
Franz, Mark P499
Franzen, Gustav E119
Franzi, Joseph P511, P767
Frappuccino drink A1326, P148
Frasch, Ronald L. A1015
Fraser, Barbara A143
Fraser, Carlyle A652
Fraser & Chalmers A96
Fraser-Gonzales, Cynthia A303
Frasier (TV show) A999, A1476
Frater, Hugh R. E157
Fraternal Assurance Society of
  America A878
FraudFinder A480
Fraunhofer Institute for Integrated
  Circuits E117
Frautschi, Roland L. E209
Frazee, Roger P413
Frazier, John R. A1177
Frazier, Kenneth C. A957
Frazier, Rick P345
Frazzitta, Bartholomew J. A489
FRD Acquisition Company A86
Fred Arbogast (fishing lures) P170
Fred B. DeBra Company, Inc. A545
Fred Krug Brewery P428
Fred Meyer Inc. A844, A845, P62,
  P462, P478, P524
Fred W. Albrecht Grocery
  Company P479
Freddie Mac A252, A580,
  A**626**-A**627**, A862, A1448, E152,
  E203, P150
Frederic Piguet (watch
  components) W562
Frederick, Douglas L. A539
Frederick, Rick P349, P570, P680
Frederickson, Philip L. A413
Fredholm, Ludwig W54

Fredrick, Francie A. P499
Fredricks, Scott P632
Fredriksen, Ole J. E73
Fred's Frozen Foods A768
Free Academy P128
Free, Brant W., Jr. A357
Freebeeb.net W522
Freeburg, F. L. P488
Freece, Robert A. A1483
Freedent gum A1526, A1527
Freedline, Robert A335
The Freedman Companies (meat
  supplier) A1350
Freedman, Tom P657
Freedom Capital
  Management E132, E306
Freedom Chemical A662
Freedom Communications,
  Inc. P611
Freedom Plan A1076
Freedom Securities. *See* Tucker
  Anthony Sutro
Freedom to Farm Act (1998) P36
Freedom-Valvoline A200
Freehold Raceway (New
  Jersey) E262
Freel, Charles W. A117
Freeland, Kevin P. A255
Freeland, Ronald L. P387
Freeman, Bruce E. A309
The Freeman Companies P611
Freeman Cosmetic A486
Freeman, David E153
Freeman, Donald S., Jr. P611
Freeman, D. S. "Buck" P611
Freeman, Graham K. A77
Freeman, James I. A491
Freeman, J. D. A373
Freeman, John P. E124, E292
Freeman, Patrick J. W67
Freeman, Phil P728
Freeman, Pliny A1016, P370
Freeman, Randall J. P560
Freeman, Russell A1113
Freeman Spogli & Company A876,
  A1084, P120, P338, P543, P676
Freeman Welwood &
  Company W112, W113
Freeman, William T. E318
Freemans (catalog business) W426
Freemantle, Richard A369
P.T. Freeport Indonesia
  Company A628, A629
Freeport Minerals A612
Freeport Oil A628
Freeport Power A1306
Freeport Studio catalog P300, P301
Freeport-McMoRan Copper & Gold,
  Inc. A**628**-A**629**, A752, A1024,
  W92, W488
Freer, Charles P450
Freer Gallery of Art P450, P451
Frees, Vincent J. A1179
Freeserve plc (Internet service
  provider) W114
Freesmeier, Eric A351
Freestyle shoes A1194

Frefcura, Thomas P638
Freia Marabou (chocolate) W410
Freidenberg, Charles C. A261
Freidman, Ira E130
Freidus, Scott D. A643
Freightliner Corporation A616,
  A1010, A1078, P152, P590
Freightliners A380, A420, W188
Freightways Manufacturing A380,
  A420
Freilich, Joan S. A419
Freimark, Jeffrey P. A1059
Freimuth, Steven P. A1501
Fremont Cooperative Creamery
  Association P58
French, Douglas D. P56, P57, P544
French Finance Ministry W480
French Fragrances W618
French, Richard L. A471
French, Theodore R. A1380
French's mustard W476
Frenchwood brand doors P541
Frenchy Frys (vending
  machines) P196
Frenzel, Michael W460, W461
Freon A1551
Frequency Electronics, Inc. E206
Frère, Baron Albert W559
Freriks, Don P694
Fresca soft drink A383
Frescala Foods E247
Freschetta pizza P436, P437, P724
Fresco, Paolo W226, W227
Frese, Calvin P121
Fresh Advantage, Inc. A1109
Fresh Brands, Inc.
  (supermarkets) P479
Fresh Express (produce
  processor) A1109
Fresh Favorites salads P722
Fresh Fields Markets P110
Fresh Fields stores A1522
Fresh Start Bakeries A316
Fresh Step cat litter A374
FreshCare A374, A375
FreshCut canned foods A471
FreshPoint Holdings A1350
Fresno State College P98
Fretz, Deborah M. A1345, P738
Freudenberg, Mark A213
Freudmann, Axel I. A151
Frevert, Mark A. A553
Frey, James A., II A1081
Frey, Robert A707
Freyman, Bruce A163
Freyman, Thomas C. A59
Fribourg, Jules A426, P140
Fribourg, Michel A426, P140
Fribourg, Paul J. A426, A427, P140,
  P141, P583
Fribourg, Rene A426, P140
Fribourg, Simon A426, P140
Frick, David (Credit Suisse
  Group) W185
Frick, David R. (Anthem
  Insurance) A179
Fricke, Howard R. P725

Fricklas, Michael D. A1477
Friday Canning A354
Friday, Michael D. P691
Fridegar Grocery Company P488
Fridge Stackables A1415
Fridgesmart containers A1415
Fried, Betty P431
Fried. Krupp AG Hoesch-Krupp W594
Fried, Samuel P. A877
Fried, Wilhelm A622
Friedberg, Barry S. A961
Friedery, John R. A225
The Friedkin Companies P624
Friedkin, Thomas P624
Friedlander, D. Gilbert A539
Friedman, Gary A176
Friedman, Howard W259
Friedman, Jack E225
Friedman, J. Kent A931
Friedman, Louis A239
Friedman, Milton P496, P756
Friedman, Neil A927
Friedman, William S. E298
Friedrich, Douglas A. A735
Friedson, Arthur S. A337
Friel, Robert F. A1111
Friendly Hills Healthcare Network, Inc. A323
Friendly, Ian R. A649
Friendly Ice Cream Corporation A708
Friends (TV show) A999
Friendship pipeline W456
Friendswood Development (builders) A862
Fries, George A81, P33
Fries, William A. A625
Frigerio, Liliana A329, P109
Frigidaire appliances A650, W210
Friner, Arlene R. P363, P684
Frisch, Ronald W. P759
Friskies cat products W388
Frissora, Mark P. A1368, A1369
Frist, Thomas F A694
Frist, Thomas F., Jr. A694, A695
Fristoe, David L. A1227
Frito-Lay, Inc. A528, A538, A814, A1062, A1106, A1404, P90, P705
Fritos snacks A1106, A1107
Fritsch, S. Frank E286
Fritschle, Stephen K. A787
Fritz, Bob A625
Fritz Companies, Inc. A1426
Fritz, John F. A1081
Fritze, Steven L. A531
Fritzky, Edward V. E71, E218
Frock Salon store W644
Froehlich, John M. E279
Froeschle, Thomas P93
Froges. *See* Société Electromélurgique Française
Frogger arcade game A692
Fröhlich, Fritz W. W73
Froimowitz, Ray P737
Frolic pet food A915, P315

From Martha's Kitchen (TV show) A918, A919
Froman, John W. A367
Fromberg, Barry A. A1339
Fromm, Ronald A. A295
Frommer, Arthur A1502
Frommer's travel books P248
Fromstein, Mitchell A910
Frontier Airlines, Inc. A428, E64, E206
Frontier cigarettes W305
Frontier Communications A1186, P434
Frontier Electronics A1140
Frontier truck W402, W403
FrontierVision (cable TV) A72
Froot Loops cereal A816, A817
Frost Hanna Capital Group. *See* Ladenburg Thalmann Financial Services Inc.
Frost Lumber Industries A1060
Frost, Philip E185
Frosted Flakes cereal A816
Frosted Mini-Wheats cereal A817
Frost-Pack Distributing (food wholesalers) A1350
FRS Capital Company E280
Fruetel, Gordon W. A843
Fruit Naturals canned foods A471
Fruit of the Loom A1474, A1498, E60, P735, W190
Fruit Pleasures canned foods A471
Fruit Roll-Ups A649
Fruit Stripe gum A708
Fruitopia beverage A384, A385
FruitRageous canned foods A471
Fruit-To-Go snacks A470
Fry, Charles P196
Fry, David P196, P197, P612
Fry, Derek A. A1481, P509
Fry, Dominic W523
Fry, George P88
Fry, John P196, P197, P612
Fry, Randy P196, P612
Fry, William R. P197
Fryda, Gary L. P423
Frydman, Dana A303
Frye boots A1194
Fry's Electronics, Inc. P196-P197, P612
Fry's Food & Drug Stores A844, A845, P196, P612
frys.com P196
FS brand grains P622
FSI International, Inc. E244
FTC. *See* US Federal Trade Commission
FT.com W430
FTD (florists) A1534, E207, P416
FTD.COM Inc. E207
The Fu Foundation School of Engineering & Applied Science P135
FUBU brand clothing E101
Fuchs, James J. A1157
Fuchs, Robert A529
Fudge Shoppe cookies A814, A815

Fuel Resources A824
Fuente, David I. A1056, A1057
Fuhrmann, Werner W151
Fuji America E181
Fuji Bank, Limited W200, W374
Fuji Electric Company, Ltd. E74, W236, W536
Fuji Heavy Industries Ltd. A650, W294, W402, W560
Fuji Iron & Steel W398
Fuji Photo Film Company, Ltd. A524, A1544, W234-W235, W368, W600
Fuji Xerox Company, Ltd. A1544
FUJIFILM Microdevices W235
Fujii, Hiroshi W369
Fujii, Takuya A917
Fujikura P535
Fujioka, Ichisuke W610
Fujisawa, Takeo W264
Fujishiro, Hideshi W305
Fujita, Den A943
Fujita, Sumitaka W297
Fujita, Takashi W409
Fujitsu Limited A82, A870, A894, A928, A1378, A1514, E28, E173, E261, E272, W60, W236-W237, W368, W386, W420, W532, W570, W610
Fujiwara, Buheita W533
Fujiya A708
Fukakusa, Janice R. W475
Fukayama, Gary P. A279
Fukuda, Mitsuaki W297
Fukuhara, Shinzo W534
Fukuhara, Yushin W534
Fukui, Takeo W265
Fukuin Shokai Denki Seisakusho W448
Fukushima, Yoshiji W527
Fulcher, Jay A1099
Fuld, Richard S., Jr. A861
Fulda tires A664
Full Circle brands P479
Full Spectrum Lending A438
Fulleon fire detection systems A431
Fuller, Arthur D. A285
Fuller brand A527
Fuller Company (cement plants) A638
Fuller, Edwin D. A913
Fuller, Jack W. A1403
Fuller Manufacturing (truck transmissions) A526
Fuller, Michael B. A1319
Fuller, Samuel H. (Analog Devices) A171
Fuller, Samuel R. (D.R. Horton) A509
Fuller, S. M. A1307
Fuller, Stephen V. E155
Fullerton, Donald W156
Fullwood, Michael P628
Fulton, J. Michael A395
Fultz, Larry A365
Funai E58
Funck-Brentano, Thierry W331

FuncoLand video games and software A232, A233
Fund Connect software A1332
Fund Navigator A94
Fund Research A944
Fundador brandy W85
Funk & Wagnalls publisher A1160
Funk Manufacturing (powertrain components) A468
Funk, Robert A. P606
Funk Seeds W414
FunScapes family entertainment centers P412
Fuqua, J. B. A1084
Fuqua School of Business P598
Furby toys A692, P486
Furman and Wolfson P230
Furman, Eric P338
Furman Lumber, Inc. A274
Furman Selz (bank) W286
Furnari, Jack A81, P33
Furniture at Work A1056
Furniture Brands International, Inc. A630-A631, P298, P659
Furniture Medic A1273
FurnitureMax A1058
Furon W506
Furr, Randy W. A1241
Furrow Building Materials stores A1090, A1091
Furrow, Sam A1090
Furrow, Sanford A1090
Furrow, Vernon A1090
Furrs Supermarkets, Inc. A606, A844, P478, P479, P612
Furr's/Bishop (cafeteria firm) A1354, P466
Furst, Jack A714, P232
Furst, Thomas P455, P734
Furth, Mark P59, P546
The Furukawa Electric Company, Ltd. A898, E258, W236, W536
Furukawa, Hideaki W199
Furukawa, Koji W371
Furuse, Yoichiro W515
Fusco, Jack E258
Fusion cigarettes W283
Fusion Group P506
Fusion Marketing Group A480
Fusion Systems (semiconductor equipment) A526
Futami, Tsuneo W599
Futcher, Jack P75
Futchko, Andrew R. A257
Futrell, Teresa E118, E284
FUTURA auto care products A1101
Future Brands A618
Future in Reservation Systems Technology (FIRST) P296
Future Metals, Inc. P313
Future Music (magazine) W239
The Future Network plc **W238-W239**
Future Shop Ltd. (consumer electronics) A254
FutureBrand (brand consulting) A773

Fuyo (*keiretsu*) W358
FVC.COM (broadband video) E55
F.W. Woolworth & Company A1470, W312
FX cable channel A528, A623
FX Energy, Inc. A184
FX Internet Trading Web A592
F.X. LaSalle shoe stores A294
Fybogel health and personal care W477
F.Y.I. Incorporated E207
Fysh, Wilmot Hudson W468

G

G. & C. Merriam P176
G. Fox department store A932
G. Heileman Brewery Company, Inc. A714, P232
G. Siegel and Company (dye and chemicals) A1212
Gabelli Asset Management Inc. E**65**, E207
Gabelli, Mario J. A446, E65, E102, E207, E263
Gabelli/Westwood Mighty Mites Fund E65
Gaberino, John A., Jr. A1065
Gaberman, Barry D. P195
Gabitril drug W416
Gable, Clark A962
Gabor, Zsa Zsa A720, P565
Gabriel auto parts A198, P112, P569
Gabriel, David G. A1369
Gabriel, Nicholas M. P195, P610
Gabrielle Studio W348
Gabrielsson, Assar W632
Gaburo, Michael P. A365
Gacek, Jon W. E23, E148
Gaddy, Bob L. A859
Gade, Michael J. A57
Gadel, Greg A. E167
al-Gadhafi, Mu'ammar abu Minyar W340
Gadiesh, Orit P64, P65, P548
Gadomski, Robert E. A101
Gadra, David M. A747
Gaertner, Frederick W. A357
GAF Corporation. *See* G-I Holdings, Inc.
Gage, Barbara Carlson P106, P567
Gage, L. Patrick A149
Gage Marketing Group A750
Gage, Terry L. E172
Gagelmann, Diethard W427
Gagliardi, Gerald A. A1013
Gagnebin, Georges W617
Gagnier, Daniel W75
Gahan, John M. A453
Gaiam.com A1522
Gail Borden, Jr. and Company P90
Gaines, Berland E231
Gaines dog food A1180
Gaines, Laurie A. A289
Gaines, Michael J. A737
The Gainesville (Florida) *Sun* A1021

Gainey, Daniel P262
Gaio, Edward J. A1141
Gaither, John F., Jr. A237
Gala Group Holdings W258, W544
Galamar Industries A188 •
Galan, Victor J. E275
Galang, Faustino F. W511
Galante, Edward G. A577
Galanti, Richard A. A437
Galasso, Michael A. A1279
Galaxy Carpet Mills A980, A981
Galaxy Food Centers P535
Galaxy Quest (movie) P167
Galbani dairy products W192, W193
Galderma (dermatology products) W342
Gale & Wentworth, L.L.C. P613
Gale Research (publishing) W592
Gale, Sam A648
Gale, Stanley C. P613
Gale, William C. A365
Galen Health Care A694, A738
Galena & Chicago Union Railroad A1422
Galeria Kaufhof department stores W364, W365
Galex, Santiago W525
Galigher (oil) A222
Galileo International, Inc. A338
Gall & Gall liquor stores W498, W499
Gallagher, Brian A. P493, P755
Gallagher, Buell P98
Gallagher, Mary E. A1061
Gallagher, Sheila E. A341
Gallagher, Thomas A. (Park Place) A1086, A1087
Gallagher, Thomas C. (Genuine Parts) A653
Gallagher, Tony W477
Gallagher, William T. A453
Gallahan, John A1455
Gallaher, Frank F. A555
Gallaher Group Plc A618, W**240**-W**241**, W282
Gallaher, Tom W240
Gallaire, Hervé J. A1545
Gallant, Peter M. A371
Gallaway, Katherine E246
Gallegos, José A. W635
Galleria shopping centers P156, P157
Galleria stores P592
Galleries of Neiman Marcus A1014, A1015
Galletas Noel biscuits W193
Galli, Giorgio W343
Galli, Joseph (Black & Decker) A264
Galli, Joseph, Jr. (Newell Rubbermaid) A1022, A1023
Gallia dairy products W193
Galliath, Andre P. A503
Galligan, Lynne M. A211
Gallina, Bennett A217
Gallina Pesada S.A. DE C.V. A1132
Gallivan, Sarah M. A263

Gallo, A. C. A1523
Gallo, Dominic P624
Gallo, Ernest A520, A521, P168, P169
Gallo, Gina A520, P168
Gallo, Giuseppe A520, P168
Gallo, Joseph E. A521, P169
Gallo, Joseph, Jr. A520, P168
Gallo, Julio A520, P168
Gallo, Michelo A520, P168
Gallo, Robert J. A521, P169
Gallo wine A520, A521, P168, P169, P600
Gallogly, Jim P574
Galls (uniforms) A190, A191
Gallucci, Vincent A853
Galoob Toys, Inc. A692
Galp (oil and gas) W216
Galt, Martin E., III A1355, P467
Galvin, Christopher B. A990, A991
Galvin, Kerry A. A901
Galvin Manufacturing A990
Galvin, Paul A990
Galvin, Robert A990
Galvin, Walter J. A547
Gamble, Clark A294
Gamble, James A1164
Gamda Trade (food retail) W322
Game & Fish (magazine) A1161
Game Blaster sound card W180
Game Boy W394, W395
Game Financial Corporation (casino services) A1478, A1479
GameCash credit card advances A1478
GameCube W394
GamePro (magazine) P249
Games.com A692
GamesMaster (magazine) W239
Gameson, Ray A1133
GameSpy (online games) P524, P525
GameStop video games A232, A233
GameWorks P166
Gamma International P318
Ganal, Michael W121
Gander, Bernard W339
Gander Mountain stores P633
G&M Stevedoring A325, P105
Gandois, Jean W559
Gandy's Dairy A466, A467
Gang, Suzanne E220
Gangl, Kenneth R. A1079
Gangl, Walter T. A195
Gangwal, Rakesh A1442, A1443
Gani, Marcel E226
Ganley, John (3Com) A55
Ganley, John P. (Burlington Industries) A307
Gannett Company, Inc. A**632**-A**633**, A832, P655
Gannett, Frank A632
Gannon, Michael J. P608
Gannon, Tom P435, P723
Ganser, Christopher D. A445
Ganslev, Stephen M. A441

Gantt, Michael P550
Ganzi, Victor F. A701, P229
Gaon, Benjamin W322
The Gap, Inc. A253, A**634**-A**635**, A790, A1530, P608, W124
GapKids A634, A635
garage.com A566, A1233
Garamycin drug A1250
Garazaglia, Mark A. P421
Garb, Sam A1490, P514
Garbacz, Gerald P68
Garban (financial services) W620
Garber, Peni P351
Garber, Robert E. A219
Garberding, Larry G. A513
Garbo, Greta A962
Garcia Candelas, Enrique W513
Garcia, Carlos M. A439
Garcia, Eduardo R. A1327
Garcia, Elisa D. A501, P163
Garcia, Ivan Ferreira A1157
Garcia, Jaime P79
Garcia, Lillian D. A1415
Garcia, Linda P716
Garcia, Pete C. A429
Garcia, Sergio P250, P251
Gardaya, Virgil P. A559
Garden Silk Mills W496
Garden Way P679
Gardeners Eden (mail order catalog) A1530
GardenSouth stores P732
Gardetto's Bakery A648
Gardiner, Bill A829, P271, P650
Gardiner, John A. W590, W591
Gardiner, Rebecca E184
Gardner, Christopher R. E136
Gardner, Dave (BAE SYSTEMS) W111
Gardner, David P. (Home Properties of New York) E214
Gardner, Frank A569
Gardner, George D. P489
Gardner, H. A. A594
Gardner, James A364
Gardner, Jeffery R. A129
Gardner, John P686
Gardner, Lisa F. A621
Gardner, Max L. P253
Gardner Merchant A1296, W546
Gardner, Paul A1481, P509
Gardner, Ricci A309
Gardner, Rick D. E296
Gardner, Steven S. A1211
Gardner, Thomas D. A1193
Gardner, Tim (Calvin Klein) P101
Gardner, Timothy S. (Credit Suisse Group) W185
Gardner-Denver Industrial Machinery A430
Garduno tequila A423
Gareeb, Nabeel E74
Garefino, Anello C. E68, E214
Garelick Farms A1338
Garey, Daniel T. A1089
Garfield, Arthur R. A599

Garfield, Sidney A810, P266
Garfinkel, Jodie R. P447
Gargano, Charles A. P399
Gargaro, Eugene A., Jr. A921
Gargaro, J. Timothy P153
Gargiulo, Jeffrey D. P464, P465, P738
Garland, Carl P35, P532
Garland, Jerry P63
Garland, Judy A962, P450
Garlick, Philip J. E100
Garling, Andrew A85
Garner, Donald A. A483
Garner, James H. E204
Garner-Klemme-Meservey (cooperative) P36
Garnet Connections (Internet service provider) W152
Garnet Point wines A521, P169
Garnett, Edward F. A161
Garnick, Robert L. A641
Garnier, Jean-Pierre W247
Garofalo, Donald P50, P51, P541
Garon, Jeffrey L. E121, E288
Garrabrant, R. Montgomery A709
Garrard, William A. E85, E234
Garraux, James D. A1463
Garret, Michael W. O. W389
Garrett, Bernard P462
Garrett, Michael D. A1307
Garrettson, Garrett A. E123
Garrido y Compañia A1338
Garrison, J. Daniel A1269
Garrison, Karen M. A1143
Garrison, Wayne A789
Garrison, William A1452, P502
Garrity, John M. A1227
Garrity, Joseph P. E147
Garrity, Thomas J. A85
Garten, Wayne P. P339
Gartley, David W. P385
Gartman, John A. A133
Gartman, Peter L. A877
Gartmore Investment Management A1008, P364
Gartner, David E244
Gartner Group (consulting) A516
Garton, Daniel P. A165
Garves W. Yates & Sons A1484
Garvey, Ellen P143
Garvey, William J. A1287
Garvis, Nate K. A1353
Gary, Elbert A1462
Gary, Ray A835, P281
Gary, Robert W. A127
Gary's Duck Inn A464
Garza, Abraham D. E168
Garza, Ramón Alberto W583
Gas 'N Go stations P225, P654
Gas Energy A824
Gas Light Company of Baltimore A424
Gas Natural W482
Gasink, Richard W. E38
Gaskamp, Roger L. A75
Gaskins, Dean C. A389

Gaspar (software) A1012
Gasparovic, John J. A1207
Gasper, Joseph J. A1009, P365
Gasser, Rupert W389
Gassler, David P333
Gaston de la Grange cognac W109
Gaston, Don A280
Gaston, Karen H. A559
Gaston, Paul E. A280, A281
Gate City Life (insurance) A794
Gately, Diane E105, E268
Gately, James H. A1469, P505
Gates (automotive products) P113
Gates, Jacquelyn A515
Gates Learning Foundation P78
Gates Ltd. (belts, couplings) W604, W605
Gates, Melinda French P78, P79, P555
Gates Rubber Company W605
Gates, Stephen F. A613
Gates, William H., III A186, A350, A972, A973, E59, E201, P78, P79, P134, P492, P510, P555, P767
Gates, William H., Sr. P79, P555
GatesMcDonald Company A1008, A1009, P364, P365, P685
Gateway Health Plan A717, P235
Gateway, Inc. A636-A637, A970, A1058, A1514, E256, P338, W180
Gateway Plaza at Battery Park City P291
Gatewood, David A. A129
Gatewood, Leonard B. A515
Gath, Phillip C. A1009, P365
Gatorade sports drink A1106, A1107, A1180, A1181, E99
Gators of University of Florida P756
Gatrixx (Internet portals) W626
Gatson, Jerry P471
Gatterman, Dave E122, E288
GATX Corporation A253, A638-A639, A1142
Gaudreau, Daniel A. E22, E148
Gauksheim, Wendy K. E213
Gaul, Hans Michael W219
Gaulin, Kevin A405
Gault, Stanley C. (Avon) A216
Gault, Stanley (Goodyear) A664
Gaunt, Ian J. A331
Gaunt, James R. A593
Gausvik, Thomas E. P761
Gautier, Jean-Francois W62
Gavin Anderson & Company (public relations) A1063
Gavin, Carol Coghlan A1363
Gavin, Moira W637
Gavin, Rupert W145
Gaviscom health and personal care W476, W477
Gavranovic, Kenneth A763
Gavrich, Lawrence J. A1433
Gawelek, Randolph J. A993
Gay City Health Project P79
Gay, Philip W429
Gay, Thomas E., III E173

Gaylans Trading Company sporting goods A876
Gaylord Container A1292
Gay-Lussac, Joseph W506
Gaymers Olde English Cyder A423
Gaynor, C. William A1519
Gaynor, Michael P. A211
Gayte, Auguste W69
Gazelle Graphics Systems W338
Gazerwitz, George R. A1425
The Gazette Newspapers, Inc. A1502, A1503
OOO Gazexport W243
OOO Gazflot W243
OAO Gazprom W116, W216, W242-W243, W346, W612
Gazzoli, Joseph J. A1355, P467
GB Foods. See Santa Barbara Restaurant Group
GB (retailer) W164, W165
GBI Capital Management. See Ladenburg Thalmann Financial Services Inc.
G.C. Murphy stores A158
G-Clef consumer electronics E58
GCS Service (commercial kitchen equipment) A530
G-CSF. See Neupogen
G. D. Searle (pharmaceuticals) A984, A1070, A1122, A1164, A1300
GE. See General Electric
GE Capitaland A790
GE Capital Services A414, A442, A646, A660, A1230, A1356, A1508, A1518, A1544, P146, P268, P390, P699, P700
GE Information Services A1070
GE Medical Systems A646, A952, E144, E218, E241
GE Specialty Heating A662
Géant hypermarkets W166, W167
Gearheard, Richard L. W67
Gearmatic A1078
Gebel-Williams, Gunther P188
Gebhardt ventilating products A921
Gebreder Kulenkampffag (tobacco) A1436
GEC Alsthom NV W76, W354
GEC Plessey Telecommunications W354
Geckle, Timothy J. A1227
GEC-Marconi Electronic Systems A342
GECO (seismic analysis) A1252
Geco-Prakla A1252
Gedeon, Charles C. A1463
Gee, David S. A1121
Gee, E. Gordan P382, P763
Geers, James H. A433
Gefco (transport) W442
Geffen, David P100, P166, P167, P510, P597
Gegare, Fred P247
Gehrig, Lou A1304, P134
Gehry, Frank P276
GEICO Corporation A252, A253
Geier, Philip H., Jr. A772

Geiger Brickel (furniture) A706
Geiger, Richard A. A653
Geigy (dyes) W414
Geigy, Johann W414
Geisel, Jean F. A235
Geiser, Edgar W563
Geiser, Thomas C. A1507
Geisler, John E. A325, P105
Geisler, Paul S. A827
Geitner, Thomas W353, W629
Gejroth, Lars W277
Gelb, Morris A901
Geldea, John P712
Gelfand, Neal A133
Geller, Laurence S. P737
Gellert, Jay M. A696, A697
Gelsinger, Patrick P. A761
Gelson's Markets P489
Geltzeiler, Michael S. A67, A1193
Gelva performance films A1301
GEMA Holdings AG A194
Gemeaz Cuzin (catering) W59
Gemey W343
Gemini car W294
Gemini Recycling Group P731
Gemini (software) W160
Gemini Submarine Cable System Limited W153
Gemma, Akira W534, W535
Gemma lingerie A1475
Gemplus (smart credit card) A1480, P474, P508
GEMS Sensors, Inc. A462, A463
Gemstar-TV Guide International A872, W390
Gemzar drug A540
Genachowski, Julius A1451
GenAmerica Corporation A964
GenCare A1434
Gencell (gene therapy) W102
GenCorp Inc. A1044
GenDerm E89
Gendron, Gerard A781
Geneal (furniture) A706
Geneen, Harold A688, W576
Geneen, Lawrence I. A183
Genentech, Inc. A540, A640-A641, E147, E217, W492
Gener S.A. A88
Generac Portable Products, Inc. A286
General America Corporation A1230
General American Tank Car A638
General American Transportation Corporation A638
General Atomic P438
General Battery A572
General Binding P655
General Brewing P428
General Cable Corporation A642-A643, P733, W450
General Casualty A1230
General Cigar Holdings, Inc. A660
General Cinema A1014, A1102
General Cologne Re A252, A253

General Crude Oil A770

Compagnie General de Geophysique A1252

General de Valores y Cambios (brokerage) W184

General Dynamics Corporation A253, A342, A404, A**644**-A**645**, A882, A990, A1044, E49, P578, W132, W290

General Electric Company A60, A264, A278, A414, A512, A642, A**646**-A**647**, A686, A724, A728, A778, A846, A882, A934, A976, A988, A992, A998, A1110, A1198, A1412, A1432, E140, E157, E251, E267, E269, E286, P106, P208, P390, P454, P572, P757, P766, W150, W226, W318, W496, W508, W610

The General Electric Company (UK). *See* Marconi plc

General Elevator A502

General Export Iron and Metal A396

General Felt (company) P276

General Film Distributors W472

General Foods Corporation A730, A842, A1126, P480

General Foods International coffee A843

General Housewares P775

General Instrument Corporation of America A872, A990, A1026, E41, E93

General Insurance Company of America A1230

General Latex and Chemical Corporation A504

General Maritime Corporation E208

General Medical A946

General Merchandise Company A790

General Microwave E68

General Mills, Inc. A70, A250, A464, A**648**-A**649**, A768, A816, A1136, A1180, A1314, P705, W192, W206, W256, W388

General Motors Acceptance Corporation A650, A651, A954

General Motors Building at Trump International Plaza A1408, A1409, P482, P483, P749

General Motors Corporation A104, A212, A256, A278, A380, A388, A400, A476, A512, A534, A538, A548, A549, A584, A616, A**650**-A**651**, A710, A736, A772, A782, A802, A856, A988, A998, A1010, A1052, A1066, A1112, A1178, A1210, A1386, A1394, A1422, E24, E104, E157, P72, P86, P92, P152, P316, P366, P417, P557, P561, P563, P590, P596, P606, P630, P644, P673, P679, P687, P695, P713, P733, P764, P767, P772, W74, W138, W188, W226, W262, W264, W294, W321, W390, W560, W614, W632

General Motors Truck Product Center P550

General Numismatics P416

General Nutrition Companies, Inc. A1202, P406

General Paint & Chemical Company A1410, P484

General Parts, Inc. A460, P112, P113, P613

General Photonics A642

General Plant Protection Company A1488

General Portland (cement) A848

General Precision Inc. E35

General Public Utilities. *See* GPU, Inc.

General Re A252

General Semiconductor, Inc. A1482

General Signal Corporation A194, A1320, E57, E81

General Supermarkets A1490, P514

General Textiles E60

General Tire P72

GeneralCologne Re W336

Société Générale (bank) P294, W104, W130, W512

Generale Biscuit W192

Société Générale de Belgique A875, W58, W558

Compagnie Générale d'Électricité W76

Compagnie Générale d'Enterprises Automobiles W624

Générale des Chauffe W624

Compagnie Générale des Eaux W58, W506, W624

Société Générale de Téléphones W232

Société Générale de Transport Aérienne W68

Compagnie Générale d'Industrie et de Participations W160

Generale Francaise de Ceramique W506

Compagnie Générales des Établissements Michelin. *See* (Compagnie Générales des Établissements) Michelin

Generali France Assurances W99

Generali Group. *See* Assicurazioni Generali S.p.A.

Generali Vita S.p.A. W98, W99

Generations Plus Northern Manhattan Health Network P369

Genesco Inc. A1384

Genesis Crude Oil E209

Genesis Entertainment A902, P304

Genesis Gas and Oil E129

Genesis Health Ventures, Inc. A908, P474, P475

Genesis (music group) W622

Genesis video game equipment W526

Genesys Telecommunications Laboratories, Inc. W76

Genetic Systems A290

Genetic Therapy W414

Genetics Institute A148

GeneTrace P454

Geneva software E25, E149

GENEX Services, Inc. A1440

Gengraf drug A58

Genho, Paul A829, P271

GENICOM E73

Genigraphics E73

Genlyte Thomas Group LLC P613

Genmar Holdings, Inc. P614

Genomyx, Inc. (DNA sequencing) A242, A243

GenRad, Inc. A1372, W600

Gensheimer, Joseph M. A1319

Genstar Land Company P96

Gent, Christopher Charles W353, W628, W629

Gentex Corporation (mirrors) A802

Gentilcore, James F. E24

Gentile, Jeffrey P339

Gentings Highlands Casino P318

Gentleman Jack Rare Tennessee Whiskey A296, A297

Gentner Communications Corporation E208

Gentry, Karen G. A785

Gentry, Mike P588

Gentry, Richard R. A1325

Gentz, Manfred W189

Gentzkow, Paul F. A1209

Genuardi's Family Markets A1234, P479

Genuine Kids clothes A1068

Genuine Parts Company A**652**-A**653**

Genuine Sonoma A838, A839

Genuity Inc. A1472, E52

Genzyme Corporation E147

Geo car P366, W294, W560

GeoCapital E149

GeoCities A1546

Geode system-on-a-chip A1002

GeoLogistics Corporation P614

The Geon Company A1054, A1072

Geophysical Service Inc. A1378

Geoppinger, William A. A1243

GeoProbe software E219

GeoQuest A1252

Georgakopoulos, Elizabeth A. A415

George A. Hormel & Company A730

George, Albert W547

George, Alex P535

George, Boyd P535

George Bush Presidential Library Center P470, P716

George, David A. (AdvancePCS) A85

George, David Lloyd (former British Prime Minister) W620

George E. Warren Corporation P614

George Foreman appliances E116

George, Howard F. E175

George II, King of England P134

George, James W. P748

George Killian's beers A78, A79

George, Lee P535

George Lucas Educational Foundation P302

George, Paul A1487

George, Peter W258
George R. Newell Company A1348
George, S. Craig E312
George, Thomas E99, E257
George, V. Carl A695
George VI, King of England W144
George V, King of England W148
George Washington Bridge P398, P399
George Weston Limited W244-W245, W618
George, William W. A953
Georgens, Thomas A895
Georgetown University P671
Georgia Baptist Medical Center P124
Georgia Blue P572
Georgia Cooperative Cotton Producers Association P200
Georgia Hardwood Lumber Company A654
Georgia Institute of Technology A1258, P124
Georgia Lighting, Inc. A724
Georgia Lottery Corporation P615
Georgia Power Company A1306, A1307
Georgia Railroad Bank & Trust A596
Georgia State Theatre chain P412
Georgiades, D. W385
Georgia-Pacific Corporation A654-A655, A848, A890, A1518, P212, P705
Georgine, Robert A. P754
Georgiopoulos, Peter C. E208
Geosafe Corporation P71
Geotek A1026
GeoVista tracking system P614
Geraghty, Gerard V. A755
Gerald R. Ford Library P758
Gerard, Peter W311
Gerard, Valerie L. W153
Gerardi, Ernest A., Jr. E175
Gerber baby products E60, P518, W414, W415
Gerber, Fritz W492, W493
Gerber, William K. A819
Gerbes Supermarkets A845
Gerges, David B. A361
Gerhard, Erwin P679
Gerhard, Lang A74
Gerhardt, Gary C. E198
Gerhardt, Kenneth W. A409
Gerharter, Thomas M. A107
Gerkens cocoa A324, P104, P566
Gerlinger, George A1524
Gerlinger, Louis A1524
Gerling-Konzern Versicherungs-Beteiligungs AG W201
Germain, Henri W182
German Allkauf (hypermarkets) W364
German Federal Cartel Office W380
German Ministry of Foreign Affairs W546
German Tip discount stores W364

German-American Car Company A638
Germania Life Insurance P214
germany.net (Internet service provider) W352
Germeshausen, Kenneth A1110
Germond, Philippe W625
Gerner, W. Cardon A1269
Geroler brand A527
Gerresheimer Glas AG A1074
Gersie, Michael H. A1163
Gerson, Elliot S. A1203
Gerstein, Irving A1552
Gerstle, Mark R. A457
Gerstman, Ned I. A357
Gerstner, Louis V., Jr. A764, A765, A948, P326
Gertmenian, Jaime L. E37, E173
Gervais Danone (yogurt and cheese) W192
GES Exposition Services A1478, A1479
Gesca Ltd. W262
Geschke, Charles M. A76, A77
Geske, Stephen A389
Gesparal (holding company) W342, W388
Gestetner Holdings W486
Gestetner Lasers A870
Compagnie de Gestion Foncière-Cogefo W183
Gestrich, Thomas E. A771
Geswein, Gregory T. A489
GET Manufacturing, Inc. A782
Getchell Mine W452, W453
GetMusic W126
Getronics NV A488, W422
GetSmart.com A1170
GetThere, Inc. (Web site) A1228, A1229
Getty Images, Inc. W621
Getty, J. Paul A1096, W592
Getty Oil A1096, A1376, P340, P416
Getty Petroleum Marketing Inc. P712, W346, W347
Getz Bros. & Company, Inc. P313
Getz, Roy C. A87
Gevaert (photography) W118
Geveda, Chester J., Jr. A517
Gexdur, Selçuk W319
Geyer, Paul R. A357
Geyres, Philippe W555
Geyser Peak Winery A618
The Geysers geothermal plant A1120
G.F. Industries A814
GF Office Furniture P741
GFO fiber packing P523
GFS Marketplace stores P618
GGT Group A1062
G.H. Besse-laar (laboratory services) A434
G. H. Mumm champagne W84
Gherini, Steven A. E128
Gherty, John E. A851, P289, P654
GHH. See Gutehoffnungshutte Aktienverein AG

Ghirardi, Jim P249, P641
Ghirga, Maurizio W555
Ghormley, Hugh M. A397
Ghosn, Carlos W402, W403
G-I Holdings, Inc. P612
G.I. Joe action figures A692, A693
Giacalone, Joseph A. E311
Giacoletto, Sergio A1067
Giacometti, Robert P415, P715
GIAG (glassmaker) W506
Giamelli, Joseph A233
Gian, Michael W195
Giancarlo, Charles H. A369
Gianelli, Deborah P662
Gianinno, Susan McManama P73
Giannetti, Steve P359
Giannissakis, G. W385
Gianopulos, Jim A623
Giant Brains; or Machines That Think (book) P248
Giant Eagle Inc. P198-P199, P478, P479, P615
Giant Food Inc. P103, W300, W498
The Giant Tire & Rubber Company A432
Giant-Carlisle stores W498, W499
Giant-Landover stores W498
Giay, Luis Vicente P421
Gibara, Samir F. A664, A665
Gibber, Robert W569
Gibbes, Asbury H. A1249
Gibbons, Alex A1137
Gibbons Goodwin van Amerongen (investments) P442
Gibbons, Green, van Amerongen A300
Gibbons, John D. A1467
Gibbons, Michael D. A1007
Gibbons, Paul F. A1015
Gibbons, Thomas E. A471
Gibbs, Dana R. A557
Gibbs, H. Jarrell A1417
Gibbs, Richard L. A1355, P467, P742
Gibraltar Casualty A1172
The Gibraltar Life Insurance Company, Ltd. A1172
Gibraltar Securities E132
Gibson, Barbara A763
Gibson, Charles S., Jr. A579
Gibson (cleaning products) A530
Gibson Electric Company, Inc. A544, A545
Gibson, F. Daniel A1329
Gibson Greetings, Inc. (cards) A146, A147
Gibson, Greg B. A1443
Gibson, J. Duncan W609
Gibson, Jean A571
Gibson, John W. A1065
Gibson, Mark P658
Gibson, Sloan D., IV A167
Gibson, Thomas R. P543
Gibson, Wayne A725
Giddings & Lewis (machine tools) A806, W594
Gienko, Glenn A. A991

Gierer, Vincent A., Jr. A1458, A1459
Giersch, Carlo A197
Giese, Al A851, P289
Gieves & Hawkes brand A691
Gifford, Charles K. A603
Gifford, Dale L. P631
Gifford, Michael B. (Danka Business Systems) W190, W191
Gifford, Michael (Rank) W472
Gifford, Randall T. A759
Gifford, Russell M. E163
Gifford, Simon W569
Gifford-Hill American (aggregates) W252
gifts.com A1192, A1193
Giga Pets toys A692
Gigante retail stores W164
Giguère, M. W377
Gil, Rosa M. P369
Gil y Carvajal (insurance broker) A182
Gilardi, Carlo W124
Gilat Satellite Networks Ltd. A528
Gilbane, Inc. P615
Gilbane, Thomas P615
Gilbane, William P615
Gilbert, Andrew J. P39
Gilbert, Barry A1274, E120
Gilbert, David (Golden State Foods) P203
Gilbert, David L. (Shoney's) A1281
Gilbert, George E28
Gilbert, H. Steven A611
Gilbert, Paul C. A433
Gilbert, Terrence M. A1207
Gilbert/Commonwealth (engineering) P386
Gilbertson, Brian P. W129
Gilchrist, David M. A897
Gilchrist, Robert A. A435
Gildersleeve, John W591
Gilead Sciences, Inc. A244
Giles, Edward F. A263
Giles, Julia E225
Gilhuly, Edward A837, P283
Gill, Daniel A234
Gill Interprovincial Lines of Canada A1454
Gill, John A. A599
Gillan, Kayla J. A315, P97
Gillen, Steve P57
Gillespie, Gilbert M. A1517
Gillespie, Robert W617
Gillespie, William A. A811, P267
Gillett, George, Jr. W376
The Gillette Company A252, A253, A**656**-A**657**, A1022, A1118, P530, P762
Gillette Dairy A994
Gillette, James R. P740
Gillette, King A656
Gilley, J. Wade P760
Gilligan, Edward P. A143
Gilliland, Sam A1229
Gilliland, Stewart W289
Gillis, Ruth Ann M. A571

Gillis, Steven E71
Gillman, Charles C. A295
Gillooly, Edward F. A263
Gilman, George A670
Gilman, Herbert A158
Gilman, Irving A158
Gilman, Kenneth B. A777
Gilman, Mark T. A267
Gilman, Milton A158
Gilman, Richard H. A1021
Gilman, Thomas F. P543
Gilmartin, Jane F. A1271
Gilmartin, Raymond V. A957
Gilmer, Gary A735
Gilmore, George H., Jr. A1005
Gilmore, Shaun P. A1187
Gilpin Hotel Casino E165
Gilroy Foods A938
Gilson, B. Nigel A453
Gilson, Jean-Marc P165
Giltin, Don P489, P752
Giltner, Philip P728
Gimson, Curtis S. A1401
Ginalski, Jan W457
Gingerella, Douglas J. A1251
Gingham brands P488, P752
Gingo, Joseph M. A665
Gingrich, Newt A626
Ginnie Mae A580, A862, E152
Ginsberg, Errol E224
Ginsberg, Gary L. W391
Ginsberg, Ruth Baden P134
Ginza fashion boutiques W534, W535
GIO Australia Holdings (insurance) W88, W89
Giordano, Richard V. W489
Giorgio Armani W342, W343
Giorgio fragrance A216
Gipson, Douglas R. A513
Gipson, Jim P634
Giraffe restaurants W315
Girard, Judy A569
Girard, Marc W471
Girl Scout cookies A814, A815
Girl Scouts of the U.S.A. P492, P493, P755
Girling, Russell K. E298
Girourd, Marvin J. A1130, A1131
Gisch, Joseph P. E191
Gish, Carl A131
Gitano jeans A1474, A1475
Git-N-Go convenience stores P624
Gittings, Brian A. A901
Gittings, David W337
Gittis, Howard A903, P305
Gittleson, Gail P549
Giuliani, Rudolph P368, P398
Giuliano, Louis J. A781
Giusti, Luis W438
Giusto, Mauro W423
Givaudan SA (fragrances) W492
Givel, Edouard E126, E299
Givenchy clothing A805, W348, W349
Givner, Elaine E97, E256

G. J. Coles & Coy A830, W172
GKH Partners E210
G.L. Kelty (window shades) A388
G. L. Ohrstrom and Company A1065
G. L. Rexroth (hydraulics) W352
Glacier auto parts A461
Glacier Park resorts A1478, A1479
Glad plastic products A374, A375
Glade air freshener A1246, A1247, P432, P433, P722
Gladiator (movie) P166, P167, P597
Gladish, Kenneth P777
Glamour (magazine) A80, P32, P33, P530
Glancy, John E. P439
Glantz, Fred A1455
Glanzmann, Thomas H. A237
Glar-Ban International (glass instrument panels) P310
Glascott, John W. A1547
Glaser, Gary A. A1001
Glashow, Sheldon P560
Glashütter watch W562
Glasier, Richard J. A1217
Glass, David D. A1494, A1495
Glass, Dennis R. A795
Glass, Donald L. A655
Glass Group (automotive information) A715, P233
Glass Idromassaggio (bath equipment) A920
Glass, John A194
Glass, Milton L. P85
Glass Plus cleaner A1246, P432, W476
Glass, Steven C. P671
Glassbook (electronic book software) A76
Glasscock, Larry C. A179
Glasser, James A638
Glassman, Karl G. A859
Glass-Steagall Act of 1933 A448, A988
Glastron boats P614
Glatch, Lisa A611
Glauber, Michael A. A859
Glauber, Robert R. A997, P353, P682
Glaverbel (glass maker) A1152, W192
Glavin, Patrick J. A293
Glaxo baby food W246
Glaxo Wellcome A242
GlaxoSmithKline plc A58, A118, A148, A242, A574, A640, E72, E89, E90, E217, P40, W118, W**246**-W**247**, W334, W336, W492
Glaze, Iris A1501
Glazer, Bennett P616
Glazer, Michael L. P649
Glazer's Wholesale Drug Company Inc. P616
GLEANER farm equipment A96, A97
Gleason, Bradley J. P43

Gleason, Larry A963
Gleason, Owen P. A345
Gleevec drug W414, W415
Gleisner, Jerry A. A1361
Glen Deveron scotch W109
Glen Moore (trucking) A1454
Glenbrook Life A126
Glencoe Butter & Produce
 Association P58
Glencoe farm equipment A97
Glencore International AG
 (commodities) W74, W340
Glendening, Brad P317
Glendronach scotch W85
Gleneagles Hotels PLC W207
Glenlivet Scotch A296, W108
Glenmorangie Scotch A297
Glenmore vodka A423
Glenn, David W. A627
Glenn, Duke A196
Glenn, John W368
Glenn, T. Michael A589
The Glens Falls Insurance
 Company A379
Glen's grocery stores A1312
Glick, Linda S. P293
Glidco, Inc. (chemicals) A974
Glidden paint A974, A1000, W252,
 W278
Glidden, Shannon K. E105
GLIDE dental floss P523
Glitsch International A620, A834,
 P280
GLL Real Estate Partners W98
Global Airlines A1442
Global Capital Markets A660
Global Companies LLC P616
Global Crossing Ltd. A866, E38,
 W152, W272, W358
Global Distribution Network
 (electronic reservations) P419
Global Election Systems Inc.
 (voting systems) A488
Global Energy Markets A114, A960
Global Express jet W132
Global Financial Information A832
Global Financial Services. See
 Bridge Information Systems, Inc.
Global Frozen Foods (food
 wholesalers) A1350
Global Health Council P78, P79
Global Imaging Systems, Inc. E208
Global Industrial Technologies Inc.
 (tools) A430
Global Information Systems A1012
Global Learning Center A911
Global Link software A1332
Global Media Services A1236
Global Metal Techologies P673
Global One A1318, W204, W232
Global Package Link A1428, P490
Global Packaging P90
Global Payments Inc. W156
Global Positioning System
 receivers A410
Global Procurement Group P208
Global Proxy Services A204

Global Steel Exchange A324
Global Sysco A1350
Global Thai Finance and
 Securities A860
Global T.H. food stores W590, W591
Global Transaction Company,
 Inc. P71
Global Travel Network P296
Global Web Advertising
 Network P248
GlobalCom (long distance) A390
GlobalNetXchange W164
Globalstar Telecommunications
 Ltd. A888, A1182, A1183
GlobalVatOnLine A1158, P400
The Globe and Mail
 (newspaper) W122, W123, W592,
 W593
Globe Aviation Services
 Corporation W525
Globe Business Furniture P222
Globe discount department
 stores A1492
Globe Feather & Down
 (pillows) A1134
Globe Furniture A306
Globe Interactive Web site W123
Globe Life and Accident Insurance
 Company A1390, A1391
GlobeGround GmbH W345
Globelle Corporation A1356
GlobeSpan (semiconductors) P475
GLOBEtrotter Software E235
Globe-Union (automotive
 batteries) A802
Globi stores W165
Globus W576
Glocer, Thomas H. W484, W485
Glore, Jodie A778
Gloria car W403
Gloria Vanderbilt brands A804,
 W342
Glory Glory Manchester
 (magazine) W239
Glosette candy A709
Gloster Aircraft W110
Glotzbach, Edward L. A1245
Glove, Brad P167
Glover, James T. A243
Glover, Richard (ABC, Inc.) A61
Glover, Richard S. (Amica Mutual
 Insurance) P540
GlucaGen drug W417
Gluck, Barry S. A1215
Gluckstern, Steven M. W653
Glucophage drug A290, A291
Glucotrol drug A1118, A1119
GlucoWatch A244
Gluth, Robert C. P313, P665
Glynn, Robert D., Jr. A1120, A1121
GM. See General Motors
GM Hughes Electronics A736
GM Locomotive Group A650
GMAC. See General Motors
 Acceptance Corporation
GMB (retailer) W164
GmC appliances P618

GMC vehicles A650, E170
GMJ Group (sleepwear and
 lingerie) A1498
GMU Group (cabinets) A920
GNA Corporation A1518
GNA (mutual fund
 wholesaler) A646
GNA (rehabilitation therapy) P748
Gnazzo, Patrick J. A1433
GNB Technologies (batteries) A572,
 W428
Gnecco, Lorraine E197
GNI Group P70
GNP. See Great Northern Paper
Gnutti Carlo SpA A1386
Go Fly Ltd. W140, W141
Go for the Green lottery game P373
Go2Net, Inc. A692, P510
Goberville, Gary J. A817, A1539
Gochnauer, Richard W. P203
GO.com. See Walt Disney Internet
 Group
Godard, Alain W103
Goddard, Rick P137
Goddess Collection body care
 products E177
Godé, Pierre W349
The Godfather (movie) P302
Godfrey, Cullen M. P499
Godfrey, Peter P338
Godfrey supermarkets A606
Godfrey, William A., III A507
Godinho, Norm E76
Godiva Chocolatier A316, A510,
 A511
Godla, Larry R. A909
Godrej & Boyce A1334
Godshalk, Ernest L., III E133
Godwin, William P485
Goedecke A1118
Goehring, Ralph J. E164
Goeken, John A1534
Goelzer, Paul P243
Goelzer, Paulo A745
Goerdeler, Reinhard A840, P286,
 W324
Goethals, Arthur W195
Goethals Bridge P398, P399
Goetz Brewing P428
Goetz, Stefan W185
Goetz, William W. A365
Gofen and Glossberg E149
Goffredo, David B. A59
GOGO Worldwide Vacations P296,
 P658
Gogono-kocha soft drink W315
Go-Gurt yogurt A648, A649
Goh Choon Phong W541
Goh, Eng Lim A1285
Goings, E. V. "Rick" A1414, A1415
Goizueta, Roberto A382
Gold & Company P120
Gold Bond Stamp Company P106,
 P567
Gold Bond wallboard P683
Gold, Charles A794
Gold Cup Trophy guns P133

Gold Dust West Casino E165
Gold Fassi beer W553
Gold Kist Inc. P200-P201, P616
Gold Medal flour A648, A649
Gold Metals Consolidated Mining
Company. *See* Tom Brown, Inc.
Gold Mines of Australia W640
Gold, P. D. A794
Gold Points Rewards (consumer
loyalty) P106, P107
Gold Quarry A1024
Gold rum W109
Gold Seal bath products W476
Gold Strike Resorts A906, A907
Goldberg, Alan A1292
Goldberg, Albert A1490, P514
Goldberg, Arthur M. A1086
Goldberg, Bruce M. E151
Goldberg, David A1189
Goldberg, Frank P501
Goldberg, Glenn S. A945
Goldberg, Lena G. A615, P191
Goldberg, Neal A635
Goldberg, Robert P752
Goldberg, William S. E210
Goldblatt Tool A1322
Goldblatt's Department Stores A158
Golden Aluminum A452
Golden Arch Hotel A942, A943
Golden Bear Golf Club (South
Carolina) P131
Golden beer W377
Golden Books A926
Golden, Charles E. A541
Golden Choice Buffet P642
Golden Classic potatoes P265
Golden Corral restaurants P642
Golden Eagle Group A1454
Golden Eagle Insurance
Company A875, P294, P295
Golden Eagle Systems A1240
Golden, Frank A313
Golden Gate Bridge A256, P643
Golden Gate Capital E97
Golden Genesis (solar
electric) W328
Golden Grain pasta A1180, A1181
Golden Guernsey Dairy P610
Golden, James A782
Golden, Jerry L. A1277
Golden, Judy E310
Golden, Michael (New York
Times) A1021
Golden, Michael P.
(Southwest) A1311
Golden Nugget (hotel and
casino) A966, A967
Golden Peanut Company P200
Golden Poultry P200
Golden, Robert C. A1173
Golden Rose A373
Golden Rule dry goods store A790
Golden Rule Insurance
Company P617
Golden State Bancorp Inc. A658,
A902, A903, P304, P305, P663

Golden State Foods
Corporation P202-P203, P524,
P525, P617, P777
Golden State Warriors (basketball
team) P355
Golden Sunlight Mine W453
Golden Virginia tobacco W282,
W283
Golden West Financial
Corporation A658-A659
Golden Wonder Crisps snack
food W282
GoldenEye 007 (video game) W395
Goldenrod Asset
Management A1509
Goldenson, Leonard A60
Golder, Thoma, Cressey,
Rauner E208
Goldfarb, David A861
Goldfinger, Solomon P371
Goldfish crackers A316
Goldfrank, Jack C. A951
Goldline cameras E184
Goldman, Alfred E. A95
Goldman, Henry A660
Goldman, Marcus A660
Goldman, Neal G. A1149
Goldman, Robert W. A413
Goldman Sachs Capital
Partners P737, W256
The Goldman Sachs Group,
Inc. A424, A660-A661, A860,
A960, A986, A1028, A1150, A1328,
E258, P398
Goldman, Steven J. (Power-
One) E269
Goldman, Steven R. (Starwood
Hotels & Resorts) A1329
Goldner, Brian A693
Goldsmith, Harry L. A209
Goldsmith, James A664, W142
Goldsmith, John H. E132, E306
Goldsmith's stores A587
Goldstar beer W255
Goldstar Company. *See* LG Group
Goldstein, I. Steven A507
Goldstein, Joe P198
Goldstein, Matthew P128, P129
Goldstein, Mitchell P. A671
Goldstein, Richard A. A766, A767
Goldstein, Samuel P542
Goldstein, Sid A458
Goldstein, Stanley A458
Goldwell (hair care) W308
Goldwyn Entertainment A962
Goldwyn Studios A962
Goldy, Susan E. P153
Golf car W631
The Golf Channel cable
network A391, A1403
Golf Digest (magazine) A80, P32,
P33
Golf Pride brand A527
Golf Properties A80
Golf World (magazine) A1020, P33
Golin/Harris A772
GoLive Systems A76, A77

Golkin, Perry A837, P283
Goller, Albert W537
Golonski, Thomas W. A1001
Golston, Allan C. P79, P555
Golub, Ben P617
Golub, Bill P617
The Golub Corporation P617
Golub, Harvey A142, A948, P326,
P670
Golub, Neil M. P617
Goman, Stanley L. P347
Gomes, W. R. P495
Gómez Chibli, Eduardo W581
Gomez, Enrique A., Jr. W511
Gomez, James H. A315, P97
Gomez, Juan Vicente W438
Gomez, Manuel W481
Gómez Martinez, Bernardo W583
Gomez-Montoy, Alejandro A1299
Gomi, Yoshifumi W531
Gompers, Samuel P34
Gone With The Wind (movie) A962,
P416
Gonggryp, Heidi P167, P597
Gonner, Renae G. A1091
Gonring, Matthew P. A173, W91
Gonsalves, Patricia E26, E151
Gonzales, Arthur L. A1077
Gonzales, Dick W. (Safeway) A1235
Gonzales, Kenda B. E309
Gonzales, Richard A. (Abbott
Laboratories) A59
Gonzáles-Adalid García-Zozaya,
Antonio W483
Gonzalez, Claudio X. A827
Gonzalez, Henry, Jr. A943
Gonzalez, Joseph P448
Gonzalez, Manolete P574
Gonzalez, Terri E305
Gonzalez, Wendy P419
Gonze, David J. P662
Good & Fruity candy A709
Good & Plenty candy A708, A709
The Good Guys (retailers) P346,
P347, P680
Good Housekeeping
(magazine) A701, P138, P229
Good Humor (ice cream) W618,
W619
Good, Michael P. P685
Good News razor A657
Good Vibrations stores E101
Goodall, Jack W. A784
Goodall, Randy P445
Goodbody Holdings Limited
Stockbroking W87
Goodby, Silverstein & Partners
(advertising) A1062, A1063
Goode, David (Duke Energy Field
Services) P598
Goode, David R. (Norfolk
Southern) A1039
Goode, William C. A723
Goodell, Elaine A881
Goodell, Roger P357
Goodfriend, M. D. A666
Goodfriend, Robert M. A666

Gooding, Harry G., III E312
Gooding's Supermarkets P479
GoodKidz clothing A666
Goodman, Bennett J. A449
Goodman, Bruce J. A739
Goodman, Edward A1218
Goodman, Harold P618
Goodman Holding Company A1190
Goodman, John B. P618
Goodman Manufacturing Company, L.P. A934, P618
Goodman, Patrick J. P341, P676
Goodman, Stephen H. P729
Goodmanson, Richard (American West) A138
Goodmanson, Richard R. (DuPont) A535
GoodMark Foods A408
Goodnight, Cecil L. A1167
Goodnight, David L. A871
Goodnight, James H. P430, P431, P721
Goodrich, Benjamin Franklin A662
Goodrich Corporation A**662**-A**663**, P691
Goodrich, David R. P387, P697
Goodrich, Denise P775
Goodrich Petroleum Corporation E209
Goodrich, T. Michael P552
Goodrich, Walter G. "Gil" E209
Goodson, Charles T. E264
Goodspeed, Linda A865
Goodwill Industries International, Inc. P618
Goodwin & Sons, Inc. P489
Goodwin, Edwin A1014
Goodwin, Everett P641
Goodwin, James E. A1420, A1421
Goodwin, John A1006
Goodwin, Paul R. A455
Goodwin, William M. A1513
Goody hair accessories A1022
Goodyby, Silverstein & Partners A1062
Goodyear Aerospace A664
Goodyear, Charles A664
The Goodyear Tire & Rubber Company A216, A522, A**664**-A**665**, A698, A1144, P238, P594, P628, W138, W366, W428
Goody's Family Clothing, Inc. A**666**-A**667**
Google (search engine) A1546, E150
Gookin, Burt A722
Goolsby, Michelle P. A1339
Goosebumps (books and TV show) A1254, A1255
Gopalakrishnan, R. W567
Gordon, Blair P255
Gordon B. Miller & Company P262
Gordon, Dan P618
Gordon, Donald M. A337
Gordon, Donna E99
Gordon Food Service P618
Gordon, Harold P. A693

Gordon, Jeff (race car driver) P681
Gordon, Jeffrey I. (Marconi) W355
Gordon, John P726
Gordon, Marc D. A255
Gordon, Milton A. P99
Gordon, Robert A. (Safeway) A1235
Gordon, Robert J. (International Flavors) A767
Gordon, Robert R., Jr. (R.J. Reynolds) A1205
Gordon, Stephen F. A155
Gordon, Susan C. A1477
Gordon's Jewelers A1552, A1553
Gordy, Berry W212
Gore, Al P34, P134, P450, P579
Gore Bank of Hamilton W156
Gore, Bill P522
Gore, Frank C. P131
Gore, Genevieve W. P523
Gore, Robert W. P522, P523, P775
Gore, Sally P775
Gorelick, Jamie S. A581
Gores, Alec P619
Gores Technology Group A762, A926, A970, P619, P676
Gores, Tom P703
GORE-SORBER exploration survey P523
GORE-TEX fabrics P522, P523, P775
Gorham (crystal and flatware) A296
Goring, Terry L. P309, P664
Gorman Eckert & Company (spices and flavorings) A938
Gorman, Joseph T. A1412
Gorman, Leon A. P300, P301
Gorman, Lon A349
Gorman, Stephen E. E80
Gormley, David W147
Gormley, Dennis A584
Gorney, Jon L. A1001
Goro Project (nickel-cobalt) W284
Gorog, Christopher E281
Gorrie, M. Miller P560
Gorrie, Thomas M. A801
Gorter, J. M. W642
Gorton's frozen seafood A648, W618
Goryainov, Yuri A. W243
Göschel, Burkhard W121
Gose, Günther W653
Gosless, Dwight J. A409
Gosnell, Thomas A. A199
Gospel Electric Works W448
Gossage, Thomas A704
Gossamer Bay wines A520, A521, P168, P169, P600
Gossigion, Rob E210
Gothic Energy E39
Gotlieb, Irwin W647
Gotlieb, Lawrence B. A813
Goto, Takuya W308, W309
Gotro, Jerry P650
Gotta, John H. A879
Götte, Klaus W351
Gottlieb, Bob A661
Gottlieb, Rachelle E115, E282

Gottlob Auwarter GmbH W350
Gottschalk, Thomas A. A651
Goudie, Peter J. W285
Gouëzel, Hervé W131
Gough, John W428
Goughenour, James P443
Gouiffés, Jean-Yves W233
Goulandris, Peter John W636, W637
Gould, Andrew A1253
Gould, Frank Jay A498
Gould, Harry E., Jr. P619
Gould, Harry, Sr. P619
Gould, Kay P565
Gould, Michael A587
Gould Paper Corporation P619
Gouldey, Glenn C. A527
Goulding, Charles R. A503
Goulds Pumps A780
Gouldthorpe, Hugh F., Jr. A1071
Gourbin, Jean-Louis W193
Gourgeon, Pierre-Henri W69
Gourio, Hervé A329, P107, P109, P567
Gourmet (magazine) P33
Gourmet Table brand A1109
Gouverneur Nursing Facility and Diagnostic & Treatment Center P369
Gove, Sue E. A1553
Goven, Gregory D. A345
Government Bond Department P374
Government National Mortgage Association. *See* Ginnie Mae
Govett, John W86
Govindji, Lisa E146
govWorks.com A172
Gowan Inc. A545
Gowans, James K. W453
Gowans, John P426, P427
Gower, Bob A900
Gowin, Mary Ellen P515
Gowland, Karen E. A275
Goya Foods, Inc. P**204**-P**205**, P619
Gozon, Richard C. A1519
GP Publications W238
GPC cigarettes W142
GP-Encore, Inc. A509
GPT Holdings W354
GPU, Inc. A253, A598, A**668**-A**669**
GQ (magazine) P33
G. R. Kinney shoes A294
GR Servicios Hoteleros W546
Graber Industries (window furnishings) A1316, P452, P453, P733
Graber, William R. A947
Graber window furnishings A1317
Grabish, Richard F. A95
Grab-It cleaning cloths A1247, P432, P433
Grabow, Karen A851, P289, P654
Grace Chemicals K.K. A1536
Grace, Joseph A1536
Grace National Bank A1536
Grace, Peter A1536

Grace, William R. A1536
Graceland P417
Graco infant products A1023
Graddick-Weir, Mirian M. A203
Grade, Jeffery A806
Gradon, R. Michael W435
Grady, Daniel A. P93, P559
Grady, Janice Stewart E312
Grady's American Grill A288
Grady's Goodtimes
  restaurants A288
Graf, A. Jay A675
Graf, Alan B., Jr. A589
Graf, Thomas J. A1163
Graff-Riccio, Rhona A1409, P483
Graffunder, Herman L. A1339
Gráficas Monte Alban (bookbinding
  and publishing) W470
Grafton, Daniel W177
Grafton, W. Robert A172, P48, W90
Graham, Allan A393
Graham, Benjamin A252
Graham, Bruce P448
Graham Composites Limited A896
Graham, Donald E. A1502, A1503
Graham, Garry A305
Graham, Ginger L. A675
Graham Group A1004
Graham, James C. A1351
Graham, John K. A909
Graham, Katharine A1502
Graham, Marc C. A1097
Graham Packaging Company,
  L.P. P620
Graham, Philip A1502
Graham School of General
  Studies P497
Graham Selects cookies A815
Graham, Thomas C., Jr. A104, A105
Graham, W. Bruce A463
Graham, William B. (Baxter) A236,
  A237
Graham, William H. (Bethlehem
  Steel) A257
Graham-Hyde, Michael E127
Graifer, Valery W347
Grain Terminal Association P122
Grainger Brothers wholesale food
  distributors A606
Grainger, David W. A1538, A1539
Grainger Export A1539
Grainger, Michael J. A759
Grainger, SA de CV A1539
Grainger, William W. A1538
Gralla (publishing and trade
  shows) W620
Gralnick, Helene E177
Gralnick, Marvin J. E177
Gram (company) A1550
Gramaglia, Jerry A567
Gramlich, Edward M. P187
Gran drug A160
Gran Federal cleaning and laundry
  products A487
Gran Llauro cleaning and laundry
  products A487
Gran Reserva Especial brandy W109

Granada plc W146, W174,
  W**248**-W**249**, W620
Granadillo, Pedro P. A541
Granaria Holdings P600
Granary Market natural
  foods A1522
Granat, David J. A1403
Granchelli, Ralph S., Jr. E55
Grand America Hotel P729
Grand Auto A1078
Grand Bank N.A. A964
Grand Bazaar Innovation Bon
  Marche W300
Grand Biotechnology Company,
  Ltd. W603
Grand Casino lottery game P666
Grand Casinos, Inc. A1086, A1087
Grand Central Terminal P334
Grand Coulee Dam A810, P266
Grand Finales frozen foods A609
Grand Forks (North Dakota)
  Herald A833
Grand Gulf nuclear plant A554
Grand Hotel (Cape Town, South
  Africa) W552
Grand Hyatt Hotel A1408, P482
Grand Ice Cream A511
Grand Manor, Inc. A347
Grand Metropolitan. *See* Diageo plc
Grand North beer W377
Grand Pequot Tower hotel P318,
  P319
Grand Rapids Coffee
  Company A1312
Grand Rapids Wholesale Grocery
  Company A1312
Grand Realty Inc. A509
Grand Rental Station A1410, P484,
  P485, P749
Grand Teton Lodge (resort) A454
Grand Theft Auto II (computer
  game) E298
The Grand Union Company P102,
  P565
Grand Union stores A1094
Grand Victoria (riverboat
  casino) A740, A907, P240
Grand Vitara car W561
Grande Auguri sparkling
  wine W109
Grande, Carlo W217
Grande Cuisine stores A1530,
  A1531
Grandma's cookies A1107
GrandMet. *See* Grand Metropolitan
Grands Moulins de Paris (flour
  milling) W134
Grandstaff, Linda A. A823
Granelli, Andrea W575
Granik, Russell T. P355
Granite City Division (steel
  mill) A1007
Granite Construction, Inc. P745
Granite Financial A590
Granite State Gas Transmission,
  Inc. A1035
Granite Steel A1006
Graniteville (textiles) A1400

Grann, Phyllis W431
Granny Smith Mine W452, W453
Granny's Buffet P562
Grano, Joseph J., Jr. W617
Grant, Alexander P206
Grant, Charles B. A585
Grant, Clark C. P562
Grant, Hugh A985
Grant, Joseph P389
Grant, Kevin C. A849
Grant, Paul A163
Grant, Steven H. E192
Grant Street National bank A954
Grant Thornton
  International A1158, P**206**-P**207**,
  P620
Granville, Irwin P291
Granville, Lord A1486
Granville Phillips E213
Granziol, Markus J. W617
Grape-Nuts cereal A842
The Grapes of Wrath (movie) A622
Grapetiser soft drink W553
GrapeVine Technologies A1342
Graphic Packaging
  International E185
Graphics Microsystems (pressroom
  equipment) A502
Grapstein, Steven H. A1375
Grasberg mine A628
Grass, Alex A1202
Grass, Martin A1202
Grass Valley Group A1358
Grassilli, Diane P119
Grasso, Richard A. A1018, A1019,
  P374, P375, P688
Grattan (mail order
  company) W426, W427
Gratton, Paul W465
Gratz, Jay M. A1225
Grauer, Peter T. P81
Graveline, Kathleen M. A799
Graver, Todd A629
Graves, Arthur C. P277
Graves, David A1547
Graves, Edward A1500
Graves, Howard D. P470, P471,
  P743
Gravy Train pet food A723
Gray & Barton A898
Gray, Bowman A1204
Gray, C. Michael A1109
Gray Drug Fair stores A1202
Gray, Elisha A898, P208
Gray, Hanna Holborn P496
Gray, Harry A1432
Gray, Herb P529
Gray, Robert C. (Highmark) A717,
  P235, P632
Gray, Robert F. (Coca-Cola
  Enterprises) A385
Gray, Shellie E287
Grayarc A1142
Graybar Electric Company,
  Inc. P**208**-P**209**, P620
Grayborn, Vandeleur W268
Gray-Felder, Denise P415, P715

Gray's Anatomy (book) P177
Graziano, Michael A. A1023
Grealis, William J. A363
Greaney, Dennis P317
Great American Ball Park A144
Great American
Communications A144
Great American Foods P122
Great American Insurance
Company A144, A145
Great American Management
Investment Inc. A560, P180
Great American Reserve A414
Great American Smokeout P40,
P41, P538
Great American Wreaths
(book) A919
The Great Atlantic & Pacific Tea
Company, Inc. A**670**-A**671**, A838,
W588, W589
*Great Books of the Western
World* P176, P177, P496, P603,
P756
Great Cedar Hotel P318, P319
Great Dane Limited
Partnership P621
Great Expectations hair
salons A1196
Great Five Cent Store A1470
The Great Gatsby (movie) A1150
The Great Indoors home decorating
store A1265
Great Lakes and Midwest Division
(steel mill) A1007
Great Lakes Cheese Company,
Inc. P588
Great Lakes Chemical
Corporation A612, A984, A1122,
P238
Great Lakes Dredge & Deck
Company A176
Great Lakes International (marine
dredging) A176
Great Lakes Pipe Line
Company A1528
Great Lakes Steel A1006
Great Northern Nekoosa A654
Great Northern Paper A284
Great Northern Railway A308
Great North Foods P243
Great Plains Reinsurance
Company A575
Great Plains Software, Inc. A972
Great Scott! supermarkets A844
Great Southern Group (funeral
homes) A1268
Great Southern Trucking A1222
The Great Universal Stores A1412
Great Western Financial
Corporation A1500
Great Western Railway A474, P154,
W196
Great Western Sugar
Company W568
Great Western Tea Company A844
Greatamerica A896
Greater All American Markets A110

Greater American Financial
Resources A144
Greater Bay Bancorp E209
Greater East Asia Co-Prosperity
Sphere W602
Greater Georgia Life
Insurance P572
The Greater New York Rental
Company A622
GreatLand Insurance P269
Great-West Assurance A124
Great-West Life Assurance A178,
A1236
Greco, Samuel A694
Greeff, Douglas A1201
Greehey, William E. A1466, A1467
Greek Shipowners Investment
Company S.A. W385
Greeley, George E235
Green Acres Foods A1132
Green, Andrew F. (Advantica) A87
Green, Andy (British
Telecom) W149
Green, Barbara P632
Green Bay Food A466
Green Bay Machinery P723
Green Bay Packaging Inc. P621
The Green Bay Packers, Inc.
(football team) A**672**-A**673**,
P**210**-P**211**, P356, P357, P621
Green Bay (Wisconsin) *Press-
Gazette* A672, P210
Green Burrito restaurants A590
Green, Colin H. W497
Green Cross W118
Green, Dana I. A1493
Green, David P632
Green, Emily Nagle E63
Green Frog restaurant A464
Green, Gary R. W175
Green, Geoffrey C. P401
Green, George A701, P229
Green Giant foods A1136, A1137,
W206
Green, Harriet A197
Green, Jack A1168
Green, James E261
Green, Jeffrey S. P399
Green, Larry J. A225
Green, Lemuel A1464
Green, Leonard A1202, P394
Green, Lorraine A. P363, P684
Green, Philip (investor) W356
Green, Philip N. (Reuters) W485
Green Power & Light A1464
Green, Ralph A1464
Green Revolution P414
Green, Richard C., Jr. A1464, A1465
Green, Robert K. A1465
Green, Roger A196
Green Shield trading stamps W590
Green Spring Health Services A904,
A905
Green Stamps P198
Green, Stephen K. (HSBC
Holdings) W269

Green, Stephen L. (SL Green
Realty) E289
Green, Stewart E. W245
Green, Thomas B. A473
Green Tree Financial
Corporation A414, A1380
Greenbaum, David R. E137
Greenberg, Alan (Carpet Co-op
Association) P568
Greenberg, Alan C. (Bear
Stearns) A238, A239
Greenberg, Evan G. A150
Greenberg, Frank A306
Greenberg, Jack M. A942, A943
Greenberg, Jeffrey W. A150, A916,
A917
Greenberg, Karen R. A881
Greenberg, Mark E. A357
Greenberg, Maurice R. A150, A151,
A916
Greenberg, Robert E289
Greenblatt, Sherwin P92
The Greenbrier (resort) A454, A455
Greenbury, Richard W356
Greene, Carolyn A219
Greene, Douglas A. (Merck) A957
Greene, Doug (Penton Media) E102
Greene, Gregory F. A1223
Greene, James H., Jr. A837, P283
Greene, Jesse J., Jr. A399
Greene, Margaret H. A249
Greene, M. S. A1417
Greene, Robert C. E157
Greenfield, Hope A445
Greenfield, Linda E266
Greenhouse Fund
(investments) W484
Greenlees, Michael A1063
GreenMark brands P479
Greeno, Ladd P55
Greenough, William A1354, P466
Greenspan, Alan P186, P187, P607,
P689
GreenStone Industries, Inc. A890
Greenville Rehabilitation Services,
Inc. A259
Greenville Steel Car A1406
Greenwald, Gerald A1420
Greenway Partners A1470
Greenwich Marine A325, P105
Greenwood, Scott A495
Greenwood Trust Company A126
Greer, Ray E. A1317, P453
Greg Norman shoes A1194, A1195
Gregg, Elaine P539
Gregg Foods P122
Gregg, Gary R. A875, P295
Gregg, Kirk P. A435
Gregg, Peter W469
Gregg, Terrance H. E241
Gregg, Walter E., Jr. A1147
Gregoire, Daniel M. A1077
Grégoire, Jean-Louis W443
Gregory, John M. E229
Gregory, Joseph M. A861
Gregory, Ramon K. A725
Gregson, Charles W621

Greif Brothers Corporation (packaging) A1302
Greig, Andy A241, P75
Greiner, Charles H. A771
Greiner, Mark T. A1335
Greisinger, James R. A467
Greka Energy Corporation E209
Grela, Peter P678
Grelle, John P754
Gremli, Alfred W185
Grenesko, Donald C. A1403
Grenex (magnetic media) A1260, P440
Grennes, Robert J. A1449
Grenson Electronics A446
Gresen Hydraulic A1088
Gresh, Philip M., Jr. A749
Gress, William J. A299
Gressette, Lawrence M., Jr. A1249
Gretzky, Wayne P251, P360
Greving, Robert C. A1441
Grewal, Randeep S. E209
Grewcock, Bruce E. A1115, P397
Grey Advertising P372
Grey Cell Systems W572
Grey, Henry A256
Grey Poupon mustard A843
Grey, Robert J. A1155
Greyhound Corporation A486, A1478, W488
Greys tobacco W283
Greystone Homes, Inc. A863
GRiD Systems (laptops) A368, A1188
Grider, D. Lynn W569
GridSouth Transco LLC A514, A1248
Grief, Gary P473
Grier, Herbert A1110
Grier, Mark B. A1173
Grier, Roosevelt P699
Griesedieck, Joseph P428
Griesmar, Andrea K. E182
Grieve, Pierson "Sandy" A530
Grieves, Robert T. A229
Griffin & Little, Chemical Engineers P54
Griffin, Bobby J. A1223
Griffin, Cornelius F. "Neal" E280
Griffin, David P736
Griffin, Donald W. A1061
Griffin, John P359
Griffin, J. Timothy A1047
Griffin, Merv A1408, P482
Griffin Pipe Products P540
Griffin, Robert G. A859
Griffin, Roger P54
Griffin, Ronald B. A725
Griffin Technology A488
Griffins biscuits W193
Griffith, Alan R. A229
Griffith, Chuck A615, P191
Griffith, D. W. A962
Griffith, Elizabeth A. P145, P585
Griffith, James W. A1387
Griffith, John D. A1353

Griffith, Patricia Hope A401
Griffith, Ray A. A65, P31
Griffith, Robert C. E250
Griffiths, John A474, P154, W196
Griffiths, Lloyd Cromwell W141
Griffiths-Kerr A1316, P452
Grigg, James L. A1071
Grigliatti, Enrico W423
Grigson, David J. W485
Grijalva, Victor E. A1253
Grilk, Thomas S. A1373
Grilla Gear barbecue tools P91
Grillo, Jeffrey A. A909
Grimes, Don A744, P242
Grimes, D. R. E251
Grimes, Frank A744, P242
Grimes, Jay A69
Grimes, Kirk D. A611
Grimland, Gene P. A1391
Grimm, Thomas R. A1495
Grimmer, Ralph P345
Grimsley, Arlene G. A819
Grimsley, J. Kevin A1549
Grinney, Jay F. A695
Grinstein, Gerald A99
Grip Printing and Publishing Company W378
Grisanti, Eugene A766
Grisé, Cheryl W. A1041
Grisik, John J. A663
Grissen, Thomas A. E88
Grissinger, Richard A. A1135
Gristede's Foods, Inc. P712
Griswell, J. Barry A1163
Grize, William W499
Grizzle, J. David A429
Groce, A. Ben A275
Groce, Greg P61
Groceries On The Go service P550
Grocers Supply Company Inc. P622, P623
Grocery Store Products A374
Grocery Supply Company Inc. See GSC Enterprises, Inc.
GroceryWorks.com Inc. A1234, W590
Groch, James R. A1399
Grode, George F. A717, P235
Grodzki, Kevin S. A299
Groebe, Louis A744, P242
Groen Manufacturing A502
Groeneveld, Oscar Y. L. W489
Groenink, Rijkman W. J. W57
Groetzinger, Jon, Jr. A147
Grogan, Ralph H. A307
Gröger, Rudolf W149
Grolier Inc. (publisher) A1254, W330
Grollier, Jean-François W343
Grolsch beer P732
Grom, Charles P. A445
Grom, Gary C. A1243
Gronlandsfly A/S W519
Groom, John A1087
Groomer Direct pet supplies A1117
Grooms, Sharon P634

Groot, Steven L. A127
Groot-Noordhollandsche W64
Grosdidier, W. Richard A621
Grose, Jan P51, P541
Grosfeld, James E45
Gros-Pietro, Gian Maria W216, W217
Gross, Bert M. A1197
Gross, Bruce E. A863
Gross, Edward H. P69, P548
Gross, Gerhard P445
Gross, Jeremy V. A1501
Gross, Loren D. A343
Gross, Richard M. A505
Gross, Robert A882
Gross, Thomas S. A463
Grossberg, Andy P639
Grosset & Dunlap A144
Grossett, James M. W377
Grossi, Pat P560
Grossi, Richard A. P645
Grossman, Ian P479
Grossman Industries (recycler) A1292
Grossman, Lawrence S. P592
Grossman, Marc A. A721
Grossman, Michael A. A1541
Grossman, Steve W493
Grosvenor Casinos W472, W473
Grosvenor, Gilbert M. P358, P359
Grosvenor, Gilbert Melville P358
Grosvenor, Melville Bell P358
Grote, Byron W137
Groundwater Technology A610
Group 4 Securitas W524
Group Health Association (HMO) A738
Group Health Cooperative of Puget Sound A810, P622
Group Maintenance America Corporation A548
Group Message paging W419
Group Sales and Service A1434
Group Technologies A1256
Group W Cable A390
Groupama W164
Groupe, Grupo, Gruppo. See entry under primary company name
Groupelec W446
GroupMAC. See Group Maintenance America Corporation
GroupWise (software) A1050, A1051
Grout, Bruce E. A103
Grove, Andrew S. A760, A761
Grove Manufacturing A1068
The Grove Park Inn Resort P720
Grove Worldwide LLC W252
Grover, Jeff I. P. W645
Grover, Stephen A. P277
Groves, Dennis "Mike" P729
Groves, Lori A249
Groves, Randall D. A473
GROWMARK, Inc. A192, P572, P622
GrowMaster Crop Services P732
Growney, Robert L. A991

Grreat Choice pet food A1117
Grubb & Ellis Company P476
Grubb, Richard N. A1483
Grubbe, Kenneth S. P37, P532
Grubbs, Robert W., Jr. A177
Gruber, Evan M. E94, E246
Grubman, Eric P. A425
Gruen, Frank P624
Gruen, Rob A1239
Gruenwald, J. Thomas A1363
Grum, Clifford A1364
Grumbacher office products A1023
Grumman Corporation A1044
Grundhofer, Jerry A. A1444, A1445
Grundhofer, John F. A1444, A1445
Grundman, Thomas K. E79, E227
Grundy, Clive W. P. W175
Grundy Worldwide (game shows
  and soap operas) W430
Grune, George A1192
Gruner + Jahr AG & Company
  (publisher) A700, P228, W126,
  W127
Grünewald, Herbert W119
Grushow, Sandy A622, A623, W391
Gruy Petroleum Management E235
Grzedzinski, Edward A1445
GS Communications (cable
  TV) A72
GS stores W165
GSC Enterprises, Inc. P622, P623
GSC Industries A856
GSD&M Advertising A1062, A1063
Gsell, Starr P681
GSM (mobile
  communications) A1026, W502
G-Smoke cigarettes E293
GS-Online A660
GTCR. See Golder, Thoma, Cressey,
  Rauner
GTCR Golder Rauner, LLC
  (investments) E286
GTE Corporation A128, A644, A758,
  A1186, A1318, A1472, P765,
  W444, W536, W628
GTE Telenet A204, A368
GTECH Holdings
  Corporation A558, P372, P472,
  P688
Groupe GTM W558
GTS Network E41
GU Markets P102
Guangdong toll road W266
Guangzhou Daily Group W565
Guangzhou Pacific Tinplate W398
The Guarantee Life Companies
  Inc. A794, A795
Guaranteed Student Loan Program
  of 1965 A1448
Guaranty Federal Bank A1364
Guardian Assurance plc W65
Guardian Industries
  Corporation P212-P213, P565,
  P623
Guardian Insurance
  Company W286

The Guardian Life Insurance
  Company of America P214-P215,
  P623
Guardian Mortgage
  Company A1227
Guardian Royal Exchange plc A875,
  P294, W64, W104, W286
Gubanich, Kathleen C. A1469,
  P505, P764
Gubbay, David A415
Gubitosi, Joan E273
Gubitosi, Robert V. E273
Gucci, Aldo W250
Gucci Group N.V. W250-W251,
  W348, W446, W447
Gucci, Guccio W250
Gucci, Maurizio W250
Gucci, Paolo W250
Gucci, Roberto W250
Gucci, Rodolfo W250
Guedon, Philippe W331
Gueguen, Franck W171
Guerin, Ray P665
Guerrera, Gloria E177
Guerrero supermarkets W498
Guest, James P138, P582
Guest Supply, Inc. (personal care
  products) A1350
Guezuraga, Robert M. A953
Guggenheim family W488
Guggenheim Museum (New York
  City) P290, W276, W514
Guglielmi, Joseph A991
Guglielmi, Peter A. A1363
Guhl Ikebana (hair care) W308
Guhse, David P145
Guichard, Antoine W167
Guichard, Geoffroy W166
Guichard, Jean W166
Guichard, Mario W166
Guichard, Yves W167
Guidant Corporation A282,
  A674-A675
Guide to Baby Products
  (book) P139
Guide to Online Shopping
  (book) P139
Guiding Light (TV show) A1164,
  A1165
Guido, Nick A81, P33
Guido, Richard L. W285
Guilbaud, Jacques W613
Guilbert S.A. (distributor) W446,
  W447
Guild Wineries & Distillers A422
GuildHouse (candles) A146, A147
Guiles, Edwin A. A1267
Guilford Pharmaceuticals A160
Guilhou, Eric W101
Guillet, Edward E. A657
Guin, James M. A307
Guinness, Arthur W206
Guinness beer W231
Guinness Book of World
  Records W206
Guinness PLC A302, A1136, P64,
  P746, W255, W289

Guinness/UDV W206, W207
Guitar Center, Inc. E66, E210
Guitar Techniques
  (magazine) W239
Guitarist (magazine) W239
Gulden's foods A409
Guldimann, Tobias W185
Gulf Air A1228
Gulf + Western Industries W526
Gulf Canada Resources
  Limited A412, A820
Gulf Coast Business
  Machines W190
Gulf Midstream Services
  Partnership (gas) A825
Gulf Oil, L.P. P438, P586, P624
Gulf Power Company A1306, A1307
Gulf States Steel A896
Gulf States Toyota, Inc. P624
GulfMark Energy, Inc. A68, A69,
  E209
Gulfstream Aerospace
  Corporation A644, A645, A1044,
  P766
Gulfstream International
  Airlines W496
Gulfstream Resources Canada A168
Gulick, Paul E73
Gull Corporation (aerospace
  electronics) A1088
Gullane Entertainment PLC W206
Gulmi, Claire M. E155
Guloso tomato products A723
Gulton (satellite data
  systems) P310
GUM department stores W310
Gum, Mary A451
Gum Tech International,
  Inc. A1526
Gummer, Charles L. A395
Gumout car care products A1096,
  A1097
Gumption cleaning products A375
Gunari, Vincent J., Jr. A445
Gund family A816
Gundersen, Gorm W55
Gunderson, Fred P517, P772
The Gunlocke Company (office
  furniture) A726
Gunn, Michael W. A165
Gunter, William J. A1319
Gunton, Howard E. A923, P321,
  P667
Gupta, Deepak A1099
Gupta, Rajat A948, A949, P326,
  P327, P670
Gupta, Rajiv L. A1212, A1213
Gupta, Ram A1099
Gupta, Yogesh A403
Gura, Thomas M. A1061
Gurassa, Charles W461
Gurin, Denise K. P413
Gurney, Peter R. P417
Gürtler, Hans-Beat W415
Gurtner, William H. P495
Gurwitch Bristow Products
  (cosmetics) A1014, A1015

Gurwitz, Norman H. E198
Gust, Anne B. A635
Gustafson, Paul A. A265
Gustafson, Robert E. A121
Gustafsson, Anders A1363
Gustin, Carl E., Jr. A525
Gut, Rainer E. W185, W389
Gutehoffnungshutte Aktienverein AG W350
Guth, Charles A1102
Guthy-Renker (infomercial producer) A902, P304
Gutierrez, Carlos M. A816, A817
Gutierrez, Phil P529
Gutnick, Michael P. P672
Gutschewski, Bernie R. A1423
Guttendorf, Richard A. A1233
Gutty, Gianfranco W99
Gutzeit, Hans W556
Guy Carpenter & Company, Inc. (reinsurance) A916, A917
Guy, Kenneth H. P479
Guy Laroche (fragrances) W343
Guyaux, Joseph C. A1147
Guyenne et Gascogne SA W164, W166
Guyette, James M. W497
Guy's Food (potato chips) P90
Guzman, Angel A305
Guzman, David R. A1071
GVC Corporation E261
GW Associates E31
Gwaltney, Eugene A1220
Gwaltney of Smithfield, Ltd. A1291
Gwaltney Packing A1290
Gydell, Hans W277
Gylling Optima Batteries A802
Gypsum Transportation Ltd. A1456

H

H. Merlyn Christie's Oil Drilling A978
H. Wilson Company (furniture) P170, P171
Ha, Joseph M. A1033
Haaf, Michael A1057
Haag, Daniel P663
Haag, Douglas G. A909
Häagen-Dazs ice cream A1136, A1137, W388
Haan, Philip C. A1047
Haank, Derk W479
Haar, Kevin A. E110
Haarmann & Reimer W568
Haas family P657
Haas, Otto A1212
Haas Outdoors A1220
Haas, Peter A868, P292
Haas, Richard J. P43
Haas, Robert D. (Levi Strauss) A868, A869, P292, P293
Haas, Robert (Furniture Brands) A631
Haas, Robert (Hicks & Haas) A714, P232
Haas, Walter A868, P292

Habano Primero tobacco A1458, A1459
Haber, Barry P580
Haber, Fritz W116
Haber, Spencer B. E224
Haberberger, William P709
Haberer, Jean-Yves W182
Habermeyer, H. William, Jr. A1167
Hachette Filipacchi Médias W330, W331
Hachette, Louis W330
Hachette (publishing) W330
Hachey, Guy C. A477
Hachiya, Kunihiko W309
Hack, Todd P113
Hackel, Kenneth E95
Hacker, Douglas A. A1421
The Hacker Group (marketing) A773
Hackerman, Willard P772
Hackett, James P. A1334, A1335
Hackett, Karen Nelson A1018, P374
Hackley, James M. A349
Hackney Petroleum P635
Hadar, Eric E34
Hadax (remote test and access) A70
Hadco A1240
Hadden, Briton A180
Haddrill, Richard M. E236
Haden, C. Roland P471
Hadfield, Mark S. P179
Hadley, Leonard A934
Hadley, Philip A. E61, E202
Hadson Energy Resources A184
Haebler, William A766
Haefele, Raymond J. A743
Haefling, Karen R. A823
Haefner, Michael E. A1229
Haefner, Walter A402
Haener, William J. A377
Haeringer, Stephan W617
Hafer, Fred D. A669
Haffner, David S. A859
Haft, Herbert A844
Hagan, James J. A497
Hagans, Bennie P389
Hagedorn, H. C. W416
Hagemann, Reiner W83
Hagemeister Park P210
Hagemeyer Group W429
Hagen, Edward L. A451
Hagen, Shella B. A743
Hagerty, Robert C. E268
Haggai, Thomas S. A744, A745, P242, P243, P638
Haggar brand A839, E60
Haggen P479
Haggerty, Charles A1514
Hägglund, Björn W557
Hagino, Michiyoshi W265
Hagio, Hiroyasu W303
Hagiwara, Toshitaka W321
Hahn, David L. A441
Hahn, Helene P167
Hahn, Rainer W491

Hahn, William K. (Ag Processing) P37
Hahn, William R. (Agilent Technologies) A99
Hahne's department store A932
Hahs, Dwain L. A235
Haig, Thomas W271
Haight, Henry Huntley P384
Haikalis, P. W385
Hail Creek Coal Project W488
Haile, Donald A. A615, P191
Haile, Kimberly M. A1183
Hailey, V. Ann A877
Haim Saban A60, A1496
Hain Food Group A722, A1180
Hain, John A1483
Hainer, Herbert W63
Haines, Helen D. A1005
Haines, Virginia E. P687
Haircrafters salons A1196
Hairston, Peyton T., Jr. A1371, P469
Haislip, Wallace G. A1259
Haj Terminal at International Airport (Jeddah, Saudi Arabia) P449
Hajela, Kuldeep E105
Hakata, Masayuki W169
Hake, Ralph F. A934, A935
Hakii, Mitsuhiko W187
Hakim, Joseph E137
Hakoshima, Shinichi W96, W97
Håkstad, Thor W411
Hakuhodo (advertising) W198
Hakunetsusha & Company W610
Hal Riney & Partners W466
Halas, George P356
Halaska, Robert H. A1493
Halatsis, George C. W285
Halbert, David D. A84, A85
Halbert, Jon S. A84, A85
Halbert, Robert E30
Halbron, Jean-Pierre W77
Haldeman, Charles E. A879
Hale, Brandon O. A699
Hale, Elmer, Jr. P624
Hale, James, Jr. (Cinergy) A363
Hale, James T. (Target) A1353
Hale, John A. A859
Hale, Lynne P303
Hale of Summit Distributors A1109
Hale, Robert N. A807
Hale, Tom P624
Hale-Halsell Company P624
Hales, Tony W84
Haley, Ann A281
Haley, John S. A129
Haley, Roy W. A1512, A1513
Half, Robert A1208
HALF TIME beverages W304
Half.com E54, E196
Halford, William P253
Halifax Banking W156
Halifax, Ian E235
Halifax (investments) W472
Halker, Gary P. A359
Hall, Arthur A878

Hall, Brian H. W593
Hall Brothers gift store A678, P216
Hall, Bruce C. P395
Hall, Charles (Alcoa) A112, W74
Hall, Charles L. (Fleming) A607
Hall, Christopher A1203
Hall, David M. (Waste
  Connections) E139
Hall, David W. (CompuCom
  Systems) A401
Hall, Dennis J. A327
Hall, Donald J. A678, A679, P216,
  P217
Hall, Donald J., Jr. A679, P217,
  P625
Hall, Eugene A. A205
Hall family P518, P625
Hall, Floyd A830
Hall, Grayson A167
Hall, Jerry D. E77
Hall, Joyce A678, P216
Hall, Kinion & Associates,
  Inc. E210
Hall, Ladd R. A1053
Hall, M. Brad A835, P281
Hall, Peggy E297
Hall, Peter W115
Hall, Richard L. A1049, P377
Hall, Rollie A678, P216
Hall, William E. (Parsons) P387
Hall, William (Hallmark) A678,
  P216
Hall, William, II (Ohio State
  University) P383
Halla, Brian L. A1003
Hallaba, Tarek S. A387
Hallam, Howard P553
Hallam, Robert P553
Hallam, Thomas F. A197
Halle, Bruce P594
Haller, Andy A1083
Halley, Paul-Auguste W164
Halliburton Company A676-A677,
  A754, A1378
Halliburton, Erle A676
Hallicrafters (electronics) A1044
Halliday, Lisa P219
Halliday, Robert E133, E310
Hallinan, Kevin M. P307
Hallmark Cards, Inc. A146, A350,
  A678-A679, E143, P216-P217,
  P518, P625
Hall-Mark Electronics A214
Hallmark Hall of Fame (TV
  show) A678, P216
Hallmark.com A678
Hallock, Richard W. A1055
Halloran, Jean (Consumers
  Union) P139
Halloran, Jean M. (Agilent
  Technologies) A99
Halloran, Kathleen L. A1031
Halls Merchandising (department
  store) A679, P217
Hallwood Energy E272
Hallworth, Richard P751
Halma plc A526

Halmi, Robert, Jr. A679, P217
Halo electrical products A431
The Haloid Company A1544, P70,
  P71
Haloid Xerox A1544, W472
Halonen, Jorma W633
Halpern, Alvin P129
Halpern, Denny P740
Halpern, Philip P497
Halpin, Stephen R. P574
Halsa hair products A1246, P432
Halsell, Hugh P624
Hälsingborgs Nattvakt W524
Halske, Johann W536
Halstead, Donald M., III A1149
Halston fragrance A766
Halter Marine A1406
Halverson, Bruce E. A667
Halverson, Duane A851, P289
Halverson, Gordon E. E30
Halvey, John K. A1233
Halvorson, William P706
HAMA Industries E48
Hamada, Hiroshi W487
Hamaguchi, Kazuya W597
Hamann, Darrel M. P107
Hamann, Dennis J. P777
Hamashbir Lata (food
  processor) W322
Hambly, Lawrence W. A1343
Hambrecht & Quist Group A348,
  A808, P238
Hambro Life Assurance W652
Hamburg, Marc D. A253
Hamburger Abendblatt
  (newspaper) W106, W107
Hamburger & Sons department
  store A932
Hamburger, Cynthia B. A517
Hamburger Helper A648
Hamburger Stahlwerks W292
Hamburg-Mannheimer
  (insurance) W380
Hamel, Dennis J. A107
Hamersley Holdings W488
Hames, Marilyn P. A. W453
Hames, Michael J. A1379
Hamid, Mohamed Nor Abdul W539
Hamilton Investments, Inc. A735
Hamill, Jeffrey S. A57
Hamilton Aero A1432
Hamilton, Alexander A228, A808,
  P134
Hamilton, Anthony W178
Hamilton Beach/Proctor-Silex,
  Inc. A992
Hamilton, Carl P88
Hamilton District Telegraph W122
Hamilton Electro A214
Hamilton, Gordon C. A1231
Hamilton, Jean D. A1173
Hamilton, John E. P620
Hamilton Lane Advisors P505
Hamilton, Lawrence W. A1357
Hamilton, Linda P706
Hamilton, Michael D. (Briggs &
  Stratton) A287

Hamilton, Michael (Ross
  Stores) A1215
Hamilton, Pamela J. A1011
Hamilton, Peter B. A299
Hamilton, Richard J. M. (ITT) A781
Hamilton, Richard K.
  (Bowater) A285
Hamilton Scientific A600
Hamilton Standard A1432
Hamilton Sundstrand
  Corporation A1432, A1433
Hamilton, Ward M. E144
Hamilton watches W563
Hamilton, W. Mark A1269
Hamilton/Hall-Mark
  (distributor) A1140
Hamje, Robert M. A1413
Hamlet cigars W240, W241
Hamlett, Harold W., Jr. A1437
Hamlin, Christopher L. A895
Hamlin, Clay W., III E187
Hamlin, Craig L. A193
Hamlin, Stephen E. P742
Hamlin, William P103
Hamm, Richard F., Jr. (Carlson
  Companies) P107
Hamm, Rick (Conoco) A413
Hammary furniture A854
Hammer, Armand A742, A1054
Hammer, Hans Jörg W427
Hammer microprocessors A82
Hammer Strength fitness
  equipment A298
Hammergren John H. A947
Hammerman, Stephen L. A961
Hammermill Paper A770
Hammon, Tim W173
Hammond, C. F., III "Kit" P621
Hammond Corporation
  (organs) P312
Hammond, Dale S. P269
Hammond Illuminating A1034
Hammond, Michael D. A636, A637
Hammond, Thomas R. A787
Hammonds, Bruce L. A937
Hamm's beer P428, P746
Hamner, Clay A1084
Hamner, W. Clay P740
Hamnett, Marty W645
Hamon, Jean-Paul W69
Hampel, Ronald W620, W621
Hampshire College P78
Hampshire Funding Inc. A795
Hampton, Claudette P69, P548
Hampton Inn A720, A721, E216
Hampton, Philip W149
Han, Bernard L. A139
Han Soo-Yang W455
Han, S. Y. A285
Hana Bank of South Korea W82
Hanaoka, Seiji W531
Hanatsuka, Hitoshi W199
Hanau (mail order company) W426
Hanauer, James D. A297
Hanawa, Akihiko W299
Hanawa, Yoshikazu W402, W403

Hance, James H., Jr. A227
Hancock, Bonnie A1167
Hancock Communities E243
Hancock, Dain M. A883
Hancock Fabrics, Inc. (stores) A796
Hancock, John A1332
Hand, Elbert O. A690, A691
Hand, Scott M. W285
Handa, Katsuo W597
Handel, Nancy H. A189
Handelgesellshaft Heinrich Heine GmbH W427
Handford, Sue W239
H&G Contractors A786
H&H Craft & Floral Company A968
Handi-Wipes cleaning product A375
Handi-Wrap plastic wrap A1247, P433
Handler, Elliott A926
Handler, Ruth A926
Handlesbanken W220
Handley, Geoffrey A. W453
Handley Page (airline) W140
Handlon, Carolyn B. A913
H&M Food Systems A742
H&R Block, Inc. A**680**-A**681**, P206
Handwerker, Ida E95
Handwerker, Nathan E95
Handy Andy home improvement stores P330
Handy City home improvement stores A1536
Handy Dan Home Improvement Centers A724
Handy-Way convenience stores A1084, A1085
Haneda, Katsuo W303
Hanes Corporation A1220, A1242, A1243, E60
Hanes Holding Company A858
Haney, Douglas W. P121
Hanf, Michael P597
Hang Seng Bank Limited W268
Hänggi, Rolf W493
Hangzhou Xin'anjiang Perfume Factory A766
Hanik, Peter P. A975
Hanjin City Gas W559
Hank, John L., Jr. P542
Hanke, Arthur E. A487
Hankin, Rockell N. E119
Hankins, Randal L. A491
Hankins, Steven A1419
Hanks, Stephen G. P769
Hanle, Robert P451
Hanley, Patrick D. A1423
Hanley, Thomas M. A1443
Hanlin, Russell P464
Hanlon, Richard E. A181
Hanman, Gary E. P148, P149, P587
Hanna Coal A416
Hanna, David G. E183
Hanna, Frank E183
Hanna, Howard A1006
Hanna, William W. A835, P281
Hannaford, Richard W283

Hannaford stores A844, W194, W195
Hannah, Steve A833
Hannemann, Timothy W. A1413
Hannen beer W163
Hannezo, Guillaume W625
Hanni, Christine E. E159
Hänni, Urs P. W185
Hannibal (movie) A962
Hannifin (cylinder maker) A1088
Hannigan, William J. A1228, A1229
Hannis, Jean M. A137
Hannity, Vincent T. A275
Hanny's clothing A690
Hanover Compressor Company E210
Hanover Group A754
The Hanover Insurance Company A124, A125
Hanower, L. David A311
Hanrahan, Paul T. A89
Hanratty, Judith C. W137
Hans Glas (cars) W120
Hans Scwarzkopf GmbH W256
Hansa Pilsner beer W552
Hansberger, Robert A274
Hanseatic Bank GmbH W426, W427
Hansell, Raymond J. E113
Hanselman, Richard W. A697
Hansen, Bill E133
Hansen, Bruce D. A1025
Hansen, Charles M., Jr. A1134
Hansen, Jean-Pierre W559
Hansen, Joy E. A1025
Hansen, Kenneth A1272
Hansen, Kurt W119
Hansen, Mark S. A606, A607, A1116
Hansen Mechanical Contractors, Inc. A545
Hansen, Peter K. E256
Hansen, Richard A. A1017, P371, P688
Hansen, Ross A1113
Hansen, Thomas J. A749
Hansmeyer, Herbert W83
Hanson, A. John A245
Hanson, Chris W177
Hanson, Clement A726
Hanson, Dale A314, P96
Hanson, James (Hanson) A974, A1446, W252, W604
Hanson, James L. (Mutual of Omaha) P349
Hanson, John Nils A806, A807
Hanson, Linda A. A1385
Hanson, Paula P355
Hanson PLC A974, A1524, W**252**-W**253**, W604
Hanson, Randall A. A307
Hanson, Richard E. A1519
Hanson, Robert A468
Hanson Trust W282
Hanson White (greeting cards) A146
Hanson-Bennett Magazine Agency P170

Hanus, Jean-Claude W443
Hanway, H. Edward A361
Hapag Touritik Union W460
Hapag-Lloyd AG W460, W461
Hapke, Wolfgang W117
Happel, Marvin H. A451
Happer, Daniel J. P692
Happy Days (TV show) A60
Happy Meals P486
Harad, George J. A275
Harada, Tadakazu W139
Harari, Eli E117, E284
Harari Page (advertising) W198
Harber, Lacy E51
Harbert, Timothy B. A1333
Harbicht, Abby Areinoff E101, E259
Harbin, Henry A904
Harbin, Henry T. A905
Harbinger carpets A981
Harbison, Rich P445
Harbison-Mahony-Higgins (contracting) P740
Harbor Capital Advisors A1074
Harbor Distributing P713
Harborview Medical Center P761
Harbour Group Industries, Inc. P625
HARCO Capital Corporation A795
Harcourt Brace Jovanovich A174
Harcourt General, Inc. A1014, W478, W479, W592
Harczak, Harry J., Jr. A337
Hard, Brian P700
Hard Disk Drive Group A1184
Hard Rock Cafe International, Inc. W472, W473
Hardage, Ginger C. A1311
Hardcast Europe (adhesives and sealants) A326
Hardee's fast food A86, A590
Harden, Donald F. A673, P211
Harder, Torrence E83
Hardiman, Roy C. A641
Hardin, Edward L., Jr. A323
Hardin, Joseph, Jr. P274
Harding & Pullein A562, P182, W222
Harding, L. Wayne P721
Harding, Tim J. R. W435
Harding, Warren G. P146
Harding's stores A1312
Hardison, Wallace A1438
Hardware Plus stores P330
Hardware Wholesalers P594
Hardwick, Christopher J. A191
Hardwick, Rhonda P768
Hardwick Stove A934
Hardy, Eva Teig A499
Hardy, Joe, Jr. P26
Hardy, Joseph A., Sr. P26, P27, P528
Hardy, Lowell P729
Hardy, Paul P26
Hardymon, James A1380
Hare, Don A493
Hare, Steve W355

Harenstam, Lars W585
Harf, Peter W477
Hargett, William G. E216
Hargreaves, David D. R. A693
Hargrow, Ralph P. A769
Harig, Hans-Dieter W219
Harig, Steven T. A1283
Harigaya, Hiroshi W529
Harker, Brian J. A493
Harker, John V. E73, E220
Harkey, Robert S. A479
Harkin, Ruth A1433
Harkness, Glenn E. E131
Harkrider-Morrison P553
Harl, R. Randall A677
Harlan, Bob A672
Harlan, Edward E. A673
Harlan, Michael W. E309
Harlan, Robert E. P210, P211, P621
Harlem Globetrotters (basketball team) P332
Harlem Hospital Center P369
Harley Davidson (video game) W527
Harley, William A682
Harley-Davidson, Inc. A682-A683, P416, P535
Harlin Holdings W230
Harline, J. C. P62
Harlow, William V. A615
Harm, Kimberly S. P349
Härmälä, Jukka W557
Harmel, Harro W459
Harmon, Brenda S. A105
Harmon, J. A. A547
Harmon, Larry A. A365
Harmon, Michael R. A1135
Harmon, Timothy M. E101
Harmount, Rusty P616
Harmsen, Daniel L. P648
Harmsworth, Andrew A284
Harner, James F. A933
Harness brand A985
Harnett, Craig P361, P684
Harnisch, Jürgen W595
Harnischfeger, Henry A806
Harnischfeger, Henry, II A806
Harnischfeger Industries A806
Harnischfeger, Walter A806
Haroche, Gilbert P296, P297, P658
Harp Lager W206
Harp, Randy E107
Harper & Row (publisher) W390
Harper, Craig A789
Harper, Donald D. A665
Harper, Hoyt A1329
Harper, James A. A541
Harper, Julia A. E109, E274
Harper, Marion A772
Harper Memorial Library P497
Harper, Mike A408
Harper, Peter J. W341
Harper, William Rainey P496
HarperCollins Inc. (publisher) A1218

HarperCollins (publisher) A700, P228, W390, W430
Harper's Bazaar (magazine) A701, P229
Harpo Entertainment A700, A701
Harpo, Inc. P218-P219, P228, P229, P625
The Harpur Group A212
Harr, Lawrence F. P349
Harrah, William A684
Harrah's Entertainment, Inc. A684-A685
Harreld, Michael N. A1147
Harrell, A. J. A1548
Harrell, Don A1355, P467
Harrell, Henry H. A1436, A1437
Harries, Robert I. A613
Harriman, E. H. A1422
Harrington, Fred P500
Harrington, Jenny E301
Harrington, Marguerite P748
Harrington, Michael F. A1293
Harrington, Richard J. (Thomson Corp.) W592, W593
Harrington, Rick A. (Conoco) A413
Harrington, Righter & Parsons A443
Harris, Alan F. A817
Harris, Alfred A686
Harris, Anthony R. W259
Harris Associates A516
Harris Automatic Press Company A686
Harris Bankcorp, Inc. W112, W113
Harris, Barbara R. A1157
Harris, Barry P429
Harris, Charles A686
Harris, Charlotte P755
Harris Chemical A752
Harris, Clarendon A124
Harris, Conrad P139, P582
Harris Corporation A686-A687, A898, E76, E274, P444
Harris, Dan P604
Harris, Don (Equity Group) A561, P181
Harris, Don S. (Wal-Mart) A1495
Harris, Duane C. A1249
Harris, Eileen P643
Harris, Elmer B. A1307
Harris Financial. *See* Waypoint Financial Corporation
Harris Graduate School of Public Policy Studies P497
Harris, Janet A597
Harris, John F. (Carlyle Group) P111, P567
Harris, John (IXYS) E76, E224
Harris, J. Wayne A791
Harris, Ken A635
Harris, King W. E102
Harris, Martee E271
Harris, Matilda A1206
Harris Methodist Health Insurance Company, Inc. A1081
Harris Methodist Health System P744

Harris, Michael (Thomson Corp.) W593
Harris, Mike (Prosperity Bancshares) E271
Harris, Mike (Prudential plc) W465
Harris, Nancy P595
Harris nuclear plant A1166
Harris, Paul P420
Harris, Peter P173
Harris, Randall C. (Nextel) A1027
Harris, Randall C. (Sodexho) A1297
Harris, Robert S. A1433
Harris Trust and Savings Bank A228
Harrison Conference Centers A721
Harrison, Gary L. A609
Harrison, Hugh A1348
Harrison, James E. A155
Harrison, Martin E244
Harrison, Sandra L. A737
Harrison Telephone A292
Harrison, Thomas L. A1063
Harrison, William B., Jr. (J.P. Morgan Chase) A809
Harrison, William (United Business Media) W620
Harriton, Richard A238
Harrod's department store W340, W426
Harrold, Mark A675
Harron Communications (cable TV) A72
Harrow Industries A754
Harry Hart and Brother clothing store A690
Harry H. Post Company P236
Harry Potter (children's books and products) A926, A927, A1254, A1255
Harry Ramsden's fish and chips W248
Harsant, Edward C. A1325
Harsco Corporation A612, P110
Harshaw/Filtrol Partnership (pigments and additives) A550
Harshfield, Elizabeth S. A581
Harshman, Richard J. A117
Hart, Alex A924, P322
Hart, Angie A93
Hart, Cathy J. A1543
Hart, Claude A432
Hart, Craig J. A743
Hart, E. Thomas E273
Hart, Harry A690
Hart, Marjorie E295
Hart, Matthew J. A721
Hart, Max A690
Hart, Michael P695
Hart Schaffner & Marx men's clothes A690, A691
Hart, Terry (Ceradyne) E175
Hart, Terry J. (Loral Space & Communications) A889
Hart, William A1322
Harte-Hanks Communications A568
Hartenstein, Eddy W. A737

Härter, Holger P. W459
The Hartford (Connecticut)
  Courant A360, A1402
The Hartford Electric Light
  Company A1040
The Hartford Financial Services
  Group, Inc. A**688**-A**689**, A780
Hartford, George A670
Hartford, George, Jr. A670
Hartford, John A670
Hartford Seguros A688
Hartig plastic blow molding A450
Hartigan, Jim A721
Hartje, Keith D. P341
Hartley, Cynthia A. A1303
Hartley, Fred A1438
Hartley, Mike P313
Hartman, Bruce L. A1471
Hartman, Ed A73
Hartman, Peter F. W317
Hartman, Raymond W379
Hartman, William P69
Hartmann, Inc. (luggage) A296
Hartmann, Ulrich W218, W219,
  W381
Hartmarx Corporation A**690**-A**691**,
  E78
Hartney, Lesley A209
Harton, Don P127
Harts Athletic Clubs P258
Harts department stores A1094
Hartsfield International Airport
  (Atlanta) P124
Hartshorn, Tom A497
Hartstang, Axel A215
Hartstone (table and cook
  ware) A326
Hartwell, Cathy E278
Harty, Linda S. A409
Hartz brand A985
The Hartz Group P626
The Hartz Mountain
  Corporation P626
Hartz, Peter W631
Hartz, Scott C. P401, W463
Haru, Hidehiko W599
Harvard Business School E258
Harvard, John P220
Harvard Medical School P697, P769
Harvard Pilgrim Health Care,
  Inc. P626
Harvard University P194,
  P**220**-P**221**, P566, P626, P761
Harvest Burgers A816
Harvest States Cooperative P122
Harvester restaurants W545
Harvey Group A1140
Harvey, James T. A721
Harvey, J. Brett A417
Harvey, Kenneth M. A735
Harvey, Kent M. A1121
Harvey, Robert W. A1199
Harvey, William G. A285
Harvey-Jones, John W278
Harveys Bristol Cream sherry W85
Harveys Casino Resorts A684
Harvey's of Bristol W84

Harvie, Thomas A665
Harville, Tom P411
Hasan, Malik A696
Hasan, Mohammed A940
Hasbro, Inc. A**692**-A**693**, A926,
  A1096, E54, E147, P302, P486
Hasegawa, Shinpachi W405
Hasegawa, Takehiko W649
Hasegawa, Toru W649
Hasek, William A639
Haseotes, Aphrodite P586
Haseotes, Vasilios P586
Hasford, Heiner W381
Hash, Thomas A241, P75
Hashimoto, Makoto W487
Hashimoto, Takeshi W371
Haskell, Robert G. P385
Haskins & Sells A474, P154, W196
Haslam, G. Edward W340, W341
Haslam, James A., II P702
Haslam, James A., III P702
Hassan, Fred A1123
Hasse, Robert F. A1135
Hassell, Gerald L. A229
Hassenfeld, Alan G. A692
Hassenfeld Brothers fabric
  remnants A692
Hassenfeld, Helal A692
Hassenfeld, Henry A692
Hassenfeld, Stephen A692
Hassey, L. Patrick A113
Hassing, Michael F. W95
Hasson, Joe A685
Hasten, Joseph E. A1445
Hastie, Neil A. A1411, P485
Hastings, Barry G. A1043
Hastings, David P711
Hastings, Phillip W587
Hastings, T. Kay P554
Hata, Kazunori W421
Hatakake, Daisuke W327
Hatch, Gilbert J. A1545
Hatch Grinding P112
Hatchel, G. Don A1079
Hatcher, Claude A1400
Hatcher, Kenneth W. E238
Hatcher, Stephen R. P753
Hatchett, Terry E. A173, P49, W91
Hateley, J. Michael A1045
Hatfield, Scott A. A443, P147
Hathaway Corporation
  (shirts) A1498
Hathaway, Peter S. A123
Hathcock, Bonnie C. A739
Hatler, Patricia R. A1009, P365
Hatley, Donald E. A515
Hatley, Mark A673, P211
Hatsopoulos, George A1382
Hatter, Edward J. A453
Hattersley Heaton Ltd. W605
Hattery, Robert R. P325
Hattori, Ganzo W530
Hattori, Kitaro W528, W530
Hattori, Reijiro W529, W530
Hattori Seiko Company W528
Hattori, Yasuo W531

Hattox, Brock A. A1005
Hatuey beer W108, W109
Haub, Christian W. E. A670, A671,
  W588, W589
Haub, Erivan Karl W588, W589
Haub, Karl-Erivan W. W589
Haubiel, Charles W., II A261
Hauck, Frank M. A543
Hauck, William P99
Hauenstein, Glen A429
Haugen, Janet Brutschea A1425
Haugh, John N. A1093
Haunschild, Robert L. A1147
Haupt, Roger A. P72, P73, P551
Haupt, Vicki A1151
Hauptfuhrer, W. Barnes A1487
Hausberg, Mark A619
Hauser, David L. A515
Hauser, Mark W161
Hausmann, Audrey P547
Hausrath, David L. A201
Hautanen, Osmo A. A1423
Hautau, Henry J. P584
Hautz, Erich W537
Hauxhurst, Sidney P422
Havana Club liquors W108
Havas Advertising W198, W646
Havas (publisher) W624
Haven (RV parks) W472
Havens, Arnold I. A455
Havens, John P. A989
Havens, Richard J. E89
Haver, William F. P171
Haverman, Marc D. A471
Havert, James R. A1055
Haverty Furniture A630
Havlicek, John A280
Havner, Ronald L., Jr. E271
Havrilla, Bettina W607
Hawaiian Grocery Stores P488
Hawaiian Pineapple Company A494
Hawaiian Punch fruit drinks A470,
  A1104, A1105, P597, W154, W155
Hawes, David W469
Hawk, Carl J. A307
Hawk, Daniel D. A311
Hawk missile A1190
Hawk, Philip A556
Hawk, Robert D. P624
Hawker Aircraft W110
Hawker jet A1190, A1191
Hawker-Siddeley Aviation W110
Hawkes, James B. E53, E195
Hawking, Stephen P251
Hawkins, Arthur A572
Hawkins, Eric P159
Hawkins, Jay L. A971
Hawkins, J. Michael W191
Hawkins, Jonathan A. P732
Hawkins, Phillip A1094
Hawkins, Richard A946
Hawks, Harry T. E212
Hawksley & Wight men's
  clothes A691
Hawksworth, Roger W111
Hawley, Greg W. A1525

Hawley, Michael C. A656
Hawn, Gates A. A449
Hawn, Jeffrey S. A271
Hawn, Joni P589
Haworth, Gerrard P222, P627
Haworth Inc. A706, **P222-P223**, P627
Haworth, Jim H. A1495
Haworth, Richard G. P222, P223
Hawthorne, Douglas D. P744
Hawthorne, H. Robert P380, P381, P692
Hawus, Rebecca E96, E251
Hay, Frederick D. A1295
Hay, Lewis, III A625
Hayakawa Electric Industry W532
Hayakawa, Tokuji W532
Hayase, Paul H. E259
Hayashi, Jun W235
Hayashi, Massaki W261
Hayashi, Nobuyuki W235
Hayashi, Tsuyoshi W327
Haydamack, William J. E57
Hayden, Donald J., Jr. A291
Hayden, James E. E96, E251
Hayden Publishing W626
Hayden, Steve W647
Hayden-Watkins, Dorothy A721
Hayek, H. C. Nicolas G. W562, W563
Hayek, Nicolas W562
Hayes, Cheryl E106, E269
Hayes, Gregory A1153
Hayes, John A. (Ball Corp.) A225
Hayes, John D. (American Express) A143
Hayes, Kristin A. A1349
Hayes Leasing A212
Hayes Lemmerz International A112
Hayes Manufacturing Group A1302
Hayes, Richard J. A315, P97
Hayes, Rutherford B. P220, P382
Hayes, Stephen L. A1089
Hayes, William M. W453
Hayes, Woody P382
Haymaker, James N. A325, P105
Haynes, Carl E. P247
Haynes, Daniel P442
Haynes, Leonard J. A1307
Haynes, Robert J. P85
The Haystack brewery W254
Hayter and Murray W604
Haythornthwaite, Richard W291
Hayton, Martin W153
Hayward, Cindy E200
Hayward, Richard A. P318, P319
Hazelhoff, Robert W255
Hazen, Paul M. (Kohlberg Kravis Roberts) A837, P283
Hazen, Paul (Vodafone) W629
Hazen, Samuel N. A695
Hazleton (laboratory services) A434
H. B. Claflin (wholesaler) P342
H. B. Zachry Company P627
hbc.com W270
HBO. *See* Home Box Office

HBO 7 Company (health care information) A946
HCA, Inc. A236, A360, A574, A**694**-A**695**, A698, A1070, A1366, E211, P629, P729
HC&B (bank) W286
HCF-Lennox A864
HCL Corporation A480
HCSC. *See* Health Care Service Corporation
H.D. Lee (jeans) A1474
H.D. Vest (financial planner) A1508
HDM Worldwide W198
H. E. Butt Foundation P224
H. E. Butt Grocery Company E313, P**224**-P**225**, P627
Head & Shoulders shampoo A1164, A1165
HeadHunter.NET (job Web site) A832, A1402
Headley, Richard D. A1009, P365
Heads and Tails animal cheese crackers A815
Headwaters Agreement (1966) A930
Headway Technologies, Inc. W572
Heafner Tire Group, Inc. P518, P628
Healey-Sedutto, Mary P570
Health Alliance Plan P630
Health Benefits America A204
Health Care and Retirement Corporation of America A908, A1074
Health Care Property Investors, Inc. E211
Health Care Service Corporation P86, P**226**-P**227**, P628
Health Care Supply Management A946
Health Choice P637
Health Group, Inc. A1074
Health Insurance Plan of Greater New York P628
Health Maintenance Life, Inc. A1081
Health Midwest P629
Health Net, Inc. A84, A**696**-A**697**
Health Network of Southern California A1506
Health Pride brand A671
Health Services Plus A155
Health Systems Design A1112
Health Systems International A696, A1506
HealthCare Equipment P706
Healthcare Informatics (magazine) A945
Healthcare Oklahoma, Inc. A695
Healthcare Plus (prescriptions by mail) A1492
Healthcare Realty Trust Inc. E211
Healthcare Solutions Group A98, W444
Healthcare Staffing Solutions E111, E277
Healthcare Ventures (venture capital) E193

Healtheon A956
Healtheon/WebMD A698, W390
HealthExtras, Inc. A1440, E211
HealthGuard A717, P235
HealthLabs A730
HealthReach PPO P694
HealthRider fitness equipment P637
Healthsource A360, A1076
HEALTHSOUTH Corporation A322, A**698**-A**699**, E211
Healthspec paint A1278
Healthtex playwear A839, A1474, A1475
HealthTrust A694
HealthWays, Inc. A323
HealthWest Foundation A1080
Healthy Choice foods A409, A510, A816
Healthy Econa cooking oil W309
Healthy Horizons brand A1135
Healthy USA brand A1109
Healy, Bernadine P. P44
Healy, Bridget M. A245
Healy, James P. A449
Healy, L. Russell P239
Healy, Robert A772
Hear Music (music retailer) A1326
Heard, William, Sr. P555
Heard, William T. P555
Hearl, Peter R. A1405
Hearn, Grant W259
Hearn, Timothy J. A577
Hearne, Graham J. W241
Hearne, Samuel W270
Hearst Castle P228
The Hearst Corporation A60, A80, A506, A568, A**700**-A**701**, E212, P32, P218, P**228**-P**229**, P248, P332, P605, P625, P629
Hearst, George A700, P228
Hearst, George R., Jr. A701, P229
Hearst, Randolph A. A700, P228
Hearst Realties A701
Hearst, William Randolph A700, A1020, E212, P228
Hearst-Argyle Television, Inc. E212, P228, P229, P629
HEART, MOON, STAR brand clothing E176
Heart Rhythm Technologies A674
Heart Technology A282
Heartbeat Theater (radio and TV shows) P426
Hearth Technologies Inc. (fireplaces) A726
Hearthside Homes E169
Heartland Capital Management, Inc. A593
Heartland Home Health Services A908
Heartland Homes A346
Heartland Industrial Partners A388, A1316, P452, P673, P733
Heartland Partners, L.P. E212
Heartport (surgery equipment) A800

Heartstream (defibrillator) A98
Heasley, Philip G. A231
Heatcraft A864
Heath candy A709
Heath, Richard W. A1415
Heathrow Airport (London) W344, W518
Heatilator fireplaces A726
Heat-N-Glo fireplaces A726
Heaton, John D. E248
Heatwole, Davis G. A1437
Heaven's Gate (movie) A962
H-E-B supermarkets P224, P225, P627
Heberling, David C. A909
Heberstreit, James B. P549
Hebert, Walter P127
Hebrew National foods A409
Hebron, Robert J. P371
Hechinger hardware stores A830
Hecht, Louis A. A983
Hecht, William F. A1154, A1155
Hecht's & Strawbridge's department stores A932
Heck, David R. A1551
Heck, John M. P724
Heckel, Gary A465
Hecker, David A1247, P433
Heckler & Koch P132
Heckman, Alton D., Jr. E297
Heckman, James P496
Hecktman, Harry A1430
Hector, Hans-Werner W516
Hedberg, Jeffrey A. W205
Hedfors, Bo A991
Hedges, William W240
Hedley, Mark F. A1541
Hedstrom (bicycles) A294
Hedstrom Corporation (playground equipment) A715, P233
Heekin Can A224
Heekin, James R., III A773
Heep, Don M. A1375
Heerema Offshore A940
Heerssen, Gary O. A82
Heet, Nancy P568
Hefes, Sylvain A661
Heffington, Joe P563
Heffner, Ralph P38
Heffner, Timothy D. E206
Heflin, Rob P393, P700
Hefner, Thomas L. E194
Heftel Broadcasting A372
Hefty plastic bags A1368
Hegarty, Michael W105
Hegarty, William F. Barry A503
Hegdal, Barbara D. A315, P97
Heggessey, Lorraine W145
Heggie, Colin P258
Hegi, Frederick B., Jr. A1431, P518, P519, P774
Hehir, Michael P408, P409, P711
HEICO Corporation A748, E**67**, E212
Heid, Werner T. A778, A779
Heide jujubes candy A709

Heidelberger Druckmaschinen AG (printing presses) W190, W191, W504
Heidelberger Zement AG W201
Heidemann, Lyle A1265
Heiden, Nancy E262
Heiden, Paul W497
Heidtke, Brian J. A387
Heifetz pickles A467
Heights Funeral Home A1268
Heijn, Albert W498
Heikkonen, Mikko W407
Heil Beauty Supply A108
Heilala, John A. A1485
Heilborn, Erik W585
Heilemann, Wilhelm W368
Heilig, W. A. A702
Heiligbrodt, William A1268
Heilig-Meyers Company A**702**-A**703**
Heilman, Leigh P59, P546
Heil-Quaker A1520
Heim Plan-Uternehmensgruppe (nursing homes) A1340
Heim, Tamara L. A277
Heimann (optoelectronic devices) A1110
Heimbold, Charles A., Jr. A290, A291
Hein, Richard J. W435
Heine, Charles F. A461
Heineken, Alfred W254
Heineken beer W231
Heineken, Gerard W254
Heineken, Henri Pierre W254
Heineken N.V. P746, W**254**-W**255**
Heineman, Benjamin W., Jr. A647
Heinemann brand A527
Heinemann Electric (circuit breakers) A526
Heinemann, Robert F. A677
Heinen, Nancy R. A187
Heinicke Instruments (lab products) E67
Heinkele, Harry J. A397
Heinrich, Claus E. W517
Heinrich, Dan A375
Heinrich Heine (clothes and household goods) W426
Heinsen, Hans H. P727
Heinsohn, Tom A280
Heintz, Frank O. A425
Heintz, Joseph E. A841, P287, P654, W325
Hein-Werner (collision repair equipment) A1294
Heinz, Curt P589
Heinz, Frederick A722
Heinz, Henry J. A722
Heinz, John A722
Heinze, Fritz W66
Heipt, J. Dennis P439
Heisen, JoAnn H. A801
Heisler, Robert B., Jr. A823
Heisse Tasse soups A316
Heivly, Chris P409

Heizer Center for Entrepreneurial Studies P379
Hekmann bakery A814
Held, John P563
Held, Valerie T. A1459
Heldman, Paul W. A845
Heldreth, Nick E. A687
Heldt, Jürgen A1003
Helen Keller International P78, P79
Helena Rubinstein (cosmetics) A386, W342, W343
Helene Curtis salon products W534, W618
Helfer, Michael S. A1009, P365
Helford, Irwin A1057
Helfrich, Thomas E. A823
Helicon (cable) A350
Hélie, Claude W471
Helios diagnostic image recording A1148
Helix Technology Corporation E213
Hella Aerospace GmbH A662
Hella KG Hueck & Company A662
Heller Financial A646
Heller, George J. W270, W271
Heller, Jeffrey M. A539
Heller, Marita P325, P668
Heller, Maurice P581
Heller, Preston A1140
Heller, Shlomo W323
Hellerstein, Mark A. E282
Helliesen, Ida W411
Hellmann's mayonnaise W618, W619
Hellmuth, Steve P355
Hello Kitty cartoon character (products) A295, E198, W534
Hellrung, Stephen A. A893
Hellström, Kurt W220, W221
Helm, Robert W. A1045
Helm, Scott B. E258
Helm, Steven M. A123
Helms, Bob (SEMATECH) P444, P445, P726
Helms, Neil P147
Helms, Robert W. (Wachovia) A1487
Helmsley Enterprises, Inc. P**230**-P**231**, P629
Helmsley, Harry P230, P629
Helmsley, Leona P230, P231, P629
Helmsley-Noyes P230
Helmsley-Spear P230
Helsby, Keith R. A1019, P375, P688
Helsel, Steve A465
Helsham, Tony W633
Helton, Mike P681
Helton, Sandra L. A1361
Helton, Tom A1431
Helvetia Complex A417
Helwick, Christine P99
Helwig, David R. (Exelon) A571
Helwig, David S. (WellPoint Health) A1507
Hely Group A1292
HemAssist A236
Hembree, R. Michael P705

Hemet Federal Savings and Load A1364
Heminger, Gary R. P664
Hemingway, Jon P737
Hemisphere Records recording label W213
Hemmady, Gokul A71
Hemp, J. Michael A879
Hemp, Peter W. A71
Hempel, Peter A635
Hempker, Carol E74, E222
Hempstead, George H., III A975
Hempstead, Peter R. A1527
Hemsley, Michael C. P115
Hemsley, Stephen J. A1435
Henderson, Alan C. E111, E277
Henderson Brothers E230
Henderson, Bruce P94, P559
Henderson, Campbell A. A1525
Henderson, Denys W472
Henderson, Frederick A. A651
Henderson, George W., III A306, A307
Henderson Global Investments W88, W89
Henderson, Greg P299
Henderson, Harold R. P357
Henderson, James A456
Henderson, J. Maarten W503
Henderson, Sherman P764
Henderson, Thomas K. A115
Henderson, William J. A1428, P490
Hendrick Automotive Group P630
Hendricks, Diane P537
Hendricks, James R., Jr. A515
Hendricks, John S. P158, P159, P594
Hendricks, Kenneth A. P537
Hendricks, Patrick C. J. W643
Hendrickson, Juanita E290
Hendrickson, Lee W. E171
Hendrix, Jimi P510
Hendrix, John L. E186
Hendrix, L. Stephen E80
Hendrix Wire & Cable, Inc. P313
Hendry, Andrew D. A387
Hendry, Robert W. A651
Hendry, Stephen J. A963
Hengerer's department store A932
Hengesbaugh, Bernard A379
Hengstler GmbH A462
Henick, Arthur P319
Henikoff, Leo M. P719
Henk, Larry D. A123
Henkel & Cie (detergent) W256
Henkel, Fritz W256
Henkel, Herbert L. A754, A755
Henkel KGaA A374, A386, A486, A530, A704, W256-W257, W322
Henkel, Konrad W256
Henkel, Robert J. P57
Henkel, Thomas R. A413
Henkel-Ecolab A530
The Henley Group A600
Henley, Jeffrey O. A1067
Henley-in-Arden manor P26

Henmi, Toshie W299
Henner, Dennis J. A641
Hennessy cognac W348, W349
Hennessy, Edward A728
Hennessy Industries Inc. (tools and components) A463
Hennessy, John P456, P457, P735
Hennessy, Richard W348
Hennessy, Sean P. A1279
Hennessy, Tim A329, P109, P567
Henney, Christopher E71
Hennig, Dieter W595
Hennigan, Thomas R. A1149
Henning, George T. A897
Henningesn, Arthur E., Jr. A531
Henredon furniture P298, P659
Henri Bendel clothing A876, A877
Henrikson, C. Robert A965
Henry and David stores P608
Henry, David C. (S.C. Johnson) A1247, P433
Henry, David J. (Logitech) W339
The Henry Ford Health Sciences Center Research Institute P630
Henry Ford Health System P630
Henry Heide (confectionery products) A708
Henry, Jack (Big Y Foods) P554
Henry, J. E. P413
Henry, John W. "Jack" (Jack Henry & Associates) E77
Henry Jones (food) W230
Henry, Joseph P451
Henry, Leonard & Thomas, Inc. (pipes) A1458
Henry, Michael E. E77, E225
Henry, Mitch A85
Henry Morgan department stores W270
Henry, Patsy P473
Henry, Richard P29
Henry, Robert K. A687
Henry, Rona Smyth P715
Henry, Suzanne P696
Henry Tate & Sons W568
Henry W. Brown and Company P480
Henry Weinhard's beer P428
Henschel, Laurel P447, P730
Hensel, Fritz W73
Hensel Phelps Construction Company P630
Henshall, Donald E80
Hensleigh, Eleo A61
Henthy Realty A144
Henwood, Stephen W111
Heparin drug W416
Hepburn, Audrey A974, A1384, W252
Her Tae-Hak W509
The Herald (Everett, WA) A1502
Heralds of Liberty A1390
The Herb Chambers Companies P631
Herb Coca-Cola A384, P577
Herb, Marvin J. P577
Herb, Robert R. A83

Herbal Care hair care A217
Herbal Essences hair care A290, A1164
Herbco Enterprises (bottlers) A384
Herberger's department stores A1238
Herbert, C. Theodore A1361
Herbert, Gavin A118
Herbert, Gavin S., Jr. A118, A119
Herbert H. Lehman College P129
Herbert, Janice E264
Herberts (can coatings) A534
Herb-Ox bouillon A730, A731
HERC. See Hertz Equipment Rental Corporation
Herceptin drug A640, A641, W492
Hercules Aircraft and Electronics Group A662
Hercules Inc. A120, A522, A704-A705
Hercules Powder A704
Herczeg, Fred P275
Herd, Alan E271
Grupo Herdez, S.A. de C.V. (Mexican food) A730, A731
Herdt, Robert W. P415
Heredia, Paul P753
Heritage Air Systems, Inc. A545
Heritage Bathrooms A920
Heritage Commerce Corporation E213
Heritage Communications A390
Heritage Financial Corporation E213
Heritage (salmon) W244
Heritage sports apparel W62
Heritage Valley (chickens) A1418
Heritage wines A422
Herl family W310
Herley Industries, Inc. E68, E214
Herlihy, Donagh A1527
Herlihy, Michael H. C. W279
Herman, Alexis M. P389
Herman, Donald G. E259
Herman, Joan E. A1507
Herman, Michael F. A393
Herman Miller, Inc. A706-A707, P222, P627
Herman, Mindy A391
Herman, Mitchell E159
Hermans sporting goods stores A1536
Hermelin, Paul W161
Hermes Express Package W426
Hermundslie, Palmer A952
Hernández Garcia, Rafael W579
Hernandez, Carlos M. A607
Hernandez, Robert M. A1461, A1463
Hernandez, William H. A1153
Herning Enterprises A1512
Héroult, Paul W432
Herramientas Eurotools SA A1294
Herrell, John H. P325
Herres, Robert T. A1452, P502, P503
Herrhausen, Alfred W200

Herrick, Dennis R. P773
Herring, Douglas G. A165
Herring, J. Andrew A1349
Herring, Leonard A892
Herrman, Ernie A1389
Herrmann, Rudolf J. A503
Herrmann, Susan A331
Herron, Jay P575
Hershberg, Howard P651
Hershenson, Jay P129
Hershey Foods Corporation A386,
  A**708**-A**709**, A914, P314, P424,
  P620, P665, P719, W154
Hershey, Milton A708
Hershman, Lawrence C. P495
Herter, Ulrich G. V. W143
Hertie department stores W310
Hertie Waren-und Kaufhaus W310
Herting, Robert P389
Hertog Jan beer W289
Hertz, Barry E221
The Hertz Corporation A212, A300,
  A616, A**710**-A**711**, A1420, P178,
  P545, P666
Hertz Equipment Rental
  Corporation A710
Hertz, John A710
Hertz Penske Truck Leasing A710,
  P390
Herwald, Kurt A1310
Herzog, David K. A415
Herzog, Doug A622
Herzog Heine Geduld A960
Hesabi-Cartwright, Sonya A529
Heschel, Michael S. A845
Hess department stores A1238
HESS gas stations A132
Hess, John B. (Amerada
  Hess) A132, A133
Hess, John C. (Engelhard) A551
Hess, John L. (Baylor Health
  Care) P551
Hess, Karl-Heinz W517
Hess, Leon A132
Hess Oil and Chemical A132
Hess, Philip W185
Hess, Steven C. P87
Hesse, Richard A64, P30
Hesser, Greg P649
Hessler, Pierre W161
Hesslewood Nursing & Residential
  Care Home A1340
Hesston farm equipment A96, A97
Hester, Jim G. A1145
Hester, Randy P127
Hester, Stephen A. M. A449
Heston, Charlton P378
Het Nieuwsblad van het Zuiden
  (publishing) W626
Het Spectrum (publishing) W626
Hetherington, Graham C. W85
Hetherington, John W. A1517
Hettinga, David A851, P289
Hetzer, G. Scott A499
Heublein (liquors) W206
Heudebert biscuits W193
Heuer, Alan J. A925, P323

Heuer, John J. P759
Heule, Hal M. A139
Hevas (automotive tubes) P310
Hevelhorst, Richard P. A347
Hevey, John A. A683
Hewes, Philip A. A393
Hewitson, Curtis E208
Hewitt Associates LLC P631
Hewitt, Nancy E270
Hewitt, Pamela A1181
Hewitt, R. Lance E247
Hewitt, Ted P631
Hewitt, William A468
Hewlett, William A98, A712, P456
Hewlett-Packard Company A54,
  A76, A98, A170, A392, A398, A400,
  A472, A524, A674, A**712**-A**713**,
  A746, A747, A760, A778, A782,
  A870, A982, A1050, A1142, A1184,
  A1186, A1256, A1284, A1298,
  A1336, A1357, A1358, A1424, E31,
  E106, E190, E206, E239, E257,
  E261, E262, E269, E281, E284,
  E297, P136, P137, P430, P444,
  P445, P580, P667, P726, P740,
  W180, W338, W554
Hexalen drug E90
HEXFET transistors E74
Heybridge (e-commerce) P308
Heyd, Stefan W381
Heyer, Steven J. A383
Heyerdahl, Thor P408
Heying, Gregory C. A1349
Heyman, Philip W162
Heyman, Samuel P612
Heyn, Christopher P355
Heyne (publishing) W107
Heyward, Andrew A335
H.F. Ahmanson A1500
HF Bancorp A1364
HFS. See Hospitality Franchise
  Systems
HG Fenton (concrete) W252
H. G. Harrison Company A1348
HGSAdministrators Medicare
  Services P235, P632
HGSAdministration A717
HGTV. See Home & Garden
  Television
H.H. Brown Shoe Company,
  Inc. A252
H.H. Cutler sports wear A1474
H.H. Scott consumer
  electronics E58
Hi & Dri deodorant A1201
Hi Brows (cards) A146
Hi Ho crackers A815
Hiatt, Jonathan P35
Hibbard, Spencer, Bartlett A1410,
  P484
Hibernia (coal) W218, W460
Hi-C fruit drinks A385
HICA Holding A1448
Hickerson, John T. A381
Hickey, Dennis J. A387
Hickey, Nancy A1335
Hickey, Patrick A1325

Hickey, William A. (Kemper
  Insurance) P269
Hickey, William V. (Sealed
  Air) A1262, A1263
Hickey-Freeman men's
  clothes A690, A691
Hickman, William E. A175
Hickory brand furniture A630
Hickory Farms A276
Hicks Communications A714, P232
Hicks, Deborah P626
Hicks, Ken C. A1092, A1093
Hicks, Larry A1285
Hicks, Muse, Tate & Furst
  Inc. A148, A372, A408, A470,
  A**714**-A**715**, A836, P**232**-P**233**,
  P282, P412, P631, P712, W84,
  W148
Hicks, R. Steven P351
Hicks, Steven A714, P232
Hicks, Thomas O. A372, A714,
  A715, P232, P233, P631
Hicks, Weston M. A357
Hi-Cone A748
Hidalgo, Hugo E185
Hidden Valley salad dressings A374,
  A375
Hidroeléctrica del Cantábrico,
  S.A. A1416, W209
Hiemenz, Duane E. A969
Hiemstra, Michael J. A1089
Hi-Fert (fertilizer) W640
HiFi buys stores E306
Hi-Fi Choice (magazine) W238
hifi.com W180
Higashi, Tetsuro W600, W601
Higashiyama, Yoshihiko W369
Higbee's department stores A490,
  P172
Hige, Dan P443
Higgins, Arthur J. E199
Higgins, James P. A625
Higgins, John J. (Hughes
  Electronics) A737
Higgins, John L. (Connetics) E184
Higgins, Michael J. A787
Higgins, Robert J. A603
Higginson, Andrew T. W591
Higgs, Jim D. E203
High Speed Access (Internet
  services provider) A350, P510
High, Thomas W. A1121
Highfield, Ashley W145
HighGround Systems A1342
Highland Appliance A254
Highland Capital Holding A794
Highland Distillers Limited A618
Highland House furniture A630
Highland Mist Scotch A423
Highland, Nick A1079
Highlander, Sharon F. A643
Highlander vehicle W615
Highlands Gold W452
Highlands Parts
  Manufacturer A1406
Highmark Inc. A**716**-A**717**,
  P**234**-P**235**, P632

HighRoad software A543
Hightower, Herma P451
Hightower, Jack D. E272
Hightower, Wanda Morris P363
Highway One P73
Higuchi, Kokei W597
HIH Insurance Limited A172, P48, W90
Hijuelos, Oscar P128
Hikaru, Utada (performer) W213
Hilander supermarkets A845
Hilber, Stefan P. W185
Hilbert, Colette P114
Hilbert, Stephen A414
Hilbrant, Veronica E209
Hilburn, Julius C. A821
Hildebrand, Phillip J. A1017, P371
Hildebrandt, E. Scott E73, E220
Hildenbrand, Wilt A313
Hildreth, Matt A607
Hiler, Edward A. P471
Hilfiger Athletics fragrance A564, A565
Hilfiger, Thomas J. A564, W606, W607
Hilfigerwear W606
Hilite Industries, Inc. A1320
HI-LITER A210
Hill, Adrian R. A735
Hill, Alan J. A431
Hill and Knowlton, Inc. (public relations) W646, W647
Hill, Barbara B. A361
Hill Brothers stores A1092
Hill, Charlie W. P655
Hill, Christie A. A1027
Hill Country Fare brands P225
Hill, David A623
Hill, Dean E. A191
Hill, Douglas E. P261
Hill, F. Trent, Jr. A1303
Hill, George Washington A618
Hill, Gregory B. E221
Hill, Herbert W., Jr. A373
Hill, Holliday, Connors, Cosmopulos A772
Hill, James A308
Hill, John A944
Hill, Kenneth A335
Hill, Kevin R. A1077
Hill, Mark C. A1189
Hill, Michael D. A1155
Hill, Otis P129
Hill, Paul J. (Yankee Candle Company) E143
Hill, Paul W. (Austin Industries) P547
Hill Phoenix (commercial refrigeration) A502
The Hill Publishing Company A944
Hill, Richard D. P726
Hill, Robb B. A1163
Hill, Stephen F. (PeopleSoft) A1099
Hill, Stephen (Pearson) W431
Hill, Steven R. (Weyerhaeuser) A1519
Hill Stores A1532

Hill, Thompson, Magid & Company (OTC trading) E132, E306
Hill, Vada A581
Hill, Vernon W., II E182
Hill, William D. A1323
Hillblom, Larry Lee A484
Hillebrand, Rainer W427
Hillenbrand, Daniel A. A718, A719
Hillenbrand, George A718
Hillenbrand Industries, Inc. **A718-A719**
Hillenbrand, John A. A718
Hillenbrand, John W. A718
Hillenbrand, Ray J. A718, A719
Hillenbrand, William A718
Hilley, John L. A997, P353
Hillhaven Corporation A1340
Hilliard Lyons A1146
Hillier Parker May & Rowden P120
Hillman, Henry P518
Hillman Minx car W294
Hillock, Michael J. A489
Hill-Rom, Inc. (health care) A718, A719
Hills, Alfred W453
Hill's Cascara Quinine A148
Hills, Lee A832
Hill's Pet Products A386, A387
Hills Stores A158
Hillsdown Holdings PLC A714, A715, P232, P233
Hillshire Farm packaged meats A1242, A1243
Hilpert, Dale W. A1470, A1530, A1531
Hilton, Barron A720, A721
Hilton, Brian A215
Hilton, Conrad A720, A1086
Hilton Group PLC E262, **W258-W259**, W472, W544
Hilton Hotels Corporation A86, A684, **A720-A721**, A740, A1086, A1328, A1420, A1540, E169, E215, P240, P318, P737
Hilton Mystic hotel P318, P319
Hilton Queen of New Orleans (riverboat casino) A720
Hilton, Steven E243
Hilton, Timothy T. A615, P191
Hilton, William Barron A1086
Hiltwein, Mark S. W379
Hilty, Wayne R. E45, E185
Hilux vehicle W615
Hilzinger, Kurt J. A155
Himan, Dennis P. A1393
Hi-Media (broadband communications) A410
Himes, John W. A535
Himes, Lawrence F. A307
Himle, Karen L. A1237
Hinchman, Steven B. A1461
Hinckley, James M. P131
Hinde & Dauch Paper Company A1516
Hindman, James M. A119
Hine, C. Clarkson A619
Hiner, Glen H. A1073

Hines, Charles A. P471
Hines Horticulture, Inc. E214
Hines, J. Susan A909
Hines, Michael P593
Hinfray, François W481
Hinky Dinky Supermarkets A994, P478
Hinman, Harvey D. A353
Hinman, Wayne A. A101
Hinnant, C. S. A1167
Hino Heavy Industries W294
Hino Motors, Ltd. (trucks) W614
Hinosawa, Akira W299
Hinrichs, Charles A. A1293
Hinrichs, Horst A152
Hinsdale Bank and Trust E318
Hinton, James H. P704
Hintz, Donald C. A555
Hippeau, Eric W549
Hi-Pure Chemicals A600
Hipwell, Arthur P. A739
HipZip (audio player) A779
Hirabayashi, Kosuke W187
Hiraide, Isao W375
Hirakawa, Tatsuo W487
Hiram Walker (liquors) W84, W85, W108
Hirata, Masayuki W419
HireCheck, Inc. A595
Hire.com A701, P229
Hires soft drink W154
Hirl, J. Roger A1055
Hirose, Sukesaburo W396
Hirose, Yuji W237
Hirsch, Barry A885
Hirsch, Gary A1094
Hirsch, Joachim V. A1380
Hirsch, Laurence E. A340, A341
Hirschberger, Max W205
Hirshhorn Museum and Sculpture Garden P449, P451
Hirst, Richard B. A303
HIS Eastern Holdings, Inc. A697
H.I.S. jeans A1474, A1475
Hisano, Katsukuni W261
Hismanal drug A800
Hispanic Broadcasting Corporation A372, A373
Hispanowin S.A. W185
Histadrut Labour Federation W322
The History Channel A61, A999, P229
Hit or Miss retail store A262, A1388
Hitachi (excavators) A468
Hitachi, Ltd. A750, A1002, E97, E142, E303, E319, W60, W236, **W260-W261**, W334, W358, W386, W398, W420
Hitachi Maxell A210
Hitchery, Regina W291
Hite beer W163
Hite, Sharon A569
Hitler, Adolf W630
Hitt, Chris A1522, A1523
Hi-Vision Static Pictures W186
Hixon, James A. A1039

H.J. Heinz Company A**722**-A**723**, A1136, A1180, P90, P512, W636
Hjorth, Hans H. A705
H. K. McCann Company A772
HKNet Company Limited W400, W401
HLB Kidsons P206
Hlista, Petr W547
HLX (laser and defense systems) E49
H. M. Spalding Electric Light Plant A1464
HMO Blue New England (managed care plan) P84, P85, P557
HMO International A360
HMO Physicians Health Services P214
HMO Sanus A574
HMV Media Group plc W212
HNB Autor Exchange, LLC A1309
Ho Cho Yin, Davy W565
Ho, Eddie P. C. W267
Ho Ho Doubler lottery game P373
Ho Oh Oolong Tea W315
Hoag, David A896
Hoagland, Ralph A458
Hoak, Jonathan S. A1013
Hoax brand clothing E259
Hobart Brothers (welding products) A748
Hobbs, Gerald S. A67, W627
Hobby Lobby Stores, Inc. P632
Hoberg, Christine B. E256
Hobgood, William P. A1421
Hobor, Nancy A. A1539
Hobson, Mark P443
Hoch, Ira J. A1355, P467
HOCHTIEF AG (construction and engineering) W504
Hock, Dee A1480, P508
Hockaday, Irvine O., Jr. A678, A679, P216
Hockenberry, John F. A1503
Hockmeyer, Wayne T. E90
Hodes, Douglas M. A875, P295
Hodge, Tommy P343, P677
Hodges, Andrew P309
Hodgman Rubber P142
Hodgson, John S. E203
Hodnik, David F. A64, A65, P30, P31, P529
Hoechst AG A504, A534, A834, A976, P280, W102, W116, W118, W278
Hoechst Celanese P238
Hoechst Marion Roussel E89
Hoechst Roussel Vet W72
Hoefer, Stephen H. P39
Hoegaarden beer W288, W289
Hoelter, Timothy K. A683
Hoenn, Dominique W131
Hoenninger, Ron A95
Hoenshell, Craig A212
Hoepner, Theodore J. A1347
Hoer, Michael A. A427, P141
Hoersch, Lori E104, E267
Hoesch AG W594

Hoesch, Eberhard W594
Hoeshen, Wayne L. A1237
Hoey, Anne W. P363
Hoff Companies (composite decking) A890
Hoff, Ted M. W339
Hoffa, James P. P35, P246, P247, P641
Hoffa, Jimmy P246
Hoffen, Howard I. A989
Hoffman, Alfred, Jr. P770
Hoffman, Carolyn E289
Hoffman Corporation P632
Hoffman, C. Steven A753
Hoffman, Floyd G. A1221
Hoffman, Gary W115
Hoffman, Harry A276
Hoffman House sauces A467
Hoffman, Jerry V. E164
Hoffman, Joyce N. A1163
Hoffman, Julie E141
Hoffman, Nina D. P359
Hoffman, Paul (Encyclopaedia Britannica) P176
Hoffman, Paul (Ford Foundation) P194
Hoffman, Ronald J. P299, P659
Hoffman, Thomas F. (CONSOL Energy) A417
Hoffman, Thomas (Performance Food Group) A1109
Hoffman, T. Scott E153
Hoffmann, Claus Dieter W491
Hoffmann-La Roche AG A640, E217, E261, W246
Hoffmann-La Roche, Fritz W492
Hoffmaster paper products P727
Hoffner, John F. A785
Hofius Steel and Equipment A1078
Hofmann, Ivan T. A589
Hofmann, Thomas W. A1345, P738
Hofmeister, John D. W501
Hofstadter, Douglas A130
Hogan, Arlene A1331, P459, P735
Hogan, David M. A117
Hogan, John E. (Clear Channel) A373
Hogan, John P. (Automatic Data Processing) A205
Hogan, Kevin P443
Hogan, Paul F. A603
Hogan, Robert P481
Hogans, Mack L. A1519
Hoganson, Scott A1027
Hoge, Charles R. A755
Hogg, Christopher A. W85, W485
Hogg, Russell A924, P322
Hoggarth, Karen P643
Hogrefe, Michael E. A1271
Hohenberg Brothers A325, P105
Hohnholt, John F. A1467
Ho-Hos snacks A774, A775
Hoiberg, Dale P177
Hoiles, R. C. P611
Hokkaido Coca-Cola Bottling W186
Holberg Industries, Inc. P**236**-P**237**, P633

Holbird, J. D. A1065
Holbrook, Diane E229
Holcomb, Keith A207
Holcomb, Robert J. P767
Holcombe, Tony G. A343
Hold Everything stores and catalogs A1530, A1531
Holden, Betsy D. A842, A843, A1127
Holden, James P. W188
Holden vehicles A650
Holden's Foundation Seeds A984, A985, A1122
Holder, Robert C. A899
Holderness, Howard A794
Holdiam (baths and whirlpools) P284
Holding company depository receipts Index options P47
Holding, Earl P729
Holding, Robert E. P729
Holditch-Reservoir Technologies A1252
HOLDRS. See Holding company depository receipts Index options
Holga Inc. (shelving and storage) A726
Holgate, Randy L. P497
Holiday Companies P633
Holiday Corporation A684, A1408, A1540, E216, E221, E231, P482, W544, W545, W552
Holiday House Travel Center P308
Holiday Inns. See Holiday Corporation
Holiday on Ice P188
Holiday Rambler (recreational vehicles) A682
Holiday (ship) A331
Holl, David P317, P666
Holl, William A. A385
Holladay, Dan P445
Holland America Line A330
Holland America Westours A330
Holland, Colin A841, P287, P654, W325
Holland, G. Edison, Jr. A1307
Holland, Jane E153
Holland, John (Electric Boat Company) A644
Holland, John L. (Vulcan Materials) A1485
Holland, Julie W485
Holland, Larry V. A1255
Holland Motor Express A1454
Holland Tunnel P398, P399, P703
Hollander, Joel E140, E317
Hollandsche Bank-Unie N.V. W56
Hollaway, David E271
Hollenbeck, John M. A595
Holleran, Charles A383
Holleran, John W. A275
Holley Automotive A278
Holley, Jean K. A1457
Holley, Ronald E. A1303
Hollick, Clive W620, W621
Holliday, Chad A534

Holliday, Charles O., Jr. A535
Holliday, K. Roger A1221
Holliday, Susan J. A335
Holliman, Wilbert G.
"Mickey" A630, A631
Hollinger Inc. W**262**-W**263**
Hollinger, William R. A813
Hollingsworth, David K. A1009,
P365
Hollinshead, John P604
Hollis Divinity Professorship P220
Hollis, M. Clayton, Jr. A1177
Hollis, Peter A158
Hollister Company stores A62
Holloman, J. Phillip A365
Holloway, Janet M. A985
Holly, Buddy P188
Holly Farms chicken A1418, A1419
Holly Hobbie (character) A146
Holly Ridge Foods (pastries) A408
Hollywood Entertainment
stores P224
Hollywood Media Corporation A334
Hollywood Park Casino (Inglewood,
CA) E178
Hollywood Park Race Track
(Inglewood, CA) E40, E178
Hollywood Pictures A1496
Holm Industries, Inc. A432
Holman, Currier A742
Holman Enterprises P633
Holman, Joseph S. P633
Holmes a Court, Robert W128
Holmes, Irvin R. A471
Holmes, Jimmy L. A605
Holmes, J. Theodore A105
Holmes, Michael R. P261, P646
Holmes, Roger W357
Holmes, Ronald H. P732
Holmes, Stephen P. A339
Holmgren, Mike A672, P210
Holmlund, Mark W. P385
Holo-Krome Company (tools and
components) A463
Holophane Corporation (outdoor
lighting) A1004
Holschuh, Laura A. A1509
Holsenbeck, G. Penn A1127
Holst, Gregg A. A1499
Holst, James E. P495
Holsum bread A609, A775
Holsum Foods P122
Holt, Allan M. P111
Holt, Alyn E223
Holt, Benjamin A332
Holt, Brian D. A1383
Holt, Donald P586
Holt Hosiery Mills W607
Holt, Janet L. E185
Holt, Richard B. A693
Holt, Thomas W88
Holt, Timothy A. A91
Holt, Vicki M. A1301
Holtaway, Edward P. E49
Holten, John V. P236, P237, P633
Holton Defense (explosives) A522

Holton, Earl D. A1335
Holtz, Clifford S. A1187
Holtzman, Don P178
Holtzman's Little Folk Shop A1470
Holy Cross Health Ministries P115
Holy Cross Health System P748
Holyoke Water Power
Company A1040, A1041
Holzer, Sy A1147
Holzwarth, Robert W. A1465
Hom, James A361
Home Plumber A921
Home Accents brand P77
Home & Garden Showplace A1410,
P484, P485, P749
Home & Garden Television
network A568
Home Baking Company A608
Home Box Office A180, A181, A312,
A1258, P166
Home Centers of America A830
Home Computer Buying Guide
(book) P139
Home ComputerWAREHOUSE
(catalogs) P338
The Home Depot, Inc. A64, A194,
A264, A270, A630, A**724**-A**725**,
A892, A920, A1278, A1410, A1454,
E214, P26, P30, P330, P484, P529,
P612, P672, W276, W376
Home Entertainment
(magazine) W238
Home HealthCare Consultant
(magazine) P611
Home Improvement (TV show) A60
Home Intensive Care A1536
Home Interiors & Gifts, Inc. A715,
P233
Home Lumber Company P655
Home (magazine) A340
Home Outfitters stores W270,
W271
Home Owners Warehouse A1270
Home PC (magazine) W238, W239
Home Planners Scrap Book P50
Home Pride bread A775
Home Products International,
Inc. A1022
Home Properties of New York,
Inc. E214
Home Savings Bank (Thomasville,
NC) E204
Home Shopping Network A872,
A1450
Home Telephone and
Telegraph A1318
Homebase home and garden
stores A262, W300
HomebuildersXchange A340
HomeCare Preferred Choice,
Inc. A259
HomeCentral brand A1264
HomeClub home improvement
warehouses A262
HomeGoods stores A1388, A1389
HomeGrocer.com A130
Homeland salami A731
Homeland Stores P62

HomeLife Furniture
Corporation A1264
Homelite (power tools) A468
Homelux hardware and tools A1023
Homemaker furniture stores A702,
A703
The Home-O-Nize Company A726
Homeplus hypermarkets W590,
W591
Homepride (cooking sauces) A316
HomePride Finance
Corporation A346, A347
HomeReach (home health
care) P694
HomeRuns.com W194
Homes of Legend, Inc. A347
Homes of Merit, Inc. A346, A347
Homescan Basket*Facts A67
HomeServices.Com Inc. (real
estate) E215, P340, P341, P676
HomeShop (online store) W645
HomeSide International,
Inc. W382, W383
Homestead Village Inc. E285
Homestore.com, Inc. A338
HomeTown Buffet P562
HomeUSA (manufactured
homes) A604
Homewood Suites by Hilton A721
Hommen, Jan H. M. W445
HON INDUSTRIES Inc. A**726**-A**727**
Honam Oil Refinery W334
Honda, Katsuhiko W304, W305
Honda Motor Company, Ltd. A286,
A1394, P561, P589, P596, P606,
P630, P631, P656, P717, P731,
P764, P767, W120, W**264**-W**265**,
W362, W402, W560, W648
Honda, Soichiro W264
Honda, Yuichi W601
Hondo (bottlers) A384
Hondo Oil & Gas A482, W340
Hondros, Paul J. A1009, P365
Honey Monster cereal A1181
Honey Stung chicken A1419
Honeycut, Van B. A404, A405
Honeycutt, Kenneth W., Jr. A1005
Honeyman, Michael A247
Honeymead (soybean
processing) P122
Honeysuckle White A324, A325,
P104, P566
Honeywell International Inc. A100,
A120, A220, A404, A526, A600,
A642, A646, A728, A**728**-A**729**,
A846, A1088, A1110, A1138,
A1152, A1190, A1344, A1432,
E128, E273, E286, P66, W150,
W290, W386, W600
Hong Kong Convention and
Exhibition Center P449
Hong Kong Dragon Airlines
Ltd. W565
Hong Kong International Trade Fair
Group W620
The Hong Kong Monetary
Authority W268

Hong Kong Stock Exchange A996, W266
Hong Kong Telecom W152
The Hongkong and Shanghai Banking Corporation W268, W269, W272
Hongkong and Whampoa Dock Company, Limited W272, W273, W564
Hongkong Bank Malaysia W268
Hongkong Bank of Canada W268
Hongkong Electric Holdings Limited W272, W273
Hongkong International Terminals W272
Hongkong Land Holdings Ltd. (real estate) W306, W307
Hongkong United Dockyards Limited W273
Honickman Affiliates P634
Honickman, Harold P634
Honickman, Jeffrey P634
The Honolulu Advertiser A633
Honorcare (nursing homes) A1340
Honse, Robert W. A582, A583, P184, P185, P606
Hood, John C. E79
Hoogasian, Seth H. A1383
Hoogendoorn, Piet A475, P155, W197
Hooghiemstra, Tjerk W445
Hook drugstores A844
Hooker Chemical A1054
Hooley, John H. A1349
Hooper, Horace P176
Hoopes, Carolyn A1189
Hoosier Park (Indiana) E40
Hootnick, Larry A928
Hoover Dam A240, A642, A810, P74, P266, P552, P643
Hoover, George L. P37
Hoover, Herbert P184, P426, P454, P456
Hoover Institution on War, Revolution and Peace P457
Hoover, R. David A224, A225
Hoover, Richard H. P165
Hoover vacuum cleaners A934, A935, P72
Hoover, William A404
Hoover's, Inc. A130, A180, P278, P279, P652
Hope cigarettes W304
Hope Creek nuclear plant A1174
Hope, David P207
Hope for African Children P78
Hope Lodge P41
HOPE scholarships P615
Hopewell Holdings Limited W**266**-W**267**
Hopfield, John J. P71
Hopkins, Curtis P622
Hopkins, John D. (Jefferson-Pilot) A795
Hopkins, John (Electric Boat) A644
Hopkins, John Jay (General Dynamics) A644
Hopkins, John R. (Conoco) A413

Hopkins Marine Station P457
Hopkins, Mark P384
Hopkins, Michael J. A1283
Hopkins, Thomas E. A1279
Hopkins, William A665
Hopkinson, Mark E26, E151
Hopp, Daniel F. A1521
Hopp, Dietmar W516
Hopp, Terry A1515
Hopper Soliday (brokerage) E132
Hoppe's gun care A298
Hopsicker, Michael R. P39
Hopson, Howard A668
Hopwood decision P498
Horace Mann Companies A360
Horace Small (transportation apparel) A1474
Horak, Brent E219, E303
Horan, John A956
Horan, Tom P621
Horchow Mail Order catalog A1014, A1015
Horden, Alan D. A677
Horder-Koop, Robin P536
Horekens, Peter A. A355
Horgan, V. J. A1417
Hori, Keuiro W405
Horiszny, Laurene H. A279
Horizon Air Industries (airline) A106
Horizon carpets A981
Horizon (computer supplies) A653
Horizon (cruise ship) A1217
Horizon Healthcare A1340
Horizon Industries (carpet mills) A980
Horizon Pipeline Company LLC A1031
Horizon tobacco W282, W283
Horizon trash bags A375
Horizon Travel W544
Horizon USA Data Supplies A652
Horizon/CMS Healthcare Corporation A698, A699
Horizons by Marriott Vacation Club A913
Groupe Horloger Breguet W562
Hormel Foods Corporation A**730**-A**731**
Hormel, George A730
Hormel, Jay A730
Horn, Alan D. W495
Horn, Charles L. P565
Horn, David C. A105
Horn, Jerry P406, P407, P709
Horn, Pat E308
Horn, Paul M. A765
Horn, Randall C. P349
Horn, Robert A. W285
Hornacek, Rudolph E. A1361
Hornbachers food stores A1348, A1349
Hornbuckle, Mertroe B. A469
Horne, Ed P361
Horne, George R. A495
Horne, John R. A1010, A1011

Horner, Matina S. A1355, P467, P742
Horne's department stores A490
Hornet tape drive P441
Hornsby's Pub Draft Cider A521, P169
Horn-Smith, Julian Michael W353, W629
Hornstein, Shirley W395
Hornstra, Peter E. A1383
Horowitz, Jeffrey R. A441
Horowitz, Joel J. W606, W607
Horowitz, Zach W625
Horseshoe Gaming Holding Corporation P634
Horst, E. B. W642
Horst, G. Paul A513
Horst, J. Robert A527
Hortarias, I. W385
Horten, Bruce C. E72
Hortex Fruit Juices A1104, A1105
Horton, Alan M. A569
Horton, Daniel E. A1247, P433
Horton, Donald R. A508, A509
Horton, Gary B. A135
Horton, Robert W136
Horton, Stanley C. A553, A556, A557
Horton, Terrill A508
Horton, Thomas W. A165
Horton, Tim A1510
Horton, William W. A699
Horvath, James J. P538
Horvath, Peter P708
Hörzu (magazine) W106
Hose, David A. E287
Hoshino, Toshio W309
Hoskins, Craig T. A769
Hoskyns Group (computer services) W160
Hosler, C. William E37, E173
Hosley, Richard A270
Hosner, Jim A1099
Hosokawa, Koichi P273, P651
Hosokawa, Osamu W535
Hospital Corporation of America A218, A360, A694
Hospital Practice (magazine) A944, A945
Hospital Services Corporation P226
Hospitality Franchise Systems A212, A338
Host Communications E140
Host Marriott Corporation A**732**-A**733**, A912, A1296
Hostess snacks A774, A775
Hostetter, Amos, Jr. A203
HostPro A762
Hot Rod (magazine) A1160
Hot Shoppe food stand A732, A912, A1296
Hot Shots lottery game P373
Hot Topic, Inc. E**69**, E215
Hot Wheels A926, A927
Hotchkiss, William A480
Hotel Astoria W466

Hotel Bar butter P149
Hotel Investors Corporation A1328
Hotel Pennsylvania (New York City) E137
Hotel Reservations Network, Inc. A1450, E215
Hotel Victoria (Johannesburg, South Africa) W552
hoteldiscount.com E215
Hotelia W58
Hotmail A973
Hotpoint appliances A646
Hotray appliance E116
Hotwire bargain air fare A138
HOTZI sandwiches P710
Hotzler, Russell K. P129
Houchens, Ervin P634
Houchens Industries Inc. A836, P282, P634
Houdry Process (chemicals) A100
Houël, Patrick W349
Hougaerdse Das beer W289
Hough, Lawrence A1448
Hough, Thomas M. A1011
Houghton, Amory A434, P164
Houghton & Richards A1386
Houghton Glass A434
Houghton International A704
Houghton, James R. A434, A435
Houghton Mifflin (publisher) P408, W624
Houk, Michael D. A179
House & Garden (magazine) P33
House Beautiful (magazine) A701, P229
House, David C. A143
House, Karen Elliott A507
House, Larry A322
House of Blues nightclub A906
House of Cerruti fragrances W619
House of Fabrics A796
House of Fraser (retailer) W340
House of the Dead (video game) W527
House of Tsang Oriental food A730, A731
House of Valentino fragrances W619
House of Windsor A1458
HouseCalls grocery service P617
Household Finance P600
Household Finance of Australia A1380
Household International, Inc. A734-A735
Householder, Joseph A. A1267
Housemart.com P739
Houser, Ronald C. P679
Housing & Commercial Bank W286
Housley, William L. E98
Houssin, Olivier W77
Houston Astrodome A984, A1122, A1300
Houston Astros (baseball team) P307
Houston Chronicle A700, A701, P228, P229, P629

Houston Comets (basketball team) P355
Houston, Daniel J. A1163
Houston Electric Lighting and Power A1198
The Houston Exploration Company (oil and gas) A824, A825, E216
Houston General Insurance W596
Houston Industries A1198
Houston, J. Wayne A1485
Houston Lighting and Power Company A1198, A1199
Houston Natural Gas A552, A556
Houston Oilers (football team) P356
Houston Pipe Line Company A140, A552
Houston Rockets (basketball team) P355
Houston Savings Bank A1198
Houston Texans (football team) P356
Hovanec, Eugene F. E136, E313
Hovde, Rob P717
Hovensa refinery A132
Hovind, David J. A1079
Hoving Corporation A1384
Hoving, Walter A1384
Hovis, John A215
How to Plan for a Secure Retirement (book) P139
Howanitz, Lawrence G. E124
Howard, Alfred J. E111
Howard, David P. A631
Howard, D. Wayne A767
Howard, Frank M. A653
Howard, Gary S. A873
Howard Hughes Medical Institute A736
Howard, J. Timothy A581
Howard, Jack (E.W. Scripps) A568
Howard, James J. A1543
Howard, John M. (Conseco) A415
Howard, John V., Jr. (Vertis) P507
Howard, John (W.W. Grainger) A1539
Howard Johnson A338, A339, A912, A1296, W282
Howard, Judy W645
Howard, Randolph L. A1439
Howard, Roy A568
Howard the Duck (movie) P303
Howard, William E46
Howard's On Scholls P489
Howdy Doody (TV show) A914, P314
Howe, Barry S. A1383
Howe commercial furniture E202
Howe, Douglas T. P131
Howe, John A1410, P484
Howe, Michael C. (Triarc) A1401
Howe, Mike (Allina Health Systems) P536
Howe Sound (aluminum) W432
Howe, Stanley M. A726
Howe, Wesley A244
Howell, A. Leo A397

Howell, Josh A867
Howell, Mary L. A1381
Howell Metal A396, A397
Howell, Robert E. P359, P683
Howells, Jeffery P. A1357
Howenstine, James D. A1411, P485
Howerton, Steve E299
Howes, William B. A1365
Howey, Bill E315
Howland, Henry W156
Howland Hook Marine Terminal P399
Howlett, C. A. A139
Howmedica (hospital products) A1118
Howmet Aluminum/Turbine Components W432
Howmet International (aerospace castings) A112, P110
Hoye, Donald J. A1410, P484
Hoyes, Louis W. A581
Hoyle, Eric N. A1221
Hoyler, Geraldine M. P117, P569
Hoynes, Louis L., Jr. A149
Hoyt, Charles B. A993
Hoyt, David A. A1509
Hoyt, Larry A276
Hoyt, Robert E. P546
Hoyt, Susan S. A1325
HP. *See* Hewlett-Packard Company
HP Books A832
H.P. Hood Inc. (dairy) P38
HP sauces W193
HPHConnect P626
H. Q. Office International A1056
HR Logic A92
HRB Business Services A680
Hritz, John G. A105
Hron, Michael G. A1361
HRT Industries shoe stores A1092
HS Administrative Services W64
HS Resources A820
HSB Group, Inc. A150
HSBC Holdings plc A596, A960, W114, W146, **W268-W269**, W382
Hsiaw, Henry W387
Hsieh, Haydn W61
Hsieh-Chih Association for the Development of Industry W570
Hsieh-Chih Industrial Publishing Company W570
HSN International A1450, A1451
Hsu, Daniel P273, P651
Hsu, George C. A551
Hsu, Robert C. P385
HT Electric P632
H.T. Hackney Company P635
HTI Health Services of North Carolina, Inc. A695
Hu, Yaw-Wen E121
Huaneng International Power Development A940
Huang, Charles E28
Huang Cheng Eng W541
Huang, George W61
Huang, Jen-Hsun E256
Huang, Robert P740

The Hub department store A578
Hubach, Joseph F. A1379
Hubba Bubba gum A1526, A1527
Hubbard, Gardiner P358
Hubbard, Will R. A469
Hubbell, Fred W287
Hubbell, M. Ward A891
Hubbert, Jürgen W189
Hubble Space Telescope A224,
A882, A1088
Hubble, Webster A258
Huber, David E41
Huber, Hunt & Nichols P635
Huber, J. Kendall A125
Huber, John U. A753
Huber, Joseph Maria P645
Huber, Nancy Bush E316
Huber, Raymond A. P199, P615
Huber, Richard A90
Huber, Rudolph P. A113
Huber, Walt P606
Hubschman, Robyn E137, E314
Huck Manufacturing
(fasteners) A112
Huck, Paul E. A101
Huckestein, Dieter H. A721
Hucklesby, Bruce W. A1159, P401,
W463
HUD. See US Department of
Housing and Urban Development
Hudak, James B. A1435
Hudepohl, James J. A593
Hudgens, Terry A1083
Hudnut, Stewart S. A749
Hudson, Calvin A689
Hudson cars P256
Hudson, C. B. A1391
Hudson Foods A742, A1418
Hudson, Harris W. A207
Hudson International
Conductors A1124
Hudson, James S. A589
Hudson, Joseph A1352
Hudson, J. Patrick A1249
Hudson, Luanne P659
Hudson Management A206
Hudson Packaging & Paper
Company A284
Hudson Pulp and Paper A654
Hudson, Ralph E117
Hudson River Rubber
Company A662
Hudson, Susan Q. E78
Hudson Valley Broadcasting A60
Hudson, William L. A1261
Hudson-Belk stores P76
Hudson's Bay Company A918,
A1090, W270-W271
Hudson's department stores A1352
Huenefeld, W. R. A897
Hueneke, Terry A. A911
Huerter, M. Jane P349
Huestis, Carolyn E37
Hueter, John P115
Huetter, Margie E192
Huff, Danny W. A655

Huff, J. Kenneth, Sr. P29
Huff, Robert C. A1505
Huff-Daland Dusters (crop
dusting) A478
Huffman, Dan P. A165
Huffman, Kenneth J. A1055
Huffy Corporation A1446
Hug, Karin R. W185
Huge, Arthur P673
Huggies diapers A826, A827
Huggins, Stephen R. A663
Hugh M. Woods Building Materials
stores A1090, A1091
Hughes Aircraft A644, A736, E24
Hughes Aircraft Pension
Fund P518
Hughes, Bill P297
Hughes Christensen (oil well drill
bits) A223
Hughes Communications W296
Hughes, Donald R. A853
Hughes Electronics
Corporation A202, A272, A476,
A528, A650, A651, A736-A737,
A1190, W390
Hughes, Gerald T. A1015
Hughes, Howard, Jr. (Baker
Hughes/Hughes Electronics) A60,
A222, A644, A736
Hughes, Howard, Sr. (Baker
Hughes) A222
Hughes, Joe P112
Hughes, Lawrence A485
Hughes, Louis R. A882
Hughes, Michael H. A689
Hughes, Patricia E192
Hughes, Robert S., II A113, P535
Hughes Shirley A343
Hughes Space and Communications
(satellite manufacturing) A736
Hughes, Timothy W. A443, P147
Hughes Tool A222
Hughes, William D. A1393
Hughes-Hallett, James W. J. W565
Hugin, Robert J. E174
Hugo Boss AG A1165
Huhtamaki Oy (candy) A708
Hui, Alex Chi-Ming E263
Huidekoper, Elizabeth P221, P626
Huijser, Ad W445
Huizenga, H. Wayne A206, A207,
A266, A1504, E59, E201, P256
Hukins, Glen E36
Hula Popper fishing lure P170
Hull, Kenneth J. P192
Hull, Stephen F. A611
Hullibarger, Gail R. P720
Hullinger, G. R. A1277
Hulme, Howard P643
Hulme, Philip W. W176
Hulse, Darcel L. A1267
Hulse, Larry E. E295
Hulseman, Leo J. P731
Hulseman, Robert L. P731
Hulsen, Mike P596
Hultenschmidt, Norbert P65
Hultsman, David R. A557

Humalog drug A540, W416
Human Affairs International,
Inc. A905
The Human Drift (book) A656
Human Genome Center P457
Human Genome Sciences W246
Human Resources Kit for Dummies
(book) A1208
Human Resources Services A342
Humana Inc. A90, A178,
A738-A739, A1434, E185, P260
Humann, L. Phillip A1346, A1347
Humbard, Charley P159
Humbert, Gustav W71
Humble Oil of Texas A576, A828,
P270
Humboldt Bancorp E216
Humboldt Bay nuclear plant A1120
Humboldt State University P98,
P99
Humenesky, Gregory A1553
Humer, Franz B. W493
Humiston-Keeling (pharmaceutical
distribution) A320
Huml, Donald S. A1295
Hummel, Joseph W. A811, P267
Hummers, William S., III E291
Humphrey, George A1006
Humphrey Hospitality Trust,
Inc. E216
Humphrey, James, Jr. E216
Humphrey Mine A417
Humphrey, Stephen M. P715
Humphreys & Glasgow
(engineering) A786
Humphreys Manufacturing A278
Humphreys, Neil A767
Humphries, Nancy C. A249
Humulin drug A540, A640
HUMVEE vehicle P712
Hund, Thomas N. A309
Hundley Frank T. A1269
Huneeus, Augustin Francisco A423
Hung, W. H. W229
Hungaria Biztosito W82
Hungate, Alex W485
Hungerford, Henry James P450
Hungle, Terry W413
Hungry Jack brand foods A768,
A1136, A1137
Hungry Minds (publishing) P248,
P641
Hunker, Chauncey A1341
Hunkin, John S. W157
Hunnell, Wayne F. A807
Hunnicutt, John O., III A493
Hunt, Alfred W74
Hunt Consolidated Inc. P635
Hunt Construction Group P635
Hunt Corporation P635
Hunt, Craig A. A1293
Hunt, Ezra C. P704
Hunt, H. L. P635
Hunt, Jack A828, A829, P270, P271,
P650
Hunt, J. Bryan, Jr. A789
Hunt, Jerri L. E139, E315

Hunt, Johnelle A789
Hunt, Johnnie Bryan A788, A789
Hunt Mexicana, S.A. de C.V. A789
Hunt, Ray L. P635
Hunt Realty Corporation P635, P648
Hunt, Robert G. (Hunt Construction) P635
Hunt, Robert J. (AutoZone) A209
Hunt, Sandy E307
Hunter Associates E131
Hunter, B. D. A1269
Hunter College P128, P129
Hunter, Eric E47
Hunter, F. Neal E47
Hunter, Jack D. (Lincoln National) A879
Hunter, John C., III (Solutia) A1300, A1301
Hunter, Larry D. A737
Hunter, Marla P525, P777
Hunter, Milton P387
Hunter Partners A238
Hunter Savings and Loan A144
Hunter, W. K. A744, P242
Hunter-Perkins, Paula A509
Hunting, David Dyer A1334
Huntington Bancshares Inc. A808
Huntington Laboratories (janitorial products) A530
Huntington, Susan L. P383
Hunt's tomato products A408
Huntsman, Blaine P238
Huntsman Cancer Institute P238
Huntsman Chemical Company A1376, P238, P239
Huntsman Corporation P238-P239, P636
Huntsman ICI Holdings W278
Huntsman, Jon Meade, Jr. P239
Huntsman, Jon Meade, Sr. P238, P239, P636
Huntsman, Peter R. P238, P239, P636
Huntway Refining A1466
Hunziker, Erich W493
Huppe bath and shower units A921
Hüppi, Rolf W653
Hurd, Mark V. A1013
Hurd Millwork (windows) P752
Hurdman Cranstoun (accounting) A840, P286, W324
Huret, Jerome P. W413
Hurlbutt, Guy A. A275
Hurley Joseph F. E231
Hurley, Norm A485
Hurn, Roger W247, W354, W355, W465
Huron Hydrocarbons, Inc. A377
Huron (Michigan) *Daily Tribune* A701, P229
Huron Steel Company, Inc. P313
Hurricane airplane W496
Hurry, Dileep E100
Hurst, F. Leon P413
Hurst, Robert J., Jr. A661
Hurwitz, Charles E. A930, A931

Hurwitz, Robert A1058
Husby, Philip G. A779
Huskies of the University of Washington P761
Husky Energy Inc. W273
Husky Injection Molding Systems Ltd. P702
Husky Oil W272
Husky tools A1322
Husqvarna chainsaws W210
Huss, Beverly A. A675
Hussain, Ishaat W567
Hussain, Tan Sri Rashid W538
Hussein, King of Jordan P324
Husserl, Jeffrey E239
Hussman International, Inc. (air compressors) A754, A755, A1104
Hutcheon, Jeff W. A75
Hutchings, Gregory W604
Hutchings, Peter L. P215, P623
Hutchins, Robert Maynard P194, P496
Hutchinson, Larry M. A1391
Hutchinson, R. Kenneth P758
Hutchinson, Ronald B. A87
Hutchison, John W272
Hutchison Whampoa Limited W272-W273, W418, W502
Huth, Johannes A837, P283
Hutschenreuther ceramics W636, W637
Hutson, Michael P. P656
Hutterly, Jane M. A1247, P433
Huttig Building Products, Inc. A446
Huttig Sash & Door A446
Huwyler, Jean-Pierre W185
Huxley, Thomas Henry P176
Huyard, Wayne A1535
Huyler, George E250
Huzl, James F. P630
HVB Group W200
Hwan Duck Yu W335
Hwang, Li-San E128, E300
Hwang Tae-Hyun W455
Hwang Teng Aun W541
Hwang Young-Key W509
H.Y. Louie (company) P243
Hyatt Center Chicago A740
Hyatt Corporation A138, A678, A732, A740-A741, A912, A1216, A1540, E231, P240-P241, P312, P636, P665
Hyatt International P636
Hyatt Legal Services A680
Hyatt Regency hotel P737
Hyatt Roller Bearing A650
Hyatt, Scott D. P255
Hybritech Inc. A243, A985
Hyco International A526
Hyde, Charles "Fritz" (Oshkosh B'Gosh) A1068
Hyde, Charles (Hy-Vee) P636
Hyde, Douglas W. A1068, A1069
Hyde, Henry A218
Hyde, Joseph "Pitt" A208

Hyde, Matt P411
Hyde Park Hotel (London) W306
Hyde Park Market A606
Hyde, Thomas D. A1495
Hyder P.L.C. (water and power) W408
Hydon, Kenneth J. W629
HYDRA-CO A1028
Hydro Agri W410
Hydro Air Industries (spa and pool) A780
Hydro Norsk W410
Hydro-Aire, Inc. (aerospace) A447
Hydrocarbon Resources A310
Hydrocare ophthalmic products A118
Hydro-Electric W522
Hydrox cookies A814
Hyland, Lawrence A736
Hylbert, Paul P655
Hyman, Steven P221
Hymel, Patricia A737
Hyne, Richard M. A245
Hynes, Mary Anne A753
Hynes, Richard A109
Hynes, Toby P624
Hynix Semiconductor Inc. A894, A928, A970, P444, P445, P726, W274, W275
Hyora, Wyatt E85
Hypak syringes A245
Hyper Photo System W158
HyperFeed Technologies, Inc. E70, E217
Hyperion (publisher) A61, A1497
Hyperion Telecommunications A72
Hypermart*USA A1494
Hypnotic (animation) P278
HypoVereinsbank W380
Hyre Electric Company of Indiana, Inc. A545
Hyster Company (forklifts) A992
Hyster-Yale materials Handling, Inc. A993
Hytec plumbing products P653
Hytrin drug A58
Hyun Myung-Kwan W509
Hyundai Electronics Industries Company, Ltd. *See* Hynix Semiconductor
Hyundai Group A150, E248, W74, W188, W274-W275, W334
Hyundai Motor Company A856, P631, W275
Hy-Vee, Inc. P636

I

I. & J. Foods Australia P264
I Can Cope cancer support P41
I Can't Believe It's Not Butter W619
I Love Lucy (TV show) A334
I. Magnin department store A564, A586
i2 Technologies, Inc. A196, A764, E242, W614
Iacobucci, Edward E42
Iacocca, Lee P747, W188

Iacon (sunglasses) E99
Iadonisi, Sally P751
The Iams Company (pet
foods) A1164, A1165, P138, P394
Iandoli, Michael J. P741
Ianna, Frank A203
Iapalucci, Samuel H. P573
IASIS Healthcare Corporation P637
iaxis Limited A518
Iba, Tamotsu W551
IBANCO A1480, P508
iBazar S.A. E54
Iberdola (utility) S.A. A624
Iberia Lineas Aereas de Espana
SA W71, W140, W141, W302
Ibero-American Media
Partners A715, P233
iBidCo (online sales system) A1227
Ibiden Company Ltd.
Corporation W506
iBiomatics (life science
information) P430
Ibis hotels W58, W59
IBM. *See* International Business
Machines Corporation
IBM Global Services A1222
IBM Personal Pension Plan
Trust E167
iBook laptop computer A186
IBOPE International (media
information) A66, W646
IBP Aerospace Group A662
IBP, Inc. A192, A324, **A742-A743**,
A1418, P104, P566
Ibuku, Masaru W550
iBusiness E179
IC Industries A440, A1104
I/C lawn equipment A287
IC Sensors A1110
Grupo ICA A1484
ICA AB (food retailer) W498, W499
ICA Group (manufactured
housing) A346
Icahn, Carl C. A584, A902, A1128,
A1204, A1376, A1406, A1460,
A1462, A1476, E154, E260
ICC Industries Inc. P637
ICD+ clothing P293
Ice Breakers A708, A709
Ice Capades P332
Ice, Carl R. A309
Ice Cream Partners USA A1136,
W388
Ice Cube (performer) W213
Ice Follies P188
Icelandair A1310, W518
Icewhite gum A1527
ICH Corporation A1368
iChain software A1051
Ichiban Shibori beer W314, W315
Ichida, Yukinori W599
Ichimasa, Takeshi W315
Ichimura, Kiyoshi W486
Ichnusa beer W255
ICI. *See* Imperial Chemical
Industries
ICI Americas A956

ICI Americas Inc. A800
ICI Swire Paints Ltd. W564, W565
icimontreal.com W470
ICL (information technology
services) W236, W406
ICM Mortgage A1178
ICO Global Communications A1026
ICO, Inc. A222
iColt (smart guns) P132
Icon CMT A1186
ICON Health & Fitness, Inc. P637
Icon Medialab International
(Internet services) A772
Icos Corporation A540
ICQ (company) A180
ICTV (cable) A350
ICX (trucking) P312
iD8 (marketing) E188
Ida, Yoshinori W295
Idanta partners A778
Idarado Mining A1024
Ide, Geoffrey F. A235
Idea Forest (Web-based arts and
crafts retailer) A796
Ideal Standard plumbing
fixtures A152, A153
idealab! (Internet incubator) A1116
Ideas Publishing Group, Inc. A80,
P32
IDEC Pharmaceuticals
Corporation E217
Idei, Nobuyuki W550, W551
Idema, Walter A1334
Idemitsu, Yasuo W309
iDEN integrated digital enhanced
network A1026
IDEO (computer mouse
maker) A1334
Idestam, Fredrik W406
IDEX Corporation (pumps) A837,
P283
IDG. *See* International Data Group
IDG Books Worldwide P248, P641
IDG Research Group P249
iDLX Technology Partners
(information to financial
institutions) A480
IDO (telecommmunications) W418
IDS A596
iECHO (Internet access to
pharmacies) A155
Iedema, Bert P600
IEM (bushings) P581
Iennaccaro, Louise R. A1091
IEX Corporation E126
iExplore travel portal P358
IFC Holdings A166
IFF. *See* International Flavors &
Fragrances Inc.
IFILM.com (film industry online
content) P166, P511
I-Flow Corporation (infusion
systems) A718
IFN Group B.V. W57
iFormation Group A596
I.G. Farben (chemicals) A576,
W116, W118, W218, W278, W414

IGA, Inc. A607, **A744-A745**, A1348,
A1349, **P242-P243**, P535, P560,
P637
Iger, Robert A. A60, A1496, A1497
Igloo Holdings A298
Ignis car W561
Ignite (Internet protocol) W148
Ignition ATMs E301
iGroup (Internet strategies) W176
IHC Physician Group P640
Ihle, Manfred W63
IHS Group A1112
IHT/Asahi Daily (newspaper) W96
Iida & Company W358
Iida, Masaaki W487
Iida, Takeshi W611
Iijima, Keiji W315
IKANO Financial Services A558
Ikawa, Masakatsu W599
IKEA International
A/S **W276-W277**
Ikebuchi, Kosuke W615
Ikeda Bussan (seat maker) A802
Ikeda, Morio W534, W535
Ikel, Kevin J. A185
IKON Office Solutions, Inc. A156,
A746-A747
IKU Group (auto controls) A526
Il Giornale coffee bar A1326
Il Giorno (Milan) W216
Il Mio Castello Editore
(publisher) W238
Ilardo, Samuel J. A1317, P453
Ilchman, Alice P414
ILEX Oncology, Inc. E72
ILEX Systems (information
technology) A846
Ilford Group A770
i.LINK hard drives A1515
Ilitch, Michael A500, P162
Illich, Jim P552
Illien, Dominique W101
Illinois Bronze A1278
Illinois Central Railroad A1104
Illinois Cereal Mills A325
Illinois Department of the
Lottery P637
Illinois Electric and Gas
Company A136
Illinois Glass Company A1074
Illinois Medical Service P226
Illinois Power Company A518, A519
Illinois Tool Works Inc. A526,
A748-A749, E67
Illinois-American Water
Company A155
Illinova Energy Partners P478
Illinova (utility holding
company) A518, A570
Illova Sugar W568
Illuminater brand A527
Illuminet Holdings, Inc. E217
Illustrator software A76, A77
iMac computer A186
Image Club Graphics A76
IMAGE fitness equipment P637
Image Industries E43

Image Information Products W368
Imagenation (machine vision components) E48
Images copying A1056
Imagica photo processing W167
Imaginarium A1396, A1397
Imagination (ship) A331
Imagine Entertainment P166
Imagine Media, Inc. W238
Imaginet (Internet service provider) A750
Imaging Technologies LLC A748
Imai, Hirokuni W397
Imai, Takashi W399, W401
Imai, Tasuku W235
Imaizumi, Retsu W373
Imaje, S.A. (ink jet printers) A502
imandi.com P511
Imari Eau de Cologne A217
Imasco A458, W142
Imation Corporation A750-A751, A976
Imatron Inc. E218
IMAX 3-D theaters P126, P412, P712
IMC Global Inc. A752-A753
iMcKesson (Web site) A946, A947
IMEC (research agency) P444
iMedium, Inc. (interactive services) A1233
IMERYS A896
IMF Steel International Ltd. A1225
IMG. *See* International Management Group
IMG Hockey Academy P251
IMG/Chase Sports Capital P250
Imhoff, Stephanie P660
IMM Office Systems A746
Immac health and personal care W477
Immelt, Jeffrey R. A647
Compagnie Immobiliere de France W131
Immunex Corporation A148, E71, E218
Immuno International A236
Immuno Serums A1202
Imo Industries Inc. P578
Imo sauces A467
i-mode Internet access W419
Imodium A-D drug A801
IMPAC Group A1516
Impacc brand A527
Impap A770
Impara, Carol P747
IMPATH Inc. E72, E218
Imperial Airways W140, W468
Imperial Bancorp A394
Imperial Bank of Canada W156
Imperial Chemical Industries PLC A100, A148, A534, A974, A1152, A1536, P238, W116, W228, W278-W279, W472, W516, W564
Imperial Eastman P310
Imperial Feather (bedding) A1134
Imperial Group PLC W252

Imperial Oil Limited W66, W280-W281
IMPERIAL plaster A1457
Imperial Sugar Company A730
Imperial Tobacco Group PLC A974, A1242, W142, W240, W282-W283, W652
Imperial Wire & Cable W412
impiric dentsu W199
Import Express A485
IMPRA (vascular grafts) A444
Imprimis (disk drives) A1260, P440
Impulse Airlines W468
Impulse stores A366
IMS Health E181
IMS International (pharmaceutical sales data) A516
Grupo Imsa, S.A. de C.V. W292
Imus, Don E140, E317
In Demand cable television A391
In Focus Systems. *See* InFocus Corporation
In Home Health A908
I/N Kote A1224, W292, W293
In Ku Kang W335
I/N Tek A1224, W292, W293
In the Company of Whales (TV show) P158
In2Focus (contract sales) E261
INA. *See* Insurance Company of North America *or* Istituto Nazionale delle Assicurazioni
INA International Finance Ltd. W99
Inada, Yoshimichi W449
Inagawa, Takahisa W421
INAMED Corporation E159, E219
Inamori Foundation W328
Inamori, Kazuo W328, W329
Inano, Kazutoshi W409
Inaoka, Minoru W299
I.N.C. brand clothing A587
Inc. (magazine) P272
INCA International A504
Incarnate Word Health System P575
Incasso Bank W56
Incentives and Marketing Services A338
Inchbrook Printers W605
INCO Electro Energy A572
Inco Limited A550, W284-W285, W640
Income Opportunity Realty Investors, Inc. E219
INCONTROL software A271
Incredible Universe stores A1188, P196
incuVest A1233
Ind Coope Brewery W84
Independence Blue Cross A716, P234
Independence Gold Mining Ltd. W341
Independent Cooperative Milk Producers Association P148
The Independent Film Channel A312, A962

Independent Financial Marketing Group A875
Independent Financial Network, Inc. E307
Independent Grocers Alliance. *See* IGA, Inc.
Independent Media A506
Independent Millwork P50
Independent Power Producer W602
Independent Television Network W144, W248
Independent Television News W249, W621
Independent Television Service P145
Inderal drug A148
InDesign software A76, A77
Indgjer, Lisa P537
Indian Gaming Regulatory Act (1988) P318
Indian Institute of Science W566
Indian in the Cupboard (movie) A1254, A1255
Indian Packing Company A672, P210
Indian Point nuclear plant A418, A554
Indiana Fever (basketball team) P355
Indiana Harbor Works A1224
Indiana Insurance Company P295
Indiana Jones Trilogy (movies) P166, P302, P303, P450, P661
Indiana Michigan Power Company A140
Indiana Pacers (basketball team) A1286, P355
Indiana Parts Warehouse P112
Indiana University P638
Indianapolis 500 (race) P262
Indianapolis Colts (football team) P357
Indianapolis Monthly (magazine) E198
Indianapolis Power & Light A88
Indigo Hills wine and champagne A521, P169
Indigo LaserOptic system A800
Inditex W426
Individual Bank A394
Indrizo A354
Induserve Supply P485
Societa Industria Meccanica e Stampaggio (auto parts) A1394
Industrial Bancorp A602
Industrial Bank of Japan, Limited W200, W374, W408
Industrial Crane & Hoist A278
Industrial Electric Supply Company A1512
Industrial Equity Limited W644
Industrial Generating A1416
Industrial Light & Magic E103, P302
Industrial Loan Act A326
Industrial Molding Corporation E254

Industrial Park at Elizabeth (New Jersey) P399
Industrial Plus lawn equipment A287
Industrial Publishing Company E102
Industrial Rubber Products A748
Industrial Tire Products A326
Industrias Arga A718
Industrias Bachoco A1132
Industrias de Maiz SA W568
Industrivarden (holding company) W220
Industry Entertainment A772
Industry Software A204
The Industry Standard (magazine) P248
Indx (fiber-optics filters) A792
Inelectra P386
Ineos Acrylics W278
Ineos Chlor W278
Inespal A112
Inet Technologies, Inc. E219
Infab (factory interface) E35
Infergen drug A160
Infineon Technologies AG E161, E229, P444, P445, P726, W536, W554
InfiNet A632
InfiNet (Internet access provider) P655
Infiniti car P633, W402
Infinity Broadcasting Corporation A334, A1476, A1477, E140, E317
Infinity (cruise ship) A1217
Infinity Outdoor A976
INFLO (holding company) A814
InFocus Corporation A778, E**73**, E220, E267
InfoGear A1002
infoMarket service Web site W484
InfoMover software A543
Infonet Services Corporation E220, W502, W503, W585
Info-Next paging service W419
Infopoint W100
Informata.com P68, P69, P548
Informatica Group A404
Information and Communication Union W642
Information and Industrial Systems W610
Information Consulting Group A948, P326
Information Dial W419
Information Partners Capital Fund E100, E258
Information Resources, Inc. E63
Information Storage Devices (recordable greeting cards) A678, P216
Information Systems & Services. *See* Experian Information Solutions
InformationWeek (magazine) W621
OOO Informgaz W243
Informission Group W470

Informix (software) A562, A764, W222
Inforte Corporation E220
Infoseek search engine P492, W106
Infostrada S.p.A. (telecommunications) W214, W352, W422, W628
InfoWeb (Internet service provider) W236
InfoWorld (magazine) P248, P249
Infusino, Thomas A1490, A1491, P514, P515, P768
Infusium hair care A1164
ING Barings (bank) E308
ING Groep N.V. A90, A1162, A1230, A1506, W56, W104, W**286**-W**287**
Ingebritson, Britt P773
Ingenix (information services) A1434, A1435
Ingerman, Mitchell P291
Ingersoll Rock Drill Company A754
Ingersoll, Roy A278
Ingersoll, Simon A754
Ingersoll Steel & Disc (agricultural blades and discs) A278
Ingersoll-Dresser Pumps A676
Ingersoll-Rand Company A96, A220, A676, A**754**-A**755**, A806, P66, P454
Ingevaldson, Paul M. A65, P31
Ingham, Greg W238, W239
Ingle, Arezu A733
Ingle, Donald B., Jr. A363
Inglenook St. Regis nonalcoholic wine A423
Inglenook wines A422, A423, A1204
Inglis appliances A1521
Inglis, Kirk A1171
ING-Principal Pension Company Limited A1163
Ingraham, James H. A681
Ingram & Kennedy (lumber) A756, P244
Ingram Barge A756, A757, P244, P245
Ingram Book Group A232, A276, A756, A757, P68, P639
Ingram, Bronson A756, A758, P244
Ingram, David B. P639
Ingram Entertainment Holdings Inc. P639
Ingram, E. W. P516, P772
Ingram, E. W., III "Bill" P516, P517, P772
Ingram, E. W., Jr. P516
Ingram, Fritz A756, P244
Ingram, Hank A756, P244
Ingram Industries Inc. A**756**-A**757**, A758, P68, P244-P**245**, P639
Ingram, Jack R. (XETA) E142, E319
Ingram, James A. W271
Ingram, John C. (Jefferson-Pilot) A795
Ingram, John (Ingram Industries) A757, P245
Ingram, Larry D. A488
Ingram Marine Group A757, P244

Ingram, Martha A756, A757, A758, P244, P245, P639
Ingram Micro Inc. A756, A**758**-A**759**, A870, A928, A1356, E148, E251, E268, E281, E290, P244, P338, P639
Ingram, Orrin H. A756, P244
Ingram, Orrin H., II A757, P245, P639
Ingram, Peter H. E76
Ingram, Robert W247
Ingram, Sharon D. A391
Ingrassia, Paul J. A507
Ingredient Technology A450
Ingulli, Alfred F. A451
Initiative Media Worldwide A772, A773
Injex (metal injection molding) W530
Inktomi Corporation A1546
Inland Container A1364
Inland Financial Services E162
Inland International A1224
Inland Paperboard and Packaging A1364
Inland Steel building (Chicago) P449
Inland Steel Industries. *See* Ryerson Tull Inc.
Inmac Corporation P338
Inmobilaria Avicola Pilgrim's Pride, S. DE R.L. DE C.V. A1132
Inmont W116
Inn on Woodlake P285
Inne W343
Innes, Jan L. W495
Innes, Roger D. A393
Innodata Corporation E221
Innogy Holdings plc A140, A1542
Innova (satellite TV) W582
Innovasive Devices (sports medicine) A800
Innovation Associates (training) P55
Innovation Telecommunications Image and Sound A686
Innovative Clinical Solutions Ltd. E72
Innovative Engineering (cheese making system) A326
Innovative Marketing Systems P80
Innovative Medical Research A84
Innovative Modular Structures E94
Innovative Systems Techniques E61
Innovative Therapeutics E89
Innovative Underwriters, Inc. P215
Innovex Inc. (consulting) E42
Innovo insulin doser W417
innowave (water purification) P349
Inntrepreneur PLC (pubs) W230, W408
Ino, Masayoshi W421
Inoh, Takeshi W295
Inoue, Chushichi W529
Inoue, Hidekazu W401
Inoue, Masayoshi W369
Inova Health System P639

InPhyNet Medical
Management A322
INRANGE Technologies
Corporation A1320
Inreon Web site W380
Insalaco's Markets A1094
Inserra, Lawrence R. P640
Inserra Supermarkets, Inc. A1491,
P515, P640
Inserra, Theresa P640
Inside Mayo Clinic
(publication) P325
Insight Capital Partners E180
Insight car W264, W265
Insight Electronics E304
Insignia Financial P120
Insilco Holding Company A1022,
P262
Instamatic camera A524
Instantiations, Inc. (software) P511
Instapak packaging A1262, A1263
Instax camera W234
InStent A952
Instinet (electronic agency
brokerage) A1018, P80, W484
Institute for Environmental
Catalysis P379
Institute for Health Services
Research and Policy Studies P379
Institute for International
Studies P457
Institute for Nonprofit
Management P520
Institute for Public Affairs P756
Institute for Research on Women
and Gender P457
Institute of Biosciences and
Technology P471
Institute of the Sisters of Mercy of
the Americas P114, P117, P118,
P119, P570, P706, P730
Institution Food House P535
Instituto Nacional de
Hidrocarburos W482
Instituto per La Ricostruzione
Industriale W574
Inston, Clive W283
Instone Air Line W140
InStore Satellite Network P350
Insull, Martin A56
Insull, Samuel A172, A362, A1034,
A1464, P48, W90
Insuman drug W103
Insurance Auto Auctions, Inc. E45
Insurance Company of North
America A360
Insurance Cooperative Association
of Wisconsin P123
Insurance Partners and Zurich
Insurance Group P268
Insurance Planners P422
Insurer Physician Services
Organization A717
Insyte. *See* Innovative Systems
Techniques
INT Media Group E263
Intabex Holdings Worldwide A492
Intabex Netherlands B.V. A493

Intec Technology E244
Integra car W265
Integra Financial A1000
Integral (publishing) W107
Integral Systems A1098
Integrated Device Technology
Inc. E76
Integrated Health Concepts A886
Integrated Health Services,
Inc. A698
Integrated Information Systems
Group A644
Integrated Material Systems E273
Integrated Measurement Systems,
Inc. (chip testing) E46
Integrated Medical Systems, Inc.
(medical communications
networks) A540
Integrated Micro Products A1342
Integrated Pharmaceutical
Services A696
Integrated Power Systems A1260,
P440
Integrated Solutions Inc. A392
Integres Global Logistics, Inc.
A1206
Integrilin drug A1251
INTEK brand A287
Intel Corporation A82, A162, A170,
A186, A188, A214, A392, A398,
A760-A**761**, A928, A1002, A1140,
A1184, A1357, A1378, A1424,
A1482, A1514, E28, E93, E98,
E109, E118, E161, E163, E182,
E190, E191, E224, E256, E267,
E274, E284, P338, P444, P445,
P662, P667, P676, P704, P726,
W180, W490, W532, W536
Intelig Telecomunicações Ltda.
(telecommunications) A1318
Intelligent Electronics A1058
IntelliQuest Information
Group W646
Intellisystems E127
Intelli-Traxx brand A527
INTELLIUM Systems &
Services W311
Intelsat, Ltd. P640, W584
Interaction office tables P277
Interactive CyberEnterprises P360
Interactive Data Corporation P350,
W430, W431
Interactive Intelligence P136, P137
Interactive Marketplace Cattle E197
Interactive Media W106
Interactive Solution Center W198
Inter-Alliance Group PLC A878
InterArt A679, P217
Interbake Foods Inc. (cookies and
crackers) W244, W245
The Interbank Card
Association A924, P322
InterBold A488
Interborough Rapid Transit P334
Interbrand (brand identity) A1063
Interbrew Italia W254
Interbrew S.A. W**288**-W**289**, W376,
W638

INTERCO A462, A496, A630, P142
Intercontinental Department Store
Group W310
Inter-Continental Hotels &
Resorts W544, W545
InterContinental Life A360
Intercontinental Mortgage A1178
Intercraft home decor
products A1023
Interface Group W548
Interfimo W183
Intergas W504
InterGen N.V. A240, A1277
Intergraph Corporation A1284
Intergroup Corporation E221
Intergroup Healthcare A696
Interhome Energy W280
Interim Services A680
Interkontinentale
Warenhausgruppe W310
Interland, Inc. A**762**-A**763**, A970,
P619, P676
Interlease A.D. W385
InterLink Communications
(cable) A350
InterLink injection system A244
Interlogic Systems (payroll) A378
Interlott Technologies, Inc. P472
Intermark A1130
Intermec Publishing A1160
Intermedia Communications
Inc. A837, A1534, P283
InterMedia Partners (cable) A350
Intermediair (publisher) W626
Intermountain Health Care P640
International Agricultural
Corporation A752
International Association of
Machinists and Aerospace
Workers P35
International Bancorporation,
Inc. A1509
International Biotechnologies A522
International Brotherhood of
Electrical Workers P35
International Brotherhood of
Teamsters A380, A420, A520,
A1206, A1426, A1548, P34, P35,
P62, P168, P**246**-P**247**, P434,
P641

International Business Machines
Corporation A54, A74, A76, A82,
A94, A98, A102, A128, A162, A170,
A176, A186, A270, A274, A336,
A342, A392, A398, A400, A402,
A404, A406, A410, A472, A488,
A538, A542, A549, A712, A736,
A746, A747, A760, A**764**-A**765**,
A792, A870, A928, A948, A972,
A990, A1002, A1050, A1066,
A1112, A1118, A1140, A1142,
A1184, A1186, A1188, A1228,
A1256, A1260, A1264, A1284,
A1298, A1336, A1356, A1357,
A1362, A1378, A1452, A1482,
A1514, E42, E77, E100, E114,
E118, E160, E167, E173, E179,
E190, E191, E196, E210,
E222, E239, E247, E256, E257,
E262, E267, E272, E284, E286,
E288, E313, P54, P92, P106,
P136, P137, P326, P338, P360,
P430, P440, P444, P445, P502,
P510, P580, P630, P662, P726,
P740, W60, W78, W150, W158,
W174, W176, W236, W260, W338,
W394, W398, W412, W422, W448,
W484, W514, W516, W530, W536,
W566, W646
International Car A1078
International Catering of
Massachusetts A1297
International Chamber of
Commerce A172, P48, W90
International Comfort
Products A1432
International Committee of the Red
Cross P44
International Computer
Group W176
International Consortium Bulgaria
AD W425
International Corporate Governance
Program A314, P96
International Dairy Queen,
Inc. A252, A253
International Data
Group P**248**-P**249**, P641
International Data
Management A590
International Delight coffee
creamers A1338, A1339
International Design Guild
(carpets) P568
International Digital
Communications W400
International Distillers &
Vintners W206
International Engine
Corporation A1010
International Family
Entertainment A622
International Fellowship
Program P194
International FiberCom, Inc. E221
International Finance
Corporation W560
International Flavors & Fragrances
Inc. A**766**-A**767**
International Game
Technology E109

International Generating. *See*
InterGen N.V.
International Grocers Alliance. *See*
IGA, Inc.
International Harvester. *See*
Navistar International
Corporation
International Herald Tribune
(newspaper) A1020, A1021,
A1502, A1503, W96
International Hockey League P361
International Home Foods A408,
A714, A1418, P232
International Hydron (contact
lenses) A118
International Labor Organization
Conference P366
International Lease Finance
Corporation A150
International Mail and Messaging
Technologies. *See* ProQuest
International Managed Care E175
International Management
Group P**250**-P**251**, P641
International Micronet
Systems A400
International Milling A768
International Mineral &
Chemical A752
International Multifoods
Corporation A648, A**768**-A**769**,
A1136, A1418, P36
International News Service A568
International Nickel
Company W284
International Olympics
Committee P251
International Organization of
Consumers Unions P138
International Outdoor
Advertising A715, P233
International Paper Company A112,
A654, A**770**-A**771**, A890, A950,
A1368, A1456, P552, P574, W556
International Performance
Institute P251
International Petroleum Investment
Company W424
International Pharmacy
Management E211
International Planned Parenthood
Federation P79
International Public Relations A772
International Publishing W478
International Rectifier
Corporation E**74**, E222
International Red Cross and Red
Crescent Movement P44, P538
International Resources Technology
Association W338
International Rock and Roll Hall of
Fame and Museum P250, P251
International Salt W72
International Space Station A272,
E284, P754
International Specialty Products
Inc. A704, A984, A1122
International Speedway
Corporation E**75**, E222

International Standard
Electric A780
International Steam Pump
Company A860
International Telecommunications
Satellite Organization. *See*
Intelsat, Ltd.
International Telephone and
Telegraph. *See* ITT Industries
International Terminal
Operating A440
International Thomson
Organization W592
International Track and Field World
Championships W572
International Trade
Commission A970
International Transmission
Company A513
International Truck and Engine
Corporation A1010
International Tuberculosis
Foundation P79
International Utilities A1222
International Vaccine Institute P78,
P79
International Western
Electric A780
International Wine & Spirits
Ltd. A1458, A1459
International Wire Holdings
Corporation A715, P233
International YMCA Training
School P354
Compagnie Internationale de
Navigation Aérienne W68
Internationale Nederland Groep.
See ING Groep N.V.
Societe Internationale Pirelli W450
Compagnie Internationale pour
l'Informatique W150
Internet Adwatch E63
Internet & Network Services
Group W260
Internet Capital Group, Inc. A1232,
A1233, E197
Internet Commerce Expo
(ICE) P248, P249
Internet Explorer software A973
Internet Gift Registries A246
Internet Movie Database A130
Internet Security Corporation E96
Internet Security Systems,
Inc. E222
Internet Travel Group P308, P664
Internet World (magazine) E102,
E263
internet.com. *See* INT Media Group
InterNetShip A588
InternetWeek (magazine) W621
INTERNEXT A866
InterNorth (natural gas) A552,
A556
Intero (wheel rims) A326
Interplak toothbrushes P580
Interpoint Corporation
(aerospace) A446, A447, E23
Interprovincial Pipe Line W280

The Interpublic Group of
Companies A252, **A772-A773**,
A1062, P72, W467, W646
Intersil Corporation
(semiconductors) A686
Interspar hypermarkets A1494
Interstate Bakeries
Corporation **A774-A775**
Interstate Distributors P236
Interstate Highway Signs P310
Interstate Hotels
Corporation A1540
Interstate Properties E137
Interstate Select Insurance Services,
Inc. A395
Interstate Stores A1396
Interstate/Johnson Lane
(brokerage) A1486
InterTAN, Inc. A1188, W644
Intertrade (feed broker) P392
Intertype (typesetter maker) A686
Interval Research P510
Interval tobacco W283
Interventional Technologies A282
inTEST Corporation E223
InteSys Technologies A1380
Intevep, SA W439
Intex Oil A1374
Intimate Beauty Corporation A877
Intimate Brands, Inc. **A776-A777**,
A876, W534
Intimate Cherry lingerie A1474,
A1475
Intimate Hotels of the
Caribbean P296
Intracoastal Health System P115
Intragastric Balloon dieting
device E219
Intranet Spider software E311
IntraServer Technology (host
adapter boards) A894
Intrepid Systems (software) A1098
INTRIA Corporation W157
Intron A drug A1250, A1251
Intruder motorcycle W561
Intrusion Detection E114
Intuit Inc. (software) A972, E220
Intuitive Surgical, Inc. (non-
invasive surgery) P454, P455
Inupiat tribe P542
Invensil (ferroalloys) W433
Invensys plc A460, A1074, A1320,
W290-W291
Inver House Scotch A423
Inverness Medical Technology, Inc.
(diabetes care) A800
Inverrary Country Club
(Florida) P131
Investcorp A1238, A1384, P262,
P647, W176, W250
Investment AB Latour W524
Investment Bank A394
Investor AB (holding
company) W210, W630, W632
Investor Select Advisors, Inc. A567
Investors Bank Corporation of
Minneapolis/St. Paul A1444
Investors Bank & Trust E223

Investors Financial Services
Corporation E223
Investors Management
Corporation P642
Investors Real Estate Trust E223
Investors Savings Bank A166
Invirase drug W492, W493
inviso (display developer) P511
IOB (regulatory publisher) W592
IoGold E254
Ioli, Nicholas L., Jr. A671
Iomega Corporation **A778-A779**,
A1357
ION (integrated on-demand
network) A1318
Ioptex Research A118
Iordanou, Constantine W653
IOS Brands Corporation E207
Iowa Beef Processors A742, A1054
Iowa Ham A743
Iowa Lumber and Supply A1090
Ip, Joseph A793
IPALCO Enterprises, Inc. A88
IPC Magazines W478
Iphotonics A1298
iPhysician Net Inc. E261
IPL Energy A518
iPlanet E-Commerce
Solutions A1500
iPower video-conferencing E268
Ippolito, Gary A521, P169
iPrint.com P274
IPSOA Francis Lefebvre (legal and
tax information) W643
Irani, Ray R. A1054, A1055
Irani, Sherry S. E171
Iraola, Manuel J. A1125
Iraq Petroleum W612
Irarrázabal, Bruno Phillippi W577
Irathane Systems (urethane
linings) A748
Irby, Mark R. A1177
Ireland, Anne B. A337
Ireland, Charles A1484
Ireland, James S., III A999
Ireland, Ross K. A1245
IRI (holding company) W78, W554
Iriarte, Luis W577
Iribe, P. Chrisman A1121
Iridio (premedia services) A1218
Iridium Satellite LLC A990, A1182
Iríondo, Ramón A1295
Iris electrical products A431
IRIS Indigo computer A1284
Iris interactive kiosks E83
Iris Power Engineering, Inc. A835
Irish, Charles P772
Irish, George B. A701, P229
Irish Ispat Limited W292, W293
Irish Red Lager beer A78
Irish Spring soap A386, A387
Irish Steel W292
Iritel (long distance, Italy) W574
P.T. IRJA Eastern Minerals A628
Iron and Steel Act of 1967
(UK) W178
Iron Skillet restaurants P701

Iroquois Gas Transmission System,
L.P. A824, A825
Irresistible Ink (handwriting
service) A679, P217
Irritrol sprinklers A1392, A1393
IRS. *See* US Internal Revenue
Service
OOO IRTsGazprom W243
Irvin, John (J.C. Penney) A791
Irvin, John W. (Spiegel) A1315
Irvine Apartment
Communities P252, P253
Irvine, Athalie P252
The Irvine Company Inc. A594,
P252-P253, P642
Irvine, James P252, P642
Irvine, James, II P252
Irvine, James, III P252
Irvine, Joan P252
Irvine, Myford P252
Irvine Ranch P642
Irving, John P757
Irving, Lee G. A823
Irving Smelting A550
Irving Trust A228
Irwin, Brad W155
Irwin, Clark A1419
Irwin, Thomas S. E67, E212
Irwin, W. G. A456
Isaacs, Jeremy A861
Isaka, Sakae W299
Isakovich, Kristina A1383
Isakow, Selwyn P695
Isaksson, Tomas W629
I.S.C. Systems (bank
automation) W422
Isco, Sheldon E70
I-Scream bar P424
ISD/Shaw (banking
consulting) A562
Iselin, John W., Jr. A1243
Iseman, Robert D. A621
Isenhower, Stephen P730
Isetta car W120
Isham, F. Lance A1151
Ishibashi, Mitsuhiro W397
Ishibashi, Shojiro W138
Ishibashi, Tadashi W261
Ishibashi, Takeru W371
Ishibashi, Tokujiro W138
Ishigaki, Kiyochika A1099
Ishige, Katsumasa W599
Ishihara, Kunio W597
Ishii, Kanji P367, P687
Ishikawajima-Harima Heavy
Industries, Ltd. A278, A1052
Ishizaka, Fumito W375
Ishizaka, Yoshio W615
Isis Pharmaceuticals, Inc. A540
Island Creek Coal A1054
The Island ECN A996, A1018, P352
Island (record company) W444
Islands in the Sun (tours) W58
Islas, Alberto W583
Isle of Capri Casinos, Inc. A720
Isle of Man TT motorcycle
race W560

ISO/Health Care Group (consulting) A773
Isomura, Iwao W615
Isotoner A1242
ISP (glass) W506
Ispat International N.V. A1224, **W292-W293**
The Israel Fuel Corporation A1528
Israelsen, Kurt W163
Isralsky, Donna H. A1531
ISS Group. *See* Internet Security Systems, Inc.
ISS Group (security) W524
Issen soft drink W315
iStar Financial Inc. E224
i-STAT Corporation point-of-care testing system A59
Istituto Nazionale delle Assicurazioni W98
Istre, M. J. A1533
(i)STRUCTURE (computer services) A866
Isuzu Motors Limited A650, A1394, P138, P767, W264, **W294-W295**, W560, W614
Isys Controls E43
Isys (financial analysis products) E100
The IT Group, Inc. A610
Italcable (intercontinental telecommunications) W574
Italenergia W208, W209
Italian Originals pizzas A500, P595
Italian Swiss Colony wine A423, A520
Società Italiana Gestione Multi Accesso. *See* Sigma-Società Italiana Gestione Multi Accesso
Italianni's restaurants A328, P106, P107, P108
Italiatour W78, W79
Italseguros Internacional A356
Italtel (telecom equipment) W574
IT&T A1200
Itanium microprocessor A82, A760
ITC^DeltaCom A1248
ITcareers.com P248
ITCO Tire (distributor) P518
Itel A176, A560, P180, W260
ITEQ Europe Ltd. A162
Ito, Kaneo W448, W449
Ito, Kigen W295
Ito, Masatoshi W298, W299
Ito, Mastoshi A57
Ito, Shuji W649
Ito, Toshiaki W409
Ito, Yasuhisa W299
ITOCHU Corporation A744, P242, P254, P574, P642, W294, **W296-W297**, W358
Itoh, Chubei W296, W358
Itoh, Eiji W305
Itoh, Josei W397
Itoh, Kensuke W329
iTouch keyboards W339
Ito-Yokado Company, Ltd. A56, **W298-W299**

ITT Industries, Inc. A60, A212, A312, A572, A584, A688, A720, A774, **A780-A781**, A802, A856, A1328, P332, W74, W76, W152, W200, W220, W386, W576, W578, W580, W626
Ittner, George D. A1315
ITT/Sheraton hotels A1326, W322
ITW. *See* Illinois Tool Works Inc.
ITX Corporation W404
Iucolano, Donna A1255
Iue, Satoshi W515
Iue, Toshimasa W515
Iue, Toshio W360, W514
iUniverse.com A232, A233
Grupo Iusacell A1472, A1473
IVAC (medical instruments) A540
iVAST, Inc. (broadband) P511
Iveco (vehicles) A456, W226, W227
Iverson, Kenneth A. (Ecolab) A531
Iverson, Kenneth (Nucor Corp.) A1052
Iverson, Mark P634
Ives, Charles A986
Ives, Nancy J. P501
Ivester, Douglas A382
Ivey, Joseph M., Jr. A549
iVillage Inc. A442, A700, A701, A999, A1146, P146, P228, P229, P629
Ivory soap A1164, A1165
IVTx, Inc. A574, A575
Ivy, Conway G. A1279
Ivy, Jim S. A1407
Ivy League P134
Ivy Mortgage E293
Iwadare, Kunihiko W386
Iwafuchi, Eric E285
Iwai, Bunsuke W404
Iwama, Yoichiro W597
Iwan, Lawrence M. A527
Iwanaga, Mitsuo W327
Iwasaki, Jiro W573
Iwasaki, Tetsui A189
Iwasaki, Yatoro W370
Iwaya, Katsuya W531
IWC Resources Corporation A1034
iWon.com A1476
IXC Communications A292
Ixia E224
IXYS Corporation **E76**, E224
IY Basics clothing label W298
IYBank W298
Iyer, Balakrishnan S. A411
IZKA lingerie A1499
I-Zone camera A1148
Izquierdo, Armando W439
Izumi, Kazumi W397
Izumi, Kunihide W405
Izumi, Norio A1285
Izvestia (newspaper) W346

J

J. and J. Colman W476
J. Aron Holdings, L.P. A660
J. Baker shoe stores A158

J. Boag & Son (brewery) W510
J. Brannam (off price stores) A1214
J. Crew Group, Inc. A1314, **P254-P255**, P474, P475, P642, P744
J. Eynard (catheters) A444
J. Lyons and Company W84
J. Ray McDermott & Company A940
J. Robert Scott (company) A615, P191
J. Roget sparkling wines A423
J Sainsbury plc **W300-W301**, W590
J. Sosnick and Son P488
J. Walter Thompson Company (advertising) A1172, W646, W647
J. Wix and Sons (cigarettes) A618, W240
J2O soft drink W545
Jaacks, James P730
Jabil Circuit, Inc. **A782-A783**, A802, E191
Jablin, Burton A569
Jacamon, Jean-Paul W521
Jachimiec, Chester J. A549
Jack, Bradley H. A861
Jack Daniel's Grilling Sauce A723
Jack Daniel's whiskey A296, A297, A922, P320, P682
Jack, D. Michael A1361
Jack Henry & Associates, Inc. **E77**, E225
Jack in the Box Inc. **A784-A785**, A1132
Jack Morton Worldwide Inc. A773
Jack Nicklaus products A690, A691, P299
Jack White & Company (discount brokerage) W608
Jackman, Brian J. A1363
Jacks stores A1282
Jackson, Alma A87
Jackson, Andrew A1428, P490
Jackson, Blair A85
Jackson Box A950
Jackson Company A1308
Jackson, Darren A255
Jackson, Dean P463
Jackson Electrical Light Works A376
Jackson, Graham A1100
Jackson, Gregory A. P497
Jackson Hewitt (tax preparation) A338, A339
Jackson, Janet (performer) W212, W213
Jackson, Jeffery M. A1229
Jackson, Jerry D. A555
Jackson, Jesse A626
Jackson, JoAnne G. P755
Jackson, John A. (Comdisco) A393
Jackson, John B. H. (Hilton Group) W258, W259
Jackson, John (BHP Billiton) W129
Jackson, John (Duke Energy Field Services) P598
Jackson, Johnnie M., Jr. (Olin) A1061

Jackson, John W. (Celgene) E174
Jackson, Julian A1084
Jackson, Kathryn A. A1371, P469
Jackson, Lawrence V. A1235
Jackson, Margaret W469
Jackson, Mark W. A529
Jackson, Martin F. E286
Jackson, Michael J.
  (AutoNation) A206, A207
Jackson, Michael L.
  (SUPERVALU) A1349
Jackson, Michael (USA
  Network) A1451
Jackson, Mike (SEMATECH) P445
Jackson National Life Insurance
  Company W464, W465
Jackson, Ralph E., Jr. A431
Jackson, Robert T. P537
Jackson, Roger A. A857
Jackson, R. Wayne P580
Jackson, Stu P355
Jackson, Sue P710
Jackson, Thomas H. P760
Jackson, Timothy E. A1369
Jackson, Walter P176
Jackson, Yvonne R. A399
Jacksonville Jaguars Ltd. (football
  team) A1488, P357
Jaclot, François W559
Jaclyn Smith clothing A831
Jacob Delafon plumbing
  products P284, P285, P653
Jacob Holm & Sons A704
Jacob, John E. A175
Jacob, Paul D. A533
Jacob Schmidt Company A1444
Jacobi Medical Center P369
Jacobs, Annette A1187
Jacob's biscuits W193
Jacobs, Charles P590
Jacobs Chuck Manufacturing
  Company A463
Jacobs Engineering Group
  Inc. A**786**-A**787**
Jacobs Entertainment E165
Jacobs, Franklin A. E202
Jacobs, Gary N. A967
Jacobs H&G (engineering) A786
Jacobs, Ilene B. P191, P609
Jacobs, Irwin (Genmar
  Holdings) P614
Jacobs, Irwin Mark
  (QUALCOMM) A1182, A1183
Jacobs, Jay R. A1131
Jacobs, Jeffrey (Harpo) P218, P219
Jacobs, Jeffrey P. (Blackhawk
  Gaming and Development) E165
Jacobs, Jeremy M. P590
Jacobs, John (Hertz) A710
Jacobs, John H. (Union Central Life
  Insurance) P753
Jacobs, Joseph J. A786, A787
Jacobs, Kenneth L. A195
Jacobs, Lance P752
Jacobs, Louis P590
Jacobs, Marcel W175
Jacobs, Marvin P590

Jacobs Matco Tools A462
Jacobs, Paul E. A1183
Jacobs, Rose E225
Jacobs, Terry S. E277
Jacobs Vehicle Systems, Inc. A463
Jacobsen, Carl W162
Jacobsen, J. C. W162
Jacobsen Manufacturers A1380
Jacobsen, Thomas H. A1445
Jacobson, Edwin E212
Jacobson, Linda E44, E182
Jacobson, Michael R. E54
Jacobson, Richard J. (Cox
  Enterprises) A443, P147
Jacobson, Richard N. (Cooper
  Tire) A433
Jacobsson, Bo W585
Jacoby, Jon E269
Jacor Communications A372, A560,
  A632, P180
Jacqueline Ferrar brand A791
Jacques Bonet sparkling
  wines A423
Jacques Borel International W58
Jacquet-Droz watch W563
Jacuzzi (bath and plumbing) A862,
  A1446, A1447
Jacuzzi, Roy A1446
Jaeger, Connie E231
Jaensen, Stephanie E166
Jaffe, Jonathan M. A863
Jaffe, Kineret S. P497
Jaffe, Robert M. E69
Jaffy, Stanley A. A251
Jagatjit Industries A296
Jager, Durk A1164
Jaggers, Jon A1087
Jagtiani, Anil A679, P217
Jaguar Cars Limited A616, E170,
  P561, P633, P717
Jaharajah, Neville J. A237
Jahnke, Jeffrey A. E51
Jahnke, Timothy J. A1023
Jain, Nirmal W567
Jain, Terri P331, P672
Jakes, John P382, P693
Jakks Pacific, Inc. E225
Jaksich, Daniel J. A253
JAL. See Japan Airlines Company,
  Ltd.
Jallos, Henry A. A407
Jamaica Fruit Distributors A494
Jamaica Water Supply
  Company A544
Jamalcan W74
Jamboree motor homes A605
James, Anthony A1307
James Bond A962
James Capel & Company
  (securities) W268
James, Catherine W207
James, Daniel A1124
James, Delwyn P612
James, Donald M. A1485
James, Donna A. A1009, P365, P685
James, Ellen P501
James Finlay of Scotland W566

James Fitzpatrick nuclear
  plant A554
James Franck Institute P497
James, Gary L. A1313
James, Hamilton E. A449
James Hardie Industries NV A1392
James, J. Bradford A753
James J. Murphy (brewery) W254
James, Julian W337
James Lees & Company
  (carpet) A306
James, Leland A380, A420
James, Michelle E94, E246
James Monroe apartments (New
  Jersey) P291
James North & Sons W290
James P. Ryan Company A1227
James, Robert A. A1399
James, Sharon L. P501
Jameson Inns, Inc. E225
Jamieson, Andrew W523
Jamieson, Douglas R. E65
Jamieson, Ian W85
Jamieson, Irene A. A1215
Jamieson, James M. A273
Jamieson, Megan S. A1215
Jamin, Gerald A. A133
Jamison, George H. A737
J&B scotch W206
jane cosmetics A564, A565
Jane (magazine) P33
Jane's Information Group W592
Janeway, Dean A1490, A1491, P514,
  P515
Janicki, James P. E243
Janitrol air conditioners P618
Janitz, John A. A1381
Jank, Michael J. A87
Janke, Kenneth S., Jr. A93
Janker, Franz A189
Jankowski, Kenneth E125
Jannard, Jim E99, E257
Janney Montgomery Scott and
  Hornor (brokerage) P698
Jannock W252
Jannotta, Edgar D. P497
Janowski, Catherine N. A1015
Jansport backpacks A1474, A1475
Janssen A800
Jantzen swimwear A1474, A1475
Janzen, Howard E. A1529
Japan Advertising W198
Japan Airlines Company, Ltd. A164,
  A484, W79, W80, W**302**-W**303**,
  W469
Japan Air Systems W71, W303
Japan Atomic Energy Research
  Institute W358
Japan COM Company,
  Limited W599
Japan Communications
  Ministry W386
Japan Communications
  Satellite W296
Japan Development Bank W402
Japan Electric Association W598
Japan Fair Trade Commission W418

Japan Health and Welfare Ministry W304
Japan Iron & Steel W398
Japan Ministry of Finance W186, W396
Japan Ministry of International Trade and Industry W236, W260, W598
Japan Musical Instruments W648
Japan Quarterly (magazine) W96
Japan Sky Broadcasting W96
Japan Telecom Company Ltd. W628, W629
Japan Telegraphic Communication Company. *See* Nihon Denpo-Tsushin Sha
Japan Tobacco and Salt Public Corporation W304
Japan Tobacco Inc. A492, A1204, **W304**-**W305**
Japan TransOcean Air Company, Ltd. W302
Japan Travel Bureau. *See* JTB Corporation
Japanese Finance Ministry W304
Japanese Ministry of Communications W400, W418
Japanese Ministry of Posts and Telecommunications W400
Japanese Navy W320
Japanese Sky Broadcasting W146
Japan-Germany Camera Company W368
Japan-US Cable Network A866
Jaques, Fred W289
Jaquinto, Roberto W217
Jarar Carrim W539
Jardieu, Paula M. A641
Jardin de Soleil fragrance A766
Jardine Matheson Holdings Limited **W306**-**W307**
Jardine, William W306
Jardot, Leo C. A149
Jarman, Terence J. W123
Jarrett, Charles E. A1169
Jarrett, Dale P681
Jarrow, Charles A401
Jarry, Philippe W165
Jartz, John G. A1181
Jarvi, Tom C. A421
Jarvis, Jeff A81, P33
Jarvis, J. Michael P153
Jarvis, Peter W638
Jarvis, Roger (King Ranch) A828, P270
Jarvis, Roger L. (Spinnaker Exploration) E292
Jarvis, Samuel A376
Jasinkiewicz, Ken A1491, P515, P768
Jaska, James M. E128, E300
Jasnoff, Jeff E295
Jasper Homes A604
Jastrow, Kenneth M., II A1364, A1365
Java programming language A972, A1342, E22, E33, E159, E210, E245

Java Records recording label W213
Javaanse Jongens tobacco W143
Javaworks brands P546
Jaws (movie) A1088, P166
Jay C supermarkets A845
Jay, John P134
Jaz drives A778, A779
J.B. Fairfax International USA A233
J.B. Hunt Transport Services, Inc. **A788**-**A789**
J.B. Lippincott (publishing) W642
JB Oxford Holdings, Inc. W474
JB Research E116
J.C. Higgins A544
J. C. Penney Company, Inc. A216, A318, A586, **A790**-**A791**, A1012, A1314, A1494
JCI (company) W340
JCPenney stores. *See* J. C. Penney Company, Inc.
J. D. Heiskell & Company W568
JDI office furniture P652
JDS FITEL (telecommunications) A792
JDS Uniphase Corporation **A792**-**A793**
J. E. Dunn Construction P599
Je Jin-Hoon W509
J.E. Morgan Knitting Mills A1242
JE Professional Resources Limited A787
JEA P643
Group Jean Didier W470
Jean, Roger L. A875, P295
Jean-Claude Darmon (sports rights) W126
Jeanne Gatineau skin care A1201
Jean-Paul Guisset (office products) A274
Jeansson, Lennart W633
Jebson, A. W. W269
Jedelhauser, Lilo P61
Jeep vehicles E170, P666, P706, P733, W188
Jeffco Manufacturing A224
Jefferies, Robert A., Jr. A859
Jefferson Electric P136
Jefferson, John P345
Jefferson Properties, Inc. *See* JPI
Jefferson Smurfit Corporation A1292, W506
Jefferson Standard Life Insurance A794
Jefferson, Thomas A1070, P450, P761
Jefferson Wells International (financial services) A910
Jefferson-Pilot Corporation A356, **A794**-**A795**, A922, P320
Jeffries, Michael S. A62, A63
Jeffs, Rohan K. S. W645
Jekel Vineyards A296, A297
Jeker, Robert A. W55
JELD-WEN, Inc. (building products) E304, P643
Jelinek, Walter C. A437
Jellison, Brian D. A755

Jell-O gelatin A842, A843, A1126
Jenifer, Franklyn G. P499
Jenkins, Alan P195
Jenkins, Ben A1487
Jenkins Canada (valves) A446
Jenkins, Charles H., Jr. (Publix) A1176, A1177, P402, P403, P707
Jenkins, Charles S. (Ryland) A1227
Jenkins, Claire W241
Jenkins, David W647
Jenkins, Francis P., Jr. P718
Jenkins, George A1176, P402
Jenkins, Howard M. A1176, P402, P403
Jenkins, J. Michael E168
Jenkins, James R. A469
Jenkins, John C. (Guidant) A675
Jenkins, John J. (Deere) A469
Jenkins, Roger A666
Jenkins, William P661
Jenks, William W. P73
Jenn-Air appliances A934, A935
Jenner, Barry W241
Jennett, Thomas R. P153
Jennie-O turkey A730, A731
Jennifer Convertibles, Inc. (furniture stores) P652
Jennings, Brian J. A483, P361
Jennings, Karen E. A1245
Jennings, Perry G. A893
Jennings Technology Corporation, LLC A463
Jenny Craig, Inc. A238
Jenoptik Aktiengesellschaft E35
Jeno's frozen pizza A1137
Jenrette, Richard A218
Jensen, Dennis G. A1539
Jensen, Jørn P. W163
Jensen, Keith A. A145
Jensen, Loren K. A1189
Jensen, Ronald E113, E280
Jensen, R. Thomas E102
JensenTools A1322
Jenson, Gail P253
Jenson, Timothy N. A959
Jenson, Warren C. A131
Jeopardy! (TV show) A334
Jeppesen, Jon A. A185
Jeppesen Sanderson (flight information) A1402
Jepsen, John R. A451
Jepson, Robert A1004
Jerbasi, James V. A245
Jergens skin care W309
Jerky Treats pet food A723
Jermoluk, Tom A1284
Jerome, Jerry K. A731
Jeronimo Martins Retail W498
Jerrell-Ash Company A600
Jerritt Canyon mine E242
Jerrold Communications A872
Jerrold Electronics A1232
The Jerry Springer Show (TV show) A1450
Jersey Cash 5 lottery game P687

Jersey Central Power & Light Company A668
Jersey Standard A352, A576
The Jerusalem Post (newspaper) W262, W263
The Jerusalem Report (newsweekly) W263
JERZEES (activewear) A1221
Jessen, Lynita A715, P233, P631
Jessick, David A1203
Jessup, Catherine K. E130, E303
Jessup, Jerome M. A635
Jester, John P350
Jet America Airlines A106
Jet Avion (jet engine parts) E67
Jet (magazine) P258, P259, P646
Jet petroleum products A412
Jet Tours Holding W170
Jet-Dry dishwashing W477
JetForm W378
Jetsave travel agency A1478
Jetset Travel A328, P108
Jett, Ernest C. A859
Jetta car W631
Jetway Systems Division A612
Jevic Transportation, Inc. A1548, A1549
Jewel Companies of Chicago W634
Jewel Cube speakers P93
Jewel Food Stores A66, A110, A111
The Jewel in the Crown (TV show) W248
Jewell, John W143
Jewell, Sally P411
Jewel-Osco stores A276
Jewett & Sherman P122
Jewett, Patrick A215
J. F. Shea Company, Inc. P643
J.F. Walker (wholesaler) A1312
J.H. Bachmann (shipping) W594
J.H. Stone & Sons A1292
J.H. Vavasseur Group W620
J. H. Williams Industrial Products A1294
Jheri Redding salon products P580
J. I. Case (tractors) A456, A1368
Jiang Baoxing W543
Jiangling Motors A856
Jiangxi Automobile Factory W294
Jif peanut butter A1164, A1165
Jiffy condoms W538
Jiffy Lube International A1096, A1097
Jiffy Mailer packaging A1262, A1263
Jiffy Pop popcorn A148, A409, A714, P232
JII Promotions, Inc. P647
Jiji Press W198
Jim Beam Distillery A618
Jim Henson Productions A730
Jim Koons Automotive P644
The Jim Moran Courtesy Hour (TV show) P256
Jim Moran & Associates P257
Jim Walter Homes A836, P282

Jimmy Dean packaged meats A1242, A1243, A1296
Jimny car W561
Jin Mao Building (Shanghai) P448, P449
Jingle Bucks lottery game P473
Jini software A1342, A1343
Jinling Dry beer W289
Jinro-Coors Brewery W288
Jinyoung Electric Machinery A1088
Jipson, Victor B. A929
Jiro software A1343
Jiskoot, Wilco G. W57
Jitney-Jungle Stores of America, Inc. A1532, P479, P644
Jitsuyo Motors W402
Jitterbug fish lure P170
Jive Coffee soft drink W315
Jiway A988
J.J. Kenny (municipal securities information) A944
J.Khakis brand P77
J. L. Kellogg Graduate School of Management P378, P379, P691
J.L. Kraft & Brothers Company A842
J.L. Turner & Son A496
JLM Industries, Inc. A1300
J.M. Bemis and Company A250
JM Family Enterprises, Inc. **P256**-**P257**, P624, P644
J. M. Huber Corporation P645
J. M. Jones Company P242
J.M. Lynne (wall coverings) A1334
The J.M. Smucker Company (jams) A608
J.M. Tull Metals A1224
JM&A Group P256, P257, P644
JMB Realty Corporation A1328, P645
JMIC Life Insurance Company P257
JNCO brand clothing E259
JNI Corporation E226
JNY Sport clothing A805
Jo Malone Limited (skin care) A564, A565
Jo-Ann Stores, Inc. **A796**-**A797**, A1058, P632
Joannes Brothers food stores A1348
Job Hunting for Dummies (book) A1208
Job, Peter W484
The Job (TV show) P166, P167, P597
Jobe, Lee A867
Jobete (company) W212
Jobs, Steven P. A76, A186, A187, E103, E266
JobUniverse.com P248
Jochum, Emil P679
Jockey International, Inc. (underwear) A839, P696, W606
Jodie, Kregg P317
Joe & Nemo's hot dog stand A1372
Joe Camel A1204
Joe Isuzu W294
Joe Notrica, Inc. P489

Joelson Taylor (concrete pipes) W252
Joeright, Daniel B. A1007
Joerres, Jeffrey A. A910, A911
Joffrion, John M. E152
Johanneson, Gerald B. P223, P627
Johansen, Jodi A1083
Johansen, Laura I. A85
Johansson, Kurt J. P311
Johansson, Lars-Goran W211
Johansson, Leif W633
John Birch Society A834, P280
John Bozzuto & Sons P560
John Brandon cigarettes W283
The John C. Groub Company P422
John Connell Dickins (stores) W172
John Crerar Library P497
John Deere A96, A1010, A1316, P452, P733
John Elway AutoNation USA A206, P563
John Fairfax Holdings Limited (publishing) W262
John F. Kennedy International Airport P398, P399, P703
John F. Kennedy School of Government P220, P221, P626
John, Francis D. E79, E227
John Hancock Center (Chicago) P448, P449, P476, P730, P745
John Hancock Financial Services, Inc. **A798**-**A799**, E315
John Hancock Mutual Life Insurance Company A1506, E132, P86
John Henry brand clothing E305
John Inglis Company (appliances) A1520
John Jay College of Criminal Justice P128, P129
John J. Nissen Baking A774
John Labatt Ltd. (brewery) W162, W288
John Laing plc (contractor) W358
John M. Bradstreet Company A516
John Miller Electric A545
John Morrell & Company A1290, A1291
The John Nuveen Company A1236, A1237
John Player cigarettes W143, W282, W283
John Rocha at Waterford Crystal W637
John Shillito Company A586
John Smith beer W282
John Swire & Sons W564
John West Foods A722, A723
John Wiley & Sons, Inc. (publishing) P248, W430
The John Zink Company P281
Johnnie Walker Scotch W206
Johnny Blaze brand clothing E101
Johns, Christopher P. A1121
Johns, David L. A1073
Johns Hopkins Medicine P645

The Johns Hopkins University P646
Johns Manville Corporation A252, A714, P232
Johnsen, Russell K. A171
Johnson, Abigail P. A614, A615, P190, P191, P609
Johnson & Higgins (insurance) A916
Johnson & Johnson A58, A160, A234, A674, A**800**-A**801**, A952, A956, A957, A1070, A1246, E105, E191, P432, P715, W416, W428, W568
Johnson, Arthur E. A883
Johnson, Ashley L. E183
Johnson, Ban P306
Johnson, Barry C. A729
Johnson, Bobby R., Jr. (Foundry Networks) E206
Johnson, Bob (Nextel) A1027
Johnson, Brad P411, P711
Johnson, Brett W469
Johnson, Bruce (Carrefour) W165
Johnson, Bruce D. (Regis) A1197
Johnson, Bruce M. E276
Johnson, Carl G. (Tyson Foods) A1419
Johnson, Carl J. (II-VI Inc.) E20, E146
Johnson, Carol Matthews (EBSCO) P171
Johnson, Carolyn A1537
Johnson, Carver L. A845
Johnson, Charles A1320
Johnson, Cheryl A123
Johnson, Christina A1239
Johnsen, Clark A1130
Johnson, Claude W496
Johnson cleaner A1247
Johnson Controls, Inc. A326, **A802**-A**803**
Johnson, Dale A1320
Johnson, Darwin A1170
Johnson, David (Campbell Soup) A316
Johnson, David (Wyndham) A1541
Johnson, Denise Thorne A1147
Johnson, Dennis (Health Midwest) P629
Johnson, Dennis R. (Burlington Northern) A309
Johnson, Dennis R. (International Multifoods) A769
Johnson (dish machine operations) A530
Johnson, Don A351
Johnson, Edward C., III (FMR) A615, P190, P191, P609
Johnson, Edward (FMR) A614, P190
Johnson, Edward Mead (Johnson & Johnson) A800
Johnson Electric Holdings Ltd. A856
Johnson Electric Service Company A802
Johnson engines W132, W133
Johnson, E. Thomas, Jr. A923, P321

Johnson, Eunice W. P258, P259, P646
Johnson, Flo E252
Johnson, Galen G. A325, P105
Johnson, Gary L. (Fleetwood) A605
Johnson, Gary R. (Xcel Energy) A1543
Johnson, Gaylen K. E215
Johnson, Geoffrey E. A1159, P401, P705, W463
Johnson, George D., Jr. (Extended Stay America) E59, E201
Johnson, George W. (SAFECO) A1231
Johnson, Glenn S. A107
Johnson, Herbert A1246, P432
Johnson, Herbert Fisk A1246, A1247, P432, P433
Johnson, Herbert, Jr. A1246, P432
Johnson Industries (auto supply distribution) A652, A653
Johnson, James A. (Wingate) P519
Johnson, James (Fannie Mae) A580
Johnson, James I. (Hon) A727
Johnson, James (Johnson & Johnson) A800
Johnson, Jay A. E69
Johnson, J. Brent P43, P538
Johnson, Jeanne E136, E313
Johnson, Jerry L. A1233
Johnson, Joe A1294
Johnson, Joel W. A730, A731
Johnson, John D. (Cenex Harvest States Coop) P122, P123, P571
Johnson, John G. (Harris) A687
Johnson, John H. (Johnson Publishing) P258, P259, P646
Johnson, John J. (Big Lots) A261
Johnson, Karl R. P381
Johnson, Keith A. P583
Johnson, Kenneth H. A455
Johnson, Larry E207
Johnson, M. Carl, III A317
Johnson, Magic P354
Johnson, Mark O. A575
Johnson, Michael A. (Chesapeake Energy) E39
Johnson, Michael O. (Andersen Corp.) P51, P541
Johnson, Michael P., Sr. (Williams Companies) A1529
Johnson, Nancy M. P43
Johnson, Ned A614, P609
Johnson, Owen C. A409
Johnson, Patricia K. A839
Johnson, Peggy A1183
Johnson, Phillip M. (Georgia-Pacific) A655
Johnson, Phillip R. (Asbury Automotive Group) P543
Johnson, Preston R., Jr. A1199
Johnson Products P258
Johnson Publishing Company, Inc. P**258**-P**259**, P646
Johnson, R. Milton A695
Johnson, Randall W. (Penske) P391, P699

Johnson, Randy (American Crystal Sugar) P538
Johnson, Ray A1036
Johnson, Richard P. (Heafner Tire) P628
Johnson, Rick R. (Smithsonian) P451, P731
Johnson, Robbin S. A325, P105
Johnson, Robert (Black Entertainment) A872
Johnson, Robert (Catholic Heathcare West) P119
Johnson, Robert D. (Honeywell) A729
Johnson, Robert (Johnson & Johnson) A800
Johnson, Robert, Jr. (Johnson & Johnson) A800
Johnson, Robert (Liberty Media) A872
Johnson, Robert Wood (Robert Wood Johnson Foundation) P715
Johnson, Roger A1514
Johnson, Ronald B. (Apple Computer) A187
Johnson, Ronald E. (Jitney Jungle) P645
Johnson, Ron (Charter Communications) A351
Johnson, Ross A1204
Johnson, Roy P422
Johnson, Russell A. A793
Johnson, S. A. A1395
Johnson, S. Curtis A1246, P432
Johnson, S. P. IV E173
Johnson, S. Sue P495
Johnson, Samuel C. (S.C. Johnson & Son) A1246, A1247, P432, P433, P722
Johnson, Samuel Curtis "Curt" (SC Johnson Commercial Markets) P722
Johnson, Samuel Curtis (S.C. Johnson & Son) A1246, P432
Johnson, Scott (Compuware) A407
Johnson, Scott W. (Bemis) A251
Johnson, Seth R. A63
Johnson, Sherwood P381
Johnson Space Center (Texas) P754
Johnson, Starlette B. A289
Johnson, Stephen L. A139
Johnson Tables commercial furniture E202
Johnson, Thomas R. (Russell) A1221
Johnson, Thomas S. (Global Imaging Systems) E208
Johnson, Tina P. A1177, P403
Johnson, Todd A247
Johnson Truck Bodies A326
Johnson, Tyson P247
Johnson, Van R. P739
Johnson, Vicki E51
Johnson, W. Martin A643
Johnson, Warren A802
Johnson wax A1246, P88, P433, P722
Johnson Wax building A1334

Johnson Wax Professional (cleaning service) W618
Johnson, William D. (Progress Energy) A1167
Johnson, William (Earle M. Jorgensen) P601
Johnson, William E. (Rohm and Haas) A1213
Johnson, William (Illinois Central Railroad) A1104
Johnson, William R. (Heinz) A722, A723
Johnson, William S. (Budget Group) A301
Johnson, Willis J. E45, E185
Johnson Worldwide Associates A1246, P432
Johnson's Baby Cream A800
Johnsson, Stefan W633
Johnston, Alistair A841, P287, W325
Johnston Coca-Cola Bottling Group A384
Johnston, Gerald E. A375
Johnston Industries, Inc. (textiles) P342
Johnston, J. Tyler A511
Johnston, Jack W. (Primus) P705
Johnston, John (Northwestern Mutual Life) A218, A1048, P376
Johnston, John (Spectrum Control) E124
Johnston, Kathy J. A1395
Johnston, Lawrence R. A110, A111
Johnston, Peter B. W641
Johnston R. Bowman Health Center for the Elderly P719
Johnston, Sean A. A641
Johnston, Stephen K. P753
Johnston, Summerfield K., III A385
Johnston, Summerfield K., Jr. A384, A385
Johnston, Vance A1059
Johnston, William R. A1019, P375
Johnstone, Rudolph G., Jr. A1517
Joint Direct Attack Munition A272
JoJo's restaurants A86
Jokerst, Thomas R. A351
Joliot, Jean-Louis W209
Jolles, Ira H. A669
Jolly Rancher candy A708, A709
Jolosky, Richard A1092
Jolson, Al A298
Jonah, Sam Esson W341
Jonas, Stephen P. A615, P191, P609
Jonathan Logan (clothes) A880
Jones & Laughlin Steel A896
Jones, Andrew B. A563, P183, W223
Jones Apparel Group, Inc. **A804-A805**, A1150, P100
Jones, Bill P694
Jones, Carolyn E. (Smithsonian) P451, P731
Jones, Carolyn (Westwood One) E140, E317
Jones, Charles E. (FirstEnergy) A599

Jones, Charles R. (Correctional Properties Trust) E187
Jones, Clayton M. A1211
Jones, Daryl A1485
Jones, David A. G. (Citrix) E42
Jones, David A. (Humana) A738
Jones, David (Allina Health Systems) P536
Jones, David (Bon Secours Health System) P557
Jones, David C. (Lafarge) A849
Jones, David (Dairy Farmers of America) P149
Jones, David (Rand McNally) P409
Jones, David (Team Health) P743
Jones, Donald F. A1363
Jones, E. J. E144
Jones, E. Laverne A1355, P467
Jones, Edward D. (Jones Financial) P260
Jones, Edward D., Jr. "Ted" (Jones Financial) P260
Jones, Edward (Dow Jones) A506
Jones, Evon L. A487
The Jones Financial Companies, L.P., LLP **P260-P261**, P646
Jones, Fletcher A404
Jones Fork Complex A417
Jones, Frank J. P215
Jones, Gareth W145
Jones, George L. (Saks) A1239
Jones, George (New York Times) A1020
Jones, Hal A1503
Jones, Helen W313
Jones, Hoyt D., III A501, P163
Jones, Ingrid Saunders A383
Jones Intercable A72, A390, W122
Jones, James (American Stock Exchange) P46
Jones, James G. (Providian) A1171
Jones, James R., III (Reebok) A1195
Jones, Janis L. A685
Jones, Jeff (Clark Retail Group) P577
Jones, Jeffrey A. (Lands' End) A853
Jones, Jerry L. P644
Jones, John M. (Green Bay Packers) A673, P211, P621
Jones, John P., III (Air Products) A101
Jones, Jonathan H. (Reckitt Benckiser) W477
Jones, K. C. A280
Jones, Kenneth E. A87
Jones Lang LaSalle Inc. (real estate investment) E231, P120
Jones Library P497
Jones, Malcolm W653
Jones, Mary Sanders A1423
Jones, Max W. A667
Jones, Melody L. A183
Jones, Michael D. (Level 3 Communications) A867
Jones, Michael D. (National Association of Security Dealers) A997, P353

Jones, Michael J. (Microchip Technology) E93, E245
Jones, Mike (Computacenter) W177
Jones, Milton H., Jr. A227
Jones, Nathan J. A469
Jones, Orlo D. A887
Jones, Patricia P457
Jones, Patrick P632
Jones, Paula A1288, A1330, P446, P458
Jones, Paul J. (American Home Products) A149
Jones, Paul W. (U.S. Can) P762
Jones, Peter C. W285
Jones Pharma E229
Jones, Randy A1341
Jones, Richard (Countrywide) A439
Jones, Richard (IGA, Inc.) A744, P242
Jones, Robert G. (KeyCorp) A823
Jones, Robert (XETA Technologies) E142
Jones, Roderick W484
Jones, Ronald H. (Waste Management) A1505
Jones, Ronald L. (Sealy) P442, P443, P725
Jones Sand W252
Jones, Stephen C. A383
The Jones Store department stores A932
Jones, Terrell B. A1229
Jones, Terri E222
Jones, Thomas C. (CIGNA) A361
Jones, Thomas L. (Ryder Systems) A1223
Jones, Thomas (Northrop) A1044
Jones, Thomas W. (Citigroup) A371
Jones, Tim E123, E292
Jones, W. O. E162
Jones, William A. (MGM) A963
Jones, William (Schnuck Markets) P723
Jonker, Terence L. A401
Jonny Cat cat litter A374
Joos, David W. A377
Jooss, Gerhard W595
Jordache Enterprises, Inc. E60
Jordan, Anne S. A1099
Jordan Automotive Group P647
Jordan, Guy J. A445
Jordan Industries, Inc. A546, P647
JORDAN instore outlets A1032
Jordan, James F. A1517
Jordan, Jeffrey D. E54
Jordan, John W., II P647
Jordan, Louis A497
Jordan Marsh stores A586
Jordan, Michael (basketball star) A1032, E99, E257, P354, P682, W62
Jordan, Michael (CBS) A948, P326, P670
Jordan, Robert L. A605
Jordan's Meats A1350
Jorgensen, Lars A. W417
Jorgensen, Paul J. P455

A=AMERICAN BUSINESS · E=EMERGING COMPANIES · P=PRIVATE COMPANIES · W=WORLD BUSINESS

Jorgenson, James A. A731
Jorndt, L. Daniel A1492, A1493
José Cuervo SA P682, W206, W207
Josefowicz, Gregory P. A276, A277
Joseph, Alfred E136
Joseph Farrow & Company W476
Joseph Leavitt stores A158
Joseph Littlejohn & Levy P637
Joseph, Mark K. E248
Joseph, Maxwell W206
Joseph Pfeifer department store A490
Joseph Regenstein Library P496, P497
Joseph T. Ryerson & Son (metal processor) A1224
Josephine Ford Cancer Center P630
Josephson, Mural R. P269, P650
Joshi, Vyomesh A713
Joshin Denki (electronics retailer) W548
Josiah Wedgwood and Sons W636
Joslin Diabetes Center P566
Joslin, John W177
Joslin, Mark W. A523
Joslin, Roger S. A1331, P459, P735
Josten, Otto P262
Jostens, Inc. P262-P263, P647
Jostensalumshop.com P262
Jotwani, Pradeep A713
Joumas, Greg A785
Jourdain, William P687
Journal Communications Inc. P648
Journal of Commerce A832
Jovanovich, Peter W431
Jowett, Richard N. A121
Joy Global Inc. A806-A807
Joy, Jim A303
Joy Mining Machinery A806
Joy, Robert J. A387
Joy, William N. A1342, A1343
JoyCam camera A1148
Joyce, John R. A765
Joyce, Julia P516
Joyce, Kenneth T. A163
Joyce, Ronald V. A1510
Joyce, William H. A704, A705
Joyner, Henry C. A165
Jozoff, Malcolm A486
JP Fire & Casualty A794
J.P. Morgan Chase & Company. See also Chase Manhattan Corporation
J.P. Morgan Chase & Company A220, A238, A348, A474, A626, A646, A660, A808-A809, A916, A954, A988, A1028, E27, E148, E154, P66, P154, P418, P537, P595, P717, W196, W200, W551, W616
J.P. Morgan H & Q A348
J.P. Morgan Partners E66, E210, P238
J.P. Taylor Company of Virginia A1436
J-Phone mobile phone operations W628

JPI P648
JPS cigarettes W282, W283
JPS Packaging W432
Jr. Foods convenience stores P634
J.R. Simplot Company A1456, E278, P264-P265, P648
JR's Mobile Homes A604
J.S. Alberici Construction Company, Inc. P649
JSB electrical products A431
JSkyB. See Japan Sky Broadcasting
JT International S.A. W304
JT Pharmaceutical W304
JTB Corporation A328, P108
JTC Acquisitions P614
JTL Corporation A384
Juaréz, Eduardo W635
Juba, Eugene D. A1443
Jubail, Saudi Arabia A240, P74
Judd, Barbara P745
Judd, James T. A659
Judel glassware A1385
Judelson, Andrew P361
Judelson, Robert P645
Judge & Dolph (liquor distributor) P774
Judges' Retirement Fund A315, P97
Judson, Arthur A334
Juelsgaard, Stephen G. A641
Juetten, George H. P769
Jufors, Staffan W633
Juice Tyme beverages A1105
The Juiceman (informercial) E116
Juicy Fruit gum A1526, A1527
Juki Corporation E189
Julian, Alexander P298
Julian, Paul C. A947
Julian, Peter J. A453
Juliana Vineyards E279
Juliber, Lois D. A387
Julius beer W289
Julius Tishman & Sons P476
JumpKing fitness equipment P637
Jung, Andrea A216, A217
Jung, Howard J. A65, P31
Jung, Volker W537
Jung water pumps A921
Jungle Adventures (ice show) P189
Junior Food Stores A845
Juniper Networks, Inc. A368, A792, E226
Junkanoo beverage A1105
Junkers Flugzeugwerke (aircraft) W344
Junkers Luftverkehr (airline) W344
Junkins, Jerry A1378
JUNOS software E226
Jupiler lager W288, W289
Jupiter Discount stores A830
Jupiter Media Metrix E251
Jupiter Partners P584
Jupiter Programming A873
Jupiter Systems (color graphics computers) A170
Jupiter Telecommunications Company Ltd. A872

Jurassic Park III (movie and products) A692
Jurassic Park (movie) P166
Jurgensen, Karen A632
Jurgensen, William G. "Jerry" A1009, P365, P685
Jurgensen's stores P777
Jurick, Geoffrey P. E58, E198
JUSCO. See AEON (retailer)
Juska, John E. E70, E217
Just Juice drinks W553
Just Right cereal A817
Juster, Andrew A. A1287
Justice, Richard J. A369
Justin Brands (footwear) A253
Justin Industries, Inc. (bricks and boots) A252
JustOn (Internet file sharing) A1050
Justrite (food wholesalers) A1350
Jutaku Ryutsu (brokerage) E227
Juvena cosmetics A1201
Juxtapose stores P539
JVC electronic products W360
J.W. Bateson (contractor) A340
J.W. Childs Associates, L.P. P406, P709
JW Foster and Sons A1194
J. W. Wilcox & Follett Company P192
JWGenesis (brokerage) A1486
JWP Information Services A544

K

K. Hattori & Company W528, W530
K Systems A1210
K12 (online learning) P278, P279
K2 Ski Company A456
KABC-TV (Los Angeles) A61
Kablanian, Adam A. E313
Kabushiki Kaisha Yokado W298
Kacza, Jeffrey A1071
Kaczorowski, Krzysztof W457
Kaczynski, Barbara A. P357, P683
Kadant Inc. (paper and pulp services) A1382
Kaden, Ellen Oran A317
Kadowaki, Tatsuo W81
Kafka, Franz W98
Kafoure, Michael D. A775
Kagan, Herman E68
Kagan World Media A1160, A1161
Kagawa, Takahiko W309
Kagen, Michael E305
Kagermann, Henning W516, W517
Kahan, James S. A1245
Kahle, Rita D. A65, P31, P529
Kahlua liqueur W84, W85
Kahn, Alfred R. E147
Kahn, Eugene S. A932, A933
Kahn, Jacob M. W553
Kahn, J. Alan A233
Kahn, Kenny P351
Kahn, Leo A1324
Kahn, Martin E100, E258
Kahn, Susan D. A1353

Kahn, Timothy F. A511
Kahn's packaged meats A1243
Kai Tak airport (Hong Kong) E32
Kailly, Darshan S. A421
Kainz, Arthur A1059
Kaiser Aerospace and
 Electronics A1210
Kaiser Aluminum
 Corporation A786, A810, A930,
 A931, P266
Kaiser beer W255
Kaiser Cement W252
Kaiser Foundation Health Plan,
 Inc. A810-A811, A1080,
 P266-P267, P597, P622, P649
Kaiser Francis Oil E264
Kaiser, Henry A810, P266
Kaiser Permanente. See Kaiser
 Foundation Health Plan, Inc.
Kaiser Steel W488
Kaiser, Thomas G. W653
Kaiser's grocery stores W588, W589
Kaiser's Kaffee-Geschaft W588
Kaisoglus, John W. P700
Kaizaki, Yoichiro W138
Kaku, Ryuzaburo W158
Kakudai, Toshikazu W597
Kal Kan (pet food) A914, P314
Kalafut, George W. A653
Kalamazoo Stamping and
 Die A1394
Kalarchian, Linda A335
Kalbfell Laboratories E44
Kale, Tom D. P471, P743
Kaleta, Paul A835, P281
Kaletra drug A58, A59
Kalgoorlie mine W640
Kalikow, Peter S. P335
Kalina, John A. A279
Kaliningradmorneftegaz (oil
 exploration) W346
Kalinowski, Andrea E217
Kalinowski, Lynn M. E241
Kalinowski, Walter P701
Kalinske, Thomas P278, P279, P652
Kalkbrenner, David L. E209
Kalkhoven, Kevin A792
Kalkwarf, Kent D. A351
Kallasvuo, Oilli-Pekka W407
Kallista plumbing fixtures P284,
 P285, P653
The Kalmanovitz Charitable
 Trust P428, P721
Kalmanovitz, Lydia P428
Kalmanovitz, Paul P428, P721
Kalmanson, Steven R. A827
Kalmbach, Lisa G. A813
KALOS software E187
Kaloski, John F. A1007
Kalpana (Ethernet switches) A368
Kam Chan W571
Kam Hing Lam W273
Kaman Industrial
 Technologies P208
Kamaz (trucks) A836, P282
Kamber, Martin A781

Kamehameha Schools/Bishop
 Estate of Hawaii A660
Kamei, Atsushi W299
Kamei, Kuniaki W187
Kamen, Charles M. P670
Kamenick, Duaine P610
Kamenitza beer W289
Kamerman, Perry E147
Kamimoto, Haruo W487
Kamins, Edward B. A215
Kaminski, Joseph J. A101
Kamkoff, Jorge W439
Kamm, Barbara B. E122
Kampen, Dan P763
Kampf, Serge W160, W161
Kampio (food retailer) W498
Kampouris, Emanuel A152
Kamprad, Ingvar W276, W277
Kan, Akitoshi A93
Kan, Alexander Rinnooy W287
Kanach, Charles A905
Kanage, Pam E169
Kanai, Hiroshi W139
Kanai, Tsutomu W260, W261
Kanak, Donald P. A151
Kanasugi, Akinobu W387
Kanasugi, Hiroshi W597
Kand, Masaki W363
Kanda, Shigueru W187
Kanders, Warren B. E29
K&L Microwave A502
K&M Electronics A780
K&R Warehouse stores A158
K&S. See Kulicke and Soffa
 Industries, Inc.
Kane, Allen R. A1429, P491
Kane, Dennis P. P269
Kane, Edward K. P215
Kane, William S. A767
Kaneb, John P624
Kaneko, Hisashi W386
Kaneko, Isao W303
Kaneko, Kokichi W531
Kaneko, Kunehide W261
Kanem, Natalia P195
Kanemaru, Shin W96
Kang Chang-Oh W455
Kangaroo convenience
 stores A1084, A1085
Kangas, Edward A474, A475, P154,
 P155, W196, W197
Kangome (foods) A722
Kangoo car W480, W481
Kanin-Lovers, Jill A217
Kann, Melvin M. A627
Kann, Peter R. A506, A507
Kansas City Automobile
 Auction A442, P146
Kansas City Chiefs Football Club,
 Inc. A672, P211, P357
The Kansas City (Missouri)
 Star A60, A832, A833
Kansas City Power & Light A1464
Kansas City Royals Baseball
 Corporation P307
Kansas Gas Service
 Company A1065

Kansas Speedway E75
The Kantar Group (market
 research) W646, W647
Kanthamneni, Sudhakar E87
Kantor, Jonathan D. A379
Kanzaki Specialty Papers A250
Kanzler, Michael W. P487, P751
Kao Corporation W308-W309
Kao skin care products A234
Kaparich, William M. P345, P679
Kaplan education and career
 services A1502, A1503
Kaplan, Herbert P769
Kaplan, Joann P689
Kaplan, Lester J. A119
Kaplan, Martin A. A793
Kaplan Thaler Group
 (advertising) P72, P73
Kaplan Thaler, Linda P73
Kappauf, Donald W. E125, E299
Kappler, David J. W155
Kapson, Craig P647
Kapson, Jordan P647
Kapustay, Rebecca A., A1507
Kaput, Jim L. A1273
Karabelas, A. W385
Karan, Donna A565
Karas, Richard A. A1009, P365
Karastan carpets A980, A981
Karatz, Bruce A812, A813
Karatzas, Theodoros B. W385
Karcher, Clarence "Doc" A1378
Kardesh, David A1315
Kareem, Arif E109
Karel, Steven A1209
KARE-TV (Minneapolis-St.
 Paul) A633
Kariya, Michio W393
Karl Oelschlager GmbH &
 Company A1380
Karlin, Jerome B. A1493
Karlsson, Sune W55
Karmanos, Peter, Jr. A406, A407
Karmazin, Mel A334, A1476, A1477
Karmoy Works (aluminium) W410
Karnes, Donald K. A1273
Karp Electric A430, A431
Karpan, John A749
Karpatkin, Rhoda H. P138
Karro, Bradley S. A323
Karson, Jamieson A. E294
Karstadt Quelle AG W310-W311,
 W344
Karstadt, Rudolph W310
Karsten Diederik W503
Kartarik, Mark A1197
Kartchner, Vickie F. P269
Karten's Jewelers A1552
Kartsimas, Lou P577
Karvinen, Jouko W55
Karvois, Paul J. A1549
KAS soft drink A1103
Kasdin, Robert A. P758
Kasenna A1284
Kash n' Karry stores W194, W195
Kashi Company A816, A817

Kashio, Kazuo W168, W169
Kashio Manufacturing W168
Kashio, Tadao W168
Kashio, Toshio W168, W169
Kashio, Yukio W168, W169
Kashkoush, Marwan A1089
Kaske, Karlheinz W536
Kasmar, Roy J. E108
Kasparov, Garry A764
Kasriel, Bernard L. A849
Kass, Daniel B. A337
Kass, Sheldon E125
Kassie, David W157
Kassner, Fred P296, P658
Kassner, Michelle P297
Kaste Allan K. E198
Kastelic, Joseph B. A891
Kasten, Jim P610
Katana 750 motorcycle W561
Katcoff, Benjamin P640
Kate Spade handbags A565, A1014, A1015
Katen, Karen L. A1119
Kathy Ireland clothing A831
Katies clothing stores W172
Kato Engineering A332, A546
Kato, Linda E22, E148
Kato, Makoto W297
Kato, Shinichi W615
Kato, Takashi W305
Kato, Toyotaro W419
Kato, Yogoru W572
Katsaros, Arthur T. A101
Katsumata, Nobuo W359
Katsumata, Tsunehisa W599
Katz, Avi A889
Katz, Karen W. A1015
Katz, Neil J. A881
Katz, Samuel L. A339
Katzenberg, Jeffrey A1496, P166, P167, P510, P597
Kaufhof AG W364
Kaufhold, David A785
Kaufman and Broad Home A508, A812, A1227
Kaufman, Donald A812
Kaufman, James B. E127
Kaufman, Joseph D. E104
Kaufman, Michael A1081
Kaufman, Scot A937
Kaufman, Stephen P. A196, A197
Kaufman, Victor A. A1451
Kaufmann, Per W447
Kaufmann's department stores A932
Kaul, Pradman P. A737
Kaupulehu Developments E163
Kautex Werke Reinold Hagen AG A1380
Kava coffee P90
Kavafian, Jane E176
Kavanaugh, John P. A125
Kawabata, Yoshifumi W409
Kawada, Takashi W361
Kawakami, Genichi W648
Kawakami, Hiroshi W648

Kawakami, Tetsuya W361
Kawalek, Polly B. A1181
Kawamoto, Nobuhiko W264
Kawano, Masabumi W515
Kawasaki (motorcycles) A286, W560
Kawasaki Steel Corporation A104, A894
Kawauchi, Hidemitsu W81
Kay Chemical A530
Kay, Christopher K. A1397
Kay, David S. E170
Kay, Kenneth J. A495
Kay Lab E44
Kay Pneumatic Valves E26
Kayama, Tetsu W527
Kay-Bee Toys stores A260, A458
Kaye, Alan A927
Kaye, Martin E221
Kayser, Paul A536
KB Home A812-A813
K-B Toys A260, E225, P649
KBkids.com A260, P649
KC Marine P574
K C Masterpiece sauce A375
KCP, Inc. (coal mining) A866
KCYY-FM (San Antonio) P147
KD drugstores W589
KDB Homes, Inc. A509
KDDI Corporation E220
K-Dur drug A1250
Kealy, Joseph P. E221
Kealy, Thomas P. E167
Kean, Steven J. A553
Keane, James P. A1335
Keane, Robert M. A391
Kearney, Albert J. A1315
Kearney, A. T. A948, P326
Kearney, Christopher J. A1321
Kearney electrical products A431
Kearney, Sandra W. P201
Kearney-National P600
Kearse, Cecil B. A831
Keate, Steven A1011
Keating, Charles A144
Keating, Mary E. A233
Keating, Michael K. A593
Keating, Susan C. W87
Keats, Jeanne A. E40, E178
Keay, Roger D. W495
Keck, Brian L. A933
Keck, Ray, III P471
Keds sneakers W62
Keebler Foods Company A608, A814-A815, A816
Keebler, Godfrey A814
Keefe Coffee and Supply P178
Keefe, Michael D. A683
Keegan, Brendan M. A913
Keegan, Francine E57, E197
Keegan, Michael P. E157
Keegan, Peter W. A885
Keegan, Robert A665
Keegel, Tom P247, P641
Keeler, Fred A882
Keeler, William A1128

Keeley, G. Chris P497, P756
Keeley, Rupert A1481, P509
KEELOQ secure data transmission E93, E245
Keely, Mary W429
Keen, Robinson & Company (spices) W476
Keenan, David J. A393
Keenan, John J., Jr. P407
Keenan, Karen C. E223
Keenan, Thomas J. P239
Keene Manufacturing (office supplies) A1022
Keener, James A. A625
Keepsake collectibles A678, A679, P217
Keeshan, Lawrence A1159, P401, W463
Keever, William L. W629
Keg Steakhouse W638
Keifer, Alan J. A223
Keightley, James J. P389
Keihin Corporation W420
Keil, Beverly R. A1503
Keillor, Garrison P144
Keillor, Larry P610
Keilman, David W. P137
Keiper Car Seating A856
Keirce, Gary E279
Keiser, John T. A1383
Keiser, Kenneth E. A1105
Keister, Richard L. P153
Keitel, Hans-Peter W505
Keith, Aram H. E226
Keith, Ben E. P553
The Keith Companies, Inc. E226
Keith, Kenneth L. A339
Keith, Robert E., Jr. (Safeguard Scientifics) A1233
Keith, Robert F. (ServiceMaster) A1273
Keith, Susan S. A677
Keithmoor men's clothes A691
Kelbel, Dundee A605
Kelbley, Stephen P. A1317, P453
Kelco A860
Keleghan, Kevin T. A1265
Keler, Marianne M. A1449
Kellagher, Thomas P. A1097
Kelleher, Daniel L. A155
Kelleher, Herbert D. A1310, A1311
Kelleher, Lawrence J. A625
Keller beer W553
Keller, Craig P. E265
Keller, David L. A941
Keller, Ed W621
Keller, James P. A432
Keller Ladders A1446
Keller, Randall W431
Keller, Robert J. A1057
Keller's butter P149
Keller's Creamery, LLC P148
Kellett, Stephen T. A1323
Kelley, Barbara M. A235
Kelley, Bernard J. A957
Kelley, Byron R. A537

Kelley, James F. A655
Kelley, Janet G. (Kmart) A831
Kelley, Janet L. (Kellogg) A817
Kelley, John M. E68
Kelley, Kevin M. P91
Kelley, Orby G., Jr. A73
Kelley, Patrick L. W377
Kelley, R. Alan A137
Kelley, Russell P. W85
Kelley, William A260
Kellner, Lawrence W. A429
Kellog, Fernanda M. A1385
Kellogg Brown & Root A676
Kellogg Company A608, A648,
A768, A814, A816-A817, A1180,
A1302, P72, P520, P551
Kellogg Environmental Research
Center P379
Kellogg, Harry W., Jr. E122
Kellogg, John Harvey (W.K. Kellogg
Foundation) P520
Kellogg, John (Kellogg) A816
Kellogg, William S. (Kohl's) A838,
A839
Kellogg, Will Keith (Kellogg) A816,
P520, P774
Kelly, Alfred F., Jr. A143
Kelly, Anastasia D. A1265
Kelly, Burnett S. P165, P596
Kelly, Carol A. A1229
Kelly, Colin P. A735
Kelly, Dan M. P615
Kelly, David H. A573
Kelly, Donald T. E125, E299
Kelly, Douglas L. A95
Kelly, Ed (American Express) A143
Kelly, Edmund F. (Liberty
Mutual) A875, P295, P658
Kelly, Eric A929
Kelly, Gary C. A1311
Kelly, Geoffrey J. A383
Kelly Girl Service A818
Kelly, Grace W250
Kelly, Henry P. A135
Kelly, Hugh Rice A1199
Kelly, James (*Chicago Daily
Tribune*) A1402
Kelly, James P. (United
Parcel) A1427
Kelly, Jeffrey D. A1001
Kelly, Jim (Ingram
Industries) A757, P245
Kelly, J. Michael A181
Kelly, John E., III (IBM) A765
Kelly, John F. (Alaska Air) A106,
A107
Kelly, John F. (Anheuser-
Bush) A175
Kelly, Kenneth A., Jr. A939
Kelly, Kevin J. A615, P191, W87
Kelly, Michael A529
Kelly, Pat E296
Kelly, Peter A896
Kelly, Ralph G. A351
Kelly, Richard C. A1543
Kelly, R. James A579
Kelly, Robert P. A1487

Kelly Services, Inc. A818-A819
Kelly, Stan A1487
Kelly, Stephen E. P71
Kelly, Thomas H. (Schering-
Plough) A1251
Kelly, Thomas M. (Loyola
University) P661
Kelly, Thomas (Nextel) A1027
Kelly, Timothy E. (Sprint) A1319
Kelly, Timothy T. (National
Geographic Society) P359
Kelly tires A664
Kelly, William Russell A818
KellyConnect (teleservices) A818
Kelly-Springfield A664, P628
Kelmar, Steven B. A953
Kelsey, Glenn B. A935
Kelso & Company A152, A358,
P601
Kelson, Richard B. A113
Kelter, Jeffrey E. E228
Keltner, Thomas L. A721
Kelty, Gibbons A388
Keltz, Hugo A. A287
Kelvinator appliances A1520
KemaNord (chemical group) W72
Kemen (office furniture) P222
Kemira A820
Kemlite Company, Inc. A447
Kemna, Wolfgang W517
Kemp, Karen P590
Kemp, Thomas L. E102, E263
Kempa, Lisa P143, P583
Kemper Corporation
(insurance) A178, A414, W512,
W652, W653
Kemper Insurance
Companies P268-P269, P650
Kemper, James P268
Kemperco P268
KEMPES (insurance) P269
Kempf, Donald G., Jr. A989
Kemsley Newspapers W592
Kem-Tone paint A1278
Ken Griffey Jr.'s Slugfest (video
game) W395
Kendall, David W. W190
Kendall, Donald A1106
Kendall (hospital supplies) A386
Kendall, Peter M. R. A79
Kendall, Rebecca O. A541
Kendall, Terry L. A361
Kendall/Amalie motor oils A1344
Kendall-Jackson Wine Estates,
Ltd. A520, P168
Kendrick, Brian E. P156
Kenin, David P217
Ken-L-Ration pet food A723
KenMar Capital E60
Kenmore appliances A1265, A1520,
A1521, E283
Kennard, William A1026
Kennard, William E. P111
Kennecott Corporation A1024,
A1344, W488
Kennedy, Alan D. A1415
Kennedy, Brian J. A711, E242

Kennedy, Bruce R. A106, A107
Kennedy, Cabot & Company W608
Kennedy Center for the Performing
Arts P450
Kennedy, Darlene E99, E257
Kennedy, Dennis G. P693
Kennedy, Donald P. (First American
Corp.) A594, A595
Kennedy, Donald (Stanford
University) P456
Kennedy, Gary W87
Kennedy, J. Paul A689
Kennedy, James C. (American
Financial) A145
Kennedy, James C. (Cox
Enterprises) A442, A443, P146,
P147, P585
Kennedy, John (Budget
Group) A300
Kennedy, John Fitzgerald (former
President) A1068, P34, P194,
P220, P258
Kennedy, John F. (RSA
Security) E114, E281
Kennedy, John (Halliburton) A677
Kennedy, John P. (Johnson
Controls) A803
Kennedy, Kerry L. P499, P761
Kennedy, Lee A. A559
Kennedy, Leonard J. A1027
Kennedy, Lesa D. E75
Kennedy, Parker S. A594, A595
Kennedy, Raymond F. A921
Kennedy Space Center
(Florida) A1110, P754
Kennedy, Ted P552
Kennedy, Wayne J. A1551
Kennedy, William A258
Kennedy-Wilson, Inc. E227
Kenner Parker Toys A648
Kenner Products (toys) A648, A692
Kenneth Cole Productions,
Inc. A690, A691, A880, E78, E227
Kenneth O. Lester Company (food
distributor) A1109
Kenney, Brian A. A639
Kenney, Crane H. A1403
Kenney, James M. A317
Kennicott, Robert W488
Kenny, Gregory B. A643
Kenny Rogers Roasters fast
food E95, E249
Ken-Ohio pipeline A978
Kensitas cigarettes A618, W240
Kent cigarettes A884, W142, W143
Kent Electronics A214
Kent, Harlan M. E143
Kent, Jerald L. A350, A351
Kent, Michael W645
Kent, William C. A73
Kentucky Blue Cross and Blue
Shield A178
Kentucky Derby E40, E178
Kentucky Fried Chicken. *See* KFC
restaurants
Kentucky Gentleman
bourbon A423
Kentucky Power Company A140

Kentucky Rib-Eye restaurants A492
Kenway (automated storage and retrieval) A526
Kenwood A170
Kenworth Truck Company A1078, A1079, P633
Kenworth Truck Company Westport Innovation A456
Kenya Airways Ltd W316, W317
Kenyon, Bruce D. A1041
Kenyon, Curt E112
Kenyon, Peter A. W271
Kenzo fashions W348
Keohane, Nannerl O. P598
Keough, Kevin J. A599
Kepler, David E. A505
Kepner, Melissa P501
Keppel TatLee Bank W86
Kératase W343
Kerbage, Omar A503
Kerfoot, Greg A1261
Kerite (power cables) P312
Kerkorian, Kirk A962, A966, P747, W188
Kerlyn Oil A820
Kermarrec, Christian A171
Kermi GmbH W461
Kermott, Gary L. A595
Kern County Land Company A1368
Kern, Dennis L. E312
Kern, Lawrence A. A495
Kern, Michael J. P239
Kern, Richard L., Jr. A1023
Kern River Gas Transmission Company A1529
Kernan, Richard M., Jr. A1017, P371
Kerns, Kim A313
KERO-TV (Bakersfield, CA) A945
Kerr, Barbara J. P542
Kerr, Darlene D. A1029
Kerr, Jim A797
Kerr, Ken A352
Kerr, K. G. W565
Kerr, Robert K. (Belk) P77
Kerr, Robert (Kerr-McGee) A820
Kerr, William R. W413
Kerrigan, Sarah E308
Kerr-McGee Corporation A482, A820-A821, A1344, A1466, W482
Kershner, Rodger A. A377
Kertel (phone cards) W446
Kerzner, Sol W552
Keskey, Michael P. A255
Kessel Food Markets A845
Kessel, Silvia P333
Kesselman, Abe A1490, P515
Kesselman, Ronald C. P91
Kessinger, George W. P618
Kessler, Bethmara A877
Kessler, Jeffrey R. P546
Kessler, Murray S. A1459
Kessler, Ronald J. A95
Kestra Ltd. E48
Kestrel Solutions (optical fiber networking) P511

Keswick, Henry W307
Keswick, Simon W306
Ketchum Communications Holdings A1062
Ketchum, Mark D. A1165
Ketchum, Richard G. A997, P353
Ketchum, Thomas B. A809
Ketner stores A1532
Kettell, Russell W. A659
Kettering, Charles F. A1012, P152
Ketting, Jaap A359
Kevco, Inc. (building products) P518, P519, P774
Kevlar A534
KEX entrance mats P343
Key Energy Services, Inc. E79, E227
Key Gardens Co-op (New York) P291
Key Pharmaceuticals A1250
Key Production Company, Inc. E228
Key3Media Group, Inc. W548
KeyCorp A794, A822-A823, A1000
Keyes, Deborah P668
Keyes Fiber P238
Keyes, James H. (Johnson Controls) A803
Keyes, James W. (7-Eleven) A56, A57
Keyport Life Insurance A875, P294
Keys, Clement Melville A1210
Keys, William M. P132, P133, P578
Keyser, Richard L. A1538, A1539
KeySpan Corporation A418, A824-A825, E216
Keystone Automotive Industries, Inc. E45
Keystone beers A78, A79
Keystone cameras E184
Keystone Complex A417
Keystone Consolidated Industries P583
Keystone Foods LLC P650
Keystone Health Plan A716, A717, P234, P235
Keystone, Inc. (investments) P518, P603, W252
Keystone Property Trust E228
Keystone Tubular Service P312
Keyte, David H. E62, E205
KEZW-AM (Denver) A1402
KFC Corporation (restaurants) A302, A694, A1106, A1204, A1404, A1405, A1510, P124, P236, P575, P633
KFSN-TV (Fresno, CA) A61
KGO-TV (San Francisco) A61, A1497
KGTV-TV (San Diego) A945
Khalifa, Armin I. A243
Khan, Ejaz A. A1485
Khan, Raymond R. P87
KHD. See Klockner-Humbolt-Deutz
Khilnani, Vinod E189
Khoba, Lubov W347
Khosla, Vinod A1342

Khosrowshahi, Dara A1451
Khoury, Kenneth F. A655
KHWB-TV (Houston) A1402
Kia Motors Company, Ltd. P631, P647, W274, W362
Kibbey, Jane W465
Kibbles 'n Bits pet food A723
Kibbon, Larry P768
KIC appliances A1521
Kick office furniture A1335
Kickham, Jill E87, E238
KICU-TV (San Francisco/San Jose) A443, P147
Kidd, Scott E45, E185
Kidde, Walter A1446
Kidder, C. Robert P91, P558
Kidder, Peabody & Company (investment banking) A646, A856
Kidder Press W378
Kids and Lead Hazards: What Every Family Should Know (educational video) P139
Kids Foot Locker stores A1470
Kid's Kitchen entrees A731
Kids Mart/Little Folks stores A1470
Kids "R" Us A1396, A1397, E60
Kidston Mine W453
Kieboom, Wilbert W101
Kiehl's Since 1851 Inc. (cosmetics) W342
Kiekhaefer Aeromarine A298
Kielar, Robert M. P477
Kieley, Kenneth E. E252
Kielly, James P480
Kiely, W. Leo, III A78, A79
Kiemle, Richard D. A1073
Kienker, James W. P309, P664
Kierans, Thomas E. W379
Kiernan, Donald E. A1245
Kierulff Electronics A196
Kiewet Brothers A1114
Kiewit, Andrew A1114
Kiewit Diversified Group A866
Kiewit, Peter A1114, P396
Kiewit, Peter, Jr. A1114, P396
Kiewit, Ralph A1114, P396
Kiggen, James D. A293
Kihara, Hanh E163
Kihara, Makoto W399
K-III Holdings (publishing) A836, A1160, P282
KiK discount stores W588, W589
Kiker, Sharon A1197
Kikkawa, Makoto W375
Kilbride, William B. A981
Kilby, Jack A1378
Kilcourse, Brian E., Sr. A887
Kile, Lon C. E270
Kilgore, Bernard A506
Kilgore (munitions) A120
Kilgore, Tom D. A1167
Kilgour, Charles A292
Kilgriff, Stephen P. A1349
Kilian, Thomas J. A415
Kilimanjaro beer W553

Killer Loop sports
equipment W124, W125
Killian, George A78
Killian, Rex P. P57
Killian's Irish Honey beer A78
Killinger, Kerry K. A1501
Killion Extruders A450
Killough, Walter P255
Killy, Jean-Claude P250
Kilts, James M. A656, A657
Kim, Agnes A162
Kim, Chang Nam A163
Kim Hyeon-Gon W509
Kim, James J. A162, A163
Kim Jing-wan W509
Kim, Jin Sun E89
Kim Joo-Jin A162
Kim lighting A1447
Kim, Peter S. A957
Kim Rogers brand P77
Kim Sung-Hwan W455
Kim Yong-Woon W455
Kimball, Christian E. P73
Kimball, Justin A268, P82, P86,
P174
Kimbell grocery stores A1532
Kimber, Michael N. W245
Kimberly, John A826
Kimberly-Clark Corporation A654,
A826-A827, A828, P270, W646
Kimble Glass A1074
Kimbrell, Curtis C., III A703
Kimbrell, Duke P696
Kimbro, Kenneth J. A743
Kimbrough, Joel R. E147
Kimes, John J. A921
Kimmel, Arnie P57
Kimmel, Sidney A804, A805
Kimmerling, Karl P. A1387
Kimmins, William J., Jr. A175
Kimmitt, Robert M. A181
Kimo (Internet portal) A1546
Kimoto, Yasuhiko W81
Kimsey, William L. A563, P183,
P605, W223
Kimura, Shinichi W373
Kimura, Toshio W531
Kimura, Yasutoshi W199
Kimwipes commercial wipes A827
Kincaid furniture A854
Kincaid, Steven M. A855
Kindelberger, James A1210
Kinder, Larry (Cendant) A339
Kinder, Lawrence E. (Avis) A213
Kinder Morgan Energy Partners,
L.P. A1030, A1065, E129, E228
Kinder, Richard D. E228
KinderCare Learning Centers,
Inc. A836, A837, P282, P283
Kindler, Jeffrey B. A943
Kinescope Interactive
(marketing) P171
Kinetic watches W529
Kin-Farm, Inc. A493
King, Allen B. A1437
King, Andrew W. A1391

King Arthur commercial
furniture E202
King, Barry A1189
King, C. Judson P495
King Companies A1488
King, David (JDS Uniphase) A793
King, David L. (PETsMART) A1117
King, David (North American
Scientific) E254
King, Diana A1085
King Edward Coronets cigars W283
King Feature Syndicate A700,
P228, P229
King, Graham A947
King, Gregory C. A1467
King, Henrietta A828, P270
King, J. Joseph A983
King, James S. W231
King, John E. A1113
King Kullen Grocery Company
Inc. A844
King of the Road Map Service P408
King, Olin B. A1256, A1257
King Pharmaceuticals, Inc. E229
King Quad ATV W561
King Ranch, Inc. A828-A829,
P270-P271, P650
King, R. Bradley A1423
King, Richard D. (Rotary
International) P421
King, Richard (King Ranch) A828,
P270, P650
King, Richard O. (EDS) A539
King, Robert J., Jr. (Fifth Third
Bancorp) A593
King, Robert (State University of
New York) P460, P461
King, Roger A335
King, Rollin A1310
King, Ruthanne A1501
King sauces A467
King, Scott L. A527
King Shipping P574
King Soopers supermarkets A844,
A845, P478
King Staffing, Inc. A1489
King Stores A1532
King, Thomas A.
(Progressive) A1169
King, Thomas B. (PG&E) A1121
King, Thomas S. (American Family
Insurance) P43
King World Productions A334,
A335, P218
King, W. Russell A629
Kingfisher plc A1324, W312-W313
King's College P134
Kings County Hospital Center P369
King's Entertainment (theme
parks) A1476
Kings River State Bank E312
King's stores A158
Kings Super Markets, Inc. P102,
P478, P479, W356, W357
Kingsborough Community
College P129
King-Seeley Thermos A734

Kingsella, Kim A491
Kingsford charcoal A374
Kingsley, Oliver D., Jr. A571
Kingsport Power A140
Kingston brands P478, P479
Kingston Cake Bakery A774
Kingston Technology
Company P272-P273, P651
Kingwood Cove Golf Club
(Texas) P131
Kinion, Todd E210
Kinkead Industries (doors) A1456
Kinkela, David P205
Kinko's, Inc. P274-P275, P651
Kinley, Thomas W178
Kinnear, James P340
Kinnear, Kendall E77
Kinnear, Peter D. A613
Kinney, Alva A408
Kinney, Catherine R. A1019, P375
Kinney, Jon C. A749
Kinney Services (funeral
homes) A1268
Kinney shoes A1470
Kinnie, D. Craig A761
Kinnune, William P. A1525
Kinoshita, Kenji W321
Kinoshita, Mikio W327
Kinoshita, Tadahiko W327
Kinray, Inc. P651
Kinschner, William H. A909
Kinsella, Geraldine A279
Kinser, Dennis P63
Kinsley, Darrell E69
Kinzler, Morton H. E163
Kiplin, Kimberly P473
Kipp, Daniel W. A549
Kipp, James E. P675
Kiraç, Suna W319
Kirby brands P204, P619
Kirby Contract Labour A910
Kirby, J. Scott A139
Kirby vacuum cleaners A252
Kirch PayTV W146, W390
KirchGruppe W106, W146, W390
Kirchoff Group (auto parts) A1394
Kirin Brewery Company,
Limited A160, A174, A175,
W314-W315, W371
Kirin Pharmaceutical A160
Kirincic, Paul E. A947
Kiriri soft drink W315
Kirk, Clifford Scott A311
Kirk, James D. P533
Kirk, Keith B. A549
Kirk Stieff (silver and pewter) A296
Kirk, William F. A535
Kirkland, George L. A353
Kirkpatrick, Lowell A., Jr. A1269
Kirkpatrick Pettis (brokerage) P349
Kirkwood, Allan K. A1115, P397
KIRO-TV (Seattle) A443, P147
Kirsch home decor products A1023
Kirsch, Steve P492
Kirstein, Louis A586
Kirsten, A. Stefan W365

Kirwan, William E. P383, P693
Kisaburo, Ikeda W375
Kiser, Gerald L. A854, A855
Kishida, Katsuhiro W649
Kishimoto (trading company) W296, W358
Kishore, Ganesh M. A985
Kislowski, Peter A1099
Kissam, Kathryn A985
Kissane, Jim P745
Kissel, W. Craig A153
KISS-FM (San Antonio) P147
Kissman, Mark E307
Kissner, Matthew S. A1143
Kist, Ewald W287
Kist, Frederick O. P269
Kistel, C. John, Jr. A1095
Kistinger, Robert F. A355
Kit Kat candy A709, W388
Kitai, Kiyoshi W397
Kitajima, Yoshitoshi W187
Kitami, Ryozo W187
Kitao, Yoshitaka W549
Kitchen Bouquet gravy A374
The Kitchen Collection, Inc. A992
Kitchen, Denise P741
KitchenAid appliances A1520, A1521
Kitchens, Deborah A. A821
Kitchens of Sara Lee A1242
Kitchin, Craig R. E225
Kitchin, Thomas W. E225
KiteKat pet food A915, P315
Kitson, John E204
Kittenbrink, Douglas A. A117
Kittredge, Michael J. E143, E320
Kitty Kit cat litter A375
Kitz, Edward G. P423
Kiviat, Randall I. A689
Kiwi shoe care A1242, A1243
A/S Kjøbenhavns Sommer-Tivoli W163
KJRH-TV (Tulsa, OK) A568, A569
KJZZ-TV (Salt Lake City) P656
KKF.net AG A837, P283
KKHK-FM (Denver) A1402
KKM&D E80
KKR. See Kohlberg Kravis Roberts & Company
KKR Associates A1074
Klaassen, Paul J. E295
Klaben, Gerald L., Jr. E200
Klaisle, Gerard M. A1455
Klane, Larry A319
Klapinsky, Raymond J. A1469, P505
Klappa, Gale E. A1307
Klare, Jeffrey T. A355
Klaristenfeld, Harry I. A1355, P467
Klatell, Robert E. A197
KLA-Tencor (chip equipment maker) A792, E46
Klatt, David A., Jr. A1023
Klaus, Robert C. A375
Klauser, N. Jeffrey A1233
Klausner, Ronald A517

Klaussner Furniture Industries, Inc. P652
Klaussner, Hans P652
KLDE-FM (Houston) P147
Klebe, Terry A. A431
Kleber, Dale E. A467
Kleber tires W367
Kleberg, Alice King A828, P270
Kleberg, Bob A828, P270
Kleberg, Richard A828, P270
Kleberg, Robert A828, P270
Kleberg, Stephen P270
Kleberg, Stephen "Tio" A828
Kleckner, Robert A. P207
Kleenex paper products A826, A827
Kleespies, J. Timothy A1361
KLegal International A840, P286, W324
Klein, Adam P89
Klein, Barbara A. A467
Klein, Calvin P100, P101, P564, W606
Klein, James M. A843
Klein, Joe A1502
Klein, Joel W127
Klein, Kenneth R. E91
Klein, Koos W259
Klein, Kurt K. E70
Klein, Michael J. W67
Klein, Richard R. W505
Klein, Roland W221
Klein, Ron A587
Klein, Thomas A1229
Klein, William M. (BEA Systems) E33, E163
Klein, William S. (Cooper Tire) A433
Kleiner, Madeleine A. A721
Kleiner Perkins Caufield & Byers A560, A918, P64, P180
Kleiner, Rolf E. A819
Kleisner, Fred J. A1540, A1541
Kleisterlee, Gerard W444, W445
Kleman, Charles J. E177
Klemann, Gilbert L., II A217
Klemens, Thomas A. A595
Klemm, Erich W189
Klepper, Kenneth O. P175
Klepser, Tanya P618
Kleveter, Lesley C. E74
Kley, Karl-Ludwig W345
Kley, Max Dietrich W117
Kliemann (tobacco) A1436
Klinck, Paul P115
Kline, Garry D. E274
Kline, Lowry F. A384, A385
Kline, Steven L. A1121
Klineberg, John A889
Klinefelter, Gary V. A135
Kling, Fred R. A1525
Kling, Lewis M. A1321
Klingel, John D. A1193
Klingele, Edward J. E293
Klingensmith, James A717, P235
Klinkhammer, Heinz W205
Klinskoye beer W289

Klintberg, Gunnar E. P236, P237
Kliogest drug W417
K-Lion beer W553
Klipper, Kenneth S. E132, E306
Klipper, Mitchell S. A233
Klitten, Martin R. A353
Klix beverage vending equipment A915, P315
KLM Royal Dutch Airlines A106, A428, A1046, W78, **W316-W317**, W518
Kloc, Thomas J. A115
Klöckner & Company AG (metals distribution) W218, W219
Klockner-ER-WE-PA (extrusion coating) A450
Klockner-Humbolt-Deutz A96
Klondike ice cream W619
Klopman Mills A306
Klopman, William A306
Kloster, Knut A330
Klotsche, John A220, P66
Kluempke, Patrick P123
Kluge, John W. P332, P333, P674
Klugman, Robert D. A79
Klum, Heidi P251
Klumb, Donald E. E236
Klump, Ron P657
Kluth, Barbara A1369
Kluttz, John L. A257
Kluwer, Abele W642
Kluwer (publishing) W642
Klyn, Steven J. A935
Klynveld Kraayenhoff (accounting) P286, W324
Klynveld Main Goerdeler (accounting) P286, W324
Klynveld Peat Marwick Goerdeler. See KPMG International
KM by Krizia brand A691
Kmart Corporation A158, A276, A458, A549, A572, A606, A664, **A830-A831**, A918, A1058, A1092, A1348, A1352, E147, E214, E225, E266, E283, E290, P390, P524, P525, P699, P777, W172, W270, W590
KMCC Western Australia Pty. Ltd. A821
KMGH-TV (Denver) A945
KMP. See Kinder Morgan Energy Partners, L.P.
KMT Semiconductor A970, A971
K N Energy A1054
Knaack-Esbeck, Jane P636
Knabusch, Charles A854
Knabusch, Edward A854
Knafaim-Arkia Holdings (tours) W323
Knapp, Dave P335, P674
Knapp Publications A80, P32
Kneale, James C. A1065
Knedlik, Ronald W. P535
Kneip, Robert C. A1489
Knell, James W. E62
Knepper, Rudolf W107
Knez, Brian J. A1014, A1015, W479

Knezevic, Miro E131
Knibbe, David M. A707
Knicely, Howard V. A1413
Knickerbocker Trust
  Company P186
Kniffen, Jan R. A933
Knight & Hale (hunting
  calls) P170, P171
Knight, Charles F. (Emerson) A546,
  A547
Knight, Charles (Knight
  Ridder) A832
Knight, Edward S. A997, P353
Knight, Glade M. E186
Knight, Guyon A1503
Knight, Jack A832
Knight, Jeffrey A. P213, P623
Knight, Jim A832
Knight Newspapers A832
Knight, Philip H. A1032, A1033
Knight Ridder Inc. A632,
  A832-A833, A1402, P655, W592
Knight, Steven F. W271
Knights and Ladies of Security
  (benefit society) P725
Knights of Labor P34
Knights Technology E57, E197
Knisely, Philip W. A463
Knobbe, Michael J. P37
Knobblock, Denise A. A407
Knoblauch, Gene A351
Knoblauch, Kathleen L. A813
Knoch, Samuel C. E302
Knoll, Florence P276
Knoll, Hans P276
Knoll, Inc. P276-P277, P652
Knoll Parmaceuticals A58, W116
Knoops, Denis W195
Knorr soups W618, W619
Knotts, Patrick W. A501, P163
Knous, Pamela K. A1349
Knowledge Learning
  Corporation P279
Knowledge Organizer
  software E311
Knowledge Universe,
  Inc. P278-P279, P652
KnowledgePlanet.com P279
Knowles, Jonathan K. C. W493
Knowles, Lucius A450
Knox, James E. A177
Knox, Leslie H. A1095
Knox Lumber stores A1090, A1091
KNOX-TV (Knoxville, TN) A568
The Knoxville (Tennessee) News-
  Sentinel A569
NV Koninklijke KNP A1368
Knudsen, Clifford E76
Knudsen, Norma A1197
Knudson, John E. W257
Knudson, Thomas C. A413
Knupp, Ralph E. E133
Knutson, Dan A851, P289, P654
Knutson Mortgage A1364
KNXV-TV (Phoenix) A568, A569
Ko Hong-sik W509

Kobacker Company stores A932,
  A1092
Kobalt tools A892, A1294
Kobayashi, Hideichiro W397
Kobayashi, Isao W299
Kobayashi, Kanji W397
Kobayashi, Koji W386
Kobayashi, Takashi W449
Kobe (oil) A222
Kobe Steel, Ltd. A970, A1463, P713
Kober, Lauri A. A1171
Kobiashvili, Zurab S. A185
Koç Holdings A.S. W318-W319
Koç, Mustafa V. W319
Koç, Ömer W319
Koç, Rahmi M. W318, W319
Koç, Vehbi W318
Koch, Charles G. A834, A835, P280,
  P281, P653
Koch, Craig R. A710, A711
Koch, David H. A834, A835, P280,
  P281, P653
Koch, Ed P368
Koch Engineering A620
Koch, Frederick A834, P280
Koch Industries, Inc. A554, A556,
  A834-A835, A1460, P54,
  P280-P281, P653
Koch, Roland W537
Koch, William A834, P280
Kocher, Joel J. A762, A763
Kochman, Edward E229
Kock, Karen E317
Kockmann, Siegfried W427
Kockums submarine yards W460
Kocol, Robert S. A1337
Koçtas stores W312, W313
Kodachrome film A524
Kodada, Toshio W600
Kodak. See Eastman Kodak
  Company
Kodera, Junichi W551
Koehler, James P337, P675
Koehler-Bright Star, Inc. P313
Koelling, Demetra A373
Koenderman, Paul P. A941
Koenemann, Carl F. A991
Koenig, Brian C. A1259
Koenig, Debra A. A943
Koenig, Mark E. A553
Koenig, Roger L. E172
Koenig, Scott E90
Koenig, William C. A1049, P377
Koep, Donna M. E269
Koeppe, Alfred C. A1175
Koff beer W163
Koffman, Christian A. A801
Koga, Nobuyuki W409
Koga, Toshihisa W449
Kogalymneftegaz (oil and gas
  exploration) W346
Kogan, Eric D. A1401
Kogan, Richard Jay A1251
Koh Boon Hwee W541
Koh, Katsuo N359
Kohl, Allen A838

Kohl, Herb A838
Kohl, Max A838
Kohlberg & Company A836, P282
Kohlberg, Jerome A238, A836,
  A870, P282
Kohlberg Kravis Roberts &
  Company A86, A208, A212, A434,
  A470, A602, A714, A836-A837,
  A844, A870, A908, A960, A1074,
  A1124, A1160, A1204, A1234,
  A1396, P90, P232, P282-P283,
  P412, P506, P558, P653, P712,
  P775
Kohlberger, Richard A. A1459
Kohler, Carl P284
Kohler Company P284-P285, P653
Kohler dairy mix P674
Kohler, Herbert V., Jr. P284, P285,
  P653
Kohler, Herbert V., Sr. P284
Kohler International Ltd. P284
Kohler, John P284
Köhler, Karl Ulrich W595
Kohler, Laura P285, P653
Kohler, Robert P284
Kohler, Ruth P284, P653
Kohler Stables P285
Kohler, Walter P284
Kohlhepp, Robert J. A364, A365
Kohli, Faqir C. W567
Kohl's Corporation A838-A839,
  A1264
Kohl's Inc. (grocery stores) A670,
  A671
Kohlsdorf, Michael E. E303
Kohner Brothers A842
Kohnstamm, Abby F. A765
Kohrt, Carl F. P70, P71, P551
Koide, Kanji W401
Koike, Nobuhiro W139
Koiwai Pure Butter W315
Kojima, Hisayoshi W403
Kojima, Kazuto W237
Kojima, Yorihiko W371
Kokanee beer W289
Kokko, Wesley P773
Kokomo Gas and Fuel
  Company A1034, A1035
Kokusai Denshin Denwa W400
Kolb, David L. A980, A981
Kolber, Jonathan W322, W323
Kolder, Kathryn P196, P197, P612
Kolding, Eivind W95
Kole Imports P524, P525
Koley's Medical Supply, Inc. A1071
Koll Real Estate Services P120
Kollmorgen Corporation (motion
  controls) A462
Kolynos oral care product A386,
  A387
Komada, Hitoshi W515
Komag, Inc. A1514
Komansky, David H. A961, A1019,
  P375
Komaromi Sorgyar (brewery) W254
Komatsu Electronic Metals
  Company W228

Komatsu Ltd. A188, A456, E43, **W320-W321**
Kombi commercial vehicle W631
OAO KomiTEK W346, W347
Komiyama, Kunihiko W321
Komori, Shigetaka W235
Kona Ranch restuarants A288
Kondo, Akira W302
Kondo, Masanobu W405
Kondo, Sadao W514
Kondo, Tasuku W373
Kondo, Tomoyoshi W405
Kondoh, Akira W551
Kondritzer, Gerald R. A355
Konen, Mark E. A795
Koney, Robert D., Jr. A663
Kong, Vincent A745, P243
Kongl. Elektriska Telegraf-Verket W584
Kongstad, Michael W585
Konica W368
König, Wolfgang W211
Koninklijke De Boer Boekhoven W626
Koninklijke Hoogovens W178
Koninklijke Luchtvaart Maatschappij voor Nederland en Kolonien (Royal Airline Company for the Netherlands and Colonies). See KLM Royal Dutch Airlines
Koninklijke Philips Electronics N.V. See Philips Electronics N.V.
Koninklijke PTT Nederland NV W502
Koninklijke Zout-Organon W72
Konishi, Hiroshi W421
Konn, Jeffrey L. P593
Konney, Paul E. A565
KONO-FM (San Antonio) P147
Konowiecki, Joseph S. A1081
Kon-Tiki (book) P408
Kontogiannis, P. W385
Kontos, Mark W. P71, P551
Konz, Ken P145
Koo Bon-Moo W335
Koo In-Hwoi W334
Koo, John W335
Koogle, Timothy A1546
Kooijmans, P. C. W643
Kool cigarettes W142, W143
Kool-Aid A843, A1126
Koolrad Design & Manufacturing (radiators) A502
Kooluris, George P. A291
Koons, James E. P644
Koons, John, Sr. P644
Koons, Linda A1255
Koontz, Bill P413
Koontz, Raymond A488
Koor Industries Ltd. **W322-W323**
Koozer, Jocelyn E261
Kopazna, Wendy P161, P595
Kopczick, Elise M. A447
Kopil, Edward A247
Kopin Corporation E229
Kopkin, Jack A1056
Koplovitz, Kay A1450

Kopnisky, Jack L. A823
Kopp Investment Advisors E123, E292
Koppel, Michael G. A1037
Koppen, Hans T. A759
Kopper, Hilmar W189, W200, W201
Koptchev, Kristine E240
Korade, Donald B. A105
Koraleski, John J. A1423
Koralu W74
Korba, Robert W. P720
Korbel champagne A296, A297, P682
Körber, Hans-Joachim W364, W365
Korda, William A1225
Korea Development Bank W454
Korean Air Lines Company, Ltd. A478, E32, E160, W68, W71, W79
Korean International Steel Associates W454
Koret of California, Inc. (sportswear) P292
Korhonen, Kai W557
Korman, Leo F. P584
Korn (band) E69
Kornafel, Peter P112, P113, P569
Kornbluh, Phillip A247
Kornblum, Warren F. A1397
Kornder, David J. E260
Kornhauser, Henry A359
A/S Korn-og Foderstof Kompagniet W411
Korrvu (packaging) A1262, A1263
Kors, Robert A. P417, P716
Korshak, Sidney A1086
Korsmeier, Gary P563
Korus, Paul J. E228
KoSa (polyester) A834, A835, P280, P281, P653
Kosche, Peter C. A1061
Kosh, Mitchell A1151
Kosich, George W270
KOSI-FM (Denver) A1402
Koslow, Larry B. A359
Kosmaler, Charles H., Jr. P423
Koson, Stanislaw W457
Koster, Steve A305
Kosterman, Gayle P. A1247, P433, P722
Kostuch, Keith A. A129
Kotex A826, A827
Kotobuki, Eiji W515
Kourey, Michael R. E268
Koutsos, M. W385
Kovacevich, Richard M. A1509
Kovacs, Gabor J. P71
Kovalchuk, Brian P429
Kovanda, Gary D. P137, P580
Kovats, Eric A1271
Kowalczyk, Barbara S. A879
Kowalk, Jeff P669
Kowalski, John P694
Kowalski, Michael J. A1384, A1385
Kowloon MTR Tower (Hong Kong) P448
Kowloon Panda hotel W266, W267

Kowon Technology E229
Koyama, Iwao W399
Kozak, Paul A. A337
Kozel, David F. P255, P642
Kozel, Edward R. A369
Kozik, Catherine E. A1363
Kozikowski, Tami A255
Kozitza, Bill P742
Kozlosky, Donna E199
Kozmetsky, George A116
Kozmo.com A1326
Kozy, William A. A245
Kozyrev, Anatoly G. W347
KPMG International A368, A404, A562, A588, A**840**-A**841**, P182, P206, P**286**-P**287**, P620, P654, W222, W**324**-W**325**
KPMG Peat Marwick A404
KPN. See Royal KPN N.V.
KPN Mobile N.V. W502
KPNQwest N.V. A764, A1186
KPR Foods A743
Krackel candy A709
Kraemer, Gerhardt A. A175
Kraemer, Harry M. Jansen, Jr. A236, A237
Kraft, Burnell D. A193
Kraft Foods Inc. A386, A408, A510, A**842**-A**843**, A850, A926, A1126, A1180, A1326, A1414, P148, P204, P288, W102, W536, W618, W646
Kraft Foods International P380, P436, P530, P588, P619, P724
Kraft, James L. A842
Kraftco A842
KraftMaid cabinets A920, A921
Krahling, Thomas J. E124
Kraines, R. Guy A641
Krajewski, Steve A1397
Krakirian, Alain E69
Kramer, Dale A1282
Kramer, Douglas C. P215, P623
Kramer, Francis J. E20
Krämer, Hartmut W447
Kramer, J. Matthew A397
Kramer, Richard J. A665
Kramer, Scott P445
Kramer, Terry A635
Kramont Realty Trust E229
Kramp, Kerry A. P562
Kranc, Lisa R. A209
Krangel, Stanley E. A297
Krannert, Herman A1364
Kransco A926
Kranzco Realty Trust E229
Kranzley, Arthur D. A925, P323
Krapek, Karl J. A1433
Krasny, Michael P. A336, A337
Kratovil, Edward D. A1459
Krauer, Alex W414
Kraus, Ann A1021
Kraus, Carl E. E266
Kraus, Eric A. A657
Kraus, Irene P56
Kraus, Mike P501
Krause, Arthur B. A1319

Krause, Brad P275
Krause, Jon E99
Krause, Morton A1100
Krause, William A54
Krauss, Alan J. A921
Krauss, Mark P732
Krauss-Maffei AG W352
Krauter, Lana Cain A666, A667
Krautsack, Dennis A497
Krautter, Jochen W257
Kravis, Henry R. A238, A836, A837, P282, P283, P653
Kravitz, Lenny W212, W213
Krazy Glue P90, P91
Krch, Cindy P774
Krebbs, Mark A797
Krebs, Robert D. A309
Krefting, Robert J. A1193
Krehbiel, Frederick A. A982, A983
Krehbiel, John H., Jr. A982, A983
Krehbiel, John H., Sr. A982
Kreindler, Peter M. A729
Kreis, Patrice W209
Kremer, Joseph K. A337
Kremer, Richard H. A415
Krenz, Doug A1277
Krenz, Scott A539
Kresa, Kent A1044, A1045
Kresge Eye Institute P591
Kresge, Sebastian A830
Kress, George P621
Kress, William F. P621
Kretzman, Robert K., III A1201
Kreuger, Ivar W220
Kreuser, Dennis P608
Kreutzjans, Michael J. E70
Kreuze, Calvin W. P223
Kriens, Scott G. E226
Krikorian, George P412
Kriloff, Israel A1430
Krim, Arthur P332
Krishna Kumar, R. K. W567
Krisowaty, Robert P693
Krispy crackers A815
Krispy Kreme Doughnuts, Inc. E80, E230
Kristiansen, Kjeld Kirk W332, W333
Krizman (auto parts) A460
KR/NYT Enterprises (purchasing consortium) A832
Kroc, Joan P426
Kroc, Ray A942, P202, P264, P426, P648
Kroeber, C. Kent A773
Kroger, Bernard A844
The Kroger Company A110, A608, A844, A844-A845, A1170, E230, E276, E290, P198, P422, P462, P524, P525, P777, W244
Krogh, August W416
Krogh, Marie W416
Krol, Jack A534
Kroll-O'Gara E29
Kromer, Mary Lou A625
Krone, Kevin A1311
Kronprinz tires W367

Kronser, J. Robert E104
Kroos, Steven R. A1415
Kropelnicki, Martin A. E210
Kropf, Susan J. A217
Krost, Margaret P229
Krott, Joseph P. A1345
Krow, Gary A. A343
KRTR-FM (Honolulu) P147
Kruczek, John P. P756
Krueger, David N. P43
Krueger, James P45
Krueger, Jody P722
Krueger, John H. A1467
Krueger, William A. P404
Kruger, Bob E42
Kruger, Charles H. P457
Kruger (forest products) A826
Krugman, Stan A786
Kruidvat (health and beauty) W312
Krumbholz, David J. A1091
Krüper, Manfred W219
Krupnick, Elizabeth P73
Krupp, Alfred W594
Krupp, Alfried W594
The Krupp Foundation W594
Krupp, Friedrich W594
Krupp Kunststofftechnik (plastic molding machines) W594
Krupp UHDE A786
Kruth, Harold E. P455
Krutter, Forrest N. A253
KRXI-TV (Reno, NV) P147
Kryder, Mark P441
Krylon paint A1278
Kryptonite Corporation A754, A755
Krysiak, Bruce A496
KSHB-TV (Kansas City, MO) A568, A569
KSL Recreation Corporation A837, P283
KS-Touristik-Beteiligungs W310
KTB Associates P506
KTRK-TV (Houston, TX) A61
KTVA-TV (Anchorage) P670
KTVU-TV (Oakland/San Francisco) A443, P147
KU. See Knowledge Universe, Inc.
OOO Kubangazprom W243
Kubasik, Christopher E. A883
Kubo, Tokuo W600
Kubo, Toshio W327
Kubodera, Masao W601
Kubota Corporation A456, A928, W326-W327
Kubota, Toshiro W326
Kucha, Michael A778
Kucharski, John A1110
Kudatgobilik, Tugrul W319
Kudos snacks A914, A915, P314, P315, P665
Kuechle, Scott E. A663
Kuehl, Joan C. A1229
Kuemmerling (spirits) W84
Kuerschner, Vaughn P741
Kugler, Ralph W619
Kuhbach, Robert G. A503

Kuhlman (diesel engine components) A278
Kuhlman, Kerry J. A1041
Kuhn, Edwin P. P748
Kuhn Loeb & Company A860
Kuhn + Bayer (scientific equipment) A600
Kuhne, Alice P624
Kuhnle, Kopp & Kaussch (turbocharger) A278
Kuhnt, Dietmar W505
Kuhura Mining W260
Kuiper, Joost Ch. L. W57
Kuipéri, Hans E. W317
Kuipers, A. S. F. W643
Kujawa, Jan W457
Kukident health and personal care W476
Kukura, Sergei P. W347
Kulicke and Soffa Industries, Inc. E81, E230
Kulicke, C. Scott E81, E230
Kulicke, Fred E81
Kulinsky, Anne A591
Kullback, William J. E262
Kullman, Conny P640
Kullman, Ellen J. A541, P637
Kumagai, Akihiko W533
Kumagai, Kazuo W261
Kumano, Yoshimaru W535
Kumar, Narendra W469
Kumar, Ram N. A1393
Kumar, Sanjay A402, A403
Kumho Group A1124
Kumho Industrial Company W138
Kum-Kleen Products A210
Kummer, Glenn F. A604, A605
Kun Hi Yu W335
Kundert, David J. A231
Kündig, Markus W617
Kundrun, Bernd W127
Kunes, Richard W. A565
Kunin, Diana A1196
Kunin, Myron A1196, A1197
Kunin, Paul A1196
Kunkel, Edward T. W230, W231
Kunnath, Rik P573
Kunz, Heidi A635
Kunz, Thomas S. A1147
Kunze, Ylisa E276
Kupp, Jeffrey A. E219
Kuppenheimer clothing A690
Kuprionis, M. Denise A569
Kureha Spinning W358
Kuritzkes, Michael S. A1345
Kuriyan, John W293
Kurland, Stanford L. A439
Kurland, Susan L. A1443
Kurlander, Lawrence T. A1025
Kuro Casting Shop W326
Kurosawa, Masami W393
Kurren, Faye W. A1375
Kurtz, Herbert E113
Kusama, Saburo W531
Kusamichi, Masatake W404
Küsel, Ottmar C. W637

Kushar, Kent A521, P169
Kushay, Kathy E147
Kushner, Jurij Z A235
Kushner, Stephanie K. A613
Kusin, Gary M. P274, P275, P651
Kusumoto, Roy A1298
Kutcher, Kenneth E. A1317, P453, P733
Kutscher, Larry A517
Kutsenda, Robert G. A173, P49, W91
Kutzman, Christopher J. A939
Kuwahara, Hiroshi W261
Kuwait Investment Authority A1286
Kuwano, Yukinori W514, W515
Kuykendall, Bill P613
Kuykendall, David P611
Kuyper, Pete P698
Kuziaev, Andrei W347
Kuzmich, Richard J. A1353
K. V. Mart Company P489
K-VA-T Food Stores, Inc. P479, P654
KVG Kesselwagen Vermietgesellschaft mbH A638, A639
Kwaishinsha Motor Car Works W402
Kwalwasser, Edward A. A1019, P375
Kwan, Allan A1547
Kwan, Mary E60
Kwan, Michael A899
Kwang Ho Cho W335
Kwanon camera W158
Kwety Ceske (publishing) W626
KWGN-TV (Denver) A1402
Kwik Shop convenience stores A844, A845
KwikFill gas stations P712
Kwik-Fit Holdings plc A616
Kwikset locks and security hardware A264, A265
Kwok, Ephraim E55, E196
KXME-FM (Honolulu) P147
Kyd, Margot A. A1267
Kyer, Maureen W. A1353
Kyle, David L. A1065
Kyle, John F. W281
Kyle, Penelope W. P766
Kynaston, David A1299
Kyocera Corporation A1182, **W328-W329**
Kyodo Tshushin (news service) W198
Kyoei Life A1172
Kyoei Mutual W596
Kyoto Ceramic W328
Kypreos, Nick M. P750
Kyser, Eric A853
Kyu Chang Park W335

L

L & C Arnold (hospital furniture) A718
L-3 Communications Holdings, Inc. A**846**-A*847*, A1190

La Barge furniture P298, P299
La Bécasse beer W289
La Cadena Investments P462, P736
La Casera (soft drinks) W154
La Centrale (electric power) W214
La Choy foods A409
La Cinq TV network W330
La Coipa mine W453
L.A. Darling Company P313
L.A. Dreyfus Company A1526, A1527
La Duc, John T. A931
La Fabrica de Cerveza de San Miguel (brewery) W510
La Farmaco A108
La Forgia, Robert M. A721
La France cleaning products A487
L.A. Gear, Inc. E289
L. A. Gift and Furniture Mart E137
La Herradura (gold mine) A1024
La Ina sherry W85
L.A., Inc. A789
La Ley (legal publisher) W592
La Mer brand A565
La Noce, Luciano W423
La Pastaria restaurants W166
La Porte Methanol Company A974
La Presse (Montreal) W470
La Redoute (catalog sales) W446
La Roche-Posay W343
La Ruche Meridionale W166
La Serenisima dairy products W193
La Spezia thermoelectric plant W214
La Terre wines A422
La Tondena Distillers W511
La Venezia Assicurazioni S.p.A. W99
Laaksonen, Pekka W557
Lab Safety Supply A1538
LaBahn, John G. P573
Labarowski, John V. A855
Labatt beer P746, W162, W288, W289, W376
Labatt, John A192
LaBode, Emmy M. P405, P708
Laboratoire Monique Remy A766
Laboratoires Decleor (cosmetics) W534, W535
Laboratoires GARNIER W342
Laboratoires Pharmaeutiques Goupil W342
Laboratoires Serobiologiques W256
LaBoskey, John E164
Labouchere N.V. W64
LaBounty Manufacturing A1322
Labov Mechanical, Inc. A545
Labrador water W192, W193
LaBranche & Company Inc. E230
LaBranche, Michael E230
Labrousse, Junien W339
Labrum, Ronald K. A321
Labtec (peripherals) W338
Labyrinth (movie) P303
Goupe Lacasse (office furniture) P222

Lacey, Barry P627
Lacey Diversified Industries. *See* LDI, Ltd.
Lacey, J. Michael A483
LaChapelle, Joseph G. E57
Lachman, Charles A1200
Lachmann, Henri W521
Lack, Andrew R. A999
Lackey, Jeffrey A. A293
Lackey, Robert E. T. A393
Lacoff, Stephen A. A239
Lacombe, Michel A973
Lacour-Gayet, Philippe A1253
Lacourt, Liliane W443
Lacquer Craft (furniture) P298
Lactaid A1338, A1339
Lacy, Alan J. A1264, A1265
Lacy, Andre B. P656
Lacy, J. Dan A201
Lacy, Kenneth W. A1427
Lacy, Linwood "Chip" A758, P338
Lada Díaz, Luis W579
Ladbroke Group PLC A720, W258, W259, W300, W472
LADD Furniture A854
Ladenburg Thalmann Financial Services Inc. E231
Ladenburger, Marsha A. P57
Lader, Philip W646, W647
Laderman, Gerald A429
Ladies' Home Journal (magazine) A1218
Ladies Professional Golf Association E184, P124
Ladish Company, Inc. (valves) A1406
Lady Aster chicken A1419
Lady Foot Locker stores A1470
Lady Guard insurance W596
Lady Mitchum cosmetics A1201
LaFare, Gilbert A. A579
Lafarge Corporation A**848**-A*849*, A1006, A1406
Lafarge S.A. A848, W278
LaFave, Arthur J. P251, P641
Lafayette Radio Electronics A366
Lafayette Steel A256
LaFerla, Donald G. A859
Laferriere, Ronald A. A263
Lafever, Dan G. A1533
Lafferty, John M. A191
Laffoon, Polk, IV A833
Lafforgue, Marcel W343
Lafley, Alan G. A1164, A1165
LaForte, Mario J. P677
Lagarde, Christine A220, A221, P66, P67, P548
Lagardère, Arnaud W330, W331
Lagardère, Jean-Luc W330, W331
Lagardère SCA A1254, W110, **W330-W331**, W622
Lagasse Brothers (distribution centers) A1430
Lagendijk, Erik W65
Lager Special Light W314, W315
Lagerfeld fragrance W618, W619

Lago, Marisa A371
Lago Systems A1336
Lagomasino, Maria Elena A809
Lagoven W438
Lagrecca, Mary E154
LaGuardia Airport P334, P398, P399
Laguna car W481
Lahey Clinic P566
LaHood, Stephen R. A747
Lahri, Rajeeva E55
Lai, Dominic K. M. W273
Lai, Michael W571
Laidlaw Inc. A122, A206, A1222, A1478, P518
Laidlaw, W. Sam H. A133
Laing, John W358
Laipple, Pam E259
L'Air Liquide SA A100, A1156
Laird, Melvin P438
Laird, William P655
Laisure, James M. A461
Lajous Vargas, Adrián W440
Lake, Charles A1218
Lake Forest Bank and Trust E318
Lake Havasu City (residential development) A930
Lake, Karen E. P521
Lake Michigan Land Company A1224
Lake Moultrie Water Agency P732
Lake, Sally J. A1313
Lake Superior Forest Products Inc. A285
Lakeland Bancorp, Inc. E231
Lakeland Square shopping center (Florida) P172
Lakelands Golf Club (Australia) P131
Lakeside Publishing and Printing A1218
Lakin, Edwin A. P559
Lal, Shirish R. A293
Lala, Dan J. P619
Lalla-Maharajh, Julia W545
Lalonde, Ron W157
Lam Research Corporation E35, E149, E166
LaMacchia, John A292
Lamacchia, Sergio W451
Lamadrid, Lorenzo P54
Lamale, Ellen Z. A1163
LaMantia, Charles P54
Lamantia, John P771
The Lamaur Corporation (salon products) W534
Lamb, Steven G. P91, P775
Lamb, Thomas (Adelphia Communications) A73
Lamb, Thomas B. (Lexmark) A871
Lambe, Mary K. P719
Lambeau, Earl "Curly" A672, P210, P621
Lambeau Field football A672, P210, P621
Lambert & Butler cigarettes W282, W283

Lambert, Joseph J. A475, P155, W197
Lambert Kay pet products A358
Lambert, Michael D. (Dell) A473
Lambert, Michael (Quantum) A1185
Lambert, Paul E. A1149
Lambert, Sandra L. A1383
Lamberti, Hermann-Josef W201
Lamberti, Nicholas P255
Lamboley, Catherine A. A1277
Lamborghini automobiles. See Automobili Lamborghini
Lambright, Stephen K. A175
Lamb's rum W85
Lameda Montero, Guaicaipuro W438, W439
Lamendola, Robert J. A1237
Lamere, David F. A955
Lamidey, Marc W69
Laminated Profiles (fiberglass panels) A446
Lamkin, Bryan A77
Lammers, Jim P151
Lamond, Pierre R. E136
Lamond, Richard A. A975
Lampe, John W138, W139
Lampert, Edward A208
Lampert, Ira B. E184
Lampert, Pam E48, E189
Lampert, Zohra P204
Lampi, Bob A1225
Lamprecht, Rudi W537
Lan, Jerry P143
Lancaster, Bill P63
Lancaster Caramel Company A708
Lancaster Company A1232
Lancaster Cotton Mills A1316, P452
Lancaster Financial Holdings W608
Lance, H. L. A546
Lancers liquors W206
LanChile (airline) W518
Lancia car A650, W226, W227
Lanciaux, Concetta W349
LANcity E30
Lanco watch W563
Lancôme cosmetics W342, W343
Lanctot, Ed A1410, P484
The Land Before Time (movie and products) A295
Land Cruiser SUV W614, W615
Land, Edwin A1148
Land O'Lakes, Inc. A466, A467, A582, A583, A850-A851, P36, P122, P123, P148, P184, P185, P288-P289, P571, P572, P622, P654, P771
Land Rover vehicle A616, W120, W538
Land Securities Trillium W148
Land Wheelwright Laboratories A1148
LandAmerica A594
Landan, Amnon E91, E242
Landau, Igor W103
Landau, Jean-Michel W171
Landau, Yvette E. A907

L&B clothing W298
LandCare USA A1272
LandCon (engineering) E131
Landegger, George P696
Landegger, Karl P696
Landel, Michel A1296, A1297, W547
Landels, William D. A1083
Landers, Ann A300
L&F Household W476
L&F Products (do-it-yourself) A524
Landis, Kennesaw Mountain P306
L&L/Jiroch A1312
L&M cigarettes A1126
Landmark Building Products P690
Landmark Communications, Inc. A632, P655
Landmark Graphics Corporation A676, A677
Landon, John R. E243
Landon, Roy D. E100, E258
Land-O-Sun Dairies A1338
Landriani, Angelo W423
Lands' End, Inc. A852-A853, P300, P696
Landstar Poole (trucking) P434
Landuyt, William M. A974, A975
L&W Supply Corporation A1456
Landy, Michael J. A1241
Lane Bryant clothing A876
Lane Company (furniture) A630
Lane, Ed A630
Lane Industries, Inc. P655
Lane, J. Gary A1039
Lane, John E124
Lane, Kent E99
Lane, Lynne L. A1205
Lane, Michael K. E219, E303
Lane Processing A1418
Lane, Raymond (Oracle) A1066
Lane, Raymond W. (Mead) A951
Lane, Richard J. A291
Lane, Robert A468, A469
Lane Rossi (textiles) W216
Lane, William, II P655
Laneco food stores A1348, A1349
Lang, Andrea A519
Lang, Charles J. P415
Lang, Linda A. A785
Lang, Sherry A1389
Lang, Steve A719
Langdon, Campbell A205
Langdon, Darby A103
Langenberg, Donald N. P762
Langenberg, Thomas P629
Langepasneftegaz (oil and gas exploration) W346
Langer, Laura L. A1121
Langfelder, Rick P369, P687
Langford, Barry P608
Langhammer, Fred H. A564, A565
Langhoff, Christopher S. A1103
Langlois, Patrick W103
Langon Rieder (tenant representative) P120
Langrand-Dumonceau, A. W64
Langsdorf, Mary C. A1081

Langsner, Scott A967
Langston, Edward P765
Langston, Nathan E. A555
Languedocienne A1252
Langwell, Dennis A875, P295
Lanham, Paul A805
Lanier, Joseph L., Jr. A493
Lanier Worldwide, Inc. A686, W486
Lanigan, Robert J. A1075
Lanigan, Susan S. A1553
Lankester, George E. C. W283
Lankford, Thomas E. A1351
Lanners, Fred, Jr. A530
Lannert, Robert C. A1011
Lanni, J. Terrence A967
Lanning, Al P223
Lanning, David B. A909
Lanning, Mark R. A719
Lanoga Corporation P655
Lansford, Gordon P599
Lansing, John F. A569
Lanterman, A. Kirk A331
Lanthorne, Rodney N. W329
Lantis Eyewear Corporation W607
Lantz, Richard D. A1073
Lanvin fashions W342, W343
Lanyado, Saul W497
Lanza, Frank C. A846, A847
Lanza, Shelley B. A1327
Lanzl, Steven G. A285
Laparte, José L. W635
LAP-BAND dieting device E219
Lapensky, Joseph A1046
LaPenta, Robert L., Jr. (Burlington Coat Factory) A305
LaPenta, Robert V. (L-3 Communications) A846, A847
Laphen, Michael W. A405
Laphroaig scotch W85
Lapidus, Stanley E50
Lapiejko, Kenneth J. A1205
Lapinsky, Joseph F. P713
LaPointe Partners (paper) A890
LaPorta, Scott A. A1087
Laporte plc A836
Lappas, Demetrios A1123
Larberg, Gregory M. A311
Lardakis, Moira A. A1169
Laredo State University P470
Laredo (Texas) *Morning Times* A701, P229
Large-Scale Retail Store Law (Japan) W298
Lariat Petroleum E253
Lark cigarettes A1126
Larkin, Bill M. E273
Larkin, James J. A415
Larkin, Lawrence P47
Larkin, Lyle N. A605
Larkin, Michael A670
Laroche, Yann W209
LaRovere, Ralph A1135
Larrabee, John A1451
Larraguivel, Sergio W635
Larrimore, Randall W. A1431
Larry Miller Advertising P656

Larry Stuart Collection shoes A294, A295
Larsen & Toubro W320
Larsen (canned and frozen vegetables) A466
Larsen, Glenn W. A365
Larsen, Jack P263
Larsen, James V. A345
Larsen, Marshall O. A663
Larsen, Ralph S. A801
Larson, Curtis E., Jr. A287
Larson, David M. A325, P105
Larson, Eric R. A163
Larson, Gustaf W632
Larson, James R. A169
Larson, John M. E172
Larson, J. T. A1341
Larson, Linda P405
Larson, Marie P640
Larson, Martin A421
Larson, Michael J. A399
Larson, Samuel G. A75
Larson, Scott G. E48, E189
Larson, Tom P123
Larson, William B. A397
Larsson, Kent A261
Lartigue, Bernard W613
Las Colinas Physical Therapy Center, Inc. A259
Las Cristinas mine W452, W453
Las Postas supermarkets W498
Las Vegas Hilton casino A1087
Lasag (lasers) W563
LaSalandra, Len P101, P564
LaSalle Bank N.A. W56, W57
LaSalle Hotel Properties E231
Lasco Fittings W605
Laser computers P336
Laser Lead Locator E189
Laser Power E20
LaserAlign sensors E189
LaserJet printer A712
Laserphoto P60
LaserTech Color P506
LaserWriter printer A76, A186
Lasezkay, George M. A119
Lash, Israel A1486
Lashutka, Gregory A1009, P365
LASIK vision correction E255
Lasker, Albert P40
Lasker, Mary P40
LASMO (oil exploration) A132, W216
Laspa, Jude A241, P75
LaSpina, Mario E147
Lassale watches W528, W529
Lasser, Lawrence J. A917
Lasseter, John A. E103
Lasso weed killer A985, A1122
Last Call Clearance Centers A1015
Last Climb: The Legendary Everest Expedition of George Mallory (book) P359
Latacha, Stanley B. A667
Latham, William N. A1467
Lathan, Kim E282

Lathe, Timothy J. A1001
Latin Trade (magazine) P611
Latitude brand A985
Latrobe Brewing W288
Latsus Group A440
Lattanzi, James R. E229
Lattice Inc. P430
Lattice Semiconductor Corporation A82, **E82**, E232, W530
Lau, Edward P419
Lau, Ross B. A1187
Laub, Philip E75
Laub, Steven A. E82, E218
LAUBAG (coal) W218
Laube, Richard W493
Laubies, Pierre A317
Lauda Air A1421
Lauder, Estée A564, A766
Lauder, Evelyn H. A565
Lauder, Joseph A564, A766
Lauder, Leonard A. A564, A565
Lauder, Ronald S. A564, A565
Lauder, William P. A565
Lauders Scotch A423
Laudick, Lawrence A. A1511
Lauer, Len A1319
Lauer, Richard M. A1315
Lauer, Stefan (Lufthansa) W345
Lauer, Steven K. (Topco Associates) P478, P479, P746
Laughlin, Mark E66
Launch Media, Inc. (digital music) A1546
Laundry By Shelli Segal clothing A881
Laun-Dry Supply (textile chemicals) A1484
Laura Ashley Holdings plc A776
Laura Mercier cosmetics A1014, A1015
Laurance, Dale R. A1055
Lauren by Ralph Lauren brand A804, A805
Lauren, Ralph A1150, A1151, W606
Laurentian Bank and Trust of the Bahamas W130
Laurentian Financial Group A878
Lauria, Christina F. A1207
Laurier sanitary napkins W308, W309
Laursen, Poul Ploughmann W333
Lausier, Ernest A127
Lautenberg, Frank A204
L'Auto-Neige Bombardier Limited W132
Laventhol & Horwath (accounting) P206
Lavenus hair care W309
Laverty, Connie H. P373
Lavigne, Louis J., Jr. A641
Lavin, Bernice E. A108, A109
Lavin, Leonard H. A108, A109
Lavine, Gary J. A1029
LaViolette, Paul A. A283
Lavoie, Luc W471

Law & Order (TV show) A999, A1450
Law Enforcement Division of Mace Security International E29
Law Enforcement Training Network A1161
Law, Kerry P623
Lawler, Joseph C. A1219
Lawler, Kathleen A. A683
Lawler, Paul J. P521
Lawless, Robert J. A938, A939
Lawn Genie irrigation products A1392, A1393
Lawn-Boy mowers A1392, A1393
Lawrence, David M. (Kaiser Foundation) A811, P267, P649
Lawrence, David W. (Mayo Foundation) P325
Lawrence, James A. A649
Lawrence, J. Rodney A1131
Lawrence Livermore National Laboratory P495
Lawrence, Ollie, Jr. A1297
Lawrence Pharmaceuticals A1006
Lawrence, Robert H., Jr. A1459
Lawrence, Sandra B. A1149
Lawrence, Steven A473
Lawrence, William B. A1413
Lawrie, J. Michael A765
Lawry's Foods W618
Lawson, A. Peter A991
Lawson, Debbie (Banner) E162
Lawson, Debra A. (Roundy's) P423, P718
Lawson, Jane E. W475
Lawson, Jim P716
Lawson, John K. A469
Lawson, Lisa B. A643
Lawson, Rodger A. A1173
Lawter International, Inc. A522
Lawyers Title A1436
Lax, Frederick M. E126
Lay, Kenneth L. A552, A553, A556
Lay, Terry L. A1475
Lay, T. Y. W61
Lay, W. P. A1306
Laybourne, Geraldine P218
Layman, David A. A855
Layman, Sharon L. A1375
Laymon, Lisa W181
Layne, Bob A497
Layne, Stuart A281
Lay's potato chips A1106, A1107
Layton, Donald H. A809
Lazar, Jack R. E251
Lazard Freres (investment bank) A212
Lazare Kaplan International W528
Lazares, Nicholas W. E170
Lazarus, Barry A. A909
Lazarus, Charles A1396
Lazarus, Franz E. A437
Lazarus, Fred A586
Lazarus, Ralph A586
Lazarus, Shelly W647
Lazarus stores A587

La-Z-Boy Inc. A854-A855, P298, P659
LB Community Bank & Trust P534
LBJ Library (University of Texas) P449
LC2 hair care W309
LCC International, Inc. E232
LCI International. A1186
LD cigarettes W241
LDDS (telecom) A1528, A1534
LDI, Ltd. P656
"Le Bebe" car W442
Le Bon Marché stores W348, W349
Le Buffet Catering W311
Le Clic cameras E184
le coq sportif shoes A294
Le Corre, Eric W367
Le Couviour (hospital beds) A718
Le Drugstore W466
Le Floch-Prigent, Loïk W102
Le Goff, Alain W477
Le Groupe Vidéotron (cable TV) W470, W471, W494
Le Journal de Montréal W471
Le Journal de Québec W471
Le Journal de Rosemont (Montreal) W470
Le Lay, Patrick W135
Le Maire, Patrice N. A709
Le Méridien hotels E231, W174, W408
Le Roux, Pierre W77
Le Tierce (betting) W258
Lea & Perrins sauces W193
Lea, Anthony W. W93
Lea, Gregory S. P263
Lea, John S. A1419
Leach, Anthony R. A1055
Leach, James A222
Leach, Thomas D. A1403
Leadbetter, F. W. A1524
Leader Mortgage Company E204
Leader Price supermarkets W166, W167
Leadership is an Art (book) A706
Leadership Jazz (book) A706
Leaf candy A708
Leafbuster A265
Leahy, John J. W71
Leahy, Terry P. W590, W591
Leamer, Marybeth H. A443, P147, P585
Leamon, Jerry A475, P155, W197
Lean, Mean Fat-Reducing Grilling Machine E116
Leap office furniture A1334, A1335
Leap Wireless International, Inc. A1182, E232
LeapFrog (toys) P278, P279
LEAPS. *See* Long-term Equity Anticipation Securities
Lear Corporation A856-A857, A1432
Lear Romec (aerospace) A446
Lear Siegler A856
Lear, William H. A605
Learjet Inc. W132

The Learning Channel P158, P159, P594
The Learning Company A926, P619
Learning Horizons A146, A147
LeaRonal (specialty chemicals) A1212
Leasco Data Processing Equipment Corporation A888
Lease International A212
Lease, Stephen L. A1231
Leasetec (computer leasing) A822
Leatherby, Dennis A1419
Leatherdale, Douglas W. A1237
LEB Communications A350
Lebel, Jean-Jacques W343
Lebensfeld, Harry P752
LeBer, Richard A1005
LeBlanc, Emery P. W75
LeBlanc, Richard Jean-Pierre W293
LeBoeuf, Raymond W. A1153
LeBow, Bennett A1204
Lech beer W553
Leche Celta (dairy) A1338
Lechene, Marc A849
Lechleiter, John C. A541
Lechner, David E. P759
LeClercq, Jacques W194
Ledbetter, Bureon E., Jr. P125
Ledbetter, Carl S. A1051
Lederer, John A. W245
Lederer, Jules A300
Lederhausen, Mats A943
Lederle Laboratories A600
Lederman, Frank L. A113
Ledford, Randall D. A547
The Ledger (Lakeland, FL, newspaper) A1021
Ledi discount stores W588
Ledman, William I. A627
LeDomaine sparkling wines A423
Lee Byung-Chull W508
Lee, Charles R. A1472, A1473
Lee Creative Research P308
Lee, C. T. W229
Lee, Denise M. P153
Lee, Dennis M. A1471
Lee Doo-Seon W275
Lee, Frank E76
Lee, Greg (Sears, Roebuck) A1265
Lee, Greg W. (Tyson Foods) A1419
Lee, Henry H. M. W267
Lee Hyung-Do W509
Lee jeans A666, A839, A1474, A1475
Lee, Jerry S. A663
Lee, J. I. W275
Lee, Joe R. A464, A465
Lee Jong-Ki W509
Lee Joong-Koo W509
Lee Kun-Hee W508, W509
Lee Ku-Taek W455
Lee Kyung-Woo W509
Lee, Mike W571
Lee Moore Oil Company A1084
Lee, Ofelia P772
Lee, Peter Y. W. W267

Lee, Randy A1261
Lee, Ray A155
Lee, Robert E. (civil war General) A828, P270
Lee, Robert E. (Millennium Chemicals) A975
Lee Soo-Bin W509
Lee, Steven J. E105, E268
Lee, Theresa K. A523
Lee, Thomas H. A836
Lee, Wanda A. A1081
Lee Won-Pyo W455
Leedham, Tom P246
Leekley, John R. A921
Leemon, Daniel O. A349
Leemputte, Peter G. A299
Leenhouts, Nelson B. E214
Leeper, Gerald A583
Leer Tokyo Pearl P662
Lees carpet and carpet tiles P568
Lees, David W569
Lee's Famous Recipe Country Chicken restaurants A1280
Leeson, Nick W286
Leewards Creative Crafts A968
Leff, Robert A958
Leffe beer W288, W289
LeFors, John D. A1525
Lefort, Neil A983
LeFrak, Harrison P291
Lefrak, Harry P290
The Lefrak Organization P290-P291, P656
LeFrak, Richard S. P290, P291
LeFrak, Samuel J. P290, P291, P656
Leftwich, Ronald W. A1277
Legacy containers A1415
Legal & General Group Plc W114
The Legal Center P399
Legend car W265
The Legend of Bagger Vance (movie) P167
Legend of the Seas (cruise ship) A1217
Legend of Zelda (video games) W394, W395
LEGENT (network software) A402, A758
Legg, Dexter R. A875, P295
Leggett & Platt, Inc. A858-A859
Leggett, Catherine S. P507, P765
Leggett family P76
Leggett, J. P. A858
L'eggs hosiery A1242, A1243
LegiSlate service A1502
Legislators' Retirement Fund A315, P97
LEGO Company W332-W333
LEGOLAND theme park W332, W333
Legrand SA (electrical products) W520
Lehel refrigerators W210
Lehigh Coal & Navigation A1154
Lehigh Navigation Electric A1154
Lehigh Valley Dairies W288

Lehigh Valley Light & Power A1154
Lehman, Alice L. A1487
Lehman Brothers Holdings Inc. A142, A596, A614, A704, A846, A856, A860-A861, A1416, E262, P88
Lehman, Durr & Company A860
Lehman, Emanuel A860
Lehman, Henry A860
Lehman, Mark E. A239
Lehman, Mayer A860
Lehman, Michael E. A1343
Lehman, Robert A860
Lehman, W. Dudley A827
Lehner, Ulrich W257
Lehnhard, Mary Nell A269, P83
Lehnkering (freight) W460
l.e.i. shoes E294
Leibler, H. Guy P449, P730
Leibovitz, Mitchell G. A1100, A1101
Leibowitz, Martin L. A1355, P467
Leibowitz, Stanley A777
Leichnitz, Leonard P. A813
Leidelmeyer, Louis E60, E202
Leiden, Jeffrey M. A59
Leidy, Mark A985
Leigh, Patricia L. P707
Leigh, Peter V. E244
Leinbach, Tracy A. A1223
Leininger, Jeffery L. A955
Leino, David L. A63
The Leisure Company A138
Leisure Lodges (nursing homes) A259
Leitch, Alexander P. W653
Leiting, Denis E. P37
Leja, Joe E247
Lejaby Euralis lingerie A1498, A1499
Leland, Douglas C. A1525
Leland, Glenn A1358
Leland, Henry P152
Leland James Service Corporation A421
Leland Stanford Junior University P456
Lemagne, Bruno W619
Leman, Eugene D. A743
Lemarchand, Francois W133
LeMay, Ronald T. A1319
Lemée, Bernard W131
Lemelson, Jerome P450
LeMenu frozen foods A316
Lemieux, Gerald J. A1075
Lemieux, Joseph H. A1075
Lemire, Denis T. A159
Lemle, Robert S. A313
Lemly, William A1486
Lemmon, Richard A. E128, E300
Lemoine, Frédéric W161
Lemoine, Gaston A491
Lemonnier, Leonor Duval W164
Lence, Robert B. P239
Lend Lease Real Estate Investments A218, W98, W382, W434
Lenderink, Gary B. P215

Lender's (bagels) A816
Lendrum, Christopher J. W115
Lenehan, James T. A801
Lenfest Communications (cable) A390
Lenhardt, David K. A1117
Lenhardt, Stephen W. P757
Lennar Corporation A862-A863, A1178
Lennar Land Partners E234
Lennon, Fred P739
Lennox, Dave A864
Lennox International Inc. A864-A865
Lennox, Susan A659
Lenny, Richard H. A708, A709
Lenoir Chair Company A630
Lenôtre (catering) W58, W59
Lenox Awards P262
Lenox (china) A296, A297, A486, P262
LensCrafters, Inc. P713
Lentini, Anthony R., Jr. A185
Lentsch, William A1047
Lentz, Thomas W. P451
Lenz, Mark R. A1553
Lenzen, Lorelei M. E70
Lenzmeier, Allen U. A255
Leo Burnett Worldwide (advertising) A1126, A1136, P72, P73, P551
The Leo Group (advertising) P72, P551, W198
Leo, Jim P771
Leon car W631
Leon Hatot watch W563
Leon, Jean P369
Leonard, Bernard J. (Burlington Industries) A307
Leonard, Bernard (Tyson Foods) A1419
Leonard Green & Partners, L.P. A830, P394, P701, W262
Leonard, J. Wayne A554, A555
Leonard N. Stern School of Business P689
Leonard, William A191
Leonardi, Anthony J. A1117
Leonard's department store A1188
Leonberger, Frederick L. A793
Leonetti, James H. P121, P571
Leonhardt, David A. E81
LEONI AG W201
Leoni, Elio W477
Leopards snacks A775
LePage (adhesive) W256
Lepley, Rick A. A1057
Lepofsky, Robert J. E213
Leponex drug W415
Lepore, Dawn G. A349
LePore, Philip T. A1191
Leprino Foods Company A768, P657
Leprino, Michael, Sr. P657
Lerch, Marie P89
Lerche-Thomsen, Kim W465
Lerer, Kenneth B. A181

Lerner, Alfred (MBNA) A936, A937
Lerner, Alfred (Progressive) A1168
Lerner New York clothing A876,
   A877
Lerner, Sandra A368
Lerner, Steven L. A1157
Leroux, Monique W471
Leroy, Pierre W331
Lerwill, Robert E. W153
Les Chais Beaucairos wine
   production W166, W167
Les Echos (newspaper
   publisher) W430
Les idées de ma maison
   (magazine) W471
Les Paperteies de la Chapelle-
   Darblay W556
Les Scwab Tire Centers P657
Lesar, David J. A676, A677
Lesch, Donna J. E316, E317
LESCO, Inc. (turf care) P38
Lescol drug W415
Lescure, Pierre W625
Leser, Lawrence A568
Lesher, Cynthia L. A1543
Leshne, Jerome A507
The Leshner Corporation A1134,
   A1135
Leshner Financial A438
Lesinski, James P. A1179
Lesko, John J. A839
Lesko, Newland A771
Leslie Hindman Auctioneers A1304
Leslie, Jonathan C. A. W489
Leslie, Matt P702
Leslie, Michael J. A663
Leslie's store A876
Lesser, Richard G. A1389
Lesser, Steven P47
Lessersohn, James C. A1021
Lessey, Bruce A122
Lessing, Stephen M. A861
Lester, James D., III A93
Lester, J. Mark E39
Lester, Larry C. A909
Lester, Michael W111
Lester, W. Howard A1530, A1531
Lester, Wilson A., Jr. A1203
Lestina, Gerald F. P422, P423, P718
Lestoil cleaning product A374,
   A375
LeStrange, Dennis P. A747
Letbetter, R. Steve A1199
Letham, Dennis J. A177
Letheby & Christopher
   (events) W175
Leto, Richard A839
Let's Go to an Amusement Park!
   software W186
Let's Talk Cellular Wireless
   stores A1026
Letterman, David A998
Lettuce Entertain You Enterprises,
   Inc. A288
L'Etude Tajan auction house W348
Letzler, Jonathan R. A1221
Leucadia National A252, E199

Leucovorin calcium drug E71
Leuenberger, Andres F. W493
Leukine drug E71, E218
Leuliette, Timothy D. P673
Leung, Sandra A291
Leuschner, Albrecht M. A573
Leustatin drug A801
Lev, Bruce L. P339
LeVan, George E152
Levangie, Daniel J. E50
Level 3 Communications,
   Inc. A**866**-A**867**, A1114, E233,
   E261, P396, P701
Level, Jacques W432
Level, Leon J. A405
Leven, Stephen H. A1379
Levenick, Stuart L. A333
Levenson, Ronald M. E153
Lever 2000 soap W618
Lever Brothers W618
Lever House (New York) P449
Lever, James W618
Lever, Ken W605
Lever, William W618
Levergood, Jay A1258
Levergood, John H. A1259
Levesley, Garry A89
Levesque, Mike P413
Levi Strauss & Company A634,
   A**868**-A**869**, A1474, P**292**-P**293**,
   P657, P735
Leviathan Gas Pipeline A536
Levin, Alan G. A1119
Levin, Gerald M. A180, A181, A312
Levin, Jay J. A1077
Levin, Ken P409
Levin, Lubbe P495, P755
Levin, Neil P398, P703
Levin, Richard C. (Yale
   University) P776
Levin, Richard (Major League
   Baseball) P307
Levin, Robert J. A581
Levin, Sandy A669
Levine, Al A578
Levine, Bernie A578
Levine, David L. E279
Levine, Howard R. A578, A579
Levine, James M. A1139
Levine, Joshua A567
Levine, Kenneth M. A987
Levine, Leon A578, A579
Levine, Lewis A578
Levine, Robert R. (USA Education,
   Inc.) A1449
Levine, Rob (National Basketball
   Association) P355
Levine, Steven E125
Levine, William I. A219
Levinson, Arthur D. A640
Levinson, Donald M. A361
Levinson, Marshall J. A239
Levinson, Milton P529
Levi's jeans A666, A838, A839,
   A868, A869, P292, P293
Levi's Outlet by M.O.S.T. P539
Levis, Salomon E193

Levit, Max P622
Levitetz, Jeff P708
Levitt, Andrea E318
Levitt, Arthur P111
Levitt, Cindy E69
Levitt, Morris R. P249
Levolor blinds A1022, A1023
Levos, Jeffrey B. A431
Levy, Alain W212, W213
Levy, Barbara A1215
Levy, Bruce L. A669
Lévy, Gilles-Pierre W433
Levy, Jacques A1325
Levy, Jeffrey M. A545
Levy, John A262
Lévy, Maurice W466, W467
Levy, Myron E68, E214
Levy, Paul D. E110
Levy, Randall D. A1365
Lévy, Raymond H.
   (Lagardère) W331
Levy, Raymond (Renault) W480
Levy Restaurants (events) W175
Levy, Richard D. A1017, P371
Lévy, Shemaya W481
Lévy-Garboua, Vivien W131
Lew, Solomon W172
Lewellen, Larry M. P383, P693
Lewent, Judy C. A957
Lewin, Dennis P357
Lewin, Luis E. A1403
Lewin, Rene R. A149
Lewinter, David J. A517
Lewis, Aylwin B. A1405
Lewis, Chris A. A783
Lewis, Claude H. A69
Lewis, Daniel C. P89
Lewis, Darlene P763
Lewis, Derek W249
Lewis, Diana D. A531
Lewis, Donald C. A225
Lewis, Everett D. A1375
Lewis, Geoffrey D. A993
Lewis, George R. A1127
Lewis, Henrietta A1246, P432
Lewis Homes A812
Lewis, Jeanne A1325
Lewis, John D. (Comerica) A395
Lewis, John L. (AFL-CIO) P34
Lewis, John (Milliken) P343, P677
Lewis, Joseph (Dave and
   Buster's) E51
Lewis, Joseph (Progressive) A1168
Lewis, Kenneth D. (Bank of
   America) A226, A227
Lewis, Kenneth O. (Stanley
   Works) A1323
Lewis, Lemuel E. P655
Lewis, Marilyn Ware A154
Lewis, Michael W87
Lewis, Peter B. A1168, A1169
Lewis, Reggie A280
Lewis, Richard A. (Anadarko
   Petroleum) A169
Lewis, Richard H. (Prima
   Energy) E270

Lewis, Robert B. (Moore) W379
Lewis, Robert E. (American
    International Group) A151
Lewis, Roderic W. A971
Lewis, Rone, III A755
Lewis, Russell T. A1020, A1021
Lewis, Salim "Cy" A238
Lewis, Shirley P720
Lewis Tappan's Mercantile
    Agency A516
Lewis, Thomas C. (Salvation Army
    USA) P427
Lewis, Thomas R., II
    (AMRESCO) E155
Lewis, Wendy P307, P663
Lewis, Yvonne A907
Lex Computer Systems A1140
Lex Electronics A196
Lexel (low-voltage products) W520
Lexent Inc. E233
Lexington Community
    College P757
Lexington Furniture P298, P299,
    P659
Lexington (Kentucky) *Herald-
    Leader* A833
LexisNexis Group (databases) A950,
    E221, P80, W478, W479
Lexmark International, Inc. A764,
    A**870**-A**871**, E239, P676
Lexus cars A1294, E170, P256,
    P589, P631, P644, P656, W614,
    W615
Ley, Mark P253, P642
Leyland Bus W632
Leyland Trucks A1078, A1079
Lezama, Fernando A217
LFE (hydraulic equipment) P310
LG Group W**334**-W**335**, W444,
    W508
LG&E Energy Corporation
    (utility) W218
LHC, Inc. P261
Lhota, William J. A141
Li & Fung Retailing A1396
Li Ka-shing A1082, W272, W273,
    W306
Li, Victor T. K. W273
Liakopulos, Nick A745, P243
Liana vehicle W561
Liang, Christine P545
Liang, Marcel P545
Libbey Glass A1074
Libbey Inc. (glass) A1022
Libbey-Owens-Ford A1152, P212
Libby's (foods) W388
Libenson, Rick A436
Liberate Technologies A1066
Liberatore, Daniel A73
Liberatore, Jorinne P597
Liberson, Dennis H. A319
Libertad hypermarkets W166, W167
Liberty Bancorp, Inc. A230
Liberty Brokerage A944
Liberty Capital Partners E282
Liberty Cellular, Inc. A128
The Liberty Corporation W474

Liberty Digital A1476
Liberty Equities A1290
Liberty Financial Companies,
    Inc. A602, P658
Liberty Hardware
    Manufacturing A920, A921
Liberty Liquor stores W644, W645
Liberty Livewire Corporation A872
Liberty Media Group A202, A338,
    A622, A**872**-A**873**, A1160, A1450,
    P158, P232, P594, W204, W390,
    W582
Liberty Media International,
    Inc. A714
Liberty Medical Supply E105, E268
Liberty Mutual Insurance
    Companies A688, A**874**-A**875**,
    A1080, P**294**-P**295**, P658
Liberty National Life Insurance
    Company A1390, A1391
Liberty Northwest Insurance
    Corporation A875, P294, P295
Liberty plan A1076
Liberty ships A810, P266
Liberty Technologies (diagnostic
    equipment) A446
Liberty Travel, Inc. P**296**-P**297**,
    P658
Liberty Wanger Asset
    Management A875, P294
Libertysurf (Internet service
    provider) W312
Libertyville Bank and Trust E318
Libonati, Berardino W574
LIBRA (software) A103
Library and Information
    Commission P79
Library at Northwestern University
    (Evanston, IL) P449
Library Server software A1336
Libris 2000 (library
    automation) P69
Librium drug W492
Librix Learning P308, P664
Lichtenberger, William A1156
Lichtenstein Pharmazeutica W342
Lichtenstein, Susan B. A1245
Lichtenthal, Peter A565
Lichtenwald, Irv H. E25, E149
Licoys, Eric W625
Liddell, Stephen C. A867
Liddy, Brian P723
Liddy, Edward M. A126, A127
LIDEX drug E89
Lidow, Alexander E74, E222
Lidow, Derek E74
Lidow, Eric E74
Liebentritt, Donald J. A561, P181
Lieberman, Pamela Forbes P484,
    P485, P749
Liebgott, Robert P485
Liedel, Christopher A. P359, P683
Liedtke, Bill A1096
Liedtke, J. Hugh A1096
Liedtke, Kurt W491
Lienhard, Jerome T. A627
Liennenbrugger, Herbert P698
Liesen, Klaus W631

Life & Health Benefits
    Management A922
Life Care Centers of America E211,
    P658
Life cereal A1107, A1180, A1181
Life Fitness equipment A298
Life Insurance Company of the
    Southwest P684
Life Investors W64
LIFE (magazine) A1218
Life Partners Group
    (insurance) A714, P232
Life Stride women's shoes A295
Lifeboat Matey (prepublication
    services) P506
Lifecast.com P130
LifeLINC annuities A794
LifePoint Hospitals, Inc. A694
LifeSavers candy A60, A843
LifeScan (diabetes
    monitoring) A800, W416
LifeStyle Furnishings International
    Ltd. A920, P**298**-P**299**, P659
Lifestyle music systems P93
Lifetime Cash lottery game P668
Lifetime Entertainment Services
    (cable network) A60, A61, A700,
    P228, P229, P629
The Lifetime Finish brass
    finish A921
LifeWorks (software) A779
Lifschitz, Frank A1150
Lifschitz, Ralph A1150
Liftin, John M. A1173
Ligand Pharmaceuticals A118
Liggero, Samuel H. A1149
Liggett & Myers A1436
Liggett Group A1126, W206
Liggett-Ducat W240
Light (electric utility) A1198
Light House stores P577
Light, John R. A1267
Light Serviços de Electricidade
    S.A. W209
Lightbridge, Inc. E**83**, E233
Lightera (fiber-optics) E41
Lightfoot, Angela P431
Lightfoot, H. Harrison P463
LIGHTHOUSE E302
Lighting Corporation of
    America A1446
Lightlife (meat alternatives) A408
Lightner, James D. E129, E302
Lightnet (fiber-
    optics/communications) A454,
    A1528
Lightning brand A527
Lightning Print P244
Lightning Source (on-demand
    printing) A756, A757, P244, P245
Lightolier lighting fixtures P613
Lightpath (local-exchange
    carrier) A312
Lightrealm A762
Light-Servicos de Eletricidade A88
LIGHTSHIP (software) A103
LightStream (ATM switches) A368

Lightstyle juice products P381
Lightworks Editing System A1358
LightWorks optical
   transmission E179
Lightyear Communications P764
Ligon, Duke R. A483
Ligon, W. Austin A367
Liguori, August J. E141, E319
Liguori, Stephen A989
LIKA (circuit boards) A1188
Lil' Champ Food Stores,
   Inc. A1084, A1085
Lila Wallace-Reader's Digest
   Fund A1192
Liles, Bob P611
Lilien, R. Jarrett A567
Lilienthal, Stephen W. A379
Lillian August funiture P299
Lillie, James E. W379
Lillie, John M. A635
Lillis, James J. A337
Lilly, Edward F. P727
Lilly, Eli A540
Lilly Endowment A540
Lilly Industries A1152
Lilly, John N. A1136, A1137
Lilly, Steven L. P685
Lily of France lingerie A1474,
   A1475
Lily paper products P727
Lily Tulip Cups A1074
Limbacher, Randy L. A311
Lime-A-Way home care W476
Limerick nuclear plant A570
The Limited, Inc. A62, A776,
   A876-A877, W124
Limol body, hair, skin care A487
Limon rum W109
Limp Bizkit (band) E69
Limzul cleaning and laundry
   products A487
LIN Broadcasting (cellular) P332
Lin, Fred W61
Lin, Fu-Kuen A160
LIN Holdings (TV stations) A715,
   P233
Lin, Maya P276, P652
Lin, Patrick W61
Lin, Shan-Chih W570
Lin, Simon W61
Lin Tingsheng W571
Lin Weishan W570, W571
Linares López, Julio W579
Linares, Nora P472
Linate airport (Milan) W518
Lincoln, Abraham A310, A688,
   A1444
Lincoln American Life
   Insurance A414
Lincoln, Bob P551
Lincoln Building (New York
   City) P231
Lincoln car P633, P647, P666, P733
Lincoln Casket A718
Lincoln Center for the Performing
   Arts, Library-Museum (New York
   City) P449

The Lincoln Company A690
Lincoln Income Life A414
Lincoln Logs A693
Lincoln Medical and Mental Health
   Center (New York City) P369
Lincoln, Murray A1008, P364
Lincoln National
   Corporation **A878-A879**, A964
Lincoln Oil Refining A1460
Lincoln Property Company P659
Lincoln, Robert A1090
Lincoln Savings A144
Lincoln Tunnel P398, P399, P703
Lincoln vehicles A616
Lind, David R. P121
Lind, Philip B. W495
Linda McCartney vegetarian
   meals A723
Lindahl, Dennis P633
Lindahl, George, III A169
Lindahl, Göran W54, W92, W93
Lindbergh, Charles A662, A1088,
   A1412
Lindbloom, Chad M. A345
Lindburg, Arthur P178
Linde AG A974, A1156, W201
Linde, Douglas T. E34, E165
Linde, Edward H. E34, E165
Lindegaard, Jørgen W519
Lindelov, Flemming W163
Lindemann, J. J. A547
Lindemood, John B. A1129
Lindenbergh, Hessel W287
Lindenmeyr family P574
Linder, Mary Carroll A1047
Linder, Wolfgang W427
Lindgren, Tim A741, P241
Lindig, Bill A1350
Lindler, Patricia T. A695
Lindman, Joanne O'Rourke P45
Lindner, Carl H. A144, A145, A355,
   P518
Lindner, Carl H., III A145, A354
Lindner family A642
Lindner, Keith E. A145, A355
Lindner, Richard G. P576
Lindner, Robert A144
Lindner, S. Craig A145
Lindquist, Gern A64, P30
Lindsay, James W. P36
Lindsay, Ronald T. A389
The Line (airline) W68
Lineage furniture P298
Linear Technology
   Corporation E**84**, E233
Linebarger, Thomas A457
Linee Aeree Italiane W78
Linen, Jonathan S. A143
Linens 'n Things stores A246, A458
LineOne (Internet service
   provider) W620
Lines diapers A826
Linfinity Microelectronics E297
Ling Electric A896
Ling, James A896
Ling, Robert M., Jr. P489

Ling, Timothy H. A1439
Ling-Temco-Vought A896
Linjeflyg (airline) W518
Link Magazine E188
Link, Raymond A. E305
Link, Walter W436
Linkabit (company) A1182
Link-Belt (power transmission
   equipment) A612
Linke, Curtis G. A469
Linkous, Ronald A381
Linn, Saundra A845
Linnert, Terrence G. A663
Linostar (diapers) A826
LINQ (data messaging) A1183
Lin's (food stores) P545
Linsco/Private Ledger
   Corporation P659
Linsdau, Anne C. A619
Linsky, Barry R. A773
Linsky, Roberta W339
Lintner, Michael J. A1407
Linton, William W. A1319
Linux Format (magazine) W239
Linux operating system A764,
   A972, E42, E170, E179, W514
LinuxWorld Conference &
   Expo P249
Linvex Technology E121
Linville, Randal L. P724
Liollio, Constantine S. A1199
Lion Expansion W183
The Lion King (movie) P166
Lion Match Company W552
Lion Nathan W84, W314
Lioncover Insurance Company
   Ltd. W337
Lione, Gail A. A683
Lionel (company) A1482
Lionel stores A1396
Lionetti, Giovanni W79
Lipe, Perry L. A199
Lipitor drug A1118, A1119
Lipobay drug W118
Lipoff, Deborah P409
Lipp, Marie P582
Lipp, Robert I. A371
Lipper Analytical Services W484
Lippert, Martin J. W475
Lippincott publishing
   imprint W642
Lippincott Williams & Wilkins
   (medical information) W643
Lips, Barbara Woodward P324
Lipschitz, Louis A1397
Lipsett, R. F. W281
Lipson, David A1196
Lipstein, Steven H. P555
Lipton P530
Lipton, Marty A1288, P446
Lipton tea A1102, A1103, A1104,
   A1105, A1106, A1107, W618,
   W619
Liquid Audio E117
Liquid Carbonic Division A1156
Liquid Paper correction fluid A656,
   A1022, A1023

Liquid-Plumr A374, A375
Liquifilm ophthalmic product A118
Liquitint dye P343
Liquorland W172
Lires Rial, Sergio A. W57
Liria, Peter, Jr. P175
Lisbon University P449
Lisenby, Terry S. A1053
Lisimachio, Louis W331
Liska, Paul J. A1265
Lisson, Kathryn W113
Lissy, David H. A159
List (publishing) W107
Listi, Frank P203
Liston, Thomas S.
  (PETsMART) A1117
Liston, Tom (Humana) A739
L'Italien, Carroll W133
Litchfield Financial
  (timeshares) A1380
Litchfield Luxury Theatres P412
Litchfield, Paul A664
Lite-Brite A693
Lite-On Power
  Semiconductor A1482, E192
Lithium Corporation of
  America A612
Litho-Krome (lithography) A679,
  P217
Lithonia Lighting A1004, A1005
Litman, David A1451, E215
Litner, Jon P361
Litt, Jay A. A1541
Litter Green cat litter A374
Little America hotel chain P729
Little & Walker P54
Little, Arthur D. P54
Little Caesar pizza A500, P162,
  P657
Little Chef restaurants W174, W248
Little Debbie snack food P669
Little Forest toys W333
Little, Gene E. A1387
Little, James M. E139
Little Mermaid statue
  (Copenhagen) W162
Little, Mitchell R. E93
Little, Paul W. E113, E280
Little, Royal A1380, P54
Little Sizzlers sausage A730
Little Swimmers diapers A827
Little Switzerland duty free
  stores A1384
Little Tikes toys A1022, A1023
Little, Vincent P422
Littlefield, Christopher J. A487
Littlefield, Warren A998
Littlejohn & Levy P565
Littlewoods Organisation
  (retailer) A436, W356
Littman, Irving A275
Littman Jewelers A844, A845
Litton Industries, Inc. A116, A408,
  A1044, A1152, W190
Littwin, Lawrence P472
Litzenich, James C. A1449
Litzsinger, Richard P192

Litzsinger, R. Mark P193
Liu, Don H. A747
Liu, Jack A1253
Liu, Tally C. A833
Liuzzi, R. C. P572
Live Wires children's shoes A295
LIVE! With Regis (TV show) A61
Lively, Dorvin A1397
Lively, Tom A340
Livengood, Scott A. E80, E230
Liveris, Andrew N. A505
Livermore, Ann M. A713
Living Well brand foods A607
living.com A130, A260
Livingston Cellars wine A521, P169
Livingston, John T. P477
LivingWell health clubs W258,
  W259
Liz & Co. A880
Liz Claiborne, Inc. A216, A690,
  A880-A881, E78
L.J. Knowles & Bros. A450
L.J. Melody & Company P120,
  P121, P571
L.L. Bean, Inc. A852, E135, P254,
  P300-P301, P660, P696
L.L. Distribution Systems P236
L.L. Kids (catalog) P300
LLOG Exploration Company
  (oil) A132
Lloyd, David M. W178
Lloyd, Donald P545
Lloyd, Edward A284, W336
Lloyd, Emily P135
Lloyd George Management E53
Lloyd, James T. P363
Lloyd, Richard L. W553
Lloyd's Act of 1871 (UK) W336
Lloyds Bank Canada W268
Lloyd's Barbeque A648
Lloyd's of London A356, A1236,
  P480, W336-W337
Lloyd's Weekly News W620
LLP A404
Llumar performance films A1301
L.M. Electronics A896
LMC (savings and loan) P268
LMR (record label) P290
LNM Group W292
LNR Properties A862
LNR Property Corporation E234
Lo, Abel S. E98
Loaf 'N Jug convenience
  stores A845
loans.com A226
LoansDirect A566
Lobbosco, Carlos A. A767
Lobeck, William A650
Lobinsky, James J. A1177, P403
Loblaw Companies Limited W244,
  W245
Local Hero hotels W172
Local Initiatives Support P194
Löchelt, Dieter W121
Lochner, James V. A743
Locke, John P176

Lockets medicated lozenges A915,
  P315
Lockhart, Eugene A924, P322
Lockhart, Gary A57
Lockhart, James P388
Lockhart, Michael D. A194, A195
Lockheed Martin
  Corporation A116, A120, A644,
  A646, A832, A846, A882-A883,
  A888, A1044, A1088, A1190,
  A1382, A1412, A1488, A1538,
  E156, E241, E277, E284, E312,
  P110, P675, P754, P766, W70,
  W110
Lockie, Paul A. E37
Lockminder locks A265
Lockridge, B. Russell A299
Locomotion P229
Locomotive Engineer A944
Loctite (adhesives) W256
Loder, Mark J. A401
The Lodge Casino E165
Loeb, David A438
Loeb, Jerome T. A932
Loeb, Rhodes E65
Loeb, Ronald M. A1531
Loebbaka, Charles R. P379
Loeffler, Tom P499
Loehmann's stores A932
Loehr, Jeff E91, E242
Loeser, David A. A401
Loew, Marcus A962
Loewe leather goods W348
Loews Cineplex Entertainment
  Corporation W550
Loews Corporation A378,
  A884-A885
Lofberg, Per G. H. A957
Loffler, Stephen J. E29
Loffredo, Nicholas L. A1295
Lofgren, Christopher B. P435
Lofredo, James A. A975
Loft Candy Company A1102, A1106,
  A1404
Loftin, Nancy C. A1139
Loftis, Harry E. P714
Loftis, Jack D. E79
Lofton, Kevin P117
Log Cabin syrup A842
Log Cabin tobacco W283
Logan, David E33
Logan, Jonathan A880
Logan, Steven W. E186
Logicom (battle
  management) A1044
LogiCorp A1222
Logidec Canada W378
LogiMetrics A846
Logistics Data Systems A66
Logitech International
  S.A. W338-W339
Logix A1454
Logli supermarkets P723
Logo Eyeware A1068
Logsdon, Linda L. A575
Logue, Ronald E. A1333
Loh Meng See W541

Lohmann, Dirk W653
Lohr, William J. P726
Lojas Americanas S.A. (retailer) A1494
Lojas Renner department stores A790
Lojdquist, Per W633
Lok, Lawrence T. S. W607
Loma Linda meat alternatives A817
Lomar Distributing P636
Lomax, Tim G. W101
Lomb, Henry A234
Lombard Brokerage A988
Lombardi, Francis J. P399
Lombardi, Paul V. P599
Lombardi, Vince A672, P210, P621
Lombardini (small engines) P310
Lommerin, Nils A1077
Lonczak, William P373
London & Edinburgh Insurance Group A688
London & Rhodesian Mining & Land Company W340
London Brick W252
London Bridge A930
London, Craig A1233
London Electricity A554, A1154, A1306, W208, W209
The London Free Press W471
London General Insurance Company Limited A182, A183
London Guarantee A1236
London Life Assurance W88, W89
London, Michael A255
London News Network W249
London Pacific Group Ltd. (investments) W86
London School of Economics P134
London, Shelly J. A153
London Stock Exchange W80, W92, W174, W190, W240, W476, W552
London *Sun* (newspaper) W390
London *Times* (newspaper) W390
London Weekend Television W248, W249
Lone Star beer P428, P721
Lone Star Pipeline A1416
Lonergan, Kevin M. A635
Long Beach Mortgage Company A1500, A1501
Long, Bruce C. P215
Long Distance Discount Services. *See* LDDS
Long, Frank A. A1155
Long, Gary A. (Northeast Utilities) A1041
Long, Gary E. (Northwestern Mutual) A1049, P377, P690
Long, Huey A1376
Long, Ian W111
Long Island Cable Communication Development A312
Long Island Jewish Medical Center P690
Long Island Lighting Company A824
Long Island Power Authority A824

The Long Island Rail Road Company P334, P335
Long Island Water Company A155
Long, John E., Jr. (Tennessee Valley Authority) A1371, P469, P743
Long, John R. (Churchill Downs) E40
Long, John W. (First American) A595
Long, Joseph A886
Long, Michael J. A197
Long Prairie Packing P717
Long, Robert M. (Longs Drug) A886, A887
Long, Robert R. (SunTrust Banks, Inc.) A1347
Long, Sandra P666
Long, Thomas A886
Long, William D. P773
The Longaberger Company P660
Longaberger, Dave P660
Longaberger, Tami P660
Long-Airdox A754
Longaker, Bruce F., Jr. A941
Longbrake, William A. A1501
Longfield, William H. A445
Longhorns of the University of Texas System P761
Longines watch W562, W563
Longman (publishing) W430
Longo, Dennis A463
Longo, Michael E. A209
Longo Toyota auto dealership P390
Longs Drug Stores Corporation **A886-A887**
Longshore, George F. P115, P569
Long-Term Capital Management (hedge fund) A226, A660, A960, P186, W114, W182, W616
Long-Term Chemical Management A808
Long-term Equity Anticipation Securities P47
Longview (Texas) *News-Journal* A443
Longwall International A806
Longwell, Harry J. A577
Lonmin Plc W92, **W340-W341**
Lonrho. *See* Lonmin Plc
Look, Bryon A895
Look Good...Feel Better cancer patient support P41
Loomis Fargo & Company P518, W524, W525
Loomis, Mark A565
Looney Tunes P424
Loose Change lottery game P373
Loose, Jacob A814
Loose, John W. A434, A435
Loose, Joseph A814
Loose-Wiles Biscuit Company A814
Lopdrup, Kim A. A303
Loper, Roland L. A657
Lopez, George A1429, P491
Lopez, Julia I. P415
Lopez, Lucille P591
Lopez, Mike A485

Lopez, Nancy P251
Lopez, Victor A741, P241
Lopienski, Thomas V. A1207
LOPROX drug E89
Lopuch, George Z. A255
Loral Corporation A616, A846, A882, A1182, A1424
Loral Space & Communications Ltd. **A888-A889**
Lorber, Howard M. E95, E249
Lorber, Matthew A170
Lorberbaum, Alan A980
Lorberbaum, Jeffrey S. A980, A981
Lord, Albert L. A1448, A1449
Lord & Taylor department stores A932
Lord Baltimore Press A770
Lord, Gerald S. A317
Lord, Jonathon T. A739
Lord, Michel W133
Lore, Crystal E105
L'Oréal SA A108, A290, A1200, **W342-W343**, W348, W388, W389
Loree, James M. A1323
Loren, Allan Z. A516, A517
Lorentz, Norman E. A1429, P491
Lorenz, Günter W121
Lorenz, William A888
Lorenzini, Paul G. A1083
Lorenzo, Frank A428
Loreti, Alberto A153
Lorick, Neville O. A1249
Lorillard, Inc. A884, A885, A1126
Lorillard Tobacco Company A492
Lorman, William A424
Lorton, Donald E. P566
Lorton, Renee L. A1099
Lorus watches W528, W529
Los Alamos National Laboratory P438, P494, P495
Los Angeles Clippers (basketball team) A623, P355
Los Angeles Convention Center P576
Los Angeles County Department of Water and Power P660
Los Angeles Daily News P670
Los Angeles Dodgers Inc. (baseball team) A622, A623, P307, W390
Los Angeles Edison Electric A532
Los Angeles Junction Railway Company A309
Los Angeles Kings (hockey team) A622, A623, P361
Los Angeles Lakers (basketball team) A622, A623, P355
Los Angeles Magazine E198
Los Angeles Olympic Organizing Committee P108
Los Angeles Sparks (basketball team) P355
Los Angeles Times A1402, A1502
Loser, Gary L. E133
Loser, Ugo P65
Loss Prevention Services A65, P31
Lotan, Ze'ev E21
Lotman, Herbert P650

LOT-Polish (airline) W79
Lotrimin AF drug A1250
Lotrisone drug A1251
Lotronex drug W246
Lott, Charles E. A605
Lott, Hamilton, Jr. A1053
Lotter, Charles R. A791
Lottes, Art E., III P112, P113
Lotto lottery game P766
Lotto Texas lottery game P472, P473, P744
Lottomatica S.p.A. (betting) W423
Lotus Development Corporation A558, A747, A764, A1112, E36, E100, E134, E170, E252, P136
Lotus food stores W590, W591
Lotzee lottery game P687
Lou lingerie A1474, A1475
Loubat-L.Frank (food distributor) A1109
Loucks, Cathy A163
Loucks, Vernon, Jr. A236
Loudermilk, Joey M. A93
Loudon, Jonkheer Aarnout A. W57, W73
Loughead, Allan A882
Loughead, Malcolm A882
Loughlin, John M. (Bausch & Lomb) A235
Loughlin, John (Primedia) A1161
Loughrey, F. Joseph A457
Loughrey, Pat W145
Louis B. Mayer Pictures A962
Louis Dreyfus et Cie E234
Louis Dreyfus Natural Gas Corporation A498, E234
Louis Harris & Associates (polling) A632
Louis Kemp Seafood A409, A1418
Louis Philippe, King of France W232
La Société Louis Renault W480
Louis Rich meats A843
Louis Vuitton. See LVMH Moët Hennessy Louis Vuitton
Louis XIV, King of France W506
Louisa Railroad A454
Louis-Dreyfus, Julia P378
Louis-Dreyfus, Robert W62
Louisiana Downs (racetrack) P172, P173
Louisiana Highway Department W292
The Louisiana Land and Exploration Company A310, A311
Louisiana Power & Light A554
Louisiana State University System P661
Louisiana-Pacific Corporation **A890-A891**
Louisiana-Pacific Timber Company A1456
Louisville & Nashville (railroad) A454
Louisville Grocery A1350
Louisville (KY) Jockey Club E40
Lounsbury, Charles B. A1223

Loup, Roland J. A1395
Lourdes Health System P115
LouverDrape home decor products A1023
Loux, P. Ogden A1539
Lovaas, Kae A1237
Lo-Vaca Gathering Company (natural gas) A1466
Love at First Bite (movie) A1286
Love Cruise (TV show) A622
Love, Dennis M. P705
Love, Howard A1006
Love, Janet P593
Love, Kathleen D. W621
Love, Michael I. A1335
Love, Spencer A306
Love, William P. A549
Lovelace, G. Thomas, Jr. A1109
Loveless, Keith A107
Lovelett, Steve P645
Lovell, Richard A329, P109
Loveman, Gary W. A685
Loveman's department stores A1238
Lovenox drug W102, W103
Loveridge Mine A417
Lovett, Keith A1203
Lovett, Michael A757, P245
Lovett, Steve A509
Lovins, Harriet P625
Lovitt, John R. E110
Lovstad, John P534
Low Rider mortorbikes A682
Low Temp 35 paint A1278
Lowber, H. Paul A1231
Lowden, Francis V., III A1437
Lowden, Steven J. A1461
The Lowe Brothers (paint maker) A1278
Lowe, Bruce E79
Lowe, Cathey S. A1227
Lowe, Challis M. A1223
Lowe, Frank B. A773
Lowe, George E252
The Lowe Group A772, A773
Lowe, Harry R. A1053
Lowe Howard-Spink (advertising) A772
Lowe, Jim A892
Lowe, John E. A1129
Lowe, Kenneth W. A569
Lowe Lintas & Partners Worldwide A772, A773
Lowe, Robert N. A173
Lowe, William M. A199, P673
Lowenberg, David A. A575
Lowenbrau beer W289
Lower, Louis G., II A127
Lowe's Companies, Inc. A64, A264, **A892-A893**, A920, A968, A1294, A1410, E214, P26, P30, P330, P484, P529, P672
Lowe's Food Stores P535
Lowman, Don P481
Lown, Andy D. P347
Loworn, Holly P597
Lowrey, F. A. P534

Lowrey, P. Lang W190, W191
Lowrider (magazine) A1161
Lowry Hill Investment Advisors, Inc. A1509
Lowry, Paul A. A1069
Loy, Bertrand E248
Loya, John P769
Loyal pet food A915, P315
Loyez, Hugues W313
Loyko, Frank, Jr. E85
Loynd, Richard A630
Loyola University of Chicago P661
Lozano, Joe J. P627
Lozano, Orland Ayala A973
L-P. See Louisiana-Pacific Corporation
LPG Services Group (propane) A518
LPGA. See Ladies Professional Golf Association
LPSO Limited W337
L.S. Ayres department stores A932
L-S Electro-Galvanizing Company A897
LS Studio shoes A295
LS&CO. See Levi Strauss & Company
L-SAT-1 satellite W110
LSG Lufthansa Service Holding AG W345
LSG Sky Chefs International W344, W345
LSI Logic Corporation **A894-A895**, A1002, E166, P444
LSU Agricultural and Mechanical College P661
LTA (company) W92
LTC Group P506, P765
The LTV Corporation **A896-A897**, A1044, P110, P388
LU biscuits W192, W193
Lu, Hong Liang E310
Lu, Keh-Shew A1379
Lu Yiping W543
Lubben, David J. A1435
Lubbers, R. Mark A415
Lubetkin, Roy S. P39
Lubin, Charles A1242
Lubman, Irving E97
Lübmann, Hartwich A841, P287, W325
The Lubrizol Corporation A1354, P466
Lubsen, S. W. W. W255
Lucas Aerospace W442
Lucas, Barbara B. A265
Lucas, Dennis C. A607
Lucas Diesel Systems A476, A1412
Lucas Digital P302
Lucas, George W., Jr. A692, E103, P302, P303, P661
Lucas Industries W354
Lucas, Tom A1179
Lucasfilm Ltd. E103, P196, **P302-P303**, P661, P719
LucasVarity A198, A332, A584, A1412

Lucci, Jenny E253
Lucci, MarySue E113
Luce, Charles A418
Luce, Henry A180
Lucent Technologies Inc. A188, A202, A242, A404, A642, A644, A686, A712, A792, **A898-A899**, A990, A1240, E118, E142, E174, E196, E244, E247, E267, E268, E284, E287, E289, E292, E302, E304, E305, E317, E318, E319, P74, P208, P589, P771, W76, W100, W412
Lucente, Francie P572
Luchessi, Ceslo F. W437
Luciani, Alfred J. P318
Luciano, Gene P738
Luciano, Robert P. A1251
Luciano, William J. W271
Lucino car W403
Lucite paint A534, A1152, W278
Lucius, Charles E. P71
Luck, Oliver P357
Luckey, Cliff A763
Lucky 7s lottery game P373
Lucky Brand clothing A880
Lucky Charms cereal A649
Lucky Chemical Company W334
Lucky Dollar grocery stores W245
Lucky Goldstar. *See* LG Group
Lucky Strike cigarettes A618, W142, W143
Lucky supermarkets A66, A110, A606, P462
Lucky-Goldstar A1072
Luczakowsky, Andrew R. E108
Luczo, Stephen J. A1260, A1261, P440, P441, P725
Ludeman, Christopher R. P121
Ludgate, Alan P165
Ludgate Office Complex (London) P449
Ludington, Callaway P179
Ludlum Steel Company A116
Ludwig, Edward J. A245
Ludwig (publishing) W107
Luechtefeld, A. Daniel A1125
Luechtefeld, Monica A1057
Lueger, Susan A. P377, P690
Luegers, William M., Jr. A467
Luethi, Jackie E174
Luetkemeyer, Mike E245
Lufkin Rule (measuring tapes) A430
The Lufkin (Texas) *Daily News* A443
Luft, Robert (Entergy) A555
Luft, Robert (Koch Industries) A835, P281
Deutsche Lufthansa AG A484, A1420, A1421, W68, W71, W78, W80, W310, **W344-W345**, W518, W540
Lugo, Miguel P205, P619
Lui, David Y. W267
Lui, Paul E121
Luigino's (foods) A722
Luikart, John F. E132

Lukash, Sergei W243
Luke, David A1516
Luke, David, III A1516
Luke, John A1516
Luke, John A., Jr. A1516, A1517
Luke, William A1516
Lukens, Max A222
Lukens (steel maker) A116, A256
Luker Inc. P200, P201
Lukes, Trevor A1333
OAO LUKOIL A412, P712, **W346-W347**
Lukowski, Stanley J. P697
Lumberjack Building Materials store A1090, A1091
Lumbermen's Building Centers P655
Lumbermen's Investment A1364
Lumbermens Life Agency P650
Lumbermens Merchandising Corporation P662
Lumbermens Mutual Casualty Company P268, P269
Lumen Technologies A1110
Lumetta, Jeffrey J. A783
Lumiere electrical products A431
Luminous Corporation (pre-press operations) A76, A750
Luminox electrical products A431
Lumisys (digital imaging) A524
Lumpkins, Robert L. A325, P105, P566
Lun Kwan Lin W571
Lunalite A1392
Lund, Constance E. P539
Lund, Mark W89, W623
Lundberg, Olof A888
Lundin, John P127
Lundy Packing Company A426, P140
Lunelle drug A1122
Lunn, Raymond C., Jr. A1533
Lupberger, Edwin A554
Lupinacci, Vince P464
Lupo car W631
Luppes, Loren W569
Lupron drug A58, P741
Lupton, Stephen D. A97
Luraschi, William R. A89
Luria Brothers (scrap metal) A440
Lurie, Robert A560, P180
Luscombe, Michael W645
Luse, Robert P587
Lushefski, John E. A975
Luskin, Meyer E285
Lussier, Marcel P478
Lussier, Rose M. P534
Lustgarten, Alvin R. E212
Lustig, Paul J. A1243
Lustig, Rick P139, P582
LUSTRA drug E89, E240
Luter, Joseph A1290
Luter, Joseph W., III A1291
Luterman, Gerald A825
Luth, Jeffrey M. A163
Luther, Siegfried W127
Lutheran Brotherhood P534

Lutheran Health Services A1080
Lutheran Health Systems P549
Lutnick, Howard W. P565
Luttrell, Barbara J. E270
Lutz, Robert A. A572, A573
Lutz, Yvonne P724
Luukko, Peter A. A391
AB Lux W210
Lux Mercantile (wholesale grocery) A606
Lux, Sam A606
Lux, Stephen D. A551
Luxo Jr. (movie) E103
Luxon Carrà (branding) A773
Luxor (electronics and computers) W406
Luxor (furniture) P170, P171
Luxor (hotel and casino) A906, A907
Luxottica (sunglasses) A234, E99, E257, P713
Luxury Linens A304, A305
Luzon, Francisco W513
LV Capital W348
LVMH Moët Hennessy Louis Vuitton SA E78, P156, P592, W206, W207, W250, **W348-W349**, W446
Lyall, Katharine C. P501, P762
Lyall, Lynn P536
Lybrand, Ross Bros. & Montgomery A1158, P400, W462
Lybrand, William A1158, P400, W462
Lycoming Turbine Engine A1380
Lycos, Inc. A614, P190, W126, W127, W578
Lycra A534
Lykes Brothers Inc. P464
Lykes Meat Group, Inc. A1290
Lykes (petroleum equipment) A896
Lyle, Abram W568
Lyle, Freeman A. E227
Lyle, Norman W307
Lyle's Golden Syrup W568, W569
Lyman, Gregory A. P521
Lyman, Ray P454
Lynch, Andrew P. W175
Lynch, Bruce E96
Lynch, Christopher W129
Lynch Corporation E207
Lynch, David A1503
Lynch, Edmund A960
Lynch G. Michael A585
Lynch, John H. (Knoll) P276
Lynch, John T. (Towers Perrin) P480
Lynch, Kevin M. E86
Lynch, Martin A247
Lynch, Mary P575
Lynch, Michael W. P675
Lynch, Patrick J. A1377
Lynch, Peter A111, A614, A1468, P190, P504
Lynch, Phil W485
Lynch, Thomas (CompuCom) A400
Lynch, Thomas C. (Safeguard Scientifics) A1233

Lynch, Thomas J. (Motorola) A991
Lynn, Kay E239
Lynn, Loretta A416
Lynn, Robert A484
Lynn, Stephen A1280
Lynx snowmobiles W132, W133
Lynx systems E316
Lyon, Deanna P675
Lyon, Edward A584
Lyon Financial Services P436, P724
Lyon, Wayne B. P298, P299
Lyondell Chemical Company A**900**-A**901**, A974, A1054, P604, W118
Lyonnaise des Eaux (engineering) A1268, W150, W558
Société Lyonnaise des Eaux et de L'Eclairage (water) W558
Lyons, Charlotte P259
Lyons, Daniel M. A465
Lyons, James E., Sr. (California State University) P99
Lyons, James W. (Advantica) A87
Lyons, Michael A1051
Lyons Physician Supply Company A1070, A1071
Lyons, Tim A877
Lyons, William M. P537
Lysol home care W476, W477
Lytle, L. Ben A179
Lytle, Walter P247
Lytton, William B. A771

M

M & G Group (investments) W464
M and M Manufacturing A432
M. Fabrikant & Sons P662
M Series defibrillators E320
M&S stores W356
M-16 guns P133
Ma, Abraham P662
Ma, Christopher A1503
M.A. Hanna (mining and transportation) A1006
MA Laboratories, Inc. P662
M. A. Mortenson Company, Inc. P663
Maack, Robert G. P425
Maag, John C. E261
Maalox over-the-counter medication W102, W414, W415
Maars Group W506
Maas, Arie W317
Maas Brothers stores A586
Maas, Cees W287
Maas, Steven P685
Maasdam (ship) A331
Maat, Stephanie E171
Mabe, Carol M. A1221
Mabe, Donald W. P201
Mabry, Rodney H. P499
Mabuchi, Takayuki W405
M.A.C. *See* Make-Up Art Cosmetics
Mac Addict (magazine) W238, W239
MAC (asset management) W548

Mac Direct P338
Mac Frugal's Bargains Close-outs stores A260, A261
Mac Plus computer A186
Mac Publications P248
MAC Specialty Coatings W72
Mac Store P338
Mac SystemsWAREHOUSE (catalogs) P338
Mac the Slasher liquor stores W172
Mac Tools A1322
Macadam, Stephen E. A655
MacAndrews & Forbes Holdings Inc. A**902**-A**903**, A1200, P**304**-P**305**, P663
Macari, Emma Espino P129
MacArthur Foundation P414
Macauley, Larry J. W289
Maccabee beer W255
MacCarthy, Mark A1481, P509
Macchia, Richard E222
MacColl, John A. A1237
MacCormack, George F. A535
MacDonald, Alan P714
MacDonald, Halsted & Laybourne A220, P66
Macdonald, John Paul W377
MacDonald, J. Randall A765
MacDonald, Laurie P167
MacDonald, Michael C. A1545
Macdonald, Roderick A643
MacDonald, William E., III A1001
MacDonnell, Robert I. A837, P283
Mace defense spray E29, E158
Mace, Larry L. A605
Mace Security International, Inc. E29
Macedonia, Richard A1297
Macenczak, Lee A. A479
Macey's (food stores) P545
Macfarlane, F. Scott A1293
Macfarquhar, Colin P176
MacFood Services P650
Mach3 razor A656, A657
Machado, Norma J. A1179
Macher, Frank E. A584, A585
Machete brand A985
Machida, Katsuhiko W532, W533
Machida, Mitsuru W375
Machine Vision International A400, A1232
Machinery and Instruments Optical by Tashima. *See* Minolta
Compagnie des Machines Bull. *See* Bull
Machribie, Adrianto A629
Macht, Michael W459
Macht, Patricia K. A315, P97
Macia, Didier W239
MacInnes, Dennis P678
MacInnis, Frank T. A544, A545
Macintosh computer A76, A186, A972, E42, E179, P336, P337, P338, P430, W338, W394, W530
Macioce, Thomas A586
Maciver, W. Kenneth A1413

Mack, Chuck P247
Mack, David S. P335
Mack Drug stores A458
Mack, John J. A448, A449, W185
Mack, Russell P317
Mack, Stephen (Inforte) E220
Mack, Stephen M. (Service Corp.) A1269
Mack Trucks, Inc. W480, W632
MacKay, A. David A817
Mackay (communications) A780
Mackay, Ernest A. Graham W552, W553
Mackay, Francis H. W174, W175
Mackay, Ian A. W475
MacKay, Inc. A251
MacKay Shields LLC A1016, A1017, P370, P371
Mackay, W. Reay W475
MacKenzie, Tod J. A1107
Mackey, Frank A734
Mackey, John P. A1522, A1523
Mackey, Marcee E289
Mackey, Patrick C. A299
Mackey, Thomas B. A1367
Mackie, Debbie E297
Mackie Designs Inc. E**85**, E234
Mackie, Gregory C. E85, E234
Mackie, Tom A1089
Mackin, Scott G. A440, A441
MacKinnon, Ian A. A1469, P505
Maclachlan, Lachlan W157
MacLane, John J. A987
MacLaurin, Ian, Lord of Knebworth W590, W629
MacLean, Ian P. A571
MacLean, Robert G. A283
Maclean-Hunter (cable TV and publishing) W494
Maclellan, R. L. A1440
Maclellan, Robert A1440
Maclellan, Thomas A1440
MacLeod, Donald A1003
MacLeod, Ivor W493
Macleod-Stedman (hardware distributor) A1410, P484
MacMahon 2M beer W553
Macmanus, Christopher P117
MacManus Group (advertising) P551, W198
MacManus, John & Adams (advertising) P72
MacManus, Theodore P72
Macmillan A1160
MacMillan Bloedel A1364, A1518
Macmillan Computer Publishing W431
MacMillan, John A324, P104
Macmillan, Neil R. W113
Macmillan Reference W592
MacMillan, Stephen P. A1123
MacMillan, Whitney A324, P104
Macmillan/McGraw Hill School Publishing A944
Macnair, David C. A317
Macnee, Walter M. A925, P323

MacNeil/Lehrer NewsHour (TV show) P144
MacNeil/Lehrer productions A873
Macnow, Joseph E137, E150, E314
M/A-COM Linkabit A1182
Macomber, John D. P408
Macomber, Scott T. E255
The Macon (Georgia) *Telegraph* A833
MacPhail, Andrew B. A1403
MacPhail, Bruce W435
MacPhee, Roddy A783
Macrides, Foster G. P586
MacRitchie, Andy A1083
Macromedia, Inc. E**86**, E235
MacroMind (software) E86
Macrotron (computer products) A758, A1356
Macrovision Corporation E192, E235
Mac's Liquor stores W644, W645
MACtac Engineered Products Inc. A250, A251
Mactas, Mark P481, P746
MacUser (magazine) P248, P338
MacWAREHOUSE (catalogs) P338
MACWORLD Expo P248, P249
Macworld (magazine) P248, P249
Macy, Rowland A586
Macy's department stores A490, A586, A587, A1068, A1286, A1470, P156, W534
Maczuzak, John A. A1007
Mad River Traders (teas and juices) A382
Madalone, Lisa E264
Madam Tussaud's wax museums W430
Madden Gas Field A310
Madden, John A64, P30, P251
Madden, Joseph E123
Madden, Nicole P27
Madden, Orval E69
Madden, Richard H. P145
Madden, Steve E294
Madden, Thomas A. A759
Maddix, Colin A1383
Maddock, Barbara B. A945
Maddocks, David P143
Maddocks, Mark E. E190
Maddox, Elton A427, P141
Maddox, Lori L. A557
Maddox, Lyndell E. A1121
Maddox, Matt A1087
Maddrey, Erwin P342
Made in Sport stores W446
Madeja, Peter A1441
Mademoiselle (magazine) A81
Madera Disposal Systems E139
Madhavpeddi, Kalidas V. A1125
Madia, William J. P71
Madigan, John W. A1402, A1403
Madio, Jane E315
Madison Capital Partners A432
Madison Dairy Produce A850, P288
Madison Dearborn Partners A1368, E214

Madison Female Academy Building P500
Madison, George W. A395
Madison, James A498
Madison Square Advisors LLC A1017, P371
Madison Square Garden A312, A313, P476, P745
Madison Square Garden Network cable channel A1450
Madison Studio brand P77
Madison, William E. A555
Madrid Stock Exchange W482
Madrona Investment Group A1036
Madsen, Dean P545
Madsen, Dennis P410, P411, P711
Maeda, Hajime W421
Maeda, Kunio W529
Maeda, Tamon W550
Maeda, Yutaka W421
Maejima, Kunihiro W649
Maeno, Shigeki W169
Maersk Air A/S Group W94, W95, W518
Maersk Line (shipping) A454
Maersk Olie og Gas AS Group W94, W95
Maersk Sealand W94, W95
Maestro debit card A924, A925, P322, P323, P668
Maestro window furnishings A1317, P453
Mafatlal Industries A306
Mafatlal Micron (connectors) A982
Mafco Consolidated Group A902, A903, P304, P305
Maffei, Susan Whirty E63, E205
Maffeo, Vincent A. A781
Maffucci, David G. A285
Mafia (computer game) E298
Maganov, Ravil U. W347
Societe des Magasins du Casino W166
Magee, John P54
Magelitz, Larry L. P593
Magellan Aerospace Corporation E35
Magellan Exploration E146
Magellan fund A614, A1468, P190, P504
Magellan Health Services, Inc. A322, A**904**-A**905**, P474, P475, P744
Magellan Holdings. *See* REBAR (investments)
Magenheimer, Richard P639
Magerko, Maggie Hardy P26, P27, P528
Maggart, Lindsay P264
Maggi brand W388
Maggiano's Little Italy restaurants A288, A289
Maggie's Building Solutions Showroom P26
Maggiotto, Rocco J. A1159, P401, W463
Maghribi, Walid A82

Magic Chef appliances A934, A935, E283
Magic Cinemas P412
Magic Kingdom (theme park) A1496
The Magic School Bus (books and TV show) A1254
Magic: The Gathering game A693
Magicuts stores A1196
Magill, William H. A1193
Magirus (distributor) A1140
Magliari, Laurane A671
Magliochetti, Joseph M. A460, A461
Maglione, Joyce P. E302
Maglione, Roberto W575
Magma Copper A1024
Magma Power P340
Magna Computer (tape storage) A542
Magna Entertainment Corporation E40
Magna International Inc. A1412
Magnavox brand W394, W444
Magnelia, Cedric W251
Magner, Jerome P681
Magness, Bob A872
Magness, Michael P672
Magnet department stores W310
Magneti Marelli S.p.A. W226, W227, W594
Magnetic Controls A70
Magnetronic Reservisor A1228
Magnivision (reading glasses) A146, A147
Magnolia Ice Cream Plant W510
Magnum brand A527
Magnum Hunter Resources, Inc. A1065, E235, E278
Magnum ice cream W619
Magnus, George C. W273
Magnusson, Carl G. P277
Magouirk, Mike P133, P578
Magowan, Peter A1234
Magowan, Robert A1234
Magrann, Robert P. A471
Magrone, James A1161
Maguire, Daniel A797
Maguire, Frances E265
Maguire, James J., Sr. (Philadelphia Consolidated Holding) E265
Maguire, James V. (R.J. Reynolds Tobacco) A1205
Maguire, Matthias D. P57
Magyar Suzuki W560
Mahadeva, Wijeyaraj "Kumar" E181
Mahasco Industries A980
Maher, Francesca M. A1421
Mahle, Stephen H. A953
Mahlke, Thomas K. A345
Mahmoud, Adel A957
Mahogany greeting cards A679, P217
Mahon, Douglas A1260, P440
Mahoney, Christopher D. A1427
Mahoney, George R., Jr. A579
Mahoney, John J. A1325
Mahoney, Robert B. A983

Mahoning Valley Mine A417
Mahony, Edward P707
Mahony, Sheila A. A313
The Mahopac National Bank E302
Mahurin, Steven L. A725
MAI (financial services) W620
Maibach, Ben C., III P550
Maich, Peter A. A1389
Maichel, Gert W505
M.A.I.D. plc A832
Maidan, Ran W323
Maiden, Benjamin G. P71
Maidenform, Inc. E60
Maidment, Karen W113
Maier Brewing Company P428
Maier, Gadi A1229
Maier, Lothar E84
Maier's Bakery W244
Mail Boxes Etc. stores A1426
Mailhot, Nancy F. A1125
Mailiao Power Corporation W229
Maillet, Jeanette P668
Mailman School of Public
    Health P135
MailMedia A1322
Main Hurdman & Cranstoun
    (accounting) A840, P286, W324
Main Lafrentz (accounting) P286,
    W324
Main Street Banks, Inc. E236
Main, Timothy L. A782, A783
Maine Bank & Trust E178
Maine Hunting Shoe P300
Maine Yankee nuclear plant A1040
MainStay Management LLC A1016,
    A1017, P370, P371
Mainstreet cigarettes E293
MainStreet department stores A838
Maintenance Warehouse A724
Mair, Dee W621
MaisGard brand A985
Maison Blanche department
    stores A490
Maistrovich, Jan P695
Maitland-Smith furniture P298,
    P659
Maitre, Michel W135
Majestic Realty A1086
Majestic Savings & Loan A658
Majesty of the Seas (cruise
    ship) A1217
Majik Mart stores P740
Majluf, Ricardo W577
Major, Drew A1051
Major Electronics E58
Major, John, CH A448, P111, P567
Major League Baseball A1220,
    E130, P108, P251, **P306-P307**,
    P486, P663
Major League Baseball Players'
    Association P306
Major Video chain A266
Major Video Concepts P656
Makarechian, Hadi E171
Makarewicz, Stephen E. A1225
Make-A-Friend-For-Life E135, E311
Mäkeläinen, Esko W557

Maker Communications A410
Maker's Mark bourbon W85
Make-Up Art Cosmetics A564, A565
Makhteshim-Agan Industries
    Ltd. W322, W323
Maki, Curt P479
Maki, Yuzuru W81
Makiba Milk W315
Makihara, Minoru W371
Makinoda, Mutsumi W305
Makinson, John C. W431
Makowski, Paul A. A735
Makro stores W364, W365
Malachowsky, Chris E256
Malahias, Angelo C. E156
Malamatinas, Dennis A302
Malanczuk, Ted E55
Malarkey, Tim A147
Malayan Airways W468, W540
Malaysia British Assurance
    Life W82
Malaysia-Singapore Airlines W540
Malcolm Baldrige Quality
    Award A1298
Malcolm in the Middle (TV
    show) A622
Malcolm, Steven J. A1529
Maldonado, Freddy E314
Malev (airline) W79
Malfitano, Ricardo A1157
Malia, Stephen P. A753
Malibu rum W206
Malinsky, Dotty W. P247
Maljers, Floris A. W317
Malkin, Judd P645
Malkin, Peter P230
Mall of America A1286, A1354,
    P466, W332
Mallamaci, Ottavio J. A665
Mallard travel trailers A605
Mallard's Food Products A1419
Mallery, Gilbert O. P363
Mallet, Rosalyn P107, P567
Mallett, Jeffrey A1547
Mallett, Robert L. A1119
Mallette, Jean S. P171
Mallinckrodt Inc. A550, A704,
    A752, A1250
Mallo, Donald A1135
Malloch, Michael P. A701, P229
Mallof, Joseph T. A1247, P433
Mallon, Joseph R., Jr. E240
Mallory, R. Mark A1403
Malmaison hotels A1540
Malone & Hyde A208, A606, A1270
Malone, Brenda Richardson P129
Malone, John C. A203, A872, A873
Malone, Patricia W251
Malone, Richie L. P261
Malone, Thomas J. P343
Malone, Wallace D., Jr. A1308,
    A1309
Maloney, Martin A570
Maloney, Sean M. A761
Maloon, James A176
Malovany, Howard A1527

Malox Company, Ltd. W363
Malson, Hunter L. A311
Maltesers candy A915, P315
Maltz, Allen P. P85, P557
Maluti beer W553
Malvern (electronic musical
    instruments) W180
MaMa Rosa's foods A409
Mammoth Micro Products (CD-
    ROM) A1502
MAN Aktiengesellschaft A754,
    W**350**-W**351**
Man To Man Prostate Cancer
    Support P41
Managed Care Indemnity, Inc. A739
Managed Care Network
    Preferred P226
Managed Dental Care of
    California P214, P215
Managed DentalGuard of
    Texas P215
Managed Health Network,
    Inc. A697
ManagedStorage
    International A1336
Management Data Processing
    Corporation A176
The Management Network Group,
    Inc. E236
ManageWise software A1051
Manbre and Garton (sugar
    refiner) W568
Manchester Development
    Corporation A591
Manchester Plastics A388
*Manchester United - The Official
    Magazine* W239
Manchester United (soccer
    team) W146, W238
Mancilla, Marcel W577
Mancino, Joseph L. E281
Manco (adhesives) W256
Mancuso, Colleen E298
Mancuso, Frank A962
Mancuso, John H. A823
Mancuso, Michael J. A645
Mancuso's Life Fitness A298
M&A Drugs A606
Mandalay Resort Group A720,
    A740, A**906**-A**907**, A966, P240
Mandaric, Milan A1240
Mandarin Magic juice
    products P381
Mandarin Oriental International
    Ltd. (hotels) W306, W307
M&D Industries A146
Mandekic, Anthony L. P747
Mandelbaum, David E137
M&F Worldwide Corporation
    (licorice extract) A902, A903,
    P304, P305, P663
M&G Investment Management
    Ltd. W465
Mandia, Albert M. E153
Mandia, Richard E164
M&M Knopf P152
M&M Restaurant Supply P650

M&M's candy A510, A511, A914, A915, P314, P315, P665
Manen, Martin G. W539
Maness, Joel H. A1345
Manetta Mills (blankets) A1134
Manetta, Richard L. A505
Manfredi, John F. A657
Mang, John C., III A897
Mangan, Michael D. A265
Manganello, Timothy M. A279
Mange, John A668
Mangiagalli, Marco W217
¡Mango Mango! juice products P381
Mangual, Evanessa P205
Mangurian, Harry A280
Manhattan Associates, Inc. E236
Manhattan Bagel E253
Manhattan Construction Company P716
Manhattan Project A360, A600, A1370, P70, P448, P468
Manheim Auctions A442, A443, P146, P147, P585
Manica beer W553
Manin, Alan E36
Manion, Jane M. A769
Maniscalco, Charles I. A1181
Manischewitz wines A422, A423
Manitoba Telecom Services W122
Manitou bike P656
Manley, Charles G. A169
Manley, Kim W85
Manley-McLennan (railroad insurance) A916
Man-Machine Interface A780
Mann, Alfred P494
Mann, David A. E71, E218
Mann, Hugo A436
Mann, Jack S. P111
Mann, Marvin L. A870
Mann, Steve W469
Manne, Kenneth W. A847
Mannelly, Patrick J. A385
Mannesmann AG A1288, P446, W232, W272, **W352-W353**, W422, W490, W628, W629
Mannesmann Arcor AG & Company KG W201
Mannesmann, Max W352
Mannesmann, Reinhard W352
Mannheimer, Michael J. A443, P147
Manning, Clark W465
Manning, David J. A825
Manning, Dennis J. P215
Manning, George E. E246
Manning, Peter J. A603
Manning, Richard W253
Manning, Selvage & Lee P73, P551
Manning, Timothy P. A345
Mannion, Martin E153
Manoogian, Alex A920
Manoogian, Richard A. A920, A921
Manor Care, Inc. **A908-A909**
Manos, Kristen P223
Manpower Inc. **A910-A911**
Mansell, Kevin B. A839

Mansfield & Company W540
Mansfield, Christopher C. A875, P295
Mansfield, Robert C. W587
Mantani, Okitsugu W399
Mantecol candy W155
Manuell, Don A1337
Manufactured Home Communities, Inc. A560, A561, P180, P181, P604
Manufacturers Bank (Chicago) E239
Manufacturer's Hanover A808
Manufacturers Hanover Trust Company Bank and Office Building P449
Manufacturers National Corporation A394
Manville Corporation P212, W228
Manweb (electricity supply) W522, W523
Manwell, Edmund R. A511
Manwich A409
Manzella, Giuseppe W423
Manzi, Jim A1112
MAP Medizin-Technologie (sleep disorder treatment) E112
MAPCO A1528
MapInfo Corporation (software) E96
Maple River brand P185
Maplehurst Bakeries Inc. W245
Maples, Marla A1408, P482
Mapp, Gordon A. A755
MapQuest.com P711
MapQuest.com, Inc. P408
Maps.com P408, P711
Mar-A-Lago (Palm Beach) A1408, A1409, P482, P483
Maranell, Mike P37
Marantz brand W444
Maratea, Michael J. A1097
Marathon Ashland Petroleum LLC A132, A200, A376, A1144, A1460, A1461, A1462, P601, P663, P702, W372
Marathon Canada Limited A1461
Marathon Equipment (waste handling equipment) A502
Marathon LeTourneau A642
Marauder motorcycle W561
Maraven W438
MARBEL Energy Corporation A598, A599
Marben Group (networking) W100
Marbert, Larry D. A833
Marble Hill nuclear plant A362
Marboro Books Corporation A232
The M/A/R/C Group (market research) A1062, A1063
Marcantonio, Richard L. A531
Marcelina wine A521, P169
Marcey, Steve E84, E233
March car W403
March, John D. A325, P105
Marchant, Richard N. W605
Marché Plus stores W164, W165
Marchegiani, Giorgio P65

Marchesano, Michael W627
marchFIRST, Inc. A1050, W198
Marchilena, Francis S. A1191
Marchioli, Nelson A87
Marchon eyewear P100
Marcilla coffee A1243
Marciniak, Jere P165
Marcinowski, Carla J. E83
Marconi Electronic Systems W110
Marconi, Guglielmo W152, W354
Marconi plc A782, W76, **W354-W355**, W490, W554
Marconi Wireless Telegraph W152
Marcopper Mine W452
Marcorp A1297
Marcos, Ferdinand W510
Marcos, Luis R. P369, P687
Marcotte, Brian W. G. A1439
Marcus, Barbara A. A1255
Marcus, Bernard A724, A725
Marcus Cable A350
Marcus, Edward A1530
Marcus, Guy T. A677
Marcus, Herbert A1014
Marcus, Joel S. E150
Marcus, Palle W163, W417
Marcus, Richard A1014
Marcus, Stanley A1014
Marcus, Stuart L. A1125
Mardi Gras paper products A654
Mardi Gras (ship) A330
Mardy, Michael P650
Marelich Mechanical Company, Inc. A544, A545
Maremont/Gabriel (automotive products) P113
Marengi, Joseph A. A473
Mares, Fidencio M. A243
Maresca, Robert A. P333, P674
Margaret Ann Stores A1532
Margareta W426
Margarine Union W618
Margetts, Rob J. W279
Margolin Evelyn E181
Margolin, Leslie A. A811, P267
Margolis, David A1389
Margolis, Jay M. A1195
Margolis, Lawrence A. E30
Margolis, Michael L. E126, E299
Mariah Associates E131
Marie Callender's foods A408, A774, A775
Marie Claire (magazine) A701, P229, W342
Marie-Jeanne Godard perfumes W348
Marie's dressings A466, A467
Marilyn Manson (band) E69
Marimac (children's bedding) A1068
Marin, Lori A815
Marina Mortgage E154
Marinaccio, Paul A475, P155
Marinangeli, Daniel A. W609
Marine Corps Association A936
Marine Midland Bank W268

Marine Transport P585
Marineau, Philip A. A868, A869, P292, P293, P657
Marinello Schools of Beauty E285
MarineMax, Inc. E237
Mariner motors A299
Mariner outboard motors A298
Mariner Post-Acute Network, Inc. A698
Marinez, Hector W181
Marino, Gary O. E275
Marino, Lelio P678
Marino, Lou P737
Marino, Roger A542
Marinopoulos stores W165
Marion Labs (pharmaceuticals) A504
Marion Merrell Dow A504
Marion, Thomas D. P751
Marion von Schröder (publishing) W107
Marionette software E103, E266
Maris, Roger P306
Maritz, Edward P308
Maritz Inc. P308-P309, P663
Maritz, James P308
Maritz, Lloyd P308
Maritz, William E. P308
Maritz, W. Stephen P308, P309, P664
Mariucci, Anne L. A1179
Mariucci, Steve P173
Mark Centers Trust E147
Mark Controls A446
Mark Cross leather goods A1242
Mark Hopkins hotel A884
Mark IV Industries, Inc. A326, P310-P311, P664
Mark, Michael A. P439
Mark, Reuben A386, A387
Mark, Robert M. (Canadian Imperial Bank) W157
Mark, Robert (PolyMedica) E105
Mark Steven (health and beauty) A458
Mark, William P455
MarkAir (airline) A106
Markborough (real estate) W270
Markee, Richard L. A1397
Markert, Stephen E., Jr. E169
Market Axess (Web site) A808
Market Basket stores P591
Market Data Center, LLC A595
Market Decisions A66
Market Express convenience stores A1084, A1085
Market Guide Inc. E61
Market Place Media E188
Market Produce Company A1132
Market Street Mortgage E251
Market Wholesale P488
Marketplace (database shopping habits) A558
Marketplace supermarkets A1532
MarketScreen (Web site) E70
MarketSmart (Web site) E70
MarketSpan A824

MarketWatch.com, Inc. A334, A1476, W430, W431
Markham, Richard J. W103
Markham, Rudy W619
Markiewicz, Mieczyslaw W457
Markley, H. J. A469
MarkNet printer servers A870
Marko International (table coverings) A326
Markoff, Steven C. P536
Markowitz, Barry G. A513
Markowski, Elizabeth M. A873
Marks & Barry (formal accessories) W607
Marks and Spencer p.l.c P102, W312, W356-W357
Marks, Ann A507
Marks, Bennett E275
Marks, Fred E135
Marks, Michael W356
Marks-A-Lot A210
MarkVision software A870
MarkWest Hydrocarbon, Inc. E237
Marland Oil A412
Marlboro cigarettes A492, A1126, W304, W305
Marlett, Wendy A813
Marlex A1128
Marley, Brian T. P77
Oy Marli W162
Marlin, George P398
Marlinski-Lehman, M. J. A797
Marlio, Louis W432
Marlite A1456
Marmaxx Group A1389
Marment, Roger E141
The Marmon Group, Inc. A558, A740, P240, P312-P313, P665
Marmon Motor Car P312
Marmon-Herrington Company P312, P313
Marolda, Janice A217
Marolt, Michael W. A255
Maroone, Michael E. A207
Marotta, Daniel A. A411
Marquand, William H. A607
Marquee brand foods A607
Marques, Clarissa C. A905
Marques, Nelson R. A. A119
Marquet, Jean-Claude W555
Marquette Medical Systems A646
Márquez, Oscar W577
Marquis by Waterford Crystal W636, W637
Marr, Daniel G. A385
Marra, Thomas M. A689
Marrakesh Express cous cous A731
Marrero, Jose A97
Marrinan, Susan F. A1295
Marriott, Alice A732, A912, A1296
Marriott, Bill A732, A912, A1296
Marriott Corporation. See Host Marriott Corporation or Marriott International, Inc.

Marriott International, Inc. A86, A732, A740, A912-A913, A1046, A1280, A1296, A1540, E142, E231, E319, P110, P240, P737, W282, W546, W638
Marriott, John A732, A912, A1296
Marriott, J. W., Jr. A732, A912, A913
Marriott Management Services A1296
Marriott, Mike W341
Marriott, Richard E. A733
Marron, Donald B. W617
Marrow, Nancy E236
Mars candy A510, A511
Mars, Forrest, Jr. A914, P314, P665
Mars, Forrest, Sr. A914, P314
Mars, Frank A914, P314
Mars, Inc. A452, A914-A915, P314-P315, P424, P665, P719, W154
Mars, Jacqueline Badger A915, P314, P315, P665
Mars, John F. P314
Mars, John Franklyn A914, A915, P315, P665
MARS music stores A1056
Mars, Robert F., III P698
Marsden, Charles J. A451
Marsee, Betty Ann A1458
Marsh & McLennan Companies, Inc. A150, A916-A917, W396
Marsh data systems W355
Marsh, Gregory A. E155
Marsh, Henry A916
Marsh, Kevin B. A1249
Marsh, Paul A1417
Marsh, R. Bruce A353
Marsh, Richard H. (FirstEnergy) A599
Marsh, Richard (Iomega) A779
Marsh Ullmann & Company A916
Marshall, Colin, Lord of Knightsbridge W140, W141, W291
Marshall, David W157
Marshall Field's department stores A1352, A1353, P496, P700, W142
Marshall, Gary (actor) P378
Marshall, Gary (United Business Media) W621
Marshall, Geoffrey A329, P109
Marshall, Gregory K. A1351
Marshall, Harold A1549
Marshall Industries A214
Marshall, Jaqui Love A833
Marshall, Laurence A1190
Marshall, Paul (Sunrise Telecom) E296
Marshall, Paul (Waste Management) A1505
Marshall, Robert R. A171
Marshall, Ron A994, A995
Marshall, Ruth Ann A925, P323
Marshall, Siri S. A649
Marshall tires W428
Marshalls stores A458, A1388, A1389

Marshell Group W240
Marsico, Dan A1207
Marson Chilena A1278
Marson (rivets) A1322
Marsteller (advertising) W198
Martahari Putra Prima Tbk P243
Marteau, Patrice W447
Martell Cognac A296
Martell liquor W108, W315
Martens, Eric P. A551
Martens, Herbert R., Jr. A1001
Martha (magazine) A918
Martha (marketing) W424
Martha Stewart Living Omnimedia
  Inc. A796, A830, A831,
  A918-**A919**, A1134
Martha White baking mixes A768,
  A1136, A1137
marthastewart.com A919
Marti, Jose W108
Martin, Brian J. (Saks) A1239
Martin, Brian T. (Avon) A217
Martin, Charles N. A1443
Martin Company. *See* Lockheed
  Martin Corporation
Martin, Craig L. A787
Martin, Duane A745, P243
Martin, Glenn A882
Martin, James A. (Engelhard) A551
Martin, James J. (Oshkosh
  B'Gosh) A1069
Martin, James L. (Westvaco) A1517
Martin, Jean W619
Martin, Jennifer P534
Martin, J. Stephen A169
Martin, Kenneth J. A149
Martin, Laura W625
Martin, Les A907
Martin Luther King, Jr. Papers
  Project P457
Martin Machine, Inc. E26
Martin Marietta. *See* Lockheed
  Martin Corporation
Martin Marietta Materials,
  Inc. A1484
Martin, Michael S. A219
Martin, Mitchell P. A959
Martin, Murray D. A1143
Martin, Patricia J. A935
Martin, Patrick J. A1336, A1337
Martin, Peter B. A551
Martin, Randal L. (Dycom) E52
Martin, Randy P. (Penn
  Traffic) A1095
Martin, R. Brad A1238, A1239
Martin Reel Company A298
Martin, Richard (Calvin
  Klein) P101
Martin, Richard J. (AT&T) A203
Martin, Richard J. (Unified Western
  Grocers) P489, P752
Martin, Robert P85, P557
Martin, Terence D. A1181
Martin, Thomas P. (Allied
  Waste) A123
Martin, Thomas R. (ITT) A781

Martin, Thomas T. (Coca-Cola
  Bottling Co. of Chicago) P577
Martin, Todd W85
Martin, William (Analog
  Devices) A171
Martin, William F., Jr. (Yellow
  Corp) A1549
Martin, William McChesney
  (NYSE) A94, A1018, P186, P374
Martin, Yves W171
Martinair Holland nv W317
The Martin-Brower Company,
  L.L.C. P665, P713
Martindale-Hubbell W478
Martineau, Eugene P. E309
Martineau, Phillip M. A727
Martinelli, James E20, E146
Martinelli, Raymond E226
Martinez, Angel R. A1194
Martinez, Annette E235
Martinez, Arthur C. A1264
Martínez del Río Petricioli,
  Eduardo W441
Martinez-Simancas, Julian W513
Martini & Rossi S.p.A. (wines and
  spirits) W108
Martini, Brent R. A155
Martini gin W109
Martini, Robert D. (Russell) A1221
Martini, Robert E.
  (AmerisourceBergen) A155
Martin-Retortillo, Teresa P65
Martins (bank) W114
Martin-Senour paints A1278
Martin/Williams
  (advertising) A1062, A1063
MartisDXX access and transport
  network system A1362, A1363
Marton, Steven G. A387
Martone, S. Michael A205
Marty Franich Auto Center P666
Marubeni Corporation A1006,
  W296, **W358**-**W359**
Marufuku Company W394
Marumo, Haruo W597
Maruta, Yoshio W308
Maruyama, Gentaro W303
Maruyama, Isao W199
Mar-Val Food Stores, Inc. P489
Marvel Carburetor A278
Marvel Entertainment Group,
  Inc. A902, P304
Marwick, James A840, P286, W324
Marwick, Mitchell &
  Company A840, P286, W324
Marx, Marcus A690
Mary Ann boutiques W299
Mary Engelbreit's Home
  Companion A443
Mary Kay Inc. **P316**-**P317**, P666
Mary Kitchen canned hash A730,
  A731
The Mary Tyler Moore Show (TV
  show) A334
Maryland Casualty Company W652
Maryland Properties A938
Maryland Square (catalog) A294

Maryland State Lottery
  Agency P666
Maryland Steel A256
Maryland-American Water
  Company A155
Marz, W. Richard A895
Marzol, Adolfo A581
Mascari, C. A. A669
Maschinenfabrik Augsburg-
  Nurnberg. *See* MAN
  Aktiengesellschaft
Masco Corporation A**920**-A**921**,
  P298, W490
Masco Home Furnishings P442
MascoTech Stamping
  Technologies A1394, P673
Masefield, Charles W111
Maselli, Peter F. A627
Maser, James E. P131
Maserati shoes A295
Maserati S.p.A. (cars) A650, W226,
  W227
*M*A*S*H* (movie and TV
  show) A1084, P740
Mashantucket Pequot Gaming
  Enterprise Inc. **P318**-**P319**, P667
Mashantucket Pequot Tribal
  Nation P318, P450, P667
Mashav (cement) W322
Mashima, Kyle A77
Masin, Michael T. A1473
Masinton, Dick P425, P719
Masius, Wynn-Williams P72
Maskel, Melanie P603
Maskey, Rebecca S. E180
Masland A856
Maslen, Peter A1327
Maslowe, Philip L. A1489
Masocotech A754
Masojara, Bronek W337
Mason & Hanger Engineering P589
Mason, George L. A429
Mason jars A224
Mason, Johnny W301
Mason, Ronald P175, P602
Mason, Steve A950
Mason Street Funds A1048, A1049,
  P376, P377
Mason, Theodore S. E216
Mason, Tim W591
Mason, William R. A147
Masonite A770, A1456
MasoTech A920
Masquerade Match Up lottery
  game P473
Mass Millions lottery game P668
Massachusetts Bank A1332
Massachusetts Financial Services
  Company A468
Massachusetts General
  Hospital P697
Massachusetts High Technology
  Council A170
Massachusetts Institute of
  Technology P54, P248, P667
Massachusetts Investors
  Trust A1332

Massachusetts Mutual Life Insurance Company A268, **A922-A923**, A1506, P82, **P320-P321**, P667
Massachusetts National Bank Of Boston A448
Massachusetts State Lottery Commission P668
Massachusetts-American Water Company A155
Massanelli, Stephen C. A1553
Massari, Chester A. A687
Massengill, Matthew H. A1514, A1515
Massey, Donald P596
Massey Energy Company A610
Massey Ferguson farm equipment A96, W156
Massey, Jack A694
Massey, Marvin P561
Massingale, Lynn P743
MassMutual. See Massachusetts Mutual Life Insurance Company
Masson, Bernard V. A871
Masson, Donald E167
Masson, Robert P696
Mast Industries (clothing) A876, A877
Mast, James P464
Mast, Kent E. A559
Mastellone dairy products W193
Masten, John P135, P579
Master Choice brand foods A671
Master Distribution W278
Master Frame windows P50
Master Lock Company A618, A754
Master Mix feed P36
Master Plan for Higher Education P494
Master Power (tool manufacturer) A430
Master Shield (vinyl building products) A462
MASTER START auto care products A1101
Master Tire & Rubber Company A432
Master vehicle W480, W481
MasterCard International Inc. A142, A262, A318, **A924-A925**, A936, A1480, E159, E312, **P322-P323**, P508, P668, P766, W608
Masterchem Industries (specialty paint products) A920
Mastercraft Pipes A1458
Mastercraft (upholstery) A388
MasterCuts hair salons A1196
Masterfeeds P36, P37
Masterfoods condiments A915, P315
Masters & Johnson A766
Masters, Kenneth H. A1069
Masters-Jackson (highway construction) A200
Masterson, Kenneth R. A589
MasterTrak software E36
Mastervac A265

Mastran, David V. E88, E238
Mastrelli, Thomas A. W627
Mastrian, James P. A1203
Mastromarino, John L. A603
Mastrov, Mark S. P258
Masuda, Isamu P689
Masuda, Yukio W371
Masujiro, Hashimoto W402
Masuko, Takashi W303
Masumoto, Teruaki W599
Mataki, Tateo W199
Match Light charcoal A374, A375
Matchbox toys A926, A927
Matchmate brand A527
Matco Tools Corporation A463
Mater, Maud A627
Material Research Corporation W600
Material Service Corporation A644
Materials Research Corporation A1156
Materna, James M. E257
Mateus, Lois A. A297
Matheis, Dieter W517
Matheney, J. Keith A891
Matheny, James T. E32
Matheny, Robert G. E305
Mather, Ann E103, E266
Mather brand A585
Mather Company (sealing products) A584
Mathers shoe stores A1470
Matheson, James W306
Mathew, Sara A517
Mathews, James G. A1047
Mathews, Sylvia P79
Mathias, Edward P110
Mathiasen, Raymond L. A1367
Mathies, William A. A259
Mathieson Chemical A290, A1060
Mathieson, Michael R. A619
Mathieu, Mark J. A1323
Mathis, Catherine J. A1021
Mathis, David B. P269, P650
Mathison, William A. A531
Mathur, Pradeep A1415
Matilda Bay beer W231
Matiuk, Gregory A353
Maton, Jérôme W171
Matos, Delores P687
Matra Automobile W330, W331
Matra BAe Dynamics W110
Matra Hachette W110
Matrisciano, James E72
Matrix Essentials hair care A290, W342
Matrix Membranes E105
Matrix partners A1372
MATRIX Rehabilitation, Inc. A259
MatrixOne, Inc. E237
MATRIXX (telemarketing) A292
Matschullat, Dale L. A1023
Matsen, Paul G. A479
Matson, Harold A926
Matson, Patricia J. A61
Matsuda, Ingiro W362

Matsui, Hidefumi A93
Matsui, Masao W359
Matsui, Takao W261
Matsummura, Norio W403
Matsumoto, Kanya W448, W449
Matsumoto, Ko W199
Matsumoto, Masaharu W395
Matsumoto, Masayuki W487
Matsumoto, Nozomu W448
Matsumoto, Satoshi W449
Matsumoto, Seiya W448
Matsumoto, Shigeo W387
Matsumoto, Shoichi A93
Matsumoto, Tadashi W611
Matsumura, Teruo W405
Matsunaga, Yasuzaemon W598
Matsuno, Haruki W401
Matsuoka, Tetsuya W373
Matsushima, Takashi W235
Matsushita Communication Industrial Company, Ltd. E117, E310
Matsushita Electric Industrial Company, Ltd. A162, A750, A1184, P300, W146, **W360-W361**, W394, W444, W514, W550, W572
Matsushita, Konosuke W360, W514
Matsushita, Masaharu W360, W361
Matsushita, Masayuki W361
Matsushita, Muneyuki W96
Matsushita-Kotobuki Electronics Industries, Ltd. A1184
Mattei, Enrico W216
Matteis, Richard J. A219
Mattel, Inc. A216, A842, **A926-A927**, E60, P188, P454, P486
Mattell P278
Matteson, Scott P675
Matthers, Edward E. A151
Matthew Clark (wines, cider and water) A422
Matthews, B. Frank, II P77
Matthews, Caroline S. A179
Matthews, Charles W., Jr. A577
Matthews, Clark J., II A56, A57
Matthews, Craig G. A825
Matthews, Daniel B. A1047
Matthews Equipment A710
Matthews, Jim P555
Matthews, John A437
Matthews, L. White, III A531
Matthews, Lynn O. A1021
Matthews, Milton T. A709
Matthews Paints A1152
Matthews, Roger W301
Matthews, Ted A1317, P453
Matthews Thompson (stores) W172
Matthiessen, Poul C. W163
Matthiessen, Robert E. E223
Mattioli, Paolo W226
Mattix, Forrest E. A1319
Mattoff, S. Charles P770
Matton, Clermont A. A1253
Mattox, William C. P349
Mattress Discounters A703, P442
Matulich, Stephanie E266

Mature Focus Radio P29
Maturity Broadcast News P29
Maturo, Michael E276
Matute, Rafael W635
Matytsin, Alexander K. W347
Matz, R. Kevin A545
Matzke, Kevin E37
Matzke, Richard H. A353
Matzkin, Katherine F. "Kitty" P776
Maucher, Helmut W388
Maudsley, Ronald R. A591
Mauerhoff, Emill W234
Maugeri, Leonardo W217
Maughan, Deryck C. A371
Mauna La'i juice products P381
Maurer, Jerald L. A1185
Maurice's stores P539
Mauro, Salvatore L. W633
Mauroy, Pierre W432
Mautner, Hans C. A1287
Maverick brand A985
Maverick cigarettes A884
Maverick jeans A1475
Maverick Tube Corporation A324,
   E**87**, E238
Maverick (TV show) A60
Mavic bicycle components W62,
   W63
Mavis, Todd W191
Mavrinac, Richard P. W245
Mavromatis, A. W385
Mawatari, Masao W315
Mawhinney, Patrick R. E249
Mawn, Peter G. A799
Mawyer, Edward A791
MAX Club stores A1348
Max Factor (cosmetics) A902,
   A1164, A1165, P304, W342
Max Foods A110, A111
Max India (asset
   management) A1016, P370
Max M. Fisher College of
   Business P382, P383
Maxalt drug A957
MaxAttach network servers A928,
   A929
MAXCOM
   (telecommunications) W580
Maxim Group (carpet) A980
Maxim (magazine) W238
Maxima Air Separation
   Center A1156
Maxima car W403
Maximum PC (magazine) W238,
   W239
MAXIMUS, Inc. E**88**, E238
Maxion International
   Motores A1010
MAXI-Papier office supply
   stores A1324
Maxoptix (computer
   memory) A928, W326
Maxson, Robert C. P99
Maxtor Corporation A**928**-A**929**,
   W274, W326
Maxtor servers A778, A1184
Maxum boats A299

Maxus Energy (oil exploration and
   production) W650
Maxus Investments A592
Maxwell Communications A944
Maxwell, David A580
Maxwell, Hamish W646
Maxwell, Harold C. A1365
Maxwell House coffee A842, A843,
   A1126
Maxwell, James Clerk P176
Maxwell Motor Car Company W188
Maxwell, Robert A1158, A1160,
   P400, W462, W470, W478, W592
Maxwell, William C. A993
MAXXAM Inc. A**930**-A**931**
MaxxiuM Worldwide (wine/spirit
   distribution) A618
MAXXUM cameras W368
May, David L. (S.C.
   Johnson) A1247, P433
May, David (May Department
   Stores) A932
The May Department Stores
   Company A490, A586, A880,
   A**932**-A**933**, A1092, A1238, W298
May, Jerry A. P383
May, Jonathon P. A1401
May, Karen J. A237
May, Lily L. A1225
May, Michael C. A627
May, Peter W. A1400, A1401
May, Tracy E181
May, William H. A243
Mayan Automation E43
Maybelline cosmetics A1200, W342,
   W343
Mayberry, Phillip H. E38
Maybin, Richard M. A415
Maydan, Dan A189
Mayer & Schmidt department
   store A490
Mayer & Schweitzer A348
Mayer, Harold A238
Mayer, Jeffrey P. P131, P577
Mayer, Louis B. A962, P428
Mayer, Stanley A. E78, E227
Mayer, W. Charles, III A167
Mayeux, David R. A1367
Mayfair cigarettes W240, W241
Mayfield dairy product A467
Mayfield, John M. P153
Mayfield Publishing A944
Mayfield Vending W282
The Mayflower Insurance Company
   Ltd. A379
Mayflower Transit P753
Maygay (amusement
   machines) W544
Mayhew, Karin D. A697
Maynard, James G. E238
Maynard, Meridee J. A1049, P377
Maynard Oil Company E238
Maynard, Peter W465
Maynard, Sue E172
Maynards candy W155
Mayo, Charles P324

*Mayo Clinic Family Health
   Book* P324, P325
Mayo Foundation P**324**-P**325**,
   P668
Mayo Graduate School of
   Medicine P324
Mayo, John W354
Mayo, Ronald A. P670
Mayo, William P324, P668
Mayo, William, Jr. P324
Mayorek, John P580
Mayr, Gerhard N. A541
Mayrhuber, Wolfgang W345
Mays, L. Lowry A372, A373
Mays, Mark P. A373
Mays, Randall T. A373
Maytag Corporation A**934**-A**935**,
   P618
Maytag, F. L. A934
Maytag, L. B. A934
Mayville Metal Products P581
Mazda Motor Corporation A616,
   A1394, P561, P606, P631, P644,
   P717, P733, W**362**-W**363**
Mazeika, Karl W439
Mazur, Daniel F. P479
Mazurkiewicz, David P630
Mazzilli, Philip J. A559
Mazzo, James V. A119
Mazzola, Mario A369
Mazzorin, Carlos E. A617
MB Financial, Inc. E239
MBC Investments
   Corporation A955
MBCH, Inc. A905
MBM Corporation P669
MBNA Corporation A**936**-A**937**
M.C. Packaging A224
MCA. *See* Music Corporation of
   America
McAdam, John D. G. (Imperial
   Chemical) W279
McAdam, John (F5 Networks) E201
McAdam, Robert A171
McAleer, John N. E80
McAleer, Joseph E80
McAlindon, Roman W. A173, P49
McAlister, Maurice E194
McAllister, Francis R. "Frank" E294
McAloon, Brian P. A171
McAndrew, Joseph P. A101
McAndrew, Kelly A1103
McAndrew, Kevin J. E36, E170
McAndrew, Mark S. A1391
McAnear, Belinda E79, E227
McArthur dairy product A467
McArthur, James W251
McArthur, Sarah E103
McArthur, Steven A. P341
McAulay, Carl D. A1439
McAuley, Catherine P114
McAuliffe, Mary E. A1423
McAusland, David W75
McBee, Judith B. A993
McBride & Son Enterprises A508
McBride, Paul F. A264, A265
MCCA (paging and cellular) A248

McCabe, Barry L. P277, P652
McCabe Company P122
McCabe, Dennis P. P471
McCabe, Dora W155
McCabe, James B. P125, P575
McCabe, John P86
McCabe, Joseph J. A1155
McCabe, Mary E100
McCabe, Michael J. A127
McCabe's Quality Foods P727
McCafferty, Michael P750
McCaffery, Mike P457
McCahill, Thomas M. A987
McCain, David B. A863
McCain Foods Limited A722
McCain, John A. A539
McCain, Lon E316
McCall, Charlie A946
McCall, David L. A351
McCall, Dawn P159
McCallion, Anne D. A439
McCallister, Kenneth A. A643
McCallister, Michael B. A739
McCallum, James R. A307
McCanless, R. William W195
McCann, Harrison A772
McCann, Mary E. A293
McCann, Steven A887
McCann, Tim A1455
McCann, Vonya B. A1319
McCanna, Pete P704
McCann-Erickson Company A772, A773, P72
McCarron, Francis T. A1401
McCarten, William W. A913
McCarter, Thomas A1174
McCarthy P669
McCarthy, Christine M. A1497
McCarthy, Cormac P760
McCarthy, Gloria M. P175
McCarthy, Jack D. A1529
McCarthy, Joseph F. A857
McCarthy, Robert J. A913
McCarthy, Timothy P669
McCartney, Stella W251
McCarty Farms (chickens) A1418
McCarty Foods chicken A1419
McCarty, Steve P706
McCarty-Holman
  supermarkets P478
McCarville, Mark J. A1243
McCaskey, Raymond F. P227, P628
McCaslin, James A. A683
McCaslin, Teresa E. A427, P141, P583
McCaughey, Gerald T. W157
McCaul, Daniel A1485
McCausland, Edwin P. A1009, P365
McCaw Cellular A202, A248, A1026, W148
McCaw, Craig A866, A1026
McCellon-Allen, Venita P551
McClafferty, Charles F. P703
McClain, Derek R. A1399
McClain International (jet engine
  parts) E67

McClain, Jackie (California State
  University) P99, P564
McClain, Jackie R. (University of
  Michigan) P758
McClain, John T. A339
McClanahan, David M. A1199
McClanahan, Jackie A865
McClatchy Company A1160
McClean, Murray R. A397
McClellan, Bobby J. A775
McClelland, Carter A227
McClelland Jeffrey D. A139
McClelland, Michael J. P595
McClelland, Norman P728
McClelland, Sarah L. A231
McClelland, Sue A521, P169
McClendon, Aubrey K. E39, E176
McClimon, David S. A381
McClintic-Marshall
  Construction A256
McClung, James A. (FMC) A613
McClung, Jim H. (National Service
  Industries) A1005
McClung, William C. W67
McClure, Charles G. A585
McClure, Gail D. P521
McClure, Lawrence D. A881
McCluskey, Eugene M. A613
McCluskey, Helen A881
McCluski, Stephen C. A235
McClusky, Karyl A307
McColgin, Jim D. A413
McColl, Hugh L., Jr. A226, A227
McCollam, Sharon L. A1531
McCollough, W. Alan A366, A367
McCollum, Mark A. A1369
McCollum, Randall H. A75
McCollum, W. Lee A1247, P433, P722
McComas, Frank A833
McComb, William H. A1429, P491
McCombs, B. J. "Red" A372, A498
McCone, John P386
McConnell, David A216
McConnell, Donald H., Jr.
  (Corning) A435
McConnell, Donald P. (Battelle) P71
McConnell, Kirk A323
McConnell, Robin W573
McConway and Torley (railcar
  couplers) A1406
McCook, Jacqueline A303
McCook Metals P675
McCook, Richard P. A1533
McCoole, Robert F. P649
McCorkindale, Douglas H. A632, A633
McCorkle, Leon M., Jr. A1511
McCormack Advisors
  International P250
McCormack & Dodge
  (software) A516
McCormack, Daniel J. A1085
McCormack, John J. A1355, P467
McCormack, June M. A1449
McCormack, Kermit E. A753

McCormack, Mark H. P250, P251, P641
McCormack, Noreen E199
McCormack, Terry R. A461
McCormick & Company,
  Inc. A938-A939, P530
McCormick, Charles A938
McCormick, Charles "Buzz" A938
McCormick, Chris P300, P301, P660
McCormick, Cyrus A1010
McCormick, Cyrus, Jr. A1010
McCormick, Patricia E204
McCormick, Richard L. P761
McCormick, Robert A1402
McCormick School of Engineering
  and Applied Science P691
McCormick, William T., Jr. A376, A377
McCormick, Willoughby A938
McCown De Leeuw &
  Company P258
McCoy, Alan H. A105
McCoy, Craig W147
McCoy, C. W. "Chuck" A230
McCoy, Deborah L. A429
McCoy, Dustan E. A299
McCoy, Fred, Jr. A675
McCoy, Holly D. A583, P185, P606
McCoy, James A928
McCoy, John B. (BANK ONE) A230
McCoy, John B., Jr. (Battelle) P71
McCoy, John G. (BANK ONE) A230
McCoy, John H. (BANK ONE) A230
McCoy, Joseph P. A311
McCoy, Kirk P189, P608
McCoy, Marilyn P379
McCoy, Michael C.
  (TranSwitch) E304
McCoy, Michael J. (Hormel
  Foods) A731
McCoy, Rob A1417
McCoy, Thomas M. A83
McCracken, Douglas M. A475, P155, W197
McCracken, Edward A1284
McCracken, Steve R. A535
McCrady, Richard, Sr. A421
McCrary, Charles D. A1307
McCraw, Leslie A610
McCrorey, John A830
McCrory Corporation A158, A830
McCulloch chainsaws W210
McCulloch Oil Corporation A930
McCulloch, Robert A930
McCulloch, Robert, Jr. A930
McCullogh, Michael P88
McCullough, Gary E. A1527
McCullough, Glenn L., Jr. P468, P469
McCullough, John P672
McCully, E. Nichol A815
McCumber, Kenneth A. A103
McCurdy, Charles G. A1161
McCusker, Thomas J. P349
McCutcheon, Jeffrey C. A455
McDaniel, Connie D. A383

McDaniel, C. William E50
McDaniel, John P. P671
McDaniel, Thomas R. A533
McDATA Corporation A542, A1514, E239
McDavid, William H. A809
McDermid, Margaret E. A499
McDermott, Eugene A1378
McDermott International, Inc. A940-A941
McDermott, Robert A1452, P502
McDermott, R. Thomas A940
McDonald & Company A822
McDonald, Debbie W115
McDonald, Dick A942
McDonald Frank J. A457
McDonald, Harry T. P201, P616
McDonald, Hugh A555
McDonald Investments Inc. A822, A823
McDonald, James F. A1258, A1259
McDonald, John A241, P75
McDonald, Ken P. E155
McDonald, Mackey J. (VF Corp.) A1474, A1475
McDonald, Mac (McDonald's) A942
McDonald, Mary Alice E170
McDonald, Robert A. A1165
McDonald, Stephen D. (Toronto-Dominion Bank) W609
McDonald, Steven L. (Household International) A735
McDonald, Wesley S. A63
McDonald William J. A319
McDonald, W. O'Neill A1349
McDonald's Corporation A302, A316, A352, A934, A942-A943, A1062, A1350, A1404, A1510, P72, P160, P202, P238, P264, P328, P354, P426, P486, P516, P524, P595, P648, P650, P665, P704, P713, P777, W206
McDonnell, Brian L. P686
McDonnell, David C. P206, P207, P620
McDonnell Douglas A190, A272, A620, W70
McDonnell, Eileen C. P215
McDonnell, John F. E239
McDonnell, Michael R. A529
McDonnell, Sue K. A951
McDonough, Bob A865
McDonough, Gerald A1551
McDonough, John J. A1022
McDonough, Joseph A171
McDonough, Kevin E76
McDonough, William E. (National Steel) A1007
McDonough, William J. (Federal Reserve Bank of New York) P607
McDougald, Don P427, P720
McDougall, Duane C. A1525
McDougall, Linda M. A681
McDougall, Ronald A. A288, A289
McDougle, Jeffery A. A1443
McDowell, Mary T. A399
McDuff Electronics A1188

MCEG Sterling (film and TV productions) P332
McElhatton, Jerry A925, P323
McElrea, Charles H. A655
McElroy, Bernard K. A1101
McElroy, Michael A. A403
McElroy Mine A417
McElwee, Andrew A., Jr. A357
McElwreath, Sally C. A1465
McElya, James S. A433
McEnery, Kevin J. A1255
McEniry, Robert W429
McEntee, Gerald W. P35
McEvoy, Thomas J. A1319
McEwan, Feona W647
McFadden, Charles B. A1249
McFadzean, Tony W645
McFarland, Keith P471
McGarr, Joseph W. P91, P775
McGarry, E. John E43
McGarry, Michael A1153
McGavick, Mike S. A1231
McGaw Medical Center P378, P691
McGee Airways A106
McGee, Dean A820
McGee, Gary L. A483
McGee, Henry L. A1129
McGee, Joseph A783
McGee, Julie A. A1255
McGee, Liam E. A227
McGee, Mac A106
McGee, Michael P. E74, E222
McGee, Ralph F. P153
McGee, Robert M. A1055
McGehee, Robert B. A1167
McGeorge, Don W. A845
McGhan, Michael J. E210
McGill, James T. P646
McGill, John F., Jr. E301
McGill, Robert A847
McGill, William H., Jr. E237
McGillivary, Christopher J. W637
McGinn, Richard A. A898
McGinnes, Paul W468
McGinnis, Carolyn P77, P553
McGinnis Farms A468
McGinnis, Kathleen A. A1511
McGinnis, Randy P149
McGinty, Jim E69, E215
McGlade, John E. A101
McGladrey & Pullen LLP (accounting) A680
McGladrey Contract Business Services, L.L.C. A681
McGlinn, John S. A727
McGlynn, Michael A945
McGoldrick, John L. A291
McGoldrick, Patrick W567
McGonigle, James J. E186
McGonigle, John P. A349
McGough, Dennis R. A1061
McGovern, Gail J. A615, P191
McGovern, John R. (Sunkist Growers) P465, P738
McGovern John W. (Silicon Laboratories) E288

McGovern Lawrence D. E213
McGovern, Patrick J. P249, P641
McGovern, Sean W337
McGovern, Thomas P., Jr. A1117
McGowan, W. Brian A1537
McGowan, William A1534
McGrath, Brian T. A147
McGrath, Eugene R. A419
McGrath, Joseph W. A1425
McGrath, J. Paul A153
McGrath, Karen P708
McGrath, Kevin N. A737
McGrath, Robert L. A625
McGrath, Tim P137
McGraw, Harold W. A944
McGraw, Harold W., III A944, A945
McGraw, James H. A944
McGraw, Jay A944
McGraw, Phil P218
McGraw, Robert J. W65
McGraw-Edison electrical products A430, A431
The McGraw-Hill Companies, Inc. A588, A944-A945, A1402
McGregor, Andrew C. P277
McGregor, Douglas J. A307
McGregor, Janet L. A883
McGregor (sporting goods) A298
McGuinn, Martin G. A954, A955
McGuire, Jim A841, P287, W325
McGuire, Joseph E306
McGuire, Michael E97
McGuire, Pamela C. A1103
McGuire small engines P284
McGuire, William W. A1434, A1435
McGuirk, Gary L. A795
McGuirk, James F., II A1425
McGurk, Christopher J. A962, A963
McGwire, Mark P306
McHale, James E. P521
McHale, Judith A. P159
McHale, Kevin A280
McHugh, Janet E. A425
McHugh, Robert (Feld Entertainment) P189
McHugh, Robert W. (Venator Group) A1471
MCI. See WorldCom, Inc.
Groupe MCI A542
MCI International E289
MCI WorldCom, Inc. See WorldCom, Inc.
McIlnay, Donald R. A1323
McIlquham, David J. P443
McInerney, Thomas E. E38
McIntire, Lee A241, P75
McIntosh, Gerald A74
McIntosh, J. David A1393
McIntosh, John L. A1061
McIntyre, David E. A1517
McIntyre, Edward J. A1543
McIntyre, J. Lawrence A1393
McIntyre, John H. P431
McIntyre, Robert C. A1259
McIntyre, Tim A501, P163
McKay, Kevin J. E132

McKay, Patricia A207
McKechnie Limited (window furnishings) A1022
McKee, E. Marie A435
McKee Foods Corporation P669
McKee, Jack P669
McKee, James E. E65
McKee, Michael D. P253
McKee, O. D. P669
McKee, Robert E., III A413
McKee, Ruth P669
McKelvey, Kerry A1535
McKenna, Charles M. E35
McKenna, Jeanne A673, P211
McKenna, John F. A401
McKenna, Matthew M. A1107
McKenna, Robert E. A653
McKenna, Timothy A1293
McKennon, Keith A1082
McKenny, John F. A775
McKenzie, Douglas P524
McKenzie, John A220, P66, P548
McKenzie, Michael K. P623
McKenzie, Peter E105
McKenzie, Reggie A673, P211
McKenzie, Ron P745
McKenzie-Swarts, Molly A721
McKeon, Aidan W87
McKeon, Mark A1327
McKerlie, Ron J. W495
McKerlie-Millen P112
McKesson Corporation A156, A320, A322, A540, A600, **A946-A947**, E240, P738
McKesson, John A946
McKesson Water W192
McKesson-Robbins A946, W246
McKey Food Services P650
McKinley, Mary Ellen E281
McKinnell, Henry A., Jr. A1119
McKinney, Harry W. A713
McKinney, William F. E64
McKinnish, Richmond D. A327
McKinnon, Paul D. A473
McKinnon, Peter A. W383
McKinsey & Company A196, A868, **A948-A949**, P94, P292, **P326-P327**, P518, P670, W626
McKinsey, James A948, P326
The McKinsey Quarterly (journal) A948, P326
McKinstry, Nancy W643
McKinzie, LeAnn P471
McKitrick, James T. P406
McKnight, William A976
McKulka, Frank E. W117
McLachlan, Neil A. A951
McLachlan, William C. A705
McLain, Robert S., Jr. E118
McLamb, Michael H. E237
McLamore, James A302
McLane Company, Inc. (wholesaler) A1084, A1458, P236, P633
McLane Distribution Centers A1494, A1495
McLane Foodservice, Inc. P236

McLane Foodservice-Temple A1109
McLane Polska P243
McLaren, Ross W301
McLaughlin, David T. P45
McLaughlin, Elizabeth M. E69, E215
McLaughlin, Eunan A1033
McLaughlin, Joseph T. A449
McLaughlin, Paul F. E282
McLaughlin, Thomas K. (Countrywide) A439
McLaughlin, Thomas M. (Publix) A1177
McLean, C. D. A429
McLean, Jim P329, P671
McLean, Ned A1502
McLeary, Wallin and Crouse (carpets) A980
McLennan, Rex J. W453
McLernon, Lawrence A. A519
McLevish, Timothy R. A951
McLintock, Michael W465
McLure, Howard A. A323
MCM Electronics E191
McMahan, James A1530
McMahan's Furniture stores A702
McMahon, Brien A339
McMahon, Christopher C. A463
McMahon, Dirk A1047
McMahon, Jesse E141
McMahon, John D. A419
McMahon, Linda E. E141, E319
McMahon, Pat A549
McMahon, Richard C. A247
McMahon, Timothy P. A409
McMahon, Vincent K. E141, E319
McMakin, Joseph H. A101
McManmon, Thomas P616
McManus, Ed A1349
The McManus Group P72
McManus, Sean A335
McMaster, Bruce D. E191
McMaster, Fergus W468
McMaster, John A1440
McMaster, Lee P. A505
McMaster, William W156
McMasters, Michael P. E177
McMillan, Cary D. A1243
McMillan, C. Steven A1242, A1243
McMillan, Henry M. P385
McMillan, J. Eddie A1525
McMillan, Joe T. A577
McMillan, John A163
McMillan, Robert S. E252
McMillan, William J. P766
McMillen, Jack A1036
McMillen, Stephen W. (Hillenbrand Industries) A719
McMillen, Steve (Truman Arnold) P749
McMonagle, Charles A. A1267
McMoRan Explorations A628, A752
McMorron, K. R. W645
McMorrow, William J. E227
McMullan, Rodney A845
McMullen, Don A1487

McMullian, Amos R. A608, A609
McMullin, Ross W62, W63
McMurphy, Edward R. E188
McMurtrie, Ron A1535
McMurtry, Vanda B. A91
MCN Corporation A900
McNabb, F. William, III A1469, P505
McNair, Robert P356
McNallen, Katherine P753
McNally, Andrew P408
McNally, Michael J. A1417
McNamara, Anne H. A165
McNamara, John D. A193
McNamara, Neil W307
McNamara, Pamela P54, P55, P543
McNamara, Robert A. A611
McNamara, William P. A933
McNaughton Apparel Group Inc. A804
McNeal, Steven C. A555
McNealy, Maverick A1342
McNealy, Scott G. A1342, A1343
McNeil, Corbin A., Jr. A571
McNeil, George W151
McNeil Labs A800
McNeil, Ronald D. A127
McNeill, Don D. A1525
McNeilly, Michael A188
McNerney, W. James A976, A977
McNish, Russ P574
McNulty, James F. P386, P387, P697
MCO Holdings A930
MCorp A230
McPaper Aktiengesellschaft W203
McPeak, Frank W190
McPheeters, Lynn A333
McPherson, George R. A573
McPherson, Samuel N. A579
McPherson, Sue E69
McQuade, Eugene A603
McQuade, J. Michael A525
McQuade, Kathryn B. A1039
McQueary, Charles E. A645
McQueeney, Michael G. A1377
McRae's department stores A1238
MCSi, Inc. E239
McSorley, John E256
McSweeney, George A480
McTernan, Bernita P119
McVay, Malcolm E. A699
McWalter, Alan W357
McWeeny, Philip A1075
McWhirter, William A., II A1407
McWhorter, Anthony L. A1391
McWhorter Technologies, Inc. (coatings) A522
McWilliams, D. Bradley A431
McWilliams, Larry S. A317
McWilliams, William A628
MDF D'Aquitaine A1524
Meachen, Edward P501
The Mead Corporation A274, **A950-A951**, A1516, P715, W478
Mead, Dana G., Jr. (Guidant) A675

Mead, Dana (Tenneco Automotive) A1368
Mead, Daniel A950
Mead (distribution) A770
Mead, Frederick W552
Mead, George (Mead) A950
Mead, George (Pratt & Whitney) A1432
Mead Johnson (drugs and infant formulas) A290
Mead, Peter W. (Omnicom Group) A1063
Meade, Peter G. (Blue Cross and Blue Shield of Massachusetts) P85
Meador, David E. A513
Meadow Brook dairy product A467
Meadow Gold milk A1339, P90
Meadows Distributing A466
Meadows, Donnie P654
Meadows, Thomas A752
Meadox Medicals A282
Meads, Mindy C. A853
MeadWestvaco A950, A1516
MEAG Munich ERGO AssetManagement W380
Meagher, David P661
Meakin, Robert I. W355
Meaney, Dick A171
Means, Barbara P455
MeansBusiness (business information) P279
Meany, George P34
Mearl Corporation (pearlescent pigments) A550
Measurement & Flow Control Division A1210
Measurement Specialties, Inc. A1412, E240
Measurex A1514
Mebane Packaging Group A1516
MECA Software A680
Mecca Bingo W472, W473
Mecca brand clothing E101
Mecca, Lorraine A758
Mechanical Technology Inc. A512, E56
Mechanics Universal Joint A278
Méchanique Aviation TRAction. See Matra Automobile
Mechas, John A1151
Mecherle, George A1330, P458
Mecherle, Ramond A1330, P458
Mecherles family P735
Mechura, Frank A453
Mecklermedia E102
MEDAES Holdings, Inc. (medical gas) A718, A719
Medalists Industries (fasteners) A748
Medallion brands P201
Medallion School Partnerships A191
MedCap Properties A694
MedCath Inc. A837, P283
MedCenterDirect.com A698
MedChem Products A444

Medco Containment Services A956
Medco Research E229
Mede, Rosemary A459
Medeco Security Locks A718
Médeias & Régies Europe (media sales) W467
Medeiros, Matthew W445
Medex (Medicare supplement) P84, P85
Medford, Mark O. A1371, P469
Medgar Evers College P128, P129
Medi Mart drug stores A1492
Media Central A1160, A1161
The Media Edge W646
Media Markt electronics stores W364, W365
Media Monitoring A66
Media Network A976
Media Play stores A254
Media4 A528
MediaBase A1284
Mediacom (cable) A312
MediaLight Inc. A170
Mediamark Research W621
Media-MOST W242
MediaNews Group, Inc. A80, A568, P32, P670
MediaOne Group, Inc. A180, A202, A390, A972, W152
Mediaring.com W180
Mediavision (movie theaters) W467
Medica Health Plans A1434, P536
Medicaid A178, A258, A538, A694, A696, A738, A886, A904, A908, A1076, A1434, A1506, E88, P368, P626, P637
Medi-Cal A1506, E88
Medical Care America A694
Medical Center for Children P566
Medical Device Technologies, Inc. P313
Medical Expense Fund P174
Medical Life Insurance Company P227
Medical Registry Services E72
Medical Research Group A952, E241
Medical Service Association of Pennsylvania A716, P234
Medicare A178, A258, A268, A360, A538, A694, A696, A716, A718, A738, A810, A904, A1076, A1080, A1340, A1366, A1390, A1434, E105, E152, E268, E309, E311, P28, P82, P83, P84, P86, P174, P226, P234, P266, P556, P557, P572, P626, P632
Medicare drugstores W312
Medicare+Choice (HMO) P266
Medicare-Glaser A574
Medicine Shoppe International, Inc. A320, A321
Medicis Pharmaceutical Corporation E89, E240
Medicode (health information) A1434
Medicus Group International P73
MediGap (insurance) A1434

Medill, Joseph A1402, P378
Medill School of Journalism P378, P379, P691
MedImmune, Inc. E90, E240
Medina Noriega, Sergio F. W581
Medina, Pedro W193
Medinol A282
MEDIOBANCA-Banca di Credito Finanziano S.p.A. W98, W208
The Mediplex Group, Inc. A1340
Medirest (health care) W175
Medis Health and Pharmaceutical Services, Inc. A946, A947
MediSense A58
MediTech (catheter) A282
MediTek (medical imaging) E67
Mediterranean Broadband Access S.A. W575
The Meditrust Companies P130
Medix (medical supply) A1070
Medline Industries, Inc. P670
Medo car care products A1096, A1097
MedPartners Managed Care, Inc. A322, A323, A698, A1366
MedPointe Inc. P110
MedQuist Inc. W444
Medscape A334
MedSelect A488
MedStar Health P671
MedTennessee, Inc. A323
Medtronic, Inc. A282, A674, A952-A953, E241
Medtronic MiniMed E241
Medusa (cement) A446
Medvidovich, Suzanne A1429, P491, P754
Medvin, Harvey N. A183
Medvyedev, Dmitri Anatolevich W242, W243
Meek, John E142
Meeker, Mary A988
Meeker, Thomas H. E40, E178
Meeks, James E. E45
MEEMIC Holdings, Inc. E241
Mees & Hope (bank) W56
Mees, David E46
Meet the Press (TV show) A998
Meeting Street brand P77
Mega Image stores W195
Mega, John S. A847
Mega Marts P422
Megalink stent A674
Megane car W480, W481
Megastores W622
Mehiel, Dennis P727
Mehigen, Karen P581
Mehlman, Charles P291
Mehrberg, Randall E. A571
Mehrotra, Sanjay E117
Mehta, James H. A1513
Mehta, Shailesh J. A1171
Mehta, Siddarth N. A735
MEI Diversified (investments) A1196
MEI (electronic bill acceptors) P315

Meier & Frank department stores A932
Meier, Arlene A839
Meier, Henri B. W492
Meier, Timothy E. A1083
Meijer, Doug P329
Meijer, Fred P328, P329
Meijer, Gezina P328
Meijer, Hendrik P328, P671
Meijer, Hendrik G. P329
Meijer, Inc. **P328-P329**, P479, P671
Meijer, Johanna P328
Meijers stores A1312
Meiji Life Insurance Company W371, W596
Meiji Mutual (insurance) W396
Meikosha (telephone equipment) W420
Meiland, Nico J. A1247, P433
Meilinger, Phillip S. P439
MEI/Micro Center mail order P336, P337, P675
Meinhardt, Hans W311
Meirdorf, Zygmunt W365
MEI-Regis Salon A1196
Meis Brothers department stores A294
Meisinger, Louis M. A1497
Meister, John H. A1457
Meister, Paul M. A601
Meitzner, Carl F. A257
Mejia, Carlos E92, E244
Melaka refinery A412
Melamine Chemicals P90
Melani, Kenneth R. A717, P235
Melard A921
Melas-Kyriazi, Theo A1383
Meldisco A458
Melendez, Lou P307
Melgar, Jose Ismael A461
Melican, James P. A771
Mellbank (holding company) A954
Mellett, Martin P. A1175
Melliar-Smith, Mark P444
Melling (automotive products) P113
Mellish, Donald L. A1049, P377
Mello Yello soft drink A385
Mellon, Andrew W. A954, P450, P541
Mellon family P110, W74
Mellon Financial Corporation A112, A228, A596, A808, **A954-A955**, A1146, W474
Mellon, Paul P541
Mellon, Richard A954
Mellon, Richard K. A954
Mellon, Thomas A954
Melman, Rich A288
Melnik, Elizabeth E. E21
Melody (records) W583
Melrose, Kendrick B. A1392, A1393
Melton, Carol A. A1477
Melton, Gary W. A1553
Melton, Louis E258
Melton, Neal P412
Melville Corporation A260, A458

Melville, Frank A458
Melville Shoe A458
Melville, Ward A458
Melvin Simon & Associates A1286
Membership B@nking (ATM operations) A142
MEMC Electronic Materials Inc. (silicon wafers) P474, P475, W218, W219
Memorex A1424, A1514, P136
Memorial Drive Trust P54
Memorial Hermann Healthcare System P671
Memorial Sloan-Kettering Cancer Center E72, P672
Memory Applications Group A762
Memory Showcase, Inc. A719
Memory Systems A542
Memphis Grizzlies (basketball team) P355
Memphis Light, Gas and Water Division P672
Memtek Products A1188
Menaker, Frank H., Jr. A883
Menard, Ellen P639
Menard, Inc. **P330-P331**, P672
Menard, John R. P330, P331, P672
Menard, Larry P331
Menarini Pharmaceutical Industries E283
Menasha Corporation P673
Mendelson, Eric A. E67
Mendelson, Laurans A. E67, E212
Mendelson, Victor H. E67
Mendez, Jeraldine P717
Menefee, Steven W. A197
Menem, Carlos W650
Menexes, Marcos A. Silva W437
Menezes, Victor J. A371
Mengozzi, Francesco W79
Menlo Logistics A380, A381
Mennen personal care products A386, A387
Meno, Philip F. A177
Mentadent toothpaste W618, W619
Mentch, René L. A1227
Mentesana, Gary A. E248
Mentor Corporation E254
Mentzer, Josephine Esther A564
Menvier electrical products A431
Menvier-Swain Group (emergency lights) A430
Menzel, Phil P665
Menzer, John B. A1495
Meow Mix pet food P626
MeraBank A1138
Mercado supermarkets P550
Mercantile and General Reinsurance Company W464
Mercantile Bancorporation A1444
Mercantile Bank P260
Mercantile Bank (Southeast Asia) W268
Mercantile Stores A490, P342
Mercasol supermarkets W498
Mercator cigars W143

Mercedes-Benz P561, P631, W120, W306, W458
Mercedes-Benz USA A206
Mercenary software E70
Mercer Consulting Group, Inc. A916, A917
Mercer, Larry M. A725
Mercer, Robert A664
Mercer, Ronnie W523
Merchandise Mart (Chicago) E137, E314
Merchant, Ismail P689
Merchant of Vino A1523
Merchants and Businessmen's Insurance Company P295
Merchants Bank (Halifax) W474
Merchants Bank of Canada W112
Merchants Bank of Prince Edward Island W156
Merchants Distributors, Inc. P243, P535
Merchants Exchange Bank A1444
Merchants Guide (consumer credit reports) A558
Merchants Parcel Delivery A1426
Merchants Union Express A142
Mercier, André W167
Mercier, Vincent W165
Merck & Company, Inc. A290, A534, A620, A640, A660, A786, A800, **A956-A957**, A984, A1122, A1250, E150, E230, W102, W334
Merck, Finck & Company (bank) W114
Merck, George A956
Merck KGaA A1156
Merck-Medco (pharmacy benefits management) A574, A956
Mercosur Agreement (South American economic union) W650
Mercosur market A344
Mercure hotels W58, W59
Mercuries Life Insurance A922, P320
Mercury car P606, P633, P647, P666, P733
Mercury Communications. *See* One 2 One
Mercury Computer Systems, Inc. E241
Mercury (cruise ship) A1217
Mercury electrical products A431
Mercury Interactive Corporation E**91**, E242
Mercury outboard motors A298, A299
Mercury vehicles A616
Mercy Center for Health Care Services (Aurora, IL) P706
Mercy Community Health (West Hartford, CT) P115
Mercy Healthcare Sacramento P118
Mercy Health Plans P730
Mercy Health Services (Michigan) P748
Mercy Health System Miami P114, P115

Mercy Health System of
Maine P115
Mercy Hospital of Pittsburgh P114
Mercy Medical (Daphne, AL) P115
Mercy Resource Management,
Inc. P115
Mercy Uihlein Health
Corporation P115
Mercycare Corporation P115
Merdek, Andrew A. A443, P147
Meredith, Thomas C., Jr. (University
of Alabama) P755
Meredith, Thomas J. (Dell
Computer) A473
Meredith, W. George P71
Merelli, F. H. E228
Merensky, Hans W92
Meriage, Lawrence P. A1055
Merial (animal health) A956
Meridian Automotive Systems,
Inc. P673
Meridian Broadcasting W249
Meridian Data A1184
Meridian filing products A707
Meridian Gold, Inc. E242
Meridian Oil A310
The Meridian Resource
Corporation E242
Meridian Sports A298
Meridian Title Insurance A590
Meridian Vineyards W230, W231
Meridiana (airline) W79
Merillat cabinets A920
Merinoff, Charles P738
Merinoff, Herman P738
Merisel, Inc. A958-A959, A1356
Merisel Open Computing
Alliance A958
Merit Electronics E97
Merit watches P308
Merita (bakery) A774, A775
Meritage Corporation E243
Meritor Academy A191
Meritor Automotive A198, A1210
Meritor WABCO A198
Merkel, Helmut W311
Merkle, Hans W490
Merkle-Korff (motors and
gears) P647
Merkley Newman Harty A1063
Merks, Nic A. P93
Merkur Direktwerbeges. mbH &
Company W203
Merle, Henri W432
Merlin engine W496
Merlin Gerin W520, W521
Merlo, Harry A890
Merlo, Larry J. A459
Merlo, Thomas P492
Merrell, Cynthia B. E47, E188
*Merriam Webster's Collegiate
Dictionary* P176, P177, P603
Merrigan, William A607
Merrild coffee A1243
Merrill, Charles A960, A1234
Merrill, John P448

Merrill Lynch Capital
Partners A278
Merrill Lynch & Company,
Inc. A114, A204, A230, A414,
A470, A560, A602, A660, A800,
A960-A961, A988, A1234, A1250,
E197, E258, P80, P180, P250,
P260, P430, P556, W56, W156,
W268, W646
Merrill, Newton P. S. A229
Merriman, Brian L. W190, W191
Merriman, Gary A. A413
Merrin Financial A204
Merritt, Allen C. P201
Merritt, Carolyn W. A753
Merritt, Sarah P. E178
Merry Maids A1272, A1273
Merry-Go-Round Enterprises A562,
P182, W222
Merryman, George P647
Mersch (picture frames) A1022
Merson, Richard W. A275
Merthiolate antiseptic A540
Mertz, Timothy R. A681
Mervyn's California (department
stores) A1352, A1353
Merzei, Geoffery W75
Mesa Air Group, Inc. E64, E206
Mesa Energy Systems, Inc. A544,
A545
Meshon, Louis P., Sr. E229
Mesquita, Jorge S. A1165
Messana, Frank P351, P681
Messer Griesham (industrial
gases) W102
Messerole, George F. A503
Messick, Andrew P355
Messier, Jean-Marie W624, W625
Messier, Michael E110, E276
Messina, Daniel A905
Messina, Grace P175
Messinger, Martin P. A335
Messiry, James B. E255
Messman, Jack L. A1050, A1051
Messmer, Harold M., Jr. A1208,
A1209
Meston, Alexander A546
Meston, Charles A546
Mestrallet, Gérard W559
Meszner-Eltrich, A. Suzanne E50,
E190
MetaFrame software E179
Metal Fabricators and
Finishers P170
Metal Office Furniture
Company A1334
Metal-Cal A210
Metaldyne Corporation (industrial
products) A754, A920, P673
Metallica (band) E69
Société Metallurgique de
Revigny W292
Metalsa (auto frames) A1394
MetalSite LP Web site A1224, W358
Metalurgica Caterina S.A. A1394
Metalwest P694
Metamucil A1164, A1165
Meta-Probe E300

MetaSolv, Inc. E243
MetaStor N-Series network
storage A895
Metatec International, Inc. (optical
media) A750
Metaxas, John A567
Metcalf, James S. A1457
Metcalfe, Robert A54
Met-Ed A669
Methotrexate sodium drug E71
MetLife. *See* Metropolitan Life
Insurance Company
MetPath (laboratory services) A434
Metra (locks) W524
MetraHealth A1162, A1434
Metraplex (airborne telemetry) E68
Metricom, Inc. (wireless data
transmission) P511
METRO AG W364-W365, W588
Metro Bancorp A1444
Metro Cash & Carry Limited P243
Metro food stores A1348, A1349
Metro Networks E140
Metro One Telecommunications,
Inc. E243
Metro Petroleum A1084
Metro Press P170
Metro Title, LLC A509
Metrobus (outdoor media) W467
Metrocall Inc. (paging) A715, P233
MetroCard P334, P674
Metro-Goldwyn-Mayer Inc. A312,
A884, A962-A963, A966, W182
MetroJet A1442
Metroliner train service P362
Metrologic Instruments E284
Metromail (mailing list
business) A1218
Metromedia Company A288, A390,
A622, A1244, P332-P333, P674,
W390
Metron Technology N.V. E244
MetroNet Communications W494
Metronix Elektronic A430
Metro-North Commuter Railroad
Company P335
Metroplex Bancshares, Inc. A1042,
A1043
MetroPlus (HMO) P368, P687
Metropole Hotels W340
Metropolis-Intercom (cable
TV) W576
Metropolitan Broadcasting P332
Metropolitan Club (Illinois) P131
Metropolitan Distributors A710
Metropolitan Edison
Company A668
Metropolitan Fiber Systems A866
Metropolitan Health Networks,
Inc. E244
Metropolitan Hospital Center P369
Metropolitan Life Insurance
Company A964-A965, A1172,
A1434, E222, P476, P737, W512
Metropolitan Property and
Casualty A964
Metropolitan State Bank E231
Metropolitan Street Railway P334

Metropolitan Suburban Bus
Authority P335
Metropolitan Transportation
Authority P674
Metropolitana (electric
utility) A1198
Metrum Information Storage A120
Metso Corporation A468, A806
Metts, J. Mark A553
Metz, Christopher T. A265
Metz, Robert C. A1161
Metzeler Kautscuk W450
Metzeler Reifen GmbH W451
Metzenbaum, Howard P236
Metzger, Blaine A. A1295
Metzger, William J. (Covanta
Energy) A441
Metzger, William L.
(Brunswick) A299
Metzinger, William (Dot
Foods) P596
Metzler, Charles M. A1317, P453
Meurs, A. Michael W499
Mevacor drug A956
Mexican Original tortillas A1419
Mexican Telephone and
Telegraph W580
Mexicana Airlines A1421, W344
Mexicana de Autobuses W632
Grupo México S.A. de C.V. A1124,
A1422
Mexpetrol Argentina W650
Mexx Group (fashion) A880
Meyer, Alan E. P43
Meyer, Eugene A728, A1502
Meyer, Fred A1202
Meyer, Henry L., III A823
Meyer International (building
materials) W506
Meyer, James B. A1312, A1313
Meyer, Jerome J. A1358, A1359
Meyer, John M. (ContiGroup) A427,
P141
Meyer, John P. (Sprint) A1319
Meyer, Karen M. A1393
Meyer, Laurence H. P187
Meyer, Marcia R. A1117
Meyer matresses P443
Meyer, Paul A373
Meyer, Ron W625
Meyer, Russ P517
Meyer, Sandra P. A515
Meyer, S. Lewis E218
Meyer, Steven J. A237
Meyer, Susan M. A1431
Meyer, Thomas C. E83
Meyer, Tony A169
Meyer, William S. A147
Meyers, David L. A471
Meyers, Geoffrey G. A909
Meyers, Howard M. P709
Meyers, Hyman A702
Meyers, Janet A. P361, P684
Meyers, Jay A373
Meyers, Jean-Pierre W343
Meyers, J. M. A702
Meyers, Kevin A1129

Meyers, Richard E. A709
Meyers, Samuel S. A513
Meyers, Scott S. A121
Meyers, Sidney A702
Meyers, Woodrow A. A1507
Meyerson, Ivan D. A947
Meyerson, Morton A1112
Meyrowitz, Carol A1389
Meyrowitz, Norman K. E86
Meysman, Frank L. A1243
Mezger, Jeffrey T. A813
OOO Mezhregiongaz W243
Mezzanine Capital A1482
MFS Communications A866,
A1114, A1534, P396
MG cars W120
mg technologies ag W201
MGDK & Associados A1058
MGI Pharma E90
MGIC Investment
Corporation A1048, P376
MGM. See Metro-Goldwyn-Meyer
Inc.; Metro-Goldwyn-Meyer Inc.
or MGM Mirage, Inc.
MGM Cinemas (UK) W622
MGM (medical supply
distributor) A947
MGM Mirage, Inc. A684, A906,
A966-A967, A1086, P747
Mi8 Corporation A1232, A1233
Miami Computer Supply. See MCSi,
Inc.
Miami Cruiseline Services dutyfree
shops P156, P157, P592, W348
Miami Daily News A442, P146
Miami Dolphins Limited (football
team) P357
Miami Heat (basketball team) A330,
P355
The Miami Herald A832, A833
Miami Sol (basketball team) P355
Miami Subs Corporation (fast food
restaurants) E95, E249
Miami Vice (TV show) A998
Miata sports car W362, W363
Micardis drug A59
Micarta (laminates) A770
Micatrotto, Joseph P. E167
Micek, Ernest S. A324, P104
Michael Foods, Inc. P674
Michael Friedman Publishing A233
Michael, Gary C. A110
Michael, George P166
Michael, J. Christopher P547
Michael, Lanny H. A103
Michael, Mark D. A55
Michael, Ralph S., III A1147
Michael, William W. A1207
Michaels, Jack D. A726, A727
Michaels, Kevin T. E106, E269
Michaels, Paul S. P315
Michaels, Randy A373
Michaels, Sam W637
Michaels Stores, Inc. A968-A969,
P632
Michaelson, L. Lynne E243
Michaelson, Michael W. A837, P283

Michaely, Yoav A911
MichCon (natural gas). See
Michigan Colsolidated Gas
Michel, Charles E51, E190
Michel, Gary A517
Michelin, André W366
Michelin, Edouard W366, W367
Michelin, François W366, W367
Compagnie Générales des
Établissements Michelin
(tires) A662, A664, P594, P628,
W366-W367, W442
Michelmore, Andrew G. W641
Michelob beer A174, A175
Michels, David M. C. W258, W259
Michie (legal publishing) A950
Michigan Avenue Partners P674
Michigan Bearings A652
Michigan Blues P86
Michigan Can and Tube A1292
Michigan Community Health
Project P520
Michigan Consolidated Gas A512
Michigan Education Employees
Mutual Insurance Company. See
MEEMIC Holdings, Inc.
Michigan Electric Power A512
Michigan Gas Storage
Company A377
Michigan International
Speedway E75, E222, P390
Michigan Light A376
Michigan Livestock Exchange P732
Michigan Lottery P675
Michigan National Bank W382
Michigan Public Service
Commission (PSC) A512
Michigan Society for Group
Hospitalization P86
Michigan State Medical Society P86
Michigan-American Water
Company A155
Michl, Michael W. A925, P323, P668
Mickey Mouse cartoon
character A382
Mickey Mouse Club A926
Mickey's brand beer P428
Micra car W403
Micrel, Inc. E92, E244
Micro Center stores P336, P337,
P675
Micro Compact Car
(company) W562
Micro Crystal W563
Micro D (computer
wholesaler) A756, A758, P244
Micro Electronics, Inc. P336-P337,
P675
Micro General Corporation A590
Micro Machines toys A692
Micro Pulse E168
Micro Warehouse, Inc. P136,
P338-P339, P676
MicroAge, Inc. W378
MicroAge Technology
Services A400, E118
MicroAire Surgical Instruments,
Inc. P313

Microamerica A958
MicroBranch (banking facilities) A488
Microchip Technology Inc. A802, E**93**, E245
Microcomputer Products Group A1514
Microcosm Communications A410
MicroDrive A779
Micro-Dynamics E68
Microdyne (telemetry receivers) A846
MicroEdge E25
Microelettronica W555
Micro-Intel (software) W470
Micromania video games W348
Micromedex (medical database) A950
MicroModule Systems E81
Micromuse Inc. E245
Micron Electronics, Inc. See Interland, Inc.
Micron Electronics, Inc. A254, A762, A970, A1514
Micron Semiconductor Products, Inc. A971
Micron Technology, Inc. A762, A**970**-A**971**, A1378, P264, P444, W508
Micron-Clean Uniform Service A364
Micronic A1188
MicronPC LLC A970, P136, P137, P676
MicroPress software E303
MicroProbe A244
Microsoft Corporation A170, A172, A186, A390, A400, A402, A406, A528, A549, A626, A636, A646, A747, A764, A798, A872, A958, A**972**-A**973**, A996, A998, A999, A1012, A1026, A1050, A1066, A1118, A1182, A1188, A1228, A1284, A1342, A1357, A1480, E36, E42, E59, E86, E91, E170, E186, E201, E235, E245, E252, E276, E298, E300, P48, P78, P134, P136, P137, P166, P176, P272, P312, P337, P353, P492, P508, P510, P545, P555, P584, P662, P719, P767, W90, W161, W168, W174, W176, W186, W290, W332, W338, W394, W418, W420, W484, W494, W526, W548, W566, W580, W586, W598, W600, W646
MicroSolutions A400
MicroStrategy Inc. A1158, P400, W462
Microtechnology A1336
Microtek International Inc. E196
MicroTouch Systems (touch-screens) A976
MicroVision, Inc. E56
Microware Systems Corporation E109
MicroWAREHOUSE (catalogs) P338
Microwave Communications, Inc. (MCI) A1534

Microwave Modules & Devices. *See* Spectrian Corporation
Microwave Semiconductor E28
Mid Ocean Reinsurance and Underwriters Capital (Merrett) Ltd. A916
Mid-Am. *See* Dairy Farmers of America
Mid-America Dairymen P58, P90, P148
MidAmerican Energy Holdings Company A1114, E215, P**340**-P**341**, P396, P676
Mid-American Waste Systems A1504
Midas International (mufflers) A198, A1104, P237
MidCity Financial E239
MidCon (natural gas) A1054
Mid-Continent Distributor P616
Mid-Continent Telephone Company A128
Middelhoff, Thomas W126, W127
Middelmann, Ulrich W595
Middle Bay Oil. *See* 3TEC Energy Corporation
Middle South Utilities A554
Middle West Utilities A362, A1464
The Middleby Company (food service eqipment) A934
Middleton, Joe P293
Middleton, Joseph A869
Middleton, Peter W114, W115
Midgal, Jane P709
Midgett, Leon, A. A225
Compagnie du Midi W98
Midland Bank Group W382
Midland Cogeneration Venture A376
Midland Financial Group, Inc. A1168
Midland Grocery Company A320
Midland Linseed Products A192
Midland Loan Services A1146
Midland (Michigan) *Daily News* A701, P229
Midland National Life Insurance P720
Midland nuclear plant A376
Midland plc W268
Midland Utilities A1034
Midlands Electricity plc A668
Midlantic Corporation A1146
Mid-Mountain Foods P654
Mido watch W563
Midway Games Inc. P681
Midwest Agri-Commodities P538
Midwest Air Charter A102
Midwest Carbon A1438
Midwest Energy Resources Company A513
Midwest Express Airlines A826
Midwest Independent System Operator (energy transmission) A136
Midwest Manufacturing and Distributing P331
Midwest Payment Systems A592

Midwest Select (hospital network) P116
Miele, Arthur R. A1125
Miele, Michael V. E21
Miercort, Clifford R. A993
Mierenfeld, Gary A367
Mierzwa, Donald A. A261
Mies van der Rohe, Ludwig P276
Mighty Ducks of Anaheim (hockey team) A1496, A1497, P361
Mignon restaurants P106
Mignone, Lou A217
Migros supermarkets W318
Mihalick, Timothy P. E223
Mihatsch, Peter W353
Mihm, John C. A1129
MIK Physics E24
Mikaliunas, Richard A. P47
Mikawa, Akikazu W235
Mike Rose Foods A1280
Miki, Sukeichi W361
Mikitarian-Bradley, Renee A125
Mikkelson, James E136
Miklosko, Jean A1141
Milan Concrete Products W252
Milbank, Jeremiah P90
Milberg, Joachim W121
Milberg, John E. P385
Milberger, Patrick A. P277
Milburn Homes A509
Milbury, Roy P757
Milcom International. *See* Powerwave Technologies, Inc.
Mild Seven cigarettes W304, W305
Mildara Blass (wines) W230
Miles, Amy P413, P712
Miles, Dan A329, P109
Miles, Fred A200
Miles Inc. A374
Miles Labs W118
Miles, Lisa P568
Miles, Mel W231
Miles, Michael A., Jr. A1405
Miles, Robert H. A1501
MileStone Healthcare, Inc. A908
Milestone Petroleum A310
Milgard Manufacturing A920
Milholland, Terence V. A539
Milhous, Paul P506
Milhous, Robert P506
Military Distributors of Virginia A994
Military Honor and Decency Act (1996) P52
Military Service Company P170, P171
Milk Chugs A466
Milk Duds candy A708, A709
Milk Marketing P58, P148
Milk-Bone pet food A843
Milken, Lowell P278, P279, P652
Milken, Michael A462, A474, A836, A902, A930, A1200, A1400, P154, P278, P279, P282, P304, P652, W196, W322
Milky Way candy A914, A915, P314, P315, P665

Mill Creek Complex A417
Millad clarifying agents P342, P343
Millar, Ian W. A951
Millar, James F. A321
Millard, Donald R. A97
Millard, Mark D. A253
Millbrook Farms bread A774, A775
Mille, Caroline W77
Millea Holdings W596
Millenbruch, Gary L. A257
Millenia car W362, W363
Millennium (cruise ship) A1217
Millennia computers A762
Millennium Chemicals, Inc. A820,
   A900, A**974**-A**975**, A1054, P604,
   W252
Millennium Millions lottery
   game P372
Millennium Pharmaceuticals,
   Inc. A235, A244, A290, A640,
   E72, W118
Miller, Alexei Borisovich W242,
   W243
Miller, Arthur P758
Miller, Barbara J. A225
Miller Brewing Company A78,
   A224, A772, A1126, P428, P721,
   W230, W231, W376
Miller, Bruce L. A1049, P377
Miller Building Systems, Inc. E94
Miller, C. Alex A1083
Miller, Carl A976
Miller, Charles C., III (Level 3
   Communications) A867
Miller, Charles E., Jr. (Ceres
   Group) E175
Miller, Charlotte L. A779
Miller, Christine E247
Miller, Christopher G. E293
Miller, Coleen P445
Miller, Craig H. A1051
Miller, D. James A629
Miller, Darren B. A549
Miller, Debra L. A195
Miller, Don P437, P724
Miller, Douglas H. (EXCO
   Resources) E200
Miller, Douglas M. (Unocal) A1439
Miller, Edward D., Jr. P645
Miller, Eugene A. A395
Miller, Eva E249
Miller, Frank, III P648
Miller Freeman (trade shows) E102,
   W620, W621, W626
Miller, Gary A. (Goodyear) A665
Miller, Gary S. (Herman
   Miller) A707
Miller, Gerald N. A1265
Miller Group (welding
   products) A748
Miller, Guy E. P379, P691
Miller, Herman A706
Miller, J. Irwin A456
Miller, James E. (Massachusetts
   Mutual) A923, P321
Miller, James G. (Utilicorp) A1465
Miller, James H. (PPL) A1155

Miller, James (Mazda Motor) W362
Miller, Jean F. A445
Miller, John Barnes (Edison
   Electric) A532
Miller, John C. (Brinker
   International) A289
Miller, Jon (USA Networks) A1451
Miller, Joseph A., Jr. A435
Miller, Kandy E191
Miller, Kirk E. A811, P267
Miller, Kristen J. E307
Miller, Larry F. (Gannett) A633
Miller, Larry H. (Larry H. Miller
   Group) P656
Miller, Leonard A862, A863, E234
Miller, Lloyd A86
Miller, Lynn C. P385
Miller, Mark C. (Stericycle) E293
Miller, Mark E. (Avis) A213
Miller, Michael E. (Solutia) A1301
Miller, Michael T.
   (AmeriCredit) E27
Miller, Paul David (Alliant
   Techsystems) A120, A121
Miller, Paul S. (Pfizer) A1119
Miller, Richard G. (Parsons) P387
Miller, Richard J. (Cardinal
   Health) A321
Miller, Richard P., Jr. (State
   University of New York) P461
Miller, Robert (DFS Group) P156,
   P592
Miller, Robert G. (Rite Aid) A1202
Miller, Robert S. (ABC) A61
Miller, Robert S., Jr. (Federal-
   Mogul) A584, A585
Miller, Robin A867
Miller, Ron A1496
Miller, Sanford "Sandy" A300, A301
Miller, Scott D. A741
Miller, Steven L. (Shell Oil) A1277,
   W501
Miller, Steve (Waste
   Management) A1504
Miller, Stewart (Whitbread) W639
Miller, Stuart A. (Lennar) A862,
   A863
Miller Tabak Hirsch +
   Company A1094
Miller Thermal A1156
Miller, Thomas B. (Ixia) E224
Miller, Thomas E. (Avery
   Dennison) A211
Miller, Thomas K. (Hon) A727
Miller, Toni P550
Miller, William H. (Harris) A687
Miller, William (Quantum) A1184
Miller, William (Textron
   Inc.) A1380
Miller, Wood A726
Miller/Howard Consulting
   Group P480
Miller's Outpost P539
Millhof, Roderick F. A433
Millhollan, Michael S. E136
Millicom International Cellular
   S.A. W628

Milligan, Ann M. A1249
Milligan, Edward C. E236
Milligan, John W. A365
Milligan, Patricia P481
Milliken & Company
   Inc. P**342**-P**343**, P677
Milliken, Christopher C. A275
Milliken (fabric maker) A306
Milliken, Gerrish P342, P677
Milliken, John T. A58
Milliken, Roger P343, P677
Milliken, Seth P342
Milliken Valves Company Inc. W605
Millinor, J. Patrick, Jr. A549
Millinor, Patrick A548
Millionaires candy P424, P425,
   P719
Millipore MicroElectronics. *See*
   Mykrolis Corporation
Millitron dye P342
Mill-Power Supply A514
Millrose Distributors A1400
Mills, Charles (Hunt
   Consolidated) P635
Mills, Charles S. (Medline
   Industries) P670
Mills, David D. A747
Mills, Edward K. A1465
Mills, Linda S. A1245
Mill's Pride cabinets A725
Mills, Rick J. A457
Mills, Robert A1375
Mills, Steven A. A765
Millsport (marketing) A1063
Millstone nuclear plant A498,
   A1040
Millward Brown (market
   research) W646
Mil-Mar chain A294
Milne & Craighead, Inc. A380,
   A420, A421
Milne Fruit Products P380
Milne, George M., Jr. A1119
Milne, Gordon A. A1227
Milne, Philip W. A1479
Milner stores A1532
Milo Beauty & Barber Supply A108
Milone, Michael D. A723
Milprint, Inc. (candy
   packaging) A250, A251
Milstar satellite A1412
Milstein, Abe A304
Milstein and Feigelson (coats) A304
Milstein, Andrew E. A304, A305
Milstein, Henrietta A304
Milstein, Monroe G. A304, A305
Milstein, Stephen E. A304, A305
Milton Bradley games A692, A693,
   P417
Milton Hershey School A708
Milton, James F. A235
Milton, Thomas H. A961
Milwaukee Brewers Baseball
   Club P306, P307
Milwaukee Bucks (basketball
   team) P355
Milwaukee Journal Sentinel P648

Mims, Joyce E. A1225
MIMS Plus W368
Mimura, Akio W399
Mina, Richard T. A1471
Minahasa (gold mine) A1024
Minami, Nobuya W599
Minami, Wesley D. E175
Minard, Guy A826
Compañia de Minas Buenaventura SA A1125
Mincato, Vittorio W217
Mincks, Jay E. A75
Mind/Body Medical Institute P566
MindShare (media planning) W646, W647
Mindspeed Technologies A410
Mindstorm toys by LEGO W332, W333
Mine No. 84 A417
Mineo, Tom A783
Miner, Robert A1066
Minera Yanacocha (gold mine) A1024
Compania Minera Zaldívar W452
Minerals & Chemical Philipp A550
Minerva (airline) W79
Mines, Raymond, Jr. A943
The Minet Group A182, A1236
Ming, Jenny J. A635
Mini Chopper convenience stores P617
MiniDiscs portable stereo W551
Minigus, Linda P673
Minikes, Michael A239
MiniMart convenience stores A844, A845, A1084, A1085
MiniMed (medical devices) A952, E241
Minipreco stores W165
Minipress drug A1118
MiniScribe (disk drives) A928, A1158, P400, W462
Minit Mart P577
Minitel online terminals W232
Minit-Lube chain A1096
Minnaugh, Mark P199, P615
Minneapolis General Electric A1542
Minnegasco A1199
Minner, Thomas O. A573
Minnesota Brush Electric A1542
Minnesota Cooperative Creameries Association A850, P288
Minnesota Life A124
Minnesota Linseed Oil P122
Minnesota Lynx (basketball team) P355
Minnesota Mining and Manufacturing Company A290, A686, A750, A**976**-A**977**, A1544, E175, E230, E262, E284, P522, P750
Minnesota Mutual Companies, Inc. P677
Minnesota Timberwolves (basketball team) P355, P742
Minnesota Twins (baseball team) P307
Minnesota Valley Canning P72

Minnesota Vikings Football Club, Inc. P357, P498
Minnesota Wild (hockey team) P360, P361, P663, P684
Minnetonka (soap) A386
Minnick, Mary E. A383
Minocin drug A149
Minolta Company, Ltd. A524, E303, W158, W**368**-W**369**, W392, W516
Minomura, Rizaemon W372
Minor, George Gilmer, III A1070
Minor, George Gilmer, IV A1070
Minor, George Gilmer, Jr. A1070
Minor, G. Gilmer, III A1070, A1071
Minorco (holding company) W92
Minority Business Development Corporation A1309
Minott, Debra A675
Grupo Minsa S.A. de C.V. (flour) A714, A715, P232, P233
Minton, Dwight C. A358, A359
Minton, Keith G. A935
Minturn, Frederick K. P679
The Minute Maid Company A384, A385, AA:386, A1106, P512, P620
Minute rice A842
Minuteman missiles A704
Minwax A1278
Minyard, Elizabeth P677
Minyard Food Stores, Inc. P677
MIPS Technologies, Inc. A1284
Miracle Bra A776
Miracle Food Mart A670
Miracle Whip sandwich spread A842, A843, A1126
Miracle-Ear hearing aids A234
Mirage Resorts A906, A966, A967, A1328
Miraglia, Salvatore J., Jr. A1387
Miramax Film Corporation A700, A701, A1496, A1497, P228, P229
Miramontes, Lou A841, P287, W325
Miranda, Bob E30
Mirant Corporation A1306
Mirante, Arthur, II P587
Mircor W470
Mirinda beverage A1103, A1105
Mirkin, Morris A300
Mirman, Richard A685
Mirra, Edward A1073
Mirrer, Louise P129
Mirro cookware A1022, A1023
Mirror Group (newspapers) W478
Mirzayantz, Nicolas A767
Misaka, Shigeo W533
Mischell, Thomas E. A145
Misenhimer, Holly P563
Mishler, Jim A865
Misima Mine W453
Misner, Jeff A429
Misrfone (mobile communications) W628
Miss Piggy A918
Miss USA/Universe pageants A1408, A1409, P482, P483, P749
Mission Beverages P746
Mission Energy Holding A532

Mission Hills Country Club (California) P130, P131, P577
Mission: Impossible 2 (movie) A1476
Mission pasta A1181
Mission Studios E298
Mission West Properties, Inc. E245
Missios, Michael H. A1257
Mississippi Lignite Mining Company A992
Mississippi Power Company A1307
Mississippi Power & Light A554, A1306
Missorten, Luc W289
Missouri and Kansas Telephone Company A1244, A1318
Missouri Edison A136
Missouri Gas & Electric A1464
Missouri Meadows, Ltd. A509
Missouri Pacific (railroad) A1422
Missouri Portland Cement A324, A848, P104
Missouri Power & Light A136
Missouri Public Service Commission A136
Missouri Public Service (utility) A1464
Missouri-American Water Company A155
Missouri-Kansas-Texas Railroad A1422
Mister Donut W84
Mister Roger's Neighborhood (TV show) P144
Misterski, Czeslaw W457
Mistic beverage A1400, W154, W155
Misty cigarettes W143
MIT. *See* Massachusetts Institute of Technology
Mita Industrial W328
MiTAC International Corporation P740
Mitarai, Fujio W158, W159
Mitarai, Hajime W158
Mitarai, Takeshi W158
Mitchell, A. Joe, Jr. P764
Mitchell & Mitchell Gas & Oil A978
Mitchell, Andrew W523
Mitchell, Connie P764
Mitchell, Debbie J. A777
Mitchell, Donald L. A855
Mitchell, Edward B. A1349
Mitchell Energy & Development Corporation A482, ʼA**978**-A**979**
Mitchell, Frederick L. A77
Mitchell, George P. A978, A979
Mitchell, James J. A1043
Mitchell, Janet D. P395, P701
Mitchell, Jay P668
Mitchell, Johnny (Mitchell Energy & Development) A978
Mitchell, John S. (Eaton) A527
Mitchell, Lee Roy P126, P127, P575
Mitchell, Linda M. (America West) A139
Mitchell, Linda Riley (Tribune) A1403

Mitchell, Mike A978
Mitchell, Pat P145
Mitchell, Paul A1033
Mitchell Repair Information A652, A1294
Mitchell, Robert W. A757, P245, P639
Mitchell, Roger A840, P286, W324
Mitchell, Sidney A140
Mitchell, Stephen F. W485
Mitchell, S. Z. A1154
Mitchell, Tandy P127
Mitchell, Thomas L. (Apache) A185
Mitchell, Tom (Seagate) A1260, P440
Mitchell, Walter A688
Mitchell, Wayne E66
Mitchell, W. E. P253
Mitchell, William E. A1299
Mitchells & Butler (brewery) W544
Mitchum deodorant A1200, A1201
Mitek Surgical Products A800
Mitel W148
Mitsubishi Bank W264, W370
Mitsubishi Chemical America E272
Mitsubishi Corporation A286, A332, A434, A750, A1212, A1344, E93, E272, E310, P606, P647, P733, W296, W314, **W370-W371**, W386, W392, W398, W420, W554, W596
Mitsubishi Estate P587
Mitsubishi Motors Corporation W188, W274, W362, W370, W371, W632
Mitsubishi Steel A198
Mitsubishi Tokyo Financial Group A860, W370, W371, W596
Mitsui & Company, Ltd. A86, A102, A1484, P122, P123, P571, W296, **W372-W373**, W404, W596, W602
Mitsui, Hachirobei W372
Mitsui Marine & Fire A144
Mitsui, Shuho W372
Mitsui, Sokubei W372
Mitsukoshi Ltd. (retailer) A1384
Mitsunaga, Hoshiro W198
Mittal, Aditya W293
Mittal, Lakshmi N. W292, W293
Mittal, Mohan W292
Mittal, Pramod W292
Mittal, Vinod W292
Mittelstaedt, Ronald J. E139, E315
Mitterrand, François W76
Mix, James P. A1263
The Mix (magazine) W238
Miyakawa, Kazuo W199
Miyake, Masao W420
Miyamoto, Gene A707
Miyamoto, Tsumoru W305
Miyamura, Satoru W401
Miyauchi, Akira W299
Miyauchi, Ken W549
Miyazu, Jun-ichiro W401
Miyoshi, Shoichi W610
Miyoshi, Susumu W615
Mizeur, Dave P638
Mizoguchi, Tetsuya W611

Mizokuchi, Makato W601
Mizuguchi, Chuichi W561
Mizuho Holdings, Inc. W200, **W374-W375**
Mizukoshi, Sakue W299
Mizuno, Masaru (Japan Tobacco) W304, W305
Mizuno, Masaru (Marubeni) W359
Mizutani, Masashi W405
M.J. Meehan & Company A602
MJDesigns, LP (retailer) A968
MKE. *See* Matsushita-Kotobuki Electronics
MKM Magyar Kabel Muvek RT (cables) W451
MKS Instruments, Inc. E246
M.L. Stern & Company, Ltd. (broker) P384, P385
Mladenovic, Rudy A85
MLC (fund management) W382
Mlekush, Kenneth C. A795
MLT Inc. (travel) A1046, A1047
MLW-Worthington Limited W132
M. M. Jones Company A744
MMA Corporation W335
MMC Enterprise Risk A916, A917
MMC Med, Inc. A323
MMI Companies A1236
MML Bay State Life Insurance Company A923, P321
MML Investors Services, Inc. A923, P321
MMT Sales A443
MNC Financial A936
Mobay W118
Moberg, Anders C. W276
Moberg, Richard P. E161
Mobic drug A59
Mobil Corporation. *See* Exxon Mobil Corporation
MobilCom AG W232
Mobile Broadcasting W360
Mobile Home Dynamics E52
Mobile Mini, Inc. E246
Mobile Q W419
MobileMedia A248
MobileOne Pte Ltd. W153
Mobimagic W418
Mobley, J. Graham A1259
Mobley, Stacey J. A535
Mobouck, Patrick C. P153
Moby Dick (book) A1326
MOCA. *See* Merisel Open Computing Alliance
Moccio, Anthony J. P554
Mocha Mix non dairy creamer A1339
Mock, Robert W. A465
Mock, Timothy S. A113
Mockett, Alfred W149
MODALGISTICS (supply chain service) A1039
MODE (magazine) P611
Model Bakery W244
Model T car A616, A1386
Grupo Modelo, S.A. de C.V. A174, W254

Modern Bride (magazine) A1160, A1161
Modern Continental Companies, Inc. P678
Modern Maid appliances P618
Modern Maturity (magazine) P28, P29, P529
Modern Plastics (magazine) A944
Modern Products P222
Modern Retail A1092
Modern Tool and Die Company P679
Moderow, Joseph R. A1427
Modicon W521
Modie, Christine M. A923, P321
Modrzejewski, Andrzej Mikolaj W457
Modtech Holdings, Inc. E**94**, E246
Modular Mates containers A415
Moduline International , Inc. A347
Modus Media International A1218
Moe, Don P253
Moe, James D. A325
Moeller, Joseph W. A835, P281
Moen (faucets) A618
Moerdyk, Carol B. A275
Moerk, Hallstein W407
Moersdorf, Gerard E157
Moersdorf, Linda E157
Moët & Chandon champagne W348, W349
Moët Hennessy. *See* LVMH Moët Hennessy Louis Vuitton
Moffat, Brian W178, W179, W269
Moffatt, David W587
Moffatt, James R. A629
Moffett, David M. A1445
Moffett, Jim Bob A628
Moffitt, Augustine E., Jr. A257
Moffitt, Donald E. A381
Mogensen, Dennis P265, P648
Mogford, Steve W111
Mogg, Jim W. P598
Mogul Metal Company A584
Mohan, Kshitij A283
Mohawk Industries, Inc. A**980-A981**, P552
Mohawk Rubber A462
Mohebbi, Afshin A1187
Mohl, Andrew W89
Mohler, Max P774
Mohn, Heinrich W126
Mohn Media Group W127
Mohn, Reinhard W126, W127
Mohney, Ralph W. A1441
Mohorovic, Jesse R. A455
Mohr, Terrence B. A1181
Moissis, Raphael W195
Moist O' Matic (irrigation products) A1392
Moisture Therapy skin care A217
MOL Magyar Olaj-és Gázipari Rt. W424
Mola-Davis, Fernando P415
Moldaw, Stuart A1214
Moldcast lighting A1447
Moler, Elizabeth Ann A571

Molés, José W577
Molex Inc. A**982**-A**983**
Molina, Debbie P635
Molinaro, Samuel L., Jr. A239
Moll, Curtis E. P679
Moll, Theo P679
Mollen, Jack A543
Moller, Andrew K. E178
Møller, A. P. W95
Møller, Arnold Peter W94
Møller, Maersk Mc-Kinney W94, W95
Møller, Per W95
Møller, Peter Maersk W94
Mollico, Mark P27
Mollie Stone's Markets P489
Molly McButter A108
Mologousis, Kristen J. E70
Moloney, Herbert W., III P507
Moloney, Monica M. E24, E149
Moloney, Thomas E. A799
Molson Centre (Montreal arena) W376, W377
Molson, Eric H. W376, W377
Molson, Fred W376
Molson, Herbert W376
Molson Inc. W230, W314, **W376**-**W377**
Molson, John W376
Molson, R. Ian W377
Molson USA A78
Molsons Bank W112
Momentum Business Applications, Inc. A1098
Momii, Katsuo W373
Monaco, AnnMarie E223
Monaco Coach Corporation A682
Monaghan, Craig T. A207
Monaghan, James A500, P162
Monaghan, Thomas A500, P162, P595
Monahan, William T. A750, A751
Monarch Brass & Copper Corporation A1060
Monarch cigarettes A1204, A1205
Monarch (cleaning products) A530
Monarch of the Seas (cruise ship) A1217
Monarch Paint Company A1152
Monarch Pharmaceuticals E229
Monarch tools A1322
Mond Nickel W284
Mondavi, Robert P474
Monday Night Football A60, A61
Mondello, Mark T. A783
Mondex International Limited (smart cash card) A924, A925, A1480, P322, P323, P508, P668
Mondragón Alarcón, Javier W581
Mondragon, Manuel A1263
Monet jewelry A648, A881
Monetary Authority of Singapore P480
Money After 50 program P29
Money Island lottery game P693
Money (magazine) P44
Money Management Institute A734

The Money Store A1486
Money Talks lottery game P666
MoneyGram Payment Systems, Inc. A596, A1478, A1479
Moneymaker, Michael B. E255
Moneypenny, Edward W. A441
Moneywise (magazine) A1193
Monfort (meat) A408
Mongoose bicycles A298
Monitor Capital Advisors LLC A1017, P371
Monitor Dealing (track foreign exchange) W484
Monk-Austin A492
Monkowski, Joseph R. E24
Monks, Donald R. A229
Monlycke A108
Monnet, Beverly A1065
Monnier, Joel W555
Monnig, Ken P445
Mono aluminum foil A375
Monolithic Memories E82
Monongahela Power Company A114
Monopoly game A692, A942, P416
Monopril drug A291
Monoprix supermarkets W166, W167
Monroe automotive products A1368
Monroe G. Milstein, Inc. A304
Monroe, Mark E. E234
Monroe, Michael J. A823
Monroe power plant A512
Monsanto Company A148, A324, A860, A**984**-A**985**, A1122, A1300, A1536, P104, P414, W118
Monsanto Kelco A704
Monsanto Oil W128
Monsters, Inc. (movie and products) A692, E103
Montage office furniture A1335
Montagner, Philippe W135
Montague, Christopher A. W609
Montague, William P. P311, P664
Montana Group (wines) W84
Montana, Joe P251
Montana, Lori P638
The Montana Power Company A1154
Montanaro, David W387
MontBell outdoor apparel and gear A852
Monte Carlo (hotel and casino) A907, A966, A967
Montecristo cigars P732
Montedison S.p.A. (chemicals) P104, W208, W209, W216, W226, W423, W574
Montefiore Medical Center P678
Monteiro Aranha W224
Monteiro, Manuel P560
Monteith, Timothy A501, P163
Montelera Riserva sparkling wine W109
Montemayor, Rogelio W440
Montemurro, Michael F. A1295

Monterey Bay Aquarium (California) P719
The Monterey County (California) *Herald* A833
Monterey Homes. *See* Meritage Corporation
Monterey Pasta Company E247
Montezuma tequila A423
Montgomerie, Colin P251
Montgomery, Ann A73
Montgomery, Boyd A1439
Montgomery Data Services E204
Montgomery, Glenn A. A357
Montgomery Mutual Insurance Company A875, P295
Montgomery, R. Lawrence A838, A839
Montgomery, Robert A1158, P400, W462
Montgomery, Rosemary J. A1391
Montgomery Securities A226
Montgomery Ward, LLC A158, A218, A254, A304, A664, A790, A932, A1264, A1286, A1314, A1428, A1456, E60, P88, P490
Montgomery's Auditing (book) A1158, P400, W462
Montgomery-Tally, La June P521, P774
Monthly Market P436
Monti, Kathleen P. E205
Monti, Roberto W483, W650
Monticello nuclear plant A1542
Montiel (retailer) A968
Montini, Enio A., Jr. A831
Montlaur retail stores W164
Montle, Paul E79
Montone, William E213
Montoya, James P457
Montoya, Jorge P. A1165
Montreal Amateur Athletic Association P360
Montreal Bank W112
Montreal Canadiens (hockey team) P360, P361, W376, W377
Montreal Expos (baseball team) P307
Montrone, Paul M. A601
Montrose Capital A1084
Montupet, J-P. L. A547
Monty, Jean C. W122, W123, W412
Monumental Corporation (insurance) W64
Monus family P198
Monus, Mickey P198
The MONY Group, Inc. A218, A**986**-A**987**
Moock, Joyce L. P415
Moody, Daniel J. A461
Moody, Dennis A905
Moody, John N. D. A1143
Moody, Wesley C. A533
Moody's Investors Service A516, A517
Moog Automotive A430, A1190, P112, P113, P569
Moomy, Charles A326
Moon, Brian P55

Moon Drops skin care A1201
Moon, Marian J. A483
Moon, Micheal P223
Mooney, Beth E. A167
Mooney, James P. E257
Mooney, Kevin W. A293
Mooney, Michael D. E134
Moonves, Leslie A334, A335
Moore, A. Bruce, Jr. A695
Moore, Bob A1329
Moore, C. Bradley P383
Moore, Charles O. A1065
Moore Corporation Limited A950,
   W378-**W379**
Moore, C. Steven A1271
Moore, Dan E. P521
Moore, Darnell P43
Moore, David P351
Moore, Ed A815
Moore, E. Kevin A1251
Moore, Francis A378
Moore, Geoffrey E. P279
Moore, Gordon E. A760, A761
Moore, Greg A1535
Moore, Jack E., Jr. (Kohl's) A839
Moore, James Brock, III A69
Moore, John (Tiffany) A1384
Moore, Laura K. A1189
Moore, Liz E280
Moore, Lord W497
Moore, Margaret D. A1107
Moore, P. A. W565
Moore, Patrick J. A1293
Moore, Paul W429
Moore, Peter A793
Moore, Robert C. (Starwood
   Hotels) A1329
Moore, Robert J. (Staples) A1325
Moore, Roger H. E217
Moore, Samuel W378
Moore, Tim A697
Moore, T. Jerald A259
Moore, Tom E101
Moore, William P202, P617
Moorehead, Don A1504
Moores, John A270
Mop & Glo home care W476
Moramarco, Jon A423
Moran, Christian E. A1125
Moran, David E. A507
Moran, Glenn J. A897
Moran, Harry J. A1303
Moran Health Care Group (nursing
   homes) A1340
Moran, James M. P256, P257, P644
Moran, Joe A1419
Moran, Michael R. A1314
Moran, Patricia P256, P257, P644
Moran, Robert A. (Bowater) A285
Moran, Robert F.
   (PETsMART) A1117
Moran, Ursula H. A1397
Morano, Kevin R. A573
Morash, David L. E277
Moravitz, Hyman P198
Morbid brand products E69, E215

More American Graffiti
   (movie) P303
More, Avery A400
More cigarettes A1204, A1205,
   W240, W241
More Excellent dishwashing
   detergent W309
More Group (outdoor
   advertising) A372
Morean, Bill A782
Morean, William D. A782, A783
Moreci, Stephen F. A283
Morecroft, Michael J. A993
Moreland, Jeffrey R. A309
Moren, Nicholas C. A889
Morenci Mine A1124
Moreno, Albert F. A869, P293
Moreno, Ernie P205, P619
Moretti beer W255
Moretti, Marco A303
Moretz, Lawrene P427
Morford, John A. P767
Morgan, Calvert A., Jr. A1147
Morgan, Carol E. A1005
Morgan, Ersel E. E264
Morgan, Geoff W337
Morgan, Glenn R. A691
Morgan Grenfell Private Equity
   Ltd. A1300, W200, W258, W638
Morgan, Henry A988
Morgan, Hugh M. W641
Morgan, James C. A188, A189
Morgan, John K. (National Service
   Industries) A1005
Morgan, John W. (Occidental
   Petroleum) A1055
Morgan, J. Pierpont A152, A202,
   A308, A418, A1010, A1462, P186,
   W92, W284, W488
Morgan, Lawrence A. A1449
Morgan, Louis E70
Morgan, Marsha K. A309
Morgan Products P50, P541
Morgan, Robert P. A775
Morgan Stanley Capital
   International E61
Morgan Stanley Dean Witter &
   Company A356, A448, A660,
   A714, A862, A960, **A988**-**A989**,
   A1158, A1292, P232, P613, W112,
   W176, W462, W636
Morgan, Stephen E.
   (FirstEnergy) A599
Morgan, Steve (Waste
   Management) A1505
Morgan, Terry W111
Morgan, Walter A1468, P504
Morgan, William F. A897
Morgensen, Jerry L. P630
Morgridge, John P. A368, A369
Mori, Akihiko W597
Mori, Atsushi W329
Mori, Yoshihiro W395
Moriarty, Gerry W587
Morici, Andrea P45
Moridera, Akio W237
Morie, G. Glen A1079

Morikis, John G. A1279
Morimoto, Yasuo W611
Morin, Charles H. W621
Morin, Gary E. A871
Morin, Louis W133
Morin, Richard A. E43, E181
Morin-Postel, Christine W559
Morio, Minoru W551
Morioka, Yoshiyuki W315
Morishita, Yoichi W360, W361
Morita, Akio W550
Morita & Company, Inc.
   (insurance) W597
Morita, Hyozo W299
Morita, Mokichi W234
Morlan, James P765
Morley, Cheryl A985
Morley, Donald M. W641
Morley, Michael P. A525
Morley, Patrick W503
Morman, Dave P568
Mormon Church. *See* Church of
   Jesus Christ of Latter-day Saints
Morning Glory Dairy P58, P610
Morningside Ventures P134
Morningstar Farms meat
   alternatives A816, A817
Morningstar Japan W548
Morningstar lactose free
   milk A1338
Moroch & Associates P73
Moroch, Tom P73
Morohashi, Yasushi W81
Moroney, Patrick E. A1273
Moroni, Alfredo W217
Morovich, Nancy A555
Morphine (performer) P167
Morpurgo, Egardo W98
Morpurgo, Giuseppe W98
Morrell (meat company) A354
Morrell, Michael P. A115
Morrell, Nicholas W340
Morrice, Robert W115
Morrill Act of 1862 P382
Morris Air A1310
Morris, Barry H. A355
Morris, Carolyn E291
Morris, Clifton H., Jr. E27
Morris, Doug W625
Morris, Gary V. A677
Morris, Herman, Jr. P672
Morris, Iain M. A713
Morris, Jack H. (Newmont
   Mining) A1025
Morris, James T. (NiSource) A1035
Morris, James T. (Pacific Mutual
   Holding) P385
Morris, Jim (Western
   Digital) A1515
Morris, John L. (Bass Pro
   Shops) P550
Morris, Ken A1098
Morris, Michael G. (Northeast
   Utilities) A1040, A1041
Morris, Michael H. (Sun
   Microsystems) A1343
Morris, Nigel W. A318, A319

Morris, Philip A1126
Morris, Stanley M. A101
Morris, Wes A1419
Morrisania Diagnostic & Treatment Center P369
Morrison, "Chick" A1206
Morrison, Colin W239
Morrison, Dale A316
Morrison, Daniel R. A467
Morrison Knudsen A1190, P769
Morrison Management Specialists Inc. (health care) W174, W175
Morrison office furniture systems P277, P652
Morrison, Robert S. A1107, A1180, A1181
Morrison, Scott C. A225
Morrison, Steve W249
Morrison, William R. P63
Morrow, George A161
Morrow, Robert H. P115
Morrow, Winston A212
Morse, Amyas C. E. A1159, P401, W463
Morse Controls P578
Morse, Edward J. P678
Morse, John B., Jr. (Washington Post) A1503
Morse, John (Encyclopaedia Britannica) P177
Morse, Lawrence J. A1325
Morse Operations, Inc. P678
Morse, Samuel A642
Morse TEC A278
Morstyn, George A161
Mort, Thomas W88
Mortal Kombat (video game) W527
Mortensen, Steven L. P612
Mortenson, M. A., Jr. P663
Mortenson, M. A., Sr. P663
MortgageSelect.com E154
Morthland, David W. A1525
Morton, David L. A1181
Morton, Donald S. A191
Morton foods A409
Morton International A1212
Morton, Leo E. A1465
Morton, Mike P635
Morton, Peter W472
Morton Salt Group A752
Morwind, Klaus W257
Mosaic Internet software P756
Mosaic Microsystems A170
Mosaic Records recording label W213
Moschino brand A1014
Mosconi, Piero W555
Moscow Magazine W626
Moseley, Debbie P742
Moser, Bobby D. P383
Moser, Eric J. E139
Moser, Kurt G. A1331, P459
Moser, Richard A155
Moses, Cornelius F., III "Neil" E161
Moses, Daniel E289
Moses, Robert J. A1077
MOSFET transistors E74, E222

Moshayedi, Manouch E289
Moshayedi, Mark E289
Moshayedi, Mike E289
Mosher, Sam A728
Mosher Steel A1406
Mosi beer W553
Moskatels (retailer) A968
Moskowitz, David K. A529
Moskowitz, Joel P. E175
Mosner, Lawrence J. A481
Moss, Andrew W337
Moss, Bob L. A341
Moss, Dale W141
Moss, James H. E315
Moss, Marcia P731
Moss, Sara E. A1143
Mossy Oak Apparel A1220, A1221
Mostek, Charles F. A743
Mosteller, Richard G. A921
Mostyn, William J., III A657
Motamed, Thomas F. A357
Motel 6 W58, W59
Motion office furniture P652
Motiva Enterprises LLC A352, A1276, A1277, A1376, A1377, **P344-P345**, P604, P679, W500
Motivational Systems E36
Motive power (batteries) E169
Motor Carrier Act (1935) A1206
Motor Carrier Act (1980) A344, P434
Motor Carriers' Road Atlas (book) P409
Motor City (casino) A906, A907
Motor Coach Industries International, Inc. A486
Motor Parcel Delivery A1426
Motor Tool Specialty Company A1294
*Motor Trend (*magazine) A1160, A1161
Motor Wheel A286, A664
MotorBook (catalog) A1538
MotorClothes A682
Motor-Columbus AG W201
Motorola, Inc. A82, A162, A186, A188, A196, A410, A524, A644, A872, **A990-A991**, A1002, A1026, A1182, A1372, A1392, A1482, A1514, A1546, E28, E41, E44, E46, E93, E106, E152, E156, E162, E179, E189, E196, E210, E220, E223, E229, E230, E244, E248, E262, E267, E277, E280, E288, E289, E316, P444, P445, P454, P474, P726, W150, W220, W338, W360, W400, W406, W490, W526, W554, W600, W610
Motorola Space and Systems E68
Motoyama, Hideyo W314
Motrin IB analgesic A801
Motroni, Hector J. A1545
Mott, David M. E90, E240
Mott, Michael R. A519
Mott, Randall D. A473
Mott's beverages P634, W154, W155
Motts, William F. A785
Moulds, Robert E. A469

Moulin Rouge (movie) A622
Moullet, Barry A465
Moulonguet, Thierry W403
Moulton, Paul G. A437
Mounds candy P314, W154
Mt. Boston brandy A423
Mount Holyoke College P78
Mount Magnet mine W640
Mount Sinai School of Medicine P128
Mount Vernon Mills P711
Mountain Biking UK (magazine) W238, W239
Mountain Dew soft drink A1102, A1103, A1105, A1106, A1107
Mountain Lake clothing A666
Mountain Safety Research. *See* MSR (mountaineering equipment)
Mountain States Blue Cross Blue Shield A716, P234
Mountain States Power A1082
Mountain Valley Spring (water) P720
Mountaineer Gas A114
Mountaineer Racetrack and Gaming Resort (Chester, West Virginia) E247
MountainGate Imaging Systems E23
Mouren, Hervé W151
Mouse Hunt (movie) P166, P167
MouseMan computer mouse W339
Mouser, Jerry H. A1375
Movado Group, Inc. (watches) W607
Move.com A338
The Movie Channel A1476
Movies.com W390
MovieTickets.com P681
Mowen, Roger K. A523
Mowi (fish farming) W410
Mowrer, James F. A843
Mox, Greg P726
Moxie, Jeffrey E. P275, P651
Moxim, Hazel A. A667
Moxley, Gregory R. E59, E201
Moxon, Jon W241
Moxonidine drug A540
Moxy software E25
Moya, Steven O. A739
Moyer, Jennifer A. A1503
Moyer, Kevin P. A461
Moylan, James E., Jr. A1257
Moynihan, Brian T. A603
Moynihan, Patricia P662
Moynot, Alain W131
Mozilo, Angelo R. A438, A439
MP Receivables Company A323
MP3.com, Inc. A442, P146, W624
MPB Corporation (precision bearings) A1386
mPower.com A348
MPRI A846
MPV van W362, W363
Mr. Clean cleanser A1165
Mr. Donut stores A768
Mr. D's seafood restaurants A1280

Mr. Gasket (auto parts) A460
Mr. Goodbar candy A709
Mr. How home improvement stores A1270
Mr. Moneysworth Inc. A320
Mr. PiBB soft drink A383, A385
Mr. Potato Head toy A692, A693
Mr. Turkey packaged meats A1243
Mrkonic, George R. A277
MRN Radio network E75, E222
Mroczkowski, Marek W457
Mrozek, Ernest J. A1273
Mrs. B's restaurants P748
Mrs. Cubbison's A774, A775
Mrs. Dash seasoning A108
Mrs. Gooch's Natural Foods Markets A1522
Mrs. Grass soup mix P91
Mrs. Paterson's Aussie Pies A731
Mrs. Paul's seafood A316
Mrs. Smith's Bakeries A608, A609
Mrs. Stover's Bungalow Candies P424
MS Contin drug P707
MSA. See Melvin Simon & Associates
MS-DOS operating system A972, P510
MSG. See Madison Square Garden
MSG Network P250
MShow.com (Web caster) P278
MSI/Canterbury (management training) E36, E170
MSLO. See Martha Stewart Living Omnimedia Inc.
MSNBC cable network A646, A972, A998, A999
MSR (mountaineering equipment) P410
MSR (outdoor clothing and equipment) P410
MSX International, Inc. P679
MTD Products Inc. A286, P679
MTR Gaming Group, Inc. E247
MTS, Inc. **P346-P347**, P680
MTV Networks A334, A1450, A1476, A1477, E69, E215
The MTVi Group, Inc. A1476, A1477
Mucci, Richard L. A923, P321
Muchmore, R. Charles, Jr. A677
Muchnick, Ed P568
Muckian, William M. A639
Mudd brand clothing E259
Mudd, Daniel H. A581
Muehleman, Frank A473
Mueller, Charles W. A136, A137
Mueller, Jim F. W291
Mueller, John E. (WestFarm Foods) P771
Mueller, John H. (Niagara Mohawk) A1029
Mueller, John J. (Broadwing) A293
Mueller, Robert J. (Bank of New York) A229
Mueller, Robert J. (International Rectifier) E74
Mueller, Thomas J. A1511

Muesli cereal A817
Muffler Warehouse P113
Mug Root Beer A1103, A1104, A1105, A1107
Muglia, Bob A973
Mühlemann, Lukas W185
Muhlhauser, Craig H. A573
Muir, James A906
Mukherjee, Malay W293
Mulally, Alan R. A273
Mulcahy, Anne M. A1544, A1545
Mulcahy, Geoffrey W313
Mulchandani, Prakash R. A199
Mulchay, Patrick J. A1035
Mulé, Ann C. A1345
Mulé, Anthony A139
Mulee, Annette E109
Mulehide brand P537
Mulet, Harold L. A1059
Mulford, David C. A449
Mulholland, Paul A1345
Mulhollem, Paul B. A193
Mullan, John H. A1045
Mullany, Hank A1235
Mullen, Lynda P415
Mullens, Thomas H., Jr. A1039
Muller, Anthony R. A793
Muller, Edward A532
Müller, Fritz W185
Müller, Horst W83
Muller, Paul W414
Muller, Warren E92, E244
Mullholland, William W112
Mulligan, Brian A623
Mulligan, Donald P591
Mulligan, Thomas M. A1297
Mullikin Medical Enterprises A322, P56
Mullin, Bernie P355
Mullin, Leo F. A478, A479
Mullin, Thomas J. A423
Mullin, W. James A1025
Mullinax, A. R. A515
Mullinix, Joseph P. P495, P755
Mullins, Anna P119
Mullins, Charles B. P499
Mullins, David R. A667
Mullins, Garrett A763
Mullins, Marc P63
Multibanco Mercantil Probursa A1112
Multibras Eletrodomesticos (appliances) A1520
Multibus (chips) E109
Multicanal (cable TV) W578
Multicare (elder care) P474
MultiCipher cable scrambling system E168
Multi-Core Aerators A1392
Multilink Technology Corporation E247
Multimedia Inc. A632
Multinet Gas/Ikon Energy A1464
Multiplex Cinemas P681
Multi-State Lottery Association P680

Multitech International W60
MultiThématiques A873, W331
MultiVendor Architecture in C software P430
MultiWave optical transmission E179
Mulva, James J. A1128, A1129
Mulva, Patrick T. W281
Mulvaney, Brian G. A191
Mulvehill, Joseph J. A345
Mumford, Catherine P426
Mumm champagne A714
Mummery, Peter W429
Mumphrey, Joseph S. A1287
Munch, Deborah A1087
Munch'ems crackers A815
Münchener Rückversicherungs-Gesellschaft AG A378, W82, W201, **W380-W381**
Münchow, Detlef W211
Munder UK, L.L.C. A395
Mundipharma P707
Mundt, G. Henry, III A925, P323
Mundt, Ray A746
Munekuni, Yoshihide W265
Muney, Alan M. A1077
Muneyuki, Masayuki W235
Munger, Charles T. A253
Munich Re. See Münchener Rückversicherungs-Gesellschaft AG
Municipal Mortgage and Equity, LLC E248
MuniMae Midland. See Municipal Mortgage and Equity, LLC
Munitz, Barry P98
Munn, Stephen A327
Munns, David W213
Munoz, Frank A1225
Muñoz Leos, Raúl W441
Muñoz Zuniga, Claudio W577
Munroe, Sharon E244
Munsell, William A. A1435
Munsingwear A1474, P388
Munson, Ronald D. A359
Munster and Leinster (banks) W86
Muppets A730
Murabito, John M. A985
Murai, Kevin M. A759
Murakami, Masatoshi W199
Muramatsu, Norimitsu W599
Murano, Koichi W529
Murase, Ryuji W419
Murashige, Mark A. E163
Muraskin, Ben E. A1115, P397
Murata, Kaichi W261
Murata, Noritoshi W299
Murata, Takashi W599
Murayama, Atsushi W361
Murayama, Ryohei W96
Murchison, Bradley D. P69
Murdoch, Elisabeth W146
Murdoch, James W391
Murdoch, K. Rupert A528, A622, A623, A736, A902, A1160, A1450, P278, P304, P332, W146, W147, W330, W390, W391, W586

Murdoch, Lachlan K. W391
Murdock, Albert A798
Murdock, David H. A494, A495
Murdock, Melvin A1358
Murdy, James L. A116, A117
Murdy, Wayne W. A1024, A1025
Mure, Christian W171
Murgel, Michele C. E86
Muriel Siebert & Company E287
Murine eye drops A58
Murjani A804
Murjani International W606
Murjani, Mohan W606
Murney, Donald W. A135
Murofushi, Minoru W297
Murphy, Cynthia Kiser A967
Murphy, Diane E151
Murphy, Edward P566
Murphy Family Farms, Inc. A1290
Murphy, F. Michael E308
Murphy, Gary A421
Murphy, Jack (OfficeMax) A1059
Murphy, James T. A517
Murphy, Jeremiah T. P532
Murphy, John H. (State University of New York) P461
Murphy, John (International Brotherhood of Teamsters) P247
Murphy, John M. (Anthem Insurance) A179
Murphy, John P. (PerkinElmer) A1111
Murphy, Judy A. (Investors Financial Services) E223
Murphy, Judy (Ceres Group) E175
Murphy, Julie E98, E257
Murphy, Kathleen A. P581
Murphy, Kenyon W. A1005
Murphy, Leslie L. A407
Murphy, Michael J. (Electro Scientific Industries) E56, E196
Murphy, Michael J. (Roadway) A1207
Murphy, Michael R. (ARAMARK) A191
Murphy, Paul B., Jr. E291
Murphy, Peter E. A1497
Murphy, Philip B. A607
Murphy, R. Craig A1229
Murphy, Reg P358
Murphy, Robert F. (Sun Healthcare) A1341
Murphy, Robert (Pemstar) E262
Murphy, Thomas A60
Murphy, Tim P573
Murphy, Vicki P589
Murphy-Brown, LLC A1291
Murphy's Irish Stout W254, W255, W289
Murphy's oil soap A386, A387
Murray, Alan W253
Murray, Andrew M. E287
Murray, Bill P729
Murray Drug A1070
Murray, George H. A423
Murray, Gerry P649
Murray, James E. (Humana) A739

Murray, James M. (FirstEnergy) A599
Murray, Jeffrey A. A1525
Murray, Michael J. (Pilgrim's Pride) A1133
Murray, Michael W. (FMC) A613
Murray Ohio (lawn mowers) W604
Murray, Patricia A761
Murray, Stephen J. A247
Murray Sugar Free cookies A814, A815
Murray, Terrence A602, A603
Murrell, Charles M. A1309
Murrell, Rick A1031
Murren, James J. A967
Murrie, Bruce A914, P314
Murry, Tom P101
Murshid, Ahmad Zubir Haji W539
Murthy, Ramesh A147
Musacchia, Mary U. P431
Muse Air A1310
Muse, John R. A714, A715, P232, P233
Muse, Lamar A1310
Muse, Michael A1310
Musesengwa, Stanley W569
Museum of Contemporary Art (Los Angeles) P553
Museum of History and Technology (Washington, DC) P450
Museum of Modern Art (New York City) P276, P284, P448, P541
Music and Video Club (MVC) W312
Music Corporation of America A1450, P166, W360, W430, W448, W472
Music Maker Publications W238
Music Plus A266
Musica, Philip A946
Musician's Friend E66, E210
Musick, Ronald E. A1511
Musicland Stores Corporation A254, P346, P680
musicmaker.com W212
MusicNet W212
Musil, Ruthellyn A1403
Musselwhite Mine W452, W453
Musser, Warren V. A400, A1232, A1233
Mussolini, Benito W574
Mustang airplane W496
Mustang cars A616
Mustang Energy A1065
Musto, Michael L. E278
Muthuraman, B. W567
Muto, Gary P. A635
Mutryn, Thomas A. A1443
Mutterperl, William C. A603
Mutual Broadcasting System E140
The Mutual Life Insurance P376
The Mutual Life Insurance Company of New York (MONY). See The MONY Group, Inc.
The Mutual of Omaha Companies P348-P349, P680
Mutual Oil A412
Mutual Service Corporation P385

Mutualité Générale W104
Mutuelle Vie W104
Mutuelles AXA W104
Mutuelles Unies W104
Muzak LLC P350-P351, P681
Muzzio, Robert J. E88
Muzzy, J. Howard A584
Muzzy-Lyon Company A584
MVC music and video stores W312, W313
MVI. See Machine Vision International
Grupo MVS SA (pay-TV) A715, P233
MW Manufacturers (building products) A1446
My Dog pet food A915, P315
My Generation (magazine) P28
Myatt, Kevin A. P768
MyChoice Inc. W113
Mycogen (seed developer) A504, A1246, P432
MyContracts.com P120
Mydland, Lars W519
Myer, David F. A65, P31
Myer Emporium (retailer) W172
Myer Grace Brothers department stores W172
Myer Home W172
Myer Megamart stores W172
Myer, Sidney W172
Myer, William P151, P588
Myers, Albert F. A1045
Myers, A. Maurice A1504, A1505, A1548
Myers, C. David A1551
Myers Electric Products A430
Myers, Glenford J. E109, E274
Myers, James M. (Petco) P395, P701
Myers, Jim (Worldcom) A1535
Myers, John (Bristol-Myers-Squibb) A290
Myers, John E. (Cintas) A365
Myers, Larry L. P769
Myer's liquor W315
Myers, Nigel E197
Myers, Robert C. (XTO Energy) E319
Myers, Robert L. (Priority Healthcare) E270
Myers, Rodney S. A185
Myers, Stuart A. E51
Myklebust, Egil W411
Mykrolis Corporation E248
Mylan Laboratories Inc. A1354, P466
Mylanta A800
Mynd Corporation A404
myplay, inc. (digital music) P511
MyPlay.com W126, W127
Mypoints.com, Inc. A1420
MYR Group Inc. A668
Myrick, Bill P27
Myrick, Julian A986
The Myrtle Beach (South Carolina) Sun News A833
mySAP.com W516

Mystic Cliffs wines A423
Mystique cars A616
Myth 3 (computer game) E298
My-World Web site W310

N

N64 (magazine) W238, W239
NAACP. *See* National Association for the Advancement of Colored People
NAB. *See* National Australia Bank Limited
NAB Asia W383
NaBANCO (credit card transaction processing) A596
Nabisco Holdings Corporation A316, A470, A656, A670, A708, A774, A814, A842, A1204, P380, P474
Nacchio, Joseph P. A1186, A1187
NACCO Industries, Inc. A**992-A993**
Nachbar, David R. A1237
Nachury, Jean-Louis W331
Corporación Nacional del Cobre de Chile A1125
Nadata, Arthur E97, E256
Naddaf, Inés W577
Nader, Ralph A688, P58
Nadro S.A. de C.V. (drug distributor) A946
OOO Nadymgazprom W243
Næss, Bjørn Erik W163
Naessens, Jerry A. E301
Naeve, Stephen W. A1199
Nafilyan, Guy A813
NAFTA. *See* North American Free Trade Agreement
Nafta Polska W456
Nafziger, Ralph Leroy A774
Nagai, Akira W527
Nagakubo, Satoshi W405
Nagarajan, Jayaraman A817
Nagase, Shin W81
Nagase, Tomiro W308
Nagata, Hiroshi W373
Nagelmackers, Georges A328, P108
Nagelmann, John P622
Naggiar, Caroline D. A1385
Nagin, Lawrence M. A1443
Nagioff, Roger B. A861
Nagler, Barry A693
Nagler, Lorna E. A831
Nagler, Steward G. A965
NagraStarr LLC A529
Nagy, Charles E. A433
Nahara, Tsuyoshi W397
NAHC (rehab hospitals) A698
Naill, Roger F. A89
Nair depilatories A358
Nair, Hari N. A1369
Nairn, William A. W93
Naismith, James P354
Naito, Hisao W599
Naito, Kotaro W561
Naitoh, Masahisa W297
Nakagawa, Makoto W611
Nakai, Kamezo W409

Nakai, Minoru A93
Nakamachi, Yoshiyuki W81
Nakamura, Ken-ichi W187
Nakamura, Kunio W361
Nakamura, Masaharu W597
Nakamura, Masao W419
Nakamura, Noboru W329
Nakamura, Shunichi W527
Nakamura, Suehiro W551
Nakamura, Takashi W601
Nakamura, Tetsu W199
Nakamura, Yuichi W561
Nakanishi, Greg A223
Nakanishi, Hirokazu W573
Nakano, Sokichi W561
Nakasone, Bob A1396
Nakatani, Kosaku W405
Nakayama, Yahuhiro W397
Naku, Rolf D. A1345
Nalco Chemical (water) W558
Naldec auto parts W362
Nalley's Fine Foods P38
Nalley's pickles A466, A467
Namath, Joe A854
Names W336
Nan Ya Plastics Corporation W228
Nandor, Ronald P. A1279
Nanik Window Coverings A1316, A1317, P452, P453
Nanjing Panda Electronics W532
Nanninga, Cherrie P399
Nanogen, Inc. A244
Nanometrics Inc. E248
Nanoteq Ltd. E93
Nantahala Power and Light A514
Nantucket Allserve P380
Nantucket Bank E285
Nantucket Nectars P380
Nanula, Richard D. A161, A1328
Nanyo Bussan (trading company) W358
NAPA. *See* National Auto Parts Association
Napier brand A805
Napier, Iain W289
Napier, James V. A1258
Napier, Robert V. A399
Napier, William A. (Inco) W285
Napier, William (Ohio State University) P383
Napoleon cognac W85
Napoleon III W624
Napoli, James A. A1287
Napp Pharmaceuticals P707
Napster, Inc. (online music service) W126
Narayen, Shantanu A77
Nardelli, Robert L. A724, A725
Nardo, Guy A507
Narita, Yutaka W199
Narragansett brewery P428
Narrondo Desarrollo S.L. W203
NAS. *See* National Advanced Systems
NASA. *See* US National Aeronautics and Space Administration

NASCAR. *See* National Association for Stock Car Auto Racing
NASCAR products A295
Nascort drug W103
NASD. *See* National Association of Securities Dealers Inc.; National Association of Securities Dealers, Inc.
NASD Regulation P682
Nasdaq. *See* National Association of Securities Dealers Automated Quotations
Nasdaq Japan W548
Nash Brothers A344, A994
Nash Coffee Company A994
Nash DeCamp (fruit and vegetable packer) A994
Nash, Edgar A994
Nash Finch Company A344, A**994-A995**, P243
Nash, Fred A994
Nash, Mary A994
Nash, Rodney R. A675
Nash, Warren A994
Nash, Willis A994
Nashville Eagle (airline) A164
The Nashville Network. *See* TNN: The National Network
Nashville Predators (hockey team) P361
NASI. *See* North American Scientific, Inc.
Nasonex drug A1251
Nassau Royale liqueur W109
Al-Nasser, Gamal Abd W558
Nasser, Jacques A. A616, A617
Nassetta, Christopher J. A733
Natale, James L. A445
Natalicio, Diana P499
Natasha vodka W109
Natchiq (oil field services) P542
NatCity Investments, Inc. A1000
Nate's pasta products E247
Nathan, Alec W246
Nathan, Badri P475
Nathan, Joseph A. (Compuware) A407
Nathan, Joseph (Glaxo) W246
Nathan's Famous, Inc. E**95**, E249
Nathanson Creek wines A422
Natiocredit W131
Natioenergie W131
National Advanced Systems A1002, W260
National Advertising (billboards) A976
National Aeronautics and Space Administration. *See* US National Aeronautics and Space Administration
National Air and Space Museum (Washington, DC) P450, P451, P615
National Airlines A684, A685
National Alliance Marketing Group, Inc. A591
National Amusements Inc. A1476, P681

National Association for Stock Car
Auto Racing A936, E75, E207,
E222, P681, P722
National Association for the
Advancement of Colored
People A86, A1280, P188, P194
National Association of Rotary
Clubs P420
National Association of Securities
Dealers Automated
Quotations A134, A348, A614,
A1018, A1424, E75, E112, P46,
P80, P190, P374, P539, W190
National Association of Securities
Dealers, Inc. A230, A**996**-A**997**,
P46, P**352**-P**353**, P539, P682,
W548
National Australia Bank
Limited W**382**-W**383**
National Auto Parts
Association A462, A572, A652,
P112
National Auto Research
(publication) P229
National Auto/Truckstops A1438
National BankAmericard
Inc. A1480, P508
National Bank of Australasia W382
National Bank of Commerce of
Seattle A1480, P508
National Bank of Greece
S.A. W**384**-W**385**
The National Bank of Sussex
County E231
National Basketball
Association A280, A1194, E130,
E257, P262, P**354**-P**355**, P682,
P767
National Bell Telephone A202,
A248, A292, W122
National Billiard P170
National Bio Systems A204
National Blind & Wallpaper
Factory A724, A725
National brand electronic
products A110
National Brands Beverage P38
National Bridle Shop
supplies A1117
National Broadcasting Company,
Inc. A60, A312, A334, A506, A507,
A622, A646, A**998**-A**999**, A1150,
A1258, E140, E141, E212, P159,
P229, P358, P681, P683
National Cancer Control
Month P40
National Cancer Institute P454,
P734
National Capital Health Plan,
Inc. A1507
National Carbon Company A1190
National Car Parks A339
National Car Rental Systems A206,
A650, A734, A896
National Cash Register Corporation.
See NCR Corporation
National Center for
Supercomputing
Applications P756
National Child Care Centers A190

National City Bank of
Cleveland A1000
National City
Corporation A**1000**-A**1001**
National Collection of Fine
Arts P450
National Collegiate Athletic
Association A334, E140, P758
National Commercial Bank and
Trust A822
National Commercial Banking
Corporation of Australia W382
National Computer Products
(satellite communications) A780
National Computer Systems W430
National Container A1074
National Cranberry
Association P380
National CSS (computer
services) A516
National Dairy A842
National Distillers Products A974
National Distributing Company,
Inc. P682
National Electric A570
National Electric Instruments
(medical instruments) A550
National Electricity Company A554
National Enquirer P330
National Enterprises A154
National Equipment Services,
Inc. E249
National Farmers
Organization P58, P148
National Fidelity Insurance A414
National Fire Insurance Company of
Hartford A379
National Football League A60, A64,
A334, A672, A692, A998, A1032,
E130, E141, E207, P30, P88,
P172, P210, P211, P**356**-P**357**,
P417, P621, P683, P767
National Fuel A1030
National Gallery of Art (Washington,
DC) P450
National General (insurance) A144
National Geographic Channel A623,
P359
National Geographic
(magazine) P358, P359, P683,
P708
National Geographic
Society P**358**-P**359**, P408, P683
National Grid Group (electric
transmission) A1028
National Grid USA P616
National Gypsum Company A848,
P683
National Hair Centers A1196
National Hand Tool A1322
National Hardlines Supply A65, P31
National Healthcare
Logistics A1350
National Highway Traffic Safety
Administration P138
National Hockey League A936,
E130, E317, P262, P**360**-P**361**,
P684, W376

National Hydrocarbon Agency. *See*
Eni S.p.A.
National Imaging Affiliates,
Inc. A699
National Indemnity Company A252,
A253
National Industrial Recovery Act
(1933) P34
National Information Group
(mortgage support) A594, A595
National Inking Appliance
Company A242
National Institute of Child Health
and Human Development P78,
P79
National Institute of Standards and
Technology P573
National Institutes of Health P769
National Intergroup A1006
National Iranian Oil Company A200
National Irish Bank W383
National Irish Holdings
Limited W382
National League baseball P306,
P307, P663
National Legal Assistance Training
Program P29
National Life Insurance
Company P684
National Linen Service A1004,
A1005
National Mall (Washington,
DC) P448, P450, P731
National Master Freight
Agreement P246
National Material P741
National Medal of Arts P769
National Medal of Science P456
National Medical Enterprises A698,
A904, A1366
National Medical Supply,
Inc. A1071
National MENTOR (foster
care) A904, A905
National Merit Scholarships P194
National Mortgage Bank of
Greece A238, W384
National Museum of African Art
(Washington, DC) P451
National Museum of American Art
(Washington, DC) P450
National Museum of American
History (Washington, DC) P450,
P451
National Museum of Natural History
(Washington, DC) P450, P451
National Museum of the American
Indian (New York City) P450,
P451
National Mutual
International W104
The National Network. *See* TNN:
The National Network
National Oats P38
National Old Line Insurance W64
National Opinion Research
Center P497
National Parking A338

National PharmPak Services, Inc. A321
National Pig Development A1290
National Portland Cement A848
National Portrait Gallery (Washington, DC) P450, P451
National Postage Meter Company A242
National Postal Museum (Washington, DC) P451
National Post (Canada) W262, W263
National Potash Company A628
National Power & Light Company A88, A668, A1154, A1166, A1198
National Processing, Inc. A1000
National Propane Partners A1400
National Provident Institution W88, W89
National Publications P170
National Public Radio, Inc. P144, P145, P585
National Railroad Passenger Corporation P362-P363, P684, W132
National Real Estate SA W385
National Realty Funding A822
National Realty Trust. *See* NRT Inc.
National Refrigeration Services A754
National Rejectors, Inc. GmbH (coin changers) A447
National Retired Teachers Association P28, P29
National Robinson, L.L.C. A1007
National Rural Utilities Cooperative Finance Corporation P685
National Science Foundation P134, P454, P769
National Security Agency A404
National Semiconductor Corporation A176, A186, A1002-A1003, E28, E84, E121, P444, W260
National Service Industries, Inc. A1004-A1005
National Specialty Services, Inc. A321
National Spirit Group P519
The National (sports newspaper) W582
National Starch W278, W279
National Steel and Shipbuilding Company A644
National Steel Corporation A1006-A1007
National Steel Pellet Company A1006, A1007
National Surgery Centers A698
National Tea (grocer) W244
National Technical Laboratories A242
National Telephone Company W148
National Testing and Research Center P138
National Titanium Dioxide Company A820

National Title Insurance Services, Inc. A591
National Underwriters P268
National Union Bank of Boston A1332
National Union Electric E58, W210
National Union Life and Limb Insurance A964
National Vendors A447
National Wildlife Federation P417
National Zoological Park (Washington, DC) P450, P451, P731
Compagnie Nationale Air France W68
Nationale Life Insurance Bank W286
Nationale-Nederland W286
Nations Title, Inc. A591
NationsBank. *See* Bank of America Corporation
NationsWay (freight hauler) A420
Nationwide A1008-A1009, E315, P364-P365, P685
Nationwide Financial Services, Inc. P364, P365
Nationwide Rubber Enterprises W604
NatSteel Electronics A1298
Natural by Garelick Farms A1339
Natural Gas Clearinghouse A518
Natural Gas Policy Act (1978) A518, A536
Natural Touch meat alternatives A817
Naturalizer shoes A294, A295
Naturals soft drink W315
The Nature Company stores P158
Nature Conservancy A1516
Nature Saver office products A652
Nature Sole shoes A295
Nature Valley snacks A649
Nature's Accents skin care products A486, A487
Nature's Finest brand foods A607
Nature's Heartland markets A1522
Nature's Own baked goods A608, A609
NatWest (bank) A910
Nauert, Peter W. E175
Naujoks, Henrik P65
Nautica Enterprises, Inc. (furniture) P299
Nautilus Insurance Company A1016, P370
Nautilus International E193
Nautilus nuclear submarine A644
Naval Research Laboratory A98
Navale (insurance) W98
Navarra, Anthony J. A889
Navarro, Richard J. A111
Navidec A1508
NAVIDEC, Inc. E249
Naviera Vizcaina (shipping) W482
Navigant International Inc. E250
Navigator toothbrush A387
Navio Communications A1066

Navis Partners A602
Navistar International Corporation A96, A332, A460, A468, A1010-A1011, A1368, P152, P342, P480, P590, W320
Navratilova, Martina P251
Navy Exchange Service Command P685
Navy Federal Credit Union P686
Navy Lodges P685
NAYA beverage A385
Naya water W192, W193
Nayden, Denis J. A647
Naylor, Craig G. A535
Naylor, Jeffrey A261
Naz, Eulogio P55
Nazem, Farzad A1547
Nazer, Hisham P340
Nazolta E263
NBA. *See* National Basketball Association
NBA Showtime (video game) W527
NBC. *See* National Broadcasting Company
NBG. *See* National Bank of Greece S.A.
NBG Balkan Fund Ltd. W385
NBGI, Inc. W385
NBT Bancorp Inc. E250
NCAA. *See* National Collegiate Athletic Association
NCL Holding A330
NCNB. *See* North Carolina National Bank
NCO Group, Inc. E250
NCR Corporation A202, A488, A764, A1012-A1013, A1142, A1298, E237, W298
NCS Pearson Inc. (educational test processing) W430, W431
nCUBE Corporation A1066
ND Cube W394
Ndovu beer W553
Neal, Diane A1353
Neal, Jane E250
Neal Manufacturing A754
Neal, Philip M. A210, A211
Neale, Gary L. A1035
Nealis, James J., III A849
Neapco (transmissions) P113, P752
Near East foods A1180, A1181
NEBCO Distribution P236
Nebedahl, Colleen A379
Nebel, Jean François W447
Nebraska Consolidated Mills A408
Nebraska Dairies A994
Nebraska Furniture Mart A252
NEC Corporation A82, A170, A782, A1284, A1372, A1514, E54, E174, E280, P137, W150, W236, W334, W386-W387, W420, W508, W526, W570, W586
NeCastro, Joseph G. E102, E263
Necco wafer candy P752
Neckermann mail order W311
Neckermann Versand mail order W310

NECX (electronics exchange) A636
Nederland B.V. A384
Nederlandsche
Kunstzijdebariek W72
Nederlandse
Middenstandsbank W286
Nedlloyd Groep W434
Nee, Thomas M. A149
NEECO (computer systems) A544
Needham (advertising) P72
Needham Harper Worldwide
(advertising) A1062
Needham, Mary Jo E247
Needlecraft (magazine) W238
Needleman, Philip A1123
Neeley, Robert L. P654
Neels, Guido J. A675
Neer, Fred J. A65, P31, P529
Neeson Meat Sales A1109
Neeves, Carole P451
Neff, Deborah J. A245
Neff, Richard B. P592
Neger, Irving A579
Negro Digest (magazine) P258
Negroponte, John D. A945
Neher, Pat P253
Nehi Corporation (soft
drinks) A1400, W155
NEI Electronics E104
Neidhart, Jerry E191
Neighborhood Entertainment
theater chain P412
Neighborhood Market A1494
Neil, David R. A117
Neil, Ian A. A767
Neil Mathieson (chemicals) A1060
Neilson Dairy W245
Neiman, A. L. A1014
Neiman, Carrie Marcus A1014
The Neiman Marcus Group,
Inc. A564, **A1014**-**A1015**, A1238,
A1530, P630
Neiman Marcus Travel
Services P107
Neisner Brothers stores A158
Nekura P364
Nelissen, Roelof J. W499
Nell, Ross B. A87
Nelles, Norbert W311
Nellie Mae Corporation (educational
loans) A1448, A1449
Nellis, Paul C. A747
Nelson & Sloan (concrete) W252
Nelson, Barbara H. A1185
Nelson, Bill A543
Nelson, Bruce S. A773
Nelson, Christian P424
Nelson Communications
Worldwide W466, W467
Nelson, Corliss J. A1223
Nelson, Curtis C. P107
Nelson, Don A280
Nelson, Douglas E. P768
Nelson, Eileen A55
Nelson, Elizabeth A. E86
Nelson filtration units A456
Nelson, Gary M. A343

Nelson, George A706
Nelson, Glen D. A953
Nelson, Gordon A1197
Nelson, Gregory M. A1179
Nelson Industries (diesel
exhaust) A456
Nelson, Jerry L. A995
Nelson, John F. (Credit
Suisse) A449
Nelson, John R. (Philip
Morris) A1127
Nelson, Marilyn Carlson P106,
P107, P567
Nelson, Maurice
(RyersonTull) A1224
Nelson, Maurice S., Jr. (Earle M.
Jorgensen Compay) P601
Nelson, M. Bruce A1056, A1057
Nelson, Peter (Coles Myer) W173
Nelson, Peter J. (Alexandria Real
Estate Equities) E150
Nelson, R. David A469
Nelson, Robert C. W379
Nelson, Ronald G. (Minnesota
Mining and Manufacturing) A977
Nelson, Ronald L. (Dreamworks
SKG) P167, P597
Nelson, Stewart G. A1051
Nelson Stud Welding A1412
Nelson, Thomas C. (AARP) P29,
P683
Nelson, Thomas E., Jr.
(Airborne) A103
Nelson Thornes (educational
information) W642, W643
Nelson, William H. P641
Nelson/Weather Rite (camping
equipment) A298
Nemacolin Woodlands resort P26
Nemerov, Jackwyn A805
Nemeth, Ken P63
Nemeti, Susie L. E258
Nemetz, Kevin M. A467
Nemirow, Arnold M. A284, A285
NEN Life Sciences A1110
NeoMagic Corporation (radio
frequency chips) A894
Neomediam plumbing
products P284, P653
NEON Systems, Inc. A270
NeoRecormon anemia W493
Neosporin ointment A1118
Neppl, Christina M. A263
Neptune (drilling company) A1252
Neptune washing machine A934
NER Auction Systems E45
Nerco (coal) W488
Nerf soft toys A692, A693
Nergaard, Leiv L. W411
Nerret, F. Arthur E88, E238
Nesbitt Burns Securities, Inc. W112
Nesbitt Lemonade A1105
Nescafé brand W388
Nesci, Mark A. A305
NESCO, Inc. P686
Nesor Alloy A1124
Nespola, Richard P. E236

Ness, Eliot A488
Nesser, John T. A941
Nessi, Marie W105
Nestea A384, A385, A1106, W388
Nestlé, Henri W388
Nestlé Purina PetCare P626
Nestlé S.A. P264, W342,
W**388**-W**389**, W466, W618
Nestlé USA A408, A452, A470, A510,
A648, A772, A1106, A1126, A1136,
P254, P474, P715, W192, W388
Nestler (office furniture) P222
Nestor Levy, Susan E. P57
.net (magazine) W238
Net2Phone, Inc. A1546
NetBank, Inc. E251
Netchvolodoff, Alexander V. A443,
P147
NetCom ASA (mobile
telephone) W584
Netcon A240, P74
Netcool suite software E245
NetCore Systems A1362
NetDispatch A67
NetDox (document delivery) W196
Netegrity, Inc. E**96**, E251
NetEngine E268
NetFlare test A1373
NetFRAME Systems (servers) A762
NetGame USA A972
Netherlands Bell Telephone W502
Netherlands Insurance
Company W286
Netherlands Trading Society W56
NetJets A252
NETLimited (dba HostPro) A762
NetLink W526
NetMedia Group W180
Neto, João Leal W437
Netolicka, Robert A803
NetOptix (optical filters) A434
Netquity E63
Netra telecommunications
servers A1343
NetRatings, Inc. A66, E63, E251
Netravali, Arun N. A899
Netromycin drug A1250
Nets Inc. A1112
Netscape Communications A76,
A130, A180, A1066, A1284, A1342,
A1546, E86, E96, P248, P456,
P756
Netscape Navigator. *See* Netscape
Communications
Netscape World: The Web
(magazine) P248
NetScheme Solutions E22
NetSolve, Inc. E252
NetSuite Development A615, P191
Nettle Creek stores A1134
Nettles, Patrick H. E41
NetWare operating system A1050,
A1051
Network Access Agents E192
Network Access Division A410
Network Appliance A542
Network Computer, Inc. A1066

Network Indiana radio network E198
Network Six (information technology) A1412
Network Solutions, Inc. (Internet domain registrar) P438
Network Systems A1336
Network World (magazine) P249
Networx SA W176
Neubauer, Joseph A190, A191
Neubürger, Joachim W537
Neue Aargauer W185
Neuger, Win J. A151
Neuharth, Allen A632
Neuhaus, Solomon A80, P32
Neukom, William H. A973
Neuleze drug A640
Neumann, Jens W631
Neumann, Spencer A61
Neumann, Wilhelm W368
Neupogen drug A160, E71
Neustadt, James C. A969
Neutrogena skin care A800, A1200
Neutzling, John R. A1287
Neuvo, Yrjö W407
Nevada Bell Telephone Company A1244, A1245
Nevada Landing Hotel and Casino A907
Nevares, Hector M., Jr. A1339
Nevares, Hector, Sr. A1338
Nevarez, Miguel A. P499
Neveu, Jean W471
Neville, Matthew E168
New America Strategies Group A773
New Balance Athletic Shoe, Inc. P686
New Book of Knowledge (encyclopedia) A1255
New Car Buying Guide (book) P139
New Carlsberg (brewery) W162
New Century Energies A140, A362, A1542
New Choices: Living Even Better After 50 (magazine) A1193
New, David A. A275
New Dawn Hair Color A108
New Dimension (software) A270
The New Ebony Cookbook (book) P258, P259
New England Cable News P229
New England Confectionery P752
New England Electric System A1120
New England Energy Group A68, A69
New England Frozen Foods P102
New England Mutual Life Insurance Company A964
New England Patriots (football team) P357
New England Telephone A202
New Enterprises Associates IV (venture capital) E252
New Hampton catalogs A1314
New Health Exchange A600

New Holland (agricultural equipment) A456, A616, W226, W227
New Horizons Wordwide, Inc. E252
New ICO A1026
New, James C. E155
New Jersey Devils (hockey team) P361
New Jersey Nets (basketball team) P355
New Jersey State Lottery Commission P687
New Line Cinema, Inc. A180, A181
New Medical (dental implants) W328
New Millennium World Atlas Deluxe Edition (software) P409
New Orleans Public Service Inc. A554
New Orleans Saints (football team) P357
New Penn Motor Express A1206
New Plan Excel Realty Trust, Inc. E252
The New Power Company A552
New Prague Flouring Mill Company A768
New Process Cork A452
New United Motor Manufacturing, Inc. A650, P366-P367, P687, W614
New Valley Corporation A596, E231
New Vanden Borre electrical stores W313
New Viesgo (electricity generation) W214
New West Energy P734
New World Coffee-Manhattan Bagel. *See* New World Restaurant Group, Inc.
New World Communications Group A902, P304
New World Pasta A708
New World Restaurant Group, Inc. E253
New World Television A902, P304
New York-American Water Company A155
New York Blue Shield P174
New York Chemical Manufacturing A808
New York, Chicago & St. Louis Railroad A1038
New York City Board of Higher Education P128
New York City Building P449
New York City Community College P128
New York City Health and Hospitals Corporation P368-P369, P687
New York City Off Track Betting E40
New York City Technical College P128, P129
New York City Transit Authority P334, P335
New York Condensed Milk P90
New York Curb Market Association P46

New York Daily News E34, E165
New York Edison Company A418
New York Federal Reserve Bank P186
New York Gas and Electric Light, Heat and Power Company A418
The New York Gas Light Company A418
New York Giants (football team) A884, P356, P357
New York Helmsley hotel P231
New York International Airport P398
New York Islanders Hockey Club, L.P. P361
New York Jets Football Club, Inc. P357
New York Knicks (basketball team) A312, A313, P355
New York Liberty (basketball team) P355
New York Life Insurance and Trust A228
New York Life Insurance Company A90, A**1016**-A**1017**, P28, **P370**-**P371**, P688
New York Life, L.P. P350
New York (magazine) A1160, A1161
New York Marine Underwriters A356
New York Mercantile Exchange. *See* NYMEX
New York Metropolitan Museum of Art P204
New York Metropolitan Opera A1062
New York Mets (baseball team) P307
New York Morning Journal A700, P228
New York-New Jersey Port P398
New York News A1402
New York-New York hotel and casino (Las Vegas) A966, A967
New York Palace hotel P230
New York Patents A452
New York Pearl Street Station A1120
New York Post P486, W390
New York Power Authority A498, A554
New York Public Library P134
New York Racing Association E40
New York Racket store P76, P553
New York Rangers (hockey team) A312, A313, P361
New York State Common Retirement Fund E271
New York State Electric & Gas A88
New York State Institute of Applied Arts and Sciences P128
New York State Lottery **P372**-**P373**, P688
New York State Public Service Commission A418
New York Steam Company A418

New York Stock Exchange,
Inc. A94, A134, A190, A204, A238,
A396, A514, A566, A602, A624,
A626, A660, A702, A710, A724,
A806, A812, A888, A892, A934,
A960, A988, A996, **A1018-A1019**,
A1070, A1090, A1130, A1136,
A1152, A1182, A1188, A1448,
A1472, A1474, A1492, E112, E132,
E230, E287, P46, P142, P352,
P374-P375, P688, W82, W194,
W286, W316, W321, W384, W448,
W474, W478, W482, W498, W516,
W536, W542, W573, W576, W612
New York Sun A1422
New York Supreme Court A1476,
P368
The New York Times Company A80,
A826, A832, **A1020-A1021**,
A1218, P32, P46
New York Transportation
Infrastructure Bond Act P334
New York Tribune A1020
New York University P689, P690
New York World A700, P228
New York Yankees (baseball
team) P250, P307
New Zealand Radio Network A373
New Zealand Shipping
Company W434
The New Yorker (magazine) A80,
P32, P33
Newage alternators A456
Newark Banking and
Insurance A1146
The Newark Group P689
Newark International Airport P399
Newbigging, David W306
Newbridge Communications A1160
Newbridge Networks W76
Newbridge partnerships P474
Newby, D. M. A915, P315
NewCap Insurance Company,
Limited P115, P116
Newcastle (steelworks) W128
Newcomb Anderson
Associates A545
Newcomb, Link E99
Newcourt Financial P208
Newell and Harrison A1348
Newell, Edgar A1022
Newell, George A1348
Newell Rubbermaid Inc. A656,
A1022-A1023, A1322
Newfield Exploration
Company A222, E253
Newfield Publication A1160
Newfoundland Brewery W376
Newgen Results Corporation (direct
marketing) E127, E300
NewHealthExchange.com A156,
A320, A1070
Newhouse Broadcasting P33
Newhouse, Donald E. A80, A81,
P32, P33, P61, P530
Newhouse, Samuel I. A80, P32
Newhouse, Samuel I., Jr. A80, A81,
P32, P33, P530
Newhouse, Stephen F. A989

Newkirk, Lyle W. E303
NewKote boxboard P689
Newland Communities P96
Newlands, David B. W604, W605
NewLeaf brand A985
Newlin, David B. P533
Newman, Andrea Fischer A1047
Newman, Deb P742
Newman, Joel H. W607
Newman, Judith A. A1255
Newman, Michael D. A1189
Newman Tonks Group A754
Newmark & James (carpets) A980
Newmark Rug Company A981
NewMedia P176
Newmont Mining
Corporation **A1024-A1025**
NewNet A70
Newport cigarettes A884
Newport City housing
development P290, P656
Newport Corporation E253
Newport Credit Group A1294
Newport Meat Company A1350
Newport News Shipbuilding
Inc. A548, A644, A1044, A1368
Newport News stores A1314, A1315
Newport Pacific Management,
Inc. P294, P295
Newport, Tom P568
NewPower Holdings, Inc. A552
News America W391
News Communications &
Media A632
The News Corporation
Limited A312, A528, A622, A700,
A736, A872, A902, A1160, A1476,
A1496, P228, P304, W96, W106,
W146, **W390-W391**, W430, W478,
W582, W586
News International W106
News of the World W390
Newsday (New York City)
newspaper A1402
NewsEdge Corporation W592,
W593
NewSouth Communications
Corporation A837, P283
Newspaper Association of
America P60
Newspaper Industry
Communication Center P60, P61
Newsprint South Inc. A284, A285
Newsquest plc A632
Newsted, Richard P673
Newsweek (magazine) A1502,
A1503, P176, P404, P708
Newton, Ashley W213
Newton handheld computer A186,
W532
Newton Management
Limited A954, A955
Newtons cookies A843, A1204
NeXagen A244
Nexans W76
Nexant (energy consulting) A240,
P74
NEXCOM Ships Stores P685

NEXIS (news database) A950,
W478, W479
Nexstar Financial
Corporation A836, A837, P282,
P283, P653
NeXT software A186
Nextel Communications, Inc. A549,
A1026-A1027, E83, E126, E233,
E243, E261, E316
Nextera Enterprises, Inc. P278,
P279, P652
Nexterna (wireless data) A1422,
A1423
NEXTLINK Communications. *See*
XO Communications, Inc.
NexTone Communications
Inc. A1233
NextWave Telecom Inc. A1026,
A1182
Nexus Fuels W346
Neylon, Paul M. A287
NFL. *See* National Football League
NFO WorldGroup, Inc. A772, A773
Ng Kai Wa W180
Ng Keh Long W181
Ng, Tony A163
NGC Oil Trading and
Transportation A88, A352, A518,
A1030
NGE A88
Ngee, Michael T. J. W541
NGTS E235
Nguyen, Anne E251
Nguyen, David E221
NHB Group (cabinets) A618
NHMG Mexico SA de CV A993
NI Finance W404
Niachlor (chlor-alkali plant) A1060
Niaga Lima Sdn. Bhd. A162
Niagara Bancorp. *See* First Niagara
Financial Group, Inc.
Niagara Falls Power A1028
Niagara Fire Insurance
Company A379
Niagara Hudson Power
Corporation A1028
Niagara Mohawk Holdings
Inc. A424, **A1028-A1029**, A1174
Niagara Seed Operations A612
Niagara Sprayer & Chemical A612
Nibblebox (animation) P278
Niblack, John F. A1119
Niblock, Robert A. A893
NIC Components E97, E256
NICACEL (wireless) A248
NICC. *See* Newspaper Industry
Communication Center
Nice 'n Easy hair care A1164
Nice 'N Fluffy A358, A359
NiceCom A54
Nichido Fire & Marine
Insurance W596
Nichi-Doku Shashinki
Shoten W368
Nichiiko Pharmaceutical W304
Nichimen Corporation W404
Nicholas, Jon O. A935
Nicholas Kiwi shoe care A1242

Nicholas, Peter M. A282, A283
Nicholas Ungar stores A1036
Nicholas-Applegate (asset
  manager) W82
Nicholls, Jonathan W253
Nichols Copper A1124
Nichols, Daniel A. A1251
Nichols, Grace A. A777
Nichols, Jean P545
Nichols, J. Larry A482, A483
Nichols, John (1-800
  CONTACTS) E146
Nichols, John (Illinois Tool
  Works) A748
Nichols, John W. (Devon
  Energy) A483
Nichols, Keith A1099
Nichols, Ken L. A65, P31
Nichols, Michael C. A1351
Nichols Research A404
Nichols, Rodney P. P664
Nichols, William A728
Nicholson, Bruce J. P534
Nicholson Group
  (investments) E26
Nicholson, Pam P179
Nicholson, Peter J. M. W123
Nick Bollettieri Tennis
  Academy P251
Nickelodeon cable network A927,
  A1450, A1476, P218, W146
Nickels, Elizabeth E. A707
Nickerson, William A656
Nicklaus, Jack P130, P382
Nicklaus, Ludovico W439
Nicoderm CQ antismoking
  patches P40, W246
Nicoderm nicotine patch A800
Nicoli, Eric L. W212, W213
Nicolle, Jean-Marc W443
NICOR Energy, L.L.C. A518
Nicor Inc. A1030-A1031
Nicorette gum smoking
  cessation A1122
Nides, Thomas R. A449
Niederberger, Jane E. A179
Niehaus, Robert P. A593
Niekamp, Randy P586
Niels Fugal Sons E52
Nielsen, Arthur Charles A66
Nielsen Dillingham
  (contractor) P593
Nielsen, Kurt Anker W417
Nielsen Media Research, Inc. A66,
  A516, E251, W626, W627
Nielsen Opportunity Explorer
  software A66
Nielsen, Steven E. E52, E195
Nielson, Patrick A. A495
Niemzyk, John A. A1455
Nien, Robert V. J. W267
Nierenberg, Nicolas C. E22
Niesmann & Bischoff (motor
  homes) A604
Nieto Bueso, Juan José W579
Nieto, Luis P. A467

Nieuwe Eerste Nederlandsche
  (insurance) W64
Nieuwenhoven, Rudy W503
Nieves, Anthony A721
Nifcalette bellows camera W368
Nifty Serve (Internet service
  provider) W236, W404
Night Train wine A521, P169
Nightingale A. J. L. W307
Nightingale, Florence P56
NightLife women's shoes A295
Nihon Card Processing A596
Nihon Denpo-Tsushin Sha W198
Nihon Keizai Shimbun W96
Nihon Koku Kabushiki
  Kaisha W302
Nihon Semiconductor A894
OOO NIIGazekonomika W243
Niijima, Akira W449
Niimura, Megumi W199
Nijko Shoji (trade company) W404
Nik Gold beer W289
NIKE, Inc. A666, A838, A839,
  A1032-A1033, A1194, P418,
  P686, P717, W62
NIKE licensed playwear A1474
Nike rockets A704
NIKEgoddess shoe stores A1032
Nikitin, Boris Alexandrovich W243
The Nikkei Weekly
  (publication) W96
Nikkel, John G. E308
Nikken Global Inc. P689
Nikko hotels W302
Nikko Securities A370
Nikkohm (passive
  components) A1482
Nikkor lenses W392
Nikols Sedgwick Group
  (insurance) A182
Nikon Corporation A524, E189,
  P137, W368, W370, W371,
  W392-W393
Niksico Pivo beer W289
Nile beer W553
Nile Spice (soup cups) A1180
Nilla cookies A843
Nilles, Richard A829, P271
Nillmij (tontine) W64
Nilsen, Jon-Harald W411
Nilsen, Robert T. A1405
Nilsen, Tore K. W525
Nilson, Bev E163
Nilsson, Sven-Christner W220
Nilsson, Torbjörn W221
Nimmy, Carolyn W161
Nin, Juan Maria W513
Nine, John E. A1251
Nine Mile Point nuclear plant A554,
  A1028
Nine West Group Inc. A804
Nineham, Rod A461
Nineteen Hundred
  Corporation A1520
Ninotchka (movie) A962
Nintendo Co., Ltd. E298,
  W394-W395, W526, W550, W600

NIOC. See National Iranian Oil
  Company
Niparko, Karen L. A1337
Nipe Bay sugar A354
Nippon Cargo Airlines W80
Nippon Credit Bank W396, W548
Nippon Dantai Life Insurance W104
Nippon Electric Company. See NEC
  Corporation
Nippon Fantasy World theme
  park W186
Nippon Gakki W648
Nippon Helicopter and Aeroplane
  Transport W80
Nippon Industries E256
Nippon Kogaku KK. See Nikon
  Corporation
Nippon Kokan. See NKK
  Corporation
Nippon Life Insurance
  Company W200, W396-W397
Nippon Mitsubishi Oil
  Corporation W370, W371
Nippon Paper A1518
Nippon Sheet Glass A612
Nippon Steel Corporation A1006,
  A1066, A1224, W292,
  W398-W399, W454
Nippon Steel Plate W404
Nippon Suisan Kaisha, Ltd.
  (seafood) W618
Nippon Telegraph and Telephone
  Corporation A596, W204, W236,
  W260, W328, W386, W400-W401,
  W418, W420, W598
Nippon Yusen Kabushiki
  Kaisha W371
NIPSCO Industries. See Northern
  Indiana Public Service Company
Nir-Sox stent A282
Nirvana (music group) P166
Nisenholtz, Martin A. A1021
Nish, David W523
Nishi, Yasumasa W603
Nishida, Yoishi W393
Nishigaki, Koji W386, W387
Nishiguchi, Yasuo W329
Nishikata, Shunpei W305
Nishimura, Hidetoshi W405
Nishimura, Koichi A1298, A1299
Nishimura, Masao W375
Nishimuro, Taizo W611
Nishinohara, Toshikuni W375
Nishizaka, Tetsuo W359
Nishizuka, Hidekazu W303
Nisita, Maurizio A531
NiSource Inc. A1034-A1035,
  A1082
Nissan Motor Company, Ltd. A548,
  A802, A992, A1394, P561, P563,
  P717, P767, P264, W358, W362,
  W402-W403, W480
Nissay. See Nippon Life Insurance
  Company
Nissay Dowa General Insurance
  Company, Ltd. W396, W397
Nisshin Printing W186
Nisshin Steel Company W398

Nissho Iwai Corporation (securities) A484, A1398, **W404-W405**, W600
Nissho Trading Company W600
Nitres (semiconductor R&D) E47
Nitro Nobel W72
Nitro-Dur drug A1251
Nitroglycerin Ltd. W72
Nitsch, Karl A. A461
Nitschke, Ray A672, P210, P621
Nivert, Marianne W585
Niwa, Norio W531
Niwa, Uichiro W297
Nix, Jerry W. A653
Nixdorf (computers) W536
Nixon, Allen M. A755
Nixon, Gordon M. W475
Nixon, Richard M. A1044, A1128, A1502, P58, P600, W542
Nizoral drug A801
NK. *See* Nederlandsche Kunstzijdebariek
NK brand grains P622
NKK Corporation A1006
NKT Holding A/S W520
NL Industries, Inc. P583, W278
NLI Properties, Inc. W397
n-LIGHTEN optical transmitter P522
NLM Dutch Airlines W316
NLRB. *See* US National Labor Relations Board
NM Direct (mail-order business) A1014
NM Properties, Inc. A1029
NMB Postbank W286
NMC/Nomanco A194
NMH Holding, BV A992, A993
NML Insurance A1236
NN Euroball ApS E254
NN, Inc. E254
no frills grocery stores W245
Noah Holding (temperature control) E24
Noah's New York Bagels E253
Nob Hill Foods P710
Nobel, Alfred W72
Nobel Educational Dynamics P278
Nobel Industries W278
Nobel Learning Communities, Inc. P278, P279, P652
Nobel prize A898, A956, A1378, P40, P128, P134, P196, P324, P378, P456, P496, P560, P667, P756, P760, P769, W116, W246, W414, W416
Noblanc, Jean-Pierre W555
Noble, Allen A970
Noble & Noble A232
Noble, Bill A685
Noble, Edward J. A60
Noble, L. C. A722
Nobles, Cy S. A835, P281
Nocito, Michael F. A285
Noda, Tadao W375
Noddle, Allan S. W499
Noddle, Jeffrey A1348, A1349

Noe, David P671
Noguchi, Isamu A706
Noha, Edward J. A379
Noia, Alan J. A115
Noilly Prat spirits W109
Noji, Kunio W321
Nokes, Jimmy W. A413
Nokia Corporation A98, A410, A982, A990, A1182, A1256, A1357, A1480, A1482, E106, E274, E276, E277, E280, E284, E305, P765, W220, W360, **W406-W407**, W554
Nolan, Frances A1355, P467
Nolan, Garry F. W383
Nolan, John A1429, P491
Nolan, Paul B. E248
Nolan, Peter M. A495
Noland, Joseph J. P427
Noland, Thomas J., Jr. A739
Nolop, Bruce P. A1143
Nolte, Reed A623
Nolvadex drug A540
Noma Industries W604
Nomad MP3 players W180, W181
Nomade.fr Web portal W312
Nomai A778
NOMECO (oil and gas) A376
Nomex (e-commerce) A406
NOMI do-it-yourself stores W312, W313
Nomura Holdings, Inc. W230, **W408-W409**, W544
Nomura International (investment bank) W174
Nomura, Kichisaburo W81
Nomura, Koichi W81
Nomura Research Institute W394
The Nomura Securities Company, Ltd. A1328
Nomura Shoten W408
Nomura, Tokushichi W408
Nomura, Tokushichi, II W408
None Such brands P90
Nonlinear Technologies (software) A76
Noon, Thomas F. A509
Noonan, Thomas E. (Internet Security Systems) E222
Noonan, Thomas N. (Crane) A447
Noorda, Raymond A1050
Noordam (ship) A331
Noordhoff (publishing) W642
Noos (cable TV) W232, W559
Nootens, Daniel J. A1457
Nooyi, Indra K. A1106, A1107
NOP Research Group W620, W621
Nopco (chemicals) W256
Nopri stores W165
NOR PAC P690
Nora Industrier P236
Noranda A112, P675
Norbitz, Wayne E95
Norbury, David A. E280
NorCal Electric Authority A1082
Norcross Safety Products W290
Nord, David G. A1433
Nordenberg, Mark A. P759

Norden-Ketay (aeronautical electronics) A1432
Nordhauser Ventil (automotive valves) A526
Nordhoff, Carroll D. A939
Nordhoff, Heinz W630
Nordic Empress (cruise ship) A1217
Nordica ski boots W124, W125
NordicTrack fitness equipment P637
NordiFine needles W417
Nordiject injection system W417
Nordisk Insulinlaboratorium W416
Norditropin drug W416, W417
Nordlund, D. Craig A99
Nordstrom, Blake W. A1036, A1037
Nordstrom, Bruce A. A1036, A1037
Nordstrom, Elmer A1036
Nordstrom, Erik B. A1037
Nordstrom, Everett A1036
Nordstrom, Inc. A586, A932, A1032, **A1036-A1037**, A1326
Nordstrom, James A1036
Nordstrom, J. Daniel A1037
Nordstrom, John A1036
Nordstrom, Lloyd A1036
Nordstrom, Peter E. A1037
Nordwestdeutsche Hefte (magazine) W106
Norelco brand W444
Norenberg, Peik W411
Norfleet, Byron D. A295
Norfolk & Southern Railway Company A1039
Norfolk & Western Railway Company A1038
Norfolk Southern Corporation A454, **A1038-A1039**, P582
Norfolkline B. V. W95
Norgate Apparel Manufacturing, Inc. W603
Norge appliances A278, A935
Norgrove, David W357
NORIC E268
Norikazu, Ishikawa W549
Norilsk Nickel W640
Noris, Peter D. A219
Norjen, John P121
Norlight Telecommunications P648
Norma Kamali clothing A804
Normal School P98
Norman, Greg A1194, P251
Norman, Stephen P. A143
Normile, Robert A927
Norminter (logistics) A344
Normua, Hideki W419
Normura Securities W249
Normura, Shinsaki W597
Norplant contraceptive A148
Norrett, Gene A163
Norris, Donna P541
Norris, D. W. A864
Norris, John W. A864
Norris, John W., Jr. A864, A865
Norris, Linda P81, P556
Norris, Michael J. W176, W177

Norris, Paul J. A1536, A1537
Norris, Richard C. E282
Norris, Stephen P110
Norris, William A342
Norseman mine W640
Norsk Hydro ASA A412, A583, **W410-W411**
Norsk Hydro-Elektrisk Kvaelstofaktieselskap W410
Norstar A602
Norte stores W164, W165
Nortel Inversora S.A. W575
Nortel Networks Corporation A170, A248, A404, A546, A782, A792, A898, A1240, A1256, A1298, A1357, A1528, E30, E106, E158, E252, E263, E267, E269, E292, E305, E318, P771, W122, W322, W323, **W412-W413**, W554
The North America Coal Corporation A992, A993
North American Aviation A198, A1210
North American Company (utility) P350
North American Company for Life and Health Insurance P720
North American Free Trade Agreement (1992) A394, A1112, P34, P342
North American Interior Systems A388
North American Mallory Controls A264
North American Philips W444
North American Rockwell A198, A1210
North American Scientific, Inc. E254
North American Title Company, Inc. A862, A863
North American Vaccine A236
North American Van Lines A1038, P535
North American Vehicle Operations A300
North Atlantic Energy Corporation A1041
North Brothers (insulation) A1004
The North Carolina Baptist Hospitals P768
North Carolina National Bank A226
North Carolina Natural Gas Corporation A1166, A1167
North Carolina State University E47
North Central Bronx Hospital P369
North Central Oil E268
North Coast Energy, Inc. E254
North Douglas Distributors (food distribution) A1350
North Electric (phone equipment) A1318
The North Face, Inc. (outdoor gear) A1474, A1475
North German Postal Confederation W204
North, Harvey A103

North, Jack W. (State Farm Insurance) A1331, P459
North, John Ringling (Ringling Bros. and Barnum & Bailey Circus) P188
North Ltd. (forestry and mining) W488
North of Scotland Hydro-Electric Board W522
North Pacific Bank E213
North Pacific Grain Growers P122
North Pacific Group, Inc. P690
North Pacific Paper Company A1518
North, Richard C. W545
North Safety Products Business W290
North Shore Community Bank and Trust E318
North Shore Health System P690
North Shore-Long Island Jewish Health System P690
North Side Foods Corporation A1290, A1291
North Star Recycling A325, P105
North Star Steel A324, A325, P104, P105
North West Company (fur trading) W270
North Western (railroad) A1422
NorthCenter Foodservice A1109
Northcutt, Scott M. A607
Northeast Airlines A478
Northeast Blanco Unit A482
Northeast Looseleaf P170
Northeast Utilities A418, A498, **A1040-A1041**
Northern & Shell plc W621
Northern Arizona Light & Power A1138
Northern Bank Limited (Ireland) W382, W383
Northern Border Partners A518
Northern Border Pipeline A552, E298
Northern California Highway A240, P74
Northern Digital, Inc. A545
Northern Electric and Gas A1114, P340, P341, P396, P676
Northern Electric and Manufacturing Company. See Nortel Networks Corporation
Northern Energy Resources Company A1082
Northern Engineering Industries W496
Northern Illinois Gas Company A1030, A1031
Northern Indiana Fuel and Light Company, Inc. A1035
Northern Indiana Public Service Company A1034, A1035
Northern Natural Gas of Omaha A552, A556, A752
Northern Ohio Power and Light A598
Northern Pacific Railway A308, A310, A1518

Northern Radio Limited A309
Northern Reflections (women's apparel) A1470
Northern Securities Company A308
Northern Star potato products P674
Northern States Power Company A418, A1028, A1040, A1542, A1543
Northern Telecom. See Nortel Networks Corporation
Northern Trust Corporation A748, **A1042-A1043**, A1048
Northfield Freezing Systems A612, A1550
Northlake Foods P512
Northland Cranberries, Inc. P380
Northland shopping center (Detroit) A1352
Northridge, Nigel W240, W241
Northrock Resources A1438
Northrop Grumman Corporation A116, A644, **A1044-A1045**, E183, E241, E277
Northrop, John A882, A1044
Northrup, King & Company W414
Northstar Energy Corporation A482
Northstar oil field A132
Northumbrian Water W558
Northwest Aerospace Training Corporation A1046, A1047
Northwest Airlines Corporation A106, A138, A302, A428, A478, **A1046-A1047**, P34, P474, W71, W79, W316
Northwest Bancorp Inc. A1508
Northwest Grocery Company P488
Northwest Investment P350
Northwest Pipeline Corporation A1529
Northwestern Flavors, Inc. A1526, A1527
Northwestern Mutual Life Insurance A218, A922, **A1048-A1049**, A1230, P320, **P376-P377**, P690
Northwestern National Bank of Minneapolis A1508
Northwestern University A948, P268, P326, **P378-P379**, P691, P700
Norton (abrasives) W506
Norton, David (Iomega) A778
Norton, David (Starwood Hotels) A1329
Norton, Matthew P655
Norton McNaughton brand A839
Norton, Mike P297
Norton, Patrick H. A855
Norton, R. P488
Norton, Robert W. A1119
Norton Simon A212
Nortrust Realty Management, Inc. A1043
Nortz, Richard A. A1051
Norvasc drug A1118, A1119
Norvik, Harald W519
Norvir drug A58, A59

Norwalk Truck Lines A1548
Norwegian Caribbean Lines A330
Norwegian Cruise Lines A330
Norwegian Hydro-Electric Nitrogen
  Corporation W410
Norwest Bank P130
Norwest Venture Capital
  Management, Inc. A1509
Norwestra (office products) A653
Norwich Inn & Spa P318, P319
Norwich Union PLC A688
Norzink Zink Smelter W488
Nosbusch, Keith D. A1211
Noski, Charles H. A203
Nosler, Peter P597
Notarnicola, James A267
Notebaert, Richard C. A1362, A1363
Nothwang, Joseph R. A711
Noticiero Financiero (TV
  show) P80
Noto, Lucio A. A576
Nottenburg, Richard N. E247
Nouvelles Frontières W460, W461
Nova car P366
NOVA Chemicals Corporation A518,
  P238, W118
NOVA Corporation A1444, A1445
NovaCare (rehab hospitals) A698
NovaCare Rehabilitation E286
Novack, Jerold E. E253
Novack, Kenneth J. A181
Novagas Clearinghouse (natural gas
  marketer) A518
Novak, David C. A1404, A1405
Novak, Paul A303
Novak, Paula P704
NovaMed Eyecare, Inc. E255
Novant Health, Inc. P691
Novantrone drug A148, E71, E218
Novartis AG A234, A640, A1180,
  E193, E255, W118, W308,
  W414-W415, W492
Novell, Inc. A747, A**1050-A1051**,
  A1232, A1357, E33, E42, E252,
  P136, P137, P337
Novelli, William D. P29, P529
Novellus E149
Novelly, P. A. "Tony" P542
Noven Pharmaceuticals, Inc. E255
Noveon, Inc. P691
Novich, Neil S. A1225
Novik, Steven P261, P646
Novikov, Anatoly W347
Novinski, Edward J. A323
NOVO Group, Inc. P73
Novo Nordisk A/S W314,
  W416-W417
Novolin drug W417
NovoNorm drug W416, W417
NovoPen injection system W417
Novopoint.com A324
NovoRapid drug W417
NovoSeven drug W416, W417
Novost cigarettes W241
Novotel hotels W58, W59
Novus A1300
NOW cigarettes A1204, A1205

Noxell A1164
Noxzema skin care A1164, A1165
Noyce, Robert A82, A760, A1378,
  P444
Nozari, Moe S. A977
Nozue, Toshiaki W199
Nozzolillo, Anthony A825
NPD/Nielsen Inc. A66
NRB (woven filaments) P342
NRG Energy, Inc. A1028, A1082,
  A1542, A1543
NRM (publishing) W626
NRT Inc. P692
NRT (real estate) A338
NSC International (binding and
  laminating) P170
NSI Chemicals Group A1004
NSM (fertilizer) W410
NSP. *See* Northern States Power
NSpire computers P545
NSS Newsagents W240
NSTAR A554
NTB National Tire & Battery A1264,
  A1265
NTC Capital A1043
NTELOS Inc. E255
NTL Inc. (cable operations) A390,
  A1473, W152, W232
NTT Corporation. *See* Nippon
  Telegraph and Telephone
  Corporation
NTT DATA Corporation W401,
  W420
NTT DoCoMo, Inc. W272, W400,
  W401, **W418-W419**, W420, W502
NTUC Fairprice Cooperative P243
NTV (television) W242
NU Enterprises, Inc. A1041
Nu Horizons Electronics
  Corporation **E97**, E256
Nuance Communications,
  Inc. P454, P455
Nuclear Corporation of
  America A1052
Nucleus (company) W428
Nucor Corporation A324,
  A**1052-A1053**
Nucorp Energy E87
Nucorp (oil and gas) A560, P180
Nuevo Energy Company A68
Nuevo Federal (laundry
  detergents) A486
Nuflor drug A1251
Nugelec fire detection
  systems A431
Nugent, Jeffrey M. A1200, A1201
Nugent, John J. A262, A263
Nugent, Robert J. A784, A785
Nugent, Ron P347
Numerical Technologies W186
NUMMI. *See* New United Motor
  Manufacturing, Inc.
Nunan, William C. A659
Nunes, John W108
Nunez, Juan A1523
Nunn, Kent A583
Nunn, Thomas W. E64

Nuns of the Third Order of St.
  Dominic P117
Nuon (utility) E254
Nuovo Pignone W216
Nuprin over-the-counter drug A148
Nur Die legwear A1243
NUR Touristik W310, W344
NURAD microwave antennae A502
NÜRNBERGER Beteiligungs-
  AG W201
Nurse Betty (movie) A1450
Nursery Rhyme brand P77
Nurseryland Garden Centers A1130
Nursoy baby formula A148
nurun Inc. (Web
  development) W470, W471
Nusbaum, Edward E. P207
Nusbaum, John P57
Nusbaum, Sandra L. A1489, E138,
  E314
Nussbaum, Aaron A1264
Nussbaum, Bennett A303
Nussbaum, David B. E102
Nussbaum, Jay H. A1067
Nussbaum, John L. E104
Nussbaum, Paul A1540
Nussbaum, Samuel R. A179
Nussdorf, Bernard P709
Nussdorf, Glenn P709
Nussdorf, Lawrence C. P576
Nussdorf, Ruth P709
Nussrallah, John R. A1407
Nusz, Thomas B. A311
Nut & Honey Crunch cereal A817
Nutmeg Industries sports
  wear A1474, A1475
The NutraSweet Company (artificial
  sweetener) A984, A1122, A1300
Nutrena Mills A324, P104
NutriGrain products A814, A816,
  A817
Nutro pet foods P394
Nutropin drug A640, A641
Nutt, Roy A404
Nutt, William J. E149
Nutter Butter cookies A843
Nuvera Fuel Cells, Inc. P55
Nu-West Industries, Inc. W66, W67
NVIDIA Corporation E256
NVision (TV distribution) A70
N. W. Ayer & Partners
  (advertising) P72, P73, P551
NWA (holding company) A1046
NY Wired (TV show) P372
Nyberg, Donald A. A1375
Nyberg, Lars A1012, A1013
NYCE Corporation (payment
  systems) A596
Nye, Bob P633
Nye, Erle A1417, P471
NYFIX, Inc. E256
NYLCare managed health A90,
  P226
NYLIFE Administration
  Corporation A1017, P371
Nylon A534
NYMEX A518

NYMU. *See* New York Marine Underwriters
Nynas Petroleum W438
NYNEX A312, A1472, W152
NYPD Blue (TV show) A60, A61
NyQuil cold medicine A1164, A1165
Nyquist, Laura K. A1013
Nyrop, Donald A1046
NYS&EB A1018
NYSE. *See* New York Stock Exchange, Inc.

O

O, The Oprah Magazine A700, A701, P218, P228, P229, P625
Oak Farms dairy A56, A1339
Oak Hill Capital Partners P748
Oak Industries (optical components) A434
Oak Ridge defense community P448, P449
Oak Ridge National Laboratory P70
Oak Ridge Research Institute A818
Oak Technology, Inc. (wireless chips) A410, E**98**, E257
Oakes, Dennis A91
Oakland Athletics (baseball team) P307
Oakland Preserving Company A470
The Oakland Raiders (football team) A64, P356, P357
Oakland University P773
Oakleaf Waste Management A548
Oakley, A. Allen A1135
Oakley, Annie A344
Oakley, Graham W357
Oakley, Inc. E**99**, E257
Oakley, Peter W117
Oakley, Robert A. A1009, P365, P685
Oakley, Ronald W. A611
Oaktree Capital Management E58, P412, P614
OakTree Health Plan A1076
O&M Funding Corporation A1071
OAO Technology Solutions, Inc. A1233
Oasis consortium A132
Oasis International Group (advertising) W198
Oasis (oil) A1460
Oasis Outsourcing, Inc. A1488
Oasis Pipe Line A1464
Oasis (resort) W472
Oates, Bill A1329
Oates, Edward A1066
OB Lager W289
O.B. McClintock Company A488
Obata, Kazuei W305
Obee, Robert W. A1207
Ober, Edgar A976
Oberland (glass maker) W506
Oberlander, Michael I. A295
Oberly, Kathryn A. A562, A563, P182, P183, W222
Obermayer, Jeffrey L. A279
Obernesser, David J. E187

Oberschmidt, Mike, Jr. A1437
Oberther Card Systems A924
Obetz, Jere E294
Obi do-it-yourself stores W588, W589
Objectif Net W312
ObjecTime Ltd. (software tools) E110
Objective Systems Integrators A98
O'Boisies potato chips A814
Obourn, Candy M. A525
O'Boyle, Thomas W. A527
O'Briant, Stonie A497
O'Brien, Beth P119
O'Brien, Bob D. P583
O'Brien, Dan (Ascencion Health) P57
O'Brien, Daniel R. (Household International) A735
O'Brien, David E55
O'Brien, George A. A771
O'Brien, James J. (Ashland) A201
O'Brien, Jim (Boston Celtics) A281
O'Brien, Jim (Texas Pacific) P475, P744
O'Brien, John F. (Allmerica Financial) A125
O'Brien, John (Mashantucket Pequot) P319, P667
O'Brien, John M. (New York Times) A1021
O'Brien, Joseph G. E302
O'Brien, Mark J. A1179
O'Brien, Michael A. (Pulte Homes) A1179
O'Brien, Michael D. (Amkor Technology) A163
O'Brien, Michael D. (Broadwing) A293
O'Brien, Morgan E. A1026, A1027
O'Brien, Patrick T. P61, P546
O'Brien, Rosanne A1045
O'Brien, Thomas R. A621
O'Brien, William (Alexander Grant) P206
O'Brien, William F. (ADC Telecommunications) A71
O'Bryan, Kathleen E211
O'Bryant, Allen A93
Observer (newspaper) W340
Obsession fragrance P100, P101
Obsidian (polishing) A188
Obst, Robert E90, E240
O'Callaghan, Mike W111
Ocarina of Time (video game) W394
Occidental Chemical Corporation A1060
Occidental Petroleum Corporation A184, A742, A900, A950, A974, A**1054**-A**1055**, A1060, A1276, E39, P604, P704, W136, W424
Occidente W568
Océ N.V. (copiers) A746, A747
Ocean Spray Cranberries, Inc. A1104, A1105, P**380**-P**381**, P692

Ocean Systems (sonar products) A846
Ochs, Adolph A1020
Ockleshaw, David J. A355
Ocoma Foods Division A1418
O'Connell, John T. P179, P603
O'Connell, Mark F. E237
O'Connell, Maureen A233
O'Connell, Robert J. A923, P321, P667
O'Connell, Tim P644
O'Connor, Carolyn E293
O'Connor, Deborah A. A1273
O'Connor, Dennis E249
O'Connor, Flannery P757
O'Connor, Jack M. (American Home Products) A149
O'Connor, J. Dennis P451
O'Connor, John J. (JPI) P648
O'Connor, John J. (State University of New York) P461
O'Connor, John J. (Texaco) A1377
O'Connor, Kevin E161
O'Connor, Thomas M. (Publix) A1177, P403
O'Connor, Thomas P. (Springs Industries) A1317, P453
O'Connor, William G. E130, E303
OCR Systems (software) A76
Octagon A772, A773
Octavia car W631
Octel Communications A898
Octopus Publishing W478
Ocuflox ophthalmic products A119
Odaira, Namihei W260
Odaka, Toshihiko W261
Odam's wharf W568
Odd Lots stores A260, A261
Odden, George C. A1211
O'Dea, Marita A1015
Odeco Drilling A884
Odeen, Philip A. A1413
Odell, Carl A126
O'Dell, Charles A1296
O'Dell, Margot E127
O'Dell, Richard A1549
O'Dell, Walden W. A488, A489
Odense Staalskibsvaerft A/S Group W95
Odeon theater chain W472
Odessa Exploration E79, E227
Odetics, Inc. A1336
Odgen, Mike W253
Odland, Steve A208, A209
Odol Saic A386
Odom, Rod D., Jr. A249
O'Donnell, Carol P686
O'Donnell, Charles P373
O'Donnell, Eugene A1059
O'Donnell, Francis E293
O'Donnell, James D. (Metropolitan Transportation Authority) P335
O'Donnell, James P. (ConAgra) A409
O'Donnell, Lawrence, III A1505
O'Donnell, Michael W. A1035
O'Donnell, Rosie A774

O'Donnell, Terrence A1381
O'Donnell-Keenan, Niamh W263
O'Donoghue, Leslie A. W67
O'Donoghue, P. Redmond W637
O'Donovan, Kathleen A. W291
O'Doul's nonalcoholic malt
  beverage A175
Odre, Steven M. A161
Odrich, Michael J. A861
O'Dwyer, Mary Ann P611
Odyssée (financial
  consulting) W100
Odyssey Investment Partners A676
Odyssey minivan W265
Odyssey Sports A1446
OEA (aerospace operations) A662
OEC Compression E210
Oehme, Rick O. A139
Oei, Gia A601
Oels, Udo W119
Oesterreicher, James E. A790
Oettinger, Julian A. A1493
O'Farrill, Romulo W582
Off 5th department stores A1238
OFF! bug repellents A1246, A1247,
  P432, P433, P722
Off-Highway Braking Systems A326
Office America stores A1324
Office Club stores A1056
Office Depot, Inc. A1056-A1057,
  A1058, A1324, E268
Office Mart office supply
  stores A1324
Office of Federal Housing
  Enterprise Oversight A626
Office of Naval Research P456
Office World stores A1058
OfficeMax, Inc. A636, A830, A870,
  A1058-A1059
OfficeTeam (temporary
  help) A1208, A1209
Officeworks stores W172
*Official PlayStation
  Magazine* W238, W239
The Official Xbox Magazine W238
Offield family A1526
OFFITBANK Holdings A1486
Offshore Pipeline A940
O'Flynn, Thomas M. A1175
OFTEL. *See* UK Office of
  Telecommunications
Ogaki, Koji W321
O'Gara-Hess & Eisenhardt (vehicle
  armoring) E29, E158
Ogden Corporation A190, A440
Ogden, Kim P65
Ogden, Peter W176
Ogden, W. B. A1422
Ogden's (tobacco) W282
Ogilvie Mills A192
Ogilvie, Scott A241, P75
Ogilvy & Mather Worldwide
  (advertising) A252, W646, W647
Ogilvy, David W646
OgilvyOne Worldwide W647
Oglethorpe Power
  Corporation P692

O'Gorman, Joseph A485
O'Grady, Barbara E192, P619
Ogura, Toshiyuki W375
Oh, Harry E123
Oh Henry! candy A709
O.H. Ingram Company
  (investments) A756, P244
Oh, Kye Hwan A189
Oh Teik Tatt W539
Oh! Zone stores P577
O'Halleran, Michael D. A183
O'Halloran, Deborah A995
O'Hanley, Ronald A955
O'Hanlon, James P. A499
O'Hara, John P425
O'Hara, Kevin J. A867
O'Hare, Dean R. A357
Ohashi, Nobuo W373
Ohashi, Tetsuro W399
Ohashi, Yoji W81
Ohboshi, Kouji W418, W419
Ohga, Norio W551
Ohio Agricultural and Mechanical
  College P382
Ohio Alloy Steels A1386
The Ohio Company (broker) A592
Ohio Edison Company A598, A599,
  A992
Ohio Farm Bureau
  Federation A1008, P364
Ohio Farmers Insurance
  Company P693
Ohio Health Choice Ventures,
  Inc. A695
Ohio Lottery Commission P693
The Ohio Mattress Company P442
Ohio No. 11 Mine A417
The Ohio Oil Company A1460
Ohio Power Company A140
Ohio Public Service A598
The Ohio State
  University P382-P383, P693
Ohio State University College of
  Medicine P44
Ohio Valley-Clarksburg
  (pharmaceuticals) A320
Ohio-American Water
  Company A155
OhioHealth P694
Ohkawa, Yoshihiko W305
Ohle, David A1277
Ohliger, Karen J. P39
Ohlsson's Lager beer W552
Ohnishi, Minoru W234, W235
O'Hoy, Trevor W231
Ohrstrom, George A502
Ohrt, Peg E187
OhSe brand P185
ÖIAG W424
Oil Center Tool A612
Oil of Olay beauty care A1164
OIS Optical Imaging Systems P212
OK Grocery P198
Oka, Takeshi W327
Okada, Shingo W397
Okada, Takahiko W237
Okamoto, Kunie W397

Okamoto, Osamu W327
Okamoto, Toshio W294
Okamura, Tadashi W611
O'Kane, Hugh E233
O'Kane, Kevin M. E233
Okarma, Jerome D. A803
Okauchi, Jitsuo W187
Okawa, Isao W526, W527
Okazaki, Yushin W297
O'Keefe, Mary A. A1163
O'Kelley, Ronald L. A1333
O'Kelly, Sean T. W539
Oken, Brian R. A727
Oken, Marc D. A227
Oki Electric Industry Company,
  Limited E173, **W420-W421**
Oki, Kibataro W420
Okidata A1357
Okihara, Yoji W327
Okla Homer Smith (cribs) P518
Oklahoma City Blazers (hockey
  team) P606
Oklahoma City Junction Railway
  Company A309
Oklahoma Natural Gas
  Company A1065
Oklahoma State Education
  Employees Group Insurance
  Board A84
Okocim beer W163
The Okonite Company (copper
  wire) A896
Okubo, Sunao W515
Okubo, Tsutomu W597
Okuda, Hiroshi W614, W615
Okumoto, Yozo W375
Okvath, John J., III A667
Olander, Stanley J., Jr. E186
Olay cosmetics A1164, A1165
Old Age & Survivors' Insurance
  Revolving Fund A315, P97
Old Bushmills Irish Whiskey A296
Old College Inn clothing A666
Old Country Buffet P562
Old Dominion Foundation P541
Old El Paso Mexican foods A1136,
  A1137
Old English home care W477
Old Forester bourbon A296
Old Guard Group, Inc. P693
Old Holborn tobacco W241
Old Jamaica Ginger Beer A1105
Old Kent Financial A592
Old Mill cereal A768
Old Milwaukee beer P428, P721
Old Mutual (financial
  services) A1236
Old Navy Clothing Company A634,
  A635, P608
Old Spice men's products A1165
Old Time brands P423
Olde English beer P428
OLDE Financial Corporation A681
Olde Financial Discount
  (broker) A680
Olde New England brownies A815
Oldenburg, William R. A511

Oldham, Larry C. E260
Olds, George R. A135
Olds Motor Works A1052
Olds, Ransom A1052, P86
Oldsmobile A476, A650, P72, P86, P555, P596, P606, P631, P706, P733
O'Leary, Christopher D. A649
O'Leary, James A1447
O'Leary, Patrick J. A1321
O'Leary, Robert C. A443, P147, P585
Olesen, Douglas E. P70
Oleszczuk, Andrew J. A1403
Olga brand lingerie A1499
Olibra appetite suppressant A648
Olien, David W. P501
Olima Holdings AG A493
OliMan (telecom holding company) W422
Olimón, Fernando W441
Olin Corporation A**1060**-A**1061**
Olin, Franklin A1060
Olin Industries A290
Olin, John A1060
Olin, Spencer A1060
Olinger Distributing P616
Oliniger, Donald D. A733
Olinkraft A1060
Oliva, L. Jay P689
Olive Garden restaurants A288, A464, A465, A648, P669
Olivennes, Denis W625
Oliver, David R. P311
Oliver, Jerry E310
Oliver, Melvin L. P195
Oliver, S. Paul A1137
Oliver, Susan M. A165
Oliver, Tom W545
Olivera, Armando J. A625
Olivetti, Camillo W422
Olivetti S.p.A. W204, W338, W**422**-W**423**, W450, W574
Olivetto, Adriano W422
Olivié, Marc R. A153
Olivier, David M. A149
Ollila, Jorma W406, W407
Olmstead, Peter J. A643
Olofsson, Lars W389
O'Loughlin, William B. P175
Olsen, Don H. P239
Olsen, Eric C. A849
Olsen, Gary L. P37
Olsen, Robert A209
Olson, Cindy K. A553
Olson, Frank A. A710
Olson, Gaylin L. A1415
Olson, Gene L. P203
Olson, Jack A. A73
Olson, Julie P79, P555
Olson, Linda A741, P241, P636
Olson, Mark W. P187
Olson, Peter W. W127
Olson, Robert W. A355
Olsson, Arne W55
Olsy (computer services) W422

Olveh (civil servants' aid group) W64
Olver, Richard L. W137
Olwen Direct Mail Limited P506
Olympia & York (property development) W156, W474
Olympia beer P428
Olympia concert hall (Paris) W624
Olympia Dam uranium deposit W640
Olympia exhibition hall (London) W434
Olympic Consolidated Industries (tires) W428
Olympic Foods (juices) P771
Olympic paint A1152
Olympic Venture Partners E287
Olympics P262
Olympus Real Estate Corporation P232, P233
OM Group, Inc. E257
Omachinski, David L. A1069
Omae, Masayoshi W531
Omae, Suguru W81
Omaha Healthcare System, Inc. A695
Omaha Property and Casualty Insurance Company P349
O'Mahoney, Conor P. E57
O'Malley, John P., III P771
O'Malley, Kevin A63
O'Malley, Thomas D. A1129
Omar, Hamed A1449
O'Mara, Frank A. A129
Ombrelle sun protection W342
O'Meara, Mark P251
O'Meara, Vicki A. A1223
Omega watch W562, W563
OMG. *See* OM Group, Inc.
OMI International, Ltd. A1071
Omicron packaging A1262
Omidyar, Pierre M. E54, E196
Ommen, Stanley R. A1331, P459
Omnes (communications) A1252
Omni Insurance Group, Inc. A688
Omnia (fiber-optics) E41
OmniAmerica Wireless LP A715, P233
Omnibus A710
Omnibus Budget Reconciliation Act (1993) A1448
OmniCell software A1340
Omnicom Group Inc. A**1062**-A**1063**, W198
OmniExpress (data messaging) A1183
Omnifax W190
Omniquip International A1380
OmniSky Corporation (Internet service provider) W390
OmniSource Corporation P694
Omnitel Pronto Italia S.p.A. (mobile communications) A1473, W352, W353, W422, W628
OmniTRACS A1182
OmniViz, Inc. P70, P71
Omo laundry soap W619

Omori, Yoshio W387
Omtvedt, Craig P. A619
OMV Aktiengesellschaft W**424**-W**425**, W456
On Cue stores A254
ON Semiconductor Corporation P474, P475
On the Border Mexican Grill & Cantina A288, A289
On The Go stores P577
On The Way convenience stores A1085
Onan generators A456
Onassis, Jacqueline Kennedy P416, P716
Oncap (investments) W110
ONCASPAR drug E199
Once and Again (TV show) A61
On-Center software E179
Oncogen (biotechnology) A290
Oncology.com P278
ONDEO Services (water) W559
Ondercik, Robert J. A1001
ONdigital (digital TV) W248, W249
One 2 One Personal Communications Ltd. (cellular service) W148, W152, W204, W628
O'Neal, E. Stanley A961
O'Neal, Kirkman P694
O'Neal, Rodney A477
O'Neal, Shaquille A1194, P661
O'Neal Steel, Inc. P694
Oneda, Gian W99
Oneida Ltd. (flatware) P262
Oneida Molded Plastics E279
Oneida Nation Electronics E104
O'Neil, Brian S. A219
O'Neil, Daniel J. W376
O'Neil, Evan A513
O'Neil, Timothy P. E304
O'Neill, Anthony W641
O'Neill, Bill A. W391
O'Neill, Brendan R. W279
O'Neill, Daniel J. W377
O'Neill, Leslee K. A63
O'Neill, Michael J., Jr. A357
O'Neill, Patricia E159
O'Neill, Paul H. A112
O'Neill, Peter J. P39, P534
O'Neill, Robert A., Jr. A231
O'Neill, Sean P. A183
O'Neill, Thomas J. (Parsons Brinckerhoff) P696
O'Neill, Thomas (Pricewaterhouse) A1159, P401, W463
O'Neill, Timothy J. W113
O'Neill's restaurants W545
O'Neil's department store A932
OneNetNow (online communities) P524
ONEOK Inc. A518, A**1064**-A**1065**, E235
OneSource Information Services, Inc. E**100**, E258

OneSource (investments) A348
OneSteel W128
OneTouch containers A1415
ONE-UP pump diaphragms P523
One-Way truck rental A1222
Oneworld A164, W68, W140, W302, W468
Ong, John A662
Onikul, Naum J. W645
Onishi, Yasuhiro W395
Onitsuka Tiger (shoes) A1032
Onken, Kristen W339
Onksen, William A247
Online Bidding (auctions) E45
Online Gamer (magazine) W239
Online Interactive P338
Online (Internet access) W586
On-Line Response. *See* HyperFeed Technologies, Inc.
Ono, Koichiro W81
Ono, Masatoshi W138
Ono, Nobuharu W419
Ono, Shigeo W392
Onoe, Shinichi W169
Onozato, Mitsura W601
Ontario Securities Commission W474
On-The-Way Foods Stores A1084
On-Trac (online procurement) W176
Ontrak Services A1297
Onustock, Michael R. A1525
Oode Casting W326
Oode, Gonshiro W326
Oogo, Norio W303
Oosterhoff, J. W64
Oozic 3-D music video player W180
Opal Fruit candy A915, P315
Opal (microscopes) A188
Opdyke, Richard P39, P534
OPEC. *See* Organization of Petroleum Exporting Countries
Opel AG W294
Opel vehicle A650
Opelika Industries, Inc. A1135
Open Board of Brokers A1018, P374
Open Pit Barbecue Sauce A714, P232
Open Systems Interconnect A866
OpenReady SAN system E239
OpenSky A54
OpenTV Corporation A528
Opera (purchasing) W166
Operation Joint Guardian P52
Opinac North America, Inc. A1028, A1029
Oppegaard, Grant E. P614
Oppenheimer, Deanna W. A1501
Oppenheimer, Ernest W92
Oppenheimer, Harry W92
Oppenheimer, Nicky W92
OppenheimerFunds, Inc. A922, A923, P320, P321, P667
Opperman, Mary George P584
The Oprah Winfrey Show (TV show) A334, A1476, P218, P219, P625

Oprah's Book Club P218
Grupo Oprimax A1058
OPTi (logic chips) W180
Optic Point Warenhandelsgesellschaft W310
Optical Coating Laboratory, Inc. A792
Optical Communication Products, Inc. E258
Optical Diodes A1298
Optical Micro Systems A118
Optical Village A102
Optim brand A527
Optima credit card A142, A924, P322
Optima Health Plan P726
Optima Petroleum. *See* PetroQuest Energy, Inc.
Optimedia W466, W467
Optimized Process Designs A620
Option Care, Inc. A574
Option One Mortgage Corporation A680, A681
OPTIPORE Sponge A291
Opti-Probe E300
Optisel (fulfillment services) A958
Optra laser printers A870
Optus Communications W586
Opus Corporation P695
OPUS360 Corporation (B2B site) A1233
OPW (gas pump nozzles) A502
Opzoomer, Mark A1547
The OR Group, Inc. A719
Oracle Corporation A402, A972, **A1066-A1067**, A1098, A1546, E249, E258, P278, P496, P652, W160, W164
Orag Inter AG A1380
Oral-B toothbrush A656, A657
Oram, John P637
Orange and Rockland Utilities, Inc. A418, A419, A1306
Orange Card discount drug plan W246
Orange County (California) *Register* (newspaper) P611
Orange County Title A594
Orange Crush drink W154
Orange SA (mobile phone) W76, W232, W272, W352, W628
Orangina soft drink W154
Oranjeboom beer W289
Oratis, M. W385
O'Ray, Patrick A. A743
ORBCOMM Global (commercial satellites) A788
ORBIS Corporation P673
Orbit 3.0 software E70
Orbit brand A527
Orbit gum A1526, A1527
Orbitrol brand A527
Orbitz.com P94
Orbot Instruments (inspection systems) A188
Orbtek (ophthalmic diagnostics) A234
Orcanta lingerie stores W446

Orchard Foods stores P422, P718
Orchard Select canned foods A471
Orchard Supply Hardware A1264, A1265
Orcofi W348
The Order People (third party fulfillment) A1430
Ordo (office furniture) P222
Ordway, Lucius A976
Oregon Craft & Supply A968
Oregon Farms frozen foods A608, A609
Oregon Metallurgical A116
The Oregonian (Portland) A81, P33
Ore-Ida potatoes A722, A723
O'Reilly, Anthony A722, W636, W637
O'Reilly, Anthony, Jr. W637
O'Reilly, David J. A352, A353
O'Reilly, Dennis E. A411
O'Reilly, Jim E165
O'Reilly, John W259
O'Reilly, Michael A357
OOO Orenburggazprom W243
Oreo cookies A842, A843, A1204
Orfalea, Paul J. P274
Orford Nickel and Copper Company W284
Organic (interactive services) A1062
Organics hair care products W619
Organizações Globo W582
Organization of Petroleum Exporting Countries A200, A352, A570, A1028, P340, W66, W130, W438, W592, W598
Ori, Danieli E91
Orica Limited A1152
Orico Life W464
Orient Express Hotels Ltd. A328, P108, P567
Oriental Brewery W288
Oriental Cotton Trading W602
Oriental Deli A730
Oriental Institute P497
Oriental Land Company A1496
Origin (computer services) W100
Origin Medsystems A674
Original Roadhouse Grill P562
Origins brand A565
Origins cosmetics A564
Orimulsion fuel W438
Oriole Park at Camden Yards P576
Orion Capital A688
Orion Food Systems P437
Orion Network Systems A888
Orion Pictures A962, P332
Orion Power Holdings, Inc. A418, A424, A425, A1028, E258, W598
Orissa Power Generation A88
Orkla P236, P633, W162
Orlando, Anthony H, A441
The Orlando (Florida) *Sentinel* A1402
Orlando, Joseph S. P369
Orlando Magic (basketball team) P355

A=AMERICAN BUSINESS · E=EMERGING COMPANIES · P=PRIVATE COMPANIES · W=WORLD BUSINESS

Orlando Miracle (basketball team) P355
Orleck, Sarah A305
Orluck, Steven G. A987
Orme, Jed A485
Ormes, James Merrill A248
Ormic (trucks) A992
Ormond, Paul A. A908, A909
OrNda HealthCorp A1366
Orndoff, C. Richard A905
Ornstein, Lawrence H. A133
Orologic E136
Oronoque Orchard frozen foods A609
ÖROP (marketing) W424
Oropon bating substitute A1212
O'Rourke Baking A774
O'Rourke, Bobbi E241
O'Rourke, John G. E138, E314
O'Rourke, Terrence E. A199
O'Rourke, Tracy E133
Oroweat baked goods A426, P140, W244, W618
Orr, Doug P680
Orr, James F., III P414, P415
Orr, John A741, P241
Orr, Michael P. A469
Orr, Sean F. A773
Orr, Thomas A328, P108
Orser, William S. A1167
Orsi, Bernard P429, P721
Ortega Mexican foods W388
Ortenberg, Arthur A880
Ortenzio, Robert A. E286
Orth, John F. A75
OrthAlliance, Inc. E259
Ortho (lawn and garden) A984, A1122
Ortho Pharmaceutical A160, A800
Ortho Tricyclen drug A801
Orthodontic Centers of America, Inc. E259
Ortho-Novum drug A801
Orthopedic Firm-O-Rest mattress P442
Ortiz, Carlos P205
Ortiz, Edgar A677
Ortner Freight (coal cars) A1406
Orullian, B. LaRae E64
Orville Redenbacher's popcorn A408
Orving, Jon A1527
Oryx Energy A820, A978, A1344, A1466
OS/2 operating system E42
Osaka Nomura Bank W408
Osar, Karen R. A1517
Osborn, A. T. A1278
Osborn, E. B. A530
Osborn, Merritt A530
Osborn, William A. A1043
Osborne, Burl P61
Osborne Mine W453
Osborne, Richard J. A515
Osborne, Shawn K. E307
Osbourn, Joseph A. A1357

Oscar de la Renta LTD A1499, W250
Oscar Mayer meats A842, A843, A1126
Oscar's restaurant A784
Oscilloquartz W563
Osco Drug stores A110, A111, A886
Osegueda Villaseñor, Roberto W441
OSHA. See US Occupational Safety and Health Administration
Osha, Thomas G. A293
O'Shaughnessy, James P. A1211
Oshawa Group P478, W244
O'Shea, William J. (Campbell Soup) A317
O'Shea, William T. (Lucent) A899
Osher, Bernard A658
Oshima, Fumio W199
OshKosh B'Gosh, Inc. A1068-A1069
Oshman's sporting goods stores A62, A1552, W298, W299
Osio (baths) P284
Oskin, David W. A771
OSMAC (irrigation products) A1392
Ospel, Marcel W616, W617
Osram GmbH (lighting) W536
Ostberg, A. Peter P237, P633
OsteoMed Corporation P312
Ostermilk fortified milk W246
Österreichische Mineralölverwaltung W424
Ostin, Mo P167
Ostling, Paul J. A563, P183, W223
Ostrander, Daryl A82
Ostrander, Gregg A. P674
Ostrov, Robert A1411, P485, P749
O'Sullivan Industries Holdings, Inc. (furniture) A1188
O'Sullivan, Michael B. P325
Oswald, Gerhard W517
Ota, Tadashi W81
Ota, Yoshiaki W299
Ota, Yoshikatsu W368, W369
Otake Trading E58
Otake, Yoshiki A93
Otard cognac W109
OTC quotation system P353
Otellini, Paul S. A761
o.tel.o Internet provider W352, W504
Otis, Clarence, Jr. A465
Otis Elevator Company A446, A1432, A1433, W570
O'Toole, J. Denis A735
O'Toole, Tom A741, P241
Otosan (cars) W318
Otoyol-Iveco (buses and trucks) W318
Otsuka, Kazuhiko W603
Ottawa Financial A592
Ottawa Senators (hockey team) P360, P361
Ottawa Sun (newspaper) W471
Ottaway family A506
Ottaway, James H., Jr. A507
Ottestad, John Ove W411
Otto family A1314

Otto, Heinz-J. A1073
Otto, Lawrence A145
Otto, Michael A1315, W426, W427
Otto, Stephanie R. A681
Otto Versand GmbH & Company A1314, W426-W427
Otto, Werner W426
Otto-Sumisho W426, W427
Ottum, Jeff P723
Ouch! gum A1527
Ouchi, Manabu W81
Ouellet, Gaston W75
Ouellette, Gilles G. W113
Ouellette, Tim P143
Our Family brand foods A994, A995
Our Own Hardware P594
Our Price music stores W622
Oursons biscuits W193
Out & Out restaurants W639
Outback Steakhouse, Inc. A1109
Outboard Marine A298, A875, P294, P614, W132
Outcault, Richard A294
Outdoor Discovery Schools (catalog) P301
Outdoor Industry Group A852
Outdoor Products W604
Outdoor Sports Industries A294
Outdoor World stores P550
Outerbridge Crossing P399
Outhwaite, Richard W336
Outlaw car care products A1096
Outlet Stores lingerie A1499
Outokumpu W488
Outsource International, Inc. E125
Outters, Maria W171
Outwin, Edson A444
Ovaciones (Mexico newspaper) W582
Ovaltine beverage W414, W415
OVATION cable network A1020
Ovations (health coverage) A1434, A1435
OvenWorks A1415
Ovenworks brands P546
Overbeck, Gregg R. A1139
Overcash, Darrell P317, P666
Overdyke, Jere C., Jr. A1145
Overend, Mark G. A1449
Overexposed (movie) P219
Overgard, Mark A255
Overhage, Chris A1359
Overland Energy (oil) A1548
Overnite Transportation Company A1422, A1423
Overseas Telecommunications Commission W586
Ovid Technologies, Inc. (information retrieval) W642
OVIDE drug E89, E240
Ovitz, Michael A1496, P524
Øvlisen, Mads W417
OW Office Warehouse A1058
Owatonna Canning A354
Owen, Claude A492
Owen, Diane A723

Owen, Gary J. E290
Owen Graduate School of Management P763
Owen Healthcare, Inc. A320, A321
Owen, Henry Clay P757
Owen, John (Avon) A217
Owen, John P. (Kmart) A831
Owen, Kim P710
Owen, Laura N. A71
Owen, Russell H. A405
Owen, Scott W. A1231
Owen Steel A396
Owen, Terry L. W285
Owen-Jones, Lindsay W342, W343
Owens & Minor, Inc. A156, A320, A444, A**1070**-A**1071**, A1112
Owens Bottle Machine Corporation A1074
Owens Corning A356, A434, A**1072**-A**1073**, A1074
Owens, Craig W195
Owens, David A1417
Owens, Donald P150
Owens, Jack B. A521, P169
Owens, James W. A333
Owens, Jesse P382, P693, W62
Owens, Marilyn E72
Owens, Michael P624
Owens, Otho A1070
Owens, Robert W. A1345
Owen's supermarkets A845
Owens, Virginia E66, E210
Owens, William T. A699
Owens Yacht A298
Owens-Illinois, Inc. A434, A836, A837, A908, A1072, A**1074**-A**1075**, P282, P283
Owings, Nathaniel P448
Owings, Steven H. E118
Ownes, Ann E232
Owyang, King A1483
Oxfam P79
Oxford Automotive, Inc. A526, P695
Oxford Health Plans, Inc. A**1076**-A**1077**, P474, P475, P744
Oxford Information Technology W621
Oxford Life Insurance Company A134, A135
Oxo bouillon A316
OXO cutlery P91, P775
Oxy Co. W476
Oxy Vinyls, LP A1054
OxyChem. See Occidental Chemical Corporation
OxyContin drug P707
Oxygen Media, Inc. P218, P510, P511
Oy. See entry under primary company name
Oyster Creek nuclear plant A668
Ozaki, Akio W97
Ozaki, Joseph P536
Ozaki, Yukitaka W599
Ozan, Terrence W161
Ozawa, Minoru W531

Özaydinli, Bülend F. W319
Ozello, Jim E227
Ozment, Tim P669
Ozujsko Pivo beer W289

P

PA Consulting Goup, Ltd. P54
Pablum baby food A723
Pabst Brewing Company P428, P721
PACCAR Inc. A456, A1010, A**1078**-A**1079**
Pace Arrow motor homes A604, A605
Pace Companies (engineering) A786
The Pace Consultants, Inc. A787
Pace, David A. A1195
PACE discount warehouse A436, A830
Pace Foods (picante sauce) A316
Pace Holdings A858
Pace, Hugh D. A665
PACE Mechanical Services, Inc. A545
Pacer Electronics A176
Pachappa Orange Growers P464
Pacheco, Luis W439
Pacheco, Manuel T. P758
Pachino, Barton P. A813
Pacific Aero Products A272
Pacific Automotive W429
Pacific Bell A1244, A1245
Pacific Brands (consumer goods) W428, W429
Pacific Car & Foundry A1078
Pacific Century CyberWorks Limited W152, W586, W602
Pacific Coast Steel A256
Pacific Color Connection P506
Pacific Corinthian Life P384
Pacific Crossing One W358
Pacific Cycle A298
Pacific Dunlop Limited A572, P264, W**428**-W**429**
Pacific Electro Dynamics A1060
Pacific Enterprises. See Sempra Energy
Pacific Far East Lines (shipping) A380, A420
Pacific Financial Products, Inc. P385
Pacific Gas & Electric Company. See PG&E Corporation
Pacific Generation A1082, A1542
Pacific Greystone (home builders) A862
Pacific Gulf Properties Inc. E259
Pacific Hydro A140
Pacific Indemnity Company A356, A357
Pacific Institute for Women's Health P78, P79
Pacific Insurance Company, Limited A379
Pacific LifeCorp P384, P385, P695
Pacific Lighting A1266

Pacific Light & Power A532
The Pacific Lumber Company A930, A931
Pacific Medical Group, Inc. A323
Pacific Metals Company W530
Pacific Mills A306
Pacific Mutual Holding Company P**384**-P**385**, P695
Pacific Northwest Laboratory P70
Pacific Power & Light Company A1082, A1083
Pacific Refining W128
Pacific Rock Products A1114, P396
Pacific Scientific (electric motors) A462
Pacific Select Distributors, Inc. P385, P695
Pacific Southwest Airlines A1442
Pacific Sunwear of California, Inc. E**101**, E259
Pacific Telecom A1082
Pacific Telecommunications Company A1186
Pacific Telesis Group A1244, A1245
Pacific Western Extruded Plastics E272
Pacific Wine Partners A422
PacifiCare Health Systems, Inc. A**1080**-A**1081**
PacifiCorp A**1082**-A**1083**, A1138, A1542, W522, W523
Pacific-Sierra Research (defense systems) A526
Pacini, Raymond J. E169
Pacioli, Luca P182, W222
Packaged Ice, Inc. A1338
Packaging Corporation of America A1368
Packard Bell A1002, W150, W386, W508, W570
Packard, David A98, A712
Packard, Ralph K. A1469, P505, P764
Packard, Susan A569
Packer, Kerry P238, W586
Packer, Richard A. E144, E320
Packwood, Geoff W. A719
PacSun. See Pacific Sunwear of California, Inc.
Pacther, Marc P451
Pac-West Telecomm, Inc. A1233
Paczkowski, George W. A413
Paddington W206
Paddock, James S. A117
Paden, A. Gayle P463
Padgett, Nick E220
Padgett, Pamela A687
Padilla, James J. A617
Padmanabham, Gobi R. A1003
Padrón, Honorio J. A571
Paganie, John E. A599
Pagano, Joe A255
Page, Charles W388
Page Communications Engineers A1044
Page, George W388
Page, Gregory R. A325, P105

Page, Mark L. A1101
Page, Stephen F. A1433
Page Time (wireless
  messaging) A72
PageMaker software A76, A77
Pagliari, Paul W523
Paglione, Vincenzo W439
Pagonis, William G. A1265
Pahl, Brian L. A705
Pai, Lou L. A553
Paine Webber Group Inc. A356,
  A394, A646
Paine Webber Inc. P290, W616
PairGain Technologies (DSL) A70
Paisano Partners Program E167
Paisley, Thomas E., III A1147
Paiz (food retailer) W498
The Palace of Auburn Hills (sports
  arena) P212
Palace of Versailles W506
Palazzo, Richard V. A381
Palchak, Joseph P. A527
Paley, Carl E95
Paley, Sam A334
Paley, William A334
Palicio, Sandy W181
Palindrome software A1260, P440
Palisades nuclear plant A376
Paliwal, Dinesh C. W55
Palka, Thomas M. E96
Pall, Brain A671
Pall Mall cigarettes A618, W143
Palladium Equity Partners P90
Pallas, Tamela E. A377
Palm Beach (Florida) *Daily
  News* P147
The Palm Beach (Florida)
  Post A443, P147
Palm Beach men's clothes A691
Palm Education Pioneers
  Program P454
Palm, Gregory K. A661
Palm, Inc. A54, A400, P454
Palma, Gianfranco A1149
Palmas del Mar Properties A930,
  A931
Palmaven, SA W439
Palmer, Arnold P250, P251, P298
Palmer, Chauncey A716, P234
Palmer G. Lewis A446
Palmer Home Collection
  furniture P299
Palmer, James F. A273
Palmer, Judith G. P638
Palmer, Kay J. A789
Palmer, Page A799
Palmer, Stanton A1294
Palmer, Vicki R. A385
Palmeri, Michael V. A1139
Palmisano, Larry A983
Palmisano, Samuel J. A764, A765
Palmolive Botanicals personal care
  products A387
The Palmolive Company A386
Palmore, Roderick A. A1243
PalmPilot A54
Palmquist, Mark P123

Palo Alto Research Center A1544
Palo Alto Technologies E31
Palo, Robert T. P577
Paloma Picasso fragrances W343
Palomar Systems E56
P.A.L.S. customer loyalty
  program P394
Palsho, Dorothea Coccoli A507
Palumbo, Thomas P769
PAM cooking spray A408, A409
Pam group W588
Pamida Holdings Corporation
  (discount stores) A1282
Pampers diapers A1164, A1165,
  W308
Pamplin Broadcasting P711
Pamplin Historical Park P711
Pamplin, Robert B., Jr. P711
Pamplin, Robert B., Sr. P711
Pan American Petroleum and
  Transport W136
Pan American World Airways A478,
  A740, A802, A1288, A1420, A1536,
  P312, P388, P446, W344, W468
Pan beer W163
Pan Glaze P164
PANACO, Inc. E260
Panama cigars W283
Pan-American Sports
  Network A715, P233
PanAmSat Corporation (satellite
  network) A736
Panasonic E117
Panasonic electronic
  products W360
Panatier, Michael J. A1129
Panavision Inc. (movie
  cameras) A902, A903, P304, P305
Panayotopoulis, Dimitri A1165
P & O (cruise operator) W249
Panda Energy International A1174
P&C Foods supermarkets A1094
P&G. *See* The Procter & Gamble
  Company
P&H Mining Equipment A806
Pandit, Vikram S. A989
P&O Nedlloyd Container
  Line W434
P&O Princess Cruises plc W434
Panduit Corporation A176
Panek, James P. A641
Panel Concepts A726
PanelBook (projection devices) E73
Panelmate brand A527
PanEnergy Corporation A514
PanEuroLife A1008, A1009, P364,
  P365
Panex (bakeware) A1022
Pangburn Candy Company P424,
  P719
Pangene Corporation (gene
  cloning) P454, P455
Panhandle Eastern Pipe Line
  Company A168, A376, A377, A514
Panke, Helmut W121
Pankey, Henry A. A1429, P491
Pankow, Charles P573

Pankow Special Projects P573
Pannier, David R. A153
Pannon GSM W502
Pantalakis, Theodoros W385
Pantaleoni, Anthony D. A447
PanTel W503
Pantepec (oil) W612
Pantex nuclear bomb plant P589
Panther Express International A102
Panthers of the University of
  Pittsburgh P759
Pantry Foods stores P627
The Pantry, Inc. A**1084**-A**1085**,
  P740
Pantry Pride grocery stores A902,
  P304
Pantry stores P224
Panza, Nicholas P. A1079
Panzani pasta W192
Panzarella, Angela J. A235
Panzer, Mark A1203
Panzerotti (stuffed pastry) P436
Paoli office furniture P652
Papa Roach (performer) P167
Papadellis, Randy P381
Papadopoulos, Gregory M. A1343
Papandreou, Andreas W384
Papanikos, I. W385
Pape, Charles A1096
Pape, Michael L. A585
Papen, Harold P149, P587
Paper Container Manufacturing
  Company P731
Paper designWAREHOUSE
  (catalogs) P338
Paper Mate pens A656, A1022,
  A1023
Paper Technology Group W290
Paperchase Products A276
PaperExchange.com, Inc. A344
Paperloop W621
Paperloop.com P434
Papesh, Patricia A. A1147
Papeteries de France A770
Papiasse, Alain W183
Pappano, Robert D. A1539
Paprocki, Ronald J. P760
Papyrus W556
Paquet cruises W58
Paquette, Paula A831
ParaBody fitness equipment A298
Paracelsus Healthcare P637
Parachute office seating P277
Paracomp (software) E86
Parade newspaper supplement A81,
  P530
Parade of Shoes A1092
Parade Publications A80, E289,
  P32, P33
Paradigm Pharmacy
  Management A84
Paradigm Technology E76
Paradise Beverages P746
Paradise, Brenda E276
Paradise Point hotels E231
Paradise (ship) A331

Paradyne Networks, Inc. (broadband accessory devices) P475
Paragon Black Leaf Counter Check Book W378
Paragon Communications A1198
Paragon Publishing P338
Paragon Trade Brands, Inc. A1518
Paraiban W56
Parallel Petroleum Corporation E260
Paramitas Foundation A1298
Paramount Citrus A494, P416, P716
Paramount Communications A1476
Paramount Farms (pistachios) P416, P417, P716
Paramount Natural Gas E264
Paramount Petroleum A556
Paramount pickles A467
Paramount Pictures A1450, A1476, A1477, A1496, P681
Paramount Planning Group A218
Paraplatin drug A291
Paraskivopoulis, Savva A978
Parati car W631
Parcel/Direct (shipping) P404, P708
Parcheesi game A692
Parden, Susannah W623
Pardun, Thomas E. A1515
Paredes, Edgar W439
Paredes, Raymond P415
Parell, Jeff E308
Parent, Louise M. A143
Parents' Institute P68
Parents (magazine) P68, W126
Paresi, Joseph S. A847
Paretti, Giancarlo A962, W182
Parfums Christian Dior W349
Parfums Givenchy W349
Parfums Stern A216
Pargo's restaurants A1280
Parham, Joseph G., Jr. A1005
Paribas. See BNP Paribas Group
Parikh, Mihir E31, E160
Paris Bourse Exchange W546
Paris, Kent E76
Paris Las Vegas hotel and casino A1086, A1087
Paris, Martin P614
Paris Match (magazine) W330
Paris Première cable channel W559
Paris, Richard E72, E218
ParisBourse W100
Parish auto parts A461
Parish, Rhonda J. A87
Parisian bread A774, A775
Parisian department stores A1238
Société Parisienne d'Enterprises et de Participations W520
Park & Save stores P422, P718
Park Avenue Life Insurance Company P215
Park Avenue Securities LLC P214, P215
Park Chong-Sup A929, W275
Park Chung Hee W334, W508

Park Chung-U W455
Park, Ernest A935
Park Inn hotels P107
Park Moon-Soo W455
Park Place Entertainment Corporation A684, A720, A1086-A1087, A1328
Park Plaza hotels P107
Park Ridge A710
Park, Robert S. A117
Park Se-Yong W275
Park Slope Co-op (New York City) P291
Park Soo-Woong W509
Park Young-Koo W509
Parkay spread A408, A409, A842
Parkdale Mills, Inc. P696
Parke-Benet (art auction house) A1304
Parke-Davis A1118
Parker, A. Joseph A1001
Parker, Alan (DFS Group) P156
Parker, Alan (Whitbread) W639
Parker, Ann P513, P767
Parker Appliance Company A1088
Parker, Arthur A1088
Parker, Bill Z. A1129
Parker Brothers (board games) A648, A692, A693, P417
Parker, C. E. A594
Parker Chemical W256
Parker, D. Wayne A1525
Parker, Elizabeth Rindskopf P501
Parker Hannifin Corporation A460, A1088-A1089, P310, P664
Parker, Helen A1088
Parker, James F. A1310, A1311
Parker, Jerry L. A493
Parker, John R., Jr. A385
Parker, Kevin T. A1099
Parker, Margo B. P766
Parker, Mark G. A1033
Parker, Michael D. A504, A505
Parker, Mitt A1351
Parker, Patrick S. A1088
Parker Pen A656, A910, A1022, A1023, A1170
Parker, Robert S. A1023
Parker, Roxanne E. A517
Parker, Sam A1116
Parker, Stan L. E80
Parker, Ted M. A1001
Parker, Wallace P., Jr. A825
Parker, W. Douglas A138, A139
Parker, William L. P39
Parker-Johnson, Toni P319
Parkes, Walter P167
Parkette drive-in restaurant A1280
Parkinson, Joe A762, A970
Parkinson, Richard A. P545
Parkinson, Ward A762, A970
ParkNet P237
Parks, Charles N. A1257
Parks, Susan B. A637
Parks, Tracy W. E60
Parmelle, Bill P683

Parmenter, Robert E. A527
Parmerica, Inc. A155
Parnell, Gordon W. E93, E245
Parodi, Dennis R. A635
Parr, Douglas A. A467
Parra, Rosendo G. A473
Parrette, Leslie J., Jr. A1465
Parretti, Giancarlo P747
Parrish, Dave P149
Parrish, D. Michael A1053
Parrish, Steven C. A1127
Parrish, Thomas C. A493
Parrott, Graham W249
Parrs, Marianne M. A771
Parry, Edward J., III A125
Parry, John R. W641
Parry, Josephine T. A1051
Parry, Michael E143
Parry, Richard M. A1375
Parry-Jones, Richard A617
PARS (TWA reservation system) A1046
Parseghian, Gregory J. A627
Parson, Kenneth R. A87
Parsons & Whittemore, Inc. P696
Parsons Bandcutter and Self Feeder Company A934
Parsons Brinckerhoff Inc. P696
Parsons Corporation P386-P387, P697
Parsons, Ralph P386
Parsons, Richard D. A181
Parsons, Robert E., Jr. A733
Parsons, William Barclay P696
Partco Group A460
Partee, Terrell A487
Partena (security and care) W546
Parthenon hotels W58
Participation (insurance) W104
Partington, Roger A1417
Partlow (controls) A462
Partners Against Pain P707
Partners Consulting Group P480
Partners HealthCare System, Inc. P697
Partners in Performance P308
PARTNERS National Health Plans of North Carolina (HMO) P691
The Partnership (advertising) A772
Parton, Mike W. J. W354, W355
Parts Plus A460
Parts Pups (magazine) A652
The Parts Source P112
Parts USA A1100
Party Express A679, P217
The Parvus Company (investigations) E29
Pascal, Philippe W349
Pascall candy W155
Pascarella, Carl A1481, P509
Pascaud, Henri W101
Pascual, Carlos A1545
Pasculano, Richard P752
Pash, Jeff P357
Paskach, Dave P437, P724
Paslode (fasteners) A748

Pass (magazine) P347
Passa, Lester M. A455
Passaretti, Robert A. E220
Passat car W630, W631
Passell, Brian J. A1169
Passmore, Malinda G. A397
Passport Research Ltd. P261
Passport SUV W265
Pasta Connection restaurants A1400
Pasta Roni A1181
Paster, Howard W647
Pasteris, Paul T. A923, P321
Pastis Casanis aperitif W109
Pastis Dubal aperitif W109
Pastor, Debbie P207, P620
Pastore, William M. A361
Pastori, Guido W99
Pataki, George A824, P128, P372, P460
Patak's Spices (Indian foods) A730, A731
Patch Kits for People wound treatments E105
Pate, James L. A1096, A1097
Pate, William C. A249
Patel, Homi B. A691
Patel, Kiran A1299
Patent Arms Manufacturing Company P132
Paterak, Joseph J. A1109
Paterno, Charles F. A1303
Paterno, Rick A1195
Paternoster Stores W312
Paterson, John E. P423
PATH. *See* Port Authority Trans-Hudson System
Pathé Communications A962, W146, W624
Pathfinder SUV W402, W403
Pathmark Stores, Inc. A994, A1490, P102, P103, P515, W498
Path.net S.p.A. W575
Pathway (ATM) A70
Pathways (fund advisory program) A94
Pathways office furniture A1334, A1335
Patina (events) W175
Patina Oil & Corporation E260
Patineau, Paula J. A121
Patio Foods A1204
Patmore, Kimberly S. A597
Patracuolla, James D. A1459
Patrick Cudahy Inc. A1290, A1291
Patrick, Deval L. A383
Patrick, Gregory S. E90, E240
Patrick, Matthew G. A1341
Patrick, Pat P390
Patrick, Sharon A918, A919
Patrick, Stephen C. A387
Patrick, Thomas H. A961
Patrikis, Ernest T. A151
Patriot American Hospitality A1540
Patriot missile A1190
PATROL software A270
Patron, Luigi W217

Patsley, Pamela H. A597
Patten, Rose M. W113
Patten, Ross M. E297
Patterson, Aubrey B., Jr. E162
Patterson, Barry P669
Patterson, Bill A1420
Patterson, James A1184
Patterson, John A1012
Patterson, Joseph A1402
Patterson, Kendall W. A705
Patterson, Kimberly S. P552
Patterson, Larry N. E142
Patterson, Robert E109
Patterson, Samuel R. A1147
Patterson, Theresa P623
Patterson, William C. A1309
Patterson, Zachary P41
Pattison, Doug P219, P625
Pattiz, Norman J. E140, E317
Patton, Gary R. E207
Patton, Greg E107, E269
Patton, Jody P510, P511, P767
Patton, Philip R. A695
Patton, William W128
Paul Allen Group P510
Paul, Gerald A1483
Paul, Judith E278
Paul Masson wines and liquor A422, A423
Paul M. Hebert Law Center P661
Paul, Rebecca P615
Paul Revere Corporation A1380, A1440
The Paul Revere Life Insurance Company A1441
Paul Revere Trust A1332
Paul, Ronald (Battelle) P70
Paul, Ronald L. (Georgia-Pacific) A655
Paul, Steven M. A541
Paul, Terrance E278
Paulachak, Stephen P492
Paulaner Weiss beer W254, W255
Paulenich, Fred A869, P293, P657
Pauley, Robin W149
Pauley, Stanley F. P568
Paulk, Pamela P645
Paull, Matthew A943
Paulsen, Thomas A. A421
Paulson, Henry M., Jr. A661
Pautler, Paul F. A95
Pauze, Jean Charles W447
Pavarini Construction P737
Paver, Robert L. A783
Pavey, Larry A. A461
Pavey, Nancy P776
Pavilions stores A1234
Pavlics, P. N. P439
Pavlis, Frank A100
Pavón, Mario W577
Pawling, Alonzo A806
Pawling and Harnischfeger A806
Pawloski, Kenneth S. A573
PAWS pet stores P394
PAX TV network A998, A999
Paxil drug W246

Paxson Communications Corporation A998, A999, P80
Pay Less Super Markets A845
PayDay candy A709
Payen brand A585
Payen, Gérard W559
Payless Cashways, Inc. A**1090**-A**1091**
PayLess Drug Stores A830
Payless Kids stores A932, A1092
Payless ShoeSource, Inc. A932, A**1092**-A**1093**
Payment First Corporation (Internet payment) W420
Paymentech (transaction processing) A596
Payne and Gunter (events) W175
Payne, Cal E. A1465
Payne, John A. A667
Payne, Nell P451
Payne, Richard B., Jr. A1001
Payne, Tommy J. A1205
Payner, Melissa J. A1315
PayPal, Inc. (online payment) A1170
Payroll Services E299
Payroll Transfers. *See* EPIX Holdings Corporation
Payson, Norman C. A1076, A1077
Payton Technology Project P272
Paz, George A575
PBG. *See* The Pepsi Bottling Group, Inc.
PBS. *See* Public Broadcasting Service
PBX, Inc. (refrigerated trucking) A743
PC Gamer (magazine) W238, W239
PC Max (magazine) W239
PC Plus (magazine) W238, W239
P.C. Richard & Son P697
PC Viewer (overhead display) E73
PC World (magazine) P248, P249, P641
PCA. *See* Pharmacy Corporation of America
PCA Property & Casualty A738
PC&E (diagnostic testing) A546
PCD Polymere W424
PCI Builders Resource (wholesale building materials) A1090
PCI Services, Inc. (pharmaceutical packaging) A320, A321
PCQuote.com, Inc. E70, E217
PCS Health Systems A84, A540, A946, A1202
PC's Limited A472
PCTEL, Inc. E261, E288
PCTV (TV/computer) A636
PdGold E254
PDI, Inc. E261
PDVSA. *See* Petróleos de Venezuela S.A.
PE Corporation A1110
Pea, Barry G. E71
Peabody Coal A416, A1024, A1416, A1528, W252

Peabody Group A532, W488
Peace Corps. *See* US Peace Corps
The Peacemaker (movie) P166, P167
Peach Bottom nuclear plant A570, A1174
Peach Bowl (football game) P124
Peachtree Center (Atlanta) A1398
Peachtree Software A204
Peak Health Care (HMO) A1434
Peak Technologies, Inc. W379
Peake Energy E254
Peale, Charles Willson A424
Peale, Rembrandt A424
Pealor, Nena I. E234
Peanuts comic strip A568, A678, P216, P424
Peapod, Inc. (online food retailing) W498, W499
Pearce, Gavin W89
Pearce, Harry J. (General Motors) A651
Pearce, Harry J. (Hughes Electronics) A736, A737
Pearce, Linda P173, P602
Pearce, Michael J. W341
Pearce, Phil A85
Pearce, Randy L. A1197
Pearce, Robert W. W113
Pearce, Vincent W177
Peare, William F. E304
Pearl beer P428, P721
Pearl Group plc (insurance) W88, W89
Pearl Meyer & Partners (compensation plans) E180
Pearl River Distribution Ltd. P243
Pearl, Suzanne J. A1479
Pearson, Charles C. E315
Pearson, Daniel R. A687
Pearson, Kevin W. A1435
Pearson plc A944, A1476, W126, W144, W145, W146, W238, W430-W431, W440, W478, W592
Pearson, Ronald D. P636
Pearson, Samuel W430
Pearson, Thomas M. A1227
Pearson, Timothy R. A841, P287, W325
Pearson TV W430
Pearson, Weetman W430, W440
Peary, Robert P358
Pease, Mark L. A169
Peat, Marwick, Mitchell, & Copartners A840, P286, W324
Peat, William A840, P286, W324
Pébereau, Michel W131
PEBSCO Nationwide Retirement Solutions A1009, P365
Pecan Delights candy P425
Pechiney, A. R. W432
Pechiney S.A. A112, W74, W432-W433
Pecht, Carrie J. A717, P235
Peck, A. John, Jr. A435
Peck, Charles A1227
Peck, Elmer A532

Peck, George A512
Peck, Jared W181
Peckham, William P422
PECO Energy Company A570, A571, A1154, A1174
PECO II, Inc. E261
PECOAdelphia A571
Pedder, Anthony P. W178
Peden, Keith J. A1191
Pedersen, Harald W416
Pedersen, Mike W157
Pedersen, Thorvald W416
Pedigree pet food A914, A915, P314, P315, P665
Pedigrees pet supplies A1117
PedoAlliance E259
Pedro Domencq (distillery) W84
Peek, David G. A667
Peek, Jeffrey M. A961
Peel, Michael A. A649
Peel-Connor Telephone Works W354
Peerless faucets A920, A921, P298
Peerless Insurance Company A875, P295
Peerless Paper Mills A1430
Peerless Pump A612
Peerless (space-venting heaters) A502
Peet Brothers (soap maker) A386
Peet's Coffee and Tea A1326
Peetz, John G., Jr. A563, P183, W223
PEGASO E232
Peg-Intron drug A1251
PEG-Intron drug E199
Pegler Ltd. W605
Pegler-Hattersley (plumbing fixtures) W604
Pehrson, Gary R. E73
Peiffer, Garry L. P664
Peiros, Lawrence S. A375
Peisner, Jonathan L. A389
Peixotto, Bob P301, P660
Pekarek, James B. A1315
Pekarsky, James R. E313
Pekin Energy A1528
Pekor, Allan J. A863
Péladeau, Érik W471
Péladeau, Pierre W470
Péladeau, Pierre Karl W470, W471
Pélata, Patrick W403
Peleaz, Cathy P297
Pelham, Judith C. P748
Pelican restaurants W639
Pélisson, Gérard W58, W59
Pell, Alfred A986
Pella Corporation P697
Pellegrini, Anthony F. A401
Peller, Clara A1510
Pelletier, Liane J. A1319
Pellicioli, Lorenzo W575
Pellissier, Gervais W151
Pellow, Barbara A. A747
Peloponnese Mediterranean foods A730, A731
Peltason, Jack P494

Peltier, Ronald J. E215
Peltz and May A1400
Peltz, Nelson A1400, A1401
Peluso, John P215
Pemberton, Francis A628
Pemberton, John A382
Pembroke Real Estate A615, P191
PEMEX. *See* Petróleos Mexicanos
Pemstar Inc. E262
Penaljo shoes A295
Pendaries Petroleum E307
Pender, Deb E215
Pender, John W152
Pender, Paul E. A1543
Pender, Robert I., Jr. E286
Pendergast, Rich A1189
Pendergrast, Leslie E42, E179
Penford (starch) A324
Peng, Philip W61
Penguin Air Conditioning Corporation A545
Penguin Group (publishing) W430, W431
Penhaligon (cosmetics) A776, A876, A1498, A1499
Penick, Derrick A. A845
Penington, Michael W239
The Peninsular and Oriental Steam Navigation Company W434-W435
Peninsular Electric Light A512
Pénisson, René W103
Penn Aluminum International, Inc. P313
Penn Central Corporation. *See* American Premier Underwriters
Penn Central (railroad) A144
Penn Fruit Company P478
Penn Machine Company P313
Penn Mutual Life Insurance Company P698
Penn National Gaming, Inc. E262
Penn National Race Course (Pennsylvania) E262
Penn Square (bank) A808
Penn State textiles A1474
The Penn Traffic Company A1094-A1095, P479
Penn Treaty E309
Penn Union (electrical connectors) P686
Penn Ventilation W605
Penn Virginia Corporation E262
Pennaco Energy A1460
Penn-Daniels stores A1282
Penney, James Cash A790
Penney Stores (Mississippi) A1532
Penneys (stores-Australia) W172
Pennington Biomedical Research Center P661
Pennington, William A906
Pennington, W. Lane A865
Penn-Ohio Edison (utility) A376, A1306
Pennstar Bank E250
Pennsylvania Blue Shield A716, P234

Pennsylvania Customer Choice Act A1154
Pennsylvania Electric Company A668
Pennsylvania Farm Bureau Cooperative Association P38
Pennsylvania Heat Light and Power A570
Pennsylvania House furniture A854
The Pennsylvania Lottery P698
Pennsylvania Medical Society A716, P234
Pennsylvania Power Company A598, A599
Pennsylvania Power & Light A1154
Pennsylvania Railroad system A1038
The Pennsylvania State University P699
Pennsylvania Steel Technologies, Inc. A256
Pennsylvania-American Water Company A155
Pennsylvania-New Jersey-Maryland Interconnection A1174
Penntech Papers A1524
Penn-Texas P132
Penny Curtiss (bakery) A1095
The Penny Press A568
PennzEnergy Brazil, Ltda. A482
Pennzoil-Quaker State Company A**1096**-A**1097**, A1376, P340, P620, W280
Penrose, George W636
Penrose, William W636
Pensabene, Gregory M. A169
Pensacola (Florida) *News Journal* A633
Penser, Erik W72
Penshorn, John S. A1435
Pension Associates, Inc. A1009, P365
Pension Benefit Guaranty Corporation P**388**-P**389**, P699
Pension Resources, Inc. A681
Pensions & Benefits Today (publication) P481
Penske Corporation A278, A652, A664, A830, A831, A1222, P**390**-P**391**, P699, P700
Penske, Gregory W. E75
Penske Motorsports E75
Penske, Roger S. E75, P390, P391, P699
Penske Truck Leasing Company A710, P699, P700
Penstock (microwave radio-frequency products) A214
The Pentagon P630
Pentagon Papers A1020
Penthouse (magazine) P52
Pentium microprocessor A82, A760
Pentland Industries A1194
Pentland, Lawrence A. A473
Penton, John E102
Penton Media, Inc. E**102**, E263
Pentothal drug A59
Penuel, William P455

People Are Talking (TV show) P218
People Express (airline) A428
People (magazine) P404, P708
Peoples Bank of Indianapolis A592
People's Choice TV A1318
Peoples Drug Stores A458
People's Gas Light Company A424
Peoples Jewellers A1552, A1553
Peoples Mortgage and Investment Company A1509
Peoples National bank A1146
Peoples Natural Gas A1464
The People's Place stores W606
Peoples Restaurants A968
Peoples stores W356
PeopleSoft, Inc. A**1098**-A**1099**, E22, E148, E220
The Pep Boys-Manny, Moe & Jack A198, A208, A**1100**-A**1101**, P112, P152, P590
Pep Valve Grinding Compound A1100
Pepcid AC antacid A801, A957
Pepcid drug A956
Pepe Jeans USA W606
Pepe Lopez tequila A296, A297
Pépin, Jocelyn W471
Peppel, Michael E. E239
Pepper Construction Group, LLC P700
Pepper, John E. A1164, A1165
Pepper, Stanley P700
Pepperidge Farm A316
The Pepsi Bottling Group, Inc. A**1102**-A**1103**, A1104, A1106
PepsiAmericas, Inc. A**1104**-A**1105**
PepsiCo, Inc. A186, A192, A224, A382, A452, A494, A648, A934, A1062, A1102, A1104, A**1106**-A**1107**, A1180, A1302, A1326, A1332, A1404, P90, P236, P292, P302, P380, P464, P634, P776, W154, W162, W254, W544, W545, W552
The Pepsi-Cola Company A1102, A1106
Pepsodent toothpaste W618, W619
Pepto-Bismol A1165
Pequivien, SA W439
Pequot Pharmaceutical Network P318, P319, P667
Pequot River Shipworks P318
Pequot Tribe. *See* Mashantucket Pequot Tribal Nation
Perceive fragrance A216, A217
Percepta (customer relations) E127
Perchick, Morton K. E81
Percival, Jennifer E167
Perclose A58
PercuSurge A952
Perdriau Rubber Company W428
Perdue, Arthur P392, P700
Perdue, David A. A1195
Perdue Farms Inc. P**392**-P**393**, P700
Perdue, Frank P392
Perdue, James A. P392, P393, P700
Perduyn, John P. A665

Peregrine Investment Holdings A860, W266
Pereira de Oliveira, Carlos A. W437
Pereirh, Maria E275
Perella, Joseph R. A989
Perelman, Alan S. W639
Perelman, Ronald O. A903, A1200, A1201, P305, P663
Peres, Albert W571
Peretti, Elsa A1384
Perez, Carlos Andres (former Venzuela President) W438
Perez, Carlos (New York City Health and Hospitals) P369
Perez, Daniel A1299
Pérez Gómez, Jaime W581
Perez, Joseph P205
Perez, Milly E275
Perez, Peter M. A1105
Perez Rios, Gustavo W583
Pérez Simón, Juan Antonio W581
Perez, William D. A1246, A1247, P432, P433, P722
Pérez-Lizaur, Ignacio W635
Perfecseal, Inc. A251
Perfecseal (medical packaging) A250
Perfect Circle auto parts A461
Perfect Copy software E278
Perfect Sleeper mattress P727
Perfection HY-Test Company P313
PerfecTV! (satellite braodcast) W296
Perfetto, Donald J. E270
Perfit, Michael A. E83
Performa by Maytag appliances A934
Performance Food Group Company A**1108**-A**1109**
Performance Friction Products A278
Performance home furnishings A1317, P453
Performance Specialties W278
Performers hard drives A1515
Pergamon (consulting) A404
Pergamon Press W478
Pericom Semiconductor Corporation E263
Perillo, John E130
Peripheral Technology Solutions W554
Periphonics (systems integrator) W412
Periquito, F. M. A1521
Perishable Distributors of Iowa P636
Perissinotto, Giovanni W99
Perkin, Gordon W. P79
PerkinElmer, Inc. A**1110**-A**1111**
Perkins, Brian D. A801
Perkins, David W377
Perkins, Edward A600
Perkins Engines A332
Perkins Group (engines) A1010
Perkins, Jim C. P630
Perkins, Marlin P348

Perkins Oil Well Cementing A676
Perkins Products A842
Perkins, R. Paul A1465
Perkins, Tom E268
Perl Pillow A1134
Perlberg, Yvonne B. A737
Perle, Richard N. W263
Perlee, Jeff P372
Perlet, Helmut W83
Perlman, Joel A. P678
Perlman, Lawrence (Ceridian) A342
Perlman, Lawrence
  (Seagate) A1261
Perlman, Richard A560, P180
Perlmutter, Barbara A917
Perlmutter, Roger A161
Perloff Brothers (food
  wholesalers) A1350
Perlyn, Donald L. E95
PermaBase cement board P683
Permanent General Insurance
  Company A756, A757, P244,
  P245, P639
Permanent University Fund P470,
  P498
Permanente Medical Groups A810,
  A811, P266, P267, P649
Perma-Shield doors P50
Permax drug A541
Permian Basin Royalty Trust E263
Permian (crude oil) A200
Permneft (oil exploration) W346
OOO Permtransgaz W243
Perna, Thomas J. A229
Pernas (trading) W538
Pernod Ricard A296, W84, W108,
  W154, W206, W624
Pero, Perry R. A1043
Peron, Juan W650
Peroni beer A423
Perot, Ross, Jr. A1112, A1113
Perot, Ross, Sr. A538, A724, A1112,
  A1113
Perot Systems Corporation A538,
  A1112-A1113
Peroxidation Systems A1484
Perrachon, Antonia W166
Perraudin, Michel W63
Perrault, Paul A. E178
Perrella, James A754
Perrier water A384, A385
Perrier-Jouët champagne A714,
  W315
Perrin, Charles (Avon
  Products) A216
Perrin, Charles (Towers
  Perrin) P480
Perrin, Jean-Claude W521
Perrin, Patrick N. E186
Perron, Linda E285
Perrone, Frank A829, P271
Perruzza, Albert L. A1193
Perry, Barry W. A551
Perry Ellis men's clothes A690,
  A691
Perry, Gregory D. A1111
Perry, Matthew C. W396

Perry, Michael W356
Perry nuclear plant A598
Perry, Pam P121, P571
Perry, Richard E207
Perry, Shirley Bird P499
Perry, Stephen A. A1387
Perry, William (AMP) W88
Perry, William (former US Secretary
  of Defense) P438, P699
Persa, Berna E132, E306
Persetel Q Data Holdings A176
Pershing A449
Persil detergent W256
Persing, David A. P333
Persing, Donna M. E255
Persona, Inc. A1233
Personal Financials Services
  Europe W185
Personal Handyphone
  Service W400, W418
Personal Handyphone
  System W328
PersonalCare HMO P706
Personalized Check Program A480
Personnel Pool of America A680
Personnel Service A818
Persons, Wallace A546
Perspex W278
Persson, Eva W633
Persson, Lars-Eric W585
Pert Plus hair care A1165
Pertamina W612
Pertz, Douglas A. A752, A753
Peru, Ramiro G. A1125
Perusse, Gary D. A441
Pervasive Software Inc. A1050
Pescatore, Peter A1161
Pesce, Peter A173, P49, W91
Pesch, Patrick K. E172
Pesci, Robert A. A1263
Peske, Sherry E. A621
Pesta pickles A467
Pester, Robert E. E34
Pet City Holdings A1116
Pet Club brands P479, P746
Pet evaporated milk A1136
Pet Food Giant stores A1116
Pet Food Supermarket A1116
Pet Inc. A1104, A1136
Pet Nosh P394
PET plastic containers A224, A225,
  A452, A453, A504, A522, A1102
Pet USA P394
PetCare Plus P394
Petco Animal Lovers Save (P.A.L.S.)
  customer loyalty program P394
Petco Animal Supplies,
  Inc. **P394-P395**, P701
Peter Jackson cigarettes W283
Peter Kiewit Sons', Inc. A866,
  A1114-A1115, P340, **P396-P397**,
  P701
Peter Pan peanut butter A408, A409
Peter Paul candy A708, A709, A914,
  P314, W154, W155
Peter Piper pickles A467
Peter Stuyvesant cigarettes W143,
  W282, W283

Peter Vella wine A521, P169
Peterbilt Motors Company A456,
  A1078, A1079
Peters, Charles A. (Emerson
  Electric) A547
Peters, Charles E., Jr.
  (Burlington) A307
Peters, Elizabeth E135, E311
Peters, James C. A1215
Peters, Lauren B. A1471
Peters, Mary O. A1145
Peters, Tom P102, P342
Peters, William E. A783
Petersen, Albert E. A1333
Petersen, Anne C. P521
Petersen, Coleman A1495
Petersen, Sheldon P685
Peterson, Denny P749
Peterson, Eric H. A513
Peterson, Gary A1059
Peterson, Gene H. A481
Peterson, Gerald O. A769
Peterson Health Care, Inc. A259
Peterson, John J. A431
Peterson, Karin P698
Peterson, Lowell P596
Peterson, Mark A. (FMR) A615,
  P191
Peterson, Mark W.
  (Broadwing) A293
Peterson, Michael C. A995
Peterson, Patti P529
Peterson, Paul T. A627
Peterson, Ralph R. P573
Peterson, Robert B. (Imperial
  Oil) W280, W281
Peterson, Robert (Jack in the
  Box) A784
Peterson, Robert L. (IBP) A743
Peterson, Ronald G. A611
Peterson, Sarah A. A1505
Peterson, Stacey M. E306
Peterson, Timothy A. E228
Petersson, Lars-Eric W585
Petersville Sleigh W428
Pete's Super Submarines P160
PetFood Warehouse stores A1116
Petford, Tony W531
Petillo, James T. A1543
Petit Casino convenience
  stores W166, W167
Petit, Jeffrey A. A147
Petit Navire tuna A723
Petite Danseuse de Quatorze Ans
  (painting) A1304
Petite Sophisticate stores P713
PetJungle.com A1116
Petopia.com P394
Petrak, Michael A833
Petram, Hans-Dieter W203
Petrelli, Frank J. W609
Petric, Velko W577
Petrillo, Alfred B., Jr. A159
Petrillo, John C. A203
Petrini, David J. A1171
Pet-Ritz frozen foods A608, A609
Petro Star P542

Petro Stopping Centers, L.P. P701
Petrobank Energy and Resources Ltd. A310
PETROBRAS. *See* PETRÓLEO BRASILEIRO S.A. - PETROBRAS
Petro-Canada A132, W410
Petrochemia Plock W456
PetroCorp Inc. E264
PetroFina W116, W612
Petrolane (petroleum services) P462
PETRÓLEO BRASILEIRO S.A. - PETROBRAS A1376, W297, **W436-W437**, W482
Petróleos de Venezuela S.A. A56, A132, A900, A1438, **W438-W439**
Petróleos Mexicanos A1466, **W440-W441**, W650
Petrolera Argentina San Jorge S.A. A352
Petroleum Development Corporation E264
Petroleum Engineering Services A676
Petroleum Geo-Services E292
Petro-Lewis A1344
Petrolite A222
Petrolot Sp. z.o.o. W457
Petro:Lube P701
Petromed (gas stations) W482
Petronas (oil and gas) A412, W612
Petronas Twin Towers (Malaysia) A1408, P448, P482
Petronor gas W482
Petroprofit Sp. z.o.o. W457
PetroQuest Energy, Inc. E264
Petroquisa W436
Petrorel refinery W346
Petro-Tex Chemicals A1368
Petrovich, Dushan A1527
Petrovich, Janice P195
Petrulio, Lynn E265
Pétry, Jacques W559
Pets At Home A1116
Pets.com A130, A1116
PETsMART, Inc. **A1116-A1117**, P394, P701, W164
Petstuff stores A1116
Petterson, David S. A437
Petterson, John S. A1385
Pettey, Tom A315, P97, P563
Pettifor, Stuart I. W178
Pettingil, Richard R. A811, P267
Pettingill, Christine A. A905
Pettinotti, Jean-Christophe P65
Pettit, Stephen R. W153
Pettit-Morry (property/casualty brokerage) A178
Pettus, Nancy Milleen A595
Petty, James R. A863
Petty, Nina B. A1189
Petty, Terry A913
Petzazz stores A1116
Peugeot, Armand W442
PSA Peugeot Citroën S.A. A1412, P695, W264, W366, **W442-W443**, W480, W546, W560, W614

Peugeot, Frédéric W442
Peugeot, Jean-Pierre W442
Peugeot, Pierre W443
Peugeot, Robert W443
Peugeot, Roland W442
Pew Charitable Trusts P414
Pew, Edgar A1344
Pew, Howard A1344
Pew, Joseph Newton A1344
Pew, Joseph Newton, Jr. A1344
Pew, Robert A1334
Peyrache, Marie-Claude W233
Peyrelevade, Jean W182, W183
Peyrer-Heimstätt, Tassilo W425
PEZ Candy, Inc. E54
Pezzoli, Robert E. P57
P.F. Chang's China Bistro, Inc. E265
P.F. Flyers sneakers W62
Pfaff, Christian J. A631
The Pfaltzgraff Company A838, A839
Pfander, Stefan A1527
Pfannschmidt, Heinz A1413
PFD Supply P704
Pfeffer, Gerald S. A1115, P397
Pfeffer, Philip A276
Pfefferl, Robert A1059
Pfeifer, Andy P702
Pfeifer, JoAnne A971
Pfeiffer, Eckhard A398
Pfeiffer, Gary M. A535
Pfeiffer Glass A600
Pfeiffer, Robert E296
Pfeifle, Jeffrey A. A635
Pfeil, Larry J. A731
Pfingsten, Linda P763
Pfister, Irwin A1253
Pfister, Ulrich W185
Pfizer, Charles A1118
Pfizer Inc. A98, A282, A320, A444, A540, A788, **A1118-A1119**, A1250, E150, E191, E220, E261, P430, W334
Pflaum, Jeffrey D. A71
PFPC Worldwide Inc. A1147
PFS (food service) P236
Pfuehler, Donald P165
Pfuntzenreuter, Richard H. P758
PGA. *See* The Professional Golfers Association of America
PGA European Tour Courses P130, P577
PG&E Corporation A240, A514, A536, **A1120-A1121**, A1138, A1306, A1466
PGE. *See* Portland General Electric Company
Phacoflexll lenses A119
Pham, Wayne N. E245
Phanstiel, Howard G. A1081
The Phantom Menace (movie) P302, P303, P661
Pharis Tire and Rubber Company A326
PharmaCare Management Services A458

Pharmaceutical Formulations, Inc. P637
Pharmacia & Upjohn A984, A1122
Pharmacia Corporation A148, A704, A800, A984, **A1122-A1123**, A1300, P414, W632
Pharmacy Corporation of America A258
Pharmacy Direct Network A1492
Pharmacy Healthcare Solutions A155, A156
Pharmacy Provider Services Corporation A156
PharmAssure A1202
PharMingen (biomedical research) A244
Phar-Mor, Inc. A1282, P198
Phasor Electronics (cable TV) A70
Phat Farm brand clothing E101
Phelan, Daniel W247
Phelizon, Jean-François W507
Phelps, Anson Greene A1124
Phelps Dodge Corporation **A1124-A1125**
Phelps, Hensel P630
Phenix cream cheese A842
PHH Fantus (corporate relocation) A338, A474, P154
PHH Group A212
PHH Vehicle Management Services A338
Philadelphia 76ers (basketball team) A390, P355
Philadelphia brand cheese A842, A843
Philadelphia Bulletin P248
Philadelphia Consolidated Holding Corporation E265
Philadelphia Daily News A833
Philadelphia Eagles (football team) A672, P210, P356, P357
Philadelphia Edison A570
Philadelphia Electric. *See* PECO Energy
Philadelphia Flyers L.P. (hockey team) A390, P361
The Philadelphia Inquirer A832, A833
Philadelphia Life Insurance Company A1368
Philadelphia (movie) A220, P66
The Philadelphia Phillies (baseball team) A390, P307
Philadelphia Suburban Corporation E265
Philip Anschutz A714
Philip Morris Companies Inc. A78, A408, A492, A549, A842, A1074, **A1126-A1127**, A1180, A1204, A1436, W100, W142, W304, W305, W516
Philipp Brothers Chemicals, Inc. A550, A1118
Philipp Holzmann AG W201
Philippine Long Distance Telephone W400, W401
Philippine Packing Corporation A470

Philips, Anton W444
Philips Electronics N.V. A98, A162, A410, A982, A1002, A1012, A1256, A1298, A1342, A1482, A1520, E189, E192, E196, E197, E203, E222, E244, E281, P444, P445, P726, P750, W100, W334, W360, **W444-W445**, W490, W514, W536, W550, W554
Philips, Gerard W444
Philips Gloeilampenfabrieken W444
Philips International Realty Corporation E266
Philips Optoelectronics (lasers) A792
Philips Products (windows and doors) W605
Philip-Sörensen, Erik W524
Philip-Sörensen, Jörgen W524
Philip-Sörensen, Sven W524
Philley, Steve A1417
PhillieCo (cable) A1318
Phillips 66 gasoline A1128
Phillips & Drew (brokerage) W616
Phillips, Anita P107
Phillips Arena (Atlanta) P550
Phillips, Chris P381
Phillips, Cindy L. E152
Phillips Coal A992
Phillips, David P. A1177, P403, P707
Phillips, Donald W284
Phillips, Frank A1128
Phillips, Gary P62, P63, P547
Phillips, Gene E219, E303
Phillips, Hoyt J. A795
Phillips, J. David P628
Phillips, Joyce W157
Phillips, Kevin A831
Phillips, L. E. A1128
Phillips, Michael C. A793
Phillips, Moira W93
Phillips, Peggy V. E71
Phillips Petroleum Company A132, A184, A352, A514, A820, **A1128-A1129**, P574, P598, P627, W136, W410, W438
Phillips, Pugh W545
Phillips, Richard B. A771
Phillips, Steven E203
Phillips, T. Danny A85
Phillips, Thomas A1190
Phillips Wire A642
Phillips, W. Norman A901
Philmus, Ken P399
Phinney, William R. A559
Phinny, T. G. A1096
Phipps, Paul E75
PHM Corporation (holding company) A1178
Phoenix AG W201
Phoenix Consortium W120
Phoenix Corporate Services A1398
Phoenix Coyotes Hockey Club P361
Phoenix Group Corporation (integrated marketing) W378
Phoenix Land Development A346

Phoenix Mercury (basketball team) P355
Phoenix Natural Gas Limited A824, A825
Phoenix Network A1186
Phoenix packaging A1302
Phoenix Resource Companies A184
Phoenix Suns (basketball team) A1138, P355
Phone Blaster W180
PhonePrint A1412
Phosphate Hill project W640
Phosphate Resource Partners Limited Partnership A752
Photo Color Systems A750
Photodyne (test instruments) A170
Photon Dynamics, Inc. E266
Photoshop software A76, A77
PhotoStress plastic coating A1482
PhotoWorks, Inc. P411
PHS. *See* Presbyterian Healthcare Services
PhyCor A322
Physical Therapeutix, Inc. A699
Physician Choice E72
Physician Practice Management Corporation A699
Physicians Corporation of America A738
Physicians Health Plan of Minnesota A1434
Physicians Health Services A696, P214
Physicians' Hospital Management Corporation A323
Physics International A1060
Physio-Control Corporation A674
Physio-Control International (defibrillators) A952
Piacentini, Diego A131
Piaggio SpA (motor scooters) P474, P475
Piasten candy W155
Piaton, René W432
P.I.B., Inc. A1445
Pic 'n Pay shoe stores A578
Pic 'N Save stores A260, A261
PIC International. *See* Sygen International
Picard, Dennis A1190
Picard Surgelés (frozen foods) W164
Picasso, Pablo A1304
Picasso, Paloma A1384
Piccinini, Mike P722
Piccinini, Robert M. P722
Pichette, Patrick W123
Pichler, Joseph A. A844, A845
Pichot, Jacques W69
Pici, Frank A. E262
Pick 'n Save Warehouse Foods stores P422, P718
Pick up Stix restaurants P106, P107
Pickard, Frank C., III A1475
Pickard, John G. A589
Pickens, T. Boone A132, A1128, A1438

Picker International Holdings W354
Pickering, Robert B. A1245
Pickford, Barry W. W123
Pickford, Mary P218
Pickford (moving company) P535
PickOmatic Systems A446
Pickron, Robert E259
Pico educational games W526, W527
PICO Holdings, Inc. (insurance/investments) E74, E213
Piconi, Louis P421
Picot, Claude W507
Pictrostate (print system) W234
The Picture People portrait studios A678, A679, P216, P217, P625
PictureTel E268
PictureVision (digital image storage) A524
Piderit, John P661
Piech, Ferdinand W630, W631
Piechoski, Michael J. A1115, P397, P701
Piecuch, John M. A848
Piedboeuf family W288
Piedmont Airlines, Inc. A1442, A1443
Piedmont Aviation A1038
Pien, Howard W247
Pieper, Dennis P479, P746
Pier 1 Imports, Inc. **A1130-A1131**
The Pier stores A1130
Pieranunzi, Richard W555
Pierce, Gerald P771
Pierce, Glenn A155
Pierce, Harvey R. P43, P538
Pierce, Nancy E172
Piercing Pagoda A1552, A1553
Piergallini, Al W415
Piergrossi, Michael N. A1537
Pieroni, Leonard P386
Pieropan, Claudia M. E214
Pierpont, Janet M. A1061
Pierre Balmain watch W563
Pierre Cardin brand A691
Pierson, François W105
Pierson, Rodney A. A1231
Pierson, Susan P511
Piesko, Michael P731
Pieszko, Christopher A943
Pieters, Marten W503
Pieterse, Robert W642, W643
Pietre, John C. A351
Pietrini, Andrew E. P752
Pietroburgo, Robert A. A95
Pifco Holdings E116
Pifer, Jay S. A115
Piggly Wiggly supermarkets A606, A607, A844, A1176, A1234, A1242, A1348, P402, P479, P654
Pignone (machinery) W216
Pigott, Charles M. A1078
Pigott, Mark C. A1078, A1079
Pigott, Paul A1078

Pigott, William A1078
Pike, David E164
Pike, Robert W. A127
Pikus, Jean Zwerlein E36, E170
Pikus, Stanton M. E36
Pilaro, Anthony P156
Pilaud, Eric W521
Pilcher, Gregory F. A821
Pilevsky, Philip E266
Pilgrim, Aubrey A1132
Pilgrim, Lindy "Buddy" A1132
Pilgrim, Lonnie "Bo" A1132, A1133
Pilgrim's Pride
  Corporation A1132-A1133
Pilkington Barnes Hind (contact
  lens) A118
Pilkington plc A1072, A1152, P212,
  W506
Pillai, Hari A1241
Pillard, Larry G. W568, W569
Pillay, Joe W540
Pillet, Erik W71
Pilliard, Jean-François W521
Pilliter, Charles J. P489
Pillmore, Eric M. E247
Pillow Pals P486, P487
Pillow, Terry R. A1195
Pillowtex
  Corporation A1134-A1135
Pillsbury, Charles A1136
The Pillsbury Company A250, A288,
  A302, A408, A648, A722, A768,
  A952, A1136-A1137, P380, W206,
  W207, W304, W388
Pillsbury, Donaldson C. A1305
Pillsbury Doughboy. See Poppin'
  Fresh Doughboy
Pillsbury, George A1136
Pillsbury Mills P72
Pillsbury Restaurant Group A288
Pilnik, Richard D. A541
Pilot computer mouse W339
Pilot Corporation P701
Pilot, Kenneth S. A635
Pilot Life Insurance Company A794
Pilsner Urquell beer W552, W553
PIMCO Advisors Holdings P384,
  P385, P695, W82
Pinault Bois & Matériaux (building
  materials) W446, W447
Pinault, François W134, W446
Pinault-Printemps-Redoute W250,
  W348, W446-W447
Pincemin, Clodine W547
Pinder, Denis W538
Pindred, R. John A1271
Pine Grove Funeral Group A1268
Pine Solutions (lumber
  distributor) A1518
Pineau, Charles A. E202
Pineau-Valencienne, Didier W521
Pineda, Patricia P367, P687
Pinehurst Collection
  furniture P299
Pinehurst Resort and Country Club
  (North Carolina) P130, P131,
  P577

Pine-Sol cleaning product A374,
  A375
Pinewild Country Club (North
  Carolina) P130
Pinewood Studios W472
Piney, Simon W131
Pink Floyd (music group) W213
Pink Panther cartoon
  character A1072
Pinkerton's, Inc. W524, W525
Pinkston, Larry D. E308
Pinnacle Entertainment, Inc. E178
Pinnacle Group Associates
  (corporate relocation) P753
Pinnacle One Partners A1416
Pinnacle Trading P599
Pinnacle West Capital
  Corporation A1138-A1139
Pinneo, Jeffrey D. A107
Pinocchio (movie) A1496
Pinochet, Augusto W576
Pinpoint Technologies E144
Pinson, Kathleen S. E107
Pinto, Charlie A1155
Pinto, Salvatore W575
Pioneer Air Cargo A102
Pioneer Airlines A428
Pioneer (auto specialty) P752
Pioneer Corporation W448-W449
Pioneer Electronics Supply A1140
Pioneer Hi-Bred International,
  Inc. A324, A534, P104
Pioneer International
  (concrete) W252
Pioneer Kabushiki Kaisha W448
Pioneer Super Save, Inc. P489
Pioneer Systems (campus ID
  cards) A488
Pioneer-Standard Electronics,
  Inc. A1140-A1141
Piotrowski, Werner W311
Pipeline Mine W452
Piper Jaffray A1444
Pipitone, Guy L. A599
Pippin, M. Lenny P436, P437, P724
Pippin, Teresa A. E126, E299
Pippins, Michael W. E35
Piqueras Bautista, Rafael W483
Piraino, Thomas A., Jr. A1089
Pirelli, Alberto W451
Pirelli & C. SAPA A642
Pirelli, Giovanni Battista W450
Pirelli S.p.A. A432, A434, A792,
  W138, W423, W450-W451, W574
Pirog, Christine R. A247
Pirotina, Susan A1375
Pirtle, Ronald M. A477
Piscatella, Michael J. A663
Pischetsrieder, Bernd W120, W630,
  W631
Piscitelli, Dawn E112, E279
Piscitelli, Meg P119
Pishotti, Nicholas J. A755
Pistachio Producers of
  California P416
Pistner, Stephen A158
Piston Ring Company A1320

Pistorio, Pasquale W554, W555
Pitcairn, John A1152
Pitco Frialator (deep fryers) A935
Pitcock, Mike P473
Pitera, Thomas G. A1141
Pitino, Rick A280
Pitman, Doug A762, A970
Pitman-Moore (animal health
  products) A752
Pitney, Arthur A1142
Pitney Bowes, Inc. A712,
  A1142-A1143, W56, W190, W486
Piton beer W255
Pitser, Tommy G. A1395
Pitt. See University of Pittsburgh of
  the Commonwealth System of
  Higher Education
Pittenger, J. C. A835
Pittenger, John C. P281
Pittle, David P139
Pittman, Michael J. A1083
Pittman, Robert W. A181
Pittock, H. L. A1524
Pitts, Ralph A. P77
Pittsburgh Coal A416
Pittsburgh Corning A434
Pittsburgh Mercy Health
  System P114, P115
Pittsburgh National Bank A1146
Pittsburgh Penquins Hockey
  Club P361
Pittsburgh Pirates (baseball
  team) A1146, P120, P307, P593
Pittsburgh Plate Glass A434, A1152
Pittsburgh Reduction
  Company A112, W74
Pittsburgh Steelers Sports, Inc.
  (football team) P356, P357, P635
Pittsburgh Testing
  Laboratories A600
Pittway E102
Pius XI, Pope W210
Piva, Gary P773
Pivara Skopje (brewery) W254
Pivirotto, Richard A656
Piwek, Brian A671
Pixar Animation Studios E103,
  E266, P597
Pixelworks, Inc. E267
Pizer, Ken A937
Pizza Beheer B.V. P162
Pizza Hut, Inc. A302, A500, A934,
  A1106, A1404, A1405, E95, E249,
  P162, P236, P595, P633, P657,
  W638, W639
Pizzey, G. John A113
P.K. gum A1527
PkMS software E236
PKN. See Polski Koncern Naftowy
  Orlen S.A.
PKN Orlen (refineries) W424
Place Two stores A1036
Placer Dome Inc. W452-W453
Plaeger, Frederick J. A311
Plaid Clothing Group A690
The Plain Dealer (Cleveland,
  OH) A80, A81, P32, P33, P530

Plains All American Pipeline LP A1144, A1460, E200
Plains Illinois Inc. A1145
Plains Resources Inc. A**1144-A1145**, E260
Plaisance, Melissa C. A1235
Plaistow wharf W568
Plakmeyer, Steve P618
Plamann, Alfred A. P488, P489, P752
Plane Crazy (cartoon) A1496
Planet Alumni, Inc. P262
Planet Automotive Group, Inc. P702
Planet Music A276
Planet of the Apes (movies and products) A622, E130, E303
Planet Sabre A1229
planetAg Web site P264
PlanetRx.com A574
Plank, Raymond A184, A185
Plank, Roger B. A185
Plankinton, William A802
Plant, John C. A1413
Plant System (railroad) A454
Plantation Foods A1350
Planters nuts A843, A1204
Plantsbrook (funeral homes) A1268
Plasmon baby food A723
Plassart, Jean-Claude W165
Plastifast fastening systems A265
Plastipak Packaging, Inc. P702
Plate Glass W552
Platinol drug A290
Platinum Equity A990, A1324
Platinum Equity Holdings A1528, P703
Platinum Software A1112
PLATINUM technology A402
Platt, C. B. A858
Platt, Jane W485
Platt, Lewis A712
Platten, Peter M., III A673, P211
Plattner, Hasso W516, W517
Platts, H. Gregory P359
Platts (magazine) A945
Platzner, Linda A1161
Plavix drug A291
Playboy (magazine) P52
Play-Doh A693
Player, Gary P250
Players Bluegrass Down (racetrack) A685
Player's cigarettes W143
Players International A684
Players Metropolis casino A685
Playlife (outdoor gear) W124
Playskool toys A692, A693
PlayStation video gaming A894, W238, W394, W550
Playtex Products, Inc. A386, A1242, A1243
Plaza Hotel A1408, P482
Pleasant Company A926
Pleasants, John A1451
Pledge furniture cleaner A1246, A1247, P432, P433, P722

Pledger, Thomas R. E52
Plénitude cosmetics W343
Plenum Publishing W642
Plescia, Gerald A. A711
Plesman, Albert W316
Plessey (telecommunications) W354
Plexiglas A1212
PLEXION drug E89
Plexus Corporation E**104**, E267
Plimpton, Thomas E. A1079
Pliner, Michael E134
Ploenzke (computer services) A404
Plotkin, Norman G. E60
Plough, Abe A1250
Plough (pharmaceutical) A1250
Plowman, Boyd R. A605
Plug Power Inc. A512
Plugra butter P149
Plum Creek Timber A654
Plum, Joseph W. A575
Plum Street Enterprises A1028
Plumb Shop A921
Plumb tools A430
Plumley, Harlan E83, E233
Plummer, William B. A113
Plummer, Wylie E119
Plumrose (meat products) W428
Plunkett, Robert F. A625
Plus Development A1184
Plus grocery and discount stores W588, W589
Plus Mark (gift wrap) A146, A147
PLUS Network P686
Plus Petrol gas stations W644, W645
Plus System (ATMs) A1480, P508
Plus Ultra W82
Plusbelle (personal care products) A487, A1200
Plusnet (fixed line phones) W594
PLX Technology, Inc. E267
Plymouth cars P666, P706, P733, W188
Plymouth Oil A1460
Plywood Reel Company A1302
P.M. Place Stores A1282
PMAC (drawn tubing) E87
PMC-Sierra (chips) E55, E247
PMD Group. *See* Noveon, Inc.
P.M.I. Comercio Internacional W440, W441
PMM&Co. A840, P286, W324
PMRealty Advisors, Inc. P385
P.N. Hirsch discount chain A496
The PNC Financial Services Group A936, A1112, A**1146-A1147**, A1500
PNC Park (baseball field) A1146, P120, P593
Pneumatic Tyre Company W428
Pneumo Abex A1088, A1104
PNJ Communications W598
Pocahontas Foods, USA, Inc. A1109
Pocahontas Gas Partnership A416
Pocahontas Land Corporation A1038, A1039

Pocket Edition tobacco W283
PocketCam camera A1148
PocketZip computer storage A778, A779
Poco Petroleums A310
Pocono Downs race course (Pennsylvania) E262
Podany, William J. A1283
Podeschi, Dave A57
Poe, John D. E119, E286
Pogo Producing Company E268
Pogue, D. Eric A317
Pogue, Mack P659
Pohang Iron & Steel Company, Ltd. W398, W**454-W455**
Pohl, W. F., Jr. P201
Pohlad, Robert C. A1104, A1105
Pohmer, Tom P697
Poindexter, Christian H. A425
Point Range Sensor E48
Point to Point Communications E52
Point.com A1324
Poirer, David F. W271
Poise undergarments A827
Pokelwaldt, Robert A1550
The Pokemon Company E147
Pokémon (movies and products) A692, A693, E130, E303, W394, W395
Pokerville Select Market P489
Pokorny, Peter W645
Pokrassa, Gary P712
Polak & Schwartz A766
Polaris missiles A704, A882
Polark, Roger L. A1493
Polaroid Corporation A614, A976, A**1148-A1149**, E184, P190
Polese Company A550
Polet, Robert W619
Poley, Paul R. A483
Policinski, Chris A851, P289
Policy Management Systems A404
Polifly Savings & Loan A658
Polimeni, Dominic A. E273
Poling, Gregory E. A1537
PolioPlus Program P421
Polish & Gas A184
Polish Oil Monopoly W456
Politically Incorrect (TV show) A61
Polk, Anthony J. P45
Polkomtel SA W456, W457
Pollak, David, Jr. A365
Pollan, Clifford M. W593
Pollard, Carl F. E40
Pollard, C. William A1272, A1273
Pollard, Frank A127
Pollard, James T. A637
Polley, R. Stephen A1407
Pollini, Laura W125
Pollis, John G. A605
Pollock, Henry T. A1135
Pollock, John A1059
Pollock, Ross H. A1059
Pollution Control Industries P70
Polly Pocket toys A927

Polo car W631
Polo Classic car W631
Polo Ralph Lauren
Corporation A804, A805, A1134,
A1150-A1151, A1194, A1195,
A1278, A1499, W342, W343
Polo, Victor Hugo, S. W439
Poloco A1150
Polski Koncern Naftowy ORLEN
S.A. W**456**-W**457**
Poly Hi Solidur polymers P673
Polycom, Inc. E268
Polyethylene terephthalate. *See* PET
plastic containers
POLYFELT Gesellschaft
m.b.H. W424, W425
Polyflex (thermoplastic
hoses) A1088
Polygon Communities (home
builders) A862
Polygon Insurance Company
Ltd. W317, W519
PolyGram Filmed
Entertainment A962
PolyGram (music) W444
PolyMask A1262
PolyMedica Corporation E**105**,
E268
Polysar (rubber) W118
Polystyrene Australia P239
Poly-T plastic A1414
Polytrap polymer P164
PolyVision Corporation (visual
communication products) A1334
Polze, Ervin G. A1553
Pomeroy, John E. A503
Pomeroy, Michelle P751
Pompa, Mark A. A545
Pompei, Shauna P347, P680
Ponce de Leon Hotel (St. Augustine,
FL) P108
Poncholito restaurants W166
Pond, Dale C. A893
Pond, Peter B. E88
Pond, Richard G. A281
Ponderosa restaurants P332, P333,
P674
Pondiumin drug A148
Pond's skin cream W619
Pong technology W394
Ponicall, Michael P481
Pons, Francis P121
Pont Securities W608
Pontal, Jean-François W233
Pont-à-Mousson W506
Pontarelli, Thomas A379
Ponte (pasta) W192
Pontiac vehicle A650, P256, P561,
P606, P706, P733
Pontikes, Kenneth A392
Pontikes, Nicholas K. A392
Pontin, Richard S. A293
Pony car W274
Ponzanelli, Enrique W635
Pool, Leonard A100
Poolawanna mine W640
Poole & Kent A544, A545

Poole, Deborah G. A1135
Poole, Fred A. A1443
Poole, Robert M. P359
Pop Secret popcorn A648, A649
Pop Top Software E298
POP.com P166
Pope, Charles C. A1261, P441, P725
Pope, C. Larry A1291
Pope, Darryl L. P261
Pope, Sharon M. E228
Popeye cartoon character A744,
P242
Popeye's Chicken & Biscuits
restaurants P124, P575
Popik, William C. A91
Popko, Kathleen P115
Popkowski, Chester J. A1005
Pople, John P378
Pop-Lok fastening systems A265
Popovits, Kimberly J. A641
Popp, Josef W120
Poppa, Ryal A1336
Poppin' Fresh Doughboy A648,
A1136
Poppin' Fresh Restaurants A288
PopShots camera A1148
Popsicle W618, W619
Pop-Tarts A814, A816, A817
Popular Club Plan (catalog
sales) P254
Popular Mechanics
(magazine) A701, P229
Popular Science (magazine) A1402
Population Council P79, P194
Porcelain Steel Building
(construction) P516
Porcello, Joseph E. E156
Groupe Porcher Industries A1072
Porcher plumbing fixtures A152,
A153
Poremba, Dave P675
Porgera Mine W452, W453
Porges, Denis H. A573
PORK PACT P36
Porky's (movie) A1286
Dr.ING.h.c.F.Porsche AG P630,
P631, P731, W**458**-W**459**
Porsche, Ferdinand W458, W630
Porsche, Ferry W458
Port Adventure, SA theme
park A175
The Port Authority of New York and
New Jersey E137, P**398**-P**399**,
P703
Port Authority of Port St. Joe E115
The Port Authority Trans-Hudson
System (PATH) P398, P399, P703
Port Dickson Power W538
Port Newark/Elizabeth Marine
Terminal P399
Port of Felixstowe Limited W273
Portal One software E134
Porter, Arthur T. P591
Porter, Jeffrey P. A511
Porter, Jim R. E70, E217
Porter, Joe P198
Porter, Michael C. A513

Porter, M. R. A1410, P484
Porter Novelli International (public
relations) A1063
Porter Paints A1152
Porter, Seton A974
Porter, Steven D. A721
Porter, Townsend H., Jr. A1261,
P441
Porter, Tracy E152
Porter, William A566
Portera, Joseph P. A437
Portland Children's Museum P79
Portland Fire (basketball
team) P355
Portland Forge A116
Portland General Electric
Company A552
Portland State University P520
Portland Trail Blazers (basketball
team) P355, P510, P511, P767
Portman, John A740, P240
Portrait of Dr. Gachet
(painting) A1304
Portsmouth & Roanoke Rail
Road A454
Portugal Telecom SGPS, S.A. W224,
W578
Porzenheim, Clifford A639
Porzig, Ullrich E. A1093
POS ProVisions E118
POSCO. *See* Pohang Iron & Steel
Company, Ltd.
Poses, Frederic M. A152, A153
Posit-Bond A1060
Positec W520
Posner, Jarrett B. A1401
Posner, Victor A1400
Post cereal A842, A843, A1126
Post, Charles A842
Post, C. W. A816
Post Exchange (PX) P52
Post, Marjorie A842
Post Shop Magazine (mail order
catalog) W426
Post Toasties cereal A842
Post, William J. A1138, A1139
Postage By Phone A1142
Postal Reorganization Act
(1970) A1428, P490
Postal Service. *See* United States
Postal Service
Postal Services and
Telegraphy W502
Postalmarket (mail order
company) W426
Postbank N.V. W286, W287
Postcheque-en Girondienst W286
Post-it Notes A976
Postl, James J. A1096, A1097
Post-Newsweek Stations
(television) A1503
PostScript computer language A76
Postum Cereal Company A842
Posturepedic mattress P442
Pot o' Gold lottery game P373,
P473
Potamkin, Alan P702

Potamkin, Robert P702
Potamkin, Victor P702
Potier, François W447
Potillo, Beth A495
The Potomac Edison
  Company A114
Potomac Electric Power
  Company A424
Potter, David R. A629
Potter, Duane W. A859
Potter, Jeff S. E64
Potter, John E. (US Postal
  Service) A1428, A1429, P490,
  P491, P754
Potter, John W. (Oxford
  Automotive) P695
Potter, Kent P574
Potter, Michael J. A260, A261
Potter, Myrtle S. A641
Potter, Nelson W. A605
Potter Production E124
Potter, Robert A1300
Pottery Barn stores and
  catalogs A1530, A1531
Pottinger, Alan W177
Pottruck, David S. A349
Potts, Charles F. A201
Potts, David B. (ARRIS Group) E30
Potts, David T. (Tesco) W591
Potucek, Elissa A. E64
Poughkeepsie Savings Bank P640
Poulain candy W155
Poulenc, Étienne W102
Poulin, Dan W339
Pouliot, Colleen M. A77
Poulson, Richard J. M. A1291
Poulter, Brian A. A775
Poulton, Lorelei E55, E196
Pounce pet food A723
Pound Puppies toys A692
Poupart-Lafarge, Olivier W135
Pour-A-Quiche A609
Pourcelot, Alain W171
Poussot, Bernard A149
Pouw, King T. A817
Pouyat, Alain W135
Powder River Basin gas
  pipeline A376
Powell, Colin P110, P128
Powell, David W. A977
Powell, George, III A1548
Powell, George, Jr. A1548
Powell, George, Sr. A1548
Powell, Hugo W288, W289
Powell, Jerome H. P111
Powell, Kendall J. A649
Powell, Lura J. P71
Powell, Patricia A383
Powell, Rod W291
Powell, Terry F A883
Power Authority of the State of New
  York P703
Power Cables Malaysia Sdn
  Bhd W451
Power Components E273
Power Computing A186, A762
Power, David J. E98

Power Electronics E169
Power House stores W644, W645
Power Investments (engines) P152
Power Markets Development A1154
Power Process Controls, Ltd. A447
Power Semiconductor
  Operations E76
Power Specialty Company A620
Power Stone (video game) W527
Power Systems Group A620
Power Transmission Group A612
POWERaDE beverage A385
Powerball - The Game Show (TV
  show) P581
Powerball Lottery P372, P581, P680
PowerBar snack W388
PowerBook computer A186, W550
PowerBridge Group P340
Powercom (reserve power
  systems) E169
Powercor A1082, W522
PowerGen plc W218
Powerlink (Internet access) A72
PowerNet (electric
  transmission) A668
Power-One, Inc. A446, E269
PowerOne Media P32
PowerPath brand A585
Powerpay (online payroll) A342
PowerPC chip A990
PowerRankings E205
Powers & Anderson A1070
Powers beer W231
Powers, Joshua A1170
Powers, Larry K. P613
Powers, Richard (SYNNEX) P740
Powers, Richard W. (ITT
  Industries) A781
Powers, Thomas W. E216
PowerSchool (software) A186
PowerShip A588
PowerSpec PC computers P336,
  P337, P675
Powerstreet online brokerage A614,
  P190
Powers-Weightman-
  Rosengarten A956
Powertel Limited A1248, W204
PowerTV A1258
Powerwave Technologies,
  Inc. E**106**, E269
Powhatan Corporation A993
Pow-R-Designer brand A527
Pozen, Robert C. A615
Pozez, Louis A1092
Pozez, Shaol A1092
Pozzi-Renati Millwork
  Products A446
PP&L Resources. *See* PPL
  Corporation
PPC Marketing, LTD. A1132
PPG Industries, Inc. A**1152**-A**1153**,
  P212, W72, W278
PPL Corporation A570,
  A**1154**-A**1155**, A1306
PPR. *See* Pinault-Printemps-
  Redoute

PPS Valley Management, Inc. A323
PR Newswire Association,
  Inc. E202, W620, W621
Prabhu, Vasant M. A1235
Prachar, William E. A1505
Pracht Spedition + Logistik
  GmbH W461
Practical Sciences E119
Practice Patterns Science,
  Inc. A574, A575
The Practice (TV show) A60, A61
Prada (fashion house) W250, W348
PRADCO (fishing tackle) P170,
  P171
Pradium (grain trading) A324
Prairie Farms Dairy Inc. P704
A Prairie Home Companion (radio
  program) P144
Prairie Island nuclear plant A1542
Prairie View A&M University P470,
  P471, P743
PRAKLA-SEISMOS A1252
Praktiker home improvement
  stores W364, W365
Pramer A873
Prandin drug W416, W417
Prandium, Inc. A86, A784
Prange, John F. E178
Prange, William J. E178
Praselj, Eduardo W439
Prasetio, John A173, P49
Pratt & Lambert (paint
  maker) A1278
Pratt & Whitney A646, A1420,
  A1432
Pratt, Edmund A1118
Pratt, Steven H. P57
Pratt, Warren A1285
Prausa, John W. P455
Pravachol drug A290, A291
Praver, Mitch P359
Praw, Albert Z. A813
Praxair, Inc. A**1156**-A**1157**
PRC-DeSoto International A1152
Precept Software A368
Prechtl, Victor L. A611
Precious Metals Development A550
Precision Blank Welding A256
Precision brand A585
Precision (bulk containers) E188
Precision Monolithics (electronic
  components) A170
Precision Optical Research
  Laboratory. *See* Seiki Kogaku
  Kenkyusho
Preckel, Rick W. E87
PRECLUDE dura substitute P523
Predator (CD-RW drives) A779
Preference paper products P727
Preferred Financial Group P226,
  P227
Preferred HealthAlliance P348
Preferred Products brand A1348
Preferred Provider Organization of
  Michigan P86, P87, P557
Preferred Selection brand
  foods A1348

Preferred Translocation Systems (logistics) A344
Prego pasta sauce A316
Preiksaitis, Raymond V. A193
Prelude car W264, W265
Prema Milmet A1386
Premarin drug A148, A149
Premark International A748, A842, A1414
Premcor Inc. P340, P704
Premier Bancorp A230
Premier Bedding P442
Premier Beverage P738
Premier Cablevision W494
Premier Car Rental (insurance replacement rentals) A300
Premier Cruise Lines A1478
Premier Diamond Mining Company W92
Premier Farnell plc A196
Premier Foodservice Distributors of America P479
Premier (health care) P115
Premier Hospitality A1297
Premier Manufacturing Support Services A1272
Premier Oil plc A132
Premier service stations W612
Premier Transco Limited (pipeline) A824, A825
Premier Trust Deed Services, Inc. A681
Premiere Cinemas P412
Premiere (magazine) A1160, W330
Premium Distributors P713
Premium fresh vegetables A355
Premium Recipe brand A1109
Premium saltines A843
Premium Standard Farms, Inc. A426, A427, P140, P583
Prentice Hall (publisher) W430
PREPA. See Puerto Rico Electric Power Authority
Pre-Paid Legal Services Inc. A474, E107, E269, P154, W196
Preparation H A148
Prep-Rite primers A1278
Presby, J. Thomas A475, P155, W197
Presbyterian Healthcare Services (New Mexico) P704
Presbyterian Healthcare System (North Carolina) P691
Presbyterian Healthcare System (Texas) P744
The Presbyterian Hospital (New York City) P44, P134
Prescolite A1447
Prescott Investors A854
Prescott, John W128
Prescott, Susan A77
Prescription Health Services, Inc. A323
Present, Randy A509
President Baking A814
President car W403
Presidential Medal of Freedom P258

Presidential Plaza apartments (New Jersey) P291
Presidio Oil E129
Presley, Elvis P416, P424
Presley, Greg P644
Presque Isle Corporation A1006
The Press Association W484
Press, Harlan I. E184
Press, Jonathan P355
Press, Terry P167
Pressey, Walter M. E165
Pressler, Paul S. A1497
Pressure Systems International A198
Presta, Kelly A1481, P509
Prestage Farms A1290
Prestige carpets P342
Prestige Fragrance & Cosmetics A1200
Prestolite Wire Corporation A572
Preston, Andrew A354
Preston, Forrest P658
Preston, Frank A389
Preston, Kasandra K. A287
Preston, Steven C. A1273
Preston, William P69
Pret A Manger Limited (sandwich shops) A942, A943
Prettejohn, Nicholas E. T. W337
Pretty Girl (retailer) W644
Pretty, Ted N. W587
Preussag AG W218, W460-W461, W594
PreussenElektra (utility) W218
Preussische Bergwerks-und Hutten-Aktiengesellschaft W460
Preussischen Elektrizitats W460
Prevacid drug A58, A59, P741
Preview Travel A1228
Prevnar drug A148
Prevo's Family Markets A1312
Prewell International E261
Prey, Richard L. A1163
PRI Automation, Inc. E35, E166
Pribilla, Peter W537
Price Chopper warehouse stores P62, P63, P547, P617
Price Club discount warehouse A262, A436
Price Company of California A1494
Price, David B., Jr. A663
Price Enterprises A436
Price, Floyd R. A185
Price, Francis D., Jr. A1095
Price, Julian A794
Price, Laurence A436
Price Mart stores P62, P63
Price, Michael A1360
Price, Pam E149
Price Pfister plumbing fixtures A264, A265, A920
Price, Robert (Ceridian) A342
Price, Robert (Price Club Warehouse) A436
Price, Samuel A1158, P400, W462
Price Saver Membership Wholesale Clubs A844

Price, Sol A436
Price, Trevor A449
Price, William P474
priceline.com Inc. A138, A1490
Priceman A67
PriceRite supermarkets A844
Price's dairy product A467
PricewaterhouseCoopers A172, A474, A562, A712, A1158-A1159, P48, P154, P182, P206, P286, P400-P401, P540, P620, P705, W90, W196, W222, W324, W462-W463
Priddy, William A., Jr. E280
Pride in Performance-Keep It Going (book) P657
Pridemark (home builders) A812
Prié, Michel W195
Priem, Curtis E256
Priest, Patricia P553
Priestly, Kay G. A173, P49, P540, W91
Prillaman, L. I. A1039
Prilosec drug W492
Prima cigarettes W241
Prima Energy Corporation E270
Primadonna Resorts, Inc. A966
Primark (financial information provider) E100, E258, W592
Primary Colors (book) A1502
Primary Energy, Inc. A1035
Primaxin drug A957
Prime, Kathleen E294
Prime Solutions A1336
PRIMEA power assemblies P523
PrimeCo (telecom) A1472, P765
PRIMEDIA, Inc. (publishing) A836, A837, A872, A873, A1160-A1161, E220, P282, P283, P460, P653
Primera car W403
Primerica Financial Services, Inc. A370
PriMerit Bank A658
PRIMESTAR (satellite TV) A650, A736, P92
Primex Technologies A644, A1060
Primex Trading A660, A988
Primis A508
Primm Valley Resort A966, A967
Primo de Rivera, Miguel W578
Primrose Asset Management, Inc. A1509
Primus beer W255
Primus Custom Publishing A944
Primus, Inc. P705
Primus Online W364, W365
Prince Automotive A802
Prince, Charles O., III A371
Prince, Gary J. W245
Prince, Jack A851, P289
Prince, James H. E295
Prince, Larry L. A653
Prince, Michael A305
The Prince of Egypt (movie) P166, P167
Prince pasta P90, P91
Prince, Steven J. A1267

Prince tennis rackets W124, W125
Prince, Thomas E. E194
Princecraft Boats A298, A299
Princess Cruises W434
Princess Hotels W340
Princeton Financial Systems,
Inc. A1333
Princeton Natural Gas E39
Princeton Packaging A250
Princeton University P378
The Principal Financial
Group A1162-A1163
Pringle of Scotland brand A691
Pringles snacks A1165
Prinivil drug A956
Print Club photo stickers W527
Printemps (department
stores) W446, W447
Printpack, Inc. P705
Prior Energy Corporation P637
Priority Healthcare
Corporation E270
Priority One W88
Priory, Richard B. A515
Pripps beer W163
Prism Communication
Services A392
Prism Financial Corporation W474
Prison Health Services E153
PRISTYNE UX filter media P523
Pritchard, Beth M. A777, A877
Pritchett, Ronald A. A643
Pritzker, A. N. A740, P240, P312
Pritzker and Pritzker (law
firm) P312
Pritzker, Bob A740, P240
Pritzker, Donald A740, P240
Pritzker family A138, A1216
Pritzker, Jay A740, A1408, P240,
P312, P482
Pritzker, Nicholas A740, P240, P312
Pritzker, Nicholas J. A741, P241
Pritzker, Penny S. A741, P241
Pritzker, Robert P312
Pritzker, Robert A. P313, P665
Pritzker School of Medicine P497
Pritzker, Thomas J. A740, A741,
P240, P241, P636
Prius car W614, W615
PrivaSeek, Inc. A1233
The Private Bank A1308
Private Brands (soup stock) P122
Private Capital Group A414
Private Client Group A960
Private Health Care Systems P214
Private Ledger. See Linsco/Private
Ledger Corporation
Private Mini Storage Realty A134,
A135
PrivateAccounts, Inc. A566, A567
Prize Energy Corporation E270
PrizeLAWN lawn spreaders P516,
P772
Prizm car P366, P367, P687
PRL Fashions of Europe A1150
PRN Holdings, Inc. A1309

PRN Services
(pharmaceuticals) A320
Pro & Son's, Inc. P489
Pro Line windows and doors P698
Pro Parts Xpress (auto parts) P518,
P519, P774
Pro Sieben Media W106
Proagro P36
ProAssurance E241
Probe Technology E81
Procard (credit card
processing) A558
Procardia XL drug A1118
Process Controls Engineering A326
Processors Unlimited A1454
Prochaska, Joseph J., Jr. A183
ProCoil Corporation A1006, A1007
Procomp Amazonia Industria
Electronica (information
technology) A488
Proconics E31
PROCOOL auto care
products A1101
Procordia AB A1110, W632
Procrit drug A801
The Procter & Gamble
Company A276, A290, A374,
A382, A386, A408, A486, A530,
A902, A1074, A1164-A1165,
A1200, A1246, A1302, A1538, P72,
P106, P304, P432, P551, P620,
W256, W273, W308, W342, W467,
W492
Procter, William A1164
Proctor, Deborah A. P57
Proctor, Georganne A241, P75,
P552
Proctor, Truby A1084
Proctor-Silex small
appliances A992, A993
ProcureNet, Inc. (software) A600
Proczko, Taras R. A691
Prodigy Communications
Corporation (online
service) A1244, A1245, A1264,
W152, W580
Producers Creamery
Company P148
Product 19 cereal A817
Production Response Systems P506
Productivity Point
International P278, P279
Productos Bard de Mexico S.A. de
C.V. A445
Productos Colombia A722
Compagnie des Produits Chimiques
et Electrométallurgiques d'Alais,
Froges et Carmargue W432
Pro-Fac Cooperative, Inc.
(vegetables) A466, P38
Profectis (customer service) W311
Profertil SA W66, W67
Professional Audio P310
Professional Claim Services,
Inc. A1506, A1507
Professional Detailing. See PDI, Inc.
Professional Employee
Management, Inc. A1488
Professional Escrow, Inc. A591

The Professional Golfers Association
of America A1220
Professional Liability Group A1169
Professional Life Underwriters
Services, Inc. A395
Professional Portfolio software E25
Professional Sports Care
Management, Inc. A699
Professional Trade Shows E102
Professionals Group Inc. E241
Proffer, Lanny M. P359
Proffer, Phyllis J. A1141
Proffitt, D. W. A1238
Proffitt, Harwell A1238
Proffitt, Jackie P716
Proffitt's department stores A1238
Proffitt's stores P76
ProForm compound P683
PROform golf, inc. P637
ProGold (corn sweeteners) P538
Prograft Medical P522
Progress Energy, Inc. A514, A515,
A1166-A1167
Progress infant nutrition A149
Progress Lighting A1446
Progress Telecommunications
Corporation A1166, A1167
Progressive American A1168
Progressive Baker A325, P105
The Progressive
Corporation A1168-A1169
Progressive Grocers P62
Progressive System
Technologies E31
Progressive Technologies E35
Progressive Toll & Industries W226
Progresso soups A1136, A1137
Project RISE P246
Prokupek, David P. E132
Pro-Lawn (turf care) P38
PROLIFT auto care A1101
PROLINE auto parts A1101
Pro-Line (personal care
products) A108
ProLogis E285
ProMarkt electrical stores W312,
W313
Prometric, Inc. (computer based
testing) W592
Promil baby formula A148
Promise margarine W618, W619
Promo Edge Company
(printing) P673
Promocash stores W164, W165
Promodata A1336
Promodès (retailer) W164, W166
Promostroibank W242
Promus Hotel Corporation A684,
A720, W544
Pronova W410
Pronto camera A1148
Prontosil drug W118
Proost, Robert L. A95
Propecia drug A957
Propel water A1107, A1181
Propeller office tables P277
Pro-Pet (pet foods) P38, P622

Prophet Score risk assessment model E108
Propulsid drug A800
Propyläen (publishing) W107
ProQuest Company A524, A1142, E100
ProSeed, Inc. A444, A445
ProSiebenSAT.1 Media AG W106
Prosise, Robert P171
Prosoft Training E36
ProSom drug A58
ProSource (restaurants) P236
ProSource Wholesale Floorcoverings P568
Prospect Farms A1418
Prospect Motors Inc. P706
Société de Prospection Electrique A1252
Prosperity Bancshares, Inc. E271
Prosser, Ian W137, W545
Prosser, John W., Jr. A787
Prosser, J. Stuart K. A1263
ProStaff Group (general staffing) A818
PRO-START auto parts A1101
Prot, Baudouin W131
PRO-TEC Coating Company A1463
Protectas S.A. W524, W525
Protection One, Inc. W494
Protection Services Industries P655
Protective Closures P310
Proteg (security) W524
Protegé car W363
Protégé hard drives A1515
Protein Technologies International A534
Proteus Airlines W68
Protex personal care products A387
Proto, Frank W. W67
Proto, Rodney A1504
Protonix drug A149
Protonotarios, D. W385
Protropin drug A640, A641
Prout, Gerald R. A613
ProVantage Health Services A956, A1282
Proven Value auto products P112
Provena Health P706
Proventil drug A1250
Provera, Marco Tronchetti W423, W574, W575
Providence Bank A602
Providence Health Systems P706
Providence (insurance) W104
Providence (TV show) A999
Provident Bank A144
Provident Companies A1380, A1440, A1441
Provident Financial Group, Inc. A144, A145
Provident National Assurance Company A126
Provident National of Philadelphia A1146
Provider Service Network P566

Providian Financial Corporation A592, A**1170**-A**1171**, W64
Provigo Inc. (grocery stores) W244, W245
Province Healthcare Company E271
Provincial Bank (Ireland) W86
Provincial Newspapers W621
Provisions (food and beverage distribution) P107
Provost, Louis W. A1189
Prowler travel trailers A605
Prowse, Robert M. C. W383
Proxi stores W165, W166
Proxima S.A. A778, A1266, E73, E220, W99
Proxy Delhaize convenience stores W194, W195
Prozac drug A220, A540, A674, P66, W72
Prozes, Andrew W479
The Pru. *See* Prudential plc
Pru Bache (securities brokerage) A1172
Prudential Annuities Ltd. W465
The Prudential Assurance Company Ltd. W465
Prudential Center (Boston) E34
Prudential Financial A**1172**-A**1173**
Prudential Florida Realty E115
Prudential Insurance Company of America A90, A204, A964, A1172, A1550, E259, P28, P120, P230, P737, W130, W464, W646
Prudential Mutual Assurance Investment and Loan Association W464
Prudential plc A150, W184, W**464**-W**465**
Prudential Securities Inc. P232
Prudential Steel E87, E238
Prudhoe Bay Royalty Trust E166
Pruett, Greg S. A1121
Prussian Mine and Foundry Company W460
Prutzman, Deborah A517
Prygocki, Mark A., Sr. E89, E240
Pryor, Daniel A. A463
PS Business Parks, Inc. E271
PSA Airlines, Inc. A1442, A1443
PSB (metal products) P516, P772
PSC. *See* Michigan Public Service Commission (PSC)
PSD Holding Corporation A323
PSEG Energy Holdings, Inc. A1174, A1175
PSEG Power A1028
PSI Energy, Inc. A362
PSI (gas marketing) A1464
PSICOR (cardiovascular perfusion) A236
PSM2 (magazine) W238
PSNC Energy A1248, A1249
PSP Swiss Property (real estate) W652
PT. *See* entry under primary company name

P. T. Barnum's Grand Traveling Museum, Menagerie, Caravan, and Circus P188
Ptachik, Robert P129
Ptak, Frank S. A749
PTT Netherland NV W502
Corporation for Public Broadcasting P**144**-P**145**
Public Broadcasting Service P144, P145, P585
Public Employees' Medical and Hospital Care Act (1962) A314
Public Policy Institute P28, P29
Public Radio International P144, P145, P585
Public Service Company of Colorado A1542
Public Service Company of Colorado (utility) A1543
Public Service Company of Indiana A362
Public Service Company of New Hampshire A1040, A1041
Public Service Company of Northern Illinois A1030
Public Service Electric and Gas Company A1174, A1175
Public Service Electric and Gas of New Jersey A1154
Public Service Enterprise Group Inc. A1028, A1154, A**1174**-A**1175**
Public Storage, Inc. E271
Public Systems and Control Software E88
Public Utility Holding Company Act (1935) A114, A154, A362, A376, A418, A498, A512, A570, A598, A624, A668, A1034, A1040, A1082, A1138, A1154, A1166, A1174, A1198, A1266, A1306, A1542
Public Utility Regulatory Policies Act (1978) A88, P340
Publicis Groupe S.A. W**466**-W**467**
Publicor W470
Publish (magazine) P249
Publishers Paper (newsprint) A1292
Publishers' Warehouse P171
Publishing and Broadcasting Limited W586
Publishing Cumbre A1255
Publix Super Markets, Inc. A**1176**-A**1177**, A1532, E276, P256, P**402**-P**403**, P707
Puca, Paul P738
Pucino, Paul J. E126, E299
Puck, Wolfgang A408
Puckett, John L. A1149
Puddister, Ann E77, E225
Pudlin, Helen P. A1147
Pueblo International P478, P479
Pueringer Distributing A768
Puerto Rico Electric Power Authority A88, P707
Pueyo, Pilar E165
Pugh, Burvin E. A923, P321
Pugsley, Trevor W177
Puhl, Chi Chi P63
Pujadas, Michelle A1233

Pulatie, David L. A1125
Puleo, J. Michael A955
Puleo, Lenore F. A825
Pulido, Mark A946
Pulitzer, Joseph A700, A1020, P134, P228
Pulitzer prize A1020, A1502, P32
Pullen, Robert W. A1363
Pullins, Jerald L. A1269
Pullman Company A1368, P310
Pullman Standard A176, A1406
Pull-Ups diapers A827
Pulmozyme drug A640, A641
Pulsar watches W528, W529, W530
Pulse Latino (magazine) P347
Pulse! (magazine) P346, P347
PulsePoint software A1424
Pulte Homes, Inc. A340, A508, A549, A862, **A1178**-A**1179**, P643
Pulte, William J. A1178
Puma athletic shoes W62
PUMA sneakers A332
Punch Taverns Ltd. P474, P475, W84, W638
Puntocash stores W165
Puorro, Michael P. E281
Pupperoni pet food A723
Purcell, Dennis J. A467
Purcell, Philip J. A989
Purcell, Steve A338
Purdue Frederick P707
Purdue Pharma L.P. P707
Purdy, Gloria E226
Pure & Natural body care A487
Pure Foods (processed meats) W511
Pure Oil A1438
Pure Resources, Inc. A1438, E272
Puregon drug W72
Pure-Pak milk containers A770
PureVision extended wear lenses A234, A235
Purex Industries A486, A487
Purina animal feeds A324, P104
Purina Mills, Inc. A834, A850, P288, W136
Puritan Fashions P100
Purity cereal A768
Purity dairy product A467
Purity supermarkets W644, W645
Purity Supreme supermarkets A1084
Purity Wholesale Grocers, Inc. P708
Purkis, Leonard C. A567
Purolator Courier A102, A380
Purolator Products (filters) A198, P310
PURPA. *See* Public Utility Regulatory Policies Act (1978)
Purple Label clothing A1150
Purse, Craig B. A463
Pursel, David G. A895
Pursell Industries A752
Pursley, Franklin E. A455
Purtell, Lawrence R. A113
Purves, Tom W121

Purvis, David M. A468
Puryear, Armistead D. E25
Puschaver, Ernest L. A603
Push Pops candy E130, E303
Pushan Power Plant A140
Pusser's of the West Indies men's clothes A691
Putin, Vladimir W242
Putnam Berkley (publishing) W430
Putnam Investments, Inc. A916, A917, W396
Putrino, John A305
Putt, Richard E. A293
Putz, Richard J. A1423
PVAC drug E89
PVX Gold W452
PW Eagle, Inc. E272
PwC. *See* PricewaterhouseCoopers
PX (Post Exchange) P52, P543
PYA/Monarch, Inc. (food service distributor) A1242, W498, W499
Pyne, Joseph M. A1427
Pyne, Vicki R. A301
Pyott, David E. I. A119
Pyra, Thomas M. E180
Pyrex housewares A1023, P90, P91, P164, P558, P775
Pyrolase 160 enzyme E193
Pyropower (boiler maker) A620
Pyrotenax A642
Pyxis Corporation (pharmaceuticals) A320, A321
Pyxsys Corporation (data storage) P54, P55

Q

Q Burgers fast food P160
Q Clubs fitness centers P258
Q Lube oil change centers A1096
Q System modular systems A707
Q8 (gas stations) W424
al-Qaddafi, Muammar. *See* al-Gadhafi, Mu'ammar abu Minyar
Qantas Airways Limited A164, W140, W141, W**468**-W**469**, W540, W541
Qatar General Petroleum A1128
QFC supermarkets A844, A845
QK Healthcare, Inc. P709
QLogic Corporation E272
QMS printers W368
Q.R.S. Company A1190
QSI Holdings P406, P709
QT convenience stores P710
Q-tips W618, W619
Quackenbush tools A430, A431
Quad/Graphics, Inc. P**404**-P**405**, P708
QuadMaster ATV W561
Quadracci, Harry R. P404
Quadracci, Harry V. P404, P405, P708
Quadracci, Thomas A. P405
Quadrapartite Cartel W414
Quadriga (publishing) W107
Quadrominium housing A1178
Quaforth, James S. E255

Quaggin, Jennifer W453
The Quaker Oats Company A426, A722, A1074, A1106, A1107, A**1180**-A**1181**, A1400, P140, P705, W244
Quaker State Corporation A1096, A1097, P390
QualChoice HMO P768
QUALCOMM Inc. A888, A**1182**-A**1183**, E92, E106, E222, E232, W220, W328, W406, W570
QualiTROL (controls) A462
Quality Chekd Dairies, Inc. P708
Quality Color Press W378
Quality Dining, Inc. A288
Quality Farm and Fleet Wholesale Supply P406
Quality Farm & Country stores P406
Quality Food Centers, Inc. A845, P479, P524
Quality Importers (liquor) A296
Quality King Distributors Inc. P709
Quality Markets supermarkets A1094
Quality Stores, Inc. P**406**-P**407**, P709
QualMed, Inc. A696, A697, A1506
Quam, Lois A1435
Quanam Medical A282
Quandt, Herbert W120
Quanta Services, Inc. A1464, A1465
Quante AG (telecom systems) A976
Quantum brand A287
Quantum Chemical (propane) A900, A974, W252
Quantum Computer Services A180, A782, A928
Quantum Corporation A928, A**1184**-A**1185**, E23, E98
Quark, Inc. A76
Quarles, W. Greyson, Jr. P431, P721
Quartet software E187
Quasar electronic products W360
Quattro lawn equipment A287
Quattro Pro software A1050
Qube software E25
Quebecor Inc. A1218, W**470**-W**471**, W494
Quebecor World Inc. (printing) W186
Queen Elizabeth 2 (ship) A330, A331
Queens College P128, P129
Queens Hospital Center P368, P369
Queensborough Community College P128, P129
Queensland and Northern Territory Aerial Services. *See* Qantas Airways Limited
Queensland National Bank W382
Queensland Phosphate W640
Queeny, Edgar A984, A1122, A1300
Queeny, John A984, A1122, A1300
Quelle mail order W310, W311
Quesnel, Gregory L. A381
Quest car W403
Quest Diagnostics Inc. A434

Quest Education A1502
Quest (fragrances and flavorings) W278
Questar Corporation E238
Questia Media E221
QuestLink Technology, Inc. A196
Questor Managment Company P614
Questor Partners A1222
Questrom, Allen I. A586, A790, A791
Questron Technology, Inc. E273
Quexco Inc. P709, W428
Quick 'n Tasty foods P710
Quick & Reilly/Fleet Securities, Inc. A602
Quick, Carla E284
Quick detachable tire A664
Quick Draw lottery game P372
Quick, John L. A237
Quick, Peter A997, P47, P353
Quick Pick lottery game P373
Quick Stop convenience stores A1085
Quick Wrench A122
QuickCam cameras W338, W339
Quickie Wiper duster W309
QuickLogic Corporation E273
QuickMAIL W202
Quicksilver Resources Inc. E273
The Quiet Company. See Northwestern Mutual Life Insurance
Quietflex P618
Quigley, Mike W77
Quik drink mix W388
Quik Stop Markets A845, A1084
Quik Sync software A779
QuikMail A102
Quiksilver brand clothing E101
QuikTrip Corporation P710
Quill Corporation (mail order distributor) A1324, A1325
Quilmes beer W255
Quilted Northern paper products A654
Quin, J. Marvin A201
Quincy Family Steakhouse A86
Quincy Hospital (Boston) P56
Quinlan, Linda E289
Quinlan, Michael R. P661
Quinlan, Thomas J., III W379
Quinn, Brian W172
Quinn, Daniel M. A1445
Quinn, David W. A341
Quinn, Douglas P357
Quinn Gary A403
Quinn, Jack F. A747
Quinn, James E. A1385
Quinn, Lochlann W87
Quinn, Patrick A1312
Quinnell, Bruce A. A277
Quint, C. Robert E108, E274
Quintero Iñiguez, Alejandro W583
Quintiles A1122
Quinton Hazell (aftermarket) A460
Quirk, Kathleen L. A629

Quirk, Raymond R. A591
Quisp cereal A1107, A1181
Quist, Steven M. E48, E189
Quixsource, Inc. A595
Quixtar P536
Quock, Les L. A1509
Quotron W484
QVC, Inc. (cable network) A390, A391, A873, A1232, A1450, P416, W146
Qwest Broadcasting A1402
Qwest Communications International Inc. A248, A368, A764, A1186-A1187, E41, E148, E179, E192, E243, E318, P412, P712, W502

R

R & H Maxxon, Inc. A1084
R. Griggs Group Limited E289
R. Hoe (printing) A452
R.18 garbage business A122
R2E (computers) W150
R. A. Graerser Chemical Works A1300
R.A. Waller and Company A916
Raab, John J. E58
Raab Karcher A1272, W506
Raab Karcher Sicherheit (guard services) W524
Rabain, Patrick W343
Rabanco Companies A122
Rabb, Kirk A640
Rabin, Edward W. A741, P241
Rabin, Stanley A. A396, A397
Rabine, Jon P247
Rabinowitz, Stephen A642, A643
Rabobank A96
Raboud, J. Frank A705
Racal Electronics Plc W628
Racamier, Henry W348
Race, Mark L. A1059
RaceTrac Petroleum, Inc. P710
Raceway convenience stores P710
Racine Cardinals (football team) P356
Rack Rite Distributors A1202
Racom Teledata W79
Racquet Club men's clothes A691
Radavitz, Moe A1100
Radcliff, Michael D. A755
Radcliffe College P220, P626
Radcliffe Institute for Advanced Study at Harvard P220, P626
Raddisson Hotels A328
Radegast beer W552, W553
Rader, Paul P426
Radian Group Inc. E108, E274
Radiance of the Seas (cruise ship) A1217
Radiant Power E67
Radianz W484
Radiation (data processing) A686
Radine, Gary D. P591
Radio 1 A373
Radio & Allied Industries W354

Radio and Television Workshop P194
Radio Bonton A373
Grupo Radio Centro W580
Radio Cine Forniture E85
Radio Cite W466
Radio City Music Hall A312, A313
Radio Corporation of America A60, A80, A646, A710, A998, A1188, A1358, A1424, A1520, P32, P88, P454, W260, W360
Radiohead (music group) W213
Radioland Murders (movie) P303
RadioShack Corporation A208, A266, A1130, A1188-A1189, P336, W180
Radisson hotels E215, E231
Radisson SAS Hotels P106, P107, P108, P567, W518
Radisson Seven Seas Cruises P106, P107
RadiSys Corporation E109, E274
Radix Microsystems. See RadiSys Corporation
Radler, F. David W263
Radley, Gordon P303, P661
Rado, Patricia A. A1175
Rado watches W562, W563
Radtke, Duane C. A499
Raduchel, William J. A181
Rady, Ernest S. E316
Radyne ComStream Inc. E274
Raeburn, Tessa W143
Raether, Paul E. A837, P283
Rafaniello, Ralph R. P47
Raff, Beryl B. A791, A1552
Raffaeli, John J. W593
Raffel, Forrest A1400
Raffel, Leroy A1400
Raffensperger, Hughes & Company A1000
Raffiani, Philip P771
Raffinato brand A1109
Rafineria Gdanska W456
Rafineria Nafty Jedlicze SA W457
Rafineria Trzebinia SA W457
Ragazzi restaurants W635
Ragen MacKenzie Group Inc. A1508, A1509
Rager, James T. W475
Raggedy Ann and Raggedy Andy dolls A693
Raghavan, Prabhakar E134
Ragland, Ronald E. E277
Ragsdale, Perry A. P125
Ragu sauces W618, W619
Rahimi, Morteza A. P379
Rahr, Joseph P651
Rahr, Stewart P651
Raid insecticide A1246, A1247, P432, P433, P722
Raiders of the Lost Ark (movie) A1450, P302, P303
Raikes, Jeffrey S. A973
Rail Passenger Service Act (1970) P362
Rail, Tom E69

RailAmerica, Inc. E275
Railroad Pass Hotel and Casino A907
Railroad Tycoon II (computer game) E298
RailTex E275
Railtrack Group PLC W176
Railway Express Agency A1104
Railway Guide (map) P408
Rain Drops water softener A359
Rainbo pickles A467
Rainbow Foods A606, A607
Rainbow Media Holdings Inc. A312, A313, A962, A999
Rainbow Production Company A746
Rainbow Programming A312
Rainbow PUSH Coalition A626
Rainbow Vanilla Wafers A815
Raines, Franklin D. A580, A581
Raines, Marjorie D. A357
Rainey, James A582, P184
Rainey, Timothy J. A1047
Rainey, William J. A1093
Rainsford, Bettis P342
Rainville, William A. A1383
Rainwater, Gary L. A137
Rainwater Management E27
Rainwater, Richard A694, A904
Rain-X car care products A1096, A1097
Rainy River Forest Products A274
Raisbeck, David W. A325, P105
Raish, Stephen F. A791
Raising the Mammoth (TV show) P158, P594
RAIT Investment Trust E275
Raithel, Michael L. A447
Rake in the Cash lottery game P473
Rakestraw, John A427, P141
Rakhmetov, Serik W347
Rakow, Jay A963
Ralcorp Holdings, Inc. A648
Raleigh carpets A980
Raleigh Electric A1166
Rales, Mitchell P. A462, A463, A630, P142
Rales, Steven M. A462, A463, A630, P142
Raley, Tom P710
Raley's Inc. (supermarkets) P479, P710
Ralgro drug A1251
Ralli Bros. and Coney A325
Rallis India (pharmaceuticals) W567
Rallye SA W166
Ralph, John T. W429, W587
Ralph Lauren brand. *See* Polo Ralph Lauren
Ralph M. Parsons Company P386
Ralph, Susan C. A557
Ralphs, George P524
Ralphs Grocery Company P172, P462, P524, P736
Ralph's supermarkets A844, A845
Ralston, Bob D. A789

Ralston, P. Eric A941
Ralston Purina Company A534, A774, A784, W389
Ram Golf A386
Ram truck A456, P695
Rama margarine W619
Ramada International hotels A338, A339, A913, E247
Ramadorai, S. W567
Ramakrishnan, Chittur W537
Ramakrishnan, S. W567
Rambach, Ralph A269, P83, P556
Rambus Inc. A760
Ramella, Daniel J. E102
Ramey, Thomas C. A875, P295
Ram-Henkel W318
Ramicone, Arthur P759
Ramirez Corzo, Luis W441
Ramirez, J. Armando A1001
Ramirez, Julio A303
Ramírez Silva, Marco W441
Ramis, Miguel W175
Ramos, Denise A1405
Ramos, Joseph M. A1023
Ramo-Wooldridge Corporation A1412
Ramp Networks W406
Rampage stores E176
Ramqvist, Lars W220, W221, W633
Ramsby, Ole W417
Ramsey Engineering A222
Ramsey, Frank A280
Ramsey, Gary W. A1283
Ramsey, J. Douglas E200
Ramsey, Roger A122
Ramstores W318
Rance, Grahame E284
Rancho Zabaco wine A521, P169
Ranco (controls) W290
Rand, A. Barry A212
Rand brothers A754
Rand McNally Road Atlas (book) P711
Rand McNally & Company P226, **P408**-**P409**, P711
Rand, Mike P63
Rand, William P408
Randall, Karen F. A87
Randall, Phillip A. A173, P49, W91
Randall Stores A1348
Randall-Barber, Bernadette M. A1095
Randall's Food Markets A606, A1234, A1494, P478, P479
Randall's Ordinary Inn P318, P319
Randazzo, Richard P. A585
Randel, Don M. P496, P497, P756
R&F pasta P91
R&G Financial Corporation E275
Randich, Steve P353
Randle, Mark D. A1267
Randolph, Ann P61
Randolph, Garry L. A137
Randolph, Jackson H. A363
Randolph, Kenneth E. A519
Random House A80, A276, P32, W126, W127

Randsworth Trust A1328
Rand-Whitney Packaging A1364
Rangan, Ashwin A411
Rangen, Eric S. A121
Ranger beer W553
Ranger, Curtis T. A513
Ranger Oil E39
Ranheim, Ron E. A1079
Ranhoff, David A. E46
Ranjit, E. K. E192
The Rank Group PLC W248, **W472**-**W473**
Rank, Joseph Arthur W472
Rank, Scot W635
Rank Xerox W472
Rankin, Alfred M., Jr. A992, A993
Rankin, Alfred M., Sr. A992
Rankin, Byron A628
Rankin, Norman J. A261
Ranks Hovis McDougall Limited (baker) W605
Ransburg Corporation (electrostatic finishing) A748
Ransom, Epaphroditus A394
Ransomes plc A1380
Ranus, Robert D. P423, P718
Rao, Santosh A1257
Rapamune drug A148
Raphael, Emanuel A1198
Rapid Fill packaging A1262
Rapid Response Survival Kit (Y2K software) A406
Rapin, Peter R. A551
Rapp, Ed A333
Rapp, Karl W120
Rapp, Ronald J. A783
Rappa, Edward J. P369
Rappaport, Alan A227
Rappaport, Neil J. E136
Rapture Television (dance club music channel) W621
Raquet, Bonnie E. A325, P105
Rare Gold/Emeralds/Rubies fragrances A217
Rasdal, Andrew A953
Rash, James T. E301
Rash, Martin S. E271
Raskind, Peter E. A1001
Rasmussen, Earl R. P331, P672
Rasmussen, Edward J. A419
Rasmussen, Jan Thieme W163
Rasmussen, Linda P638
Rasmusser, Steve S. A1009, P365
Rasner, Amy E78, E227
Rasor, John F. A655
Rasp, Charles W128
Rassi, Alan J. A333
Rastetter, William H. E217
RASTEX sewing thread P523
Rasulo, James A. A1497
Ratcliffe, Andrew A1159, P401, W463
Ratcliffe, David M. A1307
Rathbone, John P. A1039
Rather, Dan E140, E317
Rathert, Terry W. E253

Rathmann, George B. A160
Rational Rose software E276
Rational Software
  Corporation E110, E276
Ratliff, Robert J. A96, A97
Ratnathicam, Chutta A381
Rauch, Allan N. A247
Rauch beverage A1104, A1105
Rauenhorst Construction Company.
  See Opus Corporation
Rauenhorst, Gerald P695
Rauenhorst, Mark H. P695
Raufast, Jean-Charles A563, P183,
  W223
Raufer, June P634
Rauh, John M. A821
Rautenstrauch, Gary M. P69, P548
RAV4 vehicle W614, W615
Ravailhe, Serge W171
Ravelston Corporation W262
Raven Creamery P488
Raven, Gregory P103
Raven, Peter P359
Ravencroft, Thomas A. A467
Ravenscraft, Harold "Buzz" P546
Ravenswood power plant A824
Ravenswood Winery, Inc. A422
Raver, David E. A719
Ravi, Sreekanth E290
Ravi, Suhakar E290
Rawle, Robert H. A941
Rawley, Charles E., III A1405
Rawlings brand E60
Rawlings, Edwin A648
Rawlings, Hunter R., III P584
Rawlings, Michael S. A1405
Rawot, Billie K. A527
Rawson, Richard G.
  (Administaff) A74, A75
Rawson, Richard J. (Lucent) A899
Raxar drug W246
Ray, Edward J. P383
Ray, Gary A. (KB Home) A813
Ray, Gary J. (Hormel Foods) A731
Ray, Harold B. (Edison
  International) A533
Ray, Harold E. (Catholic Health
  Initiatives) P117
Ray Industries (boats) A298
Ray, Jerry M. E115
Ray, Jodie N. A289
Ray, Wendell "Windy" P329, P671
Ray-Ban sunglasses A234, E99
Raybestos auto parts A461
Raychem HTS A642
Rayco (home builder) A812
Raycom Media, Inc. A92
Rayloc (auto parts rebuilder) A652
Raymond, Henry A1020
Raymond, John T. A1145
Raymond, Lee R. A576, A577
Raymond, Roy A776
Raymond Vineyards W314
Raymund, Edward C. A1356, A1357
Raymund, Steven A. A1356, A1357
Rayner, Derek W356

Rayner, Mark R. W383
Rayonier A1292
Ray-O-Vac Company A572, A1398
Raytheon Company A650, A736,
  A846, A**1190-A1191**, A1258,
  A1372, A1378, E23, E241, E277,
  E305, P766, P769, W110, W554
Razek, Edward G. A877
Razi, Nazneen A393
Razorfish, Inc. (interactive
  services) A1062
R. B. Pamplin Corporation P711
RBC Dain Rauscher
  Corporation A394, E132
RBC Financial Group A562, E132,
  E306, W112, W156, W222,
  W**474-W475**, W608
RC Cola A1180, A1400, A1401,
  P597, W154, W155
R.C. Steele pet supplies A1117
RCA. *See* Radio Corporation of
  America
RCA Laboratories P454
RCA Records W126
RCB International A1042
RCN Corporation A715, A866,
  P233, P510, P511
RCV Entertainment (film
  distribution) W626
RD Capital E147
RDHealth.com A1192
RDM Custom Chemicals A1516
RDM Sports Group A298
Re, Michael P740
R. E. Smith (oil and gas) A978
Rea, Donald W. A743
REA Express A588
Reach America P506
Reach toothbrushes A800, A801
Reach to Recovery cancer patient
  support P41
Reactint dye P343
Reaction Kenneth Cole brand E78,
  E227
Read canned vegetables A355
Read, David A475, P155, W197
Read, Harold T. P689
Read, Randolph C. P279, P652
Reader Rabbit software A926
The Reader's Digest Association,
  Inc. A956, A**1192-A1193**, A1390,
  P138
Reader's Digest atlas P408
ReadiCare, Inc. A699
Reading, Anthony J. W605
Reading Glove and Mitten
  Manufacturing Company A1474
Ready 2 Rumble (video
  game) W527
Ready Bake Foods Inc. W245
Ready Crust piecrusts A814, A815
Ready, Set, Serve foods P618
Reagan, Martin P. P37, P532
Reagan, Nancy P324
Reagan National Airport A138
Reagan, Ronald A1042, P110, P186,
  P324, P567, W124

The Real Canadian
  Superstore W245
Real Cities (Web sites) A832
Real Color Displays E47
Real food stores W364, W365
ReaLemon juice P90
Realistic office furniture P652
Really Wild Animals (TV
  show) P359
RealNet Canada, Inc. P120
RealNetworks, Inc. E281, W212
Realogic (computer service) A402
Realsilk Hosiery P72
Reamer, David A. A677
Reardon, Andrew F. P751
Reardon, George M. A819
Reardon, Nancy A. P91, P558
Reardon, Thomas E. (Tesoro) A1375
Reardon, Thomas M. (Harvard
  University) P221
Rebane, John A851, P289
REBAR (investments) P584
Rebele, John P612
Rebell, Arthur L. A885
Rebholz, David F. A589
Rebman, Joel G. A933
Rebok, Douglas E. P530
Rebolledo, Rogelio M. A1107
Rechler, Scott H. E276
Reckitt & Colman A1246, P432,
  W476
Reckitt Benckiser plc W**476-W477**
Reckson Associates Realty
  Corporation E276
Recob, James A779
Recombivax HB drug A956
Reconstruction Finance
  Corporation A580
Record Merchandisers W312
Record watches P308
RECOVERx A155
Recreational Equipment,
  Inc. P**410-P411**, P711
Rectigraph (photocopying) A1544
Rector, Brenda B. E271
Recycla-Pak P151
Red Apple Group, Inc. P712
Red Baron pizza P436, P437, P724
Red Cell W646, W647
Red Cross. *See* The American Red
  Cross
red D marts A56
R.E.D. Electronics (data
  communications) P208
Red Heart Productions W249
Red Hook Container Terminal P399
Red Horse clothing A880
Red Hot Hearts lottery game P373
Red Jack beer W377
Red Kap work wear A1474, A1475
Red Line Agreement A576
Red Lobster restaurants A464,
  A465, A648, P236, P669
RED office furniture A706
Red Oval Family A745, P242, P243
Red Pepper Software A1098

Red River Manufacturing (custom trailers) A326
Red River Mining Company A992, A993
Red Roof Inns W58, W59
Red Rooster fast food W172
Red Seal tobacco A1458, A1459
Red Star (trucking) A1454
Red Tab Classics pants A869, P293
RED TOP plaster A1457
Red Tulip candy W155
Red Wing (food manufacturing) W605
Redbook Florist Services P416
Redbook (magazine) A700, A701, P228, P229
Redcats (catalog sales) W446, W447
Reddaway (trucking) A1454
Redden, James B. A1041
Redding (concrete) P643
Reddington Farms A1491, P515, P768
Reddi-wip topping A409
Reddy Ice A1338
Redemtech P337
Redfield, Carl A369
Redfield, Peter A176
Redgrave, Martyn R. P107, P567
Redheuil, Alain W447
Redhook Ale A174, A175
Redi-Cut Foods A1109
Redi-Seal brand A585
Redken hair care W342, W343
Redland PLC A848
Redline (magazine) W239
RedLine (medical supply distributor) A947
Redman Industries, Inc. A346, A347, P518
Redman, Tony W93
Redmond, James P. A1171
Redmond, John T. A966, A967
Redoute (catalog company) W446
Redpath (sugar) W568, W569
Redstone, Sumner M. A1476, A1477, P681
Redux drug A148
Redwood National Park A890
Redwood Systems, Inc. A420, A421
Reebok International Ltd. A666, A839, A1032, **A1194-A1195**, E60, P637, W62
Reece, Thomas L. A503
Reed, Albert E. W478
Reed, Alison W357
Reed, Barbara A281
Reed, B. Jack E129, E302
Reed Business Information W478, W479
Reed, Charles B. P98, P99, P564
Reed Crushed Stone A1484
Reed, David A. A1081
Reed, Debra L. A1267
Reed, Donald B. W153
Reed Elsevier plc A950, A1160, A1502, **W478**-W479, W592, W642
Reed, Frank W623

Reed International P.L.C. (publishing) W642
Reed, James C., Jr. A1375
Reed, Jan Stern A237
Reed, Jason H. P519
Reed, John (Citigroup) A370
Reed, John (PolyMedica) E105
Reed, Linda A863
Reed, Marc C. P765
Reed, Robert P739
Reed, Rodger V. A365
Reed, Sam K. A814, A817
Reed Terminal A1484
Reed Tool A222
Reed, William G. (SAFECO) A1231
Reed, William L. (Sempra Energy) A1267
Reeder Light, Ice & Fuel A1464
Reeder, Robert M. A107
Reedy, Herman E. E20
Reedy, John D. P674
Reedy, Timothy J. A1535
Reels, Kenneth P318, P319
Rees, James A590
Rees, Norma S. P99
Rees, W. David A1257
Reese, Michelle P475
Reese Optical A234
Reese, Richard B. A619
Reese, Robert M. A709
Reese, Stuart H. A923, P321
Reese's brand foods A708, A709
Reetz, Douglas A731
Reeve, Christopher E211
Reeve, Pamela D. A. E83, E233
Reeves, Beth P73, P551
Reeves, Joseph A., Jr. E242
Reeves, Richard W179
Reeves, Sam (Ben E. Keith) P553
Reeves, Samuel T. (Dunavant Enterprises) P599
Reeves, Stephen F. A265
Reff office furniture systems P277, P652
Ref-Fuel (waste-to-energy) A100
Refined Sugars W568
Refludan drug W103
Reforma Investments W346
Refrigeraçao Paraná W210
Regal cigarettes W282, W283
Regal Cinemas, Inc. A714, A836, A837, P126, P282, P283, **P412-P413**, P712
Regal foods P185
Regal home furnishings A1317, P453
Regal Inns W58
Regal Shoe A294
Regan, Donald A960
Regan, Hugh T., Jr. E223
Regan, Kathleen A309
Regan, Michael N. E115
Regan, Timothy J. A435
Regas, Kathi M. A983
The Regence Group P226, P628
Regency Casinos A741, P241

Regency Centers Corporation E276
Regency Health Services, Inc. A1340
Regency Homes A509
Regency hotel A884
Regency Life W64
The Regency Organization (home builder) A1227
Regency Radio A1378
Regeneron Pharmaceuticals A160
Regenstein Library (University of Chicago) P449
Regent Communications, Inc. E277
Regent International Hotels P106, P107
Regent Sheffield cutlery P91
Regie 1 (radio sales) W467
Regional Airlines W68
Regions Financial A1308
Regis Corporation **A1196-A1197**
Register.com A1324
Rego, Anthony P199
Rego Park Co-op (New York City) P291
RehabCare Group, Inc. **E111**, E277
Rehabilitation Hospital Corporation of America, Inc. A699
Rehnquist, William P450
REI. *See* Recreational Equipment, Inc.
REI Limited P120
Reich, Betty A796
Reich, Charles A977
Reich, Joni J. A1449
Reich, Victoria J. A299
Reichard, Joseph F. A717, P235
Reichenbach, Carl August W350
Reichenbach, Henry A522
Reichenberger, John F. A821
Reichenberger, Wolfgang H. W389
Reichental, Abraham N. A1263
Reichert, Jack A298
Reichmann family W474
Reichspostverwaltung W202
Reichstul, Henri P. W437
Reid, Damian W355
Reid, David W591
Reid, Donald G. W245
Reid, Frederick W. A479
Reid, Gary W645
Reid, George W108
Reid, Gregory A. A1549
Reid, James A. P121
Reid, Jocelyn E134, E311
Reid, Joseph D. E171
Reid, Rick A1357
Reid, Robert L. A1487
Reid, Ron P413
Reid-Anderson, James P587
Reider, Pieter P419
Reigel, Donald E. E142
Reigo, Britt W221
Reiling, Richard A548
Reilley, Dennis H. A1157
Reilly, Cliff P618
Reilly, Ed P506

Reilly, Paul C. P287
Reilly, Richard M. A125
Reilly, William A1160
Reily, J. P. A133
Reimer Express Lines Ltd. A1206, A1207
Rein, Catherine A. A965
Rein, Jeffrey A. A1493
Reinberg, Jeffrey D. P309
Reinebach, Thomas J. P407, P709
Reinemund, Steven S. A1106, A1107, P427
Reiner, Van R. A257
Reinertsen, James L. P566
Reinhard, J. Pedro A505
Reinhard, Keith L. A1063
Reinhardt, Erich R. W537
Reinhart, Joseph L. E56
Reinsch, Jim A241, P75
Reinsdorf, Jerry P774
Reinz Group A460
REI-Outlet.com P410
Reis, Naomi W187
Reiseland GmbH (travel agencies) W426, W427
Reising, Richard P. A193
Reiss, Joshua A. A931
Reitan, Gunnar W519
Reitano, Robert R. A799
Reiten, Eivind W411
Reiter dairy product A467
Reith, John W144
Reitman, William H. A287
Reitz, Bonnie S. A429
Reitzle, Wolfgang A617
Rejuvenique appliances E116
Rekowski, Jerry G. P43
Relais International (interlibrary loan) P171
Related Capital Company E176
Relaxor massagers E116
Relenza drug W246
Reliable furniture stores A702
Reliance Electric A1210
Reliance Group Holdings, Inc. A182, A688
Reliance Works A96
Reliant Data Systems A406
Reliant Energy, Inc. A**1198-A1199**, E243, E258, W598
Reliant Healthcare Systems, Inc. A323
Reliant Resources E258
Reliant Stadium (Houston) P716
ReliaStar Financial Corporation W286
ReliaStar Mortgage A1162
Relief Pants W309
ReLife A698
Religion News Service A81, P33
Reliure Industrielle de Barchon (bookbinding) W626
RELTEC (access technology) W354
Rely tampons A1164
REM Eyewear A926
The Remains of the Day (movie) P689

Reman, Ronald L. A931
Remar Baking A774
Rembiszewski, Jimmi W143
Rembrandt Group W142, W552
Remco toys E225
REMEC, Inc. E277
REMEDIA catalytic filter system P522, P523
Remeron drug W72
Remington Oil and Gas Corporation E235, E278
Remington Park (racetrack) P172
Remington Rand A342, A764, A1424
Remitco Management A596
Remmel, Lee A673, P211
Remmel, Manfred W505
Remnick, David A80, P32
Remón Gil, Miguel Ángel W483
Remondi, John E. A1449
Rempe, Michael T. A345
Remshard, John W. P175, P602
Remy Cointreau A618
Remy Electric P152
Remy, Frank P152
Remy Korea Ltd. P152
Rena Rowen clothing A804, A805
Renaissance Communications A1402
Renaissance Diagnostic & Treament Center P369
Renaissance Holdings A734
Renaissance Homes A862
Renaissance Hotel Group A912, A913
Renaissance Learning, Inc. E278
Renaissance media (cable) A350
Renata (batteries) W563
Renaud, Gilles A. A621
Renault Automation W226
Renault, Fernand W480
Renault, Louis W480
Renault, Marcel W480
Renault S.A. P695, W228, W330, W402, W442, W458, W**480-W481**, W508, W632
Renco Group Inc. P712
Rencoal P712
Rend Lake Mine A417
Renda, Larree M. A1235
RenderMan software E103, E266
Renewal by Andersen windows P50
Renfro, John M. A637
Renfroe, Timothy R. A719
RENK W351
Renken, Stephen P. A1039
Renna, Eugene A. A577
Renne, Paul F. A723
Renner, Troy A. A345
Rennert, Ira L. P712
Rennie drug W492, W493
Rennie, John W429
Rennie, Robert J. W67
Reno Hilton casino A1087
Renó-Dépôt do-it-yourself stores W312, W313, W376
Rensi, Edward A942

Rent Net A338
Rent-A-Wreck P178
Rentler, Barbara A1215
Rentsch, Hanspeter W563
Rentschler, Frederick A272, A1420, A1432
ReNu vision care A235
Re-Nutriv skin cream A564
Renuzit air fresheners A486, A487
Renwick Gallery P451
Renwick, Glenn M. A1169
Renyi, Thomas A. A229
Renz, Gerhard W293
Renzulli, Carmine A1241
Renzulli, Michael H. A109
Reo Car Company A1052
Replacement Benefit Fund A315, P97
Replay TV, Inc. P511
Replica Books P68, P69
Represas, Carlos E. W389
Repsol YPF, S.A. *See also* YPF, S.A.
Repsol YPF, S.A. A184, A820, P616, P635, W66, W436, W**482-W483**, W650
Reptron Electronics, Inc. E278
Republic Airlines A1046
Republic Auto P112
Republic Bancorp E251
Republic Electro E124
Republic Environmental Systems A206
Republic Freight Systems A1548
Republic Industries A206, A548, P256
Republic Motor Truck A526
Republic New York Corporation W268
Republic Steel A896
Republic Technologies International, LLC P713
Republic Western Insurance Company A134, A135
Res-Care, Inc. A238
Reschke, John A. A183
Rescoe, Michael E. A55
Rescue Industries (plumbing) A1272
Rescue Rooter A1272, A1273
RescueNet software E144, E320
The Research Business Group P308
Research Information Center P28, P29
Research Insurance Company Ltd. P71
Research Medical A236
Residence Inn Company A732, A912, A913, A1296, E169
Resinous Products A1212
Resistoflex Pte., Ltd. A447
ResMed Inc. E**112**, E279
Res-Monitor (low-fare search system) P419
Resnick, Alan H. A235
Resnick, Alice R. P455
Resnick, Lynda Rae P416, P417, P716

Resnick, Stewart A. P416, P417, P716
Resnik, Mark P524
Resolution Trust Company A1540
Resort Condominiums International A338
ResortQuest International, Inc. E279
Resorts International A1408, P482
Resorts USA (campgrounds) W473
Resource Asset Investment Trust. See RAIT Investment Trust
Resource Recycling Technologies A544
Resources Connection A474, W196
RespiGam drug E90, E240
Respini, Luciano A505
Respironics E112
Restaura (food service) A1478
Restaurant Associates (events) W175
Restrepo, Gilberto A1075
Restrepo, Robert P., Jr. A125
Restucci, Raoul A1277, W501
Retail Brand Alliance, Inc. P713
Retail Credit Company A558
Retail Financial Services W115
Retail Graphic Holding P506
Retavase drug A801
Retex (gas) E302
Retin-A drug A800, E89
Retin-A-Micro drug A801
Retirement Care Associates, Inc. A1340
Retirement Protection Act (1994) P388
Rettig, Bernd W557
Rettinger, Dale G. E264
Return of the Jedi (movie) P302, P303
Return to Midway (book) P359
Reuben H. Donnelley Corporation A516, A1218
Reuling, Michael F. A111
Reum, W. Robert P540
Reunion Industries, Inc. E279
Reuter, Herbert W484
Reuter, Lawrence G. P335
Reuter, Paul Julius W484
Reuters Group PLC A284, A506, E192, E274, P80, P556, W146, **W484-W485**
Reuther, Walter P34
Reuwer, Frank A1455
Revco D. S. (pharmacies) A458, A560, A844, A1202, A1552, P180
Revels candy A915, P315
Revere cookware P91, P775
Revere Ware A434
Reviglio, Franco W216
REVIMID drug E174
ReviveX Water and Stain Repellent P522, P523
Revlon, Inc. A902, A903, A**1200-A1201**, P258, P304, P305, P663
Revman Industries, Inc. (bedding and bath products) W607

Revolution (magazine) W238
Revolution office furniture P652
Revson, Charles A1200
Revson, Joseph A1200
Rewe (stores) W588
Rex software E25
Rexair (vacuum cleaners) A1446
Rexall Drug A1414
Rexam plc A284, W432
Rexel S.A. (electrical equipment) W446, W447
Rexona deodorant W619
Rexroth AG W352, W490
Rexsis, Inc. A1207
Reyes, Carlos E99
Reyes, David P713
Reyes, Gregory L. E166
Reyes Holdings LLC P665, P713
Reyes, J. Christopher P713
Reyes, Jorge G. A759
Rey-Giraud, Agnes A575
Reynolds Electrical & Engineering A1110
Reynolds, Gary L. A103
Reynolds, Gregory E. A627
Reynolds, James G. E211
Reynolds, Jean M. A727
Reynolds, Jennifer E283
Reynolds, John A924, P322
Reynolds Metals A112, A224, A988, P675
Reynolds, Paul W149
Reynolds (pens, pencils) A1022
Reynolds, Richard, Jr. A988
Reynolds, R. J. A1204
Reynolds, Robert A. (Graybar) P209, P620
Reynolds, Robert L. (FMR) A615, P191
Reynolds Securities A988
Reynolds, Steve P544
Reynolds Wrap A112
Reza, Rose M. A831
Rezenenko, Vladimir Ivanovich W243
RF Communications (two-way radios) A686
RF Micro Devices, Inc. E280
RF Power Products E24
RFM (company) W511
RFS Hotel Investors, Inc. A720
R.G. Dun & Company A516
R-G Premier Bank E275
R/GA Interactive (Web site development) A773
R.H. Donnelley Corporation A516
RH of Indiana LP A1227
RH of Texas LP A1227
Rhadhakrishnan, K. S. A737
Rhein, Arthur A1141
RheinHyp W200
Rheinische Aktiengesellschaft für Braunkohlenbergbau W504
Rheinisch-Westfälisches Elektrizitätswerk. See RWE Aktiengesellschaft

RHI Consulting (temporary help) A1208, A1209
Rhoads, Robert K. A1495
Compagnie Rhodanienne de Gestion W183
Rhodes, Brenda C. E210
Rhodes, Cecil W92
Rhodes, Donald V. E213
Rhodes, F. Matthew A411
Rhodes, James H., II (Publix) A1177, P403, P707
Rhodes, J. C. A1303
Rhodes, Jimmy (Texas Petrochemicals) P745
Rhodes, Michael G. E94
Rhodes, Ray A672, P210
Rhodes, Robert M. E115
Rhodes, Steve P185
Rhodes, Susan A1209
Rhodes, William C., III (Autozone) A209
Rhodes, William R. (Citigroup) A371
Rhodesian Sugar Refineries W568
Rhodia SA (chemicals) W102
Rhône-Poulenc SA. See Aventis (pharmaceuticals)
Rhoton, Wendy E243
Rhudy, Marily H. A149
Rhythms NetConnections Inc. A715, A1186
Ribar, Geoffrey G. E31, E160
Ribaudo, Michael P129
Ribeiro, Paulo E100, E258
Ribnick, Robert A1197
Riboud, Antoine W192
Riboud, Franck W192, W193
Ricci, Gilberto W575
Ricci, Renato W251
Ricciardello, Mary P. A1199
Ricciardi, Lawrence R. A765
Ricciardi, Michael P479
Ricciardi, Salvatore P708
Riccio, Dennis R. E31
Rice, Donald H. A755
Rice, George A922, P320
Rice, John D. (Archer Daniels Midlands) A193
Rice, John G. (General Electric) A647
Rice, Kapua A. A1029
Rice Krispies A816, A817
Rice, Linda Johnson P258, P259, P646
Rice, Rod W. E193
Rice, Tony W111
Rice-A-Roni A1180, A1181
Riceland Foods, Inc. P714
Ricerca W422
Rich, Bradford W. A1453, P503
Rich, Gary M. (Brown Shoe) A295
Rich, Gary S. (Reader's Digest) A1193
Rich, George A. A349
Rich, Gerry A963
Rich, Harold, Sr. E218

Rich Man, Poor Man (miniseries) A60
Rich Products Corporation P714
Rich, Robert E., Jr. P714
Richard, Bonni P697
Richard, Gary P697
Richard M. Lucas Center for Magnetic Resonance Spectroscopy & Imaging P457
Richard, Peter Christiana P697
Richard, Sherry P574
Richards, Ann P472
Richards Bay Minerals W128
Richards, Bruce S. A559
Richards, Craig M. P68
Richards, Joan P611
Richards, Joel, III A537
Richards, Margaret E. P127
Richards, Roy, Sr. P733
Richards, Stephen (Computer Associates) A403
Richards, Stephen D. (Consolidated Freightways) A421
Richards, Steven A. (Key Energy) E79
Richards, Thomas P606
Richards Wild Irish Rose A422
Richards Wine Cellar A422
Richardson, Alan V. A1082, A1083, W523
Richardson, Barbara P363
Richardson, Bryn A1531
Richardson, Cary A1419
Richardson, Chris C. W521
Richardson, Daniel J. A1533
Richardson, David H. W639
Richardson, James (Cisco Systems) A369
Richardson, Jerome A86
Richardson, Jim (Texas Lottery) P473, P744
Richardson, J. P. P188
Richardson, Paul W647
Richardson, R. Jack, Jr. A855
Richardson, Ronald J. A741, P241
Richardson, Velma L. P53
Richardson, William A. (Mandalay Resort) A906, A907
Richardson, William C. (W.K. Kellogg Foundation) P521, P774
Richardson-Vicks (health care) A1164
Richelieu brand A805
Richels, John A483
Richemont W251
Richey, Albert L. A169
Richey Electronics A196
Richey, Ellen A1171
Richfield Oil A900
Richfood Holdings, Inc. (food distributor) A1348
Richins, Darin A1051
Richland SA E21
Richman Brothers men's clothing A1470
Richman, Daniel A305
Richman, Michael S. E90

Richmond & Danville (railroad) A1038
Richmond Cedar Works (ice cream freezers) A492
Richmond cigarettes W283
Richmond College P128
Richmond International Speedway E75
Rich's stores A586, A587
Richstone, Ellen B. E35, E166
Richter, George H. A583
Richter, Glenn R. A1265
Richter, Jürgen W127
Richter Manufacturing A1368
Richter, Robert C. A461
Richton International Corporation E280
Rickard, David B. A459
Ricke, Kai-Uwe W205
Rickels, Paul A1189
Ricker, Jon J. A877
Rickershauser, Peter J. A309
Rickert, Robert A823
Rickets, James F. A759
Ricklin, Denis W195
Ricks, Ron A1311
Ricoh Company, Ltd. A746, A747, E303, W190, W191, **W486-W487**
Riconosciuto, John M. A1293
Ridder, Bernard A832
Ridder, Herman A832
Ridder, P. Anthony A832, A833
Ridder Publications A832
Riddick, Frank A., III A195
Riddiford, David M. A487
Riddle, Michael E. A351
Riddle, Raymond A1004
Riddle, W. Curtis A633
Rideout, Dewayne E. A1257
Rideout, Stanton K. A1125
Rider, Neal J. A607
Rider, Robert F. A1429, P491
Rider, Simon A1471
Riders jeans A1475
Ridge, Robert A. A1129
Ridley, Dave A1311
Ridley Inc. A426, P140
Riedel family W310
Riedel, Hans W459
Riedhammer, Thomas M. A235
Riegle-Neal Interstate Banking Act (1997) A166
Riemann, Stan A. A583, P185
Rieny, Robert P630
Rienzi, Michael P363
Rieschel, Gary E. W549
Riese-Martin, Monika A705
Riesenbeck, Ron P722
Rietz, Gary P. A467
Rietz, Gert W427
Rifkin (cable) A350
Rifkin, Irving P694
Rifkin, Leonard P694
Rigas, Gus A72
Rigas, James P. A73

Rigas, John J. (Adelphia Communications) A72, A73
Rigas, John N. (Armstrong Holdings) A195
Rigas, Michael J. A73
Rigas, Timothy J. A73
Rigby, Mark W545
Rigesa (box maker) A1516
Rigg, George P. E93
Riggers Medizintechnik (dialysis products) A1536
Riggio, Carl A562, P182, W222
Riggio, Leonard A232, A233, P549
Riggio, Stephen A233
Riggs, Mel G. E180
Right Guard deodorant A656, A657
RightCHOICE Managed Care, Inc. A574
Rightmyer, Joseph A. A1537
RIGID power tools A725
Rigsby, Robert E. A499
Rijkspostspaarbank (State Savings Bank) W286
Rikardsen, Bernhard W519
Riken Kankoshi Company W486
Riken Optical Company W486
Riken tires W367
Riker, Richard E136
Riklis Family Corporation A618
Riklis, Meshulam A158, A330
Riley, Daniel P. A227
Riley, H. John, Jr. A430, A431
Riley, James B. A355
Riley Natural Gas E264
Riley, Saxon W337
Riley, Stephen A281
Riley, Timothy M. E205
Riley, Victor A822
Rillings, Robert H. A711
Rilutek drug W103
Ring A Levio (hair accessories) A1068
Ring Dings snacks A774, A775
Ring Leader Recycling Program A748
Ring, Mitchell A. A723
Ring Pops candy E130, E303
Ring, Timothy M. A445
Ringgo news agency P60
Ringier-Taurus (publisher) W106
Ringle, William L. A117
Ringler, James M. A749
Ringling Bros. and Barnum & Bailey Circus P188, P189, P608
Ringling Brothers-Barnum & Bailey Combined Shows A926
Ringmaster software E103, E266
Ringnes beer W163
Ringo stool W276
Ringrose, Peter S. A291
Rini-Rego Stop-n-Shop stores P198
Rintamaki, John M., Jr. A617
Rio Grande, El Paso and Santa Fe Railroad Company A309
Rio Grande Foods A466, A608
Rio Grande HMO, Inc. P227

Rio Grande Servaas (inner tubes) A432
Rio Linda Chemical A1484
Rio Suite Hotel & Casino (Las Vegas) A684, A685
Rio Tinto plc A628, W488-W489, W640
Companhia Riograndense de Telecomunicaçõs W576, W578
Riordan, Lori A919
Riordan, Thomas J. A1321
Rios, Tommy E99
Ripka, David E. A1543
Ripple, Patricia L. A147
Ripple wine A520, A521, P168, P169
Ripplewood Holdings L.L.C. A912, A1160, P436, P543
Ris, William K., Jr. A165
Risch, Frank A. A577
Riscorp Health Plans A1076
Risener, Daniel M. A1177, P403
Riser Foods (wholesaler) P198, P479
Risher, John D. A131
Rishton, John W141
Rising, Nelson C. E37, E173
Rising Sun Newspaper W96
RiskAttack A182
Risley, David M. A855
Risley, Tom P766
Risoleo, James F. A732
Risseeuw, Ton W503
Rist, Larry P313, P665
Rita Ann (fragrance and cosmetics) A155
Ritalin drug W415
Ritazza restaurants W174
Ritchey, Raymond A. E34
Ritchie, James D. A1549
Ritchie, Kelly A. A853
Rite-Aid Corporation A84, A540, A790, A886, A946, A1202-A1203, A1492
Rittenberg, Stephen P135
Ritter, C. Dowd A167
Ritter Food A1350
Ritter, Keith P361
Ritts, H. James, III A1161
Rituxan drug A640, A641, E217
Ritz Camera Centers, Inc. P714
Ritz crackers A814, A842, A843
Ritz, David P714
The Ritz-Carlton Hotel Company, L.L.C. A732, A912, A913, A1328, P737
Ritzel, Joe P589
Riunione Adriatica di Sircurtà (insurance) W82
River Boat Casino A684
Rivera, Richard E. A465
Riverdeep (software) P619
Riverport Development, Inc. A787
Rivers, J. R. W497
Rivercenter shopping center (San Antonio, TX) P172
Riverside markets A1094

Riverside poultry A324, A325, P104, P105
Riverson, Renato W78
Rivertown Trading (catalogs and e-commerce) A1352, A1353
Riverwood International Corporation P715
Rivet, Jeannine M. A1435
Rivet, Robert J. A82
Riviana Foods A386
Rizla cigarette paper W282, W283
Rizzi, Lucio A1137
Rizzo, Peter J. A1015
R.J. Griffin (contractor) P599
R.J. Reynolds Tobacco Holdings, Inc. A492, A988, A1204-A1205, A1436, A1486, W304
R.J. Tower Iron Works A1394
RJR Nabisco Holdings A408, A470, A836, A960, A1204, P90, P282, W192, W240, W304
RKE (computer products) A214
RKO (movies) A222
R.L. Polk (consumer information) A558
RL restaurant A1150
RMH Teleservices, Inc. E113, E280
RMP International P386
Roaccutan drug W492, W493
Roach, Edgar M., Jr. A499
Roach, John A1188, P562
Roach, Richard G. P431
Road Champs toys E225
Road King motorbikes A682
Road Runner convenience stores P749
Road Runner (Internet service provider) A80, A81, A180, A181, P32, P33, P158
Road to Recovery cancer patient support P41
Road Trip (movie) P167
Roadmaster bicycles A298
Roadmaster Industries A298
Roadranger brand A527
Roadway Corporation A1206-A1207
Roadway Express, Inc. A420
Roaman's (catalogs) A876
Roanoke Hospital Association P566
Roark, Joseph W. A463
Roark, Stephen R. E165
Roath, Kenneth B. E211
Roath, Stephen D. A886, A887
Robb, David R. A689
Robb, Michael S. P385
Robb, Roger R. E272
Robb, Walter A1523
Robbins, Anthony K. A1285
Robbins, Daniel A946
Robbins, George W. A975
Robbins, James O. A443, P147
Robbins, Ralph W153
Robbins Resource Recovery A620
Robbins, Wayne F. A1321
Robbins, W. Clayton P692
Robeco Groep A1074

Rober, Jon P413
Robern lighting P284, P285
Robershotte, Paul J. A1015
Roberson, Dennis A. A991
Robert Allen furniture P299, P659
Robert Bosch GmbH A546, A836, A934, P282, P390, W352, W354, W490-W491, W536, W555
Robert Brown liquor W315
Robert, David P313
Robert, Elisabeth B. E135, E311
Robert Fleming Holdings Limited A808, A809, W306
Robert Half International Inc. A1208-A1209
Robert MacNeil Report (TV show) P144
Robert McCormick School of Engineering and Applied Sciences P379
The Robert Mondavi Corporation (wines) P616
Robert R. McCormick Tribune Foundation A1402
Robert W. Baird & Company Inc. (asset management) A1048, A1049, P376, P377, P690
Robert William James & Associates P606
The Robert Wood Johnson Foundation P715
Roberts, Andrew A1047
Roberts, Bert C., Jr. A1534, A1535
Roberts, Brian L. A390, A391
Roberts, Charlie P728
Roberts, Christopher G. E112
Roberts, David W115
Roberts Express A588, A1206
Roberts, Gareth E191
Roberts, George J. (Oracle) A1067
Roberts, George R. (Kohlberg Kravis Roberts) A238, A836, A837, P282, P283, P653
Roberts, Gilbert J. A1221
Roberts, Gregory B. A847
Roberts, James J. A1023
Roberts, Jan A1553
Roberts, Jeff A583
Roberts, John J. (PricewaterhouseCoopers) A1159, P401, W463
Roberts, John N., III (J.B. Hunt) A789
Roberts, John S. (UNUMProvident) A1441
Roberts, Judith A. A175
Roberts, Kevin J. W467
Roberts, Leona P230
Roberts, Leonard H. A1188, A1189
Roberts, Malcolm J. A257
Roberts, Max J. P549
Roberts, Michael J. A943
Roberts Radio A372
Roberts, Ralph J. A390, A391
Roberts, Richard T. P369
Roberts, Roger W. E42
Roberts, Vicki A. A341
Roberts, Wade H., Jr. E169

Robertshaw (appliance controls) W290
Robertson, Daryl A473
Robertson, Dave A835, P281
Robertson, Gregory P259
Robertson, James S. A469
Robertson, Julian A1442
Robertson, Pat A622
Robertson, Peter J. A353
Robertson, Sanford A566
Robertson Stephens & Company A566, A602
Robich Joseph P. A389
Robidoux, Ray A1185
Robie House P496
Robie, Richard A212
Robillard, Donald P635
Robin Hood flour A648
Robin Hood Multifoods A768, A769
Robin, Kenneth H. A735
Robino, Mary Goss A963
Robins, Ralph H. W356, W497
Robins, R. Steven P565
Robinson, Barry A1351
Robinson, Bill P385
Robinson, Bruce E. A1179
Robinson, Charles H. A344
Robinson Dairy A1338
Robinson, David (Baker & Taylor) P68
Robinson, David E. (Motorola) A991
Robinson, Dwight P. A627
Robinson, Edward R. A1301
Robinson, Errol E210
Robinson, Frank A382
Robinson, Gary A1099
Robinson, Gerry W174, W248
Robinson, Gordon W. A1387
Robinson, Ian W259
Robinson, James A142
Robinson, John N. W341
Robinson Laboratories E68
Robinson L.L.C. A1006
Robinson, Logan G. A477
Robinson, Maurice A1254
Robinson, Mel E215
Robinson, Morris A986
Robinson nuclear plant A1166
Robinson Nugent (electronic connectors) A976
Robinson, Paul A61
Robinson, Peter J. (Owens-Illinois) A1075
Robinson, Peter (Pillsbury) A1137
Robinson, Ralph A. W245
Robinson Richard A1254, A1255
Robinson Run Mine A417
Robinson Steel A1006
Robinson, Steve A. P125
Robinson, Todd A. P659
Robinson, William Sydney W640
Robinson-Humphrey (investment bank) A1346
Robinson's department stores W298, W299

Robinsons soft drink W545
Robinsons-May department stores A932
Robison, Shane V. A399
Robitussin over-the-counter drug A148
Robles, Joe, Jr. A1453, P503, P763
Robling, Sally G. A153
RoboRiders toys W333
Robson, George T. E191
Roby, Joe L. A449
Rocaltrol drug W493
Rocco Enterprises (poultry processor) A324, P104
Rocco, Vincent E131
Rocephin drug W492, W493
Roche Group W118, **W492-W493**
Roche Holding Ltd. A160, A216, A640, E89, E105
Roche, James G. A1045
Roche, John B. E252
Roche, Kevin A1435
Roche, Mark A. A619
Roche, Pat N. P533
Rochelle Canneries A470
Rochester & Pittsburgh Coal A416
Rochester Methodist Hospital P324
Rochester (New York) *Democrat and Chronicle* A633
Rochon, John P. P316
Rock, Chris P167
Rock Island Oil & Refining A834, P280
Rock N'Serve A1415
The Rock (WWFE star) E141, E319
Rockbestos-Surprenant Cable Corporation P313
Rockcor A1060
Rockefeller Center Corporation P134, P476
The Rockefeller Foundation P194, **P414-P415**, P715
The Rockefeller Group P587
Rockefeller, John D. A352, A576, A808, A992, A1000, A1010, P414, P496, P756, W136
Rockefeller, John D., III P414
Rockefeller, John D., Jr. P414
Rockefeller, Winthrop A788
Rocket Research A1060
Rockettes (Radio City Music Hall) A312
Rockford Blue Cross P226
Rockland-Atlas National Bank A1332
Rockmans women's clothing stores W644
Rockmoor Grocery store A1532
Rockport shoes A1194, A1195
Rockport Works A104
Rockresorts A454
Rockware Group A1074
Rockwell Automation A176, E43
Rockwell Collins (avionics) A1210

Rockwell International Corporation A198, A272, A410, A778, A1002, A**1210-A1211**, E136, E224, W76
Rockwell Semiconductor Systems A410
Rockwell Software A1210
Rockwell Spring and Axle Company A198
Rockwell, Willard A198, A1210
Rockwell, Willard, Jr. A198
Rockwood, Frederick W. A719
Rockwood, S. D. P439
Rockwood Specialties Inc. A836, A837, P283
Rocky Flats Closure Site Services LLC A787
Rocky Mountain Milling, LLC P123
Rocky Mount (North Carolina) *Telegram* A443
Rocky River Power A1040
Rodahl, Cindy A329, P109, P567
Roddenbery pickles A467
Roddy, Frank J. P739
Rodel (surface polishing) A1212
Rodenberg, Dan A1523
Rodeo SUV W294
Roder (office furniture) P222
Rodes, William J. E317
Rodgers, Johnathan A P159
Rodgers, Kevin E249
Rodgers, Richard P666
Rodier, Jean-Pierre W432, W433
Rodin, Judith P759
Rodionov, Pyotr Ivanovich W243
Rodkin, Gary M. A1107
Rodli, Eric G. A525
Rodono, Nick P683
Rodriguez, Antonio A625
Rodriguez Inciarte, Juan W513
Rodríguez Inciarte, Matías W513
Rodriguez, Jorge W109
Rodriguez, Michael A. A1245
Rodriguez, Ruben W108, W109
Rodriques, Kelly A. P73
Rodruan, William C. A195
Rod's sauces A467
Roe, Christian P594
Roe, George A1120
Roe, John H. A251
Roebling, Mary P46
Roebuck, Alvah A1264
Roederstein (capacitors and resistors) A1482
Roef, P. A. W. W627
Roegelein pork products P185
Roehlk, Thomas M. A1415
Roehrick, Charles T. A71
Roelf Vos food stores W644, W645
Roell, Stephen A. A803
Roels, Harry J. M. W501
Roemer, Michael K. A267
Roerig A1118
Roeth, George A375
Roferon-A drug W493
Roffi, Renato W217
Rogaine hair treatment A1122

Rogan, Sandy E294
Rogas, Edward, Jr. A1373
Rogato, Susan P143, P583
Rogel, Steven R. A1518, A1519
Rogers, Alana W109
Rogers Communications
  Inc. A1198, W288, W470,
  W494-W495
Rogers Corporation P164
Rogers, David W. A325, P105
Rogers, Donald C. W271
Rogers, Edward S. W494, W495
Rogers, Gary L. A647
Rogers, James E. (Cinergy) A362,
  A363
Rogers, James P. (Eastman
  Chemical) A523
Rogers, Jim (Allied
  Worldwide) P535
Rogers, Joe W., Jr. P512, P513,
  P767
Rogers, Joe W., Sr. P512
Rogers, Lawrence J. P443
Rogers Majestic in Toronto W494
Rogers, Melinda M. W495
Rogers, Mike A833
Rogers, Ralph A., Jr. A93
Rogers, Richard P316, P317
Rogers, Ronald G. W113
Rogers, Steven A. A499
Rogers, Susan P585
Rogers, Ted W288, W494
Rogers, Ted, Jr. W494
Rogers, Terence R. A1225
Rogers Terminal & Shipping A325
Rogers, T. Gary A510, A511
Rogers, Thomas S. A1160, A1161
Rogers, Wayne A1084, P740
Rogers, W. Brian E290
Rogers@Home Internet
  access W494
Rogers-Dierks (jet engine
  parts) E67
Rogerson, Craig A. A705
Rogge, Joyce C. A1311
Rohde, Bruce C. A408, A409
Rohde, Gilbert A706
Rohkamm, Eckhard W595
Rohm and Haas Company A504,
  A752, **A1212-A1213**, P238, W116
Rohm, Otto A1212
Rohr (airline engine nacelles) A662
Rohr, James E. A1147
Rohrbach, Alma A796
Rohrbasser, Markus W652
Rohrs, Gary P694
Rohrs, Thomas M. A189
Roiss, Gerhard W425
Rojahn, Stephan W491
Rolaids antacid A1118
Roland, Donald E. P506, P507,
  P765
Roland, Mike P550
Roland music equipment E210
Rold Gold pretzels A1107
Rolf, Gerhard P223
Rolfe, Christopher C. A515

Rolfe, Harold E. A711
Rolfe, Mark W241
Roll International
  Corporation A494, **P416-P417**,
  P716
Roll, Penni F. E151
Rollans, James O. A611
Rolldown lottery game P680
Roller, Mark P539
Rollerball (movie) A962
Rollerblade in-line skates W124,
  W125
Roller-Koater A1278
Rollier, Phillippe A849
Rolling Rock beer W288, W289
Rolling Stones (music group) W622
Rollins, Henry P166, P167, P597
Rollins, Kevin B. A473
Rollins Truck Leasing P390, P699
Rollison, John A1271
Rolls, Charles W496
Rolls-Royce plc A646, P417, P438,
  P633, W120, **W496-W497**, W630,
  W631
Rolm Corporation A888, W536
Rolo candy A709
Rolodex office supplies A1022,
  A1023
Rolscreen Company P698
Rolston, B. Fielding A523
Romaine, Aimee A1275, E120, E287
Roman Meal bread A609, A775
Romano, Massimo W215
Romano, Pamela J. A1553
Romano, Phil A288
Romano's Macaroni Grill A288,
  A289
Rombach, Sue A309
Romberg, Gotthard W491
Romeril, Barry D. A1545
Romex A642
Romiti, Cesare W226
Romney, Mitt P64
Romo, Ricardo P499
Romoser, Chris A779
Romper Room (TV show) A692
Ron Bacardi Añejo rum W109
Ronald McDonald House
  Charities A942, A943
Ronald Reagan Washington
  National Airport P593
Ronco pasta P91
Ronco Realty P422
Rondel (millwork
  distribution) A446
Roney, Michael J. A665
Rong Guangdao W543
Rongshida-Maytag A934
Ronilo, Steven C. A549
Ronningen-Petter (filter-
  strainers) A502
Ronzoni pasta A708
Roobol, Leo W503
Rood, Ken A1151
Roof, Donald C. A807
Roogow, Buddy P666
Rooke, Paul A. A871

Roomate trash cans A375
Roome, Hugh A1255
Rooms To Go P716
The RoomStore furniture A702,
  A703
Rooney Brothers Company P716
Rooney, John E. A1361
Rooney, L. H. P716
Rooney, Phillip B.
  (ServiceMaster) A1273
Rooney, Phillip B. (Waste
  Management) A1504
Rooney, Timothy P. P716
Roorda, Peter J. W. A1243
Roos, Chantal W251
Roosevelt, Franklin Delano A580,
  A998, P40, P134, P146, P220
Roosevelt Hot Springs
  geothermal P340
Roosevelt, Theodore P220
Rooster tobacco A1458, A1459
Rooster.com A324, P122
Root, Michelle P731
Rootes Group W294, W442
Roots (miniseries) A60
Roper appliances A1520, A1521
Roper, Hartwell H. A1437
Roper, Ted P265, P648
Roper, William A., Jr. P439
RoperASW W620, W621
Rorer (pharmaceuticals) W102
Rorie, Albert S. A579
Rosar (brewery) W288
Rosard, Steven J. A1233
Rosario, Hector P707
Rosato, Thomas P. A549
Rosberg, Gerald M. A1503
Roscitt, Richard R. A70, A71
Roscoe, Gary E124, E292
Rose, Anthony D., Jr. A209
Rose, Darlene A803
Rose, Gary A57
Rose, George W111
Rose, J. Donald W453
Rose, John E. V. W497
Rose, Karen M. A375
Rose, Kenneth L. A743
Rose, Kenton R. A619
Rose, Kevin N. A1313
Rose Law Firm A258
Rose, Marya M. A457
Rose, Matthew K. A309
Rose, Melissa A905
Rose, Michael E. (Anadarko) A169
Rose, Michael (Promus) A684
Rose, Michael (Royal
  Dutch/Shell) W501
Rose, Nicholas C. W207
Rose Partners P592
Rose, Tom W263
Roseanne (TV show) A60
Rosen, Andrew M. A295
Rosen, Arnold A862
Rosen, Benedict P. W329
Rosen, Benjamin M. A398, A399
Rosen, David W526

Rosen, Elaine D. A1441
Rosen, Elmer P717
Rosen Enterprises W526
Rosen, James E96
Rosen, Ludwig P717
Rosen, Michael N. (Barnes &
Noble) A233
Rosen, Michael (TruServ) P485
Rosen, Richard D. P71
Rosen, Scott M. P255, P642
Rosen, Stuart I. A1401
Rosen, Thomas J. P717
Rosenast, Hilmar A. A721
Rosenbaum, Greg P110
Rosenbaum, Robert B. A1513
Rosenberg, Bruce A721
Rosenberg, Frank B. P586
Rosenberg, Henry P586
Rosenberg, R. A. P439
Rosenberg, Sheli Z. A561, P181,
P604
Rosenberger, A. Robert A951
Rosenblum, Barbara P616
Rosenblum, Bruce P111
Rosenbluth, Hal F. P418, P419,
P717
Rosenbluth International P158,
P418-**P419**, P717
Rosenbluth, Marcus P418, P717
Rosencwaig, Allan E300
Rosendahl, Oscar W95
Rosenfeld, Emanuel A1100
Rosenfield, Andrew P496
Rosengard, Andrew B. A313
Rosen's Diversified, Inc. P717
Rosenshine, Allen A1063
Rosenthal AG W636, W637
Rosenthal, Arthur L. A283
Rosenthal Automotive
Companies P717
Rosenthal, Daniel D. E194
Rosenthal, James A. A861
Rosenthal, Robert M. P717
Rosenthal, Steve P603
Rosenwald, E. John, Jr. A239
Rosenwald, Julius A1264, P176
Rosenwas, Jeffrey S. A61
Rosenwasser, Donna A949, P327,
P670
Rosenwig, Deanna W113
Rosenzweig, Richard C. E72
Rosenzweig, Ronald E28
Rose's Lime Juice P732
Rosetta Inpharmatics A956
Rosholt, Robert A. A183
Roski, Ed, Jr. A1086
Roskin, William A. A1477
Roslyn Bancorp, Inc. E281
Rosner, William E. A1147
ROSNO (insurance) W82
Rosoff, William L. A917
Ross, Adam A1158, P400, W462
Ross, Alan (Hilton Group) W259
Ross, Allan J. (Leggett &
Platt) A859
Ross, Bob A335

Ross, Bruce E66, E210
Ross, Cathy P530
Ross, Donald L. P179
Ross, Edward A1158, P400, W462
Ross, James L. A455
Ross, Kelly P431
Ross, Mason G. A1049, P377
Ross, Paul A. A121
Ross, Peter J. A517
Ross Products A58
Ross Stores, Inc. A**1214**-A**1215**
Ross Tohmatsu A474, P154
Rossberg, Jürgen W595
Rosseau, Robert H. A349
Rossel, Cary P616
Rosser, James M. P99
Rossi, Endvar P165
Rossi, Nick A1447
Rossi, Steve A833
Rossiter, Peter L. A1043
Rossiter, Robert E. A857
Rosskamm, Alan A796
Rosskamm, Betty A796, A797
Rosskamm, Martin A796
Rosso, Louis A242
Rosso, Mario W575
Rossum, Steven A. A485
Roster, Michael A659
Rosti A/S Group W95
Rostone (plastics) E279
Rostron, Paul P275, P651
Rotaract clubs P718
Rotary International P**420**-P**421**,
P718
Rotary Lift (automotive lifts) A502
Rotella, Stephen J. A809
Rotex (embossing machines) A210
Roth Brothers A598
Roth, David E. (ONEOK) A1065
Roth, David (J.B. Hunt) A789
Roth Freres (auto
components) A802
Roth, Gregory S. A695
Roth, John A. W412, W413
Roth, Michael I. A987
Roth, Steven R. (Rudolph
Technologies) E282
Roth, Steven (Vornado Realty
Trust) E137, E150, E314
Roth, Susan N. A1441
Roth, T. Christopher A1399
Rothaupt, Daniel J. A89
Rothbury Estate wines W230, W231
Rotherham, Thomas G. A681
Rothfeld, Eric A. A805
Rothhaar, John P165
Rothkopf, Charlene E161
Rothleitner, Mark M. A265
Rothman, Thomas E. A623
Rothmans International
(cigarettes) W142, W143, W282
Rothnie, James B. A543
Rothschild family W92, W500,
W624
The Rothschild Group W170
Rothschild, Walter A586

Rothwax, Joel H. E233
Rothwell, Allan R. A523
Rothwell, Timothy A1123
Rotner, Philip R. A475, P155, W197
Rotor Tools A430
Rotring Group (cookware) A1022
Rotron A1110
Rots, David P. A831
Rotterdam Bank W56
Rotterdam Shag tobacco W283
Roub, Bryan R. A687
Roubos, Gary A502
Rouge Steel Company A1463
Rouhselang, Sandra M. A337
Rouillard, Robbin M. P107
Rouleau, R. Michael A968, A969
A/S Roulunds Fabriker Group W95
Rounds, Elizabeth A1481, P509,
P766
Rounds, Joanne M. P227
Roundup weed killer A984, A985,
A1122
Roundy, Judson P422
Roundy, Peckham &
Company P422
Roundy's, Inc. (foods) A320,
P**422**-P**423**, P718
Rounsaville, Guy A1481, P509
Roush, Carroll A1206
Roush, Galen A1206
Rousseau, Michael W271
Roussel-Uclaf
(pharmaceuticals) W102
Roussely, François W209
Route 66 cigarettes W283
Route 66 clothing A831
Routs, Rob J. P604
Routt, J. Robert A569
Roux Fine Dining W175
Roux, Olivier P64
Rouyer, Eliane W59
Rover (cars) W120
Roverstone tobacco W283
Rovetto, Gilbert W69
Rowan, James P. A1489
Rowan, Mark A. P702
Rowe, Bill A592
Rowe, Brian H. E32
Rowe, James H. A1171
Rowe, John (Fifth Third
Bancorp) A592
Rowe, John W. (Aetna) A90, A91
Rowe, John W. (Exelon) A571
Rowe, Mike P729
Rowes Wharf (Boston) P449
Rowland, Allen R. A1532, A1533
Rowland, Charles R. E142
Rowland, Joyce A1267
Rowland, Lawrence T. A879
Rowland, Marcus C. E39, E176
Rowland, Roland W340
Rowlett, Donald A1214
Rowley, Bill A1261
Rowley, Steve A55
Rowling, J. K. A1254
Rowntree (chocolate) W388

Rowntree Mackintosh A914, P314
Roxana Petroleum A1276
Roxborough-Manayunk Bank E301
Roxendal, Jan W55
Roxio, Inc. E281
Roxoil Drilling A978
Roxy brand clothing E101
Roy, Christine W473
Roy, Daniel P. E42
Roy, Peter A1522
Roy Rogers fast food A732
Royal Ahold N.V. A1242, P103, W300, **W498-W499**
Royal Air Cambodge W540
Royal & Ancient Golf Club of St. Andrews P251
Royal & Sun Alliance Insurance Group plc A356, P268, W176
Royal & SunAlliance USA A688
Royal Bank Building (Montreal) W474
Royal Bank (Ireland) W86
Royal Bank of Canada. See RBC Financial Group
Royal Bank of Scotland Group plc A228, A954, A1332, W88, W114, W512, W522, W590
Royal Canin (pet food) A914, P314
Royal Caribbean Cruises Ltd. A**1216-A1217**, W434
Royal Crest containers A1415
Royal Crown Companies A1400, W154
Royal Doulton plc (china) W636
Royal Dutch Petroleum Company W500
Royal Dutch/Shell Group A184, A240, A352, A576, A1276, A1376, W92, W136, W242, W346, W372, **W500-W501**, W612. See also Shell Oil Company
Royal Dynasty carpets P342
Royal KPN N.V. A248, A1186, E220, W272, W418, **W502-W503**, W578, W584
Royal Nedlloyd (shipping) W434
Royal Philips Electronics. See Philips Electronics N.V.
Royal Reserve whiskey W85
Royal Scandinavia A/S W162
Royal Shirt men's clothes A690, A691
Royal Soft Drinks Plant W510
Royal Trustco W474
Royal Velvet bedding and towels A1134
Royal Wessanen A994
Royale Belge W104
Royale coffee A670
Royals'. See Benson & Hedges cigarettes
Royce, Henry W496
Royco soups A316
Royer, Bernard A1297
Royer, Thomas P575
Royster (fertilizer) A1436
Royster-Clark, Inc. A752, P718
Rozelle, Mark A. A1459

Rozelle, Pete P88, P356
Rozells, Mark D. A1329
Rozenberg, Misha A929
Rozwadowski, Jean F. A925, P323
Rozwat, Charles A. A1067
RP Business Services, Inc. A681
R. P. Harding (hatmaking) A562, W222
R.P. Scherer Corporation (softgels) A320, A321
RPC Mechanical A598
RPS, Inc. A588
R. R. Donnelley & Sons Company A944, A**1218-A1219**, P584, W186
R.R. Mossison and Son A1084
R.S. Harritan & Company A545
RSA Security Inc. E**114**, E281
RSB Agency E281
RSD appliances A935
RSKCo, Claim Services A379
RSM McGladrey, Inc. (accounting) A680, A681
RSR Technologies P709
RT Capital Management W474, W616
RTE (electrical equipment) A430
RTL 4-TV W626
RTL Group S.A. (broadcasting) W126, W127, W430, W431
RTO. See Alliance Regional Transmission Organization
RTZ Corporation (mining) A628, W488
Rubbermaid, Inc. A216, A1022, A1023, A1414
Ruben, Claudio E. A657
Ruben, James A1282
Ruben-Berman, Joann E182
Rubenstein Construction A144
Rubenstein, David M. P110, P111
Ruberg, Christopher R. A719
Rubik's Cube puzzle A260
Rubin, George A666
Rubin, Gerard A804
Rubin, Jonathan M. A737
Rubin, Robert (Citigroup) A370, A371
Rubin, Robert D. (Lennar) A863
Rubin, Shelly E234
Rubino, Paolo W79
Rubinson, Harvey P429, P721
Rubinstein, Jonathan A187
Rubow, Steven P478
Rucci, Anthony J. A321
Ruch, Mike P189, P608
Ruch, Richard A706
Ruck, Walter K. A451
Rucker, Edward A590
Rudberg, Jan W585
Rudd, Stace E85, E234
Ruddon, Raymond W. A801
Ruddy, James W. A1231
Ruddy, Raymond E88
Rudenstine, Neil L. P220, P626
Rudloff, Hans-Jörg W415

Rudnick, Alan A. A455
Rudolph, Allen P719
Rudolph and Sletten, Inc. P597, P719
Rudolph Fluor & Brothers (lumber mill) A610
Rudolph Karstadt AG W310
Rudolph, Onslow "Rudy" P719
Rudolph Technologies, Inc. E282
Rudolph, Vernon E80
Rudrakshi, Charu E134
Rue, William B. E116
Rued, Scott D. A1395
Ruether, Frank W477
Ruettgers, Michael C. A542, A543
Ruffing, Robert H. A145
Ruffles, Philip C. W497
Ruffles potato chips A1106, A1107
Rufrano, Glenn J. E252
Rugama Maison, Cristobal W583
Rugby Group A446
Rugby World Cup P251
Rugg, Stephen H. A287
Ruggieri, Thomas F. A1101
Ruggiero, Anthony W. A1061
Ruggiero, Renato W216
Ruggiero, Riccardo W423, W575
Ruggirello, John R. A89
Rugrats (TV show, movie, and products) A294, A295, E60
Ruhl, Ronald F. A415
Ruhr Oel W438
Ruhrgas AG W137, W218, W242
Ruhrkohle (coal) W218
Ruiz, Hector de J. A82, A83
Ruiz-Palmer, Diego A. A1045
Rulli, John A1287
Rulo, Christina M. E316
Rumenco (animal feed supplements) W568
Rumery, Doris P681
Rummell, Peter S. E115, E282
Rummler, Ernest E. A105
Runciman, David P121
Runk, Fred J. A145
Runkel, John A723
Runkle, Donald L. A477
Runnels, Jim P179
Runners Point stores W310, W311
Running W brand A828
Running Y Ranch resort P643
Runtagh, Hellene P554
Runyon, Marvin A1370, A1428, P468, P490
Runyon, Sandra E214
Rupert, Anton W142
Rupley, Ira A340
Rupp, George P134, P135, P579
Rupp, Glenn P142
Rupp, Joseph D. A1061
Ruppel, James A. A1311
Rupprecht, Gerhard W83
Rupprecht, Rudolf W351
Ruprecht, William F. A1304, A1305
Ruputer watches W528, W529
Rural America Initiative P520

Ruscher, Robert P. E283
Rusckowski, Steve H. A99
Rush Children's Hospital P719
Rush Limbaugh (radio program) A372
Rush, Richard P99
Rush System for Health P719
Rushing, Coretha A383
Rush-Presbyterian-St. Luke's Medical Center P719
Rusk salon products P580
Rusnack, William C. P704
Rusnak, Patrick J. E216
Russ clothing A880, A881
Russack, Richard A. A309
Russell 2000 Index (stocks) A1048, P376
Russell, Benjamin A1220
Russell, Benjamin C. A1220
Russell, Bill A280, P354
Russell, C. Kent P115, P569
Russell Corporation A**1220**-A**1221**
Russell, Daniel F. P115, P569
Russell, David E307
Russell, Elizabeth P591
Russell, Ian M. A1083, W523
Russell, Israel P358
Russell, John D. (Brunswick) A299
Russell, John (Harley-Davidson) A683
Russell, John (University of Nebraska) P759
Russell Kelly Office Service A818
Russell Stover Candies Inc. A1104, P**424**-P**425**, P719
Russell, Thomas A1220
Russell, William V. A713
Russell-Newman, Inc. (sleepwear) W607
Russer Foods A742, A743
Russian Prince vodka W109
Russian Trading System W346
Russo, Christopher J. P357
Russo, Patricia F. A524, A525
Russo, Paul W. A1323
Russo, Thomas A. A861
Russomanno, Frank A751
Rust, Adlai A1330, P458
Rust, Edward A1330, P458
Rust, Edward B., Jr. A1330, A1331, P458, P459, P735
Rust, Peter A. A419
Rustler jeans A1474, A1475
Rusty brand clothing E101, E259
Rusynko, Orest P297
Ruth, Babe A744, P242
Rutherford, Alan W. A453
Rutherford, Clive W569
Rutherford, William B. A695
Rutherford-Moran Oil A352
Rutkowski, Joseph A. A1053
Rutkowski, Lawrence R. A1161
Rutledge, William A116
Rutner, Alan P708
Rutrough, James E. A1331, P459
Ruttenberg, Robert J. A777

Ruttenstorfer, Wolfgang W425
Ruys, Anthony W255
Ruzic, Ronald M. A279
RVC (fund management) W484
R. W. Sears Watch Company A1264
RWE Aktiengesellschaft A416, W218, W**504**-W**505**
RWE-DEA Aktiengesellschaft für Mineraloel und Chemie W500
RxAmerica A886
Rx.com A334
RxHub A574
Ryalls, Peter G. A1439
Ryan Aeronautical A116, A1044
Ryan, Arthur F. A1172, A1173
Ryan, Claude A1426
Ryan, Dennis J. A725
Ryan, Gerald A. E124
Ryan, Holly A501, P163
Ryan Insurance Company A182
Ryan, James J. (Carlson Companies) P107
Ryan, James N. (Petroleum Development) E264
Ryan, James (Ryland Group) A1227
Ryan, James T. (W.W. Grainger) A1539
Ryan, J. Brendan A773
Ryan, Joan E. A1363
Ryan, John J. (Parsons Brinckerhoff) P696
Ryan, John O. (Macrovision) E235
Ryan, John P. (Schering-Plough) A1251
Ryan, John W. (State University of New York) P460
Ryan, Joseph A913
Ryan, J. Stuart A89
Ryan, Marc J. W123
Ryan, Mary J. P734
Ryan Milk of Kentucky A466
Ryan, Patrick (Allied Irish Banks) W87
Ryan, Patrick G. (Aon) A182, A183
Ryan, Patrick G. (Northwestern University) P379
Ryan, Patrick M. (Yardville National) E320
Ryan, Phillip K. W185
Ryan, Robert L. A953
Ryan, Thomas L. (Service Corp.) A1269
Ryan, Thomas M. (CVS) A458, A459
Ryan, Thomas W. (Allied Waste) A123
Ryan, Tom (McDonalds) A943
Ryan, William J. A455
Ryanair Holdings (airline) P475
Rydell, Roger P. A871
Ryder, Don W478
Ryder, Jim A1222
Ryder, Myrtle V. P427, P720
Ryder System, Inc. A**1222**-A**1223**, P390, P699, P700
Ryder, Thomas O. A1192, A1193
Ryder TRS truck rental system A300, A301

Rydin, Craig W. E143, E320
Rydin, Lars W585
Ryerson de Mexico A1224
Ryerson, Martin A446, A1042
Ryerson Tull, Inc. A104, A**1224**-A**1225**, W292
Rykhoek, Phil E191
The Ryland Group, Inc. A**1226**-A**1227**
RYMAC Mortgage A1010
Rynglok brand A527
RyTEC (e-commerce) A1224
Ryu In-Gyun W275
Rzicznek, Frank P686

S

S. Pearson & Son (construction) W430
S1 Corporation (security systems) W509
Saab AB (jets) W110
Saab Automobile AB A650, A651, A856, P561, W210, W220
Saad, Anu D. E72, E218
Saari, Roger W. A1311
Saarinen, Eero P276
Saas, Jean-Paul W521
Saatchi & Saatchi (advertising) W198, W466, W467, W646
Saathoff, David P445
SAB. *See* South African Breweries plc
Saba family A834, P280, P653
Saba, Shoichi W610
SABA Trading (produce importing) A494
Sabala, James A. E294
Saban A622
Sabanci W72, W318
Sabatasso Foods P436
Sabatello, Gregory D. A393
Sabatier, James H. A1329
Sabatino, Thomas J., Jr. A237
Sabena (airline) A478, W316
Sabet, Mori P567
Sabhlok, Raj P. E197
Sabia, Michael W123
Sabin, David C. E116
Sabin polio vaccine A1118
The Sabine Mining Company A993
Sable cars A616
Sabol, Thomas B. E104, E267
Sabourin, James A139
Sabratek A236
Sabre Engines Ltd. (marine engines) A332
Sabre Holdings A538
Sabre Inc. A164, A**1228**-A**1229**, P54, P418
Sabroe (industrial refrigeration) A1551
Sabroso liqueurs A423
Saccharin sweetener A1300
Sachs (automotive) W352
Sachs, Harold L. A785
S.A.C.I. Falabella A724

Sack 'n Save warehouse stores P677
Sack & Save stores P644
Sack, Hans J. A1387
Sackler, Raymond R. P707
Saco Defense P132, P578
Sacramento Kings (basketball team) P355
Sacramento Monarchs (basketball team) P355
Sacramento Municipal Utility District P720
Saddlebred brand P77
SADE (electric power) W214
Sade, Leah E194
Sadler, David G. A958
Sadler, Edward F. A969
Sadler, Geoff W173
Sadler, Michael W. A971
Sadoff, Laurence R. A787
Sadove, Stephen I. A291
Sadowski, Charles P737
Sadowski, Peter T. A591
Sadowski, Raymond A215
Saeki, Tatsuyuki A997, P353
Saenz, Alfredo W513
SAES Getters S.p.A. A1088
Saesa (power distributor) A1174
SAES-Parker UHP Components (gas valves) A1088
Saetia Sugar A354
Safari beer W553
SAFCO Technologies (wireless) A98
Safe Harbor Hydroelectric Project A424
SAFECO Corporation A**1230**-A**1231**
SafeDisc E235
Safeguard deodorant A1165
Safeguard International Fund P54
Safeguard Scientifics, Inc. A400, A1050, A**1232**-A**1233**, E197
Safer Way Natural Foods A1522
Safeshield gloves A827
Safeskin Corporation (exam gloves) A826
SAFEsuite software E222
Safetell International Security A488
Safety Cable Company A642
Safety Fund Bank A448
Safeway, Inc. A110, A549, A836, A886, A**1234**-A**1235**, E276, P62, P103, P282, P462, P736, W156, W298, W590, W644, W645
Safeway PLC W300
Saffola Quality Foods P122
Safin, Ralif R. W347
Safirstein, Benjamin A1076
Saflex performance films A1301
Saflok hardware A921
Safra, Edmond P176, W268
Safra, Jacob E. P176, P177, P603
Safra Republic Holdings W268
Saf-T-Hammer Corporation (gun safety equipment) W605
Sag Harbor brand A666, A839
Saga Education Food Services A1297

Saga Petroleum W410
SAGAD (appliances) A1520
Sagawa, Wesley S. A197
The Sage Group plc A204
Sage, James L. A1141
Sage Tree (software) A1514
Sagem SA (automotive electronics) A802
Sagian, Inc. (robotic and genetic analysis) A243
Sahkoliikkeiden (electrical wholesaler) W406
Saia Motor Freight Lines, Inc. A1548, A1549
SAIC. See Science Applications International Corporation
Said, Dato' Mohamed Haji W539
Saigusa, Shigeo W295
Saille, Noël W151
Sainsbury, Alan John W300
Sainsbury, David W300
Sainsbury, John Benjamin W300
Sainsbury, John James W300
Sainsbury, Mary Ann W300
Sainsbury's supermarkets and bank W300
St. Bruno Ready Rubbed tobacco W283
St. Bruno tobacco W282
Ste. Chapelle wines A422
St. Charles, Sonia A481
St. Clair Paint & Wallpaper W278
St. Elizabeth Hospital (Boston) P114
Saint Group W190
St. Ives Laboratories A108
St. Ives Swiss Formula A108
St. James Mercy Health System P115
The St. Joe Company E**115**, E282
St. Joe Minerals A610
St. John, Julie A581
St. John's Bay brand A791
St. Joseph Light & Power A1464
St. Joseph of the Pines P115
St. Joseph's Healthcare System P116
St. Joseph's Health System P115
St. Joseph's University (Philadelphia) W588
St. Jude Medical A674
St. Jude Medical, Inc. A444
St. Laurent Paperboard A1292
St. Louis beer W553
St. Louis Blues Hockey Club L.L.C. P361
St. Louis Cardinals (baseball team) A174, P307
St. Louis Hawks (basketball team) A280
St. Louis Rams Football Company P357
St. Louis-San Francisco Railway A308
St. Lucie nuclear plant A624
St. Luke's Hospital (Jacksonville, FL) P325

St. Luke's Shawnee Mission Health System P629
St. Martins Healthcare A694
St. Mary Land & Exploration Company A828, E282, P270
St. Mary's bedding and towels A1134
St. Mary's Health Care System, Inc. P115
St. Marys Hospital (Rochester, NY) P324, P325
St. Mary's Hospital (San Francisco) P118
St. Michael brand W356
St. Onge, Laurence A. A103
The St. Paul Companies, Inc. A822, A964, A1172, A**1236**-A**1237**
St. Pauli Girl beer A423
St. Paul Medical Center P744
St. Paul (Minnesota) *Pioneer Press* A833
St. Paul & Pacific Railroad A308
St. Raphael spirits W109
St. Regis hotels A1328, A1329, E171
Saint Regis Mohawk Tribe A1086
St. Vincent's Health System P56
Saint-Arnaud, Louis W471
Sainte-Claire Deville, Henri W432
Saint-Geours, Frédéric W443
Compagnie de Saint-Gobain A224, W**506**-W**507**
Sainz, Jesus A441
Saiontz, Steven J. E234
Saipem SpA (oil field services) W216, W217
SAirGroup A478, A1478
Saison Group W544
Saita, Ichiro W199
Saito, Akihiko W615
Saito, Gerald H. A887
Saito, Hiroshi W603
Saito, Kanzo W572
Saito, Norio W387
Saito, Shunjiro W573
Saito, Tadakatsu W535
Saji, Hiroshi W533
Sakaguchi, Kiyofumi A1173
Sakai, Kuniya W375
Sakai, Yoshio W527
Sakaino, Kozo W295
Sakaki, Yasuo W421
Sakamoto, Kazuhiko W359
Sakane, Masahiro W321
Sakata, Masanori W309
Sakhalin Energy Investment Company Ltd. A940
Sakiya, Sachio W597
Säkl AB W524
Saks Holdings P156
Saks Inc. A564, A932, A1014, A**1238**-A**1239**, P76, W142
Sakura Bank W200, W372, W374, W396, W551
Sakura, Sumiyoshi P92, P93
Sakurai, Masamitsu W487
Sakurai, Takeshi W371

Sala, Lawrence A. E156
Salama, Eric W647
Salamon, Miklos W129
Salazar, Antonio de Oliveira W224
Saldarelli, John P. E154
Saldarini, Charles T. E261
Saldin, Thomas R. A111
Saleh, Paul A1027
Salem cigarettes A1204, A1205, W304, W305
Salem, Michael A715, P233
Salem nuclear plant A570, A1174
Salerno, Frederick V. A1473
Salerno, Robert A213
Sales, A. R. A199
Sales, William J. P477
Saliba, Joseph I. A1229
Salick, Bernard P678
Salient 3 Communications, Inc. A98
Salinas, Carlos W580
Salinas de Gortari, Carlos W440
Saline, Craig A. P775
Salins, Peter D. P461
Salisbury, Larry A287
Salix Pharmaceuticals, Ltd. E283
SALIX Technologies A1362, A1363
Salizzoni, Frank L. A680, A681
Salk, Jonas A600
Salk polio vaccine A540, A1118
Sall, John P430, P431, P721
Sall, Thomas L. A251
Sallie Mae, Inc. (student loans) A1448, A1449
Sally Beauty Company A108
Salmon & Cluckstein tobacco shops W282
Salmon, Michael C. E131
Salmon, Peter W145
Salomon and Brazil P150
Salomon, Bill P626
Salomon Brothers Asset Management A238, A252, A370, A1466, P80
Salomon skis and snowboards W62, W63
Salomon Smith Barney Holdings Inc. A1101, A1346
Salora (televisions) W406
Salow, Glen A143
Salsbury, Peter W356
Salsgiver, Jan M. A197
Salt Industry Center of Japan W304
The Salt Lake Tribune P670
Salt Lake Windustrial (pipes and valves) P705
Salt River Project. See SRP
Salto, Léon W165
Salton, Inc. E116, E283
Salton, Lewis E116
Salva, Lawrence J. A391
Salvage Lynk software E45
Salvat (encyclopedias) W330
Salvation Army USA P426-P427, P492, P493, P720, P755
Salvatore, Louis R. A857
Salvqvik bandages A109

Salzburger, Karl Heinz A1475
Salzgitter W352
Sam Goody stores A254
Sam Houston Race Park, Ltd. A931
Sam Moore Furniture Industries A854
Sama stores W195
Sämann, Heinz W537
Samaritaine stores W348
Samaritan Health System P118, P549
Samba Room restaurants P106, P107
Sambol, David A439
Sambrook, Richard W145
Sambrooks, David J. A483
Sambur, Martin R. A781
SAME Deutz-Fahr (tractors) A96
Samek, Steve M. P49
Samelman, Irwin A805
Sames Corporation (spray painting) A748
Samford, Frank A1390
SAMICA (dried fruits and nuts) A494
Samil, Dilek L. A625
SAMIMA A588
SAMM (flight systems) W442
Sammon, Maureen P341, P676
Sammons, Charles P720
Sammons, Christopher D. A629
Sammons, Elaine P720
Sammons Enterprises, Inc. P720
Sammons, Mary A1203
Sammy Sosa shoes A294, A295
Samolczyk, Mark J. A1387
Sample, Molly M. A557
Sample, Steven B. P760
Sampson, Gerald A. A1015
Sampson, Gordon W646, W647
Sam's Club A262, A436, A606, A1494, A1495, W634, W635
Samson, Nicholaas W642
Samson (publishing) W642
Samson tobacco W143
Samsonite Corporation A618, A718, W332
Samsung Electronics Company, Ltd. E248
Samsung Group A410, A434, A870, A971, E74, E166, E194, E196, E257, E292, P137, P454, P545, P627, W180, W334, W480, W486, W508-W509, W590, W632
Samsung Tesco Company Limited W591
Samuel Adams beer W289
Samuel Lawrence furniture P442
Samuel, Marcus W500
Samuel Moore (plastics and fluid power) A526
Samuels, Sandor E. A439
Samuelson, Gary M. A401
Samuelson, Paul P496
Samurai SUV W560
Samuro, Yuushi W261
San Antonio Broadcasting A372

San Antonio Express-News A701, P229, W390
San Antonio Spurs, Ltd. (basketball team) P355, P627
San Chih Semiconductor W570
San Diego Chargers Football Company P357, P532
San Diego Consolidated Gas & Electric A1266
San Diego Gas & Electric A532, A1266, A1267
San Diego Padres Baseball Club Limited Partnership A270, P307
San Diego Spirit (soccer team) A443
San Diego State University P99
San Francisco 49ers, Ltd. (football team) P172, P173, P357
San Francisco Bay Area Rapid Transit District A240, P74
San Francisco Chronicle A700, A701, P228, P229, P629
San Francisco Examiner A700, P228, P629
San Francisco French Bread A774
San Francisco Gas & Electric A1120
San Francisco Giants (baseball team) P307
San Francisco International Airport Terminal P449
The San Francisco Music Box and Gift Company A1470
San Francisco-Oakland Bay Bridge A240, P74
San Francisco Realties A701
San Francisco State University P99
San Giorgio Macaroni A708
San Joaquin Valley Dairymen P563
San Jose (California) Mercury News A832, A833
San Jose National Bank E209
San Jose Sharks L.P. (hockey team) P361
San Jose State University P99
San Juan Basin Royalty Trust E283
San Luis Resort A978
San Miguel Corporation A382, W510-W511
San Onofre nuclear plant A532
San Paolo IMI (bank) W98
San Pellegrino water W388
San Teh (rubber switches) A780
Sanborn, Grant C. A159
Sanborn (medical) A98, A712
Sanchez, Alfred A1217
Sanchez, Bart P473, P744
Sanchez Computer Associates, Inc. (software) A1233
Sanchez, Jan E97
Sanchez, Jose P369
Sanchez, Sandy E150
Sanchez-Jaimes, Jonathan A1481, P509
Sánchez-Valdepeñas W579
Sancho Rof, Juan W483
Sand Hill Advisors (investments) E165

S&A Restaurant Corporation P332.
  See also Steak & Ale Restaurant
Sandcastle sportswear A1499
Sander, Dorothy E. A1447
Sander, Drue M. A583
Sanderford, Robin A491
Sanderlin, James L. A499
Sanders (airborne
  electronics) W110
Sanders, Bernard L. A583
Sanders, Brenda A. A1135
Sanders, Daniel S. A577
Sanders, Diane Day A1351
Sanders, Harland "Colonel" A1404,
  A1510
Sanders, Jeffrey G. A85
Sanders, M. H. W643
Sanders, M. Jack A1303
Sanders, Wayne R. A826, A827
Sanders, William D. (Security
  Capital) E285
Sanders, William E.
  (Rockwell) A1211
Sanders, W. J. "Jerry", III A82, A83
Sanderson, Edward J. A1067
Sanderson, Michael O. P353
Sanderson, Randy A497
Sanderson Special Steels A1386
Sandestin Resorts (Florida) W538
S&H Green Stamps A1176, P402
Sandia National Laboratories A882
Sandies cookies A814, A815
SanDisk Corporation E117, E284
Sandler, Herbert M. A658
Sandler, Marion O. A658, A659
Sandler, Robert M. A151
Sandler, Ron W177
The SandLot Brewery A78
Sandman, Dan D. A1461, A1463
Sandman, Paul W. A283
Sandoval, Joseph R. E275
Sandoz Chemicals E20
Sandoz (dyes) W414
S&P. *See* Standard & Poor's
S&P Company P428-P429, P721
Sandridge, Leonard W. P761
Sands, Dawn M. P331
S&S Hospital Supply A1070
Sands, Marvin A422
Sands, Mordecai "Mack" A422
Sands, Richard A422, A423
Sands, Robert A423
S&S Stores P406
Sandson, Mark A401
Sandström, Per-Arne W221
Sandstrom, Richard L. E49
Sandvik AB A1294
Sandvik Saws and Tools A1294
S&W food A470, A471
Sanex body care A1243
Sanfilippe, Frank H. E204
Sanford C. Bernstein Company,
  LLC A218, A219
Sanford, Daniel A1171
Sanford, Linda S. A765
Sanford markers A1022

Sanger, Stephen W. A648
Sanger's stores A586
Sanghi, Steve E93, E245
Sanghvi, Sujata S. P626
Sani-Dairy A1094
Sanifill A1504
Sanijura bath cabinetry P284,
  P285, P653
Sanitan (bath and plumbing) A1447
Sanitary Milk Producers P148
Sanka coffee A816
Sankey, Vernon W476
Sanko Kabushiki Kaisha W296,
  W358
Sankyo (pharmaceuticals) W314
Sanmina Corporation A686,
  A1240-A1241, A1256
Sannino, Louis J. A941
Sano, Katsuhiko W421
Sanofi Beauté W250
Sanofi Diagnostics Pasteur A242,
  A243
Sanofi-Synthélabo
  (pharmaceuticals) W118, W342,
  W612, W613
SanomaWSOY (newspapers) W626
Sanrio (media) W534
SANS Fibres A1300
Sansabelt men's clothes A690, A691
Sansavera, Sanford H. A159
SANshare software A895
Sansom, William B. P635
Sansone, Thomas A. A783
Sant Ana, Armando Leal W441
Sant, Roger W. A88, A89
Santa Ana Abstract A594
Santa Barbara (California) *News-*
  Press A1021
Santa Barbara Infrared E67
Santa Barbara Restaurant
  Group A590
Santa Catalina Island A1526
Santa Clara Systems A1050
Santa Cruz cattle P270
Santa Fe Energy Resources A176
Santa Fe Financial
  Corporation E221
Santa Fe Pacific Gold A1024
Santa Fe Pacific Insurance
  Company A309
Santa Fe Pacific Railroad
  Company A308, A309, E37
Santa Fe Snyder A482
Santa Fe Southern Pacific
  Railroad A176, A788, P280
Santa Gertrudis cattle A828, P270
Santa Isabel supermarkets W498
Santa Monica Ford
  Corporation P721
Santana car W631
Santana, Carlow A294
Santanasto, James A. A1423
Santander Central Hispano
  S.A. W512-W513
Santangelo, Jim P247
Sante, William A., II A1211
Santee Cooper P732

Santee Dairies, Inc. P462, P736
Santelia, Vincenzo P65
Santiam Lumber A1524
Santilli, Anthony J., Jr. E153
Santilli, Beverly E153
Santini, Gino A541
Santiso, Guillermo R. W583
Santitas snacks A1107
Santoni, Mike P625
Santos, Hugo E226
Santoso, Prihadi A629
Santullo, Cosmo E290
Sanus Corporation Health
  Systems A1016, P370
Sanwa Bank A602, W374
Sanwa Electric A1298
Sanyo Chemical Industries
  Company, Ltd. W603
SANYO Electric Company,
  Ltd. A894, A970, A1520, E121,
  W360, W508, W514-W515
SAP Aktiengesellschaft A1098,
  A1546, E91, E311, W161,
  W516-W517
SAP America A1186
Sapac (company) W492
Sapan, Joshua W. A313
Sapirstein Greeting Card
  Company A146
Sapirstein, Jacob A146
SAPMarkets W516
Saponas, Thomas A. A99
Sapp, A. Eugene, Jr. A1256, A1257
Sapper office seating P277
Sappir, Mark Z. E169
Sapporo Breweries Limited W314
Sapsa Bedding P442
Saputo Group (cheese) A774
Sara Lee Corporation A608, A774,
  A776, A1180, A1220,
  A1242-A1243, W282, W444
Saragoza, Alex M. P495
Sarah Michaels body care A486
Sarah's Garden brand W637
Saran Wrap A504, A1247, P432,
  P433
Sarawak Trading W538
SARCOM, Inc. P336
Sareeram, Ray R. A263
Saretsky, Gregg A. A107
Sargant, Hugh L. A1263
Sargeant, Thomas J. E161
Sargent, Joseph D. P215, P623
Sargent, Ronald L. A1325
Sargrad, Lee H. P363
Sari, Robert B. A1203
Saris beer W553
Sarji bin Abdul Hamid, Tan Sri
  Dato' Seri Ahmad W539
Sarkissian, Vahé A. E203
Sarles, H. Jay A603
Sarni, Vincent A1152
Sarnoff Corporation P454, P455,
  P734
Sarnoff, David A998
Sartain, Elizabeth P. A1547
Sartorelli, Claudio W215

Saruwatari, Satoshi W187
Sarvadi, Paul J. A74, A75
Sarvary, Mark A. P254, P255, P642
SAS AB A1420, A1421, W94, W174, W**518**-W**519**, W540
SAS Institute Inc. P**430**-P**431**, P721
SAS International Hotels W519
Sasaki, Hajime W387
Sasaki, Mikio W371
Saski, Tomohiko W611
Sassa, Scott A998
Sassaby A564
Sasso, Richard E. A1217
Sasson, Gideon A349
Sasyama, Shinya W393
SAT (telephone) W220
SAT.1 (electronic media) W106
Satin Care shaving cream A657
Satinet, Claude W443
Satmex (satellite services) A888
Sato E284
Sato, Hideki W526, W527
Sato, Hiroshi W572
Sato, Kazuo W261
Sato, Masaaki W375
Sato, Michiji W187
Sato, Mitsusuke W187
Sato, Nobutake W299
Satoh, Yasuhiro W314, W315
SatoTravel E250
Satre, Philip G. A684, A685
Sattel, Darlene P303, P661
Sattler, John H. A85
Sattler, Peter V. A1321
Saturday Night Live (TV show) A999, W606
Saturday Night (magazine) W263
Saturn Corporation (automobiles) A256, A650, P606, P631, P633, W138
Saturn electronics stores W364, W365
Saturn rocket A1256
Saucona Iron A256
Saudi Aramco A1276, A1376, A1377, P340, P604, P679
The Saudi British Bank W268
Saudian Arabian Amiantit Company A1072
Sauer Drilling E129, E302
Sauer, Jon W. A185
Saul, B. Francis, II P574
Saunders, Charles H. (Dell) A473
Saunders, Charles (Masco) A920
Saunders, John (Invensys) W291
Saunders, John R. (International Speedway) E75
Saunders Karp & Megrue (investments) E176, E177
Saur S.A. (water) W134, W135
Sauza tequila W84
Sava tires A664
Sav-A-Center grocery stores A670, A671
Savacentre supermarkets W300, W301

Savage motorcycle W561
Savage, Robert G. A801
Savage, Thomas R. A287
Savane International E305
Savanna travel trailers A605
Savannah Electric and Power Company A1306, A1307
Savannah plumbing fixtures A265
Savard, Jacques W133
Sav-A-Stop stores A578
Sav-A-Ton stores P740
Save Mart Supermarkets P488, P722
Save-A-Lot stores A1348, A1349, P634, W194, W195
Saveuse, Joël W165
Savia S.A. de C.V. (insurance) W286
Saville Systems (software) A70
Savills (real estate) A1398
Savin copiers W486
Saving Private Ryan (movie) P166, P167
Savings Plus brand A671
SavMax food stores P488
Savner, David A. A645
Savoir Technology Group A214
Savol, Thomas B. E267
Sav-on drugstores A66, A110, A111, A844
Savon.com A110
Savoy Pictures A1450
Savoy, William D. P510, P511
Sawabe, Hajime W572, W573
Sawaragi, Osamu A1006
Sawi, Elizabeth G. A349
Sawtek Inc. (signal processing) E305
Sawyer, James A1157
Sawyer Lumber Company A890
Sawyers, William R. A471
Saxonville USA P690
Say, Arkan E128
Sayavedra, Leo P471
Saydun, Yuda A1357
Sayer, Kevin R. E241
Sayers, Richard A., II A1141
Sayles, Helen E. R. A875, P295, P658
Sayles, Thomas S. A1267
Saylor, Kirk C. P634
Sayonara (racing yacht) A1066
Sayre, Scott E. A1479
S-B Power Tool Company A546, W490
SBA. *See* US Small Business Administration
SBC Communications Inc. A248, A1182, A**1244**-A**1245**, E286, E296, E302, P332, P576, W122, W580
Sbona, Gary J. E134, E311
Sbrocco, Bill E200
SBS Technologies, Inc. E284
sbs.com A1341
SC Johnson Commercial Markets, Inc. P722

S.C. Johnson & Son, Inc. A234, A486, A504, A800, A**1246**-A**1247**, P88, P**432**-P**433**, P722, W476
SC Realty, Inc. A1309
Scaduto, James A. A507
Scafuri, Anna W423
Scala toys by LEGO W333
Scaldara, John A., Jr. E182
Scaldia Papier A770
Scales, Bill W587
Scales, Herbert K., III A779
Scalet, J. Chris A771
Scalice, John A. A1371, P469
Scalise, George A928
Scaminace, Joseph M. A1279
Scamp Records recording label W213
SCANA Corporation (power company) A514, A515, A**1248**-A**1249**, A1516
Scanair W518
Scandic Hotels AB W258, W259
Scandiffio, Michael P255
Scandinavian Airlines System. *See* SAS AB
Scanforms P506
Scania-Vabis (trucks) W630, W632
Scanlan, Melissa A393
Scanlon, Cathy P619
Scanlon, Edward J. A265
Scanlon, John J. A579
Scanlon, Patrick O. A605
ScanSource, Inc. E**118**, E284
Scantrack service A66, A67
Scantronic security equipment A431
Scarborough, Dean A. A211
Scarborough, Jocelyn E117, E284
Scardino, Marjorie M. W430, W431
Scarfone, Anthony C. A481
Scarpa, Michael A881
Scarpati, Ann E156
Scarpati, Stephen A. P215
Scarth, Victoria W291
Scatturo, Peter K. A371
Scavo, Anthony P291
Scavone, Anne M. A753
SCDM (holding) W134
SCE. *See* Southern California Edison
SCE&G (utility) A1248
Scenic car W480, W481
SCH. *See* Santander Central Hispano S.A.
Schaar, Richard J. A1379
Schacht, David A1287
Schacht, Henry A898
Schachter, Rozalie E68
Schadt, James A1192
Schaecher, Francis P. A853
Schaefer, Barbara W. A1423
Schaefer, Fred H. A1401
Schaefer, George A., Jr. A593
Schaefer, John A432
Schaefer, Joy E317
Schaeffer, Glenn W. A906, A907
Schaeffer, Leonard D. A1506, A1507

Schaeffer, Stephen G. A1199
Schaevitz industrial sensors A1412
Schaevitz Sensors E240
Schafer, Charles J. A847
Schafer, Glenn S. P385
Schaffer, David H. W593
Schaffer, Frederick P. P129
Schaffer, John P528
Schaffer, Michael B. A195
Schaffner, Joseph A690
Schafstall, Richard D. A1281
Schaible, Dexter E. A97
Schamberger, John P. A1475
Schandel, Susan G. E75
Schapiro, Mary L. A997, P353
Scharf, Charles W. A231
Scharff, Michael J. E113
Schatz, Douglas S. E24, E149
Schaub, Ernest F. A663
Schauf, Lawrence E. A785
Schaulandt electronics stores W311
Schaver, Steven B. A529
Schechinger, Terry A401
Schedler, Donald P. E95
Scheele, Nicholas V. A617
Scheepbouwer, A. J. W503
Scheeringa, S. Michael A1443
Scheevel, David H. A103
Scheffler, Peter M. A1257
Scheflen, John W. A937
Schehr, Barry D. A161
Scheid, Steven L. A349
Scheihing, Betty Jane A197
Schein Pharmaceutical E89
Scheinfeld, Aaron A910
Scheinman, Dan A369
Schell, Brian N. A681
Scheller, Richard H. A641
Schelling, Warren C. A1341
Schemechel, Daniel J. A531
Schenkel, Pete A1339
Schenkkan, Gerard A929
Schenley (distillery) W206
Schenz, Richard W425
Schepker, Donald P725
Schepman, Anthony W642
Schepp, Richard D. A839
Schepps brand A1339
Scher, Pat A1056
Scherb, Jeff R. A1403
Scherbarth, Ginger E277
Scherer, George F. P669
Scherer, Peter R. E129
Schering, Ernst A1250
Schering-Plough
  Corporation A956,
  A1250-A**1251**, E199, W102,
  W416
Schermerhorn, Todd C. A445
Scherr, Raymond E66
Schessler, James E. A621
Schettini, Frank E113
Scheurer, Charles B. A489
Scheurle, Walter W203
Scheyer, Steven R. A1023
Schiavo, Jacqueline J. A119

Schick shaving products A1118
Schick, Thomas (American
  Express) A143
Schick, Thomas E. (Boeing) A273
Schickedanz-Holding W310
Schiech, John W. A265
Schiefelbein, Mark A673, P211,
  P621
Schieffer, Michael P. A1097
Schiefner, Roy P101
Schiewetz, Richard P705
Schiferal, Ron P695
Schiff, Frederick S. A291
Schiffner, Robert A. A317
Schifter, Richard P474
Schiller, Phillip W. A187
Schiller, Robert R. E29, E158
Schilling, Raymond E208
Schilling Thomas L. A293
Schimberg, Henry A384
Schimkaitis, John R. E177
Schimmel, Daniel J. E100, E258
Schimmelpenninck cigars W143
Schindhelm, Klaus E112
Schindler, Andrew J. A1204, A1205
Schindler, Steven M. A1027
Schinzler, Hans-Jurgen W381
Schiola, Barbara P449, P730
Schipporeit, Erhard W219
Schirmer, R. Hamilton A921
Schiro, James J. A1159, W463
Schiro, Tom A475, P155, W197
Schivley, William W. A1041
Schjerven, Robert E. A864, A865
Schlaet, Arnold A1376
Schlais, Rudolph A., Jr. A651
Schlais, Warner F. A481
Schlapp, Herman W128
Schlede, Klaus G. W345
Schleien, Robin A329, P109
Schlert, Theodore P115
Schlesinger, Albert R. A225
Schlesinger, Leonard A. A777, A877
Schlifske, John E. A1049, P377
Schlink, Frederick P138
Schlitz beer A174, P428, P721
Schlosser, Ronald H. W593
Schlotman, J. Michael A845
Schlotzhauer, Adele E34, E165
Schlumberger, Conrad A1252
Schlumberger Limited A222, A676,
  A1252-A**1253**, E210, W100,
  W150
Schlumberger, Marcel A1252
Schlumberger, Pierre A1252
Schmalbach-Lubeca AG (plastic
  containers) A802
Schmale, Neal E. A1267
Schmalkuche, Laurie P339, P676
Schmalz, Douglas J. A193
Schmeltz, David G. A135
Schmelzer, Wilhelm A. A585
Schmidt, Andreas W127
Schmidt, Bill E99
Schmidt, E. Frank A1309

Schmidt, Eric E. A1050, A1051
Schmidt, Gary P. A109
Schmidt, Henry A992
Schmidt, Jill W. A769
Schmidt, Judy E292
Schmidt, Steven A. (Renaissance
  Learning) E278
Schmidt, Steven M.
  (ACNielsen) A67
Schmidt, Ulrich A663
Schmidt-Holtz, Rolf W127
Schmidtmann, Waldemar A752
Schmidt-Ruthenbeck family W364
Schmiesing, Sandra L. P533
Schmitt, Kurt W380
Schmitt, Michael J. P423
Schmitt stores A1094
Schmitt, Timothy J. A1025
Schmitz, Hans R. W203
Schmitz, John P123, P571
Schmitz, Louise Scholl W588
Schmitz, Ronaldo H. W201
Schmitz, William W588
Schmoldt, Hubertus W219
Schmoll, John P. W173
Schmoller, Eberhard G. H. A381
Schmutte, Daniel P. A645
Schnabel, Brian T. A1023
Schnaid, Alan M. A1329
Schnall, Peter A319
Schnapps liquor A423
Schneid, John P612
Schneidawind, Detlef W381
Schneider, Adolphe W520
Schneider, A. J. "Al" P434
Schneider, Andrea E. P389
Schneider, Antonio A563, P183,
  W223
Schneider, Charles F. (Clorox) A375
Schneider, Charles (Schneider
  Electric) W520
Schneider Corporation A1291
Schneider, Donald J. (Green Bay
  Packers) A673, P211
Schneider, Donald J. (Schneider
  National) P434, P435, P723
Schneider, Douglas H. A1407
Schneider Electric SA W**520**-W**521**
Schneider, Eugene W520
Schneider, Forrest M. P655
Schneider, George A174
Schneider, James M. A473
Schneider, Jean-Luc W225
Schneider, Jörg W381
Schneider, Jurgen W200
Schneider, Mahlon C. A731
Schneider, Manfred W119
Schneider National, Inc. A788,
  P**434**-P**435**, P723
Schneider, Pamela C. A435
Schneider, Phil E. (Pier 1
  Imports) A1131
Schneider, Phillip M. (IDEC
  Pharmaceuticals) E217
Schneider, Richard E.
  (Teradyne) A1373

Schneider, Richard P. (Tenneco Automotive) A1369
Schneider Transport & Storage P434
Schneider Worldwide (stents) A282
Schneider/NAMIC (stents) A283
Schnell, Philip G. A1527
Schnell, Scott T. E114
Schnieders, Richard J. A1351
Schnopp, Eddie K. E269
Schnuck, Craig D. P723
Schnuck Markets, Inc. P478, P479, P723
Schnuck, Todd R. P723
Schoch, Doug E21, E148
Schochet, Barry P. A1367
Schoellhorn, Robert A58
The Schoellkopf Company A1028
Schoen, Michael D. A287
Schoenbaum, Alex A1280
Schoenbaum, Raymond D. A1280
Schoenholz, David A. A735
Schoewe, Thomas M. A1495
Schoewel, Erhard W477
Schofield, Seth A1442
Schofield, S. Gene P385
Scholastic Corporation A**1254**-A**1255**, W330
Scholes, Myron P496
Scholl, Hermann W491
Scholl, Linda L. E226
Scholl, Richard A. E24
Scholten, Roger K. A935
Schonfield, Brian A857
Schöning, Georg W505
Schooley, Joyce P656
Schools, Frank J. E101
Schoonover, Philip J. A255
Schori, Jan E. P720
Schörling, Melker W524, W525
Schorr, Brian L. A1401
Schorr, Todd P535
Schoshinski, Alicia P145, P585
Schottenstein, Alvin A260
Schottenstein Center P382
Schottenstein, Jerome A260
Schottenstein, Saul A260
Schotz, John A564
Schrader Bellows (pneumatics) A1088
Schrader, Hans-Otto W427
Schrader, Richard A. P696
Schrader, William P. P734
Schraith, Jim A1185
Schram, Henry B. A357
Schrantz, Stephen J. A593
Schreiber Foods, Inc. P723
Schreiber, Pierre W185
Schreiner, Daniel G. A1227
Schreiner, Linda V. A1517
Schrempp, Jürgen E. W189
Schreyer, John Y. A133
Schrier, Eric W. A1193
Schriver, Don P149
Schrock (cabinets) A618

Schrock, Donald E. A1183
Schroder plc A750
Schroders (investment banking) A370
Schroeder, Charles F. A697
Schroeder, Edward G. P119
Schroeder, Gary P. A385
Schroeder, Gerald P499, P761
Schroeder, Paul J., Jr. A491
Schroeder, Scott C. E168
Schroeder, Stephen O. (Cooper Tire & Rubber) A433
Schroeder, Steven A. (Robert Wood Johnson Foundation) P715
Schroeder Ventures (equity) W256
Schropp, Tobin A. A1115, P397
Schroth, Richard A1113
Schrum, Harold P107
Schub, Judy P389
Schubel, Ronald L. A983
Schubert, Frank B. P648
Schubert, Klaus W351
Schueler, Charles A313
Schueler, Jacob A78
Schueller, Eugène W342
Schuessler, John T. A1510, A1511
Schuh, Dale R. P726
Schuiling, William P561
Schuitema (grocery wholesaler) W498
Schulenburg, Dianne E173
Schuler, J. Terry A211
Schuller International A1072
Schulman, Scott D. A507
Schulmeyer, Gerhard P54, P55
Schulte, David A560, P180
Schulte, Hans-Jürgen W351
Schulte, Richard L. A481
Schulte-Hillen, Gerd W127
Schulte-Noelle, Henning W83, W351, W381
Schultz, Charles L. A309
Schultz, Daniel R. P43
Schultz, Gary C. P699
Schultz, Howard A1326, A1327
Schultz, James H. (American Standard Companies) A153
Schultz, Jamie (Illuminet) E217
Schultz, Kåre W417
Schultz, Lawrence N. A1141
Schultz, Paul L. A785
Schultz, Randal P115
Schultz Sav-O Stores P479
Schultz, William A655
Schulz, Andrea M. E150
Schulz, Ekkehard W595
Schulz, Roland W257
Schulze Baking A774
Schulze, Richard M. A254, A255
Schulze, Rudiger W205
Schumacher, Diane K. A431
Schumacher, Joseph R. A103
Schumacher, Mary J. A531
Schumacher, Richard C. A295
Schumacher, William G. E100
Schuman, Allan L. A530, A531

Schuman, Donald L. A65
Schumann, William H., III A613
Schumm, Steven A. A351
Schurer, Michael M. E216
Schurmann electronics stores W311
Schurr, Eric L. E110
Schuster, James E. A1191
Schuster, Richard S. E97
Schuster, Stephen T. A235
Schutz, Larry A351
Schuylkill Silk Mills A1474
Schwab, Bob P593
Schwab, Charles R. (Charles Schwab Corp.) A349, P456
Schwab, Charles (U.S. Steel) A256, A1462
Schwab, Les P657
Schwab, Mark A679, P217
Schwäbische Hüttenwerke W351
Schwan, Alfred P436, P437
Schwan, Arthur P436
Schwan, Charles A. E44
Schwan, Marvin P436, P724
Schwan, Paul P436
Schwan's Sales Enterprises, Inc. P**436**-P**437**, P724
Schwanz, Donald K. E189
Schwappach, Nancy S. A813
Schwarte, David A. A1229
Schwartz, Alan D. A239
Schwartz, Arthur L. P696
Schwartz, Barry P100, P101, P564
Schwartz, Bernard L. A888, A889
Schwartz, Brian J. E21
Schwartz, David H. A295
Schwartz, Dick A120
Schwartz, Eric M. A495
Schwartz, Gil A335
Schwartz, H. Gerald, Jr. A787
Schwartz, Lawrence H. A847
Schwartz, Mark S. A831
Schwartz, Martin M. E300
Schwartz, Michael G. A865
Schwartz, Paul N. A931
Schwartz, Richard W. P705
Schwartz, Thomas P. A935
Schwartzer Krauser tobacco W143
Schwartzkopff TV-Productions W106
Schwarz, Randall W294, W295
Schwarzwalder, Larry P477, P745
Schwegmann Giant Super Markets A670
Schweitzer, Louis W481
Schweitzer, Peter A. W647
Schweizerische Bangesellschaft W616
Schwendler, Bill A1044
Schwenzer, Hans Joachim A1415
Schweppe, Charles P226
Schweppe, Jacob W154
Schweppes soft drinks A382, A383, A384, A385, A1103, A1105, W154, W155
Schwertfeger, Timothy R. A1237
Schwesig, Norman P309

Schwetschenau, Mark T. A1011
Schwieg, John A. A1539
Schwinn P180
Schwinn fitness equipment E193
Schwinn/GT A560, E193
SCI Systems, Inc. A1240,
  A**1256**-A**1257**, A1298, E226
SCI Television A902, P304
Scialpi, Sheryl P647
Science & Art (software) A76
Science Applications International
  Corporation P**438**-P**439**, P724
Science Diet pet food A386, A387,
  P394
ScienceDirect Web site W478
ScienceMedia P511
Scientific Advances, Inc. P71
Scientific Calculations
  (software) A686
Scientific Materials Company A600
Scientific Revolution stores P159
Scientific Supplies A600
Scientific-Atlanta, Inc. A792,
  A**1258**-A**1259**, E28, E156, E312,
  W554
Sci-Fi Channel A1450
Scifres, Don A793
SCIMED Life Systems, Inc. A282,
  A283, A674
SCIREX (pharmaceutical
  trials) A1062, A1063
Scirocco, Joseph W607
SciRox (product development) P54,
  P55
Scitex (prepress systems) A770
Sciuto, John J. E183
Sciutto, Sandra G. E169
SCM Chemicals A974
SCM Metal Products A1446
SCM (office equipment) A974,
  W252
SCOA (pharmaceuticals) W446
Scoggins, Kirk E125, E299
Scolarest (food services) W175
Scolnick, Edward M. A957
Scope Industries E285
Scope mouthwash A1164, A1165
Scorpion tape drive P441
Scotch tape A976
Scotch-Brite scouring
  products A976
Scotchgard stain repellant A976
Scotese, Peter A1316, P452
Scotia Holdings A648
Scotia Pacific Timberlands A931
Scotland, David W85
Scotsman (Edinburgh) W592
Scott, Bruce A1066
Scott, Cheryl M. P622
Scott consumer electronics E58
Scott, C. Wesley M. W123
Scott, Daniel S. A107
Scott, David J. A953
Scott, D. E. P439
Scott, Edward (BEA Systems) E33
Scott, Edward (Swire Pacific) W564

Scott Fetzer (encyclopedias) A252,
  A462
Scott Foresman W390, W430
Scott, Gregory W. A1081
Scott, H. Lee, Jr. A1494, A1495
Scott, Jack E. P269
Scott, Jeffrey E288
Scott, Jeremy A1159, P401, W463
Scott, Jonathan A670
Scott, Ken A1113
Scott, Kipling W. A1227
Scott, Michael J. A705, E257
Scott, Milton L. A519
Scott Paper A826, A827
Scott, Peter M., III A1167
Scott, Rick A694
Scott, Robert G. A989
Scott, Steve P739
Scott, Thomas G. (Atlas Air) E32
Scott, Tom (University of
  Texas) P499
Scott Transport A1454
Scott, Walter (Berkshire
  Hathaway) P340
Scott, Walter, Jr. (Level 3
  Communications) A866, A867
Scott, Walter, Jr. (Peter Kiewit
  Sons') A1114, A1115, P396, P397
Scott-Barrett, Hugh Y. W57
Scottish Amicable Life plc W464
Scottish & Newcastle
  (brewer) W192, W230
Scottish and Southern
  (utility) W523
Scottish Aviation W110
Scottish Power plc A1082, A1083,
  W144, W**522**-W**523**
Scottish Telecom. *See* Thus
  (telecommunications)
Scottish Television W592
Scott/McDuff electronics equipment
  stores A1188
Scott's cereal A1181
The Scotts Company A984, W256
Scott's Foods stores A1348, A1349
Scotts (lawn care) W102
Scotts Stores group W552
Scottsdale Insurance
  Companies A1008, A1009, P364,
  P365, P685
ScottWarren (automotive
  coatings) A1278
The Scoular Company A426, P140,
  P724
Scovanner, Douglas A. A1353
Scoville, Randy P747
Scrader-Bridgeport (automotive
  equipment) W604
Screg Group W134
Scribner's Bookstores A232, A233
Scricco, Francis M. A196, A197
Scripps, Charles A568
Scripps, Edward Willis A568, A700,
  P228
Scripps Howard Broadcasting,
  Inc. A144, A568
Scripps Howard News Service A568
Scripps, Paul K. A569

ScrippsHealth (HMO) P118, P570
Scrivani, Robert C. P607
Scrivner (wholesale foods) A606,
  A1350
Scroll Technologies A1550
Scrub Free cleanser A358
Scrubbing Bubbles cleaner A1247,
  P433
Scruggs, John E. A99
Scruggs, Samuel D. P239
Scrushy, Richard M. A322, A698,
  A699
Scubamaster watch W530
Scudder, Richard P670
Scudder Stevens & Clark (fund
  management) W652
Scull, Harvey R. A1363
Sculley, John A186
Scully, Richard W. W231
Scultz, Steven E241
Scurlock Oil A200
Scurlock Permian A1144, A1460
Scussel, Jay D. A667
Scwartz, Mark A1505
SDC. *See* Software Developer's
  Company
SDL plc
  (telecommunications) A792
Sea Breeze skin care W534
Sea Cliff Water Company A544
Sea Insurance Company of
  England A356
Sea Ray boats A298, A299, E237
Sea Robin Pipeline A536
Sea View Hospital Rehabilitation
  Center and Home P369
Sea World A1310
Seaber Corporation E209
Seaboard Air Line Railroad A454
Seaboard Coast Line
  (railroad) A454
Seaboard Corporation (packing and
  processing) A408, A426, P140
Seabourn Cruise Line A330
Seabourn Spirit (ship) A331
Seabourn Sun (ship) A331
Seabrook nuclear plant A1040
Seabrook, Raymond J. A225
Seabury & Smith, Inc. (insurance
  management) A916, A917
Seacoast (animal feed) A974, W252
Seacoast Financial Services
  Corporation E285
Sea-Doo watercraft W132, W133
Seafield Estate and Consolidated
  Plantations W538
Seaforth Corn Mills A325
Seagate Technology, Inc. A758,
  A**1260**-A**1261**, E117, E166,
  P**440**-P**441**, P725
The Seagram Company Ltd. A296,
  A385, A412, A494, A534, A618,
  A962, A1104, A1106, A1344,
  A1450, W84, W108, W146, W230,
  W360, W444, W624
Seagraves, George A509
Sea-Land Corporation (ocean
  container shipping) A454, W94

Sealand Oil Services Ltd. A638
Seale, Donald W. A1039
Sealed Air
  Corporation A**1262**-A**1263**,
  A1536
Sealed Power brand A585, A1320
Sealine International (boats) A298,
  A299
Sealol A1110
Sealy Corporation A560, P180,
  P**442**-P**443**, P652, P725, P727
Seaman Furniture Company,
  Inc. P716
Seaman, Jeffrey P716
Seaman, Morty P716
Seaman-Patrick Paper A770
SEAMGUARD staple line-
  reinforcement P523
SeaPak seafood P714
Seaport Hotel at the World Trade
  Center A615
Searchasaurus On line search
  engine P170
Searle, James A., Jr. A455
Searle, Stewart A., III A1005
Searles, Michael M. E60, E202
Sears de Mexico A1264
Sears, Gregory L. A1231
Sears, Michael M. A273
Sears Mortgage A1146
Sears PLC W426
Sears, Richard A1264
Sears, Roebuck and Company A126,
  A216, A254, A462, A490, A572,
  A660, A664, A790, A802, A860,
  A880, A932, A936, A988, A1130,
  A1218, A**1264**-A**1265**, A1278,
  A1314, A1428, A1520, A1552, E21,
  E150, E283, P88, P120, P176,
  P490, P637, W124, W164, W270,
  W298, W366, W508
Sears Tower (Chicago) A1264,
  P448, P449, P587, P730
Searson, DeVaughn D. P347, P680
Searstown Twin Theatre P412
Seashore, Eugene H., Jr. A251
SEAT Pagine Gialle S.p.A.
  (publishing & Internet
  services) W574, W575
SEAT S.A. (automobiles) W630,
  W631
Seattle Car & Foundry A1078
Seattle Computer P510
Seattle Mariners (baseball
  team) P307
Seattle Post-Intelligencer A701,
  P229
Seattle Seahawks, Inc. (football
  team) A672, P210, P357, P510,
  P511, P767
Seattle Storm (basketball
  team) P355
Seattle SuperSonics (basketball
  team) P355
Seaver, James M. A97
Seaway Food Town food and drug
  stores A1312
SeaWest W522

SeaWorld theme park A174
Seay, Larry W. E243
Seay, Scott P275
Sebastiani Vineyards, Inc. A422
Sebring, Joseph B. A1291
SEC. *See* US Securities and
  Exchange Commission
Seca petroleum products A412
Secher, Jan W55
Sechler, Susan P415
Seconal drug A540
Second National Bank
  (Boston) A1332
Second Natonal Bank of
  Pittsburgh A1146
Second Nature egg
  substitute A1338, A1339
Secor, John P69
Secret deodorant A1165
Securant Technologies E114
Secure Horizons USA, Inc. A1080,
  A1081
Securian Holding P677
Securicor Omega Holdings
  Ltd. W203
Securicor plc W148, W202, W628
SecurID E114
Securis N.V. W525
Securitas AB W**524**-W**525**
Securities Dealers Insurance
  Company, Inc. A997, P353
Securities Industry Automation
  Corporation P46
Security Bank Texas A1308
Security Benefit Group, Inc. P725
Security Capital Group Inc. E285
Security Capital U.S. Realty E276
Security Dynamics Technologies.
  See RSA Security Inc.
Security Elevator A502
Security Feed and Seed P406
Security First Group A964
Security First Technologies W474
Security National Bank A226
Security National Life
  Insurance A414
Security S&L A590
Security Savings A658
Security Title and Guarantee
  Company A590
Security Title & Trust A594
Securum (holding company) W72
Sedco Forex Drilling A1252
Sedgefield Specialties (textile
  chemicals) A306
Sedgwick Group PLC A916, A917
Sedona Golf Resort A1138
Seeber, Gerald R. P39
SEEBOARD (utility) A140
Seeger Refrigerator
  Company A1520
Seegmiller, Ray R. E168
Seelenfreund, Alan A947
Seelert, Robert Louis (Publicis
  Groupe) W467
Seelert, Robert (Topco) P478
Seelig, Sam A1234

Seeling, Ronald L. A315, P97
Seely, Timothy A. A1291
Seelye, Matthew C. A1503
Seeman, Patricia W653
SEEQ Technology
  (semiconductors) A894
See's Candies, Inc. A252
Seessel's supermarkets A111
Seeuws, Jean-Pierre W613
Seffrin, John R. P40, P41, P537
SEGA Corporation E298, P166,
  P597, W238, W394, W**526**-W**527**
Segal, Edward D. E244
Segal, Joseph P416
Segal, Steven G. P407
Segalini, Paul P399, P703
Segedin, Dan A85
Seger, Dick W525
Segin (IT services) W100
Segrets (clothing) A880
Segundo Ruiz Belvis Diagnostic &
  Treament Center P369
Seguranca ao Credito e Informacoes
  (credit information) A558
Seguros Caracas P295
Seguros Commercial America
  (insurance) A714, P232
Seguros Panamerican P295
Companhia de Seguros
  Tranquilidade SA
  (insurance) W224, W225
Segurros Monterrey A1016, P370
Sehanan, Susan E174
Sei SpA (real estate) W215
Seiberling, Charles A664
Seiberling, Frank A664
Seiberling (tires) W138
Seibert, Joseph A335
Seibold, Michael M. P227
Seibu Department Stores,
  Ltd. A1150
Seidemann, William A1294
Seidenberg, Ivan G. A1472, A1473
Seidman, Jeffery P727
Seidman, Rebecca K. E41, E179
Seifert, Kathi P. A827
Seifert, Shelley J. A1001
Seigle, C. W643
Seiki Kogaku Kenkyusho W158
Seiko Corporation E49, E189,
  E236, W**528**-W**529**, W530
Seiko Epson Corporation A778,
  E121, E267, W528, W**530**-W**531**
Seiler (vending machines) W546
Seimon A176
Seinfeld P128
Seita (tobacco manufacturer) A902,
  P304, P663
Seitz, Jane E. E237
Seitz, John N. A169
Seitz, Thomas W. A1279
The Seiyu, Ltd. (retailer) A918,
  P300, P478, P479
Seki, Kazuhira W295
Seki, Takao W305
Seki, Tetsuo W399
Sekikawa, Kazuo W405

Sekimoto, Tadahiro W386
Sekino, Hiromoto W515
Sekizawa, Tadashi W237
SEKO Worldwide A1454
Sekulic, André A925, P323
Selander, Robert W. A924, A925, P322, P323, P668
Selbach, Scott C. A327
Selby, David W. A1265
SELECT brand foods A1234
Select Energy, Inc. (marketing) A1040
Select Medical Corporation E286
Select Service Partner (food services) W175
Selecta Group W174
Selected Auto and Fire Insurance Company of America. *See* SAFECO Corporation
Selective Group (home construction) A340
Selektvracht B.V. W203
Selete (Japan semiconductor association) P444
Self, Anne Darden E273
Self (magazine) P33
Selfit cosmetics W535
Selfridges plc (stores) W172
Selig, Allan H. "Bud" P306, P307, P663
Selig Chemical Industries A1004
Selig, Clyde P. A397
Selig, Marvin A397
Selkowitz, Arthur P73
Sell, Kathleen R. P501
Sell, Robert L. W379
Sellemond, Oswald W415
Sellers, Gary A485
Sellers, Greg P696
Sellers, Mark A. A1533
Sellière, Ernest-Antoine W161
Sells-Floto (concessions) P188
Selover, R. Edwin A1175
Selsam, Robert E. E34
Selsun Blue shampoo A58
Selton insecticide A375
Seltzer, Robert W647
Seltzer, William P. A1057
Selvaggio, John N. A479
Selwanes, Raqui P47, P539
SEMATECH, Inc. E119, E286, P444-P445, P726
Semel, Terry S. A1546, A1547, P278
Semen, Barbara A797
Semenjaka, Aleksandr Nikolayevich W243
Semi-Automated Business Research Environment. *See* Sabre Inc.
The Semiconductor Industry Association P444
Semiconductor Products A98
Semiconductor Test Solutions E46
Semifab E31
Semler, Jerry D. P539
Sempra Energy A1030, A1174, A1198, A**1266**-A**1267**
Sempress Pneumatics A1088

Semrau & Sons A110
Sems (computers) W150
Semtech Corporation E**119**, E286
SEN (industrial manufacturer) E161
Sen, Laura J. A263
Senakot laxative P707
Sénard, Jean-Dominique W433
Seneca Foods Corporation A1136
Seneca Investments A1062
Senegor, Yom A1231
Senior Community Service Employment Program P29
SeniorCo, Inc. A1080, A1081
Senkler, Robert L. P677
Senkowski, Stephen J. A195
Senn, Kathy E62, E205
Sensation (ship) A331
SenSonic toothbrush P71
Sensor office furniture A1335
Sensor razor A657
Sentara Healthcare P726
Sentinel diagnostic systems E299
Sentinel Funds (investments) P684
Sentinel Products A1368
Sentra car W402, W403
Sentrachem (crop protection) A504
Sentrex Cen-Comm Communications Systems E128
Sentry Foods A606
Sentry Insurance, A Mutual Company A798, P726
Sentry Market P489
Sentry multiplexers E179
Seong Dong Kim W335
Seoul International Airport P386
Seoulbank W268
Sephora on line retailer W348, W349
Sepi S.p.A. A856
Sequa A306
SEQUEL fiber packing P523
Sequent (Internet servers) A764
Sequentia Holdings (plastic panels) A446
Sequoia Capital A368, E93, E136
Sequoia Hospital (Redwood, CA) P118
Sequoia Software E42
Ser biscuits W193
Seragnoli, Giordano W555
Sera-Tec Biologicals A236, A1202
Sereda, Peter L. A1361
Seren Innovations, Inc. (communications and data) A1542
Serena car W403
SERENA Software, Inc. E286
Serete Group (engineering) A786
Sergeant Drill A754
Sergeant, Henry Clark A754
Sero Genics A1202
Seror, Henry E21
Serota, Scott P. A269, P83, P556
Seroxat drug W416
Serra, Matthew D. A1470, A1471
Serrao, Gregory A. E153

Serta, Inc. (mattresses) P442, P727
ServantCor P706
Servants of the Holy Heart of Mary P706
Servatius, Bernhard W107
Servel A1520
Service America W174
Service Corporation International A**1268**-A**1269**
Service Employees International Union P34, P118
Service Experts (heating and air conditioning installation) A864
SErvice GAmes. *See* SEGA Corporation
Service Merchandise, Inc. A**1270**-A**1271**
Service Select stores A1270
Service Transport Company (trucking) A68, A69
OOO Servicegazprom W243
The ServiceMaster Company A**1272**-A**1273**
ServiceOne (appliance repair) A1465
Services Group of America P727
Servicios Administratios de Logistica, S.A. de C.V. A789
Servicios de Evaluacion de Riesgos, S. de R.L. de C.V. A879
Servicos de Logistica de Mexico, S.A. de C.V. A789
Servisco Sp. zo.o. W203
ServiStar Coast to Coast A64, A1322, A1410, P30, P484, P485, P749
Servus Financial Corporation (student loans) A1508
Serwa, Jan W457
Serzone drug A291
Sesa (company) W160
Sesam (IT services) W100
Sesame Street (TV show and products) A831, A927, E60, P144
Sessa, Carolyn F. P587
Sessions, F.C. A230
SET Port Processing P257
SETA (cardiovascular perfusion) A236
Seton, Elizabeth Ann (Saint) P56
Settelmyer, Scott H. A129
Setterstrom, William N. A1043
Settino, Mary Winn A1103
Seuss, James C. W251
Seuthe, Brenda P746
Sévéa dairy products W193
Sevel W442
Seven Network A962
Seven Seas salad dressings A843
Seven Stars cigarettes W304, W305
Seven Up Bottling Group, Inc. P110
Seven Up soft drink. *See* 7 UP soft drink
Seven-Eleven Japan Company, Ltd. W298, W299
Seventeen (magazine) A1160, A1161, P653

Seventh-Day Adventist Church P530
Seven-Up Pete Mine A1124
Severance Richard W. A413
Severance, Theodoric A1000
OOO Severgazprom W243
Sevin Rosen Funds E41
Sewell, George F. A1181
The Sex Pistols (music group) W212, W622
Sexton, Beth B. A747
Sexton, Mark S. E200
Seyama, Hirotada W597
Seydoux, Jerome W146
Seyfarth, Larry J. A819
Seymour, Joseph J. P703
The SF Holdings Group, Inc. P727
SF Phosphates, Limited Company A583, P185
SF Services (agricultural cooperative) A582, P184
SFAT (rail cars) A1406
Sfernice electronics A1482
SFP Pipeline Holdings, Inc. A309
SFX Entertainment A372
Sgarro, Douglas A. A459
SGI. See Silicon Graphics, Inc.
SGRM (oil exploration) A1252
SGS Communities A509
SGS Microelettronica W555
SGS-THOMSON. See STMicroelectronics N.V.
Shabel, Fred A. A391
Shachmut, Kenneth M. A1235
Shackleton: The Antarctic Challenge (book) P359
Shacknai, Jonah E89, E240
Shackouls, Bobby S. A311
Shaddix, James W. A1097
Shadwood Industries A572
Shafer, Charles L. A711
Shaff, Karen E. A1163
Shaffer, Adam P339
Shaffer, Donald D. (Heilig-Meyers) A702
Shaffer, Donald S. (Dollar General) A497
Shaffer, John N. A717, P235
Shaffet, Michael P662
Shafir, Robert S. A861
Shah, Ajay A1299
Shah, Rajesh K. A389
Shah, S. K. W567
Shaheen, Gerald L. A333
Shailor, Barbara P35
Shainman, Barry J. A451
Shake 'N Bake coatings A843
Shakeel, Arif A1515
Shakeproof fasteners A748
Shakey's Pizza Parlor W314, W315
Shallcross, Deanne J. A1355, P467
Shamrock Foods Company P728
Shamrock Group W322
Shanahan, Michael F., Sr. E198
Shanahan, William S. A387
Shan-Chih Business Association W570

Shandwick International A772
Shanghai Advanced Building Materials A194
Shanghai Automotive Industry Group A1368
Shanghai Bell W76
Shanghai Container Terminals Limited W272, W273
Shanghai GE Construction Equipment Engineering Company A468
Shanghai General Electronics E73
Shanghai Grace Semiconductor Manufacturing E121
Shanghai Petrochemical Company W542
Shanghai Radio and Television (Group) Company W532
Shanghai Ryerson Ltd. A1225
Shanghai Sharp Electronics W532
Shanghai Tyre & Rubber W366
Shanklin Corporation A1262
Shanks Ayana E224
Shanks, Earl A1013
Shanks, James R. A337
Shanks, Robert W363
Shannon, Bill F. C. W639
Shannon, Michael G. A1397
Shannon, W. Patrick A249
Shapell, James R. P387
Shaper, C. Park E228
Shapira, David S. P198, P199, P615
Shapiro, Angela A61
Shapiro, Bob P690
Shapiro, Marc J. (J.P. Morgan Chase) A809
Shapiro, Mark A. (Quaker Oats) A1181
Shapiro, Mark D. (Fleming) A607
Shapiro, Robert A984, A1122
Shapiro, Steven J. A311
Shaps, Simon W249
Shaq Attaq shoes A1194
Share Development (HMO) A1434
Share Drug stores W312
Share-Link A348
Sharer, Kevin W. A160, A161
ShareVision Technology (video conferencing) W180
Sharewave Inc. (digital wireless technology) P511
Sharifov, Vagit S. W347
Sharkey, Daniel P. E160
Sharman, Bill A280
Sharp & Dohme (drug maker) A956
Sharp & Hughes A222
Sharp, Barry J. A89
Sharp Corporation W168, W234, W532-W533
Sharp, Douglas S. A75
Sharp, Michael W469
Sharp, Richard L. A366, A367
Sharp, Steven J. E305
Sharp, Walter A222
Sharp Wizard hand held organizer W548
Sharpe, Carol P255

Sharpe, Edwin R. P499
Sharpe, Robert F., Jr. A1107
Sharpe, Stephen A. A1115, P397
Sharpe, Sylvester H. A981
Sharper Image Corporation A1274-A1275, E120, E287
Sharpie pens A1023
Sharpin, Donald H. A839
Sharples, Richard J. A169
Sharps candy W155
Shasta Networks W412
Shasteen, Julie P530
Shattuck, Frank A826
Shattuck, Shuki A119
Shaver, Russ E303
Shaw, Brad A637
Shaw Communications Inc. W494
Shaw, Curtis S. A351
The Shaw Group Inc. (piping systems) A554, A786
Shaw Industries, Inc. A252, A980, P552
Shaw, Jack A. A736, A737
Shaw, L. Edward, Jr. A91
Shaw, Marc V. P335, P674
Shaw, Ray A81, P33
Shaw, Ruth G. A515
Shaw, Steve A963
Shaw, William J. A913, A1297
Shawinigan Resins A1300
Shawk, George P208
Shawmut National Bank A602
Shaw's Supermarkets, Inc. A1116, P102, P103, P479, W300
Shea, Christina L. A649
Shea, Cornelius P246
Shea, Jim A373
Shea, John F. (J.F. Shea) P643
Shea, John (Spiegel) A1314
Shea, Ma A1477
Shea, Richard M. E157
Shean, Chris A873
Shearer, Robert K. A1475
Sheares, Bradley T. A957
Shears, Stuart C. A705
Shearson Hayden Stone E61
Shearson Lehman Brothers A142, A204, W396
Shearson Loeb Rhoades (brokerage) A142, A370, A860
Sheba pet food A915, P315, P665
Shecterle, Debra J. P595
Shedlarz, David L. A1119
Sheed, Jim C. W539
Sheehan, Jackie E168
Sheehan, James A731
Sheehan, John R. A1533
Sheehan, Kevin J. (Investors Financial Services) E223
Sheehan, Kevin M. (Avis Group) A213
Sheehan, Kevin M. (Cendant) A339
Sheehan, Robert C. A1289, P447, P730
Sheehan, Shaun M. A1403
Sheehan, Stephen G. A1383

Sheehy, Patrick A627
Sheehy, Robert H. A1435
Sheepshead Bay Co-op (New York) P291
Sheet Metal Workers Union P35
SHEETROCK panels A1456, A1457
Sheetz, Bob P728
Sheetz, Inc. P728
Sheetz, Joseph S. P728
Sheetz, Stanton R. P728
Sheffield Cellars dessert wine A521, P169
Sheffield Forgemaster's Group A116
Sheffield, Larry A1285
Sheffler, Thomas A847
Sheil, David R., Jr. A431
Sheinman, Drew A1287
Shelby Williams Industries, Inc. (commercial furniture) E202
Sheldon, Keith W320
Sheldon, Reuben A1000
Shelf Builder A67
Shelger, James M. A1269
Shell Canada Limited A184
Shell, Jeff A623, W391
Shell Oil Company A132, A352, A610, A1054, A**1276**-A**1277**, A1374, A1376, A1377, E242, P74, P238, P340, P604, P627, P679, W54, W94, W136, W424, W440, W500. *See also* Royal Dutch/Shell Group
The "Shell" Transport and Trading Company p.l.c. W500, W501
Shelley, James H. A1303
Shelnitz, Mark A. A1537
Shelton, Charles E. A1021
Shelton, Kirk A338
Shelton, Robert A828, P270
Shelton, Stanley W. A1333
Shemin, Barry L. A799
Shenandoah brands P393
Sheng, Jean A197
Shenk, Sol A260
Shenton, Joseph A183
Shenyang Brewery W314
Shenzhen Company, Ltd. W486
Shenzhen Leasing A274
Shenzhen Petrochemical Holdings A1520
Shepard, Alan A662
Shepard, Donald J. W65
Shepard, Tom A1481, P509
Shepard Warner Elevator A502
Shepards (legal citation service) W478
Shepheard-Walwyn, Tim W115
The Shepherd Group (investments) E135
Shepherd Products Inc. P313
Shepler (concrete products) A396
Shepler, Linda D. P465
Sheraton hotels A720, A780, A1326, A1328, A1329, E215
Sheraton-Moriah Israel (hotels) W323

Sherbrooke Record W262
Sherer, Paul A55
Sheridan, Diane L. A101
Sheridan, John W. W123
Sheridan, Joseph P515
Sheridan, Michael J. E290
Sheridan, William S. A1305
Sherin, Keith S. A647
Sherk, Joseph B. A849
Sherlock, William P318, P319, P667
Sherman Antitrust Act (1890) A308, A1458, P34
Sherman, Floyd F. A195, P565
Sherman, George M. A317, A462
Sherman House Corporation A719
Sherman, Jeffrey A587
Sherman, Michael A. (Guidant) A675
Sherman, Michael F. (Green Bay Packers) A672, A673, P210, P211
Sherman, Richard G. P732
Sherman, Scott A. A101
Sherrick, Jeff A553
Sherrier, Tita P393
Sherry, Nathan P428
Sherry, Yma P419
Sherwin, Henry A1278
The Sherwin-Williams Company A918, A1000, A1056, A**1278**-A**1279**, P762
Sherwood Medical Group A148
Shetler, Craig W595
Shevlin, Kelly P626
SHG Holdings Pty Limited A1341
Shibata, Katsuyoshi W139
Shibata, Noato W487
Shibata, Takumi W409
Shibaura Seisakusho Works W610
Shields, Brooke P100
Shields, Gene A739
Shields, Thomas C. E28, E156
Shiely, John S. A286, A287
Shiers, Ian J. A1149
Shiffman, Roger A693
Shiftan, Ronald P399, P703
Shiga, Yu W295
Shih, Edith W273
Shih, Elizabeth P119
Shih, Stan W60, W61
Shih, Willy C. A525
Shiina, Ringo W213
Shiley (heart valve) A1118
The Shilla Hotels & Resorts Company, Ltd. W509
Shilling, Jack W. A117
Shillman, Robert J. E43, E181
Shiloh Industries, Inc. P679
Shimagami, Kiyoaki W611
Shimamura, Teruo W393
Shimek, Daniel C. A727
Shimizu Corporation P593
Shimizu, Hisayuki W393
Shimizu, Norikatsu W369
Shimizu, Osamu W169
Shimizu, Scott E. A1135

Shimizu, Shigeo W535
Shimizu, Shinjiro W373
Shimoda, Yoshio W515
Shimura, Satoru W315
Shin Caterpillar Mitsubishi Ltd. W371
Shin Choong-Sik W455
Shin Hyun-Young W275
Shin, John E49
Shin, Kazuhisa W81
Shindelar, CarolAnn E63
Shindo, Josuke W597
Shindo, Masayoshi W531
Shinei Sangyo Pte. Ltd A1298
Shinmachi, Toshiyuki W303
Shinn, Robert W. A455
Shinohara, Iwao W387
Shinozuka, Katsumasa W421
Shinsegae Department Store Company A436
Shinsegi Telecom W454
Shiotsu, Seiji W533
Shipley, Larry A743
Shipley, Thomas A1550
Shipp, Al E33
Shirai, Kazunari W237
Shiraishi, Motoatsu W265
Shiraishi, Yoshikatsu W421
Shiramizu, Kosuke W615
Shirato, Ryoichi W599
Shire Pharmaceuticals Group plc E283
Shirey, Herb A73
Shirk, Gary P69
Shirk, Richard D. P572
Shiseido Company, Limited A776, W**534**-W**535**
Shivery, Charles W. A425
Shives, Paula J. A465
Shivley, Albert J. P185
Shkurti, William P383, P693
Shlapak, Fred A. A991
Shochiku Company Ltd. P126
Shocklely, Roger P. A495
Shockley, Thomas V., III A141
Shockrave.com E86
Shockwave Web design tool E86
Shockwave.com E235
Shoe Corporation of America A666
Shoe Works A932, A1092
Shoebox greeting cards A678, A679, P216, P217, P625
Shoemaker, Edwin A854
Shoemaker, Larry A753
Shoemaker Mine A417
Shoen, Anna Mary A134
Shoen, Edward J. "Joe" A134, A135
Shoen, James P. A135
Shoen, Leonard Samuel A134
Shoen, Mark V. A134, A135
Shoen, Sam A134
Shoen, Suzanne A134
Shoes.com A294
Shofu Industries (ceramic insulators) W328
Shoji, Norio W373

Shokrgozar, Hamid E317
Shoney's, Inc. A1280-A1281
Shonkoff, Fredi P85
Shontere, James G. P643
Shook, Mark R. A487
Shoop, Neil O. A1407
Shop 'n Go stores W195
Shop 'n Save stores A1348, A1349, W194, W195
Shopf, R. Jere A941
Shopi convenience stores W164, W165
ShopKo Stores, Inc. A1092, A1282-A1283, A1348
ShopperDirect A66
Shoppers Drug Mart Inc. A837, P283
Shoppers Food Warehouse A1348, A1349
Shoppers Value brand foods A1348
Shoppers World catalog showroom W312
Shopping.com A398
ShopRite Supermarkets A1490, A1491, P514, P515, P640, P768
Shor, Alan P. A1553
Shorewood Packaging A770, A1516
Shorin, Abram E130
Shorin, Arthur T. E130, E303
Shorin, Ira E130
Shorin, Joseph E130
Shorin, Philip E130
Short, Benjamin W88
Short Cuts chicken P393
Short, Jay M. E193
Shorts Missile Systems Ltd. W132
Shout cleaner A1246, A1247, P432, P433
SHOUTcast (Internet music) A180
Showalter, William J. A723
Showboat (casino) A684
Showcase Cinemas P681
Showerings, Vine Products and Whiteways W84
Showmaker, Rodney A. A177
Showtime Networks A1258, A1476
Shoyama, Etsuhiko W260, W261
Shrader, K. Michael P562
Shrader, Patricia B. A245
Shrader, Ralph W. P88, P89, P558
Shrek (movie) P166, P167, P597
Shrempp, Juergen W188
Shriners Hospital (Boston) P550
SHRM W174
Shroud of Turin A1156
Shu Li A411
Shueisha (printing) W186
Shugart, Alan A1260, P440
Shukan Asahi (magazine) W96, W97
Shulman, Douglas A997, P353
Shulman Transport Enterprises A1454
Shultz, Danny E. A185
Shultz, Edward J. A461
Shumejda, John M. A97
Shunk, David A. A1355, P467

SHUR GRIP auto care products A1101
Shurfine International, Inc. P479
Shurfine Markets and brands P423, P547
Shurson, Karl D. E262
Shuttle, Inc. A1443
Shuttlepoint carpets A980
Shuttleworth Brothers (carpets) A980
Shuttleworth, Herbert, II A980
Shuyler, Richard H. E32, E160
SHV Holdings N.V. W364
SI Bank & Trust E293
S.I. Finance W559
SIA Engineering Company Private Limited W541
Siam Cement Plc A1072, P212
Siam Guardian Glass Ltd. P212
Siamtyre tires W367
Sibbernsen, Richard D. A249
Sibebe beer W553
Sibirskaya Korona W289
Sibneft (oil) W346
Sibson & Company (consulting) P278
Sicard, Daniel W167
Siciliano, Arthur A. E105
Sickels, Brian D. A1083
Sickle, Dennis A1535
Sick's Brewery W376
Sicovam (French central depository) A228
OAO Sidanco (oil) W346
Sidbec-Dosco (steel) W292
Siddall, Graham J. E46, E187
Sidekicks SUV W560
Sidewinder golf products A1393
Sidgmore, John A1535
Sidler, Hans W645
Siebe, Augustus W290
Siebe Automotive A432
Siebe PLC A526, W290
Siebel Systems, Inc. A1066, A1098, E22, E148, E276
Siebert Financial Corporation E287
Siebert, Muriel F. "Mickie" E287
Sieczkarek, Mark M. A235
Siedler Verlag W127
Siefers, Robert G. A1001
Sieff, David W356
Sieff, Israel W356
Siegel, Abraham P102
Siegel, Barry E55
Siegel, Corey A975
Siegel, David B. A1537
Siegel, James A. E124
Siegel, Kenneth S., Jr. A1329
Siegel, Murray S. P131
Siegel, Patricia B. A811, P267
Siegel, Samuel A1053
Siegel, Stuart N. A1305
Siegel, Tom P133, P578
Siegelman, Jeff E151
Siegenthaler, Ronald E142

Siegfried & Roy show P188, P189, P608
Siegl, Ziv A1326
Siegle, William T. A83
Siegler Corporation A856
Siekman, Thomas C. A399
Siemens AG A82, A98, A400, A434, A544, A836, A894, A1110, A1482, E47, E160, E173, E237, E269, E286, E287, E307, E318, P282, W200, W220, W236, W318, W334, W352, W354, W406, W450, W490, W536-W537, W574, W610
Siemens & Halske W536
Siemens Components A1140
Siemens lighting A1447
Siemens Nixdorf Informationssysteme W536
Siemens USA P54
Sienna car W614, W615
Sierackis, Eric P. A439
Sierra Creative Communications W470
Sierra Health Services, Inc. A810, P266
Sierra (marine aftermarket) A460
Sierra Nevada Memorial hospital P118
Sierra On-Line (software) A338
Sierra Pacific Industries P728
Sierra Pacific Resources A518, A552
Sierra Suites hotels A1540
Sievers, James W. A1314
Sievert, Frederick, J. A1017, P371
Siew Sin, Tun Tan W538
SIFE (trust fund) A875, P294
Sige (axles) A460
Sigma Coatings A1152
SiGMA Consulting, Planning Technologies P278
Sigma-Aldrich A430
Sigma-Società Italiana Gestione Multi Accesso W78, W79
Sigmon, James E. E201
Signal Companies A728
Signal Conditioning Products Division E124
Signal Landmark E169
Signal Oil A1054
Signal Research Division E174
Signal toothpaste W619
SignalSoft Corporation E287
Signal-Stat (lighting and safety components) A584, A585
Signalware software E307
Signature Inns E225
Signature Specialties chicken A1419
Signet Bank. See First Union Corporation
Signet Banking A318
Signode Industries A748
Sigrid Olsen clothing A880, A881
Siguier, Bertrand W467
Sihler, Helmut W415, W459
SII Marketing International W528
Sikes, Alfred C. A700, A701, P228, P229

Sikorsky (helicopters) A1432, A1433
Silas, Rick P754
Silberblatt, Steven C. A375
Silberstein, Alan M. A597
Silberzahn, Charles P284
Silcrome metal valve A1412
Sileck, Mike A1451
Silence of the Lambs (movie) A962
Silenka BV A1152
Silent Systems (heat sinks) A982
Silicon Engineering W180
Silicon General E119
Silicon Graphics, Inc. A342, A**1284**-A**1285**, A1336, E86, E190, E289, P166, P592, W394
Silicon Laboratories Inc. E288
Silicon Smelters (ferroalloys) W433
Silicon Storage Technology, Inc. E**121**, E288
Silicon Studio A1284
Silicon Systems A1378, W572
Silicon Valley Bancshares E**122**, E288
Silicon Valley Chemlabs A1212
Siliconix Inc. (semiconductors) A1482
Silk, Arthur T. A263
Silk Cut cigarettes W240, W241
SilkAir Private Limited W71, W540, W541
Silkwood, Karen A820
SilkWorm switches E166
Sills, Stephen J. A357
Silva de Menezes, Antonio L. W437
Silva, Julio César W439
Silva, Stephen E. A351
Silvant, Jean-Louis W443
Silveira, Mike P722
Silver, Adam P355
The Silver Bullet A78
Silver City Casino A906
Silver Dollars lottery game P675
Silver, Gail P645
Silver Ghost car W496
Silver King Communications A1450
Silver Lake Partners A1260, P440, P725
Silver Legacy hotel and casino (Reno, NV) A907
Silver Star Automotive P746
Silver, William E43
Silverado Partners P474
Silverblatt, Pamela S. P369, P687
Silverman, Barry J. A921
Silverman, Harry J. A501, P163, P595
Silverman, Henry R. A338, A339
Silverman Jewelry A1092
Silverstar, Inc. A196
Silverstein, Arthur A81, P33, P530
Silverstein Properties P398
Silverstein, Scott E130
Silverstein, Stanley P. A1499
Silvertab pants A869, P293
Silverthorne, John A1134

Silverthorne, Mary A1134
Silvertown (company) A662
Sim, John A841, P287, W325
Sim Kay Wee W541
Sim Wong Hoo W180, W181
Simba A1161
Simca (cars) W442
Simcic, Christian A211
Sime Darby Berhad W**538**-W**539**
Sime, William W538
SimeSecurities W538
Simi Winery A422, A423
Simigrin, Patricia A. A853
Similac infant formula A58
Siminoff, Ellen A1547
Simmonds, Mary P41
Simmons, Glen P411, P711
Simmons, Hardwick A997, P353
Simmons, Harold C. P583
Simmons, Jackie P592
Simmons, Jeffrey J. A485
Simmons, Kennett A1434
Simmons (mattress) P442
Simmons, Noel E300
Simmons, Richard A116
Simms, Edward A310
Simms, Michael H. W553
Simms, Steven E. A463
Simon & Schuster Inc. (publisher) A1476, A1477, P681, W430
Simon, Barry P. A429
Simon, David A1287
Simon DeBartolo Group A1286
Simon, Heidi Locke P65
Simon, Herbert A838, A1286, A1287
Simon, Hugh P95, P559
Simon, James M. A321
Simon, Melvin A838, A1286, A1287
Simon, Nigel W241
Simon Property Group, Inc. A**1286**-A**1287**, A1354, A1398, P172, P466, P602
Simon, William (American Express) P143
Simon, William (Avis Group) A212
Simon Worldwide, Inc. A942, P486, P524, P525, P777
Simone, Joseph J. P477
Simonin, Dominique W647
Simons, Paul W644
Simonsen, Eric A. A125
Simonson, Stewart G. P363
Simpkin, Gayle P119
Simpkins, Maurice M. A1227
Simple Technology. *See* SimpleTech, Inc.
SimpleTech, Inc. E289
SimpleXx drug W416
Simplot Dairy Products P264
Simplot, J. R. "Jack" A970, A1456, P264, P265, P648
Simpson & Baker A220, P66
Simpson, Bob R. E319
Simpson, Dana A220, P66
Simpson, Daniel G. A375

Simpson, Dick W587
Simpson, George W354, W355
Simpson Industries P673
Simpson, Louis A. A252
Simpson, O. J. A710
Simpson, Timothy J. A441
Simpson, William R. A103
Simpson-Bint, Jonathan W239
Simpsons department stores W270
Sims, Frank L. A325, P105
Sims, Jeff A497
Simson, Wilhelm A219
Sinatra, Frank W212
Sinclair, Bobby P666
Sinclair Broadcast Group, Inc. E199
Sinclair, Craig P685
Sinclair, Harry P729
Sinclair Oil Corporation P729
Sinclair Oil & Refining A900
Sinebrychoff (brewery) W162
Sinegal, James D. A436, A437
Sinemet drug A541
Sinfield, Leslie J. A1227
Singapore Airlines Limited A478, A1421, W344, W518, W**540**-W**541**, W567, W622
Singapore Technologies Engineering Ltd. E274
Singapore Telecommunications Limited W152
Singer, Carlyle S. A747
Singer Controls (valves and switches) A526
Singer, Ezra A1473
Singer, Lester P247
Singer, Martin H. E261
Singer N.V. P729
Singer, Paul L. A1353
Singer, Robert W251
Singh, Jeet E159
Singh, Kuman Arun Prasad W293
Singh, Neera E232
Singh, Rajendra E232
Singin' in the Rain (movie) A962
Single Service Containers A770
Single, Thomas E. A655
Singleton, Caroline A116
Singleton, Charles A955
Singleton, Henry A116
Singleton, Knox P639
Singleton Seafood A408
Singleton, William D. P670
Singulair drug A956, A957, A1250
Sinha, Ashok K. A189
Sinn Leffers (fashions) W310
Sinnott, John T. A917
Sino Mining Alumina W640
Sinopec Shanghai Petrochemical Company Limited W**542**-W**543**
Sinotrans A1426
Sinser (management services) A182
Sinson, Alan L. A591
Sioux Oil A1374
SIP (telecom, Italy) W574
Sipols, Uldis K. A463

Sippel, David E262
Sipsy Chime Fine A1152
Sircusa, Paul J. A711
SIRIS S.A.S.
(telecommunications) W204
Sirisena, Mervyn W541
Sirkin, Stuart A. P389
SIRM (maritime
telecommunications) W574
Sirmon, Gary L. E162
Sisbarro, Pat R. P171, P601
Sisk, David A1087
Sisk, Mark D. A871
Siska, Nancy P. P105, P566
Siskind, Arthur M. A623, W391
Sisley casual wear W124, W125
Sisney, Bret P592
Sissel, George A. A225
Sist, Lynda P247, P641
Sisters of Bon Secours P557
Sisters of Charity P56
Sisters of Charity Health Care
Systems of Cincinnati P116,
P117, P569
Sisters of Charity Health System
(Texas) P575
Sisters of Charity of Leavenworth
Health Services
Corporation P729
Sisters of Charity of Nazareth
Health Care System P116, P117,
P569
Sisters of Charity of the Incarnate
Word of Houston, Texas P118,
P119
Sisters of Mercy. See Institute of the
Sisters of Mercy of the Americas
Sisters of Providence Health
System P114, P115, P706
Sisters of the Holy Family of
Nazareth P117
The Sisters of the Humility of
Mary P570
Sisters of the Presentation of the
Blessed Virgin Mary P117
Sisters of St. Catherine of Siena of
Kenosha, WI P119
Sisters of St. Dominic of Adrian,
MI P118, P119
Sisters of St. Francis of Colorado
Springs P117
Sisters of St. Francis of Penance and
Christian Charity P119
Sisters of St. Francis of
Philadelphia P116
Sisters of St. Francis of Rochester,
MN P324
Sisters of St. Francis of the
Immaculate Heart of Mary P117
Sisters of St. Francis Perpetual
Adoration P116
Sisters of St. Joseph
Carondelet P568
Sisters of St. Joseph Health
System P56, P544
Sit 'N Spin toy A693
SITA (telecommunications) A1228,
W233

SITA (waste company) A122, W558,
W559
Siteco lighting A1447
SiTel Sierra (cellular and
wireless) A1002
SiteMinder software E96, E251
Sites, Michael A1229
SiteSmith, Inc. P333
Sitework Systems A1392
Sithe Energies, Inc. A570, A571,
A668, A1198
Sitmar Cruises W434
Siudek, Richard W55
SIVEA (microelectronics) A544
Siverd, Robert J. A643
Six Continents plc A684, W84,
W258, W288, W408, W544-W545
Six Flags, Inc. (theme parks) A174,
A1452, P464, P502
Six, Robert A428
Sixt, Frank J. W273
Sixth Street Partners, Ltd. A1399
SJNB Financial E209
SJW Corporation (utility) A154
S-K Corporation A826
SK Group P635
SK Telecom Company, Ltd. W454
Skadden, Arps, Slate, Meagher &
Flom LLP A1288-A1289,
P446-P447, P730
Skadden, Marshall A1288, P446
Skaer, Susan E91
Skaggs, Leonard A110
Skaggs, L. S., Jr. A110, A1234
Skaggs, Marion A886
Skaggs, M. B. A1234
Skaggs, Robert C., Jr. A1035
Skaggs, Stephen A. E82, E232
Skaggs stores A1234
Skaggs-Albertsons food and drug
stores A110
Skala-Coop department
stores W588, W589
Skandia Insurance Company
Ltd. A182
Skandinavisk
Tobakskompagni W162
Skarholt, Amund W525
SKC (polyester film
processing) A748
Skechers U.S.A., Inc.
(shoes) A1032, E289
Skeen, Dale E313
Skelton, Robert W. A939
SKF Aktiebolegat SKF (ball
bearings) A1386, E254, W632
SKG. See Dreamworks SKG
Skidmore, Louis P448
Skidmore, Owings & Merrill,
LLP P448-P449, P730
Ski-Doo snowmobiles W132, W133
Skil tools W490
Skillern drugstore chain A1552
Skilling, Raymond I. A183
Skillman, Heidi A. A573
SkillsVillage software A1098
Skin Revival System P316

Skinner, James E. A1015
Skinner, Paul D. W501
Skinner, Peter G. A507
Skinner, Samuel K. A1454, A1455
Skinner, Stanley A1120
Skins Games (golf) P250
Skin-So-Soft skin care A216, A217
Skintastic P433
Skintimate personal care A1247,
P433
Skippy peanut butter W618, W619
Skiptunis, Raymond E125
Skittles candy A914, A915, P314,
P315, P665
Skoal tobacco A1458, A1459
SKODA automobiles W630, W631
Skoda Miada Boleslav A198
Skol vodka A423
Skoll, Jeffrey E54, E196
Skoog, Christopher R. A1065
Skopanska Banka W384
Skor candy A709
Skornicki, Eliezer A397
Skroeder, Christian E. A1415
Skrzypczak, Casimir A369
Skule, John L. A291
Skurek, John C. A897
Sky Chefs W344
Sky Courier A102
Sky Global Networks, Inc. A650,
W146, W390, W391
Sky Latin America A873
SKY Television (satellite) W146,
W582
SkyDome (ballpark) W288
Skydrol hydraulic fluid A1301
Skyfish.com A1228
Skylark Meats P717
Skyline Asset management E149
Skyline car W403
Skyline goose down jackets A1314
Skynet Satellite Services A888
SkyTeam alliance A478, W68, W78
SkyTel Communications, Inc.
(wireless messaging) A1534,
W582, W583
Skywalker Ranch P302, P719
Skywalker Sound P302
Skyway Freight Systems A1422
Skyways W518
SkyWest Airlines, Inc. A479, W132
SL Green Realty Corporation E289
Slacik, Charles P. A445
Slack, Darrel E174
Slade, Colin L. A1359
Sladnick, Clifford M. A299
Slager, Donald W. A123
Slagle, Robert F. A113
Slaner, Alfred A1482
Slaner, Luella A1482
Slark, Martin P. A983
Slate, David L. A381
Slate, John A1288, P446
Slate, Martin P388
Slater, Andy W213
Slater, Richard J. A787

Slater, William E297
Slates pants A868, A869, P292, P293, P657
Slavik, James A1538
Slavin, Steven M. A1515
Slayden, Preston W195
Sledd, Hunter A1109
Sledd, Robert C. A1109
SledgeHammer microprocessors A82
Sleep Country Canada stores P442
Sleep Disorders Center P457
Sleep Options, Inc. A718, A719
Sleeper, Mark J. E135
Sleepmaker tires W428
Sleiter, Ronald D. A407
Slepicka, Robert A. A1163
Sletten, Kenneth P719
Slevin, Jack A392
Slibailautos W183
Slibail-Société Lyonnaise de crédit-bail W183
Slice soft drink A1103, A1104, A1105
Slick 50 car care A1096, A1097
Slifka, Alfred A. P616
Sliga (data processing) W100
Groupe Sligos W100
Slim Domit, Patrick W581
Slim family A1058
Slim Helú, Carlos A366, A1238, W580, W581
Slim Jim meat snacks A408, A409
Slim Seade, Héctor W581
Slim-Fast Foods Company W618, W619
Slingerland, Stanley S. E156
Sliwa, Steven P132
Slizer Throwbots toys W333
SLM Financial Corporation A1448, A1449
SLM Holding. See USA Education, Inc.
Sloan, Alfred A650
Sloan, Jay P714
Sloan, O. Temple, Jr. P112, P613
Sloan-Kettering Institute P152, P672
Sloboda, David W. A393
Slocum, Thomas J. A479
Slodden, Toby J. A923, P321
Slolvalco (aluminum) W410
Slotkin, A. L. P439
Slots-A-Fun casino (Las Vegas) A906, A907
Slott, David A1273
Slover, Samuel P655
Slover, Thomas J. A1471
Sluimer, Hugo L. E134
Slurpee drink A56
Slusser, Mark D. E188
Slusser, Sarah A89
Sly, P. J. A547
Slyders hamburgers P516, P772
Smacks cereal A817
Smadny Mnich beer W553
Small, Harry P62

Small, Lawrence P451, P731
Small, Michael J. E38, E174
Small Order Entry System (SOES) P353
Small, Philip W. A259
Small Planet Foods A648
Small, R. Timothy P419
Small Time Crooks (movie) P167
Small, William J. E204
Small World Media (sports games Web site) P510
Smalley, Kathleen E37
Smart & Final Inc. (stores) P488, W166
Smart Card for Windows A1480, P508
Smart card payment systems A915, P315
Smart Choice Automotive Group, Inc. E188
Smart Machines (robotics) E35
SMART Modular Technologies A1298
Smart Money (magazine) A1498
Smart Ones frozen food A723
Smart, Paul A1051
SMART Refrigerated Transport P722
Smart Security Card System A1148
Smart soft drink A383
Smart Start cereal A506
S-Mart stores P722
Smart Tools business-to-business portal P404
Smart Travel, Inc. A681
SmartCores DSP chips E194
SmartCruise brand A527
SmartForce PLC A1208
SmartMoney (magazine) A701, P229
SmartRoute Systems, Inc. E140
SmartSet clock radios E198
SmartStyle hair salons A1196
Smartt, William A485
SMART-Traveler System E31, E160
SmartView Imaging Camera Network E43
smartVisa card A1481, P509
Smashing Pumpkins (music group) W213
SMATcom AG W201
SME (electric power) W214
SMED International Inc. (office furniture) P222
Smedinghoff, Mary Lynn P409, P711
Smeets (printing) W626
Smelting and Refining Company W66
Smeltzer, David P. E265
Smerge, Raymond G. A341
Smetana, Mark P601
Smethills, Harold R., Jr. P673
Smette, Darryl G. A483
SMG plc (television broadcasting) W249
SMH Automobile AG W563

SMH Immeubles SA (real estate) W563
SMH (watches) W528
Smialek, Robert L. E157
Smialowski, Joseph A. A603
Smirnoff vodka A1204, P682, W206
Smisek, Jeffery A. A429
Smith, A. J. C. A916
Smith, Adrian M. E112, E279
Smith, Alan Marc P771
Smith, Albert E. A883
Smith, Alex A1389
Smith & Wesson Corporation (guns) W604
Smith, Arthur E., Jr. A1035
Smith, Audrey P646
Smith, Barbara P535
Smith Barney, Harris Upham & Company A370
Smith, Barry W553
Smith, Bernice P219, P625
Smith, Beverly J. A263
Smith, Bill A249, P684
Smith, Blair A1228
Smith, Brad (Cinemark USA) P127, P575
Smith, Bradford K. (Ford Foundation) P195
Smith, Brad L. (Allstate) P127
Smith, Brad L. (Heritage Commerce) E213
Smith, Brian (Waterford Wedgwood) W637
Smith, Bruce A. A1375
Smith, Bryan F., Jr. (7-Eleven) A57
Smith, Byron A748, A1042
Smith, C. R. A164, A1228
Smith, C. Wesley A771
Smith, Cecil O., Jr. A515
Smith, Charles Miller W278, W279, W523
Smith, Christine P477, P745
Smith, Clyde M. P552
Smith, Colin D. W113
Smith College P78
Smith Corona. See SCM (office equipment)
Smith Corporate Living E175
Smith, Craig R. A1071
Smith, Curtis E252
Smith, Dan F. (Equistar/Lyondell) A900, A901, P604
Smith, Daniel E. (American Cancer Society) P41
Smith, Darwin A826, A828, P270
Smith, David A. (Ascension Health) P57, P544
Smith, David (Exide) A573
Smith, David N. (Tennessee Valley Authority) A1371, P469, P743
Smith, David S. (Dover) A503
Smith, David (TeleTech) E127, E300
Smith, Donald (Burger King) A302
Smith, Donnie (Tyson Foods) A1419

Smith, Doug E91
Smith, E. Follin A425
Smith, Edward A1042
Smith, Eleanor R. E285
Smith, Elisha P673
Smith, Elliott P167
Smith, Ernest D. A591
Smith, Ezra A864
Smith, Ford A1116
Smith, Frank A60
Smith, Frederick W. A588, A589, A1238
Smith, Gary B. E41, E179
Smith, Gavin H. A311
Smith, Glenn E. A625
Smith, G. Leslie P39
Smith, Gloria R. P521
Smith, Gordon R. A1121
Smith, Harold B. (Illinois Tool) A748, A749
Smith, Harold C. (Illinois Tool) A748
Smith, Harold (Northern Trust) A1042
Smith, Hope A401
Smith, Howard I. A151
Smith International A1252
Smith, Jack A. P175
Smith, James F. A1413
Smith, Janet P389
Smith, Jay R. A443, P147
Smith, John (BBC) W145
Smith, John F., Jr. (General Motors) A650, A651, W294, W295
Smith, Joseph W., Jr. A93
Smith, Kenneth M. A721
Smith Laboratories A694
Smith, L. Dennis P759
Smith, Larry (Les Schwab Tire) P657
Smith, Lawrence A. (Home Depot) A725
Smith, Lawrence S. (Comcast) A391
Smith, Lee B. E126
Smith, Lowndes A. A689
Smith, M. Lazane A401
Smith, Marie L. A235
Smith, Mark C. (Advantica) A87
Smith, Mark C. (General Cable) A643
Smith, Marschall I. A299
Smith, Matthew P. E261
Smith, Maura Abeln A1073
Smith, Maurice M., Jr. P706
Smith, Melanie P685
Smith, Michael A. (America West) A139
Smith, Michael J. (Royal Caribbean) A1217
Smith, Michael (Lands' End) A852
Smith, Michael L. (Anthem Insurance) A179
Smith, Michael T. (Hughes Electronics) A736, A737
Smith, Michelle A233

Smith, Mike (Rank Group) W472, W473
Smith, Nancy A. A57
Smith, Orin A1326, A1327
Smith, Pamela P69
Smith, Patricia A1020
Smith, Patrick N. A1319
Smith, Paul C. A993
Smith, Peter C., Jr. (AutoNation) A207
Smith, Peter F. (Baker & McKenzie) A221, P67
Smith, Peter P. (California State University) P99
Smith, Peter (Peninsular and Oriental Steam Navigation) W435
Smith, Peter (Services Group) P727
Smith, Philip B. (Prize Energy) E270
Smith, Philip S. (Mitchell Energy) A979
Smith, Philip S. (Unified Western Grocers) P489
Smith, Phillip J. (Stater Brothers Holdings) P463, P736
Smith, Quentin P480
Smith, Randy P. A755
Smith, Raymond L. P413, P712
Smith, Richard A. (Lennox) A865
Smith, Richard A. (Neiman Marcus) A1014, A1015
Smith, Richard A. (Reed Elsevier) W479
Smith, Richard A. (Wyndham) A1541
Smith, Richard (Cendant) A339
Smith, Richard C. (Science Applications) P439
Smith, Richard (Entergy) A555
Smith, Richard P. (Dairylea Coop) P588
Smith, Rick (Dairy Farmers of America) P149
Smith, Robert A. (Neiman Marcus) A1014, A1015
Smith, Robert A. (Reed Elsevier) W479
Smith, Robert L. (Spectrum Control) E124
Smith, Robert W., Jr. (Battelle) P71
Smith, Roger (General Motors) A538, A650, P366, W294
Smith, Roger (Silicon Valley Bancshares) E122
Smith, Ronald E. A417
Smith, Roundy & Company P422
Smith, Samuel A1052
Smith, Sarah Hull A985
Smith, Scott C. (Genuine Parts) A653
Smith, Scott (Tribune Company) A1403
Smith, Sharon L. P85
Smith, Shawn P694
Smith, Shelley E101
Smith, Sherry M. A1349
Smith, Solomon A1042

Smith, Stephen A. (George Weston Ltd.) W245
Smith, Stephen E. (U.S. Bancorp) A1445
Smith, Stephen J. (General Cable) A643
Smith, Stephen L. (Intel) A761
Smith, Steven C. (Greater Bay Bancorp) E209
Smith, Steven J. (Journal Communications) P648
Smith, Steven (K-VA-T Food Stores) P654
Smith, Steven O. (Home Depot) A725
Smith Stuart E252
Smith, Terrance M. A431
Smith, Thomas A. (Ogelthorpe Power) P692
Smith, Thomas L. (Waste Management) A1505
Smith, Toni P473
Smith, Trey W153
Smith, W. F. A1302
Smith, W. Randolph A1367
Smith, Wade A497
Smith, Wally P410
Smith, Wayne H. (Avery Dennison) A211
Smith, Wayne (Humana) A738
Smith, Wesley J. A471
Smith, Weston L. A699
Smith, Wilburn L. E107
Smith, William D. (Kemper Insurance) P269
Smith, William (Roundy's) P422
Smith, Winthrop H., Jr. A961
Smithburg, William A1180
Smith-Douglass (chemicals) P90
Smitherman, Marshall P201
Smithey, Roy P558
Smithfield Farms A426
Smithfield Foods, Inc. A742, A**1290**-A**1291**, A1418, P140, P583
SmithKline Beecham plc. See GlaxoSmithKline plc
Smith's Food & Drug Centers A844, A845, A1532, P478, P479, P524
Smithson, James P450
Smithsonian American Art Museum P451
Smithsonian Astrophysical Observatory P450, P451
Smithsonian Center for Latino Initiatives P451
Smithsonian Center for Materials Research and Education P451
Smithsonian Environmental Research Center P451
Smithsonian Institution A730, P134, P298, P**450**-P**451**, P731
Smithsonian Institution Building (The Castle) P451
Smithsonian Marine Station at Fort Pierce P451
Smithsonian Tropical Research Institute P451
Smith-Wagner, Jamie P333, P674

Smits, Peter W55
Smitt, J. W. W72
Smitty's Super Valu stores P524
SMO Finance A1297
Smoke Alarm: The Unfiltered Truth About Cigarettes (educational video) P139
SmokEnders A1076
Smokers Express convenience stores A1084, A1085
Smokey Bones BBQ restaurants A464, A465
Smoldt, Robert K. P325
Smolinski, Paul P740
Smorgon Steel Group A896
SMS (company) W351
SMS Services of California A1297
SMS Settlement Services, Inc. A595
Smuggler's Run (computer game) E298
Smulyan, Jeffrey H. E198
Smurfit, Jefferson A1292
Smurfit, Michael W. J. A1292, A1293
Smurfit-Stone Container Corporation A**1292**-A**1293**
Smyth, Edward I. A723
Smyth, John M. A702
Snack Ventures Europe A648
SnakeLight A265
Snam SpA (natural gas) W216, W217
Snamprogetti SpA (engineering) W216, W217
Snap Appliances, Inc. A1185
Snap car care products A1096, A1097
Snap! Web portal A998
Snape, Allan J. A619
Snap-on Inc. A652, A892, A**1294**-A**1295**
Snapp, Manco A771
Snapper lawn equipment P332, P333
Snapple Beverage Group W154
Snapple drinks A1180, A1400, P634, W155
SnapView software A543
Snausages pet food A723
Sneak Review Plus CD-ROM P192
Snecma P572
Snedker, C. William A531
Sneider, Richard A. E229
Snelgrove, Laird P479
Snell, Mark A. A1267
Snell, Richard A. (Federal-Mogul) A584
Snell, Richard (Pinnacle West) A1138
Snell, Robert M. E292
SNET. *See* Southern New England Telecommunications Corporation
Snickers P314, P315, P665
Snickers candy A510, A914, A915
Snider, Edward M. A391
Snider, Michael J. A785
Snider, Stacey W625

Snider, Timothy R. A1125
Sno Bol toilet bowl cleaner A359
Sno-Balls snacks A775
Snodgrass, S. Gary A571
Snollaerts, Etienne W167
Snoop Doggy Dog (performer) W606
Snoopy cartoon character A964
SnoPake correction fluid P71
Snoqualmie wine A1459
Snow beer W553
Snow, David B., Jr. P175
Snow, John W. A455
Snow White and the Seven Dwarfs (movie) A1496
Snowball.com, Inc. W238
Snowbasin resort P729
Snowden, David J. W605
Snowflake beer W553
SNT Group W503
SNTV sports news video service P60
Snuggle fabric softener W619
Snyder, Bruce E. A1505
Snyder, Charles E61, E202
Snyder, Howard A934
Snyder, Stuart C. (World Wrestling Federation Entertainment) E141
Snyder, Stuart (Feld Entertainment) P188
Snyder, Thomas J. P153, P590
Snyder, Tim E278
Snyder, William W. P179
SO Blue by Sigrid Olsen A881
So J.Crew bath and body products P254
Soap Opera Digest (magazine) A1160, A1161
Soap Opera Illustrated (magazine) A1160
SoapNet cable network A61
Soave, Anthony P731
Soave Enterprises L.L.C. P731
SoBe beverages A1106, P634
Sobecki, Kirk A. A1007
Sobel, Jonathan A1547
Sobel, Suzanne A919
Sobell, Michael W354
Soberana beer W289
Sobey's Inc. P243
Sobranie cigars and cigarettes W241
Socal. *See* Standard Oil Company (California)
SoCalGas. *See* Southern California Gas
The Soccer Academy P251
Social Security P466, P480
Social Security Act (1935) A916
Sociedad, Société. *See* entry under primary company name
Society Brand Ltd. men's clothes A691
Society for Savings A822
Society National A822
Socks, Greg A287
Socony Mobil Oil A352, A576
Socony-Vacuum W424

Socotab Leaf Company A1436
Sodano, Salvatore F. A997, P46, P47, P353, P539
Søderberg, Jess W95
Soderstrom, Carl A199
Soderstrom, Charlie A1426
Soderstrom, Jan A55
Sodexho Alliance A190, A912, W174, W**546**-W**547**
Sodexho, Inc. A912, A**1296**-A**1297**
Sodexho Marriott Services, Inc. *See* Sodexho, Inc.
Sodhani, Arvind A761
Sodial North America P148
Sodinforg (IT services) W100
Sodini, Peter J. A1084, A1085
Soenen, Michael J. E207
Soeprapto, Hermani A629
SOES (small order entry system) P353
Soeters, Martin W417
Sofamor Danek (spinal implants) A952
Soffa, Albert E81
Sofid (finance) W216
Sofina cosmetics W308, W309
SOFIP W439
Sofitel hotels W58, W59
Soft & Dri antiperspirant A657
Soft Scrub cleaning product A374, A375
Soft Sense lotion A234, W308, W309
Soft Sheen Products hair care W342
Soft Warehouse A472
SOFTBANK CORP. A566, A758, A830, A860, A996, A1396, A1546, E310, P272, P352, W96, W298, W**548**-W**549**, W598
Softeam A758
SoftKat (software distributor) P68
Softlan fabric care A387
SoftLens vision care A235
Softmart International A1356
Softsel Computer Products A958
Softsoap A386, A387
Software Developer's Company E96
Software Etc. A232, A233
SOFTWORKS (data storage) A542
Sofue, Mitsutaka W235
Soga, Hiroyuki W527
So.ge.gas SpA W215
Sogeres (food management) W546
Sogeti (software) W160
Sogo (retailer) W374
Soh, Tomomi W327
Sohi, Mohsen A1013
SOHIO (Standard Oil of Ohio) W136, W488
Sohn, Harold L. A225
Sohn, Young K. E98, E257
Soho, Deborah E173
SoHo office seating P277
Soi, John P381, P692
So.I.e. SpA (lighting) W215
Soignet, Michael D. A501, P163

Sokal, Steve A741, P241
Sokol & Company P264
Sokol, David (Emcor) A544
Sokol, David L. (MidAmerica
  Energy) P340, P341, P676
Sokol, Jim A1311
Sokoloff, Jonathan A1202
Sokolov, Richard S. A1287
Sokolow, Alan E. P175
Sol beer W289
Sola, Jure A1240, A1241
Solaglas (glass maker) W506
Solakoglu, Cengiz W319
Solana Gomez, Guzman W483
Solana, H. Matt, Jr. A1533
Soland, Norman R. A995
Solar Pool Blanket A1262
Solar Turbines A332
Solaris operating system A1342,
  A1343
Solaris (utility) A668
Solberg, Jeff P622
Solberg, Larry D. A459
Solcher, Stephen B. A271
Solectron Corporation A1012,
  A1298-A1299, A1378, E191,
  E226, E258, E296, E306
Solel Boneh (construction) W322
Solem, Terry S. P706
Solender, Stephen P752
Solera rum W109
Solero ice cream W619
Soles, W. Roger A794
Soliac (credit card maker) W100
Soliah, Glen A455
Solidstate Controls, Inc. P313
Soliman, Sam A835, P281, P653
Solitra Oy A70
Solkatronic Chemicals A100
Soll, Bruce A. A877
Solley, L. W. A547
Sollitto, Vincent F., Jr. E266
Solo brand A527
Solo Cup Company P731
Solomon, David A1429, P491
Solomon, Jimmie Lee P307
Solomon, Martin A1360
Solomon, Michael T. P346, P347,
  P680
Solomon, Russell M. P346, P347,
  P680
Solomon, Todd E221
Solomon Valley Milling A1464
Solomon, Vanessa A1201
Solomon, William T. P547
Solomons Company
  (pharmaceuticals) A320
Solozano, Eduardo W635
Solso, Theodore M. A456, A457
Solstice network
  management A1343
Soltam (artillery) W322
Soltz, Judith E. A361
Solutia Inc. A612, A984, A1122,
  A1300-A1301, W72
Solutions Providers Alliance P208
Solvay A1368

Solvay Duphar A450
Solvik, Peter A369
Soma.com A458
Somatogen (biotech) A236
Somekh, Sasson A189
Somera Communications,
  Inc. E290, E316
Somerhalder, John W., II A537
Somers, Daniel E. A203
Somers, John A. A1355, P467
Somers, K. Brent A823
Somerville Industries
  (packaging) W244
Somma, Rande S. A803
Sommer, Ken A1481, P766
Sommer, Ron W205
Sommerville, Donald J. A671
Sommerville, John A1313
Somnolet, Michel W343
Sompolski, Timothy A. A1127
Son, Masayoshi E310, W548, W549
Sonat A222, A536
Sonata drug A148
Sonatrach (oil and gas) A168, A310,
  W130
SONDA (information
  systems) W576
Sondius-XG sound synthesis W648
Sonera W578
Sonera Corporation E243
Sonera Group A1360
SONET/SDH interfaces E304
Song of Norway (cruise
  ship) A1216
Songbird Hearing, Inc. P455
Sonic Automotive, Inc. (auto
  dealer) E170
Sonic restaurants A1280
SonicNet.com A1476
SonicWALL, Inc. E290
Sonitech International E109
Sonneborn, John E109
Sonnen Basserman (convenience
  meals) A722
Sonnenschein, Hugo P496
Sonneveldt (distributor) P236
Sonoco Products
  Company **A1302-A1303**
Sonoda, Akira W139
Sonoma State University P99
Sonoma-Cutrer Vineyards A296,
  A297
Sonsteby, Charles M. A289
Sony Broadband
  Entertainment W550
Sony Corporation A312, A894,
  A982, A1178, A1342, A1357,
  A1482, A1520, E173, E194, E210,
  E222, E239, E262, E267, P137,
  P262, P662, W220, W234, W238,
  W360, W394, W408, W444, W526,
  W532, **W550-W551**, W554, W555,
  W600, W646
Sony Music Entertainment
  Inc. A1546, W212
Sony Pictures Entertainment A962
Sony PlayStation E298
Sooch, Navdeep S. E288

Sood, Sanjay W191
Soonwala, N. A. W567
Soosman, Barry E66
Sophie, Michael J. E310
Sophista Cat pet food A1117
SOPI petroleum products A412
Sopko, Michael D. W285
Soquimich (industrial
  minerals) W410
Sorber, Charles A. P499
Sorbo, Allen A1077
Sorensen, Erik W519
Sørensen, Lars Rebien W417
Sorensen, Norman R. A1163
Sorensen, Robert H. A1315
Sorensen, Scott K. A719
Sørensen, Vagn W518
Sorenson, Arne A913
Sorenson, Marcus E85
Sorenson, Steve P59
Soriano, Andres, III W510
Soriano, Andres, Jr. W510
Soriano y Roxas, Andres W510
Sorkin, Eric A1203
Sörme, Kjell W221
Soros Fund Management
  LLC A1094
Soros, George A1358, A1504, P110
Sorrell, Martin S. W646, W647
Sorrenson, Steve P546
Sorrentino, Franklin E. P215
Sorrentino, Neil M. A1367
Sortino, John E135
S.O.S. cleaning product A374, A375
Sosa, Sammy A294, P306
Sosiak, Jack J. A573
SOTAS, Inc. A1233
Sotheby, John A1304
Sotheby's Holdings, Inc. A130,
  A1304-A1305
sothebys.com A1305
Sotir, Mark R. A301
Sotos, Efthimios P. A805
Souchon-Neuvesel (glass
  bottles) W192
Sound Advice, Inc. (stores) E306
Sound Blaster W180, W181
The Sound of Music (movie) A622
Sound of Music stereo store A254
Sound Video Unlimited P68
Sound Warehouse A266
SoundMan speakers W339
SoundStation audio-
  conferencing E268
SoundView Technology Group,
  Inc. A566
Soup 'N Salad Unlimited P562
Soupata, Lea N. A1427
Soupline fabric care A387
The Source Information
  Management Company E290
Source Perrier W38
SourceClub warehouses P328
Soutar, Charles F. A419
South African Airways W540

The South African Bank of Athens Ltd. W385

South African Breweries plc W408, **W552-W553**

South African Nylon Spinners A1300

South Australian Land Development Scheme W88

South Beach Beverage Company A1106, P634

South Bend Gas Light Company A1034

South Carolina Canal & Rail Road A1038

South Carolina Electric & Gas Company A1248, A1249

South Carolina Power Company A1248

South Carolina Public Service Authority P732

South Center Mall (Dallas) P126

South Central Bell A248

South Deep mine W452, W453

South East Coal A416

The South Financial Group, Inc. E291

South Manhattan Healthcare Network P369

South of Scotland Electricity Board W522

South Pacific Tyres W428, W429

South Park (TV show) E69

South Penn A1096

South Shore Gas and Electric A1034

South Texas College of Law P470

South Texas Nuclear Project A676, A1198

South Umpqua Bank E307

South Western Electricity A1306

Southam, Arthur M. A811, P267

Southam (newspapers and magazines) W262, W470

Southampton apartments (New Jersey) P291

Southeast Toyota Distributors, Inc. P256, P257, P624, P644

Southeastern Asset Management A732

Southeastern Mutual Insurance A178

Southeastern Power & Light A376, A1306

Southern Australia Airlines Pty. Ltd. W468, W469

Southern Bancorp of Alabama A1308

Southern Bell Telephone and Telegraph A248

Southern Binders A1004

Southern Biscuit W244

Southern Business Group PLC (copier distribution) A746

Southern California Edison Company A532, A533

Southern California Fruit Exchange P464

Southern California Gas Company A610, A1266, A1267

Southern California Iron & Steel A256

Southern Comfort liqueurs A296, A297

Southern Communications Services, Inc. A1307

Southern Company A1154, **A1306-A1307**, P260, W266

Southern Electric Light A570

Southern Energy. *See* Mirant

Southern Envelope Manufacturers A1004

Southern Farm Fish Processors P184, P185

Southern Financial Advisors, Inc. A1309

Southern Financial Bancorp, Inc. E291

Southern Foods Group A1338, P148

Southern Hospital A1070

Southern LINC (telecommunications) A1306

Southern Living Collection furniture P299

Southern Manufacturing Company A1220

Southern Mill Creek Products A450

Southern Mineral E264

Southern Minnesota Railroad P104

Southern Natural Gas Company A536, A537

Southern New England Telecommunications Corporation A1244, A1245

Southern Novelty Company A1302

Southern Pacific Hotel Corporation W544

Southern Pacific Rail A308, A1186, A1422, A1548

Southern Pacific Railroad Internal Telecommunications. *See* Sprint Corporation

Southern Pacific Telecommunications Company A1186

Southern Pine Lumber A1364

Southern Power Company A514

Southern Public Utility Company A514

Southern Railway Company A1038

Southern Regional of Associated Milk Producers P148

Southern Sample Service A1004

Southern States Cooperative, Inc. P38, P732

Southern Sun Hotels W552

Southern Surety Company A1440

Southern Telecom, Inc. A1306, A1307

Southern Union Company A1065

Southern Water W522, W523

Southern Wine & Spirits of America, Inc. P732

Southgate, Colin W212

Southgate Plaza shopping center (Bloomington, IN) A1286

The Southland Corporation A56, A1338, W298, W438

Southland Royalty (oil and gas) A310, E283

Southmark Corporation E303

SouthTrust Corporation **A1308-A1309**

Southwell, Leonard J. P704

Southwest Airlines Company A106, A138, **A1310-A1311**, A1420, A1442

Southwest Bancorporation of Texas, Inc. E291

Southwest Gas of Las Vegas A1065

Southwest Sanitary Distributing (kitchen equipment) A530

Southwestern Bell Telephone Company A1228, A1244, A1245, A1318

Southwestern Electric Service A1416

Southwestern Public Service Company (utility) A1542, A1543

Southwestern States Portland Cement Company A848

Southwick, Peter W293

Southwind motor homes A605

Southwire Company P733

Southworth, Richard A. E124, E292

Souza, Lawrence M. A161

Souza, Stephen A847

Sovereign cigarettes W241

Sovereign of the Seas (cruise ship) A1216, A1217

Sovereign shingles P612

Sovern, Michael I. A1304, A1305

Sovey, William P. A1022, A1023

Sowa Products Company A1302

Sowers, C. Martin A579

Soybean Digest (magazine) A1161

SOYGOLD fuel additives P37

S. P. Richards Company (office products) A652, A653

SPA stores A1274

Spaarbeleg Kas N.V. W65

Space Communications Corporation W371

Space Craft Inc. A1256

Space Shuttle E206, E284, P754

Space World amusement park W398

Spacek, Leonard A172, P48, W90

Spaceman store shelf space management A66, A67

Spaceway (broadband communications) A736

Spade, Kate A565

Spadoni, Diana Simeon P177

Spageddies restaurants A288

Spain, William J. A471

Spalding Holdings Corporation (sporting goods) A836, A837, E60, P282, P283

SPAM A730, A731

Spam lottery game P687

Spanair S.A. W519

Spangler, Dick P683

Spanier, Graham B. P699

Spano, Rosemary C. A507

Spanos, Alex P532

Spanos, Dean A. P532
Spanos, Michael P532
Spar convenience stores W166, W167
Sparano, Joseph E. A1375
SPARC microprocessors A1342, A1343
Sparco office products A652
Sparkle Ice A1338
Sparkle paper products A654
Sparkletts water A946, W193
Sparrows Point Division A256, A257
Sparta Brush A326
Sparta Foods P122, P571
Spartan Coffee A1312
Spartan de Argentina (cleaning) A530
Spartan de Chile (cleaning) A530
Spartan Food Systems A86
Spartan Fund A614, P190
Spartan Stores, Inc. A1312-A1313, P422
Spartus (clocks) A1446
Spatz, Bruce P631
Spaulding, Edward P772
Spaulding lighting A1447
Spaulding, Nicky A675
Spaulding, Richard M. A1255
Spaulding, Ronald L. A1231
SPD Technologies (electronics) A846
SPDRS. See Standard & Poor's Depository Receipts
Speak & Spell toy A1378
Speakeasy Casino (Reno, NV) E247
Spear & Jackson (tools) A1446, A1447
Spear (computer systems) A244
Spear, Leeds & Kellogg A348, A614, A660, P190
Spear, Leon P230
Spearmint gum A1526, A1527
Spears, Christi E219
Specht, Uwe W257
Special Clearance Services (land mine removal) E29
Special K cereal A816, A817
Special Metals Corporation W284
Special Risk Service A1236
Special Value brands P488
Special Yarns Corporation A1380
Specialized Care Services A1435
Specialty Brands foods A743
Specialty Equipment Companies A1432
Specialty Foods Corporation A774
Specialty Hospital Group A1366
Specialty Paperboard Division A274
Specialty Products (glass beads for circuits) E57
Specialty Retail (book distributor) A757, P245
Speck, Craig P223
Speck, Eric J. A1229
The Spectator (magazine) W262, W263

SpecTek DRAM (reselling business) A762, A970
Spector, Warren J. A239
Spectra camera and film A1148
Spectra Healthcare Alliance, Inc. A259
Spectra software E219
Spectracom (optical components) A70
Spectral Dynamics A1258
Spectran Corporation A642
Spectra-Physics A792
SpectraSite Communications A1026
Spectrian Corporation E47, E123, E292
Spectrum Control, Inc. E124, E292, P750
Spectrum Group A572, P394
Spectrum Labs, Inc. P313
Spedition Pracht. See Pracht Spedition + Logistik GmbH
Speed Queen appliances A1520, A1521
Speed Slammers toys W333
Speed Stick deodorant A386, A387
Speedclip Manufacturing A572
SPEEDCOM Wireless International P454
SpeedNet (Internet service provider) W548, W598
Speedo A1498, A1499
Speedvision Networks cable channel A623
Speedway Casino (Las Vegas, NV) E247
Speedway stores P601, P664
Speedway SuperAmerica LLC A1461
Speer, David B. A749
Speleers, Allan A103
Spell, William H. E272
Spellar, Peter C. A1551
Spelling, Barrie M. A387
Spelling Entertainment A266, A1476
Spellman, Robert R. E143, E320
Spelman, Steven O., Jr. E171
Spenard Builders Supply P655
Spence, David S. P99
Spence, Will B. A1487
Spencer, Bill P444
Spencer, Christopher S. P43
Spencer, James A. A477
Spencer, Kate P777
Spencer, Kathelen V. A93
Spencer, Larry O. W263
Spencer, Robert M. (Michaels Stores) A969
Spencer, Robert S. (Baker & McKenzie) A221, P67, P548
Spencer, Simon W356
Spencer, Tom W356
Spencer, William J. P445
Spenchian, Kim R. A963
Sperduto, Michael A. A551
Sperlich, Harold K. P153

Sperling, John G. E309
Sperner, Andreas E76
Sperry Aerospace and Marine A1424
Sperry Corporation A1424
Sperry, Elmer A1424
Sperry, Margaret A923, P321
Sperry Rand A342
Speyburn Scotch A423
Speyer, Jerry P476
Sphere Corporation A1432
SPI Manufacturing (modular buildings) E94
Spic and Span cleaner A1164
Spice Girls (music group) W212, W213
Spice Islands spices A938
Spicer, Clarence A460
Spicer Manufacturing A460, A461
Spider-Man (TV show and comic books) shoes A295
Spie Batignolles (electrical contracting) W520
Spiegel, Arthur H., III (Computer Sciences) A405
Spiegel, Arthur (Spiegel) A1314
Spiegel, Inc. A1314-A1315, W426
Spiegel, John W. A1347
Spiegel, Joseph A1314
Spieker Properties A560, P180
Spielberg, Steven P166, P167, P302, P510, P597
Spielburger, Thomas C. P647
Spierings, Hubertus P. A325, P105
Spierkel, Gregory M. A759
Spiers-Lopez, Pernille W277
Spiker, Robert B. A1045
Spille, Kent P586
Spiller, Jonathan M. E29, E158
Spillers pet food W388
Spin City (TV show) A61, P166, P167, P597
Spina, David A. A1332, A1333
Spindletop oil well A1344
Spinelli, Francesca M. A1189
Spinetta, Jean-Cyril W69
Spinnaker Exploration Company E292
Spinner, Steven A1109
Spinner, Werner W119
Spinner.com A180
Spinneybeck upholstery P277
Spinozzi, Michael A277
SPINS Natural Track A67
Spira, James C. A147
Spires, William J. A1483
Spirit Cruises W546
Spirit Energy 76 A1438
Spirit (magazine) P656
The Spirit of Delta (airplane) A478
Spirit of St. Louis (airplane) A662, A1088
Spirograph A693
Spirox E187
Spitfire airplane W496
Spithill, Ron W77
Spitzer, Alan P733

Spitzer Management, Inc. P733
Splenda sugar substitute A801, W568, W569
Splendor of the Seas (cruise ship) A1217
Splinter, Michael R. A761
Splügen beer W163
Spock, Thomas E. P357
Spoehel, Ronald R. A687
Spoerle Electronic A196
Spokane, Portland & Seattle (railroad) A308
Sponyoe, John A883
Spoonemore, Brenda P355
Spooner, John P. A531, W257
Spoor, William A1136
Sporck, Charles A1002
Sporn, Philip A140
Sport Bild (magazine) W106
Sport cigarettes E293
Sport Shake beverage P149
Sport Supply Group, Inc. E198
Sport Utility Special (book) P139
SPORT1 (Web site) W106
The Sporting News (print and online sports magazine) P511
Sportline USA A566
The Sports Authority A830
Sports Illustrated (magazine) A1218, P390, P708
Sports Internet W146
SportsBusinessJournal (publication) A80, A81, P32
SportsChannel A312
Sportservice (stadium food) P590
SportsLine.com, Inc. A334, P356
SportsNet regional network A390
Sportster motorbikes A682
Sportverlag Berlin (publishing) W107
SpotLife (video sharing) W338
Spoto, James P. A411
Spra-Coupe agricultural sprayers A96, A97
Sprague, Carol Lee H. A1289, P447
Sprague, Clifford G. E81, E230
Sprague, Peter A1002
Sprang, Clark E. A665
Spray 'n Wash fabric care A1246, P432, W476, W477
Sprayon paint A1278
Sprecher + Schuh A1210
Sprenger, Gordon M. P536
Sprenger, Victor L. A551
Spring Arbor Distributors (Christian products) A756, A757, P244, P245
Spring Bock beer W377
Spring Ram (bathroom products) A1446
Spring Valley Brewery W314
Springboard office furniture A1335
Springer, Axel W106
Springer, Colby H. P131
Springer, Cora L. P415
Springer, Friede W107
Springer, Hinrich W106

Springer, Jerry P218
Springer, Paul P493, P755
Springer Verlag W126
Springfield brands P488, P752
Springfield Foodservice A1109
Springfield (Ohio) *News Sun* A443, P147
Springfield (Ohio) *Press-Republican* A442, P146
SpringHill Suites hotels A912, A913
Springhouse (assisted living) A908
Springmaid home furnishings A1316, A1317, P452, P453, P696
Springs, Elliott A1316, P452
Springs Industries, Inc. A306, **A1316-A1317**, **P452-P453**, P733
Springs, Leroy A1316, P452, P733
Springwater Farms brand P185
Sprint car W560
Sprint convenience stores A1084, A1085
Sprint Corporation A128, A248, A390, A442, A1186, A1188, **A1318-A1319**, A1362, A1534, A1546, E41, E83, E179, E233, E287, E292, E313, P146, P274, P599, W232, W580
Sprint FON Group A1318, W205
Sprint lawn equipment A287
Sprint PCS Group A292, A390, A438, A872, A873, A1318, E243, W204, W205
Sprint Spectrum A442
Sprite soft drink A382, A383, A384, A385, P577
Sprocket Systems P302
Sproul, Alan P186
Sprout Group (venture capital) A449
Sprout on demand book printing A276
Spruce Falls Power and Paper A826
Spruce Goose (airplane) A736
Sprunk, Eric A1033
Spry, Malcolm A67
Spungen, Susan A919
Spurgin, John H., II A75
Spurlock Industries P90
SPX Corporation A460, A1210, **A1320-A1321**, A1322, A1446, E57, W290
SQA (software) E110
Square Deal Milk Producers P148
Square D (electric power) W520, W521
Square Electric Company P208
Squibb. *See* Bristol-Meyers Squibb Company
Squibb, Edward A290
Squier, Carl A882
Squier, George P350
Squires, Burt A491
Squires, Stephen L. A713
Squirt soft drink W154, W155
SRDS (business information) W626
Srepco Electronics A1140

SRI International E241, **P454-P455**, P734
Srinivasan, Srinija A1547
SRP A1138, P734
S. S. Kresge Company A830, W172
S.S. Nesbitt & Company P170
Ssangyong Information & Communications Corporation P110
SSB Investments, Inc. A1333
SSC Radisson Diamond (cruise ship) P106
SSE Manufacturing P437
SSI Computer A176
SSI Container Corporation A176
SSI Food Services, Inc. P265
SSIH (watchmaker) W562
SSM Health Care System Inc. P734
SST. *See* Silicon Storage Technology, Inc.
SST (car rental) A710
SST China E121
ST Format (magazine) W238
Staats Bedrijf der Posterijen, Telegraphie, & Telephony W502
Staats-Zeitung A832
Stablein, Lawrence A. A111
Stacey, David W177
Stacey, Ron P624
Stack, Dick P593
Stack, Ed P593
Stack, Robert J. W155
Stade, Yngve W557
Stadshaug, Bob P411
Stadtlander Pharmacy A458
Stadtwerke Kiel (utility) A1416
Staffaroni, Giuseppe A895
Staffieri, Ronald S. A277
Stafford brand A791
Stafford, John R. A148, A149
Stafford, Trevor J. A611
Stafford, Walter V. P121
Staff-Rx E125
Sta-Flo cleaning products A487
Stage Rigging P611
Stagg, Amos Alonzo P496
Stagg canned chili A730, A731
Staggs, Thomas O. A1497
Staglin, Garen K. A597
Stags' Leap wines W230, W231
Staheli, Donald A426, P140
Staheli, Paul A426
Stahl, Dale E. A1365
Stairs, Harriet H. W113
Stakis (hotels) W258, W340
Staley Continental W568
Staley, Gregory R. A1397
Staley, James D. A1207
Staley, Warren R. A324, A325, P104, P105, P566
Stalin, Josef W458
Stalker, Robin W63
Stallkamp, Thomas T. P679
Stalter, J. Neil A705
Stalvey, Allan A1505
Stamey, William C. A709

Stamm, Charles H. A1355, P467
Stamm, Keith G. A1465
Stamminger, Erich W63
Stamp, Charles R., Jr. A469
Stamper, Robert P299
Stampone, Frederick A1101
Stamps.com Inc. A1142, P511
Stanbrook, Steven P. A1247, P433
Stanczak, Edmund A., Jr. A551
Standard & Poor's A944, A982, A1468
Standard & Poor's Depository Receipts P46, P47
Standard Broadcasting W494
Standard Chemicals W256
Standard Data A402
Standard Federal Bancorporation W56, W57
Standard Forgings (locomotive axles) A1406
Standard Fruit of New Orleans A494
Standard Gas & Electric A1266, A1542
Standard Manufacturing A152
Standard Media International P248
Standard Microsystems Corporation A1514
Standard Motor Products, Inc. P113
Standard Oil Company A352, A412, A576, A772, A992, A1000, A1276, A1344, A1376, A1460, E166, P236, P769, W128, W136, W280, W500
Standard Oil Company (California) A352
Standard Oil Company of Indiana W137, W438
Standard Parking Exchange P236, P237
The Standard Products Company (automotive parts) A432
Standard Radio Supply A1140
Standard Sanitary A152
Standard Slag Holding Company A848
Standard Steel and Spring A198
Standard Steel Propeller A1432
Standard Telephones & Cables W236
Standard Underground Cable A642
Standish, Ayer & Wood (asset manager) A954
Standish, Clive W617
Standish, Thomas R. A1199
Standley, John A1203
Standoff Land Attack Missile (SLAM ER) A272
Stanek, Robert V. P115
Stanford, Jane P456, P735
Stanford, Leland, Jr. P456, P735
Stanford, Leland, Sr. P384, P456, P735
Stanford Research Institute. See SRI International
Stanford Telecommunications A780

Stanford University A98, A1342, P384, P456-P457, P734, P735, W648
Stange, Richard T. A795
Stangl, Gustav R. A493
Stani candy W155
Staniar, Burton B. P277
Stanich, Lauren A919
Stanley, A. Jack A677
Stanley, Aurelia C. P41, P537
Stanley Cup (hockey) P360, W376
Stanley, David A1090
Stanley, Frederick A1322
Stanley, G. Brent A1121
Stanley, Harold A988
Stanley H. Kaplan Educational Centers A1502
Stanley Home Products A1414, P316
Stanley, Ira H. E239
Stanley, James (Scottish Power) W523
Stanley, James W. (AK Steel) A105
Stanley, Mark E. A1189
Stanley, Martin A1417
Stanley, Maxwell A726
Stanley, Neal A. E62
Stanley, Richard H. (Hon International) A727
Stanley, Richard L. (Delco Remy) P153
Stanley Rule and Level A1322
Stanley, Tim A685
The Stanley Works A1322-A1323
Stansel, Eugene A., Jr. P735
Stansi Scientific A600
Stansik, James G. A501, P163
Stansky, Robert A614, P190
Stansted airport (London) W316
Stant Corporation (windshield wipers) W604
Stant Manufacturing Inc. W605
Stanton, David P474
Stanton, John W. A625
Stanton, Kathryn A. P193, P610
Stanton, Ronald P. P748
Stanton, William H. A475, P155, W197
Stanutz, Donald J. P239
Stanworth, Tony W313
Stanzione, Robert J. E30
Staplcotn (marketing) P735
Staple Cotton Cooperative Association P735
Staples Center sports complex A622, A623, W390
Staples, David M. A1313
Staples, Inc. A1058, A1324-A1325
Sta-Prest pants A869, P293
Star Air Lines A106
Star Alliance A478, A1420, W68, W80, W344, W518, W540
Star Banc A1444
Star Bancshares, Inc. A1509
Star beer W255
Star Canyon restaurants P106, P107

Star Cruises Limited A330
Star Division (software) A1342
Star Enterprise A1376, P340
Star Forms A284
Star Furniture Company A706
Star, James A1482
Star Lake Railroad Company A309
Star Markets P102, P478, W300
Star Mart convenience stores P340
Star Scientific, Inc. E293
Star (tabloid newspaper) W390
Star Tobacco & Pharmaceuticals. See Star Scientific, Inc.
Star Trek (movies and products) P416
Star Tribune (Minneapolis) A1502
STAR (trucks) W350
STAR TV W391
Star Wars (movies and products) A294, A295, A622, A692, A693, A1404, E130, E303, P302, P303, P661, W332, W333, W395
Star Wholesale Florist A968
StarBand Communications, Inc. A528, A529
Starbucks Corporation A510, A511, A1102, A1103, A1105, A1326-A1327, P148
Starburst candy A914, A915, P314, P315, P665
Starcom MediaVest Group P72, P73, P551
Stardent Computers W326
Stargate SG-1 (movie) A962
Stark, Arthur A247
Stark, Brian J. A803
Stark, John R. E294
Stark, Robert W. W495
Starkey, James H., III A1437
Star-Kist tuna A722, A723
Starkman, Ronald P. P91
The Star-Ledger (Newark, NJ) A80, A81, P32, P33, P530
StarLink corn W102
Starlite brand A527
Starlix drug W414
StarMark cabinets A921
Starmark (health plan marketing) P750
StarMed (staffing) E111
Starnes, Debra L. A901
Starr, Bart A672, P210, P621
Starr, Cornelius A150
Starring fragrance A217
Starritt, Nick W137
StarTek, Inc. A1192
Startel (telecommunications) W576
StarTool software E286
Startpagina (Internet portal) W626
Starwave (Web services) A1496
Starwood Financial. See iStar Financial Inc.
Starwood Hotels & Resorts Worldwide A312, A688, A720, A780, A1086, A1326, A1328-A1329

Starwood Vacation Ownership, Inc. A1328
Stasior, William P88
Stata, Ray A170, A171
State Accident Fund P86
State brand cheese P58, P546
(State College, PA) *Centre Daily Times* A833
State Express 555 cigarettes W143
State Farm Insurance Companies A126, A638, A1168, A**1330**-A**1331**, P42, P**458**-P**459**, P538, P735
State Hotel Supply Company A1109
State Line Tack stores A1116, A1117
State Mutual Life Assurance Co. of America A124
State Normal Schools P98
State of Florida Department of the Lottery P736
State Peace Officers' and Firefighters' Defined Contribution Plan Fund A315, P97
State Science and Technology Institute P71
State Street Corporation A370, A**1332**-A**1333**
State Street Research & Management Company A964
State University of New York P70, P98, P**460**-P**461**, P736
Staten Island Bancorp, Inc. E293
Staten Island Community College P128
Staten Island (New York) *Advance* A80, A81, P32
Staten Island Railway P334, P674
Staten Island Rapid Transit Operating Authority P335
Staten, Reesa A1209
Statendam (ship) A331
Stater Brothers Holdings Inc. P**462**-P**463**, P524, P736
Stater, Cleo P462
Stater, Lavoy P462
Stater, Leo P462
Statewide Electrical Supply A1512
Statewide Research, Inc. A591
Statewide Savings Bank P640
Static Guard A108
Statilogie (customer relations) W100
Stationers Distributing A1430
Statler (hotel chain) A720
Statoil gas stations A132, A200, W499
Statton, Tim A241, P75
Statue of Liberty A642, P703
StatView software P430
Stauber, William A64, P30
Stauffer Chemical W102, W228
Staunton, Donna W89
Staunton, Henry W249
Stauth, Robert A606
Stavia stores W590
Stavro, William A927

Stavropoulos, William S. A504, A505
Stawarz, Raymond R. P607
Stay Alert gum A1527
Staybridge Suites by Holiday Inn W544, W545
Stayfree feminine hygiene A801
Staying Alive: A Consumer Reports Car Safety Special (educational video) P139
Stayton, Michael B. A1035
Stead, Edward B. A267
Stead, Jerre L. A758
Stead, Joel A1261
Steak & Ale restaurant A288, A1136, P332, P333, P674
Steak & Ale Restaurants. *See also* S&A Restaurant Corporation
Steakley, Joseph N. A695
Steamboat Willie (cartoon) A1496
Steamship Company of 1912. *See* Dampskibsselskabet af 1912, Aktieselskabet
Steamship Company Svendborg. *See* (Aktieselskabet) Dampskibsselskabet Svendborg
Stearman, Lloyd A882
Stearns & Foster (mattress) P442, P443, P725
Stearns, Robert A238
Stebbins, Donald J. A857
Stec, John A797
Stecher, Bernd W537
Stecher, Esta E. A661
Stecklein, Leonard F. A1049, P377
Steeg, Jim P357
Steelcase Inc. A706, A**1334**-A**1335**, P222, P613, P627
Steelcraft A152, A754, A755
Steele, Donald F. (Hertz) A711
Steele, Donald H., III (Duke Energy) A515
Steele, Glenn D., Jr. P497
Steele, John R. (Spiegel) A1315
Steele, Jon (United States Postal Service) A1429, P491
Steele, Patrick S. A111
Steenbakker, Arnold A611
Steenburgh, Eric L. A525
Steenkolen Handelsvereeniging W364
Steenland, Douglas M. A1046, A1047
Steere, William C., Jr. A1118
Stefac drug A1119
Stefan, John E. E294
Steffens, John L. A961
Steffensen, Dwight A958
Stegimen, Greg A561, P181, P604
Steginsky, Corazon A. P71
Stegman, Gary L. A93
Steiden Stores A1532
Stein, Alfred A196
Stein, Cyril W258
Stein, Heinz-Gerd W595
Stein, Helmut W407
Stein, James C. A611

Stein, Laura A723
Stein, Lawrence V. A149
Stein, Lou P716
Stein, Martin E., Jr. E276
Stein Roe & Farnham P294, P295
Stein, Shelley P207
Stein, Stanley R. A943
Stein, William C. E214
Steinberg retail A436
Steinbrecher Corporation A1362
Steiner, David P. A1505
Steiner, Jeffrey A803
Steinfeld's Products (pickles) A466, A467
Steinhafel, Gregg A1353
Steinheil Optronik W110
Steinig, Stephen N. A1017, P371
Steinkrauss, Mark A. A1361
Steinlager beer P732
Steipp, Thomas W. E297
Stejskal, Allan A207
Stelfox, Diane M. A199
Stella Artois beer W231, W288, W289
Stellarton Energy E129
Stellato, Frank A393
Stellato, Louis E. A1279
Stellenbosch Farmers' Winery W552
Stemberg, Thomas G. A1324, A1325
Stemgen drug A160, A161
Stemmons, John A1398
Stempel, Robert A650
Stena Line W434
Stenbuck, Neil L. E270
Stender, Margaret A. A1181
Stenson, Brian T. P461, P736
Sténson, Henry W519
Stensrud, Lorry J. A879
Stentorfield (vending machines) A446
Stephan, Edwin W. A1216, A1217
Stephens, Alys P170, P601
Stephens, Barrie W290
Stephens, Bobby W. A259
Stephens, Doug A85
Stephens, Elton B. P170, P171, P601
Stephens, Elton B., Jr. P171
Stephens, George A226
Stephens Group, Inc. E269
Stephens (investments) A258
Stephens, James R. (Merisel) A959
Stephens, James T. (EBSCO) P170, P171, P601
Stephens, Jim (Adobe Systems) A77
Stephens, Terry A. A775
Stephens, Timothy T. A1145
Stephenson, Dorothy L. A257
Stephenson, E. W., Jr. A167
Stephenson, William A. A451
Stepien, Ronald W. P341
Steps menswear shops W299
Steradent health and personal care W476
Sterer brand A527

Stericycle, Inc. E293
Steri-Oss (dental implants) A234
Sterling, Charlotte B. A913
Sterling Chemicals A1368
Sterling Collision Centers A126
Sterling Commerce, Inc. A1245
Sterling Communications A312
Sterling Diagnostic Imaging A1148
Sterling Digital A313
Sterling Drug A524, W118
Sterling Financial
  Corporation E294
Sterling Group A548, A654
The Sterling Group A770
Sterling Guarantee Trust W434
Sterling, Jeffrey, Lord of
  Plaistow W434, W435
Sterling, John F. A1135
Sterling Manhattan Cable A312
Sterling Newspapers W262
Sterling plastic extruders A450
Sterling plumbing products P284,
  P285, P653
Sterling Silver beef A324, P104,
  P566
Sterling Software A402, A1378
Sterling trucks P633
Sterling Vineyards A296, W108,
  W206
Sterling, Wallace P456
Sterling Winthrop (nonprescription
  drugs) W118
Stern, Arthur E159
Stern, Carl P94, P95, P559
Stern, David J. P135, P354, P355,
  P682
Stern, Gary E159
Stern, Ingrid E253
Stern, Jonathan H. E233
Stern (magazine) W126
Stern, Max P626
Stern, Mitchell A623, W391
Stern, Paul W412
Stern, Robert A. A1297
Stern, Russell A1185
Sternberg, Fred E244
Sternberg, Jan W518
Sternberg, Seymour A1017, P371,
  P688
Sternberg, Stanley A400
Sternlicht, Barry S. A1328, A1329
Sterrett, Stephen E. A1287
STET. See (Società) Finanziaria
  Telefonica
Stetz, Gordon M., Jr. A939
Steuart, David J. A285
Steuert, D. Michael A611
Steul, William M. E53, E195
Steve, Bruno W555
Steve Madden, Ltd. E294
Stevedoring Services of America
  Inc. P737
Stevens Aviation A1310
Stevens, Ben W143
Stevens, Curtis M. A891
Stevens, David C. (Smurfit-
  Stone) A1293

Stevens, David D. (Accredo
  Health) E147
Stevens, David (Freddie Mac) A627
Stevens, David (United Business
  Media) W620
Stevens, D. Richard A432
Stevens, Glenn H. A929
Stevens, Gregory W. A1125
Stevens Institute of
  Technology A1302
Stevens, Jan A117
Stevens, John M. (Hon
  Industries) A727
Stevens, John Paul (US Supreme
  Court Justice) P378
Stevens, Jonathan J. (CDW
  Computer Centers) A337
Stevens, Mark A. (Fluor) A611
Stevens, Mark (Northern
  Trust) A1043
Stevens, Robert J. A882, A883
Stevens, Sandi P258
Stevens, Scott E108, E274
Stevens, Thomas C. A823
Stevens, W. D. A979
Stevenson, Adlai P74
Stevenson, Brian E. A775
Stevenson, Catherine L. A1479
Stevenson, Dennis W431
Stevenson, Gary P637
Stevenson, Michael W145
Stevenson, Russell E41
Stevies shoes E294
Steward, Larry E. A513
Stewart, Deirdre E112
Stewart, Jackie P250
Stewart, James G. (CIGNA) A361
Stewart, Jamie B., Jr. (Federal
  Reserve Bank of New York) P607
Stewart, Jerry L. P201
Stewart, John F. (General
  Dynamics) A645
Stewart, John M. (Barclays) W115
Stewart, John O. (Pillsbury) A1137
Stewart, J. Wayne A71
Stewart, Kirk T. A1033
Stewart, Laurie K. A1097
Stewart, LeAnne M. A995
Stewart, Lee M. A1267
Stewart, Lisa A. A185
Stewart, Lyman A1438
Stewart, Martha A796, A918, A919,
  E140, E317
Stewart, Martin W147
Stewart, Robert S. A341
Stewart, Ronald P132
Stewart, Thomas J. P727
Stewart Warner Electronics E68
Stewart, William L. A1139
Stewart's sodas A1400, W154, W155
Steyr (agricultural
  equipment) W227
Sthen, Tryggve W633
STI Group A1482
STI Investment Management
  (Collateral) Inc. A1347
Stichting Ingka (foundation) W276

Sticinski, Don L. A121
Stier, Edwin P246
Stiften, Edward P555
Stigler, George P496
Stila Cosmetics A564, A565
Stiles, Allen & Company department
  store A1094
Stiles, Augustus A1094
Stiles, Mark W. A1407
Stiles, Robert B. A235
Still, John T., III A795
Still, Julie A1261
Stillwater Mining Company E294
Stillwell, Loretta P564
Stilten, Bobbi P293
Stilwell frozen foods A608, A609
Stimpert, Michael A. P201
Stimson Lane Ltd. A1459
Stimsonite A210
Stimulus Progression P350
Stinnes AG (logistics) W218, W219
Stinson, Craig A199
Stinson, J. Michael A413
Stinson, Joel T. A1037
Stinson, Kenneth E. A866, A1114,
  A1115, P396, P397, P701
Stipes, Frank C. E314
Stirek, John A. A1399
Stitle, Stephen A. A1001
Stitt, Dale E. E254
Stitzer, H. Todd W155
Stivers, William C. A1519
Stix, Baer & Fuller department
  stores A490
STMicroelectronics N.V. A162,
  A1372, E97, E161, E256, P444,
  P445, P726, W554-W555
Stoc supermarkets W164
Stock, Alan W. P127
Stock Ale beer W377
Stockam Valves & Fittings A446
Stockdale, Stewart A. A415
Stockel, Neil P113
Stocker, Michael A. P174, P175,
  P602
Stocker Resources, Inc. A1145
Stockforms Ltd. (computer
  forms) A480
Stockholms Allmanna
  Telefon W584
Stockland, Wayne L. P37
Stocklosa, Gregory A. A1219
Stockman tobacco W283
Stockmaster (financial data) W484
Stockton, Bryan A927
Stockwell, Stephen E. A195
Stodieck, Helmut W461
Stoke, Bruce E133, E310
Stokely, Ted P. E303
Stokely USA A354, A355
Stokely-Van Camp (canned
  foods) A1180
Stokes, Ken W477
Stokes, Patrick T. A175
Stokholm, Gunnar W653
Stolichnaya vodka A1106, W84,
  W85

Stolk, Marcel W339
Stoll, David E. P153, P590
Stoll, William F., Jr. P91
Stoller, John R. A1179
Stoller, Stuart A1021
Stone, Alan P221
Stone & Webster A498, A786
Stone, Bruce W. A441
Stone, Clement, Jr. A182
Stone Container
 Corporation A1292
Stone, C. W. Chuck A1231
Stone Energy Corporation E295
Stone family P142
Stone, Gary L. P387
Stone, Geoffrey R. P497
Stone, Irving A146
Stone, Jeffrey E306
Stone, Joel R. A1211
Stone, Joseph A1292
Stone, Larry D. A893
Stone Mountain Carpet Mill
 Outlets P568
Stone, Patrick F. A591
Stone, Richard C. A299
Stone, Roger A1292
Stone, Ronald P690
Stone, Theresa M. A795
Stone, W. Clement A182
Stonecipher, Charles H. E23
Stonecipher, David A. A794, A795
Stonecipher, Harland C. E107,
 E269
Stonecipher, Harry C. A273
Stonefield, Stephen E. A449
Stonegate Resources P565
Stoneham, Paul H. A109
Stoner, Janet L. A1377
Stonesifer, Patricia Q. P78, P79
Stonington Partners, Inc. A958,
 A1210
Stonkus, Alexander C. E21, E148
Stonyfield Farm yogurt W192
The Stop & Shop Companies,
 Inc. A836, A1084, W498, W499
Stop and Shop stores P103, P282
Stop-n-Shop stores P198
Stora Enso Oyj **W556**-**W557**
Stora Kopparbergs Bergslad W556
Storage Dimensions A928
Storage Technology
 Corporation A822, A**1336**-A**1337**
StorageTek. *See* Storage Technology
 Corporation
StorCare Technology P272
Storch, Gerald L. A1353
Store Opening Solutions, Inc. P313
StorEdge network storage A1343
Storhoff, Donald P610
Stork Engineering A786
Stork, Steven P612
Storm, Colin A. A302
Storm, Kees J. W65
Storm recreational vehicles A605
Storm soft drink A1105
Storm Technology W338

Storozhev, Yury W347
Stortz, Thomas C. A867
Story, Kendra P537
Story, Susan N. A1307
Storz Instrument A234
Stouffer Foods A1132, A1296, W388
Stout, David W247
Stout, Steven L. A971
Stove Top stuffing A842, A843,
 A1126
Stoveken, James E., Jr. A1517
Stover, Bruce H. A169
Stover, Clara P424
Stover, Russell William P424, P719
Stover, Wilbur G., Jr. A971
Stow, John S. A1229
Stowers, James, Jr. P537
STP auto products A374
STR (office systems) A746
STR Series audio mixers E85
Stråberg, Hans W210, W211
Strafo, Inc. P113
Strafor Facom A1334
Strafuss, David E64
Strahan, Lisa W177
Strahley, Jim P673
Strain, Clayton E56
Strain, David P619
Strain, Douglas E56
Strand, Atkinson, Williams &
 York E307
Strand, Mark A155
Strand, Steve E25
Strandwitz, Peter E104, E267
Strangfeld, John R. A1173
Stranghoener, Laurence W. P534
Strano Foodservice A1350
Strasser, Richard J., Jr. A1429,
 P491, P754
StrataCom (ATM products) A368
Strategic Advisors, Inc. A615, P191
Strategic Defense Initiative P438
Strategic Hotel Capital LLC P737
Strategic Marketing
 Corporation W621
Strategic Mortgage Services,
 Inc. A595
Strategic Resource Solutions
 Corporation A1166, A1167
Strathdee, Walker Stuart W569
Strathmore Scottish Spring
 Water A423
Stratoflex (hoses and
 fittings) A1088
Stratoliner aircraft A272
Stratosphere Casino, Hotel and
 Tower (Las Vegas, NV) E154
STRATTEC SECURITY
 CORPORATION (car and truck
 locks) A286
Stratton, Frederick P., Jr. A286,
 A287
Stratton, Harold A286
Straus Family A586
Straus, Jozef A792, A793
Strauss, Ben A1100
Strauss, Charles B. W619

Strauss, David M. P388, P389, P699
Strauss, Levi A868, P292
Strauss, Maurice A1100
Strauss, Michael E154
Strauss, Robert C. E255
Strauss, Victoria A1206
Strauss-Wieczorek, Gerlinde W351
Strautberg, Timothy E. A569
Stravinskas, Mary A403
Straw, Edward M. A565
Strawbridge's department
 stores A932
Strawn, Taylor P226
Stream International Inc. (tech
 support) A1218, A1298, P584
Stream S.p.A. (pay TV) W390,
 W575, W624
Streaming Media E102
Streamware (software) A446
Streber, Albert G. A197
Streek, Dan A1465
Streem, Craig A. A735
Streep, Meryl P776
Street & Smith (publishers) A80,
 A81, P32
Street, James E. E228
Street, Mike W141
Street, William M. A297
StreetFinder (software) P408, P711
Streets Online Limited W312,
 W313
Strehle, Etta M. E229
Streiff, Christian W507
Streisand, Barbra P290
Strellson AG (men's
 clothing) W607
Streppel, Joseph B. M. W65
Stress Relief separator stock P689
Stretmater, Robert L. A649
Strianese, Michael T. A847
Stricker, Willy W171
Strickland, Bob (SunTrust) A1346
Strickland, Robert (Lowe's
 Companies) A892
Strickler, George E. A278
Strickler, Rainer W117
The Stride Rite Corporation W606,
 W607
Strietmann bakery A814
Strigl, Dennis F. A1473, P765
Striker grenade launchers P132
Stringer, Howard W551
Stringfellow, Charles S., Jr. P561
Strobel, Pamela B. A571
Strobel, Russ A1031
Strode, Robert P. A133
Stroehmann Bakeries LC W245
Stroesser, Jim P143
Stroh Brewery P428
Stroh Company (gas
 stations) W424
Strohm, Susie S. E208
Stroh's Beer A224
Stroll, Lawrence S. W606, W607
Strom, Leonard A. A265
Strom, Peter A1150
Strömqvist, Dag W73

Strong, Benjamin P186
Strong, Gregory S. P677
Strong, James A. W645
Strong, Kevin V. A411
Strong, Steve A1553
Strong, Wendi E. A1453, P503
Stroud, Byron E. A347
Stroud, W. B. Dixon P342
Stroup, Gary A. A333
Stroup, John S. A463
Stroup, Stanley S. A1509
Strube, Jürgen F. W117
Structural Dynamics Research
  Corporation A538
Structural Metals A396
Structure clothing A876
The Structure Tone
  Organization P737
Strudler, Robert J. A863
Strumpf, Linda B. P195
Strunk, Cindy A1523
Strutt, Charles P680
Struve, Jeffrey E. A295
Stryker, Steven C. A1277
Stuart & Sons W636
Stuart crystal stemware W636,
  W637
Stuart Furniture Industries P652
Stuart F. Whitman and Son A1104
Stuart, John (IKON Office
  Solutions) A746
Stuart, John (MasterCard) P323
Stuart Medical, Inc. A1070, A1071
Stuart, Robert A1180
Stuart, Scott M. A837, P283
Stubblefield, John K., Jr. A1351
Stubkjær, Knud E. W95
Stuckey, Bruce D. P195, P610
Stuckey, Charles R. E114
Stuckey roadside candy
  stores A1104
Stucky, Nicklas D. P705
Studdert, Andrew P. A1421
Studebaker brothers A1034
Student Book Exchange NYC A232
Student Loan Funding
  Resources A1448
Student Loan Marketing
  Association A1449
Student (magazine) W622
Students' Army Training
  Corps P456
Studio Chiomenti (law firm) A1288,
  P446
StudioPLUS Deluxe Studios E59,
  E201
Studios USA LLC A1451
Study, Roy E. A289
Stuebe, David C. A727
Stuerzebecher, Gert W127
Stukas, Vitas A. A935
Stukel, James J. P756
Stull, Robert L. A1207
Stump, Harvey E119
Stump's Market, Inc. P488, P489
Stuntz, Mayo S., Jr. A181
Sturany, Klaus W505

Sturgell, Brian W. W75
Sturgeon, John A. P349
Sturgess, Tom P518
Sturken, Craig C. A671
Sturm, Fred M. E168
Stussy brand clothing E101, E259
Stutsman, Laura E85
Stutt, Carl P745
Stuttgart Municipal Gas
  Works A1212
Stutts, James F. A499
Styer, Paul A. E45
Style & Co. clothing A587
Su Casita (mortgage bank) A1178
Suárez, Coppel, José Juán W441
Suarez, Kent L. P269
Suaudeau, Calixte W467
Suave hair care W618, W619
Suavitel fabric care A387
Subaru-Isuzu Automotive A650,
  P561, P563, W294, W560
Subasi, Hasan W319
Submarino.com W582
Subotnick, Stuart P332, P333, P674
Substral (plant care) W256
Suburban Bancorp W112
Suburban Propane A974, A1248,
  W252
Suburbia apparel stores W635
Suburbia clothing W634
Subway restaurants A1084, P160,
  P161, P595, P702
Sucaryl artificial sweetener A58
Success shampoo W308, W309
Sucralose artificial sweetener W568
Sud, James P. A1523
Sud, Rahul E82
Sudafed A1118
Sudbury, David M. A397
Südzucker AG W201
Suez A122, W150, W558-W559,
  W624
Sugar Creek stores W498
Sugar Puffs cereal A1107, A1181
Sugar, Ronald A1045
Sugarland (juice) W510
Sugarman, Jay E224
SugarTwin A108
Suggs, Leo H. A1423
Sugihara, Kanji W387
Sugita, Katsuyuki W375
Sugita, Tadayasu W237
Sugiyama, Kazuhiko W361
Sugiyama, Mineo W387
Suharto, Raden A628
Suhr, Joachim W365
Societe Suisse de Microelectronique
  & d'Horlogerie W562
Suitehotel W59
Suiza Foods Corporation A466,
  A1338-A1339, P148
Sukay, Thomas J. (Commerce
  Bancorp) E182
Sukay, Thomas (Rosenbluth) P419,
  P717
Suleman, Farid E140, E317
Sulentic, Robert E. A1399

Sullivan, Austin P., Jr. A649
Sullivan, Charles A. (Interstate
  Bakeries) A774, A775
Sullivan, Charles L.
  (Sonoco) A1303
Sullivan, Colin E112
Sullivan, Daniel A. (Umpqua
  Holdings) E307
Sullivan, Daniel J.(FedEx) A589
Sullivan, Daniel L.
  (QUALCOMM) A1183
Sullivan, Dennis W. A1089
Sullivan, Donald W294
Sullivan, Douglas B. A969
Sullivan, Fred R. E280
Sullivan, G. Craig A374, A375
Sullivan, Irene A. P447
Sullivan, James M. A913
Sullivan, Jane W213
Sullivan, John L. A751
Sullivan, Kevin R. A293
Sullivan, Laura P. A1331, P459
Sullivan, Maria M. A337
Sullivan, Marion H. P423
Sullivan, Mark E. P93
Sullivan, Michael A549
SULLIVAN nasal system E112
Sullivan, Patrick J. E50, E190
Sullivan, Richard L. A725
Sullivan, Scott D. A1535
Sullivan, Shawn A281
Sullivan, Stephen G. (Liberty
  Mutual) A875, P295
Sullivan, Stephen W. (E.W.
  Scripps) A569
Sullivan, Steven R. (Amaren) A137
Sullivan, T. Dennis P541
Sullivan, Thomas H. E299
Sullivan, Timothy E. (Kaiser
  Foundation) A811, P267
Sullivan, Timothy P. (First
  American) A595
Sullivan Transfer (materials
  handling) P611
Sullivan, Trudy A881
Sullivan, Walter F. E133
Sullivan, W. Donald A1331, P459
Sullivan, William D. (Anadarko
  Petroleum) A169
Sullivan, William (Oxford Health
  Plans) A1076
Sullivan, William P. (Agilent
  Technologies) A99
Sulman, David L. A1373
Sulmon, Bruno P165
Sulnetic, Michael E. A683
Sulzbach, Christi R. A1367
Sulzberger and Company
  (meatpacking) A1212
Sulzberger, Arthur Hays A1020
Sulzberger, Arthur, Jr. A1021
Sulzberger, Arthur Ochs A1020,
  A1021
Sulzer AG W350
Sulzer Medica USA A674
Sumergrade (down
  comforters) A1134

Sumie, Hiroshi W297
Sumisho W426
Sumitomo Bank W362, W374
Sumitomo Chemical Company A58
Sumitomo Group A612, A660,
 A664, A896, A960, A1024, A1125,
 E161, E162, E174, W296, W386,
 W396, W398, W404, W598
Sumitomo Mitsui Banking
 Corporation W200, W372, W373,
 W374, W396
Summa di Arithmetica
 (book) P182, W222
Summe, Gregory L. A1110, A1111
Summer, Thomas S. A423
Summerfield Suites by
 Wyndham A1540, A1541
Summers, Lawrence H. P220,
 P221, P626
Summers, W. Dennis E259
Summers, William C. A517
Summit Acceptance
 Corporation A318
Summit Bancorp A228, A602
Summit (cruise ship) A1217
Summit Holding Southeast A875,
 P294, P295
The Summit Media Group E147
Summit Partners E290
Summit Ventures E153
Sun Apparel A804
Sun Bancorp, Inc. E295
Sun Banks A1346
Sun Brewery W288
Sun Chemical (ink maker) P608
Sun City P643
Sun Coast Industries (specialty
 resins) P90
Sun Community Bancorp
 Limited E171
Sun Company (oil) A244
Sun Country Coolers wine
 coolers A422
Sun, David P272, P273, P651
Sun Electric (automotive
 diagnostic) A1294
Sun Energy Partners A820
Sun Fire network server A1343
Sun Fresh stores P62, P63, P547
Sun Gro Horticulture E214
Sun Healthcare Group,
 Inc. **A1340-A1341**
Sun Life and Provincial
 Holdings W104
Sun Life Assurance Company of
 Canada A874, P294
Sun Life Insurance A812
Sun Life & Provincial
 Holdings A694
Sun Mart grocery stores A994,
 A995
Sun Media Corporation (newspaper
 publishing) W470, W471

Sun Microsystems, Inc. A172, A270,
 A368, A538, A636, A782, A894,
 A958, A972, A990, A1050, A1184,
 A1260, A1336, **A1342-A1343**,
 E33, E96, E97, E117, E190, E220,
 E249, E256, E272, P48, P440,
 P719, W90, W160, W260, W444,
 W550
Sun National Bank E295
Sun Oil Company of Ohio A1344,
 E62
Sun Valley Foods A325
Sun Valley resort P729
Sun warehouse markets A606
SunAmerica Inc. A150, A812
Sunbeam bread A609, A775
Sunbeam Corporation (small
 appliances) A902, A903, A1446,
 A1474, E240, P304, P305, P663
Sunbelt Beverage
 Corporation P738, P777
Sunbelt Nursery Group A1130
Sunbelt Outdoor Products A468
Sunbelt snack food P669
SunBridge Healthcare Group
 International Corporation A1341
Sunbury furniture P299
Suncoast Steel A396
Suncoast stores A254
SunCom E299
SunCor Development
 Company A1138, A1139
Suncor (petroleum) A1344
Suncorp-Metway (insurance) W88
Sund, Bjørn A. W411
Sundance Film Festival P126
SunDance Rehabilitation
 Corporation A1340
Sunday Times (UK) W592
Sundeen, John E., Jr. E315
Sunderland, John M. W154, W155
Sundgren, D. E. P593
Sundheim, Nancy Straus A1425
SunDisk A1260, E117, P440
Sundstrom, Christafor E. A1527
Sunfresh processed fruits A470,
 A471
SunGard A392
Sunglass Hut E99, E257, P713
Sunical Land & Lifestock
 Division A701
Sunkist Growers, Inc. A1204,
 P464-P465, P577, P738, W154,
 W155
Sunland brands P728
Sunland Industries (fertilizer and
 insecticides) A612
Sunlight laundry soap W618, W619
SunLite Casual Furniture A1446
Sun-Maid Growers (raisins) A774,
 A775
Sunniland Trend properties A1145
Sunny car W403
Sunny Delight juice A1105
Sunny Fresh eggs A325, P105
Sunoco, Inc. A244, **A1344-A1345**,
 P738

Sunoco Logistics Partners
 L.P. P738
Sunray DX Oil A1344
Sunrise Assisted Living, Inc. E295
Sunrise cereal A648
Sunrise healthcare A1340
Sunrise Technology A214
Sunrise Telecom, Inc. E296
Sunrise Television
 Corporation A715, P233
SunScript Pharmacy
 Corporation A1340, A1341
Sunset Limited (train) P362
Sunshine Biscuit Company A618,
 A814
Sunshine, Eugene S. P379, P691
Sunshine Travel Centers P740
SunSilk hair care W619
SunSolution, Inc. A1341
SunSource Inc. (hardware
 equipment) E151
Sunstate Airlines (Queensland) Pty.
 Ltd. W468, W469
Sun-Times Company W262
Suntory (beverages) W162, W192
SunTrust Banks, Inc. A382, A936,
 A1346-A1347, A1486
SUNY. *See* State University of New
 York
Super 1 Food stores P561
Super 6 Lotto lottery game P698
Super 8 Motels Inc. A338, A339,
 E216
Super A Foods, Inc. P489
Super Bock beer W163
Super Bowl (football game) A334,
 P211, P356, P621
Super Bubble candy A709
Super Center Concepts, Inc. P489
Super Cut-Rate Drugstore P188
Super Discount Markets W194
Super Disc (record company) P188
Super Dollar Supermarkets P654
Super Foodmart A671
Super Food Services A994
Super Fresh grocery stores A670,
 A671
Super Globo bleach A375
SUPER H supermarkets P624
Super Indo stores W195
Super K food stores W172
Super Lotto Plus lottery game P693
Super Mario (video games) W394,
 W395
Super "Melo-Ring" W649
Super Merries diapers W308
Super Mild cosmetics W535
Super Music City record store P188
Super Nintendo Entertainment
 System W394, W395
Super Pets P394
Super Rite (grocery stores) A1202
Super Saver warehouse
 stores A110, A111
Super Soaker water products A693
Super Target stores A1353

Superama supermarkets W634, W635
SuperAmerica convenience stores A200, P601, P664
SuperBeta regulators E92
SuperCalc software A402
Supercenters A1494, A1495
Supercenters auto parts stores A1100
Supercharger brand A527
Supercomputer Systems P522
Supercritical Systems W600
Supercuts hair salons A1196
Superdiplo grocery stores W498, W499
Superdrug stores W312
Superette stores W194, W195
SuperFlash memory E121, E288
Superfos A200
Superior Financial Corporation E296
Superior National Insurance companies P268
Superior Services (waste management) W624
Superior Stamps & Collectibles P536
Superkings cigarettes W282, W283
SuperLotto lottery game P564
Supermarché Delhaize "Le Lion" W195
Supermarket Developers, Inc. P62, P63
Supermarket Insurance Agency Inc. P63
Supermarkets General Corporation A1490, P514
Supermarkets Operating Company P514
SuperMontage (electronic network) A996, P353
SuperNews (publication) P481
SuPeRSaVeR stores A606
Supersweet feeds P36
Supertel Hospitality Management E216
SuperTru brand foods A607
SUPERVALU Inc. (wholesale food distributors) A606, A744, A830, A1282, **A1348**-**A1349**, P62, P202, P242, P243, P634, P638, W194, W245
SupeRX drugstores A844, A1202
Supli soft drink W315
Suppa, Gerald P. A1095
Suppes, Christine L. A1031
Support Systems International A718
Supradyn vitamins W493
Suprema Di Avellino cheese E296
Suprema Specialties, Inc. E296
Supreme Baking A774
Supreme Beauty Products P258, P259
Supreme Life Insurance Company P258
Supreme Sugar A192
Suquet, Jose S. A219

Surcouf (computer retailer) W446
Sure Start (alternators) A572
Surf laundry soap W618, W619
Surface Mount Device Placement Guidance Package E43
Surfer (magazine) A1161
Surgery Center Holding Corporation A699
Surgical Care Affiliates, Inc. A698, A699
Surgical Health Corporation A699
Surgical Specialties Corporation P313
Surgicare of Indianapolis, Inc. A695
Surgicare of Wichita, Inc. A695
Surgutneftegaz (oil) W346
Surles, Philip C. A347
Surpass gum A1526
Survey Research Group A66
Surveyor moon lander A736
Survivor: The Australian Outback (TV show) A334
Survivor (TV show) A334
Susor, Robert J. A653
Susquehanna nuclear plant A1154
Sussman, Arthur M. P497
Sustiva drug A541
Sutcliffe Catering W248
Sutcliffe, Neil W355
Suter, A. E. A546
Sutherland, Allan C. A749
Sutherland, L. Frederick A191
Sutherland Lumber Company, L. P. P739
Sutherland, Peter D. W137
Sutherland, Steve P121
Sutherland, Thomas W268
Suto, Miwa P65
Sutro & Company E132, E306
Sutter Health Systems A1070, P739
Sutter Hill Ventures E300
Sutter Laboratories A694
Suttin, Adam L. P407
Suttle Press, Inc. A1360
Sutton, Bill P355
Sutton, C. J. A101
Sutton, Michael A474, P154, W196
Sutton, Ray S. A775
Sutton, Thomas C. (Pacific Mutual) P384, P385, P695
Sutton, Thomas (Dover) A502
Sutton, Timothy A1319
Sutton, W. Kenneth, Jr. A683
Sutula, Gary L. A1219
Suver, Susan M. A1125
Suwyn, Mark A. A890, A891
Suzi Wan Chinese food A915, P315
Suzuki & Company W404
Suzuki, Bob P99
Suzuki, Iwajiro W404
Suzuki, Katsuro W265
Suzuki, Keisuke W139
Suzuki Loom Works W560
Suzuki, Masanobu W401
Suzuki, Michio W560
Suzuki, Minoru W187

Suzuki Motor Corporation A286, A650, P138, W294, **W560**-**W561**
Suzuki, Osamu W561
Suzuki, Shigehiko W401
Suzuki, Toshifumi A57, W298, W299
Suzuki, Yozo W169
Suzulight minicar W560
Svanholm, Poul W162
Svedmann, Jonie E313
Svehlak, Linda A57
Svendborg (company) W94
Svendborg Maersk (container vessel) W94
Svensk Interkontinental Luftrafik (airline) W518
Svenska Cellulosa Aktiebolaget SCA A654
Sverdrup Technology, Inc. (construction and design) A786, A787
SVGA Development E51
SVPW. See Showerings, Vine Products and Whiteways
Svyturys beer W163
Swackhamer, Roy A381
Swagelok P739
Swain, Cynthia A847
Swain, David O. A273
Swain, Robert P454
Swallow Hotels W638, W639
Swan, Dave P657
Swan, Frank J. W231
Swan, Mara A79
Swan, Peter P665
Swan, Richard A. A1055
Swan, Robert C. (Phelps Dodge) A1125
Swan, Robert H. (TRW) A1413
Swan, William E. E205
Swango, Tim P747
Swann, Joseph D. A1211
Swanson frozen foods A316, A714, P232
Swanson, Kurt R. P741
Swanson, Neil E308
Swanson, Robert (Genentech) A640
Swanson, Robert H., Jr. (Linear Technology) E84, E233
Swanson, William H. (Raytheon) A1191
Swanson, William R. (Bose) P93
Swarovski (crystals) A1552
Swartz, Steven P. A701, P229
The Swatch Group Ltd. (wrist watches) W528, **W562**-**W563**
Swatchmobile W562
Sweat, Michael T. A583, P185
Sweatt, Blaine, III A465
Sweatt, Herman P498
SWEB (utility) A1154
Swed, Patrick M. A1513
Swedin, Patricia E. P355, P682
Swedish Match Company W220, W556
Sweeney, Anne A61
Sweeney, Dawn P29

Sweeney, Douglas M. A1085
Sweeney, John J. (AFL-CIO) P34, P35, P532
Sweeney, John M. (Seacoast Financial) E285
Sweeny, Edward E313
Sweeny, Jack C. A1365
Sweet, Donald A215
Sweet, Frederic H. A1049, P377
Sweet Home Thriftway P489
Sweet Life Foods stores A1348
Sweetenham, Paul A1389
Sweetheart bread A775
Sweetheart paper products P727
Sweethearts candy P752
Swenka, Arthur J. A1351
Swenson, Doug P89, P558
Swenson, Edward J. E56
Swenson, Eric A628
Swenson, H. V. A744, P242
Swette, Brian T. E54
Swienton, Gregory T. A1222, A1223
Swift Armour Holdings P392
Swift car W560, W561
Swift, David L. A525
Swift, Dean A. E254
Swift Energy Company A1466, E297
Swift Independent Packing A408, P518
Swift, John D. A981
Swift Premium meats A409
Swift, Richard J. A620, A621
Swift, Terry E. E297
Swift Transportation Company, Inc. (trucking) A788
Swifty Mart stores P740
Swifty Serve Corporation A1084, P740
Swindells, William A1524, A1525
Swindle, Dean P691
Swinerton Inc. P740
Swinger camera A1148
Swingle, Edward R. A97
Swingline staplers A618
Swirbul, Jake A1044
Swire, John W564
Swire, John Samuel W564
Swire Pacific Limited W**564**-W**565**
Swires, Adrian W564
Swiss Bank Corporation. See UBS AG
Swiss Dairy A1338
Swiss General (chocolate) W388
Swiss Life/Rentenanstalt W616
Swiss Miss cocoa A409
Swiss Oil Company A200
Swiss Re. See Swiss Reinsurance Company
Swiss Reinsurance Company A204, A878, A964, W336, W380, W464
Swiss Timing Ltd. W563
Swissair Group A478, A1478, W469, W518, W540, W616
Swisscom AG E220, W502, W584
Swissotel hotels A732
Switchboard.com A334

Switkowski, Zygmunt E. W586, W587
Switz, Robert E. A71
Switzer, J. D. A547
Switzer, Larry W190
Switzerland Transport Insurance (reinsurance) W652
Swoboda, Charles M. E47, E188
SWT Holding, Inc. A591
Sybex, Inc. A1456
Sydec (audio products) E85
Sydran Group A288
Syed Mohamed, Syed Tamin W539
Sygen International plc P665
SYGMA Network A1350
Sykes, Richard W246, W247
Sylla, Casey J. A127
Sylvan Learning Systems W592
Sylvania (lighting) W536
Symantec Corporation A1357, E33, P584
Symbian Alliance W360
Symbios (electronics) A894
Symbiosis A282
Symington, Fife A1158, P400, W462
Symmetricom, Inc. E297
Symmetrix P278
Symmetrix RAID A542
Symmetrix storage A543
Symonds, Gardiner A1368
Sympatico Internet portal W592, W593
Symphony candy A709, A914
Symskaya Exploration E199
Synadyne E129
Synagis drug E90, E240
Synagro Technologies, Inc. E297
SYNALAR drugs E89
Syncrude W280
Synercid drug W103
Synergen A160
Synergy Semiconductor E92
Synernetics A54
Syngenta AG E193, W414
The Synkoloid Company of Canada A1456
SYNNEX Information Technologies, Inc. A958, P740
Synopsys Inc. A894
Synovus Financial E183
Syntex drug A984
Syntex (pharmaceuticals) E89
Synthélabo W342
Synthetic Pillows A1134
Syntonic (transportation communication) P438
SyQuest A778, A928
Syro Steel A1406
Syron, Richard (American Stock Exchange) P46
Syron, Richard F. (Thermo Electron) A1382, A1383
SYS-AID A404
SYSCO Corporation A**1350**-A**1351**, W568
Sysinct A746

Systech Environmental A848
System Development Laboratories A1066
System Energy Resources, Inc. A554, A555
System Fuels, Inc. A555
Systematics A128
SyStemix W414
Systems and Services Company (food wholesalers) A1350
Systems, Applications, and Projects (SAP) W516
Sytek E134
Szabo (correctional facility food services) A190
Szczerba, Tadeusz Stanislaw W457
Szeliga, Robin R. A1187
Szente, Daniel M. A315, P96
Szescila, Andrew J. A223
Szostak, M. Anne A603
Szurek, Paul E. E285
Szwed, Stanley F. A599
Szycher, Michael E105
Szymanczyk, Michael E. A1127

T

T & C Leasing E294
T. Mellon and Sons bank A954
T. Rowe Price (asset management) P110
T. Rowe Price Group, Inc. (asset management) A1398
T1msn (Web portal) W580
TA MidAtlantic E132
Taarud, Terese A. P43
TAB soft drink A382, A385, P577
Tabak, Natan P515
Tabaksblat, Morris W479
Table & Wine store P554
Tabor (grain) A192
TAC Worldwide Companies P741
Tachibana, Yusuke W401
Tachikawa, Keiji W401, W419
Taco Bell Corporation (fast food restaurants) A302, A1084, A1106, A1404, A1405, P236, P633, P702
Taco Cabana, Inc. (fast food restaurants) A288
Tacoma car W615
Tacoma truck P366, P367, P687
TAC-Trim (automotive trim) A388, A1380
Tada, Hideo W305
Tadiran Telecom W322
TAFA Group (thermal spray equipment) A1156
Taft, Claudia L. A841, P287, W325
Taft Communications A144
Taft-Hartley Act (1947) P34
TAG Heuer watches and jewelry W348, W349
TAG Manufacturing A1256
Tag Semiconductors W554
Tagamet drug W246, W492
Taggart Baking A774
Tagliabue, Paul J. P356, P357, P683
Tags stores P76

Taguchi, Wataru W397
Tahoe Joe's Famous
  Steakhouse P562
Taida, Hideya W359
Taihan Electric Wire W74
Taikoo Motors Ltd. W565
Taikoo Sugar Refinery W564
Tailien Optical W486
Taillefine biscuits W193
Taillet, Phillippe A1297
TaiMall Development E51
Taiwan Semiconductor
  Manufacturing Corporation A162,
  A170, E121, E160, E226, E248,
  E288, P444, P445, P726, W60,
  W444
Taiwan Telecommunication W570
Taiyo Kobe Bank W372
Taj Mahal Hotel (Bombay) W566
Taj Mahal resort and casino
  (Atlantic City) A1408
Takabe, Toyohiko W401
Takada, Masahiko W81
Takada, Osamu W449
Takagi, Akinori W169
Takahashi, Taira W187
Takahashi, Yosuke W393
Takanami, Koichi W187
Takano, Akiyoshi W515
Takashima, Akira W237
Takashima, Masayuki W371
Takashima, Tatsuyoshi W199
Takaya, Takashi W237
Takayama, Suguru W573
Takayama, Yasuo W305
Take Five lottery game P372, P373
Takeda Chemical Industries,
  Ltd. A58, P741
Takeiri, Masami W487
Takemoto, Shigeru W299
Takeshige, Yuzo W603
Takeshita, Noboru W96
Take-Two Interactive Software,
  Inc. E298
Takeuchi Mining Company W320
Takizawa, Haruo W339
Takla, Lars A. A1129
Talbot (cars) W442
Talbot's, Inc. (clothing) A648, P254
Tales from the Wild (TV show) P359
Taliaferro, Elizabeth W. A643
Taliens water W193
Talisman Energy Inc. A310
Talk (magazine) A700, A701, P228,
  P229
Tall, Craig E. A1501
Talladega Superspeedway
  (Alabama) E75, E222
Tallahassee (Florida)
  Democrat A833
Tallarigo, Lorenzo A541
Tallett-Williams, Michael A879
Talley, Joseph J. P538
Tallian, Peter J. E304
Tallman, Karen A. A959
Talman Home Federal Savings W56
Talonsoft E298

Talus wines A422
Tam, C. D. A991
Tam, John A197
Tamaddon, Sina A187
Tamarkin stores P198
Tambrands A1164
TAMI (food industry) W322
Tamiflu drug W492, W493
Tamke, George, Jr. P275
Tamori, Takashi W393
Tampa Bay Buccaneers (football
  team) P357
Tampa Bay Devil Rays (baseball
  team) P307
Tampa Bay Lightning Hockey
  Club P212, P361
Tampax tampons A1164, A1165
Tamura, Atsuko P411
Tamura, Masato W97
Tamura, Shigemi W599
Tamvakakis, Apostolos W385
Tan, Amy W430
Tanabe, Charles Y. A873
Tanabe, Takaharu W405
Tanaka, Hisashi A1006, A1007
Tanaka, Hisashige W610
Tanaka, Kazuo W421
Tanaka, Noburu W235
Tanaka, Nobuyoshi W159
Tanaka, Osamu W361
Tanaka Seizo-sha W610
Tanaka, Takeo W601
Tanaka, Toshizo W159
Tanaka, Yasuo W235
Tanaka, Yasusuke W515
Tanaka, Yutaka A1006
Tancer, Edward F. A625
Tanchon, James A. A819
Tandem Computers A1256
Tandem International P480
T&H Service Merchandisers
  convenience stores A994
T&N Ltd. (asbestos) A1074
T&N plc (engine bearings) A584
Tandon A1514
Tandowsky, Keith R. A375
Tandy, Charles A1130, A1188
Tandy Corporation A1188, P196,
  W180
Tandy Electronics W644
Tandycrafts, Inc. A1130
Taneichi, Takeshi W599
Taneja, Deepak E96
Tang, Cyrus P741
Tang Industries, Inc. P741
Tang, K. N. A67
Tang, Paul C. A305
Tangen, Christopher S. A769
Tangney, Michael J. A387
Tango soft drink W545
Tangram Enterprise Solutions,
  Inc. A1233
Tani, Kimio W419
Tanner, Scott S. E146
Tanqueray gin W206
Tanrei beer W314

Tansky, Burton M. A1015
Tanzberger, Eric D. A1269
TAP Pharmaceutical Products,
  Inc. A58, P741
Tapco A1412
Tapie, Bernard W62
Taplin, Frank A992
Taplin Frank, Jr. A992
Taplin, Thomas A992
Tapner, Rory W617
Tapp, Lawrence G. A1319
Tappan appliances W210
Tappan, David A610
Tappan, Lewis A516
Taqueria Canonita
  restaurants P106, P107
Tarantino, Robert V. E190
Tarbell, Anne A. A1401
Tarble, Newton A1294
Tarbutton, Allen J., Jr. A979
Tarde, Jerry A81, P33
Tardif, Yann W241
Tareyton cigarettes A618
Target Corporation A158, A549,
  A790, A802, A1270, A1316,
  A1352-A1353, E58, E198, E214,
  E225, E246, E290, P452, P733,
  W172
Target Country discount
  stores W172
Target Therapeutics, Inc. A282,
  A283
Targocid drug W103
Tarleton State University P470,
  P471, P743
Tarmac plc (facility
  management) A1272, A1484, W92
Tarnopol, Michael L. A239
Tarola, Robert M. A1537
Tarom (airline) W79
Tarozzi, Luciana W215
Tarpey, Michael P. A1187
Tarragon Realty Investors,
  Inc. E298
Tartikoff, Brandon A998
Tartikoss, Peter P41, P537
Tasher, Steven A. A149
Tashima, Hideo W368
Tashima, Kazuo W368
Tashima, Norio W369
Tashiro, Jun W373
Tashiro, Morihiko W603
Tasker, Steven W. A1029
Tasmania Independent
  Wholesalers P243
Tassis family P202
Tassopoulos, Timothy P. P125
TASTE (magazine) A1530
Tasteforliving.com P278
Tastemaker (flavors and
  fragrances) W492
Tastemaker joint venture A704
Taster's Choice coffee W388
Tastybird chicken A1418
Tata Consulting A562
Tata, Dorabji W566

Tata Engineering & Locomotive Company W567
Tata Enterprises A456, A1224, W306, **W566-W567**
Tata Iron and Steel Company W567
Tata, Jamsetji W566
Tata, J. R. D. W566
Tata, Ratan N. W566, W567
Tata Ryerson Ltd. A1225
Tata, Simone W567
Tata Timken Limited A1386
Tatar, Jerome F. A950, A951
Tatarinov, Kirill A271
Tataseo, Frank A. A375
Tate & Lyle PLC A500, P162, W564, **W568-W569**
Tate, Charles W. A714, A715, P232, P233
Tate Gallery W568
Tate, Henry W568
Tate, John W. E80, E230
Tate, Paul H. E64
Tate, Peggy P157
Tate, William Henry W568
Tatò, Francesco W215
Tato Skins snacks A814
Tatramat (appliances) A1520
Grupo TATSA A1406
Tatton-Brown, Duncan W623
OOO Tattransgaz W243
Tatum, Charles M. A1213
Tatung Company **W570-W571**
Taub, Bruce A335
Taub, Henry A204
Taub, Joe A204
Tauber, David W. P742
Tauber Oil Company P742
Tauber, O. J., Sr. P742
Taubman, A. Alfred (Sotheby's) A1304
Taubman, Alfred (Irvine Company) P252
Taukojärvi, Jouko W557
Taunton, J. T., Jr. A1221
Taunus Corporation (manufactured housing) A346
Taurel, Sidney A541
Taurone, Ralph P247
Taurus cars A616
Taurus tires W367
Tau-Tron (digital instrumentation) A170
Tavanic drug W103
Tavares, Maurice P. A793
Tavist over-the-counter medication W414, W415
Tavistock (coal) W340
Tavlarios, John P. E208
Tavola Baccano restaurants W315
Tawney, Anne E. A1097
Tax-Aide P29
Taxis family W202
TAXOL drug A290, A291
Taxotere drug W102, W103
Tayebi, Masood K. E318
Tayebi, Massih E318
Taylor, Andrew C. P178, P179, P603

Taylor & Sledd (food distribution) A1109
Taylor, Anne P221
Taylor, Chuck P142
Taylor Corporation P742
Taylor, Daniel J. A963
Taylor, Donna A. E183
Taylor, E. P. W262
Taylor, Elizabeth A766, W250
Taylor, Forrest R. P335
Taylor, Frederick A352
Taylor, Glen A. P742
Taylor, Gregory T. A1443
Taylor, Gwen E159
Taylor, Herbert P420
Taylor, Jack C. (Enterprise) P178, P179, P603
Taylor, James H., Jr. (Boston Scientific) A283
Taylor, James L. (Tesoro) A1375
Taylor, James M. (Robert Half) A1209
Taylor, Jaquelin A1436
Taylor, Jay K. W452, W453
Taylor, John C. (AMERCO) A135
Taylor, Jonathan W. (George E. Warner) P614
Taylor, Keith A. (NCR Corp.) A1013
Taylor, Keith L. (Southwest Airlines) A1311
Taylor, Larry D. A699
Taylor Made golf clubs W62, W63
Taylor, Marilyn J. P449
Taylor, Martin W114
Taylor, Marylin A1543
Taylor, Nelson P68
Taylor Packing Company P104
Taylor, Peggy P35
Taylor Publishing P262
Taylor, R. Eugene A227
Taylor Rental Center A1322, A1410, P484, P485, P749
Taylor, Richard (Burger King) A303
Taylor, Richard T. (Tellabs) A1363
Taylor, Robert A. A1279
Taylor, Russell C. A827
Taylor, S. Martin A513
Taylor, Terry A. P131
Taylor, Thomas A. (Amica Mutual Insurance) P540
Taylor, Thomas S. (Epix Holdings) P603
Taylor, Tim P630
Taylor, Trent E. A1493
Taylor, Volney A516
Taylor, W. P269
Taylor, W. M. A1417
Taylor, William L. A1437
Taylor wines A422, A423
Tazikawa, Masao W261
Tazo Tea Company A1326
Tazorac acne treatment A118, A119
TBS cable network A181
TBWA Worldwide (advertising) A1062, A1063
TC Advertising P506, P765
T.C. Farries and Company P68

T.C. Meadows & Company A752
TC New England Brokerage, Inc. A1399
TC Pipelines, LP E298
TCB hair care products A108
TCBY Enterprises, Inc. (yogurt) E95, E249
TCCC. See The Coca-Cola Company
TCD Labs (CD recording equipment) E98
T-Chek smart card fueling service A344
Tchuruk, Serge W76, W77
TCI. See AT&T Broadband & Internet Services
TCI Music. See Liberty Digital
T-Cubed A1038
TD Waterhouse Group, Inc. A348, W608, W609
T-D1 mobile phone network W204
TDK Corporation **W572-W573**
TDMarketSite W608
TDS Telecommunications Corporation A1360
T. E. Stockwell W590
Teacher Retirement System of Texas A1042
Teachers Advisors, Inc. (mutual fund management) A1355, P467
Teachers Insurance and Annuity Association-College Retirement Equities Fund **A1354-A1355**, **P466-P467**, P742
Teagle, Walter A576
Teal Bend Golf Club (California) P131
Team Air Express A1206
Team Health, Inc. P743
Team Rental Group A300
TeamOne (implementation services) A1098
TeamStaff, Inc. **E125**, E299
Teamsters. See International Brotherhood of Teamsters
Teamsters National Union P246
Teapot Dome Scandal A1502
TearDrop Golf Company A1446
Teare, Andrew W472
Tebbe, Horst A1263
TEC Worldwide (training) P279
Tecalemit (garage equipment) W290
Tecaté beer W288, W289
Tece (auto parts) A460
Tech Data Corporation A870, **A1356-A1357**, E281, E290
TECH Semiconductor Singapore Pte. Ltd. A971
Techne Systems E57
Tech-Net Professional Service P112, P569
Technical Aid Corporation P741
Technical Financial Services A542
Technical Polarizer A976
Technical Publishing A516
Technical Resource Connection A1112
Technics electronic products W360

Technip P74
Technology Capital Group E224
Technomatic P338
Technophone W406
TechSpace LLC A1233
Techy International A250
TeckCheck (skills assessment) P279
Tecnol Medical Products A826
Tecnost Sistemi S.p.A. W422, W423
Tecnotest A1320
Tec-Sem (photolithography) E35
Ted Baker brand A691
Tedeco brand A527
Teel, Joyce Raley P710
Teel, Michael J. P710
Teeley, Peter B. A161
Teen Beat (magazine) A1161
Teen (magazine) A1160, A1161
Tee-Off (video game) W527
Teeple, Richard D. A433
Teerlink, Richard A682
Teeter, Thomas C. P547
Teets, John A486
Teets, Robert W. A431
Teflon A534
Tegal Corporation W600
Tegnelia, Anthony G. A1223
Teh, K. H. A929
Tehama Bank E216
Teichelman, Christine E216
Tejas Energy A1276
Tejero-DeColli, Aida A805
Tekelec A196, E126, E299
Tekelec-Airtronic E126
TekInsight.com P599
Tekni-Plex, Inc. P310
Teksid (foundry) W226, W480
Tektronix, Inc. A1358-A1359, A1544, E46
TEL America W600
TELAV P611
Telcel Cellular A248, W580
Telco. See Tata Engineering & Locomotive Company
TelCom Semiconductor E93, E245
Telcordia Technologies, Inc. P438, P724
Tele Columbus GmbH W201, W504
Tele Sudeste Celular Participações W578
Telebanc Financial A566
Telebank A566
Télébec (phone service) W123
Telebras (phone company) W578
TeleBroker A348
Telecheck International (check authorization) A596
Telecine pay-television A623
Teleco Oilfield Services A222
Telecom Australia W586
Telecom Finland. See Sonera Group
Telecom Italia Mobile S.p.A. W418, W574, W575
Telecom Italia S.p.A. A1412, W204, W422, W423, W450, W574-W575
TelecomAsia A1473

Companhia de Telecommunicacoes de Macau S.A.R.L. W153
Telecommunications Act of 1984 (UK) W148
Telecommunications Act of 1996 (US) A140, A202, A312, A1186, A1244
Tele-Communications Inc. See AT&T Broadband & Internet Services
Telecommunications Laboratories A1362
Telecommunications Services of Trinidad & Tobago Ltd. W153
Companiá de Telecomunicaciones de Chile S.A. W576-W577
Telecorp PCS, Inc. E299
Telectronics (pacemakers) W428
Teledata Communications A70
Teledesic LLC (satellite network) A1026
Teledyne Technologies Inc. A116, A644, E92, P71
Teleflora (floral delivery) P416, P417, P716
Telefónica CTC Chile. See (Compañía de) Telecomunicaciones de Chile S.A.
Telefónica DataCorp W579
Telefónica de Argentina W578
Telefónica de España. See Telefónica, S.A.
Telefónica del Peru W578
Telefónica Internacional W576
Grupo Telefónica Media W579
Telefónica Móviles, S.A. W578, W579
Telefónica Mundo W576
Compañía Telefónica Nacional de España W578
Telefónica, S.A. E220, W430, W577, W578-W579
Telefónica Sociedad Operadora de Servicios de Telecomunicaciones en España, S.A. W579
Compañía de Teléfonos A686
Compañía de Telefonos de Chile W578
Compañía de Telefonos de Edison W576
Compañía de Teléfonos del Interior A1473
Teléfonos de México, S.A. de C.V. A1244, W232, W580-W581, W582
Teleglobe Inc. W122, W123
Telegrafverket W584
Telegraph and Texas Register P90
Telegraph Delivery Service P416
Telegraph Group (newspapers) W262, W263
Telegraphic Service Company W198
Telemecanique W520, W521
Telemedia International Italia S.p.A. W575
Telemundo Communications Group A873
Telenokia W406
Telenor ASA W148, W584

Telenor Media P474
Telephone and Data Systems, Inc. A1360-A1361
Telephone Audio Productions P350
Telephone Electronics Corporation P764
Telephone Utilities A1082
Telephones, Inc. A1360
Telepiu (pay TV) W390
Tele+ W390
Teleport Communications A202, A390
Teleprompter P350
TeleQuest Teleservices, Inc. E113
Telerate (financial data) A506
Telereal Holdings Ltd. W148
Teleregister (stock quote boards) A440
TeleRep (TV ad sales) A442, A443, P146, P147
Telergy (telecommunications) A1028
Telesat Cablevision A624
Telesat Canada W122, W123
Telescan, Inc. (online investment information) A998, P511
Telesistema Mexicana W582
Telesoft S.p.A. (software) W575
Telesp Celular Participações S.A. (phone company) W578
Telespazio S.p.A. (satellite telecommunications) W574, W575
TeleTech Holdings, Inc. E127, E300
Tele-Trip flight insurance P348
Televerket. See Telia AB
Grupo Televicentro W582
Grupo Televisa, S.A. W582-W583
Television Azteca W582
Société Television Française-1 W134, W135
Telewest Communications plc A873
Telex Communications, Inc. E142
Telfast drug W103
Telia AB E220, W502, W584-W585
Teligent, Inc. A872, W400, W401
Telkomsel W503
Tellabs, Inc. A1232, A1362-A1363, E41, E304
Tellem, Nancy A335
Tellez, Cora M. A697
Telling, Frederick W. A1119
Tellus office furniture P652
Telmark LLC P39
Telmex. See Teléfonos de México, S.A. de C.V.
Telocity A736
Telogy Networks E192
Telpner, Joel A835, P281
Telrad Networks W322, W323
Tel-Sound Electronics E58
Telstar satellite W232
Telstra Corporation Limited E220, W586-W587
TEL-Thermco Engineering Company W600
TELUS Corporation A1473

Temares, Steven H. A247
Temasek Holdings W540
Tembreull, Michael A. A1079
Temco (electronics and aerospace) A896
TEMCO (feed grains) P123
Temerlin McClain (advertising) A772
Temic Bayern-Chemie A1412
Temic GmbH W188
TEMIC Telefunken A1482
Temodar drug A1250, A1251
Temp, James A. A673, P211
Tempered Spring Company A198
Tempest, Drake S. A1187
Tempesta, John A159
Temple, Arthur A1364
Temple, Arthur, Jr. A1364
Temple, Edward A1162
Temple, Thomas A1364
Temple-Inland Inc. A**1364**-A**1365**
Templeton, Mark B. E42, E179
Templeton, Richard K. A1379
Tempo (brewery) W254
Tempo Libre (tours) W59
Tempo Research A1380
Tempra Technology A452
Tempshield packaging A1263
Temptronic E223
Tempus Group W646
ten Brick, Frank J. M. E293
TENARA fiber P523
Tenet Healthcare Corporation A322, A698, A904, A1112, A1296, A**1366**-A**1367**, E211, P568, P637
Teng, Ted A1541
Tengelmann, Emil W588
Tengelmann Group A670, W364, W**588**-W**589**
Tenholder, Edward J. A575
Tenneco Automotive Inc. A352, A388, A456, A552, A978, A**1368**-A**1369**
Tenneco Energy A536
Tennenbaum, Jeremy A1261, P441
Tennenhouse, David L. A761
Tennessee Book A756, P244
Tennessee Eastman Corporation A522
Tennessee Gas A536
Tennessee Gas and Transmission A1368
Tennessee Production Company A1368
Tennessee Titans L.L.P (football team) A68, P356, P357
Tennessee Valley Authority A**1370**-A**1371**, P**468**-P**469**, P672, P743
Tennessee Woolen Mills A1134
Tennessee-American Water Company A155
Tenovis Holding GmbH (telecom) A836, A837, P282, P283
Tenzer, Gerd W205
Teoh Tee Hooi W541

TEPCO. *See* The Tokyo Electric Power Company, Inc.
TEPPCO Partners, L.P. A376, A514, P598
Tepper, David E219
Tequiza beer A175
Tera Computer A1284
Teradata Solutions A1013
Teradyne, Inc. A**1372**-A**1373**, E46, E223, E269, W600
Terenzio, Philip A1499
Terex Corporation A116
Terino, Edward E159
Teriyaki Bowl A784, A785
Terkowitz, Ralph S. A1503
Terlixidou, M. W385
Terman, Frederick A712
Terminal Agency (insurance) P122
Terminix pest contol A1272, A1273
Terna SpA W215
Terndrup, Chris P455
Terol, Alberto E. A173, P49, W91
Terra Industries Inc. A850, P122, P288
Terra Lycos A614, P190, W578
Terra Networks W576, W578
Terracciano, Anthony P. A155
Terragrafics home decor products A1023
Terramycin drug A1118
Terrano II car W403
Terrell, James E. A655
Terrell, Mike A759
Terrion, Joe P419
Territorial University of Washington P761
Terry, Henry A688
Terry, Robert B. A583, P185
Terry travel trailers A604, A605
Terry, W. Burks A1045
Tersigni, Anthony R. P57
Tertronics E104
Teruel, Javier G. A387
Tervaert, D. G. Cohen A1437
Terwilliger, J. Ronald P747
Tesco PLC A1234, W300, W**590**-W**591**
Teske, Todd J. A287
Tesone, Antonio W423, W575
Tesoro Petroleum Corporation A556, A**1374**-A**1375**, W137
TESSAG W504
Tessler, Bernie P296
Tessler, Susan P237
Testa, Enrico W215
Testa, Justin E43
Testa, Richard J. A1373
Testec E56
TestMaster software A1372
Teter, Gordon A1510
Teterboro Airport P399
Teters Floral Products A1446
TETI W574
Teti, Nicholas L. E219
Tetley (brewery) W84, W163
Tetley tea W566

Tetra Tech, Inc. E**128**, E300
Tetra Technologies A1484
Tetrault, Roger E. A940
Teuber, William J., Jr. A543
Teutsch, Nancy P223, P627
Tevanian, Avadis, Jr. A187
Teves (brakes) A780
Texaco Inc. *See also* ChevronTexaco
Texaco Inc. A184, A352, A1096, A1130, A**1376**-A**1377**, P238, P340, P416, P604, P679, W280, W410, W438, W500
The Texas A&M University System P**470**-P**471**, P498, P743
Texas Agricultural Experiment Station P471
Texas Air A428
Texas Butadiene and Chemical A900
Texas Company A1376
Texas Eastman A522
Texas Electric Service A1416
Texas Engineering Experiment Station P471
Texas Forest Service P471
Texas Fuel A1376
Texas Gas Resources (gas pipeline) A454
Texas Gas Transmission Corporation A1529
Texas Gold Gusher lottery game P473
Texas Gulf Coast HMO, Inc. P227
Texas Health Plan, Inc. P227
Texas Health Resources P744
Texas Higher Education Coordinating Board P470
Texas Homecare stores W300
Texas Hydraulics A502
Texas Instruments, Inc. A162, A398, A636, A712, A970, A1190, A1298, A**1378**-A**1379**, E44, E117, E160, E182, E223, E240, E269, P444, P445, P470, P726, W60, W260, W572
Texas International A1310
Texas Life Insurance Company A964
Texas Lottery Commission P**472**-P**473**, P744
Texas Micro (chips) E109
Texas Million lottery game P472
Texas Monthly (magazine) E198
Texas Motor Speedway (Fort Worth) P553
Texas Oil & Gas A1460, A1462
Texas Pacific Group A138, A314, A470, A904, A1076, A1260, E191, P64, P254, P394, P440, P**474**-P**475**, P642, P725, P744, W218
Texas Pacific Oil A1344
Texas Petrochemicals LP P745
Texas Power & Light, Inc. A1416
Texas Railroad Commission A1466
Texas Rangers Baseball Club P132, P307
Texas State Board of Insurance A74

Texas State School of Mines and Metallurgy P498
Texas Supreme Court P472
Texas Transportation Institute P471
Texas T Stores A1348
Texas Two Step lottery game P472, P473, P744
Texas Utilities. *See* TXU Corporation
Texas Utilities Mining A1416
Texas Veterinary Medical Diagnostic Laboratory P471
Texas Wholesale Grocery A1350
Texas Wildlife Damage Management Service P471
Texas-New Mexico Pipe Line A556
Texmade home furnishings A1317, P453
Texstar (petroleum producer) A1374
textbooks.com P549
Textile Paper Tube Company A1302
Textron Inc. A188, A388, A468, A644, A754, **A1380**-**A1381**, A1440
Texwood Industries (cabinets) A920
TF1. *See* (Société) Television Française-1
T.G. Lee dairy product A467
TG&Y variety stores A734
T.G.I. Friday's restaurants A296, A328, P106, P107, P108, P236, P567, W174, W638, W639
T.H. International W606
TH Lee, Putnam Capital (investments) E308
Thacker, Johanna P613
Thackwray, Ian P165
Thadani, Rames P45
Thai Airways International A1420, A1421, W518
Thai International (airline) W540
Thain, John A. A661
Thales W76, W555
Thalheimer, Richard A1274, A1275, E120, E287
Thalhimers stores A932
THALOMID drug E174
Thaman, Michael H. A1073
Thames Television W430
Thames Water plc W504
Tharp, Charles G. A291
Thatcher, Margaret W148, W152
Thaw (outdoor clothing and equipment) P410
Thawerbhoy, Nazim G. A787
Thayer Capital Partners E306
Theater High Altitude Area Defense A882, A1190
THEC Holdings E216
Thedens, Reimer W647
Theede, Steven M. A413
Theiss, Sabrina P698
theLibraryPlace.com P68
Theno, David M. A785
Theophilos, Theodore J. A567
thePit.com E130
Theraphysics Corporation A259

There Are No Children Here (movie) P219
Therezien, Laurent W171
Thermador Groupe SA (ovens and ranges) A920, W490
Thermaflex A194
Thermal Structures E67
ThermaSilk hair care W618, W619
Therma-Wave, Inc. E300
Thermco Systems W600
Thermedics A1382
Therminol heat transfer fluid A1301
Thermo Electron Corporation A**1382**-A**1383**
Thermo Fax copying machine A976
Thermo King refrigeration units A754, A755
ThermoExpress Service A485
ThermoGas A1528
ThermoScan thermometer A657
Therrien, Robert J. E35, E166
Theseus Imaging E254
Theull, Bernard P439, P724
Thewes, Thomas A406, A407
Thibault, Tom P57
Thibeault, R. J. A941
Thibodeau, Lisa A1357
Thiele, Mike A241, P75
Thielen, Gunter W127
Thielen, Joanne P765
Thieme, Carl W82, W380
Thieneman, Michael D. A1521
Thier, Samuel O. P697
Thigpen, Stephen P. E214
Thimjon, Donald H. A1513
ThinAirApps, LLC A1233
ThinPrep System diagnostic test E50, E190
Thiocal drug W492
Thiokol Propulsion (rockets) A112, A120
Thioplex drug E71
Third National Bank A592, A1332, A1346
Third Watch (TV show) A999
Thirsty Hippo home care product W477
This End Up furniture stores A458
Thistle Group Holdings, Co. E301
Thistledown (racetrack) P172
Thodey, David W587
Thom, Christopher D. A925, P323
Thom McAn shoes A458, A831
Thoma, Carl E249
Thomae, Roberto R. E201
Thoman, Richard A1544
Thomas & Betts Corporation A1482
Thomas & Howard convenience stores A994
Thomas, Arthur E. A107
Thomas Barlow & Sons W552
Thomas, Benjamin A382
Thomas Brothers (maps) P408
Thomas Builders A1227
Thomas Cook AG W310, W311, W345, W460

Thomas Cook Holdings P106, P567
Thomas, David W638, W639
Thomas, Dennis A771
Thomas, Donald E. A57
Thomas Foods A1350
Thomas, Franklin P194
Thomas, Gary L. P257, P644
Thomas, Geoffrey R. M. A171
The Thomas Guides (books) P409
Thomas H. Lee Company (LBOs) A600, A1400, E132, E306, P282, P394, P506, P554, P765
Thomas, Hue, III A1071
Thomas Industries Inc. P613
Thomas, J. Grover, Jr. P750
Thomas J. Lipton W618
Thomas, Jay P339
Thomas, John P137
Thomas, Josie A335
Thomas, Kenneth A. (Triarc) A1401
Thomas, Ken (TNT Limited) A1454
Thomas, Larry E. (Cinergy) A363
Thomas, Larry (Guitar Center) E66
Thomas, Lee M. A655
Thomas Nationwide Transport Limited A1454
Thomas, R. David "Dave" A1084, A1510, A1511
Thomas, Richard L. (Willamette Industries) A1525
Thomas, Richard P. (Ashland) A201
Thomas, Sandra A. A389
Thomas, Stephen S. A321
Thomas Weisel Partners (bank) A314, P96, W408
Thomas, William D. A597
Thomas-Davis Medical Centers A696
Thomas-Graham, Pamela A999
Thomason, Don A1535
Thomason, Joel D. P700
Thomasville Furniture Industries A194, A630, A725
Thome, Kenneth L. A649
Thompson Aircraft Products Company A1412
Thompson, Barry P470
Thompson, Charles A1412
Thompson, Clifford J. A1069
Thompson, David A1099
Thompson, Donald A943
Thompson, G. Kennedy A1487
Thompson, Gary E152
Thompson, Geoff W89
Thompson, Henry R. P389
Thompson Industries (auto parts) A780
Thompson, J. Clay A611
Thompson, James Walter W646
Thompson, Joanne P373
Thompson Joe A56
Thompson, John (7-Eleven) A56
Thompson, John (EBSCO) P171
Thompson, John E. (Salton) E116, E283
Thompson, John M. (IBM) A765

Thompson, John R. (Liz Claiborne) A881
Thompson, Jon L. (Exxon) A577
Thompson, Julian Ogilvie W92
Thompson, Kirk A789
Thompson, Kurt B. A1077
Thompson Lightstone & Company P308
Thompson, Mark W145
Thompson, Michael G. A555
Thompson, Olivia M. A79
Thompson, Peter M. A1107
Thompson Ramo Wooldridge A1412
Thompson, Richard L. (Caterpillar) A333
Thompson, Rick (International Speedway) E75
Thompson, Robert (Orford Nickel) W284
Thompson, Robert (Sharper Image) A1275, E120
Thompson, Ronald D. A117
Thompson, Rosalind A797
Thompson, Rupe A1380
Thompson, Scott E127
Thompson Shipping A1030
Thompson, Simon W93
Thompson, Susan L. E77, E220
Thompson, Terry W. E77
Thompson, Tiona M. A1169
Thompson, Tommie D. (Mutual of Omaha) P349, P680
Thompson, Tommie D. (National Railroad Passenger Corp.) P362
Thompson, Trevor W89
Thompson, Westley V. A879
Thompson, William Boyce (Newmont) A1024
Thompson, William (IGA) A744, P242
Thompson's wood products A1278
Thomsen, Mads K. W417
Thomson Advisory Group P384
Thomson, Caroline W145
Thomson, Charles W. A567
Thomson Components-Mostek W554
The Thomson Corporation A632, W122, W132, W262, W478, **W592-W593**
Thomson, Kenneth R. W270, W592, W593
Thomson McLintok (accounting) A840, P286, W324
THOMSON multimedia S.A. W76, W520
Thomson, Richard W608
Thomson, Robert E. A699
Thomson, Roger F. A289
Thomson, Roy W592
Thomson, Steven M. A411
Thomson, Todd S. A371
Thomson Travel Group W460, W461
Thomson, William A1126
Thomson-CSF W76, W182, W554

Thomson-Houston Electric A646, W554
Thon, Richard M. A191
Thonier, Jacques-Henri W367
Thope and Ricks (tobacco processor) A1436
Thorazine drug W102
Thorburn, Peter A. A767
Thorco Industries, Inc. P313
Thoreau, Henry David E34
Thormann, Karen P. A1459
Thorn Apple Valley (bacon, ham) A742, A743
Thorn Electrical Industries W212
THORN EMI W212, W622
Thorn, Jules W212
Thorn, Stuart P733
Thornburgh, Richard E. A449
Thorndike, Doran, Paine and Lewis (investments) A1468, P504
Thorne, James R. A845
Thorne Riddel (accounting) A840, P286, W324
Thorner, Peter A158
Thornley, Anthony S. A1183
Thornley, G. Thomas A365
Thornton, April L. A195
Thornton Baker (accounting) P206
Thornton, Barbara E80, E230
Thornton, Felicia D. A111
Thornton, George, Jr. A702
Thornton, Herbert M. A981
Thornton, John L. A661
Thornton stores furniture A702
Thoroughbred Technology & Telecommunications, Inc. A1038, A1039
Thoroughgood stores W300
Thorpe, Jim P356
Thourot, Patrick W105
THQ, Inc. (software) E225
Thrall Car Manufacturing A1406
Thrall Car railroad cars P598
Thrash, James P387
Thrasher, Rex C. A545
Three Cities Research, Inc. (investments) E60, E202
Three Guys stores W590
Three Mile Island nuclear plant A240, A570, A668, A1166, A1248, P74
Three Rivers (activewear) A1220, A1221
Three Rivers Stadium (Pittsburgh) P635
Three Springs Talc Pty. Ltd. W640
Three-Five Systems A1002
Thresher liquor stores W84
Thrif D Discount Center A1202
Thriffiley, Donald A., Jr. A609
Thrift Drug, Inc. A790
Thrift Market P329
Thriftimart (retailer) W166
Thriftway stores A1532, P62, P63, P488, P547
Thrifty Acres stores P328

Thrifty PayLess drug stores A886, A1202
Thriving on Chaos (book) P342
Thule Air Force Base A1114, P396
Thumb Suckers candies A1527
Thunderbird wine A520, A521, P168, P169, P600
Thunderpad game controller W339
Thunman, N. Ronald W525
Thurn und Taxis (private postal system) W202, W204
Thurston Group W196
Thus plc (telecommunications) W522, W523
THX 1138 (movie) P302
THX Group (sound systems) P302, P661
Thypin Steel A1224
Thys, Patrice J. W289
Thyssen, August W594
ThyssenKrupp AG A456, A502, A806, W566, W**594-W595**
TIAA-CREF. *See* Teachers Insurance and Annuity Association-College Retirement Equities Fund
TI-Acer chips W60
Tianjin Automobile Xiali W614
Tianjin Top Power Cables Company Ltd. W451
Tiano, Linda V. P175
Tibbetts, James D. P123
TIBCO Software W484
TIBCO Software Inc. A1546
Tibey, Stephen J. A409
Tiboni, Karen H. A1141
Ti-Brook (dump bodies and trailers) A326
TIC Holdings Inc. P745
Tice, Carolyn F. A1145
Tice, Norman J. A925, P323
Ticka alarm clock W276
Ticket Restaurant (service vouchers) W59
Ticketmaster Online-CitySearch, Inc. A142, A1450, A1451, P312, P510
Tickets.com, Inc. A442, P146
Tickle Me Elmo toy A926, P486
Tide laundry product A1164, A1165
Tidel (ATMs) A488
Tidel Technologies, Inc. E301
Tidestone Technologies E22
Tideworks Technologies P737
Tiefel, William R. A913
Tieken, Robert W. A665
Tielman, Jans W101
Tiempo tires A664
Tien, Chang-Lin P494
Tien Wah Press W186
Tiencken, John H., Jr. P732
Tierney & Partners (advertising) A773
Tierney, Jack A487
Tierney, Patrick J. W593
Ties, Mark E. E308
Tiesi, Joseph A. A1127

Tiffany & Company A216, **A1384-A1385**, W250
Tiffany, Charles Lewis A1384
Tiffany, Louis Comfort A1384, P290
TIG Holdings (underwriter) A936
Tiger beer W255
Tiger biscuits W193
Tiger Electronics A692
Tiger International A588
Tiger lines test A1373
Tiger Management A1442
Tiger shoes A1032
Tighe, Steven A. P263, P647
Tikosyn drug A1118
Tilden, Bradley D. A107
Tilevitz, Harris Z. P447
Tilex cleaning product A374, A375
Tilghman, Richard G. A1347
Tiller, Marc R. E52
Tillerson, Rex W. A577
Tillie Lewis Foods A440
Tillinghast, Nelson & Warren P480
Tillinghast-Towers Perrin P480, P481, P746
Tillman, Fred A470
Tillman, Robert L. A892, A893
Tilmant, Michel W287
Tilt brand clothing E259
Tilton, Glenn F. A1377
Tilton, Michael A1059
Tim Hortons (coffee, baked goods chain) A1510, A1511
The Timber Company A654
Timber Creek jeans A1475
Timberjack forestry equipment A468
Timberlake, Bob P298
Timberline shingles P612
TimberLine tape subsystems A1337
Timberman, Terri L. E109, E274
Timbers, Stephen B. A1043
TimberWolf automated tape library A1337
Timbre Technologies W600
Time Electronic Sales A214
Time, Inc. A180, A181, A918, A1192, A1198, A1364, P32, P530
Time (magazine) A1218, A1502, P88, P94, P256
Time Saver Stores convenience stores A844
Time Stalkers (video game) W527
Time Warner Entertainment A180
Time Warner Inc. *See* AOL Time Warner Inc.
TimeFinder software A543
TimeOut candy W155
Timeplex (networks) A1424
Timera (software) A1422, A1423
Times (London) W592
The Times Mirror Company A442, A1402, P146
Times Square (New York City) A875, E188

Times Square Tower (New York City) E34, E165, P294
Times-Picayune (New Orleans, LA) A80, A81, P32, P33
The Timken Company **A1386-A1387**
Timken, Henry A310, A1386
Timken, Henry H. A1386
Timken Roller Bearing Axle Company A198
Timken, Ward J., Jr. A1386, A1387
Timken, William R., Jr. A1386, A1387
Timken, W. Robert A1386
Timken-Detroit Axle A198
Timmerman, Jose R. A1415
Timmerman, William B. A1249
Timmins, Timothy A. E243
Timmons, Ann P576
Timmons Press (newspaper) W592
Timoptic drug A956
Timpano Italian Chophouse P106, P107
Tin Fouye Tabankort (oil field) W482
Tinactin foot care A1250
Tindal, Jack A1341
Tindle Mills feeds P37
Ting, Lewis A. A563, P183, P605, W223
Tin.it (Internet service provider) W574
Tinkerbell home care product W476, W477
Tinkertoys A693
Tinnell, Greg L. A389
Tino car W403
Tinplate Holdings, Inc. A1007
Tinseltown movie theaters P126, P575
Tioga motor homes A605
Tip Top Drugstores W312
TIPC Network A636
Tippeconnic, David W438
Tippery, Miles A1358
Tippin, Ross S., Jr. A1345
TIR Holdings A566
Tiscali (Internet service provider) W312
Tisch, Andrew H. A884, A885
Tisch Hotels A884
Tisch, James S. A884, A885
Tisch, Jonathan M. A885
Tisch, Laurence A. (CNA/Loews) A378, A379, A884, A885
Tisch, Laurence (CBS) A334
Tisch, Preston R. A885
Tisch, Robert A378, A884
Tisco. *See* Tata Iron and Steel Company
Tishman, Bob P476
Tishman, Daniel R. P477
Tishman, David P476
Tishman, John L. P476, P477, P745
Tishman, Julius P476, P745
Tishman, Norman P476

Tishman, Paul P476
Tishman Realty & Construction Company Inc. **P476-P477**, P745
Tishman Speyer Properties P476
Tissot watch W562, W563
Titan Cement Company A1484, W92
TITAN digital cross-connect system A1362, A1363
Titan Exploration E272
Titan International, Inc. (tires) A326
Titan space launch rockets A644
Titan Sports E141
Titanic: Anatomy of a Disaster (TV show) P158
Titanic (movie) A1088, P302, P661
Titanium laptop computer A186
Titanium Metals Corporation P583
Title Guaranty Company of Wyoming A594
Title Source CD with Book Data P68
Title Source II P69
TitleAmerica Insurance Corporation A863
Titleist golf balls A618
Titus, Charlie P373, P688
Titus Communications A872
Titzman, Donna M. A1467
TiVo Inc. (TV technologies) A999, P511
Tivoli (computer networks) A764
Tivoli Gardens amusement park. *See* (A/S) Kjøbenhavns Sommer-Tivoli
Tizzio, Thomas R. A151
T.J. Cinnamons fast food A1400
TJ International A1518
T.J. Maxx stores A262, A1388, A1389
T. J. Morris (grocery wholesalers) A994
The TJX Companies, Inc. A158, A262, **A1388-A1389**
T.K. Maxx stores A1388, A1389
TKR Cable A832
TKS Basics brand A1265
T.L. Smith Machine A1406
TLC Beatrice W166
TM Claims Service, Inc. (insurance) W597
TM Group (vending machines) W240
TMB Industries A278
TMBR/Sharp Drilling, Inc. E129, E301
TMI. *See* Three Mile Island nuclear plant
TMNG.com E236
T-Mobile International AG (wireless telecom) W204, W205
TMT (test equipment maker) E46
TNKase drug A640, A641
TNN: The National Network A334, E319
TNT cable network A180, A181

TNT Limited (transportation) A102, A1454
TNT Post Group A454, W318, W502
To Care: A Portrait of Three Older Caregivers (educational video) P139
T.O. Haas Tire Company stores P628
Toan, Barrett A. A575
Toast software E281
Toastmaster appliances A934, E116
Tobacco Shoppe P634
Tobaccor W282
Tobata Casting W402
Tobias, Stephen C. A1039
Tobin, Daniel P246
Tobin, James R. A283
Tobin, Robert G. W499
Tobison, Gary L. A619
Toblerone chocolates A843
Tocco, Nick P722
Toda, Hiroshi W409
Toda, Masao W561
TODAY (newspaper) A632
Today (TV show) PP:590
Today's Man clothing stores A690
Todd AO. *See* Liberty Livewire
Todd Oldham clothing A804, A805
Todd, Robert K. P756
Todd, Troy W. A539
Toddy chocolate beverages A1181
ToddYnho chocolate beverages A1181
Todenhöfer, Tilman W491
Todisco, Franco A1075
Todman, Michael A. A1521
Todorov, Pierre W59
Toepel, Paul P633
Tofas (auto sales) W318
Tofel, Richard J. A507
Tofo Iron Mines A256
Toftgaard, Stig W333
Togashi, Isao W139
Togneri, Gabriel B. A1121
Togni, Alberto W617
Tognino, John N. A997, P353
Togo's Eateries W84, W85
Tohato (cookies) P130
Toho Mutual Life Insurance Company A646
Tokai Bank W374
Tokai Iron & Steel W398
Tokarz, Michael T. A837, P283
The Tokio Marine and Fire Insurance Company, Limited A348, W371, **W596-W597**
Tokunaka, Teruhisa W551
Tokuyama, Goro A983
Tokuyama Soda W404
Tokyo Broadcasting System W600
Tokyo Denkikagaku Kofyo K.K. *See* TDK Corporation
Tokyo Densetsu Services Company, Ltd. W599
Tokyo Disneyland W398
Tokyo Disney Resort A1496

Tokyo Electric Company W610
The Tokyo Electric Power Company, Inc. W400, W548, **W598-W599**
Tokyo Electron Limited **W600-W601**
Tokyo Exchange W396
Tokyo Gas and Electric Industrial W294
Tokyo Ishikawajima Shipbuilding and Engineering W294
Tokyo Motors, Inc. W294
Tokyo Sagawa Kyubin (parcel delivery) W96
Tokyo SANYO Electric W514
Tokyo Shibaura Electric Company. *See* Toshiba Corporation
Tokyo Stock Exchange W548, W572, W598
Tokyo Telecommunication Network Company W400, W598, W599
Tokyo Telecommunications Engineering W550
Toledo car W631
The Toledo Edison Company A598, A599
Toledo Trans-Kit A1320
Tolleson, Stephanie P251
Tollett, Leland A1418
Tolley (publisher) W478
Tollgrade Communications, Inc. E302
Tolliver, Mark E. A1343
Tolstyak beer W289
Tom & Co. stores W194, W195
Tom Brown, Inc. **E129**, E302
Tom Cobleigh pubs W472
Tom James Company A690
Tom Thumb Food Stores A845, P478
Toma beverage A1104, A1105
Toman W522
Tomasch, Mark R. A897
Tomasek, Ted P589
Tomasetta, Louis R. E136, E313
Tombstone pizza A843
Tome, Carol B. A725
TOMEN Corporation E194, **W602-W603**
Tomioka, Itsuki W419
Tomislav Pivo beer W289
Tomjack, Thomas J. P690
Tomkins, Mark E. A1485
Tomkins PLC A286, **W604-W605**
Tomlin, C. T. A985
Tomlinson, Lawrence J. A713
Tommy Armour Golf A1446
Tommy Bahama furniture P299
tommy girl fragrance A564
Tommy Hilfiger Corporation A564, A565, A666, A690, A691, A805, **W606-W607**
Tomnitz, Donald J. A508, A509
Tomoff, Donald A797
Tompkins Country Trustco, Inc. E302
Tompkins, Roger A1331, P459
Tompson, Graham A389

Tomsett, Peter W453
Tomsich, Robert J. P686
OOO Tomsktransgaz W243
Tom-Tracks computerized textbook system P192
Tona a.s. Pecky (tools) A1322
Tonami Transportation A102
Tone soap A486, A487
Toner, Michael W. A645
Tong, Chris E235
Tong, Lim Goh P318
Toni home permanents A656
Tonight Show with Jay Leno (TV show) A999
Tonka toys A692, A693, E60
T-Online International AG W106, W204, W205
Tonnesen, Mark K. W475
Tonomura, Naohisa W371
Tony's pizza P436, P437, P724
Too, Inc. (clothing) A876
Toohey, James F. E124
Tooker, Jeanie P455, P734
Tookes, Hansel E. II A1191
Tooley & Company, Inc. A1399
Tools of the Trade clothing A587
Toomey, Gerri P549
Toon Disney cable network A60, A61
Toopes, James A., Jr. P554
Top Care brands P478, P479
Top Crest brands P478, P479, P746
Top Dollar stores A578
Top Fin pet supplies A1117
Top, Franklin H., Jr. E90
Top Frost Foods P478, P479
Top (magazine) P347
Top Paw pet supplies A1117
Top Tier Software W516
Top Wing pet supplies A1117
Topa Equities, Ltd. P746
Topamax drug A801
Topaz software E91
Topco Associates, Inc. P198, **P478-P479**, P746
Topfer, Morton L. A473
Topic text retrieval program E134
TOPICORT drug E89
topjobs.net W262
Topol, Sidney A1258
Topp Telecom (prepaid phone service) W580
Toppan Printing A210, W186, W378
Toppen, Timothy R. A665
Toppeta, William J. A965
The Topps Company, Inc. **E130**, E303
Tops stores W498, W499
Topsy's Drive-In restaurant A784
Tora! Tora! Tora! (movie) A622
Torbensen Gear and Axle Company A526
Torbensen, Viggio A526
Torbert, Ellen A1311
Torchmark Corporation **A1390-A1391**
Tordoir, P. P. W627

Torfeaco (bedding) A1134
Torgerson, Katherine P. E102, E263
Torii Pharmaceutical W304
Toriumi, Iwao W358, W359
Tormey, Mark F. A289
The Toro Company A**1392**-A**1393**
Toro, Rafael P205
Toronto Argonauts (football team) W288
Toronto Blue Jays Baseball Club P307, W288, W494, W495
Toronto Maple Leafs Hockey Club A1510, P361
Toronto Raptors Basketball Club P354, P355
Toronto Sun (newspaper) W471
Toronto Sun Publishing W494
The Toronto-Dominion Bank W86, W156, W**608**-W**609**
Torpedo Joe clothing stores A634
Torrence, Samuel L. A1517
Torrents, Marcel W521
Torres, Gregory T. A905
Torrey Homes A509
Torrington (bearings) A754, A755, A1386
Torsone, Johnna G. A1143
Tortelli, Ronald C. A1349
Tortolano, J. Vincent E92
Tortora, Leslie M. A661
Torvund, Tore W411
Tory, John H. W495
Tosaka, Kaoru W387
Tosca, Paolo W423
Toscana bread A774, A775
Toscani, Oliviero W124
Toscano, August B. A1533
Tosco Corporation A576, A1128, A1276, A1344
Toshiba Corporation A162, A170, A782, A1002, A1357, E73, E117, E134, P136, P137, P545, P662, W158, W186, W190, W191, W210, W296, W386, W420, W422, W570, W**610**-W**611**
Toss 'N Soft fabric softener A358
Tostitos snacks A1107
Total cereal A648, A649
TOTAL FINA ELF S.A. W76, W546, W**612**-W**613**
Total Football (magazine) W238, W239
Total Guitar (magazine) W238, W239
Total Health Plan P751
Total HOMEstores A724
Total Petroleum W612
TOTAL-AUSTRIA (gas stations) W424
Totally 4 Kids stores A304, A305
TotalMRO.com A1538
Tote'm Stores A56
Totes (umbrellas and rainwear) A1242
Toth, David J. E251, W627
Toth, Michele P539
Toth, Paul P59

Toth, Robert (Avon) A217
Toth, Robert B. (Solutia) A1301
Toth, Roger W229
Toth, Stephen J. E111, E277
Totino's frozen pizza A1136, A1137
Tott's champagne A521, P169
Touch of Class bedding and towels A1134
A Touch of Frost (TV show) W249
Touche Ross A474, P154, W196
Touched by an Angel (TV show) A334
Touchstone Television A61
Touchstone/Hollywood Pictures A1496, A1497
Tough, Doug W155
Touraine, Agnès W625
Tourangeau, Kevin W. A409
TourBook guides P528
Touristik Union International W460
Toussaint Ribot, Javier W583
Towe, Dave P411
Towe, Larry J. A559
Tower Asset Management P384
Tower Automotive, Inc. A**1394**-A**1395**
Tower Cut Rate Drug Store P346
Tower Electronics E24
Tower, Francis A1394
Tower Group International (consulting) A588, A944
Tower, Michael J. A1265
Tower, Ray A1394
Tower Records P346, P347, P639, P680
Tower, Samuel A1394
Tower Semiconductor Ltd. E57
Towers Bonimart discount stores W270
Towers, John (Phoenix Consortium) W120
Towers, John R. (United Technologies) A1333
Towers, John (Towers Perrin) P480
Towers of America apartments (New Jersey) P291
Towers Perrin P**480**-P**481**, P746
Towers, Perrin, Forster & Crosby P480
Towey, Gael A919
Town & Country (magazine) A701, P229
Town & Country Supply P406
Town House crackers A815
Town Star convenience stores P740
Townley Dyestuffs Auxiliaries Company A450
Townsend, Charles H. P33
Townsend, David E. A1205
Townsend, Elihu A986
Townsend, Helen P177
Townsend, Richard J. A889
Townsend, Robert A212
Townsend, Thomas E61
Townsent & Kent (brokerage) P698
Townsley, Theresa A77
Townson, Brian P714

Toxic Clean up Systems E79
Toy Liquidators stores A260
Toy Story 2 (movie) E103, E266
Toy Story (movie and products) E103, E266, P188, P189, P608
Toya, Hiromichi W81
Toyne, J. Bret P680
Toyo Advanced Technologies Company, Ltd. W363
Toyo Cork Kogyo W362
Toyo Cotton Company W603
Toyo Engineering Works, Ltd. W371
Toyo Kogyo W362
Toyo Menka Kaisha W602
Toyo Trust and Banking W374
Toyoda Automatic Loom Works W614
Toyoda, Eiji P366
Toyoda, Kiichiro W614
Toyoda, Sakichi W602, W614
Toyoda, Shoichiro W614, W615
Toyoda, Y. P367, P687
Toyoda, Yoshiya W359
Toyopet Crown car W614
Toyota Motor Corporation A476, A572, A650, A710, A1222, A1294, A1394, P256, P366, P561, P563, P606, P624, P631, P644, P647, P656, P687, P706, P717, P733, W264, W294, W362, W402, W442, W602, W**614**-W**615**
Toyota of Orange (California) P589
Toyota Tsusho America A1222
Toys "R" Us, Inc. A130, A260, A692, A926, A1254, A**1396**-A**1397**, E225, P394, P486, P649
Toys Unlimited stores A260
toysrus.com A1396
TP2 tool performance tracking software P444
TPC Holdings P745
TPC (natural gas marketer) A1082
TPC (utility) A1034
TPG. *See* Texas Pacific Group (investments)
TPI Restaurants A1280
TPN (direct marketing) E107
TPS "La Télévision par Satellite" W559
TQ3 Travel Solutions P308, P664
T/R Systems, Inc. E303
Trac II razor A657
Trachsel, William H. A1433
Trachtenberg, Lawrence E246
Tracinda Corporation (investments) A962, P747
Tracker Marine (boats) A298, P550
TrackMan computer trackball W338, W339
Trackmobile, Inc. P313
Tracor (defense electronics) W110, W354
Tracor Holdings A222
Tractebel s.a. (utility) A624, W558, W559
Tracy, Dorothy P596

Tracy, Michael P455
Tracy, Patrick F. P596
Tracy, Robert P596
Tracy, Steven M. P351
Tradax (grain trading) A324, P104
Trade Mart (Dallas) A1398
Trade Plus (electronic brokerage) A566
Trade Secret hair salons A1196
Tradebook P80
Trademark Home Builders A812
Trader Joe's Company A110, P747
Trader Publishing A443, P147, W620
Traders Credit Bank W384
Tradigrain SA A582, A583, P184, P185
Trafalgar House W306
Traffic Alert and Collision Avoidance System A846
Traffic (broadcasting) A715, P233
Traffic (movie) A1450
traffic.com A701, P229
Trafic vehicle W480, W481
Traf-O-Data P510
Tragos, Bill A1062
Trahar, A. J. W93
Trail King Industries (low-bed trailers) A326
Traill, Gary W89
Trainer, Thomas A371
Traison, Harvey S. E230
Tramadol HCR drug P707
Tramier, Bernard W613
Trammell Crow Company A1398-A1399
Trammell Crow Residential P120, P747
Trammo Gas P748
Trammochem P748
Tran, Khanh T. P385, P695
Trane (HVAC) A152, A153, A1550
Trani, John M. A1323
Tranquilidade (insurance) W224
Trans Advantage (truck leasing) P753
Trans Pacific Insurance Company W597
Trans Union LLC (consumer credit reports) A558, P312, P313
Trans World Airlines, Inc. *See* TWA Airlines LLC
Trans World Airlines, Inc. P388
Trans World International (TV productions) P60, P250, P251, P641
Trans9 brand clothing E259
Transac (computers) W150
TransAlta A1082, A1464
Transamerica Corporation A300, A594, A734, A1520, W64, W65
TransAmerican Waste Industries A1504
Transammonia, Inc. P748
TransArt (CD ROMs) W186
Trans-Austria Gas Pipeline W424
Transavia Airlines bv W316, W317

Transax (check warranty) A558
TransCanada PipeLines A504, A1030, E298
Transcisco Industries (rail car service) A1406
Transcontinental Gas Pipe Line Corporation A1528, A1529
Transcontinental Insurance Company A379
Transcontinental Lease S.A. de C.V. A1207
Transcontinental Realty Investors, Inc. E219, E303
Transeco (motor carrier) A344
Transentric (software) A1422, A1423
TransEuropa-Reisen W310
Transflo Corporation A454, A455
Transformers toys A692, A693
Transkaryotic Therapies, Inc. A160
Transmedia Network Inc. A561, P181
Transmeta Corporation (microprocessors) P511
Transmisiones y Equipos Mecanicos A278
Transmission Pipelines (natural gas) A668
Transmould fire detection systems A431
Transocean Sedco Forex Inc. A1252
Trans-o-flex Schnell-Lieferdienst GmbH W203
Transplace.com (online trucking logistics) A788
Transport and Accident Insurance plc Zurich W652
TransPort computer notebooks A762
Transport of New Jersey A1174
Transportación Marítima Mexicana A788
Companhia Transportadora e Comercial Translor (logistics) A1222
Transportation Insurance Company A379
Transportes CF Alfi-Loder, S. de R.L. de C.V. A421
Transtar, Inc. A1462, A1463
TransTechnology Corporation A526
Transwestern Pipeline A552
Transwire (high speed network) A392
TranSwitch Corporation E304
TransWorks (information technology) A1039
Trans-World Financial Company A658
Transworld Services A86
TRANSYS Networks A1362
Tranter, Gregory D. A125
Tranzact Systems (freight payment) P434
Trapp, George J. A1017, P371
Trappler, Claire E301
Tras-Austria-Gasleitung Gesellschaft m.b.H. W425
Trasgo (poultry producer) A1418

Trask, Craig K. E72
Trask, Tallman, III P598
Traut, Christopher P192, P193, P610
Traut, Richard P192
Trautman & Shreve A545
Travel Agents International A328, P107, P108
Travel Channel P158, P159, P594
Travel Counselors International P308
Travel Information Group W478
Travel Inn W638, W639
Travel Services, Inc. A719
Travel Services of America P727
Traveland A328, P108
TravelCenters of America, Inc. P748
Traveler (magazine) P359
Travelers Cheque Group A142
Travelers Express Company (money orders) A1478, A1479
The Travelers Group Inc. A142, A370, A1434, E131
Travelers Research Center. *See* TRC Companies, Inc.
Traveler's Service P308
Traveller's Fare W174
travelnow.com E215
Travelocity.com Inc. A1228, A1229, W426
Travelodge Hotels Inc. A339, W174
Travelution (discount airline tickets) P419
Travenol Laboratories A236
Traver, Jerry E70
Traver Technologies A204
Travers, Greg W641
Traversi, Alfred A. A871
Travis County Title Company A509
Travis, Nigel A267
Travis, Tracey Thomas A777
Trayco bath and shower A921
Traylor, Linda G. A87
TRC Companies, Inc. E131, E304
Treadco (tire service centers) A664
Treadway, Gregg A497
Treanor, Mark C. A1487
Treasure Chest Advertising P404, P506
Treasure House stores A968
Treasure Island (hotel and casino) A966, A967
Treasury Bank A438
Treats shoes A295
Treaty of Utrecht W270
Trebacz, Kazimierz W457
Trebel, John M. A619
Trebor candy W154
Tréca, Laurent W131
Tree of Life products A679, P217
Treetop Enterprises P512
Treff, Donald J. A481
Tréfileurope W292
Trego, Charles R. P714
Trelleborg (hydraulic hoses) A1088
Tremec (transmissions) A460

Trench cleaning and laundry products A487
Trend Micro Inc. (software) W548
Trendwest Resorts, Inc. E304
Trent aircraft engines W496
Trepani, Joseph B. A1357
Trepp, Steven A1451
Treschow, Michael W210, W211, W220
TRESemme hair care A108
Tresierras Brothers Corporation P489
Trethewey, Virginia P383
Tretvoll, Bjørn Håkon W411
Trevathan, James E., Jr. A1505
Trevira polyester unit A834, P280
Trex Company, Inc. E305
Tri Valley Growers A452, A470
Triad Hospitals A694
Triangle Environmental E131
Triangle Pacific Corporation A194
Triangle Publications W390
Triarc Companies, Inc. A1180, **A1400-A1401**, W154
TRIAZ drug E89, E240
Tribone, Thomas A. A89
Triborough Bridge and Tunnel Authority P335
Tribune Company A832, **A1402-A1403**, P176
Tribune Education A944
Tricamo, Frank P63, P547
TRICARE (government health care contracts) A696, A738, P52
Trice, David A. E253
Trico Industries (oil drilling) A1078
Trico Ltd. (wiper blades) W605
Trico Steel Company A896
Tricoach (bus manufacturer) A1078
Tricom (acquisitions) E318
TRICON Global Restaurants, Inc. A302, A500, A1106, **A1404-A1405**, P124, P162, P236, P575, P595
Tricor drug A59
Trident ballistic missile submarine A644
Trident Fund A916
Trident International (ink jet printers) A748
Trident missiles A882
Trident NGL (natural gas liquids) A518
Trident Seafoods A1418
Trifari jewelry A881
Trigano, Gilbert W170
Trigano, Serge W170
Trigen Energy Corporation W558
Trigon Industries (packaging) A1262
Trilectron Industries (ground support equipment) A748, E67
Trilegiant Corporation A338, A339
Trill pet food A915, P315
Trimark Communities A509
Trimark Financial W608

TriMark Technologies (software) A1098
Trimble Navigation (global positioning systems) A1298, W448
Trimboli, Marie E166
TriMedia Technologies W444
Trinec (steel mill) A396
Trinidad-Tesoro Petroleum A1374
Trinitech Systems. See NYFIX, Inc.
Trinitron colorTV tube W550
Trinity Care P753
Trinity Church (New York City) P134
Trinity College of Art and Sciences P598
Trinity Contractors A548
Trinity Health P748
Trinity Industries, Inc. **A1406-A1407**, P598
Tri-Pac brand A527
TriPath Imaging, Inc. E50
Tripifoods, Inc. P243
Triple Crown (horse races) A828
Triple Crown Services Company A1038, A1039
TripMaker (software) P408, P711
Tripp, Kevin H. A111
Trippett, Lillian M. A883
TriQuint Semiconductor, Inc. E305
Triscuit crackers A843
TriStar airplane W496
TriStar Data Systems and Office Automation A400
TriStar Pictures W551
TRISTAR stent A674
Tri-Star Transportation (trucking) A1454
Tri-State Refining A200
Tritel E299
Trites, Dennis L. P101
Triton Energy Limited A132, A714, P232
Triton PCS E318
Triton Systems (ATMs) A502
Triton TBS P123
Triton Tire & Battery A583
Triumph Packaging P618
Triumph-Adler (office products) W422
Trivisonno, Nicholas L. A66
Trix cereal A649
Trofholz, Donald P213
Trojan condoms A358
Trojans of the University of Southern California P760
Troll Book Fairs Inc. A1254
Tronchetti Provera, Marco W451
Trooper SUV W294, W295
Trophy boats A298, A299
Tropical beer W553
Tropical Shipping A1031
Tropical Sportswear Int'l Corporation E305
Tropicana Products, Inc. (juice) A382, A494, A1105, A1106, P380, W314, W315

Trosino, Vincent J. A1331, P459
Trout, Deborah A905
Trout, Monroe E. E50
Trovan drug A1118
Trowbridge, Warren K. E105
Troxel, Douglas E286
Troy-Bilt tillers P679
Trubeck, William L. A1505
Truckline A460
Truck-Lite P390, P391
TruckMail (data messaging) A1183
TruckPro brand A208, A209
Trucksess, Herbert A., III A1549
Trudel, Arthur F., Jr. E158
Trudell, Cynthia M. A299
True cigarettes A884
True, Douglas K. P757
True News tabloid A1160
True North Communications A772, W466, W646
True Temper Hardware A264
True Temper Sports A264
True Temper tools A1447
True Value hardware A64, A1410, P30, P212, P484, P485, P749
Trueb, Martin R. A693
Trueheart, James L. A499
Truesdale, Anthony N. A1117
TrueSpeech software E194
Truess, Jim P622
Trueste fragrance A1385
Truett's Grill P124
TruGreen ChemLawn A1272, A1273
Truitt, Gary R. A717, P235
Truman Arnold Companies P749
Truman Hanburg (brewer) W206
Trumble, Casey J. A879
Trumbull, R. Scott A1075
Trumka, Richard L. P35, P532
Trump, Donald J. A164, A1086, A1408, A1409, E150, P230, P372, P482, P483, P629, P749
Trump, Ivana P482
The Trump Organization A1086, **A1408-A1409**, **P482-P483**, P749
Trump Shuttle A1442
Trupo, Mary P419
Trus Joist MacMillan A1518
TruServ Corporation A64, **A1410-A1411**, P30, **P484-P485**, P529, P562, P594, P749
Trusheim, H. Edwin E111
Truslow, Donald K. A1487
Trusopt drug A957
Trussler, Gary J. A619
Trust Betrayed: Inside the AARP (book) P28
Trust Company of Georgia A1346
The Trust Company of Montreal W113
The Trust Company of Washington A954
Trust, Martin A877
Trustco Capital Management, Inc. A1347

Trustees of the California State University. *See* (Trustees of the) California State University
Trustmark Insurance Company P750
Tru-Tec Services, Inc. A835, P281
Tru-Test paint A1410
TRW Inc. A278, A476, A558, A584, A780, A**1412**-A**1413**, E240, E247, E280, P152, P386, W236, W442
Trylon Corporation (metal stampings) A1394
T. S. Ragsdale (tobacco trader) A492
Tsacalis, William A. A355
Tsagarakis, N. W385
Tsai, Gerry A614, P190
Tsang, David E98
Tschira, Klaus W516
Tse, Edmund S. W. A151
TSI. *See* Tropical Sportswear Int'l Corporation
Tsingtao Brewery Company Ltd. A422, A423, W553
TSMC-Acer Semiconductor Manufacturing W60
Tsogo Sun A966
TSR Paging A1360
Tsubame car W403
Tsuboshima, Masami W305
Tsubu-Tsubu Yasai Ketchup W315
Tsuchida, Susumu W405
Tsuda, Shiro W419
Tsui, Cyrus Y. E82, E232
Tsuji, Akio W395
Tsuji, Haruo W532
Tsuji, Tohru W359
Tsujimura, Kiyoyuki W419
Tsukiyama, Muneyuki W599
Tsula Westa Hehi A1128
Tsunami systems E316
Tsuneishi, Tetsuo W601
Tsunoda, Yuji A1327
Tsuru car W403
Tsuruta, Kuniaki A429
Tsutsui, Akira W561
TSX Corporation A176
TTC Illinois, Inc. P750
TTI, Inc. P750
TTM Technologies, Inc. E306
TTNet Internet access W598
TTR Logistics A1222, A1223
TTX Company P751
Tu, John P272, P273, P651
Tuaca liqueur W85
Tubi Speciali Auto (air conditioning hoses) P310
Tuborg beer W162, W163
Tuborgs Fabrikker W162
Tuboscope A222
Tucci, Joseph M. A542, A543
Tuccillo, Dan A925, P323
Tuchman, Kenneth D. E127, E300
Tucker, Albert P120
Tucker Anthony Sutro E**132**, E306, W474
Tucker, James F. (Michaels Stores) A969

Tucker, Jim (NIKE) A1033
Tucker, John A1550
Tucker, Keith A. E315
Tucker, Lynch, & Coldwell P120
Tucker, Mark W465
Tucker Mechanical A544
Tucker, Michael J. A237
Tucker Rocky Distributing P656
Tucker: The Man and His Dream (movie) P303
Tucker, Todd E47
Tuckman, Glenn A1329
Tuckman, Mitchell E68
Tuckson, Reed V. A1435
Tucson (Arizona) *Citizen* A633
Tuesdays with Morrie (movie) P218, P219, P625
Tufano, Paul J. A929
Tüfekçioglu, Nevzat W319
Tufted Sample A1004
Tufts Associated Health Plans, Inc. P751
Tufts University P566
TUI Business Travel P308, P664
TUI Group GmbH (travel) W460, W461
Tulin, Stanley B. A219
Tull, Michael J. A891
Tully, David E85
Tully, Herbert B. P772
Tultex A1220
Tummins, Debra A271
Tundra SUV W615
Tunes lozenges A915, P315
Tung, Benson W571
Tung, Mary W273
Tunney, Francis R., Jr. A119
Tupper, Earl A1414
Tupperware Corporation A**1414**-A**1415**
Turbine Kinetics E67
Turbo Groomer Hair Trimmer E287
Turbo Sabre A1229
TurboGuard compressorless purge system A1550
TurboLinux W514
Turbotrains watercraft W133
Turcotte, Martine W123
Turcq, Dominique A911
Turfway Park racetrack A685
Türk Demir Döküm (radiators) W318
Türk Pirelli Lastikleri A.S. W451
Turkay (matches) W318
Turkey Hill Minit Markets A845
Turkey Point nuclear plant A624
Turkey Shop products A730
The Turkey Store A731
Turkish Petroleum Company W612
Turkpetrol petroleum products A412
Turley, James A563, P183, W223
Turley, Keith A1138
Turley, Robert P393
Turmes, Joe A1341
Turnbull, Andrew B. A672, P210
Turnbull, D. M. W565

Turnbull, G. Keith A113
Turner, Bill O. A709
Turner Broadcasting System, Inc. A180, A872, E141, E319
Turner, Bruce A997
Turner, Cal A496
Turner, Cal, Jr. A496, A497
Turner, Charles H. A1131
Turner, Clyde A906
Turner, Elizabeth M. A1317
Turner Entertainment Company P417
Turner Foods A624, A828, P270
Turner, Fred L. A943
Turner Home Entertainment P188
Turner, Jana L. P121
Turner, Jim L. (Dr Pepper/Seven Up) P597
Turner, Jim (media consultant) A1334
Turner, J. L. A496
Turner, John D. A897
Turner, Joseph L., Jr. A1035
Turner, Kevin A1495
Turner, Kit A907
Turner, LeBaron P772
Turner, M. Caroline A79
Turner, Marta Jones A609
Turner, Mike W111
Turner, Richard G. (Allied Domecq) W85
Turner, Richard T. (Rolls-Royce) W497
Turner Road Vintners A422
Turner, Robert Edward "Ted", III (Turner Broadcasting) A180, A181, A884, A962, P747
Turner, Robert W. (Union Pacific) A1423
Turner, Roger P513
Turner, Ronald J. (TC Pipelines) E298
Turner, Ronald L. (Ceridian) A342, A343
Turner, Russell D. P754
Turner Sports P682
Turner, Steve A496
Turner, T. J. P513, P767
Turner, Ted. *See* Turner, Robert Edward "Ted", III
Turney, Sharen Jester A777
Turning Leaf wines A520, A521, P168, P169, P600
Turnkey Services E125
Turnstone (business services) A1334
Turnstone office furniture A1334, A1335
Turpin, John E. A755
Turquands Barton Mayhew (accounting) A562, P182
Turrell, Michael W476
Tursi, Carl T. A133
Tursy, Tony P737
The Tuscaloosa (Alabama) *News* A1021
Tuscarora Gas Transmission E298
Tuttle, Allan W251

Tuttle Decision Systems A626
Tuxedo Fruit P464
Tuxedo software E33, E163
Tuzcu, Ertugrul A1353
Tuzel, Tulin A303
TV Asahi W96, W97
TV Food Network A1402
TV Guide (publication) A1218, P144, W390
TV Phone Call Center System W602
TV Times (magazine) W478
TVA. *See* Tennessee Valley Authority
Tvilum-Scanbirk (furniture) A920
TVK (chemicals) W242
TW Holdings A86
TW Recreational Services A86
TWA Airlines LLC A86, A164, A222, A478, A1046, A1442, W78
Tweddell, Edward D. W429
Tweedie, John H. A965
Tweedy, Browne E149
Tweefontein (coal) W340
Tweeter, etc. stores E306
Tweeter Home Entertainment Group, Inc. E306
Twentieth Century Fox A622, A623, P417, W390
Twentieth Century (plumbing supplies) A618
Twentsche Bank W56
Twesme, James W. A1361
Twin Bridges Marriott Hotel A912, A1296
Twin Fair stores P328
Twin Valu supercenters A1348
Twinem, Carita R. A287
Twiner, Donald H. A769
Twingo car W480, W481
Twinkies snacks A774, A775
Twix candy A914, A915, P314, P315, P665
Twizzlers candy A709
Two Guys stores E137
Two Trees Inn P318, P319
Twohy Brothers A1078
Twombly, Jay B. A1321
Twomey, Kevin M. (St. Joe Company) E115, E282
Twomey, Kevin (Rite-Aid) A1203
TWR (race cars) W124
Tx Traction shoes A295
TXU Corporation A1082, A**1416**-A**1417**, W208
Ty Inc. P**486**-P**487**, P751
Tyc, Jaroslaw Teofil W457
Tyco International Ltd. A152, A442, A444, A642, A792, A866, A898, A982, E124, E203, P146, W578
Tyco Toys A926, A927, W332
Tye farm equipment A96, A97
Tylenol over-the-counter drug A800, A801
Tyler, Lisa M. E251
Tyler Refrigeration A152
Tyler, Robert A549
Tyler Rubber Company P142
Tyler, W. Ed W378

Tylka, Patrick M. A1259
Tyndall, Gene R. A1223
Tyner, Kay E268
Tyner, Richard T. A941
Tynes, Donald P762
Tyne-Tees Television W249
Tyre, Robert A. A503
TyreMaster tires W367
Tyrolean Airways A1421
Tysdal, Craig S. E252
Tyskie beer W553
Tyson, Don A1418, A1419
Tyson Foods, Inc. A742, A1132, A1350, A**1418**-A**1419**, P200, P616
Tyson, John A1418
Tyson, John H. A1418, A1419
Tytus, John A104
Tyumen Oil Company W136
OOO Tyumentransgaz W243
Tywoniuk, Gerald A. E237
Tzagournis, Manuel P383
Tzannes, Michael A. E161
Tzoulis, A. W385

U

U S WEST, Inc. A1186, A1472
U S West Media A180, A312
U-2 spy plane A882
UA Film A962
UA-Columbia Cablevision W494
UAL Corporation A106, A164, A272, A428, A478, A1046, A1420, A**1420**-A**1421**, A1432, A1442, E64, E206, P94, P630, W68, W71, W80, W140, W258, W316, W344, W518, W540
UAP Inc. (auto parts) A652, A653
UAP (magazines) W620
UAW. *See* United Auto Workers
UB40 (music group) W213
Ubertino, Kenneth W. A725
UBS AG A226, A1112, W184, W364, W472, W**616**-W**617**
UBS PaineWebber Inc. A394, A960, P290
UBS Warburg A566
UC Industries A1072
UCAL Fuel Systems Ltd. A550
UCC-Communications Systems A686
UCCEL A402
Uchida, Kinya W159
Uchida, Saburo W158
UCLA. *See* University of California Los Angeles
Uda, Yoshinori W419
Udasin, Seth L. E177
UDI (company) W602
Udow, Marianne P87
Ueberroth, Heidi P355
Ueberroth, Peter A328, P108, P278
Ueno, Akitoshi W405
Ueno, Haruo W361
Ueno, Riichi W96
Ueno, Shoji W597
Uesaka, Yoshio W615
Ueshima, Seisuke W648

Ueshima, Shigeji W373
UFA (TV and film production) W126
UFJ Holdings W374
Ugeux, Georges A1019, P375
UGI Corporation (propane distributor) A654
Ugine-Kuhlman (chemicals) W432
Ugol, Marc L. A1363
U-Haul International, Inc. A134, A135, A300
UHC. *See* United HealthCare
Uhde (chemical plant builder) W594
UICI (insurance) E113, E280
Uihlein, Walter R. A619
UIS, Inc. P752
UJC of North America P752
Ujiie, Junichi W408, W409
UK Department of Trade and Industry W288
UK Monopolies Commission W114
UK National Health Service W246
UK National Lottery W154, W622
UK Office of Telecommunications W148
Ukrop's Super Markets, Inc. P479
UKTV news channel W144
Ullman, Myron, III P156, W349
Ullrich Copper A620
Ullstein (publishing) W107
Ulm, James P., II E268
Ulma (automotive trim) A780
Ulmann, Herbert A916
Ulrich, Rachel E204
Ulrich, Robert J. A1352, A1353
Ulsamer, James S. P69
Ulster Bank Investment Services A1042
Ulti Mate A982
Ulticom, Inc. E307
Ultima II cosmetics A1200, A1201
Ultimate Outlet stores A1315
Ultra Brite toothpaste A386
Ultra Food & Drug stores A670, A671
Ultra Mart stores P422
Ultra Petroleum Corporation E307
Ultra Plus A1415
Ultra Service Centers A1344
Ultra Spark brand A209
Ultra Wood Company W556
UltraCare ophthalmic products A119
UltraLeather A1316, P452
Ultra-Light Arms P132
Ultramar Diamond Shamrock A1128, A1344, A1466, W612
Ultrapointe (laser imaging) A792
UltraRF E47, E123
UltraSource (order management) A911
UltraSuede P452
Ultress hair care A1164
Ultrex fabrics A307
Ultronic Systems Corporation W484

Ulvac Cryogenics E213
Umansky, David J. P451
UMass. *See* University of
  Massachusetts
UMC (company) W503
Umemura, Masahiro
  (Kyocera) W329
Umemura, M. (Yamaha) W649
Umeno, Minoru W305
Umpqua Holdings
  Corporation E307
UMS Generali Marine S.p.A. W99
UMT (feed milling) W568
UNA (power generation) A1198
Unanue & Sons P204
Unanue, Andy P205
Unanue, Anthony P204
Unanue, Charles P204
Unanue, Ernesto R. A489
Unanue, Francisco J. P204, P205
Unanue, Joseph A. P204, P205,
  P619
Unanue, Prudencio P204
Uncle Ben's Rice A914, A915, P314,
  P315, P665
Undeclared (TV show) P166, P167,
  P597
Underhill, David L. A1403
Underware (software) A406
Underwood family P777
Underwood, John R. A673, P211
Underwood meat spreads A1136
Underwood Trucking A1454
Underwood (typewriters) W422
Une, Hitoshi A93
UNext (online training) P278, P279,
  P496
Unfried, Charles O. A491
Unhjem, Michael B. A268, P83
UNIASS S.p.A. W99
Unic stores W165
UNICARE Life & Health Insurance
  Company A1506, A1507
UNICEF E289, P79
Unicenter software A402
Unicer-Uniao Cervejeira
  (brewery) W162
Unicom Corporation A532, A570
Unicorn International W506
Uni-Dur drug A1250
Uniejewski, Joseph E114
Unifab International A940
Unifi, Inc. P696
Unified FoodService
  Purchasing A1404
Unified Western Grocers,
  Inc. P488-P489, P752
Unifile filing cabinets A726
Uniform Federal Fund-Raising
  Program (1957) P492
Uniform Support Centers P685
Uniforms To You A364
Unify Corporation (database
  company) E22
Unigraphics Solutions A538
UniGroup, Inc. (moving
  company) P753

Uni-Group office panels P222
UniHealth Foundation A1080,
  P118, P753
UniKix Technology (software) A600
Unilever A108, A316, A374, A510,
  A648, A984, A1107, P100, P530,
  W244, W256, W278, W308, W476,
  W546, **W618-W619**, W646
Unilloyd (company) P574
UniMark Group A470
UniMédia W262
Unimétal W292
Union Bank A1332
Union Bank of Canada W474
Union Bank of Switzerland. *See* UBS
  AG
Union Bottling Works A1400
Union Camp A770
Union Carbide Corporation A504,
  A704, A900, A1156, W102, W542
The Union Central Life Insurance
  Company P753
Union College of Law P378
Union Company (utility) A136
Union de Queretaro A1132
Union des Assurances de
  Paris W104
Union des Assurances
  Fédérales W182
Union de Transports Aériens W68
Union Electric (phone
  equipment) A1318
Union Electric (utility) A136
Union Gas & Electric A1030
The Union Labor Life Insurance
  Company P754
Union Minière W559
Union National Bank of
  Charlotte A1486
Union National Bank & Trust A822
Union Oil Company A582, P184
Union Oil of California A1438
Union Pacific Corporation A308,
  A514, A1096, A1186,
  A**1422-A1423**, A1548, P751
Union Pacific Resources A168,
  E308
Union Potash A752
Union Savings Bank and Trust
  Company A592
Union Switch and Signal A152
Union Tank Car Company P313
Union Texas Natural Gas A728
Union Theological Seminary P134
Union Trust Company A592, A954
Unionamerica Holdings A1236
Unionbay brand A839
Unipath diagnostics W619
Uniphase Corporation A792
Unipiston brand A585
Uniprise (corporate health
  care) A1434, A1435
Unique Wheel (steel wheels) A326
Uniroyal Chemical
  Corporation A450
Uniroyal Goodrich Tire
  Company A662, P594, W318,
  W366, W367

Unison Capital Corporation,
  Inc. P261
Unisource (global
  communication) W502, W578,
  W584
Unisource Worldwide, Inc. A654,
  A746
Unistar Radio Networks E140
Unisys Corporation A342, A400,
  A404, A**1424-A1425**, E77
Unit Companies A638
Unit Corporation E308
Unitary Products (heating and
  cooling) A1551
United Advertising
  Publications W620
United Agri Products A408
United Aircraft and Transport A272,
  A1044, A1432
United Airlines. *See* UAL
  Corporation
United Alkali (chemicals) W278
United American Insurance
  Company A1390, A1391
United Artists Corporation A962
United Artists Theatre Circuit
  (movie chain) P412
United Asset Management
  Corporation P414, W596
United Audio Centers stores E306
United Auto Parts A652
United Auto Workers A332, A476,
  A1010, P35, P222, P366
United Bankshares A954
United Biscuit Company of
  America A814
United Biscuits (UK) A714, A715,
  P232, P233, W192, W212
United Brands A144
United Breweries W162, W552
United Building Centers P655
United Bulgarian Bank W384,
  W385
United Business Company A680
United Business Media plc W248,
  W620-W621, W626
United Carbon A200
United Center arena P774
United Chair (office furniture) P222
United Cigar Manufacturers A660
United Cinemas
  International A1477
United Coconut Planters
  Bank W510
United Colors of Benetton casual
  wear W124, W125
United Community Funds and
  Councils P492
United Concordia Companies A716,
  A717
United Concordia Companies,
  Inc. P234, P235
United Dairy Farmers A144
United Defense Industries
  Inc. A612, P110, P567
United Distillers Glenmore A422
United Dollar Stores A496

United Dominion Industries Limited A1320

United Dry Goods A932

United Electric Securities Company A1198

United Energy Limited A1464, A1465

United Estates (property development) W538

Groupe United European Bank W131

United Express airline P534

United Facility Supply A1430

United Farm Workers A520, P168

United Financial Casualty Company A1169

United Financial Group A930

United Food and Commercial Workers Union A110, A742, A1176, P402

United Fruit Company A354

United Gas Improvement A570

United Gas Pipe Line A834, A1096

United Gas & Electric Company of New Albany, IN A362

United Grain Growers A192

United Grocers of Oregon P488, P752

United Harvest P123, P571

United HealthCare A574, A738, A794, A1434

United Independent Broadcasters A334

United Investors Life Insurance Company A1390, A1391

United Israel Appeal P752

United Jewish Appeal P752

United Liberty Life Insurance A144

United Malayan Banking W538

United Media Publishing A1160

United Media (syndication) A568

United Medical Service P174

United Microelectronics Corporation E160, W398

United Mine Workers A84, A416, A716, P234

United Molasses W568

United Mortgage Servicing A438

United Mutual Fire Insurance Company A875, P294

United Mutual Life Insurance P539

United Nations P414, P420, P482, W304

United Negro College Fund P78, P79

United News & Media plc. See United Business Media

United NewVentures A1420

United of Omaha Life Insurance Company P349, P680

United Oil A412

United Paramount Network A60, A1476, A1477

United Parcel Service, Inc. A102, A484, A549, A588, **A1426-A1427**, A1428, A1548, P34, P246, P404, P490, P641, W71

United Press International, Inc. A568, A700, P60, P228, W198

United Refining P712

United Savings Association of Texas A930

United Services Automobile Association. See USAA

United Shipping & Technology, Inc. E308

United Shuttle A106, A1420

United Space Alliance P754

United States Agricultural Corporation A752

United States Army Automobile Insurance Association A1452, P502

United States Cellular Corporation A1360

United States Electric Light and Power Company A424

United States Electric Lighting Company A570

United States Exploration, Inc. E308

United States Golf Association P251

United States Gypsum A1456

United States Pension Services A596

United States Postal Service A102, A210, A380, A478, A484, A588, A802, A1012, A1112, A1426, **A1428-A1429**, E198, P254, P404, P454, **P490-P491**, P754

United States Satellite Broadcasting A736

United States Shipbuilding A256

United States Steel Corporation A256, A716, A1158, P234, P400, W462

United States Tobacco Company. See UST Inc.

United Stationers Inc. **A1430-A1431**, P518

United Sugars P538

United Technologies Corporation A646, A728, A792, A856, **A1432-A1433**, A1550, W554

United Technologies Photonics A792

United Telecommunications A1318

United Telephone A1318

United Van Lines P753

United Video Satellite Group. See Gemstar-TV Guide International

United Waste Systems E139

United Water Resources W558

United Way of America **P492-P493**, P755

United Westburne (distributor) A1140

United Wholesale A1312

United Wisconsin Insurance Company A1282

United World Life Insurance Company P349

United-A.G. Cooperative (grocery distributor) A994

UnitedAuto Group, Inc. A206, P390, P391, P699

UnitedGlobalCom, Inc. A872, W586

UnitedHealth Group Inc. A738, A1162, **A1434-A1435**

UnitedNetworks Limited (electric utility) A1465

Unitek E175

Unitel W494

Unitog A364

Unitrin (insurance) A116, P258

Unitrode E74

UNIVAC computers A342, A764, A1424, P248

Universal American Financial Corporation E309

Universal American Mortgage Company A863

Universal Cooperatives P123

Universal Corporation A492, **A1436-A1437**

Universal (entertainment) W146

Universal Fastener A662

Universal Furniture P298

Universal Gym Equipment A1446

Universal Instruments A502

Universal Leaf Tobacco Company A1436

Universal Mercantile Schedule A378

Universal Music Group A1546, W126, W212, W624, W625

Universal Ogden Services W546

Universal Outdoor Holdings A372

Universal Pictures P302

Universal Pioneer Corporation W448

Universal Product Code P70, P71

Universal Rim for tires A664

Universal Silicones & Lubricants P164

Universal Sodexho W546

Universal Stamping Machine A1142

Universal Studios, Inc. A1450, A1477, P166, P597, W360, W472, W624, W625

Compagnie Universelle du Canal Maritime de Suez W558

The University of Alabama System A674, P755

University of Buffalo P460

University of California A1110, P98, P252, P456, **P494-P495**, P667, P755, P761

University of California at San Diego E49

University of California Los Angeles P495, P746

The University of Chicago P176, P194, P414, **P496-P497**, P756

University of Florida A1180, P756

University of Illinois A1182, P449, P756

The University of Iowa P757

The University of Kentucky P757

University of Massachusetts P78, P757

The University of Michigan P758

University of Michigan Medical School P773
University of Minnesota E48, P663, P758
University of Missouri System P758
The University of Nebraska P759
University of New Mexico P704
University of North Carolina P683
The University of Pennsylvania A948, P326, P759
University of Pennsylvania Health System P116
University of Phoenix Online E309
University of Pittsburgh of the Commonwealth System of Higher Education P759
University of Riyadh (Saudi Arabia) W134
University of Rochester P760
University of Southern California P760
University of Tennessee P70, P192, P760
University of Texas-Houston Medical School P671
University of Texas Investment Management Company P498, P761
The University of Texas System P192, P470, P**498**-P**499**, P518, P693, P744, P761
University of Virginia P541, P761
University of Washington P761
The University of Wisconsin System P**500**-P**501**, P762
University System of Maryland P762
Univex Licensing Group A1274, E120
Univision A1450, W582
Uniwide (food retailer) W166
Uniwill (notebook computers) A1256
UniWorld Group, Inc. (advertising) W646
UNIX operating system A712, A1012, A1050, A1342, E42, E179, E190, P430, W60, W290
Unlisted brand E78, E227
Unmacht, Brian P411
Uno cosmetics W535
Uno, Ikuo W397
Unocal Corporation A200, A1212, A**1438**-A**1439**, E272, E302, W66, W438, W500
Unocal Indonesia W612
UNO-VEN (refining and marketing) A1438, W438
Unruh, Jesse A314, P96
Unruh, Paul A241, P75
Unser, Al, Sr. P390
Unternehmensbeteiligungs-gesellschaft W201
The Untouchables (TV show and movie) A488
UNUMProvident Corporation A126, A878, A1380, A**1440**-A**1441**, E315
Unwin, Geoff W160, W161
UP. *See* Union Pacific Corporation

Upco (veterinary supply) P394
Updegrove, Mark K. A1503
Updyke, Rick A57
UPI. *See* United Press International
Upjohn A704
UPMC Health System P759
UPM-Kymmene A770
UPN Network A334, A335, A1476, A1477, E319, P681
Upper Appomattox Company (canal operation) A498
Upper Crust restaurants W174
Uprima drug A59, P741
UPS. *See* United Parcel Service, Inc.
Upshaw, Gene P357
Upstart office furniture line P276
Upton, Fred A1520
Upton, Lou A1520
Upton Machine Company A1520
Uptons stores P276
Uraineftegaz (oil and gas exploration) W346
OOO Uraltransgaz W243
Uram, Lynn P593
Urann, Marcus P380
Urbach, Michael H. P703
The Urban League P493
Urban, Stanley P115
Urban, Wolfgang W311
Urbani, David D. E42
UrCarco E27
U'Ren, L. J. P734
OOO Urengoygazprom W243
Uriarte Santamarina, Pedro L. W579
Urkiel, William S. A747
Urquhart, Ernie P119, P570
Urquhart, Richard P642
URS Corporation A504
Ursu, John J. A977
Ursus beer W553
Urvan car W403
US Air Force A224, A736, A1412, P88, P132, P156, P160
US Air Force Academy P449
US Airways Group, Inc. A138, A164, A1222, A1228, A1420, A**1442**-A**1443**, W71, W140
US Army A120, A548, A644, A676, A826, A982, A984, A1122, A1428, A1452, P132, P136, P160, P454, P502, P543, P772, W294, W378, W403
US Army Air Corps A234
US Army Corps of Engineers A1370, P468
US Atomic Energy Commission A1488
U.S. Bancorp A954, A**1444**-A**1445**, E172, W474
U.S. Beef A1400
U.S. BioScience E90
U.S. Borax W488
U.S. Can Corporation P762
U.S. Central Capital Markets P763
U.S. Central Credit Union P763
US Civil Aeronautics Board A106

U.S. Concrete, Inc. E309
US Congressional Budget Office A626
U.S. Corrugated-Fiber Box Company P656
US Department of Agriculture E203, P58, P430
US Department of Defense A224, A696, A736, A738, A1110, E110, E312, E317, P52, P70, P88, P438, P444, P454, P543, P734
US Department of Education E250
US Department of Energy A512, A882, A1110, A1370, A1488, E128, P70, P438, P454, P468, P558
US Department of Health and Human Services A1366, P70, P380
US Department of Housing and Urban Development A580, A626, A812, A1330, P458
US Department of Justice A122, A142, A164, A174, A282, A406, A448, A568, A728, A774, A846, A888, A898, A924, A972, A1026, A1046, A1142, A1202, A1304, A1338, A1382, A1412, A1420, A1424, A1442, A1480, A1488, E138, P42, P68, P78, P148, P212, P246, P322, P464, P479, P508, W412, W492
US Department of Labor P386, P512
US Department of State A1284, W578
US Department of Transportation A484, P362, P684
US Department of Treasury A626, P70, P71, P186
U.S. Design (computer storage) A928
U.S. Diagnostic Inc. E67
U.S. Envelope A1516
US Environmental Protection Agency A140, A192, A362, A456, A598, A1290, A1370, A1466, A1524, P36, P70, P468, W102
US Equal Employment Opportunity Commission A988, A1470
US Farm Bureau P288
US Federal Aviation Administration A106, A138, A380, A588, A846
US Federal Bureau of Investigation A192, W260
US Federal Communications Commission A60, A72, A202, A248, A372, A528, A700, A998, A1026, A1244, A1472, A1476, A1496, A1534, P144, P228, P336, W390, W580
US Federal Courthouse, Boston P576
US Federal Deposit Insurance Corporation A226, A602, A930, A1486
US Federal Drug Administration A282, A540, A640, A648, A800, A952, A956, A1118, A1122, A1164, A1250

US Federal Energy
  Administration A88
US Federal Energy Regulatory
  Commission A168, A362, A518,
  A532, A598, A1120, A1248
US Federal Housing
  Administration A580, A626, P476
US Federal Reserve System A172,
  A326, A438, A480, A626, A658,
  A964, A1000, A1042, A1380, P48,
  P186-P187, P607, W90, W474
US Federal Trade Commission A58,
  A110, A156, A190, A320, A374,
  A490, A520, A540, A558, A576,
  A654, A756, A844, A890, A938,
  A946, A994, A1202, A1250, A1268,
  A1322, A1324, A1396, A1532,
  A1544, P118, P160, P168, P244,
  P366, P442, P462, W206
U.S. Financial Life Insurance
  Company A986
US Food and Drug
  Administration A58, A148, A234,
  A674, A1506, E50, E71, E112,
  E144, E150, E174, E190, E199,
  E217, P40, P44, P70, P164, P382,
  P741, W102, W246, W414, W416,
  W428, W492
U.S. Foods A769
U.S. Foodservice A1242, W498,
  W499
US Fund for UNICEF P79
US General Accounting Office A888
US General Services
  Administration A1514, P88
U.S. Generating A424, A1120
U.S. Gypsum P88
U.S. Healthcare A90
U.S. HealthWorks A698
U.S. Home Corporation A862, A863
US Immigration and Naturalization
  Service A1488, E138
US Industrial Chemicals A974
U.S. Industries, Inc. A1320,
  A1446-A1447, W252
US Internal Revenue Service A80,
  A404, A688, A1426, E53, P28, P32,
  P88, P150, P256
US Interstate Commerce
  Commission A308, P434
US Interstate Highway
  system A1114, P396
U.S. Link, Inc. A1360
US Marine Corps A1452, P502,
  P686
US McCafe coffee house A942
US National Aeronautics and Space
  Administration A100, A112, A224,
  A404, A542, A572, A1256, A1284,
  A1294, A1488, A1550, P88, P438,
  P439, P454, P754, P766
US National Guard and the
  Reserve P52
US National Highway Traffic Safety
  Administration W294
US National Labor Relations
  Board A258

US Navy A272, A538, A548, A572,
  A644, A940, A1256, A1334, A1452,
  E42, E179, P70, P156, P160,
  P240, P502, P543, P686, W284
U.S. News & World Report
  (magazine) E34, E165, P496,
  P500, P598, P756, P761
US Nuclear Regulatory
  Commission A140, A624, A668,
  A1370, A1416, P468
US Occupational Safety and Health
  Administration A742
US Office of Management and
  Budget P110
US Office Products Company A274,
  E250
US Oncology, Inc. E71
US Open golf tournament P577
U.S. Paper Mills Corporation A1302
US Patent Office P208, P450
US Peace Corps P492
US Pentagon A1442, A1472
US Post Office. See United States
  Postal Service
US Pressed Steel A278
U.S. Robotics Corporation A54
US Securities and Exchange
  Commission A62, A90, A144,
  A172, A226, A234, A238, A248,
  A338, A348, A448, A474, A544,
  A562, A570, A572, A742, A796,
  A840, A926, A954, A996, A1158,
  A1306, A1354, A1418, A1498,
  A1504, A1536, E100, E258, E269,
  P46, P48, P80, P154, P182, P206,
  P278, P286, P338, P352, P400,
  P466, P590, W196, W324, W462
US Small Business
  Administration E213, E236
U.S. Smokeless Tobacco
  Company A1458, A1459
U.S. Software Resource A1356
US Sound (speakers) P92
U.S. Steel Corporation. See USX-
  U.S. Steel Group
U.S. Steel Kosice sro A1462, A1463,
  W292
US Supreme Court A154, A376,
  A412, A536, A576, A618, A1072,
  A1422, A1438, A1456, A1458,
  A1460, A1486, P40, P42, P52, P58,
  P92, P126, P318, P342, P388,
  P420, P442, P478, P498, P512,
  P709
US Supreme Court Building A256
U.S. Technologies Systems E142
U.S. Trust Corporation A228, A348,
  A349, P290
US Veterans Administration A156,
  A236, A580, A626
US Weekly LLC A1496
U S WEST, Inc. W152
USA. See United Space Alliance
USA Cafes P332
USA Convenience Foods
  Division A816
USA Detergents, Inc. A358
USA Education, Inc. A1448-A1449
USA Films A1450

USA Flex (direct marketing) P136,
  P338
U.S.A. Floral Products, Inc. A492
USA Group A1448
USA Networks, Inc. A872, A873,
  A1450-A1451, E215, P511, W624
USA Olympic brand A791
USA TODAY A506, A632, A633,
  A1020
USA Waste Services A1504, E139
USAA A1452-A1453, P502-P503,
  P763
USAir. See US Airways Group, Inc.
USAR Systems E119
USB Trade Services Limited A1445
USC/Canterbury (network
  services) E36
USDATA Corporation A1232
Used Car Buying Guide
  (book) P139
Uselton, James C. A787
Usertech (training) A343
USF Holland Inc. A1454, A1455
USF&G Financial Services
  Corporation A822, A1236, A1237
USFilter W624
USFreightways
  Corporation A1454-A1455
USG Corporation A252,
  A1456-A1457
Usher, Thomas J. A1461, A1463
Usher, William A311
Usher's Scotch A297
U-Ship. See United Shipping &
  Technology, Inc.
Usinor (steel) W292, W398
Usioda, Kunio W419
Uskup, Ergin A1431
USPS. See United States Postal
  Service
USS-POSCO Industries A1463
UST Inc. A1458-A1459
Ustian, Daniel C. A1011
USX Corporation A1460, A1462
USX-Delhi Group P280
USX-Marathon Group A200,
  A1460-A1461, A1462
USX-U.S. Steel Group A916, A988,
  A1052, A1460, A1462-A1463,
  E96, P713, W284
Utah Copper Company W488
Utah Jazz (basketball team) P355,
  P656
Utah Power & Light
  Company A1082, A1083
Utah Retail Grocers
  Association P545
Utah Starzz (basketball team) P355,
  P656
Utel (company) W503
Uthoff, Stephen J. A1269
UtiliCorp United Inc. A114, A668,
  A1464-A1465
Utility Stationery Stores A1430
Utility Supply Company A1430
UTStarcom, Inc. E310
UUNET (Internet backbone) A866,
  A1534, P274

UVa. *See* University of Virginia
Uvholt, Espen W411
Uzzi, Donald A539

V

V & V Associates A746
V2 Music Group (recordings) W623
V8 beverages A316
VA. *See* US Veterans Administration
Vaccarino, Simone W423
Vachey, François W343
Vacutainer blood collection
  products A244
Vacuum Oil A576
Vadasz, Leslie L. A761
Vagelos, Roy A956
Vagifem drug W417
Vagitrol drug W493
Vagnini, Michael F. A451
Vahlkamp, Cynthia A. A1327
Vail Banks, Inc. E310
Vail Resorts, Inc. A454
Vail, Theodore A248
Vaill, Timothy L. E165
Valade, Gary C. W189
Valanju, Subbash A803
Valdes, Max O. A595
Valdiva, Eunice A565
Valeika, Ray A479
Valens, Ritchie P188
Valentine, Donald T. A368, A369
Valentine, Linda J. A691
Valentino brand lingerie A1498
Valeo A780
Valerio, Martha M. A1049, P377
Valero Energy Corporation A576,
  A1466-A1467
Valhi, Inc. A1524, P583
Valium drug W492
Valkenaar, Lee A1523
Vallecitos nuclear plant A1120
Vallee, Roy A214, A215
Vallejo, Juan W525
Vallen Corporation P208
Valley Fare brands P488
Valley Forge Group A1320
Valley Forge Insurance
  Company A379
Valley Gas Production A552
Valley Independent Bank E312
Valley Joist (construction
  materials) P170, P171
Valley Line (barges) A454
Valley National Bank A1490
Valley of the Rogue Bank E307
Valley of Virginia Milk Producers
  Association A1338
Valley Race Park Inc. (greyhound
  racing) A930, A931
Valley Recreational Products A1446
Valleydale Foods A1290
Vallier, Herb A903, P305, P663
Vallina-Laguera, Eloy E305
Valmac (chickens) A1418
Valpre water W553

Valssis Communications A500,
  P162
Valstorp, Per W417
Valu Merchandisers Company P62,
  P63
Valu Time brands P478, P479
Valucraft brand A209
Value America (online
  retailer) A958
Value & Service P484
Value Health Inc. (pharmacy
  benefits) A575, A694
Value Partners (consulting) P64
ValueRx of Michigan, Inc. A574,
  A575
ValueVision International A999
valu-mart grocery stores W245
Valutas, Charles K. A1345
ValuTerm insurance P617
The Valvoline Company A200
van Ameringen, A. L. A766
van Ameringen-Haebler
  company A766
Van Andel, Jay P536
Van Atta, Dale P28
Van Bebber, David L. A1419
Van Ben Bossche, Patrick E94
Van Berkem, Tom A1507
Van Biesbroeck, Jo W289
van Boxmeer, Jean François W255
Van Brunt, Gary P594
Van Brunt, John M. W67
Van Brunt, William P107
Van Bueuren, Archbold D. A317
Van Camp's foods A409
van Cleave, Donna P766
Van Damme, Albert W288
van de Aast, Gerard W479
van de Geijn, Paul W65
Van de Kamp frozen seafood A1104
van de Meent, Henk W75
van den Berg, Ruurd A. W65
van den Bergh, Albertus J. A541
Van den Berghe, Dirk W195
van den Bergh, Maarten A. W501
van den Bergh, Rob F. W626, W627
van den Brink, R. G. C. W57
van den Heijkant, H. W. M. W503
van den Hoeven, Cees H. W498,
  W499
van der Meer, Rudy M. J. W73
van der Merwe, Robert P. A827
Van der Minne, Frank W255
van der Poel, Arthur P. M. W445
van der Veer, Ada W503
van der Veer, Jereon W501
van der Velde, Johannes I. A1481,
  P509
van der Wansem, Paul J. E167
Van De Velde, James D. A719
van de Vijver, Walter W501
van de Winkel, Jack M. M. A1437
van Dieter, J. E. M. W643
Van Doorselaere, Ignace W289
Van Dorn (plastic containers) A452
van Duyne, J. Fokko W179
Van Duyne, Richard A1123

Van Dyke, Steven A544
Van Eijle BV (forklift trucks) A992
Van Faasen, William C. P84, P85,
  P557
Van Gelder, John M. A835, P281
van Gemert, Lo A1027
Van Gend & Loos B.V. W203
Van Gessel, John A1505
Van Gogh, Vincent A1304
Van Graafeiland, Gary P. A525
Van Hall, Thomas A. A1313
Van Handel, Michael J. A911
van Heemstra, André W619
van Hellemond, Andy P361
Van Hise, David W. A921
Van Hoof, Paul A803
Van Hoose, David A1132, A1133
Van Hooser, David G. A1075
Van Houten, C. David, Jr. A385
Van Ingen, Chris A99
Van Kaldekerken, Rolf A1057
van Katwijk, C. Michiel W65
van Kempen, Casper W642
van Kerchem, C. F. W. Wiggers W64
Van Kleef, William T. A1375
van Lanschot, Ito A1199
van Lede, Cees J. A. W73
van Leent, Paul J. M. A1159, P401,
  W463
van Liemt, Hans W57
Van Loan, David R. A503
Van Lopik, William H. A1247, P433
van Maldeghem, Todd P563
van Munching, Leo W254
Van Nelle Tabak W282
Van Nelle tobacco A1242, W283
van Oppen, Peter H. E23, E148
van Oppen, Shannon E23, E148
Van Ossel, Marc W507
Van Oss, Stephen A. A1513
van Paasschen, Frits D. A1033
Van Pelt, Jack F. P209, P620
Van Raalte lingerie A1499
Van Ripper, Daniel S. A1263
Van, Ronald P., Jr. A1513
van Schoonenberg, Robert G. A211
Van Slyke, Gary K. P39
Van Stedum, Edward J. A653
Van Steenwyck, E. A. A268, P82
van Tets, Rijnhard W. F. W57
van Tielraden, A. H. P. M. W499
Van Tran, Muoi E258
Van Tuyl, Cecil P767
Van Tuyl, Larry P767
van Vissingen, Frits H.
  Fentener W73
van Vlissingen, John Fentener P776
Van Wagenen, Paul G. E268
Van Weelden, Thomas H. A122,
  A123
Van Wie, William A. A483
van Wijk, Leo M. W317
van Woudenberg, Cees W317
Van Zile, John R. A573
Vanaselja, Siim W123

Vance, James P581
Vance, Myrna B. A539
Vance Sanders & Company E53
Vance, Walter R. P718
Vance, Wesley B. A488
Vanceril drug A1250, A1251
Vanco, Radu M. E173
Vancouver Canucks (hockey
  team) P361
Vancouver Grizzlies (basketball
  team) P354
Vande Steeg, Nickolas W. A1089
Vanden Dorpel, Ronald D. P379
Vandenberghe, James H. A857
Vander Ark, Tom P79
Vanderbeek, Jeffrey A861
Vanderbilt, Cornelius P763
Vanderbilt, Gloria W606
Vanderbilt University P94, P763
Vanderford, Allyson A959
VanderLind, Merwyn R. P71
Vanderlinde, Daisy L. A209
Vanderslice, James T. A473
Vandervell auto parts A461
Vanderwist, Kathryn K. A1141
VanDeVeer, Alicia E70, E217
Vandevelde, Luc W356, W357
Vandiver, F. William, Jr. A227
V&S variety stores A1410, P484
Vanette Cargo car W403
Vangard Labs A1070
Vanguard 500 Index Fund A1468
Vanguard Financial A592
The Vanguard Group, Inc. A614,
  A**1468**-A**1469**, P190, P**504**-P**505**,
  P764
Vanguard lawn equipment A287
Vanguard Technologies A292
Vanillin A1300
Vanish household products A1247,
  P433, W476, W477
Vanity Fair lingerie A1474, A1475
Vanity Fair (magazine) A80, P32,
  P33, P530
VanLandingham, Donald W. A225
Vanlev drug A290
Vanliner Group (insurance) P753
VanLuvanee, Donald R. E56, E196
Vann, Kyle D. A835, P281
Vannieuwenhoven, Vicki A673,
  P211
Vans shoes E101
VanSpronsen, Gary A707
VanStone, Donald L. A925, P323
Vantage cigarettes A1204, A1205
Vantage hard drives A1515
Vantage Healthcare
  Corporation A259
Vantis (logic chips) A82, E82
The Vantive Corporation
  (software) A1098
VanWestenbrugge, Isaac P618
VanWoerkom, Jack A. A1325
Vapor (doors for trains and
  buses) P310
Vaqta drug A957
Varasano, Frank A. A1067

Varcom Corporation A1320
Vardanega, Roland W443
Vargas, Getúlio W436
Varhol, James A. A159
Varian, Russell E133
Varian Semiconductor Equipment
  Associates, Inc. E**133**, E310
Varian, Sigurd E133
Variance lingerie A1474, A1475
Variant car W631
VARIG A1421, W79, W80, W518
Varin, Philippe W433
Varley, John S. W115
Varmus, Harold P672
Varner, Bruce D. P463
Varney, David W149
Varney Speed Lines A428
Varney, Walter A428
Varon, Gil E290
Varra, Susan A873
VarTec Telecom, Inc. P764, W122
Vas-Cath, Inc. A445
Vascellaro, Jerome A949, P327,
  P670
Vasco (heating systems) A920
Vasconcellos, Anthony A. E277
Vaseline W618, W619
Vasella, Daniel W414, W415
Vaskevitch, David A973
Vasomedical, Inc. E311
Vasotec drug A956, A957
Vasques, Gary A839
Vasquez, Felix A509
Vásquez Oria, Pablo W583
Vassalluzzo, Joseph S. A1325
Vassarette lingerie A1474
Vastar Resources W136
Vastola, Eugene L. A397
The Vatican P416, P417
Vatistas, Robert G. A453
Vaugh, Robert H., Jr. E80
Vaughan, Alan P677
Vaughan, Richard C. A879
Vaughn, Donald C. A677
Vaughn, William T. A483
Vaughn-Lee, Mark W190
Vaux, Robert W245
Vauxhall Motors Limited A650
VAW Aluminum AG W219
Vaz Moreira, Ronnie W437
Vazquez del Mercado Benshimol,
  Andres R. W581
Vázquez, José Luis A173, P49
VCI (electronic
  entertainment) W312
V-Crest (auto dealer systems) A204
VDO Control Systems, Inc. W352
VEAG (utility) W218
Veal, Ian W429
Veale, Tinkham A156, A746
Veasman, Louise P113, P569
VEBA Oel AG (oil and gas
  exploration) W137, W218, W219,
  W438, W460, W504
Vecchione, Maurizio A1451
Vecci, Raymond J. A1047

Veckstett, Doug P671
Vector Group Ltd. W240
Vector SCM (supply chain
  management) A380, A381
Vectrix.com (software) P126
Vedomosti (Russian business
  newspaper) A506, A507
Veeck family A982
Veeder Root (controls) A462
Veet health and personal care W477
Vega airplane A882, A1044
Vega Precision Laboratories E68
Vegas cigarettes E293
VehiCROSS SUV W294, W295
Veitch, Arthur J. A645
Veitsiluoto W556
Velamints A1526
Velanovich, Bogoljub A803
Velasquez, Gary S. A697
Velda Farms (dairy products) A1338
Velez, Pete P369
Velli, Joseph M. A229
Velocity A348
Velouté dairy products W193
Velox Retail Holdings W498
Velveeta cheese A842, A843, A1126
Velvet carpets A980
Venable, Thomas E124
Venator Group Inc. A**1470**-A**1471**,
  A1530
Vendamerica A490
Vendange wines A422
Vendepac vending machines W174,
  W240
Vendex International A232, A490
Vendor Management Services,
  Inc. A595
Vendors Supply of America A768
Venechanos, Steven E296
Venezuelan Petroleum
  Corporation W438, W439
Venick, Shelley J. A309
Venn, Richard E. W157
Vennootschap Nederland
  (tontine) W64
VennWorks A1233
VENTAK (defibrillator) A674
Ventech Controls (valve
  repair) A446
Vento, Gerald T. E299
Ventratech A674
Ventro (B2B online firm) A142
Ventura County (California)
  Star A569
Ventura, Elizabeth A239
Ventura Foods, LLC P122, P123
Venture Industries P764
Venture Stores A932
Ver Hager, J. K. A547
Veranth, Joseph P93
Verbatim (computer disks) A524
Verburg, Harriet D. P389
Verdix (Ada tools) E110
Verdoorn, D. R. "Sid" A344, A345
Vereinigte Elektrizitatswerk
  Westfalen W504
Vereinigte Glanzstoff-Fabriken W72

Vereniging AEGON W64
Verfaillie, Hendrik A. A985, A1123
Vergel brandy W109
Vergne, Jean-Luc W443
Vergnes, Bernard P. A973
Verhagen, Adri A97
Verhagen, Timothy J. A363
Verheij, Richard H. A1459
Verifi online shopping
  technology A750
Verifine dairy product A467
Veriflo (valves and
  regulators) A1088
VeriFone, Inc. (electronic
  commerce) A712
Verio Inc. (Internet services) W400,
  W401
VeriSign, Inc. A596, E217, P438
Verissimo, Marc J. E122, E288
Veritas Capital Management P713
VERITAS Software
  Corporation A1260, E23, P440
Veritus Medicare Services A716,
  A717, P234, P235, P632
Verity, George A104
Verity, Inc. E**134**, E311
VERITY voice quality
  enhancement A1363
Verizon Communications,
  Inc. A202, A248, A1244, A1372,
  A**1472**-A**1473**, E269, E290, E318,
  P535, P765, W628
Verizon Wireless Inc. A248, A1026,
  A1188, A1472, E38, E126, P576,
  P765, W628, W629
Verlag H. Stam (educational
  information) W643
Vermeulen, Jean-Luc W613
The Vermont Teddy Bear Company,
  Inc. E**135**, E311
Vermont Yankee nuclear
  plant A554, A1040
Vermylen, David B. A814, A815,
  A817
Vernon Pools (betting) W259
Vero, Ryan T. A1059
Veronis Suhler (banking) W144
Veronis Suhler Stevenson &
  Associates (trade shows) A944
Verougstraete, Chris W289
Verrecchia, Alfred J. A693
Verri, Carlo W78
Versace brand A1014, W637
VERSAPAK power tools A265
Versatile (agricultural
  equipment) A616
VERSUS Technologies, Inc. A566,
  A567
Vertbaudet (children's wear) W446
VerticalNet, Inc. A1232
Vertis Inc. P**506**-P**507**, P765
Verwaayen, Bernardus J. A899
Vesce, Vincent P703
Vesey, Edward C. A453
Vespoli, Leila L. A599
Vessey, Paul A1481, P509
Vest, Charles M. P667
Vesta Fire Insurance A688

Vesta Insurance Group, Inc. A178,
  A688, A1390
Vetri (glass) W506
Vette (magazine) A1161
Vetter, David R. A1357
Vettier, Paul W613
Veuve Amiot champagne W109
Veuve Clicquot Ponsardin
  spirits W349
VEW. *See* Vereinigte
  Elektrizitatswerk Westfalen
VF Corporation A**1474**-A**1475**
VH1 cable network A1476
VHS video W550
Via Banque SA W224, W225
Vía Digital (satellite TV) W578
VIA Technologies, Inc. A1002
Viação Aérea Rio-Grandense S.A.
  See VARIG
Viacom Inc. A266, A334, A872,
  A1258, A1450, A**1476**-A**1477**,
  E140, E317, P218, P332, P681,
  W146, W430
Viacore A196
Viad Corporation A486,
  A**1478**-A**1479**
VIAG AG A802, A1356, W218
VIAG Interkom AG W148
Viagra drug A540, A1118, A1119
Viana, Luiz Antonio W437
Vianova Resins A1300
ViaSat, Inc. A1258, E312
Viasoft (software) A406
Viasys Healthcare Inc. A1382
Viasystems Group Inc. A715, P233
Viault, Raymond G. A649
Viaweb software A1546
VIB Corporation E312
Vibramycin drug A1118
Viceroy cigarettes W143
Vichy skin care products W342,
  W343
Vick, Daniel D. A1241
Vicker-Armstrong (aircraft) W110
Vickers brand A527
Vickers (cars) A1386, W120, W630
Vickers, John A. P477
Vickers Turbine Components W496
Vickery, David P618
Vicks cold medicine A1165
Vicks Vapor Rub A1164
Groupe Victoire W558
Victor Company of Japan W360
Victor Microcomputer A1188
Victor Reinz auto parts A461
Victoria + Co. A804
Victoria AG (insurance) W380
Victoria & Company, Ltd.
  (jewelry) W607
Victoria Bitter beer W230, W231
Victoria, Justin R. A149
Victoria, Queen of England W240
Victoria Wine stores W84
Victoria's Secret Stores, Inc. A776,
  A777, A876, P404, P708, W534
Victory Oil A1344
Victory Supermarket P554

Vida Corporation S.A. P321
Vidal Sassoon hair care A1165
Viden drug A291
Video Blaster WebCam W181
Video Central stores P224
Video News International A1020
VideoConcepts stores A1188
Videojet data systems W355
Le Groupe Vidéotron (cable
  TV) W152
Vidra, Carla W423
Grupo Vidrio Formas (glass
  containers) A715
Viegas, Leslie A. P87
Viehbacher, Chris W247
Vieillard, Georges W150
Viejo Vergel brandy W109
Vienna Finger cookies A815
Vienot, Marc W103
Viens, Daniel A. E61, E202
Vieth, Christopher W. A507
Vietmeier, David G. A117
Vietnam Airlines W303, W469
Vietnam Insurance Company A798
Vietnam War Memorial P276
Vietze, Mary J. P253
Vieujant, Jules W194
Vieux Temps beer W289
View Master A927
ViewCam camcorder W532
Vieweg, Cecilia W211
Views word processor W180
ViewSonic Corporation A1357,
  P765
ViewStation video-
  conferencing E268
Viewtron A832
Vigdal, David P614
Vigilant Insurance Company A356
Vigilante (marketing) P73
Vigoro fertilizer A725, A752
Vijayaraghavan, Ravi P65
Vikase (plastic films) A250
Viking Food Stores P422
Viking Freightways A588
Viking Gas Transmission
  Company A1542, A1543
Viking Homes A604
Viking Office Products A1056
Viking (publishing) W430
Viking Serenade (cruise
  ship) A1217
Viktora, Richard P449
Vilá Boix, Angel W579
Vila Olimpica (Barcelona,
  Spain) P449
Vilarasau Salat, José W483
Viljoen, J. Neil W355
Vill, Robert A881
Villa, Joyce P461
Villa Markets JP Company P243
Villa Mt. Eden wine A1458, A1459
Villa, Stephen P. P351, P681
Villa-Abrille, Alberto O., Jr. W511
Village Banc of Naples W112
Village Homes A862

Village Super Market, Inc. A1491,
  P515
Villager clothing A804, A839, A880,
  A881
Villager's Hardware A724
Villa-Komaroff, Linda P379
Villalonga, Juan W578
Villanova Capital A1009
Villas-Boas, Manuel W225
Villeneuve, André-Francois
  H. W485
VILPAC A1078
Vilucci, Gerard P570
Vin & Spirit A618
Vinana Baptista, Antonio W579
The Vincam Group A204
Vincent, Fay P306
Vincent, Gregory M. A1371, P469
Vincent, Jacques W193
Vincent, Paul E. E152
VINCI (construction) W558
Vinciguerra, Jean-Louis W233
Vindasius, Al E55
Viner, Anthony B. W495
Vingaarden A/S W162
Viniar, David A. A661
Vinik, Jeffrey A614, P190
Vintage Inns W545
Vintage Petroleum, Inc. E312
Vintner's Choice wines A422, A423
Vintner's Reserve wine P168
Viotty, Michelle E. A657
Viper tape drive P441
Vips restaurants W635
Virage Logic Corporation E313
Vireo Software A406
Virgil, Robert, Jr. P261
Virgin Atlantic Airways A428, W71,
  W140, W540, W541, W622
Virgin beverages W622
Virgin Group Ltd. P274, W88,
  W330, W622-W623
Virgin Megastores W331
Virgin One (online financial
  services) W88
Virgin Records America W212,
  W213
Virginia Electric and Power
  Company A498, A499
Virginia Folding Box
  Company A1516
Virginia Foodservice Group,
  Inc. A1109
Virginia Gold tobacco W283
Virginia Mason Medical
  Center P622
Virginia Natural Gas A498
Virginia Polytechnic Institute and
  State University P566
Virginia Railway and Power
  Company A498
Virginia Slims cigarettes A1126
Virginia State Lottery P766
Virginia Surety Company,
  Inc. A182, A183

Virginia Tech. *See* Virginia
  Polytechnic Institute and State
  University
Virginia-American Water
  Company A155
Virginian Railway A1038
Virgo Optics Division. *See* VLOC
Virgulak, Christopher F. A643
Viridian Fertilizers Ltd. W66, W67
Vironda, Jean-Jacques W547
Virtually There destination
  guides A1229
Viry, Alain W447
Visa Buxx prepaid card A1480
Visa International A142, A230,
  A318, A596, A924, A936, A1146,
  A**1480**-A**1481**, E157, E159, E312,
  P322, P348, P454, P**508**-P**509**,
  P668, P686, P734, P766, W114,
  W464
Visa table linens P342, P343
Visagis (candy) A708
VisaNet P766
Vishay Intertechnology,
  Inc. A**1482**-A**1483**, P750
Vishay Lite-On Power
  Semiconductor E192
Visine eye care A1118
Vision Advantage optical
  outlets A1282
Vision camera A1148
Vision Group
  (semiconductors) W554
Vision Management Services A908
VisionLand theme park P560
Visions cooking ware P91, P775
VisionStar, Inc. A529
Visnews W484
Visosky, Michelle P676
Vista Energy Resources E270
Vistana A1328
Vistant Corporation A321
Visteon Corporation (car
  components) A616, W362
Visual Communications
  Group W621
Vital Insurance Protection plan P85
Vitale, Dick P212
Vitale, Nickolas P591
Vitale, Vivian M. E114, E281
Vitali, Cheryl L. A1201
Vitalic containers A1415
Vitalinea biscuits W193
Vitelle, Richard K. E168
Viterbi, Andrew A1182
Viterra (real estate) W219
Vitesse Semiconductor
  Corporation E**136**, E313
Vitex Systems, Inc. P71
Vitramon (ceramic chip
  capacitor) A1482
Vitria Technology, Inc. E313
Vitronic (promotional
  products) P170
Vitronics Soltec (soldering
  equipment) A502
Vittadini, Adrienne P713
Vittel water A385

Vittor, Kenneth M. A945
Vittoria, Joseph A212
Viva detergent A386
Viva paper towels A827
Vival convenience stores W166,
  W167
Vivanco, Edgar E. A243
Vivendi Environnement SA W208,
  W558
Vivendi Universal S.A. A1450, E265,
  P278, W58, W146, W230, W390,
  W504, W622, W**624**-W**625**, W628,
  W629
Vivian, Robert T. E265
Vivian, Simon W253
Vivid cleaner A1246, P432
Vivid Technologies A1110
Vivona, Joseph F. P762
Vivre dairy products W193
Vizzavi Europe Ltd. (Internet
  portal) W624, W628, W629
Vlahakis, Nicholas G. A121
Vlasic Foods International A316,
  A714, P232
VLOC E20, E146
VLSI Technology A162, W444
VNU N.V. A66, E251, W620,
  W**626**-W**627**
VO Canadian whiskies W206
Vobis Microcomputer AG W364
Voblo (exhibit company) A1478
Voda One P771
Vodafone Group plc A248, A1288,
  A1472, A1473, P446, P765, W204,
  W232, W272, W352, W418, W422,
  W624, W**628**-W**629**
Voelker, Raymond M. A1169
Voelker, Ruthann P591
Vogel, Ben P544
Vogel, Carl E. A350, A351
Vogel, Chuck P544
Vogel, Jacqueline Mars A914
Vogel, Jennifer A429
Vogel, Peter H., Jr. A951
Vogel Peterson (office
  partitions) A618
Vogel, Thomas E279
Vogelsand, Günter W219
Vogue (magazine) A80, P32, P33,
  P100
Vöhringer, Klaus-Dieter W189
Voice for the Voiceless P56
VoiceStream Wireless
  Corporation A1360, E126, E316,
  W204, W272
VoIP Blaster Internet
  telephony W180, W181
Volanakis, George B. A693
Volanakis, Peter F. P165
Volcker, Paul P186
Vold, Bjørn W411
Volera, Inc. (networking) A1050
OOO Volgogradtransgaz W243
OOO Volgotransgaz W243
Volk, Stephen R. A449
Volkart Brothers W566
Volkema, Michael A. A706, A707

Volkert, Jon D. A469
Volkswagen AG A170, A342, A572, A584, A856, A1062, A1112, E170, P561, P717, P733, P764, W58, W120, W188, W340, W422, W442, W458, W497, W614, **W630-W631**, W632
Vollrath, Frederick E. A405
Vollum, Charles Howard A1358
Volpe, Richard P247
Volpi, Michelangelo A369
Volta appliances W210
Voltas Limited W566
Voltolina, Frank A. A199
Volume Distribution shoe stores A1092
Volume Shoe Corporation A932, A1092
Volunteer Fabricators (furniture) P635
Volunteer Firefighters' Length of Service Award System A315, P97
Volvic water W192, W193
AB Volvo A198, A616, A710, P644, P647, P701, P717, W188, W370, W480, W508, W546, W564, W630, **W632-W633**
Von Ballestrem, Ferdinand Graf W351
von Bernuth, Carl W. A1423
Von Braun, Wernher A1256
von Dehn, Hyatt A740, P240
von der Nahmer, Paul W82
Von Durpin exit devices A755
Von Eschenbach, Andrew C. P41
Von Furstenberg, Diane A216
von Glahn, William G. A1529
von Haeften, Jan W365
Von Hauske Solís, Oscar W581
von Heydebreck, Tessen W201
Von Krannichfeldt, Thomas W. A1157
von Kuhn, Geoffrey A. A167
von Linde, Karl A1156
von Menges, Klaus W351
Von Ohlen, Jack A975
von Pierer, Heinrich W536, W537
von Prondzynski, Heino W493
von Reininghaus, Eberhard W380
von Schimmelmann, Wulf W203
von Siemens, Georg W200
von Siemens, Werner W536
von Zuben, Fred G. P689
Vonderheide, Scott D. A557
Vonesh, John A1113
Vonnegut Industrial Products A1538
Vonnegut, Kurt P496
The Vons Companies, Inc. (supermarkets) A784, A1234, P462
Vorad brand A527
Gesellschaft zur Vorbereitung des Volkswagen W630
Vornado Realty Trust **E137**, E150, E314, P398
Vortex Sound Communications P350

Vorwaller, Gregory P121
Vorwerk & Company A1414
Vos beer W255
Vosicky, John J. A393
Voss, Arthur T. E64
Voss, Scott A163
Voss, Terry J. P37
Voss, Thomas R. A137
Voss, William H. A453
Vossloh AG W201
Vought Aircraft Industries, Inc. A1044, P766
Vowles, Ken L. W523
Voyage expedition E206
Voyager of the Seas (cruise ship) A1217
Voyageur Fund Managers A878
Voyageur Travel Insurance W474
VPSI van leasing A300
Vranas, Andreas W385
VRB Corporation A395
Vredenburg, David P636
Vrins, Henk A. M. W178
VSEA. *See* Varian Semiconductor Equipment Associates, Inc.
V.SHOP stores W623
VSOP cognac W85
VSZ. *See* U.S. Steel Kosice; U.S. Steel Kosice sro
VT Inc. P767
VTech Holdings Limited A898
VTG-Lehnkering AG (freight) W460, W461
VTM-TV W626
VTR Larga Distancia W576
VTR (video distributor) P68
VTR-Celular W576
Vuitton, Georges W348
Vuitton, Louis W348
Vuitton stores W348
Vujovich, Christine M. A457
Vulcan Industries (displays) P170, P171
Vulcan Materials Company A**1484**-A**1485**
Vulcan Northwest Inc. P**510**-P**511**, P593, P767
Vulcan Service/Periodical Sales P171
Vulcan Spice Mills A358
Vulcan Ventures P166, P510, P511
Vulcanite eyeglass frames A234
Vulcraft (steel joists) A1052
VU/TEXT (online service) A832
Vuursteen Karel W254, W255
VWR Scientific Products P208
VWR Textiles & Supplies A858
Vyakhirev, Rem W242

W

W. & O. Bergmann W460
W. Duke and Sons A618
W. Flagler Investment A624
Aktiebolaget W. Gutzeit & Company W556
W Holding Company E314
W Hotels A1328

W. Lee Flowers & Company, Inc. P243
W. Lowenstein (home furnishings) A1316, P452
W. Lyman Case (mortgage banker) A592
W (magazine) P33
W.A. Bechtel & Co. A240, P74
Waack, William A. P407
Waaser, R. Ernest A719
Waban (warehouse club sales) A262, A1388
Wabash Alloys P581
Wabash Railroad A1038
Wabasso home furnishings A1317, P453
WABCO (railroad brakes) A152, A153
WABC-TV (New York City) A61
Wachi, Masatada W649
Wachner, Linda J. A1498, A1499
Wachovia Banks A549
Wachovia Corporation A230, A270, A1332, A1346, A**1486**-A**1487**, E148, E249. *See also* First Union Corporation
Wachtel, Michael D. A1069
Wachtell, Lipton, Rosen & Katz A1288, P446
The Wackenhut Corporation A190, A**1488**-A**1489**
Wackenhut Corrections Corporation E**138**, E187, E314
Wackenhut, George R. A1488, A1489, E138
Wackenhut, Richard R. A1489
Wackenhut, Ruth J. A1489
Wacker-Chemie (semiconductors) W102
Waco (Texas) *Tribune-Herald* A443
Wada, Hiroyoshi W597
Wada, Hisashi W321
Wada, Norio W401
Waddell & Reed Financial, Inc. A1390, E315
Waddell, John C. A196, A197
Waddell, M. Keith A1209
Waddell Ranch E263
Wade, Craig G. A1429, P491
Wade, Daniel M. A966, A967
Wade, Dennis A699
Wade, Gregory L. W377
Wade, Marion A1272
Wadlington, Cuba, Jr. A1529
Wadworth 6X beer W289
Waechter, Thomas H. E123, E292
Waegelin, Robert A. E309
Waesche, Horst W103
Waesche, Roger A., Jr. E187
Wafer ID E43
WaferGage E48
WaferTech A170
Waffle House Inc. P**512**-P**513**, P767
Wager, Deidra A1327
Wagman, David A958
Wagner Act (1936) P34

Wagner, Barry J. A1063
Wagner brand A585
Wagner, David L. P379
Wagner, Gretchen P541
Wagner, Harold A. A101
Wagner, Ivan P748
Wagner, Jeanette S. A565
Wagner, John E180
Wagner, Klaus W350
Wagner, Mark A673, P211
Wagner Mining Equipment A1078
Wagner, Paul P679
Wagner, Peter W203
Wagner, Robert B. E142, E319
Wagner Stott Bear Specialists A238
Wagner Stott Mercator A238
Wagoner, G. Richard, Jr. A650, A651
Wagonlit Travel. *See* Carlson Wagonlit Travel
Wagons-Lits P108, P567, W58, W59
Wagstaff, Caroline W337
Waguespack, Hickley M. E111
Wahaha water W193
Wahl, Andrew D. E261
Wahl, Dale N. E243
Wahl, John C. E204
Wahl, Robert G. A73
Wahlström, Mats W525
Wahrenbrock, Jim A851, P289
Waialua Agricultural Company A494
Waichunas, Ann P213
Wainscott, James L. A105
Waisanen, Larry J. A849
Waite, Brad A. A261
Waite, Donald L. A1261, P441
Waite-Lusk, Debbra A1087
Waitt, Norm A636
Waitt, Theodore W. A636, A637
Waitukaitis, Mike P203, P617
Wakasa, Tokuji W80
Wake Forest University Baptist Medical Center P768
Wake, Richard P601
Wake, Tom P601
Wake, William P601
Wakefern Food Corporation A**1490**-A**1491**, P479, P**514**-P**515**, P554, P640, P768
Wakefield, Bernard P587
Wakefield, Stephen A. A1307
Waki, Eitaro W397
Wakuya, Nobuo W235
Walcott, Derek P560
Waldbaum's grocery stores A670, A671
Waldek, David P. E150
Walden Book Company A276, A830
Walden, John C. A255
Walden Pond E34
Walden Residential Properties P232, P233
Waldman, David L. P715
Waldo, Ladd P718
Waldo, Mary Helen E286

Waldoks, Phillip H. A693
Waldorf-Astoria hotel A720
Waldron, Anne P67
Waldron, Maureen P581
Waldrop, Robert L. A1199
Walenczyk, Bruce E. A115
Walgreen, Charles A1492
Walgreen, Charles, III A1492
Walgreen Company A1202, A**1492**-A**1493**, A1494, P639
Walgren, Shari L. E94, E246
Walker & Associates E172
Walker automotive products A1368
Walker, Brian C. A707
Walker Brothers Grocery P488
Walker, Cecil L. A633
Walker, Dan A187
Walker, David A. (Morgan Stanley) A989
Walker, David A. (Pier 1) A1131
Walker, David N. (LCC International) E232
Walker, David P. (Credit Suisse First Boston) A449
Walker, Debra A797
Walker Drug stores A156
Walker, Edmund W156
Walker, Edward V. P363
Walker F. Borden A133
Walker, Gary G. A1321
Walker, Henry G. P706
Walker, Jeffrey C. A809
Walker, John E. (Continental Airlines) A429
Walker, John H. W. (Tate & Lyle) W569
Walker, John P. (Emerson Radio) E58
Walker, Kelly E146
Walker, Kenneth L. P443
Walker Manufacturing A1368
Walker, Mark (C.H. Robinson Worldwide) A345
Walker, Mark (Klaussner Furniture) P652
Walker, Mervyn W141
Walker, Norman W415
Walker, Paul D. A411
Walker, R. A. E146
Walker, Richard W201
Walker, Rob (Compaq) A399
Walker, Robert C. (Associated Wholesale Grocers) P63, P547
Walker, Robert R. (Agilent) A99
Walker, Robert (U.S. Concrete) E309
Walker, Ronald C. (Imperial Oil) W281
Walker, Ronald E. (Shoney's) A1281
Walker, Samuel P132
Walker Stainless (trailers) A326
Walker, Todd A. A1459
Walker, William (Arthur D. Little) P54
Walker, William (TeleTech) E127
Walking (magazine) A1192

Walking With Dinosaurs (TV show) P158, P594
Walkman personal stereo W550
Walkup's Merchant Express A1454
Walkush, J. P. P439
Wall, Charles A1127
Wall, James H. A475, P155, P590, W197
Wall, John C. (Cummins Engine) A457
Wall, John T. (NASD) A997, P353
Wall, Malcolm W621
The Wall Street Journal A506, A507, A632, A1020, A1202, P80
Wallac Group (diagnostic systems) A1110
Wallace, Brian W259
Wallace, Chris A281
Wallace Computer Services, Inc. A274
Wallace, DeWitt A1192
Wallace, Eugene C. P566
Wallace, Graham M. W152, W153
Wallace, Henry D. G. A617
Wallace, James B. E129
Wallace, Janet B. A1425
Wallace, Jean B. A821
Wallace Law Registry A818
Wallace, Lila A1192
Wallace Manufacturing (paneling) A1456
Wallace, Ronald G. A1427
Wallace Sanders Business Consulting, L.P. A681
Wallace, Stephen P. E37
Wallace, Timothy G. (Healthcare Realty Trust) E211
Wallace, Timothy R. (Trinity Industries) A1406, A1407
Wallace, W. Ray A1406, A1407
Wallach, Abraham A1409, P483
Wallach Brothers clothing A690
The Wallach Company A822
Wallach, Dan P27, P528
Wallach, Kenneth L. P571
Wallaesa, Harry A401, A1233
Wallau, Alex A61
Wallenberg family W220
Wallenberg, Jacob W211
Wallenberg, Marcus W72, W210, W518
Waller, Jeffrey M. A1247, P433
Waller, Robert A916
Wallerstein A236
Waller-Sutton Media Partners E277
Wallin & Nordstrom shoe store A1036
Wallin, Carl A1036
Wallin, Winston A952
Wallinger, R. Scott A1517
Wallis, Stan (AMP) W89
Wallis, Stanley D. M. (Coles Myer) W173
Wallman, Richard F. A729
Wallsten Lloyd P143
Wal-Mart de México, S.A. de C.V. A1494, W**634**-W**635**

Wal-Mart Stores, Inc. A66, A158, A208, A260, A262, A266, A436, A470, A496, A520, A548, A549, A572, A578, A596, A606, A630, A664, A692, A708, A788, A802, A830, A926, A992, A1000, A1022, A1092, A1134, A1148, A1196, A1220, A1264, A1270, A1282, A1312, A1316, A1348, A1352, A1374, A1396, A1458, A1470, A1474, **A1494-A1495**, A1532, A1553, E58, E198, E201, E214, E225, E246, E283, E298, P102, P103, P168, P198, P236, P260, P346, P394, P452, P486, P565, P595, P632, P633, P644, P646, P733, W164, W234, W270, W300, W312, W528, W606, W608, W634

Walsh, Bill P173

Walsh, David J. A1255

Walsh, Ed A317

The Walsh Group P768

Walsh, Jim P329, P671

Walsh, Matthew M. P768

Walsh, Patricia E68, E214

Walsh, Paul S. A1136, W206, W207

Walsh, Richard F. (PerkinElmer) A1111

Walsh, Richard J. (Darden Restaurants) A465

Walsh, Tim P610

Walsh, William D. A421

Walsh, W. S. W88

The Walt Disney Company A60, A80, A252, A312, A334, A382, A390, A622, A692, A700, A701, A712, A720, A830, A831, A832, A926, A927, A1284, A1316, A1328, A1346, **A1496-A1497**, E60, E103, E135, E266, P32, P166, P176, P228, P229, P296, P360, P452, P476, P524, P597, P605, P682, P733, P745, W332, W390

Walt Disney Internet Group A60, A1496, E54, P492, P524, W106

Walt Disney Studios A98

Walter, Elisse Barbara A997

Walter, Henry A766

Walter Industries, Inc. (builders) A836, A837, P282, P283

Walter, John A1218

Walter Kidde & Company A1446

Walter, Michael D. A409

Walter Reed Army Hospital E90

Walter, Robert D. A320, A321

Walter, W. Edward A733

Walter, William G. A613

WALTERMART SUPERMARKETS P243

Walters, Beth A. A783

Walters, Daniel B. A687

Walters, Eric G. E105

Walters, James A1541

Walters, Kirk W. E178

Walters, Louis M. A441

Walters, Paul F. P391

Walters, Robert F. A799

Walters, William (CSX Corp.) A454

Walthall, William L. (Goodrich) A663

Waltham pet food A915, P315

Walthie, Theo A505

Waltman, Howard L. A575

Walton 5 & 10 store A1494

Walton, Bill R. P77

Walton, James "Bud" A1494

Walton, Jerry W. A789

Walton, Jon D. A117

Walton, Joseph F. A543

Walton, R. Keith P135

Walton, Robert D. A315, P97

Walton, Sam A1092, A1494, P198, P260

Walton, S. Robson A1495

Walton, William L. E151

Waltrip, Robert L. A1268, A1269

Waltrip, William H. A234, A235

Waltzinger, G. William, Jr. A247

Wamberg, W. T. E180

Wamhoff, Richard H. A723

Wampler Foods A1132

Wamsutta home furnishings A1316, A1317, P452, P453

WaMu. See Washington Mutual, Inc.

Wan, David W431

Wan, Tracy A1275, E120

Wanadoo (Internet service provider) W232

Wandell, Keith E. A803

Wander group (dietetic products) W414

W&L Technologies, Inc. A567

Wandmacher, William N. A1293

W&R Funds E315

Wandschneider, Gary K. A1103

Wanek, Ron P544

Wanek, Todd P544

Wang, Caden P157, P592

Wang, Charles B. A402, A403

Wang, David N. K. A189

Wang, J. T. W61

Wang, Stanley L. A391

Wang, Susan (Formosa Plastics) W229

Wang, Susan S. (Solectron) A1299

Wang, Yung-ching W228, W229

Wangurd, Debra P764

WAPE-FM (Jacksonville) P147

War Damage Corporation A1236

Warburg Dillon Read (investments) W616

Warburg Pincus Funds W184, W185

Warburg Pincus LLC A1434, E33, P276, P652

Warburg, Pincus Ventures E292

Ward Baking Company A774

Ward, Brian F. E124

Ward, Charles G., III A449

Ward, Germaine A779

Ward, Jim P303

Ward, John F. (Russell) A1220, A1221

Ward, Jonathan P. (ServiceMaster) A1273

Ward, Lloyd D. A934

Ward, Louis P424

Ward Paper Box Company P424

Ward, Scott H. P424, P425, P719

Ward, S. E. A1277

Ward stores A932

Ward, Thomas S. (Russell Stover) P424, P425, P719

Ward, Tom L. (Chesapeake Energy) E39, E176

Ward, William A774

Warde, George W70

Warden, Gail L. P630

Warden, William C., Jr. A893

Wardley (investment banking) W268

Wardrip, Rocky D. A135

Wardrop, Richard M., Jr. A104, A105

Wards Company A366

Ware, Carl A383

Ware, John H., Jr. A154

Ware, John, III A154

Ware, Marilyn A155

Wäreby, Jan W221

Wareham, James L. A105

Wareham, John P. A242, A243

Warehouse.com P338

Waremart Foods P773

Warener Brothers A1546

Warga, Thomas J. A1017, P371

Warhol, Andy A316

Warka beer W255

Warlick, Anderson D. P696

Warm Wishes greeting cards A678, P216

The Warnaco Group, Inc. **A1498-A1499**, P100

Warner, Abe A180

Warner, Bob A497

Warner, Bradford H. A603

Warner Brothers A180, A181, A622, A962, A1274, A1496, E120, E147, P278, P350, P417, W296

Warner Brothers Worldwide Publishing A1254

Warner Communications W342. See AOL Time Warner Inc.

Warner, DeVer A1498

Warner, Douglas A., III A809

Warner Electric Group, Ltd. A460

Warner Gear A278

Warner, Harry A180

Warner (hotels and resorts) W472

Warner, H. Ty A487, P751

Warner, Jack (Warner Bros.) A180

Warner, John D. (Boeing) A273

Warner, John H., Jr. (Science Applications) P439

Warner, Lucien A1498

Warner, M. Richard A1365

Warner Music Group A180, A181, W212

Warner, Sam A180

Warner, Tim P127

Warner, Ty P486

Warner-Ishi A278

Warner-Lambert. *See* Pfizer Inc.
Warner-Pioneer W448
Warner's brand lingerie A838, A839, A1498, A1499
Warning: Dieting May Be Hazardous To Your Health (educational video) P139
Warnock, Dan W. A1465
Warnock, John E. A76, A77
Warnshuis, Glenn E124
Warren Bank A602
Warren, Benjamin S. A743
Warren, David P. P353
Warren Electric Group, Ltd. P578
Warren Equities Inc. P769
Warren, George E. P614
Warren, Jeffrey S. A1263
Warren, John E., III E28, E156
Warren, Joseph G., Jr. E185
Warren, Robert J. A489
Warren, V'Ella P761
Warren Walker (educational resources) A191
Warrin, Catherine P554
Warrington, George D. P362, P363, P684
Warshauer, Myron P236, P237
Warshaw, Steven G. A354, A355
Warson, Toby A120
Wartsila NSD A456
Warwick Electronics A1520
Wasa crackers W414
Wasai, Hiromi W401
Wasall A1456
Wasatech Electric Company A545
Wascoe, Thomas M. A59
Wash 'n Dri cleaning product A375
Washburn, Cadwallader A648
Washburn Crosby Company A648
Washburn, Frank A148
Washburn, W. D. A1348
Washington Capitals (hockey team) P361
Washington Central Railroad A308
The Washington Companies. *See* Washington Group International, Inc.
Washington Counsel (lobbying) A562, P182, W222
Washington County Light and Power Company. *See* Consumers Power Company
Washington County Light & Power Company. *See* Monongahela Power Company
Washington Group International, Inc. A1190, P769
Washington, Lawrence J., Jr. A505
Washington Mutual, Inc. A488, A658, A1146, A**1500**-A**1501**
Washington Mutual Life Insurance A1230
Washington Mystics (basketball team) P355
Washington National Bank A1500
Washington National Building Loan and Investment Association A1500

The Washington Post Company A252, A253, A728, A1020, A1021, A**1502**-A**1503**, P176
Washington Redskins (football team) P357
Washington Specialty Metals A1224
Washington University in St. Louis P769
Washington University Medical Center P555
Washington Wizards (basketball team) P354, P355
Washkewicz, Donald E. A1088, A1089
Wasilov, Alex P419
Wassall PLC A642, A836, P282
Wasser, Marilyn J. A203
Wasserman, David S. A687
Wasserstein Perella & Company A388, A630, W408
Wasson, Gregory D. A1493
Wasson, Pam E267
Wasson, Ted P773
Waste Connections, Inc. E**139**, E315
Waste Control Specialties P583
Waste Management, Inc. A122, A206, A1272, A**1504**-A**1505**, A1548, E297
Waste Material Recycling E285
Waste Recycling Group PLC W252
Watanabe, Akira W305
Watanabe, August M. A541
Watanabe, Kazuhide W363
Watanabe, Kenichi W409
Watanabe, Shigeo W138, W139
Watanabe, Toshizo "Tom" P689
Watari, Sugichiro W610
Watchmaker, Kenneth I. A1195
Watchung Hills Bank for Savings A658
Water Pik Technologies, Inc. A116, P71
Water Resources International E163
Water Works Supply A620
Waterford Wedgwood plc W**636**-W**637**
Watergate A1502
Waterhouse, Edwin A1158, P400, W462
Waterhouse Investor Services W608
Waterhouse National Bank W608
Waterloo Industries A618
Waterman, Bruce W67
Waterman office products A1023, P262
Waterman pens A656
Waterman, Robert A. A695
Waters, John F., Jr. A867
Waters, Ronald V. A1527
Waters, Tom P. A719
Waterstone bookstores W212
Watford, Michael D. E307
Watjen, Thomas R. A1441
Watkins Associated Industries P770
Watkins, Aurmond, A. A1055

Watkins, Bill (Watkins Associated Industries) P770
Watkins, Carole S. A321
Watkins, George E. A413
Watkins, H. Thomas P741
Watkins, Ian J. A235
Watkins, James W307
Watkins, John P770
Watkins, Peter A945
Watkins, William D. (Seagate) A1260, A1261, P440, P441
WATL-TV (Atlanta) A1402
Watney Mann (brewer) W206
WATS Marketing (telemarketing) A292
Watsmann, Judy P291, P656
Watson, Anne N. A145
Watson, Anthony L. P628
Watson, Charles E. (Jack in the Box) A785
Watson, Charles L. (Dynegy) A518, A519
Watson, Craig M. A613
Watson Foodservice A1350
Watson, Gary L. A633
Watson, I. Benjamin A1319
Watson, John S. A353
Watson, Mary A1541
Watson, Max P., Jr. A270
Watson, Noel G. A786, A787
Watson Pharmaceuticals, Inc. E89
Watson, Robert A., IV A1485
Watson, Solomon B., IV A1021
Watson, Thomas A764, A1378
Watson, Weldon L. A1065
Watson-Wilson Transportation System A1548
Watt, Andrew R. A819
Watt, David J. W495
Watt, Graeme A1357
Watt, James A. E278
Watt, Linda M. A887
Watterson, Scott R. P637
Wattier, Philippe W183
Wattie's Limited (food processing) A722
Watts, Christie E237
Watts, Harry W644
Watts, Howard P115
Watts, Jeffrey E171
Watts, Peter E85
Watts, Philip B. W501
Watts, Richard H. A1169
Waugh, Richard B., Jr. A1045
Wausau A875, A1008, P364
Wausau Commercial Insurance Market P295
Wausau Paper Mills A284
Wauth, Ed P644
Wave radio P92, P93, P559
Wave Technologies International W592
Wavefront Technologies A1284
Waverly furniture P299
Waverly (publishing) W642
WaveRunners W648

Wavish, William P. R. W645
Wavtrace (wireless access equipment) A686, P511
Wawa Inc. P770
Wawak, Wladyslaw W457
Wawersich, Thomas R. A595
Wax, Charles J. P53, P543
WAXN-TV (Charlotte, NC) A443, P147
Way, Kenneth L. A856, A857
Waycaster, Bill P745
Wayfoong (mortgage) W268
Waylung Waste Collection Ltd. W565
Wayman, Robert P. A713
Wayne Farms, LLC A427
Wayne Foods A426, P140
Wayne Homes A340
Wayne State University P591
Wayne State University School of Medicine P773
Waypoint Financial Corporation E315
The WB Television Network A180, A181, A1402, A1403
WBAB-FM (Long Island, NY) P147
WBAL-TV (Baltimore) A700, P228
WBDC-TV (Washington, DC) A1402
WBLI-FM (Long Island, NY) P147
WBNT-TV (New York) A998
WBTS-FM (Atlanta) P147
WBZL-TV (Miami) A1402
W.C. Bradley & Company A298
W.C. Norris (oil well components) A502
WCI Communities, Inc. P770
WCI Steel, Inc. P712
WCPO-TV (Cincinnati, OH) A568, A569
WDUV-FM (Tampa, FL) P147
We Care Hair Salons A1196, P160
WE: Women's Entertainment cable network A313, A962
The Weakest Link (TV show) A998, A999
WealthBuilder annuities P617
Wear Products A1406
WearEver-ProctorSilex A992
WearGuard-Crest (uniforms) A191
Weather Channel P655
Weatherall, Bob E221
Weatherall, Percy W307
WeatherBeater brand A1265
Weatherhead Company (auto parts) A460, A461
Weatherholtz, Karen D. A939
Weatheringon, Carman P177
Weatherley, Sue E301
Weatherly, E. Mitchell A1131
Weatherup, Craig E. A1102, A1103, A1107
Weaver chicken A1419
Weaver Corporation (automotive lifts) A502
Weaver, Don A. A1533
Weaver, Greg H. E101, E259
Weaver, H. Pratt P480

Weaver, Philip G. A433
Weaver, William F. A107
Webauction.com P338
Webb, Chris W177
Webb, Del P643
Webb, Maynard G. E54
Webb, Michael G. (Kerr-McGee) A821
Webb, Michael R. (Service Corp.) A1269
Webb, Robert W141
Webb, Thomas J. A817
Webb, William H. A1127
Webber, Henry P497
WebCal Internet scheduling products A1546
WebCam Freestyle W181
Webcraft P506, P765
Webegg S.p.A. (consulting) W423
Weber, Arnold R. P379
Weber, Jürgen W345
Weber, Larry A773
Weber, Lisa M. A965
Weber, Mark R. A477
Weber, Paul P642
Weber, Peter E. A613
Weber, Robinn S. P425, P719
Weber, Ronald A. A977
Weber Shandwick Worldwide A772, A773
Weber, Tom P704
Weber's bread A774, A775
WebForce Suite software E191
WebLogic software E33, E163
WebMD Corporation A60, A698, A952, A1192, W390
WEBS. *See* World Equity Benchmark Shares
Webster, Bill P549
Webster, Holt A102
Webster, Michael S. A819
Webster, Steven E173
WebTV Networks, Inc. A928, A972, A973
Webvan P266
Wechsler Coffee A1242
Weckx, André W289
The Wedding (movie) P219
WeddingChannel.com A586, A587, A902, A903, A1552, P305, P663
WeddingNetwork Web site A246
Wedge, Michael T. A263
Wedgwood, Alan W636
Wedgwood Group W636, W637
Wedgwood, Josiah W636
Wedo, Anthony D. E253
WEDR-FM (Miami) P147
Weebles toys A693
Weebok shoes A1194, A1195
Weed, David G. A1235
Weed Eater garden tools W210
Weed, Joe K. P171
Weeker, J. T. A1429, P491
Weekley, David P588
Weekly, John W. P349, P680
Weekly Reader (magazine) A1160
Weeks Corporation E194

Weeks, Darwin J. A785
Weeks, Mark S. A323
Weetman, Geoffrey A. W485
Weg, Kenneth E. A291
Wega flat screen TV W550
Wege, Peter M. A1334
Wege, Peter M., II A1334
Wege, Peter, Sr. A1334
Weger, Hans S. E231
Wegman, John P771
Wegman, Robert B. P771
Wegmans Food Markets, Inc. P771
Wegworth, Glen A. A803
Wehmeier, Helge H. W119
Wehmer, Edward J. E318
Wehmeyer clothing stores W310, W311
Wehrli, Cary P536
Wehrnyak, Ronald J. A1007
Weich, Barbara Jane A262
Weich, Mervyn A262
Weicher, Richard E. A309
Weicker, Theodore A956
Weida, Katherine S. A387
Weidemeyer, Thomas H. A1427
Weider Health & Fitness P637
Weight Watchers International, Inc. A722, A723, A1498, A1499
Weigner, Ronald C. E246
Weigold, Franklin A. A171
Weikel, M. Keith A909
Weil, Gilles W343
Weil, William S. A859
Weiland, John H. A445
Weill, Sanford I. A370, A371, A860
Weimer, Linda P501
Weinbach, Arthur F. A204, A205
Weinbach, Lawrence A. A172, A1424, A1425, P48, W90
Weinberg, Alan S. A1263
Weinberg College of Arts and Sciences P379
Weinberg, David E289
Weinberg, D. Mark A1507
Weinberg, Harvey A690
Weinberg, John A660
Weinberg, Peter A. A661
Weinberg, Richard A. P612
Weinberg, Serge W446, W447
Weinberg, Sidney A660
Weinberger, Alan D. P544
Weinberger, Carlyle P544
Weinberger, Robert A. A681
Weiner, Edward G. P748
Weiner, Robert B. A573
Weiner, Steven P455
Weinshilboum, Richard M. P325
Weinstein, David C. A615, P191
Weinstein, Elaine A825
Weinstein family A1004
Weinstein, Norman E60
Weinstein, Steven I. A621
Weinstock, Arnold W354
Weintraub Entertainment Group A238
Weintraub, William H. A79

Weinzierl, Mark E219
Weir, Colin H. W267
Weir, E. K. W475
Weir Group A222
Weir, Helen W313
Weir, Thomas T. A139
Weirton Steel Corporation A100, A1006
Weis, Gerald R. "Gary" P580
Weis Markets, Inc. P479
Weisbarth, Michael A1059
Weisberg, Marc B. A1187
Weisenburger, Randall J. A1063
Weisheimer Companies (pet stores) A1116
Weismüller, Albert W353
Weiss, Daniel E. E217
Weiss, David A1336
Weiss, Douglas A. P145
Weiss, Erwin A147
Weiss, Jeffrey M. A147
Weiss, Judy E. A965
Weiss, Kenneth E114
Weiss, Louis A1490, P514
Weiss, Michael A877
Weiss, Morry A146, A147
Weiss, Peck & Greer P738
Weiss, Scott A. A375
Weiss, Wojciech Jerzy W457
Weisselberg, Allen A1409, P483, P749
Weisser, Alberto P565
Weissman, Jerry P174
Weitman, Gary A1403
Weitzen, Jeffrey A636
Weizenbaum, Morris P198
Wejman, Janet P. A429
Welborn, R. Michael A231
Welch, Dennis E. A1041
Welch, James S., Jr. (Brown-Forman) A297
Welch, James (Yellow Corp.) A1549
Welch, John F., Jr. "Jack" (General Electric) A646, A728, P757
Welch, John K. (General Dynamics) A645
Welch, Joseph L. A513
Welch, Kevin A1341
Welch, Kimberly A. A585
Welch, Michael T. A1181
Welch, Patrick P684
Welch's fruit drink A1104, A1105
Welch's juice P577, W154, W155
Weldcraft Products A502
Welded Tube Company of America A896
Welding, Robert D. A279
Weldon, William C. A801
Weliky, Charles (Consolidated Edison) A419
Weliky, Charles (PPL) A1155
Well Care HMO A738
Welland, David E288
Wellauer, Thomas W185
Wellcome, Henry W246
The Wellcome Trust W246

Wellcraft boats P614
Welle, Bernhard J. A487
Weller, H. S. P348
Weller soldering equipment A430
Welles, Judith P389
Wellferon drug W246
Wellington Management Group A688, A1468, P504
Wellington, Susan D. A1181
Wellmark Health Networks P226
WellPoint Health Networks Inc. A268, A**1506**-A**1507**, P82, P572
Wells BDDP (advertising) A1062
Wells, Ben K. A399
Wells Fargo & Company A142, A228, A252, A253, A594, A626, A**1508**-A**1509**, E27, E54, E154, E172, E249, P110, P518
Wells, Frank A1496
Wells, Harry A938
Wells, Henry A142
Wells, James M., III A1347
Wells, Jeffrey S. A367
Wells, Joel A1346
Wells Lamont Corporation P312, P313
Wells Manufacturing Corporation (automotive products) P113, P752
Wells, Norman E., Jr. P408, P409
Wells, Robert B. W113
Wells, William P565
Wellspring Grocery A1522
Welsbach Electric Corporation A544, A545
Welsh, Carson, Anderson & Stowe (venture capital) E38, E174, E286
Welsh, George A. A717, P235
Welsh, Kelly R. A1043
Welsh, Mark A141
Welt am Sonntag (newspaper) W107
Welton, Julie E249
Welty, Eudora A1182
Welty, John D. P99
Wenck, David H. A751
Wendlandt, Gary E. A1017, P371
Wendt, Gary A414
Wendt, Gary C. A414, A415
Wendt, Richard L. P643
Wendy's International, Inc. A302, A942, A1084, A1132, A1350, A**1510**-A**1511**, P702
Wengert's dairy product A467
Wenig, Devin N. W485
Wenner-Gren, Axel W210
Wenning, Werner W119
Wenninger, Fred A778
Wenstrom, Jonas W54
Wentworth art galleries A614, P190
Wenz, George A. A147
Werbin, Dan W633
Werndl BuroMobel (office furniture) A1334
Werner, Earl K. A683

Werner Enterprises (trucking) A788
Werner, Jon A1227
Werner, Mary Ann A1355, P467
Werner, Olle W73
Wertheim Schroder & Co. (broker) A158
Werthén, Hans W210, W220
Wertkauf (hypermarket chain) A1494
Wertz, Carl E192
WESCO International, Inc. A**1512**-A**1513**, W536
Wescom (telecom) A1362
Wesendonck, Hugo P214
WeServeHomes.com A1272
Wesley Jessen VisionCare A234, W414
Wesley, Norman H. A619
Wesley-Clough, Marita A679, P217
Weslo fitness equipment P637
Wesray Capital Corporation A212
Wesser Fruit Juices A1105
Wessex Water PLC A552
Wessner, Kenneth A1272
Wesson oil A408, A409
West, Barry A1027
West Bend (appliances) A748
West, Catherine A319
West Coast Hockey League P361
West Coast Life Insurance A1008, P364
West, David J. A709
West, George E. A1079
West, Gloria E312
West, Henry J. P313
West Indies Sugar Company W568
West Instruments A462
West Kootenay Power Limited A1464, A1465
West Lynn Creamery A1339
West, Mary C. A959
West Missouri Power A1464
West Musgrave mine W640
West Penn Electric Company A114
West Penn Power Company A114
West, Richard P. P99, P564
West, Robert A1374
West Side Lighting A532
West, Stephen O. P201, P616
West Texas A&M University P470
West Texas Health Plans, L.C. P227
West Texas Pipeline Partnership A519, A1466
West Virginia Management Services Organization, Inc. A695
West Virginia Pulp and Paper Company A1516
Westab (school and office supplies) A950
Westbrock, Leon P123
Westcon Group, Inc. P771
Westcorp E316
Westcott Communications A1160
Westdeutsche Landesbank W364, W460
Westech Mobile Solutions E144

Westenberger, Richard F. A1265
Westendorf, Alan J. A1157
Westerburgen, Jos W619
Westerlaken, Arie W445
Westerling, Dick P413
Westerlund, David A. A225
Western AG-Minerals A752
Western Air Lines A478
Western Aluminum NL W640
Western Areas Ltd. W452
Western Atlas A222
Western Auto stores A1100, A1264, E21
Western, B. Curtis A697
Western Cartridge A1060
Western Counties (utility) A1040
Western Dairymen Cooperative P58, P148
Western Digital Corporation A410, A1357, A**1514**-A**1515**
Western Drug Distributors A886
Western Electric Manufacturing Company A202, A898, A1378, E81, P208, W386, W412, W550
Western Family Foods, Inc. (grocery wholesaler) P488, P545, P752
Western Farm Credit Bank P534
Western Farm Service, Inc. W66, W67
Western Feed Division P771
Western Fiberglass Group A1072
Western Financial Bank E316, E317
Western Financial Trust Company A591
Western Fruit Express Company A309
Western Gas Resources, Inc. E200
Western GECO A222, A223, A1252
Western Grocers W244
Western International Media A772
Western Kraft Corporation A1524
Western Maryland Railway A454
Western Massachusetts Electric Company A1040, A1041
Western Mining Group (WMC) W640
Western Mobile of New Mexico (road construction) A848
Western Multiplex Corporation E316
Western National Life Insurance A414
Western National Warranty A378
Western Nuclear (uranium mining) A1124
Western Pacific (railroad) A1422
Western Paper A770
Western Pennsylvania Caring Foundation A716, P234, P632
The Western Pennsylvania Scholastic newspaper A1254
Western Platinum Ltd. W340, W341
Western Power Distribution A1154, A1155, A1306
Western Professional Hockey League P361
Western Publishing A926

The Western Reserve Telephone Company A128
Western Resources, Inc. A1065, A1464
Western Summit Constructors P745
Western Textbook Exchange P192
Western Union A202, A248, A404, A484, A596, A898, A1362, A1478, A1480, A1544, P508
Western Universal Life Insurance A696
Western Veneer and Plywood A1524
Western Waste Industries A1504
Western Wireless Corporation E38, W272
WesternBank Puerto Rico E314
Westervelt, Conrad A272
WestEx, Inc. A1548
Westfall, Kevin P. A207
Westfall, Timothy C. A509
WestFarm Foods P771
Westfield Bank P693
Westfield Capital Management E165
Westfield Insurance P693
Westies clothing A805
Westin, David A61
Westin hotels A1328, A1329
Westinghouse P94, P276, P350
Westinghouse Air Brake. *See* WABCO
Westinghouse Electric Company A334, A526, A646, A754, A954, A998, A1512, W444
Westinghouse Electric Supply Company. *See* WESCO International, Inc.
Westinghouse, George A642, A1512
Westinghouse Process Control Division A546
Westlake, W. James W475
WestLB. *See* Westdeusche Landesbank
Westley's car care products A1097
Westling, Jon P560
Westman, Bob P614
Westmark Realty P120
Westmiller, Michael A1341
Westminster Health Care A1366
Westoil Marine P574
Weston Bakeries Limited W245
Weston, Garfield W244
Weston, George W244
Weston, John W111
Weston, Josh A204
Weston, W. Galen W244, W245
Westpac Banking Corporation W382
WestPoint Stevens Inc. (home textiles) A1134, A1150
Westport Resources Corporation E316
Westport travel trailers A605
Westralian Sands Ltd. W252
Westronic (control systems) A686
WestStar Bank E310

Westvaco Corporation A612, A950, A1248, A1364, A**1516**-A**1517**
Westwood One, Inc. E**140**, E317
Westwood Swinerton (contracting) P740
Wet 'n Wild theme park A440
Wet Seal, Inc. A1014
Wetair.com E188
Wetheim, Herbert E67, E212
Wethington, Charles T., Jr. P757
Wetle, Michael D. E48
Wetmore, Douglas J. A767
Wetterau Associates (food wholesalers) A1348, P202, P524, P617
Wetterau, Mark S. P202, P203, P617
Wetz, Byron A. A1361
WEWS-TV (Cleveland, OH) A568, A569
Wexner, Leslie H. A776, A777, A876, A877
Weyerhaeuser Company A756, A**1518**-A**1519**, P244, P574
Weyerhaeuser, Frederick A756, A1518, P244
Weyerhaeuser, George H., Jr. A1518, A1519
Weyerhaeuser Headquarters (Tacoma, WA) P449
Weyerhaeuser, J. P., Jr. "Phil" A1518
Weyman & Brothers A1458
Weyman, George A1458
Weyman-Bruton A1458
Weymuller, Bruno W613
W.F. Linton Company A1022
WFAN E140
WFS Financial Inc. E316, E317
WFTS-TV (Tampa, FL) A568, A569
WFTV-TV (Orlando, FL) A443, P147
WFYV-FM (Jacksonville) P147
WGAY radio (Silver Springs, MD) P332
WGNO-TV (New Orleans) A1402
WGN-TV (Chicago) A1402
WGRT radio station (Chicago) P258
WH Smith PLC W622
W. H. Snyder & Sons (cigar company) A1458
Whalen & Company (site development) E128
Whalen, Wayne W. P447
Whaley, Bobby A667
Whaley, Ronald L. P731
Whalley, Greg A553
Wharton, Clifton A1354, P466
Wharton, L. Carole P451
Wharton School P759
What Lies Beneath (movie) P166, P167
Whataburger, Inc. (fast food restaurants) A608
Whatchamacallit candy A709
Whatcott, Lee A. E316, E317
Whatley, Tom P317
Whatman (purification products) A1088
whatyoucrave.com P516

Whealy, Michael T. A597
Wheat, Allen D. A448
Wheat Thins crackers A843
Wheatable crackers A815
Wheaties A648, A649
Wheel Horse (mowers) A1392
Wheel of Fortune (TV show) A334
Wheeler, Arnie P549
Wheeler, Clifton A620
Wheeler Condenser &
  Engineering A620
Wheeler, Frederick A620
Wheeler Group (office
  supplies) A1142
Wheeler Group (tube
  distributor) P312
Wheeler, John E., Jr. (Crown Central
  Petroleum) P586
Wheeler, John (Tribune
  Company) A1402
Wheeler, Linda K. A1025
Wheeler, Paul P281, P653
Wheeler, R. Channing A1435
Wheeler, Robert C. A387
Wheeler, Steven A1139
Wheeler, William M. P706
Wheelers (farm goods) P406
Wheeling-Pittsburgh Steel
  Corporation A256
Wheels (auto leasing) P611
Wheelwright, George, III A1148
Whelan, John P617
Whelan, Karen M. A1437
Whelton, Robert E92
Wherehouse Entertainment,
  Inc. A1476, P524
Whiddon, Thomas E. A893
Whilden, Robert H., Jr. A271
Whinney, Frederick A562, P182,
  W222
Whinney Murray
  (accounting) A562, P182, W222
Whinney, Smith & Whinney A562,
  W222
WHIO-AM, FM, and TV (Dayton,
  OH) A442, P146, P147
WhipperSnapple drinks A1400
Whipple, Arthur O. E273
Whirlpool Corporation A368, A934,
  A1520-A1521
Whirlwind (mowers) A1392
Whiskas pet food A914, A915, P314,
  P315, P665
Whiskey Pete's hotel and casino
  (Primm, NV) A966, A967
Whisler, J. Steven A1125
Whistler (radar detection) A1322
Whistling Straits golf course P285
Whitacre, Naomi E318
Whitacre, Edward E., Jr. A1244,
  A1245
Whitacre, John A1036
Whitacre, Mark A192
Whitaker & Company P260
Whitaker, Wharton P. E53
Whitbread PLC W84, W200, W288,
  W544, **W638-W639**

Whitbread, Robin W301
Whitbread, Samuel W638
Whitbread, Samuel, II W638
Whitbread, W. H. W638
White, Alex W177
White Barn Candle Company A776,
  A876
White, Bill A163
White Bridge
  Communications A757, P245
White, Britton, Jr. A537
White Castle System, Inc. A1296,
  P516-P517, P772
White Consolidated
  Industries W210
White, David A., Jr. (Cooper
  Industries) A431
White, David R. (IASIS
  Healthcare) P637
White, Edward W. A107
White, Eileen B. A433
White Electronic Designs
  Corporation E317
White, Gordon A974, A1446, W252,
  W604
White, Harvey P. E232
White Hen Pantry stores P577
White, H. Katherine A1263
White House Conference on Child
  Health and Protection P520
White, James M., III A1437
White, Jeffrey P307, P663
White, Jeremy E320
White, Jo Jo A280
White, Kathy Brittain A321
White Labs A1250
White, Miles D. A59
White Motors W632
White Mountain DSP A170
White Outdoor lawn
  equipment P679
White, Patricia E228
White, Peter W262
White Rain hair care A656
White, Raymon M. A687
White, Reed A. A389
White, Reggie P210
White, Richard (Ross Stores) A1215
White, Richard S., Jr.
  (SouthTrust) A1309
White River (insurance) P220
White Rose brands P478, P592
White, Samuel Elliott A1316, P452
White Stag brand lingerie A1499
White, Thomas (Agilent
  Technologies) A99
White, Thomas E. (Enron) A553
White, Tommi A. (Kelly
  Services) A819
White, Tony L. P542
White Tractor A96, A97
White Wave Inc. (soy foods) A466
White, W. Brett P121
White, William (CNF Inc.) A380
White, William K. (Pure
  Resources) E272
White, W. Ward A1049, P377

Whited, Beth A1423
Whitehall-Robins Healthcare A148
Whitehead, Dane E. A311
Whitehead, David W. A599
Whitehead, John A382
Whitehead, Robert C. A1347
Whitehouse, Mark A487
Whitehouse, Rebekah A1081
Whiteley, David A. A137
White-New Idea farm
  equipment A96, A97
Whitesell, Shirley P540
Whiteside, Arthur A516
Whitespoon (sugar) W569
White-Westinghouse
  appliances A831, E283
Whitfield, Charles D., Jr. A1309
Whitford, Nancy E250
Whitford, Thomas K. A1147
Whiting, G. W. C. P772
Whiting, Jack C. A1511
Whiting, Susan D. W627
The Whiting-Turner Contracting
  Company P772
Whitman, Charles P498
Whitman Corporation A1102,
  A1104
Whitman, Margaret C. "Meg" E54,
  E196
Whitman, William E. A441
Whitman's Candies P424, P719
Whitmer, Richard E. P86, P87,
  P557
Whitmer, W. Carl P637
Whitmire Distribution (drug
  wholesaler) A320
Whitmire, John L. A417
Whitmire, Melburn A320
Whitney & Company P54
Whitney, Sara S. A515
Whiton, A. Ernest E144, E320
Whitson, Clay M. E186
Whitson, Keith R. W269
Whittaker, Sheelagh D. A539
Whittemore, George R.
  "Randy" E216
Whittle, Mack I., Jr. E291
Whittman-Hart A1050
Whitton, Barbara A. E260
Whitwam, David R. A1520, A1521
Whitworth, Clark P656
Whitworth, J. Bryan A1129
Whitworth, Ralph A1504
Who Wants To Be A Millionaire (TV
  show) A60, A61, A334
Whole Foods Market,
  Inc. **A1522-A1523**
Whole Kids brand foods A1522
WholePeople.com A1522
Wholesale Alliance
  Cooperative P651
Wholesale Food outlets A995
Whopper sandwich A302, A303
Whoppers candy A709
Whorley, John F. A1449
WHP Health Initiatives A1492
WHQT-FM (Miami) P147

WHTQ-FM (Orlando, FL) P147
WHX Corp. (holding company) A116, A256
Whybrow, John W. W445
Whyte & Mackay Distillers A618, W240
Wiater, Patrick J. P461
Wibawa, Sugiyanto W195
Wibben, Sharon I. A479
The Wichita (Kansas) *Eagle* A833
Wichita Wranglers (baseball team) P714
Wichlacz, Wayne A673, P211
Wick, Philip P657
Wicker (food distribution) A1350
Wicker Mart convenience stores A1084, A1085
Wicker, Robert A. A307
Wicker, William M. A1377
Wickersham, David A1261, P441
Wickes Companies A1072
Wickes Lumber A388
Wickham, Michael W. A1207
Wickus, James D. A1351
Wickwire, Lane C. A1525
Widder-Lowry, Barbara R. A1069
WideOpenWest LLC (broadband) E128
Wider, John J., Jr. A905
Wideroe's Flyveselskap (airline) W518
Widmer wine A422, A423
Widows and Orphans Friendly Society A1172
Wieckse Witte beer W255
Wiedeking, Wendelin W458, W459
Wiehoff, John P. A345
Wiele, Andreas W107
Wielkopolski Bank Kredytowy S.A. W86, W87
Wielkopolski, Kathleen P613
Wieman, Roberta A495
Wien, Lawrence P230
Wienberger, Peter A81, P33
Wiens, Harold J. A977
Wiersbe, Dale A1224
Wiese Equine Supply A1117
Wiese, Jon E142
Wiesel, Elie P560
Wiest, Barbara G. A745, P243
Wiest, Christian W521
Wiggans, Thomas G. E184
Wiggenhorn, A. William A1171
Wiggett, James P157, P592
Wiggins, Mike P733
Wiggins, Stephen A1076
Wigglesworth, Margaret P578
Wiggs, David A., Jr. P660
Wight, Marshall A. P69
Wight, Wayne A. A1479
Wightman, David W. A503
Wijnberg, Sandra S. A917
Wilbur, Brayton, Sr. P772
Wilbur Chocolate Company A325, P105

Wilbur-Ellis Company (chemicals) A582, A583, P184, P185, P772
Wilcher, Larry K. A497
Wilcox, Gregory G. A219
Wilcox, John P192
Wilcox, Kenneth P. E122, E288
Wild Card 2 lottery game P680
Wild Cherry Pepsi soft drink A1104, A1105
Wild File (recovery software) E281
Wild Irish Rose wine A422, A423
Wild Kingdom (TV show) P348, P680
Wild Oats Markets, Inc. A1522
Wild Vines wine A521, P169
Wild West Shootout (game) P132
WildBlue Communications Inc. A528, A529
Wildcats of Northwestern University P378
Wilde, Alexander P195
Wilder, Gene P757
Wilder, John A555
Wilderness travel trailers A605
Wildfire restaurants A288
Wildflower Productions (topographic maps) P358
Wildhorse Energy Partners E129
Wilding Division P308
Wiles Group (fertilizer) A974, W252
Wiles, John A814
Wiles, Paul M. P691
Wiley, Michael E. A223
WILFARM, LLC A582, A583, P184, P185
Wilford, Dan S. P671
Wilgus, Carol F. A263
Wilh. Schmitz Scholl coffeehouse W588
Wilhelm, Edward W. A277
Wilhelmina, Queen of The Netherlands W316
Wilhelmsen, Arne A1216
Wilhelmsson, Fredrik P65
Wilhold cleaning and organizing products A1023
Wilk, Gerald A1233
Wilke, Jeffrey A. A131
Wilke, Jerry G. A683
Wilkening, Garry A. E282
Wilkerson, Gary C. A891
Wilkerson, Patricia A. A499
Wilkerson, Randolph A1281
The (Wilkes-Barre, PA) *Times Leader* A833
Wilkie, Wendell (CMS Energy) A376
Wilkie, Wendell L., II (Westvaco) A1517
Wilkin, Alexander A1236
Wilkins, William P694
Wilkinson, Bruce W. A940, A941
Wilkinson, Charles A. A605
Wilkinson, Desmond W539
Wilkinson, Gregory J. A1361
Wilkinson, Kathleen A. P703

Wilkinson, Terry L. A1075
Wilkinson, Walt P634
Wilkinson, William J. A1497
Wilkirson, John P. A1439
Wilks, David M. A1543
Wilks, Lewis O. A1187
Will & Grace (TV show) A999
Will Ross A1070
Willamette Industries, Inc. A1518, A**1524**-A**1525**
Willard, Judith P550
Willard, Richard K. A657
Willard, Wynn A. A709
Willardson, Thomas D. E232
Willcox, Brodie W434
Wille, David P631
Wille, Howard E. E61, E202
Willey, David M. A319
Willey, Dick P393
Willey, Frank P. A590, A591
Willhite, Colleen R. A751
Willhite, Deborah K. A1429, P491
William A. Krueger (printing) P404
William, Alan E245
William Arthur (stationery) A679, P217
William Beaumont Hospital P773
William Benton Foundation P176
William Blair & Company, L.L.C. E100, E237, E258
William Duff & Son (trade company) W404
William D. Witter E65
William E. Simon & sons P614
William H. Gates Foundation P78
William Hill (betting) W408
William Hill Winery W85
William J Hough Company P573
William J. Pulte, Inc. A1178
William Lawson's Finest Blend scotch W109
William M. Mercer Companies LLC A916
William Morris Agency, Inc. (talent agency) A1450
William Morrow (publisher) A700, P228
William Neilson (chocolate and dairy products) W244
The William Pears Group W148
Wm. Wrigley Jr. Company A**1526**-A**1527**
William Wycliff Vineyards A521, P169
Williams Act (1968) A1288, P446
Williams, Alan (Coles Myer) W173
Williams, Al (Sunkist) P465
Williams & Wilkins publishing imprint W642
Williams, Anthony T. A1135
Williams Brothers Corporation A1528
Williams Brothers grocery stores P488
Williams, Bruce N. A1083
Williams, Carl C. A1163

Williams, Charles E. (Waste Management) A1505
Williams, Charles E. (Williams-Sonoma) A1530, A1531
Williams, Charles F. (Georgia-Pacific) A655
Williams, Charles M. (Bank of America) A227
Williams, Charles (Williams Companies) A1528
Williams, Clayton W. E180
Williams Communications Group, Inc. A1244
The Williams Companies, Inc. A88, A482, A1276, A**1528**-A**1529**, P122, W500
Williams Company (gas) A552
Williams, Dale P453
Williams, David, Jr. (Williams Companies) A1528
Williams, David R. (H.J. Heinz) A723
Williams, David (Williams Companies) A1528
Williams, Derek A1067
Williams, Diane A1359
Williams, Donald D. A347
Williams, Douglas E. (Immunex) E71
Williams, Doug (Polo Ralph Lauren) A1151
Williams, Edward (Sherwin-Williams) A1278
Williams, Edward W. (ITT) A781
Williams, Elliot J. A875, P295
Williams, E. Michael A1167
Williams, Gareth W207
Williams Gas Pipeline Central Inc. A1528, A1529
Williams, George A. A1155
Williams, Glen D. A1391
Williams, Gretchen Minyard P677
Williams, Jackie (J.B. Hunt) A789
Williams, Jack L. (Comcast) A391
Williams, Jack L. (Royal Caribbean Cruises) A1217
Williams, James (Golden State Foods) P202
Williams, James (SunTrust) A1346
Williams, J. Douglas A905
Williams, Jim (Beaulieu of America) P552
Williams, Jim (TeamStaff) E125, E299
Williams, J. McDonald A1398, A1399
Williams, Joe A1275, E120
Williams, John A. (Burlington Resources) A311
Williams, John C. (Cox Enterprises) A443, P147
Williams, John (Williams Companies) A1528
Williams, Jonnie R. (Star Scientific) E293
Williams, J. Spencer A923, P321
Williams, K. C. W281
Williams, Keith E. A953

Williams, Kenneth R. A785
Williams, Kevin D. E77, E225
Williams, Larry (Irvine Company) P253
Williams, Larry P. (Pennsylvania Lottery) P698
Williams, Mark P171
Williams, Miller A1528
Williams, Noel B. A695
Williams, Patricia P618
Williams, Paul S. A321
Williams, Peter W191
Williams, Phil (Computacenter) W177
Williams, Phillip (Vodafone) W629
Williams PLC W524
Williams, Robbie (performer) W212, W213
Williams, Rob (Clear Channel) A373
Williams, Robert T. (Progressive) A1169
Williams, Roger L. A787
Williams, Ronald A. A91
Williams, Rose Marie A753
Williams, Serena P250, P251
Williams, Stephen W619
Williams, Susan Larson A1475
Williams, Tennessee P757
Williams, Thomas E. (Allegheny Technologies) A117
Williams, Thomas L. (Vivendi Universal) W625
Williams, Thomas W., Jr. (Manhattan Assoc.) E236
Williams, Venus P250, P251
Williams, Wayne B. A1179
Williams, Wilbert A221, P67, P548
Williams, W. Michael A1515
Williamsburg Paper Manufacturing A1516
Williams-Gulfmark Energy E183
Williams-Labadie Advertising P73
Williamson, Charles R. A1439
Williamson, Garland S. A523
Williamson, Jan L. A737
Williamson, Malcolm A1481, P509, P766
Williamson, Musselwhite & Main Street Insurance E236
Williamson, R. Phillip C. P773
Williamson, R. Max A1009, P365
Williamson, Scott H. A1361
Williamson, Steve E107, E269
Williamson, Telan, Jr. P757
Williamson-Dickie Manufacturing Company P773
Williams-Sonoma, Inc. A**1530**-A**1531**
Williford, John H. A381
Willingham, Deborah A973
Willis Corroon Group (insurance) A837, P283
Willis, Donald R. A169
Willis Stein & Partners, L.P. E188
Williston, Peter G. E310
Willits, John A444

Willmar farm equipment A96, A97
Willoughby, John P713
Willow Brook Foods (turkeys) A1418
Willow (movie) P303
Wills, Richard H. A1358, A1359
Wills (tobacco) W282
Willson, John M. W452
Willson, Prentiss, Jr. W223
Willson, Richard D. A775
Willumstad, Robert B. A371
Wilmington (North Carolina) *Morning Star* A1021
Wilmington, W. Phillip A1099
Wilmoski, Scott P63
Wilmot, Patricia A. A501, P163, P595
Wilsey Foods P122, P123
Wilshire Financial Services Group Inc. A592
Wilson, Alex W279
Wilson & Bennet Manufacturing A1224
Wilson, Bernard M. A681
Wilson, Carl A913
Wilson, Dale T. A483
Wilson Dam A1370, P468
Wilson, David (David Wilson's Automotive Group) P589
Wilson, David E. (Eagle-Pilcher Industries) P600
Wilson, David (Hasbro, Inc.) A693
Wilson, Dean M. A267
Wilson, F. Lee A279
Wilson, Floyd C. E146
Wilson, Gary L. (Northwest Airlines) A1046, A1047
Wilson, Gary (Micro Warehouse) P338, P676
Wilson, Gene A606
Wilson, Harold A. A261
Wilson, Irene A1315
Wilson, James C. (OrthAlliance) E259
Wilson, James H. (R.J. Reynolds) A1205
Wilson, Joan P564
Wilson, John P149
Wilson, Keith, Jr. A461
Wilson, Kemmons W544
Wilson, Kemp & Associates, Inc. A395
Wilson, L. Duane A413
Wilson, Lawrence A. (Beck Group) P553
Wilson, Lawrence (Rohm and Haas) A1212
Wilson, Lee A219
Wilson, Lynton R. W412, W413
Wilson, Mark L. P481, P746
Wilson, Michael L. (Ross Stores) A1215
Wilson, Michael M. (Agrium) W67
Wilson, Newton W., III E62
Wilson, Paige H. A703
Wilson, Pete (California governor) A314, P96

Wilson, Peter (Gallaher) W241
Wilson, Ray W71
Wilson, Richard A. A1003
Wilson, Rita P. A127
Wilson, Robert N. (Johnson & Johnson) A801
Wilson, Robert P. (Rio Tinto) W489
Wilson, Roger G. A269, P83
Wilson, S. Liane A1501
Wilson, Shanna P739
Wilson, Stephen R. P572
Wilson Tabor, Susan A. A1037
Wilson, Thomas J., II A127
Wilson, William L. P77
WilTel A1528
Wilton carpets A980
Wilton Foods A743
Wiltrakis, John N. A775
Wilver, Peter M. A1383
Wiman, Charles A468
Wimberly, James C. A1311
Wimbledon (tennis) P250, W144
Wimer, Mark G. A1341
Wimpey fast food A302
Win Ben Stein's Money (Comedy Central) A61
Winamp (Web music) A180
Winarsky, Norman P455
Winberg, Håkan W525
WinBook Computer Corporation P336, P337
Winbook computers P675
Wincanton Engineering (food processing equipment) A326
Winchester Repeating Arms A1060
WinCo Foods, Inc. P773
Wincor Nixdorf Holding GmbH & Company A837, P283
Wind Song (ship) A331
Wind Surf (ship) A331
Wind Telecomunicazioni SpA W214, W215
Windex cleaner A1246, A1247, P432, P433, P722
Windhover Fund P404
Windmere-Durable Holdings (small appliances) A264
Windmöller, Rolf A1159, P401, W463
Windowed Persons Service P29
Windows operating system A186, A472, A636, A972, A973, E23, E25, E91, E190, E281, P272, P338, W168, W176, W186
Windrow, Kimberly G. A987
Windsor Fund A1468, P504
Windsor Vineyards W230
Windstar Cruises A330
Windswept Pacific (music) W212
Windward Capital Partners P612
Wine Planet Holdings Limited (Web site) W230
Wine World Estates P474
Winebarger, Paul P445
Wines International A296
WineToday.com A1020
Winfield cigarettes W143

Winfield, John V. E221
Winfrey, Oprah A700, A701, P219, P228, P229, P625
Wingate Partners A1430, P**518**-P**519**, P774
Winger, Dennis L. P542
Wingert, Michael J. A929
Winget, Larry J., Sr. P764
Wingfoot Commercial Tire Systems A664
WingMan input devices W338, W339
Wingroad car W403
Wings Alliance A428, A1046, W316
WingspanBank.com A230
Winik, Gregg P355
Winiter, Richard W545
Winjum, Stephen J. E255
Wink Communications, Inc. P511
Wink (interactive TV) A350
Winkel, Michael W. A1219
Winkelhaus, Kathryn L. A277
Winkelried, Jon A661
Winkhaus, Hans-Dietrich W205
Winkleman, Dennis R. A807
Winkler, Michael J. A399
Winmar (real estate development) A1230
Winn & Lovett Grocery Company A1532
Winn, Marilyn A685
Winn, Penny W645
Winncrest Homes A862
Winn-Dixie Stores, Inc. A608, A698, A844, A1176, A**1532**-A**1533**, E290, P402, P644, W156
Winners Apparel stores A1388, A1389
Winnie the Pooh (TV show, books, and products) A927, E60, W332, W333
Winning, Norma E203
Winnipeg Sun (newspaper) W471
Winograd, Charles M. W475
Winograd, Les P161
Winokur, Steven L. E250
Winona Bridge Railway Company A309
Winowiecki, Ron L. A1321
Winrock (grass company) A788
Winslow, Larry P393
Winstead, Barry J. A311
Winston & Newell Company (grocery distributor) A744, A1348, P242
Winston cigarettes A1204, A1205, W304, W305
Winston Cup Series racing circuit P681
Wintel P338
Winter, Elmer A910
Winter, Matthew E. A923, P321
Winter, Peter M. A443, P147
Winter Velvet Barbie doll A216
Winterfresh gum A1526, A1527
Winters, James K. P53, P543
Winters, Phil P431

Winterthur (insurance) W184, W185, W464
Winthrop Laboratories W118
Winton, Alexander A662
Wintrust Financial Corporation E318
Winvick, Stanley A83
WinView software E42
Wire and Plastic Products (WPP Group) W646
The WIRE (online news service) P60, P61, P546
Wired (magazine) A80, P32, P33
wiredscholar.com A1449
Wireless Facilities, Inc. E318
Wireless Web A1318
WirelessKnowledge A1182
Wirex (plastics) A534
Wirfs, Walter M. A891
Wirichs home improvement centers W364
Wirta, Raymond E. P120, P121, P571
Wirth, Michael I. E176
Wirth, Thomas E. E289
Wirtz, Arthur P774
Wirtz Corporation P774
Wirtz, William W. P774
Wis-Con Total Power P686
Wisconsin Employers Group, Inc. A739
Wisconsin Energy Corporation A1542
Wisconsin Parts Company A198, A1210
Wisconsin Retail Hardware Association P726
Wisconsin State Universities P500
Wisconsin's State Normal School A802
Wisdom (online service) A1070
Wise, Brownie A1414
Wise, Bud A1153
Wise Foods P90, P558
Wise, Joan P29
Wise, Michael V. P137
Wise, William A. A537
Wiseman, Eric A1475
Wiseman, Stacy E186
Wiser Oil E235, E278
Wiser's gin W85
Wish-Bone salad dressing W618, W619
Wisk laundry soap W618, W619
Wisner, Frank G. A151
WISSOLL (candy maker) W589
Wistrand, Richard A1417
Wit Capital A660
Wit Soundview A566
Witaszak, Richard B. A1091
Witcher Construction P599
Witco Corporation A450, A1344
Withers, Bruce A978
Withington, Neil W143
Withrington, John W501
Withrow, J. Paul E297
Witt, Rick P349

Witt, Robert E. P499
Witten, Peer W427
Wittenberg, Bill P299
Witter, Dean A988
Wittlov, Arne W633
Wittmann, Karl W381
Wittwer, Herman P42
Witty, Tim E. P37
WIX (automotive products) P113
Wix auto parts A461
Wix Filtron A460
The Wiz electronics retailer A312,
  P697
The Wizard of Oz (movie) A962,
  P450
Wizard System rental car
  reservation A212
Wizards of the Coast (trading
  cards) A692, A693
Wizota, Janice E213
WJ Communications, Inc. E318
W.J. Powell (food
  distributor) A1109
WJPC-FM (Lansing, IL) P258
WJRT-TV (Flint, MI) A61
WJZ-TV (Baltimore, MD) P218
W.K. Kellogg Foundation A816,
  P520-P521, P774
WKI Holding Company, Inc. P775
WKK Semiconductor A214
WKQL-FM (Jacksonville) P147
W. L. Gore and Associates,
  Inc. P522-P523, P775
W.L. Ross (investments) A150
WLNR-FM (Lansing, IL) P258
WLOU radio station (Louisville,
  KY) P258
WLR Foods A1132
WLS-TV (Chicago) A61, P218
WLVI-TV (Boston) A1402
WM Financial Services, Inc. A1501
WMAR-TV (Baltimore, MD) A569
WMC Holding Corporation E316
WMC Limited W640-W641
WMF Group (motgages) A1172
WMF Württembergische
  Metallwarenfabrik AG W201
WMS Industries P681
WMX Technologies A1504
WNBA. See Women's National
  Basketball Association
Wochomurka, C. F. A457
Woehl, Juergen P445
Woehlk Contact Lens GmbH A234
Woerner, John E21
Woertz, Patricia A353
Woeste, Albrecht W257
Woghin, Stephen M. A403
Wohl Leased Shoe
  Department A294
Wohl, Ronald A. A1067
Wohl Shoe stores A294
Wohleber, Robert M. A821
Wohleen, David B. A477
Woitkoski, Jerry P373, P688
Wojciechowski, Susan E231

Wojcik, Walt J. A1049, P377
Wolande, Chuck P136, P137, P580
Wold, Mary A511
Wold-Olsen, Per A957
Wolf, Abe P231, P629
Wolf Blass wines W230, W231
Wolf Brothers Cigar A1458
Wolf Camera P714
Wolf, Chuck P714
Wolf, Donald D. E316
Wolf, Ellen C. A155
Wolf GmbH W461
Wolf, Gregory A738
Wolf, Henry C. A1039
Wolf, Howard A1430
Wolf, James A. A1355, P467
Wolf, John W. P209, P620
Wolf, Linda S. P73
Wolf, Morris A1430
Wolf, Ron A672, P210
Wolf, Stephen M. (US
  Airways) A1442, A1443
Wolf, Steven (UAL) A1420
Wolf, Timothy V. A79
Wolfe, Carrie A. E207
Wolfe, Daniel E. A1231
Wolfe Frostop (salad bars) A502
Wolfe Industries A908
Wolfe, Kenneth L. A708, A709
Wolfe, Lee W. A1187
Wolfe, R. Dean A933
Wolfe, Russel P479
Wolfe, S. David P277, P652
Wolfe, Stephen P. A1393
Wolfenberger, Mary P420
Wolfe's Nursery A1130
Wolff, Sherman M. P227, P628
Wolfgang Puck frozen foods A408
Wolfgram, David A289
Wolfinger, F. Mark W191
Wolfinger, Russ P431
Wolford, Richard G. A470, A471
Wolfovski, Michel W171
Wolf's Head motor oil A1097
Wolfson, Bernardo A1181
Wolgemuth, Samuel P611
Wolin, Neal S. A689
Wollen, Foster A241, P75
Wolpert, Richard P524
Wolseley plc W294
Wolters, J. B. W642
Wolters Kluwer nv W642-W643
Wolters Plantyn Educatieve
  Uitgevers W643
Wolters-Noordoff (educational
  information) W643
Woltil, Robert D. A1341
Wolverine Equities A458
Wolverine Packing Company P775
Wolynic, Edward T. A551
WOM World of Music stores W311
Womack, Carl W. E101, E259
Womack, Christopher C. A1307
Womack, E. Allen, Jr. A941
Women & Success (magazine) P316

The Women of Brewster Place
  (movie) P219
Women of Earth fragrance A216,
  A217
Women.com Networks, Inc. A700,
  P228
Women's Field Army
  (volunteers) P40
Women's Financial Information
  Program P29
Women's National Basketball
  Association A1194, P354, P355,
  P682
Women's Wear Daily A80, P32, P33
Wometco Enterprises A836, P282
Won Dae-Yun W509
Wonder bread A774, A775
Wonderbra A776, A1242, A1243
Wonderware (software) W290
Wonderwear cosmetics A1201
Wonfor, Andrea W249
Wong & Leow (attorneys) A220,
  P66
Wong, Ernest S. E61, E202
Wong, Michael F. A1527
Wong, Stephen R. E197
Wong, Vicki W267
Wong, Wai A403
Wonish, Robert G. E260
Wood, Alison W111
Wood, David P93
Wood Dining (food
  management) W546
Wood, E. Jenner, III A1347
Wood Fiberboard A1524
Wood, George P770
Wood Group ESP A1078
Wood Gundy (investments) W156
Wood, Howard A350
Wood, James A670
Wood, Ken P247
Wood, Mark W465
Wood, Michael B. P325, P668
Wood, Morrell & Company A1094
Wood, Philip P127
Wood, Phoebe A. A297
Wood, Richard D., Jr. P770
Wood River Oil & Refining A834,
  P280
Wood, Robert (Bozzuto's) P560
Wood, Robert (Sears,
  Roebuck) A126
Wood, Roger J. A279
Wood, Steven H. A935
Wood, Word A226
Woodard, William M. P395
Woodcock, Kenneth R. A89
Woodford, Brent A. A1405
Woodhaven Foods A1350
Woodhead, Robin A1305
Woodhouse, John F. A1351
Woodhull Medical and Mental
  Health Center P369
Woodland Healthcare P118
The Woodlands (residential
  development) A978
Woodley, Graeme P431

A=AMERICAN BUSINESS · E=EMERGING COMPANIES · P=PRIVATE COMPANIES · W=WORLD BUSINESS

Woodlief, Philip K. P595
Woodrow, David M. A1187
Woodruff, Ernest A382
Woods, Allan P. A955
Woods, Douglas P597
Woods, Emily Cinader P254, P255, P642
Woods, Gary W. A1039
Woods, John A166
Woods, Robert B. W435
Woods, Tiger A1032, P250, P251, P641
Woodside Co-op (New York City) P291
Woodstuff Manufacturing P442
Woodward & Lothrop stores A304
Woodward, Bob A1502
Woodward, David A. P489
Woodward, Jimmy M. A609
Woodward, Joanne P661
Woodward, Mark E286
Woodward, Robert J., Jr. A1009, P365
Woodward, Samuel A. A421
Woodward, William Peter A821
Woodward-Walker Lumber Company A1524
Woodworth, Patricia P497, P756
Woodworth, Richie P361
Woolco (discount chain) A1470, A1494, W312
Woolford, Cator A558
Woolford, Guy A558
Woolies. *See* Woolworths Limited
Woolite fabric care W476
Woolman, C. E. A478
Woolson, Tyler A655
Woolsy, J. Rod A941
Woolverton, Barbara E234
Woolwich plc A438, W114
Woolworth Corporation A294, A1022, A1214
Woolworth, Frank A1470, W312, W644
Woolworth Holdings W312, W313
Woolworths Limited **W644**-**W645**
Wooster Brush Company P71
Wooster Rubber (balloons) A1022
Wooten's Department Store A490
Wooton, Michael P465
Worcester (Massachusetts) *Telegram & Gazette* A1020, A1021
Worcester Mutual Fire Insurance A124
Word software A973
Worden, Jeffrey A. A1153
WordPerfect software A1050
Wordsworth, Jerry L. P669
Wordsworth, J. R. P669
Work.com A506, A507
WorkHealth (workers' compensation management) P694
Workman, John L. P762
Workman, Larry E. A1221
Workmate power tools A265

Workout Warehouse (catalog) P637
Workstage P613
World 4 Kids stores W172
World Air Network Charter W80
World Almanac A1160
World Asset Management A395
World Bank W650
World Basketball League P198
World Book (encyclopedias) A252, A253
World Call international calling W419
World Carpets A980, A981
World Championship Wrestling E141, E319
World Classics brands P478
World Color Press W470
World Equity Benchmark Shares P46, P47
World Food Production Conference A752
World Health Organization P414, W304, W388
World Hockey Association P360
The World Is Not Enough (movie) A962
World Kitchen (housewares) P90, P91, P558, P775
World (magazine) P359
World MasterCard A924, P322
World Mortgage Investors, Inc. A659
World of Music stores W310, W311
World Omni Financial Corporation P256, P257, P644
World Peace Industrial (distributor) A1140
World Savings Bank A658, A659
World Series (baseball) P306
World Trade Center (Boston) A615, P191, P609
World Trade Center (New York City) A860, A988, A1222, A1388, A1442, A1472, E96, E137, E251, P134, P334, P398, P399, P476, P565, P703, P745, W82, W174, W336, W380, W468
World Trade Organization A150, E32, W234, W400, W542, W581, W630
World Wide (starters and alternators) P152
World Wrestling Federation Entertainment, Inc. A998, E**141**, E225, E319
WorldCom, Inc. A160, A202, A248, A528, A538, A548, A549, A866, A898, A996, A1026, A1186, A1318, A1356, A1528, A**1534**-A**1535**, E52, E192, E219, E226, E232, E233, E261, E290, P274, P332, P352, P396, P597, W122, W148, W152, W578, W581
WorldCrest Group A837, P283
WorldFreight A485
WorldGate Communications, Inc. A350
worldlyinvestor.com A150
WorldMark E304

WorldNet A202, E309
WORLDSPAN, L.P. (reservation system) A478, A479, A1046
WorldTravel BTI P776
Worldwide Ceilings A1456
Worldwide Insurance Company A144, W64
Worldwide Pay and Benefits Headlines (publication) P481
Worldwide Plaza (New York) P449
World-Wide Reassurance Company Limited P384, P385
Worldwide Television News P60
WORM disk W448
Wormington, Stephen L. A1375
Wornom, Sam A1084
Worobow, Robert R. P750
Worroll, David P161
Worsley alumina refinery A112
Worth, Christine E201
Worth (magazine) A614, P190
Worthington & Company (brewery) W544
Worthington brand A791
Worthington, Bruce R. A1121
Worthington Foods A816, A817
Worthington Industries Inc. A194, A1463
Worthington Specialty Processing A1463
Wortzman, Mitchell S. E89
Woven Interlock carpets A980
WOW! snacks A1107
WOW! stores P346, P347, P680
Wozniak, Curtis S. E57, E197
Wozniak, Steve A186
WPG Corporate Development E277
WPHL-TV (Philadelphia) A1402
WPIX-TV (New York) A1402
WPP Group plc (advertising) A1062, P72, W198, W**646**-W**647**
WPS Resources A1542
WPVI-TV (Philadelphia) A61
WPXI-TV (Pittsburgh, PA) A443, P147
WPXN-TV (New York) P80
W. R. Grace & Company A192, A804, A1262, A**1536**-A**1537**, P68, W278
Wrabel, R. Richard A1097
Wraight, Stanley G. E32
Wrangler jeans A1474, A1475, E60
Wrather Corporation P350
WRDQ-TV (Orlando, FL) A443, P147
Wredberg, Conrad, Jr. A1259
Wren, John D. A1062, A1063
Wrico Packaging A1527
Wright, Alan M. A377
Wright Amendment (1979) A1310
Wright Brand Foods A743
Wright Brothers P451
Wright, Bruce E35, E166
Wright, Charles R. A1331, P459
Wright, Chris A1439
Wright, Daniel E177

Wright, Donald A. (Toronto-Dominion Bank) W609
Wright, Donald E. (Saks) A1239
Wright, Donald P. (Safeway) A1235
Wright, Doreen A. A317
Wright, Eduardo Castro W635
Wright, Elease E. A91
Wright Express A212
Wright, Felix E. A858, A859
Wright, Frank Lloyd A500, A1246, A1334, P162, P432, P496
Wright, Gregory A. A1375
Wright, James T. A285
Wright, Joseph R., Jr. A737
Wright, Michael W. A1348, A1349
Wright, Pandit P159, P594
Wright, Robert C. (GE) A647
Wright, Robert C. (NBC) A999
Wright, Robert E. (Unocal) A1439
Wright, Robert S. (International Multifoods) A769
Wright, Russell E137
Wright, Steve P558
Wright, Tom A555
Wrighton, Mark Stephen P769
Wright's Foodliner P489
Wrightson, Robert E. A421
Wrigley Building A1526
Wrigley, Philip A1526
Wrigley, William A1526
Wrigley, William, Jr. A1402, A1526, A1527
Wrigley's gum A656
Write-Once Read-Many optical disk W448
Wroe, Thomas, Jr. A1379
WRTV-TV (Indianapolis) A945
WSB-AM, FM, and TV (Atlanta) P146, P147
WSB-TV (Atlanta) A442, A443
WSJ.com A506, A507
WSK Gorzyce (pistons) A584
WSOC-TV (Charlotte, NC) A443, P147
wswedding.com A1530
W.T. Reynolds Company (grocery distributor) A744, P242
W.T. Rogers (office supplies) A1022
WTVD-TV (Raleigh-Durham, NC) A61
WTVF-TV (Nashville, TN) P218
WTVG-TV (Toledo, OH) A61
Wu, Gordon Y. S. W266, W267
Wu, James Man Hon W267
Wu, Jeanne E33, E163
Wu, Shareen P662
Wu, Thomas Jefferson W267
Wu Wear brand clothing E101
Wubbolding, Christine A975
Wuellner, Charleen A1553
Wuffli, Peter A. W617
Wulf, Gene C. A251
Wulf, Jerold P50
Wulff, Harald W257
Wuliger, Ernest P442
Wunder, Rich A405
Wuori, Richard P770

Wurtzel, Alan A366
Wurtzel, Samuel A366
W.V. Bowater & Sons A284
W.W. Grainger, Inc. A**1538**-A**1539**
W.W. Hansen Experimental Physics Laboratory P457
WWAV Group A1062
WWF Raw is War (TV show) E141, E319
WWF Smackdown! (TV show) E141, E319
WWFE. *See* World Wrestling Federation Entertainment, Inc.
WWKA-FM (Orlando, FL) P147
WWRM-FM (Tampa, FL) P147
www.nordstrom.com A1037
www.StockHouse.com W262
WXYZ-TV (Detroit) A568, A569
Wyandotte Chemicals W116
Wyatt, E. Lee P443, P725
Wyatt, Joe P763
Wyatt, Lance B. A59
Wyatt, Oscar A1466
Wyche, Jimmie E64
Wyeth-Ayerst Laboratories A148
Wyker, Kenneth E. A373
Wyle Components/Systems A196
Wyle Laboratories A214
Wyler's bouillon and soup A723, P90, P91
Wylie Company Stores A1532
Wylie, W. Gill A514
Wyllie, Bill W272
Wyly, Charles J., Jr. A968, A969
Wyly, Sam A402, A968, A969
Wyman family A1068
Wyman, Georgina W123
Wyman, G. Mead E241
Wyman, Malcolm I. W553
Wyman, Samuel D. A687
Wyman, William F. A1069
Wynant, Wilbur A878
Wyndham International Inc. A1398, A**1540**-A**1541**
Wyner, James D. W379
Wynn, Steven (Mirage Resorts) A966, A1328
Wynne, John O. "Dubby" P655
Wynne, Margaret W339
Wynne, Steve W62
Wynn's International (industrial sealing) A1088
WypAll commercial wipes A827
Wypych, Ireneusz W457
Wysher, David B. A339
Wysocki, Pawel W457
Wyszomierski, Jack L. A1251

X

Xalt fabrics A307
Xanax drug A1122
Xbox video game consoles A972, E298
Xceed Mortgage Corporation W113
Xcel Energy Inc. A140, A362, A**1542**-A**1543**
Xcert International E114

XCL (oil) A184
Xebec (disk controllers) E98
Xeloda drug W493
Xenical drug W493
Xerox Corporation A54, A76, A212, A472, A614, A888, A982, A1142, A1336, A1358, A**1544**-A**1545**, P70, P137, P190, P444, W158, W190, W234, W472
XETA Technologies, Inc. E**142**, E319
Xfab E173
XFL (football league) A998, E141, E319
Xicor, Inc. (chips) E121
Xilinx, Inc. E57, E97
Xionics (digital office equipment) E98
XIOtech network storage A1260, P440, P441, P725
XL Vision (electronic imaging) A1232
XL/Datacomp (computer distributor) A1336
XO Communications, Inc. A1026
Xoma (pharmaceuticals) A640
Xomed Surgical Products A952
Xomox (valves) A446
Xpect (first aid and safety equipment) A364
xpedx (graphic art supplies) A770
Xterra SUV W402, W403
XTO Energy, Inc. E319
Xtra detergent A358
Xtra Mart convenience stores P769
X-Trode (stents) A444
Xu Kaicheng W543
Xuzhou Construction Machinery A198
Xytron pacemakers A952

Y

Yabuki, Jeffrey W. A681
Yaffe, Ken P361
Yagi, Isao W81
Yagi, Yoshiki W261
Yahoo! Inc. A830, A832, A**1546**-A**1547**, E220, P138, P456, W516, W548
Yahtzee game A692
Yakabindie mine W640
Yale & Towne Manufacturing (locks and forklifts) A526
Yale Materials Handling (forklifts) A992
Yale University E147, P356, P518, P626, P761, P776
Yali Dry beer W289
Yam! (online magazine) W106
Yamada, Masayoshi W187
Yamada, Shoichi W449
Yamada, Tadataka W247
Yamada, Tomohisa W597
Yamaguchi, Kanji W371
Yamaguchi, Takashi W295
Yamaguchi, Tokuichi W405

Yamaha Corporation W560, W614, **W648-W649**
Yamaha music equipment E210, E281
Yamaha, Torakusa W648
Yamahatsu Sangyo (hair coloring) W256
Yamaichi Securities W408
Yamaji, Hiromi W409
Yamaji, Susumu W302
Yamal-Europe pipeline W242
Yamami, Todd K. E134, E311
Yamamoto, Kosuke W615
Yamamoto, Masakatsu W327
Yamamoto, Masaru W599
Yamamoto, Michihisa W329
Yamamoto, Mineo W81
Yamamoto, Mitsuku W327
Yamamoto, Tadashi W81
Yamamoto, Yoshiro W375
Yamani, Sheikh P340
Yamashita, Yukio W159
Yamate, Gordon T. A833
Yamato Kogyo A1052
Yamauchi, Hiroshi W394, W395
Yamauchi, Keiji W561
Yamazaki, Teiichi W572
Yamazaki, Yuji W531
Yanacocha Mine A1024
Yanagito, Seijiro W302
Yanai, Yuval W323
Yancey, Carol B. A653
Yandoo, Greg P149
Yang, Charles C. A901
Yang In-Mo W509
Yang, Jerry A1546, A1547, P456
Yankee Book Peddler P68
The Yankee Candle Company, Inc. E**143**, E320
Yankee Energy System, Inc. A1040, A1041
Yankee Oil & Gas E79
Yankowski, Carl A1194
Yanmar (tractors) A468
Yanney, John R. P573
Yannias, Don P176, P177
Yannotta, Pat P580
Yano, Junichiro W515
Yano, Kaoru W387
Yantai Timken A1386
Yard Machines lawn equipment P679
Yard-Man lawn equipment P679
Yardville National Bancorp E320
Yarick, Paul E. A775
Yarno, Wendy A957
Yarrington, Hugh J. W643
Yaruss, Howard S. E108
Yashica (cameras) W328
Yasukawa, Hideaki W531
Yasumoto, Masayoshi W548
Yasutake, Shiro W404, W405
Yates, Bradley W. A411
Yates, Philip R. P620
Yates, Roger W89
Yates, Ronald L. P501

Yavorsky, William D. E73
Yawata Steel Works W398, W404
YBP Library Services P68, P69
Yee, Yangwei P449
Yeh, Bing E121, E288
Yell Publishing W548
Yell (yellow pages) A714, P232, W148, W149
Yellin, Neil P335
Yellow Corporation A420, A1206, A1504, A**1548**-A**1549**
Yellow Pages A516
Yellow Rental (leasing service) A1222
Yellow Truck and Coach Manufacturing A710
Yellowave A1196
Yellowglen wines W230
Yeltsin, Boris W346
Yelverton, Jerry W. A555
Yemenidjian, Alex A962, A963
Yentob, Alan W145
Yeomans, Janet L. A977
Yerkes Observatory P496, P497
Yes cleaner A1246, P432
Yesco P350
Yeshua, Ilan P176, P177, P603
Yes!Less food stores A606, A607
yesmail.com inc. E222
YieldGard brand A985
Yip Jon Khiam W539
YMCA of the USA P777
YNB Financial Services E320
Yochum, Jerry W. A503
Yoda toys A693
Yodels snacks A775
Yoder, Stephen A. A167
Yoh, Harold L., III P589
Yohe, D. Scott A479
Yokely, John M. W67
Yokich, Stephen P. P35
Yokota, Akira W297
Yokote, Yasunori W373
Yomiuri Shimbun (newspaper) W96
Yoneda, Terumasa W533
Yonel, Ömer E254
Yong AK Ro W335
Yoo Bok-Yeol W275
Yoo Sang-Boo W455
Yoo-Hoo beverage A1105, W154
Yoplait yogurt A648, A649, W192
York Benimaru supermarkets W299
York College P128, P129
York, Denise DeBartolo P172
York Factory W270
York Financial E315
York International Corporation A278, A**1550**-A**1551**
York, Jerome B. P338, P339, P676
York, Jill E. E239
York, John C., II P173
York, Marie Denise DeBartolo P173, P602
York Mart supermarkets W298, W299
York peppermint patties A709, W154, W155

York Safe A488
Yorkshire Bank PLC W382, W383
Yorkshire Electricity A1542
Yorkshire Food Group A470
Yorkshire Group (dyes) A450
Yorkshire Power Group A140, A1542
Yorkshire Television W249
Yorkshire Tyne-Tees Television W248, W620
Yorkshire Water A440
Yorozu Corporation (auto parts) A1394
Yoshi (video games) W395
Yoshida Asian sauces A723
Yoshida, Hideo W198
Yoshida, Katsumi W487
Yoshida, Mitsutaka W601
Yoshida, Shoichiro W392, W393
Yoshikawa, Atsushi W409
Yoshikawa, Eiichi W387
Yoshikawa, Yoji W603
Yoshikawa, Yoshikazu W397
Yoshino, Hiroyuki W264, W265
Yost, Larry D. A199
Yost, R. David A155
Yost, Timothy L. A573
Youga, Tony A521, P169, P600
Young 'n Tender brands P200, P201
Young, Adriane E89, E240
Young & Rubicam Inc. (advertising) A852, W198, W646, W647
Young, Arthur A562, P182, W222
Young, Charles E. P756
Young, Daniel P253
Young, Frederick C. E164
Young, George P357
The Young Indiana Jones Chronicles (movies) P303
Young, James F. (MedImmune) E90
Young, James R. (Union Pacific) A1423
Young, John A. (Colfax) P578
Young, John A. (Novell) A1050
Young, John (Hewlett-Packard) A712
Young, John (Lloyd's of London) W337
Young, John (Tiffany) A1384
Young, John (Young's Market) P777
Young, Larry D. A1105
Young, Mary E. P702
Young, Michael R. A1550, A1551
Young, Nancy N. A1221
Young Pecan Company P200, P201, P616
Young, Philip E. (International Brotherhood of Teamsters) P247
Young, Philip W. (Lands' End) A853
Young, R. Blake A519
Young, Roger A. A1035
Young, Russell A. A1181
Young, Stephen W. (Verity) E134
Young, Steven D. (Albertson's) A111
Young, Thomas L. A1075

A=AMERICAN BUSINESS · E=EMERGING COMPANIES · P=PRIVATE COMPANIES · W=WORLD BUSINESS

Young, Walter R., Jr. A346, A347
Young, William C. P702
Younger, Laurie A61
Youngman, David A389
Young's Market Company, LLC P777
Youngs, Peter P341
Youngstown Sheet & Tube A896
Younker, Doug P637
Younkers department stores A1238
Younkin, Floyd E52
Your Father's Mustache barbers A1196
Your Independent Grocer W245
Your Staff (employee leasing) A818
YourPharmacy.com, Inc. A574, A575
Youth Dew fragrance A564, A766
Yoyodyne Internet direct marketing A1546
YPF, S.A. See also Repsol YPF, S.A.
YPF, S.A. W482, W483, **W650-W651**
YSL Beauté W251
Yuan, Crystal P545
Yuasa, Hisao W487
Yuba Heat Transfer P581
Yuca chips P204
The Yucaipa Companies LLC A606, P202, P462, **P524-P525**, P617, P777
Yudkovitz, Martin J. A999
Yudkuff, Royce G. P351
Yudof, Mark G. P758
Yuejin Motor W226
OOO Yugtransgaz W243
Yuhanrox bleach A375
Yukon Pacific Corporation (pipelines) A455
Yukos (oil) A1460, W346
Yun Jong-Yong W509
Yundt, Jeffrey W. A1035
Yungchia Chemical Industries Corporation W229
Yurko, Allen M. W290
Yusko, David P702
Yusoff, Datuk Othman W539
Yuspeh, Alan A695
Yusuf, Yasmin W357
Yves Saint Laurent A902, P304, W250

Z

Z Frank Chevrolet dealership P611
Zaadunie (seeds) W414
Zaandam (ship) A331
Zaban, Erwin A1004, A1005
Zaby, Gottfried W119
Zaccaria, Adrian A241, P75
Zachry, Henry Bartell, Jr. P627
Zachwieja, Patrick A. A107
Zacks, David M. P41
Zacky Farms P610
Zadel, C. William E248
Zadoorian, Ken A85
Zaepfel, Martin W427
Zafirovski, Mike S. A991

ZAG Industries Ltd. (plastics) A1322
Zagnut candy A709
Zagorka beer W255
Zahler, Eric J. A889
Zahn, Philipp J. W351
Zahr, Andrew A. A691
Zahra, E. Ellis, Jr. A1533
Zakin, Jonathan N. E316
Zaklady Azotowe Anvil SA W457
Zaklady Piwowarskie W. Zywcu (brewery) W254
Zaldivar Mine W453
Zale Corporation A**1552**-A**1553**
Zale, Donald A1552
Zale, Morris A1552
Zalman, David E271
Zalzneck, Robert J. A1437
Zambelli, Jean-Claude E119
Zambesi beer W553
Zambia Sugar W568
Zamora, Gloria A309
Zamora, Nassry G. E38, E174
Zamora, Rafael W577
Zamoyski, James J. A585
Zampieri, Gianni W125
Zander, Edward J. A1343
Zander, Winfried W257
Zanders A770
Zandman, Felix A1482, A1483
Zane, Robert J. A881
Zanesville (pharmaceuticals) A320
Zannino, Richard F. A507
Zantac drug W246, W492
Zanuck, Darryl A622
Zanuck, Richard A622
Zanxx (auto lighting components) A430, A585
Zany Brainy, Inc. (toy stores) E135
Zanzibar International Film Festival P610
Zaoui, Yoel A661
Zapata Petroleum A1096
ZapMail A588
Zappacosta, Pierluigi W338
Zar, Ira H. A403
Zara Deutschland W426
Zarafshan-Newmont (gold mine) A1024
Zarate, Antonio R. A1395
Zarb, Frank G. A996, A997, P352
Zarchin, Jim A569
Zarcone, Donna F. A683
Zarella, Ronald L. A651
Zaremba, James W. E102
Zarkin, Herbert J. A262, A263
Zarnikow, Eric R. A1273
Zaurus personal digital assistant W532
Zayadi, Hani W173
Zayre Corporation A158, A262, A1388
ZCMI department stores A932
ZDNet W548
Zebco fishing equipment A298

Zebra Technologies Corporation E284
Zech, Ronald H. A638, A639
Zechman, R. S. A669
Zeckhauser, Sally H. P221
ZED lighting P613
Zedillo, Ernesto W440
Zee Medical, Inc. (first aid products) A947
Zehrs Markets W244, W245
Zeichner, Bernard E176
Zeigler, Charles E., Jr. A1249
Zeigler Coal A1276, W500
Zeitler, William M. A765
Zeitlin, Allan R. A1005
Zeitoun, Alain W151
Zelayeta, Joseph M. A895
Zelda (video games) W395
Zelencik, Stephen J. A83
Zeleny, Dennis A541
Zelisko, Judith P. A299
Zelkowitz, Steven L. A825
Zell, Samuel A176, A177, A560, A561, P180, P181, P604, P659
Zell/Chilmark Fund L.P. A560, A561, P180, P181, P442
Zeller, Dick E305
Zeller, Paul R. (Imation) A751
Zellerbach (paper) A950
Zellers discount stores A918, W270, W271
Zellmer, Jeffrey A1285
Zelmac drug W414, W415
Zelnicek, Ivana A1408, P482
Zelnick, Moshe E194
Zema Foods P713
Zeman, Gregory C. A337
Zemba, Karen A417
Zemsky, Howard A. A743
Zemurray, Samuel A354
Zencke, Peter W517
Zendan, Michael F., II P351
Zeneca (pharmaceuticals) W278
Zengine (e-commerce) E239
Zenith (cruise ship) A1217
Zenith Data Systems W150
Zenith Electronics Corporation A894, P92, W334
Zenith Media W467
Zenith Products bath and shower A921
Zenith Radio P258
Zeno Manufacturing A1526
Zentmyer, Hugh J. A749
Zentronics (distributor) A1140
ZENworks (software) A1050, A1051
ZEOS International, Ltd. A762, A970
Zep Manufacturing A1004
Zerbe, Darell R. A1225
Zerbst, Robert P121
Zereski, Don W151
Zerex antifreeze A200
Zeringue, Ike A1371, P469
Zeringue, Oswald "Ike" P743
Zerit drug A291

Zero candy A709
Zero Foods A1350
Zerza, Fred P265
Zest soap A1165
Zesta crackers A814, A815
Zetsche, Dieter W188, W189
Zettler, Michael E. P53
Zeumer, James P. A1179
ZEVALIN drug E217
ZFS. *See* Zurich Financial Services
Zhang Zhiliang W543
Zhejiang Acrylic Fibre Plant W542
Zhone Technologies, Inc. (data
  networking equipment) A837,
  P283, P475
Zhong Shan Zhonglong Aquatic
  Company, Ltd. (eel
  processing) W603
Zhongbei Building Material
  Products Company A1456
Zhou Enlai W542
Zhu Rongji W306
Zhuhai Hiwin Boise Cascade A274
Ziai, Said A571
Ziegfeld theater A312
Ziegler, Albert R. A243
Ziegler, Ann E. A1243
Ziegler, Flo E295
Ziegler, Steve P658
Ziemer, James L. A683
Ziff family (Starwood Hotels &
  Resorts Worldwide) A1328
Ziff-Davis Inc. P170, P248, P338,
  W390, W548
Zigarelli, Lawrence J. A459
Ziggy (cartoon character) A146
Zigrossi, Norm A. A1371, P469
Zijlker, Aeilko W500
Zilinskas, M. J. P600
Zilius, Jan W505
Zilkha & Company P132, P578
Zilkha, Donald P133
Zillions (magazine) P138, P139,
  P582
*Zillions TV: A Kid's Guide to the
  Best Toys and Games* (educational
  video) P139
Zillmer, John J. A191
ZiLOG Inc. (semiconductors) P474,
  P475, P744
Zils, Joseph C. A793
Zima carbonated malt
  beverage A78, A79
Zimmer nuclear plant A140
Zimmer (orthopedic
  implants) A290
Zimmer, P. Joseph A857
Zimmer Station power plant A362
Zimmerlin, Edward L. A1091
Zimmerman, Alma A796, A797
Zimmerman, Freddy A796

Zimmerman, Gary A1349
Zimmerman, Harry A1270
Zimmerman, James M. A586
Zimmerman, Jane D. P369
Zimmerman, John P329
Zimmerman, Justin A797
Zimmerman, Mary A1270
Zimmerman, Michael J. A427,
  P141, P583
Zimmerman Partners
  (advertising) A1063
Zimmerman, Raymond A1270
Zimmerman, Rolf A417
Zimmerman, Ronald D. E273
Zimmerman, S. LaNette A1035
Zimmerman, Stewart E152
Zimmerman, Thomas L. A681
Zimmermann, Winfried W427
Zimpleman, Larry D. A1163
Zinc Corporation W488
Zinderman, Dana E258
Zine, Larry J. A267
Zing Technologies E74
Zingers snacks A775
Zingraff, René W366, W367
Zink, Darell E., Jr. "Gene" E194
Zinn, Raymond D. E92, E244
Zinn, Thomas T., Sr. A147
ZIP code P490
Zip drives and disks A778, A779
Zip hair care A217
Zip Mart convenience stores A1084,
  A1085
Ziploc plastic bags A504, A1246,
  A1247, P432, P433, P722
Zirnkilton, Frank P542
Ziskin, Ian A1187
Zithromax drug A1118
Zitzer, Gerald E. A287
Zitzner, Duane E. A713
Zizzo, Lawrence F., Jr. A1007
Zlatkus, Lizabeth H. A689
Zlaty Bazant (brewery) W254
Zobel, Enrique W510
Zoch, Margaret R. P399
Zocor drug A956, A957, A1250
Zodiac Maritime Agencies W434
Zodtner, Steven A1233
Zohouri, Saeed A1299
Zoley, George C. A1489, E138, E314
Zolintakis, Peter N. A873
ZOLL Medical Corporation E**144**,
  E320
Zoll, Paul E144
Zollars, William D. A1548, A1549
Zoloft drug A1118, A1119
Zolotaya Boshka beer W553
Zomax drug A800
Zomax Optical Media W308

Zombie Revenge (video
  game) W527
Zommer, Nathan E76, E224
Zone Publishing W238
Zonis, Meshulam A331
Zoo brand cookies A814, A815
Zook, Dennis R. A437
Zook, J. Randolph A1005
ZoomTown.com Inc. A293
Zorbo, Vita A441
Zore, Edward J. A1049, P377, P690
Zorro cleaning products A487
Zostrix drug E89
Zotos hair products W534
Zout cleaning products A487
Zovant drug A540
Zovirax drug W246
Zowie Intertainment W332
ZSR (company) W568
Zuanich, Anthony J. E106
Zubrow, Barry L. A661
Zuccaro, Robert S. E65, E207
Zuckerman, Michael T. E134
Zuckerman, Mitchell A1305
Zuckerman, Mortimer B. E34, E165
Zuerblis, Kenneth J. E199
Zühlsdorff, Peter W589
Zuker, Aron W323
Zulkey, Edward J. A221, P67
Zumtobel AG A837, P283
Zumwalt, Deborah P457
Zumwinkel, Klaus W202, W203
Zurich Allied W142
Zurich American Insurance E211
Zurich Financial Services A226,
  A1440, P268, W82, W200, W512,
  W**652**-W**653**
Zurich Scudder Investments W200
Zurich US A182
ZURITEL W653
Zurkow, Peter L. A1094, A1095
Zurn (bath and plumbing) A1446,
  A1447
Zutz, Denise M. A803
Zwach, Colleen A345
Zwan, Bryan E192
Zweckform Buro-Produkte A210
Zweier, Tonya A1233
Zweig, John W647
Zweigert, Erich W504
Zwickel, Klaus W353, W631
Zwiener, David K. A689
Zwolsche Algemeene A688
ZX cattle ranch P264
Zych, John W281
ZymoGenetics, Inc. W416
Zyprexa drug A540
Zyrtec drug A1507
Zyvox drug A1122
Zywiec beer W254, W255

HOOVER'S MEANS BUSINESS